PRAISE FOR THE ULTIMATE SCHOLARSHIP BOOK
BY GEN AND KELLY TANABE

"Upbeat, well-organized and engaging, this comprehensive tool is an exceptional investment for the college-bound."

—*PUBLISHERS WEEKLY*

"Gen and Kelly Tanabe are by far the best experts on winning scholarships. Not only will their books help you find scholarships that you qualify for, they will show you how to win them. Soon after applying the strategies in their book, I won a $1,000 scholarship. I couldn't have done it without them. The Tanabes can help you win scholarships too!"

—*DOUG WONG, UNIVERSITY OF CALIFORNIA, SAN DIEGO*

"A present for anxious parents."

—*THE HONOLULU ADVERTISER*

"Upbeat tone and clear, practical advice."

—*BOOK NEWS*

"Unlike other authors, the Tanabes use their experiences and those of other students to guide high school and college students and their parents through the scholarship and financial aid process."

—*PALO ALTO DAILY NEWS*

"If the Tanabes could earn over $100,000 in scholarships and graduate from an Ivy League institution owing nothing, others can, too."

—*STAR-BULLETIN*

"This is a helpful, well-organized guide. A good resource for all students."

—*KLIATT*

"A common sense approach to scholarship searches. *The Ultimate Scholarship Book* gives a down to earth step by step method of finding, applying for and winning scholarships. The scholarship list has many opportunities for students to showcase their talents for financial reward."

—*LYNDA MCGEE, COLLEGE COUNSELOR, DOWNTOWN MAGNETS HIGH SCHOOL, LOS ANGELES*

"Getting into college is only half of the game. How to pay for it offers the second big challenge. Whether they qualify for financial need or are just looking for ways to help their parents with this heavy burden, all students will profit from *The Ultimate Scholarship Book* which both outlines the process of finding financial help for college as well as it provides an extensive and up to date list of current scholarship sources.

"Take these important tips from two experienced writers who are nationally recognized for their expertise on all facets of the college application process. Both members of this impressive husband and wife team paid for their Harvard educations by following the precepts which they share with you now in this easy to read guidebook."

—*DAVID MILLER, DIRECTOR OF COLLEGE COUNSELING, STEVENSON SCHOOL, PEBBLE BEACH, CALIFORNIA*

Dedication

To our families for shaping who we are.

To Harvard for four of the best years of our lives.

To the many students and friends who made this book possible by sharing their scholarship experiences, secrets, successes and failures.

To all the students and parents who understand that paying for college is a challenging but worthwhile endeavor.

The Ultimate Scholarship Book 2010

Billions of Dollars in Scholarships, Grants and Prizes

Gen and Kelly Tanabe

Winners of over $100,000 in college scholarships and award-winning authors of
Get Free Cash for College and *How to Write a Winning Scholarship Essay*

- Comprehensive scholarship directory to over 1.5 million awards worth more than $2 billion

- Scholarships for high school and college students of every background, talent and achievement level

- Easy to use indexes to quickly find the best matching scholarships

The Ultimate Scholarship Book 2010: Billions of Dollars in Scholarships, Grants and Prizes

By Gen and Kelly Tanabe

Published by SuperCollege, LLC
3286 Oak Court
Belmont, CA 94002
650-618-2221
www.supercollege.com

ISBN-13: 978-1-9326-6236-8
ISBN-10: 1-932662-36-7

Manufactured in the United States of America
10 9 8 7 6 5 4 3 2 1

Library of Congress Cataloging-in-Publication Data

Tanabe, Gen S.
  The ultimate scholarship book 2010 : billions of dollars in scholarships, grants, and prizes / Gen Tanabe and Kelly Tanabe.
     p. cm.
  Includes indexes.
  ISBN-13: 978-1-9326-6236-8 (alk. paper)
  ISBN-10: 1-932662-36-7 (alk. paper)
  1. Scholarships--United States--Directories. I. Tanabe, Kelly Y. II. Title.
  LB2338.T36 2009
  378.3'402573--dc22
                              2009014761

CONTENTS

How to Use the Ultimate Scholarship Book

A Scholarship Book That's Better Than a Website

Is it crazy to say that a bound stack of paper and glue is superior to the high speed bits and bytes of a scholarship website? Absolutely not! Because it is true.

Let us explain.

Unless you're starting out, you've probably used a scholarship website. Typically you fill out a profile questionnaire to provide information about yourself before hitting the "search" button. So far, this seems much easier than using a book.

Until you get your results.

No matter what website you use, there will be an unusually large number of scholarships that aren't good matches. After reading the eligibility requirements, you will discover that only a small handful are worth your time to apply.

You've just discovered the first major weakness of every scholarship website: your life (background, experiences, goals, talents, awards, interests and accomplishments) cannot be defined or summarized by a computer-generated questionnaire.

Your Life is MORE Than a 30-Question Profile

The simple truth is that no computer can match you to scholarships as well as you can. You are a complex individual with a variety of passions, interests and goals. Nothing—person or machine—knows you better than you know yourself.

And think about that profile form. That's the only information the computer has about you. But what if you don't know all the answers? Are you really set on becoming an orthopedic surgeon, or did that just sound cool? Even worse, you are limited by the choices provided on that profile questionnaire. Imagine that you wrote a poem that was published in your town's community newspaper. Should you select "poet" as a future career? Will that trigger a great poetry scholarship? Or maybe under hobbies, you should select "writing and journalism"? Of course, that might trigger a flood of journalism scholarships that wouldn't apply to you. Or maybe, even though your school doesn't have a poetry club, you should still tell the computer that you are a member of one in order to trick it into showing you a sweet poetry award?

Do you see where we're going?

The very fact that you need to give the computer information about yourself while only using the choices the computer provides, without any clue about how those answers will affect your results, almost guarantees that you are going to miss out on some good scholarships. How do you know that because you answered a single question in the way that you did, that you are not missing out on some fantastic scholarship opportunities?

The answer is, you don't.

About Your Authors

What makes us qualified to write *The Ultimate Scholarship Book*? Primarily it's because at one time we were exactly where you are now. We needed money to pay for college, and scholarships turned out to be our only answer. Not only did we do pretty well (winning more than $100,000 in free cash for college) but since then, we've continued to help thousands of students do the same.

Here's our story:

Kelly grew up in Los Angeles and when she got accepted to Harvard (which costs about $45,000 per year!), her family just didn't have the money to pay for it. Gen grew up in Hawaii and faced a similar financial crunch when he got into Harvard. In fact, his father even tried to bribe him to attend his state university by offering him a new car if he would give up his idea of attending the ivy-league college. Even considering the cost of a brand new car, it would have been cheaper for Gen's family to make car payments than pay Harvard tuition!

Since we both had our hearts set on attending a very expensive college that our families could not afford, we had little choice but to become fanatics about applying for scholarships. While we made a lot of beginner mistakes and it was by no means a quick or easy process, we were ultimately successful in winning more than $100,000 in scholarships. It was only because of this money that we were able to attend Harvard and were both able to graduate from college debt free.

As you may have guessed by now, we met while at college. We were actually next door neighbors in the dorm, and we were married a few years after we graduated from Harvard. Knowing first-hand how hard it can be for families to pay for college, we decided to share what we had learned as a result of our own pursuits to find funds for tuition. Our first books were about how to win scholarships and get financial aid. In fact, you can find *1001 Ways to Pay for College* and *How to Write a Winning Scholarship Essay* in bookstores. But despite the success of these books, we found that whenever we spoke to groups of students or parents, the number one question they asked was, "Do you know of scholarships for such-and-such a student?"

At the same time, we were also noticing a growing dissatisfaction from students who only relied on websites for scholarship information. This was somewhat of a mystery to us since we knew of thousands of great scholarships that were available. Why weren't these awards being found? Why wasn't every student applying for these scholarships?

All of this led to our decision to build our own database of scholarships and publish the results in *The Ultimate Scholarship Book*. We have a team of researchers who help us investigate scholarships, verify awards and ensure that the scholarships that make it into the book are the best and most up-to-date possible.

So that's our story and why we feel so passionate about what we write in this book. It's not just a collection of words on paper; it's really the collective experience and intelligence of our own quest for scholarships along with thousands of hours of research by our scholarship staff.

How This Book Overcomes the Disadvantages of Websites

A book has certain advantages over websites; for example, a book can work for you without the necessity of input. In many ways, a book is more flexible than a computer site because you are not penalized for not having an answer to a specific question that is worded in a narrow and inflexible way. Likewise, you are not forced to fit yourself into a predetermined, inflexible category. A book also lets you do the matching, a tool which we have found to be far better than outsourcing that work to some machine.

The Ultimate Scholarship Book is designed to be browsed. Spend an hour with this book and you will be able to evaluate hundreds of scholarships quickly and efficiently. By scanning the descriptions, you (not some computer) can decide if you have the right combination of background, interests or skills to qualify. By seeing all of the possibilities, you remain in control of how you prioritize which awards are right for you.

Now it is true that this is a slower process than using a website. But the trade-off is that it is far more accurate, and accuracy is what it's all about. You're not trying to find hundreds of awards that you may or may not win. Who has time to apply for that many scholarships anyway?! Your goal is to find the best awards that you have highest chances of winning. So while you'll invest more time in the finding of scholarships by using a book, we guarantee that the payoff (which in this case is literally thousands of extra dollars in scholarships) will be worth it.

If the time aspect of using a book versus a website still bothers you, here's one more thought. You can use books practically anywhere—especially when you have downtime. Try using a scholarship website while you're waiting for the bus, hanging out at school or even in the bathroom! In other words, you can transform the natural wasted time during your day into highly productive scholarship time.

A Dirty Secret of Websites: They're Out-of-Date

It's natural to assume that anything online is more current than something printed on paper. But is this really true? Use a few scholarship websites and you'll soon realize that many are horribly out of date. Does it make you angry? Do you want to demand a refund? Of course not! Most scholarship websites are free services! Now it is true that many so-called "free" websites do actually make money by reselling your information; and once they get this from your profile form, you are of little value to the site. This is very annoying. However, we digress. Our point is that as a free service, there is really very little incentive for the website to maintain a high level of accuracy in their data. You really do get what you pay for with most scholarship websites!

It's a lot different with a book. There are two strong incentives that ensure the data in this book is up-to-date and accurate. The first is that we know once we commit something to paper, it's permanent. That creates a very strong desire to get it right the first time. This degree of permanence—the finality of words on paper—is a huge responsibility for us. Once the book goes to press, it is very difficult and expensive to update a mistake. The second powerful incentive is that you're paying hard earned money for this book! It's not free. Because of this, you expect to receive only the best product. If we don't deliver, we'll hear from you!

Together, these two incentives guarantee that each award in this book has been checked and re-checked. We have a small army of researchers whose only job is to verify each award in the book before it goes to press. We also send out letters twice a year to every scholarship listed to ask the providers themselves to verify and update their information. The end result is that this book is extremely accurate and up-to-date.

We also never keep this book in print for longer than a year—which is what we have found to be the typical time in which scholarships change. So as long as you are buying this book new, you are guaranteed to have the latest information possible.

Given how diligent and thorough our researchers are and the rigorous process we apply to every award we publish, we would happily pit this book against any website!

Another Dirty Secret of Websites: They Don't Actually List Millions of Awards

Here's a controversial statement: Websites often claim to list millions of awards worth billions of dollars, but the truth is that these numbers are just marketing hype. To arrive at these numbers, the websites use the most liberal definitions possible. For example, the Coca-Cola Foundation awards $3.4 million per year to over 1,400 students. So the website counts their single listing of the Coca-Cola Foundation Scholarship as being 1,400 awards valued at $3.4 million. Or consider that each Target department store gives a scholarship to a student in the community. Even though you can apply only at the store in your community, the website still counts each individual award, which totals into the thousands. The results are highly inflated numbers.

Now before we claim the high road in this debate, we have to admit that we do the exact same thing! Take a look at the front cover of this book. Our numbers are just as impressive as many scholarship websites. But unlike the websites, we don't hide reality. All you need to do is pick up our book and see how thick it is to know how many awards we have inside. But you can't do this with a website. There is no way to know (and the website will never tell you) how many actual awards they have. They want you to think that they have millions when in reality they often contain no more—and often much less—than what you'll find in this book!

The Bottom Line: Books Can Beat Websites

It should be obvious by now that we are just a little bothered when we hear that websites—just because they are online—are superior to books.

It's just not true.

This is not to say that websites don't have any value. They absolutely do and inside this book, we list a number of websites that we think are worth your time. However, you need to understand that you must go beyond websites if you hope to find the best scholarships. In fact, you need to go beyond books too! The entire next chapter is dedicated to places in which to find scholarships other than books and websites. We highly recommend that you explore all these sources in order to find the best scholarships for you.

Why Choose *This* Book?

We know that there are other books that provide directories of scholarships, so why choose this one?

- Discover the best scholarships for you with awards in the humanities, academics, public service, extracurricular activities, talents, athletics, religion, ethnicity, social science and science based on career goals and more.

- Find scholarships that are not based on grades.

- Get all the information you need in one place with the application details, eligibility requirements, deadlines, contact information and website addresses.

- Find scholarships you can use at any college.

- Avoid wasting money on scholarship competitions that require a fee to enter.

- Save time and find the best scholarships that fit you with the easy-to-use indexes.

- Access the most up-to-date information that has been checked and double-checked.

- Learn not only how to find scholarships but how to win them! Get insider advice from judges and scholarship winners.

Common Scholarship Myths Busted

Now that we've cleared up some of the misconceptions about books and websites, let's debunk some of the common scholarship myths. We hate these myths because not only are they untrue, but they often prevent students from applying for scholarships.

Myth: You need to be financially destitute to be eligible to apply for scholarships.

Busted: While it is true that financial need is a consideration for some scholarships, the definition of "need" varies considerably. Given the cost of a college education, many families who consider themselves to be "middle class" actually qualify for some need-based scholarships. In addition, there are many scholarships where financial need is not even a factor. These "merit-based" scholarships are based on achievements, skills, career goals, family background and a host of other considerations that have nothing to do with a family's financial situation. You could actually be the son or daughter of Donald Trump and still win a "merit-based" scholarship.

Myth: You can only win scholarships as a high school senior.

Busted: It is never too early or too late to apply for scholarships. There are awards for students as young as seventh grade. If you win, the money is usually held in an account until it is time for you to actually go to college. But even if there are not as many awards for younger students as there are for seniors, it doesn't mean it's not important to look. Finding awards that you can apply for next year or even two years from now is a huge advantage. Keep a list of these awards since you are going to be super busy as a senior (think college apps and AP classes!) and you are going to be so thankful when you can just refer to your file of previously found awards and don't have to spend time searching. At the same time, you also don't want to stop applying for scholarships after you graduate from high school. There are many awards for college students. Once you are in college, you should continue to apply for scholarships, especially those geared toward specific majors and careers.

Myth: Only star athletes get college scholarships.

Busted: While star running backs receiving full-tuition scholarships are often what make the news, the majority of scholarships awarded by colleges are not for athletics. As you will see in this book, there are literally thousands of scholarships for those of us who don't know the difference between a touchdown and a touchback. Even if you are an athlete, you might also be surprised to know that many colleges give scholarships to student athletes who may not be destined to become the next Michael Jordan. The needs of a college's athletic program depend on the level of their competition. You may find that at one college your soccer skill wouldn't earn you a place on the team as a bench warmer; but at another school, you might not only be a starter but also earn a half-tuition scholarship.

Myth: You need straight A's to win money for college.

Busted: While straight A's certainly don't hurt, most students mistakenly assume that grades are the primary determinate for selecting scholarship winners. This is just not true. Most scholarships are based on criteria other than grades and reward specific skills or talents such as linguistic, athletic or artistic ability. Even for scholarships in which grades are considered, GPAs are often not the most important factor. What's more relevant is that you best match the qualities the scholarship committee seeks. Don't let the lack of a perfect transcript prevent you from applying for scholarships.

Myth: You should get involved in as many extracurricular activities as possible to win a scholarship.

Busted: Scholarship competitions are not pie eating contests where you win through volume. They are more like baking contests in which you create an exquisite dessert with an appearance and flavor that matches the tastes of the judges. Scholarships are won by quality, not quantity. Scholarship judges are looking for students who have made quality contributions. For example, for a public service scholarship, the judges would be more impressed if you organized a school-wide volunteer day than if you were a member of 20 volunteer organizations but did little to distinguish yourself in any one of them.

Myth: If you qualify for financial aid, you don't need to apply for scholarships.

Busted: Financial aid and scholarships are not mutually exclusive but complimentary. You need to do both—apply for financial aid and scholarships—at the same time! Relying only on financial aid is dangerous. First, financial aid is "need based" which means if you're a middle or upper middle class family, you may not receive any free money (i.e. grants) but only student loans which you need to pay back. Even if you do qualify for grants, it may not be enough. The maximum Pell Grant, for example, is $4,050 per year, which is still far short of what tuition plus room and board costs at most schools. While financial aid is important, we consider scholarships to be far superior. With few, if any, strings attached, scholarships represent free cash that does not have to be paid back and which you can use at almost any school. Best of all, you can win scholarships regardless of your family's income!

Myth: You should apply to every scholarship that you find.

Busted: When you turn 35, you technically are eligible to run for President of the United States. This hardly means you should start packing your bags for the White House. Let's apply that same logic to scholarships. Just because you are technically eligible for a scholarship does not mean you should start filling out the paperwork for it. Why? You have a limited amount of time to spend on scholarship applications. It is necessary to allocate your time to those that you have the best chance of winning. You may find that you are eligible for 500 scholarships. Unless you're willing to make applying to scholarships your full-time avocation, it's unlikely that you can apply for more than several dozen awards. Thus, you need to be selective about which scholarships fit you the best. One caveat: This does not mean that you should only apply to two or three scholarships. You should still apply to as many scholarships as you can—just make sure you have them prioritized.

How a Solid Scholarship Strategy Helps Win You Money

Back in high school, Kelly applied for a scholarship from her father's employer. She was confident she would win since academically she had both high grades and test scores—which she diligently listed on the application. After turning in her application, she eagerly waited for the check to arrive. But the check never came. In fact, when Kelly found out who did win, she was surprised to learn that he had lower grades and lower test scores. What happened? How did this guy win instead of Kelly?

The answer was that Kelly relied solely on grades and test scores to win while the other applicant clearly used the entire application to stand out. That was when Kelly learned the importance of having a strategy.

So what does it take to win a scholarship?

The answer is that scholarship winners are not superstars. Rather, they are the students who have prepared—those young men and women that have invested the time to create applications that highlight their strengths. It's really sad to see students who don't apply for scholarships because they mistakenly assume that they don't have a chance to win.

Unlike a lottery, scholarships are not based on luck. To win scholarships, you need to show the scholarship judges how you fit the award. Often this is through the scholarship application, essay and interview. In fact, almost all scholarship competitions come down to one key factor—how well you can show that you fit the purpose of the scholarship. In this respect, you have power over the outcome. Through what you choose to highlight (and ignore) in the scholarship application, you are able to construct a case for why you deserve to win.

In the following chapters we will lay out what we found to be the keys to a winning strategy. Now turn the page and let's get started!

Where to Find the Best Scholarships

Scholarships Beyond this Book

We know you bought this book because it's the largest and most up-to-date directory of scholarships available. However, we do want to show you how to find even more scholarships above and beyond the ones listed in this book.

We learned how to find scholarships through trial and often painful error. For example, when we first started to search for scholarships, we spent a lot of time tracking down scholarships that we later discovered were listed in our high school counseling office. But we did learn from each mistake and slowly developed an efficient strategy for finding scholarships.

Our approach to finding scholarships consists of two important steps. First, you must create a list of as many scholarships as possible that fit you. Second, once you have a big list of scholarships, prioritize the awards. Here is where you will do some detective work that will show you which scholarships are worth your time to fill out.

By following this two-step approach, you will end up with a prioritized list of scholarships that are closely matched to your background and achievements. So, even before you fill out a single scholarship application form, you will have greatly improved your chances of winning. Plus, you saved time by not wasting energy on awards that you won't win.

Start Your Scholarship Search in Your Own Backyard

When we began looking for scholarships, we made what is perhaps the biggest mistake of the novice scholarship hunter—we started by looking as far away as possible. We were mesmerized by the big prizes of the large (and often well-publicized) national awards. We thought, "If I won just one of these national scholarship competitions, I'd be set and could end

17

my search." This turned out to be a big mistake and an even bigger time-waster. It seemed that everyone and his brother, sister and cousin were also applying to these competitions. The Coca-Cola scholarship competition, for example, receives more than 100,000 applications each year.

It turned out that the last place we looked for scholarships was our most lucrative source. Best of all, this place turned out to be in our own backyard!

What are backyard scholarships and where do you find them? Think about all the civic groups, clubs, businesses, churches and organizations in your community. Each of these is a potential source for scholarships. (If you are already in college, you have two communities: your hometown and the city in which you go to school.) Since these awards are usually only available to students in your community, the competition is a lot less fierce.

You may be thinking, "What good is a $500 Lions Club scholarship when my college costs 20 grand a year?" It's true that local scholarships don't award the huge prizes that some of the national competitions do. You already know that we won over $100,000 in scholarships. What we haven't told you is that the majority of this money came from local scholarships! We literally won $500 here and $1,500 there. By the time we graduated from Harvard and added up all the awards, it turned out to be a huge amount. Plus, some of the local scholarships that we won were "renewable," which meant that we received that money each year we were in college. So a $500 renewable scholarship was really worth $2,000 over four years.

If you still can't get excited because these local awards seem small compared to the cost of tuition, try this exercise: Take the amount of the award and divide it by the time you invested in the application. For the $500 Lions Club award, let's say that you spent one hour each night for three days to complete the application and write the essay. Take $500 and divide it by three hours. That works out to a little over $166 per hour. (Now imagine that the award was for $1,000 instead. That would make it $333 per hour!) Not bad by any measure. If you can find a job that pays you more than $166 an hour, then take it and forget applying to scholarships. If not, get back to applying for scholarships—even the little ones!

Let's get specific and look at all of the places in your backyard to find scholarships.

✓ High school counselor or college financial aid officer

If you are a high school student, start with your counselor. Ask if he or she has a list of scholarship opportunities. Most counselors have a binder filled with local scholarships. It's helpful if before your meeting, you prepare information about your family's financial background as well as special interests or talents you have that would make you eligible for scholarships. Don't forget that your own high school will have a variety of scholarships from such places as the parent-teacher organization, alumni group and athletic booster clubs.

If you are a college student, make an appointment with your school's financial aid office. Before the appointment, think about what interests and talents you have and what field you may want to enter after graduation. Take a copy of your Free Application for Federal Student Aid (FAFSA) as background (www.fafsa.ed.gov). Mention any special circumstances about your family's financial situation. Ask the financial aid officer for recommendations of scholarships offered by the college or by community organizations.

Also, if you have already declared a major, check with the department's administrative assistant or chair for any awards that you might be eligible to win.

It's important whenever you speak to a counselor (either in high school or college) that you inquire about any scholarships that require nomination. Often these scholarships are easier to win since the applicant pool is smaller. You have nothing to lose by asking, and if anything, it shows how serious you are about financing your education.

 High school websites

You may not visit your school's website daily, but when you are looking for scholarships, it pays to search the site for lists of scholarships. Most high schools post scholarship opportunities for students on their websites. (You may have to dig down a few levels to find this list.)

 Other high school websites

If your school does not post scholarship opportunities, surf over to the websites of other high schools in the area. You'll find that many offer a wealth of scholarship resources.

 Nearby colleges

While your college has great scholarship resources, wouldn't it be great if you had double or triple these resources? You can. Simply seek the resources of other local colleges. Ask permission first, but you'll find that most neighboring schools are more than willing to help you. If you are in high school, nothing prevents you from visiting a local college and asking for scholarship information. Because you are a prospective student, the college will often be happy to provide whatever assistance it can.

 Student clubs and organizations

Here's a reason to enjoy your extracurricular activities even more. One benefit of participating may be a scholarship sponsored by the organization. Inquire with the officers or advisors of the organization about scholarship funds. Bands, newspapers, academic clubs, athletic organizations and service organizations often have scholarships that are awarded to outstanding members. If the organization has a national parent organization (e.g. National Honor Society) visit the national organization website. There are often awards that are given by the parent organization for members of local chapters.

 Community organizations

Maybe you've wondered why community organizations have so many breakfast fundraisers—one reason is that some provide money for scholarships.

You usually don't have to be a member of these organizations to apply. In fact, many community groups sponsor scholarships that are open to all students who live in the area. As we have mentioned, college students really have two communities: their hometown and where they go to college. Don't neglect either of these places.

How do you find these organizations? Many local government websites list them. Visit the websites for your town, city and state. Also visit or call your community association or center. You can use the phone book to look up organizations. Some phone books even have a calendar of annual events that are sponsored by various civic groups. Finally, don't forget to pay a visit to the public library and ask the reference librarian for help. Here is a brief list of some of the more common civic groups to track down:

- Altrusa
- American Legion and American Legion Auxiliary
- American Red Cross
- Association of Junior Leagues International
- Boys and Girls Clubs
- Boy Scouts and Girl Scouts
- Circle K
- Civitan
- Elks Club
- Lions Club
- 4-H Clubs
- Fraternal Order of Eagles
- Friends of the Library
- Kiwanis International
- Knights of Columbus
- National Exchange Club
- National Grange
- Optimist International
- Performing Arts Center
- Rotary Club
- Rotaract and Interact
- Ruritan
- Sertoma International

- Soroptimist International of the Americas
- U.S. Jaycees
- USA Freedom Corps
- Veterans of Foreign Wars
- YMCA and YWCA
- Zonta International

 Local businesses

Businesses like to return some of their profits to employees and students in the community. Many offer scholarships as a way to reward students who both study and work. Ask your manager if your employer has a scholarship fund and how you can apply. Some companies—particularly large conglomerates that have offices, distributorships or factories in your community—offer scholarships that all students in the community are eligible to win. Check with the chamber of commerce for a list of the largest companies in the area. You can call the public relations or community outreach department in these companies to inquire about any scholarship opportunities. Visit the large department and chain stores in the area and ask the store manager or customer service manager about scholarships.

 Parents' employer

Your parents may hate their jobs, but they'll love the fact that many companies award scholarships to the children of employees as a benefit. They should speak with someone in the human resources department or with their direct managers about scholarships and other educational programs offered by their company.

 Parents' or grandparents' military service

If your parents or grandparents served in the U.S. Armed Forces, you may qualify for a scholarship from a military association. Each branch of the service and even specific divisions within each branch have associations. Speak with your parents and grandparents about their military service and see if they belong to or know of these military associations.

 Your employer

Flipping burgers may have an up side. Even if you work only part-time, you may qualify for an educational scholarship given by your employer. For example, McDonald's offers the National Employee Scholarship to reward the accomplishments of its student-employees. There is even a McScholar of the Year prize that includes a $5,000 scholarship. If you have a full- or part-time job, ask your employer about scholarships.

Parents' union

Don't know if your parents are in a union? Ask and find out. Some unions sponsor scholarships for the children of their members. Ask your parents to speak with the union officers about scholarships and other educational programs sponsored by their union.

 Interest clubs

Performing arts centers, city orchestras, equestrian associations and amateur sports leagues are just a few of the many special interest clubs that may offer scholarships. While some limit their awards to members, many simply look for students who are interested in what they support. A city performing arts center, for example, may offer an award for a talented performing artist in the community.

 Professional sports teams

They may not have won a World Series since the 1950s, but don't discount them as a viable scholarship source. Many local professional athletic teams offer community awards (and not necessarily for athletes) as a way to contribute to the cities in which they are based.

 Church or religious organizations

Religious organizations may provide scholarships for members. If you or your parents are members of a religious organization, check with the leaders to see if a scholarship is offered.

 Local government

Some cities and counties provide scholarships specifically designated for local students. Often, local city council members and state representatives sponsor a scholarship fund. Even if you didn't vote for them, call their offices and ask if they offer a scholarship.

 Local newspaper

Local newspapers often print announcements about students who win scholarships. Keep a record of the scholarships featured or go to the library or look online at back issues of the newspaper. Check last year's spring issues (between March and June) for announcements of scholarship recipients. Contact the sponsoring organizations to see if you're eligible to enter the next competition.

Is There a Magic Number of Scholarships?

We often are asked, "How many scholarships should I apply to?" The truth is that there is no magic number of scholarships for which you should apply. But you should avoid the extremes. Don't select only a couple of scholarships with the intention of spending countless hours crafting the perfect application. While it is true that to win you need to turn in quality applications, there is also a certain amount of subjective decision making. So even with the perfect application, you may not win. This means that you need to apply to more than a few scholarships. On the other hand, don't apply for 75 awards, sending in the same application to each. You'll just waste your time. You need to strike a balance between quantity and quality.

Searching Beyond Your Backyard

Once you have exhausted the opportunities in the community, it is time to broaden your search. Although the applicant pool is often larger with national awards, you shouldn't rule them out. Because many national award programs have marketing budgets, finding these awards may actually be easier than local awards. Most national awards will be advertised and the following places will help you track them down:

 Internet

Forget the time-wasting social networks, and let's use the Internet for something productive. We recommend that you use as many online scholarship databases as possible as long as they are free. There are enough quality free databases that you should not have to pay for any online search. Here are a few we recommend:

- SuperCollege (www.supercollege.com)
- Sallie Mae (www.salliemae.com/scholarships)
- BrokeScholar (www.brokescholar.com)
- Careers and Colleges (www.careersandcolleges.com)
- The College Board (www.collegeboard.com)
- Free Scholarship Information (www.freschinfo.com)
- Scholarships.com (www.scholarships.com)
- AdventuresinEducation (www.adventuresineducation.org)
- CollegeNet (www.collegenet.com)
- Mario Einaudi Center for International Studies (www.einaudi.cornell.edu/funding/search.asp)

Just remember that while many online databases claim to have billions of dollars in scholarships listed, they represent only a tiny fraction of what is available. We have personally used nearly every free scholarship database on the Internet and know from experience that none of them (including our own at www.supercollege.com) lists every scholarship that you might win. Think of these databases as starting points, and remember that they are not the only places to find awards.

 Professional associations

There is an association for every profession you can imagine. Whether you want to be a doctor, teacher or helicopter pilot, there are professional organizations that exist not only to advance the profession, but also to encourage students to enter that field by awarding grants and scholarships.

To find these associations, contact people who are already in the profession. If you think you want to become a computer programmer, ask computer programmers about the associations to which they belong. Also look at the trade magazines that exist for the profession since they have advertisements for various professional organizations.

Another way to find associations is through books like *The Encyclopedia of Associations*. This multi-volume set found at most college libraries lists nearly every professional association in the United States. Once you find these associations, contact them or visit their websites to see if they offer scholarships.

Professional associations often provide scholarships for upper-level college students, graduate school or advanced training. But even high school students who know what they want to do after college can find money from associations.

 Big business

If you've never received a personal "thank you" from large companies like Coca-Cola, Tylenol or Microsoft, here it is. A lot of these have charitable foundations that award scholarships. Companies give these awards to give something back to the community (and the positive PR sure doesn't hurt either). When you visit company websites, look for links to their foundations, which often manage the scholarship programs.

Many companies offer similar types of scholarships. What if you're a student film maker? Think about all the companies that make money or sell products to you from cameras to editing software to tripods. Are you into industrial music? What special equipment or instruments do you use? Consider the companies that will benefit from more people using their products and services. Some companies also offer awards to attract future employees. For example, Microsoft, the software company, sponsors a scholarship program for student programmers. Be sure to investigate companies that employ people in your field of study—especially if it is highly competitive—to see if they offer scholarships.

Colleges

You may think that checks only travel from your pocket to your college to pay for tuition. But colleges actually give a lot of money to students. Some of this money comes from the college itself while other money is from generous donations of alumni. Every college administers a number of scholarships, some based on financial need and some based on merit. What many students don't know is that often a student's application for admission is also used by the college to determine if he or she may win a scholarship. This is one reason it is worth the submission of any optional essay suggested on a college application. Even if the essay does not impact your admission, it could be used to award you some scholarship dollars.

Don't Look for Scholarships Alone

One of the biggest mistakes we made when looking for scholarships was that we did so alone. Maybe we didn't want to share what we found with our friends and thereby increase competition, or perhaps we just didn't see the benefits of working in groups. Whatever the reason, it probably cost us a ton of money.

Since then we've met thousands of students who have won scholarships. Of these the most successful are those who did not look for scholarships alone. In fact, they made it the biggest group project imaginable.

Take for example the three guys we met in Los Angeles. Essentially, all three young men are going to college for free because they were able to win way more money than they could ever use! How did they do it? They formed a "scholarship group". Every Saturday morning they met at Starbucks and one of their parents agreed to pick up the tab for Frappuccinos. The only rule was that each had to bring at least two new scholarships. What happened was that one guy might find an award that was not right for him but was perfect for someone else in the group. This sharing of information was a tremendous advantage over laboring individually and literally tripled their chances of finding scholarships.

Another benefit was that working in a group kept these guys motivated. There certainly must have been weeks when searches were fruitless and the scholarship pickings were slim. The guys might have been tempted to give up, but being in a group brings with it a sense of responsibility not to disappoint the other members of the unit. Searching for scholarships alone is very difficult and it's so easy to just quit. But when you work in a group, you keep one another motivated and you have a natural support base that keeps you going when you feel like quitting.

So did these guys increase the competition by sharing scholarships? In some cases they did. But this was far outweighed by the sheer number of scholarships that they found collectively that they never would have found working alone.

As a general rule, students who worked with others discovered that by sharing the awards they found and pooling their resources, they were able to find more scholarships in less time than they would have found individually. The end result was that these students had more scholarships to apply to and more time to focus on their applications. Hence, they won more money.

Let this be a lesson to all of us. Look around you and find others who are also hunting for scholarships. Convince them that the way to really win lots of free money for college is to work in groups.

Prioritize the Scholarships You Find

Until now, we have focused on where to find scholarships. If you invest time exploring these areas, you should have a fairly long list of potential scholarships. It may be tempting to start cranking out applications. We actually have a name for the methodology used by students that apply to anything and everything they find—it's called the "shotgun" approach and it never works. Just because you find an award for which you qualify does not mean that you should immediately apply. You want to focus your energies (and limited time) only on those awards that you have the best chance of winning.

It would save a lot of time if you knew beforehand which scholarships you'd win and which you wouldn't. With this information, you'd only spend time applying for the scholarships that you knew would result in cash in your pocket. While there is no way to be 100 percent certain that you'll win any scholarship, you can do some research and make an educated guess.

Here are the steps you should take with each scholarship to determine if you have a reasonable chance of winning it. By prioritizing your list based on these criteria, you'll be able to focus time on awards that you have the best odds of winning while not wasting time on the ones where being a match is a long shot.

Step 1   Learn the Purpose

Nobody, and we mean nobody, gives away money without a reason. Every sponsor of a scholarship has a concrete reason for giving away their hard-earned cash to students like you. For example, a teachers' organization might award a scholarship to encourage students to enter the teaching profession. An environmental group might sponsor a scholarship with the purpose of promoting environmental awareness, or it might reward students who have done environmental work in school. A local bank might give money to a student who has done a great deal of public service as a way to give back to the community in which it does business.

Your job is to uncover the purpose of every scholarship on your list. If you're lucky, it will be stated in the description of the award. Look at the eligibility requirements to see what kind of questions the scholarship sponsors are asking. Is there a GPA requirement? If there is and it's relatively high, academic achievement is probably important. If the GPA requirement is low, then grades are probably not important. Does the application ask for a list of extracurricular activities? If so, they are probably a significant part of the selection criteria. Do you need to submit an essay on a specific topic or a project to demonstrate proficiency in a field of study? All these requirements are clues about what the scholarship judges think will (and won't) be important.

For example, the sole purpose of a public service scholarship may be to reward a student's philanthropic acts. If that is the case, the application will most likely be focused on descriptions of a student's selfless deeds. On the other hand, a scholarship given by a major corporation may be based on a combination of grades, leadership and character.

If you cannot determine the purpose of the scholarship by reading its description and eligibility requirements, then you need to look for the purpose of the group that sponsors the award. For example, even if the scholarship description does not directly state it, you can be sure that an award given by an organization that is composed of local physicians will probably prefer that the winner have a connection with medicine or an intention to enter the medical field.

The membership of the organization can be a big clue. Just as your friends are a reflection of who you are, most clubs and organizations want to reach students who are similar to their membership. If you don't know much about the organization, contact them to learn background information regarding the history, purpose or contributions of the group. Visit the organization's website. Read their brochures or publications. The more you know about why the organization is giving the award, the better you'll understand how you may or may not fit.

Somewhere on your list of potential scholarships, note in a few words its purpose. You'll be using this information in the next step which is to determine if you can make a case that you are the type of person the scholarship committee is looking for.

Beware of Scholarship Scams

While the great majority of scholarship providers and services have philanthropic intentions, not all do. There are some scholarship services and even scholarships themselves that you need to avoid. According to the Federal Trade Commission, in one year there were more than 175,000 cases reported of scholarship scams, costing consumers $22 million. And this is a low estimate since most scholarship scams go unreported!

While we were fortunate to have not been victims of a scholarship scam, we have to admit that the offers we received were tempting. We both received letters in high school and college from companies that promised to help us find and win "unclaimed" scholarships. The pitch was tempting: There is money out there that no one is claiming. All we needed to do was purchase their service to get a list of these awards. Had we done so, we would have been $400 poorer and certainly none the richer. In this chapter, we will describe some of the common scams that you may encounter. You must avoid these offers, no matter how glamorous they seem.

The key to avoiding a scholarship scam is to understand the motivation of the people behind these scams. Those who operate financial aid rip-offs know that paying for college is something that makes you extremely nervous. They also know that most people don't have extensive experience when it comes to scholarships and may therefore believe that there are such things as "hidden" or "unclaimed" scholarships. These charlatans take advantage of your fears and discomfort by offering an easy answer with a price tag that seems small compared to the promised benefits. Be aware that you are vulnerable to these kinds of inducements. Think about it this way. If you have a weakness for buying clothes, you need to be extra vigilant when you are at the shopping mall. Similarly, because you need money for college, you are more susceptible to tempting scholarship offers. Acknowledging that these fears make you a target of scam artists is the first step to spotting their traps.

Step 2   Think Like a Judge

Once you know the purpose of the scholarship, you need to see if you are a match for the organization that sponsors it. At this point students often make one of two mistakes. Either they 1) overestimate how well they fit the purpose or, more commonly, 2) underestimate their qualifications and don't apply. After working with thousands of students, we have learned that students more often underestimate their abilities than overestimate. Try to be realistic, but also don't sell yourself short. Remember that scholarship judges are not looking for the perfect match. There are a lot of factors that will influence their decision, and many of these things—like personality, character and motivation—are difficult to measure.

Let's look at an example. If you are your school's star journalist, naturally you should apply for journalism scholarships. But if all you have done is write a single letter to the editor, then spend your time applying to scholarships that better match what you have accomplished. You can still apply for a journalism scholarship, especially if you only recently realized that you want to become a journalist, but you will be at a disadvantage compared to the other applicants and therefore should prioritize this award below other awards on your to-do list.

As you go through your list of scholarships, move to the bottom those which are the weakest matches to the goal of the scholarships. Make those awards that fit you best your highest priority. These are the ones that you want to focus on first.

Step 3   Take a Reality Check

Scholarship deadlines are not like tax deadlines, where there is a single day when all forms are due. The deadlines for scholarships vary. Be aware of these crucial dates. Unless you plan carefully, you may miss out on a scholarship simply because you don't have the time to create a decent application. Sandwiched among studying, sleeping and everything else in your busy life, there is limited time to spend on applying for scholarships. If you find a great scholarship that is due next week but requires a yet to-be-written original composition that would take a month, you should probably pass on the competition. If you know that, given the amount of time available, you won't be able to do an acceptable job, it's better to pass and move on to awards in which you have the time to put together a winning application. Remember too that you may be able to apply for the award next year.

Review Your List Daily

After you prioritize your scholarships with the ones you feel fit you best at the top of the list, push yourself to apply to as many as you can, working from top to bottom. You probably won't get to the end. This is okay since you have the least chance of winning the awards at the bottom anyway. By prioritizing and working methodically down your list, you will have hedged your bets by making sure that your first applications are for the scholarships that you have the best chance of winning while also not limiting yourself to only a handful of awards.

How to Win the Scholarships You Find

Attacking the Scholarship Application

At first glance, scholarship applications look easy—most are only a single page in length. Piece of cake, right? Don't let their diminutive size fool you. The application is a vital part of winning any scholarship. Scholarship judges must sift through hundreds or even thousands of applications, and the application form is what they use to determine which applicants continue to the next stage. It's crucial that you ace your application to make this first cut.

In this chapter, we'll look at strategies you can use to transform an ordinary scholarship application form into a screaming testament of why you deserve to win free cash for college.

Five Steps to Crafting a Winning Application

Step 1   Strategically Choose What to List

Imagine that you need to give a speech to two groups of people. Without knowing who your audience is, you would have a difficult time composing a speech that would appeal to them, right? It would make a huge difference if one were a group of mathematicians and the other a group of fashion designers. To grab the attention of each of these audiences, you'd need to adjust your speech accordingly. References to mathematical theorems would hardly go over well with the designers, just as the mathematicians probably couldn't care less about how black the "new" black really is.

In much the same way, you need to decide what to highlight on your scholarship application based on the purpose of the award. When you know what the scholarship judges are looking for, it makes it easier to decide what to include or omit. As we mentioned earlier, organizations don't give away scholarships and expect nothing in return. Behind their philanthropic motives lies an ulterior motive—to promote their organization's purpose. If you prioritized your list of scholarships correctly, you've already uncovered the purpose for each award. Now look at all your activities, interests, hobbies and achievements. Ask yourself which ones fit the purpose of each award and would make a positive impression on the scholarship judges.

Let's imagine that you are applying for an award given by an organization of professional journalists. In visiting their website, you learn that print and broadcast journalists join this group because they are passionate about the profession of journalism and want to encourage public awareness about the importance of a free press. Immediately, you know that you need to highlight those experiences that demonstrate your zeal for journalism and, if applicable, your belief in the value of a free press.

Among your activities and accomplishments are the following:

- Soccer team captain

- Vice President of the Writers' Club

- Key Club treasurer

- Columnist for your high school newspaper

- English essay contest winner

- Summer job working at a pet store

- Summer internship at a radio station

As you look at this list, you can eliminate some activities outright. Your involvement on the soccer team, with the Key Club, and your job at the pet store are not relevant and don't show how you fit with the purpose of the scholarship.

However, even looking at what's left, you still have to decide which ones to list first. As you think about the purpose of the scholarship, you remember that in the Writers' Club you participated in a workshop that helped a local elementary school start its own newspaper. Since this achievement almost perfectly matches the mission of our hypothetical journalism organization, use your limited space in the application to list it first and to add an explanation.

You might write something like this:

```
Writers' Club, Vice President, organized "Writing Counts"
workshop at Whitman Elementary School, which resulted in the
launch of the school's first student-run newspaper.
```

Think of the impact this would have on the scholarship judges. "Look here, Fred!" one journalist on the judging committee would say. "This student does what we do! Definitely someone we should interview!"

When choosing accomplishments to list, don't be afraid to eliminate any that don't fit—even good ones. You have limited space in which to cram a lot of information. As you fill out the application, you may find that you are trying to squeeze in too many details or simply too many things. You need to be ruthless in trimming down what you submit to the judges. Make sure to include the accomplishments that *best fit* the purpose of the award.

At the same time you are picking which things to include in your application, be sure to also be aware of what might be offensive to the organization's members. Just imagine what would happen if you thoughtlessly mentioned that you were the author of an economics project entitled "How Labor Unions Make the U.S. Unable to Compete and Lower Our Standard of Living" to judges who are members of the International Brotherhood of Teamsters.

Clearly you can't use the same list of activities and accomplishments for every scholarship. You must take the time to craft a unique list that matches what each of the scholarships is intended to reward.

Create a Timeline

Every scholarship has a deadline. Even though you have created a prioritized list of awards, you need also be aware of the deadlines. In fact, the due date for an award may also influence how you prioritize it. It's also helpful to set yourself deadlines and create a schedule for applying. Set deadlines for when you will have the application forms completed, essays written and any required recommendations submitted. Post this schedule where you can see it every day. We also recommend that you share it with your parents. Moms and dads are great at nagging (we mean reminding) you to meet deadlines, so you might as well use their nagging (we mean motivating) skills to your advantage.

Step 2   List Important Accomplishments First

In movies, the most dare-devilish car chase, the most harrowing showdown and the most poignant romantic revelations are usually saved until the end. While this works for Hollywood, it does not for scholarship applications. Since scholarship judges review so many applications and the space on the form is limited, you must learn to highlight your most impressive points first.

If you have listed four extracurricular activities, assume that some judges won't read beyond the first two. This doesn't mean that all judges will be this rushed, but there are always some who are. It's extremely important that you prioritize the information that you present and rank your accomplishments according to the following criteria—which should not come as too much of a surprise.

Fit: The most important factor in ordering your achievements is how they fit with the purpose of the scholarship. This is, after all, why these kind people want to hand you some free dough. Emphasize accomplishments that match the purpose of the scholarship. If you are applying for an award that rewards athleticism, stress how well you've done in a particular sport before listing your volunteer activities.

Scope: Next prioritize your accomplishments by their scope, or how much of an impact they have made. How many people have been affected by your work? To what extent has your accomplishment affected your community? Did your contribution produce measurable results? In simple terms, put the big stuff before the small stuff.

Uniqueness: Since your application will be compared to those of perhaps thousands of others, include accomplishments that are uncommon. Give priority to those that are unique or difficult to win. Being on your school's honor roll is certainly an achievement, but it is an honor that many others have received. Try to select honors that fewer students have received—you want to stand out in order to be selected.

Timeliness: This is the least-important criterion, but if you get stuck and aren't sure how to arrange some of your accomplishments, put the more recent achievements first. Having won an election in the past year is more relevant than having won one three years ago. Some students ask us if they should list junior high or even elementary school achievements. Generally, stick to accomplishments from high school if you're a high school student and to college if you're a college student. An exception is if your accomplishment is extremely impressive and relevant—such as publishing your own book in the eighth grade. Of course, if you run out of recent achievements and there is still space on the form, go ahead and reach back to the past—but try to limit yourself to only one or two items.

You want your application to be as unforgettable as the best Hollywood movies. The only difference between your work and Spielberg's—besides the millions of dollars—is that you need to place the grand finale first.

You Can Recycle Your Applications

The first scholarship for which you apply will take the most time. But with each application you complete, it will get easier. This is because for each successive application, you can draw on the materials you developed for the previous one. To complete your first application, you need to think about your activities and recall achievements that you have forgotten. If there is an essay component, you will need to find a topic and craft an articulate essay. When you work on your second application, you can benefit from the work you've already done for the first. As you're building your timeline, look for scholarships in which you can recycle information from one application to another.

Recycling will save you time. In addition, you can improve on your work each time that you use it. For example, the second time you answer a question about your plans after graduation, you can craft your response more effectively than the first. As you recycle information, don't just reuse it—improve it!

Step 3	Spin Your Application to Impress the Judges

Politicians are notorious for telling voters what they want to hear. Good politicians never lie, but they do put a flattering "spin" on their words depending on whom they're addressing. While you must never lie on your application forms, you do want to present yourself in the best possible way so that you appeal to your audience. In other words, employ a little spin.

We know that some politicians have a difficult time distinguishing between lying and spinning. You shouldn't. Let's say you are applying for a scholarship that rewards students who are interested in promoting literacy. You have been a volunteer at your local library where, aside from typical page duties each week, you also read stories to a dozen children for story time. Here are three ways you could describe this activity on your application:

Non-spin description:
```
Library volunteer.
```

Lie:
```
Library reading program founder. Started a national program
that reaches thousands of children every day to promote
literacy.
```

Spin:
```
Library volunteer. Promoted literacy among children through
weekly after-school reading program at public library.
```

At one extreme, you can see that a lie exaggerates well beyond the truth. At the other extreme, the non-spin description is not very impressive because it does not explain how the activity relates to the purpose of the scholarship. The spin version is just right. It does not stretch the truth, but it does make clear how this activity fits within the context of the purpose of the scholarship. It focuses on what is important to the judges while at the same time, it ignores other aspects of your job that are not relevant—such as shelving books.

To take this example one step further, let's say that now you are applying for a scholarship that rewards student leaders. One of your other responsibilities as a library volunteer is to maintain the schedule for volunteers and help with the recruitment of new volunteers. Your description for this scholarship might read something like this:

```
Library volunteer. In charge of volunteer schedule and re-
cruitment of new members.
```

Notice how you have "spun" your activity so that it highlights a different aspect of what you did and better shows the judges how you fit their criteria. In the application, you should use the opportunity to spin your accomplishments to match the purpose of the award.

To be able to spin effectively, you need to know your audience. When you prioritized your scholarships earlier, you should have discovered the purpose of each scholarship. Remember that in most cases the scholarship judges want to give their money to students who are the best reflections of themselves. For example, the Future Teachers of America judges will want to fund students who seem the most committed to pursuing a teaching career. The American Congress of Surveying and Mapping judges, on the other hand, want to award their money to students who have the strongest interest in cartography.

Step 4   Write to Impress

The inspiring words of Martin Luther King Jr.'s "I Have a Dream" speech were punctuated with his dramatic, emotion-filled voice, hopeful expression and confident presence. His delivery would not have been as forceful had he spoken in a drab, monotone, with hands stuffed into his pockets and eyes lowered to avoid contact with the audience. Nor would his dramatic presentation have been as effective had his message been unimportant. The lesson? Both content and delivery count. While you don't have the opportunity for person-to-person delivery with your scholarship applications, you can and should present information in a compelling way. Here are some time-tested writing strategies for creating a positive impression through your applications:

Showcase Your Smarts. There's a reason why your parents wanted you to study and do well in school. In addition to the correlation between studying and success in college, almost all scholarship judges (even those of athletic awards) are impressed by academic achievement. College is, after all, about learning (at least that's what you want your parents to believe).

As you are completing your applications, keep in mind that while you may be applying for a public service scholarship, you should also include at least one academic achievement. For example, it does not hurt to list on an athletic scholarship form that you also came in second place at the science fair. This should not be the first thing you list, but it should be included somewhere to show the committee that you have brains in addition to brawn.

Extracurricular Activities and Hobbies Show Your Passion. If your only activity were studying, your life would be severely lacking in excitement. Scholarship organizers recognize this and thus the criteria for many scholarships include extracurricular activities or hobbies. Scholarship committees want evidence that you do more than read textbooks, take exams and watch television. They want to know that you have other interests. This makes you a more well-rounded person.

As always, when completing your applications, select extracurricular activities and hobbies that fit with the scholarship's mission. If you are applying for a music scholarship, describe how you've been involved in your school's orchestra or how you've taken violin lessons. By showing that you not only have taken classes in music theory but have also been involved with music outside of your studies, the scholarship committee will get a more complete picture of your love for music. Remember to use your activities and hobbies to illustrate your passion for a subject.

Leadership Is Always Better Than Membership. If you've ever tried to motivate a group of peers to do anything (without taking the easy way out—bribery) you know that it takes courage, intelligence and creativity to be a leader. Because of this, many scholarships give extra points to reward leadership. Scholarship judges want to know that the dollars will be awarded to someone who will not only make a difference in the future but who will also be a leader and motivate others to do the same. Think of it this way: If you were a successful businessperson trying to encourage entrepreneurship, wouldn't you want to give your money to a young person who is not only an entrepreneur but who also motivates others to become entrepreneurs?

Describing leadership in your activities or hobbies will also help set you apart from the other applicants. Many students are involved with environmental groups, but what if you are the only one to actually help increase recycling on your campus? Wouldn't that make your application a standout?

To show scholarship judges that you are a leader, list any activities in which you took responsibility for a specific project. Use action verbs when describing your work:

- Organized band fundraiser to purchase new instruments

- Led a weeklong nature tour in Yosemite Valley

- Founded first website to list volunteer activities

- Directed independent musical performance

Remember that you don't need to be an elected officer to be a leader. Many students have organized special projects, led teams or helped run events. Even if you didn't have an official title, you can include these experiences. Here's an example:

```
Environmental Action Committee Member. Spearheaded sub-
committee on reducing waste and increasing recycling on
campus.
```

When describing your leadership, include both formal and informal ways you have led groups. This shows the scholarship committee that you are a worthy investment.

Honors and Awards Validate Your Strengths. There's a reason why all trophies are gold and gaudy. They shout to the world in a deafening roar, "Yes, this glittery gold miniature figure means I am the best!" For applications that ask for your honors and awards, impart some of that victorious roar and attitude. In no way are we recommending that you ship your golden statuettes off with your applications. We are saying that you should highlight honors and awards in a way that gets the scholarship committee to pay attention to your application. What makes an award impressive is scope. Not a minty mouthwash, scope in this case is the impact and influence of the award. You worked for the award and earned every golden inch of it. Show the committee that they don't just hand these statuettes out to anybody. One way to do this is to point out how many awards are given:

```
English Achievement Award. Presented to two outstanding ju-
niors each year.
```

By itself, the English Achievement Award does not tell the scholarship committee very much. Maybe half the people in your class were given the award. By revealing the scope of the award (particularly if it was given to only a few) it becomes much more impressive.

In competitions that reach beyond your school, it is important to qualify your awards. For example, while everyone at your school may know that the Left Brain Achievement Award is given to creative art students, the rest of the world does not.

Don't write:
```
Left Brain Achievement Award.
```

Do write:
```
Left Brain Achievement Award. Recognized as an outstanding
creative talent in art as conferred upon by vote of art de-
partment faculty.
```

You've worked hard to earn the honors and awards that you have received, and you should not hesitate to use them in your applications to help you win scholarships.

Know when to leave a space blank. An official mom rule from childhood is this: "If you don't have anything nice to say, don't say it." While this is a good lesson on self-restraint, it does not always hold true for scholarship applications. In general, it is not a good idea to leave any area blank. You don't need to fill the entire space, but you should make an effort to list something in every section. However, before you try to explain how the handmade certificate that your mom presented you for being Offspring of the Year qualifies as an "award," realize that there are limits. If you've never held a job, don't list anything under work experience. If, however, you painted your grandmother's house one summer and got paid for it, you might consider listing it if you don't have any other options.

Perfect every sentence. Succinct and terse, scholarship application forms bear the well-earned reputation for having less space than you need. Often offering only a page or less, scholarship and award forms leave little room for much more than just the facts. As you are completing your applications, remember to abbreviate where appropriate and keep your sentences short. Often judges are scanning the application form. If they want an essay, they will ask for one. However, you do not want to take instructions so literally that you miss their intent. For instance, if the instructions say to list your awards, don't feel like you can't add explanation if you need to. And, as always, be selective in what you list. If you have three great awards, it is better to use your space to list those three with short explanations rather than cram in all 15 awards that you've won in your life. (No argument can be made for the timeliness of your Perfect Attendance Award from kindergarten.) You are trying to present the most relevant information that shows the scholarship judges why you deserve their money. Use the space to explain how each award, job or activity relates to the scholarship.

Also, feel free to interpret some instructions. Work experience does not have to be limited to traditional jobs. Maybe you started your own freelance design business or cut lawns on the weekends—those count! The same goes for leadership positions. Who said that leadership has to be an elected position within an organization? Just be sure to explain the entry if the relationship is not totally clear. Here's an example:

```
Volunteer Wilderness Guide. Led clients through seven-day
trek in Catskills. Responsible for all aspects of the trip
including group safety.
```

Always remember that the application is you. A scholarship application is more than a piece of paper. In the eyes of the scholarship judges, it is *you*. It may not be fair, but in many cases the application is the only thing that the judges will have as a measurement standard. The last thing you want to be is a dry list of academic and extracurricular achievements. You are a living, breathing person. Throughout the application, take every opportunity—no matter how small—to show the judges who you really are. Use descriptions and vocabulary that reveal your passion and commitment. Always remember that the application is a reflection of you.

Step 5   Separate Yourself from the Competition

Think of the scholarship competition as a reverse police lineup where you want to stand out and be picked by the people behind the one-way mirror. You want the judge to say without hesitation, "That's the one!" The only way this will happen is if your application is noticed and doesn't get lost in the stack. One of the best ways to accomplish this is to know what you're up against—in other words, think about who else will be in the lineup with you.

Try to anticipate your competition—even if it's just an educated guess. Depending on to whom the scholarship is offered, you may have a limited or broad pool of competitors. If the award is confined to your school, you may know everyone who will enter on a first-name basis. If it's national, all you may know is that all the applicants have a similar interest in a broad field. For a medical scholarship, for instance, the applicants might be students interested in becoming doctors or nurses. More important than the scope of the competition is the type of students who will apply. One of the biggest challenges in any competition is to break away from the pack. If 500 pre-med students are applying for a $10,000 scholarship from a medical association, you need to make sure that your application stands out from those of the 499 other applicants. If you are lucky, you may have done something that few have done. (Inventing a new vaccine in your spare time would certainly set you apart!) Unfortunately, most of us will have to distinguish ourselves in more subtle ways, such as through the explanation of our activities and accomplishments.

Say you are applying for a scholarship given by a national medical association that seeks to promote the medical sciences. It just so happens that you are considering a pre-med major and you have interned at a local hospital. If you hadn't read this book, you might have listed under activities something like this entry:

```
Summer Internship at Beth Israel Children's Hospital.
```

But you did read this book! So you know that this is a great activity to elaborate on since it demonstrates your commitment to medicine and shows that you truly are interested in entering the medical field. You also know that you need to stand out from the competition; and as great as this activity is, you know that a lot of other applicants also will have volunteered at hospitals. So instead of simply listing the internship, you add detail to make the experience more unique. You could write it this way:

```
Summer Internship at Beth Israel Children's Hospital; assisted with clinical trial of new allergy medication.
```

This description is much more unique and memorable. By providing details, you can illustrate to the judges how your volunteer work is different from that of other students. Remember that you can add short descriptions in most applications even if the instructions do not explicitly ask for them.

If you can anticipate who your competition will be and what they might write in their applications, you will be able to find a way to go one step further to distinguish yourself from the crowd. Even the simple act of adding a one-sentence description to an activity can make the difference between standing out or being overlooked.

Now that you know the five steps to insure that your application is a winner, here is our Top Ten list of application form do's and don'ts which will serve as a final reminder of how to create that stunning application!

Be a Neat Freak

You may have dirty laundry strewn across your room and a pile of papers large enough to be classified as its own life form, but you don't want the scholarship judges to know that. When it comes to applications, neatness does count. We would not ordinarily be neatness zealots—we admit to having our own mountains of life-imbided papers—but submitting an application with globs of correction fluid, scratched out words or illegible hieroglyphics will severely diminish your message. Think how much less impressive the Mona Lisa would be if da Vinci had painted it on a dirty old bed sheet. You may have the most incredible thoughts to convey in your applications, but if your form is filled with errors, none of it will matter. In a sea of hundreds and even thousands of other applications, you don't want yours to be penalized by sloppy presentation.

Top Ten Application Do's and Don'ts

With money on the table, it's much better to learn from others' successes and mistakes before you risk your own fortunes. From interviews with students and scholarship judges and firsthand experience reviewing scholarship applications, we've developed our Top Ten list of scholarship application do's and don'ts. Let's shed the negative energy first and start with the don'ts.

Don'ts

1. DON'T prioritize quantity over quality. It's not the quantity of your accomplishments that is important. It's the quality of your contributions.

2. DON'T stretch the truth. Tall tales are prohibited.

3. DON'T squeeze to the point of illegibility. Scholarship applications afford minimal space. It's impossible to fit in everything that you want to say. Don't try by sacrificing legibility.

4. DON'T write when you have nothing to say. If you don't have something meaningful to present, leave it blank.

5. DON'T create white-out globs. If it's that sloppy, start over.

6. DON'T procrastinate. Don't think you can finish your applications the night before they're due.

7. DON'T settle for less than perfect. You can have imperfections. Just don't let the selection committee know.

8. DON'T miss deadlines. No matter the reason, if you miss the deadline, you won't win the scholarship.

9. DON'T turn in incomplete applications. Make sure your application is finished before sending it.

10. DON'T underestimate what you can convey. Scholarship applications may appear to be short and simple. Don't undervalue them. In a small space, you can create a powerful story of why you should win.

And now the good stuff.

Do's

1. DO understand the scholarship's mission. Know why they're giving out the dough.

2. DO remember who your audience is. You need to address animal rights activists and retired dentists differently.

3. DO show how you fit with the scholarship's mission. You're not going to win unless you have what the selection committee wants.

4. DO be proud of your accomplishments. Don't be afraid to brag.

5. DO focus on leadership and contributions. Make your contributions known.

6. DO make your application stand out.

7. DO practice to make sure everything fits. Make practice copies of the original form before you begin filling it out. Then use your spare copies for trial and error.

8. DO get editors. They'll help you create the best, error-free applications you can.

9. DO include a resume. Whether they ask for it or not, make sure you include a tailored scholarship resume. See the next chapter for how to create a great resume.

10. DO make copies of your finished applications for reference. Save them for next year when you do this all over again.

Double Check Your App

Once you've completed your applications, check and double-check for accuracy. Look at every line and every question to make sure you've filled out all the information that is requested on the form. Make sure you have someone else take a look at your application. A second set of eyes may catch mistakes that you invariably will miss. Remember that presentation affects how scholarship judges view applications. You want to convey that you are serious about winning the scholarship by submitting an application that is complete and error-free.

Finally, before handing your applications off to the post office, make application twins. Photocopy all your application materials. If for some reason your scholarship form is lost in the mail, you have a copy you can resend. Plus, by saving this year's applications, you have recycling possibilities (especially the essays: you'll see what we mean in Chapter 4!) and a great starting place for next year's scholarships.

How to Write a Winning Scholarship Essay

The Essay Can Make or Break Your Chances of Winning

Here's a situation repeated a million times each year. A student receives a scholarship application and quickly glances over the form. It looks pretty straightforward, so it's tossed into the "to do" pile. The day before it's due, the student finally gets around to filling it out. Breezing through the application form, the student is about to celebrate finishing when he or she encounters the final requirement. It reads as follows:

In 1894 Donald VonLudwig came to America with 10 cents in his pocket and within a decade built an empire. Write an 800-word essay on how you would incorporate the lessons of VonLudwig's success into your life.

Uh, oh. Life just got harder. Meet the dreaded scholarship essay. The hypothetical student described above—the one we are poking fun at—was one of us! After a few experiences like this one, (which were usually accompanied by all night writing sessions), we learned to work on the essay first and never underestimate how much time it requires.

For most scholarship competitions, it is the essay that will make or break your chances of winning. Why? Because the essay offers you the best chance to show the scholarship judges why you deserve to win. While your application form will get you to the semifinals, it is the essay that will carry you into the winner's circle.

Since the essay is so important, you must not assume that you can crank out a quality essay the night before it's due. A quality essay will take both time and effort. In this chapter we will take you step by step through the process of crafting a winning essay—don't worry, it's easier than you may have imagined. Plus, you will read examples of essays that won thousands of dollars in scholarships. From these, you can see firsthand how the strategies presented in this chapter are actually put to use in real life.

All Essays Ask the Same Underlying Question

Regardless of the specific wording, the underlying question for almost all essay questions is the same: "Why do you deserve to win?" (Your answer should *not* be, "Because I need the money!")

Think about these questions: The Future Teachers of America scholarship asks you to write about the "future of education". The Veterans of Foreign Wars asks you to define "patriotism". The National Sculpture Society asks you to "describe your extracurricular passions". Believe it or not, all these seemingly different questions are asking for the same answer: Why do you deserve to win our money?

Your answers to each must address this underlying question. When writing the Future Teachers of America essay, you can discuss the general state of education and quote a few facts and figures, but you'd better be sure to include how you personally fit into the future of education. If you are planning to be a teacher, you might elaborate on how you will contribute to shaping students' lives. Similarly use the topic of patriotism to impress the VFW judges with not only what you perceive patriotism to be but also how you have actually acted upon those beliefs. And if you answer the National Sculpture Society question with an essay on how much you love to play the guitar, then you really don't deserve to win!

Six Steps to Writing a Winning Scholarship Essay

By now you should be tired of hearing us repeat our mantra of knowing the purpose of the scholarship. You have used this to guide your selection of those scholarships you are most likely to win and how to complete the application form for them. It shouldn't surprise you that you must also use it to guide your essay. Remember, when you are writing about why you deserve to win, the answer and all the examples that you use should show how you fulfill that mission of the scholarship. With this in mind, let's begin our six steps to writing a winning scholarship essay.

Step 1   Find the Right Topic and Approach

You will encounter two types of essay questions. The first asks you to write about a specific topic. For example, "Why is it important to protect our natural environment?" The second type of question gives you a very broad topic such as, "Tell us about yourself." In the first case you don't need to think about a topic, but you do need to develop an approach to answering the question. In the latter you need to come up with both a topic and an approach. Let's look at how this is done, starting with the more difficult task of finding a topic.

Finding a Topic

Let's imagine that you are applying for a scholarship that presents an essay question so broad that you can essentially choose your own topic. To get the ideas flowing, you should use that idea-generating technique you learned in fifth grade—brainstorming. Take out a notebook or start a new file on your computer and just start listing possible topics and themes. Ask yourself questions like these:

- What was a significant event in my life?

- What teacher, relative or friend has influenced who I am?

- What have I learned from my experiences?

- What are my goals for the future?

- Where will I be ten years from now?

- What motivates me to achieve my goals?

When brainstorming, don't be critical of the topics you unearth—just let the creativity flow. Ask parents and friends for suggestions.

Once you have a list of topics, you can start to eliminate those that don't help you answer the question of why you deserve to win. For example, if you apply to a scholarship that rewards public service, you would not want to write about the time you got lost in the woods for three days and had to survive on a single candy bar and wild roots. While that might make an interesting and exciting essay, it does not show the scholarship judges why you are the epitome of public service. This topic, however, may come in handy when you need to write an essay for a scholarship based on character or leadership or why you love Snickers bars.

After you whittle down your list to a few topics that will help show why you deserve to win this particular scholarship, then choose the topic that is the most interesting to you or that you care about the most. It seems self-evident, but surprisingly many students do not select topics that excite them. Why is it important to pick a topic that you are passionate about? Because if you truly like your topic, you will write a better essay. In fact, your enthusiasm and excitement will naturally permeate your writing, which will make it interesting and memorable. It's so much easier to stay motivated writing about something you enjoy rather than something you find boring.

How to Develop a Unique Approach

Whether you have to think of a topic yourself or one is given to you, the next task is to figure out how you are going to approach it. For any given topic there are probably a hundred ways you could address the subject matter in an essay. Most topics are also way too large to completely cover in an 800- to 1,000-word essay, so you are going to have to narrow it down and only share a small part of the larger story. All this involves coming up with an approach to what you will present in your essay—an approach that must convince the judges that you deserve to win their money.

The Ultimate
Scholarship Book
2010

Let's take a look at writing about the traumatic experience of being lost in the woods for three days. You choose this topic since the scholarship wants to reward students with strong character and leadership and this is an experience that you believe shows both. But how do you write about it? If you just retell the story of the ordeal, it will not help the judges see why such an experience reveals the quality of your character or leadership. You need to dig deeper and think about how this experience revealed your strengths. To do this, ask yourself questions like these:

- What does this topic reveal about me?

- How has my life been changed by this experience?

- Why did I do what I did?

- What is the lesson that I learned from this experience?

- What aspect of this topic is most important to making my point?

In thinking about your experience alone in the woods, you may realize that on the second day you came close to breaking down and losing all hope of being rescued. This was the critical point where you had to make a decision to give up or push forward. You decide to focus your essay only on this small sliver of time, what went through your mind and how you decided that you were not going to give up. The details of how you got lost and of your eventual rescue would be unimportant and may be mentioned in only a sentence or two. Focusing your essay on just the second day—and more particularly on how you were able to conquer your fears and not lose hope—would clearly demonstrate to the judges that even under extreme pressure, your true character was revealed. Since you also need to address the leadership aspect, you decide to focus on how you took charge of your fears on the second day. To do this, your essay will describe specific actions you took to lead yourself successfully through this ordeal.

Finding the right approach is just as important as finding the right topic. This is especially true if you answer a question that provides a specific topic. With every scholarship applicant writing about the same topic, you need to be sure that your approach persuasively shows the judges why you deserve to win more than anyone else.

Step 2   Share a Slice of Life

Now that you have a topic and an idea for your approach, you need to decide how you are going to convey your message on paper. Keep in mind that scholarship judges are going to read hundreds if not thousands of essays. Often the essays will be on similar topics, particularly if the topic was given in the scholarship application. Therefore, you need to make sure that your writing is original. The best way to do this is to share a "slice of your life" in the essay.

Imagine that you are writing about your summer trip to Europe. Travel is a very common topic. If you decide to write about how your trip made you realize people from around the world are really quite similar, then you run the real risk of sounding just like every other travel essay. The same would be true for writing about sports. If you tell the story of how your team rallied and came from behind to win the game, you can be sure that it will sound like many other essays about sports. To make sure your essay is original, you need to share a "slice of life." Find one incident that happened during your travels or pick one particular moment in the game and use that to make your point. By focusing on a single day, hour or moment, you greatly reduce your chances of having an essay that sounds like everyone else's. Plus, essays that share a slice of life are usually a lot more interesting and memorable.

Let's look at an example. What if you choose to write about how your mom has been your role model? Moms are one of the most popular role models for essays (and they should be, considering the pain of childbirth). How do you make your mom distinct from all the other applicants writing about their moms? Go ahead and take a moment to think about your mom. Be very specific. Can you find one character trait or incident that really influenced you? Let's say your mom has an obsession with collecting porcelain figurines and this passion led to you becoming interested in collecting baseball cards. Because of this, you are now considering a career in sports management. Now we have something! Imagine that first day when you realized how much your mom loved collecting figurines. Maybe you even bought her one as a present and now she cherishes it above all others. Perhaps it was that moment that jump-started your love for baseball cards, which has now developed into a full blown obsession with sports to the point that you intend to make it a career. You've just succeeded in turning a very popular topic—Mom—into an entirely original essay by finding that slice of life. No two people share the exact same slice of life, so by finding one to share, you are almost always guaranteed to have an original essay.

Want another example? Let's set the stage. Imagine that you are applying to a scholarship for students who major in psychology. The question posed on the application is this: "Tell us about an influential person who inspired you to pursue psychology." As you brainstorm, you list the authors of books you've read and some professors whose classes you have enjoyed. But how many students will be writing about these same people? You could even wager money that every other essay will be about Freud!

As you brainstorm, you recall the worst fight you have ever had with your best friend Susan. As you think about this fight that nearly destroyed a 10-year friendship, you realize that it was one of the first times you applied classroom knowledge to a real life experience. In analyzing the fight, you realize that those psychology principles you studied have practical applications beyond the textbook. So for your essay you decide to write about the fight and how it made you even more committed than ever to become a psychology major.

You don't have to look far to find originality. We all have experiences that are unique to us. Even common experiences can be made original, depending on how you approach them. So don't exclude a topic just because it is common.

By spending some time thinking about how you will write about it, you may be surprised at how original it could be.

Step 3   Stop Thinking, Start Writing

The most challenging part of writing a scholarship essay is getting started. Our advice: Just start writing. The first words you put down on paper may not be brilliant, but don't worry. You can always return to edit your work. It's easier to edit words you've already written than words that don't exist.

Do you think you have a bad case of writer's block? If so, the cure may surprise you. The best cure for writer's block is to just start writing!

We all have different writing styles, but certain points should be kept in mind as you are writing something that is focused on winning over a scholarship committee. Think about these things as you craft that winning essay:

Write for the Scholarship Judges. Let's pretend you're a stand-up comedian who has two performances booked: one at the trendiest club in town where all cool college students congregate and the other at a retirement home. As a skilled comedian, you would prepare different material aimed at the different audiences. The college crowd would be able to relate to jokes about relationships and dating, while your jokes about dentures and arthritis would probably—and this is a hunch—go over better with the senior citizens. The same goes for writing your essays. Since many are given by specialized organizations or for specific purposes, you need to write an essay that is appropriate for the audience. Think about who is going to read your essay. Is your audience natural science professors, circus performers or used car salesmen? Write your essay so it appeals to that audience. This should guide not only your selection of topics but also your word choice, language and tone.

Be Yourself. While you want to present yourself in a way that attracts the attention of the scholarship judges, you don't want to portray yourself as someone you are not. It's okay to present selected highlights from your life that fit with the award, but it's not ethical to exaggerate or outright lie. If you apply for a scholarship to promote the protection of animals, don't write about your deep compassion for helping animals when you've never ventured closer than 10 feet to one because of your allergies. Feel comfortable about everything you write, and don't go overboard trying to mold yourself into being the student you think the scholarship judges want to read about. If you've done your job of picking scholarships that match you best, you already know that you are a good fit. Your task in the essay is to demonstrate this to the judges.

Personalize Your Essay. Think of the scholarship judges as an audience that has come to see your Broadway show. You are the star. To keep them satisfied, give them what they want. In other words, the scholarship judges want to know about your life and experiences. When you write your essay, write about what has happened to you personally or about how you personally have been affected by something. If you are writing about drug abuse for an essay about a problem that faces college students today, do more than recite the latest national drug use statistics and the benefits of drug rehabilitation programs. Otherwise, your essay may be informative, but it won't be interesting. Instead, write about how a friend nearly overdosed on drugs, how others tried to pressure you into trying drugs or about your volunteer work at a rehabilitation clinic. Instantly, your essay will be more interesting and memorable. Plus, the judges really do want to learn more about you, and the only way for them to do this is if you share something about yourself in your essay.

Make Sure You Have a Point. Try this exercise: See if you can encapsulate the point of your essay into a single sentence. If you can't, you don't have a main point. So, you'd better get one! You may think this is obvious, but many students' essays don't have a main point. Use that most basic lesson from Composition 101: Have a thesis statement that states the main point of your essay. Let's say you are writing about growing up in the country. You might structure your essay around the idea that growing up in the country gave you a strong work ethic. This is the essay's main point. You can describe all the flat land and brush you like, but unless these descriptions help to support your point, you don't have a quality essay.

Support Your Statement. Once you put your main point out there, you can't abandon it. Like a baby learning to walk, you have to support your thesis statement because it can't stand on its own. This means you have to provide reasons why your statement is true. You can do this by giving detailed and vivid examples from your personal experiences and accomplishments.

Use Examples and Illustrations. When a reader can visualize what you are writing, it helps to make an impression. Anecdotes and stories accomplish this very effectively. Examples and illustrations also make your ideas clearer. If you want to be a doctor, explain how you became interested in becoming one. You might describe the impact of getting a stethoscope from your father when you were a child. Or maybe you can write about your first day volunteering at the hospital. Examples help readers picture what you are saying and even relate to your experiences. The scholarship judge may have never volunteered at a hospital; but by reading your example, that judge can easily understand how such an experience could be so influential. The one danger of examples is that you need to be sure to keep them concise. It is often too easy to write a long and detailed example when only a few sentences are sufficient. Remember, in an example you are not retelling an entire story but just pulling out a few highlights to illustrate the point you are trying to make.

Show Activity. If you were forced to sit in an empty room with nothing but a bare wall to stare at, you would probably get bored pretty quickly. The same goes for an essay. Don't force the scholarship judges to read an essay that does nothing. Your essay needs activity and movement to bring it to life. This may consist of dialogue, action, stories and thoughts. The last thing you want to do is bore your readers. With action, you won't have to worry about that!

Highlight Your Growth. You may not have grown an inch since seventh grade, but scholarship judges will look for your growth in other ways. They want to see evidence of emotional and intellectual growth, what your strengths are and how you have developed them. Strengths may include—but certainly aren't limited to—mastery of an academic course, musical talent, a desire to help others, athletic ability, leadership of a group and more. Overcoming adversity or facing a challenge may also demonstrate your growth.

Be Positive. You don't need to break out the pompoms and do a cheer, but you need to convey a positive attitude in your essay. Scholarship committees want to see optimism, excitement and confidence. They prefer not to read essays that are overly pessimistic, antagonistic or critical. This doesn't mean that you have to put a happy spin on every word written or that you can't write about a serious topic or problem. For example, if you were a judge reading the following essays about the very serious topic of teen pregnancy, to which author's education fund would you rather make a contribution?

Thesis 1:
We could reduce the number of pregnant teens if we shifted our efforts away from scare tactics to providing responsible sex education combined with frank discussions regarding the responsibilities of caring for a child.

Thesis 2:
Teen pregnancy is incurable. Teenagers will always act irresponsibly and it would be futile for us to believe that we can control this behavior.

Scholarship committees favor authors who not only recognize problems but also present potential solutions. Leave being pessimistic to adults. You are young, with your entire future ahead of you. Your optimism is what makes you so exciting and why organizations want to give you money to pursue your passion for changing the world. Don't shy away from this opportunity.

Be Concise. The scholarship essay may not have the strict limits of a college admission essay, but that does not give you a license to be verbose. Keep your essay tight, focused and within the recommended length of the scholarship guidelines. If no parameters are given, one or two pages should suffice. You certainly want the readers to get through the entirety of your masterpiece. Remember that most scholarship selection committees are composed of volunteers who are under no obligation to read your entire essay. Make your main points quickly and keep your essay as brief and to the point as possible.

Step 4   Don't Neglect Your Introduction and Conclusion

Studies have found that the most important parts of a speech are the first and last minutes. In between, listeners fade in and out rather than constantly pay attention. It is the introduction and conclusion that leave a lasting impact. This holds true for scholarship essays as well. You need to have a memorable introduction and conclusion. If you don't, the readers may not make it past your introductory paragraph or they may discount your quality essay after reading a lackluster ending. Spend extra time making sure these two parts deliver the message you want. Here are some tips to create knockout introductions and conclusions:

For Introductions

Create action or movement. Think of the introduction as the high-speed car chase at the beginning of a movie that catches the audience's attention.

Pose a question. Questions draw the readers' attention for two reasons. First, they think about how they would answer the query as you have posed it. Second, they are curious to see how you will answer or present solutions to the question in your essay.

Describe. If you can create a vivid image for readers, they will be more likely to want to read on.

For Conclusions

Be thoughtful. Your conclusion should make the second most powerful statement in your essay because this is what your readers will remember. (The most powerful statement should be in your introduction.)

Leave a parting thought. The scholarship committee members have already read your essay (we hope), so you don't need to rehash what you have already said. It's okay to summarize in one sentence, but you want to do more than just "wrap it up". You have one final opportunity to make an impression, so add a parting thought. This should be one last observation or idea that ties into the main point of your essay.

Don't be too quick to end. Too many students tack on a meaningless conclusion or even worse, don't have one at all. Have a decent conclusion that goes with the rest of your essay. Never end your essay with the two words, "The End."

Step 5   Find Editors

Despite what you may think, you're not infallible. Stop gasping—it's true. This means it's important to get someone else to edit your work. Roommates, friends, family members, teachers, professors or advisors make great editors. When you get another person to read your essay, he or she will find errors that eluded you, as well as parts that are unclear to someone reading your essay for the first time. Ask your editors to make sure your ideas are clear, that you answer the question appropriately and that your essay is interesting. Take their suggestions seriously. The more input you get from others and the more times you rewrite your work, the better.

You want your essay to be like silk—smooth and elegant. When you read your work, make sure the connections between ideas are logical and the flow of your writing is understandable. (This is where editors can be extremely helpful.) Also check that you have not included any unnecessary details that might obscure the main point of your essay. Be careful to include any information that is vital to your thesis. Your goal is to produce an essay with clear points and supporting examples that logically flow together.

You also want to make sure that your spelling and grammar are perfect. Again, the best way to do this is to have someone else read your work. If you don't have time to ask someone, then do it yourself—but do it carefully. Read your essay at least once with the sole purpose of looking for spelling and grammatical mistakes. (Your computer's spell check is not 100 percent reliable and won't catch when you accidentally describe how you bake bread with one cup of "flower" instead of "flour.") Try reading your work out loud to listen for grammatical mistakes.

Step 6   Recycle Your Essays

This has no relation to aluminum cans or newspapers. In this case recycling means reusing essays you have written for college applications, classes or even other scholarships. Because colleges and scholarship committees usually ask very broad questions, this is generally doable and saves you a tremendous amount of time. Later in this chapter you will read an example essay. You may be surprised to learn that the author recycled her essay with minimal changes to answer such differing questions as these: "Tell us about one of your dreams," "What is something you believe in strongly?" and "What past experience continues to influence you today?"

However, be careful not to recycle an essay when it just doesn't fit. It's better to spend the extra time to write an appropriate essay than to submit one that doesn't match the scholarship or answer the question.

Seven Sins of the Scholarship Essay

Instead of writing an essay, one student placed the sheet of paper on the floor and tap danced on it. She then wrote that she hoped the scuff marks on the paper were evidence of her enthusiasm. In the judges' eyes, this was a silly stunt and, of course, her application was sent to the rejection pile. While you may not make such an egregious error, there are common mistakes that you need to avoid. Most of these lessons were learned the hard way—through actual experience.

1. DON'T Write a Sob Story

Everyone who applies for a scholarship needs money. Many have overcome obstacles and personal hardships. However, few scholarships are designed to reward students based on the "quantity" of hardships. Scholarship judges are not looking to give their money to those who have suffered the most. On the contrary, they want to give money to students who came up with a plan to succeed despite an obstacle. Therefore, if you are writing about the hardships you have faced, be sure that you spend as much time, if not more, describing how you have overcome or plan to rise above those challenges.

2. DON'T Use the Shotgun Approach

A common mistake is to write one essay and submit it without any changes to dozens of scholarships—hoping that maybe one will be a winner. While we do recommend that you recycle your essays, you should not just photocopy your essays and blast them out to every scholarship committee. This simply does not work. Unless the scholarships have identical questions, missions and goals, your essay cannot be reused verbatim. Spend the time to craft an essay for each scholarship, and you will win more than if you write just one and blindly send it off to many awards.

3. DON'T Be Afraid to Get Words on Paper

One common cause of writer's block is the fear of beginning. When you sit down to write, don't be afraid to write a draft, or even ideas for a draft, that are not perfect. You will have time to revise your work. What you want to do is get words on paper. They can be wonderfully intelligent words or they can be vague concepts. The point is that you should just write. Too many students wait until the last minute and get stuck at the starting line.

4. DON'T Try to Be Someone Else

Since you want to be the one the scholarship judges are seeking to reward with money, you need to highlight achievements and strengths that match the criteria of the scholarship. But you don't want to lie about yourself or try to be someone you are not. Besides being dishonest, the scholarship judges will probably pick up on your affectation and hold it against you.

5. DON'T Try to Impress with Feats of Literary Gymnastics

You won't get any bonus points for overusing clichés, quotes or words you don't understand. Too many students think that quotes and clichés will impress scholarship judges; but unless they are used sparingly and appropriately, they will win you no favors. (Remember that quotes and clichés are not your words and are therefore not original.) The same goes for overusing the thesaurus.

Do experiment with words that are less familiar to you, but do not make the thesaurus your co-author. It's better to use simple words correctly than to make blunders with complicated ones.

6. DON'T Stray Too Far from the Topic

A mistake that many students make is that they don't actually answer the question. This is especially true with recycled essays. Make sure that your essays, whether written from scratch or recycled from others, address the question asked.

7. DON'T Write Your Stats

A common mistake is to repeat your statistics from your application form. Often these essays begin with "My name is" and go on to list classes, GPAs and extracurricular activities. All this information is found in your application. On top of that, it's boring. If you are going to write about a class or activity, make it interesting by focusing on a specific class or activity.

Example Winning Scholarship Essays

It's one thing to study the theory behind the pheromones of love, but it is entirely a different thing to experience the euphoria, quickened heartbeat and walking-on-clouds feeling that goes with love. In a similar way, you have seen the theory behind writing a powerful scholarship essay. It is now time to see this theory in action.

The following two essays were written by students who won scholarships. In each essay you will see how winning principles are put to use. The results are essays that inspire, provoke and most important, win money. As with any example essay, please remember that this is not necessarily the way your essay should be written. Use these sample essays as illustrations of how a good essay might look. Your essay will naturally be different and unique to your own style and personality.

Winning Essay: My Two Dads

This essay was written by Gregory James Yee, a graduate of Whitney High School in Cerritos, California. Although Gregory is a student at Stanford University, he wrote this essay as part of his application to the University of Southern California. Besides garnering an acceptance to USC, this essay also earned him a $7,500 per year Trustee Scholarship. Remember that many colleges use your college application to automatically consider you for scholarships they offer.

The topic of the essay is Gregory's musical talent, which was discovered early in his life. At the age of two, he could hum *The Star-Spangled Banner* in perfect rhythm and pitch; and at age four, he began piano lessons. Throughout his 15 years of lessons, he won numerous awards, including the Raissa Tselentis Award given to one student nationwide for outstanding performance in the Advanced Bach category of the National Guild Audition. He is also a composer.

My Two Dads

I have two fathers. My first and biological father is the one who taught me how to drive a car, throw a baseball and find the area under a curve using integral calculus, among the innumerable other common duties of a good dad. He has been there for me through the ups of my successful piano career and the downs of my first breakup, and has always offered his insightful hand of guidance. My second father is who I connect with on a different level; he is the only person I know who thinks like I do. My second dad is my music composition teacher, Tony Fox, and he shares the one passion that has been a part of my life since the age of two: music.

Tony is a hardworking professor who can spend hours illustrating the meaning of a particular chord in a famous classical composition or ease an extraordinarily stressful situation with his colorful wit. He may appear intimidating to a new student at USC as the Assistant Band Director, but once someone mentions music, there is no one more adept, more creative or more dedicated to making music for the world to hear than Tony.

Tony has touched my life in a way few people have experienced. At my lessons with him, I bring compositions I am in the progress of perfecting, and with a few words of his guidance, I can almost see the changes needed before he mentions them. Almost instantly after I ask a question - such as which chord progression works best at a certain point in the music or why a certain counter melody sounds so beautiful—we agree on what is best for the music. It is almost as if we know what the other is thinking and merely state aloud our thoughts just in case one or the other is caught off guard. It is truly rare to find two people who agree with each other on what it is exactly that makes compositions aesthetically pleasing. Last year when I was working on a composition, I ran into a discouraging roadblock that could have delayed my progress significantly. No one in my family and none of my friends could help.

However, as soon as I shared the piece with Tony, he made some suggestions and together we made the necessary amendments to the music. The result was a finished project, a beautiful mosaic of our collective design, and it was debuted last year by my high school wind ensemble. When I first heard my music performed, I thought back to the hours I had spent tinkering at my piano and Tony's thoughtful guidance. This is how Tony and I relate. It's a common frequency upon which the most advanced radio cannot even begin to comprehend.

Tony has filled in areas of my life where few people, including my real father, could understand. He is the teacher of lessons big and small, from looking into the eyes of those whose hands I shake to recognizing that time is the most valuable gift one can give or receive. Whereas many of my peers have only one father, I have been fortunate enough to have two of them.

Why This Essay Won

An accomplished musician like Gregory could have written an essay that was simply a retelling of all the musical awards he had won. Instead, Gregory gives insight into what music means to him and takes us into his mind to see the creative and learning process at work. Writing about what he goes through to create a composition allows even those of us who are tone deaf to experience vicariously what it is like to create music.

Notice how Gregory uses powerful imagery to show us how he interacts with his music teacher and overcomes difficulties while composing. Gregory also subtly includes some of his most important musical accomplishments. Although he listed many of his awards in his application, this essay takes us beyond those achievements and really lets us see the wonderful person behind those awards.

Winning Essay: Leadership

Donald H. Matsuda, Jr. is the kind of person who doesn't just act. He inspires others to act as well. In his application for the Truman Scholarship, Donald shared how he directed community leaders and health professionals to start a series of health insurance drives. This is one of the essays that he wrote to become one of 80 Truman Scholars in the country.

From Sacramento and a graduate of Stanford University, Donald also founded the San Mateo Children's Health Insurance Program, directed the United Students for Veterans' Health and founded the Nepal Pediatric Clinical Internship.

Leadership

A few years ago, I saw a shocking headline on the front page of the New York Times that read: "Forty-Four Million Americans Without Health Insurance." Upon reading the article, I was stunned to discover that one-third of these uninsured Americans were children. Such figures made it clear to me that work needed to be done to remedy this problem, and I was ready to take action.

At this time, I was working at the Health for All Clinic as a public health and community outreach intern, and I decided to approach the director about this problem. He clearly agreed that immediate action needed to be taken to control the growing numbers of America's uninsured. However, he admitted that the clinic did not have the time, energy or the funds to invest in such an ambitious endeavor. I was not discouraged by his response. Instead, I saw this challenge as an opportunity to gain firsthand experience as a change agent in the field of public policy.

After completing extensive research, I discovered a unique program called Healthy Families. The ultimate goal of this government program is to provide low-cost insurance coverage to children who do not qualify for traditional insurance plans. I decided to develop my own project from scratch, proposing to launch a sustainable series of Healthy Families insurance drives at the Health for All Clinic. I applied for funding through the Haas Center for Public Service Fellowship program, and the clinic director signed on as my community partner for the project.

During the next six months, I worked very closely with the clinic staff to organize and plan this series of insurance drives. I recruited various ethnic community leaders and healthcare professionals to help generate support for the program and assembled several advertising campaigns in the surrounding communities. The clinic director and I also developed a workshop on immigrant health to attract more diverse populations to our insurance drives. After holding three Healthy Families drives, the clinic managed to sign up over 150 children for this program. The director was elated by this turnout and established an entire Healthy Families division to build upon the success of this project. Upon completion of this project, I started directing other insurance drives with the hope of improving the health and well-being of America's children.

Why This Essay Won

Donald's essay only scratches the surface of his accomplishments, which is exactly how it should be. Instead of listing every leadership role he has ever had, Donald explains how he created a health care program in his community. He begins with his motivation for starting the program and then recounts the initial skepticism that he faced when he first proposed the idea. Donald's essay describes the various difficulties and ultimate success of his project.

Notice that Donald does not describe a typical leadership role, one in which he was elected as a leader. This is an excellent example of how you can take a project in which you played a significant role and show how it demonstrates your leadership abilities. Remember, leadership is not just an elected position.

Where to Find More Winning Scholarship Essays

We believe that reading real essays is the best way for you to really see what works, and these essays are certainly a start. Unfortunately, we could not include more than two examples in this book. If you want more scholarship essay examples, take a look at our book, *How to Write a Winning Scholarship Essay*. In it you will find 30 additional winning essays from students who tested the waters of many topics and wrote in a variety of styles. Also, take a look at our website, SuperCollege (www.supercollege.com), where we post additional example essays. We think you'll be inspired.

The Scholarship Resume

Write Your Own One-Page Autobiography

If you want to say that your life is a book, then be ready to follow with the analogy that your scholarship resume is the *CliffsNotes* summary. A scholarship resume is your opportunity to tout your greatest achievements and life's accomplishments. The only catch is that you are limited to one page. Some scholarship committees require resumes as a part of the application process so that they can use them to get a quick overview of your achievements. Others don't, but including a resume will always enhance your application.

A scholarship resume is not the same as one that you would use to get a job. It's unlikely that your work experience (if you have any) will be the focus. However, the principles and format are the same. A good resume that scores you a job shows employers that you have the right combination of work experience and skills to be their next hire. Similarly, your scholarship resume should show the committee why you are the most qualified student to win their award.

Think of the scholarship resume as a "cheat sheet" that you give to the judges. By looking at your resume, the judges get a quick overview of your achievements and interests. The resume is not an exhaustive list of everything you have done. It rather highlights and summarizes the most impressive and relevant achievements.

To make sure that it really focuses on the crème de la crème, your resume should fit on a single sheet of paper. This is sometimes harder than it sounds.

Here is the information you need for a scholarship resume:

● **Contact information:** Your vital statistics, including name, address, phone number and email.

- **Education:** Schools you've attended beginning with high school, expected or actual graduation dates.

- **Academic achievements:** Relevant coursework, awards and honors received.

- **Extracurricular experience.** Relevant extracurricular activities, locations and dates of participation, job titles, responsibilities and accomplishments.

- **Work experience:** Where and when you've worked, job titles, responsibilities and accomplishments on the job.

- **Skills and interests:** Additional relevant technical, lingual or other skills or talents that do not fit in the categories above.

Don't worry if your resume presents the same information that's in the application form. Some judges will read only the application or your resume, so it's important your key points are in both. However, in the resume, try to expand on areas that you were not able to cover fully in the application.

Example Resume that Worked

There are many good ways to format a resume. Most important, your resume should be easy to skim and be organized in a logical manner. Here is an example of a well-written scholarship resume. Remember that there are other equally good formats in which to present this information.

Melissa Lee
1000 University Drive
San Francisco, CA 94134
(415) 555-5555
melissa@email.com

Education
University of San Francisco; San Francisco, CA
B.A. candidate in sociology. Expected graduation in 2013.
Honor roll.

Lowell High School; San Francisco, CA
Graduated in 2009 with highest honors. Principal's Honor
Roll, 4 years.

Activities and Awards
SF Educational Project; San Francisco, CA
Program Assistant. Recruited and trained 120 students for
various community service projects in semester-long program.
Managed and evaluated student journals, lesson plans and
program participation.
2007-present.

Lowell High School Newspaper; San Francisco, CA
Editor-In-Chief. Recruited and managed staff of 50. Oversaw
all editorial and business functions.
Newspaper was a finalist for the prestigious Examiner Award
for excellence in student
journalism. 2005-2009.

Evangelical Church; San Francisco, CA
Teacher. Prepared and taught weekly lessons for third grade
Sunday School class. Received dedication to service award
from congregation. 2005-2009.

Asian Dance Troupe; San Francisco, CA
Member. Performed at community functions and special events.
2007-present.

Employment
Palo Alto Daily News; Palo Alto, CA
Editorial Assistant. Researched and wrote eight feature ar-
ticles on such topics as education reform, teen suicide and
summer fashion. Led series of teen-reader response panels.
Summer 2009.

Russian Hill Public Library; San Francisco, CA
Library Page. Received "Page of the Month" Award for outstanding performance. Summers 2007-2008.

Interests
Fluent in Mandarin and HTML. Interests include journal writing, creative writing, photography, swimming and aerobics.

Some points to note about this resume:

- Notice how this resume is concise and very easy to read. By limiting herself to a single page, Melissa makes sure that even if you just scan her resume, you will pick up her key strengths.

- See how each description includes examples of leadership as well as awards or special recognition.

- Melissa conveys the impact of her work by pointing out concrete results (which you should also do on the application form).

- Notice how her description of summer jobs highlights some of her key accomplishments.

- The final section adds a nice balance by describing some of her other hobbies and interests.

Elements of a Powerful Resume

Your resume should be descriptive enough for the judges to understand each item but not so wordy that they can't find what they need. It should be neatly organized and easy to follow. Having reviewed hundreds of resumes, here are some simple strategies that we've developed to help you:

Include only the important information. Remember to incorporate only the most relevant items and use what you know about the scholarship organization to guide how you prioritize what you share in your resume. Only include things that support your fit with the scholarship's mission. For each piece of information, ask yourself these two questions: Will including this aid the selection committee in seeing that I am a match for the award? Is this information necessary to convince them that I should receive the award?

Focus on responsibilities and achievements. In describing your experiences in work and activities, focus on the responsibilities you held and highlight measurable or unique successes such as starting a project, reaching goals or implementing one of your ideas. For example, if you were the treasurer of the Literary Club, you would want to include that you were responsible for managing a $10,000 annual budget.

Demonstrate in your resume how you showed leadership. Leadership could include leading a project or team, instructing others or mentoring your peers. What's more important than your title or where you worked is the quality of your involvement. Explaining your successes and your role as a leader will provide concrete evidence of your contribution.

Be proud. Your resume is your time to shine. Don't be afraid to draw attention to all that you've accomplished. If you played a key role in a project, say so. If you exceeded your goals, advertise it. No one else is going to do your bragging for you.

Use action verbs. When you are describing your achievements, use action verbs such as these: founded, organized, achieved, created, developed, directed and (our personal favorite) initiated.

Don't tell tall stories. On the flip side of being proud is being untruthful. It's important that you describe yourself in the most glowing way possible, but stay connected with the truth. If you developed a new filing system at your job, don't claim that you single-handedly led a corporate revolution. With your complete scholarship application, selection committees can see through a resume that is exaggerated and doesn't match the rest of the application, essay and recommendations.

Get editors. After the hundredth time reading your resume, you'll probably not notice an error that someone reading it for the first time will catch. Get others to read and edit your resume. Editors can let you know if something doesn't make sense, offer you alternative wording and help correct your boo-boos. Some good choices for editors may be teachers or professors, work supervisors or parents. Work supervisors may be especially helpful since part of their job is to review resumes of job applicants. Your school may also offer resume help in the counseling department or career services office.

Avoid creating an eye test. In trying to squeeze all the information onto a single page, don't make your font size so small that the words are illegible. Try to leave space between paragraphs. The judges may have tired, weary eyes from reading all those applications. Don't strain them even more.

Strive for perfection. It's a given that your resume should be error-free. There's no excuse for mistakes on a one-page document that is meant to exemplify your life's work.

Include Your Resume in Every Application

Once you have a resume, include it with every scholarship application. In addition, you should also give it to your recommenders so that they have a "cheat sheet" that highlights your accomplishments when it comes time to write those letters of recommendations. They will no doubt want to mention some of your successes to make their letters on point and personal. Remember, your resume is *you*!

Getting Great Recommendations

Chapter 6

Letters of Recommendation Count

If you need a reason to kiss up to your teachers or professors, here's one: recommendations. Scholarships sometime require that you submit recommendations from teachers, professors, school administrators, employers or others who can vouch for your accomplishments. Scholarship judges use these testaments to get another perspective of your character and accomplishments. Viewed together with your application and essay, the recommendation helps the judges get a more complete picture of who you are. Plus, it's always impressive when someone else extols your virtues.

Many students believe that they have no control over the recommendation part of their application. This isn't true. You actually can have a lot of input regarding the letters that your recommenders write. In this chapter we will explore several ways—all perfectly ethical—to ensure that you get great recommendations.

A recommendation is an important opportunity for someone else to tell scholarship judges why you deserve to win. You may assume that because others do the actual writing, recommendations are completely out of your control. Banish that thought. The secret is to not only pick the right people but to also provide them with all of the information they need to turn out a great letter of recommendation. Many applicants overlook this fact. But not you, right? Armed with superb recommendations, your scholarship application is sure to rise to the top.

Find People to Say Nice Things about You

Your first task is to find recommenders. Unfortunately, Mom, Dad and anyone else related to you is excluded. So, how do you get those recommendations without familial ties to sing your praises?

First, think about all the people in your life who can speak meaningfully about you and your accomplishments. Your list may include teachers, professors, advisors, school administrators, employers, religious leaders, coaches or leaders of organizations and activities in which you are involved. While some scholarships require recommendations from specific people (like a teacher or professor), most are pretty liberal and allow you to select anyone who knows you.

Second, once you have a list of potential recommenders, analyze which of these people could present information about you that best matches the goals of the scholarships.

If you apply for an academic scholarship, you'll want at least one teacher or professor to write a recommendation. If you apply for an athletic scholarship, a coach would be a good choice. Select people who are able to write about the things that are most important to the scholarship judges. A good exercise is to imagine what your potential recommender would write and whether or not this would enhance your case for winning the scholarship.

After considering these two questions, you should be left with only a few people from which to choose. If you can't decide between two equally qualified people, choose the one who knows you the best as a person. For example, if you got A's in three classes and are trying to decide which professor to ask for a recommendation, pick the one who can write *more* than a testament to your academic ability. This is important because a recommendation that contains comments on your character is extremely memorable. Maybe one of the professors knows you well enough to include a few sentences on your drive to succeed or your family background. Ideally, your recommender is able to describe not only your performance in the classroom but also the values and character traits that make you special.

Give Your Recommender the Chance to Say "No"

Once you've selected those you'd like to write your recommendations, ask them to do so—early. A general rule is to allow at least three weeks before the recommendation is due. Explain that you are applying for scholarships and are required to submit recommendations from people who know you and who can comment on some of your achievements.

It's important to ask the person a question like this: "Do you feel comfortable writing a recommendation letter for me?" This allows the person the opportunity to decline your request if he or she doesn't feel comfortable or doesn't have the time. If you get a negative or hesitant response, don't assume that it's because he or she has a low opinion of you. It could simply be that the person doesn't know you well enough or is too busy to write a thoughtful recommendation. It's much better to have the recommender decline to write a letter than to get one that is rushed or not entirely positive. In most cases, however, potential recommenders are flattered and happy to oblige.

Don't Play the Name Game

From being recognized by strangers to getting preferential reservations at the hottest restaurants, there are a lot of perks to being famous. You might think that this special treatment carries over to recommendations, and that scholarship judges will be star-struck by a letter from someone with a fancy title. However, don't assume that just because you ask someone well known to write your recommendations that you are a shoo-in for the scholarship. In fact, you might be surprised to learn that doing so could actually hurt your chances of winning.

So the question is this: "Should I try to find someone famous to write a letter of recommendation for me?" The answer comes down to the principles outlined above. How well does the person know you, and can he or she write about you in a way that presents you as a viable candidate for the scholarship? If the answer is "yes," then by all means ask the person to help you. However, if you don't know the person very well or if what he or she will write could lack a connection to the qualities that the scholarship committee is looking for, it's better to forgo the value of high name recognition and ask someone who can address what's most important in a letter of recommendation.

For example, if you work as a summer intern for your state senator, you may think that a letter from such a political luminary would give your application the star power to set it apart from others with recommendations from mere mortals. However, if you spent more time photocopying or stuffing envelopes than you did developing keen political strategies, and you saw the senator as many times as you have fingers on your left hand, chances are that he or she would have very few meaningful things to say about your performance. "A skilled photocopier" and "brewed a mean cup of coffee" are not compliments you want sent to the scholarship judges.

If you ask someone well known to write your recommendations, make sure that he or she really knows you and can speak about your accomplishments personally and meaningfully. The quality of what is said in the recommendations is much more important than whose signature is at the bottom of the page.

Do the Grunt Work for Your Recommenders

Once you've selected your recommenders, give them everything they need to get the job done. Since they are doing you a favor, make the process as easy as possible for them. This is also where you can most influence what they write and actually direct what accomplishments they highlight. But before we delve into the specifics, here is an overview of what you need to provide each recommender:

Cover letter: This describes the scholarships you are applying for. In the letter, you should list deadlines and give the recommenders direct guidance on what to write. More on this in a bit.

Resume: A resume provides a quick overview of your most important achievements in an easy to follow one-page format. It is also what your recommenders will use as they cite your important achievements.

Recommendation form: Some scholarships provide an actual form that your recommenders need to complete. Fill in the parts that you can, such as your name and address.

Pre-addressed, stamped envelopes: Read the application materials to find out if you need to submit your recommendations separately or with the rest of your application. For letters that are to be mailed separately, provide your recommenders with envelopes that are stamped and have the scholarship's mailing address on them. If you are supposed to submit the letters with your application, provide your recommenders with envelopes on which you have written your name. Many recommenders prefer to write letters that are confidential and that you don't get to read. Once you have everything, place it in a folder or envelope and label it with your recommender's name.

Give Your Recommenders a Script

Because you know yourself better than anyone else, you would probably receive the best recommendations if you sat down and wrote them yourself. Unfortunately, this practice is frowned upon by scholarship judges. Short of writing your own recommendations, you can influence how they turn out by providing your recommenders with detailed descriptions of your accomplishments that can help them decide which aspects of you to highlight in their letters. This is best done through the cover letter that you send to the prospective recommender.

Your cover letter provides your recommenders with all the information that they need to write your recommendations, including details about the scholarships and suggestions for what you'd like the recommendations to address. Since the cover letter also includes other essentials like deadlines, mailing instructions and a thank you, you will not sound as if you are giving orders but rather that you are providing helpful assistance. In fact, your recommenders will appreciate your reminding them what's important and what they should include.

Here are the elements to include in your cover letter:

Details on the scholarships: List the scholarships for which you will use their letters. Give a brief one-paragraph description of the mission of each of the awards and what qualities the scholarship committee seeks. This information will help your recommenders understand which of your qualities are important to convey and who will read the letters.

How you fit the scholarship: This is the most important part of your cover letter because it's your chance to remind your recommenders of your accomplishments and to offer suggestions for what to write. Make sure that you highlight how you match the goals of the scholarships. For example, if you are applying for a scholarship for future teachers, include information about your student teaching experience and the coursework you've taken in education. Leave out the fact that you were on the tennis team.

Deadlines: Inform your recommenders of how long they have to compose the letters. If time permits, ask them to mail the letters a week before the actual deadlines.

What to do with the letters when they're done: Give your recommenders instructions about what to do with the completed letters. You may want to offer to pick them up, or you might explain that you have included addressed, stamped envelopes so that the letters can be mailed.

Thank you: Recommendations may take several hours to complete, and your recommenders are very busy people. Don't forget to say thank you in advance for writing you a great letter of recommendation.

To illustrate the power of a good cover letter, read the example on the following page as if you were a recommender. Remember that this is only one example and your cover letter will naturally be different. However, regardless of your individual writing style, your cover letter should include the same points as the following example.

**Some notes about
this cover letter:**

- Beth describes
  each scholarship
  she is applying
  for, its goal and
  deadline, and
  why she feels she
  is a match for
  the award.

- The heart of the
  cover letter is
  here, where Beth
  gives a quick
  summary of infor-
  mation she sug-
  gests her profes-
  sor include in the
  letter.

- Beth provides in-
  structions about
  what to do with
  the letters when
  completed.

- This is a well-writ-
  ten cover letter that is brief
  and easy to
  understand.

Dear Dr. Louis,

Thank you again for writing my scholarship recommendations. I want to do my best to be competitive for these awards. They are very important for my family as they will help me to pay for my education. Here are the scholarships I am applying for:

SuperCollege.com Scholarship Deadline: July 31
This is a national scholarship based on academic and non-academic achievement, including extracurricular activities and honors. I believe I'm a match for this scholarship because of my commitment to academics (I currently have a 3.85 grade point average) and because of the volunteer work I do with the Youth Literacy Project and the PLUS program.

Quill & Scroll Scholarship Deadline: April 20
This scholarship is for students who want to pursue a career in journalism. As you know, I am an editor for our school newspaper, contributing a column each week on issues that affect our student body. Journalism is the field I want to enter after graduation.

Community Scholarship Deadline: May 5
This scholarship is for students who have given back to their communities through public service. I have always been committed to public service. Outside of class, I not only formed the Youth Literacy Project but have also volunteered with the PLUS program.

To help you with your recommendation, I've enclosed a resume. Also, here are some highlights of specific accomplishments that I was hoping you might comment on in your letter:

* The essay I wrote for your class that won the Young Hemingway competition

* How I formed the Youth Literacy Project with you as the project's advisor

* My three years of volunteer work with the PLUS program

* The weekly column I've written for the newspaper on school issues

After you've finished, please return the recommendations to me in the envelopes I've enclosed. If you have any questions, please feel free to contact me at 555-5555. Again, thank you very much for taking the time to help me.

Sincerely,

Beth

Don't Let Your Recommenders Miss Deadlines

All recommenders have one thing in common: Too much to do and not enough time. It's important that you check with your recommender a couple of weeks before the letters are due. You need to monitor the progress of your recommendations. You may find that they're complete and already in the mail. A more common discovery is that they won't have been touched. Be polite yet diligent when you ask about the progress. It's crucial that you work with your recommenders to get the letters in on time.

The "You Can't Spell Success Without U" Mug

You now have everything you need to receive stellar recommendations. It's important to remember that even if it is a part of their job description, your recommenders are spending their time to help you. Remember this as you ask others to write recommendation letters and be sure to let them know that you appreciate their efforts.

Sometimes, a thank you gift is appropriate. Every time my (Kelly) mother wants to say thank you to a friend or acquaintance, she writes a note and gives a small token gift. My favorite is the "You Can't Spell Success Without U" mug because of its campy play on words.

Whether or not you select an equally campy token of appreciation, it's important that you thank your recommenders. After all, they are dedicating their free time to help you win funds for college.

Ace the Scholarship Interview

The Face-to-Face Encounter

A judge for the Rotary International Ambassadorial Scholarship shared with us the following true story. For the last phase of the scholarship competition for his region, the finalists met with the selection committee for an interview. The interview was very important and was the final step in determining who would win the $25,000 scholarship.

One finalist was an Ivy League student who flew across the country for the interview. Within the first five minutes, it was painfully clear to all the judges that the applicant didn't have the foggiest idea what the Rotary Club stood for. It's as if the applicant thought that his resume and Ivy League pedigree would make him a winner. As you can guess, this applicant had a very disappointing flight back to his college. Lesson number one for the scholarship interview: At the very least, know what the organization stands for.

Many students dread the interview. If your heart beats faster or your palms moisten when you think about the prospect of sitting face to face with the judges, you are not alone. While the other parts of the scholarship application take time and effort, they can be done in the privacy of your home. Interviews, on the other hand, require interaction with—gasp—a real live human.

The good news is that the interview is usually the final step in the scholarship application process and if you make it that far, you're a serious contender. In this chapter, we show you what most scholarship committees are looking for and how you should prepare to deliver a winning interview. We also show you how to make the most of your nervousness and how to turn it into an asset rather than a liability.

There are two secrets for doing well in scholarship interviews. The first is this: Remind yourself over and over again that scholarship interviewers

are real people. Repeat it until you believe it. As such, your goal is to have as normal a conversation as possible, despite the fact that thousands of dollars may hang in the balance. It's essential that you treat interviewers as real people, interact with them and ask them questions.

The second secret is just as important: The best way to have successful interviews is to train for them. The more you practice interviewing, the more comfortable you'll be during the real thing. Don't worry—we'll tell you what kinds of questions to expect and how to perfect your answers.

Why Human Interaction Is Necessary

The first step to delivering a knockout interview is to understand why some scholarships require interviews in the first place. With the popularity of technology like e-mail and instant messaging, there seems to be less need for human interaction. (Believe it or not, there was a time when telephones were answered by a person instead of a maze of touchtone options.)

For some scholarship committees, a few pieces of paper with scores and autobiographical writing are not enough to get a full picture of who the applicants really are. They are giving away a lot of cash and the judges are responsible for making sure they are giving it to the most deserving students possible.

Scholarship judges use interviews as a way to learn how you compare in person versus on paper. Having been on both sides of the interview table, we can attest to the fact that the person you expect based on the written application is not always the person you meet at the interview. It's important to know that the purpose of interviews is not to interrogate you, but rather for the scholarship committee to get to know you better and probe deeper into the reason that you deserve their money.

Interviewers Are Real People Too

If you've ever met someone famous, you've probably realized that while celebrities' faces may grace the covers of magazines and they have houses big enough to merit their own ZIP code, they eat, drink and sleep and have likes and dislikes just like other people. The same thing holds true for interviewers.

Interviewers can be high-profile professors or high-powered businesspeople, but they are all passionate about some topics and bored with others. They enjoy speaking about themselves and getting to know more about you. Acknowledging this will help keep your nerves under control. Throughout the interview, remind yourself that your interviewer is human, and strive to make the interview a conversation, not an interrogation.

Interview Homework

You'd never walk into a test and expect to do well without studying the material. The same is true for interviews. Don't attempt them without doing your homework. There is basic information you need to know before starting your interviews so that you appear informed and knowledgeable. It's not difficult information to obtain, and it goes a long way in demonstrating that you care enough about winning to have put in some effort. Here are some things you should know before any interview:

Purpose of the scholarship: What is the organization hoping to accomplish by awarding the scholarship? Whether it's promoting students to enter a certain career area, encouraging a hobby or interest or rewarding students for leadership, every scholarship has a mission.

Criteria for selecting the winner: From the scholarship materials, you can get information about what the judges are hoping to find in a winner. From the kinds of information they request in the application to the topic of the essay question, each piece is a clue about what is important to the judges. Scholarships can be based on academic achievement, nonacademic achievement or leadership, to name a few criteria. Understand what kind of student the organization is seeking and stress that side of yourself during the interview.

Background of the awarding organization: Do a little digging on the organization itself. Check out its website or publications. Attend a meeting or speak with someone who's a member. From this detective work, you will get a better idea of who the organization's members are and what they are trying to achieve. It can also be a great topic of conversation during the interview.

Background of your interviewer: If possible, find out as much as you can about who will be interviewing you. In many cases, you may know little more than their names and occupations, but if you can, find out more. You already have one piece of important information about your interviewers: You know that they are passionate about the organization and its mission. They wouldn't be volunteering their time to conduct interviews if they weren't.

Use Your Detective Work to Create an Advantage
Once you've done your detective work on the above topics, it's time to use the information you've uncovered. For example, if you are in front of a group of doctors and they ask you about your activities, you would be better off discussing your work at the local hospital than your success on the baseball diamond. As much as possible, focus the conversation on areas where your activities, goals, interests and achievements match the goal of the awarding organization. By discussing what matters most to the scholarship judges, you will insure that this will be a memorable conversation—one that will set you apart from the other applicants that are interviewed.

By knowing something about your interviewers beforehand, you can think of topics and questions that will be interesting to them. Most interviewers allow some time for you to ask questions. Here again your detective work will come in handy since you can ask them about their background or the history of the organization. By asking intelligent questions (i.e. not the ones that can be answered by simply reading the group's mission statement) you will demonstrate that you've done your homework.

You'll also give interviewers something interesting to talk about—either themselves or their organization. The more information you can get before the interview, the better you will perform. Having this background material will also allow you to answer unexpected questions better and come up with thoughtful questions for the judges if you are put on the spot.

You Are Not the Center of the Universe

Despite what Mom or Dad says, the Earth revolves around the sun, not you. It helps to remember this in your interviews. Your life may be the most interesting ever lived, but this is still no excuse for speaking only about yourself for the duration of the interview.

The secret to successful interviews is simply this: They should be *interactive*. The surest way to bore your interviewers is to spend the entire time speaking only about yourself. You may have had the unfortunate experience of being on the receiving end of a conversation like this if you have a friend who speaks nonstop about herself and who never seems to be interested in your life or what you have to say. Don't you just hate this kind of conversation? So will your scholarship interviewers.

To prevent a self-centered monologue, constantly look for ways to interact with your interviewers. In addition to answering questions, ask some yourself. Ask about their experiences in school or with the organization. Inquire about their thoughts on some of the questions they pose to you. Take time to learn about your interviewers' experiences and perspectives.

Also, speak about topics that interest your interviewers. You can tell which topics intrigue them by their reactions and body language. From the detective work you've done, you also have an idea of what they are passionate about.

Try to make your interviews a two-way conversation instead of a one-way monologue. Engage your interviewers and keep them interested. If you do this, they will remember your interview as a great conversation and you as a wonderful, intelligent person deserving of their award.

Look and Sound the Part

Studies on the effectiveness of speeches have shown that how you sound and how you look when you present your material is more important than what you actually say. From that, we can learn that it is positively essential that you make a good visual presentation. Here are some tips to make sure that you look and sound your best, an important complement to what you actually say to the judges:

Dress appropriately: A backward-turned baseball cap and baggy jeans slung down to your thighs may be standard fare for the mall (at least they were last season), but they are not appropriate for interviews.

You probably don't have to wear a suit unless you find out through your research that the organization is very conservative, but you should dress appropriately. No-no's include the following: hats, bare midriffs, short skirts or shorts, open-toe shoes and iron-free wrinkles. Think about covering obtrusive tattoos or removing extra ear/nose/tongue/eyebrow rings. Don't dress so formally that you feel uncomfortable, but dress nicely. It may not seem fair, but your dress will affect the impression you make and influence the decision of the judges. Save making a statement of your individuality for a time when money is not in question.

Sit up straight: During interviews, do not slouch. Sitting up straight conveys confidence, leadership and intelligence. It communicates that you are interested in the conversation. Plus, it makes you look taller.

Speak in a positive tone of voice: One thing that keeps interviewers engaged is your tone. Make sure to speak in a positive one. This will not only maintain your interviewers' interest but will also suggest that you have an optimistic outlook. Of course, don't try so hard that you sound fake.

Don't be monotonous: If you've ever had a teacher or professor who speaks at the same rate and tone without variation, you know that this is the surest reason for a nap. Don't give your interviewers heavy eyelids. Tape record yourself and pay attention to your tone of voice. There should be natural variation in your timbre.

Speak at a natural pace: If you're like most people, the more nervous you are, the faster you speak. Be aware of this so that you don't speed talk through your interview.

Make natural gestures: Let your hands and face convey action and emotions. Use them as tools to illustrate anecdotes and punctuate important points.

Make eye contact: Eye contact engages interviewers and conveys self-assurance and honesty. If it is a group interview, make eye contact with all your interviewers—don't just focus on one. Maintaining good eye contact can be difficult, but just imagine little dollar signs in your interviewers' eyes and you shouldn't have any trouble. Ka-ching!

Smile: There's nothing more depressing than having a conversation with someone who never smiles. Don't smile nonstop, but show some teeth at least once in a while. If you use these tips, you will have a flawless look and sound to match what you're saying. All these attributes together create a powerful portrait of who you are. Unfortunately, not all these things come naturally, and you'll need to practice so that they can become unconscious actions.

The Practice Interview

One of the best ways to prepare for an interview is to do a dress rehearsal. This allows you to run through answering questions you might be asked and to practice honing your interview skills, including demeanor and style. You will feel more comfortable when it comes time for the actual interview. If anything will help you deliver a winning interview, it's practice. It may be difficult, but force yourself to set aside some time to run through a practice session at least once. Here's how:

Find a mock interviewer. Bribe or coerce a friend or family member to be your mock interviewer. Parents or teachers often make the best interviewers because they are closest in age and perspective to most actual scholarship interviewers.

Prep your mock interviewer. Share with your interviewer highlights from this chapter such as the purpose of scholarship interviews, what skills you want to practice and typical interview questions, which are described in the next section. If you're having trouble with eye contact, for example, ask them to take special notice of where you are looking when you speak and to make suggestions for correcting this.

Set up a video camera. If you have access to a tape recorder or camcorder, set it up to tape yourself so that you can review your mock interview afterward. Position the camera behind your interviewer so you can observe how you appear from their perspective.

Do the dress rehearsal. Grab two chairs and go for it. Answer questions and interact with your mock interviewer as if you were at the real thing. Get feedback. After you are finished, get constructive criticism from your mock interviewer. Find out what you did well and what you need to work on. What were the best parts of the interview? Which of your answers were strong, and which were weak? When did you capture or lose your mock interviewer's attention? Was your conversation one-way or two-way?

Review the tape. Evaluate your performance. If you can, watch or listen to the tape with your mock interviewer so you can get additional feedback. Listen carefully to how you answer questions so you can improve on them. Pay attention to your tone of voice. Watch your body language to see what you are unconsciously communicating.

Do it again. If you have the time and your mock interviewer has the energy or you can find another mock interviewer, do a second interview. If you can't find anyone, do it solo. Practice your answers, and focus on making some of the weaker ones more interesting. The bottom line is the more you practice, the better you'll do.

How to Answer to the Most Common Interview Questions

The best way to ace an exam would be to know the questions beforehand. The same is true for interview questions. From interviewing dozens of judges and applicants as well as having judged dozens of scholarship competitions ourselves, we've developed a list of commonly asked questions along with suggestions for answering them. This list is by no means comprehensive. There is no way to predict every question you will be asked, and in your actual interviews, the questions may not be worded in exactly the same way. However, the answer that interviewers are seeking is often the same.

Before your interviews, take the time to review this list. Add more questions particular to the specific scholarship to which you are applying. Practice answering these questions to yourself and in your mock interviews with friends and family. You will find that the answers you prepare to these questions will be invaluable during your real interviews. Even though the questions you are asked may be different, the thought that you put in now will help you formulate better answers. To the interviewer, you will sound incredibly articulate and thoughtful. Let's take a look at those questions.

Why did you choose your major?

- For major-based scholarships and even for general scholarships, interviewers want to know what motivated you to select the major, and they want a sense of how dedicated you are to that area of study. Make sure you have reasons for your decision. Keep in mind that an anecdote will provide color to your answer.

- If you are still in high school, you will probably be asked about your intended major. Make sure you have reasons for considering this major.

Why do you want to enter this career field?

- For scholarships that promote a specific career field, interviewers want to know your inspiration for entering the field and how committed you are to it. You will need to articulate the reasons and experiences that prompted your interest in this career and also anything you have done to prepare yourself for associated studies in this area.

- Be prepared to discuss your plans for after graduation, i.e. how will you use your education in the field you have chosen. You may be asked what kind of job you plan to have and why you would like it.

- Know something about the news in the field associated with the scholarship. For example, if you are applying for an information technology award, read up on the trends in the IT industry. There may be some major changes occurring that you will be asked to comment on.

What are your plans after graduation?

- You are not expected to know precisely what you'll do after graduation, but you need to be able to respond to this common question. Speak about what you are thinking about doing once you have that diploma in hand. The more specific you can be, the better.

- Provide reasons for your plans. Explain the process in which you developed your plans and what your motivation is.

- It's okay to discuss a couple of possible paths you may take, but don't bring up six very different options. Even if you are deciding among investment banking, the Peace Corps, banana farming and seminary, don't say so. The interviewer will think that you don't have a clear direction of what you want to do. This may very well be true, but it's not something you want to share. Select the one or two possible paths that you are most likely to take.

Why do you think you should win this scholarship?

- Focus your answer on characteristics and achievements that match the mission of the scholarship. For example, if the scholarship is for biology majors, discuss your accomplishments in the field of biology. Your answer may include personal qualities as well as specific accomplishments.

- Be confident but not arrogant. For this type of question, be careful about balancing pride and modesty in your answer. You want to be confident enough to have reasons why you should win the scholarship, but you don't want to sound overly boastful. To avoid sounding pompous, don't say that you are better than all the other applicants or put down your competition. Instead, focus on your strengths independent of the other people who are applying.

- Have three reasons. Three is the magic number that is not too many or too few. To answer this question just right, offer three explanations for why you fulfill the mission of the scholarship.

Tell me about times when you've been a leader.

- Interviewers ask this type of question (although sometimes worded a little differently) to gauge your leadership ability and your accomplishments as a leader. They want to award scholarships to students who will be leaders in the future. When you answer, try to discuss leadership you've shown that matches what the scholarship is meant to achieve.

- Don't just rattle off the leadership positions you've held. Instead, give qualitative descriptions of what you accomplished as a leader. Did your group meet its goals? Did you start something new? How did you shape the morale of the group you led? For this kind of question, anecdotes and short stories are a good way to illustrate how you've been effective.

- Remember that leadership doesn't have to be a formally elected position. You can describe how you've informally led a special project or group. You could even define how you are a leader among your siblings.

- Be prepared to discuss what kind of leader you are. Your interviewer may ask about your approach to leadership or your philosophy on being a good leader. Have examples ready that show how you like to lead. For example, do you lead by example? Do you focus on motivating others and getting their buy-in?

What are your strengths? Weaknesses?

- As you are applying for jobs, you will answer this question more times than you will shake hands. It is a common job interview question that you may also get asked in scholarship interviews. Be prepared with three strengths and three weaknesses. Be honest about your weaknesses.

- Your strengths should match the mission of the scholarship and should highlight skills and accomplishments that match the characteristics the judges are seeking.

- You should be able to put a positive spin on your weaknesses. (And you'd better say you have some!) For example, your perfectionism could make you frustrated when things don't go the way you plan but could also make you a very motivated person. Your love of sports could detract from your studies but could provide a needed break and be representative of your belief in balance for your life. Just make sure that the spin you put on your weakness is appropriate and that your weakness is really a weakness.

Where do you see yourself ten years from now?

- We know that nobody knows exactly what he or she is going to be doing in ten years. The interviewers don't need specific details. They just want a general idea of what your long-term goals are and what you aspire to become. If you have several possibilities, at least one should be in line with the goals of the scholarship.

- Try to be as specific as possible without sounding unrealistic. For example, you can say that you would like to be working at a high-tech company in marketing, but leave out that you plan to have a daughter Rita, son Tom and dog Skip. Too much detail will make your dreams sound too naive.

Tell me about yourself. Or, is there anything you want to add?

- The most difficult questions are often the most open-ended. You have the freedom to say anything. For these kinds of questions, go back to the mission of the scholarship and shape your answer to reflect the characteristics that the judges are seeking in the winner. Practice answering this question several times because it is the one that stumps applicants the most.

- Have three things to say about yourself that match the goal of the scholarship. For example, you could discuss three personal traits you have, such as motivation, leadership skills and interpersonal skills. Or, you could discuss three skills applicable to academics, such as analytical skills, problem-solving skills and your love of a good challenge.

- The alternative, "Is there anything you want to add?" is typically asked at the end of the interview. In this case, make your response brief but meaningful. Highlight the most important thing you want your interviewer to remember.

Other Questions

In addition to these, here are some more common questions:

- What do you think you personally can contribute to this field?

- How do you plan to use what you have studied after graduation?

- Do you plan to continue your studies in graduate school?

- What do you want to specifically focus on within this field of study?

- Do you plan to do a thesis or senior project?

- Who are your role models in the field?

- What do you see as the future of this field?

- How do you see yourself growing in your career?

- What can you add to this field?

- What do you think are the most challenging aspects of this field?

- What is your ideal job after graduating from college?

- Tell me about a time that you overcame adversity.

- What are your opinions about (fill in political or field-related issue)?

- Tell me about your family.

- What do you hope to gain from college?

- Who is a role model for you?

- What is your favorite book? Why?

- What is the most challenging thing you have done?

Remember that with all these questions your goal is to demonstrate that you are the best fit for the scholarship. Be sure to practice these with your mock interviewer. The more comfortable and confident you feel answering these questions, the better you'll do in your interviews.

Questions for the Questioner

There is a huge difference between an interview and an interrogation. In an interview, you also ask questions. Make certain that your interview does not become an interrogation. Ask questions yourself throughout the conversation. Remember that you want to keep the conversation two-way.

Toward the end of your interview, you will probably have the opportunity to ask additional questions. Take this opportunity. If you don't ask any questions, it will appear that you are uninterested in the conversation or haven't put much thought into your interview. Take time before the interview to develop a list of questions you may want to ask. Of course you don't have to ask all your questions, but you need to be prepared to ask a few.

To get you started, we've developed some suggestions. Adapt these questions to the specific scholarship you are applying for and personalize them.

- How did you get involved with this organization?

- How did you enter this field? What was your motivation?

- Who do you see as your mentors in this field?

- What do you think are the most exciting things about your career?

- What advice do you have for someone starting out?

- What do you see as the greatest challenges for this field?

- What do you think will be the greatest advancements in ten years?

- What effect do you think technology will have on this field?

- I read that there is a (insert trend) in this field. What do you think?

The best questions are those that come from your detective work. Let's say that in researching an organization you discover that they recently launched a new program to research a cure for diabetes. Inquiring about this new program would be a perfect question to ask. It not only shows that you have done your homework, but it is also a subject about which the organization is deeply concerned.

Use Time to Your Advantage

The best time to ask Mom or Dad for something is when they're in a good mood. It's all about timing. Timing is also important in interviews. If you have more than one scholarship interview, time them strategically. Schedule less important and less demanding interviews first. This will allow you the opportunity to practice before your more difficult interviews. You will improve your skills as you do more interviews. It makes sense to hone your skills on the less important ones first.

If you are one of a series of applicants who will be interviewed, choose the order that fits you best. If you like to get things over with, try to be interviewed in the beginning. If you need more time to prepare yourself mentally, select a time near the end. We recommend that you don't choose to go first because the judges will use your interview as a benchmark for the rest. They may not recognize you as the best applicant even though it turns out to be true.

The Long-Distance Interview

If you've ever been in a long-distance relationship, you know there's a reason why most don't last. You simply can't communicate over the telephone in the same way you can in person. Scholarship interviews are the same. You may find that an interview will not be face to face but over the telephone instead. If this happens, here are some strategies to help bridge the distance:

Find a quiet place to do the interview where you won't be interrupted. You need to be able to give your full attention to the conversation you are having.

Know who's on the other end of the line. You may interview with a panel of people. Write down each of their names and positions when they first introduce themselves to you. They will be impressed when you are able to respond to them individually and thank each of them by name.

Use notes from your practice interviews. One of the advantages of doing an interview over the telephone is that you can refer to notes without your interviewers knowing. Take advantage of this.

Look and sound like you would in person. Pretend that your interviewers are in the room with you, and use the same gestures and facial expressions that you would if you were meeting in person. It may sound strange, but your interviewers will actually be able to hear through your voice when you are smiling, when you are paying attention and when you are enthusiastic about what you're saying. Don't do your interview lying down in your bed or slouched back in a recliner.

Don't use a speaker phone, cordless phone or cell phone. Speaker phones often echo and pick up distracting surrounding noise. Cordless and cell phones can generate static, and the battery can die at the worst possible moment.

Turn off call waiting. Nothing is more annoying than hearing the call waiting beep while you are trying to focus and deliver an important thought. (And, this may sound obvious, never click over to take a second call.) Use the techniques of regular interviews. You'd be surprised how much is translated over the telephone. Don't neglect good speaking and delivery points just because the interviewers can't see you!

Secrets to the Group Interview

So it's you on one side of the table and a panel of six on the other side. It's certainly not the most natural way to have a conversation. How do you stay calm when you are interviewed by a council of judges?

Think of the group as individuals. Instead of thinking it's you versus the team, think of each of the interviewers as an individual. Try to connect with each person separately.

Try to get everyone's name if you can. Have a piece of paper handy that you can use to jot down everyone's name and role so that you can refer to them in the conversation. You want to be able to target your answers to each of the constituents. If you are interviewing with a panel of employees from a company and you know that Ms. Sweeny works in accounting while Mr. Duff works in human resources, you can speak about your analytical skills to appeal to Ms. Sweeny and your people skills to appeal to Mr. Duff.

Make eye contact. Look into the eyes of each of the panelists. Don't stare, but show them that you are confident. Be careful not to focus on only one member of the group.

Respect the hierarchy. You may find that there is a leader in the group like the scholarship chair or the CEO of the company. Pay a little more attention to stroke the ego of the person or persons in charge. They are used to it, they expect it and a little kissing up never hurt anyone.

Include everyone. In any group situation, there are usually one or two more vocal members who take the lead. Don't focus all your attention only on the loud ones. Spread your attention among the panelists as evenly as possible.

The Disaster Interview

Even if you do your interview homework and diligently practice mock interviewing, you may still find that you and your interviewer(s) just don't connect or that you just don't seem to have the right answers. For students who spend some time preparing, this is a very rare occurrence. Interviewers are not trying to trick you or make you feel bad. They are simply trying to find out more about you and your fit with the award. Still, if you think that you've bombed, here are some things to keep in mind:

Avoid should have, would have, could have. Don't replay the interview in your head again and again, thinking of all the things you should have said.

It's too easy to look back and have the best answers. Instead, use what you've learned to avoid making the same mistakes in your next interview.

There are no right answers. Remember that in reality there really are no right answers. Your answers may not have been perfect, but that doesn't mean that they were wrong. There are countless ways to answer the same question.

The toughest judge is you. Realize that you are your own greatest critic. While you may think that you completely bombed an interview, your interviewer will most likely not have as harsh an opinion.

The Post-Interview

After you complete your interviews, follow up with a thank you note. Remember that interviewers are typically volunteers and have made the time to meet with you. If you feel that there is very important information that you forgot to share in your interview, mention it briefly in your thank you note. If not, a simple note will suffice. You will leave a polite, lasting impression on your interviewer(s).

Final Thoughts

How to Keep the Money You Win

When you learn to skydive, your first lesson does not start with jumping out of an airplane. First you go through training in which you learn techniques and safety measures—on the ground. Only after practicing on the ground can you take to the sky. In your scholarship education, you have just completed the ground training and are ready to take the plunge. As you move from the *strategies* for applying for scholarships to actually *applying* for them, we have a few words of advice on how to keep the dollars you earn and how to stay motivated.

Let's jump ahead to after you win a cache of scholarship dollars. It would be nice once the scholarship checks were written if you could run off for that well-deserved trip to the Bahamas. Alas, there are restrictions on how you can spend the cash and how you must maintain your scholarship. (Besides, everyone knows that Hawaii is the place to go.) Here are some tips to keep in mind:

Get to know your scholarship and financial aid administrators. These people will be able to answer questions about your award and make sure you are spending it in the way that you should.

Give the scholarship committee members proof if they want it. Some awards require that you provide proof of enrollment or transcripts. Send the committee whatever they need.

Be aware of your award's requirements and what happens if something changes. How long does the award last? What happens if you take a leave of absence, study part time, study abroad, transfer schools or quit your studies? College is full of possibilities! Do you have to maintain a minimum grade point average or take courses in a certain field?

Know if there are special requirements for athletic scholarships. If you've won an athletic scholarship, you are most likely required to play the sport. (You didn't get that full ride scholarship for nothing!) Understand the implications of what would happen if you were not able to play because of circumstances such as an injury or not meeting academic requirements.

Find out if the award is a cash cow (renewable). If an award is renewable, you are eligible to get it every year that you are in school. If so, find out what you need to do, and when you need to do it, to renew your scholarship. Some awards just require a copy of your transcript, while others require you to submit an entirely new application.

Understand restrictions for spending the dough. Some awards are limited to tuition. Others can be used for books, travel or even living expenses. Some provide the money directly to your school; others provide a check made out to you. Be aware of what you can spend the money on and what sort of records you need to keep.

Learn the tax implications of your award. Speak with the award administrator or your pals at the IRS (www.irs.gov or 800-829-1040). Be aware of requirements after you graduate. Some awards such as ROTC scholarships require employment after graduation. Because these arrangements can drastically affect your future, learn about the requirements now.

Keep the awarding organization up to date on your progress as a student. Write the organization a thank you note, and keep them updated on your progress at the end of the year. This is not only good manners, but it will also help ensure that the award is around in the future.

Parting Words

I (Gen) remember when I won the Sterling Scholarship, one of the highest honors for students in Hawaii. The awards ceremony was televised live throughout the state. For weeks before submitting my application, I prepared for the competition, compiling a 50-page application book, practicing for the eight hours of interviews and enlisting the help of no less than three teachers from my high school. Even though the scholarship was only $1,000, my parents still keep the trophy on display and share with unwitting visitors the videotape of my triumph. I realize now that I was able to put in such extensive effort because of my outlook on the award. I knew whether I won or lost, I would gain the experience of building a portfolio, becoming a skilled interviewee, working closely with my teachers and meeting some incredible students.

While scholarships are primarily a source of funding for your education, approach them in the same way you do your favorite sport or hobby. I also played for my school's tennis team—and lost just about every match. Yet, I continued because I enjoyed the sport and found the skills a challenge. If you approach your scholarships in this manner, you'll probably win more of them and have fun in the process. Treat them like a chore, and you'll hate every minute, neglecting to put in the effort required to win.

The bottom line is that if you are going to take the time to apply, you should take the time to win. The secrets, tips and strategies in this book will put you within striking distance. Follow them and you'll win more and more often. This book is unique in that it really is two books in one. Now that you know how to win, it's time to begin finding scholarships to put these strategies to use. The second half of this book is a complete listing of scholarships and awards and is indexed by various criteria so you can quickly find those that match your interests and qualifications. And, because we know you just can't get enough of us, we also encourage you to visit our website, SuperCollege. com, for the most up-to-date information on scholarships and financial aid.

We both wish you the best of luck.

A SPECIAL REQUEST

As you jump headlong into the wonderful world of scholarships, we have a special request. We would love to hear about your experiences with scholarships and how this book has helped you. Please send us a note after you've finished raking in your free cash for college.

Gen and Kelly Tanabe
c/o SuperCollege
3286 Oak Court
Belmont, CA 94002

Onward! Flip the page and start finding scholarships. It's time to put all the strategies and tips you've just learned to work for you!

The Ultimate Scholarship Directory

Now it's time to put into action all that you learned in the first half of the book. We've done the hard work of scouring the country to find the best scholarships that you can win. We've made a special effort to select awards with broad eligibility requirements, which means you'll find plenty of scholarships that fit your background, goals and interests.

Before you jump into the directory, spend a few moments to learn how the scholarships are organized so you don't miss out on any awards for which you might be a good fit.

To help find the awards that match you best, we've conveniently organized our directory of scholarships into eight major categories.

Below is the complete list of categories and descriptions of the types of awards you'll find in each one. Remember to also use the various indexes in the back of the book to help you zero in on more scholarships.

General

This section lists scholarships that have the broadest eligibility requirements. Included are awards based on **academics**, **leadership** and **community service** to name a few. While some of the scholarships have GPA requirements, you'll be surprised at how many are not based on grades. Some are even awarded by random drawing.

Humanities / Arts

This section includes awards for students interested in **English** and **writing** as well as **foreign language** and **area studies**. It also includes all of the **visual and performing arts** such as **dancing**, **singing**, **acting**, **music**, **drawing**, **painting**, **sculpture**, **photography** and **graphic art**.

Social Sciences

This section deals with the study of the human aspects of the world. Often called the "soft sciences" it includes:

- Anthropology
- Accounting / Finance
- Archaeology
- Business Management
- Communications
- Criminology
- Economics
- Education / Teaching
- Geography
- History
- Hospitality / Travel
- International Relations
- Journalism / Broadcasting
- Law / Legal Studies
- Marketing / Sales
- Political Science
- Psychology
- Public Administration / Social Work
- Sociology
- Urban Studies

Sciences

Typically known as the "hard sciences," this category includes:

- Aerospace / Aviation
- Agriculture / Horticulture / Animals
- Anatomy
- Architecture
- Astronomy
- Biological Sciences / Life Sciences
- Biochemistry
- Chemistry
- Computer and Information Science
- Dentistry
- Earth and Planetary Sciences
- Ecology
- Engineering
- Forestry / Wildlife
- Geology
- Health Professions / Medicine
- Mathematics
- Neuroscience
- Nursing
- Oceanography
- Paleontology
- Pathology

- Pharmacology
- Physics
- Zoology

State of Residence

Here's your opportunity to get something back from your (or your parents') state tax dollars. Every state offers scholarships and grants for their residents. Some states even offer awards to out-of-state students who study in their states. Be sure to look at both your home state as well as any of the states you are planning to go to college in to find the most awards.

Membership

Many large **companies**, **unions**, **organizations** and **religious organizations** give awards to their members. If you or your parents are members of any of the groups in this category, you may qualify for a scholarship.

Ethnicity /Race/Gender/Family Situation/Sexual Orientation

There are a lot of awards for members of minority and nonminority ethnic groups, women and students with unique family situations.

Disability / Illness

This section has awards for students with physical, hearing, vision, mental and learning disabilities. It also includes awards for students who have been afflicted with certain illnesses.

"Take Off the Blinders" to Find the Most Scholarships

Now that you know the categories, the best way to find scholarships is to jump right in and head to the sections that fit you best.

Do you remember when your elementary school teacher used to say, "Take off the mental blinders"? Ours did to encourage us to think broadly. In the same way, we want to encourage you to "take off the scholarship blinders" and not think about yourself too narrowly. Consider your accomplishments, activities, goals and background as broadly as possible. Look through some of the categories even if you don't immediately see a fit. You might discover that you actually fit one of the leadership scholarships even if you haven't held a formal leadership position. Or you may find an award in the sciences category in a field that you love but never realized was a science.

Don't be afraid to be forward-thinking. Write down any scholarships that fit, even if you have to wait a year to apply. The awards we have selected are from the larger organizations and businesses, so you can be certain that they are going to be around for a long time.

We are really excited that you can now put everything that you learned to good use to help you find and win some free cash for college.

Happy scholarship hunting!

GENERAL

(1) · $1,000 Gen and Kelly Tanabe Parent Scholarship

Gen and Kelly Tanabe Parent Scholarship Program
3286 Oak Court
Belmont, CA 94002
Phone: 650-618-2221
Email: tanabe@gmail.com
Website: http://www.parentscholarship.com
Purpose: To help parents of junior high school, high school and college students pay for their child's education.
Eligibility: Applicants must be legal U.S. residents, and their children may attend or plan to attend any U.S. college or university.
Target applicant:
  Parents of junior high students or younger
  Parents of high school students
  Parents of college students
  Parents of graduate school students
  Parents of adult students
Minimum GPA: None.
Amount: $1,000.
Deadline: June 15.
How to apply: Applications are available online.

(2) · $1,000 Gen and Kelly Tanabe Student Scholarship

Gen and Kelly Tanabe Scholarship Program
3286 Oak Court
Belmont, CA 94002
Phone: 650-618-2221
Email: tanabe@gmail.com
Website: http://www.genkellyscholarship.com
Purpose: To assist high school, college and graduate school students with educational expenses.
Eligibility: Applicants must be 9th-12th grade high school students, college students or graduate school students who are legal U.S. residents. Students may study any major and attend any college in the U.S.
Target applicant:
  High school students
  College students
  Graduate school students
  Adult students
Minimum GPA: None.
Amount: $1,000.
Deadline: July 31.
How to apply: Applications are available online.

(3) · Academic Competitiveness Grant

Federal Student Aid
U.S. Department of Education
400 Maryland Avenue, SW
Washington, DC 20202
Phone: 800-433-3243
Website: http://studentaid.ed.gov
Purpose: To help students who have finished a rigorous secondary school program of study.
Eligibility: Applicants must be full-time students eligible for Federal Pell Grants who have enrolled or been accepted by a two- or four-year degree-granting institution of higher education. The grants are available to students for the first and second years of college with up to $750 for the first year and up to $1,300 for the second year. Second year students must also have a minimum 3.0 GPA.
Target applicant:
  High school students
  College students
  Adult students
Minimum GPA: None.
Amount: Up to $1,300.
Number of awards: Varies.
Scholarship may be renewable.
Deadline: Varies.
How to apply: Contact the program for more information.

(4) · AFSA National Essay Contest

American Foreign Service Association (AFSA)
2101 East Street NW
Washington, DC 20037
Phone: 202-944-5504
Fax: 202-338-6820
Email: dec@afsa.org
Website: http://www.afsa.org/essaycontest
Purpose: To support students interested in writing an essay on foreign service.
Eligibility: Students must attend a public, private, parochial school, home school or participate in a high school correspondence program in any of the 50 states, the District of Columbia or U.S. territories or must be U.S. citizens attending schools overseas. Students must be the dependent of a US government Foreign Service employee (active, retired with pension, deceased or separated). The current award is $2,500 to the student, $500 to his/her school and all expenses paid trip to Washington, DC, for the winner and parents.
Target applicant:
  High school students
Minimum GPA: None.
Amount: $2,500.
Number of awards: 1.
Deadline: February 6.
How to apply: The registration form is available online. Applicants must write a 750- to 1,000 word essay on the topic provided.

(5) · Akademos / TextbookX.com Scholarship

Akademos
TextbookX.com
25 Van Zant Street
Norwalk, CT 06855
Phone: 203-866-0190
Fax: 203-866-0199
Website: http://www.textbookx.com/scholarship
Purpose: To support students who are pursuing undergraduate or graduate degrees.
Eligibility: Applicants must submit an essay based on the provided topic and that references at least one book. Students must be U.S. citizens or legal residents and undergraduate or graduate students attending a U.S. college of university.
Target applicant:
  College students
  Graduate school students
  Adult students
Minimum GPA: None.
Amount: Up to $2,000.

Number of awards: Varies.
Deadline: October 31.
How to apply: Applications are available online.

(6) · All-Ink Scholarship

All-Ink.com
1460 N. Main Street
Suite 2
Spanish Fork, UT 84660
Phone: 888-567-6511
Fax: 801-794-0124
Email: csp@all-ink.com
Website: http://www.all-ink.com/scholarship.aspx
Purpose: To help students who want to pursue higher educational goals.
Eligibility: Applicants must be U.S. citizens or legal residents who are enrolled in or plan to attend an accredited college or university. Students must be high school seniors, college students or graduate students. To be considered, a student must have a 2.5 GPA or better, must complete an online application and write a pair of 50 to 200 word essays about what they hope to accomplish after they complete their college degree and about who their greatest influence has been.
Target applicant:
　High school students
　College students
　Graduate school students
　Adult students
Minimum GPA: 2.5
Amount: $5000.
Number of awards: Varies.
Deadline: December 31.
How to apply: Applications are available online.

(7) · Alpha Kappa Alpha Financial Need Scholars

Alpha Kappa Alpha
5656 S. Stony Island Avenue
Chicago, IL 60637
Phone: 800-653-6528
Fax: 773-947-0277
Email: akaeaf@akaeaf.net
Website: http://www.akaeaf.org
Purpose: To assist undergraduate and graduate students who have overcome hardships to achieve educational goals.
Eligibility: Applicants must be studying full-time at the sophomore level or higher at an accredited institution and have a GPA of 2.5 or higher. Students must also demonstrate leadership, volunteer, civic or academic service. The program is open to students without regard to sex, race, creed, color, ethnicity, religion, sexual orientation or disability. Students do NOT need to be members of Alpha Kappa Alpha.
Target applicant:
　College students
　Graduate school students
　Adult students
Minimum GPA: 2.5
Amount: $750-$1,500.
Number of awards: Varies.
Deadline: April 15 for college students, August 15 for graduate students.
How to apply: Applications are available online.

(8) · American Darts Organization Memorial Scholarships

American Darts Organization
230 N. Crescent Way
Suite K
Anaheim, CA 92801
Phone: 714-254-0212
Fax: 714-254-0214
Email: adooffice@aol.com
Website: http://www.adodarts.com
Purpose: To support participants in the American Darts Organization Youth Playoff Program.
Eligibility: Applicants must be ADO members, and they must have been at least quarter-finalists in the ADO Youth Playoff Program. Students must be under 21 years old on December 1 of the year in which they intend to start school. They must be enrolled or accepted in a degree-granting program on a full-time basis with at least a 2.0 GPA.
Target applicant:
　High school students
　College students
Minimum GPA: 2.0
Amount: $500-$1,500.
Number of awards: 8.
Deadline: Varies.
How to apply: Applications are available online.

(9) · American Fire Sprinkler Association Scholarship Program

American Fire Sprinkler Association
12750 Merit Drive
Suite 350
Dallas, TX 75251
Phone: 214-349-5965
Fax: 214-343-8898
Email: afsainfo@firesprinkler.org
Website: http://www.afsascholarship.org
Purpose: To provide financial aid to high school seniors and introduce them to the fire sprinkler industry.
Eligibility: Applicants must be high school seniors who plan to attend a U.S. college, university or certified trade school. Students must read the "Fire Sprinkler Essay" available online and then take an online quiz. Applicants receive one entry in the scholarship drawing for each question answered correctly.
Target applicant:
　High school students
Minimum GPA: None.
Amount: $2,000.
Number of awards: 10.
Scholarship may be renewable.
Deadline: April 11.
How to apply: Applications are available online.

(10) · American Legion Baseball Scholarship

American Legion Baseball
700 N. Pennsylvania Street
Indianapolis, IN 46204
Fax: 317-630-1369
Email: baseball@legion.org
Website: http://www.baseball.legion.org

Purpose: To award scholarships to members of American Legion-affiliated baseball teams.

Eligibility: Applicants must be graduating high school seniors and be nominated by a head coach or team manager. One player per department (state) will be selected. Nominations should be sent to the local Department Headquarters. Scholarships may be used to further education at any accredited college, university or other institution of higher education.

Target applicant:
  High school students

Minimum GPA: None.

Amount: $1,000.

Number of awards: 51.

Deadline: July 15.

How to apply: Applications are available online.

---

(11) · Americorps National Civilian Community Corps

AmeriCorps
1201 New York Avenue NW
Washington, DC 20525
Phone: 202-606-5000
Fax: 202-606-3472
Email: questions@americorps.org
Website: http://www.americorps.org

Purpose: To strengthen communities and develop leaders through community service.

Eligibility: Applicants must be U.S. citizens who are at least 17 years of age. They must relocate to one of four Americorps campuses and commit to 10 months of service.

Target applicant:
  High school students
  College students
  Graduate school students
  Adult students

Minimum GPA: None.

Amount: $4,725.

Number of awards: Varies.

Deadline: Varies.

How to apply: Applications are available online.

---

(12) · Americorps Vista

AmeriCorps
1201 New York Avenue NW
Washington, DC 20525
Phone: 202-606-5000
Fax: 202-606-3472
Email: questions@americorps.org
Website: http://www.americorps.org

Purpose: To provide education assistance in exchange for community service.

Eligibility: Applicants must be United States citizens who are at least 17 years of age. They must be available to serve full-time for one year and submit to a criminal background check.

Target applicant:
  High school students
  College students
  Graduate school students
  Adult students

Minimum GPA: None.

Amount: $4,725.

Number of awards: Varies.

Deadline: Varies.

How to apply: Applications are available online.

---

(13) · Arlene Schlosser Memorial Endowment

Epsilon Sigma Alpha Foundation
P.O. Box 270517
Fort Collins, CO 80527
Phone: 970-223-2824
Fax: 970-223-4456
Email: kloyd@knoxy.net
Website: http://www.esaintl.com/esaf

Purpose: To provide financial assistance to students who demonstrate scholastic ability, financial need and leadership.

Eligibility: Applicants may be residents of any state. They may pursue any major at any institution of higher learning. Selection is based on the following criteria: scholastic ability (30 percent), financial need (30 percent), leadership (20 percent), character (10 percent) and service (10 percent).

Target applicant:
  High school students
  College students
  Adult students

Minimum GPA: None.

Amount: $500.

Number of awards: 1.

Deadline: February 1.

How to apply: Applications are available online.

---

(14) · AWSEF Scholarship

American Water Ski Educational Foundation (AWSEF)
1251 Holy Cow Road
Polk City, FL 33868-8200
Phone: 863-324-2472
Email: info@waterskihalloffame.com
Website: http://www.waterskihalloffame.com

Purpose: To support those involved in USA WATER SKI.

Eligibility: Applicants must be full-time undergraduates at a two- or four-year college as incoming sophomores to incoming seniors. Applicants must also be active members of USA WATER SKI all divisions: AWSA-ABC-AKA-WSDA-NSSA-NCWSA-NCWSRA-USAWB-HYD. Students should submit applications, two reference letters, essays and transcripts.

Target applicant:
  College students
  Adult students

Minimum GPA: None.

Amount: $1,500.

Number of awards: 6.
Scholarship may be renewable.

Deadline: April 1.

How to apply: Applications are available online.

---

(15) · AXA Achievement Scholarships

AXA Achievement Scholarship c/o Scholarship America
One Scholarship Way
P.O. Box 297
St. Peter, MN 56082
Phone: 800-537-4180

Email: axaachievement@scholarshipamerica.org
Website: http://www.axa-equitable.com
Purpose: To provide financial assistance to ambitious students.
Eligibility: Applicants must be U.S. citizens or legal residents who are current high school seniors and are planning to enroll full-time in an accredited college or university in the fall following their graduation. They must show ambition and drive evidenced by outstanding achievement in school, community or workplace activities. A recommendation from an unrelated adult who can vouch for the student's achievement is required.
Target applicant:
    High school students
Minimum GPA: None.
Amount: $10,000-$25,000.
Number of awards: 52.
Deadline: December 15.
How to apply: Applications are available online.

---

(16) · Ayers/Gallatin Endowment

Epsilon Sigma Alpha Foundation
P.O. Box 270517
Fort Collins, CO 80527
Phone: 970-223-2824
Fax: 970-223-4456
Email: kloyd@knoxy.net
Website: http://www.esaintl.com/esaf
Purpose: To provide financial assistance to students.
Eligibility: Applicants may be from any state, attend any school and pursue any major. Selection is based on character (10 percent), leadership (20 percent), service (10 percent), financial need (30 percent) and scholastic ability (30 percent).
Target applicant:
    High school students
    College students
    Adult students
Minimum GPA: None.
Amount: $500.
Number of awards: 2.
Deadline: February 1.
How to apply: Applications are available online.

---

(17) · Babe Ruth League Scholarships

Babe Ruth League Inc.
1770 Brunswick Avenue
P.O. Box 5000
Trenton, NJ 08638
Website: http://www.baberuthleague.org/scholarship.html
Purpose: To provide educational assistance to players in the Babe Ruth Baseball and Softball divisions.
Eligibility: Applicants must be members or former members of the Babe Ruth Baseball or Softball leagues. They must be graduating seniors. A short essay, copy of high school transcript and a letter of recommendation are required.
Target applicant:
    High school students
Minimum GPA: None.
Amount: $1,000.
Number of awards: Varies.
Deadline: July 1.
How to apply: Applications are available online.

(18) · Barbara Wiedner and Dorothy Vandercook Memorial Peace Scholarship

Grandmothers for Peace International
Wiedner and Vandercook MSF
c/o Leal Portis, President
301 Redbud Way
Nevada, CA 95949
Phone: 530-265-3887
Email: portis.leal@gmail.com
Website: http://www.grandmothersforpeace.org
Purpose: To reward students who have exhibited their commitment to peace and justice through volunteer work and have plans to help create a more peaceful and just world.
Eligibility: Applicants must be high school seniors or college freshmen and provide an autobiography of activities relating to nuclear disarmament, conflict resolution or community service and describe their plans for contributing to a healthy planet. Applicants must also provide information on community activities and include two letters of recommendation.
Target applicant:
    High school students
    College students
    Adult students
Minimum GPA: None.
Amount: $250-$500.
Number of awards: Varies.
Deadline: March 1.
How to apply: Applications are available online.

---

(19) · Best Buy Scholarships

Best Buy Children's Foundation
7601 Penn Avenue S.
Richfield, MN 55423
Phone: 612-292-6397
Email: bestbuy@scholarshipamerica.org
Website: http://www.bbycommunications.com/crnew/scholarships.asp
Purpose: To assist students in obtaining a higher education.
Eligibility: Applicants must be graduating seniors residing in the U.S. or Puerto Rico, live within 75 miles of a Best Buy store, have a minimum GPA of 2.5 and have community service or work experience.
Target applicant:
    High school students
Minimum GPA: 2.5
Amount: $1,500-$10,000.
Number of awards: 1,551.
Deadline: February 15.
How to apply: Students may apply online only.

---

(20) · Billy Welu Scholarship

United States Bowling Congress
5301 S. 76th Street
Greendale, WI 53129
Phone: 800-514-2695 x3168
Email: smart@bowl.com
Website: http://www.bowl.com/scholarships
Purpose: To recognize exemplary qualities in amateur bowlers who are in college.
Eligibility: Applicants must be amateur bowlers who are currently attending college. They must have a 2.5 or higher GPA.

Target applicant:
  College students
  Graduate school students
  Adult students
Minimum GPA: 2.5
Amount: $1,000.
Number of awards: 1.
Deadline: May 31.
How to apply: Applications are available online.

(21) · Blogging for Progress

ProgressiveU.org
Email: info@progressiveu.org
Website: http://www.progressiveu.org
Purpose: To support students who contribute to the online dialogue for students.
Eligibility: Applicants must attend any regionally or nationally affiliated college, university or vocational school. Winners are selected based on points awarded for each blog entry and comment accepted for posting to the website and for each read of a participant's blog entry by members or visitors.
Target applicant:
  College students
  Adult students
Minimum GPA: None.
Amount: $500-$1,000.
Number of awards: 3.
Deadline: October 15.
How to apply: Students must register online by October 15.

(22) · Blogging Scholarship

CollegeScholarships.org
150 Caldecott Lane #8
Oakland, CA 94618
Phone: 888-501-9050
Email: info@collegescholarships.org
Website: http://www.collegescholarships.org
Purpose: To provide financial assistance for students who blog.
Eligibility: Applicants must maintain blogs with unique and interesting information. They must be U.S. citizens or permanent residents who are currently enrolled full-time in a U.S. institution of higher learning. Winners must agree to have their name and blog listed on the website.
Target applicant:
  College students
  Adult students
Minimum GPA: None.
Amount: Up to $10,000.
Number of awards: Varies.
Deadline: October 30.
How to apply: Applications are available online.

(23) · Bob Warnicke Scholarship

National Bicycle League (NBL)
3958 Brown Park Drive
Suite D
Hilliard, OH 43026
Phone: 614-777-1625
Fax: 614-777-1680

Email: administration@nbl.org
Website: http://www.nbl.org
Purpose: To help students who have participated in BMX racing events.
Eligibility: Applicants must be members, have a current NBL competition license or officials license and have participated in BMX racing events for at least a year. Students must also be high school graduates and plan to or currently attend a postsecondary institution full- or part-time.
Target applicant:
  College students
  Graduate school students
  Adult students
Minimum GPA: None.
Amount: Varies.
Number of awards: Varies.
Deadline: November 1.
How to apply: Applications are available online, by mail or by phone.

(24) · Bobby Sox High School Senior Scholarship Program

Bobby Sox Softball
P.O. Box 5880
Buena Park, CA 90622-5880
Phone: 714-522-1234
Fax: 714-522-6548
Website: http://www.bobbysoxsoftball.org/scholar.html
Purpose: To provide educational assistance for Bobby Sox softball players.
Eligibility: Applicants must be eighth grade girls who have participated in Bobby Sox for four or more seasons, or high school seniors who have participated for five or more seasons. They must have a GPA of 2.0 or higher.
Target applicant:
  Junior high school students or younger
  High school students
Minimum GPA: 2.0
Amount: Up to $2,500.
Number of awards: 45.
Deadline: April 5.
How to apply: Applications are available online.

(25) · Bonner Scholarship

Bonner Foundation
10 Mercer Street
Princeton, NJ 08540
Phone: 609-924-6663
Fax: 609-683-4626
Email: info@bonner.org
Website: http://www.bonner.org
Purpose: To award four-year community service scholarships to students planning to attend one of 27 participating colleges.
Eligibility: Students must complete annual service requirements as stipulated by the organization. Awards are geared toward students demonstrating significant financial need. Scholarship recipients are named Bonner Scholars.
Target applicant:
  High school students
Minimum GPA: None.
Amount: Varies.

Number of awards: 1,500.
Deadline: Same date as college application deadline.
How to apply: Contact the admission office at each participating school to request an application.

(26) · Buddy Pelletier Surfing Foundation Scholarship

Buddy Pelletier Surfing Foundation Fund
5121 Chalk Street
Moorehead City, NC 28557
Phone: 252-727-7917
Fax: 252-727-7965
Email: lynne.pelletier@bbandt.com
Website: http://www.buddy.pelletier.com
Purpose: To support the education and humanitarian needs of the East Coast surfing community.
Eligibility: Applicants must be members of the East Coast surfing community. Rising high school seniors, current undergraduate college students and returning students may apply regardless of age. Two letters of recommendation and a 500-word essay are required. Previous applicants and winners may reapply each year.
Target applicant:
   High school students
   College students
   Adult students
Minimum GPA: None.
Amount: $1,000.
Number of awards: Varies.
Deadline: June 1.
How to apply: Applications are available online.

(27) · Burger King Scholars Program

Burger King Scholars Program c/o International Scholarship and Tuition Services
P.O. Box 23737
Nashville, TN 37202
Phone: 305-378-3186
Email: bdorado@whopper.com
Website: http://www.bk.com/companyinfo/community/scholarships. aspx
Purpose: To provide financial assistance for high school seniors who have part-time jobs.
Eligibility: Applicants may apply from public, private, vocational, technical, parochial and alternative high schools in the United States, Canada and Puerto Rico and must be U.S. or Canadian residents. Students must also have a minimum 2.5 GPA, work part-time an average of 15 hours per week unless there are extenuating circumstances, participate in community service or other activities, demonstrate financial need and plan to enroll in an accredited two- or four-year college, university or vocational/technical school by the fall term of the graduating year. Applicants do NOT need to work at Burger King, but Burger King employees are eligible.
Target applicant:
   High school students
Minimum GPA: None.
Amount: $1,000.
Number of awards: Varies.
Deadline: February 2.
How to apply: Applications are available online.

(28) · Carpe Diem Foundation Scholarship

Carpe Diem Foundation of Illinois
P.O. Box 3194
Chicago, IL 60690-3194
Email: glevine@carpediemfoundation.org
Website: http://www.carpediemfoundation.org
Purpose: To provide financial assistance to students who are most likely to improve the quality of human life.
Eligibility: Applicants must be U.S. citizens who are or will be undergraduate students at accredited institutions of higher learning. Priority is given to students from families who have been employed in public service positions. There is a $10 application fee. It is highly recommended that you research the scholarship and awarding organization before applying for a scholarship with a fee. There are many scholarships that do not require a fee.
Target applicant:
   High school students
   College students
   Adult students
Minimum GPA: None.
Amount: Up to $5,000.
Number of awards: 20.
Deadline: May 13.
How to apply: Applications are available online.

(29) · Challenge Scholarship

National Strength and Conditioning Association (NSCA) Foundation
1885 Bob Johnson Drive
Colorado Springs, CO 80906
Phone: 800-815-6826
Fax: 719-632-6367
Email: nsca@nsca-lift.org
Website: http://www.nsca-lift.org
Purpose: To support NSCA members pursuing studies related to strength and conditioning.
Eligibility: Applicants must be NSCA members for one year before applying and be pursuing careers in strength and conditioning. Students must submit an essay detailing their course of study, career goals and financial need. Applications are evaluated based on grades, courses, experience, honors, recommendations and involvement in the community and with NSCA.
Target applicant:
   College students
   Graduate school students
   Adult students
Minimum GPA: None.
Amount: $1,000.
Number of awards: Varies.
Deadline: March 15.
How to apply: Applications are available with membership.

(30) · Chinese American Citizens Alliance Foundation Essay Contest

Chinese American Citizens Alliance
1044 Stockton Street
San Francisco, CA 94108
Phone: 415-434-2222
Website: http://www.cacanational.org
Purpose: To provide a forum for expression for future leaders of the United States.

Eligibility: Applicants must be high school students in grades 9 through 12. Students do NOT need to be Chinese Americans. They must write a 500-word essay on a topic chosen by the Chinese American Citizens Alliance. The essay must be written on a given date at the student's local lodge or other designated location.

Target applicant:
    High school students

Minimum GPA: None.

Amount: Up to $1,000.

Number of awards: 13.

Deadline: March 4.

How to apply: Applications are available online.

---

(31) · Church Hill Classics "Frame My Future" Scholarship

Church Hill Classics
594 Pepper Street
Monroe, CT 06468
Phone: 800-477-9005
Email: info@diplomaframe.com
Website: http://www.framemyfuture.com

Purpose: To help success-driven students attain their higher education goals.

Eligibility: Applicants must be high school seniors or otherwise eligible for graduation in the school year of application or current college students. They must plan to enroll in college full-time the following academic year. Applicants must be residents of the United States, including APO/FPO addresses but excluding Puerto Rico. Employees of Church Hill Classics and affiliated companies, their family members and individuals living in the same household are not eligible. A photograph, essay, painting or other creative entry is required to demonstrate what the applicants want to achieve in their personal and professional life after college.

Target applicant:
    High school students
    College students
    Adult students

Minimum GPA: None.

Amount: $1,000.

Number of awards: 5.

Deadline: March 31.

How to apply: Applications are available online. Applicants may enter by mail or online.

---

(32) · CIA Undergraduate Scholarship Program

Central Intelligence Agency
Office of Public Affairs
Washington, DC 20505
Phone: 703-482-0623
Fax: 703-482-1739
Website: http://www.cia.gov

Purpose: To encourage students to pursue careers with the CIA.

Eligibility: Applicants must be high school students or college sophomores. High school students must have an SAT score of 1000 or higher or an ACT score of 21 or higher, while all applicants must have a GPA of at least 3.0. Applicants must demonstrate financial need, defined as a household income of less than $70,000 for a family of four or $80,000 for a family of five or more. They must meet all criteria for regular CIA employees, including security checks and medical examinations. Applicants must commit to a work experience each

summer during college and agree to CIA employment for at least 1.5 times the length of their CIA-sponsored scholarship.

Target applicant:
    High school students
    College students
    Adult students

Minimum GPA: 3.0.

Amount: Annual salary including benefits and up to $18,000 for tuition.

Number of awards: Varies.

Scholarship may be renewable.

Deadline: November 1.

How to apply: There is no application form; applicants may submit a resume online.

---

(33) · CKSF Intern Challenge

Common Knowledge Scholarship Foundation
P.O. Box 290361
Davie, FL 33329-0361
Phone: 954-262-8553
Email: info@cksf.org
Website: http://www.cksf.org

Purpose: To support high school and college students.

Eligibility: Applicants must register online with CKSF and complete quizzes on various topics. The student with the most points from correct answers and the shortest time that it takes to answer the questions wins the scholarship.

Target applicant:
    High school students
    College students
    Graduate school students
    Adult students

Minimum GPA: None.

Amount: Varies.

Number of awards: 1.

Deadline: Monthly.

How to apply: Applications are available online.

---

(34) · CKSF Movie Scholarships

Common Knowledge Scholarship Foundation
P.O. Box 290361
Davie, FL 33329-0361
Phone: 954-262-8553
Email: info@cksf.org
Website: http://www.cksf.org

Purpose: To reward students and parents for movie knowledge.

Eligibility: Applicants must be high school or college students or their parents and complete the free online registration. The contest is based on a series of short multiple choice quizzes about a movie. Participants receive 500 points for each correct answer and lose one point for each second taken to finish a question. The top 25 percent of the highest scoring students in the first quiz will be automatically entered into a second quiz round. The highest scoring student at the end of the second quiz wins the scholarship.

Target applicant:
    High school students
    College students
    Graduate school students
    Adult students

Minimum GPA: None.

Amount: $250.

Number of awards: 1.
Deadline: June 1.
How to apply: Applicants must complete the free online registration.

(35) · Coca-Cola Scholars Program

Coca-Cola Scholars Foundation
P.O. Box 442
Atlanta, GA 30301
Phone: 800-306-2653
Email: questions@coca-colascholars.org
Website: http://www.coca-colascholars.org
Purpose: Begun in 1986 to celebrate the Coca-Cola Centennial, the program is designed to contribute to the nation's future and to assist a wide range of students.
Eligibility: Applicants must be high school seniors in the U.S. and must use the awards at an accredited U.S. college or university. Selection is based on character, personal merit and commitment. Merit is shown through leadership, academic achievement and motivation to serve and succeed.
Target applicant:
    High school students
Minimum GPA: None.
Amount: $4,000-$20,000.
Number of awards: 250.
Scholarship may be renewable.
Deadline: October 31.
How to apply: Applications are available online.

(36) · Coca-Cola Two-Year College Scholarship

Coca-Cola Scholars Foundation
P.O. Box 442
Atlanta, GA 30301
Phone: 800-306-2653
Email: questions@coca-colascholars.org
Website: http://www.coca-colascholars.org
Purpose: To recognize students enrolled in two-year programs for their academic achievement and community service.
Eligibility: Applicants/nominees should be first- or second-year post-secondary students who intend to complete their education at a two-year degree school. Applicants must be U.S. citizens or permanent residents, but may NOT be children of Coca-Cola employees. Students must have maintained a 2.5 GPA and performed 100+ hours of community service within the 12 months previous to application. Applicants must be planning to enroll in at least two courses at a two-year institution.
Target applicant:
    College students
    Adult students
Minimum GPA: 2.5
Amount: Varies.
Number of awards: Varies.
Scholarship may be renewable.
Deadline: May 31.
How to apply: Applications are available online.

(37) · College Insider TV $500 Scholarship

College Insider TV
925 Adobe Drive
Billings, MT 59105
Phone: 406-670-3866
Email: cirtoms@yahoo.com
Website: http://www.collegeinsider.tv
Purpose: To provide financial assistance to college students and promote College Insider TV.
Eligibility: Applicants must be upcoming or current college students. A high school GPA of 2.0 or higher and/or a college GPA of 2.5 or higher is required. One scholarship is given away each month.
Target applicant:
    High school students
    College students
    Adult students
Minimum GPA: 2.0 for high school students; 2.5 for college students
Amount: $500.
Number of awards: 12.
Deadline: Varies.
How to apply: Applications are available online. Each application is good for six months.

(38) · College Match Program

QuestBridge
P.O. Box 20054
Stanford, CA 94309
Phone: 888-275-2054
Fax: 650-653-2516
Website: http://www.questbridge.org
Purpose: To help low-income students who have academic achievement to find the right college, QuestBridge matches students with the colleges of their choice and provides scholarships.
Eligibility: Applicants should familiarize themselves with the participating colleges' requirements and will be required to answer essay questions. In addition to the application, students must send two teacher recommendations, one counselor recommendation, a transcript, SAT or ACT score reports and a copy of the family tax return. Selected applicants will be required to submit a list of colleges they want to attend and a CSS Profile to those colleges.
Target applicant:
    High school students
Minimum GPA: None.
Amount: Varies.
Number of awards: 75.
Scholarship may be renewable.
Deadline: October 1.
How to apply: Applications are available online in August of each year.

(39) · College Prep Scholarship for High School Juniors

QuestBridge
P.O. Box 20054
Stanford, CA 94309
Phone: 888-275-2054
Fax: 650-653-2516
Website: http://www.questbridge.org
Purpose: To award high school juniors based on academic merit and financial need.
Eligibility: Applicants must submit essays and transcripts. Scholarship packages include one of the following: tuition and room and board for attending the summer school programs of Harvard, Stanford or Yale; SAT prep courses and materials or a computer. Assistance may also include expenses to visit colleges.
Target applicant:
    High school students
Minimum GPA: None.

Amount: Varies.
Number of awards: 500.
Deadline: March 31.
How to apply: Applications are available online.

(40) · College Prowler Essay Scholarship

College Prowler Inc.
5001 Baum Boulevard
Suite 750
Pittsburgh, PA 15213
Phone: 800-290-2682
Fax: 412-697-1396
Email: scholarship@collegeprowler.com
Website: http://www.collegeprowler.com
Purpose: To award students for their advice on entering college.
Eligibility: Applicants must be high school sophomores, juniors or seniors or college freshmen or recent transfer students. Students must write essays based on the topics stated on the website. There are monthly and annual winners.
Target applicant:
  High school students
  College students
  Adult students
Minimum GPA: None.
Amount: $2,000.
Number of awards: 1.
Deadline: Monthly.
How to apply: Applications are available online.

(41) · CollegeNET Scholarship

CollegeNET Scholarship Review Committee
805 SW Broadway
Suite 1600
Portland, OR 97205
Phone: 503-973-5200
Fax: 503-973-5252
Email: scholarship@collegenet.com
Website: http://www.collegenet.com
Purpose: To assist college applicants.
Eligibility: Applicants must sign up at the website and visit and participate in forums. Recipients are determined by votes on the website.
Target applicant:
  High school students
  College students
  Adult students
Minimum GPA: None.
Amount: $1,000-$5,000.
Number of awards: 4.
Deadline: February 24.
How to apply: Applications are available online.

(42) · CollegeWeekLive.com $3,500 Scholarship

CollegeWeekLive
Website: http://www.collegeweeklive.com
Purpose: To support collegebound high school students.
Eligibility: Applicants must be high school freshmen, sophomores, juniors or seniors at the time of application and be international or U.S. students. Students must enroll no later than the fall of 2012 in an accredited U.S. post-secondary institution of higher education.

Target applicant:
  High school students
Minimum GPA: None.
Amount: $3,500.
Number of awards: 1.
Deadline: March and November.
How to apply: Applicants must submit an online short written response (150 words or less) for the question: "Going to college is a big, important step in one's life. What are you looking forward to the most about going college, and why?" More information is available at http://www.scholarshipexperts.com/showApp.htx?appId=10440&src=super

(43) · Congressional Black Caucus Spouses Education Scholarship

Congressional Black Caucus Foundation
1720 Massachusetts Avenue NW
Washington, DC 20036
Phone: 202-263-2800
Fax: 202-775-0773
Email: info@cbcfinc.org
Website: http://www.cbcfinc.org
Purpose: To support students who are pursuing undergraduate or graduate degrees.
Eligibility: Applicants do NOT need to be African American but must reside or attend school in a congressional district represented by a CBC member. Students must be attending or planning to attend school on a full-time basis. Students must have at least a 2.5 GPA, and they must demonstrate leadership and community service participation.
Target applicant:
  High school students
  College students
  Graduate school students
  Adult students
Minimum GPA: 2.5
Amount: Varies.
Number of awards: Varies.
Deadline: May 1.
How to apply: Applications are available online.

(44) · CrossLites Scholarship Contest

CrossLites
Email: crosslites@gmail.com
Website: http://crosslites.com/scholarship.aspx
Purpose: To encourage students to learn about Dr. Charles Parker.
Eligibility: Applicants must be high school, undergraduate or graduate students. There are no minimum GPA, SAT, ACT, GMAT, GRE or any other test score requirements. Students must write a reflective essay of 400 to 600 words based on one of Dr. Charles Parker's quotes or messages, which are listed on the website. There are winners for the high school, undergraduate and graduate school levels. Selection is based on the judges' score (10 percent) and votes from website visitors (90 percent).
Target applicant:
  High school students
  College students
  Graduate school students
  Adult students
Minimum GPA: None.
Amount: $300-$1,500.
Number of awards: 9.
Deadline: March 1.
How to apply: Applications are available online.

(45) · Cultural Ambassadorial Scholarships

Rotary International
One Rotary Center
1560 Sherman Avenue
Evanston, IL 60201
Phone: 847-866-3000
Fax: 847-328-8554
Email: scholarshipinquiries@rotaryintl.org
Website: http://www.rotary.org
Purpose: The scholarship aims to improve international understanding while encouraging friendly relations between people in different countries.
Eligibility: Students must have completed at least two years of college, including at least one year of college-level study of the focus language. Ideal candidates will have excellent leadership skills, demonstrate academic or vocational success, display a commitment to community service and be willing to fulfill their obligations to Rotary according to the terms of the scholarship. Applicants must be citizens of a country containing Rotary clubs, and applications can only be made through a local Rotary club. Rotarians, direct family members of Rotarians and employees or Rotary International or a Rotary district are not eligible for scholarships.
Target applicant:
    College students
    Graduate school students
    Adult students
Minimum GPA: None.
Amount: Varies.
Number of awards: Varies.
Deadline: Varies by Rotary district.
How to apply: Applications are available online.

(46) · Curt Greene Memorial Scholarship

Harness Horse Youth Foundation
16575 Carey Road
Westfield, IN 46074
Phone: 317-867-5877
Fax: 317-867-5896
Email: ellen@hhyf.org
Website: http://www.hhyf.org
Purpose: To support students who are interested in harness racing.
Eligibility: Students must demonstrate financial need, and they must be at least in their senior year of high school. Applicants must submit an essay and two letters of reference.
Target applicant:
    High school students
    College students
    Adult students
Minimum GPA: None.
Amount: Varies.
Number of awards: Varies.
Deadline: April 30.
How to apply: Applications are available online.

(47) · Davidson Fellows Award

Davidson Institute for Talent Development
9665 Gateway Drive
Suite B
Reno, NV 89521
Phone: 775-852-3483
Email: davidsonfellows@ditd.org
Website: http://www.davidson-institute.org
Purpose: To award young people for their works in mathematics, science, technology, music, literature, philosophy or "outside the box."
Eligibility: Applicants must be under the age of 18 and be able to attend the awards reception in Washington, DC. In addition to the monetary award, the institute will pay for travel and lodging expenses. Three nominator forms, three copies of a 15-minute DVD or VHS videotape and additional materials are required.
Target applicant:
    Junior high students or younger
    High school students
Minimum GPA: None.
Amount: $50,000.
Number of awards: Varies.
Deadline: March 30.
How to apply: Applications are available online.

(48) · Davis-Putter Scholarship Fund

Davis-Putter Scholarship Fund
P.O. Box 7307
New York, NY 10116
Email: information@davisputter.org
Website: http://www.davisputter.org
Purpose: To assist students who are both academically capable and who aid the progressive movement for peace and justice both on campus and in their communities.
Eligibility: Applicants must be undergraduate or graduate students who participate in the progressive movement, acting in the interests of issues such as expansion of civil rights and international solidarity, among others. Applicants must also have demonstrated financial need as well as a solid academic record.
Target applicant:
    College students
    Graduate school students
    Adult students
Minimum GPA: None.
Amount: Up to $6,000.
Number of awards: Varies.
Deadline: April 1.
How to apply: Applications are available online.

(49) · Dell Scholars Program

Michael & Susan Dell Foundation
P.O. Box 163867
Austin, TX 78716
Phone: 512-329-0799
Email: act@dellscholars.org
Website: http://www.dellscholars.org
Purpose: To support underprivileged high school seniors.
Eligibility: Students must be participants in an approved college readiness program, and they must have at least a 2.4 GPA. Applicants must be pursuing a bachelor's degree in the fall directly after graduation. Students must also be U.S. citizens or permanent residents and demonstrate financial need. Selection is based on "individual determination to succeed," future goals, hardships that have been overcome, self motivation and financial need.
Target applicant:
    High school students
Minimum GPA: 2.4
Amount: Varies.

Number of awards: Varies.
Scholarship may be renewable.
Deadline: January 15.
How to apply: Applications are available online.

(50) · Dennis Schlosser Endowment

Epsilon Sigma Alpha Foundation
P.O. Box 270517
Fort Collins, CO 80527
Phone: 970-223-2824
Fax: 970-223-4456
Email: kloyd@knoxy.net
Website: http://www.esaintl.com/esaf
Purpose: To provide financial assistance students, especially those with academic achievements.
Eligibility: Applicants may be residents of any state. They may attend any college or university and pursue any major. Selection is based on the following criteria: service (5 percent), character (10 percent), leadership (10 percent), financial need (25 percent) and scholastic ability (50 percent).
Target applicant:
    High school students
    College students
    Adult students
Minimum GPA: None.
Amount: $500.
Number of awards: 1.
Deadline: February 1.
How to apply: Applications are available online.

(51) · Dinah Shore Scholarship

Ladies Professional Golf Association
100 International Golf Drive
Daytona Beach, FL 32124-1092
Phone: 386-274-6200
Fax: 386-274-1099
Website: http://www.lpga.com/content_1.aspx?mid=6&pid=55
Purpose: To honor the late Dinah Shore.
Eligibility: Applicants must be female high school seniors who have been accepted into a full-time course of study at an accredited U.S. institution of higher learning. They must have played golf regularly for the past two years but not played on a competitive collegiate golf team. A minimum GPA of 3.2 is required.
Target applicant:
    High school students
Minimum GPA: 3.2
Amount: $5,000.
Number of awards: 1.
Deadline: May 15.
How to apply: Applications are available online.

(52) · Discover Card Tribute Award Scholarships

Discover Card
c/o American Association of School Administrators
801 N. Quincy Street
Suite 700
Arlington, VA 22203
Phone: 703-528-0700
Fax: 703-841-1543
Email: tributeaward@aasa.org

Website: http://www.discoverfinancial.com/community
Purpose: To recognize high school juniors for their accomplishments beyond academics.
Eligibility: Applicants must be high school juniors at an accredited U.S. high school and have a minimum cumulative 2.75 GPA for their 9th and 10th grades. Applicants must also demonstrate accomplishments in community service and leadership and have faced a significant roadblock or challenge.
Target applicant:
    High school students
Minimum GPA: 2.75
Amount: $30,000.
Number of awards: 10.
Deadline: January 31.
How to apply: Requests for applications are available online.

(53) · DiscoverScholars.org Scholarship

DiscoverScholars.org
5062 27th Street N.
Arlington, VA 22207
Phone: 413-454-5233
Email: mail@discoverscholars.org
Website: http://www.discoverscholars.org
Purpose: To distribute scholarship funds to the types of students that individual donors wish to support.
Eligibility: Applicants must be United States citizens or permanent residents. They must be high school seniors who have accepted an offer to attend a four-year institution of higher learning or current undergraduate students at a four-year college or university.
Target applicant:
    High school students
    College students
    Adult students
Minimum GPA: None.
Amount: Varies.
Number of awards: Varies.
Deadline: December 15.
How to apply: Applications are available online. Deadlines are March 15, June 15, September 15 and December 15 of each year.

(54) · Dixie Boys Baseball Scholarship Program

Dixie Boys Baseball
P.O. Box 8263
Dothan, AL 36304
Phone: 334-793-3331
Fax: 334-793-3331
Email: jjones29@sw.rr.com
Website: http://www.dixie.org
Purpose: To help high school seniors who have participated in a franchised Dixie Boys Baseball Inc. program.
Eligibility: Applicants must plan to pursue undergraduate studies at a college or university. An application, financial statement, two recommendation letters, proof of baseball participation, transcript and essay are required. Selection is based on class rankings, strong school and community leadership and financial need. Programs are located in Alabama, Arkansas, Florida, Georgia, Louisiana, Mississippi, North Carolina, South Carolina, Tennessee, Texas and Virginia.
Target applicant:
    High school students
Minimum GPA: None.
Amount: $1,500.

Number of awards: 11.
Deadline: March 15.
How to apply: Applications are available online.

(55) · Dixie Youth Scholarship Program

Dixie Youth Baseball
P.O. Box 877
Marshall, TX 75671
Phone: 903-927-2255
Email: dyb@dixie.org
Website: http://www.dixie.org
Purpose: To help high school seniors who have participated in a franchised Dixie Youth Baseball league.
Eligibility: Applicants must have been registered on a Dixie Youth Baseball team participating in a franchised Dixie Youth Baseball Inc. league prior to reaching age thirteen. Selection is based on financial need, scholastic record and citizenship. Programs are located in Alabama, Arkansas, Florida, Georgia, Louisiana, Mississippi, North Carolina, South Carolina, Tennessee, Texas and Virginia.
Target applicant:
    High school students
Minimum GPA: None.
Amount: $2,000.
Number of awards: 60.
Deadline: March 1.
How to apply: Contact your local league officials or a district, state or national director for an application, and applications are also available online.

(56) · Do Something Awards

Do Something
24-32 Union Square East
4th Floor
New York, NY 10003
Phone: 212-254-2390
Website: http://www.dosomething.org/awards
Purpose: To award scholarships and community grants to young social entrepreneurs who make a measurable difference in their communities.
Eligibility: Young community leaders up to age 25 may apply. Emphasis is on those who take a leadership role in creating a positive, lasting impact on the community. Focus areas include health, environment and community building.
Target applicant:
    High school students
    College students
    Graduate school students
Minimum GPA: None.
Amount: Up to $25,000.
Number of awards: 9.
Deadline: February 1.
How to apply: Applications are available online.

(57) · Dollars for Scholars Scholarship

Citizens' Scholarship Foundation of America
One Scholarship Way
P.O. Box 297
St. Peter, MN 56082
Phone: 800-537-4180
Website: http://scholarshipamerica.org/dollars_for_scholars.php
Purpose: To encourage students to aim for and achieve loftier educational goals.
Eligibility: Applicants must be members of a local Dollars for Scholars chapter. There are more than 1,200 Dollars for Scholars chapters that award more than $29 million in awards each year.
Target applicant:
    High school students
Minimum GPA: None.
Amount: Varies.
Number of awards: Varies.
Deadline: Varies.
How to apply: Contact your local Dollars for Scholars chapter for more information. A list of chapters is available online.

(58) · Dorothy Harris Endowed Scholarship

Women's Sports Foundation
Eisenhower Park
1899 Hempstead Turnpike, Suite 400
East Meadow, NY 11554
Phone: 800-227-3988
Fax: 516-542-4716
Email: info@womenssportsfoundation.org
Website: http://www.womenssportsfoundation.org
Purpose: To support female students who are majoring in physical education, sport management, sport psychology or sport sociology.
Eligibility: Students must be enrolled full-time in a graduate program. Applicants must submit two letters of recommendation.
Target applicant:
    Graduate school students
    Adult students
Minimum GPA: None.
Amount: $1,500.
Number of awards: 3.
Deadline: December 31.
How to apply: Applications are available online.

(59) · Dr. Arnita Young Boswell Scholarship

National Hook-Up of Black Women Inc.
1809 East 71st Street
Suite 205
Chicago, IL 60649
Phone: 773-667-7061
Fax: 773-667-7064
Email: nhbwdir@aol.com
Website: http://www.nhbwinc.com
Purpose: To reward adult students for their academic achievement.
Eligibility: Applicants must be undergraduate or graduate continuing education students. Selection is based on academic accomplishments as well as involvement in school and community activities and an essay.
Target applicant:
    Graduate school students
    Adult students
Minimum GPA: 2.75
Amount: $1,000.
Number of awards: Varies.
Scholarship may be renewable.
Deadline: March 20.
How to apply: Applications are available by mail and must be requested by March 1.

(60) · Dr. Wynetta A. Frazier "Sister to Sister" Scholarship

National Hook-Up of Black Women Inc.
1809 East 71st Street
Suite 205
Chicago, IL 60649
Phone: 773-667-7061
Fax: 773-667-7064
Email: nhbwdir@aol.com
Website: http://www.nhbwinc.com
Purpose: To assist women who are returning to school without the support of a spouse or family.
Eligibility: Applicants may have taken a break in their educations to seek employment, care for their children or because of financial burden.
Target applicant:
   Graduate school students
   Adult students
Minimum GPA: None.
Amount: $500.
Number of awards: At least 2.
Deadline: April.
How to apply: Applications are available by mail.

(61) · Earl Anthony Memorial Scholarships

United States Bowling Congress
5301 S. 76th Street
Greendale, WI 53129
Phone: 800-514-2695 x3168
Email: smart@bowl.com
Website: http://www.bowl.com/scholarships
Purpose: To honor legendary professional bowler Earl Anthony.
Eligibility: Applicants must be USBC members in good standing who are high school seniors or current college students. They must have a GPA of 2.5 or higher. Community involvement, academic achievement and financial need are considered.
Target applicant:
   High school students
   College students
   Adult students
Minimum GPA: 2.5
Amount: $5,000.
Number of awards: 5.
Deadline: May 1.
How to apply: Applications are available online.

(62) · Educational Advancement Foundation Merit Scholarship

Alpha Kappa Alpha
5656 S. Stony Island Avenue
Chicago, IL 60637
Phone: 800-653-6528
Fax: 773-947-0277
Email: akaeaf@akaeaf.net
Website: http://www.akaeaf.org
Purpose: To support academically-talented students.
Eligibility: Applicants must be full-time undergraduate sophomores or graduate students at an accredited school. They must have a GPA of at least 3.0 and demonstrate involvement and community service. The program is open to students without regard to sex, race, creed, color, ethnicity, religion, sexual orientation or disability. Students do NOT need to be members of Alpha Kappa Alpha.
Target applicant:
   College students
   Graduate school students
   Adult students
Minimum GPA: 3.0
Amount: $1,000.
Number of awards: Varies.
Deadline: April 15 for undergraduate, September 15 for graduate.
How to apply: Applications are available online.

(63) · ESA Foundation Endowment

Epsilon Sigma Alpha Foundation
P.O. Box 270517
Fort Collins, CO 80527
Phone: 970-223-2824
Fax: 970-223-4456
Email: kloyd@knoxy.net
Website: http://www.esaintl.com/esaf
Purpose: To provide financial assistance to students.
Eligibility: Applicants may be residents of any state. They may attend any college or university and major in any field. Selection is based equally on character, leadership, service, financial need and scholastic ability.
Target applicant:
   High school students
   College students
   Adult students
Minimum GPA: None.
Amount: $1,500.
Number of awards: 1.
Deadline: February 1.
How to apply: Applications are available online.

(64) · Ethnic Minority and Women's Enhancement Scholarship

National Collegiate Athletic Association
700 W. Washington Street
P.O. Box 6222
Indianapolis, IN 46206
Phone: 317-917-6222
Fax: 317-917-6888
Email: ahightower@ncaa.org
Website: http://www.ncaa.org
Purpose: To assist minority and female students in intercollegiate athletics with postgraduate scholarships at the NCAA national office.
Eligibility: Applicants must be planning to attend a sports administration program and plan to pursue a career in intercollegiate athletics such as athletic administration, coaching or athletic training.
Target applicant:
   College students
   Graduate school students
   Adult students
Minimum GPA: None.
Amount: $6,000.
Number of awards: 16.
Deadline: Varies.
How to apply: Application details are available online.

(65) · Family Common Knowledge Challenge

Common Knowledge Scholarship Foundation
P.O. Box 290361
Davie, FL 33329-0361
Phone: 954-262-8553
Email: info@cksf.org
Website: http://www.cksf.org
Purpose: To reward students for working together with generations of family members.
Eligibility: Applicants must be high school students, college students or parents. They must participate in a quiz challenge made up of questions from the 1950s through the present. The four rounds of quizzes run in January.
Target applicant:
　High school students
　College students
　Graduate school students
　Adult students
Minimum GPA: None.
Amount: $250.
Number of awards: 1.
Deadline: The first quiz starts January 3.
How to apply: Applications are available online.

(66) · FiSCA Scholarship

Financial Service Centers of America
Attn.: FiSCA Scholarship Program
Court Plaza South, East Wing
21 Main Street, 1st Floor, P.O. Box 647
Hackensack, NJ 07602
Phone: 201-487-0412
Fax: 201-487-3954
Email: info@fisca.org
Website: http://www.fisca.org
Purpose: To help collegebound high school seniors from areas served by FiSCA centers.
Eligibility: Applicants must be high school seniors. Selection is based on leadership, academic achievement and financial need. There are more than 7,000 locations nationwide.
Target applicant:
　High school students
Minimum GPA: None.
Amount: $2,000.
Number of awards: 2.
Deadline: April 3.
How to apply: Applications are available online.

(67) · Floyd Gray Endowment

Epsilon Sigma Alpha Foundation
P.O. Box 270517
Fort Collins, CO 80527
Phone: 970-223-2824
Fax: 970-223-4456
Email: kloyd@knoxy.net
Website: http://www.esaintl.com/esaf
Purpose: To provide financial assistance to students who demonstrate scholastic ability and leadership.
Eligibility: Applicants may be from any state, attend any school and pursue any major. They must have a GPA of 3.0 to 3.5. Criteria for selection include financial need (30 percent), scholastic ability (30 percent), leadership (20 percent), service (10 percent) and character (10 percent).
Target applicant:
　High school students
　College students
　Adult students
Minimum GPA: 3.0
Amount: $1,000.
Number of awards: 1.
Deadline: February 1.
How to apply: Applications are available online.

(68) · Frank Newman Leadership Award

Campus Compact
P.O. Box 1975
Brown University
Providence, RI 02912
Phone: 401-867-3950
Email: campus@compact.org
Website: http://www.compact.org
Purpose: To provide scholarships and opportunities for civic mentoring to students with financial need.
Eligibility: Emphasis is on students who have demonstrated leadership abilities and significant interest in civic responsibility. Students must attend one of the 1,000 Campus Compact member institutions and be nominated by the Campus Compact member president.
Target applicant:
　College students
　Adult students
Minimum GPA: None.
Amount: Varies.
Number of awards: Varies.
Deadline: Varies.
How to apply: Nominations must be made by the Campus Compact member president.

(69) · Fulbright Grants

U.S. Department of State
Office of Academic Exchange Programs, Bureau of Educational and Cultural Affairs
U.S. Department of State, SA-44
301 4th Street SW, Room 234
Washington, DC 20547
Phone: 202-619-4360
Fax: 202-401-5914
Email: academic@state.gov
Website: http://exchanges.state.gov
Purpose: To increase the understanding between the people of the United States and the people of other countries.
Eligibility: Applicants must be graduate students, scholars or professionals. Funds are generally used to support students in university teaching, advanced research, graduate study or teaching in elementary and secondary schools.
Target applicant:
　College students
　Graduate school students
　Adult students
Minimum GPA: None.
Amount: Varies.
Number of awards: 4,500.

Deadline: August 1.
How to apply: Applications are available online.

(70) · Gatorade Leadership Awards

American Legion Baseball
700 N. Pennsylvania Street
Indianapolis, IN 46204
Fax: 317-630-1369
Email: baseball@legion.org
Website: http://www.baseball.legion.org
Purpose: To provide educational assistance for American Legion League players.
Eligibility: Applicants must be high school seniors nominated by their state American Legion department. One nominee from each region is chosen to receive a $1,000 scholarship. Out of the regional winners, one player is selected as Player of the Year and wins an additional $2,000.
Target applicant:
High school students
Minimum GPA: None.
Amount: $1,000-$3,000.
Number of awards: 8.
Deadline: Varies.
How to apply: Applications are available online. Three letters of recommendation are required.

(71) · General Scholarships

Epsilon Sigma Alpha Foundation
P.O. Box 270517
Fort Collins, CO 80527
Phone: 970-223-2824
Fax: 970-223-4456
Email: kloyd@knoxy.net
Website: http://www.esaintl.com/esaf
Purpose: To provide financial assistance for students pursuing higher education.
Eligibility: Applicants may pursue any major at any institution of higher learning. Selection is based equally on character, leadership, service, financial need and scholastic ability. There are three categories of general scholarships: those for students with a GPA of 2.5 to 3.0, those for students with a GPA of 2.0 to 2.5 and those without GPA restrictions.
Target applicant:
High school students
College students
Adult students
Minimum GPA: None.
Amount: $1,000.
Number of awards: Varies.
Deadline: February 1.
How to apply: Applications are available online.

(72) · Generation E Scholarship

WHOmentors.com Inc.
110 Pacific Avenue, Suite 250
San Francisco, CA 94111
Phone: 888-946-6368
Email: rauhmel@whomentors.com
Website: http://www.whomentors.com
Purpose: To support students with academic merit and financial need.

Eligibility: Students must have at least a 2.0 GPA. They must be graduating high school seniors or full-time college students. Preference will be given to graduates of the CEO@18 Youth and College Development Program. Selection is based on academic record, academic goals, financial need, community service, essay and letter of recommendation.
Target applicant:
High school students
College students
Adult students
Minimum GPA: 2.0
Amount: $1,500.
Number of awards: Varies.
Deadline: May 15.
How to apply: Applications are available online.

(73) · Gift for Life Scholarships

United States Bowling Congress
5301 S. 76th Street
Greendale, WI 53129
Phone: 800-514-2695 x3168
Email: smart@bowl.com
Website: http://www.bowl.com/scholarships
Purpose: To provide financial assistance to high school students with financial need.
Eligibility: Applicants must be USBC Youth members who are current high school students in grades 9-12. They must have a GPA of 2.0 or higher and demonstrate financial need. Two awards each year are reserved for children of fire department, emergency rescue or police personnel. Candidates may win once per year up until graduation.
Target applicant:
High school students
Minimum GPA: 2.0
Amount: $1,000.
Number of awards: 6.
Deadline: April 1.
How to apply: Applications are available online.

(74) · Global Action Awards

NetAid Foundation
75 Broad Street, Suite 2410
New York, NY 10004
Phone: 212-537-0500
Fax: 212-537-0501
Email: gaa@netaid.org
Website: http://www.netaid.org
Purpose: To support high school students who have helped the poor at home or abroad.
Eligibility: Applicants must be in high school, live in the U.S. and have led projects on issues such as hunger, HIV/AIDS or education in developing countries.
Target applicant:
High school students
Minimum GPA: None.
Amount: $5,000.
Number of awards: Varies.
Deadline: November 30.
How to apply: Applications are available online.

(75) · Global Citizen Awards

EF Educational Tours
EF Center Boston
One Education Street
Cambridge, MA 02141
Phone: 617-619-1300
Fax: 800-318-3732
Email: marisa.talbot@ef.com
Website: http://www.eftours.com
Purpose: To help students reflect on their place in the world through writing and then have a chance to experience it first-hand.
Eligibility: Applicants must be college-bound high school sophomores and juniors in the U.S. or Canada nominated by their schools and must write an essay on a topic related to global citizenship. The award involves a paid educational trip to Europe.
Target applicant:
     High school students
Minimum GPA: None.
Amount: Trip to Europe.
Number of awards: 12 (10 American, 2 Canadian).
Deadline: January 1.
How to apply: Applications are available online.

(76) · GNC Nutritional Research Grant

National Strength and Conditioning Association (NSCA) Foundation
1885 Bob Johnson Drive
Colorado Springs, CO 80906
Phone: 800-815-6826
Fax: 719-632-6367
Email: nsca@nsca-lift.org
Website: http://www.nsca-lift.org
Purpose: To fund nutrition-based research.
Eligibility: Applicants must be NSCA members for one year before applying and pursuing careers in strength and conditioning. Students must also plan a research project that falls within the mission of the NSCA and submit a proposal describing the rationale, purpose and methods of the planned research. Applications are evaluated based on grades, courses, experience, honors, recommendations and involvement in the community and with NSCA.
Target applicant:
     College students
     Graduate school students
     Adult students
Minimum GPA: None.
Amount: $2,500.
Number of awards: 1.
Deadline: March 15.
How to apply: Applications are available with membership.

(77) · GPA Isn't Everything Scholarship

Cappex
600 Laurel Avenue
Highland Park, IL 60035
Website: http://www.vhmnetwork.com/trackingcode.php?aid=2659&linkid=N139&subid=1
Purpose: To assist high school and college students with college expenses.
Eligibility: Applicants must be current high school or college students or be planning to enroll within the next 12 months.

Target applicant:
     High school students
     College students
     Adult students
Minimum GPA: None.
Amount: $1,000.
Number of awards: Varies.
Deadline: March 31.
How to apply: Applications are available online.

(78) · Graduate Research Grant - Master and Doctoral

National Strength and Conditioning Association (NSCA) Foundation
1885 Bob Johnson Drive
Colorado Springs, CO 80906
Phone: 800-815-6826
Fax: 719-632-6367
Email: nsca@nsca-lift.org
Website: http://www.nsca-lift.org
Purpose: To support research in strength and conditioning.
Eligibility: Applicants must be master's or doctoral students and submit a proposal for a research project in the field of strength and conditioning that fulfills the mission of the NSCA. Students must be NSCA members for one year before applying and pursuing careers in strength and conditioning. Applications are evaluated based on grades, courses, experience, honors, recommendations and involvement in the community and with NSCA.
Target applicant:
     Graduate school students
     Adult students
Minimum GPA: None.
Amount: $2,500-$5,000.
Number of awards: Varies.
Deadline: March 15.
How to apply: Applications are available with membership.

(79) · Graduate Scholarship

Jack Kent Cooke Foundation
44325 Woodridge Parkway
Lansdowne, VA 20176
Phone: 800-498-6478
Fax: 703-723-8030
Email: jkc-u@act.org
Website: http://www.jackkentcookefoundation.org
Purpose: To help students with academic merit and financial need attend graduate school.
Eligibility: Applicants must be college seniors or recent graduates of an accredited U.S. college or university who plan to attend full-time graduate or professional programs for the first time. Applicants may not apply directly to the foundation but must be nominated by the Jack Kent Cooke Foundation faculty representatives at their institutions. The award is based on academic merit and unmet financial need.
Target applicant:
     College students
     Adult students
Minimum GPA: 3.5
Amount: $50,000.
Number of awards: 65.
Scholarship may be renewable.
Deadline: May 1.
How to apply: Nomination forms are available online and by phone.

(80) · Graduate Studies Scholarship

Epsilon Sigma Alpha Foundation
P.O. Box 270517
Fort Collins, CO 80527
Phone: 970-223-2824
Fax: 970-223-4456
Email: kloyd@knoxy.net
Website: http://www.esaintl.com/esaf
Purpose: To provide financial assistance for graduate students.
Eligibility: Applicants may pursue any major at any accredited graduate school in the United States. They must have a GPA of 3.5 or higher. Selection is based equally on character, leadership, service, financial need and scholastic ability.
Target applicant:
    Graduate school students
    Adult students
Minimum GPA: 3.5
Amount: $7,500.
Number of awards: 2.
Deadline: February 1.
How to apply: Applications are available online.

(81) · HANDS Essay Contest

Hands Along the Nile Development Services Inc.
1601 North Kent Street
Suite 1014
Arlington, VA 22209
Phone: 703-875-9370
Fax: 703-875-9371
Email: contest@handsalongthenile.org
Website: http://www.handsalongthenile.org
Purpose: To promote the work of HANDS Along the Nile Development Services.
Eligibility: Applicants must be enrolled in an undergraduate or graduate program at an accredited institution of higher learning or high school students who will enter college in the fall semester following application. They must be United States citizens. An essay of 2,500 words or fewer is required.
Target applicant:
    High school students
    College students
    Graduate school students
    Adult students
Minimum GPA: None.
Amount: $1,500-$5,000.
Number of awards: 5.
Deadline: July 4.
How to apply: Applications are available online.

(82) · Harness Racing Scholarship

Harness Horse Youth Foundation
16575 Carey Road
Westfield, IN 46074
Phone: 317-867-5877
Fax: 317-867-5896
Email: ellen@hhyf.org
Website: http://www.hhyf.org
Purpose: To encourage the education of young people about harness racing.
Eligibility: Applicants must be pursuing a horse-related career, have financial need, demonstrate scholastic achievements and have experience with horses and harness racing. Applicants must also be at least a high school senior and under the age of 25.
Target applicant:
    High school students
    College students
    Graduate school students
Minimum GPA: None.
Amount: Varies.
Number of awards: Varies.
Deadline: April 30.
How to apply: Applications are available by mail.

(83) · Hayek Fund for Scholars

Institute for Humane Studies at George Mason University
3301 N. Fairfax Drive
Suite 440
Arlington, VA 22201
Phone: 800-697-8799
Fax: 703-993-4890
Email: ihs@gmu.edu
Website: http://www.theihs.org
Purpose: To make awards of up to $1,000 to graduate students and untenured faculty members for career-enhancing activities.
Eligibility: Applicants must be graduate students or untenured faculty members and must submit a cover letter explaining how participation will advance their careers and how their understanding of the classical liberal/libertarian tradition will be broadened. Applicants must also submit an abstract of the paper they are going to present (if applicable), an itemized expense list and resume.
Target applicant:
    Graduate school students
    Adult students
Minimum GPA: None.
Amount: $1,000.
Number of awards: Varies.
Deadline: Applications accepted year round.
How to apply: There is no application form.

(84) · High School Internet Challenge

Common Knowledge Scholarship Foundation
P.O. Box 290361
Davie, FL 33329-0361
Phone: 954-262-8553
Email: info@cksf.org
Website: http://www.cksf.org
Purpose: To reward high school students for learning.
Eligibility: Students must attend school in a sponsored county and participate in a quiz competition. There are four cycles in the academic year of eight weeks each from September to April. Local winners advance to compete in the national competition.
Target applicant:
    High school students
Minimum GPA: None.
Amount: $100-$500.
Number of awards: 16.
Deadline: Varies.
How to apply: Applications are available online.

(85) · High School Scholarship

National Strength and Conditioning Association (NSCA) Foundation
1885 Bob Johnson Drive
Colorado Springs, CO 80906
Phone: 800-815-6826
Fax: 719-632-6367
Email: nsca@nsca-lift.org
Website: http://www.nsca-lift.org
Purpose: To support high school students entering the strength and conditioning field.
Eligibility: Applicants must be high school seniors planning to graduate with a degree related to strength and conditioning with a current 3.0 GPA. Students must be NSCA members, although applicants may enroll at the time of application, and pursuing a career in strength and conditioning. Applications are evaluated based on grades, courses, experience, honors, recommendations and involvement in the community and with NSCA.
Target applicant:
    High school students
Minimum GPA: 3.0
Amount: $1,000.
Number of awards: 2.
Deadline: March 15.
How to apply: Applications are available by contacting the organization.

(86) · Horatio Alger Association Scholarship Program

Horatio Alger Association
Attn.: Scholarship Department
99 Canal Center Plaza
Alexandria, VA 22314
Phone: 703-684-9444
Fax: 703-684-9445
Website: http://www.horatioalger.com
Purpose: To assist students who are committed to pursuing a bachelor's degree and have demonstrated integrity, financial need, academic achievement and community involvement.
Eligibility: Applicants must enter college the fall following their high school graduation, be in need of financial aid ($50,000 or less adjusted gross income per family is preferred) and be involved in extracurricular and community activities.
Target applicant:
    High school students
Minimum GPA: 2.0
Amount: Varies.
Number of awards: Varies.
Deadline: October 30.
How to apply: Applications are available online.

(87) · Howard R. Swearer Student Humanitarian Award

Campus Compact
P.O. Box 1975
Brown University
Providence, RI 02912
Phone: 401-867-3950
Email: campus@compact.org
Website: http://www.compact.org
Purpose: Awards granted to college students for use in strengthening or maintaining a service program/project. Emphasis is on college students who work to improve their communities while encouraging others to do the same.
Eligibility: Applicants must be undergraduate students attending institutions that are Campus Compact members and must be nominated by the Campus Compact member president. Students of any class year are eligible.
Target applicant:
    College students
    Adult students
Minimum GPA: None.
Amount: Varies.
Number of awards: 5.
Deadline: February.
How to apply: Nominations must be made by the Campus Compact member president.

(88) · Humane Studies Fellowships

Institute for Humane Studies at George Mason University
3301 N. Fairfax Drive
Suite 440
Arlington, VA 22201
Phone: 800-697-8799
Fax: 703-993-4890
Email: ihs@gmu.edu
Website: http://www.theihs.org
Purpose: To award scholarships to students who are interested in the classical liberal/libertarian tradition of individual rights and market economies and wish to apply these principles in their work.
Eligibility: Applicants must be one of the following: undergraduates who will be juniors or seniors during the academic year of funding, graduate students who are in any field and at any stage before completion of the Ph.D., law students, MBA students or other professional students. The fellowships can be used for study in the U.S. or abroad. Applicants must also be enrolled as full-time students at an accredited degree-granting institution.
Target applicant:
    College students
    Graduate school students
    Adult students
Minimum GPA: None.
Amount: Up to $12,000.
Number of awards: Varies.
Scholarship may be renewable.
Deadline: December 31.
How to apply: Applications are available online.

(89) · ISIA Education Foundation Scholarship

Ice Skating Institute of America (ISIA) Education Foundation
17120 N. Dallas Parkway, Suite 140
Dallas, TX 75248
Phone: 972-735-8800
Fax: 972-735-8815
Website: http://www.skateisi.com
Purpose: To encourage skaters to make athletic and educational achievements.
Eligibility: Applicants must have completed at least three years of high school with a minimum 3.0 GPA during the last two years and enroll as full-time undergraduate students. Applicants must also have been members of the Ice Skating Institute (ISI) and have participated in the ISI Recreational Skater Program for at least four years, have participated in ISI competitions or classes within the last two years, and have completed

240 hours of verified service, with 120 hours volunteered. Applicants must also submit two evaluation forms and an essay of 500 words or less explaining why they should receive the award.

Target applicant:
　High school students
　College students
　Adult students
Minimum GPA: 3.0
Amount: $4,000.
Number of awards: 4.
Deadline: March 1.
How to apply: Applications are available online.

(90) · James M. and Virginia M. Smyth Scholarship

Community Foundation for Greater Atlanta Inc.
50 Hurt Plaza
Suite 449
Atlanta, GA 30303
Phone: 404-688-5525
Email: info@atlcf.org
Website: http://www.atlcf.org/GrantsScholarships/Scholarships/NancyPennLyons.aspx
Purpose: To support students who are pursuing undergraduate degrees.
Eligibility: Students must have at least a 3.0 GPA, and they must have community service experience. Applicants must plan to obtain a degree in the arts and sciences, music, ministry or human services. Preference will be given to students from the following states: Missouri, Mississippi, Georgia, Illinois, Oklahoma, Texas and Tennessee. Applicants must demonstrate financial need. Adult students may also apply.
Target applicant:
　High school students
　College students
　Adult students
Minimum GPA: 3.0
Amount: $2,000.
Number of awards: 12-15.
Scholarship may be renewable.
Deadline: March 26.
How to apply: Applications are available online.

(91) · Jeanne Parker Honorarium Endowment

Epsilon Sigma Alpha Foundation
P.O. Box 270517
Fort Collins, CO 80527
Phone: 970-223-2824
Fax: 970-223-4456
Email: kloyd@knoxy.net
Website: http://www.esaintl.com/esaf
Purpose: To provide financial assistance for outstanding students.
Eligibility: Applicants may be residents of any state and may pursue any major at any college or university. They must have a GPA of 3.0 to 3.5 on a 4.0 scale. Selection is based equally on character, leadership, service, financial need and scholastic ability.
Target applicant:
　High school students
　College students
　Adult students
Minimum GPA: 3.0
Amount: $800.
Number of awards: 1.

Deadline: February 1.
How to apply: Applications are available online.

(92) · John Jowdy Scholarship

Columbia 300
P.O. Box 746
Hopkinsville, KY 42241
Phone: 800-531-5920
Email: columbiainfo@columbia300.com
Website: http://www.columbia300.com
Purpose: To support graduating high school seniors who are involved in bowling.
Eligibility: Students must submit an essay and two letters of recommendation. Recipients must maintain at least a 3.0 GPA for award renewal.
Target applicant:
　High school students
Minimum GPA: None.
Amount: $500.
Number of awards: 1.
Scholarship may be renewable.
Deadline: April 1.
How to apply: Applications are available online.

(93) · Joseph P. Lipman Scholarships

National High School Coaches Association
3276 Nazareth Road
Easton, PA 18045
Phone: 610-923-0900
Fax: 610-923-0800
Email: nhsca@nhsca.com
Website: http://www.nhsca.com
Purpose: To assist high school athletes who have overcome adversity.
Eligibility: Applicants must be graduating high school seniors who have been involved in sports and overcome a disability or other adversity. They must plan to attend a college or university.
Target applicant:
　High school students
Minimum GPA: None.
Amount: $1,000.
Number of awards: 5.
Deadline: May 1.
How to apply: Applications are available online.

(94) · Josephine De Karman Fellowship

Josephine De Karman Fellowship Trust
P.O. Box 3389
San Dimas, CA 91773
Phone: 909-592-0607
Email: info@dekarman.org
Website: http://www.dekarman.org
Purpose: To recognize students who demonstrate academic achievement.
Eligibility: Applicants must be undergraduate students entering their senior year or Ph.D. candidates nearing completion of their degree (all requirements except for the dissertation must be completed by January 31). Applicants may not be post-doctoral students. Special consideration is given to doctoral students in the humanities. The award is open to international students living in the U.S.

Target applicant:
College students
Adult students
Minimum GPA: None.
Amount: $16,000.
Number of awards: 10.
Deadline: January 31.
How to apply: Applications are available online.

(95) · KFC Colonel's Scholars Program
KFC Kentucky Fried Chicken
P.O. Box 725489
Atlanta, GA 31139
Phone: 866-532-7240
Website: http://www.kfcscholars.org
Purpose: To assist students with financial need in obtaining a college education.
Eligibility: Applicants must be high school seniors who are enrolling in a public college or university within their state of residence and pursuing a bachelor's degree. They must also have a GPA of 2.75 or higher and demonstrate financial need. The award is up to $5,000 per year and renewable for up to four years. To renew the scholarship, recipients must maintain a 2.75 minimum GPA, take a minimum of 12 credit hours per semester and during the second year of funding work an average of 10 hours per week.
Target applicant:
High school students
Minimum GPA: 2.75
Amount: Up to $5,000 per year.
Number of awards: 50.
Scholarship may be renewable.
Deadline: February 10.
How to apply: Applications are available online.

(96) · Kiwanis International Foundation Scholarships
Kiwanis International
Key Club International
Youth Funds Specialist
Phone: 800-549-2647
Website: http://www.kiwanis.org
Purpose: To recognize Key Club members for their outstanding service and leadership.
Eligibility: Applicants must be high school seniors who have been active, dues-paying Key Club members in good standing for two years or more. Students must plan to attend a post-secondary institution and have a 3.0 GPA or "B" average. A high school transcript is required. Applications must be submitted to the Key Club district administrator.
Target applicant:
High school students
Minimum GPA: 3.0
Amount: Typically $1,000 but can vary by Key Club district.
Number of awards: 1-10 per Key Club district.
Deadline: Varies.
How to apply: Applications are available online. More information is available from Key Club districts, which are listed online.

(97) · Kohl's Kids Who Care Scholarship
Kohls Corporation
N56 W17000 Ridgewood Drive
Menomonee Falls, WI 53051

Phone: 262-703-7000
Fax: 262 703-7115
Email: community.relations@kohls.com
Website: http://www.kohlscorporation.com
Purpose: To recognize young people who volunteer in their communities.
Eligibility: Applicants must be nominated by parents, educators or community members. There are two categories: one for kids ages 6-12 and another for ages 13-18.
Target applicant:
Junior high students or younger
High school students
Minimum GPA: None.
Amount: Varies.
Number of awards: Varies.
Deadline: March 15.
How to apply: Applications are available online and at Kohl's stores.

(98) · Lauretta M. Roberts Memorial Endowment
Epsilon Sigma Alpha Foundation
P.O. Box 270517
Fort Collins, CO 80527
Phone: 970-223-2824
Fax: 970-223-4456
Email: kloyd@knoxy.net
Website: http://www.esaintl.com/esaf
Purpose: To assist students who demonstrate scholastic ability, financial need and leadership.
Eligibility: Applicants may be residents of any state. They may attend any college or university and pursue any major. Selection is based on the following criteria: scholastic ability (30 percent), financial need (30 percent), leadership (20 percent), character (10 percent) and service (10 percent).
Target applicant:
High school students
College students
Adult students
Minimum GPA: None.
Amount: $500.
Number of awards: 1.
Deadline: February 1.
How to apply: Applications are available online.

(99) · Leaders and Achievers Scholarship Program
Comcast
1500 Market Street
Philadelphia, PA 19102
Website: http://www.comcast.com
Purpose: To provide one-time scholarship awards of $1,000 each to graduating high school seniors. Emphasis is on students who take leadership roles in school and community service and improvement.
Eligibility: Students must have a minimum 2.8 GPA, be nominated by their high school principal and attend school in a Comcast community. See the website for a list of eligible communities by state. Comcast employees, their families or other Comcast affiliates are not eligible to apply.
Target applicant:
High school students
Minimum GPA: 2.8
Amount: $1,000.
Number of awards: 1,300.

Deadline: December 14.
How to apply: Applicants must be nominated by their high school principal.

(100) · Life Lessons Essay Contest

Life and Health Insurance Foundation for Education
1655 N. Fort Myer Drive
Suite 610
Arlington, VA 22209
Phone: 202-464-5000
Fax: 202-464-5011
Email: info@lifehappens.org
Website: http://www.lifehappens.org
Purpose: To support students who have been affected financially and emotionally by the death of a parent.
Eligibility: Applicants must submit either a 500-word essay or a three-minute video describing the impact of losing a parent at a young age. The grand prize winner of the video contest is selected by an online public vote.
Target applicant:
    High school students
    College students
    Adult students
Minimum GPA: None.
Amount: Up to $5,000.
Number of awards: 25.
Deadline: March 31.
How to apply: Applications are available online.

(101) · Linda Riddle/SGMA Scholarship

Women's Sports Foundation
Eisenhower Park
1899 Hempstead Turnpike, Suite 400
East Meadow, NY 11554
Phone: 800-227-3988
Fax: 516-542-4716
Email: info@womenssportsfoundation.org
Website: http://www.womenssportsfoundation.org
Purpose: To help young women athletes with financial need to pursue their sports passion in addition to their college studies.
Eligibility: Applicants must be female high school student athletes with financial need. Selection is based on academic and athletic achievement.
Target applicant:
    High school students
Minimum GPA: None.
Amount: $1,500.
Number of awards: Varies.
Deadline: Varies.
How to apply: Applications are available online.

(102) · Margaret Jesser Memorial Endowment

Epsilon Sigma Alpha Foundation
P.O. Box 270517
Fort Collins, CO 80527
Phone: 970-223-2824
Fax: 970-223-4456
Email: kloyd@knoxy.net
Website: http://www.esaintl.com/esaf
Purpose: To honor the memory of Margaret Jesser.
Eligibility: Applicants may be residents of any state and pursue any major at any college or university. Applicants are selected using the following criteria: scholastic ability (30 percent), financial need (30 percent), leadership (20 percent), service (10 percent) and character (10 percent).
Target applicant:
    High school students
    College students
    Adult students
Minimum GPA: None.
Amount: $500.
Number of awards: 1.
Deadline: February 1.
How to apply: Applications are available online.

(103) · Markley Scholarship

National Association for Campus Activities
13 Harbison Way
Columbia, SC 29212
Phone: 803-732-6222
Fax: 803-749-1047
Email: info@naca.org
Website: http://www.naca.org
Purpose: To support undergraduate and graduate students who have made exceptional contributions in the field of student activities. The focus is on involvement with NACA Central, along with contributions to other activities-based organizations.
Eligibility: Applicants must attend a college/university in the former NACA South Central Region (AR, LA, NM, OK, TX); must be enrolled as juniors, seniors or graduate students at a four-year institution or as sophomores at a two-year institution and must have a minimum 2.5 GPA.
Target applicant:
    College students
    Graduate school students
    Adult students
Minimum GPA: 2.5
Amount: Varies.
Number of awards: 2.
Deadline: September 1.
How to apply: Applications are available online.

(104) · Marsh Scholarship Fund

Eastern Surfing Association
P.O. Box 321
Ormond Beach , FL 32175
Phone: 386-672-4905
Email: scholastics@surfesa.org
Website: http://www.surfesa.org
Purpose: To assist Eastern Surfing Association (ESA) student surfers.
Eligibility: Applicants must be current ESA members. Transcripts, a recommendation letter, purpose letters and applications are required. The award is based on academics and citizenship, not athletic ability.
Target applicant:
    College students
    Graduate school students
    Adult students
Minimum GPA: None.
Amount: Varies.
Number of awards: Varies.

Deadline: May 15.
How to apply: Applications are available online and by email.

(105) · Marshall Memorial Fellowship

German Marshall Fund of the United States
1744 R Street NW
Washington, DC 20009
Phone: 202-745-3950
Fax: 202-265-1662
Email: info@gmfus.org
Website: http://www.gmfus.org
Purpose: To provide fellowships for future community leaders to travel in Europe and to explore its societies, institutions and people.
Eligibility: Applicants must be between 28 and 40 years of age and demonstrate achievement within their profession, civic involvement and leadership. Candidates should have little or no previous experience traveling through Europe. Fellows visit five or six cities and meet with policy makers, business professionals and other community leaders.
Target applicant:
    Graduate school students
    Adult students
Minimum GPA: None.
Amount: Varies.
Number of awards: 100.
Deadline: June 23.
How to apply: Applications are available online.

(106) · Maxine Wirth Graduate Studies Endowment

Epsilon Sigma Alpha Foundation
P.O. Box 270517
Fort Collins, CO 80527
Phone: 970-223-2824
Fax: 970-223-4456
Email: kloyd@knoxy.net
Website: http://www.esaintl.com/esaf
Purpose: To provide financial assistance for graduate students.
Eligibility: Applicants must be graduate students pursuing any major at any accredited graduate school in the United States. They must have a GPA of 3.5 or higher. Selection is based equally on character, leadership, service, financial need and scholastic ability.
Target applicant:
    Graduate school students
    Adult students
Minimum GPA: 3.5
Amount: $2,000.
Number of awards: 1.
Deadline: February 1.
How to apply: Applications are available online.

(107) · Mensa Education & Research Foundation Scholarship Program

Mensa Education & Research Foundation
1229 Corporate Drive West
Arlington, TX 76006-6103
Website: http://www.mensafoundation.org
Purpose: The purpose of the foundation is to "pursue excellence in the areas of intelligence."
Eligibility: Applicants must write an essay, which is used to determine the winners. Grades, academic achievement and financial need are not considered. Students need to reside in a participating Mensa group's

area but do not need to be members of Mensa. A list of participating groups is listed online.
Target applicant:
    High school students
    College students
    Adult students
Minimum GPA: None.
Amount: $60,000 in total awards.
Number of awards: Varies.
Deadline: January 15.
How to apply: Application information is available online during the first week of September.

(108) · Most Valuable Student Scholarships

Elks National Foundation (IL)
2750 North Lakeview Avenue
Chicago, IL 60614
Phone: 773-755-4732
Fax: 773-755-4733
Email: scholarship@elks.org
Website: http://www.elks.org
Purpose: To support high school seniors who have demonstrated scholarship, leadership and financial need.
Eligibility: Applicants must be graduating high school seniors who are U.S. citizens and who plan to pursue a four-year degree on a full-time basis at a U.S. college or university. Male and female students compete separately.
Target applicant:
    High school students
Minimum GPA: None.
Amount: $1,000-$15,000.
Number of awards: 500.
Scholarship may be renewable.
Deadline: January 9.
How to apply: Contact the scholarship chairman of your local Lodge or the Elks association of your state.

(109) · My Turn Essay Competition

Kaplan/Newsweek
888 7th Avenue, 22nd floor
New York, NY 10106
Phone: 800-526-2595
Email: classroom.service@newsweek.com
Website: http://www.kaptest.com/essay
Purpose: To assist high school students who write a personal essay for the publication.
Eligibility: Applicants must be high school students planning to attend a college or university following high school who write a personal essay that shares an opinion or experience. Selection is based on criteria including creativity, organization and effectiveness.
Target applicant:
    High school students
Minimum GPA: None.
Amount: $1,000-$5,000.
Number of awards: 10.
Deadline: February 1.
How to apply: Applications are available online.

(110) · NAA College Scholarship

National Archery Association
One Olympic Plaza
Colorado Springs, CO 80906
Phone: 719-866-4576
Fax: 719-632-4733
Email: info@usarchery.org
Website: http://www.usarchery.org
Purpose: To support student archers.
Eligibility: Applicants must be full-time students at two- or four-year institutions and compete in the NAA College Division. A minimum 2.5 GPA is required.
Target applicant:
    College students
    Adult students
Minimum GPA: 2.5
Amount: $500.
Number of awards: 8.
Deadline: December 31.
How to apply: Applications are available online.

(111) · NABF Scholarship Program

National Amateur Baseball Federation
Awards Committee Chairman
P.O. Box 705
Bowie, MD 20718
Phone: 301-464-5460
Fax: 301-352-0214
Email: nabf1914@aol.com
Website: http://www.nabf.com
Purpose: To support students who have been involved with the federation.
Eligibility: Applicants must be enrolled in an accredited college or university, must have participated in a federation event and must be sponsored by a member association. Selection is based on grades, financial need and previous awards.
Target applicant:
    College students
    Adult students
Minimum GPA: None.
Amount: Varies.
Number of awards: Varies.
Deadline: Varies.
How to apply: Applications are available online.

(112) · NACA Regional Council Student Leader Scholarships

National Association for Campus Activities
13 Harbison Way
Columbia, SC 29212
Phone: 803-732-6222
Fax: 803-749-1047
Email: info@naca.org
Website: http://www.naca.org
Purpose: To provide educational assistance to students in each of NACA's regions.
Eligibility: Applicants must be undergraduate college students in good standing, hold leadership positions on campus and have made significant contributions to their respective campuses.
Target applicant:
    College students
    Adult students
Minimum GPA: None.
Amount: Varies.
Number of awards: Varies.
Deadline: May 1.
How to apply: Applications are available online.

(113) · Nancy Reagan Pathfinder Scholarships

National Federation of Republican Women
124 N. Alfred Street
Alexandria, VA 22314
Phone: 703-548-9688
Fax: 703-548-9836
Email: mail@nfrw.org
Website: http://www.nfrw.org/programs/scholarships.htm
Purpose: To honor former First Lady Nancy Reagan.
Eligibility: Applicants must be college sophomores, juniors, seniors or master's degree students. Two one-page essays and three letters of recommendation are required. Winners may not reapply.
Target applicant:
    College students
    Graduate school students
    Adult students
Minimum GPA: None.
Amount: $2,500.
Number of awards: 3.
Deadline: June 1.
How to apply: Applications are available online.

(114) · NATA Scholarship

National Athletic Trainers' Association
National Athletic Trainer's Association Research and Education Foundation Inc.
2952 Stemmons Freeway
Dallas, TX 75247
Phone: 214-637-6282
Fax: 214-637-2206
Email: barbaran@nata.org
Website: http://www.nata.org
Purpose: To encourage study among athletic trainers.
Eligibility: Applicants must be at least a junior in college with a minimum 3.2 GPA, be sponsored by a certified athletic trainer and be a member of the NATA.
Target applicant:
    College students
    Graduate school students
    Adult students
Minimum GPA: 3.2
Amount: $2,000.
Number of awards: 60.
Deadline: February 10.
How to apply: Applications are available online.

(115) · National Junior Girls Scholarships

Ladies Auxiliary VFW
406 West 34th Street
10th Floor
Kansas City, MO 64111

Phone: 816-561-8655 x19
Fax: 816-931-4753
Email: jmillick@ladiesauxvfw.org
Website: https://www.ladiesauxvfw.org
Purpose: To award Junior Girls who excel academically, are actively involved in Junior Girls and demonstrate leadership at school.
Eligibility: Applicants must be Junior Girls ages 13 to 16 and active members of a Ladies Auxiliary VFW Junior Girls Unit for at least a year who have held an office. Applicants must also submit letters of recommendation, a transcript and a list of activities.
Target applicant:
    Junior high students or younger
    High school students
Minimum GPA: None.
Amount: $100-$10,000.
Number of awards: 2.
Deadline: March 11.
How to apply: Applications are available online.

---

(116) · National Merit Scholarship Program and National Achievement Scholarship Program

National Merit Scholarship Corporation
1560 Sherman Avenue, Suite 200
Evanston, IL 60201
Phone: 847-866-5100
Fax: 847-866-5113
Website: http://www.nationalmerit.org
Purpose: To provide scholarships through a merit-based academic competition.
Eligibility: Applicants must be enrolled full-time in high school, progressing normally toward completion and planning to enter college no later than the fall following completion of high school, be U.S. citizens or permanent legal residents in the process of becoming U.S. citizens and take the PSAT/NMSQT no later than the 11th grade. Participation in the program is based on performance on the exam.
Target applicant:
    High school students
Minimum GPA: None.
Amount: Varies.
Number of awards: Varies.
Scholarship may be renewable.
Deadline: Varies.
How to apply: Application is made by taking the PSAT/NMSQT test.

---

(117) · National Oratorical Contest

American Legion
Attn.: Americanism and Children and Youth Division
P.O. Box 1055
Indianapolis, IN 46206
Phone: 317-630-1249
Fax: 317-630-1369
Website: http://www.legion.org
Purpose: To reward students for their knowledge of government and oral presentation skills.
Eligibility: Applicants must be high school students under the age of 20 who are U.S. citizens or legal residents. Students first give an oration within their state and winners compete at the national level. The oration must be related to the Constitution of the United States focusing on the duties and obligations citizens have to the government. It must be in English and be between eight and ten minutes. There is also an assigned topic which is posted on the website, and it should be between three and five minutes.
Target applicant:
    High school students
Minimum GPA: None.
Amount: $18,000.
Number of awards: Varies.
Deadline: December 1.
How to apply: Contact your local American Legion post or state headquarters.

---

(118) · National Scholarship Program

National Scholastic Surfing Association
P.O. Box 495
Huntington Beach, CA 92648
Phone: 714-378-0899
Fax: 714-964-5232
Email: jaragon@nssa.org
Website: http://www.nssa.org
Purpose: To assist NSSA members in their pursuit of post-high school education.
Eligibility: Applicants must be competitive student NSSA members and have a minimum 3.0 GPA in the current school year. Scholastic achievement, leadership, service, career goals and recommendations are considered.
Target applicant:
    High school students
    College students
    Adult students
Minimum GPA: 3.0
Amount: Varies.
Number of awards: Varies.
Deadline: Varies.
How to apply: Applications are available with organization membership.

---

(119) · Navin Narayan Scholarship

American Red Cross
National Headquarters
2025 E Street NW
Washington, DC 20006
Phone: 202-303-4498
Website: http://www.redcross.org
Purpose: The scholarship is named after Navin Narayan, a former youth volunteer with the Red Cross who died from cancer at the age of 23. In his honor, the Red Cross awards this scholarship to youth volunteers who have made significant humanitarian contributions to the organization and who have also achieved academic excellence in high school.
Eligibility: Applicants must plan to attend a four-year college or university and have volunteered a minimum of two years with the Red Cross.
Target applicant:
    High school students
Minimum GPA: None.
Amount: $2,500.
Number of awards: 1.
Deadline: Varies.
How to apply: Application forms are available online.

(120) · NCAA Postgraduate Scholarship

National Collegiate Athletic Association
700 W. Washington Street
P.O. Box 6222
Indianapolis, IN 46206
Phone: 317-917-6222
Fax: 317-917-6888
Email: ahightower@ncaa.org
Website: http://www.ncaa.org
Purpose: To reward student athletes who perform well in both sports and academics.
Eligibility: Student athletes must show achievement in their last year of varsity-level intercollegiate athletics at an NCAA school. Applicants must be nominated by the faculty athletic representative or athletic director and be enrolling as a full- or part-time graduate student.
Target applicant:
　College students
　Adult students
Minimum GPA: 3.2
Amount: $7,500.
Number of awards: Up to 174.
Deadline: December 12.
How to apply: Applications are available online.

(121) · Nelnet $1 Million Scholarship Giveaway

Nelnet
121 South 13th Street Suite 201
Lincoln, NE 68508
Phone: 888-486-4722
Email: scholarships@nelnet.net
Website: http://www.nelnet.com
Purpose: To provide financial assistance to students and to promote Nelnet's student loans.
Eligibility: Applicants must be U.S. students age 16 or older and high school juniors or seniors or undergraduate college students. The college attended must participate in the federal loan program.
Target applicant:
　High school students
　College students
　Adult students
Minimum GPA: None.
Amount: Up to $25,000.
Number of awards: 760.
Deadline: August 7.
How to apply: Applications are available online.

(122) · New America Foundation Essay Contest

New America Foundation
Workforce and Family Program
1630 Connecticut Avenue NW
7th Floor
Washington, DC 20009
Phone: 202-986-2700
Fax: 202-986-3696
Website: http://www.newamerica.net/programs/workforce_and_family/essay_contest
Purpose: To encourage high school seniors to voice their opinions about improving the lives of children.
Eligibility: Applicants must be public or private high school seniors. They must write an essay of 600 words or less about what they would do as President of the United States to improve the lives of children. Submissions must be verified as original works by a parent and a teacher.
Target applicant:
　High school students
Minimum GPA: None.
Amount: $2,500.
Number of awards: 1.
Deadline: February 20.

(123) · North American Rolex Scholarship

Our World-Underwater Scholarship Society
P.O. Box 4428
Chicago, IL 60680
Phone: 630-969-6690
Fax: 630-969-6690
Email: info@owuscholarship.org
Website: http://www.owuscholarship.org
Purpose: To support students planning careers in underwater world or associated disciplines.
Eligibility: Applicants must be certified scuba divers with a minimum of 25 open-water dives, be academically excellent, not have earned graduate degrees and be at least 21 and no older than 26 at the time of the application deadline. Applicants must also pass a preliminary medical examination for diving fitness and pass a NOAA diving physical if selected. A personal interview will be required of all scholarship finalists. There is a $25 fee. It is highly recommended that you research the scholarship and awarding organization before applying for a scholarship with a fee. There are many scholarships that do not require a fee.
Target applicant:
　College students
　Adult students
Minimum GPA: None.
Amount: $20,000.
Number of awards: Varies.
Deadline: December 31.
How to apply: Applications are available online.

(124) · NRA Outstanding Achievement Youth Award

National Rifle Association
11250 Waples Mill Road
Fairfax, VA 22030
Phone: 703-267-1505
Email: youth_programs@nrahq.org
Website: http://www.nrahq.org
Purpose: To recognize NRA Junior Members who actively participate in shooting sports.
Eligibility: Applicants must be NRA Junior Members (or Regular or Life Members under 18 years old) and have completed five core and five elective requirements. Core requirements are being current members of the NRA, attending and completing an NRA Basic Firearm Training Course, earning a rating in a shooting discipline and submitting an essay. Applicants must also complete five elective requirements from those listed on the website.
Target applicant:
　High school students
Minimum GPA: None.
Amount: $5,000.
Number of awards: 3.

Deadline: May 1.
How to apply: Applications are available online.

(125) · Off to College Scholarship Sweepstakes

SunTrust
P.O. Box 27172
Richmond, VA 23261-7172
Phone: 800-786-8787
Website: http://www.suntrusteducation.com/sweeps/
Purpose: To assist a student for the first year of expenses at any accredited college.
Eligibility: Applicants must be high school seniors who are at least 13 years old and plan to attend a college accredited by the U.S. Department of Education the following fall. U.S. residency is required. Financial need and academic achievement are not considered. Note that this is a sweepstakes drawing every two weeks.
Target applicant:
  High school students
Minimum GPA: None.
Amount: $1,000.
Number of awards: 15.
Deadline: May 15.
How to apply: Applications are available online. Mail-in entries are also accepted.

(126) · Parent Answer Scholarship Sweepstakes

Parent Answer Scholarship Sweepstakes--$10,000
P.O. Box 9500
Wilkes-Barre, PA 18773-9500
Website: http://www.parentanswerservice.com
Purpose: To support the parents of undergraduate college students.
Eligibility: This $10,000 sweepstakes is open to all U.S. residents who are parents of undergraduate college students. Applicants must have children who are undergraduate students at a Title IV school. The children must be born in 1982 or later.
Target applicant:
  Graduate school students
  Adult students
Minimum GPA: None.
Amount: $10,000.
Number of awards: 1.
Deadline: May 30.
How to apply: Applicants may enter the sweepstakes online or by mail.

(127) · Past International Council President's Endowment

Epsilon Sigma Alpha Foundation
P.O. Box 270517
Fort Collins, CO 80527
Phone: 970-223-2824
Fax: 970-223-4456
Email: kloyd@knoxy.net
Website: http://www.esaintl.com/esaf
Purpose: To provide assist students who demonstrate scholastic ability and financial need.
Eligibility: Applicants may be residents of any state and may pursue any major at any institution of higher learning. Selection is based on the following criteria: scholastic ability (30 percent), financial need (30 percent), leadership (20 percent), character (10 percent) and service (10 percent).

Target applicant:
  High school students
  College students
  Adult students
Minimum GPA: None.
Amount: $500.
Number of awards: 1.
Deadline: February 1.
How to apply: Applications are available online.

(128) · Patricia M. McNamara Memorial Scholarship

Ropage Group LLC
8877 N. 107th Avenue
Suite 302
Box 287
Peoria, AZ 85345
Email: questions@patricias-scholarship.org
Website: http://www.patricias-scholarship.org
Purpose: To honor the memory of Patricia McNamara.
Eligibility: Applicants must be attending or plan to attend an institution of higher education in the school year following application. An essay is required.
Target applicant:
  High school students
  College students
  Adult students
Minimum GPA: None.
Amount: $1,000.
Number of awards: 1.
Deadline: May 31.
How to apply: Applications are available online.

(129) · Patriot's Pen Essay Contest

Veterans of Foreign Wars
406 W. 34th Street
Kansas City, MO 64111
Phone: 816-756-3390
Fax: 816-968-1149
Email: info@vfw.org
Website: http://www.vfw.org
Purpose: To give middle school students the opportunity to express their views on democracy.
Eligibility: Students must be 6th, 7th or 8th graders. They must write a 300-400 word essay based on a theme chosen by the VFW related to patriotism.
Target applicant:
  Junior high students or younger
Minimum GPA: None.
Amount: Up to $10,000.
Number of awards: Varies.
Deadline: November 1.
How to apply: Applications are available from your local VFW Post, VFW State Headquarters or VFW National Programs.

(130) · Paul and Daisy Soros Fellowships for New Americans

Paul and Daisy Soros
400 W. 59th Street
New York, NY 10019
Phone: 212-547-6926

Fax: 212-548-4623
Email: pdsoros_fellows@sorosny.org
Website: http://www.pdsoros.org
Purpose: Named after Hungarian immigrants, the Paul and Daisy Soros Fellowships are designed to assist the graduate studies of immigrant children.
Eligibility: Applicants must be immigrants who are resident aliens, have been naturalized or are the children of two parents who have been naturalized. The potential winner of a fellowship must already have a bachelor's degree or be a college senior and must not be over the age of 30 by the application deadline.
Target applicant:
    College students
    Graduate school students
    Adult students
Minimum GPA: None.
Amount: $20,000.
Number of awards: 30.
Scholarship may be renewable.
Deadline: November 1.
How to apply: Applications are available online.

(131) · Phillips Foundation Ronald Reagan Future Leaders Program

Penguin Group (USA)
Academic Marketing Department
Signet Classic Student Scholarship
375 Hudson Street
New York, NY 10014
Website: http://us.penguingroup.com/static/html/services-academic/essayhome.html
Purpose: To recognize students who demonstrate leadership on behalf of freedom, American values and constitutional principles.
Eligibility: Applicants must be enrolled full-time at any accredited, four-year degree-granting institution in the U.S. or its territories. Applicants may apply for a Ronald Reagan Future Leaders Program grant during their sophomore or junior year in high school. Selection is based on merit and financial need.
Target applicant:
    High school students
Minimum GPA: None.
Amount: $1,000-7,500.
Number of awards: Varies.
Scholarship may be renewable.
Deadline: January 15.
How to apply: Applications are available online.

(132) · Phoenix Scholarship Program

Phoenix Scholarship Program
159 Concord Avenue
Suite 1C
Cambridge, MA 02138
Email: phoenixawards@gmail.com
Purpose: To provide financial assistance to deserving high school seniors who plan to seek higher education.
Eligibility: Applicants must be U.S. high school seniors or they must have graduated within 13 months prior to the application deadline. They must have a 2.75 or higher GPA and have already taken the SAT or ACT. They must be in good standing with their high school, possess

good moral character and plan to enroll in an accredited college or university upon graduation.
Target applicant:
    High school students
Minimum GPA: 2.75
Amount: Varies.
Number of awards: Up to 4.
Deadline: April 30.
How to apply: Applications are available via email.

(133) · Principal's Leadership Award

Herff Jones
c/o National Association of Secondary School Principals
1904 Association Drive
Reston, VA 20191
Phone: 800-253-7746
Email: carrollw@principals.org.
Website: http://www.principals.org/awards/
Purpose: To recognize students for their leadership.
Eligibility: Applicants must be seniors and nominated by their high school principal. Each principal can nominate one student leader from the senior class. Application packets are mailed each fall to every secondary school.
Target applicant:
    High school students
Minimum GPA: None.
Amount: $1,000.
Number of awards: 150.
Deadline: December 3.
How to apply: Nomination forms are available online.

(134) · Prudential Spirit of Community Award

Prudential Spirit of Community Awards
751 Broad Street, 16th Floor
Newark, NJ 07102
Phone: 888-450-9961
Email: spirit@principals.org
Website: http://www.prudential.com/community
Purpose: To recognize students for their self-initiated community service.
Eligibility: Applicants must be middle and high school students in the U.S. or Puerto Rico and involved in volunteer work that was completed during the year prior to date of application.
Target applicant:
    Junior high students or younger
    High school students
Minimum GPA: None.
Amount: $1,000-$5,000.
Number of awards: 104.
Deadline: October 29.
How to apply: Applications are available online.

(135) · Rhodes Scholar

Rhodes Scholarship Trust
Attn.: Elliot F. Gerson
8229 Boone Boulevard, Suite 240
Vienna, VA 22182
Email: amsec@rhodesscholar.org
Website: http://www.rhodesscholar.org

Purpose: To recognize qualities of young people that will contribute to the "world's fight."

Eligibility: Applicants must be U.S. citizens between the ages of 18 and 24 and have a bachelor's degree at the time of the award. The awards provides for two to three years of study at the University of Oxford including educational costs and other expenses. Selection is extremely competitive and is based on literary and scholastic achievements, athletic achievement and character.

Target applicant:
    College students

Minimum GPA: None.

Amount: Varies.

Number of awards: 32.

Deadline: October.

How to apply: Applications are available online.

---

(136) · RMHC National Scholarship Program

Ronald McDonald House Charities
One Kroc Drive
Oak Brook, IL 60523
Phone: 630-623-7048
Fax: 630-623-7488
Email: scholarships@us.mcd.com
Website: http://www.rmhc.org

Purpose: To help high school seniors attend college.

Eligibility: Applicants must be high school seniors less than 21 years of age who are eligible to attend a two- or four-year institution of higher learning full-time. They must be U.S. residents who live in a participating Ronald McDonald House Charities chapter's geographic area. A list of chapters is on the website.

Target applicant:
    High school students

Minimum GPA: None.

Amount: Varies.

Number of awards: Varies.

Deadline: February 15.

How to apply: Applications are available online.

---

(137) · Rosagene Huggins Memorial Endowment

Epsilon Sigma Alpha Foundation
P.O. Box 270517
Fort Collins, CO 80527
Phone: 970-223-2824
Fax: 970-223-4456
Email: kloyd@knoxy.net
Website: http://www.esaintl.com/esaf

Purpose: To provide funds for students based on scholastic ability, financial need and leadership.

Eligibility: Applicants may be from any state and may pursue any major at any institution of higher learning. Selection is based upon the following criteria: scholastic ability (30 percent), financial need (30 percent), leadership (20 percent), character (10 percent) and service (10 percent).

Target applicant:
    High school students
    College students
    Adult students

Minimum GPA: None.

Amount: $1,300.

Number of awards: 1.

Deadline: February 1.

How to apply: Applications are available online.

---

(138) · Russ Griffith Memorial Scholarship

Datatel
4375 Fair Lakes Court
Fairfax, VA 22033
Phone: 800-486-4332
Email: scholars@datatel.com
Website: http://www.datatelscholars.org

Purpose: To support students returning to Datatel client institutions after an extended absence.

Eligibility: Applicants must be currently attending an eligible Datatel school after an absence of at least five years. Both full-time and part-time (at least six credit hours) students may apply. Applicants must provide a personal statement that includes the impact of being a returning student, the challenges of combining school with such things as work and family and the importance of receiving the scholarship to help achieve a dream.

Target applicant:
    College students
    Graduate school students
    Adult students

Minimum GPA: None.

Amount: $2,000.

Number of awards: 50.

Deadline: January 31.

How to apply: Applications are available online.

---

(139) · Ruth Gregg Memorial Endowment

Epsilon Sigma Alpha Foundation
P.O. Box 270517
Fort Collins, CO 80527
Phone: 970-223-2824
Fax: 970-223-4456
Email: kloyd@knoxy.net
Website: http://www.esaintl.com/esaf

Purpose: To provide financial assistance to students who demonstrate scholastic ability and leadership.

Eligibility: Applicants may be residents of any state and may major in any field at any college or university. Selection criteria include character (10 percent), service (10 percent), leadership (20 percent), financial need (30 percent) and scholastic ability (30 percent).

Target applicant:
    High school students
    College students
    Adult students

Minimum GPA: None.

Amount: $1,500.

Number of awards: 1.

Deadline: February 1.

How to apply: Applications are available online.

---

(140) · Sallie Mae $1,000 Scholarship

College Answer
Sallie Mae
12061 Bluemont Way
Reston, VA 20190
Website: http://www.collegeanswer.com

Purpose: To help students pay for college.

Eligibility: Applicants may be high school, undergraduate or graduate students and must register on the CollegeAnswer website. Each month one registered user is selected in a random drawing to receive the scholarship. When you are registered for the website or the Sallie Mae Scholarship Search, you are automatically entered into the scholarship drawing.

Target applicant:
    High school students
    College students
    Graduate school students
    Adult students
Minimum GPA: None.
Amount: $1,000.
Number of awards: 1 per month.
Deadline: Monthly.
How to apply: Enter the scholarship by registering on the website. If you have already registered on the website or have a screen name and password, you are already entered for the scholarship.

(141) · Salvatore J. Natoli Dissertation Award in Geographic Education

National Council for Geographic Education
Jacksonville State University
206-A Martin Hall
700 Pelham Road North
Jacksonville, AL 36265-1602
Phone: 256-782-5293
Fax: 256-782-5336
Email: ncge@jsu.edu
Website: http://www.ncge.org
Purpose: To recognize outstanding doctoral research.
Eligibility: This award is not restricted to dissertations in geography. Applicants must have received the doctoral degree within the previous two years and are expected to present their research at the annual meeting. Applicants must submit papers drawn from the dissertation, plus abstracts; cover letters that state the title of the dissertation, date of the degree, major professor's name and institution and applicant's social security number; verification letters from the major professors and applications for program participation for the NCGE Annual Meeting. The meeting registration fee will be refunded to finalists and winners after the meeting.
Target applicant:
    Graduate school students
    Adult students
Minimum GPA: None.
Amount: $500.
Number of awards: 2.
Deadline: March 15.
How to apply: Application materials are stated online.

(142) · Sam Walton Community Scholarship

Wal-Mart Foundation
c/o Scholarship Program Administrators
P.O. Box 22117
Nashville, TN 37202
Phone: 866-851-3372
Fax: 615-523-7100
Website: http://www.walmartfoundation.org
Purpose: To support local communities and to help students achieve their educational dreams.
Eligibility: Applicants must be high school seniors. Selection is based on academic record, test scores, community and extracurricular involvement, work experience and financial need. Each Wal-Mart Store

and Sam's Club awards up to two scholarships. Wal-Mart employees and the children of employees are not eligible.
Target applicant:
    High school students
Minimum GPA: None.
Amount: $1,000.
Number of awards: 3,000.
Deadline: February 1.
How to apply: Applications are only available at your local Wal-Mart Store or Sam's Club during the first week of December.

(143) · Samuel Huntington Public Service Award

National Grid
25 Research Drive
Westborough, MA 01582
Phone: 508-389-2000
Website: http://www.nationalgridus.com
Purpose: To assist students who wish to perform one year of humanitarian service immediately upon graduation.
Eligibility: Applicants must be graduating college seniors, and must intend to perform one year of public service in the U.S. or abroad. The service may be individual work or through charitable, religious, educational, governmental or other public service organizations.
Target applicant:
    College students
    Adult students
Minimum GPA: None.
Amount: $10,000.
Number of awards: 1.
Deadline: February 15.
How to apply: Applications are available online.

(144) · Scholar Athlete Milk Mustache of the Year Award (SAMMY)

National Fluid Milk Processor Promotion Board
Scholar Athlete Milk Mustache of Year
P.O. Box 9249
Medford, NY 11763
Website: http://www.whymilk.com
Purpose: To reward outstanding student athletes.
Eligibility: Applicants must be legal residents of the 48 contiguous United States or the District of Columbia, high school seniors and participate in a high school or club sport. Applicants must describe in 75 words or less how drinking milk has been a part of their life and training regimen.
Target applicant:
    High school students
Minimum GPA: None.
Amount: Varies.
Number of awards: Varies.
Deadline: March 7.
How to apply: Applications may be obtained online, and only applications submitted online will be accepted.

(145) · Scholarship Drawing for $1000

Edfinancial Services
eCampusTours c/o Edsouth
P.O. Box 31549
Knoxville, TN 37930
Website: http://www.ecampustours.com

Purpose: Ten entrants will each receive a $1,000 scholarship to help pay for college. Winners will be selected through a random drawing by Edfinancial Services.

Eligibility: Eligible students include U.S. citizens, U.S. nationals and permanent residents or students enrolled in a U.S. institution of higher education. Winners must be enrolled in an eligible institution of higher education, as stipulated in the eligibility requirements, within one year of winning the award. Scholarship awards will be paid directly to the college.

Target applicant:
  High school students
  College students
  Graduate school students
  Adult students
Minimum GPA: None.
Amount: $1,000.
Number of awards: 10.
Deadline: March 31.
How to apply: Entries are available online, and registration is required. Entries may be submitted by mail.

(146) · Scholarship Lucky Draw

GoCollege.com
Email: giovanna@gocollege.com
Website: http://www.gocollege.com/lucky-draw-scholarship.html
Purpose: To provide scholarship opportunities to students who register on the website.
Eligibility: This is a monthly drawing for a $250 college scholarship award.
Target applicant:
  High school students
  College students
  Graduate school students
  Adult students
Minimum GPA: None.
Amount: $250.
Number of awards: 1.
Deadline: Monthly.
How to apply: Enter by registering online and completing a questionnaire.

(147) · Scholarship Program for Students in Cargill Communities

National FFA Organization
P.O. Box 68960
6060 FFA Drive
Indianapolis, IN 46268-0960
Phone: 317-802-6060
Fax: 317-802-6051
Email: scholarships@ffa.org
Website: http://www.ffa.org
Purpose: To provide financial support to students who are living in Cargill communities.
Eligibility: Students must obtain a signature from a Cargill or Cargill joint-venture employee from their community. Applicants must be high school students who are planning to pursue two-year or four-year degrees. Children of Cargill employees are not eligible.
Target applicant:
  High school students
Minimum GPA: None.
Amount: $1,000.

Number of awards: 350.
Deadline: February 15.
How to apply: Applications are available online.

(148) · Scholarships for Student Leaders

National Association for Campus Activities
13 Harbison Way
Columbia, SC 29212
Phone: 803-732-6222
Fax: 803-749-1047
Email: info@naca.org
Website: http://www.naca.org
Purpose: The NACA foundation is committed to developing professionals in the field of campus activities.
Eligibility: Students must hold a significant campus leadership position, have made significant contributions to their campus communities and have demonstrated leadership skills and abilities.
Target applicant:
  College students
  Adult students
Minimum GPA: None.
Amount: Varies.
Number of awards: Varies.
Deadline: November 1.
How to apply: Applications are available online.

(149) · September 11th Scholarship

Jack Kent Cooke Foundation
44325 Woodridge Parkway
Lansdowne, VA 20176
Phone: 800-498-6478
Fax: 703-723-8030
Email: jkc-u@act.org
Website: http://www.jackkentcookefoundation.org
Purpose: To help spouses and dependents of those disabled or killed by the September 11 events.
Eligibility: Applicants must currently be enrolled at any two-year, four-year, technical or trade school in the United States; demonstrate financial need and be spouses or dependents of those disabled or killed by the September 11 events: United Airlines Flight 93, American Airlines Flight 77, American Airlines Flight 11, United Airlines Flight 175, World Trade Center, Pentagon or September and October 2001 anthrax attacks. Applications for summer funding must be postmarked by July 7, and applications for fall funding must be postmarked by October 13.
Target applicant:
  College students
  Adult students
Minimum GPA: None.
Amount: $15,000.
Number of awards: Varies.
Deadline: July 7 and October 13.
How to apply: Applications are available online.

(150) · Shepherd Scholarship

Ancient and Accepted Scottish Rite of Freemansonry Southern Jurisdiction
1733 16th Street NW
Washington, DC 20009-3103
Phone: 202-464-3579
Fax: 202-464-0487

Website: http://www.srmason-sj.org

Purpose: To provide financial assistance to students pursuing degrees in fields associated with service to country.

Eligibility: Applicants must have accepted enrollment in a U.S. institution of higher learning. No Masonic affiliation is required. Up to four letters of recommendation will be considered. Selection is based on "dedication, ambition, academic preparation, financial need and promise of outstanding performance at the advanced level."

Target applicant:
   High school students
   College students
   Graduate school students
   Adult students

Minimum GPA: None.

Amount: $1,500.

Number of awards: Varies.

Scholarship may be renewable.

Deadline: April 1.

How to apply: Applications are available online.

---

(151) · Simon Youth Foundation Community Scholarship

Simon Youth Foundation
c/o Scholarship America
One Scholarship Way
P.O. Box 297
St. Peter, MN 56082
Phone: 800-537-4180
Email: syf@simon.com
Website: http://simonyouth.scholarshipamerica.org

Purpose: To assist promising students who live in communities with Simon properties.

Eligibility: Applicants must be high school seniors who plan to attend an accredited two- or four-year college, university or technical/vocational school. Scholarships are awarded without regard to race, color, creed, religion, gender, disability or national origin, and recipients are selected on the basis of financial need, academic record, potential to succeed, participation in school and community activities, honors, work experience, a statement of career and educational goals and an outside appraisal. Awards are given at every Simon mall in the U.S. A list of malls is online at www.simon.com/find_mall.

Target applicant:
   High school students

Minimum GPA: None.

Amount: $1,500.

Number of awards: 382.

Scholarship may be renewable.

Deadline: January 31.

How to apply: Applications are available online each year from October 15 to January 31.

---

(152) · Skateboard Scholarship

Patrick Kerr Skateboard Scholarship
P.O. Box 2054
Jenkintown, PA 19046
Fax: 215-663-5897
Email: info@skateboardscholarship.org
Website: http://www.skateboardscholarship.org

Purpose: To provide scholarships for skateboarders.

Eligibility: Applicants must be skateboarders who are high school seniors with at least a 2.5 GPA. They must be U.S. citizens and be planning to enroll full-time at a post-secondary school. Applicants must submit an essay on how skateboarding has influenced their lives, two letters of recommendation and a high school transcript. Special consideration will be given to students who are involved in skateboarding activism. Skateboarding skill will not be considered in awarding the scholarship.

Target applicant:
   High school students

Minimum GPA: 2.5

Amount: $1,000-$5,000.

Number of awards: 4.

Deadline: April 20.

How to apply: Applications are available online.

---

(153) · Stokes Educational Scholarship Program

National Security Agency (NSA)
9800 Savage Road, Suite 6779
Ft. George G. Meade, MD 20755-6779
Phone: 410-854-4725
Website: http://www.nsa.gov/careers/

Purpose: To recruit those with skills useful to the NSA, especially minority high school students.

Eligibility: Students must be seniors at the time of application, be U.S. citizens, have a 3.0 GPA, have a minimum ACT score of 25 or a minimum SAT score of 1600 and demonstrate leadership skills. Applicants must be planning to major in one of the following fields: computer science, electrical or computer engineering, languages, mathematics or intelligence analysis.

Target applicant:
   High school students

Minimum GPA: 3.0

Amount: Tuition, fees, salary and summer employment.

Number of awards: Varies.

Scholarship may be renewable.

Deadline: November 30.

How to apply: Applications are available online.

---

(154) · Stonehouse Golf Youth Scholarship

Stonehouse Publishing Company
Scholarship Committee
1508 Leavenworth Street
Omaha, NE 68102
Phone: 800-949-7274
Fax: 402-344-3563
Email: pseina@stonehousegolf.com
Website: http://www.stonehousegolf.com

Purpose: To recognize individuals who throughout their high school careers have shown outstanding academic and golf achievements.

Eligibility: Applicants must be seniors in high school, participate in at least two seasons on high school golf teams and have a minimum 3.5 GPA. Students must be intending to pursue a 2 or 4 year degree and must have participated with their school in the Stonehouse Golf Fundraiser.

Target applicant:
   High school students

Minimum GPA: 3.5

Amount: $500.

Number of awards: 20.

Deadline: May 30.

How to apply: Applications are available online.

(155) · Stuck at Prom Scholarship

Henkel Consumer Adhesives
32150 Just Imagine Drive
Avon, OH 44011-1355
Website: http://www.stuckatprom.com/contests
Purpose: To reward students for their creativity with duct tape.
Eligibility: Applicants must attend a high school prom as a couple in the spring wearing the most original attire that they make from duct tape. Photographs of past winners are available on the website.
Target applicant:
High school students
Minimum GPA: None.
Amount: $6,000.
Number of awards: 3.
Deadline: June 9.
How to apply: Applications are available online.

(156) · Student Activist Awards

Freedom from Religion Foundation
P.O. Box 750
Madison, WI 53701
Phone: 608-256-5800
Email: info@ffrf.org
Website: http://www.ffrf.org
Purpose: To assist high school and college student activists.
Eligibility: Selection is based on activism for free thought or separation of church and state.
Target applicant:
High school students
College students
Adult students
Minimum GPA: None.
Amount: $1,000.
Number of awards: Varies.
Deadline: Varies.
How to apply: Contact the organization for more information.

(157) · Study Abroad Grants

Honor Society of Phi Kappa Phi
P.O. Box 16000
Louisiana State University
Baton Rouge, LA 70893
Phone: 800-804-9880
Fax: 225-388-4900
Email: awards@phikappaphi.org
Website: http://www.phikappaphi.org
Purpose: To provide scholarships for undergraduate students who will study abroad.
Eligibility: Applicants do not have to be members of Phi Kappa Phi but must attend an institution with a Phi Kappa Phi chapter, have between 56 and 90 credit hours and have at least two semesters remaining at their home institution upon return. Students must have been accepted into a study abroad program that demonstrates their academic preparation, career choice and the welfare of others.
Target applicant:
College students
Adult students
Minimum GPA: 3.5
Amount: $1,000.
Number of awards: 38.

Deadline: February 15.
How to apply: Applications are available online.

(158) · Summer Graduate Research Fellowships

Institute for Humane Studies at George Mason University
3301 N. Fairfax Drive
Suite 440
Arlington, VA 22201
Phone: 800-697-8799
Fax: 703-993-4890
Email: ihs@gmu.edu
Website: http://www.theihs.org
Purpose: To support graduate students who are interested in scholarly research in the classical liberal tradition.
Eligibility: Applicants must be graduate students in areas related to the classical liberal tradition and should be focusing on a discrete writing project. Selection is based on resume, GRE or LSAT scores and graduate transcripts, writing sample and research proposal and bibliography for thesis chapter or publishable paper.
Target applicant:
Graduate school students
Adult students
Minimum GPA: None.
Amount: $3,000 + travel allowance.
Number of awards: Varies.
Deadline: February 15.
How to apply: Applications are available online.

(159) · SuperCollege.com Student Scholarship

SuperCollege.com
Scholarship Dept. 673
3286 Oak Court
Belmont, CA 94002
Website: http://www.supercollege.com/about/about.cfm?area=7
Purpose: Each year SuperCollege.com uses a portion of the proceeds from the sales of its books to award a scholarship to an outstanding high school or college student.
Eligibility: Applicants must be high school students, college undergraduates or graduate students, be U.S. citizens or legal residents and may study any major and attend or plan to attend any accredited college or university in the U.S. Selection is based on academic and extracurricular achievement and an essay.
Target applicant:
High school students
College students
Graduate school students
Adult students
Minimum GPA: None.
Amount: $500-$2,500.
Number of awards: Varies.
Deadline: July 31.
How to apply: Applications are only available online. Please do not call or write for an application.

(160) · Talbots Women's Scholarship Fund

Talbots
Scholarship Management Services, Scholarship America
One Scholarship Way
P.O. Box 297
Saint Peter, MN 56082

Phone: 507-931-1682
Website: http://www.talbots.com/about/scholar/scholar.asp
Purpose: To provide scholarships for women returning to college.
Eligibility: Applicants must be female U.S. residents who have earned their high school diploma or GED at least 10 years ago and who are now enrolled or planning to attend undergraduate study at a two- or four-year college or university or vocational-technical school. The deadline is January 2 or when the first 1,000 applications are received, whichever is earlier.
Target applicant:
  College students
  Adult students
Minimum GPA: None.
Amount: $1,000-$10,000.
Number of awards: 55.
Deadline: January 2 or until 1,000 applications are received.
How to apply: Applications are available online.

---

(161) · Telluride Association Summer Programs

Telluride Association
217 West Avenue
Ithaca, NY 14850
Phone: 607-273-5011
Fax: 607-272-2667
Email: telluride@cornell.edu
Website: http://www.tellurideassociation.org
Purpose: Summer program to provide high school students with a college-level, intellectually enriching experience.
Eligibility: Applicants must be high school juniors. The association seeks applicants from a variety of socio-economic backgrounds and provides for their tuition and room and board during summer programs in New York, Texas and Michigan. Students are invited to apply either by receiving a score on the PSAT/NMSQT that is usually in the top 1 percent or by nomination by a teacher or counselor.
Target applicant:
  High school students
Minimum GPA: None.
Amount: Summer program tuition.
Number of awards: Varies.
Deadline: January.
How to apply: Applications are sent to nominated students.

---

(162) · The 50k Giveaway Scholarship

Academic Finance Corporation
One W. Boylston Street, Chadwick Court
Worcester, MA 01605
Phone: 877-232-4322
Fax: 508-854-9972
Email: info@afclending.com
Website: http://www.afclending.com/50k
Purpose: To assist first-year college or trade-school students with expenses.
Eligibility: This is a random drawing. Entries must be from those entering their first year of an accredited two-year or four-year college or trade school.
Target applicant:
  High school students
  College students
  Adult students
Minimum GPA: None.
Amount: $5,000.

Number of awards: 10.
Deadline: May 31.
How to apply: Applications are available online.

---

(163) · The Lowe's Scholarship

Lowe's Company
1000 Lowe's Boulevard
Mooresville, NC 28117
Phone: 800-44-LOWES
Website: http://www.lowes.com
Purpose: To help young people in the communities where Lowe's does business to get a strong educational foundation.
Eligibility: Applicants must be high school seniors who will enroll in an accredited two- or four-year college or university in the United States. Leadership ability, community involvement and academic achievement are considered when making the selection for the scholarships.
Target applicant:
  High school students
Minimum GPA: None.
Amount: $15,000.
Number of awards: Varies.
Scholarship may be renewable.
Deadline: March 15.
How to apply: Applications are available online.

---

(164) · Top Ten College Women Competition

Glamour
The Conde Nast Publications Inc.
4 Times Square
New York, NY 10036
Phone: 800-244-4526
Fax: 212-286-6922
Email: ttcw@glamour.com
Website: http://www.glamour.com
Purpose: To recognize outstanding leaders among women who are college juniors.
Eligibility: Applicants must be female junior-year students in an undergraduate program. Judging is based on academics, community service and leadership skills.
Target applicant:
  College students
  Adult students
Minimum GPA: None.
Amount: $1,500.
Number of awards: 10.
Deadline: January 15.
How to apply: Applications are available by email to ttcw@glamour.com.

---

(165) · Toyota Community Scholars

Toyota
Scholarship and Recognition Programs
Educational Testing Service
P.O. Box 6730
Princeton, NJ 08541
Phone: 609-771-7878
Fax: 609-734-5410
Website: http://www.toyota.com/about/our_commitment/philanthropy/education/scholarships/

Purpose: To recognize students for their academic achievement and community involvement.
Eligibility: Applicants must be high school seniors with at least at 3.0 GPA, be nominated by their high school, and be involved in community service.
Target applicant:
    High school students
Minimum GPA: 3.0
Amount: $10,000-$20,000.
Number of awards: 100.
Scholarship may be renewable.
Deadline: December.
How to apply: Contact your high school guidance counselor.

(166) · Transatlantic Community Foundation Fellowship

German Marshall Fund of the United States
1744 R Street NW
Washington, DC 20009
Phone: 202-745-3950
Fax: 202-265-1662
Email: info@gmfus.org
Website: http://www.gmfus.org
Purpose: To provide fellowships for community foundation staff to exchange experiences with European colleagues.
Eligibility: The fellowships provide a two-week program including roundtrip airfare, a daily stipend and reimbursement for car rental expenses.
Target applicant:
    Graduate school students
    Adult students
Minimum GPA: None.
Amount: Varies.
Number of awards: 5.
Deadline: Varies.
How to apply: Contact the organization for application information.

(167) · Truman Scholar

Truman Scholarship Foundation
712 Jackson Place NW
Washington, DC 20006
Phone: 202-395-4831
Fax: 202-395-6995
Email: office@truman.gov
Website: http://www.truman.gov
Purpose: To provide college junior leaders who plan to pursue careers in government, non-profits, education or other public service with financial support for graduate study and leadership training.
Eligibility: Applicants must be juniors, attending an accredited U.S. college or university and be nominated by the institution. Students may not apply directly. Nominated applicants must be U.S. citizens or U.S. nationals, complete an application and write a policy recommendation.
Target applicant:
    College students
    Adult students
Minimum GPA: None.
Amount: $30,000.
Number of awards: 70-75.
Deadline: February 7.

How to apply: See your school's Truman Faculty Representative or contact the foundation.

(168) · U.S. Bank Internet Scholarship Program

U.S. Bank
U.S. Bancorp Center
800 Nicollet Mall
Minneapolis, MN 55402
Phone: 800-242-1200
Website: http://www.usbank.com/studentbanking
Purpose: To support graduating high school seniors who plan to attend college.
Eligibility: Applicants must be high school seniors who plan to attend full-time an accredited two- or four-year college and be U.S. citizens or permanent residents. Recipients are selected through a random drawing.
Target applicant:
    High school students
Minimum GPA: None.
Amount: $1,000.
Number of awards: up to 30.
Deadline: February 28.
How to apply: Applications are only available online.

(169) · Ultimate Scholarship Giveaway

Next Step Magazine
86 W. Main Street
Victor, NY 14565
Phone: 800-771-3117
Email: members@nextstepmag.com
Website: http://www.nextstepmagazine.com
Purpose: A sweepstakes for scholarship prize money given out by a random drawing from applicants.
Eligibility: The drawing is open to residents of the U.S. or Canada (except for Puerto Rico and Quebec) who are at least 14 and currently in college or will be enrolled in college within the next two years.
Target applicant:
    High school students
    College students
    Adult students
Minimum GPA: None.
Amount: $20,000.
Number of awards: 1.
Deadline: June 20.
How to apply: Applications are available online.

(170) · Undergraduate Research Grant

National Strength and Conditioning Association (NSCA) Foundation
1885 Bob Johnson Drive
Colorado Springs, CO 80906
Phone: 800-815-6826
Fax: 719-632-6367
Email: nsca@nsca-lift.org
Website: http://www.nsca-lift.org
Purpose: To support undergraduate research in strength and conditioning.
Eligibility: Applicants must be undergraduate students planning to undertake a research project related to strength and conditioning that fits in with the mission of the NSCA. Students must submit a proposal with rationale, study methods and purpose and find a faculty advisor.

Applicants must be NSCA members for one year before applying and be pursuing careers in strength and conditioning. Applications are evaluated based on grades, courses, experience, honors, recommendations and involvement in the community and with NSCA.

Target applicant:
    College students
    Adult students
Minimum GPA: None.
Amount: Up to $1,500.
Number of awards: Varies.
Deadline: March 15.
How to apply: Applications are available with membership.

---

(171) · Undergraduate Transfer Scholarship

Jack Kent Cooke Foundation
44325 Woodridge Parkway
Lansdowne, VA 20176
Phone: 800-498-6478
Fax: 703-723-8030
Email: jkc-u@act.org
Website: http://www.jackkentcookefoundation.org
Purpose: To help community college students attend four-year universities.
Eligibility: Applicants must be students or recent alumni from accredited U.S. community colleges or two-year institutions who plan to pursue bachelor's degrees at four-year institutions. Applicants may not apply directly to the foundation but must be nominated by the Jack Kent Cooke Foundation faculty representatives at their institutions. The award is based on academic merit and unmet financial need.
Target applicant:
    College students
    Adult students
Minimum GPA: 3.5
Amount: $30,000.
Number of awards: 35.
Scholarship may be renewable.
Deadline: February 1.
How to apply: Nomination forms are available online and by phone.

---

(172) · University Writing Scholarship

Elder & Leemaur Publishers
115 Garfield Street #4953
Sumas, WA 98295
Website: http://www.elpublishers.com
Purpose: To promote students to explore career opportunities in professional writing.
Eligibility: Applicants must be high school seniors or current undergraduate students in North America and must submit an essay up to 500 words on one of the provided topics. Students must attend or plan to attend a college/university in either Canada or the United States. Some essays will be featured in the publication. There are numerous competitions with deadlines spread throughout the year.
Target applicant:
    High school students
    College students
    Adult students
Minimum GPA: None.
Amount: Varies.
Number of awards: Varies.
Deadline: July 1.
How to apply: Essays should be submitted online.

---

(173) · Unmet Need Scholarship

Sallie Mae Fund Unmet Need Scholarship Program
Scholarship America
One Scholarship Way
P.O. Box 297
Saint Peter, MN 56082
Phone: 507-931-1682
Website: http://www.thesalliemaefund.org
Purpose: To assist students whose financial aid packages are not enough.
Eligibility: Applicants must have a minimum 2.5 GPA, family incomes of $30,000 or less and financial aid packages with unmet need of $1,000 or more. Applicants must also be accepted or enrolled as full-time undergraduate students at two- or four-year schools in the U.S. or Puerto Rico. The application must include a transcript, Student Aid Report and financial aid award letter from the school the student plans to attend.
Target applicant:
    High school students
    College students
    Adult students
Minimum GPA: 2.5
Amount: $1,000-$3,800.
Number of awards: Varies.
Deadline: May 31.
How to apply: Applications are available online.

---

(174) · USA Funds Access to Education Scholarships

USA Funds
Scholarship Management Services, CSFA
1505 Riverview Road
St. Peter, MN 56082
Phone: 888-537-4180
Email: scholarship@usafunds.org
Website: http://www.usafunds.org
Purpose: To assist students in achieving their higher education goals.
Eligibility: This is a need-based scholarship program with aid for full-time and half-time students. Applicants must be high school seniors or other individuals who plan to enroll or are enrolled in full- or half-time undergraduate or graduate coursework at an accredited two- or four-year college, university or vocational or technical school. Students must be U.S. citizens or eligible noncitizens and must have an adjusted gross family income of $35,000 or less. Selection is based on academic performance, leadership, activities, work experience and career and educational goals.
Target applicant:
    High school students
    College students
    Graduate school students
    Adult students
Minimum GPA: None.
Amount: Varies.
Number of awards: Varies.
Deadline: February 15.
How to apply: Applications are available online.

---

(175) · USBC Alberta E. Crowe Star of Tomorrow

United States Bowling Congress
5301 S. 76th Street
Greendale, WI 53129
Phone: 800-514-2695 x3168

Email: smart@bowl.com
Website: http://www.bowl.com/scholarships
Purpose: To recognize star qualities in female students in high school or college who are competitive bowlers.
Eligibility: Applicants must be female high school seniors or college students 22 years of age or younger and USBC members who compete in certified events. They must hold an average of 175 or higher and must not have competed in professional tournaments except for Pro-AM's. They must also have a GPA of 2.5 or higher.
Target applicant:
   High school students
   College students
Minimum GPA: 2.5
Amount: $1,500.
Number of awards: 1.
Deadline: October 1.
How to apply: Applications are available online.

(176) · USBC Annual Zeb Scholarship

United States Bowling Congress
5301 S. 76th Street
Greendale, WI 53129
Phone: 800-514-2695 x3168
Email: smart@bowl.com
Website: http://www.bowl.com/scholarships
Purpose: To reward USBC Youth members with high academic achievement who have participated in community service.
Eligibility: Applicants must be high school juniors or seniors who are USBC Youth members in good standing. They must have a GPA of 2.0 or higher and must not have competed in any professional bowling tournament except for Pro-Am's.
Target applicant:
   High school students
Minimum GPA: 2.0
Amount: $2,500.
Number of awards: 1.
Deadline: April 1.
How to apply: Applications are available online.

(177) · USBC Chuck Hall Star of Tomorrow

United States Bowling Congress
5301 S. 76th Street
Greendale, WI 53129
Phone: 800-514-2695 x3168
Email: smart@bowl.com
Website: http://www.bowl.com/scholarships
Purpose: To recognize star qualities in male high school and college students who are competitive bowlers.
Eligibility: Applicants must be United States Bowling Congress members who compete in certified events, are age 22 or younger and are high school seniors or college students with a GPA of 2.5 or higher. They must also have a bowling average of 175 or greater and not have competed in a professional bowling tournament except for Pro-AM's.
Target applicant:
   High school students
   College students
Minimum GPA: 2.5
Amount: $1,500.
Number of awards: 1.
Scholarship may be renewable.

Deadline: October 1.
How to apply: Applications are available online.

(178) · USBC Earl Anthony Memorial Scholarships

United States Bowling Congress
5301 S. 76th Street
Greendale, WI 53129
Phone: 800-514-2695 x3168
Email: smart@bowl.com
Website: http://www.bowl.com/scholarships
Purpose: To recognize USBC members for community involvement and academic achievement.
Eligibility: Applicants must be high school seniors or college students who are USBC members in good standing. They must have never competed in a professional bowling tournament, excluding Pro-AMs. They must also have a minimum GPA of 2.5.
Target applicant:
   High school students
   College students
   Adult students
Minimum GPA: 2.5
Amount: $5,000.
Number of awards: 5.
Deadline: May 1.
How to apply: Applications are available online.

(179) · USBC Gift for Life Scholarships

United States Bowling Congress
5301 S. 76th Street
Greendale, WI 53129
Phone: 800-514-2695 x3168
Email: smart@bowl.com
Website: http://www.bowl.com/scholarships
Purpose: To assist USBC Youth members with financial need in attending college.
Eligibility: Applicants must be high school students with a minimum GPA of 2.0 who are current USBC members. They must also demonstrate and explain in an essay their financial hardship. Students may apply and win each year from grades 9-12.
Target applicant:
   High school students
Minimum GPA: 2.0
Amount: $1,000.
Number of awards: Up to 12.
Deadline: April 1.
How to apply: Applications are available online.

(180) · USBC Youth Ambassador of the Year

United States Bowling Congress
5301 S. 76th Street
Greendale, WI 53129
Phone: 800-514-2695 x3168
Email: smart@bowl.com
Website: http://www.bowl.com/scholarships
Purpose: To recognize contributions to the sport of bowling, academic achievement, and community service.
Eligibility: Students must be USBC Youth members who will be 18 years of age or older by August 1 of the year of their selection. They must also be high school seniors and be nominated by a USBC member.

Target applicant:
　High school students
Minimum GPA: None.
Amount: $1,500.
Number of awards: 2.
Deadline: November 1.
How to apply: Applications are available online.

---

(181) · Violet Richardson Award

Soroptimist International
1709 Spruce Street
Philadelphia, PA 19103
Phone: 215-893-9000
Fax: 215-893-5200
Email: siahq@soroptimist.org
Website: http://www.soroptimist.org
Purpose: To recognize young women who contribute to the community through volunteer efforts.
Eligibility: Applicants must be young women between the ages of 14 and 17 who make outstanding contributions to volunteer efforts. Efforts that benefit women or girls are of particular interest. This award is administered by local, participating Soroptimist clubs and is not available in all communities.
Target applicant:
　High school students
Minimum GPA: None.
Amount: Varies.
Number of awards: Varies.
Deadline: Varies.
How to apply: Contact your local Soroptimist club.

---

(182) · Virginia Taylor Honorarium Scholarship

Epsilon Sigma Alpha Foundation
P.O. Box 270517
Fort Collins, CO 80527
Phone: 970-223-2824
Fax: 970-223-4456
Email: kloyd@knoxy.net
Website: http://www.esaintl.com/esaf
Purpose: To assist students who are continuing an interrupted education.
Eligibility: Applicants may pursue any major at any school. Selection is based on the following characteristics: character (10 percent), leadership (20 percent), service (10 percent), financial need (30 percent) and scholastic ability (30 percent).
Target applicant:
　College students
　Adult students
Minimum GPA: None.
Amount: $500.
Number of awards: 1.
Deadline: February 1.
How to apply: Applications are available online.

---

(183) · Voice of Democracy Audio Essay Contests

Veterans of Foreign Wars
406 W. 34th Street
Kansas City, MO 64111
Phone: 816-756-3390
Fax: 816-968-1149

Email: info@vfw.org
Website: http://www.vfw.org
Purpose: To encourage patriotism with students creating audio essays expressing their opinion on a patriotic theme.
Eligibility: Applicants must submit a three- to five-minute audio essay on tape or CD focused on a yearly theme. Students must be in the 9th to 12th grade in a public, private or parochial high school, home study program or overseas U.S. military school. Foreign exchange students are not eligible for the contest, and students who are age 20 or older also may not enter. Previous first place winners on the state level are ineligible.
Target applicant:
　High school students
Minimum GPA: None.
Amount: $1,000-$30,000.
Number of awards: Varies.
Deadline: November 1.
How to apply: Applications are available online but must be submitted to a local VFW post.

---

(184) · VRG Scholarship

Vegetarian Resource Group
P.O. Box 1463
Baltimore, MD 21203
Phone: 410-366-8343
Email: vrg@vrg.org
Website: http://www.vrg.org
Purpose: To award high school seniors who promote vegetarianism.
Eligibility: Applicants must be graduating U.S. high school students who have promoted vegetarianism in their schools or communities. Vegetarians do not eat meat, fish or fowl. The award is based on compassion, courage and commitment to promoting a "peaceful world through a vegetarian diet or lifestyle." Applicants should submit transcripts and at least three recommendations.
Target applicant:
　High school students
Minimum GPA: None.
Amount: $5,000.
Number of awards: 2.
Deadline: February 20.
How to apply: Applications are available online, by mail, by phone or by email. A typed document containing the application's information will be accepted.

---

(185) · Wallace and Margaret Shaw Endowment

Epsilon Sigma Alpha Foundation
P.O. Box 270517
Fort Collins, CO 80527
Phone: 970-223-2824
Fax: 970-223-4456
Email: kloyd@knoxy.net
Website: http://www.esaintl.com/esaf
Purpose: To provide financial assistance to outstanding students.
Eligibility: Applicants may be residents of any state. They may attend any college or university and major in any field. Selection is based equally on the following criteria: character, leadership, service, financial need and scholastic ability.
Target applicant:
　High school students
　College students
　Adult students
Minimum GPA: None.

Amount: $500.
Number of awards: 1.
Deadline: February 1.
How to apply: Applications are available online.

(186) · Watson Travel Fellowship

Thomas J. Watson Foundation
810 7th Avenue, 31st Floor
New York, NY 10019
Phone: 212-245-8859
Fax: 212-245-8860
Email: tjw@watsonfellowship.org
Website: http://www.watsonfellowship.org
Purpose: To award one-year grants for independent study and travel outside the U.S. to graduating college seniors.
Eligibility: Applicants must be nominated by participating colleges or universities and submit proposals for a project, personal statements, application forms, photos, transcripts and letters of recommendation. An interview with a representative may follow. Recipients must graduate before the fellowship can begin.
Target applicant:
    College students
    Adult students
Minimum GPA: None.
Amount: $35,000.
Number of awards: 50.
Deadline: Varies.
How to apply: Applicants should contact the local Watson liaison for any local deadlines or additional information.

(187) · Wendy's High School Heisman Award

Wendy's Restaurants
c/o National Association of Secondary School Principals
1904 Association Drive
Reston, VA 20191
Phone: 800-205-6367
Email: dsa@principals.org
Website: http://www.wendyshighschoolheisman.com
Purpose: To recognize scholarship, citizenship and athletic ability.
Eligibility: Applicants must be entering their high school senior year and participate in one of 32 officially sanctioned sports. Eligible students have a minimum 3.0 GPA. Selection is based on academic achievement, community service and athletic accomplishments.
Target applicant:
    High school students
Minimum GPA: 3.0
Amount: Varies.
Number of awards: Varies.
Deadline: October 1.
How to apply: Nomination forms are available online.

(188) · Willow C. Gray Endowment

Epsilon Sigma Alpha Foundation
P.O. Box 270517
Fort Collins, CO 80527
Phone: 970-223-2824
Fax: 970-223-4456
Email: kloyd@knoxy.net
Website: http://www.esaintl.com/esaf

Purpose: To provide funds for students who demonstrate scholastic ability and leadership.
Eligibility: Applicants may be from any state and may pursue any major at any institution of higher learning. They must have a GPA of 3.0 to 3.5. Selection criteria include scholastic ability (30 percent), financial need (30 percent), leadership (20 percent), service (10 percent) and character (10 percent).
Target applicant:
    High school students
    College students
    Adult students
Minimum GPA: 3.0
Amount: $1,000.
Number of awards: 1.
Deadline: February 1.
How to apply: Applications are available online.

(189) · Win Free Tuition Giveaway

Next Step Magazine
86 W. Main Street
Victor, NY 14565
Phone: 800-771-3117
Email: members@nextstepmag.com
Website: http://www.nextstepmagazine.com
Purpose: To support higher education.
Eligibility: Entrants must be legal residents of the U.S. and Canada (except for Puerto Rico or Quebec) who are age 14 or older. They must also be planning to enroll or currently enrolled in college by September 30 three years after the application date. This is a sweepstakes drawing for one year's tuition up to $20,000.
Target applicant:
    Junior high students or younger
    High school students
    College students
    Graduate school students
    Adult students
Minimum GPA: None.
Amount: Up to $20,000.
Number of awards: 1.
Deadline: June 27.
How to apply: Applications are available online. Students may also apply by mailing a 3x5 postcard with their name, address, city, state, zip code, age, phone number and email address or using a reply card found in Next Step Magazine.

(190) · Women's Western Golf Foundation Scholarship

Women's Western Golf Foundation
393 Ramsay Road
Deerfield, IL 60015
Phone: 608-274-0173
Email: cocomc2000@comcast.net
Website: http://www.wwga.org
Purpose: To support female students who are involved in golf.
Eligibility: Applicants must be in their senior year of high school. Students must demonstrate academic excellence, good character and financial need. Recipients must maintain a 3.0 GPA for award renewal.
Target applicant:
    High school students
Minimum GPA: None.
Amount: $2,000.

Number of awards: Varies.
Scholarship may be renewable.
Deadline: March 1.
How to apply: Applications are available by mail.

---

(191) · Word Nerd High School Essay Contest
Confessions of a Word Nerd
69 Brookview Avenue
Delmar, NY 12054
Phone: 518-432-4323
Email: wordnerdheadquarters@gmail.com
Website: http://www.confessionsofawordnerd.com
Purpose: To encourage young writers to share funny stories about high school.
Eligibility: Applicants must be United States high school students. Home-schooled students are eligible. Applicants must write a humorous essay of 1,500 to 3,000 words with a minimum of 60 SAT words.
Target applicant:
    High school students
Minimum GPA: None.
Amount: $500.
Number of awards: 1.
Deadline: November 15.
How to apply: Applicants should submit their essays in word format via email along with their name, address, phone number, email address, name of high school and name of sponsoring English or literature teacher.

---

(192) · Yoshiyama Award
Hitachi Foundation
1215 17th Street NW
Washington, DC 20036
Phone: 202-457-0588
Fax: 202-296-1098
Website: http://www.hitachifoundation.org
Purpose: To recognize exemplary service and community involvement.
Eligibility: Applicants must be graduating high school seniors in the U.S. and U.S. territories, demonstrate outstanding community service and have shown leadership, self-motivation, creativity, dedication and commitment to the community. Applicants' service should impact a socially, economically or culturally isolated area. Applicants must also be nominated by someone familiar with their service; family members may not nominate their relatives, and students may not nominate themselves.
Target applicant:
    High school students
Minimum GPA: None.
Amount: $5,000 over two years.
Number of awards: 10.
Deadline: April 1.
How to apply: Applicants must be nominated.

---

(193) · Young American Award
Explorers Learning for Life
P.O. Box 152079
Irving, TX 75015
Phone: 972-580-2433
Fax: 972-580-2137
Email: pchestnu@lflmail.org

Website: http://www.learningforlife.org/exploring
Purpose: To support exceptional students who have served their community, state or country.
Eligibility: Applicants must be between 15 and 25 years of age. Students must have an above-average academic record and exceptional achievements in art, athletics, business, community service, education, government, humanities, literature, math, music, religion or science. Applicants must provide three to six letters of recommendation. They must be nominated by a Boy Scout troop, Explorer post, Learning for Life group or other approved community youth organization but do not need to have participated in the Learning for Life or Exploring program.
Target applicant:
    Junior high students or younger
    High school students
    College students
Minimum GPA: None.
Amount: $7,500.
Number of awards: 5.
Deadline: December 1.
How to apply: Applications are available online.

---

(194) · Young Authors Head Start Program
Elder & Leemaur Publishers
115 Garfield Street #4953
Sumas, WA 98295
Website: http://www.elpublishers.com
Purpose: To encourage students to explore career opportunities in professional writing.
Eligibility: Applicants must be high school seniors or current undergraduate students in North America and must write an essay of up to 500 words on one of the provided topics. Students must attend or plan to attend a college/university in either Canada or the United States. Some essays will be featured in the publication.
Target applicant:
    High school students
    College students
    Adult students
Minimum GPA: None.
Amount: Varies.
Number of awards: Varies.
Deadline: July 1.
How to apply: Essays should be submitted online.

---

(195) · Young Scholars Program
Jack Kent Cooke Foundation Young Scholars Program
301 ACT Drive
P.O. Box 4030
Iowa City, IA 52243
Phone: 800-498-6478
Fax: 703-723-8030
Email: jkc@jackkentcookefoundation.org
Website: http://www.jackkentcookefoundation.org
Purpose: To help high-achieving students with financial need and provide them with educational opportunities throughout high school.
Eligibility: Applicants must have financial need, be in the 7th grade and plan to attend high school in the United States. Academic achievement and intelligence are important, and students must display strong academic records, academic awards and honors and a letter of recommendation. The award is also based on students' will to succeed, leadership and public service, critical thinking ability and participation

in the arts and humanities. During two summers, recipients must participate in a Young Scholars Week and Young Scholars Reunion in Washington, DC.

Target applicant:
    Junior high students or younger
Minimum GPA: None.
Amount: Varies.
Number of awards: 50.
Scholarship may be renewable.
Deadline: May 1.
How to apply: Applications are available online and at regional talent centers.

HUMANITIES/ARTS

(196) · Academic Fellowships and Grants

American-Scandinavian Foundation
58 Park Avenue
New York, NY 10016
Phone: 212-879-9779
Email: grants@amscan.org
Website: http://www.amscan.org
Purpose: To encourage research projects related to Scandinavia.
Eligibility: Applicants must have completed their undergraduate educations and have a research or study project requiring a stay in Scandinavia. Some language proficiency is required.
Target applicant:
    Graduate school students
    Adult students
Minimum GPA: None.
Amount: $4,000-$20,000.
Number of awards: Varies.
Scholarship may be renewable.
Deadline: November 1.
How to apply: Applications are available online and by written request.

(197) · Actors' Work Program

Actors' Fund of America/Actors' Work Program
729 Seventh Avenue
11th Floor
New York, NY 10019
Phone: 800-221-7303
Fax: 212-921-4295
Email: info@actorsfund.org
Website: http://www.actorsfund.org
Purpose: To assist members of the entertainment industry with finding sideline work and pursuing new careers.
Eligibility: Applicants must be members in good standing of an entertainment industry union and have a referral from the Fund's social service department or other organization able to document entertainment industry work.
Target applicant:
    Junior high students or younger
    High school students
    College students
    Graduate school students
    Adult students
Minimum GPA: None.
Amount: Varies.
Number of awards: Varies.
Deadline: Varies.
How to apply: Applicants must attend an Actors' Work Program Orientation to learn more about the program.

(198) · AMCA Music Scholarship

Associated Male Choruses of America
Robert H. Torborg, Scholarship Chair
P.O. Box 342
Cold Spring, MN 56320
Phone: 320-685-3848
Email: scholarship@amcofa.net
Website: http://www.amcofa.net

Purpose: To promote the study of chorus and music studies in college.

Eligibility: Applicants must be full-time students obtaining their bachelor's degree in a music-related field (with preference given to voice or choral concentrations) and be sponsored by a chorus of the Associated Male Choruses of America. Applicants must submit references and a personal letter.

Target applicant:
    College students
    Adult students

Minimum GPA: None.

Amount: Varies.

Number of awards: Varies.

Deadline: March 1.

How to apply: Applications are available online or by contacting your local AMCA chorus.

---

(199) · American Theatre Organ Society Scholarships

American Theatre Organ Society
Carlton B. Smith, Director
2175 N. Irwin Street
Indianapolis, IN 46219
Phone: 317-356-1240
Fax: 317-322-9379
Email: smith@atos.org
Website: http://www.atos.org

Purpose: To provide students with an opportunity to study with professional theatre organ teachers or to further their organ performance education in college.

Eligibility: Applicants must be between the ages of 13 and 27 as of July 1 and either working toward college organ performance degrees or be studying with professional organ instructors. Students' names must be submitted by their present organ instructor or the school's music department head. An essay is also required.

Target applicant:
    Junior high students or younger
    High school students
    College students
    Adult students

Minimum GPA: None.

Amount: Up to $1,000.

Number of awards: Varies.

Deadline: April 15.

How to apply: Applications are available online.

---

(200) · Amy Lowell Poetry Travelling Scholarship

Choate, Hall and Stewart
Two International Place
Boston, MA 02110
Phone: 617-248-5253
Email: amylowell@choate.com
Website: http://www.amylowell.org

Purpose: To support travel abroad for American-born poets.

Eligibility: Applicants should submit applications, curriculum vitae and poetry samples. Recipients should not accept another scholarship during the scholarship year, must travel outside North America and should have three poems by the end of scholarship year.

Target applicant:
    College students
    Graduate school students
    Adult students

Minimum GPA: None.

Amount: $47,000.

Number of awards: 1.

Deadline: October 15.

How to apply: Applications are available online.

---

(201) · Animoids 3D Animation Contest

Troy Studios
Loomis , CA Email: support@animoids.com
Website: http://www.animoids.com

Purpose: To support students interested in graphic design.

Eligibility: Applicants may be anyone who creates animated characters, props, movie sets and movie scenes using ANIMOIDS. The judges recommend that entries have sound, action and a good story and that applicants use creativity. Employees of Troy Studios may not enter.

Target applicant:
    Junior high students or younger
    High school students
    College students
    Graduate school students
    Adult students

Minimum GPA: None.

Amount: $500.

Number of awards: 2.

Deadline: May 31 and November 30.

How to apply: Get software from the site and send the finished product back to the site.

---

(202) · Annual Young Artist Competition

Fort Collins Symphony
FCSO Young Artist Competition
P.O. Box 1963
Fort Collins, CO 80522
Phone: 970-482-4823
Fax: 970-482-4858
Email: note@fcsymphony.org
Website: http://www.fcsymphony.org

Purpose: To support student pianists.

Eligibility: Contestants must be age 25 or younger and must compete in piano or orchestral performance.

Target applicant:
    Junior high students or younger
    High school students
    College students
    Graduate school students

Minimum GPA: None.

Amount: $300-$6,000.

Number of awards: 6.

Deadline: January 12.

How to apply: Applications are available online.

---

(203) · Anthem Essay Contest

Ayn Rand Institute Anthem Essay Contest
Department W
P.O. Box 57044
Irvine, CA 92619-7044
Phone: 949-222-6550
Fax: 949-222-6558
Email: essay@aynrand.org
Website: http://www.aynrand.org

Purpose: To honor high school students who distinguish themselves in their understanding of Ayn Rand's novel Anthem.

Eligibility: Applicants must be eighth graders or high school freshmen or sophomores who submit a 600-1200 word essay that will be judged on both style and content, with an emphasis on writing that is clear, articulate and logically organized. Winning essays must demonstrate an outstanding grasp of the philosophic meaning of Anthem.

Target applicant:
    Junior high students or younger
    High school students
Minimum GPA: None.
Amount: $30-$2,000.
Number of awards: 236.
Deadline: March 20.
How to apply: Application request information is available online.

---

(204) · ARS Recorder Workshop Scholarships

American Recorder Society
1129 Ruth Drive
St. Louis, MO 63122-1019
Phone: 800-491-9588
Fax: 314-966-4649
Email: recorder@americanrecorder.org
Website: http://www.americanrecorder.org
Purpose: To support workshop attendance by recording players.
Eligibility: Applicants should apply at least two months before funds are needed and must submit an application, essay and letter of recommendation.
Target applicant:
    College students
    Graduate school students
    Adult students
Minimum GPA: None.
Amount: Varies.
Number of awards: Varies.
Deadline: April 15.
How to apply: Applications are available online.

---

(205) · Art Awards

Scholastic
557 Broadway
New York, NY 10012
Phone: 212-343-6100
Fax: 212-389-3939
Email: a&wgeneralinfo@scholastic.com
Website: http://www.artandwriting.org
Purpose: To reward America's best student artists.
Eligibility: Applicants must be in grades 7 through 12 in American or Canadian schools and must submit artwork in one of the following categories: art portfolio, animation, ceramics and glass, computer art, design, digital imagery, drawing, mixed media, painting, photography, photography portfolio, printmaking, sculpture or video and film. There are regional and national levels.
Target applicant:
    Junior high students or younger
    High school students
Minimum GPA: None.
Amount: Up to $10,000.
Number of awards: Varies.
Deadline: Varies by location; November through January.
How to apply: Applications are available online.

(206) · Arts Recognition and Talent Search Scholarships

National Foundation for Advancement in the Arts
444 Brickell Avenue
P-14
Miami, FL 33131
Phone: 800-970-ARTS
Fax: 305-377-1149
Email: info@nfaa.org
Website: http://www.nfaa.org
Purpose: To reward talented young individuals in the arts.
Eligibility: Applicants must be either high school seniors or 17 or 18 years old by December 1 of the year of application. Students must be U.S. citizens or permanent residents. The disciplines included are cinematic arts, dance, jazz, music, photography, theater, visual arts, voice and writing. Those applying in the discipline of jazz music may be registered aliens. There is a nonrefundable fee. It is highly recommended that you research the scholarship and awarding organization before applying for a scholarship with a fee. There are many scholarships that do not require a fee.
Target applicant:
    High school students
Minimum GPA: None.
Amount: $100-$10,000.
Number of awards: Varies.
Deadline: October 1.
How to apply: Applications are available online.

---

(207) · Atlas Shrugged Essay Contest

Ayn Rand Institute Atlas Shrugged Essay Contest
Department W
P.O. Box 57044
Irvine, CA 92619-7044
Phone: 949-222-6550
Fax: 949-222-6558
Email: essay@aynrand.org
Website: http://www.aynrand.org
Purpose: To honor high school seniors and college students who distinguish themselves in their understanding of Ayn Rand's novel Atlas Shrugged.
Eligibility: Applicants must be college students and high school seniors who submit an 800-1,600 word essay which will be judged on both style and content with an emphasis on writing that is clear, articulate and logically organized. Winning essays must demonstrate an outstanding grasp of the philosophic meaning of Atlas Shrugged.
Target applicant:
    High school students
    College students
    Adult students
Minimum GPA: None.
Amount: $50-$10,000.
Number of awards: 49.
Deadline: September 17.
How to apply: Application request information is available online.

---

(208) · BEEM Foundation Scholarships

Beem Foundation for the Advancement of Music
309 E. Hillcrest Boulevard, Suite 350
Inglewood, CA 900301
Phone: 301-677-6793

Fax: 310-677-6664
Email: info@beemfoundation.org
Website: http://www.beemfoundation.org
Purpose: To support winners of an annual music competition.
Eligibility: Applicants must be vocal or instrumental music students under the age of 25 and must perform in the annual Scholarship and Showcase Competition at the Los Angeles Center for Enriched Studies.
Target applicant:
   Junior high students or younger
   High school students
   College students
Minimum GPA: None.
Amount: Varies.
Number of awards: Varies.
Deadline: May 2.
How to apply: Applications are available online.

(209) · Bill Gove Scholarship

National Speakers Association
1500 S. Priest Drive
Attn: Scholarship Committee
Tempe, AZ 85281
Phone: 480-968-2552
Fax: 480-968-0911
Website: http://www.nsaspeaker.org
Purpose: To encourage study in the field of professional speaking.
Eligibility: Applicants must be full-time students majoring or minoring in speech. Selection is based on application, essay, recommendation and college transcript.
Target applicant:
   College students
   Graduate school students
   Adult students
Minimum GPA: None.
Amount: $1,000.
Number of awards: 1.
Deadline: June 1.
How to apply: Applications are available online or by written request.

(210) · Bridging Scholarships for Study in Japan

Association of Teachers of Japanese
Bridging Project Clearinghouse
Campus Box 279
240 Humanities Building, University of Colorado
Boulder, CO 80309
Phone: 303-492-5487
Fax: 303-492-5856
Email: atj@colorado.edu
Website: http://www.colorado.edu/ealld/atj
Purpose: To assist students with travel and living expenses while studying in Japan.
Eligibility: Applicants must be undergraduates, U.S. citizens or permanent residents and be enrolled in a U.S. college. Students must submit a letter of recommendation and an essay on their interest in studying in Japan.
Target applicant:
   College students
   Adult students
Minimum GPA: None.

Amount: $2,500-$4,000.
Number of awards: 100.
Deadline: October 5.
How to apply: Applications are available online.

(211) · Bronislaw Kaper Award

Los Angeles Philharmonic
Education Department
151 S. Grand Avenue
Los Angeles, CA 90012
Phone: 213-972-3454
Fax: 213-972-7650
Email: education@laphil.org
Website: http://www.laphil.org
Purpose: To encourage the development of young musicians.
Eligibility: Applicants must be current residents of the state of California and are required to prepare and perform a piano or string piece for competition. The category alternates between piano and string each year. The maximum level in school is a senior in high school.
Target applicant:
   Junior high students or younger
   High school students
Minimum GPA: None.
Amount: $1,000-$2,500.
Number of awards: 4.
Deadline: December 17.
How to apply: Applications are available online.

(212) · Broome and Allen Boys Camp and Scholarship Fund

American Sephardi Federation
15 W. 16th Street
New York, New York 10011
Phone: 212-294-8350
Fax: 212-294-8348
Website: http://www.americansephardifederation.org
Purpose: To help those of Sephardic origin or those working in Sephardic studies.
Eligibility: Applicants must be undergraduate or graduate students or those doing research projects. Two letters of recommendation, a family tax return and transcripts are required. Applicants do not have to be United States citizens or living in the United States but they should be conducting their research in the United States.
Target applicant:
   High school students
   College students
   Graduate school students
   Adult students
Minimum GPA: None.
Amount: Varies.
Number of awards: Varies.
Scholarship may be renewable.
Deadline: May 15.
How to apply: Applications are available online.

(213) · Carl A. Ross Student Paper Award

Appalachian Studies Association Carl A. Ross Student Paper Award
William Schumann
Emory and Henry College

P.O. Box 947
Emory, VA 24327
Phone: 304-696-2904
Fax: 276-944-6170
Website: http://www.appalachianstudies.org
Purpose: To promote Appalachian studies.
Eligibility: Applicants must submit a 20- to 30-page research paper on an Appalachian studies topic. Selections will be made from two categories: middle/high school and undergraduate/graduate.
Target applicant:
　　Junior high students or younger
　　High school students
　　College students
　　Graduate school students
　　Adult students
Minimum GPA: None.
Amount: $100.
Number of awards: 2.
Deadline: December 9.
How to apply: Submission of research paper is the application.

(214) · Caroline H. Newhouse Scholarship Fund

Career Transition for Dancers
Caroline and Theodore Newhouse Center for Dancers
165 West 46th Street, Suite 701
The Actors' Equity Building
New York, NY 10036
Phone: 212-764-0172
Fax: 212-764-0343
Email: info@careertransition.org
Website: http://www.careertransition.org
Purpose: To provide educational grants for dancers seeking second careers.
Eligibility: Applicants must provide documentation of 100 weeks or more of paid employment as a dance performer in the U.S. over at least seven years. For work not performed under union jurisdiction, applicants must also provide documentation of total gross earnings of at least $56,000. Choreographers and dance teachers are not eligible for this program.
Target applicant:
　　College students
　　Graduate school students
　　Adult students
Minimum GPA: None.
Amount: Up to $2,000.
Number of awards: Varies.
Deadline: Varies.
How to apply: Applicants must call to confirm their eligibility.

(215) · Cavett Robert Scholarship

National Speakers Association
1500 S. Priest Drive
Attn: Scholarship Committee
Tempe, AZ 85281
Phone: 480-968-2552
Fax: 480-968-0911
Website: http://www.nsaspeaker.org
Purpose: To encourage study in the field of professional speaking.
Eligibility: Applicants must be full-time students majoring or minoring in speech. Selection is based on application, essay, recommendation and college transcript.

Target applicant:
　　College students
　　Graduate school students
　　Adult students
Minimum GPA: None.
Amount: $1,000.
Number of awards: 1.
Deadline: June 1.
How to apply: Applications are available online or by written request.

(216) · ChiGems Art and Poetry Scholarship

ChiGems
24695 Monita Circle
Laguna Niguel, CA 92677
Phone: 949-547-9427
Email: info@chigems.com
Website: http://www.chigems.com/scholarshipapplication.htm
Purpose: To reward artistically and academically talented students who contribute to their schools and communities.
Eligibility: Applicants must be students in grades 9 through 12 who are enrolled in any U.S. public or private school or adult non-professionals who want to continue their art education. Financial need and merit are considered. An art or poetry submission is required.
Target applicant:
　　High school students
Minimum GPA: None.
Amount: $250.
Number of awards: 6.
Deadline: Varies.
How to apply: Applications are available online. There are six deadlines per year, with one award distributed every other month.

(217) · Chopin Piano Competition

Thomas Pniewski, Director of Cultural Affairs
Kosciuszko Foundation
15 East 65th Street
New York, NY 10021-6595
Phone: 212-734-2130 x214
Fax: 212-628-4552
Email: tompkf@aol.com
Website: http://www.kosciuszkofoundation.org
Purpose: To encourage young pianists to continue their studies and to perform Polish composers' works.
Eligibility: Applicants must be U.S. citizens or permanent residents or international full-time students with valid student visas and must be between the ages of 16 and 22. Applicants are required to prepare a repertoire of works by designated composers. There is a $50 nonrefundable application fee. It is highly recommended that you research the scholarship and awarding organization before applying for a scholarship with a fee. There are many scholarships that do not require a fee.
Target applicant:
　　High school students
　　College students
Minimum GPA: None.
Amount: $1,500-$5,000.
Number of awards: 3.
Deadline: March 5.
How to apply: Applications are available online.

(218) · Christianson Grant

InterExchange Inc.
161 Sixth Avenue
New York, NY 10013
Phone: 212-924-0446
Fax: 212-924-0575
Email: grants@interexchange.org
Website: www.interexchange.org
Purpose: To further international understanding and promote cultural awareness by supporting young Americans in working abroad.
Eligibility: Applicants must have arranged their own work abroad programs and be U.S. citizens or permanent residents aged 18 to 28.
Target applicant:
　High school students
　College students
　Graduate school students
　Adult students
Minimum GPA: None.
Amount: $2,500-$10,000.
Number of awards: 8.
Deadline: March 15.
How to apply: Applications are available online.

(219) · Clan MacBean Foundation Grant Program

Clan MacBean Foundation
441 Wadsworth Boulevard, Suite 213
Denver, CO 80226
Website: http://www.clanmacbean.net
Purpose: To provide financial assistance to those studying Scottish culture.
Eligibility: Applicants must be pursuing a course of study related directly to Scottish culture. If pursuing a project, applicants must pick a project that reflects direct involvement in the preservation or enhancement of Scottish culture.
Target applicant:
　College students
　Adult students
Minimum GPA: None.
Amount: Varies.
Number of awards: Varies.
Deadline: Varies.
How to apply: Applications are available by written request.

(220) · College Television Awards

Academy of Television Arts and Sciences Foundation
5220 Lankershim Boulevard
North Hollywood, CA 91601
Phone: 818-754-2800
Fax: 818-761-2827
Email: collegeawards@emmys.org
Website: http://www.emmys.org
Purpose: To award college student film or video producers.
Eligibility: Applicants must produce an original film or video in one of the following categories: drama, comedy, music, documentary, news, magazine show, traditional or computer-generated animation, children's programming, or commercials. Professionals may not be involved in the production of the piece, including producers, directors, camera operators, lighting or sound technicians, and production managers. Applicants must also be full-time students who have produced their

video for course credit at an American college or university from January 1 to December 31 of the current year.
Target applicant:
　College students
　Graduate school students
　Adult students
Minimum GPA: None.
Amount: $500-$4,000.
Number of awards: Varies.
Deadline: January 15.
How to apply: Applications are available online from September 1 to January 15 and are also sent to college film and television departments.

(221) · Computer Graphic Design Scholarships

Armed Forces Communications and Electronics Association
4400 Fair Lakes Court
Fairfax, VA 22033
Phone: 800-336-4583
Fax: 703-631-4693
Email: scholarship@afcea.org
Website: http://www.afcea.org
Purpose: Monetary assistance is awarded to full-time graduate or undergraduate students majoring in computer graphic design or related fields.
Eligibility: Applicants must be full-time students working toward an undergraduate or graduate degree in computer graphic design or a related field at an accredited U.S. college or university, be U.S. citizens and be at least college sophomores. Selection is based on a single sample of digital artwork. Applicants do not need to be affiliated with the military.
Target applicant:
　College students
　Graduate school students
　Adult students
Minimum GPA: None.
Amount: $2,000.
Number of awards: Varies.
Deadline: October 15.
How to apply: Applications are available online.

(222) · Congressional Black Caucus Spouses Performing Arts Scholarship

Congressional Black Caucus Foundation
1720 Massachusetts Avenue NW
Washington, DC 20036
Phone: 202-263-2800
Fax: 202-775-0773
Email: info@cbcfinc.org
Website: http://www.cbcfinc.org
Purpose: To support students who are pursuing careers in performing arts.
Eligibility: Applicants do NOT need to be African American but must reside or attend school in a congressional district represented by a CBC member. Students must have at least a 2.5 GPA, and they must be enrolled or accepted into a full-time undergraduate degree program. Applicants must show leadership qualities and community service participation.
Target applicant:
　High school students
　College students
　Adult students

Minimum GPA: 2.5
Amount: $3,000.
Number of awards: Up to 10.
Deadline: May 1.
How to apply: Applications are available online.

(223) · Congressional Black Caucus Spouses Visual Arts Scholarship

Congressional Black Caucus Foundation
1720 Massachusetts Avenue NW
Washington, DC 20036
Phone: 202-263-2800
Fax: 202-775-0773
Email: info@cbcfinc.org
Website: http://www.cbcfinc.org
Purpose: To support students who are pursuing careers in visual arts.
Eligibility: Applicants do NOT need to be African American but must reside or attend school in a congressional district represented by a CBC member. Students must have at least a 2.5 GPA, and they must be enrolled or accepted into a full-time undergraduate degree program. Applicants must show leadership qualities and community service participation.
Target applicant:
    High school students
    College students
    Adult students
Minimum GPA: 2.5
Amount: Up to $3,000.
Number of awards: Up to 5.
Deadline: May 1.
How to apply: Applications are available online.

(224) · Constance Eberhardt Memorial Award, AIMS Graz Experience Scholarship and Banff Center School of Fine Arts Scholarship

National Opera Association
Vocal Competition
P.O. Box 60869
Canyon, TX 79016-0001
Phone: 806-651-2857
Email: rhansen@mail.wtamu.edu
Website: http://www.noa.org
Purpose: To provide financial support for young opera singers.
Eligibility: Applicants must be enrolled in undergraduate or graduate programs or the equivalent and be between the ages of 18 and 24. The applicants' teachers must be members of the National Opera Association. Selection is based on a recording of two arias for preliminary hearings and a live audition of four arias for the final judging. There is a $20 entry fee. It is highly recommended that you research the scholarship and awarding organization before applying for a scholarship with a fee. There are many scholarships that do not require a fee.
Target applicant:
    High school students
    College students
    Graduate school students
Minimum GPA: None.
Amount: $500-$2,000.
Number of awards: Varies.
Deadline: October 15.
How to apply: Applications are available online.

(225) · Corporate Leadership Scholarships

Gravure Education Foundation
1200-A Scottsville Road
Rochester, NY 14624
Phone: 315-589-8879
Fax: 585-436-7689
Email: lwshatch@gaa.org
Website: http://www.gaa.org
Purpose: To provide scholarships to undergraduate and graduate students pursuing degrees in printing or graphic arts.
Eligibility: Applicants must be enrolled full-time at a GEF Learning Resource Center at Arizona State University, California Polytechnic State University, Clemson University, Murray State, Rochester Institute of Technology, University of Wisconsin - Stout or Western Michigan University. Students must major in printing, graphic arts or graphic communications and be a sophomore, junior or senior at the time the scholarship is awarded.
Target applicant:
    College students
    Graduate school students
    Adult students
Minimum GPA: 3.0
Amount: $1,500.
Number of awards: 6.
Deadline: May 31.
How to apply: Applications are available online.

(226) · Council on International Educational Exchange (CIEE) Scholarships

Council on International Educational Exchange
7 Custom House Street, 3rd Floor
Portland, ME 04101
Phone: 800-40-STUDY
Fax: 207-553-7699
Email: scholarships@ciee.org
Website: http://www.ciee.org
Purpose: To make the study abroad program available to a wider audience and to provide assistance to CIEE Study Center (CSC) members who have demonstrated academic talent and financial need in order to study abroad.
Eligibility: Applicants must plan to participate in a CIEE study abroad program. Financial need is strongly considered along with other materials from the study abroad application. Other eligibility requirements vary according to the specific scholarship. If awarded a scholarship, applicants are required to submit a one-page essay on their experiences after returning.
Target applicant:
    College students
    Graduate school students
    Adult students
Minimum GPA: None.
Amount: $500-$1,000.
Number of awards: Varies.
Deadline: April 1 and November 1.
How to apply: Applications are available online.

(227) · Critical Need Language Supplement

Institute of International Education
809 United Nations Plaza
New York, NY 10017

Phone: 212-883-8200
Fax: 212-984-5452
Email: gilman@iie.org
Website: http://www.iie.org
Purpose: To support recipients of the Gilman International Scholarship who need language training.
Eligibility: Students must plan to study from one of the following critical need language groups: Arabic, Chinese, Turkic, Persian, Indic, Korean or Russian.
Target applicant:
 College students
 Adult students
Minimum GPA: None.
Amount: $3,000.
Number of awards: 25.
Deadline: April 15.
How to apply: Applications are available online.

(228) · DAAD/AICGS Research Fellowship Program

American Institute for Contemporary German Studies - (AICGS)
1755 Massachusetts Avenue NW
Suite 700
Washington, DC 20036
Phone: 202-332-9312
Fax: 202-265-9531
Email: kverclas@aicgs.org
Website: http://www.aicgs.org
Purpose: To encourage the research of modern and contemporary postwar Germany.
Eligibility: Applicants must be Ph.D. candidates, recent Ph.D.s or junior faculty who hold U.S. or German citizenship. The grant provides summer residency at AICGS.
Target applicant:
 Graduate school students
 Adult students
Minimum GPA: None.
Amount: $4,600.
Number of awards: 1-2.
Deadline: September 30.
How to apply: Applications are available by mail.

(229) · DiversityAbroad.com Blog Abroad Grant

Diversity Abroad
1731 Delaware Street
Berkeley, CA 94703
Phone: 510-647-5100
Fax: 510-647-5032
Email: feedback@diversityabroad.com
Website: http://www.diversityabroad.com
Purpose: To support students who study abroad and are willing to share their experiences online.
Eligibility: Applicants must be African American, Asian American, Hispanic or Native American. Recipients must contribute regularly to a blog on DiversityAbroad.com.
Target applicant:
 College students
 Adult students
Minimum GPA: None.
Amount: $250.
Number of awards: Varies.

Deadline: Varies.
How to apply: Applications are available online.

(230) · DiversityAbroad.com Summer Abroad Scholarship

Diversity Abroad
1731 Delaware Street
Berkeley, CA 94703
Phone: 510-647-5100
Fax: 510-647-5032
Email: feedback@diversityabroad.com
Website: http://www.diversityabroad.com
Purpose: To support minority students who plan to study abroad in a summer session.
Eligibility: Applicants must be African American, Asian American, Hispanic or Native American. Students must have at least a 2.5 GPA in a full-time undergraduate program. Applicants must submit an essay and one letter of recommendation. Recipients must enroll in a study abroad program sponsored by a Diversity Abroad member organization, and they must be willing to share their experiences through blogs and online forums at DiversityAbroad.com.
Target applicant:
 College students
 Adult students
Minimum GPA: 2.5
Amount: $2,000.
Number of awards: 5.
Deadline: April 15.
How to apply: Applications are available online.

(231) · Donna Reed Performing Arts Scholarships - National Scholarship

Donna Reed Foundation for the Performing Arts
1305 Broadway
Denison, IA 51442
Phone: 712-263-3334
Fax: 712-263-8026
Email: info@donnareed.org
Website: http://www.donnareed.org
Purpose: To recognize students who demonstrate excellence and a high level of interest in the performing arts.
Eligibility: Applicants must graduate or have graduated from high school between September 1 and August 31 of the award year. Applicants must be registered as full-time students in the Donna Reed Performing Arts Workshop Program. Finalists must take part in a live competition at the workshop. Available categories are acting and musical theater, with each category requiring a separate audition tape. Two of the available scholarships are set aside for Iowa residents.
Target applicant:
 High school students
Minimum GPA: None.
Amount: $500-$1,000.
Number of awards: 8.
Deadline: June 1.
How to apply: Applications are available online.

(232) · Doodle 4 Google

Google
1600 Amphitheatre Parkway
Mountain View, CA 94043

Phone: 650-253-0000
Fax: 650-253-0001
Email: doodle4google-team@google.com
Website: http://www.google.com/doodle4google
Purpose: To encourage creativity in United States school students through a logo contest.
Eligibility: Participants must be elementary or secondary school students in the 50 U.S. states or the District of Columbia who have registered for the contest. They must be U.S. residents who have obtained parental consent to enter. Employees, interns, contractors, and office-holders of Google Inc. and their immediate families are not eligible.
Target applicant:
    Junior high students or younger
    High school students
Minimum GPA: None.
Amount: $10,000.
Number of awards: 1.
Deadline: May 22.
How to apply: Applications are available from participating schools.

(233) · Dumbarton Oaks Fellowships

Dumbarton Oaks
1703 32nd Street NW
Washington, DC 20007
Phone: 202-339-6401
Fax: 202-339-6419
Email: dumbartonoaks@doaks.org
Website: http://www.doaks.org
Purpose: To provide fellowships to scholars engaged in Byzantine studies, Pre-Columbian studies and garden and landscape studies.
Eligibility: Applicants must hold a doctorate (or appropriate final degree) or have established themselves in their field and wish to pursue their own research or expect to have the Ph.D. in hand prior to taking up residence at Dumbarton Oaks. The fellowships are in the following areas: Byzantine Studies (including related aspects of late Roman, early Christian, western medieval, Slavic and Near Eastern Studies), Pre-Columbian Studies (of Mexico, Central America and Andean South America) and garden and landscape studies. Fellowships are based on demonstrated scholarly ability and preparation (including knowledge of the required languages), interest and value of the study or project and its relevance to Dumbarton Oaks.
Target applicant:
    Graduate school students
    Adult students
Minimum GPA: None.
Amount: $43,400.
Number of awards: Varies.
Deadline: November 1.
How to apply: Applicants must submit ten complete, collated sets of the application letter, proposal and personal and professional data. Applicants must also submit three recommendation letters.

(234) · Earl Nightengale Scholarship

National Speakers Association
1500 S. Priest Drive
Attn: Scholarship Committee
Tempe, AZ 85281
Phone: 480-968-2552
Fax: 480-968-0911
Website: http://www.nsaspeaker.org
Purpose: To encourage study in the field of professional speaking.
Eligibility: Applicants must be full-time undergraduate juniors, seniors or graduate students majoring or minoring in speech. Selection is based on application, essay, recommendation and college transcript.
Target applicant:
    College students
    Graduate school students
    Adult students
Minimum GPA: None.
Amount: $5,000.
Number of awards: 4.
Deadline: June 1.
How to apply: Applications are available online or by written request.

(235) · Edna Meudt Memorial Award and the Florence Kahn Memorial Award

National Federation of State Poetry Societies
NFSPS College/University-Level Competition
N. Colwell Snell
P.O. Box 520698
Salt Lake City, UT 84152
Phone: 801-484-3113
Email: SBSenior@juno.com
Website: http://www.nfsps.com
Purpose: To recognize the importance of poetry on the nation's culture.
Eligibility: Applicants can be college students at any level.
Target applicant:
    College students
    Adult students
Minimum GPA: None.
Amount: $500.
Number of awards: 2.
Deadline: February 1.
How to apply: Applications are available online.

(236) · Elizabeth Greenshields Foundation Grants

Elizabeth Greenshields Foundation
1814 Sherbrooke Street West Suite #1
Montreal
Quebec, Canada H3H 1E4
Phone: 514-937-9225
Fax: 514-937-0141
Website: http://www.calarts.edu
Purpose: To promote an appreciation of painting, drawing, sculpture and the graphic arts by supporting art students, artists or sculptors.
Eligibility: Applicants must have already started or completed training at an established school of art, and/or demonstrated, through past work and future plans, a commitment to make art a lifetime career. Applicants must be in the early stages of their careers working in painting, drawing, printmaking or sculpture. Abstract work will not be considered.
Target applicant:
    High school students
    College students
    Graduate school students
    Adult students
Minimum GPA: None.
Amount: $10,000 CDN.
Number of awards: Varies.
Deadline: None.

How to apply: Applications are available by phone or written request.

(237) · FALCON - Full Year Asian Language CONcentration

FALCON Program
Department of Asian Studies, Cornell University
338 Rockefeller Hall
Ithaca, NY 14853
Phone: 607-255-6457
Fax: 607-255-1345
Email: falcon@cornell.edu
Website: http://lrc.cornell.edu/falcon/
Purpose: To provide scholarships for undergraduate and graduate students seeking intensive, long-term instruction in Chinese and Japanese.
Eligibility: The program is conducted at Cornell University, and students receive Cornell credits.
Target applicant:
  College students
  Graduate school students
  Adult students
Minimum GPA: None.
Amount: Varies.
Number of awards: Varies.
Deadline: Varies.
How to apply: Applications are available online.

(238) · Federal Junior Duck Stamp Program and Scholarship Competition

U.S. Fish and Wildlife Service
Federal Duck Stamp Office
4401 N. Fairfax Drive
MBSP-4070
Arlington, VA 22203
Phone: 877-887-5508
Email: duckstamps@fws.gov
Website: http://www.fws.gov/duckstamps
Purpose: To introduce children to an important part of the natural world.
Eligibility: Applicants must be in kindergarten to 12th grade and submit a 9- by 12-inch original artwork picturing one of several duck species. The first place national winner receives a $5,000 cash award and a free trip to Washington, DC. Applicants must submit their artwork to their state or local department.
Target applicant:
  Junior high students or younger
  High school students
Minimum GPA: None.
Amount: $100-$5,000.
Number of awards: 100.
Deadline: August 15.
How to apply: Applications are available online.

(239) · Fellowships for Regular Program

American School of Classical Studies at Athens
6-8 Charlton Street
Princeton, NJ 08540
Phone: 609-683-0800
Fax: 609-683-0800
Email: ascsa@ascsa.org
Website: http://www.ascsa.edu.gr
Purpose: The institution is devoted to allowing American students to study the language, literature, art, history, archaeology and philosophy of Greece and the Greek world.
Eligibility: Applicants must take exams in Greek language, history and either literature or art and archaeology. Students must be able to read French, German, ancient Greek and Latin with an ability to also read modern Greek and Italian considered helpful. Applicants must be graduate students who are preparing for an advanced degree in classical and ancient Mediterranean studies or a related field. Preference is given to current graduate students, but highly qualified applicants with bachelor's degrees will be considered.
Target applicant:
  Graduate school students
  Adult students
Minimum GPA: None.
Amount: $10,000.
Number of awards: 13.
Deadline: March 15.
How to apply: Applications are available online.

(240) · FFTA Scholarship Competition

Flexographic Technical Association
900 Marconi Avenue
Ronkonkoma, NY 11779
Phone: 631-737-6020
Fax: 631-737-6813
Email: education@flexography.org
Website: http://www.flexography.org
Purpose: To advance the state of the flexographic industry.
Eligibility: Applicants must demonstrate interest in a career in flexography and must be high school seniors with plans to attend a post-secondary institution or be presently enrolled at a post-secondary institution offering a course of study in flexography. Applicants must exhibit exemplary performance in their studies, particularly in the area of graphic communications and must have a minimum 3.0 GPA.
Target applicant:
  High school students
  College students
  Adult students
Minimum GPA: 3.0
Amount: $2,000.
Number of awards: 19.
Scholarship may be renewable.
Deadline: February 11.
How to apply: Applications are available online.

(241) · Film and Fiction Scholarships

Institute for Humane Studies at George Mason University
3301 N. Fairfax Drive
Suite 440
Arlington, VA 22201
Phone: 800-697-8799
Fax: 703-993-4890
Email: ihs@gmu.edu
Website: http://www.theihs.org
Purpose: To support promising young filmmakers and writers with an interest in classical liberal ideas and their contemporary application.
Eligibility: Applicants must be pursuing a Master of Fine Arts (M.F.A.) degree in filmmaking, fiction writing or playwriting. Applicants must

also have a demonstrated interest in classical liberal ideas and must show their commitment to their profession through desire, motivation and creative ability.

Target applicant:
    Graduate school students
    Adult students
Minimum GPA: None.
Amount: Up to $10,000.
Number of awards: Varies.
Deadline: January 15.
How to apply: Applications are available online.

(242) · Fountainhead Essay Contest

Ayn Rand Institute Fountainhead Essay Contest
Department W
P.O. Box 57044
Irvine, CA 92619-7044
Phone: 949-222-6550
Fax: 949-222-6558
Email: essay@aynrand.org
Website: http://www.aynrand.org
Purpose: To honor high school students who distinguish themselves in their understanding of Ayn Rand's novel The Fountainhead.
Eligibility: Applicants must be high school juniors or seniors who submit a 800-1,600 word essay which will be judged on both style and content with an emphasis on writing that is clear, articulate and logically organized. Winning essays must demonstrate an outstanding grasp of the philosophic and psychological meaning of The Fountainhead.
Target applicant:
    High school students
Minimum GPA: None.
Amount: $50-$10,000.
Number of awards: 236.
Deadline: April 25.
How to apply: Application request information is available online.

(243) · GEF Resource Center Scholarships

Gravure Education Foundation
1200-A Scottsville Road
Rochester, NY 14624
Phone: 315-589-8879
Fax: 585-436-7689
Email: lwshatch@gaa.org
Website: http://www.gaa.org
Purpose: To award scholarships to undergraduate and graduate students majoring in printing, graphic arts or graphic communications.
Eligibility: Applicants must be enrolled at one of the following GEF Learning Resource Centers: Arizona State University, California Polytechnic State University, Clemson University, Murray State University, Rochester Institute of Technology, University of Wisconsin - Stout or Western Michigan University.
Target applicant:
    College students
    Graduate school students
    Adult students
Minimum GPA: 3.0
Amount: Varies.
Number of awards: Varies.
Deadline: May 31.
How to apply: Applications are available online.

(244) · General Heritage and Culture Grants

Sons of Norway
1455 W. Lake Street
Minneapolis, MN 55408
Phone: 800-945-8851
Fax: 612-827-0658
Email: foundation@sofn.com
Website: http://www.sofn.com
Purpose: To preserve Norwegian heritage.
Eligibility: Applicants may be individuals, groups or organizations dedicated to the preservation of Norwegian heritage. Selection is based on applicants' record or activities and adherence to the goals and objectives of the Sons of Norway Foundation.
Target applicant:
    High school students
    College students
    Adult students
Minimum GPA: None.
Amount: Up to $3,000.
Number of awards: Varies.
Deadline: January 15.
How to apply: Applications are available online.

(245) · German Studies Research Grant

German Academic Exchange Service
DAAD
871 UN Plaza
New York, NY 10017
Phone: 212-758-3223
Fax: 212-755-5780
Email: graaff@daad.org
Website: http://www.daad.org
Purpose: To encourage the research of cultural, political, historical, economic and social aspects of modern and contemporary German affairs.
Eligibility: Applicants must be junior or senior undergraduates pursuing a German studies major or minor, or master's degree students or Ph.D. candidates in the humanities or social sciences who are working on a certificate in German studies at U.S. or Canadian institutions of higher education or a dissertation on a modern German topic, respectively. Applicants must be nominated by their department and must have completed two years of college German and a minimum of three courses in German studies (literature, history, politics or other fields). Applicants should submit applications, resumes, project descriptions, budget reports, lists of German courses taken, two recommendation letters, language evaluation forms and transcripts.
Target applicant:
    College students
    Graduate school students
    Adult students
Minimum GPA: None.
Amount: $1,500-$2,500.
Number of awards: Up to 5.
Deadline: May 1 and November 1.
How to apply: Applications are available online.

(246) · Gilman International Scholarship

Institute of International Education
809 United Nations Plaza
New York, NY 10017

Phone: 212-883-8200
Fax: 212-984-5452
Email: gilman@iie.org
Website: http://www.iie.org
Purpose: To support students with financial need who are planning to study abroad.
Eligibility: Students must be recipients of a Pell Grant. They must be currently attending a two-year or four-year college in the United States. Recipients must study abroad for at least four weeks in any country excluding Cuba and the countries on the Travel Warning list.
Target applicant:
    College students
    Adult students
Minimum GPA: None.
Amount: Up to $5,000.
Number of awards: 820.
Deadline: April 15.
How to apply: Applications are available online.

(247) · Glenn Miller Scholarship Competition

Glenn Miller Birthplace Society
107 East Main Street
P.O. Box 61
Clarinda, IA 51632
Phone: 712-542-2461
Fax: 712-542-2461
Email: gmbs@heartland.net
Website: http://www.glennmiller.org
Purpose: To honor Glenn Miller by recognizing future musical leaders.
Eligibility: Applicants may apply as instrumentalists or vocalists. They must be high school seniors or college freshmen who plan to focus on music in their future lives. Applicants must submit an audition CD or tape in addition to an application form. High school seniors may reapply as college freshmen as long as they weren't first-place winners the previous year.
Target applicant:
    High school students
    College students
    Adult students
Minimum GPA: None.
Amount: $1,000-$3,000.
Number of awards: 6.
Deadline: March 15.
How to apply: Applications are available online.

(248) · Graduate and Postgraduate Study and Research in Poland

Thomas Pniewski, Director of Cultural Affairs
Kosciuszko Foundation
15 East 65th Street
New York, NY 10021-6595
Phone: 212-734-2130 x214
Fax: 212-628-4552
Email: tompkf@aol.com
Website: http://www.kosciuszkofoundation.org
Purpose: To allow American graduate students and university faculty members to conduct research at universities in Poland.
Eligibility: Applicants must be U.S. citizens or Polish permanent residents and be graduate students or university faculty members. Applicants must also possess a level of Polish language proficiency

appropriate for their proposed research projects. Selection is based on academic excellence and motivation for pursuing research in Poland. Host institutions must fall under the jurisdiction of the Polish Ministry of National Education. There is a nonrefundable application fee of $50. It is highly recommended that you research the scholarship and awarding organization before applying for a scholarship with a fee. There are many scholarships that do not require a fee.
Target applicant:
    Graduate school students
    Adult students
Minimum GPA: None.
Amount: Stipend.
Number of awards: Varies.
Deadline: January 16.
How to apply: Applications are available online.

(249) · Gravure Catalog and Insert Council Scholarship

Gravure Education Foundation
1200-A Scottsville Road
Rochester, NY 14624
Phone: 315-589-8879
Fax: 585-436-7689
Email: lwshatch@gaa.org
Website: http://www.gaa.org
Purpose: To support undergraduate students to help them enter the printing industry.
Eligibility: Applicants must major in printing, graphic arts or graphic communications and be at least a junior at the time the scholarship is awarded. Applicants should be interested in promoting gravure as the preferred method in high-quality printing.
Target applicant:
    College students
    Adult students
Minimum GPA: 3.0
Amount: Varies.
Number of awards: Varies.
Deadline: May 31.
How to apply: Applications are available online.

(250) · Hallmark Graphic Arts Scholarship

Gravure Education Foundation
1200-A Scottsville Road
Rochester, NY 14624
Phone: 315-589-8879
Fax: 585-436-7689
Email: lwshatch@gaa.org
Website: http://www.gaa.org
Purpose: To provide a scholarship to an undergraduate student in printing or graphic arts who exhibits leadership through involvement in clubs, associations, sports, community involvement or volunteering.
Eligibility: Applicants must be enrolled full-time at a GEF Learning Resource Center at Arizona State University, California Polytechnic State University, Clemson University, Murray State, Rochester Institute of Technology, University of Wisconsin - Stout or Western Michigan University. Students must major in printing, graphic arts or graphic communications and be a junior or senior at the time the scholarship is awarded.
Target applicant:
    College students
    Adult students

Minimum GPA: 3.0
Amount: Up to $1,500.
Number of awards: 1.
Deadline: May 31.
How to apply: Applications are available online.

(251) · HAPCO Music Scholarship

HAPCO Music Foundation Inc.
P.O. Box 784581
Winter Garden, FL 34778
Phone: 407-877-2262
Fax: 407-654-0308
Email: info@hapcopromo.org
Website: http://www.hapcopromo.org
Purpose: To encourage students to pursue their interest in music while attending college.
Eligibility: Applicants must be accepted at a college or university. They may major in any area but must participate in a music organization at their school. Students must have at least a 3.0 GPA, have taken a set of required core credits and earn a score of 970 on the SAT or 20 on the ACT. Home-schooled students must earn a score or 1070 on the SAT or 23 on the ACT unless they can provide proof of the college-preparatory credits. Applicants must include a letter of recommendation, a high school transcript, a photo and an essay on their future educational goals.
Target applicant:
    High school students
Minimum GPA: 3.0
Amount: $250-$1,000.
Number of awards: Varies.
Deadline: December 31.
How to apply: Applications are available online.

(252) · Harvie Jordan Scholarship

American Translators Association
225 Reinekers Lane
Suite 590
Alexandria, VA 22314
Phone: 703-683-6100
Fax: 703-683-6122
Email: ata@atanet.org
Website: http://www.atanet.org
Purpose: To support members of the Spanish Language Division of the American Translators Association.
Eligibility: Applicants must have been ATA Spanish Language Division members for at least two years. They must also be able to show that they have made important contributions to translation and interpretation.
Target applicant:
    College students
    Graduate school students
    Adult students
Minimum GPA: None.
Amount: Varies.
Number of awards: Varies.
Deadline: September 18.
How to apply: Applications are available online.

(253) · Henry Luce Foundation/ACLS Dissertation Fellowships in American Art

American Council of Learned Societies (ACLS)
633 Third Avenue
New York, NY 10017-6795
Phone: 212-697-1505
Fax: 212-949-8058
Email: sfisher@acls.org
Website: http://www.acls.org
Purpose: To support Ph.D. candidates working on art history dissertations.
Eligibility: Applicants must be Ph.D. candidates in an art history department in the U.S. who are working on dissertations about American visual arts history. All the Ph.D. requirements should be met except the dissertation before taking the fellowship. Applicants should submit an application, a proposal, a bibliography, illustrations (optional), a publications list (optional), three reference letters and an official transcript of graduate record. The fellowship lasts for a year.
Target applicant:
    Graduate school students
    Adult students
Minimum GPA: None.
Amount: $22,500.
Number of awards: 10.
Deadline: November 10.
How to apply: Applications are available online.

(254) · IACI/NUI Visiting Fellowship in Irish Studies

Irish-American Cultural Institute (IACI)
AN FORAS CULTUIR GAEL-MHEIRCHEANACH
1 Lackawanna Place
Morristown, NJ 07960
Phone: 973-605-1991
Fax: 973-605-8875
Website: http://www.iaci-usa.org
Purpose: To award fellowships to Irish studies scholars to spend one semester at the University of Ireland-Galway.
Eligibility: Applicants must provide a description of how the fellowship will be used and a curriculum vitae with a list of publications.
Target applicant:
    Graduate school students
    Adult students
Minimum GPA: None.
Amount: $13,000.
Number of awards: Varies.
Deadline: December 31.
How to apply: Application is available online.

(255) · IDSA Undergraduate Scholarships

Industrial Designers Society of America
45195 Business Court
Suite 250
Dulles, VA 20166
Phone: 703-707-6000
Fax: 703-787-8501
Email: idsa@idsa.org
Website: http://www.idsa.org
Purpose: To help industrial design students in their final year of schooling.

Eligibility: Applicants must be full-time students enrolled in an IDSA-listed program in their next-to-last year of the program, have a minimum 3.0 GPA, be members of an IDSA Student Chapter and be U.S. citizens or residents. Applicants must submit a letter of intent, 20 visual examples of their work and a transcript. Awards are based solely on the excellence of the submitted works.

Target applicant:
 College students
 Adult students
Minimum GPA: 3.0
Amount: Varies.
Number of awards: 2.
Deadline: May 2.
How to apply: Applications are available online.

---

(256) · Illustrators of the Future

L. Ron Hubbard
P.O. Box 3190
Los Angeles, CA 90078
Email: contests@authorservicesinc.com
Website: http://www.writersofthefuture.com
Purpose: To discover deserving amateur aspiring illustrators.
Eligibility: Applicants must not have published more than three black-and-white story illustrations or more than one color painting in national media. Applicants must also submit three original illustrations done in a black-and-white medium in three different themes.
Target applicant:
 High school students
 College students
 Graduate school students
 Adult students
Minimum GPA: None.
Amount: $500-$4,000.
Number of awards: 3 awards are given quarterly with a grand prize awarded annually.
Deadline: December 31, March 31, June 30, September 30.
How to apply: There is no application form.

---

(257) · International Scholarships

American Institute for Foreign Study
AIFS College Division
River Plaza
9 W. Broad Street
Stamford, CT 06902
Phone: 800-727-2437
Fax: 203-399-5597
Email: info@aifs.com
Website: http://www.aifsabroad.com
Purpose: To promote international understanding through study abroad.
Eligibility: Applicants must be currently enrolled college undergraduates with a minimum 3.0 GPA who show leadership potential and are involved in extra-curricular activities centered on multicultural or international issues. Applicants must submit a 1,000-word essay on how study abroad will change their lives.
Target applicant:
 College students
 Adult students
Minimum GPA: 3.0
Amount: $1,000.

Number of awards: Up to 100.
Deadline: April 15 for fall semester, October 15 for spring semester.
How to apply: Applications are available online.

---

(258) · International Trumpet Guild Conference Scholarship

International Trumpet Guild
John Irish, Department of Music
Angelo State University
ASU Station #10906
San Angelo, TX 76909
Email: confscholarships@trumpetguild.org
Website: http://www.trumpetguild.org
Purpose: To improve the artistic level of trumpet players.
Eligibility: Applicants must be students and record audition songs onto a tape or CD. There are different age group categories, and each category has its own performance requirements. Applicants must be ITG members.
Target applicant:
 Junior high students or younger
 High school students
 College students
 Graduate school students
 Adult students
Minimum GPA: None.
Amount: $200 + conference registration fee.
Number of awards: Varies.
Deadline: February 15.
How to apply: Applications are available online.

---

(259) · Jeanne S. Chall Research Fellowship

International Reading Association
The Jeanne S. Chall Research Fellowship
Division of Research and Policy
800 Barksdale Road, P.O. Box 8139
Newark, DE 19714
Phone: 302-731-1600
Fax: 302-731-1057
Website: http://www.reading.org
Purpose: To support dissertation research in reading.
Eligibility: Applicants must be doctoral students planning or beginning their dissertation on one of the following topics in the field of reading: beginning reading, readability, reading difficulty, stages of reading development, the relation of vocabulary to reading and diagnosing and teaching adults with limited reading ability. Applicants must also be members of the International Reading Association.
Target applicant:
 Graduate school students
 Adult students
Minimum GPA: None.
Amount: $6,000.
Number of awards: 1.
Deadline: January 15.
How to apply: Applications are available online.

---

(260) · Joel Polsky Academic Achievement Award

American Society of Interior Designers (ASID) Educational Foundation Inc.
608 Massachusetts Avenue NE
Washington, DC 20002-6006

Phone: 202-546-3480
Fax: 202-546-3240
Website: http://www.asid.org
Purpose: To recognize an interior design student's project.
Eligibility: Applicants must be undergraduate or graduate students in interior design and should submit entry forms and projects such as research papers or doctoral and master's theses that focus on interior design topics. The projects are judged on content, breadth of material, coverage of the topic, innovative subject matter, bibliography and references. The society may exhibit any entry for two years.
Target applicant:
  College students
  Graduate school students
  Adult students
Minimum GPA: None.
Amount: $1,000.
Number of awards: 1.
Deadline: May 15.
How to apply: Applications are available online.

(261) · John Lennon Scholarship Competition

BMI Foundation Inc.
320 W. 57th Street
New York, NY 10019
Phone: 212-586-2000
Email: info@bmifoundation.org
Website: http://www.bmifoundation.org
Purpose: Established in 1997 by Yoko Ono in conjunction with the BMI Foundation, the John Lennon Scholarship recognizes the talent of young songwriters.
Eligibility: Applicants must be age 15 to 25 and write an original song to be reviewed by a prestigious panel of judges. Entries are to be submitted by music schools, universities, youth orchestras and the Music Educators National Conference (MENC).
Target applicant:
  Junior high students or younger
  High school students
  College students
  Graduate school students
Minimum GPA: None.
Amount: $5,000-$10,000.
Number of awards: 3.
Deadline: January 26.
How to apply: Please see the website for a full list of eligible organizations that may submit entries.

(262) · JTG Scholarship in Scientific and Technical Translation or Interpretation

American Translators Association
225 Reinekers Lane
Suite 590
Alexandria, VA 22314
Phone: 703-683-6100
Fax: 703-683-6122
Email: ata@atanet.org
Website: http://www.atanet.org
Purpose: To support students in the fields of translation and interpretation.
Eligibility: Applicants must be enrolled or planning to enroll in a graduate or undergraduate degree program for either scientific and technical translation or interpretation. Students must be attending school full-time, and they must have completed one year of post-secondary schooling. Applicants should also have at least a 3.0 overall GPA and a 3.5 GPA in translation or interpretation courses.
Target applicant:
  College students
  Graduate school students
  Adult students
Minimum GPA: 3.0
Amount: $2,500.
Number of awards: 1.
Deadline: June 1.
How to apply: Applications are available online.

(263) · Junior Competition

Gina Bachauer International Piano Foundation
138 W. Broadway, Suite 220
Salt Lake City, UT 84101
Phone: 801-297-4250
Fax: 801-521-9202
Email: info@bachauer.com
Website: http://www.bachauer.com
Purpose: To reward top piano prodigies, ages 11 to 13.
Eligibility: Applicants must perform at this competition in Salt Lake City, Utah. Students are provided with housing but must provide own transportation to and from Salt Lake City. Applicants must perform a 20-minute program of solo music and a 30-minute program of solo music.
Target applicant:
  Junior high students or younger
Minimum GPA: None.
Amount: Up to $7,000.
Number of awards: Varies.
Deadline: The competition is in June.
How to apply: Applications are available online.

(264) · Junior Competition

Fort Collins Symphony
FCSO Young Artist Competition
P.O. Box 1963
Fort Collins, CO 80522
Phone: 970-482-4823
Fax: 970-482-4858
Email: note@fcsymphony.org
Website: http://www.fcsymphony.org
Purpose: To reward student pianists.
Eligibility: Applicants must be between 12 and 18 and perform one movement of a standard, published solo concerto or similar work. The competition is limited to the first 20 applicants and 2 alternates in each division.
Target applicant:
  Junior high students or younger
  High school students
  College students
Minimum GPA: None.
Amount: $300-$500.
Number of awards: 2.
Deadline: January 12.
How to apply: Applications are available online.

(265) · Junior Composers Award

National Federation of Music Clubs Junior Composers Award
Jan Hill
1503 Wellington Road
Homewood, AL 35209
Phone: 205-871-1532
Fax: 317-638-0503
Email: jkhill@bellsouth.net
Website: http://www.nfmc-music.org
Purpose: To support young composers.
Eligibility: There are four age classes: 9 and under; 10-12; 13-15 and 16-18. Applicants must be members of the National Federation of Music Clubs. Selection is based on content and musicianship. There is a $1.25 entry fee plus state entry fee. It is highly recommended that you research the scholarship and awarding organization before applying for a scholarship with a fee. There are many scholarships that do not require a fee.
Target applicant:
    Junior high students or younger
    High school students
Minimum GPA: None.
Amount: $50-$200.
Number of awards: Varies.
Deadline: February 1.
How to apply: Applications are available online.

(266) · Junior Fellowships

Dumbarton Oaks
1703 32nd Street NW
Washington , DC 20007
Phone: 202-339-6401
Fax: 202-339-6419
Email: dumbartonoaks@doaks.org
Website: http://www.doaks.org
Purpose: To provide fellowships to scholars engaged in Byzantine studies, Pre-Columbian studies, and garden and landscape studies.
Eligibility: Applicants at the time of application should have fulfilled all preliminary requirements for a Ph.D.and be willing to work on a dissertation or final project at Dumbarton Oaks under the direction of a faculty member at their own university. The fellowships are in the following areas: Byzantine Studies (including related aspects of late Roman, early Christian, western medieval, Slavic and Near Eastern Studies), Pre-Columbian Studies (of Mexico, Central America and Andean South America) and garden and landscape studies. Fellowships are based on demonstrated scholarly ability and preparation of the candidate (including knowledge of the required languages) and value of the study or project and its relevance to Dumbarton Oaks.
Target applicant:
    Graduate school students
    Adult students
Minimum GPA: None.
Amount: $22,110.
Number of awards: Varies.
Deadline: November 1.
How to apply: Applicants must submit ten complete, collated sets of: application letter, proposal and personal and professional data. They must also submit an official transcript and three recommendation letters, with one from the faculty advisor.

(267) · King Olav V Norwegian-American Heritage Fund

Sons of Norway
1455 W. Lake Street
Minneapolis, MN 55408
Phone: 800-945-8851
Fax: 612-827-0658
Email: foundation@sofn.com
Website: http://www.sofn.com
Purpose: To promote educational exchange between Norway and North America.
Eligibility: Applicants must be Americans, 18 years or older, who would like to further their interest in Norwegian heritage or in modern Norway at an institution of higher learning. The fund also welcomes applications from Norwegians who desire to further their studies in North America. Selection is based on grade point average, participation in school and community activities, work experience, education and career goals and personal and school references.
Target applicant:
    High school students
    College students
    Adult students
Minimum GPA: None.
Amount: $1,000-$1,500.
Number of awards: Varies.
Deadline: March 1.
How to apply: Applications are available online.

(268) · KOR Memorial Scholarship

Klingon Language Institute
P.O. Box 634
Flourtown, PA 19031
Website: http://www.kli.org/scholarship
Purpose: To encourage language study.
Eligibility: Applicants must be full-time undergraduate or graduate students pursuing a degree in the field of language study. They must be nominated by the chair, head or dean of their department. Nominating faculty must submit a nominating letter, two additional faculty letters of recommendation and a personal statement and resume from the nominee. Knowledge of Klingon is not required.
Target applicant:
    College students
    Graduate school students
    Adult students
Minimum GPA: None.
Amount: $500.
Number of awards: 1.
Deadline: June 1.
How to apply: There is no application form.

(269) · Lions International Peace Poster Contest

Lions Club International
300 W. 22nd Street
Oak Brook, IL 60523-8842
Website: http://www.lionsclubs.org
Purpose: To award creative youngsters with cash prizes for outstanding poster designs.
Eligibility: Students must be 11, 12 or 13 years old as of the deadline and must be sponsored by their local Lions club. Entries will be judged at the local, district, multiple district and international levels. Posters will

be evaluated on originality, artistic merit and expression of the assigned theme, "Celebrate Peace."

Target applicant:
Junior high students or younger

Minimum GPA: None.
Amount: $500-$2,500.
Number of awards: 24.
Deadline: November 15.
How to apply: Applicants must be sponsored by the local Lions club.

(270) · Lotte Lenya Competition for Singers

Kurt Weill Foundation for Music
7 East 20th Street
3rd Floor
New York, NY 10003
Phone: 212-505-5240
Fax: 212-353-9663
Email: kwfinfo@dwf.org
Website: http://www.kwf.org
Purpose: To recognize excellence in music theater performance.
Eligibility: Applicants must be between 18 and 32 years old and attend a regional competition, performing four selections. If contestants are unable to participate in any of the scheduled regional auditions, they may instead submit a videotape or DVD, which must contain all four of the required repertoire selections. Finalists will be chosen, based on vocal beauty and technique, interpretation, acting, repertoire variety and presence.

Target applicant:
High school students
College students
Graduate school students
Adult students

Minimum GPA: None.
Amount: $500-$10,000.
Number of awards: Varies.
Deadline: January 14.
How to apply: Applications are available online.

(271) · Mabelle Wilhelmina Boldt Scholarship

American Society of Interior Designers (ASID) Educational Foundation Inc.
608 Massachusetts Avenue NE
Washington, DC 20002-6006
Phone: 202-546-3480
Fax: 202-546-3240
Website: http://www.asid.org
Purpose: To help interior designers continue their education.
Eligibility: Applicants must be enrolled in or have applied for admission to a graduate-level interior design program at a degree-granting institution. Students must have been active designers for at least five years before returning to graduate school. The scholarship is based on academic and creative accomplishment. Applicants must submit undergraduate transcripts, a statement and a letter of recommendation. Preference is given to students with a focus on design research. ASID may publish some of the research.

Target applicant:
Graduate school students
Adult students

Minimum GPA: None.
Amount: $2,000.

Number of awards: 1.
Deadline: May 15.
How to apply: Applications are available online.

(272) · Malmberg Scholarship and Fellowship

American Swedish Institute
2600 Park Avenue
Minneapolis, MN 55407
Phone: 612-870-3374
Fax: 612-871-8682
Email: ninac@americanswedishinst.org
Website: http://www.americanswedishinst.org
Purpose: To provide funds for students who wish to perform research in Sweden.
Eligibility: Applicants must be U.S. residents who are enrolled in a degree-granting program or qualified scholars whose study or research could be enhanced by studying in Sweden.

Target applicant:
College students
Adult students

Minimum GPA: None.
Amount: Up to $10,000.
Number of awards: Varies.
Deadline: November 15.
How to apply: Applications are available online.

(273) · Metchie J.E. Budka Award

Thomas Pniewski, Director of Cultural Affairs
Kosciuszko Foundation
15 East 65th Street
New York, NY 10021-6595
Phone: 212-734-2130 x214
Fax: 212-628-4552
Email: tompkf@aol.com
Website: http://www.kosciuszkofoundation.org
Purpose: To honor works that contribute significantly to the knowledge and understanding of Polish literature, Polish history and Polish-American relations.
Eligibility: Applicants may be either graduate students who are working in the fields of Polish literature, Polish history, or Polish-American relations at American colleges and universities, or postdoctoral candidates who received their Ph.D. degrees for work in these fields and who apply during or at the close of the first three years of their postdoctoral careers in the field.

Target applicant:
Graduate school students
Adult students

Minimum GPA: None.
Amount: $3,000.
Number of awards: 1.
Deadline: Third Wednesday in July.
How to apply: Applications are available online.

(274) · Microsoft Live@edu Film Contest

Microsoft Live@edu
One Microsoft Way
Redmond, WA 98052
Phone: 800-642-7676
Email: info@filmatedu.com
Website: http://www.filmatedu.com

Purpose: To reward student filmmakers.
Eligibility: Applicants must be college or university students who are residents of, and attend school in, one of the 50 U.S. states or the District of Columbia. They must be 18 years of age or older. Employees of Microsoft and its affiliates and their families are ineligible. Awards consist of high-definition video cameras and cash.
Target applicant:
    College students
    Adult students
Minimum GPA: None.
Amount: Varies.
Number of awards: 8.
Deadline: March 31.
How to apply: Applications are available online.

---

(275) · Mildred and Albert Panowski Playwriting Award

Forest Roberts Theatre at Northern Michigan University
1401 Presque Isle Avenue
Marquette, MI 49855
Phone: 906-227-2553
Email: bowersr1@chartermi.net
Website: http://www.nmu.edu/theatre/
Purpose: To provide students and faculty the opportunity produce an original work on the university stage.
Eligibility: This award is available to any playwright, and entries must be original, full-length productions.
Target applicant:
    Junior high students or younger
    High school students
    College students
    Graduate school students
    Adult students
Minimum GPA: None.
Amount: $2,000.
Number of awards: 1.
Deadline: November.
How to apply: There is no application form. The play is the application.

---

(276) · MMT New Play Competition

Mill Mountain Theatre
Literary Coordinator
One Market Square SE
Roanoke, VA 24011
Phone: 540-342-5749
Email: outreach@millmountain.org
Website: http://www.millmountain.org
Purpose: To promote play-writing.
Eligibility: Applicants must submit an act that should be 25 to 35 minutes long. The script must be agent-submitted or accompanied by a professional letter of recommendation by a director or literary manager. Film or TV scripts, translations or adaptations are not accepted. Plays that have received developmental workshops or musicals accompanied by a demo tape or CD are accepted.
Target applicant:
    High school students
    College students
    Graduate school students
    Adult students
Minimum GPA: None.

Amount: $1,000.
Number of awards: Varies.
Deadline: January 1.
How to apply: There is no official application.

---

(277) · Morton Gould Young Composer Award

ASCAP Foundation
One Lincoln Plaza
New York, NY 10023
Phone: 212-621-6219
Website: http://www.ascapfoundation.org
Purpose: To encourage young composers early in their careers.
Eligibility: Applicants must be composers who have not turned 30 before January 1 of the current year. They must be U.S. citizens or permanent residents or enrolled students with a student visa. Applicants must submit an original composition.
Target applicant:
    Junior high students or younger
    High school students
    College students
    Graduate school students
    Adult students
Minimum GPA: None.
Amount: Varies.
Number of awards: Varies.
Deadline: March 1.
How to apply: Applications are available online.

---

(278) · National High School Essay Contest

United Nations Association of the United States of America
801 Second Avenue, 2nd Floor
New York, NY 10017
Phone: 212-907-1300
Fax: 212-682-9185
Email: unahq@unausa.org
Website: http://www.unausa.org
Purpose: To encourage thought on issues of international importance.
Eligibility: Applicants must submit an essay of no more than 1,500 words on a designated topic. The contest is open to all students in grades 9 to 12. Applicants must submit essays to a local chapter for the first level of judging.
Target applicant:
    High school students
Minimum GPA: None.
Amount: $750-$3,000 + trip to UN Headquarters.
Number of awards: 3.
Deadline: January 3.
How to apply: Applications are available from UNA-USA chapters.

---

(279) · National High School Poetry Contest/ Easterday Poetry Award

Diet-Live Poets Society
P.O. Box 8841
Turnersville, NJ 08012
Website: http://www.geocities.com/diet-lps
Purpose: To provide a venue for young poets to be recognized.
Eligibility: Applicants must be U.S. high school students. Submitted poems must be 20 lines or less, in English, unpublished and not simultaneously submitted to any other competition. Applicants may

only submit one poem during any 90-day span and must include a self-addressed, stamped envelope with each mailed entry, or applicants may submit their poems online.

Target applicant:
    High school students
Minimum GPA: None.
Amount: $100-$1,000 + publication.
Number of awards: 12.
Deadline: October 31 and March 31.
How to apply: There is no application form.

(280) · National Italian American Foundation Scholarship

National Italian American Foundation
1860 19th Street NW
Washington, DC 20009
Phone: 202-387-0600
Fax: 202-387-0800
Email: scholarships@niaf.org
Website: http://www.niaf.org
Purpose: To support Italian American students and students of any ethnic background studying Italian language or studies.
Eligibility: Applicants must either be Italian American students who demonstrate outstanding academic achievement or be students from any ethnic background majoring or minoring in Italian language, Italian studies, Italian American studies or a related field and demonstrate outstanding academic achievement. Applicants must also plan to be or currently be enrolled in an accredited institution of higher education, have a minimum 3.25 GPA and be U.S. citizens or permanent residents.
Target applicant:
    High school students
    College students
    Adult students
Minimum GPA: 3.5
Amount: $2,000-$10,000.
Number of awards: Varies.
Deadline: March 6.
How to apply: Applications are available online.

(281) · National Junior Classical League (NJCL) Scholarships

National Junior Classical League
1122 Oak Street North
Fargo, ND 58102
Phone: 513-529-7741
Fax: 513-529-7742
Email: administrator@njcl.org
Website: http://www.njcl.org
Purpose: To support students studying the classics.
Eligibility: Applicants must be NJCL members in good standing, entering college the upcoming year, and studying the classics. Special consideration is given to those planning to teach Latin, Greek or classical humanities. Selection is based on financial need, JCL service, academics and recommendations.
Target applicant:
    High school students
Minimum GPA: None.
Amount: $1000-$2,000.
Number of awards: 9.
Deadline: May 1.

How to apply: Applications are available online or by written request.

(282) · National Latin Exam Scholarship

National Latin Exam
University of Mary Washington
1301 College Avenue
Fredericksburg, VA 22401
Phone: 888-378-7721
Email: nle@umw.edu
Website: http://www.nle.org
Purpose: To reward students for their Latin proficiency.
Eligibility: Applicants must be gold medal winners in Latin III-IV Prose, III-IV Poetry or Latin V-VI on the National Latin Exam. Applicants must be high school seniors who agree to take at least one Latin or classical Greek each semester during their first year of college. A classics in translation course does not count.
Target applicant:
    High school students
Minimum GPA: None.
Amount: $1,000.
Number of awards: 21.
Scholarship may be renewable.
Deadline: September 15.
How to apply: Applications are mailed to eligible students. Renewal applications are available online.

(283) · National Literature Scholarship - Siddhartha

Common Knowledge Scholarship Foundation
P.O. Box 290361
Davie, FL 33329-0361
Phone: 954-262-8553
Email: info@cksf.org
Website: http://www.cksf.org
Purpose: To support students who are interested in literature.
Eligibility: Applicants must register online with CKSF. Students must read "Siddhartha" by Herman Hesse and take four online quizzes about the novel. The student with the most points from correct answers and the shortest time that it takes to answer the questions wins the scholarship.
Target applicant:
    High school students
    College students
    Graduate school students
    Adult students
Minimum GPA: None.
Amount: $500.
Number of awards: 1.
Deadline: January 26.
How to apply: Applications are available online.

(284) · National Sculpture Society Scholarship

National Sculpture Society
237 Park Avenue
Ground Floor
New York, NY 10017
Phone: 212-764-5645
Email: nss1893@aol.com
Website: http://www.nationalsculpture.org

Purpose: To award scholarships to students of figurative or representative sculpture.
Eligibility: Applicants must provide brief biographies and an explanation of their background in sculpture, two recommendation letters and photographs of their sculpture work. Students must also demonstrate financial need.
Target applicant:
    College students
    Adult students
Minimum GPA: None.
Amount: $2,000.
Number of awards: Varies.
Deadline: May 31.
How to apply: Follow the application guidelines listed on the website.

(285) · National Security Education Program David L. Boren Undergraduate Scholarships

Institute of International Education
809 United Nations Plaza
New York, NY 10017
Phone: 212-883-8200
Fax: 212-984-5452
Email: gilman@iie.org
Website: http://www.iie.org
Purpose: To provide an opportunity for undergraduate students to study abroad in countries vital to future American security interests.
Eligibility: Applicants must prove that they have a serious interest in pursuing academic study in a foreign country. Applicants must also be well-versed in foreign languages and be willing to commit up to a year living overseas.
Target applicant:
    College students
    Adult students
Minimum GPA: None.
Amount: $2,500-$6,000.
Number of awards: Varies.
Deadline: Varies.
How to apply: Applications are available online.

(286) · National Ten Minute Play Contest

Actors Theatre of Louisville
National Ten Minute Play Contest
316 W. Main Street
Louisville, KY 40202-4218
Phone: 502-584-1265
Website: http://www.actorstheatre.org
Purpose: To identify emerging playwrights.
Eligibility: Each playwright may only submit one script no more than 10 pages in length that has not been previously submitted.
Target applicant:
    Junior high students or younger
    High school students
    College students
    Graduate school students
    Adult students
Minimum GPA: None.
Amount: $1,000.
Number of awards: Varies.
Deadline: December 1.
How to apply: No application is necessary.

(287) · NFMC Claire Ulrich Whitehurst Piano Award

National Federation of Music Clubs Claire Ulrich Whitehurst Piano Award
Claire-Frances Whitehurst
3360 SW 18th Street
Miami, FL 33145-1853
Phone: 305-445-2128
Fax: 317-638-0503
Email: info@nfmc-music.org
Website: http://www.nfmc-music.org
Purpose: To support young piano players.
Eligibility: Applicants must be high school sophomores, juniors or seniors under age 18 and members of the National Federation of Music Clubs and must submit taped piano solo performances. There is a $10 entry fee. It is highly recommended that you research the scholarship and awarding organization before applying for a scholarship with a fee. There are many scholarships that do not require a fee.
Target applicant:
    High school students
Minimum GPA: None.
Amount: $750.
Number of awards: 1.
Deadline: March 1 on even numbered years.
How to apply: Applications are available online.

(288) · NFMC Lynn Freeman Olson Composition Awards

National Federation of Music Clubs Olson Awards
James Schnars
6550 Shoreline Drive
Suite 7505
St. Petersburg, FL 33708
Phone: 317-638-4003
Fax: 317-638-0503
Email: info@nfmc-music.org
Website: http://www.nfmc-music.org
Purpose: To support student composers.
Eligibility: Applicants must be at least in grade 7 and no older than age 25. Three awards are given, one for each category: intermediate (grades 7 to 9), high school (grades 10 to 12) and advanced (high school graduates through age 25). Applicants must be members of the National Federation of Music Clubs and must submit an original piano composition to be judged. This biennial award is given in odd numbered years.
Target applicant:
    Junior high students or younger
    High school students
    College students
Minimum GPA: None.
Amount: $500-$1,500.
Number of awards: 3.
Deadline: March 1.
How to apply: Applications are available online.

(289) · NFMC Wendell Irish Viola Award

National Federation of Music Clubs (AR)
Dr. George Keck
421 Cherry Street
Arkadelphia, AR 71923
Phone: 317-638-4003
Fax: 317-638-0503

Email: keckg@obu.edu
Website: http://www.nfmc-music.org
Purpose: To recognize musically talented students.
Eligibility: Applicants must be between the ages of 12 and 18 and must be Individual Junior Special members or Active Junior Club members of the National Federation of Music Clubs. Applicants must enter in their state of residence by submitting a taped performance.
Target applicant:
   Junior high students or younger
   High school students
Minimum GPA: None.
Amount: $1,000.
Number of awards: 4.
Deadline: February 1.
How to apply: Applications are available online.

(290) · Nido Qubein Scholarship

National Speakers Association
1500 S. Priest Drive
Attn: Scholarship Committee
Tempe, AZ 85281
Phone: 480-968-2552
Fax: 480-968-0911
Website: http://www.nsaspeaker.org
Purpose: To encourage study in the field of professional speaking.
Eligibility: Applicants must be full-time students majoring or minoring in speech. Selection is based on application, essay, recommendation and college transcript.
Target applicant:
   College students
   Graduate school students
   Adult students
Minimum GPA: None.
Amount: $1,000.
Number of awards: 1.
Deadline: June 1.
How to apply: Applications are available online or by written request.

(291) · Omaha Symphony Guild International New Music Competition

Omaha Symphony Guild
c/o Susan Woodford
9925 Broadmoor
Omaha, NE 68114
Phone: 402-342-3836
Fax: 402-342-3819
Email: bertese@aol.com
Website: http://www.omahasymphony.org
Purpose: Created in 1978, the Omaha Symphony Guild International New Music Competition offers not only a monetary award to amateur composers but also the opportunity to hear their contemporary classical work performed by a professional orchestra, the Omaha Symphony.
Eligibility: The New Music Competition is open to any composer over the age of 25. The entry must not have been published or performed previously and must not exceed 20 minutes in length. Compositions intended for small ensembles do not qualify for submission.
Target applicant:
   College students
   Graduate school students
   Adult students

Minimum GPA: None.
Amount: $3,000.
Number of awards: 1.
Deadline: April 15.
How to apply: Applications and further submission rules are available online.

(292) · Optimist International Essay Contest

Optimist International
4494 Lindell Boulevard
St. Louis, MO 63108
Phone: 314-371-6000
Fax: 314-371-6006
Email: programs@optimist.org
Website: http://www.optimist.org
Purpose: To reward students based on their essay-writing skills.
Eligibility: Applicants must be under 19 years of age as of December 31 of the current school year and application must be made through a local Optimist Club. The essay topic is, "I want to make a difference because..." Applicants compete at the club, district and international level. District winners receive a $650 scholarship, and three international winners receive prizes up to $6,000. Scoring is based on organization, vocabulary and style, grammar and punctuation, neatness and adherence to the contest rules.
Target applicant:
   High school students
Minimum GPA: None.
Amount: $650-$6,000.
Number of awards: Varies.
Deadline: February 28.
How to apply: Contact your local Optimist Club.

(293) · Pat Roberts Intelligence Scholars Program for Language Analysts

National Security Agency (NSA)
9800 Savage Road, Suite 6779
Ft. George G. Meade, MD 20755-6779
Phone: 410-854-4725
Website: http://www.nsa.gov/careers/
Purpose: To support students who plan to work in language analysis after graduation.
Eligibility: Applicants must be within two years of completing a master's or doctorate degree in a language or language-related field. Recipients are expected to enter the NSA Language Analysis New Hire Program after graduation.
Target applicant:
   Graduate school students
   Adult students
Minimum GPA: None.
Amount: Up to $25,000 per year.
Number of awards: Varies.
Deadline: October 30.
How to apply: Applications are available online.

(294) · Patriot's Pen Youth Essay Contest

Veterans of Foreign Wars
406 W. 34th Street
Kansas City, MO 64111
Phone: 816-756-3390
Fax: 816-968-1149

Email: info@vfw.org
Website: http://www.vfw.org
Purpose: To give students in grades 6 through 8 an opportunity to write essays that express their views on democracy.
Eligibility: Applicants must be enrolled as a 6th, 7th or 8th grader in a public, private or parochial school in the U.S., its territories or possessions. Home-schooled students and dependents of U.S. military or civilian personnel in overseas schools may also apply. Foreign exchange students and former applicants who placed in the national finals are ineligible. Students must submit essays based on an annual theme to their local VFW posts. If an essay is picked to advance, the entry is judged at the District (regional) level, then the Department (state) level and finally at the National level. Essays are judged 30 percent on knowledge of the theme, 35 percent on development of the theme and 35 percent on clarity.
Target applicant:
   Junior high students or younger
Minimum GPA: None.
Amount: Up to $10,000.
Number of awards: Varies.
Deadline: November 1.
How to apply: Applications are available online or by contacting the local VFW office. Entries must be turned into the local VFW office. Contact information for these offices can be found online or by calling the VFW National Programs headquarters at 816-968-1117.

(295) · Pete Carpenter Fellowship for Aspiring Film Composers
BMI Foundation Pete Carpenter Fellowship
Ms. Linda Livingston, Director
8730 Sunset Boulevard, 3rd Floor West
Los Angeles, CA 90069
Email: carpenterfellowship@bmifoundation.org
Website: http://www.bmifoundation.org
Purpose: Established by the BMI Foundation and Mr. Carpenter's family, colleagues and friends to honor the late co-composer of television themes and scores.
Eligibility: Applicants must be under the age of 35 and submit an original one- to three- minute composition or part of a score that they consider appropriate as the theme of a film or series with the application. The winner can work for one month in Los Angeles on a day-to-day basis with distinguished theatrical film and television composers and receives a $3,000 stipend for travel and expenses.
Target applicant:
   Junior high students or younger
   High school students
   College students
   Graduate school students
   Adult students
Minimum GPA: None.
Amount: $3,000.
Number of awards: 1.
Deadline: January 26.
How to apply: Applications are available online.

(296) · Playwright Discovery Award
VSA Arts
818 Connecticut Avenue NW
Suite 600
Washington, DC 20006
Phone: 800-933-8721

Fax: 202-429-0868
Email: info@vsarts.org
Website: http://www.vsarts.org
Purpose: To award promising young writers with scholarship funds and a chance to have one of their scripts professionally produced at the John F. Kennedy Center for the Performing Arts.
Eligibility: Applicants must be students in grades 6-12. Applicants are to create an original one-act script of less than 40 pages that documents the experience of living with a disability. Applicants themselves need not be disabled, but the script must address the issue. Selected scripts will be performed for middle school, high school, and adult audiences. First and second place winners will have their plays performed at the JFK Performing Arts Center.
Target applicant:
   Junior high students or younger
   High school students
Minimum GPA: None.
Amount: $1,000 + Washington, DC trip.
Number of awards: 2.
Deadline: April 15.
How to apply: Applications are available online.

(297) · Poster Contest for High School Students
Christophers
12 E. 48th Street
New York, NY 10017
Website: http://www.christophers.org
Purpose: To reward students for interpreting a given theme through poster art.
Eligibility: Entrants must be high school students. Students must work individually to create posters of original content. Posters are judged by a panel based on overall impact, expression of the year's theme, artistic merit and originality.
Target applicant:
   High school students
Minimum GPA: None.
Amount: $250-$1,000.
Number of awards: 8.
Deadline: January 23.
How to apply: Applications are available online.

(298) · Princess Grace Awards
Princess Grace Awards
150 E. 58th Street
21st Floor
New York, NY 10155
Phone: 212-317-1470
Fax: 212-317-1473
Email: pgfusa@pgfusa.com
Website: http://www.pgfusa.com
Purpose: To assist emerging young artists in theater, dance and film to realize their career goals.
Eligibility: Applicants must submit an example of their work in the category in the category in which they apply: theatre, dance, film or playwriting. Theatre and dance applicants require the sponsorship of a professional company or school, one nominee per institution. Awards are based on the artistic quality of the artist's work, potential for future excellence and activities.

Target applicant:
    High school students
    College students
    Adult students
Minimum GPA: None.
Amount: Varies.
Number of awards: Varies.
Deadline: Varies.
How to apply: Applications are available online.

---

(299) · Print and Graphics Scholarship

Graphic Arts Information Network
Print and Graphics Scholarship Foundation
Scholarship Competition
200 Deer Run Road
Sewickley, PA 15143
Phone: 412-741-6860
Fax: 412-741-2311
Email: pgsf@gatf.org
Website: http://www.gain.org
Purpose: To provide financial assistance for postsecondary education to students interested in graphic communications careers.
Eligibility: Applicants must be high school seniors or high school graduates who have not started college yet, or college students enrolled in a two- or four-year college program. Applicants must be full-time students, be interested in a career in graphic communications and able to maintain a 3.0 GPA.
Target applicant:
    High school students
    College students
    Adult students
Minimum GPA: 3.0
Amount: $1,000-$1,500.
Number of awards: 300.
Scholarship may be renewable.
Deadline: March 1 for high school.
How to apply: Applications are available online.

---

(300) · Prize in Ethics Essay Contest

Elie Wiesel Foundation for Humanity
555 Madison Avenue, 20th Floor
New York, NY 10022
Phone: 212-490-7788
Fax: 212-490-6006
Email: info@eliewieselfoundation.org
Website: http://www.eliewieselfoundation.org
Purpose: To promote the thought and discussion of ethics and their place in education.
Eligibility: Applicants must be registered full-time juniors and seniors at accredited colleges and universities in the U.S. Students must write an essay dealing with ethics and have a faculty sponsor review their essay and sign the entry form.
Target applicant:
    College students
    Adult students
Minimum GPA: None.
Amount: $500-$5,000.
Number of awards: 5.
Deadline: December 7.
How to apply: Applications are available online.

---

(301) · Rotary International Ambassadorial Scholarship Program

Rotary International
One Rotary Center
1560 Sherman Avenue
Evanston, IL 60201
Phone: 847-866-3000
Fax: 847-328-8554
Email: scholarshipinquiries@rotaryintl.org
Website: http://www.rotary.org
Purpose: To further international understanding and friendly relations among people of different countries.
Eligibility: Applicants must be citizens of a country in which there are Rotary clubs and have completed at least two years of college-level coursework or equivalent professional experience before starting their scholarship studies. Initial applications are made through local clubs. Students must be proficient in the language of the proposed host country.
Target applicant:
    College students
    Graduate school students
    Adult students
Minimum GPA: None.
Amount: Varies.
Number of awards: Varies.
Deadline: As early as March for club deadlines.
How to apply: Applications are available through your local Rotary club or online.

---

(302) · Scholarship Program for Young Pianists

Chopin Foundation of the United States, Inc.
1440 79th Street Causeway
Suite 117
Miami, FL 33141
Phone: 305-868-0624
Fax: 305-865-5150
Email: info@chopin.org
Website: http://www.chopin.org
Purpose: To support pianists to prepare and qualify for the American National Chopin Piano Competition.
Eligibility: The program is available to any qualified American pianists age 14 to 17 who are enrolled in secondary or undergraduate institutions as full-time students. Applicants also must study music and major in piano. They must submit applications, statements of career goals, two references, audio tapes, and $25 fees. It is highly recommended that you research the scholarship and awarding organization before applying for a scholarship with a fee. There are many scholarships that do not require a fee.
Target applicant:
    High school students
    College students
Minimum GPA: None.
Amount: $1,000.
Number of awards: Up to 10.
Scholarship may be renewable.
Deadline: February 15.
How to apply: Applications are available online.

(303) · Scholarships to Oslo International Summer School

Sons of Norway
1455 W. Lake Street
Minneapolis, MN 55408
Phone: 800-945-8851
Fax: 612-827-0658
Email: foundation@sofn.com
Website: http://www.sofn.com
Purpose: To give financial support to students who attend Oslo International Summer School.
Eligibility: Applicants who are admitted to Oslo International Summer School and who are Sons of Norway members or children or grandchildren of current members are eligible. Selection is based on financial need, essay, GPA and letters of recommendation. Extra consideration is given to students who are members of Sons of Norway.
Target applicant:
    High school students
    College students
    Adult students
Minimum GPA: None.
Amount: $1,500.
Number of awards: 2.
Deadline: March 1.
How to apply: Applications are available online.

(304) · Senior Fellowship Program

National Gallery of Art
2000B South Club Drive
Landover, MD 20785
Phone: 202-842-6482
Fax: 202-789-3026
Website: http://www.nga.gov/resources/casva.htm
Purpose: To award fellowships to scholars in the visual arts.
Eligibility: Applicants should have held the Ph.D. for five years or more or possess an equivalent record of professional accomplishment at the time of application. They must submit application forms, proposals, copies of publications and three letters of recommendation. Fellowships are for full-time research, and scholars are expected to reside in Washington and to participate in the activities of the Center. One Paul Mellon Fellowship, one Frese Senior Fellowship and four to six Ailsa Mellon Bruce and Samuel H. Kress Senior Fellowships will be awarded for the academic year. The Paul Mellon and Ailsa Mellon Bruce Senior Fellowships support research in the history, theory and criticism of the visual arts of any geographical area and of any period. The Samuel H. Kress Senior Fellowships support research on European art before the early nineteenth century. The Frese Senior Fellowship is for study in the history, theory and criticism of sculpture, prints and drawings or decorative arts of any geographical area and of any period. Applications are also accepted from scholars in other disciplines whose work is related.
Target applicant:
    Graduate school students
    Adult students
Minimum GPA: None.
Amount: $50,000.
Number of awards: Varies.
Deadline: October 1.
How to apply: Applications are available online.

(305) · Short-Term Travel Grants (STG)

International Research and Exchanges Board (IREX)
2121 K Street NW
Suite 700
Washington, DC 20037
Phone: 202-628-8188
Fax: 202-628-8189
Email: irex@irex.org
Website: http://www.irex.org
Purpose: To provide travel grants for U.S. postdoctoral scholars and holders of other graduate degrees to travel to Europe and Eurasia.
Eligibility: Applicants must be U.S. citizens or permanent residents for at least three consecutive years before applying for the grant and must hold a Ph.D. or other terminal degree. The grant is for up to eight weeks for independent research projects. Projects must contribute to the knowledge of political, economic or cultural development of the region and how that knowledge is relevant to U.S. foreign policy.
Target applicant:
    Graduate school students
    Adult students
Minimum GPA: None.
Amount: Up to $5,000.
Number of awards: Varies.
Deadline: February 1.
How to apply: Applications are available online.

(306) · Signet Classic Student Scholarship Essay Contest

Penguin Group (USA)
Academic Marketing Department
Signet Classic Student Scholarship
375 Hudson Street
New York, NY 10014
Website: http://us.penguingroup.com/static/html/services-academic/essayhome.html
Purpose: To reward high school students for their essays on literature.
Eligibility: Applicants must be high school juniors or seniors or equivalent home schooled students and write an essay on one of four selected topics based on a piece of literature. Each English teacher may only submit one junior and one senior essay. Selection is based on style, content, grammar and originality.
Target applicant:
    High school students
Minimum GPA: None.
Amount: $1,000.
Number of awards: 5.
Deadline: April 15.
How to apply: English teachers submit entries.

(307) · Sinfonia Foundation Scholarship

Sinfonia Foundation
Scholarship Committee
10600 Old State Road
Evansville, IN 47711-1399
Phone: 800-473-2649 x110
Email: sef@sinfonia.org
Website: http://www.sinfonia.org/SEF/
Purpose: To assist the collegiate members and chapters of Sinfonia.
Eligibility: Applicants must be in college for at least two semesters with good academic standing and submit references and an essay.

Target applicant:
College students
Adult students
Minimum GPA: None.
Amount: $2,500-$5,000.
Number of awards: 2.
Deadline: February 1.
How to apply: Applications are available online.

(308) · Sorantin Competition

San Angelo Symphony
Sorantin Award
P.O. Box 5922
San Angelo, TX 76902
Phone: 325-658-5877
Fax: 325-653-1045
Email: assistant@sanangelosymphony.org
Website: http://www.sanangelosymphony.org
Purpose: To promote musical performances.
Eligibility: There are two divisions of the competition: piano and strings. A winner and a runner-up are selected in each division, and an overall winner is selected to perform with the San Angelo Symphony and will receive an extra $3,000. Applicants cannot have reached their 28th birthday by November 15. There is a $50 application fee. It is highly recommended that you research the scholarship and awarding organization before applying for a scholarship with a fee. There are many scholarships that do not require a fee.
Target applicant:
Junior high students or younger
High school students
College students
Graduate school students
Adult students
Minimum GPA: None.
Amount: $1000-$3,000.
Number of awards: Varies.
Deadline: October 9.
How to apply: Applications are available online.

(309) · Stacey Scholarship Fund

John F. and Anna Lee Stacey Scholarship Fund
1700 N.E. 63rd Street
Oklahoma City, OK 73111
Phone: 405-478-2250
Fax: 405-478-4714
Email: emuno@nationalcowboymuseum.org
Website: http://www.cowboyhalloffame.org
Purpose: To educate young men and women who aim to enter the art profession.
Eligibility: Applicants must be between the ages of 18 and 35 and must submit not more than 10 35mm slides of their painting or drawing work for judging along with a letter outlining the applicants' ambitions and plans. Letters of recommendation will also be taken into account during selection.
Target applicant:
High school students
College students
Graduate school students
Adult students
Minimum GPA: None.
Amount: $5,000.

Number of awards: Varies.
Deadline: February 1.
How to apply: Applications are available online.

(310) · Stella Blum Research Grant

Costume Society of America (CSA)
Ann Wass
5903 60th Avenue
Riverdale, MD 20737
Phone: 800-272-9447
Fax: 908-359-7619
Email: national.office@costumesocietyamerica.com
Website: http://www.costumesocietyamerica.com
Purpose: To support a CSA student member working in the field of North American costume.
Eligibility: Applicants must be accepted into an undergraduate or graduate degree program at an accredited university for the time during which the grant would apply, conduct a research project in the area of North American costume and be members of the Costume Society of America (CSA) in good standing. Applications are judged according to significance of topic, feasibility, time frame, methodology, bibliography, budget, applicants' qualifications and how the research might further the field of costumes.
Target applicant:
High school students
College students
Graduate school students
Adult students
Minimum GPA: None.
Amount: $2,000 plus a travel component of up to $500 to attend National Symposium.
Number of awards: 1.
Deadline: May 1.
How to apply: Applications are available by email or phone.

(311) · Stillman-Kelley Awards

National Federation of Music Clubs Stillman-Kelley Award
Sue Breuer
4404 Travis Country
Circle B4
Austin, TX 78735
Phone: 512-892-5633
Website: http://www.nfmc-music.org
Purpose: To support young musicians and composers.
Eligibility: Applicants must be instrumentalists under the age of 17 and be members of the National Federation of Music Clubs. This award rotates by region with the Northeastern and Southeastern regions in even years and Central and Western regions in odd years.
Target applicant:
High school students
Minimum GPA: None.
Amount: $500-$1,000.
Number of awards: 2.
Deadline: February 1.
How to apply: Applications are available online.

(312) · Student Academy Awards

Academy of Motion Picture Arts and Sciences
8949 Wilshire Boulevard
Beverly Hills, CA 90211

Phone: 310-247-3000
Email: rmiller@oscars.org
Website: http://www.oscars.org
Purpose: To support student filmmakers with no previous professional experience who are enrolled as full-time students.
Eligibility: Applicants must be full-time students at an accredited U.S. college, university, film school or art school. Films must be made as a part of a school curriculum in the categories of alternative, animation, documentary or narrative. Entries must have been completed after April 1 of the previous year. In case of graduation or other departure from a program, a film may be submitted up to one year from that date. All entries must be submitted on DVD-R format. Selection is based on originality, entertainment, production quality and resourcefulness.
Target applicant:
    College students
    Graduate school students
    Adult students
Minimum GPA: None.
Amount: $2,000-$5,000.
Number of awards: 3 per category.
Deadline: April 2.
How to apply: Applications are available online.

---

(313) · Student Design Competition
International Housewares Association
6400 Shafer Court, Suite 650
Rosemont, IL 60018
Phone: 847-292-4200
Fax: 847-292-4211
Website: http://www.housewares.org
Purpose: To honor and encourage young, up-and-coming designers to enter careers in the housewares industry.
Eligibility: Applicants must be enrolled as an undergraduate or graduate student at an IDSA-affiliated college or university.
Target applicant:
    College students
    Graduate school students
    Adult students
Minimum GPA: None.
Amount: Varies.
Number of awards: Varies.
Deadline: December 19.
How to apply: Applications are available online.

---

(314) · Student Translation Award
American Translators Association
225 Reinekers Lane
Suite 590
Alexandria, VA 22314
Phone: 703-683-6100
Fax: 703-683-6122
Email: ata@atanet.org
Website: http://www.atanet.org
Purpose: To encourage translation projects by students.
Eligibility: Applicants must be graduate or undergraduate students or a group of students attending an accredited U.S. college or university. The project should have post-grant results such as a publication, conference presentation or teaching material. Computer-assisted translations, dissertations and theses are not eligible, and students who are already published translators are not eligible. Translations must be from a foreign language into English. Preference is given to students who have

been or are currently enrolled in translator training programs. There is a limit of one entry per student. Applicants should submit entry forms, statements of purpose, letter of recommendation, translation sample with corresponding source-language text, proof of permission to publish from copyright holder, and sample outline or other material demonstrating the nature of the work (if the project is not a translation).
Target applicant:
    College students
    Graduate school students
    Adult students
Minimum GPA: None.
Amount: $500.
Number of awards: 1.
Deadline: April 17.
How to apply: Applications are available online.

---

(315) · Swackhamer Peace Essay Contest
Nuclear Age Peace Foundation
1187 Coast Village Road
PMB 121, Suite 1
Santa Barbara, CA 93108-2794
Phone: 805-965-3443
Fax: 805-568-0466
Website: http://www.wagingpeace.org
Purpose: To encourage high school create a video on world peace.
Eligibility: Students must be in any high school in the world and submit a video on the provided topic. Selection is based on analysis of the subject matter, originality, development of point of view, insight, clarity of expression, organization and grammar.
Target applicant:
    High school students
Minimum GPA: None.
Amount: $500-$1,500.
Number of awards: 3.
Deadline: June 1.
How to apply: Applications are available online.

---

(316) · Taylor/Blakeslee University Fellowships
Council for the Advancement of Science Writing (CASW)
P.O. Box 910
Hedgesville, WV 25427
Phone: 304-754-5077
Email: diane@nasw.org
Website: http://www.casw.org
Purpose: To help graduate students in science writing.
Eligibility: Applicants must be U.S. citizens who are enrolled in U.S. graduate-level science writing programs.
Target applicant:
    Graduate school students
    Adult students
Minimum GPA: None.
Amount: $2,000.
Number of awards: Varies.
Deadline: Varies.
How to apply: Contact the organization for more information.

---

(317) · Thelma A. Robinson Award in Ballet
National Federation of Music Clubs (Coral Gables, FL)
Anne Cruxent
5530 Lajeune Road
Coral Gables, FL 33146

Phone: 330-638-4003
Fax: 317-638-0503
Email: acruxent@bellsouth.net
Website: http://www.nfmc-music.org
Purpose: To support students who are ballet dancers.
Eligibility: Applicants must be between the ages of 13 and 16. There is no entry fee, but applicants must be members of the NFMC.
Target applicant:
    Junior high students or younger
    High school students
Minimum GPA: None.
Amount: $2,000.
Number of awards: 1.
Deadline: October 1.
How to apply: Applications are available online.

(318) · Thespian Scholarships

Educational Theatre Association
2343 Auburn Avenue
Cincinnati, OH 45219
Phone: 513-421-3900
Website: http://www.edta.org
Purpose: To support student thespians.
Eligibility: Applicants must be seniors in high school, active members of the International Thespian Society and planning to major or minor in communicative arts. Most of the scholarships require an audition or tech portfolio.
Target applicant:
    High school students
Minimum GPA: None.
Amount: $1,500-$4,500.
Number of awards: Varies.
Deadline: May 8.
How to apply: Applications are available online.

(319) · Translation Prize

American-Scandinavian Foundation
58 Park Avenue
New York, NY 10016
Phone: 212-879-9779
Email: grants@amscan.org
Website: http://www.amscan.org
Purpose: To encourage the English translation of Scandinavian literature.
Eligibility: The award is given to the best English translation of poetry, fiction, drama or literary prose written by a Scandinavian author in Danish, Finnish, Icelandic, Norwegian or Swedish after 1800. Translations may not previously have been published in the English language.
Target applicant:
    Junior high students or younger
    High school students
    College students
    Graduate school students
    Adult students
Minimum GPA: None.
Amount: $1,000-$2,000.
Number of awards: 2.
Scholarship may be renewable.

Deadline: June 1.
How to apply: There is no application form. Please see website for submission details.

(320) · Tuition Scholarship Program

Thomas Pniewski, Director of Cultural Affairs
Kosciuszko Foundation
15 East 65th Street
New York, NY 10021-6595
Phone: 212-734-2130 x214
Fax: 212-628-4552
Email: tompkf@aol.com
Website: http://www.kosciuszkofoundation.org
Purpose: To provide funding to qualified students for full-time graduate studies in the United States and several graduate programs in Poland.
Eligibility: Applicants must be U.S. citizens or permanent residents of Polish descent, beginning or continuing graduate students and have a minimum 3.0 GPA. U.S. citizens who are majoring in Polish studies are also eligible. Selection is based on academic performance, achievements, motivation, interest in Polish subjects or involvement in the Polish community and financial need.
Target applicant:
    College students
    Graduate school students
    Adult students
Minimum GPA: 3.0
Amount: $1,000-$7,000.
Number of awards: Varies.
Scholarship may be renewable.
Deadline: January 16.
How to apply: Applications are available online.

(321) · U.S. Department of Education Fulbright-Hays Project Abroad Scholarship for Programs in China

Council on International Educational Exchange
7 Custom House Street, 3rd Floor
Portland, ME 04101
Phone: 800-40-STUDY
Fax: 207-553-7699
Email: scholarships@ciee.org
Website: http://www.ciee.org
Purpose: To assist students who are participating in the Chinese language programs offered by the Council Study Centers.
Eligibility: Applicants must participate in the Council Study Centers Chinese language programs at Beijing, Shanghai, Nanjing, or Taipei, have completed two years of college level Mandarin Chinese, be a U.S. citizen or U.S. permanent resident, be a junior, senior, or graduate student who plans to pursue further studies or a career related to China, demonstrate high merit, and demonstrate financial need.
Target applicant:
    College students
    Graduate school students
    Adult students
Minimum GPA: None.
Amount: Varies.
Number of awards: Varies.
Deadline: April 1 or November 1.
How to apply: Applications are available online.

(322) · Undergraduate Scholarships

Sigma Alpha Iota Philanthropies
Director, Undergraduate Scholarships
One Tunnel Road
Asheville, NC 28805
Phone: 828-251-0606
Fax: 828-251-0644
Email: saiphxalum@joetapscott.com
Website: http://www.sai-national.org
Purpose: To assist members of the Sigma Alpha Iota organization who have demonstrated outstanding leadership abilities, musical talent and scholastic achievement.
Eligibility: Applicants must be active members of at least one year of the Sigma Alpha Iota organization, be in good standing and demonstrate financial need.
Target applicant:
    College students
    Adult students
Minimum GPA: None.
Amount: $1,500-$2,000.
Number of awards: 15.
Deadline: March 15.
How to apply: Applications are available online.

(323) · Urban Outreach Grants

American String Teachers Association (ASTA) with National School Orchestra Association
4153 Chain Bridge Road
Fairfax, VA 22030
Phone: 703-279-2113
Fax: 703-279-2114
Email: asta@astaweb.com
Website: http://www.astaweb.com
Purpose: To help economically disadvantaged urban school children study stringed instruments.
Eligibility: Applicants must be economically disadvantaged urban school children through grade 12 who want to study stringed instruments. There are two projects, individual and group. Funds given by the Urban Outreach Program must be matched by state and/or local sources. Project coordinator(s) must be active members of ASTA. Applicants should submit an application signed by the state chapter president, project description and proposed budget.
Target applicant:
    Junior high students or younger
    High school students
Minimum GPA: None.
Amount: $500.
Number of awards: Varies.
Deadline: April 1.
How to apply: Applications are available online.

(324) · Visiting Senior Fellowship Program

National Gallery of Art
2000B South Club Drive
Landover, MD 20785
Phone: 202-842-6482
Fax: 202-789-3026
Website: http://www.nga.gov/resources/casva.htm
Purpose: To award fellowships to scholars in visual arts.

Eligibility: Applicants must have held their Ph.D. for five years or more or who possess an equivalent record of professional accomplishment at the time of application. Applications are considered for research in the history, theory and criticism of the visual arts of any geographical area and of any period. Applicants must submit application forms, proposals, copies of a publication and two letters of recommendation. Fellowships are for full-time research, and scholars are expected to reside in Washington and to participate in the activities of the Center. Applications are also accepted from scholars in other disciplines whose work is related. The Center awards up to twelve short-term Paul Mellon and Ailsa Mellon Bruce Visiting Senior Fellowships. The deadlines are March 21 for the fellowship from September to February and September 21 for March through August.
Target applicant:
    Graduate school students
    Adult students
Minimum GPA: None.
Amount: $8,000.
Number of awards: Up to 12.
Scholarship may be renewable.
Deadline: Varies.
How to apply: Applications are available online.

(325) · Werner B. Thiele Memorial Scholarship

Gravure Education Foundation
1200-A Scottsville Road
Rochester, NY 14624
Phone: 315-589-8879
Fax: 585-436-7689
Email: lwshatch@gaa.org
Website: http://www.gaa.org
Purpose: To award scholarships to college juniors and seniors majoring in printing, graphic arts or graphic communications.
Eligibility: Applicants must be enrolled full-time at one of the GEF Learning Resource Centers: Arizona State University, California Polytechnic State University, Clemson University, Murray State, Rochester Institute of Technology, University of Wisconsin - Stout or Western Michigan University.
Target applicant:
    College students
    Adult students
Minimum GPA: 3.0
Amount: $1,250.
Number of awards: 2.
Deadline: May 31.
How to apply: Applications are available online or by mail.

(326) · Women Band Directors International College Scholarships

Women Band Directors International
Diane Gorzycki
WBDI Scholarship Chair
7424 Whistlestop Drive
Austin, TX 78749
Email: dgorzycki@austin.rr.com
Website: http://www.womenbanddirectors.org
Purpose: To support future female band directors.
Eligibility: Applicants must be studying instrumental music with the intention of becoming a band director. One scholarship will be available to all-level college and graduate students, while the other three are designated for undergraduate upperclassmen.

Target applicant:
    College students
    Graduate school students
    Adult students
Minimum GPA: None.
Amount: $300.
Number of awards: 4.
Deadline: December 1.
How to apply: Applications are available online.

(327) · Working Abroad Grant

InterExchange Inc.
161 Sixth Avenue
New York, NY 10013
Phone: 212-924-0446
Fax: 212-924-0575
Email: grants@interexchange.org
Website: www.interexchange.org
Purpose: To further international understanding and promote cultural awareness by supporting young Americans in working abroad.
Eligibility: Applicants must be accepted to any InterExchange Working Abroad program except for language schools. They must also be U.S. citizens or permanent residents age 18 to 28.
Target applicant:
    High school students
    College students
    Graduate school students
    Adult students
Minimum GPA: None.
Amount: Varies.
Number of awards: Varies.
Deadline: 8 weeks prior to program start date.
How to apply: Applications are available online.

(328) · Worldstudio Foundation Scholarship Program

Worldstudio Foundation
200 Varick Street
Suite 507
New York, NY 10014
Phone: 212-807-1990
Fax: 212-807-1799
Email: scholarshipcoordinator@worldstudio.org
Website: http://www.worldstudio.org
Purpose: To support art and design students who need financial assistance.
Eligibility: Applicants must be full-time undergraduate or graduate students of fine or commercial art, design or architecture. They must have a GPA of at least 2.0 and demonstrate financial need. Applicants must be U.S. citizens or permanent residents. Minority students will be given special consideration.
Target applicant:
    High school students
    College students
    Graduate school students
    Adult students
Minimum GPA: 2.0
Amount: Varies.
Number of awards: Varies.
Deadline: April 13.
How to apply: Applications are available online.

(329) · Writers of the Future

L. Ron Hubbard
P.O. Box 3190
Los Angeles, CA 90078
Email: contests@authorservicesinc.com
Website: http://www.writersofthefuture.com
Purpose: To discover deserving amateur aspiring writers.
Eligibility: Applicants must not have professionally published more than three short stories or one novelette and must submit an original English work of prose.
Target applicant:
    High school students
    College students
    Graduate school students
    Adult students
Minimum GPA: None.
Amount: $500-$4,000.
Number of awards: 3 awards are given quarterly with a grand prize awarded annually.
Deadline: December 31, March 31, June 30, September 30.
How to apply: There is no application form.

(330) · Writing Awards

Scholastic
557 Broadway
New York, NY 10012
Phone: 212-343-6100
Fax: 212-389-3939
Email: a&wgeneralinfo@scholastic.com
Website: http://www.artandwriting.org
Purpose: To reward creative young writers
Eligibility: Applicants must be in grades 7 through 12 in U.S. or Canadian schools and must submit writing pieces or portfolios in one of the following categories: dramatic script, general writing portfolio, humor, journalism, nonfiction portfolio, novel, personal essay/memoir, poetry, science fiction/fantasy, short story and short short story.
Target applicant:
    Junior high students or younger
    High school students
Minimum GPA: None.
Amount: Up to $10,000.
Number of awards: Varies.
Deadline: Varies based on location; November through January.
How to apply: Applications are available online.

(331) · Year Abroad Program

Thomas Pniewski, Director of Cultural Affairs
Kosciuszko Foundation
15 East 65th Street
New York, NY 10021-6595
Phone: 212-734-2130 x214
Fax: 212-628-4552
Email: tompkf@aol.com
Website: http://www.kosciuszkofoundation.org
Purpose: To allow an American student to study and live in Poland for a year or a semester.
Eligibility: Applicants must be U.S. citizens or permanent residents of Polish descent, be current undergraduate sophomores, juniors, seniors or graduate students and have a minimum 3.0 GPA. Selection is based on academic excellence, motivation for pursuing Polish studies and interest

in Polish subjects or involvement in Polish American communities. There is a non-refundable application fee of $50. It is highly recommended that you research the scholarship and awarding organization before applying for a scholarship with a fee. There are many scholarships that do not require a fee.

Target applicant:
  College students
  Graduate school students
  Adult students
Minimum GPA: 3.0
Amount: Tuition waiver and stipend.
Number of awards: Varies.
Deadline: January 16.
How to apply: Applications are available online.

(332) · Young American Creative Patriotic Art Awards Program

Ladies Auxiliary VFW
406 West 34th Street
10th Floor
Kansas City, MO 64111
Phone: 816-561-8655 x19
Fax: 816-931-4753
Email: jmillick@ladiesauxvfw.org
Website: https://www.ladiesauxvfw.org
Purpose: To encourage patriotic art.
Eligibility: Applicants must be high school students in the same state as the sponsoring Ladies Auxiliary. They must submit one piece of patriotic art on paper or canvas. Art must have been completed during the current school year and must be accompanied by a teacher's signature. Applicants must participate in a local Auxiliary competition before advancing to the national level.
Target applicant:
  High school students
Minimum GPA: None.
Amount: $2,500-$10,000.
Number of awards: 3.
Deadline: March 31.
How to apply: Applications are available online.

(333) · Young Jazz Composer Award

ASCAP Foundation
One Lincoln Plaza
New York, NY 10023
Phone: 212-621-6219
Website: http://www.ascapfoundation.org
Purpose: To recognize the talent of young jazz composers.
Eligibility: Applicants must be under the age of 30 and U.S. citizens or permanent residents. They must submit one original composition, including a score and performance, if possible.
Target applicant:
  Junior high students or younger
  High school students
  College students
  Graduate school students
  Adult students
Minimum GPA: None.
Amount: Varies.
Number of awards: Varies.
Deadline: December 1.
How to apply: Applications are available online.

(334) · Youth Free Expression Network Film Contest

National Coalition Against Censorship (NCAC)
275 Seventh Avenue
15th Floor
New York, NY 10001
Phone: 212-807-6222
Fax: 212-807-6245
Email: ncac@ncac.org
Website: http://www.ncac.org
Purpose: To reward students who create films on war and free speech.
Eligibility: Awards are given for the top three films addressing the topic "War and (Free) Speech: Can They Co-exist?" Entries must be four minutes or less and may include documentary, animation, experimental and/or music. Winners will receive cash stipends and will be flown to New York for a gala awards ceremony. Applicants must be age 19 and under.
Target applicant:
  Junior high students or younger
  High school students
  College students
Minimum GPA: None.
Amount: Up to $1,000.
Number of awards: 3.
Deadline: August 14.
How to apply: Applications are available online.

SOCIAL SCIENCES

(335) · 1st Marine Division Association Scholarship

1st Marine Division Association Inc.
410 Pier View Way
Oceanside, CA 92054
Phone: 877-967-8561
Fax: 760-967-8567
Email: oldbreed@sbcglobal.net
Website: http://www.1stmarinedivisionassociation.org
Purpose: To provide financial aid to undergraduate students who are the dependents of deceased or disabled veterans of the 1st Marine Division.
Eligibility: Applicants must be dependents of honorably discharged veterans of the 1st Marine Division or units attached to or supporting the Division who are now deceased or totally and permanently disabled for any reason. Applicants must attend an accredited university as full-time undergraduate students.
Target applicant:
   College students
   Adult students
Minimum GPA: None.
Amount: Up to $1,500.
Number of awards: Varies.
Scholarship may be renewable.
Deadline: Varies.
How to apply: Applications are available online.

(336) · A. Harry Passow Classroom Teacher Scholarship

National Association for Gifted Children
1707 L Street NW
Suite 550
Chair, Awards Committee
Washington, DC 20036
Phone: 202-785-4268
Fax: 202-785-4248
Email: nagc@nagc.org
Website: http://www.nagc.org
Purpose: To award excellent teachers of gifted students of grades K-12.
Eligibility: Applicants must be teachers of gifted students of grades K-12 and be continuing their education. Applicants must also have been members of NAGC for at least one year. Selection is based on commitment to teaching as shown by reviews from students, parents, principal and peers and admission into a graduate or certification program in gifted education.
Target applicant:
   Graduate school students
   Adult students
Minimum GPA: None.
Amount: $2,000.
Number of awards: Varies.
Deadline: April 1.
How to apply: Applications are available online.

(337) · AALL Educational Scholarships

American Association of Law Libraries
53 W. Jackson Boulevard
Suite 940
Chicago, IL 60604
Phone: 312-939-4764
Fax: 312-431-1097
Email: scholarships@aall.org
Website: http://www.aallnet.org
Purpose: To encourage students to pursue careers as law librarians.
Eligibility: There are five levels of awards: 1. Library Degree for Law School Graduates, awarded to a law school graduate with law library experience pursuing a degree at an accredited library school. 2. Library School Graduates Attending Law School, awarded to a library school graduate pursuing a degree at an accredited law school who has law library experience and no more than 36 semester credit hours left before obtaining the law degree. 3. Library Degree for Non-Law School Graduates, awarded to a college graduate with law library experience who is seeking a degree involving law librarianship courses at an accredited library school. 4. Library School Graduates Seeking A Non-Law Degree, awarded to library school graduates who are seeking degrees in fields other than law. 5. Law Librarians in Continuing Education Courses, awarded to law librarians with a degree from an accredited library or law school who are continuing their education. Preference is given to AALL members, but a non-member can apply. All applicants must intend to have careers as law librarians. There must be financial need for awards 1-4.
Target applicant:
   Graduate school students
   Adult students
Minimum GPA: None.
Amount: Varies.
Number of awards: Varies.
Scholarship may be renewable.
Deadline: April 1.
How to apply: Applications are available online, by mail with a self-addressed, stamped envelope, by fax, by phone or by email.

(338) · ABA Essay and Writing Competitions

American Bar Association
321 North Clark Street
Chicago, IL 60610
Phone: 312-988-5000
Email: abalsd@abanet.org
Website: http://www.abanet.org/lsd/
Purpose: To support and recognize achievement among law students.
Eligibility: The ABA sponsors a variety of essay and writing competitions for law students. Each is centered on a specific legal topic. Topics include: affordable housing and community, community development law, law and aging, antitrust, business law, criminal justice, dispute resolution, entertainment and sports law, family law, health care, labor and employment, liability, education, public contracts, real estate, tort and insurance and children.
Target applicant:
   Graduate school students
   Adult students
Minimum GPA: None.
Amount: $1,000-$5,000.
Number of awards: Varies.
Deadline: Varies.
How to apply: Applications and specific deadlines for each competition are available online.

(339) · ABC-CLIO America: History and Life Award

Organization of American Historians
112 N. Bryan Avenue
P.O. Box 5457
Bloomington, IN 47408
Phone: 812-855-9852
Fax: 812-855-0696
Email: awards@oah.org
Website: http://www.oah.org
Purpose: The Organization of American Historians promotes the teaching and learning of history.
Eligibility: The History and Life Award grants money to an author of a published journal article that meets the organization's mission. Judges look for articles that suggest and explore new interpretations of historical events, places or people. The winning entry is presented at the OAH annual meeting. Both editors and authors may submit entries. This is a biennial award.
Target applicant:
   Junior high students or younger
   High school students
   College students
   Graduate school students
   Adult students
Minimum GPA: None.
Amount: $750.
Number of awards: 1.
Deadline: December 1.
How to apply: No application is required. Submit one copy of each entry (clearly labeled "ABC-CLIO America: History and Life Award Entry") directly to each of the judges. Their names and addresses are available online.

(340) · Abe Schechter Graduate Scholarship

Radio and Television News Directors Association
1600 K Street NW
Suite 700
Washington, DC 20006
Phone: 202-659-6510
Fax: 202-223-4007
Email: rtnda@rtnda.org
Website: http://www.rtnda.org
Purpose: To honor professional achievements in electronic journalism.
Eligibility: Applicants must be full-time or incoming graduate students. Applicants may be enrolled in any major as long as their career intent is television or radio news. Applicants may only apply for one RTNDA scholarship.
Target applicant:
   Graduate school students
   Adult students
Minimum GPA: None.
Amount: $2,000.
Number of awards: Varies.
Deadline: May 3.
How to apply: Applications are available online.

(341) · Above and Beyond Scholarship

California School Library Association
1001 26th Street
Sacramento, CA 95816

Phone: 916-447-2684
Fax: 916-447-2695
Email: csla@pacbell.net
Website: http://www.schoollibrary.org
Purpose: To support library media teachers pursuing advanced degrees or National Board Certification.
Eligibility: Applicants must be professional members of the California School Library Association and California residents intending to continue working in California in the school library profession after completing their additional education. Students must submit a 500-word essay describing their professional goals and how an advanced degree or certification applies to those goals and three letters of recommendation.
Target applicant:
   Graduate school students
   Adult students
Minimum GPA: None.
Amount: $1,000.
Number of awards: 1.
Deadline: June 30.
How to apply: Applications are available online.

(342) · Academic Scholarship for High School Seniors

National Restaurant Association Educational Foundation
175 W. Jackson Boulevard
Suite 1500
Chicago, IL 60604-2702
Phone: 800-765-2122
Fax: 312-715-1010
Email: scholars@naref.org
Website: http://www.nraef.org/scholarships/
Purpose: To support students majoring in food services.
Eligibility: Applicants must have been accepted into an accredited restaurant or food service related program, have had at least 250 hours of restaurant or food service-related work experience, submit a letter of recommendation and have a minimum 2.75 GPA.
Target applicant:
   High school students
Minimum GPA: 2.75
Amount: $2,000.
Number of awards: Varies.
Deadline: May 16.
How to apply: Applications are available online.

(343) · Academic Scholarship For Undergraduate College Students

National Restaurant Association Educational Foundation
175 W. Jackson Boulevard
Suite 1500
Chicago, IL 60604-2702
Phone: 800-765-2122
Fax: 312-715-1010
Email: scholars@naref.org
Website: http://www.nraef.org/scholarships/
Purpose: To assist restaurant and food service students.
Eligibility: Applicants must be currently majoring in a restaurant or foodservice program and submit a transcript, proof of restaurant or foodservice-related work experience of a minimum of 750 hours and a letter of recommendation.
Target applicant:
   College students
   Adult students

Minimum GPA: 2.75
Amount: $2,000.
Number of awards: Varies.
Deadline: November 19 and April 8.
How to apply: Applications are available online.

---

(344) · Accountemps/American Institute Of Certified Public Accountants Student Scholarship

American Institute Of Certified Public Accountants
American Institute of CPAs--Team 046
1211 Avenue of the Americas
New York, NY 10036-8775
Phone: 212-596-6224
Website: http://www.aicpa.org
Purpose: To provide financial assistance to students pursuing careers in business or accounting.
Eligibility: Applicants must be currently enrolled full-time undergraduate or graduate students at an accredited university, major in accounting, finance or information systems, have completed 30 semester or 45 quarter hours with six semester hours in accounting and be AICPA student affiliate members.
Target applicant:
    College students
    Graduate school students
    Adult students
Minimum GPA: 3.0
Amount: $2,500.
Number of awards: 2.
Deadline: April 1.
How to apply: Applications are available online.

---

(345) · Achievement Award

National Council of Teachers of English
1111 W. Kenyon Road
Urbana, IL 61801
Phone: 877-369-6283
Fax: 217-328-9645
Email: pyw@ncte.org
Website: http://www.ncte.org
Purpose: To recognize outstanding student writers.
Eligibility: Applicants must be current high school juniors who will graduate the following school year, and they must be nominated for the award by their high school English department. Nominees must provide two writing samples: one timed response to a prompt written under the supervision of a teacher and one sample of their best work.
Target applicant:
    High school students
Minimum GPA: None.
Amount: Certificate of commendation.
Number of awards: Up to 876.
Deadline: February 2.
How to apply: Applications are available online. However, students must be nominated by their high school English departments.

---

(346) · ACJA/Lambda Alpha Epsilon Scholarship

American Criminal Justice Association
P.O. Box 601047
Sacramento, CA 95860-1047
Phone: 916-484-6553
Fax: 916-488-2227

Email: acjalae@aol.com
Website: http://www.acjalae.org
Purpose: To assist criminal justice students.
Eligibility: Applicants must be undergraduate or graduate students who are studying criminal justice. Students must be ACJA/LAE members, but they may submit a membership form at the time of application. Applicants must have completed at least two semesters or three quarters of their education while earning at least a 3.0 GPA. Applicants must submit transcripts, letters of enrollment, and goals statements.
Target applicant:
    College students
    Graduate school students
    Adult students
Minimum GPA: 3.0
Amount: $100-$400.
Number of awards: Varies.
Deadline: December 31.
How to apply: Applications are available online and by written request.

---

(347) · ACLS Digital Innovation Fellowships

American Council of Learned Societies (ACLS)
633 Third Avenue
New York, NY 10017-6795
Phone: 212-697-1505
Fax: 212-949-8058
Email: sfisher@acls.org
Website: http://www.acls.org
Purpose: To support humanities scholars who work on digital projects.
Eligibility: Applicants must be scholars in the humanities fields and have Ph.D. degrees. An application, a proposal, a project plan, a budget plan, a bibliography, a publications list, three reference letters and one institutional statement are required. In addition to the stipend, there are also funds for project costs. The fellowship should last an academic year.
Target applicant:
    Graduate school students
    Adult students
Minimum GPA: None.
Amount: $55,000.
Number of awards: 5.
Deadline: November 10.
How to apply: Applications are available online.

---

(348) · ACLS Fellowships

American Council of Learned Societies (ACLS)
633 Third Avenue
New York, NY 10017-6795
Phone: 212-697-1505
Fax: 212-949-8058
Email: sfisher@acls.org
Website: http://www.acls.org
Purpose: To support a scholar in the study of humanities.
Eligibility: Applicants must have a Ph.D. degree and at least a three year period since their last supported research. An application, a proposal, bibliography, publications list and two reference letters are required. The award levels are based on the position of the applicant: professor and equivalent, associate professor and equivalent and assistant professor and equivalent. The ACLS fellowships include ACLS/SSRC/NEH

International and Area Studies Fellowships and ACLS/New York Public Library Fellowships.
Target applicant:
  Graduate school students
  Adult students
Minimum GPA: None.
Amount: $50,000.
Number of awards: Varies.
Deadline: September 28.
How to apply: Applications are available online.

(349) · ACOR-CAORC Fellowships

American Center of Oriental Research (ACOR)
656 Beacon Street, 5th Floor
Boston, MA 02215
Phone: 617-353-6571
Fax: 617-353-6575
Email: acor@bu.edu
Website: http://www.bu.edu/acor
Purpose: To assist master's and pre-doctoral students conducting research in Jordan.
Eligibility: Applicants must be graduate students researching topics involving scholarship in Near Eastern studies. Recipients are required to engage in scholarly and cultural activities while residing at the American Center of Oriental Research (ACOR) in Jordan. The fellowships last from two to six months. The award includes room and board at ACOR, transportation, a stipend and research funds.
Target applicant:
  Graduate school students
  Adult students
Minimum GPA: None.
Amount: $19,400.
Number of awards: At least 5.
Deadline: February 1.
How to apply: Applications are available online.

(350) · Adelle and Erwin Tomash Fellowship in the History of Information Processing

Charles Babbage Institute
Center for the History of Information Processing
211 Andersen Library, University of Minnesota
222 - 21st Avenue South
Minneapolis, MN 55455
Phone: 612-624-5050
Email: yostx003@tc.umn.edu
Website: http://www.cbi.umn.edu
Purpose: To support a graduate student who is researching the history of computing.
Eligibility: Applicants must be graduate students who have completed all doctoral degree requirements except the research and writing of the dissertation. Students must submit a curriculum vitae and a five-page statement and justification of the research program.
Target applicant:
  Graduate school students
  Adult students
Minimum GPA: None.
Amount: $14,000 stipend.
Number of awards: 1.
Deadline: January 15.
How to apply: Visit the website for more information.

(351) · Admiral Mike Boorda Scholarship Program

Navy-Marine Corps Relief Society
875 North Randolph Street Suite 225
Arlington, VA 22203
Phone: 703-696-4960
Fax: 703-696-0144
Email: education@hq.nmcrs.org
Website: http://www.nmcrs.org
Purpose: To help eligible Navy and Marine Corps members.
Eligibility: Applicants must be enrolled or planning to enroll as full-time undergraduate students at an eligible post-secondary, technical or vocational institution. Applicants must have a minimum 2.0 GPA and be active duty servicemembers accepted to the Enlisted Commissioning Program, the Marine Enlisted Commissioning Education Program or the Medical Enlisted Commissioning Program.
Target applicant:
  College students
  Adult students
Minimum GPA: 2.0
Amount: Varies.
Number of awards: Varies.
Scholarship may be renewable.
Deadline: May 1.
How to apply: Applications are available online.

(352) · Adult Students in Scholastic Transition (ASIST)

Executive Women International (EWI)
515 South 700 East Suite 2A
Salt Lake City, UT 84102
Phone: 801-355-2800
Fax: 801-355-2852
Email: ewi@executivewomen.org
Website: http://www.executivewomen.org
Purpose: To assist adult students who face major life transitions.
Eligibility: Applicants may be single parents, individuals just entering the workforce or displaced workers.
Target applicant:
  College students
  Adult students
Minimum GPA: None.
Amount: Varies.
Number of awards: Varies.
Deadline: March 1.
How to apply: Contact your local EWI chapter.

(353) · AFCEA General Emmett Paige Scholarships

Armed Forces Communications and Electronics Association
4400 Fair Lakes Court
Fairfax, VA 22033
Phone: 800-336-4583
Fax: 703-631-4693
Email: scholarship@afcea.org
Website: http://www.afcea.org
Purpose: To offer scholarships to members of the armed forces.
Eligibility: Applicants must be on active duty in the uniformed military services, honorably discharged veterans, or their spouses or dependents who are full-time students in an accredited four-year U.S. college or university. Applicants must also be U.S. citizens, majoring in electrical, computer, chemical or aerospace engineering, computer science, physics or mathematics and have a minimum 3.4 GPA. Veterans may apply for

the scholarship as college freshmen. All others must apply as college sophomores or juniors.

Target applicant:
 College students
 Adult students
Minimum GPA: 3.4
Amount: $2,000.
Number of awards: Varies.
Deadline: March 1.
How to apply: Applications are available online.

---

(354) · AFCEA ROTC Scholarships

Armed Forces Communications and Electronics Association
4400 Fair Lakes Court
Fairfax, VA 22033
Phone: 800-336-4583
Fax: 703-631-4693
Email: scholarship@afcea.org
Website: http://www.afcea.org
Purpose: To assist ROTC sophomores or juniors who are majoring in aerospace engineering, electronics, computer science, computer engineering, physics or mathematics.
Eligibility: Applicants must major in electrical or aerospace engineering, electronics, computer science, computer engineering, physics or mathematics at an accredited U.S. four-year college or university. Applicants must also be enrolled full-time as college sophomores or juniors and be nominated by professors of military science, naval science or aerospace studies. Applicants must be U.S. citizens enrolled in ROTC, have good moral character, demonstrate academic excellence and the potential to serve as an officer in the U.S. Armed Forces and have financial need.
Target applicant:
 College students
 Adult students
Minimum GPA: None.
Amount: $2,000.
Number of awards: Varies.
Deadline: April 1.
How to apply: Applications are available online.

---

(355) · AFCEA Sgt Jeannette L. Winters, USMC Memorial Scholarship

Armed Forces Communications and Electronics Association
4400 Fair Lakes Court
Fairfax, VA 22033
Phone: 800-336-4583
Fax: 703-631-4693
Email: scholarship@afcea.org
Website: http://www.afcea.org
Purpose: To support active duty Marine Corps members or veterans.
Eligibility: Applicants must be on active duty in the U.S. Marine Corps or honorably discharged veterans of the U.S. Marine Corps. Applicants must also be current undergraduate sophomores, juniors or seniors attending an accredited U.S. college or university majoring in electrical, aerospace or computer engineering, computer science, physics or mathematics with a minimum 3.4 GPA.
Target applicant:
 College students
 Adult students
Minimum GPA: 3.4
Amount: $2,000.

Number of awards: 1.
Deadline: September 15.
How to apply: Applications are available online.

---

(356) · Affirmative Action Scholarship

Special Libraries Association
331 S. Patrick Street
Alexandria, VA 22314
Phone: 703-647-4900
Fax: 703-647-4901
Email: sla@sla.org
Website: http://www.sla.org
Purpose: To support minority students who show an interest in special librarianship.
Eligibility: Applicants must be college seniors or graduates who are members of a minority group admitted by a recognized library school or information science program and demonstrate financial need. Preference is given to SLA members and those who show an interest in special library work. Applicants must submit an essay on their contribution to special librarianship.
Target applicant:
 College students
 Graduate school students
 Adult students
Minimum GPA: None.
Amount: $6,000.
Number of awards: 1.
Deadline: October 31.
How to apply: Applications are available online.

---

(357) · AGA Scholarships

Association of Government Accountants (AGA)
2208 Mount Vernon Avenue
Alexandria, VA 22301-1314
Phone: 800-242-7211
Email: rortiz@agacgfm.org
Website: http://www.agacgfm.org
Purpose: To support public financial management students.
Eligibility: Applicants for full-time or part-time scholarships must be an AGA member or family member (spouse, child or grandchild), and scholarships must be used for full-time or part-time undergraduate study in a financial management academic area such as accounting, auditing, budgeting, economics, finance, electronic data processing, information resources management or public administration. Essays and transcripts are required. There are two categories for high school students/graduates and undergraduates/graduates. The Academic Scholarships are based on academic achievement and the student's potential for making a contribution to public financial management. A reference letter from an AGA member and from another professional such as a professor, guidance counselor or employer are required. Applicants to the Community Service Scholarships do not have to be AGA members, must be pursuing a degree in a financial management academic discipline and must be actively involved in community service projects. The awards are based on community service and accomplishments. A letter of recommendation from a community service organization and from another professional are required.
Target applicant:
 High school students
 College students
 Graduate school students
 Adult students

Minimum GPA: 2.5
Amount: $1,000.
Number of awards: 9.
Deadline: March 31.
How to apply: Applications are available online.

(358) · Air Force ROTC ASCP

Air Force Reserve Officer Training Corps
AFROTC Admissions
551 E. Maxwell Boulevard
Maxwell AFB, AL 36112-5917
Phone: 866-423-7682
Fax: 334-953-6167
Website: http://www.afrotc.com
Purpose: To allow active duty Air Force personnel to earn a commission while completing their bachelor's degree.
Eligibility: Applicants must be active-duty Air Force personnel who are U.S. citizens under the age of 31, with the exception of nurses, who must be under the age of 42. They must also meet all testing and waiver requirements and be recommended by their commanding officer.
Target applicant:
    College students
    Adult students
Minimum GPA: 2.5
Amount: Up to $15,750.
Number of awards: Varies.
Scholarship may be renewable.
Deadline: Varies.
How to apply: Application details are available online.

(359) · Air Force ROTC Enhanced HBCU Scholarships

Air Force Reserve Officer Training Corps
AFROTC Admissions
551 E. Maxwell Boulevard
Maxwell AFB, AL 36112-5917
Phone: 866-423-7682
Fax: 334-953-6167
Website: http://www.afrotc.com
Purpose: To increase enrollment at Historically Black Colleges or Universities and to meet officer production requirements.
Eligibility: Applicants must be college freshmen or sophomores enrolled at Jackson State University, Tuskegee University, Alabama State University, Howard University, Grambling State University, North Carolina A&T University, Fayetteville State University or Tennessee State University.
Target applicant:
    College students
    Adult students
Minimum GPA: None.
Amount: Up to $15,900.
Number of awards: Up to 120.
Deadline: Varies.
How to apply: Applications are available from your school's Air Force ROTC detachment.

(360) · Air Force ROTC Enhanced Hispanic Serving Institutions (HSI) Scholarships

Air Force Reserve Officer Training Corps
AFROTC Admissions

551 E. Maxwell Boulevard
Maxwell AFB, AL 36112-5917
Phone: 866-423-7682
Fax: 334-953-6167
Website: http://www.afrotc.com
Purpose: To enhance enrollment at Hispanic Serving Institutions and to meet officer production requirements.
Eligibility: Applicants must be college freshmen or sophomores at California State University (Fresno or San Bernardino), New Mexico State University, University of Miami, University of New Mexico, University of Puerto Rico (Rio Piedras or Mayaguez) or University of Texas-San Antonio.
Target applicant:
    College students
    Adult students
Minimum GPA: None.
Amount: Up to $15,900.
Number of awards: Up to 120.
Scholarship may be renewable.
Deadline: Varies.
How to apply: Applications are available from your school's Air Force ROTC detachment.

(361) · Air Force ROTC Express Scholarships

Air Force Reserve Officer Training Corps
AFROTC Admissions
551 E. Maxwell Boulevard
Maxwell AFB, AL 36112-5917
Phone: 866-423-7682
Fax: 334-953-6167
Website: http://www.afrotc.com
Purpose: To meet Air Force ROTC officer production requirements.
Eligibility: Applicants must be U.S. citizens who are college students, have passed the Air Force ROTC Physical Fitness Test and have either passed the Air Force Officer Qualifying Test or had their failing scores waived. Students must have a GPA of 2.5 or higher and major in computer engineering, electrical engineering, environmental engineering, aeronautical engineering, aerospace engineering, astronautical engineering, civil engineering, mechanical engineering or meteorology/atmospheric sciences.
Target applicant:
    College students
    Adult students
Minimum GPA: 2.5
Amount: Up to $15,900.
Number of awards: Varies.
Scholarship may be renewable.
Deadline: Varies.
How to apply: Applications are available from your school's Air Force detachment.

(362) · Air Force ROTC HBCU Minority School Scholarships

Air Force Reserve Officer Training Corps
AFROTC Admissions
551 E. Maxwell Boulevard
Maxwell AFB, AL 36112-5917
Phone: 866-423-7682
Fax: 334-953-6167
Website: http://www.afrotc.com

Purpose: To assist students who are attending minority institutions that offer Air Force ROTC programs.

Eligibility: Applicants must be U.S. citizens who are college students and have passed the Air Force ROTC Physical Fitness Test and have either passed the Air Force Officer Qualifying Test or had their failing scores waived. They must also have a 2.5 or higher GPA.

Target applicant:
  College students
  Adult students
Minimum GPA: 2.5
Amount: Up to $15,900.
Number of awards: Varies.
Scholarship may be renewable.
Deadline: Varies.
How to apply: Applications are available from your school's Air Force ROTC detachment.

(363) · Air Force ROTC High School Scholarship Program

Air Force Reserve Officer Training Corps
AFROTC Admissions
551 E. Maxwell Boulevard
Maxwell AFB, AL 36112-5917
Phone: 866-423-7682
Fax: 334-953-6167
Website: http://www.afrotc.com
Purpose: To help students with financial need who are also interested in joining the Air Force pay for college.
Eligibility: Applicants must pass the physical fitness assessment and demonstrate academic achievement or outstanding leadership skills. There are three types of award: one that pays full tuition, most fees and for books, one that pays tuition up to $15,000, most fees and for books and one that pays full tuition at a college or university that costs less than $9,000 per year. In return for the scholarship, recipients must serve in the Air Force.
Target applicant:
  High school students
Minimum GPA: None.
Amount: Varies.
Number of awards: Varies.
Scholarship may be renewable.
Deadline: December 1.
How to apply: Applications are available online.

(364) · Air Force ROTC Hispanic Serving Institutions (HSI) Minority School Scholarships

Air Force Reserve Officer Training Corps
AFROTC Admissions
551 E. Maxwell Boulevard
Maxwell AFB, AL 36112-5917
Phone: 866-423-7682
Fax: 334-953-6167
Website: http://www.afrotc.com
Purpose: To increase enrollment at Hispanic Serving Institutions and to meet officer production requirements.
Eligibility: Applicants must be college freshmen or sophomores enrolled at a Hispanic Serving Institution that hosts an Air Force ROTC detachment or is a crosstown of another school with a detachment.

Target applicant:
  College students
  Adult students
Minimum GPA: None.
Amount: Up to $15,900.
Number of awards: Varies.
Scholarship may be renewable.
Deadline: Varies.
How to apply: Applications are available from your school's Air Force ROTC detachment.

(365) · Air Force ROTC In-College Program

Air Force Reserve Officer Training Corps
AFROTC Admissions
551 E. Maxwell Boulevard
Maxwell AFB, AL 36112-5917
Phone: 866-423-7682
Fax: 334-953-6167
Website: http://www.afrotc.com
Purpose: To promote the Air Force ROTC program.
Eligibility: Applicants must be U.S. citizens who have passed the Air Force Officer Qualifying Test, the Air Force ROTC Physical Fitness Test and a Department of Defense medical examination. Students must also be college freshmen or sophomores and have a GPA of 2.5 or higher.
Target applicant:
  College students
  Adult students
Minimum GPA: 2.5
Amount: Up to $15,000.
Number of awards: Varies.
Scholarship may be renewable.
Deadline: Varies.
How to apply: Applications are available from your school's Air Force ROTC detachment.

(366) · Air Force ROTC Professional Officer Course-Early Release Program

Air Force Reserve Officer Training Corps
AFROTC Admissions
551 E. Maxwell Boulevard
Maxwell AFB, AL 36112-5917
Phone: 866-423-7682
Fax: 334-953-6167
Website: http://www.afrotc.com
Purpose: To allow active duty Air Force personnel the opportunity for early release in order to complete their bachelor's degrees.
Eligibility: Applicants must be active-duty Air Force personnel who are U.S. citizens under the age of 31, with the exception of nurses, who must be under the age of 42. They must also meet all testing and waiver requirements, be recommended by their commanding officer and not be within one year of receiving their degree.
Target applicant:
  College students
  Adult students
Minimum GPA: 2.5
Amount: Up to $750.
Number of awards: Varies.
Scholarship may be renewable.
Deadline: October 15.
How to apply: Application details are available online.

(367) · Air Force ROTC SOAR Program

Air Force Reserve Officer Training Corps
AFROTC Admissions
551 E. Maxwell Boulevard
Maxwell AFB, AL 36112-5917
Phone: 866-423-7682
Fax: 334-953-6167
Website: http://www.afrotc.com
Purpose: To give active duty Air Force personnel the opportunity to earn their commissions while completing their bachelor's degrees.
Eligibility: Applicants must be active-duty Air Force personnel who are U.S. citizens under the age of 31, with the exception of nurses, who must be under the age of 47. They must also meet all testing and waiver requirements and be recommended by their commanding officer. Students must also have a minimum college GPA of 2.5 or a minimum ACT score of 24 or minimum SAT reading comprehension and math score of 1100.
Target applicant:
    College students
    Adult students
Minimum GPA: 2.5
Amount: Up to $15,750.
Number of awards: Varies.
Scholarship may be renewable.
Deadline: Varies.
How to apply: Application details are available online.

(368) · Air Force Spouse Scholarship

Aerospace Education Foundation
1501 Lee Highway
Arlington, VA 22209
Phone: 800-291-8480
Fax: 703-247-5853
Email: aefstaff@aef.org
Website: http://www.afa.org
Purpose: This scholarship provides aid to Air Force spouses who plan to pursue associate's, bachelor's or graduate degrees.
Eligibility: Applicants must be the spouses of members of the Air Force Active Duty, Air National Guard or Air Force Reserve and attend a college or university in the current academic year. However, spouses who are themselves Air Force members or in ROTC are not eligible.
Target applicant:
    College students
    Graduate school students
    Adult students
Minimum GPA: 3.5
Amount: $1,000.
Number of awards: 30.
Deadline: January 30.
How to apply: Applications are available online.

(369) · Airmen Memorial Foundation Scholarship Program

Air Force Sergeants Association
5211 Auth Road
Suitland, MD 20746
Phone: 301-899-3500
Fax: 301-899-8136
Email: staff@afsahq.org
Website: http://www.afsahq.org

Purpose: To assist dependents of Air Force enlisted personnel in obtaining higher education.
Eligibility: Applicants must be dependents of Air Force enlisted personnel who are attending high school or college. They must have a GPA of 3.5 or higher and be accepted to the college of their choice.
Target applicant:
    High school students
    College students
    Adult students
Minimum GPA: 3.5
Amount: $1,000-$2,000.
Number of awards: Varies.
Deadline: March 31.
How to apply: Applications are available online.

(370) · Al Neuharth Free Spirit Scholarship and Conference Program

Freedom Forum
1101 Wilson Boulevard
Arlington, VA 22209
Phone: 703-284-2814
Fax: 703-284-3529
Email: freespirit@freedomforum.org
Website: http://www.freedomforum.org/freespirit
Purpose: To provide assistance to students who meet the criteria of being a "free spirit."
Eligibility: Applicants must be high school seniors who plan to pursue a career in journalism and who are "free spirits," defined as those who "dream, dare and do."
Target applicant:
    High school students
Minimum GPA: None.
Amount: $1,000-$50,000.
Number of awards: 102.
Deadline: October 15.
How to apply: Applications are available online.

(371) · Allstudentloan.org College Scholarship Program for Business Students

All Student Loan Corporation
HS Scholarship Program
6701 Center Drive
Suite 500
Los Angeles, CA 90045-1547
Phone: 888-271-9721
Fax: 310-979-4714
Email: faoss@allstudentloan.org
Website: http://www.allstudentloan.org
Purpose: To reward members of business-related student organizations.
Eligibility: Applicants must be graduating high school seniors or post-secondary students who are active members of one of these vocational student organizations: Future Business Leaders of America-Phi Beta Lambda (FBLA-PBL), Business Professionals of America (BPA) or DECA for the current academic year. They must be enrolled in post-secondary institutions that participate in the Federal Family Education Loan Program.
Target applicant:
    High school students
    College students
    Adult students

Minimum GPA: None.
Amount: $500.
Number of awards: 4.
Deadline: June 1.
How to apply: Applications are available online.

(372) · Alphonso Deal Scholarship Award

National Black Police Association
NBPA Scholarship Award
3251 Mt. Pleasant Street NW
Washington, DC 20010
Phone: 202-986-2070
Fax: 202-986-0410
Email: nbpanatofc@worldnet.att.net
Website: http://www.blackpolice.org
Purpose: To support students who plan careers in law enforcement.
Eligibility: Applicants must be collegebound high school seniors planning to study law enforcement who are U.S. citizens and are recommended by their high school principal, counselor or teacher.
Target applicant:
   High school students
Minimum GPA: None.
Amount: Varies.
Number of awards: Varies.
Deadline: June 1.
How to apply: Applications are available online.

(373) · American Bar Association-Bar/Bri Scholarships

BAR/BRI Bar Review
ABA Scholarship Committee
111 W. Jackson Boulevard
Chicago, IL 60604
Email: abalsd@abanet.org
Website: http://www.abanet.org/lsd/
Purpose: To defer the cost of study for graduating law students who must take the BAR/Bri exam.
Eligibility: Applicants must be ABA Law Student Division members who will be December or May graduates and will use the award toward their BAR/BRI tuition. Scholarships will vary in amount depending upon the applicant's financial condition and the size of the applicant pool.
Target applicant:
   Graduate school students
   Adult students
Minimum GPA: None.
Amount: Varies.
Number of awards: Varies.
Deadline: October 31 or February 1.
How to apply: Applications are available online.

(374) · American Express Scholarship Competition

American Hotel and Lodging Educational Foundation (AH&LEF)
1201 New York Avenue NW
Suite 600
Washington, DC 20005-3931
Phone: 202-289-3188
Fax: 202-289-3199
Email: chammond@ahlef.org
Website: http://www.ahlef.org
Purpose: To provide financial assistance to students pursuing a degree in hospitality management.
Eligibility: Applicants must be enrolled in an accredited undergraduate program resulting in a degree in hospitality management. Students or their parents must be employed in the lodging industry by an American Hotel & Lodging Association member facility.
Target applicant:
   College students
   Adult students
Minimum GPA: None.
Amount: Up to $2,000.
Number of awards: Varies.
Deadline: June 15.
How to apply: Applications are available online.

(375) · American Express Travel Scholarship

American Society of Travel Agents (ASTA) Foundation Inc.
1101 King Street
Suite 200
Alexandria, VA 22314
Phone: 703-739-2782
Fax: 703-684-8319
Email: scholarship@astahq.com
Website: http://www.astanet.com
Purpose: To encourage the growth and development of the future travel and tourism work force.
Eligibility: Applicants must be enrolled in a travel and tourism program in either a two- or four-year college or university or proprietary travel school, have a minimum 2.5 GPA and write a 500-word paper detailing their plans in travel and tourism and their views of the travel industry's future. Applicants must be a resident, citizen or legal alien of the U.S. or Canada.
Target applicant:
   College students
   Adult students
Minimum GPA: 2.5
Amount: Varies.
Number of awards: 1.
Deadline: July 27.
How to apply: Applications are available online.

(376) · American Heroes - U.S. Military Challenge

Common Knowledge Scholarship Foundation
P.O. Box 290361
Davie, FL 33329-0361
Phone: 954-262-8553
Email: info@cksf.org
Website: http://www.cksf.org
Purpose: To reward students for learning about the U.S. Military.
Eligibility: Applicants must be high school students, college students or parents. They must compete for the scholarship by taking quizzes online.
Target applicant:
   High school students
   College students
   Adult students
Minimum GPA: None.
Amount: $250.
Number of awards: 1.
Deadline: September 14.
How to apply: Applications are available online.

(377) · American History Scholarship, Enid Hall Griswold Memorial Scholarship, J.E. Caldwell Centennial Scholarship

National Society Daughters of the American Revolution
1776 D Street NW
Washington, DC 20006-5303
Phone: 202-628-1776
Website: http://www.dar.org
Purpose: To promote the study of history, political science, government and economics.
Eligibility: Applicants to the American History Scholarship must be high school students planning to major in American history. The award is up to $2,000 each year for up to four years. Applicants for the Enid Hall Griswold Memorial Scholarship must be juniors or seniors majoring in political science, history, government or economics. The award is $1,000. Applicants to the J.E. Caldwell Centennial Scholarship must be graduate students in historic preservation. The award is $2,000. All applicants must obtain a letter of sponsorship from their local DAR chapter.
Target applicant:
  High school students
  College students
  Graduate school students
  Adult students
Minimum GPA: None.
Amount: $1,000-2,000.
Number of awards: 5.
Scholarship may be renewable.
Deadline: February 15.
How to apply: Applications are available by written request.

(378) · American Police Hall of Fame Educational Scholarship Fund

American Police Hall of Fame and Museum
6350 Horizon Drive
Titusville, FL 32780
Phone: 321-264-0911
Email: info@aphf.org
Website: http://www.aphf.org/scholarships.html
Purpose: To provide financial assistance for children of fallen law enforcement officers.
Eligibility: Applicants must be sons or daughters of law enforcement officers who were killed in the line of duty. They may attend a public, private or vocational school. A current transcript, letter of acceptance to an institution of higher learning or a student ID is required.
Target applicant:
  High school students
  College students
  Adult students
Minimum GPA: None.
Amount: $1,500.
Number of awards: Varies.
Scholarship may be renewable.
Deadline: Varies.
How to apply: Applications are available online.

(379) · AMVETS National Scholarship for Veterans

AMVETS National Headquarters
4647 Forbes Boulevard
Lanham, MD 20706-4380
Phone: 877-726-8387
Fax: 301-459-7924
Email: thilton@amvets.org
Website: http://www.amvets.org
Purpose: To provide financial assistance for veterans.
Eligibility: Applicants must be United States citizens and veterans who demonstrate financial need. They must have been honorably discharged or be on active duty and eligible for release. They must agree to allow AMVET to publicize their award if selected.
Target applicant:
  High school students
  College students
  Adult students
Minimum GPA: None.
Amount: $4,000.
Number of awards: 3.
Deadline: April 15.
How to apply: Applications are available online.

(380) · AMVETS National Scholarships for Entering College Freshman

AMVETS National Headquarters
4647 Forbes Boulevard
Lanham, MD 20706-4380
Phone: 877-726-8387
Fax: 301-459-7924
Email: thilton@amvets.org
Website: http://www.amvets.org
Purpose: To provide education assistance for graduating JROTC cadets.
Eligibility: Applicants must be high school seniors with a minimum GPA of 3.0 or documented extenuating circumstances. They must be United States citizens and children or grandchildren of U.S. veterans. They must show academic potential and financial need.
Target applicant:
  High school students
Minimum GPA: 3.0
Amount: $1,000.
Number of awards: 1.
Deadline: April 15.
How to apply: Applications are available online.

(381) · Anchor Scholarship Foundation Scholarship

Anchor Scholarship Foundation
P.O. Box 9535
Norfolk, VA 23505
Phone: 757-374-3769
Email: admin@anchorscholarship.com
Website: http://www.anchorscholarship.com
Purpose: To assist the dependents of current and former members of the Naval Surface Forces, Atlantic and Naval Surface Forces, Pacific.
Eligibility: Applicants must be high school seniors or college students planning to attend or currently attending an accredited, four-year college or university full-time. Applicants must also be dependents of service members who are on active duty or retired and have served a minimum of six years in a unit under the administrative control of Commander, Naval Surface Forces, U.S. Atlantic Fleet or U.S. Pacific Fleet. The award is based on academics, extracurricular activities, character, all-around ability and financial need.
Target applicant:
  High school students
  College students
  Adult students

Minimum GPA: None.
Amount: Varies.
Number of awards: 35.
Deadline: March 15.
How to apply: Applications are available online.

(382) · Annual Logistics Scholarship Competition

International Society of Logistics
Chairman, Scholarships Review Committee
Logistics Education Foundation
8100 Professional Place, Suite 111
Hyattsville, MD 20785
Phone: 301-459-8446
Fax: 301-459-1522
Email: solehq@sole.org
Website: http://www.sole.org
Purpose: The organization is dedicated to upgrading the quality and availability of logistics education.
Eligibility: Applicants must be pursuing a bachelor's or master's degree in logistics or a logistics-related major and be full-time students with a full-time course load. Applicants' intention to pursue a logistics-related career, scholastic achievements and current and potential contributions to the logistics profession are considered.
Target applicant:
   College students
   Graduate school students
   Adult students
Minimum GPA: None.
Amount: $1,000.
Number of awards: Varies.
Deadline: May 15.
How to apply: Applications are available online.

(383) · APF/COGDOP Graduate Research Scholarships

American Psychological Foundation
750 First Street NE
Washington, DC 20002
Phone: 800-374-2721
Website: http://www.apa.org
Purpose: To assist graduate psychology students.
Eligibility: Applicants must attend a school whose psychology department is a member in good standing of Council of Graduate Departments of Psychology (COGDOP). Applicants are nominated by their schools' departments with no more than three nominees at each school.
Target applicant:
   Graduate school students
   Adult students
Minimum GPA: None.
Amount: $1,000-$3,000.
Number of awards: Up to 13.
Deadline: May 28.
How to apply: Applicants must be nominated.

(384) · APF/TOPSS Scholars Competition

American Psychological Foundation
750 First Street NE
Washington, DC 20002
Phone: 800-374-2721

Website: http://www.apa.org
Purpose: To assist students who are studying psychology.
Eligibility: Applicants must be high school students who have been or are presently enrolled in a psychology course and must write an essay answering a question from the APA. A Teachers of Psychology in Secondary Schools (TOPSS) member must sponsor all candidates, and each school may submit no more than ten papers.
Target applicant:
   High school students
Minimum GPA: None.
Amount: $1,000.
Number of awards: 3.
Deadline: February 16.
How to apply: There is no official application.

(385) · APTF Transit Hall of Fame Scholarship Award

American Public Transportation Foundation
1666 K Street NW
Suite 1100
Washington, DC 20006
Phone: 202-496-4800
Fax: 202-496-4321
Email: info@apta.com
Website: http://www.apta.com
Purpose: To encourage students to enter the transit field.
Eligibility: Applicants must be enrolled in an accredited undergraduate or graduate institution, have a minimum 3.0 GPA, be employed by or demonstrate an interest in entering the public transportation industry and be nominated by a member organization of American Public Transportation Association (APTA) with which recipients must participate in an internship. Selection is based on this, as well as academic achievement, essay, financial need and extracurricular and leadership activities. There is also a $500 award for the best application essay.
Target applicant:
   College students
   Graduate school students
   Adult students
Minimum GPA: 3.0
Amount: At least $2,500.
Number of awards: 7.
Scholarship may be renewable.
Deadline: June 16.
How to apply: Applications are available from your local APTA member organization or by email.

(386) · Arc Welding Awards

James F. Lincoln Arc Welding Foundation
Secretary
P.O. Box 17188
Cleveland, OH 44117-9949
Website: http://www.jflf.org
Purpose: To award prizes for arc welding projects made by the applicant or a group of applicants.
Eligibility: Projects may fit into one of the following categories: home, recreational or artistic equipment; shop tool, machine or mechanical device; a structure; agricultural equipment or a repair. Applicants must submit a paper about the creation of the project and be enrolled in a shop class. Applicants must also be enrolled in high school, adult evening classes, two-year/community college, vocational school, apprentice program, trade school, in-plant training or technical school and may not be college students enrolled in a bachelor's or master's program.

Target applicant:
    High school students
    College students
    Adult students
Minimum GPA: None.
Amount: Up to $2,000.
Number of awards: 95.
Deadline: June 1.
How to apply: Applications are available online.

(387) · ARIT Fellowships for Research in Turkey

American Research Institute in Turkey (ARIT)
3260 South Street
Philadelphia, PA 19104-6324
Phone: 215-898-3474
Fax: 215-898-0657
Email: leinwand@sas.upenn.edu
Website: http://ccat.sas.upenn.edu/ARIT
Purpose: To support scholars in their research in Turkey.
Eligibility: Applicants must be scholars or advanced graduate students involved in research on ancient, medieval or modern times in Turkey, in any field of the humanities and social sciences. Student applicants must have completed all requirements for the doctorate except the dissertation before beginning any ARIT-sponsored research. Non-U.S. applicants must be connected to an educational institution in the U.S. or Canada. Applicants should submit applications, three letters of recommendation and graduate transcripts.
Target applicant:
    Graduate school students
    Adult students
Minimum GPA: None.
Amount: Varies.
Number of awards: Varies.
Deadline: November 1.
How to apply: Applications are available online.

(388) · Armed Services YMCA Annual Essay Contest

Armed Services YMCA
6359 Walker Lane
Suite 200
Alexandria, VA 22310
Phone: 703-313-9600
Fax: 703-313-9668
Email: essaycontest@asymca.org
Website: http://www.asymca.org
Purpose: To promote reading among children of service members and civilian Department of Defense employees.
Eligibility: Applicants must be K-12 students who are children of active duty or Reserve/Guard military personnel. Entrants up to eighth grade should write an essay of 300 words or less. High school entrants should write an essay of 500 words or less.
Target applicant:
    Junior high students or younger
    High school students
Minimum GPA: None.
Amount: Up to $1,000.
Number of awards: Varies.
Deadline: March 20.
How to apply: Applications are available online.

(389) · Army ROTC Four-Year Scholarship Program

Headquarters
U.S. Army Cadet Command
55 Patch Road
Fort Monroe, VA 23651
Email: atccps@monroe.army.mil
Website: http://www.rotc.monroe.army.mil
Purpose: To bolster the ranks of the Army, Army Reserve and Army National Guard by providing monetary assistance to eligible student candidates.
Eligibility: Applicants must be U.S. citizens and high school seniors, graduates or college freshmen with at least four years of college remaining who wish to attend one of 600 colleges and earn a commission. Recipients must serve in the Army for four to eight years after graduation.
Target applicant:
    High school students
    College students
    Adult students
Minimum GPA: 2.5
Amount: Varies.
Number of awards: Varies.
Scholarship may be renewable.
Deadline: November 15.
How to apply: Applications are available online.

(390) · Army ROTC Green To Gold Scholarship Program

Headquarters
U.S. Army Cadet Command
55 Patch Road
Fort Monroe, VA 23651
Email: atccps@monroe.army.mil
Website: http://www.rotc.monroe.army.mil
Purpose: To provide scholarship funds for Army enlisted soldiers.
Eligibility: Applicants must be active duty enlisted members of the Army who wish to complete their baccalaureate degree requirements and obtain a commission. Recipients are required to serve in the U.S. Army.
Target applicant:
    College students
    Adult students
Minimum GPA: None.
Amount: Varies.
Number of awards: Varies.
Deadline: Varies.
How to apply: Applications are available online.

(391) · Arnold Rigby Scholarship

Tourism Cares
585 Washington Street
Canton, MA 02021
Phone: 781-821-5990
Fax: 781-821-8949
Email: carolynv@tourismcares.org
Website: http://www.tourismcares.org
Purpose: To assist graduate students who are studying travel and tourism in paying for their education.
Eligibility: Applicants must be enrolled in a travel and tourism-related graduate program at an accredited college or university in the U.S. or Canada. They must have a GPA of 3.0 or higher.

Target applicant:
  Graduate school students
  Adult students
Minimum GPA: 3.0
Amount: $1,000.
Number of awards: 1.
Deadline: April 2.
How to apply: Applications are available online.

(392) · Arnold Sobel Endowment Fund Scholarships

Coast Guard Foundation
2100 Second Street SW
Washington, DC 20593
Website: http://www.uscg.mil
Purpose: To provide financial assistance to children of Coast Guard members.
Eligibility: Applicants must be dependent children of men or women who are enlisted in the Coast Guard or who are in the Coast Guard Reserve on extended active duty. Children of retired or deceased Coast Guard members are also eligible.
Target applicant:
  High school students
  College students
  Adult students
Minimum GPA: None.
Amount: $2,500-$5,000.
Number of awards: 4.
Deadline: April 1.
How to apply: Applications are available online after January 2.

(393) · ARRL Scholarship Honoring Senator Barry Goldwater, K7UGA

American Radio Relay League Foundation
225 Main Street
Newington, CT 06111
Phone: 860-594-0397
Fax: 860-594-0259
Email: foundation@arrl.org
Website: http://www.arrl.org
Purpose: To assist ham radio operators in furthering their educations.
Eligibility: Applicants must have at least a novice ham radio license, be studying for a bachelor's or graduate degree and attend a regionally-accredited institute.
Target applicant:
  High school students
  College students
  Graduate school students
  Adult students
Minimum GPA: None.
Amount: $5,000.
Number of awards: 1.
Deadline: February 1.
How to apply: Applications are available online.

(394) · Aspiring Educator Scholarship

Teachers-Teachers.com
P.O. Box 2519
Columbia, MD 21045
Phone: 877-812-4071
Email: scholarship@teachers-teachers.com

Website: http://www.teachers-teachers.com/scholarship
Purpose: To support students majoring in some area of special education.
Eligibility: Students must be at least a college junior majoring in special education, speech pathology/therapy, occupational therapy, physical therapy or school psychology.
Target applicant:
  College students
  Graduate school students
  Adult students
Minimum GPA: None.
Amount: $1,000.
Number of awards: 5.
Deadline: June 30.
How to apply: Applications are available online.

(395) · Avis Scholarship

American Society of Travel Agents (ASTA) Foundation Inc.
1101 King Street
Suite 200
Alexandria, VA 22314
Phone: 703-739-2782
Fax: 703-684-8319
Email: scholarship@astahq.com
Website: http://www.astanet.com
Purpose: To promote management skills in current travel professionals.
Eligibility: Applicants must have two years of full-time travel industry experience or an undergraduate degree in travel/tourism and submit proof of current employment in the travel industry. Students must be enrolled in a minimum of two courses per semester in an accredited undergraduate or graduate level program in business, have a minimum 3.0 GPA and write a brief essay (500-750 words) explaining how the degree program relates to their future career in the travel industry. Applicants must also be a resident, citizen or legal alien of the United States or Canada.
Target applicant:
  College students
  Graduate school students
  Adult students
Minimum GPA: 3.0
Amount: $2,000.
Number of awards: 1.
Scholarship may be renewable.
Deadline: July 27.
How to apply: Applications are available online.

(396) · Begun Scholarship

California Library Association
717 20th Street, Suite 200
Sacramento, CA 95814
Phone: 916-447-8541
Fax: 916-447-8394
Email: info@cla-net.org
Website: http://www.cla-net.org
Purpose: To assist California library or information sciences graduate students at California schools.
Eligibility: Applicants must be California graduate students attending an American Library Association accredited school and have completed core coursework toward a master's of library and science or information studies degree. Recipients must also plan to become a children's or young

adult librarian in a California public library and to join the California Library Association if not already a member.
Target applicant:
  Graduate school students
  Adult students
Minimum GPA: None.
Amount: $3,000.
Number of awards: 1.
Deadline: July 15.
How to apply: Applications are available online.

---

(397) · Betsy Plank/PRSSA Scholarship

Public Relations Student Society of America
33 Maiden Lane
11th Floor
New York, NY 10038
Phone: 212-460-1474
Fax: 212-995-0757
Email: prssa@prsa.org
Website: http://www.prssa.org
Purpose: To assist public relations students.
Eligibility: Applicants must be PRSSA members enrolled in an undergraduate public relations program and be college juniors or seniors. One eligible student may be nominated from each PRSSA chapter. Selection is based on academic achievement, leadership, experience and commitment to public relations. Applicants need to include a 300-word statement of commitment to public relations.
Target applicant:
  College students
  Adult students
Minimum GPA: None.
Amount: Varies.
Number of awards: 3.
Deadline: June 4.
How to apply: Applications are available online.

---

(398) · Better Chance Scholarship

Associates of Vietnam Veterans of America
8605 Cameron Street
Suite 400
Silver Spring, MD 20910-3710
Phone: 800-822-1316
Fax: 301-585-0519
Email: pvarnell@avva.org
Website: http://www.avva.org/better_chance.htm
Purpose: To provide financial assistance to the families of veterans.
Eligibility: Applicants must be VVA or AVVA members or their spouses, children or grandchildren, or spouses, children or grandchildren of KIA or MIA Vietnam Veterans. They must be registered at an accredited institution of higher learning, and they must demonstrate financial need according to an official FAFSA printout.
Target applicant:
  High school students
  College students
  Adult students
Minimum GPA: None.
Amount: Up to $1,000.
Number of awards: 3.
Deadline: June 17.
How to apply: Applications are available online.

---

(399) · Bill Salerno, W2ONV, Memorial Scholarship

American Radio Relay League Foundation
225 Main Street
Newington, CT 06111
Phone: 860-594-0397
Fax: 860-594-0259
Email: foundation@arrl.org
Website: http://www.arrl.org
Purpose: To provide financial assistance to amateur radio operators with high academic achievement.
Eligibility: Applicants must hold an active Amateur Radio License of any class and attend an accredited four-year college or university. They must have a GPA of 3.7 or higher, and their household income may not exceed $100,000 per year. They must not have previously received the Salerno Scholarship.
Target applicant:
  High school students
  College students
  Adult students
Minimum GPA: 3.7
Amount: $1,000.
Number of awards: 1.
Deadline: February 1.
How to apply: Applications are available online.

---

(400) · Bob East Scholarship

National Press Photographers Foundation Bob East Scholarship
Chuck Fadely
The Miami Herald
One Herald Plaza
Miami, FL 33132
Phone: 305-376-2015
Website: http://www.nppa.org
Purpose: To encourage newcomers in photojournalism.
Eligibility: Applicants must either be an undergraduate in the first three and one half years of college or be planning to pursue postgraduate work.
Target applicant:
  College students
  Graduate school students
  Adult students
Minimum GPA: None.
Amount: $2,000.
Number of awards: 1.
Deadline: March 1.
How to apply: Applications are available online.

---

(401) · Bodie McDowell Scholarship

Outdoor Writers Association of America
121 Hickory Street
Suite 1
Missoula, MT 59801
Phone: 406-728-7434
Fax: 406-728-7445
Email: krhoades@owaa.org
Website: http://www.owaa.org
Purpose: To support students in outdoor communications fields.
Eligibility: Applicants must be students of outdoor communications fields including print, film, art or broadcasting and must be either

undergraduate students entering their junior or senior year or graduate students.

Target applicant:
- College students
- Graduate school students
- Adult students

Minimum GPA: None.
Amount: $1,000-$4,000.
Number of awards: 3 or more.
Deadline: March 1.
How to apply: Applicants are available online.

(402) · Bound to Stay Bound Books Scholarship

Association for Library Service to Children
50 E. Huron Street
Chicago, IL 60611
Phone: 800-545-2433
Fax: 312-944-7671
Email: alsc@ala.org
Website: http://www.ala.org/alsc
Purpose: To support students pursuing their MLS degrees.
Eligibility: Applicants must intend to pursue an MLS or advanced degree, plan to work in children's librarianship and be U.S. or Canadian citizens. Selection is based on academic excellence, leadership and a desire to work with children in any type of library.

Target applicant:
- College students
- Graduate school students
- Adult students

Minimum GPA: None.
Amount: $6,500.
Number of awards: 4.
Deadline: March 1.
How to apply: Applications are available online.

(403) · Bowfin Memorial Academic Scholarships

Pacific Fleet Submarine Memorial Association
11 Arizona Memorial Drive
Honolulu, HI 96818
Phone: 808-423-1341
Fax: 808-422-5201
Email: info@bowfin.org
Website: http://www.bowfin.org
Purpose: To provide financial assistance to submariners and their families.
Eligibility: Applicants must be children of submarine force personnel who are on active duty, retired or deceased. They must be less than 23 years of age, and their surviving parent or sponsor must live in Hawaii. They must demonstrate financial need, scholastic proficiency and community involvement.

Target applicant:
- High school students
- College students

Minimum GPA: None.
Amount: Up to $2,500.
Number of awards: Up to 40.
Deadline: March 1.
How to apply: Applications are available from the Pacific Fleet Submarine Memorial association.

(404) · Bowfin Memorial Continuing Education Scholarships

Pacific Fleet Submarine Memorial Association
11 Arizona Memorial Drive
Honolulu, HI 96818
Phone: 808-423-1341
Fax: 808-422-5201
Email: info@bowfin.org
Website: http://www.bowfin.org
Purpose: To provide financial assistance for submariners and their families.
Eligibility: Applicants must be active duty or retired submariners, their spouses, or spouses of deceased submariners. They must live in Hawaii when they apply and while receiving scholarship benefits. They must demonstrate financial need and community involvement.

Target applicant:
- High school students
- College students
- Adult students

Minimum GPA: None.
Amount: Up to $2,500.
Number of awards: Up to 40.
Deadline: March 1.
How to apply: Applications are available from the Pacific Fleet Submarine Memorial Association.

(405) · Broadcast Education Association Scholarship Program

Broadcast Education Association
1771 North Street NW
Washington, DC 20036
Phone: 888-380-7222
Email: beainfo@beaweb.org
Website: http://www.beaweb.org
Purpose: To honor broadcasters and the broadcast industry.
Eligibility: Applicants must be college juniors or seniors or graduate students at BEA member universities, students pursuing freshman and sophomore instruction only or students who have already completed BEA two-year programs at a four-year college.

Target applicant:
- College students
- Graduate school students
- Adult students

Minimum GPA: None.
Amount: Varies.
Number of awards: Varies.
Deadline: September 15.
How to apply: Applications are available online.

(406) · BSA Research Fellowship

Bibliographical Society of America
P.O. Box 1537
Lenox Hill Station
New York, NY 10021
Phone: 212-452-2710
Email: bsa@bibsocamer.org
Website: http://www.bibsocamer.org
Purpose: To provide financial assistance to those pursuing bibliographical studies.

Eligibility: Applicants must submit proposals for studying books as historical evidence or an examination of the history of book trades or publishing history.

Target applicant:
   College students
   Graduate school students
   Adult students

Minimum GPA: None.

Amount: $2,000.

Number of awards: Varies.

Deadline: December 1.

How to apply: Applications are available online.

---

(407) · CaGIS Scholarships

American Congress on Surveying and Mapping (ACSM)
6 Montgomery Village Avenue
Suite 403
Gaithersburg, MD 20879
Phone: 240-632-9716
Fax: 240-632-1321
Website: http://www.acsm.net

Purpose: To support excellence in cartography or GIScience.

Eligibility: Applicants must be enrolled full-time in a four-year undergraduate or graduate degree program in cartography or geographic information science. Prior scholarship winners may apply. Applicants are judged on their records, statements, letters of recommendation and professional activities.

Target applicant:
   College students
   Graduate school students
   Adult students

Minimum GPA: None.

Amount: $1,000.

Number of awards: Varies.

Scholarship may be renewable.

Deadline: January 22.

How to apply: Applications are available online.

---

(408) · California - Hawaii Elks Association Vocational Grants

California-Hawaii Elks Association
5450 E. Lamona Avenue
Fresno, CA 93727-2224
Phone: 559-222-8071
Fax: 559-222-8073
Website: http://www.chea-elks.org

Purpose: To provide assistance to those pursuing vocational/technical education.

Eligibility: Applicants must be U.S. citizens and California or Hawaii residents. They must plan to pursue a vocational or technical course of study above and supplemental to high school or preparatory school. A high school diploma or equivalent is not required. Students planning to transfer into a bachelor's degree program upon completion of vocational studies are not eligible.

Target applicant:
   High school students
   College students
   Adult students

Minimum GPA: None.

Amount: Varies.

Number of awards: Varies.

Scholarship may be renewable.

Deadline: Varies.

How to apply: Applications are available online.

---

(409) · Capt. James J. Regan Scholarship

Explorers Learning for Life
P.O. Box 152079
Irving, TX 75015
Phone: 972-580-2433
Fax: 972-580-2137
Email: pchestnu@lflmail.org
Website: http://www.learningforlife.org/exploring

Purpose: To support students who are Law Enforcement Explorers.

Eligibility: Students must be at least in their senior year of high school. Applicants must submit three letters of recommendation and an essay.

Target applicant:
   High school students
   College students
   Adult students

Minimum GPA: None.

Amount: $500.

Number of awards: 2.

Deadline: March 31.

How to apply: Applications are available online.

---

(410) · Captain Caliendo College Assistance Fund Scholarship

U.S. Coast Guard Chief Petty Officers Association
5520-G Hempstead Way
Springfield, VA 22151-4009
Phone: 703-941-0395
Fax: 703-941-0397
Email: cgcpoa@aol.com
Website: http://www.uscgcpoa.org

Purpose: To provide financial assistance for children of CPOA/CGEA members.

Eligibility: Applicants must be dependents of a living or deceased USCG CPOA/CGEA member who are under the age of 24 as of March 1 of the award year. The age limit does not apply to disabled children. Proof of acceptance or enrollment in an institution of higher learning is required.

Target applicant:
   High school students
   College students

Minimum GPA: None.

Amount: $5,000.

Number of awards: 1.

Deadline: March 1.

How to apply: Applications are available online.

---

(411) · Carole J. Streeter, KB9JBR Scholarship

American Radio Relay League Foundation
225 Main Street
Newington, CT 06111
Phone: 860-594-0397
Fax: 860-594-0259
Email: foundation@arrl.org
Website: http://www.arrl.org

Purpose: To support students who are involved in amateur radio.

Eligibility: Applicants must have an amateur radio license of Technician Class or higher. Preference will be given to applicants with Morse Code proficiency and those studying health and healing arts.
Target applicant:
High school students
College students
Adult students
Minimum GPA: None.
Amount: $750.
Number of awards: 1.
Deadline: February 1.
How to apply: Applications are available online.

(412) · Carole Simpson Scholarship

Radio and Television News Directors Association
1600 K Street NW
Suite 700
Washington, DC 20006
Phone: 202-659-6510
Fax: 202-223-4007
Email: rtnda@rtnda.org
Website: http://www.rtnda.org
Purpose: To honor professional achievements in electronic journalism.
Eligibility: Applicants must be full-time college sophomores or higher with at least one full academic year remaining. Applicants may be enrolled in any major as long as their career intent is television or radio news. Applicants may only apply for one RTNDA scholarship. Preference is given to students of color.
Target applicant:
College students
Adult students
Minimum GPA: None.
Amount: $2,000.
Number of awards: 1.
Deadline: May 3.
How to apply: Applications are available online.

(413) · Chain des Rotisseurs Scholarship

American Academy of Chefs
180 Center Place Way
St. Augustine, FL 32095
Phone: 800-624-9458
Fax: 904-825-4758
Email: educate@acfchefs.net
Website: http://www.acfchefs.org
Purpose: To assist students attending culinary programs.
Eligibility: Applicants must be enrolled in an accredited post-secondary school of culinary arts or AAC-approved post-secondary culinary training program, be excellent students and have completed at least one grading period. Applicants should submit applications, two recommendation letters, financial aid release forms, transcripts, and signed photo releases. Selection is based on application, financial need, references and transcript.
Target applicant:
College students
Adult students
Minimum GPA: None.
Amount: Varies.
Number of awards: Varies.
Deadline: December 1.
How to apply: Applications are available online.

(414) · Chair's Scholarship

American Academy of Chefs
180 Center Place Way
St. Augustine, FL 32095
Phone: 800-624-9458
Fax: 904-825-4758
Email: educate@acfchefs.net
Website: http://www.acfchefs.org
Purpose: To assist students attending culinary programs.
Eligibility: Applicants must be enrolled in accredited, post-secondary schools of culinary arts, be excellent students, have completed at least one grading period and plan to become either chefs or pastry chefs. Applicants should submit applications, two recommendation letters, financial aid release forms, and transcripts. Selection is based on application, references, financial need and transcript.
Target applicant:
College students
Adult students
Minimum GPA: None.
Amount: Varies.
Number of awards: Varies.
Deadline: July 1.
How to apply: Applications are available online.

(415) · Charles & Lucille King Family Foundation Scholarship

Charles and Lucille King Family Foundation
366 Madison Avenue
10th Floor
New York, NY 10017
Phone: 212-682-2913
Email: info@kingfoundation.org
Website: http://www.kingfoundation.org
Purpose: To assist film and television students.
Eligibility: Applicants must be undergraduate juniors or seniors and demonstrate academic ability, financial need and professional potential. Applicants must also major in film and television. Applicants must submit applications, personal statements, three recommendation letters and transcripts.
Target applicant:
College students
Adult students
Minimum GPA: None.
Amount: up to $2,500.
Number of awards: Varies.
Scholarship may be renewable.
Deadline: April 15.
How to apply: Applications are available online or by written request between September 1 and April 1.

(416) · Charles A. Ryskamp Research Fellowships

American Council of Learned Societies (ACLS)
633 Third Avenue
New York, NY 10017-6795
Phone: 212-697-1505
Fax: 212-949-8058
Email: sfisher@acls.org
Website: http://www.acls.org
Purpose: To support scholars researching the humanities field.

Eligibility: The fellowships are for advanced assistant professors and untenured associate professors. By the application deadline, the applicants should have finished their institution's last reappointment review before tenure review, and their tenure review is not finished. The applicants should have a Ph.D. or equivalent and be in a tenure-track position at degree-granting U.S. institutions during the fellowship. Previous supported research leaves do not affect eligibility. The application process involves the application, proposal, bibliography, publications list and four reference letters.

Target applicant:
 Graduate school students
 Adult students
Minimum GPA: None.
Amount: $64,000.
Number of awards: 12.
Deadline: September 28.
How to apply: Applications are available online.

(417) · Charles Clarke Cordle Memorial Scholarship

American Radio Relay League Foundation
225 Main Street
Newington, CT 06111
Phone: 860-594-0397
Fax: 860-594-0259
Email: foundation@arrl.org
Website: http://www.arrl.org
Purpose: To assist ham radio operators in furthering their educations.
Eligibility: Applicants must have any class of ham radio license, have a minimum 2.5 GPA and be residents of and attend school in Georgia or Alabama.
Target applicant:
 High school students
 College students
 Graduate school students
 Adult students
Minimum GPA: 2.5
Amount: $1,000.
Number of awards: 1.
Deadline: February 1.
How to apply: Applications are available online but may not be completed electronically. All completed applications must be mailed.

(418) · Charles Earp Memorial Scholarship

National Society of Accountants Scholarship Program
Scholarship America
One Scholarship Way
P.O. Box 297
Saint Peter, MN 56082
Phone: 507-931-1682
Website: http://www.nsacct.org
Purpose: To provide financial assistance to college students majoring in accounting. The Charles Earp Memorial Scholarship is awarded to the most outstanding applicant in the larger scholarship competition.
Eligibility: Applicants must be U.S. or Canadian citizens enrolled in an accredited college or university in the United States and have a GPA of 3.0 or better. Students in two-year and four-year programs are eligible. Scholarships are awarded on the basis of academics, leadership, honors, participation in school and community events, work experience, goals, unusual family or personal circumstances and an outside evaluation. Applicants must demonstrate financial need.

Target applicant:
 College students
 Adult students
Minimum GPA: 3.0
Amount: $700-$1,200+plaque.
Number of awards: 1.
Deadline: March 10.
How to apply: Applications are available online.

(419) · Charles Foy Jr. Scholarship Fund

Epsilon Sigma Alpha Foundation
P.O. Box 270517
Fort Collins, CO 80527
Phone: 970-223-2824
Fax: 970-223-4456
Email: kloyd@knoxy.net
Website: http://www.esaintl.com/esaf
Purpose: To provide financial assistance to business majors.
Eligibility: Applicants may be residents of any state and may attend any institution of higher learning. Selection is based on the following criteria: character (25 percent), leadership (25 percent), service (20 percent), financial need (15 percent) and scholastic ability (15 percent).
Target applicant:
 High school students
 College students
 Adult students
Minimum GPA: None.
Amount: $500.
Number of awards: 1.
Deadline: February 1.
How to apply: Applications are available online.

(420) · Charles G. Koch Summer Fellow Program

Institute for Humane Studies at George Mason University
3301 N. Fairfax Drive
Suite 440
Arlington, VA 22201
Phone: 800-697-8799
Fax: 703-993-4890
Email: ihs@gmu.edu
Website: http://www.theihs.org
Purpose: To encourage the understanding of market-based solutions to social and economic problems, especially through public policy.
Eligibility: Applicants must be current college students, graduates, graduate students or professional students and have a demonstrated interest in public policy issues and in learning how a market-based approach might help solve social and economic problems.
Target applicant:
 College students
 Graduate school students
 Adult students
Minimum GPA: None.
Amount: $1,500 and internship.
Number of awards: 40.
Deadline: February 15.
How to apply: Applications are available online.

(421) · Charles N. Fisher Memorial Scholarship

American Radio Relay League Foundation
225 Main Street
Newington, CT 06111

Phone: 860-594-0397
Fax: 860-594-0259
Email: foundation@arrl.org
Website: http://www.arrl.org
Purpose: To assist ham radio operators in furthering their educations.
Eligibility: Applicants must have any class of ham radio license, be residents of the ARRL Southwestern Division (Arizona, Los Angeles, Orange County, San Diego or Santa Barbara), attend a regionally-accredited college or university and study electronics, communications or a related field.
Target applicant:
    College students
    Graduate school students
    Adult students
Minimum GPA: None.
Amount: $1,000.
Number of awards: 1.
Deadline: February 1.
How to apply: Applications are available online. Completed applications must be submitted by mail, not electronically.

(422) · Charlie Logan Scholarship Program for Seamen

Seafarers International Union of North America
Mr. Lou Delma, Administrator
Seafarers Welfare Plan Scholarship Program
5201 Auth Way
Camp Springs, MD 20746
Phone: 301-899-0675
Fax: 301-899-7355
Website: http://www.seafarers.org
Purpose: To offer scholarships to members of the SIU.
Eligibility: Applicants must be active seamen who are high school graduates or its equivalent, are eligible to receive Seafarers Plan benefits and have credit for two years (730 days) of employment with an employer who is obligated to make contributions to the Seafarers' Plan on the employee's behalf prior to the date of application. Recipients may attend any U.S. accredited institution (college or trade school). Selection is based on high school equivalency scores or secondary school records, college transcripts, if any, SAT/ACT scores, references on character or personality and autobiography. The $6,000 scholarships are for two-year study, and the $20,000 scholarship is for four-year study.
Target applicant:
    College students
    Adult students
Minimum GPA: None.
Amount: $6,000-$20,000.
Number of awards: 3.
Scholarship may be renewable.
Deadline: April 15.
How to apply: Applications are available by written request.

(423) · Chicago FM Club Scholarships

American Radio Relay League Foundation
225 Main Street
Newington, CT 06111
Phone: 860-594-0397
Fax: 860-594-0259
Email: foundation@arrl.org
Website: http://www.arrl.org
Purpose: To assist ham radio operators in furthering their educations.

Eligibility: Applicants must have at least a technician ham radio license, be residents of the FCC Ninth Call District (Illinois, Indiana or Wisconsin) and be students at an accredited post-secondary two- or four-year college or trade school.
Target applicant:
    College students
    Adult students
Minimum GPA: None.
Amount: $500.
Number of awards: Varies.
Deadline: February 1.
How to apply: Applications are available online but must be sent in by mail.

(424) · Chief Master Sergeants of the Air Force Scholarships

Air Force Sergeants Association
5211 Auth Road
Suitland, MD 20746
Phone: 301-899-3500
Fax: 301-899-8136
Email: staff@afsahq.org
Website: http://www.afsahq.org
Purpose: To provide financial assistance to the families of Air Force enlistees.
Eligibility: Applicants must be dependents of enlisted Air Force members, either on active duty or retired. They must meet the eligibility requirements and participate in the Airmen Memorial Foundation Scholarship Program. An unweighted GPA of 3.5 or higher is required. Extenuating circumstances are considered.
Target applicant:
    High school students
    College students
    Adult students
Minimum GPA: 3.5
Amount: Varies.
Number of awards: Varies.
Deadline: March 31.
How to apply: Applications are available online.

(425) · CLA Reference Services Press Fellowship

California Library Association
717 20th Street, Suite 200
Sacramento, CA 95814
Phone: 916-447-8541
Fax: 916-447-8394
Email: info@cla-net.org
Website: http://www.cla-net.org
Purpose: To support college seniors and graduates pursuing master's degrees in library science.
Eligibility: Applicants must either be California residents enrolled in a master's program at an American Library Association-approved library school in any state or residents of any state enrolled in an ALA-approved library school master's program in California. Recipients are expected to pursue a career in reference or information service librarianship and take at least three classes about reference or information service.
Target applicant:
    College students
    Graduate school students
    Adult students
Minimum GPA: None.

Amount: $3,000.
Number of awards: 1.
Deadline: June 15.
How to apply: Applications are available online.

(426) · CLA Scholarship for Minority Students in Memory of Edna Yelland

California Library Association
717 20th Street, Suite 200
Sacramento, CA 95814
Phone: 916-447-8541
Fax: 916-447-8394
Email: info@cla-net.org
Website: http://www.cla-net.org
Purpose: To assist minority California graduate students who are pursuing degrees in library or information science.
Eligibility: Applicants must be California residents, be American Indian, African American, Mexican American, Latino, Asian American, Pacific Islander or Filipino and be accepted into or enrolled in an American Library Association accredited state library school. The award is based on financial need, and an interview is required.
Target applicant:
  Graduate school students
  Adult students
Minimum GPA: None.
Amount: $2,500.
Number of awards: 3.
Deadline: May 31.
How to apply: Applications are available online.

(427) · CNF Professional Growth Scholarship

Child Nutrition Foundation
Scholarship Committee
700 S. Washington Street, Suite 300
Alexandria, VA 22314
Phone: 703-739-3900
Email: jcurtis@schoolnutrition.org
Website: http://www.schoolnutrition.org
Purpose: To support the continuing education of School Nutrition Association members.
Eligibility: Applicants must be members of the School Nutrition Association for at least one year who are enrolled in an undergraduate or graduate program in a school foodservice related field.
Target applicant:
  College students
  Graduate school students
  Adult students
Minimum GPA: None.
Amount: Tuition, fees and books.
Number of awards: Varies.
Scholarship may be renewable.
Deadline: April 15.
How to apply: Applications are available online.

(428) · Coast Guard Foundation Scholarship Fund

Coast Guard Foundation
2100 Second Street SW
Washington, DC 20593
Website: http://www.uscg.mil

Purpose: To provide financial assistance to children of Coast Guard members.
Eligibility: Applicants must be unmarried dependent children of U.S. Coast Guard members, living, retired or deceased or Coast Guard reservists on extended active duty. They must be high school seniors or full-time undergraduate students in a four-year program or vocational/technical program. They must be under 23 years old.
Target applicant:
  High school students
  College students
Minimum GPA: None.
Amount: $2,500-$5,000.
Number of awards: 4.
Scholarship may be renewable.
Deadline: April 1.
How to apply: Applications are available online.

(429) · Coca-Cola USA Scholarship

DECA Inc.
1908 Association Drive
Reston, VA 20191-1594
Phone: 703-860-5000
Fax: 703-860-4013
Email: kathy_onion@deca.org
Website: http://www.deca.org
Purpose: To reward DECA members who are committed to leadership and community service.
Eligibility: Applicants must be active DECA members showing leadership, scholastic ability and community involvement. They must be planning to attend a 2-year or 4-year school to study marketing, business or marketing education.
Target applicant:
  High school students
Minimum GPA: None.
Amount: $1,000.
Number of awards: Up to 6.
Deadline: February 17.
How to apply: Applications are available from DECA advisors.

(430) · College Photographer of the Year

National Press Photographers Foundation College Photographer of the Year
David Rees
CPOY Director, School of Journalism, The University of Missouri
106 Lee Hills Hall
Columbus, MO 65211
Phone: 573-882-4442
Fax: 919-383-7261
Email: jourdlr@showme.missouri.edu
Website: http://www.nppa.org
Purpose: To award outstanding student work in photojournalism and provide a forum for student photographers to gauge their skills.
Eligibility: Applicants must be currently enrolled in a full-time four-year college or university, provide a portfolio and demonstrate financial need. Applicants can apply to as many NPPA scholarships as desired, but only one award will be granted.
Target applicant:
  College students
  Adult students
Minimum GPA: None.
Amount: $500-$1,000.

Number of awards: 2.
Deadline: October 1.
How to apply: Applications are available by written or email request.

(431) · College Scholarships
Insurance Scholarship Foundation of America,
P.O. Box 866
Hendersonville, NC 28793-0866
Phone: 828-890-3328
Fax: 828-891-2667
Email: billie@inssfa.org
Website: http://www.inssfa.org
Purpose: To promote studies in the insurance industry.
Eligibility: Applicants must major in insurance, risk management or actuarial science, have completed two insurance or risk management-related courses, be currently attending a college or university and be completing or have completed the third year of college, have a minimum 3.75 GPA and be a NAIW Student Member.
Target applicant:
College students
Graduate school students
Adult students
Minimum GPA: 3.75
Amount: $2,500-$5,000.
Number of awards: Varies.
Deadline: February 15.
How to apply: Applications are available online.

(432) · College/University Excellence of Scholarship Awards
National Council for Geographic Education
Jacksonville State University
206-A Martin Hall
700 Pelham Road North
Jacksonville, AL 36265-1602
Phone: 256-782-5293
Fax: 256-782-5336
Email: ncge@jsu.edu
Website: http://www.ncge.org
Purpose: To recognize senior geography majors.
Eligibility: Every college or university geography department in North America may submit the name of its outstanding graduating senior geography majors. The students receive certificates.
Target applicant:
College students
Adult students
Minimum GPA: None.
Amount: Varies.
Number of awards: Varies.
Deadline: April 1.
How to apply: Nomination materials are described online.

(433) · Congressional Medal of Honor Society Scholarships
Congressional Medal of Honor Society
40 Patriots Point Road
Mount Pleasant, SC 29464
Phone: 843-884-8862
Fax: 843-884-1471

Email: medalhq@earthlink.net
Website: http://www.cmohs.org
Purpose: To provide education assistance to children of Congressional Medal of Honor recipients.
Eligibility: Applicants must be natural or adopted children of Congressional Medal of Honor recipients or of other combat veterans if recommended by a Medal of Honor recipient.
Target applicant:
High school students
College students
Adult students
Minimum GPA: None.
Amount: Up to $500.
Number of awards: Varies.
Deadline: Varies.
How to apply: Applications are available from the Congressional Medal of Honor Society.

(434) · Contemplative Practice Fellowship Program
American Council of Learned Societies (ACLS)
633 Third Avenue
New York, NY 10017-6795
Phone: 212-697-1505
Fax: 212-949-8058
Email: sfisher@acls.org
Website: http://www.acls.org
Purpose: To support scholars interested in contemplative practices.
Eligibility: There are two awards, Contemplative Practice Fellowships and Contemplative Program Development Fellowships. The first is for $10,000, and the second is for $20,000. Applicants for the Contemplative Practice Fellowships must be scholars who are full-time faculty members at accredited U.S. academic institutions who want to integrate contemplative practices into their courses. Preferred applicants will have experience with contemplative practice. The fellowship is for a summer or semester. The Contemplative Program Development Fellowships is for scholars who are full-time faculty members and faculty-status administrators at accredited U.S. academic institutions who want to develop academic courses involving contemplative studies. The fellowship lasts for an academic year.
Target applicant:
Graduate school students
Adult students
Minimum GPA: None.
Amount: $20,000.
Number of awards: Varies.
Deadline: November 10.
How to apply: Applications are available online.

(435) · Council on Approved Student Education's Scholarship Fund
National Court Reporters Association
8224 Old Courthouse Road
Vienna, VA 22182-3808
Phone: 800-272-6272
Email: dgaede@ncrahq.org
Website: http://www.ncraonline.org
Purpose: To support the reporting profession.
Eligibility: Applicants must be in good academic standing at an approved court-reporting program, be members of the NCRA, write 140 to 180 words per minute and submit a two-page essay with references.

Target applicant:
    College students
    Adult students
Minimum GPA: None.
Amount: $500-$1,500.
Number of awards: 3.
Deadline: April 1.
How to apply: Applications are available by email.

---

(436) · Darrel Hess Community College Geography Scholarship

Association of American Geographers (AAG) Hess Scholarship
1710 Sixteenth Street NW
Washington, DC 20009-3198
Phone: 202-234-1450
Fax: 202-234-2744
Email: grantsawards@aag.org
Website: http://www.aag.org
Purpose: To support geography majors.
Eligibility: Applicants must be currently enrolled at a U.S. community college, junior college, city college or similar two-year educational institution, have completed at least two transfer courses in geography and plan to transfer to a four-year institution as a geography major. The award is based on academic excellence and promise. Applications, personal statements, two recommendation letters and transcripts are required.
Target applicant:
    College students
    Adult students
Minimum GPA: None.
Amount: $1,000.
Number of awards: 2.
Deadline: May 1.
How to apply: Applications are available online.

---

(437) · Daughters of the Cincinnati Scholarship

Daughters of the Cincinnati
National Headquarters
122 East 58th Street
New York, NY 10022
Phone: 212-319-6915
Website: http://fdncenter.org/grantmaker/cincinnati/
Purpose: To support daughters of Armed Services commissioned officers.
Eligibility: Applicants must be daughters of career officers in the United States Army, Navy, Air Force, Coast Guard or Marine Corps (active, retired or deceased). Daughters of reserve officers or enlisted personnel cannot apply. Applicants must also be high school seniors.
Target applicant:
    High school students
Minimum GPA: None.
Amount: $1,000-$3,000.
Number of awards: Varies.
Scholarship may be renewable.
Deadline: March 15.
How to apply: Applications are available by mailing the organization your parent's rank and branch of service and enclosing a self-addressed, stamped envelope.

---

(438) · Dayton Amateur Radio Association Scholarship

American Radio Relay League Foundation
225 Main Street
Newington, CT 06111
Phone: 860-594-0397
Fax: 860-594-0259
Email: foundation@arrl.org
Website: http://www.arrl.org
Purpose: To provide financial assistance to students who are amateur radio operators.
Eligibility: Applicants must be accepted or enrolled at an accredited four-year institution of higher learning. They must possess an Amateur Radio License of any class.
Target applicant:
    High school students
    College students
    Adult students
Minimum GPA: None.
Amount: $1,000.
Number of awards: 4.
Deadline: February 1.
How to apply: Applications are available online.

---

(439) · Distinguished Service Award for Students

Society for Technical Communication
Manager of the Distinguished Community Awards Committee
7107 Paradise Park Bend
Richmond , TX 77469
Phone: 703-522-4114
Email: stc@stc.org
Website: http://www.stc.org
Purpose: To assist students who are pursuing degrees in an area of technical communication.
Eligibility: Applicants must be full-time undergraduate or graduate students who have completed at least one year of post-secondary education and who have at least one full year of academic work remaining to complete their degree programs. Students must also be in the field of communication of information about technical subjects and be student members of the STC. Applicants must be nominated by student chapters.
Target applicant:
    College students
    Graduate school students
    Adult students
Minimum GPA: None.
Amount: $1,000.
Number of awards: 7.
Deadline: November 30.
How to apply: Applications are available online.

---

(440) · Distinguished Student Scholar Award

Pi Lambda Theta
P.O. Box 6626
Bloomington, IN 47407
Phone: 800-487-3411
Fax: 812-339-3462
Email: office@pilambda.org
Website: http://www.pilambda.org
Purpose: To recognize education majors with leadership potential and a dedication to education.

Eligibility: Applicants must be education majors of at least sophomore level who demonstrate leadership skills and a strong dedication to education. They must be nominated for the scholarship by an instructor or supervisor. Applicants must have a GPA of at least 3.5 and demonstrate significant contributions to local or national education efforts. This scholarship is only available in odd years.
Target applicant:
  College students
  Adult students
Minimum GPA: 3.5
Amount: $500.
Number of awards: 1.
Deadline: February 10 of odd years.
How to apply: Applications are available online.

(441) · DJNF Summer Internships
Dow Jones Newspaper Fund
P.O. Box 300
Princeton, NJ 08543-0300
Phone: 609-452-2820
Fax: 609-520-5804
Email: newsfund@wsj.dowjones.com
Website: http://www.dj.com/Careers/Internships/Internships.htm
Purpose: To assist student journalists.
Eligibility: Applicants must be college students interested in pursuing journalism careers and paid summer internships. The three programs have their own requirements. Applicants to the Newspaper Copy Editing Program and the Sports Copy Editing Program must be juniors, seniors or graduate students and must take copy editing exams and seminars. Candidates must submit the application form, a resume, a list of courses and grades and a 500-word essay. Applicants for the Business Reporting Internship Program must be minority college sophomores and juniors who are African American, Hispanic, Asian American/Pacific Islander or American Indian/Alaskan Native. Candidates should submit application forms, resumes, three to five recent clips, a list of courses and grades and 500-word essays. They must also take the business reporting tests.
Target applicant:
  College students
  Graduate school students
  Adult students
Minimum GPA: None.
Amount: $1,000.
Number of awards: Varies.
Deadline: November 1.
How to apply: Applications are available online.

(442) · Dolphin Scholarship
Dolphin Scholarship Foundation
5040 Virginia Beach Boulevard
Suite 104A
Virginia Beach, VA 23462
Phone: 757-671-3200
Fax: 757-671-3330
Email: info@dolphinscholarship.org
Website: http://www.dolphinscholarship.org
Purpose: To assist the children of members of the Navy Submarine Force and other Navy submarine support personnel.
Eligibility: Applicants must be the unmarried children or stepchildren of navy submariners or navy members who have served in submarine support activities and must be under 24 years old at the time of the application deadline. The parents must have been part of the Submarine

Force for at least eight years, have served in submarine support activities for at least 10 years or died on active duty while in the Submarine Force. The children of submariners who served less than the required number of years due to injury or illness occurring in the line of duty may also be eligible. Applicants must attend an accredited four-year college, working for a bachelor's degree.
Target applicant:
  High school students
  College students
Minimum GPA: None.
Amount: $3,250.
Number of awards: 137.
Scholarship may be renewable.
Deadline: March 15.
How to apply: Applications are available online.

(443) · Donald Groves Fund
American Numismatic Society
96 Fulton Street
New York, NY 10038
Phone: 212-571-4470
Fax: 212-571-4479
Email: info@numismatics.org
Website: http://www.amnumsoc.org
Purpose: To support publication in the field of early American numismatics, which involves materials created no later than 1800.
Eligibility: Funding is available for travel, research and publication costs. Applicants must submit an outline of the proposed research, research methods, funding amount requested and how the funds will be used.
Target applicant:
  Graduate school students
  Adult students
Minimum GPA: None.
Amount: Varies.
Number of awards: Varies.
Deadline: Varies.
How to apply: Application instructions are available online. Applications should be mailed to the ANS, Attn.: Secretary of the Society.

(444) · Donald Riebhoff Memorial Scholarship
American Radio Relay League Foundation
225 Main Street
Newington, CT 06111
Phone: 860-594-0397
Fax: 860-594-0259
Email: foundation@arrl.org
Website: http://www.arrl.org
Purpose: To assist ham radio operators in furthering their educations.
Eligibility: Applicants must have at least a technician ham radio license, be undergraduate or graduate students in international studies at an accredited post-secondary institution and be members of ARRL.
Target applicant:
  College students
  Graduate school students
  Adult students
Minimum GPA: None.
Amount: $1,000.
Number of awards: 1.
Deadline: February 1.
How to apply: Applications are available online. Completed applications must be mailed in. They cannot be completed electronically.

(445) · Donald W. Fogarty International Student Paper Competition

APICS-The Educational Society for Resource Management
5301 Shawnee Road
Alexandria, VA 22312
Phone: 800-444-2742
Fax: 703-354-8106
Email: service@apicshq.org
Website: http://www.apics.org
Purpose: To aid students interested in operations management.
Eligibility: Applicants must be full- or part-time college students, undergraduate or graduate and submit a paper on a topic related to operations management.
Target applicant:
    College students
    Graduate school students
    Adult students
Minimum GPA: None.
Amount: $100-$1,000.
Number of awards: Varies.
Deadline: May 15.
How to apply: Papers must be submitted to a local APICS chapter.

(446) · Dr. James L. Lawson Memorial Scholarship

American Radio Relay League Foundation
225 Main Street
Newington, CT 06111
Phone: 860-594-0397
Fax: 860-594-0259
Email: foundation@arrl.org
Website: http://www.arrl.org
Purpose: To assist ham radio operators in furthering their educations.
Eligibility: Applicants must have at least a general ham radio license, be residents of and attend post-secondary institutions in the New England states (Connecticut, Maine, Massachusetts, New Hampshire, Rhode Island or Vermont) or New York state and be pursuing a bachelor's or graduate degree in electronics, communications or a related field.
Target applicant:
    College students
    Graduate school students
    Adult students
Minimum GPA: None.
Amount: $500.
Number of awards: 1.
Deadline: February 1.
How to apply: Applications are available online but cannot be completed electronically. All applications must be mailed.

(447) · Dr. Tom Anderson Scholarship

Tourism Cares
585 Washington Street
Canton, MA 02021
Phone: 781-821-5990
Fax: 781-821-8949
Email: carolynv@tourismcares.org
Website: http://www.tourismcares.org
Purpose: To provide financial assistance to graduate students who are studying travel and tourism.

Eligibility: Applicants must be entering or returning graduate students at a four-year college or university in the U.S. or Canada who are studying travel and tourism. They must have a minimum GPA of 3.0.
Target applicant:
    Graduate school students
    Adult students
Minimum GPA: 3.0
Amount: $1,000.
Number of awards: 1.
Deadline: April 2.
How to apply: Applications are available online.

(448) · Earl I. Anderson Scholarship

American Radio Relay League Foundation
225 Main Street
Newington, CT 06111
Phone: 860-594-0397
Fax: 860-594-0259
Email: foundation@arrl.org
Website: http://www.arrl.org
Purpose: To assist ham radio operators with furthering their educations.
Eligibility: Applicants must have some form of ham radio operating license, be residents of Florida, Illinois, Indiana or Michigan, major in electronic engineering or a related technical field and be ARRL members.
Target applicant:
    College students
    Graduate school students
    Adult students
Minimum GPA: None.
Amount: $1,250.
Number of awards: 3.
Deadline: February 1.
How to apply: Applications are available online. Completed applications must be submitted by mail.

(449) · Ecolab Scholarship Competition

American Hotel and Lodging Educational Foundation (AH&LEF)
1201 New York Avenue NW
Suite 600
Washington, DC 20005-3931
Phone: 202-289-3188
Fax: 202-289-3199
Email: chammond@ahlef.org
Website: http://www.ahlef.org
Purpose: To provide scholarships for students who intend to earn a degree in hospitality management.
Eligibility: Applicants must be enrolled or intend to enroll full-time in a two- or four-year U.S. college or university.
Target applicant:
    High school students
    College students
    Adult students
Minimum GPA: None.
Amount: Up to $2,000.
Number of awards: Varies.
Deadline: May 1.
How to apply: Applications are available online.

(450) · Ed Bradley Scholarship

Radio and Television News Directors Association
1600 K Street NW
Suite 700
Washington, DC 20006
Phone: 202-659-6510
Fax: 202-223-4007
Email: rtnda@rtnda.org
Website: http://www.rtnda.org
Purpose: To honor professional achievements in electronic journalism.
Eligibility: Applicants must be full-time college sophomores or higher with at least one full academic year remaining. Applicants may be enrolled in any major as long as their career intent is television or radio news. Applicants may only apply for one RTNDA scholarship. Preference will be given to undergraduate students of color.
Target applicant:
   College students
   Adult students
Minimum GPA: None.
Amount: $10,000.
Number of awards: 1.
Deadline: May 3.
How to apply: Applications are available online.

(451) · Edmond A. Metzger Scholarship

American Radio Relay League Foundation
225 Main Street
Newington, CT 06111
Phone: 860-594-0397
Fax: 860-594-0259
Email: foundation@arrl.org
Website: http://www.arrl.org
Purpose: To assist ham radio operators in furthering their educations.
Eligibility: Applicants must have at least a novice ham radio license, be undergraduate or graduate students in electrical engineering, be residents of and attend schools in the ARRL Central Division (Illinois, Indiana or Wisconsin) and be members of ARRL.
Target applicant:
   College students
   Graduate school students
   Adult students
Minimum GPA: None.
Amount: $500.
Number of awards: 1.
Deadline: February 1.
How to apply: Applications are available online. Completed applications must be mailed in. They cannot be completed electronically.

(452) · Edmund S. Muskie Graduate Fellowship Program

International Research and Exchanges Board (IREX)
2121 K Street NW
Suite 700
Washington, DC 20037
Phone: 202-628-8188
Fax: 202-628-8189
Email: irex@irex.org
Website: http://www.irex.org
Purpose: To provide fellowships to encourage graduate students and professionals from Eurasia to study in the United States.
Eligibility: Applicants must hold an undergraduate degree and be a citizen, national or permanent resident of Armenia, Azerbaijan, Belarus, Georgia, Kazakhstan, Kyrgyzstan, Moldova, Russian Federation, Tajikistan, Turkmenistan, Ukraine or Uzbekistan. Students must also be able to obtain and retain a U.S. J-1 visa. Applicants must be in one of the following fields of study: business administration, economics, education, environmental management, international affairs, journalism/mass communication, law, library/information science, public administration, public health or public policy.
Target applicant:
   Graduate school students
   Adult students
Minimum GPA: None.
Amount: Varies.
Number of awards: Varies.
Deadline: Varies.

(453) · Education Memorial Scholarship Awards / George and Rosemary Murray Scholarship Award

25th Infantry Division Association (TIDA)
P.O. Box 7
Flourtown, PA 19031
Website: http://www.25thida.com
Purpose: To aid in the education of the members of the 25th Infantry Division Association or the children and grandchildren of active and former members of the association.
Eligibility: Applicants must be high school seniors who are the child or grandchild of an active association member, the child of a former member who died during combat with the Division or an active member who will be discharged before the end of the award year. Applicants must be entering a four-year college or university as a freshman. Selection is based on future plans, school activities, interests, financial status and academic achievement.
Target applicant:
   High school students
Minimum GPA: None.
Amount: Up to $1,500.
Number of awards: Varies.
Deadline: April 1.
How to apply: Applications are available throughout the year in Tropic Lightning Flashes, the quarterly newsletter of the 25th Infantry Division Association.

(454) · Edward J. Nell Memorial Scholarships in Journalism

Quill and Scroll Society
University of Iowa School of Journalism and Mass Communications
100 Adler Journalism Building
Iowa City, IA 52242
Phone: 319-335-3457
Fax: 319-335-3989
Email: quill-scroll@uiowa.edu
Website: http://www.uiowa.edu/~quill-sc/
Purpose: To aid high school journalists seeking to improve their skills and techniques.
Eligibility: Applicants to the Nell Scholarship must have been national winners in the Yearbook Excellence Contest or the International Writing/Photography Contest.
Target applicant:
   High school students

Minimum GPA: None.
Amount: $500-$1,500.
Number of awards: 9-10.
Deadline: May 10.
How to apply: Applications are available online.

(455) · Eileen J. Garrett Scholarship

Parapsychology Foundation
P.O. Box 1562
New York, NY 10021-0043
Phone: 212-628-1550
Fax: 212-628-1559
Email: office@parapsychology.org
Website: http://www.parapsychology.org
Purpose: To aid a student attending an accredited school in the academic study of parapsychology.
Eligibility: Applicants must be college undergraduates or graduate students and include a sample of writings on parapsychology, three references and application form.
Target applicant:
　　College students
　　Graduate school students
　　Adult students
Minimum GPA: None.
Amount: $3,000.
Number of awards: 1.
Deadline: July 15.
How to apply: Applications are available online or by email.

(456) · Electronic Document Systems Foundation Scholarship Awards

Electronic Document Systems Foundation
608 Silver Spur Road, Suite 280
Rolling Hills Estates, CA 90274
Phone: 310-265-5510
Fax: 310-265-5588
Email: info@edsf.org
Website: http://www.edsf.org
Purpose: To support students interested in pursuing careers in document management and communication.
Eligibility: Applicants must be full-time students interested in a career in the preparation, production or distribution of documents. Possible areas of study include marketing, graphic arts, e-commerce, imaging science, printing, web authoring, electronic publishing, computer science, telecommunications or business. For most scholarships, applicants must be junior, senior or graduate students; however opportunities exist for students at all levels, including those attending two-year colleges. Specific scholarships are available for U.S. and Canadian citizens.
Target applicant:
　　College students
　　Graduate school students
　　Adult students
Minimum GPA: None.
Amount: $250-$5,000.
Number of awards: Varies.
Deadline: May 15.
How to apply: Applications are available online.

(457) · Entrepreneurial Scholarship from the McKelvey Foundation

McKelvey Foundation
200 Park Ave, 44th Floor
New York, NY 10166
Website: https://www.mckelveyfoundation.org
Purpose: The McKelvey Foundation awards $40,000 scholarships to young entrepreneurs who have started their own businesses. Each scholar is awarded up to $10,000 per year to attend any four-year college.
Eligibility: Applicant must be a graduating senior of a U.S. high school or home-school program and plan to attend a four-year college in the U.S. Applicant must also own and operate a business for at least one year (non-profits are OK) and have at least one paid employee. Winners attend an all-expense paid three-day summer e-Venture program (June 28-July 1) to meet other scholars, business leaders and to take part in exciting workshops activities.
Target applicant:
　　High school students
Minimum GPA: None.
Amount: $40,000.
Number of awards: 10.
Deadline: January 25.
How to apply: Applications are available online.

(458) · EOD Memorial Scholarship

Explosive Ordnance Disposal (EOD) Memorial Committee
P.O. Box 594
Niceville, FL 32588
Phone: 850-729-2401
Fax: 850-729-2401
Email: admin@eodmemorial.org
Website: http://www.eodmemorial.org
Purpose: To support those connected to Explosive Ordnance Disposal (EOD) technicians.
Eligibility: Applicants must be accepted or enrolled as full-time undergraduates in a U.S. accredited two-year, four-year, or vocational school. Students must also be the family member of an active duty, guard/reserve, retired or deceased EOD technician. The award is based on academic achievement, community involvement and financial need. Applicants should submit the Free Application for Federal Student Aid form.
Target applicant:
　　High school students
　　College students
　　Adult students
Minimum GPA: None.
Amount: Varies.
Number of awards: Varies.
Deadline: March 1.
How to apply: Applications are available online.

(459) · Eric Friedheim Scholarship

Tourism Cares
585 Washington Street
Canton, MA 02021
Phone: 781-821-5990
Fax: 781-821-8949
Email: carolynv@tourismcares.org
Website: http://www.tourismcares.org

Purpose: To assist graduate students who are studying travel and tourism in paying for their education.

Eligibility: Applicants must be U.S. residents who are studying travel and tourism at the graduate level at an accredited four-year college or university in the U.S. They must have a GPA of 3.0 or higher.

Target applicant:
   Graduate school students
   Adult students

Minimum GPA: 3.0

Amount: $1,000.

Number of awards: 1.

Deadline: April 2.

How to apply: Applications are available online.

---

(460) · Esther R. Sawyer Scholarship Award

Institute of Internal Auditors
247 Maitland Avenue
Altamonte Springs, FL 32701-4201
Phone: 407-937-1100
Fax: 407-937-1101
Email: research@theiia.org
Website: http://www.theiia.org

Purpose: To award internal auditing students.

Eligibility: Applicants should be accepted to or currently enrolled in a graduate program in internal auditing at an IIA-endorsed school or have taken internal auditing undergraduate courses at an IIA-endorsed school and be enrolled in any graduate program in internal auditing or business. An original manuscript on a topic related to modern internal auditing is required. The award is based on the topic, value to the audit profession, originality and the quality of writing.

Target applicant:
   Graduate school students
   Adult students

Minimum GPA: None.

Amount: $5,000.

Number of awards: 1.

Deadline: March 1.

How to apply: Application materials are described online.

---

(461) · Eugene Gene Sallee, W4YFR Memorial Scholarship

American Radio Relay League Foundation
225 Main Street
Newington, CT 06111
Phone: 860-594-0397
Fax: 860-594-0259
Email: foundation@arrl.org
Website: http://www.arrl.org

Purpose: To support students who are involved in amateur radio.

Eligibility: Applicants must have an FCC amateur radio license at the level of Technician Plus or higher. Students must have at least a 3.0 GPA.

Target applicant:
   High school students
   College students
   Adult students

Minimum GPA: 3.0

Amount: $500.

Number of awards: 1.

Deadline: February 1.

How to apply: Applications are available online.

---

(462) · Executive Women International Scholarship Program

Executive Women International (EWI)
515 South 700 East Suite 2A
Salt Lake City, UT 84102
Phone: 801-355-2800
Fax: 801-355-2852
Email: ewi@executivewomen.org
Website: http://www.executivewomen.org

Purpose: To assist high school students in achieving their academic goals.

Eligibility: Applicants must be high school juniors who plan to pursue four-year degrees at accredited colleges or universities. Selection is based on application materials, communication skills, academic record, extracurricular activities and leadership.

Target applicant:
   High school students

Minimum GPA: None.

Amount: $500-$10,000.

Number of awards: Varies.

Deadline: Varies.

How to apply: Contact your local EWI chapter.

---

(463) · Federal Criminal Investigators' Service Award

Explorers Learning for Life
P.O. Box 152079
Irving, TX 75015
Phone: 972-580-2433
Fax: 972-580-2137
Email: pchestnu@lflmail.org
Website: http://www.learningforlife.org/exploring

Purpose: To support students who are Law Enforcement Explorers.

Eligibility: Students must by nominated by the sponsoring agency of their Explorer post. Applicants must submit three letters of recommendation and an essay.

Target applicant:
   High school students
   College students
   Adult students

Minimum GPA: None.

Amount: $500.

Number of awards: Varies.

Deadline: March 31.

How to apply: Applications are available online.

---

(464) · Felix Morley Journalism Competition

Institute for Humane Studies at George Mason University
3301 N. Fairfax Drive
Suite 440
Arlington, VA 22201
Phone: 800-697-8799
Fax: 703-993-4890
Email: ihs@gmu.edu
Website: http://www.theihs.org

Purpose: To support young writers whose work demonstrates an appreciation of classical liberal principles.

Eligibility: Applicants must be young writers who are 25 years or younger and full-time students. Applicants must submit three to five articles, editorials, opinion pieces, essays or reviews published in student newspapers or other periodicals. Submissions are judged on the basis of writing ability, potential to succeed and appreciation of liberty.

Target applicant:
  College students
  Graduate school students
Minimum GPA: None.
Amount: $250-$2,500.
Number of awards: 6.
Deadline: December 1.
How to apply: Applications are available online.

(465) · First Cavalry Division Association Scholarship

Foundation of the First Cavalry Division Association
Alumni Of The First Team
302 North Main Street
Copperas Cove, TX 76522
Phone: 254-547-6537
Email: firstcav@1cda.org
Website: http://www.1cda.org
Purpose: To assist the children of 1st Cavalry troopers who have become disabled or who died while serving in the Division.
Eligibility: Applicants must be First Cavalry Division troopers who have become totally disabled while serving in the division or active duty members, their spouses or children. Applicants may also be the spouses or children of First Cavalry Division troopers who have died while serving in the division.
Target applicant:
  High school students
  College students
  Adult students
Minimum GPA: None.
Amount: $1,000.
Number of awards: Varies.
Deadline: Varies.
How to apply: Applications are available by request.

(466) · Fisher Broadcasting Scholarships for Minorities

Fisher Communications Inc.
100 4th Avenue N.
Suite 440
Seattle, WA 98109
Phone: 206-404-7000
Email: info@fsci.com
Website: http://www.fsci.com
Purpose: To attract minority students into careers in broadcasting.
Eligibility: Applicants must be college sophomores enrolled in a broadcast, marketing or journalism curriculum at a college or vocational-technical school, be of non-white origin, and have a minimum 2.5 GPA. Residents outside of Washington, Oregon, Idaho, Montana and must apply scholarship funds to colleges in those states. Residents of those states may apply scholarship awards to out-of-state schools.
Target applicant:
  College students
  Adult students
Minimum GPA: None.
Amount: Varies.
Number of awards: Varies.
Deadline: April 30.
How to apply: Applications are available online.

(467) · Florence C. and Robert H. Lister Fellowship

Crow Canyon Archeological Center
23390 Road K
Cortez, CO 81321-9908
Phone: 800-422-8975
Email: schoolprograms@crowcanyon.org
Website: http://www.crowcanyon.org
Purpose: To assist graduate students in the archeology of American Indian cultures of the Southwest.
Eligibility: Applicants must be enrolled in a North American Ph.D. program and have projects based on archaeological, ethnoarchaeological or paleoenvironmental research in the southwestern United States and northern Mexico.
Target applicant:
  Graduate school students
  Adult students
Minimum GPA: None.
Amount: $5,000.
Number of awards: Varies.
Deadline: Varies.
How to apply: Applications are available online.

(468) · Frances M. Schwartz Fellowship

American Numismatic Society
96 Fulton Street
New York, NY 10038
Phone: 212-571-4470
Fax: 212-571-4479
Email: info@numismatics.org
Website: http://www.amnumsoc.org
Purpose: To award fellowships in support of the study of numismatics and museum methodology at the American Numismatic Society.
Eligibility: Applicants must hold a B.A. or equivalent.
Target applicant:
  Graduate school students
  Adult students
Minimum GPA: None.
Amount: Up to $5,000.
Number of awards: Varies.
Deadline: Varies.
How to apply: Applications are available online or by mail.

(469) · Francis Walton Memorial Scholarship

American Radio Relay League Foundation
225 Main Street
Newington, CT 06111
Phone: 860-594-0397
Fax: 860-594-0259
Email: foundation@arrl.org
Website: http://www.arrl.org
Purpose: To assist ham radio operators in furthering their educations.
Eligibility: Applicants must have at least five words per minute certification, be residents of the ARRL Central Division (Illinois, Indiana or Wisconsin) and pursue a bachelor's or graduate degree at a regionally-accredited institution.
Target applicant:
  High school students
  College students
  Graduate school students
  Adult students

Minimum GPA: None.
Amount: $500.
Number of awards: Varies.
Deadline: February 1.
How to apply: Applications are available online but must be mailed in.

(470) · Fraternal Order of Eagles Memorial Foundation

Fraternal Order of Eagles
1623 Gateway Circle S.
Grove City, OH 43123
Phone: 614-883-2200
Fax: 614-883-2201
Email: assistance@foe.com
Website: http://www.foe.com
Purpose: To provide financial support for post-secondary education to the children of Eagles.
Eligibility: Applicants must be the children of Eagles who lost their lives while serving in the military or in the commission of their daily employment. Applicants must have a 2.0 minimum GPA.
Target applicant:
    High school students
    College students
    Graduate school students
Minimum GPA: 2.0
Amount: Up to $6,000.
Number of awards: Varies.
Scholarship may be renewable.
Deadline: Varies.
How to apply: Eligible juniors in high school will be sent a form requesting post high school plans, and eligible seniors will be mailed the scholarship application form.

(471) · Fred R. McDaniel Memorial Scholarship

American Radio Relay League Foundation
225 Main Street
Newington, CT 06111
Phone: 860-594-0397
Fax: 860-594-0259
Email: foundation@arrl.org
Website: http://www.arrl.org
Purpose: To assist ham radio operators in furthering their educations.
Eligibility: Applicants must have at least a general ham radio license, be residents of and attend a post-secondary institution in the FCC Fifth Call District (Texas, Oklahoma, Arkansas, Louisiana, Mississippi or New Mexico) and be studying for a bachelor's or graduate degree in electronics, communications or a related field. Preference is given to applicants with a 3.0 GPA or higher.
Target applicant:
    College students
    Graduate school students
    Adult students
Minimum GPA: None.
Amount: $500.
Number of awards: 1.
Deadline: February 1.
How to apply: Applications are available online but must be sent in by mail.

(472) · Frederic G. Melcher Scholarship

Association for Library Service to Children
50 E. Huron Street
Chicago, IL 60611
Phone: 800-545-2433
Fax: 312-944-7671
Email: alsc@ala.org
Website: http://www.ala.org/alsc
Purpose: To support students who want to become children's librarians.
Eligibility: Applicants must intend to pursue an MLS degree, plan to work in children's librarianship and be U.S. or Canadian citizens. Selection is based on academic excellence, leadership and desire to work with children in any type of library.
Target applicant:
    College students
    Graduate school students
    Adult students
Minimum GPA: None.
Amount: $6,000.
Number of awards: 2.
Deadline: March 1.
How to apply: Applications are available online.

(473) · Frederick Burkhardt Residential Fellowships for Recently Tenured Scholars

American Council of Learned Societies (ACLS)
633 Third Avenue
New York, NY 10017-6795
Phone: 212-697-1505
Fax: 212-949-8058
Email: sfisher@acls.org
Website: http://www.acls.org
Purpose: To support scholars researching in the humanities field.
Eligibility: Applicants must be recently tenured humanists and must be employed in tenured positions at U.S. degree-granting institutions during the fellowship. An application, a proposal, a bibliography, a publications list, three reference letters and one institutional statement are required. Previous supported research leaves does not affect eligibility.
Target applicant:
    Graduate school students
    Adult students
Minimum GPA: None.
Amount: $75,000.
Number of awards: 11.
Deadline: September 28.
How to apply: Applications are available online.

(474) · FSF Scholarship Program

Funeral Service Foundation
13625 Bishop's Drive
Brookfield, WI 53005
Phone: 877-402-5900
Fax: 262-789-6977
Email: kbuenger@funeralservicefoundation.org
Website: http://www.funeralservicefoundation.org
Purpose: To provide financial assistance for higher education to those working in fields related to funeral service.
Eligibility: Applicants must be undergraduate students enrolled in funeral science programs.

Target applicant:
    College students
    Adult students
Minimum GPA: None.
Amount: Varies.
Number of awards: Varies.
Deadline: March.
How to apply: Applications are available online.

(475) · Fund for American Studies Internships

Fund for American Studies
1706 New Hampshire Avenue NW
Washington, DC 20009
Phone: 800-741-6964
Email: admissions@tfas.org
Website: http://www.dcinternships.org
Purpose: To provide scholarships for students attending one of the Fund's internship programs.
Eligibility: There are programs in comparative political and economic systems, political journalism, business and government, philanthropy and international institutes. Each program includes classes, an internship and special events. Students take classes at Georgetown University and live in downtown Washington, DC. Summer and school-year programs are available.
Target applicant:
    College students
    Adult students
Minimum GPA: None.
Amount: Varies.
Number of awards: Varies.
Deadline: Varies.
How to apply: Applications are available online.

(476) · Future Teacher of America Scholarship--High School

Common Knowledge Scholarship Foundation
P.O. Box 290361
Davie, FL 33329-0361
Phone: 954-262-8553
Email: info@cksf.org
Website: http://www.cksf.org
Purpose: To help high school students interested in teaching.
Eligibility: Applicants must be in grades 9-12 and should be interested in teaching or education as a career. Students first register for free at the website. On specified dates, there is a multiple-choice, online quiz competition that tests the student's knowledge in subjects related to teaching: math, language arts, science, history and common knowledge, with some questions from the sponsor's website. Applicants receive 500 points for each correct answer and lose one point for each second taken to complete a question. The person with the most points at the end is the scholarship winner.
Target applicant:
    High school students
Minimum GPA: None.
Amount: $250.
Number of awards: 2.
Deadline: December 4.
How to apply: Applicants may register online.

(477) · Future Teacher Scholarship

Journalism Education Association Future Teacher Scholarship
Kansas State University
103 Kedzie Hall
Manhattan, KS 66506
Phone: 330-672-8297
Email: cbowen@kent.edu
Website: http://www.jea.org
Purpose: To provide scholarships for upper-level or master's students who intend to teach scholastic journalism.
Eligibility: Applicants must be education majors focusing on learning to teach scholastic journalism at the secondary school level.
Target applicant:
    College students
    Graduate school students
    Adult students
Minimum GPA: None.
Amount: $1,000.
Number of awards: Up to 3.
Deadline: October 1.
How to apply: Application information is available online.

(478) · Gamma Theta Upsilon-Geographical Honor Society

Gamma Theta Upsilon
Dr. Donald Zeigler
Old Dominion University
1181 University Drive
Virginia Beach, VA 23453
Website: http://www.gtuhonors.org
Purpose: To support geography knowledge and awareness by awarding monetary assistance to college and graduate students.
Eligibility: Applicants must be initiated through a Gamma Theta Upsilon chapter.
Target applicant:
    College students
    Graduate school students
    Adult students
Minimum GPA: None.
Amount: $500.
Number of awards: 5.
Deadline: July.
How to apply: Applications are available online.

(479) · Gary Wagner, K3OMI Scholarship

American Radio Relay League Foundation
225 Main Street
Newington, CT 06111
Phone: 860-594-0397
Fax: 860-594-0259
Email: foundation@arrl.org
Website: http://www.arrl.org
Purpose: To support engineering students who are involved in amateur radio.
Eligibility: Applicants must have an amateur radio license of Novice Class or higher. Students may be pursuing a bachelor's degree in any field of engineering. They must be residents of one of the following states: North Carolina, Virginia, West Virginia, Maryland or Tennessee. Preference will be given to students with financial need.

Target applicant:
    High school students
    College students
    Adult students
Minimum GPA: None.
Amount: $1,000.
Number of awards: 1.
Deadline: February 1.
How to apply: Applications are available online.

---

(480) · Gary Yoshimura Scholarship

Public Relations Student Society of America
33 Maiden Lane
11th Floor
New York, NY 10038
Phone: 212-460-1474
Fax: 212-995-0757
Email: prssa@prsa.org
Website: http://www.prssa.org
Purpose: To assist public relations students.
Eligibility: Applicants must be PRSSA members with a minimum 3.0 GPA in the pursuit of higher education in the public relations field. Applicants must submit an essay on personal or professional challenges and a statement on financial need.
Target applicant:
    College students
    Graduate school students
    Adult students
Minimum GPA: 3.0
Amount: $2,400.
Number of awards: 1.
Deadline: January 16.
How to apply: Applications are available online.

---

(481) · GED Jump Start Scholarship

Child Nutrition Foundation
Scholarship Committee
700 S. Washington Street, Suite 300
Alexandria, VA 22314
Phone: 703-739-3900
Email: jcurtis@schoolnutrition.org
Website: http://www.schoolnutrition.org
Purpose: To support School Nutrition Association members in earning a GED.
Eligibility: Applicants must be School Nutrition Association members who do not currently have a GED or high school diploma and plan on earning a GED within a year of receiving the scholarship.
Target applicant:
    College students
    Adult students
Minimum GPA: None.
Amount: $200.
Number of awards: Approximately 20.
Deadline: Applications are accepted throughout the year.
How to apply: Applications are available online.

---

(482) · Gene Carte Student Paper Competition

American Society of Criminology Gene Carte Student Paper Competition
Nancy Rodriguez

Department of Criminology and Criminal Justice, Arizona State University West
4701 W. Thunderbird Road
Glendale, AZ 85306
Phone: 602-543-6601
Fax: 602-543-6658
Email: nancy.rodriguez@asu.edu
Website: http://www.asc41.com
Purpose: To recognize outstanding student works in criminology.
Eligibility: Applicants must be full-time undergraduate or graduate students. The writing competition requires applicants to write on a topic directly related to criminology and must be accompanied by a letter signed by the dean or department chair. Other paper formatting requirements are listed on the website. The first place winner also receives a travel award.
Target applicant:
    College students
    Graduate school students
    Adult students
Minimum GPA: None.
Amount: $200-$500.
Number of awards: 3.
Deadline: April 15.
How to apply: There is no application form. Paper must be mailed in. The paper specifications are on the website.

---

(483) · General Fund Scholarships

American Radio Relay League Foundation
225 Main Street
Newington, CT 06111
Phone: 860-594-0397
Fax: 860-594-0259
Email: foundation@arrl.org
Website: http://www.arrl.org
Purpose: To assist ham radio operators in furthering their educations.
Eligibility: Applicants must have any level of ham radio license.
Target applicant:
    High school students
    College students
    Graduate school students
    Adult students
Minimum GPA: None.
Amount: $1,000.
Number of awards: Varies.
Deadline: February 1.
How to apply: Applications are available online. Completed applications must be submitted by mail.

---

(484) · General Henry H. Arnold Education Grant Program

Air Force Aid Society Inc.
Education Assistance Department
241 18th Street S, Suite 202
Arlington, VA 22202
Phone: 800-429-9475
Fax: 703-607-3022
Website: http://www.afas.org
Purpose: To help Air Force members and their families realize their academic goals.
Eligibility: Applicants must be the dependent sons and daughters of Air Force members, spouses of active duty members or surviving spouses of

Air Force members who died while on active duty or in retired status. They must also be high school seniors or college students enrolled or accepted as full-time undergraduates for the following school year and maintain a minimum 2.0 GPA.

Target applicant:
High school students
College students
Adult students

Minimum GPA: 2.0

Amount: $2,000.

Number of awards: Varies.

Scholarship may be renewable.

Deadline: March 9.

How to apply: Applications are available online.

(485) · George A. Strait Minority Scholarship

American Association of Law Libraries
53 W. Jackson Boulevard
Suite 940
Chicago, IL 60604
Phone: 312-939-4764
Fax: 312-431-1097
Email: scholarships@aall.org
Website: http://www.aallnet.org

Purpose: To encourage minorities to enter careers as law librarians.

Eligibility: Applicants must be a member of a minority group as defined by U.S. government rules, degree candidates in an accredited library or law school, and intend to pursue a career as law librarians. Law library experience is preferred. Applicants must also have financial need and have at least one quarter or semester left after the scholarship is given.

Target applicant:
Graduate school students
Adult students

Minimum GPA: None.

Amount: Varies.

Number of awards: Varies.

Scholarship may be renewable.

Deadline: April 1.

How to apply: Applications are available online, by mail with a self-addressed, stamped envelope, by fax, by phone or by email.

(486) · George and Viola Hoffman Award

Association of American Geographers (AAG) Hoffman Award
Frostburg State University
101 Braddock Road
c/o George White
Frostburg, MD 21532-2303
Phone: 301-687-4000
Email: gwhite@frostburg.edu
Website: http://www.aag.org

Purpose: To support graduate research in Eastern Europe.

Eligibility: Applicants must research toward a master's thesis or doctoral dissertation on a geographical subject in Eastern Europe which includes the countries of East Central and Southeast Europe from Poland south to Romania, Bulgaria and the successor states of the former Yugoslavia. The research topics may be historical or contemporary, systematic or regional, limited to a small area or comparative. Applicants must submit applications including a statement of the research topic, research methods, field of study, schedule and bibliography. Applicants should also submit a letter describing professional achievements and the goals and a letter of support from a sponsoring faculty member.

Target applicant:
Graduate school students
Adult students

Minimum GPA: None.

Amount: $500.

Number of awards: 1.

Deadline: December 31.

How to apply: Application materials are described online.

(487) · George M. Brooker Collegiate Scholarship for Minorities

Institute of Real Estate Management
IREM Foundation Administrator
430 N. Michigan Avenue
Chicago, IL 60611
Phone: 800-837-0706
Fax: 800-338-4736
Website: http://www.irem.org

Purpose: To increase minority participation in the real estate industry.

Eligibility: Applicants must be minorities, be U.S. citizens, declare a major in real estate or a related field, have a minimum 3.0 GPA in the major and have completed two courses in real estate or plan to finish them. Applicants must submit a 500-word essay explaining their reason for pursuing a real estate career. Applicants must also submit three general letters of recommendation and a letter of recommendation from a local IREM chapter officer.

Target applicant:
College students
Graduate school students
Adult students

Minimum GPA: 3.0

Amount: $1,000-$2,500.

Number of awards: 3.

Deadline: March 31.

How to apply: Applications are available online.

(488) · Giles Sutherland Rich Memorial Scholarship

Federal Circuit Bar Association
1620 I Street NW
Suite 900
Washington, DC 20006
Phone: 202-466-3923
Fax: 202-833-1061
Website: http://www.fedcirbar.org

Purpose: To support promising law students who demonstrate financial need.

Eligibility: Applicants must be undergraduate or graduate law students who demonstrate academic ability and financial need. They must submit a one-page statement describing their financial need, their interest in law and their qualifications for the award. Applicants must also submit transcripts and a curriculum vitae.

Target applicant:
College students
Graduate school students
Adult students

Minimum GPA: None.

Amount: $10,000.

Number of awards: 1.

Deadline: April 30.

How to apply: There is no application form.

(489) · Golden Gate Restaurant Association Scholarship

Golden Gate Restaurant Association
Scholarship Foundation
120 Montgomery Street, Suite 1280
San Francisco, CA 94104
Phone: 415-781-5348
Fax: 415-781-3925
Email: ggra@ggra.org
Website: http://www.ggra.org
Purpose: To provide scholarships for college students who wish to pursue a career in the restaurant/food service industry.
Eligibility: Applicants must be California residents at time of application submission and pursue a major in food service.
Target applicant:
  High school students
  College students
  Adult students
Minimum GPA: None.
Amount: Up to $5,000.
Number of awards: Varies.
Deadline: March 31.
How to apply: Applications are available online or by mail.

(490) · Grades 7-12 Excellence of Scholarship Awards

National Council for Geographic Education
Jacksonville State University
206-A Martin Hall
700 Pelham Road North
Jacksonville, AL 36265-1602
Phone: 256-782-5293
Fax: 256-782-5336
Email: ncge@jsu.edu
Website: http://www.ncge.org
Purpose: To recognize outstanding geography students.
Eligibility: Nominators must be NCGE members who teach grades 7-12 geography courses and who nominate students in their classes. Only one student in each section or class may be nominated.
Target applicant:
  Junior high students or younger
  High school students
Minimum GPA: None.
Amount: Varies.
Number of awards: Varies.
Deadline: March 25.
How to apply: Nominating materials are described online.

(491) · Grants for Research in Broadcasting

National Association of Broadcasters
1771 N Street NW
Washington, DC 20036
Phone: 202-429-5300
Fax: 202-429-4199
Email: kfox@nab.org
Website: http://www.nab.org
Purpose: To support academic research on economic, business, policy and social issues important to policy makers and station managers in the network broadcast industry.
Eligibility: Applicants may be academic faculty, graduate students or undergraduate seniors. Research issues may include the economic and social dynamics of digital TV multicasting, broadcasting's public service role during natural disasters, adoption of HD radio, impact of new regulations, analysis of audience response to digital broadcasting, impact of new technologies, consumer media habits, effectiveness of local news programs, trends in audience measurement technologies, commercial advertising effectiveness, impact of non-response on media research, training future broadcasters and the importance of television and radio advertising on local and national economies.
Target applicant:
  College students
  Graduate school students
  Adult students
Minimum GPA: None.
Amount: Varies.
Number of awards: 4-6.
Deadline: Varies.
How to apply: Applications are available online.

(492) · Hagley-Winterthur Fellowships in Arts and Industries

Hagley Museum and Library
Center for the History of Business, Technology and Society
P.O. Box 3630
Wilmington, DE 19807-0630
Phone: 302-655-2400
Fax: 302-658-3188
Website: http://www.hagley.org
Purpose: To support research fellowships for projects focusing on the relationship between economic life and the arts, including design architecture, crafts and the fine arts.
Eligibility: Fellowships last for one to six months and are available to students and independent professionals to perform serious scholarly research. Fellows may use collections of the Winterthur Museum, Gardens and Library and the Hagley Museum and Library.
Target applicant:
  High school students
  College students
  Graduate school students
  Adult students
Minimum GPA: None.
Amount: Up to $1,400 per month.
Number of awards: Varies.
Deadline: December 1.
How to apply: Applications are available online. For more information, contact Dr. Philip Scranton at the museum at pscranton@hagley.org.

(493) · Harrell Family Fellowship

American Center of Oriental Research (ACOR)
656 Beacon Street, 5th Floor
Boston, MA 02215
Phone: 617-353-6571
Fax: 617-353-6575
Email: acor@bu.edu
Website: http://www.bu.edu/acor
Purpose: To assist a graduate student with expenses on an archaeological project in Jordan.
Eligibility: Applicants must be graduate students in a program approved by a recognized academic review body.
Target applicant:
  Graduate school students
  Adult students

Minimum GPA: None.
Amount: $1,500.
Number of awards: 1.
Deadline: February 1.
How to apply: Applications are available online.

(494) · Harry A. Applegate Scholarship

DECA Inc.
1908 Association Drive
Reston, VA 20191-1594
Phone: 703-860-5000
Fax: 703-860-4013
Email: kathy_onion@deca.org
Website: http://www.deca.org
Purpose: To reward current active members of DECA, the high school division or Delta Epsilon Chi, the college division of DECA.
Eligibility: Applicants must plan to be full-time students at a two-year or four-year program in marketing, entrepreneurship or management. This award is based on merit, not financial need, but applicants may include financial need statements for review. Applicants should submit transcripts, test scores, a statement of club participation, proof of leadership outside DECA, three recommendation letters and proof of membership.
Target applicant:
　High school students
　College students
　Adult students
Minimum GPA: None.
Amount: Varies.
Number of awards: Varies.
Deadline: Check with your state or provincial advisor about deadlines.
How to apply: Applications are available online and should be submitted to state/provincial DECA advisors.

(495) · Harry S. Truman Research Grant

Harry S. Truman Library Institute for National and International Affairs
Grants Administrator
500 W. U.S. Highway 24
Independence, MO 64050
Phone: 816-268-8248
Fax: 816-268-8299
Email: lisa.sullivan@nara.gov
Website: http://www.trumanlibrary.org
Purpose: To promote the Truman Library as a center for research.
Eligibility: Graduate students and post-doctoral scholars are most encouraged to apply, but others completing advanced research will be considered. Preference is given to research dealing with enduring public policy and foreign policy issues that have a high chance of being published or otherwise shared publicly. Applicants can receive up to two research grants in a five-year period. Grant winners must submit a report at the end of their studies.
Target applicant:
　Graduate school students
　Adult students
Minimum GPA: None.
Amount: Up to $2,500.
Number of awards: Varies.

Deadline: April 1 and October 1.
How to apply: Applications are available online.

(496) · Harry S. Truman Undergraduate Student Grant

Harry S. Truman Library Institute for National and International Affairs
Grants Administrator
500 W. U.S. Highway 24
Independence, MO 64050
Phone: 816-268-8248
Fax: 816-268-8299
Email: lisa.sullivan@nara.gov
Website: http://www.trumanlibrary.org
Purpose: To promote the Truman Library as a center for research.
Eligibility: Applicants must be writing a senior thesis on an aspect of the life and career of Harry S. Truman or public and foreign policy issues that were prominent during the Truman years, describe in writing the proposed project and show how using the Truman Library for research will help their future development. Grant winners must submit a written report on their research.
Target applicant:
　College students
　Adult students
Minimum GPA: None.
Amount: Up to $1,000.
Number of awards: 1.
Deadline: September 30.
How to apply: There is no application form.

(497) · Healy Scholarship

American Society of Travel Agents (ASTA) Foundation Inc.
1101 King Street
Suite 200
Alexandria, VA 22314
Phone: 703-739-2782
Fax: 703-684-8319
Email: scholarship@astahq.com
Website: http://www.astanet.com
Purpose: To encourage study in the field of travel and tourism.
Eligibility: Applicants must be admitted to or enrolled in a four-year college or university, be enrolled in travel and tourism classes, have a minimum 2.5 GPA and write a 500-word paper suggesting improvements in the travel industry. Applicants must be residents, citizens or legal aliens of the U.S. or Canada.
Target applicant:
　College students
　Adult students
Minimum GPA: 2.5
Amount: $2,000.
Number of awards: 1.
Deadline: July 27.
How to apply: Applications are available online.

(498) · Henry B. Gonzalez Award

Financial Markets Center
Gonzalez Award
P.O. Box 334
Philomont, VA 20131
Phone: 540-338-7754
Fax: 540-338-7757
Website: http://www.fmcenter.org

Purpose: To promote institutional reforms that make the central bank more effective.

Eligibility: Applicants must submit a paper on the subject of central bank reform. Paper should be no longer than 15,000 words, not including footnotes, endnotes and references. Preference is given to clearly written entries accessible to a broad audience.

Target applicant:
College students
Graduate school students
Adult students

Minimum GPA: None.

Amount: $2,500.

Number of awards: Varies.

Deadline: Varies.

How to apply: There is no official application form.

(499) · Henry Belin du Pont Dissertation Fellowship

Hagley Museum and Library
Center for the History of Business, Technology and Society
P.O. Box 3630
Wilmington, DE 19807-0630
Phone: 302-655-2400
Fax: 302-658-3188
Website: http://www.hagley.org

Purpose: To provide four-month fellowships for doctoral students performing dissertation research.

Eligibility: Applicants must be doctoral students who have completed all course work and are performing dissertation research. Research topics should involve historical questions and should relate to the collections in the Hagley Library. Fellows will receive housing, office space, a computer and Internet access. A presentation is required at the end of the residence period.

Target applicant:
Graduate school students
Adult students

Minimum GPA: None.

Amount: $6,000.

Number of awards: Varies.

Deadline: November 15.

How to apply: Applications are available online. For more information contact Dr. Roger Horowitz at rhorowitz@hagley.org.

(500) · Henry J. Reilly Memorial Scholarship

Reserve Officers Association of the U.S.
Ms. Chandra Oliphant
One Constitution Avenue NE
Washington, DC 20002
Phone: 202-479-2200
Fax: 202-479-0416
Email: coliphant@roa.org
Website: http://www.roa.org

Purpose: To help Reserve Officers Association members and their families.

Eligibility: Applicants must have registered for the draft and be members of the ROA or be the children or grandchildren of members.

Target applicant:
High school students
College students
Graduate school students
Adult students

Minimum GPA: None.

Amount: $500.

Number of awards: Varies.

Scholarship may be renewable.

Deadline: April.

How to apply: Contact the ROA offices for application information.

(501) · Herbert Hoover Presidential Library Association Travel Grant Program

Herbert Hoover Presidential Library Association
P.O. Box 696
West Branch, IA 52358
Phone: 800-828-0475
Fax: 319-643-2391
Email: scholarship@hooverassociation.org
Website: http://www.hooverassociation.org

Purpose: To provide financial aid to individuals to research at the Herbert Hoover Presidential Library in West Branch, Iowa.

Eligibility: Applicants must be current graduate students, post-doctoral scholars or independent researchers. Applicants must also ensure that the library's contents will meet their research needs before applying.

Target applicant:
Graduate school students
Adult students

Minimum GPA: None.

Amount: $500 - $1,500.

Number of awards: Varies.

Deadline: March 1.

How to apply: Applications are available online.

(502) · Holland America Line-Westours Inc. Research Grant

American Society of Travel Agents (ASTA) Foundation Inc.
1101 King Street
Suite 200
Alexandria, VA 22314
Phone: 703-739-2782
Fax: 703-684-8319
Email: scholarship@astahq.com
Website: http://www.astanet.com

Purpose: To fund research projects in the travel and tourism field.

Eligibility: Applicants must be enrolled at a travel school, community or junior college, college or university with proof of enrollment in travel courses, have a minimum 2.5 GPA and be residents, citizens or legal aliens of the U.S. or Canada. Research proposals must be based on one of five areas listed on the website. Funds are awarded based on proposals submitted by students which include an abstract/summary on the intended topic of research, purpose of study, methodology, cost of research, objectives and timeline. This may be a school, class or individual project.

Target applicant:
College students
Adult students

Minimum GPA: 2.5

Amount: Varies.

Number of awards: 2.

Deadline: July 27.

How to apply: Applications are available online.

(503) · Holocaust Remembrance Project Essay Contest

Holland and Knight Charitable Foundation
P.O. Box 2877
Tampa, FL 33601
Phone: 866-HK-CARES
Email: holocaust@hklaw.com
Website: http://www.holocaust.hklaw.com
Purpose: To reward high school students who write essays about the Holocaust.
Eligibility: Applicants must be age 19 and under who are currently enrolled as high school students in grades 9 to 12 (including home-schooled students), high school seniors or students who are enrolled in a high school equivalency program and be residents of either the United States or Mexico or United States citizens living abroad. Applicants should submit essays about the Holocaust and entry forms. Every essay must include works cited, a reference page or a bibliography. First place winners will receive free trips to Washington, DC.
Target applicant:
   High school students
Minimum GPA: None.
Amount: $10,000.
Number of awards: Varies.
Deadline: May 1.
How to apply: Essays may be submitted online.

(504) · Horace Mann Scholarship

Horace Mann Insurance Companies
1 Horace Mann Plaza
Springfield, IL 62715
Phone: 800-999-1030
Website: http://www.horacemann.com
Purpose: To help public and private K-12 educators.
Eligibility: Applicants must be an educator currently employed by a U.S. public or private school and planning to enter a two- or four-year college or university. Applicants must also have at least two or more years of teaching experience. Selection is based on an essay and school and community activities. The program is not open to residents of Hawaii, New Jersey and New York.
Target applicant:
   College students
   Adult students
Minimum GPA: None.
Amount: $1,000-$5,000.
Number of awards: 16.
Deadline: March 12.
How to apply: Applications are available online.

(505) · Horace Samuel and Marion Galbraith Merrill Travel Grants in Twentieth-Century American Political History

Organization of American Historians
112 N. Bryan Avenue
P.O. Box 5457
Bloomington, IN 47408
Phone: 812-855-9852
Fax: 812-855-0696
Email: awards@oah.org
Website: http://www.oah.org

Purpose: Named after a University of Maryland political historian and his wife, the Horace Samuel and Marion Galbraith Merrill Travel Grants seek to perpetuate the couple's desire to assist fledgling scholars and authors.
Eligibility: The award provides stipends, access to research collections and opportunities to interview current and former public figures in Washington, DC. Only applications from current OAH members are accepted.
Target applicant:
   Junior high students or younger
   High school students
   College students
   Graduate school students
   Adult students
Minimum GPA: None.
Amount: $500-$3,000.
Number of awards: Varies.
Deadline: December 1.
How to apply: A copy of a completed submission package (clearly labeled "Merrill Travel Grants") must be mailed directly to each selector. The required contents of the package and the names and addresses of the selectors are available online.

(506) · HORIZONS Foundation Scholarship

Women In Defense
HORIZONS Foundation
c/o National Defense Industrial Association
2111 Wilson Boulevard, Suite 400
Arlington, VA 22201
Phone: 703-247-2552
Fax: 703-527-6945
Email: jcasey@ndia.org
Website: http://wid.ndia.org
Purpose: To encourage women to pursue careers related to the national security interests of the United States and to provide development opportunities to women already working in national security fields.
Eligibility: Applicants must be full- or part-time female students at an accredited university or college and must have reached at least junior level status. Applicants must also demonstrate an interest in a career related to national security and defense, have a minimum GPA of 3.25 and demonstrate financial need. Preference is given to students in security studies, military history, government relations, engineering, computer science, physics, mathematics, business, law, international relations, political science, or economics.
Target applicant:
   College students
   Graduate school students
   Adult students
Minimum GPA: 3.25
Amount: Varies.
Number of awards: Varies.
Deadline: November 1 and July 1.
How to apply: Applications are available online.

(507) · HSMAI Foundation Scholarship

Hospitality Sales and Marketing Association International (HSMAI)
8201 Greensboro Drive, Suite 300
McLean, VA 22102
Phone: 703-610-9024
Fax: 703-610-9005
Email: info@hsmai.org

Website: http://www.hsmai.org
Purpose: To assist students pursuing a career in hospitality sales and marketing.
Eligibility: For the $2,000 scholarships, applicants must be full-time undergraduate or graduate students pursuing a career in hospitality sales and marketing. For the $500 scholarships, applicants must be part-time associate's, bachelor's or graduate students pursuing a career in hospitality sales and marketing.
Target applicant:
    College students
    Graduate school students
    Adult students
Minimum GPA: None.
Amount: $500-$2,000.
Number of awards: 4.
Deadline: May 31.
How to apply: Applications are available online.

(508) · Huntington Fellowships

Huntington Library, Art Collections and Botanical Gardens
1151 Oxford Road
San Marino, CA 91108
Phone: 626-405-2194
Fax: 626-449-5703
Email: cpowell@huntington.org
Website: http://www.huntington.org
Purpose: To provide fellowships to doctoral students and recipients in British and American history, literature, art history and the history of science and medicine.
Eligibility: Applicants must have a Ph.D. or equivalent or be doctoral candidates at the dissertation stage. Cover sheets, project descriptions, curriculum vitae and three letters of recommendation are required.
Target applicant:
    Graduate school students
    Adult students
Minimum GPA: None.
Amount: $10,000.
Number of awards: More than 100.
Deadline: December 15.
How to apply: Application materials are described online.

(509) · Huntington-British Academy Fellowships for Study in Great Britain

Huntington Library, Art Collections and Botanical Gardens
1151 Oxford Road
San Marino, CA 91108
Phone: 626-405-2194
Fax: 626-449-5703
Email: cpowell@huntington.org
Website: http://www.huntington.org
Purpose: To offer scholars exchange fellowships to research British and American history, literature, art history and the history of science and medicine.
Eligibility: Applicants must have a Ph.D. or equivalent. Applicants must submit cover sheets, project descriptions, curriculum vitae and three letters of recommendation.
Target applicant:
    Graduate school students
    Adult students
Minimum GPA: None.
Amount: Varies.

Number of awards: Varies.
Deadline: December 15.
How to apply: There is no application form, and application materials are described online.

(510) · IAFC Foundation Scholarship

International Association of Fire Chiefs Foundation
4025 Fair Ridge Drive
Fairfax, VA 22033-2868
Phone: 571-344-5410
Email: iafcfoun@msn.com
Website: http://www.iafcf.org
Purpose: To assist students in fire sciences or related academic programs.
Eligibility: Applicants must be active members with a minimum of three years volunteer work, two years paid work or a combination of paid and volunteer work of three years with a state, county, provincial, municipal, community, industrial or federal fire department who will use the scholarship at an accredited institution of higher education. Students must submit application forms, statements, a list of credits and a transcript. Preference is given to those demonstrating need, desire and initiative.
Target applicant:
    College students
    Graduate school students
    Adult students
Minimum GPA: None.
Amount: $4,000.
Number of awards: Varies.
Deadline: August 1.
How to apply: Applications are available online.

(511) · IEHA Scholarship

International Executive Housekeepers Association (IEHA) Education Foundation
1001 Eastwind Drive, Suite 301
Westerville, OH 43081-3361
Phone: 800-200-6342
Fax: 614-895-1248
Email: excel@ieha.org
Website: http://www.ieha.org
Purpose: To support IEHA members who are pursuing undergraduate or associate's degrees or IEHA certification.
Eligibility: Applicants must submit a 2,000-word manuscript about an issue in the housekeeping industry. The winning manuscript will be selected by a panel of judges and published.
Target applicant:
    College students
    Adult students
Minimum GPA: None.
Amount: Up to $800.
Number of awards: Varies.
Deadline: January 10.
How to apply: Applications are available online.

(512) · IFEC Scholarships Award

International Foodservice Editorial Council (IFEC)
P.O. Box 491
Hyde Park, NY 12538
Phone: 845-229-6973

Email: ifec@aol.com
Website: http://www.ifec-is-us.com
Purpose: To assist students interested in foodservice combined with communication arts.
Eligibility: Applicants must be enrolled at a post-secondary, degree-granting educational institution and must demonstrate training, skill and interest in the foodservice industry and communication arts. Eligible majors from foodservice and communications areas include culinary arts, hotel/restaurant/hospitality management, dietetics, nutrition, food science/technology, journalism, public relations, mass communication, English, broadcast journalism, marketing, photography, graphic arts and related studies.
Target applicant:
　College students
　Graduate school students
　Adult students
Minimum GPA: None.
Amount: Varies.
Number of awards: Varies.
Deadline: March 15.
How to apply: Applications are available online.

---

(513) · IFSEA Worthy Goal Scholarship

International Food Service Executives Association
Joseph Quagliano
8824 Stancrest Drive
Las Vegas, NV 89134
Phone: 502-589-3602
Website: http://www.ifsea.com
Purpose: To help students receive food service management training beyond the high school level.
Eligibility: Applicants must be enrolled or accepted at a college as a full-time student in a food service related major. Students must provide a financial statement, personal statement, list of work experience and professional activities, transcripts, recommendations and a statement describing how the scholarship would help them reach their goals.
Target applicant:
　High school students
　College students
　Graduate school students
　Adult students
Minimum GPA: None.
Amount: $500-$1,000.
Number of awards: Varies.
Scholarship may be renewable.
Deadline: February 1.
How to apply: Applications are available online.

---

(514) · IHS Journalism Internships

Institute for Humane Studies at George Mason University
3301 N. Fairfax Drive
Suite 440
Arlington, VA 22201
Phone: 800-697-8799
Fax: 703-993-4890
Email: ihs@gmu.edu
Website: http://www.theihs.org
Purpose: To offer students reporting experience.
Eligibility: Applicants must be current college students, graduates, graduate students or professional students and demonstrate interest in journalism and an understanding of the principles of a free society.

Target applicant:
　College students
　Graduate school students
　Adult students
Minimum GPA: None.
Amount: $1,500 + internship, travel and lodging expenses.
Number of awards: Varies.
Deadline: January 30.
How to apply: Applications are available online.

---

(515) · IMA Memorial Education Fund Scholarship

Institute of Management Accountants (IMA)
10 Paragon Drive
Montvale, NJ 07645-1760
Phone: 800-638-4427
Email: students@imanet.org
Website: http://www.imanet.org
Purpose: To support students in fields related to management accounting.
Eligibility: Applicants must be full- and part-time undergraduate and graduate students, be IMA student members and declare which four- or five-year management accounting, financial management or information technology related program they plan to pursue as a career or list a related field. Candidates should submit applications, resumes, transcripts, two recommendations and statements. Advanced degree students must pass one part of the CMA/CFM certification.
Target applicant:
　College students
　Graduate school students
　Adult students
Minimum GPA: 2.8
Amount: $2,500.
Number of awards: Varies.
Deadline: February 15.
How to apply: Applications are available online.

---

(516) · Imagine America scholarship

Imagine America Foundation
1101 Connecticut Avenue NW
Suite 901
Washington, DC 20036
Phone: 202-336-6724
Fax: 202-408-8102
Email: kerryt@career.org
Website: http://www.imagine-america.org
Purpose: To help high school seniors pursue a postsecondary career education.
Eligibility: Applicants must have a minimum 2.5 high school GPA, demonstrate financial need and have demonstrated community service during their senior year.
Target applicant:
　High school students
Minimum GPA: 2.5
Amount: $1,000.
Number of awards: Varies.
Deadline: October 31.
How to apply: Applications are available online.

(517) · IMCEA Scholarships

International Military Community Executives Association (IMCEA)
1530 Dunwoody Village
Parkway Suite 203
Atlanta, GA 30338
Phone: 770-396-2101
Fax: 770-396-2198
Email: imcea@imcea.com
Website: http://www.imcea.com
Purpose: To provide scholarships for high school students and military welfare and recreation professionals seeking to further their educations.
Eligibility: High school or college applicants must be children of IMCEA members. Candidates must provide information about their activities, honors and awards and submit an essay on the provided topic.
Target applicant:
    High school students
    College students
    Graduate school students
    Adult students
Minimum GPA: None.
Amount: Varies.
Number of awards: Varies.
Deadline: Varies.
How to apply: Applications are available online.

(518) · Indianhead Division Scholarships

Second Indianhead Division Association
P.O. Box 460
Buda, TX 78610
Phone: 512-295-5324
Email: warriorvet@verizon.net
Website: http://www.2ida.org
Purpose: To support the children and grandchildren of veterans from the Second Indianhead Division Association.
Eligibility: Applicants' parents or grandparents must have been members of the association for at least three years, or they must have been killed while serving with the Second Infantry Division.
Target applicant:
    High school students
    College students
    Adult students
Minimum GPA: None.
Amount: $1,000.
Number of awards: Varies.
Scholarship may be renewable.
Deadline: Varies.
How to apply: Applications are available by phone.

(519) · Institute for Court Management Scholarship

American Association of Law Libraries
53 W. Jackson Boulevard
Suite 940
Chicago, IL 60604
Phone: 312-939-4764
Fax: 312-431-1097
Email: scholarships@aall.org
Website: http://www.aallnet.org
Purpose: To support education at the Institute for Court Management.
Eligibility: Applicants must belong to the AALL and be a member of the State, Court & County Law Libraries Special Interest Section. Applicants should submit a resume, a registration form and a statement explaining why they want to continue their education with the Institute for Court Management and the seminar or conference they want to attend.
Target applicant:
    Graduate school students
    Adult students
Minimum GPA: None.
Amount: $1,700.
Number of awards: 2.
Deadline: April 1.
How to apply: Applications are available online.

(520) · International Association of Fire Chiefs Foundation Scholarship

Explorers Learning for Life
P.O. Box 152079
Irving, TX 75015
Phone: 972-580-2433
Fax: 972-580-2137
Email: pchestnu@lflmail.org
Website: http://www.learningforlife.org/exploring
Purpose: To support students who are pursuing careers in fire sciences.
Eligibility: Students must be graduating high school seniors, active fire service Explorers and members of a fire department. Applicants must submit three letters of recommendation and an essay.
Target applicant:
    High school students
Minimum GPA: None.
Amount: $500.
Number of awards: 2.
Deadline: July 1.
How to apply: Applications are available online.

(521) · International Order of Alhambra Scholarship

International Order of Alhambra
4200 Leeds Avenue
Baltimore, MD 21229
Phone: 410-242-0660
Fax: 410-536-5729
Email: hq@orderalhambra.org
Website: http://www.orderalhambra.org
Purpose: To provide financial assistance to undergraduate students who wish to become special education teachers or to those who give care to the permanently disabled.
Eligibility: One of the purposes of the organization is to provide assistance, education and residences to the developmentally disabled.
Target applicant:
    High school students
    College students
    Adult students
Minimum GPA: None.
Amount: Varies.
Number of awards: Varies.
Deadline: Varies.
How to apply: Contact the organization for more information.

(522) · IRARC Memorial Joseph P. Rubino WA4MMD Scholarship

American Radio Relay League Foundation
225 Main Street
Newington, CT 06111
Phone: 860-594-0397
Fax: 860-594-0259
Email: foundation@arrl.org
Website: http://www.arrl.org
Purpose: To provide financial assistance to amateur radio operators who are seeking an undergraduate degree or electronic technician certification.
Eligibility: Applicants must hold an active Amateur Radio License in any class and be studying at an accredited institution. They must have a minimum GPA of 2.5. Preference is given to Florida residents, particularly those of Brevard County, and those with need and lower GPAs.
Target applicant:
  High school students
  College students
  Adult students
Minimum GPA: None.
Amount: $750.
Number of awards: Varies.
Deadline: February 1.
How to apply: Applications are available online.

(523) · Isabel M. Herson Scholarship in Education

Zeta Phi Beta Sorority Inc. National Educational Foundation
1734 New Hampshire Avenue NW
Washington, DC 20009
Email: ihq@zphib1920.org
Website: http://www.zphib1920.org
Purpose: To support education students.
Eligibility: Applicants must be current or future full-time undergraduate or graduate education students. They must submit three letters of recommendation, transcripts and a personal essay.
Target applicant:
  High school students
  College students
  Graduate school students
  Adult students
Minimum GPA: None.
Amount: $500-$1,000.
Number of awards: 1.
Deadline: February 1.
How to apply: Applications are available online or by sending a self-addressed, stamped envelope.

(524) · J. Franklin Jameson Fellowship in American History

American Historical Association
400 A Street SE
Washington, DC 20003
Phone: 202-544-2422
Fax: 202-544-8307
Email: info@historians.org
Website: http://www.historians.org
Purpose: To support one semester of scholarly research in the Library of Congress collections.

Eligibility: Applicants must hold a Ph.D. or equivalent, must have earned the degree within the past seven years and may not have published a book-length historical work. Projects should focus on American history.
Target applicant:
  Graduate school students
  Adult students
Minimum GPA: None.
Amount: $5,000.
Number of awards: Varies.
Deadline: March 15.
How to apply: Application instructions are available online.

(525) · Jack Kinnaman Scholarship

National Education Association
NEA-Retired, Room 410
1201 16th Street NW
Washington, DC 20036
Phone: 202-822-7149
Website: http://www.nea.org
Purpose: To honor the memory of NEA-retired vice president and former advisory council member Jack Kinnaman.
Eligibility: Applicants must be NEA student members, major in education and have a minimum 2.5 GPA. An essay describing activities in NEA, a brief paragraph describing financial need, two letters of recommendation and a copy of the most recent transcript are required.
Target applicant:
  College students
  Adult students
Minimum GPA: 2.5
Amount: Varies.
Number of awards: 1.
Deadline: April 7.
How to apply: Applications are available online.

(526) · James A. Turner, Jr. Memorial Scholarship

American Welding Society Foundation
550 NW LeJeune Road
Miami, FL 33126
Phone: 800-443-9353
Email: info@aws.org
Website: http://www.aws.org
Purpose: To aid those interested in a management career in welding store operations or distributorship.
Eligibility: Applicants must be full-time students pursuing a four-year bachelor's of business degree, plan to enter management careers in welding store operations or distributorship, be high school graduates at least 18 years of age and be employed a minimum of 10 hours per week at a welding distributorship. Preference is given to members of the American Welding Society.
Target applicant:
  College students
  Adult students
Minimum GPA: None.
Amount: $3,000.
Number of awards: 1.
Deadline: January 15.
How to apply: Applications are available online.

(527) · James F. Connolly LexisNexis Academic and Library Solutions Scholarship

American Association of Law Libraries
53 W. Jackson Boulevard
Suite 940
Chicago, IL 60604
Phone: 312-939-4764
Fax: 312-431-1097
Email: scholarships@aall.org
Website: http://www.aallnet.org
Purpose: To support a librarian interested in becoming a law librarian.
Eligibility: Preference will be given to librarians who are interested in government documents. Applicants must be library school graduates with experience working in a law library who intend to obtain a degree at an accredited law school and have careers as law librarians. Applicants should have no more than 36 semester credit hours left before qualifying for the degree and should have financial need.
Target applicant:
    Graduate school students
    Adult students
Minimum GPA: None.
Amount: $3,000.
Number of awards: 1.
Scholarship may be renewable.
Deadline: April 1.
How to apply: Applications are available online, by mail with a self-addressed, stamped envelope, by fax, by phone and by email.

(528) · James J. Hill Research Grants

James J. Hill Research Library
80 W. Fourth Street
Saint Paul, MN 55102
Phone: 651-265-5500
Email: manuscripts@jjhill.org
Website: http://www.jjhill.org
Purpose: To assist scholars whose research requires them to use the business information manuscript collections at the Hill Library.
Eligibility: Applicants must be college or university professors, independent scholars, or Ph.D. candidates who are working on their dissertations. Applications must include a research proposal, projected budget and three letters of recommendation.
Target applicant:
    Graduate school students
    Adult students
Minimum GPA: None.
Amount: $2,000.
Number of awards: Varies.
Deadline: November 1.
How to apply: Applications are available by email, phone or online at http://www.jjhill.org/History/grant_program.html.

(529) · Jane M. Klausman Women in Business Scholarship Fund

Zonta International
557 West Randolph Street
Chicago, IL 60661-2206
Phone: 312-930-5848
Fax: 312-930-0951
Email: zontafdtn@zonta.org
Website: http://www.zonta.org
Purpose: To help female business management majors overcome gender barriers.
Eligibility: Applicants must be eligible to enter their junior or senior year in an undergraduate degree program at an accredited institution when funds are received. Applicants must also have an outstanding academic record in their college career, and they must show intent to complete a business program.
Target applicant:
    College students
    Adult students
Minimum GPA: None.
Amount: $5,000.
Number of awards: 6.
Deadline: April.
How to apply: Applications are available online or from your local Zonta Club.

(530) · Jean Cebik Memorial Scholarship

American Radio Relay League Foundation
225 Main Street
Newington, CT 06111
Phone: 860-594-0397
Fax: 860-594-0259
Email: foundation@arrl.org
Website: http://www.arrl.org
Purpose: To provide scholarship assistance to amateur radio operators.
Eligibility: Applicants must hold a Technician Class Amateur Radio License or higher, and they must be attending a four-year college or university.
Target applicant:
    High school students
    College students
    Adult students
Minimum GPA: None.
Amount: $1000.
Number of awards: 1.
Deadline: February 1.
How to apply: Applications are available online.

(531) · Jennifer C. Groot Fellowship

American Center of Oriental Research (ACOR)
656 Beacon Street, 5th Floor
Boston, MA 02215
Phone: 617-353-6571
Fax: 617-353-6575
Email: acor@bu.edu
Website: http://www.bu.edu/acor
Purpose: To assist students with expenses on an archaeological project.
Eligibility: Applicants must be undergraduate or graduate students with little or no archaeological field experience. Recipients will travel to Jordan for the project.
Target applicant:
    College students
    Graduate school students
    Adult students
Minimum GPA: None.
Amount: $1,500.
Number of awards: At least 2.

Deadline: February 1.
How to apply: Applications are available online but must be submitted by mail.

(532) · Jessica King Scholarship

Association for International Practical Training (AIPT)
10400 Little Patuxent Parkway
Suite 250
Columbia, MD 21044-3519
Phone: 410-997-2200
Fax: 410-992-3924
Email: aipt@aipt.org
Website: http://www.aipt.org
Purpose: To help students in the international hospitality field.
Eligibility: Applicants must be between 18 and 35 years old, have a degree in the hospitality industry or be currently employed for at least one year in the hospitality industry and be fluent in the host country's language. Applicants must also have been offered an overseas position and be participating in an AIPT-sponsored program. The scholarship is based on merit.
Target applicant:
  College students
  Graduate school students
  Adult students
Minimum GPA: None.
Amount: $1,000.
Number of awards: Varies.
Deadline: June 1.
How to apply: Applications are available by email.

(533) · Jewell Hilton Bonner Scholarship

Navy League Foundation
2300 Wilson Boulevard
Arlington, VA 22201
Phone: 800-356-5760
Fax: 703-528-2333
Email: lhuycke@navyleague.org
Website: http://www.navyleague.org
Purpose: To support the dependents and descendants of sea personnel.
Eligibility: Service personnel may be active, reserve, retired or honorably discharged members of the U.S. Navy, Coast Guard, U.S. Flag Merchant Marine, Marine Corps or U.S. Naval Sea Cadet Corps. Students must be high school seniors who plan to enter a college or university in the fall.
Target applicant:
  High school students
Minimum GPA: None.
Amount: $10,000.
Number of awards: 23.
Deadline: March 3.
How to apply: Applications are available online.

(534) · Joe Francis Haircare Scholarship Program

Joe Francis Haircare Scholarship Foundation
P.O. Box 50625
Minneapolis, MN 55405
Phone: 651-769-1757
Fax: 651-459-8371
Website: http://www.joefrancis.com

Purpose: To provide barber and cosmetology students with financial aid.
Eligibility: Applicants must be sponsored by one of the following: a fully accredited, recognized barber or cosmetology school, a licensed salon owner or manager, a full-service distributor or a member of the International Chain Association, Beauty and Barber Supply Institute, Cosmetology Advancement Foundation or National Cosmetology Association. Applicants must be actively enrolled in cosmetology school or planning to enroll during or after the award month of August. Judging is based on financial need, motivation and character.
Target applicant:
  High school students
  College students
  Adult students
Minimum GPA: None.
Amount: $1,000.
Number of awards: Varies.
Deadline: June 1.
How to apply: Applications are available online.

(535) · Joe Perdue Scholarship

Club Foundation
1733 King Street
Alexandria, VA 22314
Phone: 703-739-9500
Fax: 703-739-0124
Email: schaverr@clubfoundation.org
Website: http://www.clubfoundation.org
Purpose: To support students pursuing careers in private club management.
Eligibility: Applicants must be pursuing managerial careers in the private club industry, have completed their freshman year of college, have a minimum 2.5 GPA and be enrolled full-time for the following year. An essay and letters of recommendation are also required.
Target applicant:
  College students
  Adult students
Minimum GPA: 2.5
Amount: $2,500.
Number of awards: Varies.
Deadline: April 13.
How to apply: Applications are available online.

(536) · John Bayliss Radio Scholarship

John Bayliss Radio
P.O. Box 51126
Pacific Grove, CA 93950
Phone: 831-655-5229
Website: http://www.baylissfoundation.org
Purpose: To promote interest in the broadcasting industry.
Eligibility: Applicants must be college juniors, seniors or graduate students majoring in broadcast communications who have a minimum 3.0 GPA.
Target applicant:
  College students
  Graduate school students
  Adult students
Minimum GPA: 3.0
Amount: Varies.
Number of awards: Varies.
Deadline: Varies.
How to apply: Applications are available online.

(537) · John F. Duffy Scholarship/Grant Program

California Peace Officers' Memorial Foundation
P.O. Box 2437
Fair Oaks, CA 95628
Email: cpomf@camemorial.org
Website: http://www.camemorial.org
Purpose: To provide financial assistance to survivors of California peace officers who have died in the line of duty.
Eligibility: Applicants must be spouses, children, stepchildren or adopted children of peace officers who died in the line of duty and are enrolled on the California memorial monument. They must carry no less than six units per quarter or eight units per semester at an accredited college or university, and they must maintain a 2.5 or higher GPA.
Target applicant:
  High school students
  College students
  Graduate school students
  Adult students
Minimum GPA: 2.5
Amount: Varies.
Number of awards: Varies.
Deadline: June 1.
How to apply: Applications are available online.

(538) · John F. Kennedy Profile in Courage Essay Contest

John F. Kennedy Library Foundation
Columbia Point
Boston, MA 02125
Phone: 617-514-1691
Email: profiles@nara.gov
Website: http://www.jfkcontest.org
Purpose: To encourage students to research and write about politics and John F. Kennedy.
Eligibility: Applicants must be in grades 9 through 12 in public or private schools or be home-schooled and write an essay about politics as it relates to John F. Kennedy's book "Profiles in Courage." Essays must have source citations. Applicants must register online before sending essays and have a teacher help with the essay. The winner and teacher will be invited to the Kennedy Library to accept the award, and the winner's teacher will receive a grant.
Target applicant:
  High school students
Minimum GPA: None.
Amount: $500-$3,000.
Number of awards: 7.
Deadline: January 7.
How to apply: Essays may be sent online or by mail.

(539) · John R. Johnson Memorial Scholarship Endowment

American Association of Law Libraries
53 W. Jackson Boulevard
Suite 940
Chicago, IL 60604
Phone: 312-939-4764
Fax: 312-431-1097
Email: scholarships@aall.org
Website: http://www.aallnet.org
Purpose: To encourage current and future law librarians in memory of John Johnson, a prominent law librarian.
Eligibility: Applicants who apply for any of the AALL Educational Scholarships become automatically eligible to receive this award. No separate application is necessary. Applicants must intend to have careers as law librarians. Preference is given to AALL members, but a non-member may apply.
Target applicant:
  Graduate school students
  Adult students
Minimum GPA: None.
Amount: Varies.
Number of awards: Varies.
Scholarship may be renewable.
Deadline: April 1.
How to apply: Applications are available online, by mail with a self-addressed, stamped envelope, by fax, by phone or by email.

(540) · Jolly Green Memorial Scholarship

Jolly Green Association
P.O. Box 965
O'Fallon, IL 62269
Email: bill6100@aol.com
Website: http://www.jollygreen.org/jolly_green_memorial_scholarship.htm
Purpose: To provide financial assistance to dependents of present or former Air Force Combat Rescue or rescue support organization members.
Eligibility: Applicants must be eligible for admission to a college or university and must have demonstrated aptitude for college-level study.
Target applicant:
  High school students
Minimum GPA: None.
Amount: Varies.
Number of awards: Varies.
Deadline: April 15.
How to apply: Applications are available by mail or email.

(541) · Jonathan Jasper Wright Award

National Association of Blacks in Criminal Justice
North Carolina Central University
P.O. Box 19788
Durham, NC 27707
Phone: 919-683-1801
Fax: 919-683-1903
Email: office@nabcj.org
Website: http://www.nabcj.org
Purpose: To award regional and national leadership in the field of criminal justice.
Eligibility: Award recipients will be involved in affecting policy change. Nominator should be a member of NABCJ.
Target applicant:
  College students
  Graduate school students
  Adult students
Minimum GPA: None.
Amount: Varies.
Number of awards: Varies.
Deadline: May 1.
How to apply: Nomination applications are available online.

(542) · Joseph R. Stone Scholarship

American Society of Travel Agents (ASTA) Foundation Inc.
1101 King Street
Suite 200
Alexandria, VA 22314
Phone: 703-739-2782
Fax: 703-684-8319
Email: scholarship@astahq.com
Website: http://www.astanet.com
Purpose: To aid students whose parents work in the travel industry.
Eligibility: Applicants must be undergraduates at a four year college or university, have a minimum 2.5 GPA, provide proof that one parent is employed in the travel industry and submit a 500-word paper on their goals. Applicants must be a resident, citizen or legal alien of the U.S. or Canada.
Target applicant:
    College students
    Adult students
Minimum GPA: 2.5
Amount: $2,400.
Number of awards: 3.
Deadline: July 27.
How to apply: Applications are available online.

(543) · Joseph S. Rumbaugh Historical Oration Contest

National Society of the Sons of the American Revolution
1000 S. Fourth Street
Louisville, KY 40203
Phone: 502-589-1776
Email: contests@sar.org
Website: http://www.sar.org
Purpose: To encourage students to learn more about the Revolutionary War and its impact on modern America.
Eligibility: Applicants must prepare a speech of five to six minutes on some aspect of the Revolutionary War. The contest is open to high school sophomores, juniors and seniors at public, private and parochial high schools, as well as home-schooled students. Eligibility for the national contest is determined by contests on the state and local level.
Target applicant:
    High school students
Minimum GPA: None.
Amount: $200-$3,000.
Number of awards: Varies.
Deadline: Varies.
How to apply: Applications are available from local chapters of Sons of the American Revolution.

(544) · Junior Fellowships

American Institute of Indian Studies
1130 E. 59th Street
Chicago, IL 60637
Phone: 773-702-8638
Email: aiis@uchicago.edu
Website: http://www.indiastudies.org
Purpose: To support doctoral candidates at U.S. universities who wish to travel to India to conduct dissertation research on Indian aspects of their academic discipline.

Eligibility: Applicants must be doctoral candidates at a U.S. university. Junior fellows are affiliated with Indian universities and research mentors. Awards may last up to 11 months.
Target applicant:
    Graduate school students
    Adult students
Minimum GPA: None.
Amount: Varies.
Number of awards: Varies.
Deadline: July 1.
How to apply: Applications are available by mail or email.

(545) · K2TEO Martin J. Green, Sr. Memorial Scholarship

American Radio Relay League Foundation
225 Main Street
Newington, CT 06111
Phone: 860-594-0397
Fax: 860-594-0259
Email: foundation@arrl.org
Website: http://www.arrl.org
Purpose: To provide financial assistance to students who are amateur radio operators.
Eligibility: Applicants must hold a general class or higher amateur radio license. Preference is given to students from ham families.
Target applicant:
    High school students
    College students
    Graduate school students
    Adult students
Minimum GPA: None.
Amount: $1,000.
Number of awards: 1.
Deadline: February 1.
How to apply: Applications are available online.

(546) · Kathern F. Gruber Scholarship Program

Blinded Veterans Association (BVA)
477 H Street, NW
Washington, DC 20001-2694
Phone: 202-371-8880
Email: bva@bva.org
Website: http://www.bva.org
Purpose: To assist the spouses and children of blinded veterans with their higher-learning goals.
Eligibility: Applicants must be the spouses or children of a blind veteran and be accepted or enrolled at an accredited, higher learning institution.
Target applicant:
    High school students
    College students
    Graduate school students
    Adult students
Minimum GPA: None.
Amount: $1,000-$2,000.
Number of awards: 4.
Deadline: April.
How to apply: Contact the BVA for application materials.

(547) · Ken Kashiwahara Scholarship

Radio and Television News Directors Association
1600 K Street NW
Suite 700
Washington, DC 20006
Phone: 202-659-6510
Fax: 202-223-4007
Email: rtnda@rtnda.org
Website: http://www.rtnda.org
Purpose: To honor professional achievements in electronic journalism.
Eligibility: Applicants must be full-time college sophomores or higher with at least one full academic year remaining. Applicants may be enrolled in any major as long as their career intent is television or radio news. Applicants may only apply for one RTNDA scholarship. Preference is given to students of color.
Target applicant:
    College students
    Adult students
Minimum GPA: None.
Amount: $2,500.
Number of awards: 1.
Deadline: May 3.
How to apply: Applications are available online.

(548) · Kit C. King Graduate Scholarship Fund

National Press Photographers Association Kit C. King Graduate Scholarship Fund
Scott R. Sines
Managing Editor, Memphis Commercial-Appeal
495 Union Avenue
Memphis, TN 38103
Phone: 901-529-5843
Email: sines@commercialappeal.com
Website: http://www.nppa.org
Purpose: To support photojournalism students.
Eligibility: Applicants must provide a portfolio, be pursuing an advanced degree in journalism with an emphasis in photojournalism and demonstrate financial need. Applicants may apply to as many NPPA scholarships as desired, but only one award may be granted per applicant.
Target applicant:
    Graduate school students
    Adult students
Minimum GPA: None.
Amount: $1,000.
Number of awards: 1.
Deadline: March 1.
How to apply: Applications are available online.

(549) · L. Phil Wicker Scholarship

American Radio Relay League Foundation
225 Main Street
Newington, CT 06111
Phone: 860-594-0397
Fax: 860-594-0259
Email: foundation@arrl.org
Website: http://www.arrl.org
Purpose: To assist ham radio operators in furthering their educations.
Eligibility: Applicants must have at least a general ham radio license, be residents of and attending school in the ARRL Roanoke Division (North Carolina, South Carolina, Virginia, West Virginia) and be undergraduate or graduate students in electronics, communications or another related field.
Target applicant:
    College students
    Graduate school students
    Adult students
Minimum GPA: None.
Amount: $1,000.
Number of awards: 1.
Deadline: February 1.
How to apply: Applications are available online. Completed applications must be submitted by mail.

(550) · La Fra National President's Scholarship

Ladies Auxiliary of the Fleet Reserve Association
125 N. West Street
Alexandria, VA 22314
Phone: 800-372-1924 x123
Email: mserfra@fra.org
Website: http://www.la-fra.org
Purpose: To support the descendants of sea personnel.
Eligibility: Students must have a father or grandfather who was in the Marine Corps, Coast Guard, Navy, Fleet Reserve, Coast Guard Reserve or Fleet Marine Corps Reserve.
Target applicant:
    High school students
    College students
    Adult students
Minimum GPA: None.
Amount: Varies.
Number of awards: Varies.
Deadline: April 15.
How to apply: Applications are available online.

(551) · La Fra Scholarship

Ladies Auxiliary of the Fleet Reserve Association
125 N. West Street
Alexandria, VA 22314
Phone: 800-372-1924 x123
Email: mserfra@fra.org
Website: http://www.la-fra.org
Purpose: To support the female descendants of sea personnel.
Eligibility: Students must have a father or grandfather who was in the Marine Corps, Coast Guard, Navy, Fleet Reserve, Coast Guard Reserve or Fleet Marine Corps Reserve.
Target applicant:
    High school students
    College students
    Adult students
Minimum GPA: None.
Amount: Varies.
Number of awards: Varies.
Deadline: April 15.
How to apply: Applications are available online.

(552) · La Macchia Family Scholarship

Tourism Cares
585 Washington Street
Canton, MA 02021
Phone: 781-821-5990
Fax: 781-821-8949
Email: carolynv@tourismcares.org
Website: http://www.tourismcares.org
Purpose: To honor the memory of William E. La Macchia, founder of Mark Travel Corporation.
Eligibility: Applicants must be entering their junior or senior year at an accredited four-year institution in Wisconsin, have a GPA of 3.0 or higher and have completed 50 percent or more of the degree requirements in a travel- and tourism-related major.
Target applicant:
    College students
    Adult students
Minimum GPA: 3.0
Amount: $1,000.
Number of awards: 1.
Deadline: April 2.
How to apply: Applications are available online.

(553) · Laurel Fund

Educational Foundation for Women in Accounting
P.O. Box 1925
Southeastern, PA 19399
Phone: 610-407-9229
Fax: 610-644-3713
Email: info@efwa.org
Website: http://www.efwa.org
Purpose: To provide scholarships to women pursuing advanced degrees in accounting.
Eligibility: This award is available to women pursuing a Ph.D. in accounting. The awardees are selected based on scholarship, service and financial need. Applicants must have completed their comprehensive exams before the previous fall semester.
Target applicant:
    Graduate school students
    Adult students
Minimum GPA: None.
Amount: Up to $5,000.
Number of awards: Varies.
Deadline: May 1.
How to apply: Applications are available online.

(554) · Lawrence G. Foster Award for Excellence in Public Relations

Public Relations Student Society of America
33 Maiden Lane
11th Floor
New York, NY 10038
Phone: 212-460-1474
Fax: 212-995-0757
Email: prssa@prsa.org
Website: http://www.prssa.org
Purpose: To assist public relations students.
Eligibility: Applicants must be undergraduate students majoring in public relations who are committed to careers in public relations.

Applicants must submit an essay on what excellence in public relations is and how they plan to achieve excellence in their own careers.
Target applicant:
    College students
    Adult students
Minimum GPA: None.
Amount: $1,500.
Number of awards: 1.
Deadline: June 4.
How to apply: Applications are available online.

(555) · Learning and Leadership Grants

NEA Foundation
1201 16th Street NW
Suite 416
Washington, DC 20036
Phone: 202-822-7840
Fax: 202-822-7779
Email: info-neafoundation@list.nea.org
Website: http://www.neafoundation.org
Purpose: To support public school teachers, public education support professionals and faculty or staff in public institutions of higher education in professional development experiences such as summer institutes or action research.
Eligibility: Applicants must be current public school teachers in grades K-12, public school education support professionals or faculty and staff at public higher education institutions. The professional development must improve practice, curriculum and student achievement. Funds may be used for fees, travel expenses, books or materials. There is also a grant for groups for $5,000.
Target applicant:
    Graduate school students
    Adult students
Minimum GPA: None.
Amount: $2,000.
Number of awards: Varies.
Deadline: February 1, June 1, October 15.
How to apply: Applications are available online. Applications may be submitted at any time and are reviewed three times each year on February 1, June 1 and October 15.

(556) · Legal Opportunity Scholarship Fund

American Bar Association
321 North Clark Street
Chicago, IL 60610
Phone: 312-988-5000
Email: abalsd@abanet.org
Website: http://www.abanet.org/lsd/
Purpose: To encourage members of underrepresented ethnic groups to enter the legal profession.
Eligibility: Applicants must be members of a racial and/or ethnic minority that has been underrepresented in the legal profession. Applicants must be entering, first-year law students, demonstrate financial need and show participation in community service activities. Applicants who have not yet been accepted by a law school may also apply.
Target applicant:
    College students
    Graduate school students
    Adult students
Minimum GPA: None.

Amount: $5,000.
Number of awards: 20.
Scholarship may be renewable.
Deadline: February 22.
How to apply: Applications are available online.

(557) · Lewis A. Kingsley Foundation Scholarship

Naval Sea Cadet Corps
2300 Wilson Boulevard
Arlington, VA 22201-3308
Phone: 800-356-5760
Email: alewis@seacadets.org
Website: http://www.seacadets.org
Purpose: To provide financial assistance to Sea Cadets.
Eligibility: Applicants must be former Sea Cadets attending college full-time at the sophomore level or higher. They musts be employed, earning at least $5,000 per year and maintain a 2.0 or higher GPA. A one- to two- page personal statement, a letter of recommendation and a resume are required.
Target applicant:
   College students
   Adult students
Minimum GPA: 2.0
Amount: $5,000.
Number of awards: Varies.
Deadline: October 22.
How to apply: Applications are available online.

(558) · Litherland Scholarship

International Technology Education Association
Foundation for Technology Education
1914 Association Drive, Suite 201
Reston, VA 20191
Phone: 703-860-2100
Fax: 703-860-0353
Email: bmongold@iteaconnect.org
Website: http://www.iteaconnect.org
Purpose: To provide scholarships for undergraduate students pursuing a career in teaching technology.
Eligibility: Applicants must be members of ITEA, be full-time undergraduate students majoring in technology education teacher preparation and have a minimum 2.5 GPA.
Target applicant:
   College students
   Adult students
Minimum GPA: 2.5
Amount: $1,000.
Number of awards: Varies.
Deadline: December 1.
How to apply: Application information is available online.

(559) · Lodging Management Program (LMP)

American Hotel and Lodging Educational Foundation (AH&LEF)
1201 New York Avenue NW
Suite 600
Washington, DC 20005-3931
Phone: 202-289-3188
Fax: 202-289-3199
Email: chammond@ahlef.org
Website: http://www.ahlef.org
Purpose: To recognize high school students who have completed the two-year LMP curriculum and who have intent to pursue a career in hospitality management.
Eligibility: Applicants must be graduating seniors who have completed the two-year LMP high school program. Students must be employed in the lodging industry or have applied to a post-secondary hospitality institution.
Target applicant:
   High school students
Minimum GPA: 2.0
Amount: $1,000.
Number of awards: Varies.
Deadline: April 15.
How to apply: Applications are available online.

(560) · Lou and Carole Prato Sports Reporting Scholarship

Radio and Television News Directors Association
1600 K Street NW
Suite 700
Washington, DC 20006
Phone: 202-659-6510
Fax: 202-223-4007
Email: rtnda@rtnda.org
Website: http://www.rtnda.org
Purpose: To provide monetary assistance to a student pursuing a career as a sports reporter for radio or television.
Eligibility: Applicants must be full-time college sophomores or higher with at least one full academic year remaining. Applicants may be enrolled in any major but must have a career goal of becoming a sports reporter for television or radio. Applicants may only apply for one RTNDA scholarship.
Target applicant:
   College students
   Adult students
Minimum GPA: None.
Amount: $1,000.
Number of awards: 1.
Deadline: May 3.
How to apply: Applications are available online.

(561) · Lou Hochberg Awards

Orgone Biophysical Research Laboratory
P.O. Box 1148
Ashland, OR 97520
Phone: 541-522-0118
Fax: 541-522-0118
Email: info@orgonelab.org
Website: http://www.orgonelab.org
Purpose: The Orgone Biophysical Research Lab offers a number of awards to students, scholars and journalists through a program set up by Louis Hochberg, a social worker who was dedicated to the sociological discoveries of Wilhelm Reich.
Eligibility: The Lou Hochberg Awards are given to winning theses and dissertations, university and college essays, high school essays and published articles that focus on Reich's sociological work. There are categories for students, scholars or journalists beginning at high school age through adulthood. A suggested list of topics and a bibliography is available online.

Target applicant:
High school students
College students
Graduate school students
Adult students
Minimum GPA: None.
Amount: $500-$1,500.
Number of awards: 5.
Deadline: Varies.
How to apply: Each award has a specific set of instructions for submitting a package for consideration. Guidelines are listed online.

(562) · LTG and Mrs. Joseph M. Heiser Scholarship
U.S. Army Ordnance Corps Association
P.O. Box 377
Aberdeen Proving Ground, MD 21005
Phone: 410-272-8540
Fax: 410-272-8425
Website: http://www.usaocaweb.org/scholarships.htm
Purpose: To honor the memory of LTG Joseph M. Heiser.
Eligibility: Applicants must be active or reserve Ordinance soldiers or OCA members or members or their immediate family. They must write a 300- to 500- word essay about the reasons they are seeking the grant and why they feel they deserve it and a 1,000- to 1,500-word essay on the missions, heritage or history of the U.S. Army Ordnance Corps.
Target applicant:
High school students
College students
Adult students
Minimum GPA: None.
Amount: Varies.
Number of awards: Varies.
Deadline: June 30.
How to apply: Applications are available online.

(563) · Luray Caverns Graduate Research Grant
Tourism Cares
585 Washington Street
Canton, MA 02021
Phone: 781-821-5990
Fax: 781-821-8949
Email: carolynv@tourismcares.org
Website: http://www.tourismcares.org
Purpose: To promote and provide financial assistance for the completion of tourism-related research.
Eligibility: Applicants must be enrolled in a graduate program at an accredited college or university in the U.S. or Canada and be conducting tourism-related research. Students must include an abstract of the research project which includes the purpose, hypothesis, objectives, scope, literature review, applicability of results and methodology.
Target applicant:
Graduate school students
Adult students
Minimum GPA: None.
Amount: $3,000.
Number of awards: 1.
Deadline: April 2.
How to apply: Applications are available online.

(564) · Lyndon B. Johnson Foundation Grants-in-Aid Research
Lyndon B. Johnson Foundation
2313 Red River Street
Austin, TX 78705
Phone: 512-478-7829
Fax: 512-478-9104
Email: webmaster@lbjlib.utexas.edu
Website: http://www.lbjlib.utexas.edu
Purpose: To assist with the travel and room-and-board expenses of those wishing to conduct research at the Lyndon B. Johnson Foundation Library.
Eligibility: Applicants must first contact the library to determine if their topic is appropriate for study at the facility. Applicants must also calculate the estimated amount of the grant before making a request.
Target applicant:
College students
Adult students
Minimum GPA: None.
Amount: $500-$2,000.
Number of awards: Varies.
Deadline: February 28.
How to apply: Applications are available online.

(565) · Maley Teacher Scholarship
International Technology Education Association
Foundation for Technology Education
1914 Association Drive, Suite 201
Reston, VA 20191
Phone: 703-860-2100
Fax: 703-860-0353
Email: bmongold@iteaconnect.org
Website: http://www.iteaconnect.org
Purpose: To support technology education teachers.
Eligibility: Applicants must be members of ITEA and plan to pursue or continue graduate study. Candidates must provide their plans for graduate study, description of need, college transcript and three recommendation letters.
Target applicant:
Graduate school students
Adult students
Minimum GPA: None.
Amount: $1,000.
Number of awards: Varies.
Deadline: December 1.
How to apply: Application information is available online.

(566) · Marine Corps League Scholarships
Marine Corps League
P.O. Box 3070
Merrifield, VA 22116
Phone: 800-625-1775
Fax: 703-207-0047
Website: http://www.mcleague.org
Purpose: To provide educational opportunities to spouses and descendants of Marine Corps League members.
Eligibility: Applicants must be Marine Corp League or Auxiliary members in good standing, their spouses or their descendants, children of Marines who died in the line of duty or honorably discharged

Marines who need rehabilitation training that is not being subsidized by government programs.

Target applicant:
High school students
College students
Adult students

Minimum GPA: None.

Amount: Varies.

Number of awards: Varies.

Scholarship may be renewable.

Deadline: July 1.

How to apply: Applications are available online.

(567) · Marine Corps Scholarship Foundation Scholarship

Marine Corps Scholarship Foundation
P.O. Box 3008
Princeton, NJ 08543-3008
Phone: 800-292-7777
Fax: 609-452-2259
Email: mcsfnj@mcsf.org
Website: http://www.marine-scholars.org

Purpose: To provide financial assistance to sons and daughters of U.S. Marines and children of former Marines in their pursuit of higher education.

Eligibility: Applicants must be children of one of the following: an active duty or reserve U. S. Marine, a U.S. Marine who has received an Honorable Discharge, Medical Discharge or was killed while serving in the U.S. Marine Corps, an active duty or reserve U.S. Navy Corpsman who is serving, or has served, with the U.S. Marine Corps, a U.S. Navy Corpsman who has served with the U.S. Marine Corps and has received an Honorable Discharge, Medical Discharge or was killed while serving in the U.S. Navy. Applicants can also be grandchildren of one of the following: A U.S. Marine who served with the 4th Marine Division during World War II and is/was a member of their association, a U.S. Marine who served with the 6th Marine Division during World War II and is/was a member of their association, or a U.S. Marine who served in the 531 Gray Ghost Squadron and is/was a member of their association. Applicants must be either high school graduates or undergraduate students. There is a family income limit.

Target applicant:
College students
Adult students

Minimum GPA: 2.0

Amount: Varies.

Number of awards: Varies.

Deadline: March 3.

How to apply: Applications are available online.

(568) · Mary Church Terrell Award

National Association of Blacks in Criminal Justice
North Carolina Central University
P.O. Box 19788
Durham, NC 27707
Phone: 919-683-1801
Fax: 919-683-1903
Email: office@nabcj.org
Website: http://www.nabcj.org

Purpose: To award activism for positive change in criminal justice on city and state levels.

Eligibility: Nominator should be a member of NABCJ. Awarded to an individual who has initiated relationships with churches, courts, councils and assemblies.

Target applicant:
College students
Graduate school students
Adult students

Minimum GPA: None.

Amount: Varies.

Number of awards: Varies.

Deadline: May 1.

How to apply: Nomination applications are available online.

(569) · Mary Lou Brown Scholarship

American Radio Relay League Foundation
225 Main Street
Newington, CT 06111
Phone: 860-594-0397
Fax: 860-594-0259
Email: foundation@arrl.org
Website: http://www.arrl.org

Purpose: To assist ham radio operators with furthering their educations.

Eligibility: Applicants must have at least a general ham radio license, be residents of the ARRL Northwest Division (Alaska, Idaho, Montana, Oregon or Washington), be working for a bachelor's or graduate degree, have a minimum 3.0 GPA and have demonstrated interest in promoting the Amateur Radio Service.

Target applicant:
High school students
College students
Graduate school students
Adult students

Minimum GPA: 3.0

Amount: $2,500.

Number of awards: Varies.

Deadline: February 1.

How to apply: Applications are available online. Completed applications must be submitted by mail.

(570) · Medal of Honor AFCEA ROTC Scholarships

Armed Forces Communications and Electronics Association
4400 Fair Lakes Court
Fairfax, VA 22033
Phone: 800-336-4583
Fax: 703-631-4693
Email: scholarship@afcea.org
Website: http://www.afcea.org

Purpose: To support students who are members of the ROTC and committed to serving in the United States armed forces.

Eligibility: Applicants must be enrolled in college full-time, and they must be in their sophomore or junior year. Students must have at least a 3.0 GPA.

Target applicant:
College students
Adult students

Minimum GPA: 3.0

Amount: $4,000.

Number of awards: Varies.

Deadline: April 1.

How to apply: Applications are available online.

(571) · Medger Evers Award

National Association of Blacks in Criminal Justice
North Carolina Central University
P.O. Box 19788
Durham, NC 27707
Phone: 919-683-1801
Fax: 919-683-1903
Email: office@nabcj.org
Website: http://www.nabcj.org
Purpose: To award efforts to ensure that all people, including those in institutions, receive equal justice under the law.
Eligibility: This award honors the slain civil rights leader. Nominator should be a member of NABCJ.
Target applicant:
    College students
    Graduate school students
    Adult students
Minimum GPA: None.
Amount: Varies.
Number of awards: Varies.
Deadline: May 1.
How to apply: Nomination applications are available online.

(572) · Melvin and Anne Tracy Endowment

Epsilon Sigma Alpha Foundation
P.O. Box 270517
Fort Collins, CO 80527
Phone: 970-223-2824
Fax: 970-223-4456
Email: kloyd@knoxy.net
Website: http://www.esaintl.com/esaf
Purpose: To provide financial assistance to education majors.
Eligibility: Applicants may study teaching at any college or university. Selection is based on the following characteristics: character (10 percent), leadership (20 percent), service (10 percent), financial need (30 percent) and scholastic ability (30 percent).
Target applicant:
    High school students
    College students
    Adult students
Minimum GPA: None.
Amount: $500.
Number of awards: 1.
Deadline: February 1.
How to apply: Applications are available online.

(573) · Memorial Scholarship Fund

Third Marine Division Association
MFySgt. James G. Kyser, USMC (Ret)
15727 Vista Drive
Dumfries, VA 22025-1810
Phone: 352-726-2767
Email: scholarship@caltrap.org
Website: http://www.caltrap.com
Purpose: To assist veterans and their families.
Eligibility: Applicants must be the children of Marines (Corpsman or other) who served with the Third Marine Division or in support of the Division at any time and who have been members of the Third Marine Division Association for at least two years. Applicants must be 16-23

and unmarried dependents. Applicants must attend school in the U.S. or Canada.
Target applicant:
    High school students
    College students
Minimum GPA: None.
Amount: Varies.
Number of awards: Varies.
Scholarship may be renewable.
Deadline: April 15.
How to apply: Applications are available by written request after September 1.

(574) · MG James Ursano Scholarship Fund

Army Emergency Relief (AER)
200 Stovall Street Rm. 5N13
Alexandria, VA 22332
Phone: 703-428-0035
Fax: 703-325-7183
Email: education@aerhq.org
Website: http://www.aerhq.org
Purpose: To assist the children of Army families with their undergraduate education, vocational training and service academy education.
Eligibility: Applicants must be dependent children of Army soldiers who are unmarried and under the age of 22. Students must also be registered with the Defense Eligibility Enrollment Reporting System, have a minimum 2.0 GPA and be enrolled and accepted or pending acceptance as full-time students in post-secondary educational institutions. Awards are based primarily on financial need.
Target applicant:
    High school students
    College students
Minimum GPA: 2.0
Amount: Varies.
Number of awards: Varies.
Scholarship may be renewable.
Deadline: March 1.
How to apply: Applications are available online and by mail.

(575) · Mike Nash Memorial Scholarship Fund

Vietnam Veterans of America
8605 Cameron Street
Silver Spring, MD 20910
Phone: 800-882-1316
Email: finance@vva.org
Website: http://www.vva.org/scholarship.html
Purpose: To provide financial assistance to Vietnam veterans, their widows and their children.
Eligibility: Applicants must be Vietnam Veterans of America members or their spouses, children, stepchildren or grandchildren, or spouses, children, stepchildren or grandchildren of Vietnam veterans who are deceased, MIA or KIA. They must enroll at least half time at an accredited institution of higher learning.
Target applicant:
    High school students
    College students
    Adult students
Minimum GPA: None.
Amount: Varies.
Number of awards: Varies.
Deadline: May 31.
How to apply: Applications are available online.

(576) · Mike Reynolds Scholarship

Radio and Television News Directors Association
1600 K Street NW
Suite 700
Washington, DC 20006
Phone: 202-659-6510
Fax: 202-223-4007
Email: rtnda@rtnda.org
Website: http://www.rtnda.org
Purpose: To honor professional achievements in electronic journalism.
Eligibility: Applicants must be full-time college sophomores or higher with at least one full academic year remaining. Applicants may be enrolled in any major as long as their career intent is television or radio news. Applicants may only apply for one RTNDA scholarship. Preference is given to students who demonstrate financial need by describing media-related jobs held and contributions made to funding their own education.
Target applicant:
    College students
    Adult students
Minimum GPA: None.
Amount: $1,000.
Number of awards: 1.
Deadline: May 3.
How to apply: Applications are available online.

(577) · Military Award Program (MAP)

Imagine America Foundation
1101 Connecticut Avenue NW
Suite 901
Washington, DC 20036
Phone: 202-336-6724
Fax: 202-408-8102
Email: kerryt@career.org
Website: http://www.imagine-america.org
Purpose: To help those who have served in the military with their education and make the transition from military to civilian life.
Eligibility: Applicants must be active duty members or honorably discharged veterans of a United States military service branch, have financial need and plan to attend one of the 500 participating career colleges. There is a list of career colleges on the website. Before applying, the applicant selects a career college and program of study. The application is sent electronically to the career college, and the career college notifies the applicant if an award is available.
Target applicant:
    College students
    Graduate school students
    Adult students
Minimum GPA: None.
Amount: $1,000.
Number of awards: Varies.
Deadline: June 30.
How to apply: Applications are available online.

(578) · Military Officers' Benevolent Corporation Scholarships

Military Officers' Benevolent Corporation
1010 American Eagle Boulevard
Box 301
Sun City Center, FL 33573
Phone: 813-634-4675
Fax: 813-633-2412
Email: president@mobc-online.org
Website: http://www.mobc-online.org
Purpose: To provide financial assistance to children and grandchildren of military members and others who have served their country.
Eligibility: Applicants must be children or grandchildren of current or former military members, federal employees of GS-7 or higher equivalent officer grade, foreign services officers (FSO-8 and below) and honorably discharged or retired foreign military officers of Allied Nations living in the U.S. The applicant must be a high school senior who has been recommended by his or her principal and have a minimum score of 21 on the ACT, 900 on the two-part SAT or 1350 on the three-part SAT. The minimum GPA required is 3.0.
Target applicant:
    High school students
Minimum GPA: 3.0.
Amount: $2,000-$8,000.
Number of awards: 12.
Scholarship may be renewable.
Deadline: March 1.
How to apply: Applications are available online.

(579) · Military Order of the Purple Heart Scholarship

Military Order of the Purple Heart
MOPH National Headquarters
5413-B Backlick Road
Attn.: Scholarship Committee
Springfield, VA 22151
Phone: 703-642-5360
Fax: 703-642-1841
Email: scholarship@purpleheart.org
Website: http://www.purpleheart.org
Purpose: To recognize outstanding achievement.
Eligibility: Applicants must be children, step-children, grandchildren or great grandchildren of a member of the Military Order of the Purple Heart or a veteran killed in action or a veteran who died of injuries but did not have the chance to join the Military Order of the Purple Heart. Applicants must also be U.S. citizens, be high school graduates or high school seniors, have a 2.75 minimum GPA and be enrolled in a full-time program in a college. Applicants must write an essay and send a non-refundable $10 fee. It is highly recommended that you research the scholarship and awarding organization before applying for a scholarship with a fee. There are many scholarships that do not require a fee.
Target applicant:
    High school students
    College students
    Graduate school students
    Adult students
Minimum GPA: 2.75
Amount: $3,000.
Number of awards: 50.
Deadline: February 19.
How to apply: Applications are available online.

(580) · Miller Brewing Scholarship

Adelante U.S. Educational Leadership Fund
8415 Datapoint Drive
Suite 400
San Antonio, TX 78229
Phone: 877-692-1971

Fax: 210-692-1951
Email: info@adelantefund.org
Website: http://www.adelantefund.org
Purpose: To assist students attending participating institutions who are pursuing degrees in business, economics, finance, accounting, marketing, public relations or sales.
Eligibility: Applicants must be full-time rising juniors or seniors, have a GPA of 3.0 or higher, provide two letters of recommendation and participate in Adelante's Annual Leadership Institute and possibly a paid internship.
Target applicant:
    College students
    Adult students
Minimum GPA: 3.0
Amount: Up to $3,000.
Number of awards: Varies.
Deadline: May 31.
How to apply: Applications are available online starting March 1.

(581) · Minorities and Women Educational Scholarship

Appraisal Institute
550 W. Van Buren Street
Suite 1000
Chicago, IL 60607
Phone: 312-335-4100
Fax: 312-335-4400
Email: wwoodburn@appraisalinstitute.org
Website: http://www.appraisalinstitute.org
Purpose: To assist minority and women college students in pursuing degrees in real estate appraisal or related fields.
Eligibility: Applicants must be women or American Indians, Alaska Natives, Asians, African Americans, Hispanics or Latinos, Native Hawaiians or other Pacific Islanders. Applicants must be full- or part-time students enrolled in real estate courses and working toward degrees, have a minimum 2.5 GPA and demonstrate financial need.
Target applicant:
    College students
    Adult students
Minimum GPA: 2.5
Amount: $1,000.
Number of awards: Varies.
Deadline: April 15.
How to apply: Applications are available online.

(582) · Minority Fellowship Program

American Sociological Association
1307 New York Avenue NW
Suite 700
Washington, DC 20005
Phone: 202-383-9005
Fax: 202-638-0882
Email: minority.affairs@asanet.org
Website: http://www.asanet.org
Purpose: To provide pre-doctoral graduate education for sociology students.
Eligibility: Applicants must be enrolled in a Ph.D. program in sociology departments that have National Institute of Mental Health (NIMH) and National Institute of Drug Abuse (NIDA) relevant research programs and/or faculty who are currently engaged in research focusing on topics important to the NIMH and NIDA. Students may be earlier

in their graduate career but must be accepted into a Ph.D. program in sociology. Recipients are selected on the basis of their commitment to research, the focus of their research experience, academic achievement, scholarship, writing ability, research potential, financial need and racial/ethnic minority background. Applicants must be members of one of the following racial/ethnic groups: African American, Latino, American Indian or Alaskan Native or Asian or Pacific Islander. An application, essay, three recommendation letters and transcripts are required.
Target applicant:
    Graduate school students
    Adult students
Minimum GPA: None.
Amount: $20,772.
Number of awards: Varies.
Deadline: January 31.
How to apply: Applications are available online.

(583) · Minority Scholarship Program

Fredrikson and Byron, P.A.
200 S. Sixth Street
Suite 4000
Minneapolis, MN 55402-1425
Phone: 612-492-7000
Fax: 612-492-7077
Email: market@fredlaw.com
Website: http://www.fredlaw.com
Purpose: To provide opportunities for law students from diverse backgrounds.
Eligibility: In addition to the financial award, scholarship winners are also invited to serve as summer associates at the firm.
Target applicant:
    Graduate school students
    Adult students
Minimum GPA: None.
Amount: $5,000.
Number of awards: 2.
Deadline: Varies.
How to apply: Applications are available online.

(584) · MLA Scholarship

Medical Library Association
65 East Wacker Place
Suite 1900
Chicago, IL 60601-7246
Phone: 800-545-2433 x4276
Fax: 312-419-8950
Email: spectrum@ala.org
Website: http://www.mlanet.org
Purpose: To aid a student with finishing their education at an ALA-accredited library school.
Eligibility: Applicants must be either entering or less than half-way through an accredited graduate school program in a field relevant to library science and be U.S. or Canadian citizens or permanent residents.
Target applicant:
    Graduate school students
    Adult students
Minimum GPA: None.
Amount: $5,000.
Number of awards: 1.
Deadline: December 1.
How to apply: Applications are available online.

(585) · MLA Scholarship for Minority Students

Medical Library Association
65 East Wacker Place
Suite 1900
Chicago, IL 60601-7246
Phone: 800-545-2433 x4276
Fax: 312-419-8950
Email: spectrum@ala.org
Website: http://www.mlanet.org
Purpose: To aid minority students entering or currently attending graduate library school.
Eligibility: Applicants must be African-American, Hispanic, Asian, Native American or Pacific Islander and entering or currently attending an ALA-accredited library school and be no more than halfway through the program. Applicants must also be citizens or permanent residents of the United States or Canada.
Target applicant:
    Graduate school students
    Adult students
Minimum GPA: None.
Amount: $5,000.
Number of awards: 1.
Deadline: December 1.
How to apply: Applications are available online. Eligibility URL does not work.

(586) · MLA/NLM Spectrum Scholarship

Medical Library Association
65 East Wacker Place
Suite 1900
Chicago, IL 60601-7246
Phone: 800-545-2433 x4276
Fax: 312-419-8950
Email: spectrum@ala.org
Website: http://www.mlanet.org
Purpose: To aid minority students in becoming health sciences information professionals.
Eligibility: Applicants must be American Indian/Alaska Native, Asian, Black/African American, Hispanic/Latino or Native Hawaiian/Other Pacific Islander students attending accredited library schools who are studying fields relevant to library science and who plan to enter the health sciences information field.
Target applicant:
    College students
    Graduate school students
    Adult students
Minimum GPA: None.
Amount: Varies.
Number of awards: Varies.
Deadline: March 1.
How to apply: Applications are available online.

(587) · MOAA Base/Post Scholarships

Military Officers Association of America
201 N. Washington Street
Alexandria, VA 22314
Phone: 800-234-6622
Email: msc@moaa.org
Website: http://www.moaa.org
Purpose: To provide financial assistance for children of active duty military personnel.
Eligibility: Applicants must be dependents of an active duty military member, including the National Guard and drilling reserve, and be under the age of 24. Recipients are selected at random.
Target applicant:
    High school students
    College students
Minimum GPA: None.
Amount: $1,000.
Number of awards: 25.
Deadline: March 3.
How to apply: Applications are available online.

(588) · Montgomery GI Bill - Active Duty

Department of Veterans Affairs
Veterans Benefits Administration
810 Vermont Avenue NW
Washington, DC 20420
Phone: 888-442-4551
Website: http://www.gibill.va.gov
Purpose: To provide educational benefits to veterans.
Eligibility: Applicants must have an Honorable Discharge and high school diploma and meet other service requirements. The bill provides up to 36 months of educational benefits to veterans for college, technical or vocational courses, correspondence courses, apprenticeship/job training or flight training, high-tech training, licensing and certification tests, entrepreneurship training and certain entrance examinations. In most cases the award must be used within 10 years of being discharged.
Target applicant:
    College students
    Graduate school students
    Adult students
Minimum GPA: None.
Amount: Varies.
Number of awards: Varies.
Deadline: None.
How to apply: Applications are available online.

(589) · Montgomery GI Bill - Selected Reserve

Department of Veterans Affairs
Veterans Benefits Administration
810 Vermont Avenue NW
Washington, DC 20420
Phone: 888-442-4551
Website: http://www.gibill.va.gov
Purpose: To support members of the United States military Selected Reserve.
Eligibility: Applicants must have a six-year commitment to the Selected Reserve signed after June 30, 1985. The Selected Reserve includes the Army Reserve, Navy Reserve, Air Force Reserve, Marine Corps Reserve and Coast Guard Reserve, and the Army National Guard and the Air National Guard. Applicants must have completed basic military training, meet the requirements to receive a high school diploma or equivalency certificate and may use the funds for degree programs, certificate or correspondence courses, cooperative training, independent study programs, apprenticeship/on-the-job training, and vocational flight training programs.
Target applicant:
    High school students
    College students

Graduate school students
Adult students
Minimum GPA: None.
Amount: Varies.
Number of awards: Varies.
Scholarship may be renewable.
Deadline: Varies.
How to apply: Applications are available online.

---

(590) · Montgomery GI Bill Tuition Assistance Top-Up

Department of Veterans Affairs
Veterans Benefits Administration
810 Vermont Avenue NW
Washington, DC 20420
Phone: 888-442-4551
Website: http://www.gibill.va.gov
Purpose: To support students who are receiving tuition assistance from the military that doesn't cover the full cost of courses.
Eligibility: Applicants must be eligible for MGIB-Active Duty benefits, and they must have served on active duty in the United States military for at least two years.
Target applicant:
College students
Graduate school students
Adult students
Minimum GPA: None.
Amount: Varies.
Number of awards: Varies.
Scholarship may be renewable.
Deadline: Varies.
How to apply: Applications are available online. Contact your education services officer or education counselor for more information.

---

(591) · NACA East Coast Graduate Student Scholarship

National Association for Campus Activities
13 Harbison Way
Columbia, SC 29212
Phone: 803-732-6222
Fax: 803-749-1047
Email: info@naca.org
Website: http://www.naca.org
Purpose: To provide assistance to graduate students who are attending a college or university on the East Coast.
Eligibility: Applicants must be enrolled in master's or doctorate degree programs in student personnel services or a related area. Applicants must be attending a graduate school in Washington DC, Delaware, Maryland, New Jersey, New York or Eastern Pennsylvania, be involved in campus activities and plan to pursue a career in campus activities.
Target applicant:
Graduate school students
Adult students
Minimum GPA: None.
Amount: Varies.
Number of awards: Up to 2.
Deadline: May 30.
How to apply: Applications are available online.

---

(592) · Nancy Curry Scholarship

Child Nutrition Foundation
Scholarship Committee
700 S. Washington Street, Suite 300
Alexandria, VA 22314
Phone: 703-739-3900
Email: jcurtis@schoolnutrition.org
Website: http://www.schoolnutrition.org
Purpose: To support students wishing to enter the school foodservice industry.
Eligibility: Applicants or the parents of applicants must be School Nutrition Association members for at least one year and be enrolled in a school foodservice-related program at an educational institution.
Target applicant:
High school students
College students
Graduate school students
Adult students
Minimum GPA: None.
Amount: Tuition, fees and books.
Number of awards: 1.
Deadline: April 15.
How to apply: Applications are available online.

---

(593) · National Business School College Scholarship

Common Knowledge Scholarship Foundation
P.O. Box 290361
Davie, FL 33329-0361
Phone: 954-262-8553
Email: info@cksf.org
Website: http://www.cksf.org
Purpose: To support college students who are interested in business.
Eligibility: Students must register with CKSF and take online quizzes in business and economics. The student with the most points from correct answers and the shortest time that it takes to answer the questions wins the scholarship.
Target applicant:
College students
Graduate school students
Adult students
Minimum GPA: None.
Amount: $250.
Number of awards: 1.
Deadline: November 16.
How to apply: Applications are available online.

---

(594) · National Business School High School Scholarship

Common Knowledge Scholarship Foundation
P.O. Box 290361
Davie, FL 33329-0361
Phone: 954-262-8553
Email: info@cksf.org
Website: http://www.cksf.org
Purpose: To reward high school students in grades 9-12 who are interested in attending business school.
Eligibility: Applicants must complete the free online registration and compete by taking a series of short multiple-choice quizzes online. Each week, the quiz will consist of 15 to 20 questions. Five hundred points are awarded for each correct answer, and one point is deducted for each

second taken to complete each question. After rounds one and two, a percentage of the high scorers from each state advance to the next round. The winner is determined through a combination of time and accuracy in answering the questions.

Target applicant:
High school students

Minimum GPA: None.

Amount: $500.

Number of awards: 1.

Deadline: October 2.

How to apply: Applicants must complete the free online registration and then answer questions.

(595) · National D-Day Museum Online Essay Contest

National D-Day Museum Foundation
945 Magazine Street
New Orleans, LA 70130
Phone: 504-527-6012
Fax: 504-527-6088
Email: info@nationalww2museum.org
Website: http://www.ddaymuseum.org

Purpose: To increase awareness of World War II by giving students the opportunity to compete in an essay contest.

Eligibility: Applicants must be high school students in the United States. They must prepare an essay of up to 1,000 words based on a topic specified by the sponsor. Only the first 500 valid essays will be accepted.

Target applicant:
High school students

Minimum GPA: None.

Amount: $500-$1,000.

Number of awards: 3.

Deadline: March.

How to apply: Applications are available online.

(596) · National Defense Transportation Association, St. Louis Area Chapter Scholarship

National Defense Transportation Association-Scott St. Louis Chapter
Attention: Scholarship Committee
P.O. Box 25486
Scott Air Force Base, IL 62225-0486
Website: http://www.ndtascottstlouis.org

Purpose: To promote careers in business, transportation logistics and physical distribution.

Eligibility: Preference is given to students majoring in business, transportation logistics and physical distribution or a related field. High school students must live in Illinois or Missouri. College students must attend school in Colorado, Iowa, Illinois, Indiana, Kansas, Michigan, Minnesota, Missouri, Montana, North Dakota, Nebraska, South Dakota, Wisconsin or Wyoming.

Target applicant:
High school students
College students
Adult students

Minimum GPA: None.

Amount: $2,500.

Number of awards: 6.

Deadline: March 1.

How to apply: Applications are available online.

(597) · National History Day Contest

National History Day
0119 Cecil Hall
University of Maryland
College Park, MD 20742
Phone: 301-314-9739
Fax: 301-314-9767
Email: info@nhd.org
Website: http://www.nationalhistoryday.org

Purpose: To reward students for their scholarship, initiative and cooperation.

Eligibility: Applicants must be in grades 6-12 and prepare throughout the school year history presentations based on an annual theme. Around February or March students compete in district History Day contests. District winners then prepare for the state contests, held usually in April or May. Those winners advance to the national contest held in June at the University of Maryland.

Target applicant:
Junior high students or younger
High school students

Minimum GPA: None.

Amount: Varies.

Number of awards: Varies.

Deadline: February-March.

How to apply: Applications are available online.

(598) · National President Scholarship

American Legion Auxiliary
8945 N. Meridian Street
Indianapolis, IN 46260
Phone: 317-569-4500
Fax: 317-569-4502
Email: alahq@legion-aux.org
Website: http://www.legion-aux.org

Purpose: To support students who are the children and stepchildren of veterans who served in the Armed Forces.

Eligibility: Applicants must be high school seniors, complete 50 hours of volunteer service and be the sons or daughters of veterans who served in the Armed Forces during eligibility dates for membership in the American Legion. Applicants should submit applications, four recommendation letters, essays, proof of volunteering, transcripts, ACT or SAT scores, and parents' military service description. Awards are based on character, essay, application, leadership, financial need and scholarship.

Target applicant:
High school students

Minimum GPA: None.

Amount: $1,000-$2,500.

Number of awards: 10.

Deadline: March 1.

How to apply: Applications are available online.

(599) · National President's Scholarship

American Legion Auxiliary
8945 N. Meridian Street
Indianapolis, IN 46260
Phone: 317-569-4500
Fax: 317-569-4502
Email: alahq@legion-aux.org
Website: http://www.legion-aux.org

Purpose: To award scholarships to children of veterans who served in the Armed Forces.

Eligibility: Applicants must be the daughters or sons of veterans who served in the Armed Forces for membership in The American Legion, be high school seniors and complete 50 hours of community service. Selection is based on character, application/essay, scholastic achievement, leadership and financial need.

Target applicant:
   High school students

Minimum GPA: None.

Amount: $2,000-$2,500.

Number of awards: 2 per Division.

Deadline: March 10.

How to apply: Applications are available online.

(600) · National Scholarship Program

American Board of Funeral Service Education
Scholarship Committee
3432 Ashland Avenue, Suite U
St. Joseph, MO 64506
Phone: 816-233-3747
Fax: 816-233-3793
Email: scholarships@abfse.org
Website: http://www.abfse.org

Purpose: To assist students enrolled in funeral service or mortuary science programs.

Eligibility: Applicants must be undergraduate students who have completed at least one semester or quarter of study in funeral service or mortuary science education at an accredited school and have at least one term remaining in their study. Applicants must be U.S. citizens.

Target applicant:
   College students
   Adult students

Minimum GPA: None.

Amount: $500-$2,500.

Number of awards: Varies.

Deadline: March 1 or September 1.

How to apply: Applications are available online.

(601) · National Society of Hispanic MBAs Scholarship

National Society of Hispanic MBAs
1303 Walnut Hill Lane Suite 100
Irving, TX 75038
Phone: 877-467-4622
Fax: 214-596-9325
Email: scholarships@nshmba.org
Website: http://www.nshmba.org

Purpose: To provide financial support to Hispanic students pursuing an MBA.

Eligibility: Applicants must be U.S. citizens or legal permanent residents of Hispanic heritage (defined as having at least one parent of full Hispanic heritage or both parents of half-Hispanic heritage). Students must be members of the NSHMBA, but they may enroll at a special application rate. Applicants must be enrolled or planning to enroll in master's programs in business or management at an accredited college or university. Scholarships are based on academic achievement, work experience, personal statement, community service, recommendations and financial need.

Target applicant:
   College students
   Graduate school students
   Adult students

Minimum GPA: None.

Amount: $1,500-$5,000.

Number of awards: Varies.

Deadline: June 12.

How to apply: Applications are available online.

(602) · National Tour Association State Scholarship

Tourism Cares
585 Washington Street
Canton, MA 02021
Phone: 781-821-5990
Fax: 781-821-8949
Email: carolynv@tourismcares.org
Website: http://www.tourismcares.org

Purpose: To assist undergraduate and graduate students who are studying travel and tourism.

Eligibility: Applicants must be in their junior or senior year of undergraduate study or entering or returning year of graduate study at an accredited four-year college or university in the U.S. or Canada and enrolled in a travel and tourism-related program. They must have a GPA of 3.0 or higher.

Target applicant:
   College students
   Graduate school students
   Adult students

Minimum GPA: 3.0

Amount: $1,000.

Number of awards: 11.

Deadline: April 2.

How to apply: Applications are available online. In addition to the application form, a resume, recommendation letter, essay and transcript are required.

(603) · National Washington Crossing Foundation Scholarship

Washington Crossing Foundation
P.O. Box 503
Levittown, PA 19058
Phone: 215-949-8841
Fax: 215-949-8843
Email: info@gwcf.org
Website: http://www.gwcf.org

Purpose: To support students who are planning careers in government service.

Eligibility: Students must be in their senior year of high school. Applicants must submit an essay and a letter of recommendation.

Target applicant:
   High school students

Minimum GPA: None.

Amount: Varies.

Number of awards: Varies.
Scholarship may be renewable.

Deadline: January 15.

How to apply: Applications are available online.

(604) · Naval Enlisted Reserve Association Scholarships

Naval Enlisted Reserve Association
6703 Farragut Avenue
Falls Church, VA 22042-2189
Phone: 800-776-9020
Email: secretary@nera.org
Website: http://www.nera.org
Purpose: To recognize the service and sacrifices made by Navy, Marine and Coast Guard members, retirees and their families.
Eligibility: Applicants must be members of the Naval Enlisted Reserve Association in good standing or their spouses, children or grandchildren. Children and grandchildren of members must be single and under 23 years of age on the application deadline. Applicants must be graduating high school seniors or students who are already pursuing an undergraduate degree.
Target applicant:
High school students
College students
Adult students
Minimum GPA: None.
Amount: $2,500-$3,000.
Number of awards: 4.
Deadline: May 30.
How to apply: Applications are available online.

(605) · Naval Helicopter Association Undergraduate Scholarships

Naval Helicopter Association
P.O. Box 180578
Coronado, CA 92178-0578
Phone: 619-435-7139
Fax: 619-435-7354
Email: nhascholars@hotmail.com
Website: http://www.nhascholarship.org
Purpose: To assist those who wish to pursue educational goals.
Eligibility: Applicants must be members of or dependents of members of the association or have an affiliation with naval aviation. Students may pursue undergraduate degrees in any field.
Target applicant:
High school students
College students
Adult students
Minimum GPA: None.
Amount: $1,500.
Number of awards: 5.
Deadline: Varies.
How to apply: Applications are available by mail.

(606) · Navy College Fund

U.S. Navy Personnel
5720 Integrity Drive
Millington, TN 38055
Phone: 866-827-5672
Email: bupers_webmaster@navy.mil
Website: http://www.npc.navy.mil/CareerInfo/Education/GIBill/NavyCollegeFundProgam.htm
Purpose: To encourage entry into the Navy for recruits who have skills and specialties for which there is a critical shortage.

Eligibility: Applicants must be Navy recruits who are qualified for training in selected Navy ratings as non-prior service enlistees and agree to serve on active duty for at least three years. They must have graduated from high school, be 17 to 30 years old, agree to a $1,200 pay reduction and receive an "Honorable" Character of Service.
Target applicant:
High school students
College students
Adult students
Minimum GPA: None.
Amount: Varies.
Number of awards: Varies.
Scholarship may be renewable.
Deadline: Varies.
How to apply: Applications are available from Navy recruiters.

(607) · Navy League Endowed Scholarships

Navy League Foundation
2300 Wilson Boulevard
Arlington, VA 22201
Phone: 800-356-5760
Fax: 703-528-2333
Email: lhuycke@navyleague.org
Website: http://www.navyleague.org
Purpose: To help military dependents attend college.
Eligibility: Applicants must be dependents or direct descendants of an active, reserve, retired or honorably discharged member of the U.S. Navy, Coast Guard, U.S.-Flag Merchant Marine, Marine Corps or U.S. Naval Sea Cadet Corps; be high school seniors or the equivalent and enter an accredited college or university. Students should submit a list of scholastic and extracurricular activities, transcripts, no more than two recommendations, SAT or ACT scores, FAFSA information, proof of qualifying sea service duty and personal statement. There are various scholarships available.
Target applicant:
High school students
College students
Adult students
Minimum GPA: None.
Amount: $10,000.
Number of awards: 22.
Scholarship may be renewable.
Deadline: March 1.
How to apply: Applications are available online.

(608) · Navy Supply Corps Foundation Scholarship

Navy Supply Corps Foundation Inc.
1425 Prince Avenue
Athens, GA 30606-2205
Phone: 706-354-4111
Fax: 706-354-0334
Email: evans@usnscf.com
Website: https://www.usnscf.com
Purpose: To provide financial aid for undergraduate studies to family members of Supply Corp members and enlisted Navy personnel.
Eligibility: Applicants must be family members of a Navy Supply Corps officer or an enlisted member, active duty, reservist or retired. Awards are based on character, leadership, academic performance and financial need.

Target applicant:
    Junior high students or younger
    High school students
    College students
    Adult students
Minimum GPA: None.
Amount: Varies.
Number of awards: Varies.
Deadline: April 11.
How to apply: Applications are available online.

(609) · Navy-Marine Corps ROTC College Program

U.S. Navy
NSTC OD2
250 Dallas Street Suite A
Pensacola, FL 32508-5268
Phone: 800-NAV-ROTC
Email: pnsc_nrotc.scholarship@navy.mil
Website: https://www.nrotc.navy.mil/scholarships_application.cfm
Purpose: To provide education opportunities for NROTC students.
Eligibility: Applicants must be accepted to or attending a college with an NROTC program. They must complete naval science and other specified university courses and attend a summer training session. Scholarships are available for two or four years, depending on time of application.
Target applicant:
    College students
    Adult students
Minimum GPA: None.
Amount: Varies.
Number of awards: Varies.
Scholarship may be renewable.
Deadline: Varies.
How to apply: Applications are available online.

(610) · Navy-Marine Corps ROTC Four-Year Scholarships

U.S. Navy
NSTC OD2
250 Dallas Street Suite A
Pensacola, FL 32508-5268
Phone: 800-NAV-ROTC
Email: pnsc_nrotc.scholarship@navy.mil
Website: https://www.nrotc.navy.mil/scholarships_application.cfm
Purpose: To provide education opportunities for ROTC members.
Eligibility: Applicants must plan to attend an eligible college or university. They must commit to eight years of military service, four of which must be on active duty. The scholarship pays full tuition and fees plus a stipend for textbooks.
Target applicant:
    High school students
Minimum GPA: None.
Amount: Tuition plus stipend.
Number of awards: Varies.
Scholarship may be renewable.
Deadline: Varies.
How to apply: Applications are available online.

(611) · Navy-Marine Corps ROTC Two-Year Scholarships

U.S. Navy
NSTC OD2
250 Dallas Street Suite A
Pensacola, FL 32508-5268
Phone: 800-NAV-ROTC
Email: pnsc_nrotc.scholarship@navy.mil
Website: https://www.nrotc.navy.mil/scholarships_application.cfm
Purpose: To provide education opportunities for NROTC students.
Eligibility: Applicants must be attending a college with an NROTC program as a freshman or sophomore. They must complete naval science and other specified university courses and attend a summer training session. They must also attend a Naval Science Institute program during the summer between their sophomore and junior year.
Target applicant:
    College students
    Adult students
Minimum GPA: None.
Amount: Varies.
Number of awards: Varies.
Scholarship may be renewable.
Deadline: Varies.
How to apply: Applications are available online.

(612) · NCCPAP Scholarship

National Conference of CPA Practitioners NCCPAP Scholarship
Attention: Scholarship Committee
22 Jericho Turnpike, Suite 110
Mineola, NY 11501
Phone: 888-488-5400
Email: lanak.nccpap@verizon.net
Website: http://www.nccpap.org
Purpose: To assist future certified public accountants.
Eligibility: Applicants must be graduating high school seniors with a minimum GPA of 3.3 planning to become certified public accountants. They must be full-time students applying to or accepted at a two- or four-year college.
Target applicant:
    High school students
Minimum GPA: 3.3
Amount: $1,000.
Number of awards: Varies.
Deadline: December 15.
How to apply: Applications are available online.

(613) · NCDXF Scholarship

American Radio Relay League Foundation
225 Main Street
Newington, CT 06111
Phone: 860-594-0397
Fax: 860-594-0259
Email: foundation@arrl.org
Website: http://www.arrl.org
Purpose: To provide financial assistance to amateur radio operators with interest in DXing.
Eligibility: Applicants must hold a Technician Class or higher Amateur Radio License and demonstrate activity and interest in DXing. They must attend a junior college, trade school or four-year college or university in the United States.

Target applicant:
    High school students
    College students
    Adult students
Minimum GPA: None.
Amount: $1,500.
Number of awards: 2.
Deadline: February 1.
How to apply: Applications are available online.

(614) · NCGE Cram Scholarships

National Council for Geographic Education
Jacksonville State University
206-A Martin Hall
700 Pelham Road North
Jacksonville, AL 36265-1602
Phone: 256-782-5293
Fax: 256-782-5336
Email: ncge@jsu.edu
Website: http://www.ncge.org
Purpose: To award K-12 teachers for exemplary annual meeting materials presentations.
Eligibility: Applicants must be K-12 teachers (or group of teachers) who submit descriptions of classroom presentations that they have created. The presentation must show current trends in geographic education and display an original approach to teaching geography. Formats may include lessons, simulations, workshops or other learning activities. Winners of a CRAM scholarship award are required to present their lessons during the NCGE meeting in order to receive the scholarship. Applicants must submit the Call for Proposal, NCGE/CRAM Scholarship application, abstracts, three letters of recommendation, lesson plan, proof of use of the lesson in the classroom, presenter registration form and registration and AV fees. For winners, the registration and applicable AV fees will be refunded.
Target applicant:
    College students
    Graduate school students
    Adult students
Minimum GPA: None.
Amount: $750.
Number of awards: Varies.
Deadline: April 1.
How to apply: Applications are available online.

(615) · NEMAL Electronics Scholarship

American Radio Relay League Foundation
225 Main Street
Newington, CT 06111
Phone: 860-594-0397
Fax: 860-594-0259
Email: foundation@arrl.org
Website: http://www.arrl.org
Purpose: To provide scholarship assistance to amateur radio operators from the Southeast United States who are studying electronics and communications.
Eligibility: Applicants must possess a General Class or higher Amateur Radio License and attend an accredited college or university. They must demonstrate financial need and have a GPA of 3.0 or higher. Preference is given to residents of the Southeastern United States and those who participate in community service or civic volunteer organizations.

Target applicant:
    High school students
    College students
    Adult students
Minimum GPA: 3.0
Amount: $1,000.
Number of awards: 1.
Deadline: February 1.
How to apply: Applications are available online.

(616) · New England FEMARA Scholarships

American Radio Relay League Foundation
225 Main Street
Newington, CT 06111
Phone: 860-594-0397
Fax: 860-594-0259
Email: foundation@arrl.org
Website: http://www.arrl.org
Purpose: To assist ham radio operators in furthering their educations.
Eligibility: Applicants must have at least a technician ham radio license and be residents of the New England States (Connecticut, Maine, Massachusetts, New Hampshire, Rhode Island, Vermont).
Target applicant:
    High school students
    College students
    Graduate school students
    Adult students
Minimum GPA: None.
Amount: $1,000.
Number of awards: Varies.
Deadline: February 1.
How to apply: Applications are available online. Completed applications must be mailed in. They cannot be completed electronically.

(617) · New Horizons Kathy LeTarte Scholarship

Tourism Cares
585 Washington Street
Canton, MA 02021
Phone: 781-821-5990
Fax: 781-821-8949
Email: carolynv@tourismcares.org
Website: http://www.tourismcares.org
Purpose: To assist Michigan residents in obtaining degrees in travel and tourism.
Eligibility: Applicants must be permanent residents of Michigan who are entering their junior or senior year in a travel and tourism related major at a college or university in the United States or Canada. They must have a GPA of 3.0 or higher.
Target applicant:
    College students
    Adult students
Minimum GPA: 3.0
Amount: $1,000.
Number of awards: 1.
Deadline: April 2.
How to apply: Applications are available online.

(618) · NFMC Gretchen E. Van Roy Music Education Scholarship

National Federation of Music Clubs (FL)
Mrs. Ralph Suggs
412 Greening Way
Roswell , GA 30076
Phone: 317-638-4003
Fax: 317-638-0503
Email: rose331s@bellsouth.net
Website: http://www.nfmc-music.org
Purpose: To support students majoring in music education.
Eligibility: Applicants must be college juniors majoring in music education and must be affiliated with the National Federation of Music Clubs. There is no application fee to apply.
Target applicant:
　College students
　Adult students
Minimum GPA: None.
Amount: $1,000.
Number of awards: 1.
Deadline: April 1.
How to apply: Applications are available online.

(619) · NLUS Stockholm Scholarship Fund

Naval Sea Cadet Corps
2300 Wilson Boulevard
Arlington, VA 22201-3308
Phone: 800-356-5760
Email: alewis@seacadets.org
Website: http://www.seacadets.org
Purpose: To provide financial assistance to a selected cadet.
Eligibility: Applicants must have been Sea Cadets for at least two years and be a member at the time of application. They must be rated NSCC E-3 or higher and receive a recommendation from their commanding officer, NSCC Committee Chairman and a high school principal or counselor. A B+ average or better is required, and SAT/ACT scores and class rank are considered. Applicants must present evidence of acceptance from an accredited institution of higher learning. Stockholm Scholars are selected every four years or when the previous scholar ceases to meet continuation criteria.
Target applicant:
　High school students
Minimum GPA: 3.3
Amount: Varies.
Number of awards: 1.
Scholarship may be renewable.
Deadline: May 15.
How to apply: Applications are available online.

(620) · Non-Commissioned Officers Association Scholarships

Non-Commissioned Officers Association
10635 IH 35 N
San Antonio, TX 78233
Phone: 800-662-2620
Email: membsvc@ncoausa.org
Website: http://www.ncoausa.org
Purpose: The scholarships are given to help the children and spouses of members of the Non-Commissioned Officers Association.

Eligibility: Students must be children or spouses of members of the Non-Commissioned Officers Association. Children must be under 25 to receive the scholarship.
Target applicant:
　High school students
　College students
　Adult students
Minimum GPA: None.
Amount: $900-$1,000.
Number of awards: 16.
Scholarship may be renewable.
Deadline: March 31.
How to apply: Applications are available online.

(621) · NPPF Television News Scholarship

National Press Photographers Foundation Television News Scholarship
Ed Dooks
5 Mohawk Dr
Lexington, MA 02421-6217
Phone: 781-861-6062
Email: dooks@verizon.net
Website: http://www.nppa.org
Purpose: To support students with television news photojournalism potential but with little opportunity and great need.
Eligibility: Applicants must be full-time juniors or seniors at a four-year college or university, provide a portfolio and demonstrate financial need. Applicants must also have courses in TV news photojournalism and continue in this program towards a bachelor's degree. Applicants can apply to as many NPPA scholarships as desired, but only one award will be granted.
Target applicant:
　College students
　Adult students
Minimum GPA: None.
Amount: $1,000.
Number of awards: Varies.
Deadline: March 1.
How to apply: Applications are available online.

(622) · NROTC Scholarship Program

Chief of Naval Education and Training/NROTC
Phone: 800-NAV-ROTC
Website: https://www.nrotc.navy.mil
Purpose: To prepare young men and women for leadership roles in the Navy and Marine Corps.
Eligibility: Applicants must be U.S. citizens who are at least 17 years old as of September 1 of their first year of college, no older than 23 on June 30 of that first year and must be younger than 27 at the time of anticipated graduation. Students must attend an NROTC college and have no moral or personal convictions against military service. Those interested in the Navy program, including Nurse-option, must have an SAT critical reading score of 530 and a math score of 520 or an ACT score of 22 in English and 22 in math. For the Marine Corps option, students must have an SAT composite score of 1000 or an ACT composite score of 22. Applicants must also meet all Navy or Marine Corps physical standards.
Target applicant:
　High school students
　College students
Minimum GPA: None.

Amount: Full tuition and fees, books, uniforms and monthly stipend.
Number of awards: Varies.
Scholarship may be renewable.
Deadline: January 31.
How to apply: Applications are available online. Contact information for regional offices is available online.

(623) · NSA Scholarship Foundation

National Society of Accountants Scholarship Program
Scholarship America
One Scholarship Way
P.O. Box 297
Saint Peter, MN 56082
Phone: 507-931-1682
Website: http://www.nsacct.org
Purpose: To support students entering the accounting profession.
Eligibility: Applicants must be undergraduate students majoring in accounting with a minimum 3.0 GPA and be U.S. or Canadian citizens.
Target applicant:
    College students
    Adult students
Minimum GPA: 3.0
Amount: $500-$2,000.
Number of awards: Varies.
Deadline: March 10.
How to apply: Applications are available online.

(624) · NSCC Scholarship Funds

Naval Sea Cadet Corps
2300 Wilson Boulevard
Arlington, VA 22201-3308
Phone: 800-356-5760
Email: alewis@seacadets.org
Website: http://www.seacadets.org
Purpose: To provide financial assistance for Sea Cadets.
Eligibility: Applicants must have been Sea Cadets for at least two years and be members at the time of application. They must have attained the rate of NSCC E-3 or higher and be recommended by their commanding officers, NSCC Committee Chairmen and principals or counselors. They must have a B+ or higher GPA and present evidence of acceptance to an accredited institution of higher learning. SAT or ACT scores and class rank are considered.
Target applicant:
    High school students
Minimum GPA: 3.3
Amount: Varies.
Number of awards: Varies.
Deadline: May 15.
How to apply: Applications are available online.

(625) · Optimist International Oratorical Contest

Optimist International
4494 Lindell Boulevard
St. Louis, MO 63108
Phone: 314-371-6000
Fax: 314-371-6006
Email: programs@optimist.org
Website: http://www.optimist.org
Purpose: To reward students based on their oratorical performance.

Eligibility: Applicants must be students in the U.S., Canada or Caribbean under the age of 16 as of December 31st of the entry year. Selection is based on an oratorical contest.
Target applicant:
    Junior high students or younger
    High school students
Minimum GPA: None.
Amount: $500-$1,500.
Number of awards: Varies.
Deadline: June 15.
How to apply: Contact your local Optimist Club.

(626) · Otto M. Stanfield Legal Scholarship

Unitarian Universalist Association
25 Beacon Street
Boston, MA 02108
Phone: 617-742-2100
Email: info@uua.org
Website: http://www.uua.org
Purpose: To help Unitarian Universalist students entering or attending law school.
Eligibility: Applicants should be planning to attend or currently attending law school at the graduate level. The award is based on activity with Unitarian Universalism and financial need. Applicants should submit transcripts and recommendations.
Target applicant:
    Graduate school students
    Adult students
Minimum GPA: None.
Amount: Varies.
Number of awards: Varies.
Deadline: February 15.
How to apply: Applications are available online.

(627) · Overseas Press Club Foundation Scholarships

Overseas Press Club Foundation
40 W. 45 Street
New York, NY 10036
Phone: 212-626-9220
Fax: 212-626-9210
Email: foundation@opcofamerica.org
Website: http://www.opcofamerica.org
Purpose: To encourage undergraduate and graduate students attending American colleges and universities to pursue careers as foreign correspondents.
Eligibility: Scholarships are open to undergraduate and graduate students with an interest in a career as a foreign correspondent. Eligible students must be attending American colleges or universities.
Target applicant:
    College students
    Graduate school students
    Adult students
Minimum GPA: None.
Amount: $2,000.
Number of awards: 11.
Deadline: December 1.
How to apply: Applications are available online.

(628) · Parsons Brinckerhoff –Golden Apple Scholarship

Conference of Minority Transportation Officials
818 18th Street NW, Suite 850
Washington, DC 20006
Phone: 202-530-0551
Fax: 202-530-0617
Email: comto@comto.org
Website: http://www.comto.org
Purpose: To support students who are pursuing careers in transportation in the fields of communications, marketing or finance.
Eligibility: Applicants must be graduating high school students who have been members of COMTO for at least one year. They must have at least a 2.0 GPA and be accepted into a college or technical school program.
Target applicant:
    High school students
Minimum GPA: 2.0
Amount: $2,500.
Number of awards: Varies.
Deadline: April 4.
How to apply: Applications are available online.

(629) · Pat Roberts Intelligence Scholars Program for Global Network Analysts

National Security Agency (NSA)
9800 Savage Road, Suite 6779
Ft. George G. Meade, MD 20755-6779
Phone: 410-854-4725
Website: http://www.nsa.gov/careers/
Purpose: To support students who plan to work in global network analysis after graduation.
Eligibility: Applicants must be college sophomores or juniors pursuing one of the following fields related to global network analysis: technical studies (computer science major with a minor in political science or international relations); topical studies (telecommunications and information systems networks, terrorism, proliferation or related sciences, international banking and finance) or disciplines (technical intelligence analysis, information assurance, network and telecommunications). Recipients are expected to become full-time employees of NSA's Global Network Analysis Intern Program after graduation. One- and two-year scholarships are offered.
Target applicant:
    College students
    Adult students
Minimum GPA: None.
Amount: Up to $25,000 per year.
Number of awards: Varies.
Deadline: November 30.
How to apply: Applications are available online.

(630) · Pat Roberts Intelligence Scholars Program for Intelligence Analysts

National Security Agency (NSA)
9800 Savage Road, Suite 6779
Ft. George G. Meade, MD 20755-6779
Phone: 410-854-4725
Website: http://www.nsa.gov/careers/
Purpose: To support students who plan to work in intelligence analysis.

Eligibility: Applicants must be college juniors who are pursuing the following specialties related to intelligence work: regional studies (Middle East, South, East or Central Asia); topical studies (terrorism, proliferation or related sciences, international banking and finance or telecommunications and information systems networks) and disciplines (intelligence analysis, philosophy or international relations). Familiarity with foreign languages, particularly Arabic, Chinese, Dari, Farsi, Hindi, Korean, Pashto, Urdu or a Central Asian language is preferred. Applicants studying social network analysis, library science or geographic information systems may also be considered. Recipients are expected to become full-time employees of NSA's Intelligence Analysis Development Program after graduation.
Target applicant:
    College students
    Adult students
Minimum GPA: None.
Amount: Up to $25,000.
Number of awards: Varies.
Deadline: October 30.
How to apply: Applications are available online.

(631) · Paul and Helen L. Grauer Scholarship

American Radio Relay League Foundation
225 Main Street
Newington, CT 06111
Phone: 860-594-0397
Fax: 860-594-0259
Email: foundation@arrl.org
Website: http://www.arrl.org
Purpose: To assist ham radio operators in furthering their educations.
Eligibility: Applicants must have at least a novice ham radio license, be residents and attend school in the ARRL Midwest Division (Iowa, Kansas, Missouri, Nebraska) and be undergraduate or graduate students in electronics, communications or another related field.
Target applicant:
    College students
    Graduate school students
    Adult students
Minimum GPA: None.
Amount: $1,000.
Number of awards: 1.
Deadline: February 1.
How to apply: Applications are available online. Completed applications must be submitted by mail.

(632) · Pentagon Assistance Fund

Navy-Marine Corps Relief Society
875 North Randolph Street Suite 225
Arlington, VA 22203
Phone: 703-696-4960
Fax: 703-696-0144
Email: education@hq.nmcrs.org
Website: http://www.nmcrs.org
Purpose: To provide financial assistance to spouses of military personnel who died as a result of the September 11, 2001 terrorist attack on the Pentagon.
Eligibility: Applicants must be spouses of deceased victims of the 9/11/2001 terrorist attack on the Pentagon who have not remarried. They must be pursuing an undergraduate degree and demonstrate financial need. They must have a Dependent's Uniformed Services Identification and Privilege Card and maintain a GPA of 2.0 or higher.

They must also be enrolled or accepted to an eligible institution of higher learning.
Target applicant:
   High school students
   College students
   Adult students
Minimum GPA: None.
Amount: Varies.
Number of awards: Varies.
Deadline: Varies.
How to apply: Applications are available online.

(633) · Perry F. Hadlock Memorial Scholarship

American Radio Relay League Foundation
225 Main Street
Newington, CT 06111
Phone: 860-594-0397
Fax: 860-594-0259
Email: foundation@arrl.org
Website: http://www.arrl.org
Purpose: To assist students who are involved in amateur radio and seeking a bachelor's degree or higher in a technology-related field.
Eligibility: Applicants must hold Technician Class Amateur Radio License or higher in the ARRL Atlantic or Hudson Division. They must be seeking a bachelor's degree or higher in a technology related field with preference given to electrical and electronics engineering students.
Target applicant:
   High school students
   College students
   Graduate school students
   Adult students
Minimum GPA: None.
Amount: $2,000.
Number of awards: 1.
Deadline: February 1.
How to apply: Applications are available online.

(634) · PHD ARA Scholarship

American Radio Relay League Foundation
225 Main Street
Newington, CT 06111
Phone: 860-594-0397
Fax: 860-594-0259
Email: foundation@arrl.org
Website: http://www.arrl.org
Purpose: To assist ham radio operators in furthering their educations.
Eligibility: Applicants must have any class of ham radio license, be residents of the ARRL Midwest Division (Iowa, Kansas, Missouri, Nebraska) and be studying journalism, computer science or electronic engineering. Applicants may also be the children of deceased amateur radio operators.
Target applicant:
   College students
   Graduate school students
   Adult students
Minimum GPA: None.
Amount: $1,000.
Number of awards: 1.
Deadline: February 1.
How to apply: Applications are available online but may not be completed electronically. All completed applications must be mailed.

(635) · Pi Sigma Alpha Washington Internship Scholarships

Pi Sigma Alpha
The Washington Center
2301 M Street NW, Fifth Floor
Washington, DC 20037-1427
Email: info@twc.edu
Website: http://www.apsanet.org/~psa/
Purpose: To provide Pi Sigma Alpha members with scholarships to participate in summer or fall term internships in Washington, DC.
Eligibility: Applicants must belong to Pi Sigma Alpha and be nominated by their local chapter. The award is for a political science internship is based on academic achievement and service to the organization.
Target applicant:
   College students
   Graduate school students
   Adult students
Minimum GPA: None.
Amount: $2,000.
Number of awards: 4.
Deadline: April 15.
How to apply: Applications are available online.

(636) · Pierre and Patricia Bikai Fellowship

American Center of Oriental Research (ACOR)
656 Beacon Street, 5th Floor
Boston, MA 02215
Phone: 617-353-6571
Fax: 617-353-6575
Email: acor@bu.edu
Website: http://www.bu.edu/acor
Purpose: To help graduate students in an archaeological project at the American Center of Oriental Research.
Eligibility: Applicants must be graduate students. The fellowship includes room and board at ACOR and $400 a month and may be combined with the Harrell and Groot fellowships. The fellowship does not support field work or travel. Recipients must live at the ACOR center in Jordan from June of one year to May of the next.
Target applicant:
   Graduate school students
   Adult students
Minimum GPA: None.
Amount: $400 plus room and board.
Number of awards: Varies.
Deadline: February 1.
How to apply: Applications are available online.

(637) · Predoctoral Fellowships for Historians of American Art to Travel Abroad

National Gallery of Art
2000B South Club Drive
Landover, MD 20785
Phone: 202-842-6482
Fax: 202-789-3026
Website: http://www.nga.gov/resources/casva.htm
Purpose: To award fellowships to doctoral students in art history who are studying aspects of art and architecture of the United States, including native and pre-Revolutionary America.
Eligibility: Applicants must be nominated by the chair of a graduate department of art history or other appropriate department. Each

department may support two candidates. Applicants should submit proposals, itineraries, a curriculum vitae, two letters of support from professors and an additional letter of nomination from the chair. The fellowship is for a period of six to eight weeks of continuous travel abroad in areas such as Africa, Asia, South America or Europe to sites of historical and cultural interest. The travel fellowship is intended to encourage art-historical experience beyond the applicant's major field not for the advancement of a dissertation. Preference is given to those who have had little opportunity for professional travel abroad.

Target applicant:
　Graduate school students
　Adult students
Minimum GPA: None.
Amount: $4,500.
Number of awards: Up to 6.
Deadline: February 15.
How to apply: Application materials are described online.

(638) · Princess Cruises and Princess Tours Scholarship

American Society of Travel Agents (ASTA) Foundation Inc.
1101 King Street
Suite 200
Alexandria, VA 22314
Phone: 703-739-2782
Fax: 703-684-8319
Email: scholarship@astahq.com
Website: http://www.astanet.com
Purpose: To encourage study in the field of travel and tourism.
Eligibility: Applicants must be admitted or enrolled in a travel and tourism curriculum at a two- or four-year college or university or proprietary travel school, have a minimum 2.5 GPA and write a 300-word paper on the two features cruise ships will need to offer passengers in the next 10 years. Applicants must be a resident, citizen, or legal alien of the United States or Canada.
Target applicant:
　High school students
　College students
　Adult students
Minimum GPA: 2.5
Amount: $2,000.
Number of awards: 2.
Deadline: July 27.
How to apply: Applications are available online.

(639) · Professional Scholarships

Insurance Scholarship Foundation of America,
P.O. Box 866
Hendersonville, NC 28793-0866
Phone: 828-890-3328
Fax: 828-891-2667
Email: billie@inssfa.org
Website: http://www.inssfa.org
Purpose: To promote excellence in the insurance industry by helping in the education of its employees.
Eligibility: Applicants must have been employed in the industry for at least three years, must be NAIW member for a minimum of three years, must have the CPIW/M designation, demonstrated active involvement in NAIW leadership activities, and engaged in a course of study designed to improve knowledge and skills in performing employment responsibilities.

Target applicant:
　College students
　Graduate school students
　Adult students
Minimum GPA: None.
Amount: $1,000-$2,000.
Number of awards: Varies.
Deadline: December 1, August 1.
How to apply: Applications are available online.

(640) · Professor Sidney Gross Memorial Award

Public Relations Student Society of America
33 Maiden Lane
11th Floor
New York, NY 10038
Phone: 212-460-1474
Fax: 212-995-0757
Email: prssa@prsa.org
Website: http://www.prssa.org
Purpose: To assist public relations undergraduate students.
Eligibility: Applicants must be undergraduate students who demonstrate superior understanding of ethical principles in public relations. Applicants need to write a response to a given scenario and must be members of the PRSSA.
Target applicant:
　College students
　Adult students
Minimum GPA: None.
Amount: $1,000.
Number of awards: Varies.
Deadline: April 16.
How to apply: Applications are available online.

(641) · ProStart National Certificate of Achievement Scholarship

National Restaurant Association Educational Foundation
175 W. Jackson Boulevard
Suite 1500
Chicago, IL 60604-2702
Phone: 800-765-2122
Fax: 312-715-1010
Email: scholars@naref.org
Website: http://www.nraef.org/scholarships/
Purpose: To support students who have been recognized in the HBA/ProStart School-to-Career Initiative.
Eligibility: Applicants must be graduating high school seniors and must have received the ProStart national Certificate of Achievement from participation in the HBA/ProStart School-to-Career Initiative. Applicants must also submit a copy of the National Restaurant Association Educational Foundation's ProStart National Certificate of Achievement, GPA and acceptance into a culinary and/or restaurant/foodservice management related program.
Target applicant:
　High school students
Minimum GPA: 2.75
Amount: $2,000.
Number of awards: Varies.
Deadline: August 15.
How to apply: Applications are available online.

(642) · Public Relations Scholarship

Common Knowledge Scholarship Foundation
P.O. Box 290361
Davie, FL 33329-0361
Phone: 954-262-8553
Email: info@cksf.org
Website: http://www.cksf.org
Purpose: To reward college students majoring in public relations, journalism, advertising or communications.
Eligibility: Applicants must complete the free online registration. This scholarship contest has two rounds: Round One is a short, multiple choice online quiz based on questions from college-level public relations courses. The top 20 students progress to Round Two. Participants in Round Two submit articles on one of three topics. Articles can be no more than two pages and are judged on creativity, accuracy and spelling/punctuation/correct use of Associated Press style. There are first, second and third places. Second and third place winners receive $50 gift certificates.
Target applicant:
 College students
 Adult students
Minimum GPA: None.
Amount: $250.
Number of awards: 3.
Deadline: February 4.
How to apply: Applicants must complete the free online registration.

(643) · Ray, NRP & Katie, WKTE Pautz Scholarship

American Radio Relay League Foundation
225 Main Street
Newington, CT 06111
Phone: 860-594-0397
Fax: 860-594-0259
Email: foundation@arrl.org
Website: http://www.arrl.org
Purpose: To provide financial assistance to amateur radio operators from the ARRL Midwest Division.
Eligibility: Applicants must be ARRL members with a General Class or higher Amateur Radio License. They must be residents of Iowa, Kansas, Missouri or Nebraska and should major in electronics, computer science or a related field at a four-year institution.
Target applicant:
 High school students
 College students
 Adult students
Minimum GPA: None.
Amount: $500-$1,000.
Number of awards: 1.
Deadline: February 1.
How to apply: Applications are available online.

(644) · Reid Blackburn Scholarship

National Press Photographers Foundation Blackburn Scholarship
Fay Blackburn
The Columbian
P.O. Box 180
Vancouver, WA 98666
Phone: 360-759-8027
Fax: 919-383-7261
Email: fay.blackburn@columbian.com
Website: http://www.nppa.org
Purpose: To support photojournalism students.
Eligibility: Applicants must have completed one year at a full-time four-year college or university, provide a portfolio, demonstrate financial need and must have courses in photojournalism and have at least half a year of undergraduate study left. Applicants may apply to as many NPPA scholarships as desired, but only one award may be granted per applicant.
Target applicant:
 College students
 Adult students
Minimum GPA: None.
Amount: Varies.
Number of awards: Varies.
Deadline: March 1.
How to apply: Applications are available online.

(645) · René Campbell Memorial Scholarship

Tourism Cares
585 Washington Street
Canton, MA 02021
Phone: 781-821-5990
Fax: 781-821-8949
Email: carolynv@tourismcares.org
Website: http://www.tourismcares.org
Purpose: To assist residents of North Carolina who are pursuing degrees in tourism.
Eligibility: Applicants must be rising juniors or seniors at an accredited four-year college or university and permanent residents of the state of North Carolina. They must have a GPA of 3.0 or higher.
Target applicant:
 College students
 Adult students
Minimum GPA: 3.0
Amount: $1,000.
Number of awards: 1.
Deadline: April 2.
How to apply: Applications are available online.

(646) · Retiree's Association of the Bureau of Alcohol, Tobacco, Firearms and Explosives (ATFAR) Scholarship

Explorers Learning for Life
P.O. Box 152079
Irving, TX 75015
Phone: 972-580-2433
Fax: 972-580-2137
Email: pchestnu@lflmail.org
Website: http://www.learningforlife.org/exploring
Purpose: To support students who are pursuing careers in law enforcement.
Eligibility: Students must be at least in their senior year of high school, and they must be active members of a Law Enforcement Explorer post. Applicants must submit three letters of recommendation and an essay.
Target applicant:
 High school students
 College students
 Adult students
Minimum GPA: None.
Amount: $1,000.
Number of awards: Varies.

Deadline: March 15.
How to apply: Applications are available online.

(647) · Richard W. Bendicksen Memorial Scholarship

American Radio Relay League Foundation
225 Main Street
Newington, CT 06111
Phone: 860-594-0397
Fax: 860-594-0259
Email: foundation@arrl.org
Website: http://www.arrl.org
Purpose: To provide financial assistance to amateur radio operators.
Eligibility: Applicants must hold an active amateur radio license of any class, and they must be attending a four-year institution of higher learning.
Target applicant:
    High school students
    College students
    Adult students
Minimum GPA: None.
Amount: $1,000.
Number of awards: 1.
Deadline: February 1.
How to apply: Applications are available online.

(648) · Ritchie-Jennings Memorial Scholarship

Association of Certified Fraud Examiners
Scholarships Program Coordinator
The Gregor Building
716 West Avenue
Austin, TX 78701
Phone: 800-245-3321
Fax: 512-276-8187
Email: memberservices@acfe.com
Website: http://www.cfenet.com
Purpose: To support the college education of accounting and criminal justice students who may become Certified Fraud Examiners in the future.
Eligibility: Applicants must be full-time undergraduate or graduate students with a declared major or minor in criminal justice or accounting. Applicants must submit three letters of recommendation, with at least one from a Certified Fraud Examiner or local CFE Chapter and must write an essay on why they deserve the scholarship and how fraud awareness will help their career.
Target applicant:
    College students
    Graduate school students
    Adult students
Minimum GPA: None.
Amount: $1,000.
Number of awards: Varies.
Deadline: April 20.
How to apply: Applications are available online.

(649) · Rolling Stone Annual College Journalism Competition

Rolling Stone
College Journalism Competition
1290 Avenue of the Americas, 2nd Floor
New York, NY 10104
Website: http://www.rollingstone.com
Purpose: To reward outstanding college journalism in the fields of entertainment reporting, feature writing and essays and criticism.
Eligibility: Awards are available in the categories of entertainment reporting, feature writing and essays and criticism. Applicants must submit a piece published between June 1 and May 30 of the current school year in a college student newspaper or magazine. Applicants must have been full- or part-time students at the time the entries were published. Only one entry is allowed per category, but students may submit to more than one category. Each entry must be submitted separately with a completed entry form, and the submitted piece must be a tearsheet from the magazine or newspaper with the date of publication shown.
Target applicant:
    College students
    Graduate school students
    Adult students
Minimum GPA: None.
Amount: $2,500.
Number of awards: 3.
Deadline: June 15.
How to apply: Applications are available online.

(650) · Rural Poverty Research Center Undergraduate Fellowships

Rural Poverty Research Center
Oregon State University
213 Ballard Hall
Corvallis, OR 97331-3601
Phone: 541-737-1442
Fax: 541-737-2563
Email: rprc@oregonstate.edu
Website: http://www.rprconline.org
Purpose: To provide research opportunities for undergraduate students interested in rural poverty.
Eligibility: Applicants must have an interest in pursuing a career in rural poverty research or policy, be U.S. citizens or permanent residents, have a minimum 3.0 GPA in their major and be entering their final year of undergraduate study.
Target applicant:
    College students
    Adult students
Minimum GPA: 3.0
Amount: $500.
Number of awards: Varies.
Deadline: Varies.
How to apply: Contact RPRC for application information.

(651) · Samuel H. Kress Foundation Paired Fellowship for Research in Conservation and the History of Art

National Gallery of Art
2000B South Club Drive
Landover, MD 20785
Phone: 202-842-6482
Fax: 202-789-3026
Website: http://www.nga.gov/resources/casva.htm
Purpose: To award fellowships for research in conservation and the history of art.
Eligibility: Applicants should be teams consisting of two scholars with the appropriate terminal degree for five years or more: one in the field of art history, archaeology or another related discipline in

the humanities or social sciences and one in the field of conservation or materials science. Applications will be considered for study in the history and conservation of the visual arts in Europe before the early nineteenth century. Applicants should submit the application forms; proposals; tentative travel schedule indicating the site(s), collection(s) or institution(s) for the proposed research; two publications and two letters of recommendation. The fellowship is a two- to three-month period for field, collections and/or laboratory research followed by a two-month residency at the Center.

Target applicant:
Graduate school students
Adult students
Minimum GPA: None.
Amount: $12,000.
Number of awards: Varies.
Deadline: March 21.
How to apply: Applications are available online.

(652) · Scholarships for Military Children

Defense Commissary Agency
Attn: OC
1300 E Avenue
Fort Lee, VA 23801-1800
Phone: 804-734-8860
Email: info@militaryscholar.org
Website: http://www.militaryscholar.org
Purpose: To provide educational opportunities for children of military personnel.
Eligibility: Applicants must be unmarried dependents under the age of 21 (23 if full-time students) of active duty, reserve, retired or deceased members of the military. They must be enrolled in the Defense Enrollment Eligibility Reporting System database. Applicants must be enrolled or plan to enroll in a full-time undergraduate degree-seeking program and have a minimum GPA of 3.0. Community or junior college students must be in a program that will allow transfer directly into a four-year program. Applicants also must not be accepted to a U.S. Military Academy or be the recipients of full scholarships at any accredited institution.
Target applicant:
High school students
College students
Minimum GPA: None.
Amount: $1,500.
Number of awards: Varies.
Deadline: February 20.
How to apply: Applications are available online or from military commissaries.

(653) · Schwan's Food Service Scholarship

Child Nutrition Foundation
Scholarship Committee
700 S. Washington Street, Suite 300
Alexandria, VA 22314
Phone: 703-739-3900
Email: jcurtis@schoolnutrition.org
Website: http://www.schoolnutrition.org
Purpose: To support those entering the school foodservice industry.
Eligibility: Applicants or parents of applicants must be School Nutrition Association members for at least one year and be pursuing a field of study related to school foodservice.

Target applicant:
High school students
College students
Graduate school students
Adult students
Minimum GPA: None.
Amount: Tuition, fees and books.
Number of awards: Varies.
Scholarship may be renewable.
Deadline: April 15.
How to apply: Applications are available online.

(654) · Scripps Howard Top Ten Scholarship

Scripps Howard Foundation
Top Ten Scholarship
P.O. Box 5380
Cincinnati, OH 45201
Phone: 513-977-3035
Fax: 513-977-3800
Email: vlmartin@scripps.com
Website: http://www.scripps.com
Purpose: To recognize the top journalism students in the country.
Eligibility: Applicants are nominated by their college and must be full-time college students entering their junior or senior year and studying journalism. Selection is based on academic achievement, commitment to a career journalism and essay.
Target applicant:
College students
Adult students
Minimum GPA: None.
Amount: $10,000.
Number of awards: 10.
Deadline: Varies.
How to apply: Applications are available by request.

(655) · Seabee Memorial Scholarship

Seabee Memorial Scholarship Association
P.O. Box 6574
Silver Spring, MD 20916
Phone: 301-570-2850
Email: smsa@erols.com
Website: http://www.seabee.org
Purpose: To provide scholarships for sons, daughters and grandchildren of Seabees, both past and present, active, reserve or retired.
Eligibility: Applicants must be sons, daughters, step-children or grandchildren of Regular, Reserve, Retired or deceased officers or enlisted members who have served or are now serving with the Naval Construction Force or Naval Civil Engineer Corps, or who have served but have been honorably discharged. Scholarships are for bachelor's degrees.
Target applicant:
High school students
College students
Adult students
Minimum GPA: None.
Amount: $1,500.
Number of awards: 94.
Deadline: April 15.
How to apply: Applications are available online or by written request.

(656) · Sergeant Major Douglas R. Drum Memorial Scholarship Fund

American Military Retirees Association
5436 Peru Street
Suite 1
Plattsburgh, NY 12901
Phone: 800-424-2969
Fax: 518-324-5204
Email: info@amra1973.org
Website: http://www.amra1973.org
Purpose: To provide funds for members of the AMRA or their dependents, children or grandchildren for tuition, room and board or books.
Eligibility: Applicants must be current members of the AMRA or the dependent, child or grandchild of a current member.
Target applicant:
    Junior high students or younger
    High school students
    College students
    Graduate school students
    Adult students
Minimum GPA: None.
Amount: Varies.
Number of awards: Varies.
Deadline: April 4.
How to apply: Applications are available online.

(657) · Seth Horen, K1LOM Memorial Scholarship

American Radio Relay League Foundation
225 Main Street
Newington, CT 06111
Phone: 860-594-0397
Fax: 860-594-0259
Email: foundation@arrl.org
Website: http://www.arrl.org
Purpose: To provide scholarship assistance to active amateur radio operators.
Eligibility: Applicants must hold an active Amateur Radio License in any class and must be attending a four-year institution of higher learning.
Target applicant:
    High school students
    College students
    Adult students
Minimum GPA: None.
Amount: $500.
Number of awards: 1.
Deadline: February 1.
How to apply: Applications are available online.

(658) · Sheryl A. Horak Memorial Scholarship

Explorers Learning for Life
P.O. Box 152079
Irving, TX 75015
Phone: 972-580-2433
Fax: 972-580-2137
Email: pchestnu@lflmail.org
Website: http://www.learningforlife.org/exploring
Purpose: To support students who are pursuing careers in law enforcement.

Eligibility: Students must be in their senior year of high school, and they must be members of a Law Enforcement Explorer post. Applicants must submit three letters of recommendation and an essay.
Target applicant:
    High school students
Minimum GPA: None.
Amount: $1,000.
Number of awards: Varies.
Deadline: March 31.
How to apply: Applications are available online.

(659) · Shields-Gillespie Scholarship

American Orff-Schulwerk Association (AOSA)
P.O. Box 391089
Cleveland, OH 44139-8089
Phone: 440-543-5366
Email: info@aosa.org
Website: http://www.aosa.org
Purpose: To assist pre-K and kindergarten teachers with program funding, including instruments and training.
Eligibility: Applicants must be a member of AOSA. Applicants must be U.S. citizens or have lived in the United States for the past five years. Programs should focus on music/movement learning.
Target applicant:
    College students
    Graduate school students
    Adult students
Minimum GPA: None.
Amount: Varies.
Number of awards: Varies.
Deadline: Varies.
How to apply: Applications are available online for AOSA members.

(660) · Simmons Scholarship

American Society of Travel Agents (ASTA) Foundation Inc.
1101 King Street
Suite 200
Alexandria, VA 22314
Phone: 703-739-2782
Fax: 703-684-8319
Email: scholarship@astahq.com
Website: http://www.astanet.com
Purpose: To aid graduate study in travel and tourism.
Eligibility: Applicants must have a minimum 2.5 GPA, be residents, citizens or legal aliens of the U.S. or Canada and be graduate students pursuing master's or doctorate degrees with an emphasis in travel and tourism. Applicants must also submit a travel and tourism-related paper or thesis.
Target applicant:
    Graduate school students
    Adult students
Minimum GPA: 2.5
Amount: $2,000.
Number of awards: Up to 2.
Deadline: July 27.
How to apply: Applications are available online.

(661) · SLA Scholarship

Special Libraries Association
331 S. Patrick Street
Alexandria, VA 22314

Phone: 703-647-4900
Fax: 703-647-4901
Email: sla@sla.org
Website: http://www.sla.org
Purpose: To support students who wish to pursue careers in special librarianship.
Eligibility: Applicants must be college graduates or college seniors with an interest in special librarianship who are admitted by a recognized library school or information science program and demonstrate financial need. Preference is given to SLA members and those who show an interest in special library work.
Target applicant:
    College students
    Graduate school students
    Adult students
Minimum GPA: None.
Amount: $6,000.
Number of awards: 3.
Deadline: October 31.
How to apply: Applications are available online.

(662) · Sons of Union Veterans of the Civil War Scholarships

Sons of Union Veterans of the Civil War
John R. Ertell, Chair
654 Grace Avenue
Spring City, PA 19475
Phone: 610-948-1278
Email: jertell@verizon.net
Website: http://www.suvcw.org/scholar.htm
Purpose: To assist students connected with the Sons of Union Veterans of the Civil War in obtaining higher education.
Eligibility: Male applicants must be members or associates of the Sons of Union Veterans of the Civil War. Female applicants must be daughters or granddaughters of members or associates and must be current members of the Women's Relief Corps, Ladies of the Grand Army of the Republic, Daughters of Union Veterans of the Civil War 1861-1865 or Auxiliary to the Sons of Union Veterans of the Civil War. All applicants must rank in the upper quarter of their graduating class, have a record of school and community service and provide three letters of recommendation.
Target applicant:
    High school students
    College students
    Adult students
Minimum GPA: None.
Amount: $1,000.
Number of awards: 2.
Deadline: March 31.
How to apply: Applications are available online.

(663) · Southern California Chapter/Pleasant Hawaiian Holidays Scholarship

American Society of Travel Agents (ASTA) Foundation Inc.
1101 King Street
Suite 200
Alexandria, VA 22314
Phone: 703-739-2782
Fax: 703-684-8319
Email: scholarship@astahq.com
Website: http://www.astanet.com
Purpose: To encourage students to enter the profession of travel and tourism.
Eligibility: Applicants must be enrolled in a four-year college or university and be enrolled in travel and tourism classes, have a minimum 2.5 GPA and write a 500-word paper entitled, "My Goals in the Travel Industry." Students should also include why they should be selected and must be U.S. citizens. One winner from the Southern California area and one winner from anywhere in the U.S. will be chosen.
Target applicant:
    College students
    Adult students
Minimum GPA: 2.5
Amount: $2,500.
Number of awards: 2.
Deadline: July 27.
How to apply: Applications are available online.

(664) · Specialty Equipment Market Association (SEMA) Memorial Scholarship

Specialty Equipment Market Association
1575 S. Valley Vista Drive
Diamond Bar, CA 91765
Phone: 909-396-0289
Fax: 909-860-0184
Email: education@sema.org
Website: http://www.sema.org
Purpose: To support the education of students pursuing careers in the automotive aftermarket.
Eligibility: Applicants must show financial need, have a minimum 2.5 GPA and pursue a career in the automotive aftermarket or related field.
Target applicant:
    College students
    Adult students
Minimum GPA: 2.5
Amount: $1,000-$4,000.
Number of awards: Varies.
Deadline: May 1.
How to apply: Applications are available online.

(665) · SPS Future Teacher Scholarship

Society of Physics Students
One Physics Ellipse
College Park, MD 20740
Phone: 301-209-3007
Fax: 301-209-0839
Email: sps@aip.org
Website: http://www.spsnational.org
Purpose: To provide scholarships to physics majors who are participating in a teacher education program and who intend to pursue a career in physics education.
Eligibility: Applicants must be members of SPS and intend to pursue a career in teaching physics. Students must be undergraduate physics majors, at least in their junior year of study at the time of application.
Target applicant:
    College students
    Adult students
Minimum GPA: None.
Amount: $2,000.
Number of awards: 1.
Deadline: February 15.

How to apply: Applications are available online or from chapter advisors.

(666) · SSPI Scholarship Program

Society of Satellite Professionals International (SSPI)
Tamara Bond
55 Broad Street
14th Floor
New York, NY 10004
Phone: 212-809-5199
Fax: 212-825-0075
Email: rbell@sspi.org
Website: http://www.sspi.org
Purpose: To help high school and university graduates with undergraduate and post-graduate study in satellite-related disciplines.
Eligibility: Applicants must be high school seniors, undergraduate or graduate students who are members of SSPI (membership is free) studying satellite-related technologies, policies or applications. Some scholarships have requirements such as interests, financial need, residency, gender, race or GPA. The award is based on commitment to education and careers in the satellite fields, academic and leadership achievement, potential for contribution to the satellite communications industry and a scientific, engineering, research, business or creative submission.
Target applicant:
    High school students
    College students
    Graduate school students
    Adult students
Minimum GPA: None.
Amount: $5,000.
Number of awards: Varies.
Deadline: April 30.
How to apply: Applications are available online.

(667) · Steven Hymans Extended Stay Scholarship

American Hotel and Lodging Educational Foundation (AH&LEF)
1201 New York Avenue NW
Suite 600
Washington, DC 20005-3931
Phone: 202-289-3188
Fax: 202-289-3199
Email: chammond@ahlef.org
Website: http://www.ahlef.org
Purpose: To provide scholarships to help educate students on the needs of extended stay visitors in the lodging industry.
Eligibility: Applicants must be undergraduate students who have experience working at an extended stay facility and must pursue a career in that segment of the lodging industry.
Target applicant:
    College students
    Adult students
Minimum GPA: None.
Amount: Up to $2,000.
Number of awards: Varies.
Deadline: June 15.
How to apply: Applications are available online.

(668) · Still Photographer Scholarship

National Press Photographers Association Still Photographer Scholarship
Bill Sanders
Photo Editor, Asheville Citizen-Times
P.O. Box 2090
Asheville, NC 28802
Email: wsanders@citizen-times.com
Website: http://www.nppa.org
Purpose: To honor the profession of photojournalism.
Eligibility: Applicants must have completed one year in a full-time four-year college or university with courses in photojournalism, provide a portfolio and demonstrate financial need. Applicants can apply to as many NPPA scholarships as desired, but only one award will be granted.
Target applicant:
    College students
    Adult students
Minimum GPA: None.
Amount: $2,000.
Number of awards: Varies.
Deadline: March 1.
How to apply: Applications are available online.

(669) · Stuart Cameron and Margaret McLeod Memorial Scholarship

Institute of Management Accountants (IMA)
10 Paragon Drive
Montvale, NJ 07645-1760
Phone: 800-638-4427
Email: students@imanet.org
Website: http://www.imanet.org
Purpose: To help management accounting students.
Eligibility: Applicants must be full- and part-time undergraduate and graduate students, be IMA student members and declare which four- or five-year management accounting, financial management or information technology related program they plan to pursue as a career or list a related field. Candidates should submit applications, resumes, transcripts, two recommendations and statements. Advanced degree students must pass one part of the CMA/CFM certification.
Target applicant:
    College students
    Graduate school students
    Adult students
Minimum GPA: 2.8
Amount: $5,000.
Number of awards: 1.
Deadline: February 15.
How to apply: Applications are available online.

(670) · Student Achievement Grants

NEA Foundation
1201 16th Street NW
Suite 416
Washington, DC 20036
Phone: 202-822-7840
Fax: 202-822-7779
Email: info-neafoundation@list.nea.org
Website: http://www.neafoundation.org

Purpose: To promote the academic achievement of students in U.S. public schools and public higher education institutions by providing funds for teachers.

Eligibility: Applicants must be current public school teachers in PreK-12, public school education support professionals or faculty or staff at public higher education institutions. Preference is given to those who work with economically disadvantaged students and NEA members. The grants may be used for materials, supplies, equipment, transportation, software or scholars-in-residence and in some cases professional development. The work should "engage students in critical thinking and problem solving that deepens their knowledge of standards-based subject matter."

Target applicant:
 Graduate school students
 Adult students

Minimum GPA: None.

Amount: $5,000.

Number of awards: Varies.

Deadline: February 1, June 1, October 15.

How to apply: Applications are available online and may be submitted at any time. Applications are reviewed three times each year on February 1, June 1 and October 15.

(671) · Student Journalist Impact Award

Journalism Education Association
Kansas State University
103 Kedzie Hall
Manhattan, KS 66506
Phone: 785-532-5532
Email: jea@spub.ksu.edu
Website: http://www.jea.org

Purpose: To award scholarships to secondary school students who have made a difference in their own lives, the lives of others or their community or school through journalism.

Eligibility: Applicants must have a teacher who is a member of JEA. Submitted works must have been published within the past two years.

Target applicant:
 High school students

Minimum GPA: None.

Amount: $1,000.

Number of awards: 1.

Deadline: March 1.

How to apply: Applications are available online.

(672) · Student Paper Competition

American Criminal Justice Association
P.O. Box 601047
Sacramento, CA 95860-1047
Phone: 916-484-6553
Fax: 916-488-2227
Email: acjalae@aol.com
Website: http://www.acjalae.org

Purpose: To encourage scholarship in criminal justice students.

Eligibility: Applicants must be student members (undergraduate or graduate) of the American Criminal Justice Association-Lambda Alpha Epsilon and submit an original paper on criminology, law enforcement, juvenile justice, courts, corrections, prevention, planning and evaluation or career development and education in the field of criminal justice. Students may apply for membership along with their paper submission. Applicants should submit applications and three copies of the paper.

Target applicant:
 College students
 Graduate school students
 Adult students

Minimum GPA: None.

Amount: $50-$150.

Number of awards: 3.

Deadline: January 31.

How to apply: Applications are available online and by written request.

(673) · Student Travel Award

American Sociological Association
1307 New York Avenue NW
Suite 700
Washington, DC 20005
Phone: 202-383-9005
Fax: 202-638-0882
Email: minority.affairs@asanet.org
Website: http://www.asanet.org

Purpose: To help students with travel expenses to the ASA annual meeting.

Eligibility: Applicants must be pursuing an undergraduate or graduate sociology degree in an academic institution and current student members of ASA. Awards are based on participation in the annual meeting, purpose for attending, student need, availability of other forms of support, matching funds and the potential benefit to the student.

Target applicant:
 College students
 Graduate school students
 Adult students

Minimum GPA: None.

Amount: $200.

Number of awards: 25.

Deadline: May 1.

How to apply: Applications are available online.

(674) · Student with a Disability Scholarship

American Speech-Language-Hearing Foundation
2200 Research Boulevard
Rockville, MD 20850
Phone: 301-296-8700
Email: foundation@asha.org
Website: http://www.ashfoundation.org

Purpose: To support a graduate student with a disability studying communication sciences and disorders.

Eligibility: Master's degree candidates must be in programs accredited by the Council on Academic Accreditation for Audiology and Speech Pathology, but doctoral programs do not have to be accredited. The applicants should submit a transcript, essay, reference form and statement of good standing; be recommended by a faculty or workplace committee and have not received scholarships from the ASHA Foundation. Students must attend their programs full-time.

Target applicant:
 Graduate school students
 Adult students

Minimum GPA: None.

Amount: $4,000.

Number of awards: 1.

Deadline: January 13.

How to apply: Applications are available online.

(675) · Summer Fellowship Program

American Institute for Economic Research
P.O. Box 1000
Attn.: Susan Gillette, Assistant to the President
Great Barrington, MA 01230
Phone: 413-528-1216
Fax: 413-528-0103
Email: fellowship@aier.org
Website: http://www.aier.org
Purpose: To provide summer fellowships for college seniors entering a doctoral program in economics or economics-related studies.
Eligibility: Applicants must be college seniors who will enter a doctoral program in economics or an affiliated program.
Target applicant:
　　College students
　　Adult students
Minimum GPA: None.
Amount: Room and board, $250 per week.
Number of awards: 12.
Deadline: March 31.
How to apply: Applications are available online.

(676) · Tailhook Educational Foundation Scholarship

Tailhook Association
The Tailhook Educational Foundation
9696 Businesspark Avenue
San Diego, CA 92131-1643
Phone: 800-269-8267
Email: thookassn@aol.com
Website: http://www.tailhook.org
Purpose: To assist the members of and the children of the members of the United States Navy carrier aviation.
Eligibility: Applicants must be high school graduates who are accepted at an undergraduate institution and are the natural or adopted children of current or former Naval Aviators, Naval Flight Officers or Naval Aircrewmen. Applicants may also be individuals or children of individuals who are serving or have served on board a U.S. Navy Aircraft Carrier in the ship's company or the air wing. Educational and extracurricular achievements, merit and citizenship will be considered.
Target applicant:
　　High school students
　　College students
　　Adult students
Minimum GPA: None.
Amount: Varies.
Number of awards: Varies.
Deadline: March 15.
How to apply: Applications are available online.

(677) · Teacher Education Scholarship Fund

American Montessori Society
281 Park Avenue South
New York, NY 10010
Phone: 212-358-1250
Fax: 212-358-1256
Email: info@amshq.org
Website: http://www.amshq.org
Purpose: To support future Montessori teachers.

Eligibility: Applicants must be accepted into but not yet attending an AMS teacher education program. Financial need, the applicant's personal statement and letters of recommendation are considered.
Target applicant:
　　High school students
　　College students
　　Adult students
Minimum GPA: None.
Amount: Tuition.
Number of awards: Varies.
Scholarship may be renewable.
Deadline: May 1.
How to apply: Applications are available online.

(678) · Teacher of the Year Award

Veterans of Foreign Wars
406 W. 34th Street
Kansas City, MO 64111
Phone: 816-756-3390
Fax: 816-968-1149
Email: info@vfw.org
Website: http://www.vfw.org
Purpose: To salute the nation's top elementary, junior high and high school teachers who educate their students about citizenship and American history and traditions.
Eligibility: Applicants must be current classroom teachers who teach at least half of the school day in a classroom environment, grades K-12. Previous winners from the state or national levels are not eligible. Fellow teachers, supervisors or other interested individuals who are not related to the nominee may send in nominations; no self-nominations will be accepted.
Target applicant:
　　College students
　　Graduate school students
　　Adult students
Minimum GPA: None.
Amount: $1,000.
Number of awards: 3.
Deadline: November 1.
How to apply: Applications are available online but initial nominations must be sent to the local VFW office. Visit the website for more information.

(679) · The FBI Common Knowledge Challenge

Common Knowledge Scholarship Foundation
P.O. Box 290361
Davie, FL 33329-0361
Phone: 954-262-8553
Email: info@cksf.org
Website: http://www.cksf.org
Purpose: To educate students about the Federal Bureau of Investigation.
Eligibility: Applicants must be high school students, college students or parents. They must participate in an online quiz competition for a chance to win.
Target applicant:
　　High school students
　　College students
　　Adult students
Minimum GPA: None.
Amount: $250.

Number of awards: 1.
Deadline: November 16.
How to apply: Applications are available online.

(680) · Thomas H. Steel Fellowship Fund

Pride Law Fund
P.O. Box 2602
San Francisco, CA 94104
Email: info@pridelawfund.org
Website: http://www.pridelawfund.org
Purpose: To support law students with a project that serves the lesbian, gay, bisexual and transgendered community.
Eligibility: Applicants must be students in their last year of law school or lawyers within three years of graduating from law school. The award is based on the quality and scope of the project, proposal, public service activities, and relation to the LGBT community. Applicants should submit applications, resumes, project descriptions, two reference letters, budget, timetable and law school transcript.
Target applicant:
　　Graduate school students
　　Adult students
Minimum GPA: None.
Amount: $25,000-$35,000.
Number of awards: 1.
Deadline: December 31.
How to apply: Applications are available online.

(681) · TLMI Four Year Colleges/Full-Time Students Scholarship

Tag and Label Manufacturers Institute Inc.
40 Shuman Boulevard, Suite 295
Naperville, IL 60563
Phone: 630-357-9222
Fax: 630-357-0192
Website: http://www.tlmi.com
Purpose: To assist upper-level students planning to pursue a career in tag and label manufacturing.
Eligibility: Applicants must demonstrate an interest in the tag and label manufacturing industry while taking appropriate courses at an accredited four-year college. They must be full-time sophomores or juniors with a GPA of at least 3.0. Applicants must submit a personal statement and three letters of recommendation attesting to their character.
Target applicant:
　　College students
　　Adult students
Minimum GPA: 3.0
Amount: $5,000.
Number of awards: 6.
Deadline: March 31.
How to apply: Applications are available online and by phone.

(682) · Tobin Sorenson Physical Education Scholarship

Pi Lambda Theta
P.O. Box 6626
Bloomington, IN 47407
Phone: 800-487-3411
Fax: 812-339-3462
Email: office@pilambda.org
Website: http://www.pilambda.org

Purpose: To support future K-12 physical education teachers.
Eligibility: Applicants must be pursuing a career as a physical education teacher, adapted physical education teacher, coach, recreational therapist, dance therapist or related profession at the K-12 level. They must be at least college sophomores with a GPA of 3.5 or higher. Applicants must also demonstrate leadership abilities and involvement in extracurricular activities related to their chosen profession. This scholarship is only awarded in odd years.
Target applicant:
　　College students
　　Adult students
Minimum GPA: None.
Amount: $1,000.
Number of awards: 1.
Deadline: February 10 of odd years.
How to apply: Applications are available online.

(683) · Tom and Judith Comstock Scholarship

American Radio Relay League Foundation
225 Main Street
Newington, CT 06111
Phone: 860-594-0397
Fax: 860-594-0259
Email: foundation@arrl.org
Website: http://www.arrl.org
Purpose: To assist ham radio operators in furthering their educations.
Eligibility: Applicants must have any class of ham radio license, be residents of Texas or Oklahoma and be high school seniors accepted at a two- or four-year college or university.
Target applicant:
　　High school students
Minimum GPA: None.
Amount: $1,000.
Number of awards: 1.
Deadline: February 1.
How to apply: Applications are available online but may not be completed electronically. All completed applications must be mailed.

(684) · Tourism Cares Sustainable Tourism Scholarship

Tourism Cares
585 Washington Street
Canton, MA 02021
Phone: 781-821-5990
Fax: 781-821-8949
Email: carolynv@tourismcares.org
Website: http://www.tourismcares.org
Purpose: To promote sustainable tourism and to assist graduate students who are studying tourism.
Eligibility: Applicants must be enrolled in a tourism program at the graduate level at an accredited college or university in any country and have a GPA of 3.0 or higher. Students in developing countries are encouraged to apply.
Target applicant:
　　Graduate school students
　　Adult students
Minimum GPA: 3.0
Amount: $1,000.
Number of awards: 1.
Deadline: April 2.
How to apply: Applications are available online.

(685) · Transatlantic Fellows Program

German Marshall Fund of the United States
1744 R Street NW
Washington, DC 20009
Phone: 202-745-3950
Fax: 202-265-1662
Email: info@gmfus.org
Website: http://www.gmfus.org
Purpose: To research topics of foreign policy, international security, trade and economic development and immigration.
Eligibility: Fellowships are by invitation from GMF and are issued to senior policy-practitioners, journalists, academics and businesspeople. Fellows work in residence in Washington, DC and Brussels, Belgium.
Target applicant:
    Graduate school students
    Adult students
Minimum GPA: None.
Amount: Varies.
Number of awards: Varies.
Deadline: Varies.
How to apply: Contact John K. Glenn at the organization for more information.

(686) · Travel Leaders Scholarship

Tourism Cares
585 Washington Street
Canton, MA 02021
Phone: 781-821-5990
Fax: 781-821-8949
Email: carolynv@tourismcares.org
Website: http://www.tourismcares.org
Purpose: To assist graduate students who are studying travel and tourism.
Eligibility: Applicants must be entering or returning graduate students at accredited colleges or universities in the U.S. or Canada. They must be enrolled in a travel and tourism-related program and have a minimum GPA of 3.0.
Target applicant:
    Graduate school students
    Adult students
Minimum GPA: 3.0
Amount: $1,000.
Number of awards: 2.
Deadline: April 2.
How to apply: Applications are available online.

(687) · TROA Scholarship

Military Officers Association of America
201 N. Washington Street
Alexandria, VA 22314
Phone: 800-234-6622
Email: msc@moaa.org
Website: http://www.moaa.org
Purpose: To award scholarships to children of military families.
Eligibility: Applicants must have a minimum 3.0 GPA, be under the age of 24 and be the children of a member of the uniformed services. Children of enlisted personnel are also eligible for the scholarship. Recipients are selected on the basis of scholastic ability, potential, character, leadership and financial need. Students accepting a military academy appointment are not eligible for the grants, but recipients who

join the armed forces during college may have their maximum age for eligibility raised by as much as five years.
Target applicant:
    High school students
    College students
Minimum GPA: 3.0
Amount: $3,000.
Number of awards: 25.
Scholarship may be renewable.
Deadline: March 1.
How to apply: Applications are available online.

(688) · TSA-Sponsored ITEA Scholarship

International Technology Education Association
Foundation for Technology Education
1914 Association Drive, Suite 201
Reston, VA 20191
Phone: 703-860-2100
Fax: 703-860-0353
Email: bmongold@iteaconnect.org
Website: http://www.iteaconnect.org
Purpose: To provide scholarships for TSA students who plan to pursue a career in teaching technology to students in grades K-12.
Eligibility: Applicants must be TSA members and have participated in a local chapter for at least two years; served as a TSA officer at the local, state, or national level for at least one academic year and attended at least one TSA state or national conference.
Target applicant:
    High school students
    College students
    Graduate school students
    Adult students
Minimum GPA: None.
Amount: $500.
Number of awards: 1.
Deadline: December 31.
How to apply: Application information is available online.

(689) · UDT-SEAL Scholarship

Naval Special Warfare Foundation
P.O. Box 5965
Virginia Beach, VA 23471
Phone: 757-363-7490
Email: info@nswfoundation.org
Website: http://www.nswfoundation.org
Purpose: To assist the dependents of UDT-SEAL Association members.
Eligibility: Students must be single dependents of a UDT-SEAL Association member who has served in or is serving in the U.S. Armed Forces and the Naval Special Warfare community. Selection is based on academic achievement, a written essay and extracurricular involvement.
Target applicant:
    High school students
    College students
Minimum GPA: None.
Amount: Varies.
Number of awards: Varies.
Deadline: First quarter of the year.
How to apply: Applications are available by contacting the NWSF.

(690) · Undergraduate Scholarship

International Technology Education Association
Foundation for Technology Education
1914 Association Drive, Suite 201
Reston, VA 20191
Phone: 703-860-2100
Fax: 703-860-0353
Email: bmongold@iteaconnect.org
Website: http://www.iteaconnect.org
Purpose: To support undergraduate students majoring in technology education teacher preparation.
Eligibility: Applicants must be members of ITEA, be full-time undergraduate students and have a minimum 2.5 GPA.
Target applicant:
    College students
    Adult students
Minimum GPA: 2.5
Amount: $1,000.
Number of awards: 1.
Deadline: December 1.
How to apply: Application information is available online.

(691) · Undergraduate Scholarships

Radio and Television News Directors Association
1600 K Street NW
Suite 700
Washington, DC 20006
Phone: 202-659-6510
Fax: 202-223-4007
Email: rtnda@rtnda.org
Website: http://www.rtnda.org
Purpose: To honor professional achievements in electronic journalism.
Eligibility: Applicants must be full-time college sophomores or higher with at least one full academic year remaining. Applicants may be enrolled in any major as long as their career intent is television or radio news. Applicants may only apply for one RTNDA scholarship.
Target applicant:
    College students
    Adult students
Minimum GPA: None.
Amount: Varies.
Number of awards: Varies.
Deadline: May 3.
How to apply: Applications are available online.

(692) · United States Senate Youth Program

William Randolph Hearst Foundation
90 New Montgomery Street, Suite 1212
San Francisco, CA 94105
Phone: 800-841-7048
Fax: 415-243-0760
Email: ussyp@hearstfdn.org
Website: http://www.hearstfdn.org/ussyp/
Purpose: To expose students to their government in action.
Eligibility: Applicants must be high school juniors or seniors in an elected position at school or in civic or educational offices. Award winners must attend an educational program in Washington, DC.
Target applicant:
    High school students

Minimum GPA: None.
Amount: $5,000.
Number of awards: 104.
Deadline: December 1.
How to apply: Contact your school principal, counselor or state-level education administrator.

(693) · VADM E. P. Travers Scholarship and Loan Program

Navy-Marine Corps Relief Society
875 North Randolph Street Suite 225
Arlington, VA 22203
Phone: 703-696-4960
Fax: 703-696-0144
Email: education@hq.nmcrs.org
Website: http://www.nmcrs.org
Purpose: To aid Navy and Marine Corps families.
Eligibility: Applicants must be enrolled or planning to enroll as full-time undergraduate students at an eligible post-secondary, technical or vocational institution. Applicants must also have a minimum 2.0 GPA and be unmarried dependent sons or daughters of active duty or retired Navy or Marine Corps service members or spouses of active duty Navy or Marine Corps service members.
Target applicant:
    College students
    Adult students
Minimum GPA: 2.0
Amount: $2,000.
Number of awards: Varies.
Scholarship may be renewable.
Deadline: March 1.
How to apply: Applications are available online.

(694) · W.M. Keck Foundation Fellowships for Young Scholars

Huntington Library, Art Collections and Botanical Gardens
1151 Oxford Road
San Marino, CA 91108
Phone: 626-405-2194
Fax: 626-449-5703
Email: cpowell@huntington.org
Website: http://www.huntington.org
Purpose: To provide fellowships to non-tenured faculty or doctoral candidates in British and American history, literature, art history and the history of science and medicine.
Eligibility: Applicants should be non-tenured faculty or doctoral candidates at the dissertation stage. Cover sheets, project descriptions, curriculum vitae and three letters of recommendation are required.
Target applicant:
    Graduate school students
    Adult students
Minimum GPA: None.
Amount: $11,500.
Number of awards: Varies.
Deadline: December 15.
How to apply: There is no application form, and application materials are listed online.

(695) · Wesley-Logan Prize

American Historical Association
400 A Street SE
Washington, DC 20003
Phone: 202-544-2422
Fax: 202-544-8307
Email: info@historians.org
Website: http://www.historians.org
Purpose: To award a prize to a scholarly/literary book focusing on the history of dispersion, relocation, settlement or adjustment of people from Africa, or on their return to that continent.
Eligibility: Books must have been published between May 1 of the previous year and April 30 of the entry year. Entries are mailed directly to committee members.
Target applicant:
　Junior high students or younger
　High school students
　College students
　Graduate school students
　Adult students
Minimum GPA: None.
Amount: Varies.
Number of awards: Varies.
Deadline: May 15.
How to apply: Application information is available on approximately March 30.

(696) · William B. Ruggles Right to Work Scholarship

National Institute for Labor Relations Research (NILRR)
William B. Ruggles Scholarship Selection Committee
5211 Port Royal Road, Suite 510
Springfield, VA 22151
Phone: 703-321-9606
Fax: 703-321-7342
Email: research@nilrr.org
Website: http://www.nilrr.org
Purpose: To support students who are dedicated to high journalistic standards.
Eligibility: Applicants must be undergraduate or graduate students majoring in journalism and demonstrate an understanding of the principles of voluntary unionism and the economic and social problems of compulsory unionism.
Target applicant:
　College students
　Graduate school students
　Adult students
Minimum GPA: None.
Amount: $2,000.
Number of awards: 1.
Deadline: December 31.
How to apply: Applications are available online.

(697) · William L. Hastie Award

National Association of Blacks in Criminal Justice
North Carolina Central University
P.O. Box 19788
Durham, NC 27707
Phone: 919-683-1801
Fax: 919-683-1903

Email: office@nabcj.org
Website: http://www.nabcj.org
Purpose: To award demonstrations of national leadership in criminal justice and the pursuit of policy change within the field.
Eligibility: The award honors the first African American appointed to the bench in 1937 by President Franklin Roosevelt. Nominator should be a member of NABCJ.
Target applicant:
　College students
　Graduate school students
　Adult students
Minimum GPA: None.
Amount: Varies.
Number of awards: Varies.
Deadline: May 1.
How to apply: Nomination applications are available online.

(698) · William R. Goldfarb Memorial Scholarship

American Radio Relay League Foundation
225 Main Street
Newington, CT 06111
Phone: 860-594-0397
Fax: 860-594-0259
Email: foundation@arrl.org
Website: http://www.arrl.org
Purpose: To provide financial assistance to high school seniors who are amateur radio operators and are seeking a bachelor's degree in business, computers, medical, nursing, engineering or science.
Eligibility: Applicants must have demonstrated financial need and be planning to attend a regionally accredited institution of higher learning.
Target applicant:
　High school students
Minimum GPA: None.
Amount: Up to $10,000.
Number of awards: 1.
Deadline: February 1.
How to apply: Applications are available online.

(699) · William S. Bullinger Scholarship

Federal Circuit Bar Association
1620 I Street NW
Suite 900
Washington, DC 20006
Phone: 202-466-3923
Fax: 202-833-1061
Website: http://www.fedcirbar.org
Purpose: To support financially needy but academically promising law students.
Eligibility: Applicants must be undergraduate or graduate law student who demonstrate financial need and academic promise. They must submit a one-page statement describing their financial circumstances, their interest in law and their qualifications for the scholarship along with transcripts and a curriculum vitae. Applicants will be considered for the William S. Bullinger Scholarship when applying for the Giles Sutherland Rich Memorial Scholarship.
Target applicant:
　College students
　Graduate school students
　Adult students
Minimum GPA: None.

Amount: $5,000.
Number of awards: Varies.
Deadline: April 30.
How to apply: There is no application form.

---

(700) · Women in Geographic Education Scholarship

National Council for Geographic Education
Jacksonville State University
206-A Martin Hall
700 Pelham Road North
Jacksonville, AL 36265-1602
Phone: 256-782-5293
Fax: 256-782-5336
Email: ncge@jsu.edu
Website: http://www.ncge.org
Purpose: To aid undergraduate or graduate women planning careers in geographic education.
Eligibility: Applicants must be enrolled in a program leading to a career in geographic education, submit an essay on the provided topic and have an overall GPA of 3.0 and a geography GPA of 3.5. The winner receives an additional $300 travel stipend if she attends the NCGE Annual Meeting.
Target applicant:
    College students
    Graduate school students
    Adult students
Minimum GPA: 3.0
Amount: $300.
Number of awards: 1.
Deadline: March 15.
How to apply: Applications are available online.

---

(701) · Women in Need Scholarship

Educational Foundation for Women in Accounting
P.O. Box 1925
Southeastern, PA 19399
Phone: 610-407-9229
Fax: 610-644-3713
Email: info@efwa.org
Website: http://www.efwa.org
Purpose: This scholarship was established to provide financial assistance to female reentry students who are pursuing degrees in accounting.
Eligibility: Applicants must be female students pursuing a degree in accounting. This award is directed toward incoming, current or reentering juniors. Selection criteria include commitment to the study of accounting, accounting aptitude, established goals and financial need.
Target applicant:
    College students
    Adult students
Minimum GPA: None.
Amount: Up to $2,000.
Number of awards: 1.
Scholarship may be renewable.
Deadline: April 15.
How to apply: Applications are available online.

---

(702) · Women in Transition Scholarship

Educational Foundation for Women in Accounting
P.O. Box 1925
Southeastern, PA 19399
Phone: 610-407-9229

Fax: 610-644-3713
Email: info@efwa.org
Website: http://www.efwa.org
Purpose: This scholarship was established to provide financial assistance to female reentry students who are pursuing degrees in accounting.
Eligibility: Applicants must be female students pursuing a degree in accounting. The award is directed toward incoming, current or reentering freshmen. Selection criteria include commitment to the study of accounting, aptitude, and financial need.
Target applicant:
    High school students
    College students
    Adult students
Minimum GPA: None.
Amount: Up to $4,000.
Number of awards: 1.
Scholarship may be renewable.
Deadline: April 15.
How to apply: Applications are available online.

---

(703) · Worda Russell Memorial Endowment

Epsilon Sigma Alpha Foundation
P.O. Box 270517
Fort Collins, CO 80527
Phone: 970-223-2824
Fax: 970-223-4456
Email: kloyd@knoxy.net
Website: http://www.esaintl.com/esaf
Purpose: To provide financial assistance for teaching majors.
Eligibility: Applicants may be residents of any state and attend any institution of higher learning. Selection is based on scholastic ability (30 percent), financial need (30 percent), leadership (20 percent), character (10 percent) and service (10 percent).
Target applicant:
    High school students
    College students
    Adult students
Minimum GPA: None.
Amount: $1,000.
Number of awards: 1.
Deadline: February 1.
How to apply: Applications are available online.

---

(704) · Yasme Foundation Scholarship

American Radio Relay League Foundation
225 Main Street
Newington, CT 06111
Phone: 860-594-0397
Fax: 860-594-0259
Email: foundation@arrl.org
Website: http://www.arrl.org
Purpose: To support science and engineering students who are involved in amateur radio.
Eligibility: Applicants must have an active amateur radio license. Students must be enrolled in a four-year college or university. Preference will be given to students in the top 10 percent of their class and those who have participated in community service and local amateur radio clubs.
Target applicant:
    High school students
    College students
    Adult students

Minimum GPA: None.
Amount: $2,000.
Number of awards: 5.
Scholarship may be renewable.
Deadline: February 1.
How to apply: Applications are available online.

(705) · Yellow Ribbon Scholarship

Tourism Cares
585 Washington Street
Canton, MA 02021
Phone: 781-821-5990
Fax: 781-821-8949
Email: carolynv@tourismcares.org
Website: http://www.tourismcares.org
Purpose: To provide financial assistance to travel and tourism students who have physical or sensory disabilities.
Eligibility: Applicants must be enrolled in a travel and tourism-related program at an accredited two- or four- year college or university in the U.S. or Canada at the undergraduate or graduate level. They must enter the undergraduate level with a 3.0 or higher GPA or maintain a 2.5 or higher GPA at the undergraduate or graduate level.
Target applicant:
    High school students
    College students
    Graduate school students
    Adult students
Minimum GPA: 2.5
Amount: $3,500.
Number of awards: 1.
Deadline: April 2.
How to apply: Applications are available online.

(706) · Young Communicators Fellowships

Institute for Humane Studies at George Mason University
3301 N. Fairfax Drive
Suite 440
Arlington, VA 22201
Phone: 800-697-8799
Fax: 703-993-4890
Email: ihs@gmu.edu
Website: http://www.theihs.org
Purpose: To help students pursue careers which involve the communication of ideas.
Eligibility: Applicants must be college juniors or seniors, graduate students or recent graduates, have a clearly demonstrated interest in the classical liberal tradition of individual rights and market economies and pursue careers in journalism, film, writing (fiction or nonfiction), publishing or market-oriented public policy. Applicants must also have arranged or applied for an internship, training program or other short-term opportunity related to the intended career. Applicants must submit a written proposal, cover letter, resume, writing sample and two references.
Target applicant:
    College students
    Graduate school students
    Adult students
Minimum GPA: None.
Amount: $2,500 and housing and travel assistance up to $2,500.
Number of awards: Varies.

Deadline: March 15 for summer positions or 10 weeks in advance for others.
How to apply: There is no application form.

(707) · Youth Scholarship

Society of Broadcast Engineers
9102 N. Meridian Street
Suite 150
Indianapolis, IN 46260
Phone: 317-846-9000
Fax: 317-846-9120
Email: mclappe@sbe.org
Website: http://www.sbe.org
Purpose: To help students who plan to pursue a career in the technical aspects of broadcasting.
Eligibility: Applicants must be graduating high school seniors who plan to enroll in a technical school, college or university and should pursue studies leading to a career in broadcasting engineering or a related field. Preference is given to members of SBE, but any student may apply. Applicants should submit applications, transcripts, biographies and statements. Recipients must write a paper about broadcast engineering.
Target applicant:
    High school students
Minimum GPA: None.
Amount: $3,000.
Number of awards: Varies.
Deadline: July 1.
How to apply: Applications are available online.

(708) · Zachary Taylor Stevens Memorial Scholarship

American Radio Relay League Foundation
225 Main Street
Newington, CT 06111
Phone: 860-594-0397
Fax: 860-594-0259
Email: foundation@arrl.org
Website: http://www.arrl.org
Purpose: To support students who are involved in amateur radio.
Eligibility: Applicants must have an amateur radio license of Technician Class or higher. Preference will be given to students residing in call areas in Michigan, Ohio and West Virginia. Students may be enrolled in a two-year or four-year college or technical school.
Target applicant:
    High school students
    College students
    Adult students
Minimum GPA: None.
Amount: $750.
Number of awards: 1.
Deadline: February 1.
How to apply: Applications are available online.

SCIENCES

(709) · A.O. Putnam Memorial Scholarship

Institute of Industrial Engineers (IIE)
3577 Parkway Lane
Suite 200
Norcross, GA 30092
Phone: 800-494-0460
Fax: 770-441-3295
Email: bcameron@iienet.org
Website: http://www.iienet.org/studentcenter
Purpose: To help undergraduate Institute members who plan to pursue careers in management consulting.
Eligibility: Applicants must be undergraduate students enrolled in a college in the United States, Canada or Mexico with an accredited industrial engineering program, major in industrial engineering and be active members. Preference is given to students who plan to work in management consulting. Students may not apply directly for this scholarship and must be nominated. The award is based on academic ability, character, leadership, potential service to the industrial engineering profession and financial need.
Target applicant:
    College students
    Adult students
Minimum GPA: 3.4
Amount: $600.
Number of awards: 1.
Deadline: February 15.
How to apply: Nomination forms are available online.

(710) · AAAE Foundation Scholarship

American Association of Airport Executives
601 Madison Street
Alexandria, VA 22314
Phone: 703-824-0500
Fax: 703-820-1395
Email: member.services@aaae.org
Website: http://www.aaae.org
Purpose: To support students of aviation.
Eligibility: Applicants must be enrolled in an aviation program with at least junior standing and at least a 3.0 GPA for a chance at 10 of the scholarships. Applicants must be pursuing any degree and be recommended by an active AAAE member for a chance at the remaining 15 scholarships.
Target applicant:
    High school students
    College students
    Graduate school students
    Adult students
Minimum GPA: 3.0
Amount: $1,000.
Number of awards: 25.
Deadline: May 31.
How to apply: Applicants should email the organization for more information.

(711) · AACN Educational Advancement Scholarship

American Association of Critical-Care Nurses
101 Columbia
Aliso Viejo, CA 92656
Phone: 800-899-2226
Fax: 949-362-2020
Email: info@aacn.org
Website: http://www.aacn.org
Purpose: To advance critical care nursing and promote nursing professionalism.
Eligibility: Applicants must be AACN members in good standing with active RN licenses, have a minimum 3.0 GPA, be junior status or higher, be currently working in critical care or have worked in critical care for one full year in the last three years and be currently enrolled in a nursing program accredited by the State Board of Nursing in their state.
Target applicant:
    College students
    Adult students
Minimum GPA: None.
Amount: $1,500.
Number of awards: Varies.
Scholarship may be renewable.
Deadline: April 1.
How to apply: Applications are available online.

(712) · Abel Wolman Fellowship

American Water Works Association
6666 W. Quincy Avenue
Denver, CO 80235-3098
Phone: 303-347-6201
Fax: 303-795-7603
Email: swheeler@awwa.org
Website: http://www.awwa.org
Purpose: To support doctoral students pursuing advanced training and research in the field of water supply and treatment.
Eligibility: Applicants must obtain a Ph.D. within two years of the award, must be citizens of the U.S., Canada or Mexico and should submit applications, transcripts, GRE scores, three recommendation letters, course of study and description of the dissertation research study and how it pertains to water supply and treatment. The award is based on academics, the connection between the research and water supply and treatment and the applicant's research skills.
Target applicant:
    Graduate school students
    Adult students
Minimum GPA: None.
Amount: $20,000.
Number of awards: 1.
Scholarship may be renewable.
Deadline: January 15.
How to apply: Applications are available online.

(713) · Academic Achievement Award

American Water Works Association
6666 W. Quincy Avenue
Denver, CO 80235-3098
Phone: 303-347-6201
Fax: 303-795-7603
Email: swheeler@awwa.org
Website: http://www.awwa.org
Purpose: To recognize contributions to the field of public water supply.
Eligibility: Master's theses and doctoral dissertations that are relevant to the water supply industry are eligible. Unbound manuscripts must be the work of a single author and be submitted during the competition

year in which they were submitted for the degree. Students may major in any area as long as the research is directly related to the drinking water supply industry. In addition to the application, students must submit a one-page abstract of the manuscript and a letter of endorsement from the major professor or department chair. The doctoral dissertation awards are $3,000 and $1,500. The master's thesis awards are $3,000 and $1,500.

Target applicant:
   Graduate school students
   Adult students

Minimum GPA: None.

Amount: $1,500 and $3,000.

Number of awards: 4.

Deadline: October 1.

How to apply: Applications are available online.

(714) · Academic Study Award

American Association of Occupational Health Nurses (AAOHN) Foundation
2920 Brandywine Road
Suite 100
Atlanta, GA 30341
Phone: 770-455-7757
Fax: 770-455-7271
Email: ann@aaohn.org
Website: http://www.aaohn.org

Purpose: To provide further education for occupational and environmental health professionals.

Eligibility: Applicants must be registered nurses enrolled full- or part-time in a nationally accredited school of nursing baccalaureate program with an interest in occupational and environmental health or be registered nurses enrolled full- or part-time in a graduate program that has application to occupational and environmental health. Applicants should submit a narrative and letters of recommendation.

Target applicant:
   College students
   Graduate school students
   Adult students

Minimum GPA: None.

Amount: $3,500.

Number of awards: 4.

Scholarship may be renewable.

Deadline: December 1.

How to apply: Applications are available online.

(715) · ACI Student Fellowship Program

American Concrete Institute Student Fellowship Program
38800 Country Club Drive
Farmington Hills, MI 48331
Phone: 248-848-3700
Fax: 248-848-3701
Email: scholarships@concrete.org
Website: http://www.concrete.org

Purpose: To encourage careers in the concrete field.

Eligibility: Applicants must be full-time undergraduate or graduate students nominated by a faculty member who is also a member of the ACI. Students must be studying engineering, construction management or another relevant field. Applicants may live anywhere in the world, but actual study must take place in the U.S. or Canada. Finalists for a fellowship must attend an ACI convention for an interview. In addition

to the monetary award, the scholarship also includes conference fees, mentoring and a potential internship.

Target applicant:
   College students
   Graduate school students
   Adult students

Minimum GPA: None.

Amount: $10,000.

Number of awards: Varies.

Scholarship may be renewable.

Deadline: November 15.

How to apply: Applicants must be nominated by ACI-member faculty in order to receive an application.

(716) · ACI-James Instruments Student Award for Research on NDT of Concrete

American Concrete Institute ACI-James Instruments Student Award
F. Dirk Heidbrink
Wiss Janney, Elstner Associates, Inc
330 Pfingsten Road
Northbrook, IL 60062
Phone: 248-848-3700
Fax: 248-848-3701
Email: fheidbrink@wje.com
Website: http://www.aci-int.org

Purpose: To recognize outstanding research in the area of concrete and concrete materials using NDT methods.

Eligibility: Applicants must submit an original research paper on a topic related to the nondestructive testing (NDT) of concrete. The research must have been done by applicants while enrolled either as an undergraduate or a graduate student in an accredited institution of higher education.

Target applicant:
   College students
   Graduate school students
   Adult students

Minimum GPA: None.

Amount: $800.

Number of awards: 1.

Deadline: December 5.

How to apply: There is no application form. Papers must be submitted by mail.

(717) · ACIL Scholarship

American Council of Independent Laboratories
1629 K Street NW, Suite 400
Washington, DC 20006-1633
Phone: 202-887-5872
Fax: 202-887-0021
Email: jallen@acil.org
Website: http://www.acil.org

Purpose: To encourage students to enter the laboratory testing community.

Eligibility: Applicants must be college juniors or higher attending a four-year university or graduate school program and must major in physics, chemistry, engineering, geology, biology or environmental science. In addition to the applications, applicants should submit resumes, two recommendation letters, transcripts and any information about other scholarships received.

Target applicant:
  College students
  Graduate school students
  Adult students
Minimum GPA: None.
Amount: $1,000-$4,000.
Number of awards: Varies.
Deadline: April 4.
How to apply: Applications are available online.

(718) · ACSM - AAGS - NSPS Scholarships

American Congress on Surveying and Mapping (ACSM)
6 Montgomery Village Avenue
Suite 403
Gaithersburg, MD 20879
Phone: 240-632-9716
Fax: 240-632-1321
Website: http://www.acsm.net
Purpose: To award excellent surveying and mapping students.
Eligibility: There are several different types of awards. The first is for students enrolled in two-year degree programs in surveying technology. The second is for students enrolled in or accepted to a graduate program in geodetic surveying or geodesy. The third is for students enrolled in four-year degree programs in surveying (or in related areas such as geomatics or surveying engineering). The last type is for students enrolled in a two-year or four-year surveying (and closely related) degree program, either full or part-time. All awards are based on academic record, statement, recommendation letters and professional activities.
Target applicant:
  College students
  Graduate school students
  Adult students
Minimum GPA: None.
Amount: $500-$5,000.
Number of awards: Varies.
Deadline: December 1.
How to apply: Applications are available online.

(719) · ADAF Student Scholarship

American Dietetic Association Foundation
120 South Riverside Plaza
Suite 2000
Chicago, IL 60606-6995
Phone: 800-877-1600
Email: education@eatright.org
Website: http://www.eatright.org
Purpose: To encourage students in a dietetic program.
Eligibility: Applicants should be American Dietetic Association members and enrolled in their junior or senior year of a baccalaureate or coordinated program in dietetics or the second year of study in a dietetic technician program, a dietetic internship program or a graduate program. One application form is used for all ADAF scholarships.
Target applicant:
  College students
  Graduate school students
  Adult students
Minimum GPA: None.
Amount: Varies.
Number of awards: Varies.
Deadline: February.
How to apply: Applications are available online.

(720) · Adams Scholarship Grant

American Society of Agricultural Engineers Foundation
Administrator
Scholarship Fund
2950 Niles Road
St. Joseph, MI 49085
Phone: 269-429-0300
Fax: 269-429-3852
Website: http://www.asae.org
Purpose: To aid undergraduate students with an interest in agricultural machinery product design and development.
Eligibility: Applicants must be biological or agricultural engineering majors in eligible accredited programs in the U.S. or Canada. Applicants must also have completed at least one year of undergraduate study and have at least one year of undergraduate study remaining, have a minimum 2.5 GPA, have an interest in agricultural machinery product design and development and demonstrate financial need.
Target applicant:
  College students
  Adult students
Minimum GPA: 2.5
Amount: $1,000.
Number of awards: 1.
Deadline: March 15.
How to apply: Application is by formal letter.

(721) · ADDC Education Trust Scholarship

Desk and Derrick Educational Trust
5153 E 51st Street, Suite 107
Tulsa, OK 74135
Phone: 918-622-1749
Fax: 918-622-1675
Email: adotulsa@swbell.net
Website: http://www.addc.org
Purpose: To promote studies in the energy industry.
Eligibility: Applicants must be U.S. or Canadian citizens, have completed two years of undergraduate study, have a minimum 3.0 GPA and demonstrate financial need. Students must be pursuing a degree in a field related to the petroleum, energy or allied industries and plan to work full-time in the petroleum, energy or allied industry or research alternative fuels such as coal, electric, solar, wind hydroelectric, nuclear or ethanol.
Target applicant:
  College students
  Adult students
Minimum GPA: 3.0
Amount: Varies.
Number of awards: Varies.
Deadline: April 1.
How to apply: Applications are available online.

(722) · ADHA Institute Scholarship Program

American Dental Hygienists' Association (ADHA) Institute for Oral Health
444 N. Michigan Avenue
Suite 3400
Chicago, IL 60611
Phone: 800-735-4916
Email: institute@adha.net
Website: http://www.adha.org/institute

Purpose: To assist students pursuing a career in dental hygiene.

Eligibility: Applicants should be enrolled full-time (unless applying for a part-time scholarship) in an accredited dental hygiene program in the U.S., be finishing their first year and have a minimum 3.0 GPA. Undergraduate students should be active members of the Student American Dental Hygienists' Association or the American Dental Hygienists Association. Graduate students should be active members of the Student American Dental Hygienists' Association or the American Dental Hygienists Association, have a valid dental hygiene license and a bachelor's degree. There should be financial need of at least $1,500, with the exception of the merit-based scholarships.

Target applicant:
College students
Graduate school students
Adult students

Minimum GPA: 3.0

Amount: $1,000-$2,000.

Number of awards: Varies.

Deadline: June 30.

How to apply: Applications are available online.

---

(723) · AFCEA General John A. Wickham Scholarships

Armed Forces Communications and Electronics Association
4400 Fair Lakes Court
Fairfax, VA 22033
Phone: 800-336-4583
Fax: 703-631-4693
Email: scholarship@afcea.org
Website: http://www.afcea.org

Purpose: Monetary assistance for college is awarded to sophomores and juniors who are studying electrical, computer, chemical or aerospace engineering, computer science, physics or mathematics.

Eligibility: Applicants must be full-time college sophomores or juniors in accredited four-year U.S. colleges or universities, be U.S. citizens, be working toward a degree in electrical, computer, chemical or aerospace engineering, computer science, physics or mathematics and have a minimum 3.5 GPA. Applicants do not need to be affiliated with the U.S. military.

Target applicant:
College students
Adult students

Minimum GPA: 3.5

Amount: $2,000.

Number of awards: Varies.

Deadline: May 1.

How to apply: Applications are available online.

---

(724) · AFCEA Ralph W. Shrader Scholarships

Armed Forces Communications and Electronics Association
4400 Fair Lakes Court
Fairfax, VA 22033
Phone: 800-336-4583
Fax: 703-631-4693
Email: scholarship@afcea.org
Website: http://www.afcea.org

Purpose: Monetary assistance is awarded to graduate students studying electrical, computer, chemical or aerospace engineering, mathematics, physics, computer science, computer technology, electronics, communications technology or engineering or information management systems.

Eligibility: Applicants must be U.S. citizens, full-time postgraduate students working toward a master's degree in electrical, computer, chemical or aerospace engineering, mathematics, physics, computer science, computer technology, electronics, communications technology, communications engineering or information management at an accredited U.S. university. Primary consideration will be given for demonstrated excellence. Applicants do not need to be affiliated with the U.S. military.

Target applicant:
Graduate school students
Adult students

Minimum GPA: None.

Amount: $3,000.

Number of awards: Varies.

Deadline: February 1.

How to apply: Applications are available online.

---

(725) · AfterCollege/AACN Nursing Scholarship Fund

American Association of Colleges of Nursing
One Dupont Circle NW
Suite 350
Washington, DC 20036
Phone: 202-463-6930
Fax: 202-785-8320
Email: anniea@aacn.nche.edu
Website: http://www.aacn.nche.edu

Purpose: To assist students pursuing careers in nursing.

Eligibility: Applicants must be enrolled in a bachelor's, master's or doctoral program in nursing at an AACN member institution and have a minimum 3.25 GPA.

Target applicant:
College students
Graduate school students
Adult students

Minimum GPA: 3.25

Amount: $2,500.

Number of awards: 4.

Deadline: Varies.

How to apply: Applications are available online. There are four deadlines: January 31, April 30, July 31 and October 31. Winners are announced within 60 days of each deadline.

---

(726) · AGC Graduate Scholarships

Associated General Contractors of America
333 John Carlyle Street
Suite 200
Alexandria, VA 22314
Phone: 703-837-5342
Fax: 703-837-5402
Email: sladef@agc.org
Website: http://www.agc.org

Purpose: Monetary assistance is awarded to college seniors pursuing graduate degrees that will lead to careers in construction or civil engineering.

Eligibility: Applicants must be college seniors enrolled in an undergraduate construction or civil engineering degree program or college graduates with a degree in construction or civil engineering. Applicants must also be enrolled or planning to enroll full-time in a graduate level construction or civil engineering degree program.

Target applicant:
College students
Graduate school students
Adult students
Minimum GPA: None.
Amount: $7,500.
Number of awards: 2.
Deadline: November 1.
How to apply: Applications are available online.

(727) · AGC Undergraduate Scholarships

Associated General Contractors of America
333 John Carlyle Street
Suite 200
Alexandria, VA 22314
Phone: 703-837-5342
Fax: 703-837-5402
Email: sladef@agc.org
Website: http://www.agc.org
Purpose: To assist students pursuing studies that lead to a career in construction or civil engineering.
Eligibility: Applicants must be sophomores or juniors enrolled in or planning to enroll in ABET- or ACCE-accredited construction or civil engineering programs at four- or five-year colleges.
Target applicant:
College students
Adult students
Minimum GPA: None.
Amount: $2,000.
Number of awards: Varies.
Scholarship may be renewable.
Deadline: November 1.
How to apply: Applications are available online.

(728) · AIA/AAF Minority/Disadvantaged Scholarship

American Architectural Foundation
1799 New York Avenue NW
Washington, DC 20006
Phone: 202-626-7318
Fax: 202-626-7420
Email: info@archfoundation.org
Website: http://www.archfoundation.org
Purpose: To provide scholarships for students who intend to study architecture and who could not otherwise afford to enter a degree-seeking program.
Eligibility: Applicants must be high school seniors or college freshmen who intend to study architecture in an NAAB-accredited program. Students must be nominated by a high school counselor, AIA component, architect or other person aware of student's aptitude.
Target applicant:
High school students
College students
Adult students
Minimum GPA: None.
Amount: Up to $2,500.
Number of awards: 20.
Scholarship may be renewable.
Deadline: January.
How to apply: Applications are available by email.

(729) · AIAA Foundation Undergraduate Scholarship Program

American Institute of Aeronautics and Astronautics
1801 Alexander Bell Drive
Suite 500
Reston, VA 20191-4344
Phone: 800-639-AIAA
Fax: 703-264-7551
Email: stephenb@aiaa.org
Website: http://www.aiaa.org
Purpose: AIAA advances the arts, sciences and technology of aeronautics and astronautics.
Eligibility: Applicants must be enrolled in an accredited college or university and have completed at least one semester or quarter of college work with a minimum 3.3 GPA. Applicants must plan to enter a career in science or engineering related to the technical activities of the AIAA. Applicants do not have to be AIAA student members to apply but must join before accepting scholarships. Selection is based on scholarship, career goals, recommendations and extracurricular activities.
Target applicant:
College students
Adult students
Minimum GPA: 3.3
Amount: $2,000-$2,500.
Number of awards: 30.
Scholarship may be renewable.
Deadline: January 31.
How to apply: Applications are available online.

(730) · Air Traffic Control Association Scholarship Program

Air Traffic Control Association
Attn.: Scholarship Fund
1101 King Street, Suite 300
Alexandria, VA 22134
Phone: 703-299-2430
Fax: 703-299-2437
Email: info@atca.org
Website: http://www.atca.org
Purpose: To assist students enrolled in aviation-related courses and full-time air traffic control employees and their children.
Eligibility: Applicants must be enrolled or accepted into an accredited college or university and have coursework leading to a bachelor's or graduate degree related to an aviation related career, be full-time aviation employees pursuing advanced study in air traffic control or aviation or be the children of air traffic control specialists.
Target applicant:
High school students
College students
Graduate school students
Adult students
Minimum GPA: None.
Amount: $1,500-$2,500.
Number of awards: Varies.
Deadline: May 1.
How to apply: Applications are available online.

(731) · AIST Benjamin F. Fairless Scholarship (AIME)

Iron and Steel Society
Attn.: Lori Wharrey

AIST Foundation
186 Thorn Hill Road
Warrendale, PA 15086
Phone: 724-776-6040 x621
Fax: 724-776-1880
Email: lwharrey@aist.org
Website: http://www.aistfoundation.org
Purpose: To honor the memory of Benjamin F. Fairless, former Chairman of the Board of U.S. Steel Corporation.
Eligibility: Applicants must be enrolled full-time in an accredited university in North America and majoring in engineering, metallurgy or materials science. Applicants must also have a GPA of 3.0 or higher and plan to pursue a career in the iron and steel industry.
Target applicant:
    College students
    Graduate school students
    Adult students
Minimum GPA: 3.0
Amount: $2,000.
Number of awards: 3.
Deadline: March 2.
How to apply: Applications are available online.

(732) · AIST Ronald E. Lincoln Memorial Scholarship

Iron and Steel Society
Attn.: Lori Wharrey
AIST Foundation
186 Thorn Hill Road
Warrendale, PA 15086
Phone: 724-776-6040 x621
Fax: 724-776-1880
Email: lwharrey@aist.org
Website: http://www.aistfoundation.org
Purpose: To honor the memory of Ronald Lincoln and to reward students who demonstrate leadership and innovation.
Eligibility: Applicants must be enrolled full-time in an accredited university in North America and majoring in engineering, metallurgy or materials science. Applicants must also have a GPA of 3.0 or higher and plan to pursue a career in the iron and steel industry.
Target applicant:
    College students
    Adult students
Minimum GPA: 3.0
Amount: $3,000.
Number of awards: 2.
Deadline: March 2.
How to apply: Applications are available online.

(733) · AIST William E. Schwabe Memorial Scholarship

Iron and Steel Society
Attn.: Lori Wharrey
AIST Foundation
186 Thorn Hill Road
Warrendale, PA 15086
Phone: 724-776-6040 x621
Fax: 724-776-1880
Email: lwharrey@aist.org
Website: http://www.aistfoundation.org
Purpose: To honor the memory of William E. Schwabe, steelmaking pioneer.

Eligibility: Applicants must be enrolled full-time in an accredited university in North America and majoring in engineering, metallurgy or materials science. Applicants must also have a GPA of 3.0 or higher and plan to pursue a career in the iron and steel industry.
Target applicant:
    College students
    Adult students
Minimum GPA: 3.0
Amount: $3,000.
Number of awards: 1.
Deadline: March 2.
How to apply: Applications are available online.

(734) · AIST Willy Korf Memorial Fund

Iron and Steel Society
Attn.: Lori Wharrey
AIST Foundation
186 Thorn Hill Road
Warrendale, PA 15086
Phone: 724-776-6040 x621
Fax: 724-776-1880
Email: lwharrey@aist.org
Website: http://www.aistfoundation.org
Purpose: To honor the memory of the late Willy Korf, the founder of the Korf Group and to assist students who plan to enter the fields of engineering, metallurgy or materials science in the iron and steel industry.
Eligibility: Applicants must be enrolled full-time in an accredited university in North America, and majoring in engineering, metallurgy or materials science. Applicants must also have a GPA of 3.0 or higher and plan to pursue a career in the iron and steel industry.
Target applicant:
    College students
    Adult students
Minimum GPA: 3.0
Amount: $3,000.
Number of awards: 3.
Deadline: March 2.
How to apply: Applications are available online.

(735) · Alice / Jeanne Wagner Endowment

Epsilon Sigma Alpha Foundation
P.O. Box 270517
Fort Collins, CO 80527
Phone: 970-223-2824
Fax: 970-223-4456
Email: kloyd@knoxy.net
Website: http://www.esaintl.com/esaf
Purpose: To provide financial assistance for nursing students.
Eligibility: Applicants may attend any college or university. Selection is based on the following characteristics: character (10 percent), leadership (20 percent), service (10 percent), financial need (30 percent) and scholastic ability (30 percent).
Target applicant:
    High school students
    College students
    Adult students
Minimum GPA: None.
Amount: $500.
Number of awards: 3.
Deadline: February 1.
How to apply: Applications are available online.

(736) · Alice T. Schafer Prize

Association for Women in Mathematics
4114 Computer and Space Sciences Building
University of Maryland
College Park, MD 20742
Phone: 301-405-7892
Fax: 301-314-9074
Email: awm@math.umd.edu
Website: http://www.awm-math.org
Purpose: To support female students who are studying mathematics.
Eligibility: Nominees must be female college undergraduates and either be U.S. citizens or have a school address in the U.S. Selection is based on performance in advanced mathematics courses and special programs, interest in mathematics, ability to conduct independent work and performance in mathematical competitions at the local or national level.
Target applicant:
   College students
   Adult students
Minimum GPA: None.
Amount: Varies.
Number of awards: 1-2.
Deadline: October 1.
How to apply: Applicants must be nominated.

(737) · Alice W. Rooke Scholarship and Irene And Daisy MacGregor Memorial Scholarship

National Society Daughters of the American Revolution
1776 D Street NW
Washington, DC 20006-5303
Phone: 202-628-1776
Website: http://www.dar.org
Purpose: To assist students in becoming medical doctors.
Eligibility: Applicants must be accepted into or enrolled in a graduate course of study to become a medical doctor. Those pursuing study in psychiatric nursing at the graduate level at a medical school may also apply to the Irene and Daisy MacGregor Memorial Scholarship, and preference is given to females. All applicants must obtain a letter of sponsorship from their local DAR chapter.
Target applicant:
   Graduate school students
   Adult students
Minimum GPA: None.
Amount: $5,000.
Number of awards: Varies.
Scholarship may be renewable.
Deadline: April 15.
How to apply: Applications are available by written request.

(738) · Allied Dental Health Scholarships

American Dental Association Foundation
211 East Chicago Avenue
Chicago, IL 60611
Phone: 312-440-2763
Fax: 312-440-3526
Email: famularor@ada.org
Website: http://www.ada.org
Purpose: To encourage students to pursue careers in dental hygiene, dental assisting, dentistry and dental laboratory technology.

Eligibility: Applicants must be either in their final year of study in an accredited dental hygiene program, entering students in an accredited dental assisting program or in their final year of study in an accredited dental laboratory technician program. Selection is based on minimum financial need of $1,000, academic achievement, a biographical sketch and references. A minimum 3.0 GPA is required. Only two scholarship applications per school are allowed, so schools may set their own in-school application deadlines that are earlier.
Target applicant:
   College students
   Graduate school students
   Adult students
Minimum GPA: 3.0
Amount: $1,000.
Number of awards: 30.
Deadline: October 16.
How to apply: Applications are available from dental school officials.

(739) · Alpha Mu Tau Fraternity Scholarships

American Society for Clinical Laboratory Science
6701 Democracy Boulevard, Suite 300
Bethesda, MD 20817
Phone: 301-657-2768
Fax: 301-657-2909
Email: ascls@ascls.org
Website: http://www.ascls.org
Purpose: To support new professionals in the clinical laboratory sciences.
Eligibility: Applicants must be undergraduate students entering or in their last year of study in an NAACLS-accredited program in Clinical Laboratory Science/Medical Technology or Clinical Laboratory Technician/Medical Laboratory Technician. Applicants must be a U.S. citizen or a permanent resident of the U.S.
Target applicant:
   College students
   Adult students
Minimum GPA: None.
Amount: Up to $1,500.
Number of awards: Varies.
Deadline: April 1.
How to apply: Applications are available online.

(740) · AMBUCS Scholars

AMBUCS
P.O. Box 5127
High Point, NC 27262
Phone: 800-838-1845
Fax: 336-852-6830
Email: janiceb@ambucs.org
Website: http://www.ambucs.com
Purpose: To provide more opportunities for the disabled by encouraging students to become therapists.
Eligibility: Applicants must be undergraduate juniors or seniors or graduate students pursuing their master's or doctoral degrees and must have been accepted into an accredited program in physical therapy, occupational therapy, speech language pathology or hearing audiology. Assistant programs are ineligible. Selection is based on financial need, U.S. citizenship, community service, academic achievement, character and career plans.

Target applicant:
College students
Graduate school students
Adult students
Minimum GPA: None.
Amount: $500-$6,000.
Number of awards: Varies.
Deadline: April 15.
How to apply: Applications are available online.

(741) · Amelia Earhart Fellowships

Zonta International
557 West Randolph Street
Chicago, IL 60661-2206
Phone: 312-930-5848
Fax: 312-930-0951
Email: zontafdtn@zonta.org
Website: http://www.zonta.org
Purpose: To support women in science and engineering.
Eligibility: Applicants must be pursuing graduate doctoral degrees in aerospace-related sciences and engineering.
Target applicant:
Graduate school students
Adult students
Minimum GPA: None.
Amount: Up to $100,000.
Number of awards: Varies.
Deadline: Varies.

(742) · American Architectural Foundation and Sir John Soane's Museum Foundation Traveling Fellowship

American Architectural Foundation
1799 New York Avenue NW
Washington, DC 20006
Phone: 202-626-7318
Fax: 202-626-7420
Email: info@archfoundation.org
Website: http://www.archfoundation.org
Purpose: To provide scholarships enabling graduate students to travel to England and to study the work of Sir John Soane (or Sir John Soane's Museum and its collections).
Eligibility: Applicants must be enrolled in graduate programs focusing on the history of art, architecture, decorative arts or interior design.
Target applicant:
Graduate school students
Adult students
Minimum GPA: None.
Amount: $5,000.
Number of awards: 1.
Deadline: March 1.
How to apply: Applications are available online.

(743) · American Electroplaters and Surface Finishers Society Scholarship

National Association for Surface Finishing
1155 Fifteenth Street NW
Washington, DC 20005
Phone: 202-457-8401

Fax: 202-530-0659
Website: http://www.nasf.org
Purpose: To award students whose education or research is related to surface finishing and plating technologies.
Eligibility: For the undergraduate scholarship program, applicants must be full-time undergraduates of at least junior standing majoring in chemistry, chemical engineering, environmental engineering, metallurgy, metallurgical engineering or materials science or engineering with the focus of the curriculum in surface science subjects. Applicants for the graduate scholarship program must have completed an undergraduate program leading to a master's or Ph.D. degree. Selection is based on motivation and interest in finishing technologies, scholarship potential and achievement.
Target applicant:
College students
Graduate school students
Adult students
Minimum GPA: None.
Amount: $1,500.
Number of awards: Varies.
Scholarship may be renewable.
Deadline: April 15.
How to apply: Applications are available online.

(744) · American Plastics Council (APC)/SPE Plastics Environmental Division Scholarship

Society of Plastics Engineers
14 Fairfield Drive
Brookfield, CT 06804
Phone: 203-740-5447
Fax: 203-775-1157
Email: foundation@4spe.org
Website: http://www.4spe.org
Purpose: To aid students who have an interest in the plastics industry.
Eligibility: Applicants must have an interest in the plastics industry, major in or take courses leading to a career in the plastics industry and be in good academic standing. Financial need is considered.
Target applicant:
College students
Graduate school students
Adult students
Minimum GPA: None.
Amount: $2,500.
Number of awards: 1.
Deadline: January 15.
How to apply: Applications are available online.

(745) · American Quarter Horse Foundation Scholarship

American Quarter Horse Foundation
Attn.: Scholarship Coordinator
2601 I-40 East
Amarillo, TX 79104
Phone: 806-378-5034
Fax: 806-376-1005
Email: lowens@aqha.org
Website: http://www.aqha.com
Purpose: To encourage future Quarter Horse industry professionals.
Eligibility: Applicants must demonstrate involvement in equine-related activities and be members of American Quarter Horse Association (AQHA) or American Quarter Horse Youth Association (AQHYA) for

a minimum of up to three years, depending on the scholarship. Selection is based on financial need, academic achievement, equine involvement, references and career plans. A transcript and three references are required for all scholarships. All other requirements vary by scholarship.

Target applicant:
  High school students
  College students
  Graduate school students
  Adult students
Minimum GPA: None.
Amount: $8,000.
Number of awards: 30.
Scholarship may be renewable.
Deadline: January 2.
How to apply: Applications are available online.

(746) · AMS Graduate Fellowship in the History of Science

American Meteorological Society
Macelwane Award
45 Beacon Street
Boston, MA 02108-3693
Phone: 617-227-2426 x246
Fax: 617-742-8718
Email: dfernand@ametsoc.org
Website: http://www.ametsoc.org/AMS/
Purpose: To support students writing dissertations on the history of atmospheric or related oceanic or hydrologic sciences.
Eligibility: Applicants must be graduate students who plan to write dissertations on the history of atmospheric or related oceanic or hydrologic sciences. Students must submit a cover letter with vitae, official transcripts, a typed description of the dissertation topic and three letters of recommendation.
Target applicant:
  Graduate school students
  Adult students
Minimum GPA: None.
Amount: $15,000.
Number of awards: Varies.
Deadline: February 10.
How to apply: Submit materials to address listed.

(747) · AMS Undergraduate Scholarships

American Meteorological Society
Macelwane Award
45 Beacon Street
Boston, MA 02108-3693
Phone: 617-227-2426 x246
Fax: 617-742-8718
Email: dfernand@ametsoc.org
Website: http://www.ametsoc.org/AMS/
Purpose: To encourage undergraduate students to pursue careers in the atmospheric and related oceanic and hydrologic sciences.
Eligibility: Applicants must be full-time students majoring in the atmospheric or related oceanic or hydrologic science and entering their final undergraduate year, show intent to make the atmospheric or related sciences their career and have a minimum 3.25 GPA. For the Schroeder scholarship, applicants must demonstrate financial need. For the Murphy scholarship, applicants must demonstrate interest in weather forecasting through curricular or extracurricular activities and for the Crow scholarship, applicants must demonstrate interest in applied

meteorology. The Glahn scholarship will be awarded to a student with a strong interest in statistical meteorology.
Target applicant:
  College students
  Adult students
Minimum GPA: 3.25
Amount: Varies.
Number of awards: Varies.
Deadline: February 20.
How to apply: Applications are available online.

(748) · AMS/Industry Minority Scholarships

American Meteorological Society
Macelwane Award
45 Beacon Street
Boston, MA 02108-3693
Phone: 617-227-2426 x246
Fax: 617-742-8718
Email: dfernand@ametsoc.org
Website: http://www.ametsoc.org/AMS/
Purpose: To support minority students who have been traditionally underrepresented in the sciences, especially Hispanic, Native American and African American students.
Eligibility: Applicants must be minority students who will be entering their freshman year of college in the following fall and must plan to pursue degrees in the atmospheric or related oceanic and hydrologic sciences. Applicants must submit applications, transcripts, recommendation letters, and SAT or equivalent scores. Original materials should be mailed to the closest AMS Local Chapter listed at the bottom of the application, and copies should be mailed to headquarters.
Target applicant:
  High school students
Minimum GPA: None.
Amount: $3,000.
Number of awards: Varies.
Scholarship may be renewable.
Deadline: February 10.
How to apply: Applications are available online.

(749) · AMS/Industry/Government Graduate Fellowships

American Meteorological Society
Macelwane Award
45 Beacon Street
Boston, MA 02108-3693
Phone: 617-227-2426 x246
Fax: 617-742-8718
Email: dfernand@ametsoc.org
Website: http://www.ametsoc.org/AMS/
Purpose: To attract students to prepare for careers in the meteorological, oceanic and hydrologic fields.
Eligibility: Applicants must be entering their first year of graduate study the following year and plan to pursue advanced degrees in the atmospheric and related oceanic and hydrologic sciences. Awards are based on undergraduate performance. References, transcripts, and GRE scores may be sent under separate cover. References can be sent to dfernand@ametsoc.org.
Target applicant:
  College students
  Adult students
Minimum GPA: 3.25

Amount: $22,000.
Number of awards: Varies.
Deadline: February 15.
How to apply: Applications are available online.

---

(750) · AmSECT Scholarship

American Society of Extra-Corporeal Technology (AmSECT)
2209 Dickens Road
P.O. Box 11086
Richmond, VA 23230-1086
Phone: 804-565-6363
Fax: 804-282-0090
Email: patelpump@sbcglobal.net
Website: http://www.amsect.org
Purpose: To support academic achievement in the study of cardiovascular perfusion.
Eligibility: Applicants must be current student members of AmSECT, be in a CAAHEP-accredited perfusion education program, have finished 25 percent of the coursework, have a minimum 2.75 GPA and submit an application, essay and a transcript.
Target applicant:
   College students
   Graduate school students
   Adult students
Minimum GPA: 2.75
Amount: $1,000.
Number of awards: Varies.
Deadline: December 15.
How to apply: Applications are available online.

---

(751) · AMT Student Scholarship

American Medical Technologists
10700 W. Higgins Road
Rosemont, IL 60018
Phone: 800-275-1268
Fax: 847-823-0458
Website: http://www.amt1.com
Purpose: To provide financial assistance to students interested in medical technology careers.
Eligibility: Applicants must be high school graduates or current seniors planning to attend an accredited institution to pursue an American Medical Technologists-certified career, which includes medical laboratory technology, medical assisting, dental assisting, phlebotomy and office laboratory technician.
Target applicant:
   High school students
Minimum GPA: None.
Amount: $500.
Number of awards: 5.
Deadline: April 1.
How to apply: Applications are available online.

---

(752) · Amtrol Inc. Scholarship

American Ground Water Trust
16 Centre Street
Concord, NH 03301
Phone: 603-228-5444
Fax: 603-228-6557
Website: http://www.agwt.org

Purpose: To provide scholarships for high school seniors to pursue a career in a ground water-related field.
Eligibility: Applicants must be high school seniors with intentions to pursue a career in ground water management or a related field. Students must be entering their freshman year at a four-year accredited institution. Prior research or experience with the field is required.
Target applicant:
   High school students
Minimum GPA: 3.0
Amount: Up to $2,000.
Number of awards: Varies.
Deadline: June 1.
How to apply: Applications are available online.

---

(753) · Angus Foundation Scholarship

American Foundation
3201 Frederick Avenue
St. Joseph, MO 64506
Phone: 816-383-5100
Fax: 816-233-9703
Email: angus@angus.org
Website: http://www.angusfoundation.org
Purpose: To provide scholarships to youth active in the Angus breed.
Eligibility: Applicants must have been members of the National Junior Angus Association and must be junior, regular or life members of the American Angus Association at the time of application. Applicants must be high school seniors or enrolled in a junior college, four-year college, or other accredited institution of post-secondary education in an undergraduate program and have a minimum 2.0 GPA. Students may not have reached their 25th birthday by January 1 of the year of application.
Target applicant:
   High school students
   College students
Minimum GPA: 2.0
Amount: $1,000-$5,000.
Number of awards: 52.
Deadline: May 1.
How to apply: Applications are available online or by written request.

---

(754) · Annual NBNA Scholarships

National Black Nurses Association
8630 Fenton Street
Suite 330
Silver Spring, MD 20910
Phone: 800-575-6298
Fax: 301-589-3223
Email: nbna@erols.com
Website: http://www.nbna.org
Purpose: To promote excellence in education and in continuing education programs for African American nurses and allied health professionals.
Eligibility: Applicants must be African Americans currently enrolled in a nursing program and be in good academic standing, be members of the NBNA, be members of a local chapter and have at least a full year of school remaining. Applicants must submit with their application an essay, references, an official transcript and evidence of participation in student nurse activities and involvement in the African American community.

Target applicant:
 College students
 Adult students
Minimum GPA: None.
Amount: $500-$2,000.
Number of awards: Varies.
Deadline: April 15.
How to apply: Applications are available online.

(755) · ANS Graduate Scholarship

American Nuclear Society
555 North Kensington Avenue
La Grange Park, IL 60526
Phone: 708-352-6611
Fax: 708-352-0499
Email: hr@ans.org
Website: http://www.ans.org
Purpose: To assist full-time graduate students who are pursuing advanced degrees in a nuclear-related field.
Eligibility: Applicants must be full-time students at an accredited graduate school in a program leading to an advanced degree in nuclear science, nuclear engineering or a nuclear-related field. There are also individual graduate scholarships. Applicants should submit applications, transcripts, recommendation letter and three reference forms.
Target applicant:
 Graduate school students
 Adult students
Minimum GPA: None.
Amount: Varies.
Number of awards: Up to 29.
Deadline: February 1.
How to apply: Applications are available online.

(756) · ANS Undergraduate Scholarship

American Nuclear Society
555 North Kensington Avenue
La Grange Park, IL 60526
Phone: 708-352-6611
Fax: 708-352-0499
Email: hr@ans.org
Website: http://www.ans.org
Purpose: To assist undergraduate students who are pursuing careers in the field of nuclear science.
Eligibility: Applicants must be at least sophomores or students who have completed two or more years and will be entering as juniors or seniors in an accredited university and must be enrolled in a program leading to a degree in nuclear science, nuclear engineering or a nuclear-related field. Applicants should submit applications, transcripts, recommendation letter, and three reference forms. There are individual undergraduate scholarships for students who have completed two or more years in a course of study leading to a degree in nuclear science, nuclear engineering, or a nuclear-related field.
Target applicant:
 College students
 Adult students
Minimum GPA: None.
Amount: Varies.
Number of awards: Up to 4 for sophomores, up to 21 for juniors and seniors.
Deadline: February 1.
How to apply: Applications are available online.

(757) · Antoinette Lierman Medlin Scholarship

Geological Society of America
Program Officer
Grants, Awards and Recognition
P.O. Box 9140
Boulder, CO 80301-9140
Phone: 303-357-1028
Fax: 303-357-1070
Email: awards@geosociety.org
Website: http://www.geosociety.org
Purpose: To assist full-time students involved in research in coal geology.
Eligibility: Applicants must be full-time students who are conducting research in coal geology pertaining to origin, occurrence, geologic characteristics, or economic implications.
Target applicant:
 Graduate school students
 Adult students
Minimum GPA: None.
Amount: Up to $3,000.
Number of awards: 2.
Deadline: February 15.
How to apply: No application is necessary. Students must send a cover letter, proposal, and letter of recommendation.

(758) · AOC Scholarships

Association of Old Crows
1000 N. Payne Street
Suite 300
Alexandria, VA 22314-1652
Phone: 703-549-1600
Fax: 703-549-2589
Email: richetti@crows.org
Website: http://www.myaoc.org
Purpose: To encourage students interested in strong defense capability emphasizing electronic warfare and information operations.
Eligibility: Applicants should consult their AOC chapters for scholarship guidelines.
Target applicant:
 College students
 Graduate school students
 Adult students
Minimum GPA: None.
Amount: Varies.
Number of awards: Varies.
Deadline: December 1.
How to apply: Applications are available online.

(759) · AORN Foundation Scholarship Program

Association of Perioperative Registered Nurses
2170 S. Parker Road
Suite 300
Denver, CO 80231
Phone: 800-755-2676
Email: sstokes@aorn.org
Website: http://www.aorn.org
Purpose: To encourage the education of nurses and future nurses.
Eligibility: Applicants must be current nursing students or AORN members accepted to an accredited program and have a minimum 3.0 GPA. Applicants must also demonstrate financial need.

Target applicant:
    College students
    Graduate school students
    Adult students
Minimum GPA: 3.0
Amount: $500-$4,000.
Number of awards: Varies.
Deadline: June 1.
How to apply: Applications are available online.

(760) · AOS Master's Scholarship Program

American Orchid Society
16700 AOS Lane
Delray Beach, FL 33446-4351
Phone: 561-404-2000
Fax: 561-404-2045
Email: theaos@aos.org
Website: http://www.aos.org
Purpose: To provide a two-year scholarship for completing a master's thesis on orchid education, orchidology or a related topic.
Eligibility: Applicants must be enrolled in a master's program at an accredited institution. The thesis project must focus on orchid education, applied science or orchid biology. The scholarship is limited to two consecutive years.
Target applicant:
    Graduate school students
    Adult students
Minimum GPA: None.
Amount: $10,000.
Number of awards: Varies.
Scholarship may be renewable.
Deadline: February 1.
How to apply: Applications are available online.

(761) · Appaloosa Youth Association Art Contest

Appaloosa Horse Club
Appaloosa Youth Foundation Scholarship Committee
2720 W. Pullman Road
Moscow, ID 83843
Phone: 208-882-5578
Fax: 208-882-8150
Email: acaap@appaloosa.com
Website: http://www.appaloosa.com
Purpose: To allow students to showcase their artistic talents with Appaloosa-themed projects.
Eligibility: Applicants age 18 and under should submit drawings, paintings and hand-built ceramics or sculptures with the Appaloosa theme. There are two age divisions: 13 and under and 14 to 18. Awards are based on originality, creativity and the theme.
Target applicant:
    Junior high students or younger
    High school students
Minimum GPA: None.
Amount: $250.
Number of awards: Varies.
Deadline: May 1.
How to apply: Applications are available online.

(762) · Appaloosa Youth Association Essay Contest

Appaloosa Horse Club
Appaloosa Youth Foundation Scholarship Committee
2720 W. Pullman Road
Moscow, ID 83843
Phone: 208-882-5578
Fax: 208-882-8150
Email: acaap@appaloosa.com
Website: http://www.appaloosa.com
Purpose: To reward students for essays that demonstrate their love of the Appaloosa breed.
Eligibility: Applicants must be 18 and under and should submit entry forms and essays on the provided themes. There are two age divisions: 13 and under and 14 to 18. Awards are based on originality and accuracy.
Target applicant:
    Junior high students or younger
    High school students
Minimum GPA: None.
Amount: $250.
Number of awards: Varies.
Deadline: May 1.
How to apply: Applications are available online.

(763) · Appaloosa Youth Association Junior Journalist Contest

Appaloosa Horse Club
Appaloosa Youth Foundation Scholarship Committee
2720 W. Pullman Road
Moscow, ID 83843
Phone: 208-882-5578
Fax: 208-882-8150
Email: acaap@appaloosa.com
Website: http://www.appaloosa.com
Purpose: To encourage students to become familiar with the Appaloosa industry.
Eligibility: Applicants must be current AYA members and aspiring writers between the ages of 14 and 18 who would like to report on news related to the AYA and the World Championship Appaloosa Youth Show. Applicants must submit an application and essay.
Target applicant:
    Junior high students or younger
    High school students
Minimum GPA: None.
Amount: Varies.
Number of awards: Varies.
Deadline: April 1.
How to apply: Applications are available online.

(764) · Appaloosa Youth Association Speech Contest

Appaloosa Horse Club
Appaloosa Youth Foundation Scholarship Committee
2720 W. Pullman Road
Moscow, ID 83843
Phone: 208-882-5578
Fax: 208-882-8150
Email: acaap@appaloosa.com
Website: http://www.appaloosa.com
Purpose: To reward students for their speeches on Appaloosa.

Eligibility: Applicants should be 18 and under and can enter two divisions: a speech on a pre-determined topic or an impromptu speech. Age groups are 13 and under and 14 to 18. The speech is given at the World Championship Appaloosa Youth World Show.

Target applicant:
Junior high students or younger
High school students
Minimum GPA: None.
Amount: $250.
Number of awards: Varies.
Deadline: June 1.
How to apply: Applications are available online.

(765) · APS Minority Scholarship

American Physical Society
One Physics Ellipse
College Park, MD 20740-3844
Phone: 301-209-3200
Fax: 301-209-0865
Email: wilson@aps.org
Website: http://www.aps.org
Purpose: To assist minorities studying physics.
Eligibility: Applicants must be African-American, Hispanic American or Native American U.S. citizens or permanent residents who plan to or are majoring in physics. Applicants must be high school seniors, college freshmen or college sophomores.

Target applicant:
High school students
College students
Adult students
Minimum GPA: None.
Amount: $2,000-$3,000.
Number of awards: Varies.
Scholarship may be renewable.
Deadline: February 1.
How to apply: Applications are available online.

(766) · ARC-ST Scholarships

Association of Surgical Technologists
6 W. Dry Creek Circle
Littleton, CO 80120
Phone: 800-637-7433
Fax: 303-694-9169
Email: kfrey@ast.org
Website: http://www.ast.org
Purpose: To support the continuing education of surgical technology students.
Eligibility: Applicants should be AST members in CAAHEP-accredited surgical technology programs. Applications, transcripts, a minimum 3.0 GPA, essays and recommendation letters are required.

Target applicant:
College students
Graduate school students
Adult students
Minimum GPA: 3.0
Amount: $1,000.
Number of awards: 1.
Deadline: April 1.
How to apply: Applications are available online.

(767) · ARM Undergraduate Student Fellowships

Academia Resource Management
535 E 4500 S, Suite D120
Salt Lake City, UT 84107-2988
Phone: 801-273-8911
Fax: 801-277-5632
Email: info@armanagement.org
Website: http://www.armanagement.org
Purpose: To support scientific and technological study in non-academic settings under the guidance of mentors at sponsoring facilities.
Eligibility: Applicants must plan to be science or technology interns or fellows at national laboratories and sponsoring institutions and be undergraduates in any accredited institution within six months of the start of their award. The award is based on academic performance, career goals, recommendations and compatibility with the host facility. Applications, a recommendation letter and transcripts are required. Applicants do not need to be enrolled in an ARM member institution to apply.

Target applicant:
College students
Adult students
Minimum GPA: None.
Amount: Varies.
Number of awards: Varies.
Deadline: February 15.
How to apply: Applications are available online.

(768) · ASAE Foundation Scholarship

American Society of Agricultural Engineers Foundation
Administrator
Scholarship Fund
2950 Niles Road
St. Joseph, MI 49085
Phone: 269-429-0300
Fax: 269-429-3852
Website: http://www.asae.org
Purpose: To assist student members of ASAE.
Eligibility: Applicants must have completed at least one year of undergraduate study and have at least one year of undergraduate study remaining, major in agricultural or biological engineering at an eligible accredited degree program in the U.S. or Canada, have a minimum 2.5 GPA and demonstrate financial need.

Target applicant:
College students
Adult students
Minimum GPA: 2.5
Amount: $1,000.
Number of awards: 1.
Deadline: March 15.
How to apply: Application is by formal letter.

(769) · ASAE Student Engineer of the Year Scholarship

American Society of Agricultural Engineers Foundation
Administrator
Scholarship Fund
2950 Niles Road
St. Joseph, MI 49085
Phone: 269-429-0300
Fax: 269-429-3852
Website: http://www.asae.org

Purpose: To award outstanding agricultural or biological engineering undergraduate students in the U.S. or Canada.

Eligibility: Applicants must be biological or agricultural engineering students and have completed at least one year of undergraduate study with at least one year of undergraduate study remaining. Applicants must also be enrolled in an eligible accredited engineering program and have a minimum 3.0 GPA. Selection is based on academic performance, character, student membership in ASAE, activities, leadership, paper and some financial need.

Target applicant:
   College students
   Adult students
Minimum GPA: 3.0
Amount: $1,000.
Number of awards: 1.
Deadline: March 15.
How to apply: Applications are available online.

(770) · ASCLS Student Award

American Society for Clinical Laboratory Science
6701 Democracy Boulevard, Suite 300
Bethesda, MD 20817
Phone: 301-657-2768
Fax: 301-657-2909
Email: ascls@ascls.org
Website: http://www.ascls.org

Purpose: To reward outstanding student case studies and research papers.

Eligibility: Applicants must be current ASCLS members. For research papers, they must have been enrolled in a NAACLS-accredited CLS/CLT program at the time the research was conducted. For case studies, they must be currently attending a NAACLS-accredited CLS/CLT program. Case studies must represent actual patient cases.

Target applicant:
   College students
   Graduate school students
   Adult students
Minimum GPA: None.
Amount: $500 for case studies and travel expenses for research papers.
Number of awards: 1 for research papers and 1 for case studies.
Deadline: May 1.
How to apply: Applications are available online.

(771) · ASDSO Dam Safety Scholarships

Association of State Dam Safety Officials
450 Old Vine Street
2nd Floor
Lexington, KY 40507
Phone: 859-257-5140
Fax: 859-323-1958
Email: info@damsafety.org
Website: http://www.damsafety.org

Purpose: To increase awareness of careers in dam safety.

Eligibility: Applicants must be full-time seniors in an accredited civil engineering program or a related field and show an interest in a career related to dam design, construction or operation. Students must have a minimum 2.5 GPA for the first two years of college, be recommended by their academic advisor and write an essay on what ASDSO is and why dam safety is important. Financial need is considered.

Target applicant:
   College students
   Adult students
Minimum GPA: 2.5
Amount: Up to $5,000.
Number of awards: Varies.
Deadline: March 31.
How to apply: Applications are available online.

(772) · ASEV Scholarships

American Society for Enology and Viticulture
P.O. Box 1855
Davis, CA 95617-1855
Phone: 530-753-3142
Fax: 530-753-3318
Email: society@asev.org
Website: http://www.asev.org

Purpose: To support those seeking a degree in enology, viticulture or in a curriculum focusing on a science basic to the wine and grape industry.

Eligibility: Applicants must be undergraduate or graduate students enrolled in or accepted into a full-time accredited four-year university program, must reside in North America (Canada, Mexico or the U.S.) and must be at least juniors for the upcoming academic year. Undergraduate students must have a minimum 3.0 GPA, and graduate students must have a minimum 3.2 GPA. Applicants must be enrolled in a major or in a graduate group concentrating on enology or viticulture or in a curriculum with a focus on a science basic to the wine and grape industry. The application, transcripts and two letters of recommendation are required.

Target applicant:
   College students
   Graduate school students
   Adult students
Minimum GPA: 3.0
Amount: Varies.
Number of awards: Varies.
Deadline: March 1.
How to apply: Applications are available online, by phone or by email.

(773) · ASF Olin Fellowships

Atlantic Salmon Federation
P.O. Box 807
Calais, ME 04619-0807
Phone: 506-529-1033
Fax: 506-529-4438
Email: asfweb@nbnet.nb.ca
Website: http://www.asf.ca

Purpose: To help fund projects that focus on solving problems in Atlantic salmon biology, management and conservation.

Eligibility: Applicants must be studying or actively engaged in salmon management or research. The award is open to U.S. and Canadian applicants.

Target applicant:
   College students
   Graduate school students
   Adult students
Minimum GPA: None.
Amount: $1,000-$3,000.
Number of awards: Varies.

Deadline: March 15.
How to apply: Applications are available by mail.

(774) · ASHA Youth Scholarships

American Saddlebred Horse Association Foundation
4083 Iron Works Parkway
Lexington, KY 40511
Phone: 859-259-2742 x343
Fax: 859-259-1628
Website: http://www.saddlebred.com
Purpose: To help youths involved with Saddlebreds.
Eligibility: This award is based on academic excellence, financial need, extracurricular activities, community service, involvement with American Saddlebred horses and personal references. An interview may be part of the selection process. Applicants should write an essay about school experiences, special interests, hobbies and American Saddlebred Horse Association activities. Scholarships are given only to high school seniors or recent graduates.
Target applicant:
    High school students
Minimum GPA: None.
Amount: $5,000.
Number of awards: Varies.
Deadline: April 30.
How to apply: Applications are available online.

(775) · ASHRAE Scholarship Program

American Society of Heating, Refrigerating and Air-Conditioning Engineers Inc.
Lois Benedict
Scholarship Administrator, ASHRAE Inc.
1791 Tullie Circle NE
Atlanta, GA 30329
Phone: 404-636-8400
Fax: 404-321-5478
Email: benedict@ashrae.org
Website: http://www.ashrae.org
Purpose: To encourage heating, ventilating, air conditioning and refrigeration education.
Eligibility: Applicants must be full-time undergraduates majoring in engineering or engineering technology or graduate students in a related course of study approved by the Accreditation Board for Engineering and Technology (ABET) or another accrediting agency recognized by ASHRAE with a minimum 3.0 GPA. Selection is based on financial need, leadership, character and potential contribution to the heating, ventilating, air conditioning or refrigeration profession. Applicants must also submit recommendations from instructors.
Target applicant:
    College students
    Graduate school students
    Adult students
Minimum GPA: 3.0
Amount: Varies.
Number of awards: Varies.
Deadline: December 1.
How to apply: Applications are available online.

(776) · ASM Foundation Scholarship Awards

ASM International Foundation
9639 Kinsman Road
Materials Park, OH 44073-0002
Phone: 440-338-5151
Fax: 440-338-4634
Email: crhayes@asminternational.org
Website: http://www.asminternational.org
Purpose: To support undergraduates studying metallurgy or materials science engineering.
Eligibility: Applicants must be student members of ASM International, major in metallurgy or materials science engineering and be juniors or seniors at a North American university that has a bachelor's degree program in science and engineering. Applications, personal statements, transcripts, two recommendation forms and photographs are required. The award is based on academics, interest in the metallurgy/materials engineering field and character.
Target applicant:
    College students
    Adult students
Minimum GPA: None.
Amount: $1,000.
Number of awards: 12.
Deadline: May 1.
How to apply: Applications are available online.

(777) · ASM Foundation Technical and Community College Scholarship Awards

ASM International Foundation
9639 Kinsman Road
Materials Park, OH 44073-0002
Phone: 440-338-5151
Fax: 440-338-4634
Email: crhayes@asminternational.org
Website: http://www.asminternational.org
Purpose: To support community college students in engineering fields.
Eligibility: Applicants must be student members who are majoring in metallurgy or materials science engineering at technical or community colleges, are training to be technicians in various engineering fields and have completed at least one year of college. Applications, personal statements, transcripts, two recommendation forms and photographs are required. The award is based on academics, interest in the metallurgy/materials engineering field and character.
Target applicant:
    College students
    Adult students
Minimum GPA: None.
Amount: $500.
Number of awards: 10.
Deadline: May 1.
How to apply: Applications are available online.

(778) · ASM Outstanding Scholars Awards

ASM International Foundation
9639 Kinsman Road
Materials Park, OH 44073-0002
Phone: 440-338-5151
Fax: 440-338-4634
Email: crhayes@asminternational.org
Website: http://www.asminternational.org
Purpose: To recognize distinguished scholars in metallurgy or materials science engineering.
Eligibility: Applicants must be student members of ASM International, major in metallurgy or materials science engineering and be juniors

or seniors at a North American university that has a bachelor's degree program in science and engineering. Applications, personal statements, transcripts, two recommendation forms and photographs are required. The award is based on academics, interest in the metallurgy/materials engineering field and personal character.

Target applicant:
    College students
    Adult students
Minimum GPA: None.
Amount: $2,000.
Number of awards: 3.
Deadline: May 1.
How to apply: Applications are available online.

(779) · ASME Foundation Scholarships

American Society of Mechanical Engineers
Three Park Avenue
New York, NY 10016
Phone: 800-843-2763
Fax: 973-882-1717
Email: infocentral@asme.org
Website: http://www.asme.org
Purpose: To support mechanical engineering students.
Eligibility: Applicants must be ASME student members in good standing and enrolled in an ABET-accredited (or equivalent) program of study. Eligible candidates must be in their sophomore, junior or senior years.
Target applicant:
    College students
    Adult students
Minimum GPA: None.
Amount: $1,500.
Number of awards: 15.
Deadline: March 15.
How to apply: Applications are available online.

(780) · ASNE Scholarship Program

American Society of Naval Engineers
1452 Duke Street
Alexandria, VA 22314-3458
Phone: 703-836-6727
Fax: 703-836-7491
Email: dwoodbury@navalengineers.org
Website: http://www.navalengineers.org
Purpose: To encourage college students to enter the field of naval engineering and to provide support to naval engineers pursuing advanced education.
Eligibility: Applications must be for the last year of a full-time or co-op undergraduate program or for one year of full-time graduate study for a designated engineering or physical science degree at an accredited school. Applicants must be U.S. citizens pursuing careers in naval engineering. Graduate student applicants must be members of ASNE. An applicant's academic record, work history, professional promise and interest, extracurricular activities and recommendations are considered. Financial need may be considered.
Target applicant:
    College students
    Graduate school students
    Adult students
Minimum GPA: None.
Amount: $3,000-$4,000.

Number of awards: Varies by year.
Deadline: February 15.
How to apply: Applications are available online or by written request.

(781) · ASNT Fellowship

American Society for Nondestructive Testing
1711 Arlingate Lane
P.O. Box 28518
Columbus, OH 43228
Phone: 800-222-2768
Fax: 614-274-6899
Email: sthomas@asnt.org
Website: http://www.asnt.org
Purpose: To fund research in nondestructive testing.
Eligibility: The award is given to an educational institution accredited by ABET to fund research in nondestructive testing (NDT) at the postgraduate level. One proposal per faculty member will be considered annually. Applicants should submit research proposal, program of study, description of facilities, budget, background on faculty advisor and background on graduate student.
Target applicant:
    Graduate school students
    Adult students
Minimum GPA: None.
Amount: $15,000.
Number of awards: Varies.
Deadline: October 15.
How to apply: Applications are available online.

(782) · Association for Women in Science College Scholarship

Association for Women in Science
1200 New York Avenue NW
Suite 650
Washington, DC 20005
Phone: 202-326-8940
Fax: 202-326-8960
Email: awisedfd@awis.org
Website: http://www.awis.org
Purpose: To assist female students who plan to study science.
Eligibility: For the undergraduate scholarship, applicants must be in their first, second or third year of college and expect to major in science or a related field. For the graduate scholarship, students must be enrolled in a life or physical science or engineering program leading to a Ph.D. degree. Selection is based on academic achievement, the importance of the research question addressed, quality of the research, reference letters and the applicants' potential for future contributions to science and related fields.
Target applicant:
    College students
    Graduate school students
    Adult students
Minimum GPA: None.
Amount: Varies.
Number of awards: 2-5.
Deadline: January 19.
How to apply: Applications are available online.

(783) · Association for Women in Science Predoctoral Awards

Association for Women in Science
1200 New York Avenue NW
Suite 650
Washington, DC 20005
Phone: 202-326-8940
Fax: 202-326-8960
Email: awisedfd@awis.org
Website: http://www.awis.org
Purpose: To recognize female students enrolled in a behavioral, life, physical or social science or engineering program leading to a Ph.D. degree.
Eligibility: Three of the awards have limitations for students in certain fields and one is reserved for a student who interrupted her education for at least three years to raise a family. Awards are given based on academic achievement, the importance of the research question addressed, the quality of the research and the applicant's potential for future contributions to science or engineering.
Target applicant:
  Graduate school students
  Adult students
Minimum GPA: None.
Amount: $1,000.
Number of awards: 5-10.
Deadline: January 26.
How to apply: Applications are available online.

(784) · Association of Food and Drug Officials Scholarship Award

Association of Food and Drug Officials
2550 Kingston Road
Suite 311
York, PA 17402
Phone: 717-757-2888
Fax: 717-755-8089
Email: afdo@afdo.org
Website: http://www.afdo.org
Purpose: To support college students who are studying food, drug or consumer product safety.
Eligibility: Applicants must be in their third or fourth year of college at an accredited institution and demonstrate a desire to work in a career of research, regulatory work, quality control or teaching in an area related to food, drug or consumer product safety. Applicants must also have demonstrated leadership capabilities, a minimum 3.0 GPA and submit two letters of recommendation from faculty.
Target applicant:
  College students
  Adult students
Minimum GPA: 3.0
Amount: $1,500.
Number of awards: 2.
Deadline: February 1.
How to apply: Applications are available online.

(785) · AST National Honor Society Scholarship

Association of Surgical Technologists
6 W. Dry Creek Circle
Littleton, CO 80120
Phone: 800-637-7433
Fax: 303-694-9169
Email: kfrey@ast.org
Website: http://www.ast.org
Purpose: To help members of the AST National Honor Society.
Eligibility: Applicants must be members of the AST National Honor Society, plan to attend or currently attend a CAAHEP-accredited surgical assisting program and have a minimum 3.0 GPA. The award is given after the completion of one semester of classes.
Target applicant:
  College students
  Adult students
Minimum GPA: 3.0
Amount: $1,000.
Number of awards: Varies.
Deadline: September 1.
How to apply: Applications are available online.

(786) · Astronaut Scholarship

Astronaut Scholarship Foundation
6225 Vectorspace Boulevard
Titusville, FL 32780
Phone: 321-269-6101
Fax: 321-264-9176
Email: linnleblanc@astronautscholarship.org
Website: http://www.astronautscholarship.org
Purpose: To ensure the United States' continued leadership in science by assisting promising physical science and engineering students.
Eligibility: Applicants must be junior or senior undergraduate or graduate students in physical science or engineering at Georgia Institute of Technology, Harvey Mudd College, Miami University, North Carolina A&T State University, North Carolina State University, North Dakota State University, Pennsylvania State University, Purdue University, Syracuse University, Texas A&M University, Tufts University, University of Central Florida, University of Colorado, University of Kentucky, University of Minnesota, University of Oklahoma, University of Washington or Washington University and must be nominated by faculty or staff. Applicants may not directly apply for the scholarship. Students must have excellent grades and performed research or lab work in their field.
Target applicant:
  College students
  Graduate school students
  Adult students
Minimum GPA: None.
Amount: $10,000.
Number of awards: One per school.
Deadline: Varies.
How to apply: Applicants must be nominated.

(787) · AUA Foundation Research Scholars Program

American Foundation for Urologic Disease Inc.
1000 Corporate Boulevard
Linthicum, MD 21090
Phone: 410-689-3750
Fax: 410-689-3850
Email: grants@auafoundation.org
Website: http://www.auafoundation.org
Purpose: To help young men and women who intend to pursue careers in urologic research.
Eligibility: Applicants must be researchers who conduct their research in the U.S. or Canada. Funding is provided for post-doctoral research only.

Target applicant:
    Graduate school students
    Adult students
Minimum GPA: None.
Amount: Varies.
Number of awards: Up to 12.
Deadline: August 10.
How to apply: Applications are available online.

(788) · Autism Awareness Scholarship

Common Knowledge Scholarship Foundation
P.O. Box 290361
Davie, FL 33329-0361
Phone: 954-262-8553
Email: info@cksf.org
Website: http://www.cksf.org
Purpose: To support students who are knowledgeable about autism and communication disorders.
Eligibility: Applicants must register online with CKSF. Students must take several online quizzes about autism and related disorders. The student with the most points from correct answers and the shortest time that it takes to answer the questions wins the scholarship.
Target applicant:
    High school students
    College students
    Graduate school students
    Adult students
Minimum GPA: None.
Amount: $250.
Number of awards: 1.
Deadline: April 20.
How to apply: Applications are available online.

(789) · Automotive Hall of Fame Scholarships

Automotive Hall of Fame
Award and Scholarship Programs
21400 Oakwood Boulevard
Dearborn, MI 48124
Phone: 313-240-4000
Fax: 313-240-8641
Website: http://www.automotivehalloffame.org
Purpose: To assist students interested in automotive careers.
Eligibility: Applicants must be interested in automotive careers. Other requirements vary depending on the specific scholarship.
Target applicant:
    High school students
    College students
    Adult students
Minimum GPA: None.
Amount: Varies.
Number of awards: Varies.
Deadline: May 30.
How to apply: Applications are available online or by sending a self-addressed, stamped envelope.

(790) · AWM Biographies Contest

Association for Women in Mathematics
4114 Computer and Space Sciences Building
University of Maryland
College Park, MD 20742

Phone: 301-405-7892
Fax: 301-314-9074
Email: awm@math.umd.edu
Website: http://www.awm-math.org
Purpose: To increase awareness of women's contributions to the mathematical sciences.
Eligibility: Applicants must interview a woman working in a mathematical career and write an essay based on the interview. Applicants may be from the sixth grade to graduate students.
Target applicant:
    Junior high students or younger
    High school students
    College students
    Adult students
Minimum GPA: None.
Amount: Varies.
Number of awards: Varies.
Deadline: October 29.
How to apply: Applications are available online.

(791) · Bachelor's Scholarships

Oncology Nursing Society
ONS Foundation
125 Enterprise Drive
Pittsburgh, PA 15275-1214
Phone: 412-859-6100
Fax: 412-859-6163
Email: foundation@ons.org
Website: http://www.ons.org
Purpose: To improve oncology nursing by assisting RNs in furthering their education.
Eligibility: Applicants who are registered nurses must have a current license to practice as an RN, have more than a high school diploma and be currently enrolled in an undergraduate nursing degree program in a school of nursing recognized by the National League for Nursing or the Commission on Collegiate Nursing Education. Applicants who are not registered nurses must be currently enrolled in an undergraduate nursing degree program in a school of nursing recognized by the National League for Nursing or the Commission on Collegiate Nursing Education. Non-RN applicants must be in the nursing component of the program and must have an interest in and commitment to oncology nursing. At least one Bachelor Scholarship is available to a non-RN applicant living in Ohio and West Virginia. There is a $5 application fee. It is highly recommended that you research the scholarship and awarding organization before applying for a scholarship with a fee. There are many scholarships that do not require a fee.
Target applicant:
    College students
    Adult students
Minimum GPA: None.
Amount: $2,000.
Number of awards: Varies.
Deadline: October 15.
How to apply: Applications are available online or by email request.

(792) · Baroid Scholarship

American Ground Water Trust
16 Centre Street
Concord, NH 03301
Phone: 603-228-5444
Fax: 603-228-6557
Website: http://www.agwt.org

Purpose: To support high school seniors intending to pursue a career in a ground water-related field.

Eligibility: Applicants must be high school seniors entering an accredited four-year college or university and intending to pursue a career in a ground water-related field.

Target applicant:
   High school students

Minimum GPA: 3.0

Amount: Up to $2,000.

Number of awards: Varies.

Deadline: June 1.

How to apply: Applications are available online.

---

(793) · Barry M. Goldwater Scholarship and Excellence in Education Program

Barry M. Goldwater Scholarship and Excellence in Education Foundation
6225 Brandon Avenue, Suite 315
Springfield, VA 22150
Phone: 703-756-6012
Fax: 703-756-6015
Email: goldwater@act.org
Website: http://www.act.org/goldwater/

Purpose: To assist college students who pursue studies that lead to careers as scientists, mathematicians and engineers.

Eligibility: Applicants must be full-time college sophomores or juniors, U.S. citizens or resident aliens, have a minimum "B" GPA and be in the upper fourth of their class. Award must be used during the junior or senior year of college. Selection is based on potential and intent to pursue careers in mathematics, the natural sciences or engineering.

Target applicant:
   College students
   Adult students

Minimum GPA: 3.0

Amount: $7,500.

Number of awards: Up to 300.

Deadline: February 1.

How to apply: Institutions nominate college sophomores or juniors. Applicants may not apply directly to the foundation.

---

(794) · Battery Division Student Research Award

Electrochemical Society
65 South Main Street, Building D
Pennington, NJ 08534-2839
Phone: 609-737-1902
Fax: 609-737-2743
Email: awards@electrochem.org
Website: http://www.electrochem.org

Purpose: To recognize young engineers and scientists in the field of electrochemical power sources.

Eligibility: Applicants must be accepted or enrolled in a college or university and must submit transcripts, an outline of the proposed research project, a description of how the project is related to the field of electrochemical power sources, a record of achievements in industrial work and a letter of recommendation from the research supervisor. Awards are based on academic performance, past research, proposed research and the recommendation.

Target applicant:
   High school students
   College students
   Graduate school students
   Adult students

Minimum GPA: None.

Amount: $1,000.

Number of awards: Varies.

Deadline: March 15.

How to apply: Application materials are described online.

---

(795) · Behavioral Sciences Student Fellowship

Epilepsy Foundation
8301 Professional Place
Landover , MD 20785
Phone: 301-459-3700
Email: researchwebsupport@efa.org
Website: http://www.epilepsyfoundation.org

Purpose: To encourage students to pursue careers in epilepsy research or practice settings.

Eligibility: Applicants must be undergraduate or graduate students in the behavioral sciences, have an epilepsy-related study, have a qualified mentor who can supervise the project and have an interest in careers in epilepsy research or practice settings. The project must be in the U.S. and should not be for dissertation research. The award is based on the quality of the project, relevance to epilepsy, interest in epilepsy, and the quality of the proposed lab or facility. Applicants must submit three recommendation letters, statement of intent, biographical sketch and research plan.

Target applicant:
   College students
   Graduate school students
   Adult students

Minimum GPA: None.

Amount: $3,000.

Number of awards: Varies.

Deadline: March 1.

How to apply: Application materials are described online.

---

(796) · Ben Everson Scholarship

American Ground Water Trust
16 Centre Street
Concord, NH 03301
Phone: 603-228-5444
Fax: 603-228-6557
Website: http://www.agwt.org

Purpose: To provide scholarships to high school seniors pursuing a career in a ground water-related field.

Eligibility: Applicants must be high school seniors entering a four-year accredited institution and intending to pursue a career in a ground water-related field.

Target applicant:
   High school students

Minimum GPA: 3.0

Amount: $2,500.

Number of awards: 1.

Deadline: June 1.

How to apply: Applications are available online.

---

(797) · Benjamin Willard Niebel Scholarship

Institute of Industrial Engineers (IIE)
3577 Parkway Lane
Suite 200
Norcross, GA 30092
Phone: 800-494-0460

Fax: 770-441-3295
Email: bcameron@iienet.org
Website: http://www.iienet.org/studentcenter
Purpose: To award students majoring in industrial engineering.
Eligibility: Applicants must be full-time undergraduate or graduate students enrolled in a college in the United States, Canada or Mexico with an accredited industrial engineering program, major in industrial engineering and be active members. Students may not apply directly for this scholarship and must be nominated. The award is based on academic ability, character, leadership, potential service to the industrial engineering profession and financial need.
Target applicant:
    College students
    Graduate school students
    Adult students
Minimum GPA: 3.4
Amount: $1,000.
Number of awards: 1.
Deadline: February 15.
How to apply: Nomination forms are available online.

(798) · Bill Kane Scholarship, Undergraduate

American Association for Health Education
1900 Association Drive
Reston, VA 20191
Phone: 703-476-3437
Fax: 703-476-6638
Email: aahe@aahperd.org
Website: http://www.aahperd.org/aahe
Purpose: To support health education students.
Eligibility: Applicants must be full-time undergraduate health majors in their sophomore, junior or senior years. They must have a GPA of at least 3.25 and write an essay about what they hope to accomplish as a health educator.
Target applicant:
    College students
    Adult students
Minimum GPA: 3.25
Amount: $1,000.
Number of awards: 1.
Deadline: November 15.
How to apply: Applications are available online.

(799) · Black and Veatch Scholarships

Black and Veatch
11401 Lamar Avenue
Overland Park, KS 66211
Phone: 913-458-2000
Fax: 913-458-2934
Website: http://www.bv.com
Purpose: To assist students at select universities, technical schools and engineering colleges.
Eligibility: Black and Veatch is an engineering, consulting and construction company that specializes in infrastructure development in energy, water, information and government markets. For information on eligibility, please contact the endowment or financial aid office at your university, engineering college or technical school.
Target applicant:
    College students
    Adult students
Minimum GPA: None.

Amount: Varies.
Number of awards: Varies.
Deadline: Varies.
How to apply: Contact the financial aid office for application information.

(800) · BSN Scholarship

Association of Rehabilitation Nurses
4700 W. Lake Avenue
Glenview, IL 60025
Phone: 800-229-7530
Fax: 888-458-0456
Email: gelliott@connect2amc.com
Website: http://www.rehabnurse.org
Purpose: To help nurses pursuing a bachelor's of science in nursing.
Eligibility: Applicants must be members of and involved in ARN, enrolled in a bachelor's of science in nursing (BSN) program, have completed at least one course, be currently practicing rehabilitation nursing and have a minimum of two years' experience in rehabilitation nursing. Applications, transcripts, a summary of professional and educational goals and achievements and two recommendation letters are required. Applications should be submitted by fax or email.
Target applicant:
    College students
    Adult students
Minimum GPA: None.
Amount: $1,000.
Number of awards: Varies.
Deadline: June 1.
How to apply: Applications are available online.

(801) · Bud Glover Memorial Scholarship

Aircraft Electronics Association
4217 South Hocker
Independence, MO 64055
Phone: 816-373-6565
Fax: 816-478-3100
Email: info@aea.net
Website: http://www.aea.net
Purpose: To support students who wish to pursue a career in avionics and aircraft repair.
Eligibility: Applicants must be high school seniors or college students who plan to or are attending an accredited school in an avionics or aircraft repair program.
Target applicant:
    High school students
    College students
    Adult students
Minimum GPA: None.
Amount: $1,000.
Number of awards: 1.
Deadline: February 15.
How to apply: Applications are available by contacting the organization for more information.

(802) · C.B. Gambrell Undergraduate Scholarship

Institute of Industrial Engineers (IIE)
3577 Parkway Lane
Suite 200
Norcross, GA 30092

Phone: 800-494-0460
Fax: 770-441-3295
Email: bcameron@iienet.org
Website: http://www.iienet.org/studentcenter
Purpose: To help undergraduate industrial engineering students from the U.S.
Eligibility: Applicants must be full-time undergraduate students who have completed their freshman year in an accredited industrial engineering program, major in industrial engineering and be active members. Students may not apply directly for this scholarship and must be nominated. The award is based on academic ability, character, leadership, potential service to the industrial engineering profession and financial need.
Target applicant:
    College students
    Adult students
Minimum GPA: 3.4
Amount: $600.
Number of awards: 1.
Deadline: February 15.
How to apply: Nomination forms are available online.

(803) · Cadbury Adams Community Outreach Scholarships

American Dental Hygienists' Association (ADHA) Institute for Oral Health
444 N. Michigan Avenue
Suite 3400
Chicago, IL 60611
Phone: 800-735-4916
Email: institute@adha.net
Website: http://www.adha.org/institute
Purpose: To reward students committed to improving oral health in their communities.
Eligibility: Applicants must have completed one year in an accredited dental hygiene program and demonstrate financial need of at least $1,500. They must also demonstrate through an essay a commitment to improving oral health in their communities. Applicants must be active SADHA or ADHA members and submit a goals statement.
Target applicant:
    College students
    Adult students
Minimum GPA: None.
Amount: $1,500.
Number of awards: Varies.
Deadline: May 1.
How to apply: Applications are available online.

(804) · Campus Safety Health and Environmental Management Association Scholarship

National Safety Council
CSHEMA, Scholarship Committee
CSHEMA Division, National Safety Council
12100 Sunset Hills Road ,Suite 130
Reston , VA 20190-3221
Phone: 703-234-4141
Fax: 703-435-4390
Email: info@cshema.org
Website: http://www.nsc.org
Purpose: To encourage the study of safety.

Eligibility: Applicants must be full-time undergraduate or graduate students with at least one year left in their degree program. Applicants must also write an essay about health, safety or environmental issues relevant to the university or college campus.
Target applicant:
    College students
    Adult students
Minimum GPA: None.
Amount: $2,000.
Number of awards: 1.
Deadline: March 31.
How to apply: Applications are available online.

(805) · Canadian Section Student Award

Electrochemical Society
65 South Main Street, Building D
Pennington, NJ 08534-2839
Phone: 609-737-1902
Fax: 609-737-2743
Email: awards@electrochem.org
Website: http://www.electrochem.org
Purpose: To support a student at a Canadian university who is pursuing an advanced degree related to electrochemical science and technology and/or solid state science and technology.
Eligibility: Applicants must be nominated in writing by a university faculty member of a Canadian university. Nominations must then be supported by letters of recommendation from personnel at the university, in industry or in government. The nomination should have a student curriculum vitae, a letter of recommendation from the nominating professor and a brief outline of the proposed and completed research project written by the student.
Target applicant:
    Graduate school students
    Adult students
Minimum GPA: None.
Amount: $1,500.
Number of awards: 1.
Deadline: February 28.
How to apply: Application materials are described online.

(806) · Caroline E. Holt Nursing Scholarship

National Society Daughters of the American Revolution
1776 D Street NW
Washington, DC 20006-5303
Phone: 202-628-1776
Website: http://www.dar.org
Purpose: To support students who are studying to become nurses.
Eligibility: Applicants must demonstrate financial need and attend a school of nursing. All applicants must obtain a letter of sponsorship from their local DAR chapter.
Target applicant:
    High school students
    College students
    Adult students
Minimum GPA: None.
Amount: $1,000.
Number of awards: Varies.
Deadline: February 15.
How to apply: Applications are available by written request.

(807) · Carville M. Akehurst Memorial Scholarship

American Nursery and Landscape Association
Horticultural Research Institute
1000 Vermont Avenue NW
Suite 300
Washington, DC 20005
Phone: 202-789-5980 x3014
Fax: 202-789-1893
Email: tjodon@anla.org
Website: http://www.anla.org
Purpose: To provide scholarships for undergraduate and graduate students who plan to pursue careers in horticulture.
Eligibility: Applicants must be enrolled full-time in a landscaping or horticultural program at a two- or four-year accredited institution and be residents of Maryland, Virginia or West Virginia.
Target applicant:
 College students
 Graduate school students
 Adult students
Minimum GPA: 2.7
Amount: $1,000.
Number of awards: 1.
Scholarship may be renewable.
Deadline: April 1.
How to apply: Applications are available online.

(808) · Charlotte McGuire Scholarship

American Holistic Nurses' Association
P.O. Box 2130
Flagstaff, AZ 86003-2130
Phone: 800-278-2462 x10
Fax: 928-526-2752
Email: info@ahna.org
Website: http://www.ahna.org
Purpose: To provide scholarships to nurses in undergraduate or graduate nursing programs or other graduate programs related to holistic nursing.
Eligibility: Applicants must be pursuing an education in holistic nursing and be members of the AHNA.
Target applicant:
 College students
 Graduate school students
 Adult students
Minimum GPA: 3.0
Amount: Varies.
Number of awards: 2.
Deadline: March 15.
How to apply: Applications are available online or from AHNA Headquarters.

(809) · Charlotte Woods Memorial Scholarship

Transportation Clubs International Scholarships
Attn.: Bill Blair
Zimmer Worldwide Logistics
15710 JFK Boulevard
Houston, TX 77032
Phone: 877-858-8627
Email: bblair@zimmerworldwide.com
Website: http://www.transportationclubsinternational.com

Purpose: To support students who want to enter the transportation industry.
Eligibility: Applicants must be enrolled in an accredited institution of higher learning in a vocational or degree program in the fields of transportation logistics or traffic management and must be TCI members or dependents of members. The awards are based upon scholastic ability, potential, professional interest and character. Financial need is also considered.
Target applicant:
 College students
 Adult students
Minimum GPA: None.
Amount: $1,000.
Number of awards: 1.
Deadline: April 30.
How to apply: Applications are available online.

(810) · Chemistry Common Knowledge Challenge

Common Knowledge Scholarship Foundation
P.O. Box 290361
Davie, FL 33329-0361
Phone: 954-262-8553
Email: info@cksf.org
Website: http://www.cksf.org
Purpose: To support high school students who are knowledgeable about chemistry.
Eligibility: Applicants must register with CKSF and take eight online quizzes about chemistry. Students must attend a high school in a sponsored county. The student with the most points from correct answers and the shortest time that it takes to answer the questions wins the scholarship.
Target applicant:
 High school students
Minimum GPA: None.
Amount: $100-$500.
Number of awards: Varies.
Deadline: Varies.
How to apply: Applications are available online.

(811) · Chicago Mercantile Exchange FFA Scholarship

National FFA Organization
P.O. Box 68960
6060 FFA Drive
Indianapolis, IN 46268-0960
Phone: 317-802-6060
Fax: 317-802-6051
Email: scholarships@ffa.org
Website: http://www.ffa.org
Purpose: To assist students who are pursuing degrees in agricultural business management and agricultural economics.
Eligibility: Applicants must be current FFA members and high school seniors or college students planning to enroll or currently enrolled full-time. Students only need to complete the online application one time to be considered for all FFA-administered scholarships. The application requires information about the students' activities and a 1,000-word essay. Awards may be used for books, supplies, tuition, fees and room and board. Applicants from families connected to the commodity brokerage industry may also be considered.
Target applicant:
 College students
 Adult students

Minimum GPA: None.
Amount: $1,000.
Number of awards: 1.
Deadline: February 15.
How to apply: Applications are available online.

---

(812) · Clinical Research Pre-Doctoral Fellowship

American Nurses Association (ANA)
8515 Georgia Avenue, Suite 400
Attn.: Janet Jackson, Program Manager
Silver Spring, MD 20910-3492
Phone: 301-628-5247
Fax: 301-628-5349
Website: http://www.nursingworld.org
Purpose: To provide stipends and tuition assistance to nurses studying minority psychiatric-mental health and substance abuse.
Eligibility: Applicants must be members of the ANA, have their master's degree and plan to pursue doctoral degrees. Fellowships may last from three to five years.
Target applicant:
  Graduate school students
  Adult students
Minimum GPA: None.
Amount: Varies.
Number of awards: Varies.
Deadline: March 1.
How to apply: Applications available online.

---

(813) · Colgate "Bright Smiles, Bright Futures" Minority Scholarships

American Dental Hygienists' Association (ADHA) Institute for Oral Health
444 N. Michigan Avenue
Suite 3400
Chicago, IL 60611
Phone: 800-735-4916
Email: institute@adha.net
Website: http://www.adha.org/institute
Purpose: To support members of groups underrepresented in dental hygiene programs.
Eligibility: Applicants must have completed one year of an accredited dental hygiene curriculum and be a member of a group that is underrepresented in the field of dental hygiene. Examples of eligible groups include African-American, Hispanic, Asian, Native American and male students. Applicants must also demonstrate financial need of at least $1,500, be active members of SADHA or ADHA and submit a goals statement.
Target applicant:
  College students
  Adult students
Minimum GPA: None.
Amount: $1,250.
Number of awards: Varies.
Deadline: May 1.
How to apply: Applications are available online.

---

(814) · Collegiate Inventors Competition

National Inventors Hall of Fame
221 S. Broadway
Akron, OH 44308-1505

Phone: 330-849-6887
Email: collegiate@invent.org
Website: http://www.invent.org
Purpose: To encourage college students in science, engineering, mathematics, technology and creative invention and to stimulate interest in technology and economic leadership.
Eligibility: Applicants must have been full-time college or university students during part of the 12-month period prior to the entry date. Up to four students may work as a team, and at least one student must meet the full-time criteria. Judging is based on originality and inventiveness, as well as the invention's potential value to society.
Target applicant:
  College students
  Graduate school students
  Adult students
Minimum GPA: None.
Amount: $5,000-$25,000.
Number of awards: Varies.
Deadline: June 1.
How to apply: Applications are available online.

---

(815) · Collins Scholarship

Autism Society of America
7910 Woodmont Avenue, Suite 300
Bethesda, MD 20814-3067
Phone: 800-328-8476
Email: chapters@autism-society.org
Website: http://www.autism-society.org
Purpose: To fund graduate and post-doctoral study in the prevention and cure of autism.
Eligibility: ASA members must submit nominations, and preference is given to students who are ASA members. Accomplishments must have been achieved within the previous year.
Target applicant:
  Graduate school students
  Adult students
Minimum GPA: None.
Amount: $1,000.
Number of awards: 1.
Deadline: March 14.
How to apply: Applications available online.

---

(816) · Composites Division/Harold Giles Scholarship

Society of Plastics Engineers
14 Fairfield Drive
Brookfield, CT 06804
Phone: 203-740-5447
Fax: 203-775-1157
Email: foundation@4spe.org
Website: http://www.4spe.org
Purpose: To aid undergraduate and graduate students who have an interest in the plastics industry.
Eligibility: Applicants must have an interest in the plastics industry, major in or take courses leading to a career in the plastics industry and be in good academic standing. Financial need is considered.
Target applicant:
  College students
  Graduate school students
  Adult students
Minimum GPA: None.

Amount: $1,000.
Number of awards: 1.
Deadline: January 15.
How to apply: Applications are available online.

(817) · Congressional Black Caucus Spouses Cheerios Brand Health Initiative Scholarship

Congressional Black Caucus Foundation
1720 Massachusetts Avenue NW
Washington, DC 20036
Phone: 202-263-2800
Fax: 202-775-0773
Email: info@cbcfinc.org
Website: http://www.cbcfinc.org
Purpose: To support minority students who are studying health-related fields.
Eligibility: Applicants do NOT need to be African American. Students must attend school or reside in a district represented by a Congressional Black Caucus member. Students must have at least a 2.5 GPA, and they must be enrolled or accepted into a full-time undergraduate degree program. Applicants must show leadership qualities and community service participation.
Target applicant:
    High school students
    College students
    Adult students
Minimum GPA: 2.5
Amount: Varies.
Number of awards: Varies.
Deadline: May 1.
How to apply: Applications are available online.

(818) · Continuing Education Award

American Association of Occupational Health Nurses (AAOHN) Foundation
2920 Brandywine Road
Suite 100
Atlanta, GA 30341
Phone: 770-455-7757
Fax: 770-455-7271
Email: ann@aaohn.org
Website: http://www.aaohn.org
Purpose: To support the continuing education of occupational and environmental health professionals.
Eligibility: Applicants must be employed in the field of occupational and environmental health nursing and demonstrate an interest in occupational and environmental health. A narrative, a letter of support from the employer and material describing the continuing education activity are required. This scholarship is for continuing education activities not tuition for an academic program.
Target applicant:
    Graduate school students
    Adult students
Minimum GPA: None.
Amount: $1,500.
Number of awards: 13.
Deadline: December 1.
How to apply: Applications are available online.

(819) · Corrosion Division Morris Cohen Graduate Student Award

Electrochemical Society
65 South Main Street, Building D
Pennington, NJ 08534-2839
Phone: 609-737-1902
Fax: 609-737-2743
Email: awards@electrochem.org
Website: http://www.electrochem.org
Purpose: To recognize graduate research in corrosion science and/or engineering.
Eligibility: Applicants must be graduate students who have completed all the requirements for their degrees within two years prior to the nomination deadline. Nomination may be made by the applicant's research supervisor or someone familiar with the applicant's research work. A summary of the applicant's master's or Ph.D. research work, reports, memberships and involvement with scientific societies, awards, an academic record and reprints of publications are required.
Target applicant:
    Graduate school students
    Adult students
Minimum GPA: None.
Amount: $1,000.
Number of awards: 1.
Deadline: December 15.
How to apply: Application materials are listed online.

(820) · D.W. Simpson Actuarial Science Scholarship

D.W. Simpson and Company
1800 Larchmont Avenue
Chicago, IL 60613
Phone: 800-837-8338
Fax: 312-951-8386
Email: actuaries@dwsimpson.com
Website: http://www.dwsimpson.com/scholar.html
Purpose: To assist college students interested in an actuarial science career.
Eligibility: Eligible students must be college seniors majoring in actuarial science who are eligible to work in the U.S. and have taken and passed a minimum of one actuarial examination.
Target applicant:
    College students
    Adult students
Minimum GPA: 3.0
Amount: $1,000.
Number of awards: 2.
Deadline: April 30 and October 31.
How to apply: Applications are available online.

(821) · Dade-Behring/Coordinating Council on the Clinical Laboratory Workforce Scholarship

American Society for Clinical Laboratory Science
6701 Democracy Boulevard, Suite 300
Bethesda, MD 20817
Phone: 301-657-2768
Fax: 301-657-2909
Email: ascls@ascls.org
Website: http://www.ascls.org
Purpose: To assist students in the second year of a Clinical Laboratory Technician (CLT/MLT) program.

Eligibility: Applicants must be currently enrolled in a NAACLS-accredited Clinical Laboratory Technician (CLT/MLT) program and planning to complete their final year of study by the end of the following August. Applicants must have a GPA of at least 2.5.

Target applicant:
College students
Adult students

Minimum GPA: 2.5

Amount: $1,000.

Number of awards: 50.

Deadline: October 1.

How to apply: Applications are available online.

(822) · Dairy Student Recognition Program

National Dairy Shrine
1224 Alton Darby Creek Road
Columbus, OH 43228-9792
Phone: 614-878-5333
Fax: 614-870-2622
Email: shrine@cobaselect.com
Website: http://www.dairyshrine.org

Purpose: To recognize graduating seniors planning careers related to dairy.

Eligibility: Applicants must be planning to enter the fields such as dairy production agriculture, marketing, agricultural law, business, veterinary medicine or environmental science. Selection is based on leadership skills, academic achievement and interest in dariy cattle.

Target applicant:
High school students

Minimum GPA: None.

Amount: At least $5,000.

Number of awards: Varies.

Deadline: March 15.

How to apply: Applications are available online, and two applicants per college or university are accepted each year.

(823) · Dan L. Meisinger Sr. Memorial Learn to Fly Scholarship

National Air Transportation Foundation Meisinger Scholarship
4226 King Street
Alexandria, VA 22302
Phone: 703-845-9000
Fax: 703-845-8176
Website: http://www.nata.aero

Purpose: To provide an annual flight training scholarship.

Eligibility: Applicants must be enrolled in an aviation program with a B or better GPA and be a resident of Kansas, Missouri or Illinois. Students should be recommended by an aviation professional; independent applications are also considered.

Target applicant:
College students
Graduate school students
Adult students

Minimum GPA: None.

Amount: $2,500.

Number of awards: Varies.

Deadline: Last Friday in November.

How to apply: Applications are available online.

(824) · Darling International Inc. FFA Scholarship

National FFA Organization
P.O. Box 68960
6060 FFA Drive
Indianapolis, IN 46268-0960
Phone: 317-802-6060
Fax: 317-802-6051
Email: scholarships@ffa.org
Website: http://www.ffa.org

Purpose: To assist students of land grant colleges in Colorado, Iowa, Illinois, Indiana, Kansas, Nebraska and Wisconsin in obtaining a degree in agriculture.

Eligibility: Applicants must be current FFA members and high school seniors or college students planning to enroll or currently enrolled full-time. Students only need to complete the online application one time to be considered for all FFA-administered scholarships. The application requires information about the students' activities and a 1,000-word essay. Awards may be used for books, supplies, tuition, fees and room and board.

Target applicant:
College students
Adult students

Minimum GPA: None.

Amount: $2,000.

Number of awards: 1.

Deadline: February 15.

How to apply: Applications are available online.

(825) · David Alan Quick Scholarship

EAA Aviation Center
P.O. Box 2683
Oshkosh, WI 54903
Phone: 877-806-8902
Fax: 920-426-6865
Email: scholarships@eaa.org
Website: http://www.youngeagles.org

Purpose: To support students in aerospace or aeronautical engineering.

Eligibility: Applicants must be in their junior or senior year at an accredited college or university pursuing a degree in aerospace or aeronautical engineering. Applicants must be involved in school and community activities as well as aviation and be EAA members or be recommended by an EAA member.

Target applicant:
College students
Adult students

Minimum GPA: None.

Amount: Varies.

Number of awards: 1.
Scholarship may be renewable.

Deadline: March 1.

How to apply: Applications are available online.

(826) · David Arver Memorial Scholarship

Aircraft Electronics Association
4217 South Hocker
Independence, MO 64055
Phone: 816-373-6565
Fax: 816-478-3100
Email: info@aea.net

Website: http://www.aea.net
Purpose: To support students who wish to pursue a career in avionics or aircraft repair.
Eligibility: Applicants must be high school seniors or college students who plan to or are attending an accredited school in an avionics or aircraft repair program.
Target applicant:
    High school students
    College students
    Adult students
Minimum GPA: None.
Amount: $1,000.
Number of awards: 1.
Deadline: February 15.
How to apply: Applications are available by contacting the organization for more information.

(827) · David S. Bruce Awards for Excellence in Undergraduate Research

American Physiological Society
Education Office
9650 Rockville Pike
Bethesda, MD 20814-3991
Phone: 301-634-7787
Fax: 301-634-7241
Email: education@the-aps.org
Website: http://www.the-aps.org
Purpose: To award undergraduate students for excellence in experimental biology research.
Eligibility: Applicants must be enrolled as an undergraduate at time of application and at time of meeting. Students must be first authors of the abstract and must be working with an APS member who will confirm the authorship. Applicants must submit a one-page paper discussing research and career plans and an abstract to be reviewed by a committee at the annual Experimental Biology meeting.
Target applicant:
    College students
    Adult students
Minimum GPA: None.
Amount: $500.
Number of awards: Up to 4.
Deadline: October.
How to apply: Applications are available online.

(828) · Delta Faucet Company Scholarships

Plumbing-Heating-Cooling Contractors–National Association
P.O. Box 6808
180 South Washington Street
Falls Church, VA 22046
Phone: 800-533-7694
Fax: 703-237-7442
Email: scholarships@naphcc.org
Website: http://www.phccweb.org
Purpose: To elevate the technical and business competence of the plumbing-heating-cooling (p-h-c) industry by awarding scholarships to students who are enrolled in a p-h-c-related major.
Eligibility: Applicants must be students who are currently enrolled or plan to be enrolled in a p-h-c-related major at an accredited four-year college or university or two-year technical college, community college or trade school. Apprentice program students must also be working full-time for a licensed plumbing or HVAC contractor who is a member of

the PHCC. Two $2,500 scholarships are awarded to students who are enrolled in either a PHCC-approved apprentice program or a full-time certificate or degree program at an accredited two-year community college, technical college or trade school. Four $2,500 scholarships are awarded to students who are enrolled in an undergraduate degree program at an accredited four-year college or university.
Target applicant:
    High school students
    College students
    Adult students
Minimum GPA: None.
Amount: $2,500.
Number of awards: 6.
Deadline: May 1.
How to apply: Applications are available online, by email or by phone.

(829) · Denny Lydic Scholarship

Transportation Clubs International Scholarships
Attn.: Bill Blair
Zimmer Worldwide Logistics
15710 JFK Boulevard
Houston, TX 77032
Phone: 877-858-8627
Email: bblair@zimmerworldwide.com
Website: http://www.transportationclubsinternational.com
Purpose: To support students in the field of transportation.
Eligibility: Applicants must be enrolled in an accredited institution of higher learning in a vocational or degree program in the fields of transportation, logistics or traffic management. The awards are based upon scholastic ability, potential, professional interest and character. Financial need is also considered.
Target applicant:
    College students
    Adult students
Minimum GPA: None.
Amount: $500.
Number of awards: 1.
Deadline: April 30.
How to apply: Applications are available online.

(830) · Dental Student Scholarship

American Dental Association Foundation
211 East Chicago Avenue
Chicago, IL 60611
Phone: 312-440-2763
Fax: 312-440-3526
Email: famularor@ada.org
Website: http://www.ada.org
Purpose: To encourage students to pursue careers in dental hygiene, dental assisting, dentistry and dental laboratory technology.
Eligibility: Applicants must be full-time entering second-year students in an accredited dental program and demonstrate a minimum financial need of $2,500. Applicants must submit applications, two reference forms and biographies. Selection is based on financial need, academic achievement, biographical sketch and references. A minimum 3.0 GPA is required. Only two scholarship applications are allowed per school, so schools may set their own in-school application deadlines that are earlier.
Target applicant:
    College students
    Graduate school students
    Adult students

Minimum GPA: 3.0
Amount: Up to $2,500.
Number of awards: 25.
Deadline: October 16.
How to apply: Applications are available from dental school officials.

(831) · Doctoral Scholars Forgivable Loan Program

Society of Automotive Engineers (SAE)
400 Commonwealth Drive
Warrendale, PA 15096-0001
Phone: 724-776-4841
Fax: 724-776-0790
Email: customerservice@sae.org
Website: http://www.sae.org
Purpose: To provide funding to assist promising engineering graduate students to pursue careers in teaching at the college level.
Eligibility: Applicants must hold an undergraduate degree from an engineering program and have been admitted to a doctoral program with the purpose of teaching engineering at the college level. Selection is based on scholastic achievement, desire to teach, interest in mobility technology and support of the SAE Collegiate Chapter Faculty advisor.
Target applicant:
   Graduate school students
   Adult students
Minimum GPA: None.
Amount: $5,000.
Number of awards: 2.
Scholarship may be renewable.
Deadline: April 1.
How to apply: Applications are available online.

(832) · Don King Student Fellowship

Huntington's Disease Society of America
505 Eighth Avenue, Suite 902
New York, NY 10018
Phone: 800-345-4372
Fax: 212-239-3430
Email: rgraze@hdsa.org
Website: http://www.hdsa.org
Purpose: To sponsor Huntington's Disease research.
Eligibility: Applicants must be current undergraduate life science or pre-medical students or first-year medical students attending accredited institutions in the United States where HDSA sponsors HD research. Recipients will conduct full-time research for 10 weeks. A letter of support and project plan are required. The award is based on academic achievement, scientific merit of the project and the relevancy to HD.
Target applicant:
   College students
   Graduate school students
   Adult students
Minimum GPA: None.
Amount: $3,000.
Number of awards: Varies.
Deadline: May 1.
How to apply: Applications are available by email, by mail or online.

(833) · Donald Burnside Memorial Scholarship

AOPA Air Safety Foundation
421 Aviation Way
Frederick, MD 21701
Phone: 301-695-2000
Fax: 301-695-2375
Email: aopahq@aopa.org
Website: http://www.aopa.org
Purpose: To assist students in non-engineering aviation programs.
Eligibility: Applicants must be college juniors or seniors and have at least one semester or quarter to be completed, have a minimum 3.25 GPA and be enrolled in a baccalaureate level, non-engineering aviation degree program at a four-year institution. Applicants must also submit an essay on a topic provided on the website.
Target applicant:
   College students
   Adult students
Minimum GPA: 3.25
Amount: $1,000.
Number of awards: 1.
Deadline: March 31.
How to apply: Applications are available online.

(834) · Donald F. and Mildred Topp Othmer Foundation

American Institute of Chemical Engineers - (AIChE)
3 Park Avenue
New York, NY 10016
Phone: 212-591-7634
Fax: 212-591-8890
Email: awards@aiche.org
Website: http://www.aiche.org
Purpose: To support AIChE student members.
Eligibility: Applicants must be members of an AIChE Student Chapter or Chemical Engineering Club. Applicants must be nominated by their student chapter advisors. Awards are presented on the basis of academic achievement and involvement in student chapter activities.
Target applicant:
   College students
   Graduate school students
   Adult students
Minimum GPA: None.
Amount: $1,000.
Number of awards: 15.
Deadline: May 7.
How to apply: Applications are available online.

(835) · Dorothy Budnek Memorial Scholarship

American Radiological Nurses Association
7794 Grow Drive
Pensacola, FL 32514
Phone: 866-486-2762
Fax: 850-484-8762
Email: arna@puetzamc.com
Website: http://www.arna.net
Purpose: To help ARNA members continue their nursing education.
Eligibility: Applicants must be active members of the American Radiological Nurses Association for three years, have a current nursing license and be enrolled in an approved academic program. Students should submit the application, a statement of purpose, two recommendation letters, a transcript which shows a minimum 2.5 GPA, a statement of financial support and a copy of the nursing license.
Target applicant:
   Graduate school students
   Adult students

Minimum GPA: 2.5
Amount: $600.
Number of awards: 1.
Deadline: December 1.
How to apply: Applications are available online.

(836) · Dorothy Dyer Vanek Endowment

Epsilon Sigma Alpha Foundation
P.O. Box 270517
Fort Collins, CO 80527
Phone: 970-223-2824
Fax: 970-223-4456
Email: kloyd@knoxy.net
Website: http://www.esaintl.com/esaf
Purpose: To provide financial assistance for architecture and interior design students.
Eligibility: Applicants may attend any college or university with an architecture or interior design program. They must have a GPA of 3.0 to 3.5. Selection is based equally on character, leadership, service, financial need and scholastic ability.
Target applicant:
  High school students
  College students
  Adult students
Minimum GPA: 3.0
Amount: $1,000.
Number of awards: 1.
Deadline: February 1.
How to apply: Applications are available online.

(837) · Dorothy M. and Earl S. Hoffman Award

American Vacuum Society
120 Wall Street, 32nd Floor
New York, NY 10005-3993
Phone: 212-248-0200
Fax: 212-248-0245
Email: angela@avs.org
Website: http://www.avs.org
Purpose: To recognize excellence in continuing graduate studies in the sciences and technologies related to AVS.
Eligibility: Applicants must be graduate students in an accredited academic institution. An application, summary of research, letters of recommendation and transcript are required. The award is based on achievement in research and academic record. The top five student nominees are invited to present talks on their research to the trustees at the international symposium. The trustees then select one recipient for the Dorothy M. and Earl S. Hoffman Award. The award covers travel expenses to the symposium.
Target applicant:
  Graduate school students
  Adult students
Minimum GPA: None.
Amount: $1,500.
Number of awards: 1.
Deadline: March 31.
How to apply: Applications are available online.

(838) · Dr. Alfred C. Fones Scholarship

American Dental Hygienists' Association (ADHA) Institute for Oral Health
444 N. Michigan Avenue
Suite 3400
Chicago, IL 60611
Phone: 800-735-4916
Email: institute@adha.net
Website: http://www.adha.org/institute
Purpose: To provide support to dental hygiene educators.
Eligibility: Applicants must be undergraduate or graduate students planning to become a teacher of dental hygienists and submit a goals statement. They must also be active members of SADHA or ADHA and demonstrate financial need of at least $1,500.
Target applicant:
  College students
  Graduate school students
  Adult students
Minimum GPA: None.
Amount: $1,500.
Number of awards: 1.
Deadline: May 1.
How to apply: Applications are available online.

(839) · Dr. Harold Hillenbrand Scholarship

American Dental Hygienists' Association (ADHA) Institute for Oral Health
444 N. Michigan Avenue
Suite 3400
Chicago, IL 60611
Phone: 800-735-4916
Email: institute@adha.net
Website: http://www.adha.org/institute
Purpose: To support outstanding dental hygiene students.
Eligibility: Applicants must have completed one year of an accredited dental hygiene program with a GPA of at least 3.5. They must demonstrate excellence in both academics and clinical performance. Applicants must also demonstrate financial need of at least $1,500, be active members of SADHA or ADHA and submit a goals statement.
Target applicant:
  College students
  Adult students
Minimum GPA: 3.5
Amount: $1,500.
Number of awards: 1.
Deadline: May 1.
How to apply: Applications are available online.

(840) · DuPont Challenge Science Essay Award

DuPont
The DuPont Challenge
Science Essay Awards Program, c/o General Learning Communications
900 Skokie Boulevard, Suite 200
Northbrook, IL 60062
Phone: 847-205-3000
Website: http://thechallenge.dupont.com/students.html
Purpose: To promote interest in scientific studies.

Eligibility: Applicants must be full-time students between grades 7 and 12 in a U.S. or Canadian school and write a 700- to 1,000-word essay about a scientific or technological development that interests them.
Target applicant:
    Junior high students or younger
    High school students
Minimum GPA: None.
Amount: $100-$3,000.
Number of awards: 10 plus honorable mentions.
Deadline: February 12.
How to apply: Applications are available online.

(841) · Dutch and Ginger Arver Scholarship

Aircraft Electronics Association
4217 South Hocker
Independence, MO 64055
Phone: 816-373-6565
Fax: 816-478-3100
Email: info@aea.net
Website: http://www.aea.net
Purpose: To support students who wish to pursue a career in avionics or aircraft repair.
Eligibility: Applicants must be high school seniors or college students who plan to or are attending an accredited school in avionics or aircraft repair.
Target applicant:
    High school students
    College students
    Adult students
Minimum GPA: None.
Amount: $1,000.
Number of awards: 1.
Deadline: February 15.
How to apply: Applications are available by contacting the organization for more information.

(842) · Dwight D. Gardner Scholarship

Institute of Industrial Engineers (IIE)
3577 Parkway Lane
Suite 200
Norcross, GA 30092
Phone: 800-494-0460
Fax: 770-441-3295
Email: bcameron@iienet.org
Website: http://www.iienet.org/studentcenter
Purpose: To award undergraduate members.
Eligibility: Applicants must be undergraduate students enrolled in a college in the United States, Canada or Mexico with an accredited industrial engineering program, major in industrial engineering and be active members. Students may not apply directly for this scholarship and must be nominated. The award is based on academic ability, character, leadership, potential service to the industrial engineering profession and financial need.
Target applicant:
    College students
    Adult students
Minimum GPA: 3.4
Amount: $1,000.
Number of awards: 2.
Deadline: February 15.
How to apply: Nomination forms are available online.

(843) · E.J. Sierieja Memorial Fellowship

Institute of Industrial Engineers (IIE)
3577 Parkway Lane
Suite 200
Norcross, GA 30092
Phone: 800-494-0460
Fax: 770-441-3295
Email: bcameron@iienet.org
Website: http://www.iienet.org/studentcenter
Purpose: To award graduate students pursuing advanced studies in the area of transportation.
Eligibility: Applicants must be full-time graduate students, majoring in transportation and active members. Students may not apply directly for this scholarship and must be nominated. The award is based on academic ability, character, leadership, potential service to the industrial engineering profession and financial need. Preference is given to students focusing on rail transportation.
Target applicant:
    Graduate school students
    Adult students
Minimum GPA: 3.4
Amount: $600.
Number of awards: 1.
Deadline: February 15.
How to apply: Nomination forms are available online.

(844) · Eight and Forty Lung and Respiratory Nursing Scholarship Fund

American Legion
Attn.: Americanism and Children and Youth Division
P.O. Box 1055
Indianapolis, IN 46206
Phone: 317-630-1249
Fax: 317-630-1369
Website: http://www.legion.org
Purpose: To assist registered nurses.
Eligibility: Applicants must plan to be employed full-time in hospitals, clinics or health departments in a position related to lung and respiratory control.
Target applicant:
    College students
    Graduate school students
    Adult students
Minimum GPA: None.
Amount: $2,500.
Number of awards: Varies.
Deadline: May 15.
How to apply: Applications are available by written request.

(845) · ENA Foundation Undergraduate Scholarship

Emergency Nurses Association
915 Lee Street
Des Plaines, IL 60016
Phone: 847-460-4100
Fax: 847-460-4004
Email: foundation@ena.org
Website: http://www.ena.org
Purpose: To promote research and education in emergency care.
Eligibility: Applicants must be nurses pursuing baccalaureate degrees in nursing and must have been ENA members for at least 12 months

before applying. Selection is based on application, statement of goals, references and transcript.

Target applicant:
    College students
    Adult students
Minimum GPA: None.
Amount: $2,000-$5,000.
Number of awards: 7.
Deadline: June 1.
How to apply: Applications are available online.

(846) · Engineering Undergraduate Award

American Society for Nondestructive Testing
1711 Arlingate Lane
P.O. Box 28518
Columbus, OH 43228
Phone: 800-222-2768
Fax: 614-274-6899
Email: sthomas@asnt.org
Website: http://www.asnt.org
Purpose: To support students studying nondestructive testing.
Eligibility: Applicants must be undergraduate students enrolled in an engineering program of an accredited university and specialize in nondestructive testing (NDT). A nominating letter, transcript, three letters of recommendation and an essay describing the role of NDT/NDE in their career are required.
Target applicant:
    College students
    Adult students
Minimum GPA: None.
Amount: $3,000.
Number of awards: Varies.
Deadline: December 15.
How to apply: Applications are available online.

(847) · Eugene S. Kropf Scholarship

University Aviation Association Eugene S. Kropf Scholarship
Kevin R. Kuhlmann, Professor of Aviation and Aerospace Science
Metropolitan State College of Denver
Campus Box 30, P.O. Box 173362
Denver, CO 80217
Phone: 334-844-2434
Fax: 334-844-2432
Website: http://www.uaa.aero
Purpose: To support students studying an aviation-related curriculum.
Eligibility: Applicants must be U.S. citizens enrolled in an aviation-related curriculum of a two-year or a four-year degree at a UAA member college or university. Students must have a 3.0 GPA and write a 250-word paper on how they can improve aviation education.
Target applicant:
    College students
    Adult students
Minimum GPA: 3.0
Amount: $500.
Number of awards: 1.
Deadline: May 31.
How to apply: Applications are available online.

(848) · F.W. Beichley Scholarship

American Society of Mechanical Engineers
Three Park Avenue
New York, NY 10016
Phone: 800-843-2763
Fax: 973-882-1717
Email: infocentral@asme.org
Website: http://www.asme.org
Purpose: To support mechanical engineering students.
Eligibility: Applicants must be ASME student members enrolled in an eligible accredited mechanical engineering baccalaureate program. Selection is based on leadership, scholastic ability, potential contribution to the mechanical engineering profession and financial need. The scholarship is only applicable for study in the junior or senior year.
Target applicant:
    College students
    Adult students
Minimum GPA: None.
Amount: $2,000.
Number of awards: 1.
Deadline: March 15.
How to apply: Applications are available online.

(849) · FA Davis Student Award

American Association of Medical Assistants' Endowment
20 North Wacker Drive
Suite 1575
Chicago, IL 60606
Phone: 800-228-2262
Email: info@aama-ntl.org
Website: http://www.aama-ntl.org
Purpose: To reward aspiring medical assistants for ad design.
Eligibility: Applicants must be enrolled in and have finished a quarter or a semester at an accredited postsecondary medical assisting program. Students must create one ad that supports the medical assisting profession, the CMA credential and the AAMA. The ad must have a slogan, body copy and a call to action and can be designed using any medium.
Target applicant:
    College students
    Graduate school students
    Adult students
Minimum GPA: None.
Amount: $1,000.
Number of awards: 1.
Deadline: July 1.
How to apply: Applications are available online.

(850) · Fellowship Award

Damon Runyon Cancer Research Foundation
675 Third Avenue, 25th Floor
New York, NY 10017
Phone: 212-455-0520
Fax: 212-455-0529
Email: awards@drcrf.org
Website: http://www.drcrf.org
Purpose: To support the training of postdoctoral scientists as they start their research careers.
Eligibility: Applicants must have completed one or more of the following degrees or its equivalent: M.D., Ph.D., M.D./Ph.D., D.D.S.

or D.V.M. Applicants should submit an application cover sheet, sponsor's biographical sketch, CV, degree certificate, letter, research proposal, summary of research form, up to three reprints of work and four letters of reference. This is a three-year award with various deadlines and funding. The research must be conducted at a university, hospital or research institution. International candidates may apply to do their research only in the United States.

Target applicant:
  Graduate school students
  Adult students
Minimum GPA: None.
Amount: $174,000 over three years.
Number of awards: Varies.
Deadline: March 15.
How to apply: Applications are available online.

(851) · Fellowship in Aerospace History

American Historical Association
400 A Street SE
Washington, DC 20003
Phone: 202-544-2422
Fax: 202-544-8307
Email: info@historians.org
Website: http://www.historians.org
Purpose: To provide funding for an academic research project related to aerospace history.
Eligibility: Applicants must possess a doctorate degree in history or a related field or be enrolled in a doctorate program (all coursework completed). One fellow will be appointed for one academic year. The fellow will be expected to write a report and present a paper or lecture on the research at the end of the term.

Target applicant:
  Graduate school students
  Adult students
Minimum GPA: None.
Amount: $20,000.
Number of awards: 1.
Deadline: March 1.
How to apply: Applications are available online.

(852) · Ferrous Metallurgy Education Today (FeMET)

Iron and Steel Society
Attn.: Lori Wharrey
AIST Foundation
186 Thorn Hill Road
Warrendale, PA 15086
Phone: 724-776-6040 x621
Fax: 724-776-1880
Email: lwharrey@aist.org
Website: http://www.aistfoundation.org
Purpose: To increase the number of metallurgy and materials science students in North America and to encourage them to pursue careers in the iron and steel industry.
Eligibility: Applicants must be college juniors who are majoring in metallurgy or materials science at a North American University, and they must show interest in the iron and steel industry. Applicants must also have a minimum GPA of 3.0 and be eligible for and commit to a paid summer internship at a North American steel company.

Target applicant:
  College students
  Adult students

Minimum GPA: 3.0
Amount: $5,000.
Number of awards: 10.
Scholarship may be renewable.
Deadline: March 2.
How to apply: Applications are available online.

(853) · FIRST Scholarship

Floriculture Industry Research and Scholarship Trust
P.O. Box 280
East Lansing, MI 48826
Phone: 517-333-4617
Fax: 517-333-4494
Email: scholarship@firstinfloriculture.org
Website: http://endowment.org
Purpose: To promote the floriculture industry by assisting qualified students with education expenses.
Eligibility: Applicants must be high school senior, college undergraduate, vocational or graduate students pursuing a horticulture-related field. Applicants must also have a minimum 3.0 GPA or outstanding extracurricular activities and be U.S. citizens or residents or Canadian citizens.

Target applicant:
  High school students
  College students
  Graduate school students
  Adult students
Minimum GPA: 3.0
Amount: $500-$2,000.
Number of awards: 25.
Deadline: May 1.
How to apply: Applications are available online.

(854) · Foundation for Surgical Technology Advanced Education/Medical Mission Scholarship

Association of Surgical Technologists
6 W. Dry Creek Circle
Littleton, CO 80120
Phone: 800-637-7433
Fax: 303-694-9169
Email: kfrey@ast.org
Website: http://www.ast.org
Purpose: To help practitioners with continuing education or medical missionary work.
Eligibility: Applicants must be active AST members, document the educational program or mission program and provide two recommendation letters.

Target applicant:
  College students
  Graduate school students
  Adult students
Minimum GPA: None.
Amount: Varies.
Number of awards: Varies.
Deadline: Varies.
How to apply: Applications are available online.

(855) · Foundation for Surgical Technology Student Scholarship

Association of Surgical Technologists
6 W. Dry Creek Circle
Littleton, CO 80120
Phone: 800-637-7433
Fax: 303-694-9169
Email: kfrey@ast.org
Website: http://www.ast.org
Purpose: To help surgical technology students in CAAHEP-accredited surgical technology programs.
Eligibility: Applicants must be currently enrolled in a surgical technology program accredited by the Commission on Accreditation of Allied Health Education Programs (CAAHEP). Applicants must also demonstrate academic achievement and financial need. Applications, transcripts and an instructor evaluation are required.
Target applicant:
　College students
　Adult students
Minimum GPA: None.
Amount: Varies.
Number of awards: Varies.
Deadline: April 1.
How to apply: Applications are available online.

(856) · Frank and Brennie Morgan Prize for Outstanding Research in Mathematics by an Undergraduate Student

American Mathematical Society
Dr. Martha J. Siegel, MAA Secretary
Mathematics Department, Towson University
Stephens Hall 302, 8000 York Road
Towson, MD 21252
Phone: 410-704-2980
Email: siegel@towson.edu
Website: http://www.ams.org
Purpose: Awarded to an undergraduate student (or students who have collaborated) for research in the field of mathematics.
Eligibility: Applicants must be undergraduate students at colleges or universities in the United States or its possessions, Canada and Mexico. Students must be nominated.
Target applicant:
　College students
　Adult students
Minimum GPA: None.
Amount: $1,000-$2,000.
Number of awards: 1.
Deadline: Varies.
How to apply: Nomination information is available by email. Questions should be directed to Dr. Martha J. Siegel at the address above. Nominations and submissions should be sent to: Morgan Prize Committee, c/o Robert J. Daverman, American Mathematical Society, 312D Ayres Hall, University of Tennessee, Knoxville, TN 37996.

(857) · Frank and Dorothy Miller ASME Auxiliary Scholarships

American Society of Mechanical Engineers
Three Park Avenue
New York, NY 10016
Phone: 800-843-2763
Fax: 973-882-1717
Email: infocentral@asme.org
Website: http://www.asme.org
Purpose: To support mechanical engineering students.
Eligibility: Applicants must be ASME student members, be enrolled in an eligible accredited mechanical engineering baccalaureate program, be North American residents and U.S. citizens and demonstrate character and integrity.
Target applicant:
　College students
　Adult students
Minimum GPA: None.
Amount: $1,500.
Number of awards: 2.
Deadline: March 15.
How to apply: Applications are available online.

(858) · Freshman and Sophomore Scholarships

Institute of Food Technologists (IFT)
525 W. Van Buren
Suite 1000
Chicago, IL 60607
Phone: 312-782-8424
Email: ejplummer@ift.org
Website: http://www.ift.org
Purpose: To help young food scientists who plan to work in industry, government and academia.
Eligibility: Applicants for the freshman scholarships must be academically outstanding high school graduates or seniors who will enter college for the first time in an approved program in food science/technology. The deadline for the freshman scholarships is February 15. Applicants for the sophomore scholarships must be academically outstanding college freshman with a minimum 2.5 GPA in an approved program in food science/technology. The deadline for the sophomore scholarships is March 1. All candidates must submit applications, transcripts and a recommendation.
Target applicant:
　High school students
　College students
　Adult students
Minimum GPA: 2.5
Amount: $1,500.
Number of awards: 46.
Deadline: February 15 for freshmen, March 1 for sophomores.
How to apply: Applications are available online.

(859) · Freshman Undergraduate Scholarship

American Meteorological Society
Macelwane Award
45 Beacon Street
Boston, MA 02108-3693
Phone: 617-227-2426 x246
Fax: 617-742-8718
Email: dfernand@ametsoc.org
Website: http://www.ametsoc.org/AMS/
Purpose: To encourage high school students to pursue careers in the atmospheric and related oceanic and hydrologic sciences.
Eligibility: Applicants must enter as full-time freshmen the following fall and major in the atmospheric or related oceanic and hydrologic sciences. Applicants should submit applications, transcripts, recommendation letter, and SAT or equivalent scores.

Target applicant:
  High school students
Minimum GPA: None.
Amount: $5,000.
Number of awards: Varies.
Scholarship may be renewable.
Deadline: February 10.
How to apply: Applications are available online.

(860) · Gaige Fund Award

American Society of Ichthyologists and Herpetologists
Maureen Donnelly, Secretary
Department of Biological Sciences, Florida International University
11200 SW 8th Street
Miami, FL 33199
Phone: 305-348-1235
Fax: 305-348-1986
Email: asih@fiu.edu
Website: http://www.asih.org
Purpose: To support young herpetologists.
Eligibility: Applicants must be members of ASIH and studying for an advanced degree. The award may be used for museum or laboratory study, travel, fieldwork, or other activities that will enhance their careers and their contributions to the science of herpetology. Both merit and need will be considered.
Target applicant:
  Graduate school students
  Adult students
Minimum GPA: None.
Amount: $400-$1,000.
Number of awards: Varies.
Deadline: March 1.
How to apply: Applications are available by email or written request.

(861) · Garland Duncan Scholarships

American Society of Mechanical Engineers
Three Park Avenue
New York, NY 10016
Phone: 800-843-2763
Fax: 973-882-1717
Email: infocentral@asme.org
Website: http://www.asme.org
Purpose: To support mechanical engineering students.
Eligibility: Applicants must be ASME student members, be enrolled in an eligible accredited mechanical engineering baccalaureate program, have strong academic performance and be college juniors or seniors. Selection is based on character, integrity, leadership, scholastic ability, potential contribution to the mechanical engineering profession and financial need.
Target applicant:
  College students
  Adult students
Minimum GPA: None.
Amount: $3,500.
Number of awards: 2.
Deadline: March 15.
How to apply: Applications are available online.

(862) · Garmin Scholarship

Aircraft Electronics Association
4217 South Hocker
Independence, MO 64055
Phone: 816-373-6565
Fax: 816-478-3100
Email: info@aea.net
Website: http://www.aea.net
Purpose: To support students who wish to pursue a career in avionics and aircraft repair.
Eligibility: Applicants must be high school seniors or college students who plan to or are attending an accredited school in an avionics or aircraft repair program.
Target applicant:
  High school students
  College students
  Adult students
Minimum GPA: None.
Amount: $2,000.
Number of awards: 1.
Deadline: February 15.
How to apply: Applications are available online.

(863) · Gary Kiteley Executive Director Scholarship

University Aviation Association (UAA)
David NewMeyer
College of Applied Sciences and Arts, Southern Illinois University Carbondale
1365 Douglas Drive, Rm 126
Carbondale , IL 62901-6623
Phone: 618-453-8898
Fax: 618-453-7286
Email: newmyer@siu.edu
Website: http://www.uaa.aero
Purpose: To support aviation students at UAA institutions.
Eligibility: Applicants must be enrolled at a UAA member college or university in an aviation-related curriculum and be a UAA student member. Fifteen hours in an associate degree program or 30 hours in a bachelor's degree program should have been completed.
Target applicant:
  College students
  Adult students
Minimum GPA: 3.0
Amount: $500.
Number of awards: 1.
Deadline: Varies.
How to apply: Applications are available online.

(864) · GBT Student Support Program

National Radio Astronomy Observatory (NRAO)
NRAO Headquarters
520 Edgemont Road
Charlottesville, VA 22903
Phone: 434-296-0211
Fax: 434-296-0278
Email: info@nrao.edu
Website: http://www.nrao.edu
Purpose: To support student research at the Robert C. Byrd Green Bank Telescope (GBT).

Eligibility: GBT is the largest fully steerable single aperture antenna. Students begin the application process by completing a preliminary funding proposal form. If the proposal is accepted, they will be informed of further requirements.

Target applicant:
College students
Graduate school students
Adult students

Minimum GPA: None.

Amount: Varies.

Number of awards: Varies.

Deadline: Varies.

How to apply: Applications are available online.

---

(865) · GCSAA Scholars Program

Golf Course Superintendents Association of America Foundation
GCSAA Career Development Department
GCSAA Scholars Competition
1421 Research Park Drive
Lawrence, KS 66049
Phone: 800-472-7878
Email: infobox@gcsaa.org
Website: http://www.gcsaa.org

Purpose: To recognize outstanding students who plan careers in golf course management or a related field.

Eligibility: Applicants must be GCSAA members who are enrolled in an undergraduate turf management program or related field and have completed their first year or 24 credit hours.

Target applicant:
College students
Adult students

Minimum GPA: None.

Amount: $500-$6,000.

Number of awards: Varies.

Deadline: June 1.

How to apply: Applications are available by contacting Pam Smith, 800-472-7878 x3678.

---

(866) · GCSAA Student Essay Contest

Golf Course Superintendents Association of America Foundation
GCSAA Career Development Department
GCSAA Scholars Competition
1421 Research Park Drive
Lawrence, KS 66049
Phone: 800-472-7878
Email: infobox@gcsaa.org
Website: http://www.gcsaa.org

Purpose: To support students pursuing degrees in golf course management.

Eligibility: Applicants must be undergraduate or graduate students pursuing degrees in turfgrass science, agronomy or any other golf course management-related field. Applicants must be members of GCSAA and write an essay on golf course management.

Target applicant:
College students
Graduate school students
Adult students

Minimum GPA: None.

Amount: Varies.

Number of awards: Varies.

Deadline: March 31.

How to apply: Applications are available by contacting Pam Smith, 800-472-7878 x3678.

---

(867) · GeoEye Award

American Society for Photogrammetry and Remote Sensing
5410 Grosvenor Lane
Suite 210
Bethesda, MD 20814
Phone: 301-493-0290 x101
Fax: 301-493-0208
Email: scholarships@asprs.org
Website: http://www.asprs.org

Purpose: To support remote sensing education and stimulate the development of applications of high-resolution digital satellite imagery for applied research by undergraduate or graduate students.

Eligibility: Applicants must be full-time undergraduate or graduate students at an accredited college or university with proper image processing facilities. Selection is based on the application, letters of recommendation and a brief two-page proposal. The structure for the proposal can be found on the website.

Target applicant:
College students
Graduate school students
Adult students

Minimum GPA: None.

Amount: $2,000.

Number of awards: 1.

Deadline: December 1.

How to apply: Applications are available online.

---

(868) · George A. Hall / Harold F. Mayfield Award

Wilson Ornithological Society
Dr. Robert B. Payne
Museum of Zoology, University of Michigan
1109 Gedes Avenue
Ann Arbor, MI 48109
Email: rbpayne@umich.edu
Website: http://www.wilsonsociety.org

Purpose: To assist those who are conducting avian research.

Eligibility: Applicants must be independent researchers without access to funds available at colleges, universities or government agencies and must be non-professionals currently conducting avian research. Applicants must also be willing to present their research results at an annual meeting of the Wilson Ornithological Society.

Target applicant:
High school students
College students
Graduate school students
Adult students

Minimum GPA: None.

Amount: $1,000.

Number of awards: 1.

Deadline: February 1.

How to apply: Applications are available online.

---

(869) · George A. Roberts Scholarships

ASM International Foundation
9639 Kinsman Road
Materials Park, OH 44073-0002

Phone: 440-338-5151
Fax: 440-338-4634
Email: crhayes@asminternational.org
Website: http://www.asminternational.org
Purpose: To help students interested in the metallurgy or materials engineering field.
Eligibility: Applicants must be student members of ASM International, plan to major in metallurgy or materials science engineering and be juniors or seniors at a North American university that has a bachelor's degree program in science and engineering. Applications, personal statements, transcripts, two recommendation forms, photographs and financial aid officers' contact information are required. The award is based on academics, interest in the field, character and financial need.
Target applicant:
    College students
    Adult students
Minimum GPA: None.
Amount: $6,000.
Number of awards: 7.
Deadline: May 1.
How to apply: Applications are available online.

(870) · Gertrude Cox Scholarship For Women In Statistics

American Statistical Association
Dr. Amita Manatunga, Gertrude Cox Scholarship Committee Chair
Department of Biostatistics, Emory University
1518 Clifton Road NE #374
Atlanta, GA 30322
Phone: 404-727-1309
Fax: 404-727-1370
Email: amanatu@sph.emory.edu
Website: http://www.amstat.org
Purpose: To encourage women to pursue education for careers in statistics.
Eligibility: Applicants must be women who are full-time students in a graduate-level statistics programs.
Target applicant:
    Graduate school students
    Adult students
Minimum GPA: None.
Amount: $1,000.
Number of awards: Varies.
Deadline: April 1.
How to apply: Applications are available online.

(871) · Gilbreth Memorial Fellowship

Institute of Industrial Engineers (IIE)
3577 Parkway Lane
Suite 200
Norcross, GA 30092
Phone: 800-494-0460
Fax: 770-441-3295
Email: bcameron@iienet.org
Website: http://www.iienet.org/studentcenter
Purpose: To support graduate student Institute members.
Eligibility: Applicants must be graduate students at an institution in the United States, Canada or Mexico, majoring in industrial engineering or its equivalent and active members. Students may not apply directly for this scholarship and must be nominated. The award is based on

academic ability, character, leadership, potential service to the industrial engineering profession and financial need.
Target applicant:
    Graduate school students
    Adult students
Minimum GPA: 3.4
Amount: $1,000.
Number of awards: 2.
Deadline: February 15.
How to apply: Nomination forms are available online.

(872) · Gladys Anderson Emerson Scholarship

Iota Sigma Pi (ISP) ND
Professor Kathryn A. Thomasson, Iota Sigma Pi Director for Student Awards
University of North Dakota, Department of Chemistry
P.O. Box 9024
Grand Forks, ND 58202-9024
Phone: 701-777-3199
Fax: 701-777-2331
Email: kthomasson@chem.und.edu
Website: http://www.iotasigmapi.info
Purpose: To award achievement in the fields of chemistry and biochemistry by women.
Eligibility: Applicants must have attained junior status at an accredited college or university, be female and be nominated by a member of Iota Sigma Pi.
Target applicant:
    College students
    Graduate school students
    Adult students
Minimum GPA: None.
Amount: $2,000.
Number of awards: 1.
Deadline: February 15.
How to apply: Applications are available online.

(873) · Graduate Fellowships

Institute of Food Technologists (IFT)
525 W. Van Buren
Suite 1000
Chicago, IL 60607
Phone: 312-782-8424
Email: ejplummer@ift.org
Website: http://www.ift.org
Purpose: To award graduate students researching food science or technology.
Eligibility: Applicants should be graduate students pursuing an M.S. and/or Ph.D. at the time the fellowship becomes effective and should research an area of food science or technology. Applications, transcripts and three recommendation letters are required.
Target applicant:
    Graduate school students
    Adult students
Minimum GPA: None.
Amount: $5,000.
Number of awards: Varies.
Deadline: February 1.
How to apply: Applications are available online.

(874) · Graduate Research Award (GRA)

American Vacuum Society
120 Wall Street, 32nd Floor
New York, NY 10005-3993
Phone: 212-248-0200
Fax: 212-248-0245
Email: angela@avs.org
Website: http://www.avs.org
Purpose: To support graduate studies in the sciences and technologies related to the AVS.
Eligibility: Applicants must be graduate students in an accredited academic institution. Awards are based on research and academic record. The awards cover travel expenses to the international symposium. Applicants should submit applications, recommendation letters, research summaries and transcripts.
Target applicant:
    Graduate school students
    Adult students
Minimum GPA: None.
Amount: $1,000.
Number of awards: 10.
Deadline: March 31.
How to apply: Applications are available online.

(875) · Graduate Student Research Grants

Geological Society of America
Program Officer
Grants, Awards and Recognition
P.O. Box 9140
Boulder, CO 80301-9140
Phone: 303-357-1028
Fax: 303-357-1070
Email: awards@geosociety.org
Website: http://www.geosociety.org
Purpose: To support thesis and dissertation research for graduate students in geological science.
Eligibility: Applicants must currently be enrolled in a geological science graduate program at an institution in the United States, Canada, Mexico or Central America. Applicants must also be members of the Geological Society of America (GSA).
Target applicant:
    Graduate school students
    Adult students
Minimum GPA: None.
Amount: Varies.
Number of awards: Varies.
Deadline: February 1.
How to apply: Applications are available online.

(876) · Graduate Student Scholarship

American Speech-Language-Hearing Foundation
2200 Research Boulevard
Rockville, MD 20850
Phone: 301-296-8700
Email: foundation@asha.org
Website: http://www.ashfoundation.org
Purpose: To support graduate students in communication sciences and disorders.
Eligibility: Applicants must be full-time graduate students in U.S. communication sciences and disorders programs. Master's degree candidates must be in programs accredited by the Council on Academic Accreditation for Audiology and Speech Pathology, but doctoral programs do not have to be accredited. Transcripts, an essay, a reference form and a statement of good standing are required.
Target applicant:
    Graduate school students
    Adult students
Minimum GPA: None.
Amount: $4,000.
Number of awards: Varies.
Deadline: January 13.
How to apply: Applications are available online.

(877) · Graduate Summer Student Research Assistantship

National Radio Astronomy Observatory (NRAO)
NRAO Headquarters
520 Edgemont Road
Charlottesville, VA 22903
Phone: 434-296-0211
Fax: 434-296-0278
Email: info@nrao.edu
Website: http://www.nrao.edu
Purpose: To allow graduate students to perform astronomical research at National Radio Astronomy Observatory (NRAO) sites.
Eligibility: Applicants must be first- or second-year graduate students interested in astronomical research. Recipients work on-site for 10 to 12 weeks, beginning in late May or early June.
Target applicant:
    Graduate school students
    Adult students
Minimum GPA: None.
Amount: $510 per week stipend.
Number of awards: Varies.
Deadline: January 23.
How to apply: Applications are available online.

(878) · Grotto Scholarships

DeMolay Foundation
10200 NW Ambassador Drive
Kansas City, MO 64153
Phone: 800-336-6529
Fax: 816-891-9062
Email: demolay@demolay.org
Website: http://www.demolay.org
Purpose: To assist medical students.
Eligibility: Applicants must be enrolled in a dental, medical or pre-medical program at an accredited institution but do not need to be active members of DeMolay. Students should complete an application and submit it to the DeMolay Service and Leadership Center.
Target applicant:
    College students
    Graduate school students
    Adult students
Minimum GPA: None.
Amount: $1,500.
Number of awards: 4.
Deadline: April 1.
How to apply: Applications are available online.

(879) · H.P. Milligan Aviation Scholarship

EAA Aviation Center
P.O. Box 2683
Oshkosh, WI 54903
Phone: 877-806-8902
Fax: 920-426-6865
Email: scholarships@eaa.org
Website: http://www.youngeagles.org
Purpose: To support excellence among individuals studying aviation.
Eligibility: Applicants must be enrolled in an accredited college, aviation academy or technical school pursuing a course of study focusing on aviation. Applicants must also be involved in school and community activities as well as aviation and be an EAA member or be recommended by an EAA member.
Target applicant:
High school students
College students
Adult students
Minimum GPA: None.
Amount: $1,000.
Number of awards: 1.
Scholarship may be renewable.
Deadline: March 1.
How to apply: Applications are available online.

(880) · Hansen Scholarship

EAA Aviation Center
P.O. Box 2683
Oshkosh, WI 54903
Phone: 877-806-8902
Fax: 920-426-6865
Email: scholarships@eaa.org
Website: http://www.youngeagles.org
Purpose: To support excellence among individuals studying the technologies and the skills needed in the field of aviation.
Eligibility: Applicants must be enrolled in an accredited college or university pursuing a degree in aerospace engineering or aeronautical engineering and must be involved in school and community activities as well as aviation. Applicants must be in good academic standing. Financial need will be considered. Applicants must also be EAA members or be recommended by an EAA member.
Target applicant:
College students
Graduate school students
Adult students
Minimum GPA: None.
Amount: $1,000.
Number of awards: 1.
Scholarship may be renewable.
Deadline: March 1.
How to apply: Applications are available online.

(881) · Harness Tracks of America Scholarship Fund

Harness Tracks of America
4640 E. Sunrise, Suite 200
Tucson, AZ 85718
Phone: 520-529-2525
Fax: 520-529-3235
Email: info@harnesstracks.com
Website: http://www.harnesstracks.com
Purpose: To provide assistance to students who are involved in the harness racing industry.
Eligibility: Applicants must have a parent or parents involved in harness racing or must be active in the business. Applicants must also demonstrate active merit or financial need.
Target applicant:
Junior high students or younger
High school students
College students
Adult students
Minimum GPA: None.
Amount: $7,500.
Number of awards: 6.
Deadline: Varies.
How to apply: Applications are available by telephone.

(882) · HDSA Research Fellowships

Huntington's Disease Society of America
505 Eighth Avenue, Suite 902
New York, NY 10018
Phone: 800-345-4372
Fax: 212-239-3430
Email: rgraze@hdsa.org
Website: http://www.hdsa.org
Purpose: To help postdoctoral researchers in the early stages of their careers.
Eligibility: Applicants must have M.D. or Ph.D. degrees and work on clinical or basic research projects related to Huntington's Disease. Candidates should submit a research and training plan summary, budget, biography and letter of support.
Target applicant:
Graduate school students
Adult students
Minimum GPA: None.
Amount: $40,000.
Number of awards: Varies.
Scholarship may be renewable.
Deadline: May 1.
How to apply: Applications are available online.

(883) · Health Careers Scholarship

International Order of the King's Daughters and Sons
Director
P.O. Box 1040
Chautauqua, NY 14722
Website: http://www.iokds.org
Purpose: To assist students interested in pursuing health careers.
Eligibility: Applicants must be full-time students pursuing a career in medicine, dentistry, nursing, pharmacy, physical or occupational therapy or medical technologies. R.N. students and those pursuing an M.D. or D.D.S must have completed at least one year of schooling at an accredited institution. All others must be entering at least their third year of school. Pre-med students are not eligible. Applicants must be U.S. or Canadian citizens.
Target applicant:
College students
Graduate school students
Adult students
Minimum GPA: None.
Amount: $1,000.
Number of awards: Varies.

Deadline: April 1.
How to apply: Applications are available by sending a self-addressed, stamped legal size envelope.

(884) · Health Resources and Services Administration-Bureau of Health Professions Scholarships for Disadvantaged Students

United States Public Health Service
Health Resources and Services Administration
5600 Fishers Lane
Rockville, MD 20857
Website: http://bhpr.hrsa.gov/dsa
Purpose: To support students from disadvantaged backgrounds who are pursuing health-related careers.
Eligibility: Applicants must be full-time students, be from a disadvantaged background, demonstrate financial need and be studying in a health field, including medicine, nursing, veterinary medicine, dentistry, pharmacy and others. They must be U.S. citizens, nationals or permanent residents. All other criteria are set by individual schools.
Target applicant:
   High school students
   College students
   Graduate school students
   Adult students
Minimum GPA: None.
Amount: Up to the full cost of schooling plus living allowance.
Number of awards: Varies.
Deadline: Varies.
How to apply: Applications are available from participating schools.

(885) · Health Sciences Student Fellowship

Epilepsy Foundation
8301 Professional Place
Landover , MD 20785
Phone: 301-459-3700
Email: researchwebsupport@efa.org
Website: http://www.epilepsyfoundation.org
Purpose: To encourage students to pursue careers in epilepsy in either research or practice settings.
Eligibility: Applicants must be enrolled in medical school, a doctoral program or other graduate program, have an epilepsy-related study, have a qualified mentor who can supervise the project and have access to a lab or clinic to conduct the project. The project must be in the U.S. and should not be for dissertation research. The award is based on the quality of the project, relevance of the project to epilepsy, applicant's interest in epilepsy, applicant's qualifications and the quality of the lab or clinic. Applicants should submit three recommendation letters, statement of intent, biographical sketch and research plan.
Target applicant:
   Graduate school students
   Adult students
Minimum GPA: None.
Amount: $3,000.
Number of awards: Varies.
Deadline: March 1.
How to apply: Applications are available online.

(886) · Henry Hecaen and Manfred Meier Neuropsychology Scholarships

American Psychological Foundation
750 First Street NE
Washington, DC 20002
Phone: 800-374-2721
Website: http://www.apa.org
Purpose: To assist neuropsychology graduate students.
Eligibility: Applicants must demonstrate need and potential for a promising career in the field of neuropsychology. Applicants should also submit a letter that documents their scholarly and research accomplishments, financial need and how the award will be used.
Target applicant:
   Graduate school students
   Adult students
Minimum GPA: None.
Amount: $2,500.
Number of awards: 2.
Deadline: June 1.
How to apply: There is no official application.

(887) · Herbert L. Cox Memorial Scholarship

EAA Aviation Center
P.O. Box 2683
Oshkosh, WI 54903
Phone: 877-806-8902
Fax: 920-426-6865
Email: scholarships@eaa.org
Website: http://www.youngeagles.org
Purpose: To support aviation students.
Eligibility: Applicants must be enrolled in an accredited college or university pursuing a course of study focusing on aviation and involved in school and community activities as well as aviation. Recipient of award must show need for financial support. Applicants must also be EAA members or be recommended by an EAA member.
Target applicant:
   High school students
   College students
   Adult students
Minimum GPA: None.
Amount: $500.
Number of awards: 1.
Deadline: March 1.
How to apply: Applications are available online.

(888) · Herbert Levy Memorial Scholarship

Society of Physics Students
One Physics Ellipse
College Park, MD 20740
Phone: 301-209-3007
Fax: 301-209-0839
Email: sps@aip.org
Website: http://www.spsnational.org
Purpose: To provide financial assistance for physics students in any year of undergraduate study.
Eligibility: Applicants must be physics majors, be members of SPS and demonstrate scholarly achievement and financial need.
Target applicant:
   College students
   Adult students

Minimum GPA: None.
Amount: $2,000.
Number of awards: 1.
Deadline: February 15.
How to apply: Applications are available online or from SPS Chapter Advisors.

(889) · Hertz Foundation's Graduate Fellowship Award

Fannie and John Hertz Foundation
2456 Research Drive
Livermore, CA 94550-3850
Phone: 925-373-1642
Fax: 925-373-6329
Email: askhertz@hertzfoundation.org
Website: http://www.hertzfoundation.com
Purpose: To help graduate students in the applied physical and engineering sciences.
Eligibility: Applicants must be college seniors planning to pursue or graduate students currently pursuing a Ph.D. in the applied physical and engineering sciences or modern biology which applies the physical sciences. Successful applicants must attend one of the foundation's approved schools. The award is based on merit, creativity and potential for research.
Target applicant:
  College students
  Graduate school students
  Adult students
Minimum GPA: None.
Amount: $33,000.
Number of awards: Varies.
Scholarship may be renewable.
Deadline: October 28.
How to apply: Applications are available online, by phone or by email.

(890) · HHMI-NIH Research Scholars (Cloister Program)

Howard Hughes Medical Institute Research Scholars
1 Cloister Court, Building 60
Bethesda, MD 20814-1460
Phone: 800-424-9924
Email: research_scholars@hhmi.org
Website: http://www.hhmi.org/research/cloister/
Purpose: To award fellowships to medical students.
Eligibility: Applicants must be enrolled in a U.S. medical school or dental school but not in M.D./Ph.D., D.D.S./Ph.D. or Ph.D. programs or have an M.D. or Ph.D. in lab-based biological sciences. Recipients will conduct research at the National Institutes of Health in Bethesda, MD. Research experience is not required. Applicants should submit research areas of interest, personal statements, professional activities, awards, publications (optional), letters of reference, undergraduate and medical or dental school transcripts and MCAT or DAT scores.
Target applicant:
  Graduate school students
  Adult students
Minimum GPA: None.
Amount: $25,000.
Number of awards: Varies.
Deadline: January 10.
How to apply: Applications are available online.

(891) · HIMSS Foundation Scholarship

Healthcare Information and Management Systems Society
230 E. Ohio Street, Suite 500
Chicago, IL 60611-3269
Phone: 312-664-4467
Fax: 312-664-6143
Website: http://www.himss.org
Purpose: To provide scholarships based on academic achievement and leadership in the field of healthcare information and management systems.
Eligibility: Applicants must be members of HIMSS and study healthcare information and management systems. Scholarships are also available from individual chapters listed on the HIMSS website.
Target applicant:
  College students
  Adult students
Minimum GPA: None.
Amount: Varies.
Number of awards: 7.
Deadline: October 31.
How to apply: Application details are available online.

(892) · Holly Cornell Scholarship

American Water Works Association
6666 W. Quincy Avenue
Denver, CO 80235-3098
Phone: 303-347-6201
Fax: 303-795-7603
Email: swheeler@awwa.org
Website: http://www.awwa.org
Purpose: To support female and/or minority master's students pursuing advanced training in the field of water supply and treatment.
Eligibility: Applicants must be females and/or minorities who have been accepted to or are current master's degree students in engineering. Applications, transcripts, GRE scores, three recommendation letters, statements and course of study are required. The award is based on academics and leadership.
Target applicant:
  Graduate school students
  Adult students
Minimum GPA: None.
Amount: $5,000.
Number of awards: 1.
Deadline: January 15.
How to apply: Applications are available online.

(893) · Hooper Memorial Scholarship

Transportation Clubs International Scholarships
Attn.: Bill Blair
Zimmer Worldwide Logistics
15710 JFK Boulevard
Houston, TX 77032
Phone: 877-858-8627
Email: bblair@zimmerworldwide.com
Website: http://www.transportationclubsinternational.com
Purpose: To support students who want to enter the transportation industry.
Eligibility: Applicants must be enrolled in an accredited institution of higher learning in a vocational or degree program in the fields of transportation logistics or traffic management. The awards are based

upon scholastic ability, potential, professional interest and character. Financial need is also considered.

Target applicant:
College students
Adult students
Minimum GPA: None.
Amount: $1,500.
Number of awards: 1.
Deadline: April 30.
How to apply: Applications are available online.

(894) · HSA Research Grants

Herb Society of America
Attn.: Research Grant
9019 Kirtland Chardon Road
Kirtland, OH 44094
Phone: 440-256-0514
Fax: 440-256-0541
Email: herbs@herbsociety.org
Website: http://www.herbsociety.org
Purpose: To educate about herbs and contribute to the fields of horticulture, science, literature, history, art and/or economics.
Eligibility: Applicants must have a proposed program of scientific, academic or artistic investigation of herbal plants. Applicants must describe their research needs in 500 words or less and include a proposed budget with specific budget items listed. This grant may not be used in combination with funding from another source and may not be used to pay for salaries, tuition or private garden development.
Target applicant:
College students
Graduate school students
Adult students
Minimum GPA: None.
Amount: Up to $5,000.
Number of awards: Varies by year.
Deadline: January 31.
How to apply: Applications are available online or by written request.

(895) · IEEE Presidents' Scholarship

Institute of Electrical and Electronics Engineers History Center
445 Hoes Lane
Piscataway, NJ 08854
Phone: 732-562-3860
Email: supportieee@ieee.org
Website: http://www.ieee.org/history_center
Purpose: To award a student for a project relevant to electrical engineering, electronics engineering, computer science or other IEEE fields of interest.
Eligibility: Applicants must be high school students planning to study engineering or engineering-related fields and must compete in the Intel ISEF competitions beginning at the state/local level and advance to the international competition.
Target applicant:
High school students
Minimum GPA: None.
Amount: $10,000.
Number of awards: Varies.
Scholarship may be renewable.
Deadline: Varies.
How to apply: Contact the organization for more information.

(896) · IIE Council of Fellows Undergraduate Scholarship

Institute of Industrial Engineers (IIE)
3577 Parkway Lane
Suite 200
Norcross, GA 30092
Phone: 800-494-0460
Fax: 770-441-3295
Email: bcameron@iienet.org
Website: http://www.iienet.org/studentcenter
Purpose: To support undergraduate student members.
Eligibility: Applicants must be full-time undergraduate students enrolled in a college in the United States, Canada or Mexico with an accredited industrial engineering program, major in industrial engineering and be active members. Students may apply directly for this scholarship and do not need to be nominated. The award is based on academic ability, character, leadership, potential service to the industrial engineering profession and financial need.
Target applicant:
College students
Adult students
Minimum GPA: 3.4
Amount: $1,000.
Number of awards: 2.
Deadline: February 15.
How to apply: Applications are available online.

(897) · Industrial Electrolysis and Electrochemical Engineering Division H.H. Dow Memorial Student Award

Electrochemical Society
65 South Main Street, Building D
Pennington, NJ 08534-2839
Phone: 609-737-1902
Fax: 609-737-2743
Email: awards@electrochem.org
Website: http://www.electrochem.org
Purpose: To recognize young engineers and scientists in the fields of electrochemical engineering and applied electrochemistry.
Eligibility: Applicants must be accepted to or enrolled in a graduate program. The application requires transcripts, a description of the research project, a description of how the project relates to electrochemical engineering or applied electrochemistry, a biography, a resume or curriculum vitae and a letter of recommendation from the research supervisor. The award is based on academic performance, research and the recommendation.
Target applicant:
Graduate school students
Adult students
Minimum GPA: None.
Amount: $1,000.
Number of awards: Varies.
Deadline: September 15.
How to apply: Application materials are described online.

(898) · Industrial Electrolysis and Electrochemical Engineering Division Student Achievement Awards

Electrochemical Society
65 South Main Street, Building D
Pennington, NJ 08534-2839

Phone: 609-737-1902
Fax: 609-737-2743
Email: awards@electrochem.org
Website: http://www.electrochem.org
Purpose: To recognize young engineers and scientists in electrochemical engineering and to encourage the recipients to enter careers in the field.
Eligibility: Applicants must be accepted by or enrolled in a college or university and propose a research project. The application must include transcripts, research outline, statement describing how the project relates to electrochemical engineering, record of industrial work and letter of recommendation from the research supervisor. The award is based on academic performance, research and the recommendation.
Target applicant:
  High school students
  College students
  Graduate school students
  Adult students
Minimum GPA: None.
Amount: $1,000.
Number of awards: Varies.
Deadline: September 15.
How to apply: Application materials are described online.

(899) · Intel Science Talent Search

Intel Corporation and Science Service
1719 North Street NW
Washington, DC 20036
Phone: 202-785-2255
Fax: 202-785-1243
Email: sciedu@sciserv.org
Website: http://www.societyforscience.org/sts/
Purpose: To recognize excellence in science among the nation's youth and encourage the exploration of science.
Eligibility: Applicants must be high school seniors in the U.S., Puerto Rico, Guam, Virgin Islands, American Samoa, Wake or Midway Islands or the Marianas. U.S. citizens attending foreign schools are also eligible. Applicants must complete college entrance exams and complete individual research projects and provide a report on the research.
Target applicant:
  High school students
Minimum GPA: None.
Amount: $1,000-$100,000.
Number of awards: 300.
Deadline: November.
How to apply: Applications are available by request.

(900) · International Science and Engineering Fair

Intel Corporation and Science Service
1719 North Street NW
Washington, DC 20036
Phone: 202-785-2255
Fax: 202-785-1243
Email: sciedu@sciserv.org
Website: http://www.societyforscience.org/sts/
Purpose: To reward outstanding high school science fair projects.
Eligibility: Students must participate in a regional science fair affiliated with Intel ISEF and be selected to advance to the Intel ISEF. The competition is open to students in the ninth to twelfth grade and has 18 categories: Animal Sciences, Behavioral and Social Sciences, Biochemistry, Cellular and Molecular Biology, Chemistry, Computer Science, Earth Science, Engineering: Electrical and Mechanical, Engineering: Materials and Bioengineering, Energy and Transportation, Environmental Management, Environmental Science, Mathematical Sciences, Medicine and Health, Microbiology, Physics and Astronomy, Plant Sciences and Team Projects.
Target applicant:
  High school students
Minimum GPA: None.
Amount: Up to $50,000.
Number of awards: 600.
Deadline: Varies.
How to apply: Required forms are available online.

(901) · International Student Scholarship

American Speech-Language-Hearing Foundation
2200 Research Boulevard
Rockville, MD 20850
Phone: 301-296-8700
Email: foundation@asha.org
Website: http://www.ashfoundation.org
Purpose: To support an international graduate student in communication sciences and disorders.
Eligibility: Applicants must be full-time students in the U.S. Master's degree candidates must be in programs accredited by the Council on Academic Accreditation for Audiology and Speech Pathology, but doctoral programs do not have to be accredited. The applicants should submit transcripts, an essay and a reference form.
Target applicant:
  Graduate school students
  Adult students
Minimum GPA: None.
Amount: $4,000.
Number of awards: 1.
Deadline: January 13.
How to apply: Applications are available online.

(902) · Irene E. Newman Scholarship

American Dental Hygienists' Association (ADHA) Institute for Oral Health
444 N. Michigan Avenue
Suite 3400
Chicago, IL 60611
Phone: 800-735-4916
Email: institute@adha.net
Website: http://www.adha.org/institute
Purpose: To support students interested in public health or community dental health.
Eligibility: Applicants must be undergraduate or graduate students interested in public health or community dental health. They must also demonstrate financial need of at least $1,500, submit a goals statement and be active members of SADHA or ADHA.
Target applicant:
  College students
  Graduate school students
  Adult students
Minimum GPA: None.
Amount: $1,500.
Number of awards: 1.
Deadline: May 1.
How to apply: Applications are available online.

(903) · IRF Fellowship Program

International Road Federation
Madison Place
500 Montgomery Street, 5th Floor
Alexandria, VA 22314
Phone: 703-535-1001
Fax: 703-535-1007
Email: info@internationalroadfederation.org
Website: http://www.irfnet.org
Purpose: To provide fellowships in support of graduate study in a transportation-related field.
Eligibility: Applicants must demonstrate potential leadership in the highway industry in financing, administration, planning, design, construction, operations or maintenance. They must also have three to 15 years of work experience in transportation, a bachelor's of science degree (or equivalent) in a transportation-related discipline and a commitment to full-time study for a minimum of nine months.
Target applicant:
Graduate school students
Adult students
Minimum GPA: None.
Amount: Varies.
Number of awards: Varies.
Deadline: Varies.
How to apply: More information is available online.

(904) · ISS Scholarship Foundation

Iron and Steel Society
Attn.: Lori Wharrey
AIST Foundation
186 Thorn Hill Road
Warrendale, PA 15086
Phone: 724-776-6040 x621
Fax: 724-776-1880 ·
Email: lwharrey@aist.org
Website: http://www.aistfoundation.org
Purpose: To attract talented and dedicated students to careers within the iron and steel and steel-related industries.
Eligibility: Applicants must be full-time college juniors or seniors majoring in metallurgy, metallurgical engineering or materials science. Other related majors are considered with a letter from the academic adviser. Applicants must have a minimum 3.0 GPA in the major or a minimum 3.25 GPA if they are undeclared and be ISS student members or submit an application for membership with the scholarship application.
Target applicant:
College students
Adult students
Minimum GPA: 3.0 in the major; 3.25 if undeclared
Amount: $2,000.
Number of awards: 5.
Deadline: April 30.
How to apply: Applications are available online.

(905) · Jack Horkheimer Award

Astronomical League
7241 Jarboe
Kansas City, MO 64114
Phone: 816-444-4878
Email: carroll-iorg@kc.rr.com
Website: http://www.astroleague.org
Purpose: To assist young Astronomical League members.
Eligibility: Applicants must be Astronomical League members under the age of 19 on the date of the application. The award is based on involvement in the organization.
Target applicant:
Junior high students or younger
High school students
Minimum GPA: None.
Amount: $1,000.
Number of awards: Varies.
Deadline: March 31.
How to apply: Applications are available online.

(906) · James P. Dearing Scholarship

American Society of Extra-Corporeal Technology (AmSECT)
2209 Dickens Road
P.O. Box 11086
Richmond, VA 23230-1086
Phone: 804-565-6363
Fax: 804-282-0090
Email: patelpump@sbcglobal.net
Website: http://www.amsect.org
Purpose: To support perfusion education.
Eligibility: Applicants must be current student members of AmSECT, be in a CAAHEP accredited perfusion education program, have finished 25 percent of the coursework, have a minimum 2.75 GPA and submit an application, essay and transcript.
Target applicant:
College students
Graduate school students
Adult students
Minimum GPA: 2.75
Amount: $2,000.
Number of awards: Varies.
Deadline: December 15.
How to apply: Applications are available online.

(907) · Jean Theodore Lacordaire Prize

Coleopterists Society
Anthony I. Cognato, Chair
Texas A & M University
College Station, TX 77845-2475
Phone: 979-458-0404
Email: a.cognato@tamu.edu
Website: http://www.coleopsoc.org
Purpose: To recognize the work of coleopterists.
Eligibility: Applicants must be graduate students whose papers are nominated for the competition. The papers must be about coleoptera (beetle) systematics or biology published in a journal or book. Self-nominations are not accepted.
Target applicant:
Graduate school students
Adult students
Minimum GPA: None.
Amount: $300.
Number of awards: Varies.
Deadline: August 1.
How to apply: Application materials are described online.

(908) · Jerry W. Richmond Memorial Scholarship

American Society of Extra-Corporeal Technology (AmSECT)
2209 Dickens Road
P.O. Box 11086
Richmond, VA 23230-1086
Phone: 804-565-6363
Fax: 804-282-0090
Email: patelpump@sbcglobal.net
Website: http://www.amsect.org
Purpose: To support perfusion education.
Eligibility: Applicants must be current student members of AmSECT, be in a CAAHEP accredited perfusion education program, have finished 25 percent of the coursework, have a minimum 2.75 GPA and submit an application, essay and transcript.
Target applicant:
   College students
   Graduate school students
   Adult students
Minimum GPA: 2.75
Amount: $1,000.
Number of awards: Varies.
Deadline: December 15.
How to apply: Applications are available online.

(909) · Jimmy A. Young Memorial Education Recognition Award

American Association for Respiratory Care
9425 North MacArthur Boulevard
Suite 100
Irving, TX 75063-4706
Phone: 972-243-2272
Fax: 972-484-2720
Email: info@aarc.org
Website: http://www.aarc.org
Purpose: To recognize outstanding minority students in respiratory care education programs.
Eligibility: Applicants must be enrolled in an accredited respiratory care education program and have a minimum 3.0 GPA. Students must submit an original paper on respiratory care. Preference is given to minority students.
Target applicant:
   College students
   Graduate school students
   Adult students
Minimum GPA: 3.0
Amount: Up to $1,000.
Number of awards: 1.
Deadline: June 15.
How to apply: Applications are available online.

(910) · John and Elsa Gracik Scholarships

American Society of Mechanical Engineers
Three Park Avenue
New York, NY 10016
Phone: 800-843-2763
Fax: 973-882-1717
Email: infocentral@asme.org
Website: http://www.asme.org
Purpose: To support mechanical engineering students.

Eligibility: Applicants must be ASME student members, enrolled in an eligible accredited mechanical engineering baccalaureate program and be U.S. citizens. Selection is based on scholastic ability, financial need, character, leadership and potential contribution to the mechanical engineering profession.
Target applicant:
   College students
   Adult students
Minimum GPA: None.
Amount: $1,500.
Number of awards: 18.
Deadline: March 15.
How to apply: Applications are available online.

(911) · John and Muriel Landis Scholarship

American Nuclear Society
555 North Kensington Avenue
La Grange Park, IL 60526
Phone: 708-352-6611
Fax: 708-352-0499
Email: hr@ans.org
Website: http://www.ans.org
Purpose: To assist disadvantaged students to seek careers in a nuclear-related field.
Eligibility: Applicants must be undergraduate or graduate students enrolled or planning to enroll in a U.S. college or university who are also planning a career in nuclear science, nuclear engineering or another nuclear-related field. High school seniors may apply. Students must have greater than average financial need. Applicants must submit applications, transcripts, sponsor forms and three reference forms.
Target applicant:
   High school students
   College students
   Graduate school students
   Adult students
Minimum GPA: None.
Amount: Varies.
Number of awards: Up to 8.
Deadline: February 1.
How to apply: Applications are available online.

(912) · John Culver Wooddy Scholarships

Actuarial Foundation
475 North Martingale Road
Suite 600
Schaumburg, IL 60173
Phone: 847-706-3535
Fax: 847-706-3599
Email: scholarships@actfnd.org
Website: http://www.aerf.org
Purpose: To assist students who plan to become actuaries.
Eligibility: Applicants must be undergraduate students who will receive their degrees by August 31 of the year following the application deadline. Students must be in the top quartile of their class and have completed a minimum of one actuarial examination. A recommendation from a professor is required. Only one applicant per school is permitted. Preference is given to applicants who have demonstrated leadership ability in extracurricular activities.
Target applicant:
   College students
   Adult students

Minimum GPA: None.
Amount: $2,000.
Number of awards: Varies.
Deadline: June 23.
How to apply: Applications are available online.

(913) · John Henry Comstock Graduate Student Awards

Entomological Society of America
10001 Derekwood Lane
Suite 100
Lanham, MD 20706
Phone: 301-731-4535
Fax: 301-731-4538
Email: esa@entsoc.org
Website: http://www.entsoc.org
Purpose: To encourage graduate students interested in entomology to attend the Annual Meeting of the Entomological Society of America.
Eligibility: Applicants must be graduate students and members of the ESA. Each ESA branch has its own eligibility requirements, so an interested student must contact their Branch Secretary-Treasurer for more information.
Target applicant:
 Graduate school students
 Adult students
Minimum GPA: None.
Amount: $100.
Number of awards: 5.
Deadline: September 1.
How to apply: Applications are available online.

(914) · John J. McKetta Scholarship

American Institute of Chemical Engineers - (AIChE)
3 Park Avenue
New York, NY 10016
Phone: 212-591-7634
Fax: 212-591-8890
Email: awards@aiche.org
Website: http://www.aiche.org
Purpose: To support chemical engineering students.
Eligibility: Applicants must be chemical engineering incoming undergraduate juniors or seniors and be planning a career in the chemical engineering process industries. Applicants must also have a minimum 3.0 GPA and be attending an ABET accredited school in the U.S., Canada or Mexico. Selection is based on an essay outlining career goals, leadership in an AIChE student chapter or other university sponsored activity and letters of recommendation. Preference is given to members of AIChE.
Target applicant:
 College students
 Adult students
Minimum GPA: 3.0
Amount: $5,000.
Number of awards: 1.
Deadline: April 15.
How to apply: Applications are available online.

(915) · John L. Imhoff Scholarship

Institute of Industrial Engineers (IIE)
3577 Parkway Lane
Suite 200
Norcross, GA 30092
Phone: 800-494-0460
Fax: 770-441-3295
Email: bcameron@iienet.org
Website: http://www.iienet.org/studentcenter
Purpose: To award a student who has contributed to the development of the industrial engineering profession through international understanding.
Eligibility: Applicants must be pursuing a B.S., master's or doctorate degree in an accredited IE program and have at least two years of school remaining. Students may not apply directly for this scholarship and must be nominated. An essay describing the candidate's international contributions to industrial engineering and three references are required. IIE membership is not required.
Target applicant:
 College students
 Graduate school students
 Adult students
Minimum GPA: 3.4
Amount: $1,000.
Number of awards: 1.
Deadline: February 15.
How to apply: More information is available online.

(916) · John S.W. Fargher Scholarship

Institute of Industrial Engineers (IIE)
3577 Parkway Lane
Suite 200
Norcross, GA 30092
Phone: 800-494-0460
Fax: 770-441-3295
Email: bcameron@iienet.org
Website: http://www.iienet.org/studentcenter
Purpose: To award graduate students in industrial engineering who have demonstrated leadership.
Eligibility: Applicants must be full-time graduate students with at least one full year left who are enrolled in a college in the United States with an accredited industrial engineering program. Candidates must also major in industrial engineering or engineering management and be active members who have demonstrated leadership in industrial engineering-related activities. Students may not apply directly for this scholarship and must be nominated.
Target applicant:
 Graduate school students
 Adult students
Minimum GPA: 3.0
Amount: $1,000.
Number of awards: 1.
Deadline: September 11.
How to apply: More information is available online.

(917) · Johnny Davis Memorial Scholarship

Aircraft Electronics Association
4217 South Hocker
Independence, MO 64055
Phone: 816-373-6565

Fax: 816-478-3100
Email: info@aea.net
Website: http://www.aea.net
Purpose: To support students of avionics and aircraft repair.
Eligibility: Applicants must be high school seniors or college students who plan to or are attending an accredited school in an avionics or aircraft repair program.
Target applicant:
  High school students
  College students
  Adult students
Minimum GPA: None.
Amount: $1,000.
Number of awards: 1.
Deadline: February 15.
How to apply: Applications are available by contacting the organization for more information.

(918) · Joseph C. Johnson Memorial Grant

American Society of Certified Engineering Technicians (ASCET)
P.O. Box 1536
Brandon, MS 39043
Phone: 601-824-8991
Email: general-manager@ascet.org
Website: http://www.ascet.org
Purpose: To support engineering technology students.
Eligibility: Applicants must have a minimum 3.0 GPA, be U.S. citizens or legal residents of the country in which they are currently living, be either a student, certified, regular, registered or associate member of the American Society of Certified Engineering Technicians (ASCET) and be full- or part-time students in an engineering technology program. Students in a two-year program should apply in the first year to receive the grant for their second year. Students in a four-year program who apply in the third year may receive the grant for their fourth year. Applicants must show financial need and submit three letters of recommendation.
Target applicant:
  College students
  Adult students
Minimum GPA: 3.0
Amount: $750.
Number of awards: 1.
Deadline: April 1.
How to apply: Applications are available online.

(919) · Joseph Frasca Excellence in Aviation Scholarship

University Aviation Association (UAA)
David NewMeyer
College of Applied Sciences and Arts, Southern Illinois University Carbondale
1365 Douglas Drive, Rm 126
Carbondale , IL 62901-6623
Phone: 618-453-8898
Fax: 618-453-7286
Email: newmyer@siu.edu
Website: http://www.uaa.aero
Purpose: To encourage students to reach the highest level of achievement in their aviation studies.
Eligibility: Applicants must be juniors or seniors enrolled at a UAA member college or university with at least a 3.0 GPA. Students must

demonstrate excellence in all areas related to aviation and have FAA certification in either aviation maintenance or flight. Applicants must be a member of at least one aviation organization and be involved in aviation activities that demonstrate interest in and enthusiasm for aviation.
Target applicant:
  College students
  Adult students
Minimum GPA: 3.0
Amount: $2,000.
Number of awards: 2.
Deadline: April 9.
How to apply: Applications are available online.

(920) · Joseph M. Parish Memorial Grant

American Society of Certified Engineering Technicians (ASCET)
P.O. Box 1536
Brandon, MS 39043
Phone: 601-824-8991
Email: general-manager@ascet.org
Website: http://www.ascet.org
Purpose: To help engineering technology students.
Eligibility: Applicants must have a minimum 3.0 GPA, be U.S. citizens or legal residents of the country in which they are currently living, be student members of the American Society of Certified Engineering Technicians (ASCET) and be full-time students in an engineering technology program. Applicants in a two-year program should apply in the first year to receive the grant for their second year. Students in a four-year program who apply in the third year may receive the grant for their fourth year. Applicants must show financial need. Students pursuing a BS degree in engineering are not eligible for this grant.
Target applicant:
  College students
  Adult students
Minimum GPA: 3.0
Amount: $500.
Number of awards: 1.
Scholarship may be renewable.
Deadline: April 1.
How to apply: Applications are available online.

(921) · Junior and Senior Scholarships

Institute of Food Technologists (IFT)
525 W. Van Buren
Suite 1000
Chicago, IL 60607
Phone: 312-782-8424
Email: ejplummer@ift.org
Website: http://www.ift.org
Purpose: To encourage undergraduate students in food science or technology.
Eligibility: Applicants must be college sophomores, juniors or seniors pursuing an approved program in food science or food technology. Applications, transcripts and a recommendation letter are required.
Target applicant:
  College students
  Adult students
Minimum GPA: None.
Amount: $2,500.
Number of awards: 62.
Deadline: February 1.
How to apply: Applications are available online.

(922) · Junior Scholarship Program

American Kennel Club
260 Madison Avenue
New York, NY 10016
Phone: 212-696-8200
Website: http://www.akc.org
Purpose: To assist students who are involved with AKC purebred dogs.
Eligibility: Applicants must be under age 18 with an AKC registered purebred dog. Selection is based on involvement with AKC registered dogs, academic achievement and financial need. The scholarship program awards a total of $150,000 annually.
Target applicant:
    Junior high students or younger
    High school students
Minimum GPA: None.
Amount: Varies.
Number of awards: Varies.
Deadline: February 20.
How to apply: Applications are available online.

(923) · Karen O'Neil Endowed Advanced Nursing Practice Scholarship

Emergency Nurses Association
915 Lee Street
Des Plaines, IL 60016
Phone: 847-460-4100
Fax: 847-460-4004
Email: foundation@ena.org
Website: http://www.ena.org
Purpose: To promote advanced degrees in emergency nursing.
Eligibility: Applicants must be nurses pursuing an advanced degree and must have been ENA members for at least 12 months before applying.
Target applicant:
    Graduate school students
    Adult students
Minimum GPA: None.
Amount: $3,000.
Number of awards: 1.
Deadline: June 1.
How to apply: Applications are available online.

(924) · Kenneth Andrew Roe Scholarship

American Society of Mechanical Engineers
Three Park Avenue
New York, NY 10016
Phone: 800-843-2763
Fax: 973-882-1717
Email: infocentral@asme.org
Website: http://www.asme.org
Purpose: To support students who are studying mechanical engineering.
Eligibility: Applicants must be ASME student members, be enrolled in an ABET accredited mechanical engineering baccalaureate program, be North American residents and be U.S. citizens. Applicants must also be juniors or seniors in college with strong academic performance, character and integrity.

Target applicant:
    College students
    Adult students
Minimum GPA: None.
Amount: $10,000.
Number of awards: 1.
Deadline: March 15.
How to apply: Applications are available online.

(925) · Klussendorf Scholarship

National Dairy Shrine
1224 Alton Darby Creek Road
Columbus, OH 43228-9792
Phone: 614-878-5333
Fax: 614-870-2622
Email: shrine@cobaselect.com
Website: http://www.dairyshrine.org
Purpose: To honor students in dairy husbandry fields.
Eligibility: Applicants must be first, second or third year college students at two- or four-year universities, must major in a dairy husbandry field and plan to enter the dairy field.
Target applicant:
    College students
    Adult students
Minimum GPA: None.
Amount: $1,000.
Number of awards: 2.
Deadline: March 15.
How to apply: Applications are available online.

(926) · Larry Williams Photography and AYA Photo Contest

Appaloosa Horse Club
Appaloosa Youth Foundation Scholarship Committee
2720 W. Pullman Road
Moscow, ID 83843
Phone: 208-882-5578
Fax: 208-882-8150
Email: acaap@appaloosa.com
Website: http://www.appaloosa.com
Purpose: To support students who express their love of the Appaloosa through photography.
Eligibility: Applicants must submit multiple photographs in three divisions: 13 and under, 14 to 18 and 4H/FFA youths 18 and under.
Target applicant:
    Junior high students or younger
    High school students
Minimum GPA: None.
Amount: $150.
Number of awards: 9.
Deadline: May 1.
How to apply: Applications are available online.

(927) · Larson Aquatic Research Support (LARS)

American Water Works Association
6666 W. Quincy Avenue
Denver, CO 80235-3098
Phone: 303-347-6201
Fax: 303-795-7603
Email: swheeler@awwa.org
Website: http://www.awwa.org

Purpose: To support doctoral and master's students interested in careers in the fields of corrosion control, treatment and distribution of domestic and industrial water supplies, aquatic chemistry and/or environmental chemistry.

Eligibility: Applicants must pursue an advanced (master's or doctoral) degree at an institution of higher education located in Canada, Guam, Puerto Rico, Mexico or the U.S. Applications, resumes, transcripts, GRE scores, three recommendation letters and a course of study are required. Master's students also must submit a statement of educational plans and career objectives or a research plan. Ph.D. students must submit research plans. The master's grant is $5,000, and the doctoral grant is $7,000. The award is based on academics and leadership.

Target applicant:
 Graduate school students
 Adult students
Minimum GPA: None.
Amount: $7,000.
Number of awards: 2.
Deadline: January 15.
How to apply: Applications are available online.

(928) · Leadership Development Award
American Association of Occupational Health Nurses (AAOHN) Foundation
2920 Brandywine Road
Suite 100
Atlanta, GA 30341
Phone: 770-455-7757
Fax: 770-455-7271
Email: ann@aaohn.org
Website: http://www.aaohn.org
Purpose: To reward volunteer leadership development in occupational and environmental health nursing.
Eligibility: Applicants must work in the field of occupational and environmental health nursing and demonstrate an interest in occupational and environmental health. The funds may be used for leadership development activity/program registration, travel and/or associated travel-related expenses. Applicants must submit a narrative and letter of support from their employer.
Target applicant:
 College students
 Graduate school students
 Adult students
Minimum GPA: None.
Amount: $1,500.
Number of awards: 3.
Deadline: August 1.
How to apply: Applications are available online.

(929) · Lee Tarbox Memorial Scholarship
Aircraft Electronics Association
4217 South Hocker
Independence, MO 64055
Phone: 816-373-6565
Fax: 816-478-3100
Email: info@aea.net
Website: http://www.aea.net
Purpose: To support students of avionics and aircraft repair.
Eligibility: Applicants must be high school seniors or college students who plan to or are attending an accredited school in an avionics or aircraft repair program.

Target applicant:
 High school students
 College students
 Adult students
Minimum GPA: None.
Amount: $2,500.
Number of awards: 1.
Deadline: February 15.
How to apply: Applications are available by contacting the organization for more information.

(930) · Len Assante Scholarship Fund
National Ground Water Association
601 Dempsey Road
Westerville, OH 43081-8978
Phone: 800-551-7379
Fax: 614-898-7786
Email: ngwa@ngwa.org
Website: http://www.ngwa.org
Purpose: To support students in fields related to the ground water industry.
Eligibility: Applicants must be high school graduates or college students with a minimum 2.5 GPA who are studying fields related to the ground water industry including geology, hydrology, hydrogeology, environmental sciences or microbiology or well drilling two-year associate degree programs.
Target applicant:
 High school students
 College students
 Adult students
Minimum GPA: 2.5
Amount: Varies.
Number of awards: Varies.
Deadline: April 1.
How to apply: Applications are available by mail or e-mail.

(931) · Liberty Mutual Safety Research Fellowship Program
American Society of Safety Engineers
1800 East Oakton Street
Des Plaines, IL 60018
Phone: 847-699-2929
Fax: 847-768-3434
Email: mgoranson@asse.org
Website: http://www.asse.org
Purpose: To award research fellowships to promote safety research.
Eligibility: Applicants must be U.S. citizens and either have their Ph.D. or be working toward a masters or Ph.D. Preference is given to applicants working within an ABET-accredited safety program. The selection committee prefers applied safety/health research with a broad appeal and gives special consideration to ASSE members. Recipients must spend four to six weeks during the summer at the Liberty Mutual Research Center, in Hopkinton, MA, and write an article on their research or an outline for a grant proposal to continue the research.
Target applicant:
 Graduate school students
 Adult students
Minimum GPA: None.
Amount: Up to $9,500 stipend.
Number of awards: 2.

Deadline: February 1.
How to apply: Applications are available online.

(932) · Linda Craig Memorial Scholarship Presented by St. Vincent Sports Medicine

Pacers Foundation
125 S. Pennsylvania Street
Indianapolis, IN 46204
Phone: 317-917-2864
Fax: 317-917-2599
Email: foundation@pacers.com
Website: http://www.nba.com/pacers/news/Foundation_Index.html
Purpose: To support students interested in sports medicine, physical therapy and related fields.
Eligibility: Applicants must U.S. citizens who have completed at least four semesters of an undergraduate program majoring in medicine, sports medicine, physical therapy or a related area. They must have a GPA of at least 3.0 and demonstrate outstanding character, integrity and leadership. Applicants may not have received a full scholarship from any other organization.
Target applicant:
  College students
  Adult students
Minimum GPA: 3.0
Amount: Varies.
Number of awards: Varies.
Deadline: July 1.
How to apply: Applications are available online.

(933) · Linda Moore Scholarship

Epsilon Sigma Alpha Foundation
P.O. Box 270517
Fort Collins, CO 80527
Phone: 970-223-2824
Fax: 970-223-4456
Email: kloyd@knoxy.net
Website: http://www.esaintl.com/esaf
Purpose: To provide financial assistance for nursing majors.
Eligibility: Applicants must be residents of Alabama, Arkansas, Florida, Georgia, Kentucky, Louisiana, Maryland, Mississippi, North Carolina, South Carolina, Tennessee or Virginia. They may study nursing at any school. Selection is based on scholastic ability (30 percent), financial need (30 percent), leadership (20 percent), character (10 percent) and service (10 percent).
Target applicant:
  High school students
  College students
  Adult students
Minimum GPA: None.
Amount: $1,000.
Number of awards: 1.
Deadline: February 1.
How to apply: Applications are available online.

(934) · Lisa Zaken Award For Excellence

Institute of Industrial Engineers (IIE)
3577 Parkway Lane
Suite 200
Norcross, GA 30092
Phone: 800-494-0460
Fax: 770-441-3295
Email: bcameron@iienet.org
Website: http://www.iienet.org/studentcenter
Purpose: To award excellence in scholarly activities and leadership related to the industrial engineering profession on campus
Eligibility: Applicants must be undergraduate or graduate students with at least one year remaining, major in industrial engineering and be active members who have been leaders in IIE. Students may not apply directly for this scholarship and must be nominated. The award is based on academic ability and leadership related to industrial engineering.
Target applicant:
  College students
  Graduate school students
  Adult students
Minimum GPA: 3.0
Amount: $600.
Number of awards: 1.
Deadline: February 15.
How to apply: Nomination forms are available online.

(935) · Long-Term Member Sponsored Scholarship

Society of Automotive Engineers (SAE)
400 Commonwealth Drive
Warrendale, PA 15096-0001
Phone: 724-776-4841
Fax: 724-776-0790
Email: customerservice@sae.org
Website: http://www.sae.org
Purpose: This scholarship recognizes outstanding SAE student members who actively support SAE and its activities.
Eligibility: Applicants must be college juniors and student members of SAE, major in engineering and actively support SAE and its programs. The scholarship will be awarded purely on the basis of the student's support for SAE and its programs.
Target applicant:
  College students
  Adult students
Minimum GPA: None.
Amount: $1,000.
Number of awards: Varies.
Deadline: April 1.
How to apply: Applications are available online.

(936) · Louis Agassiz Fuertes Award

Wilson Ornithological Society
Dr. Robert B. Payne
Museum of Zoology, University of Michigan
1109 Gedes Avenue
Ann Arbor, MI 48109
Email: rbpayne@umich.edu
Website: http://www.wilsonsociety.org
Purpose: To support ornitholigists' research.
Eligibility: Applicants must be students or young professionals doing avian research. Applicants must be willing to report their research results at an annual meeting of the Wilson Ornithological Society.
Target applicant:
  High school students
  College students
  Graduate school students
  Adult students
Minimum GPA: None.

Amount: $2,500.
Number of awards: 1.
Deadline: February 1.
How to apply: Applications are available online.

(937) · Lowell Gaylor Memorial Scholarship

Aircraft Electronics Association
4217 South Hocker
Independence, MO 64055
Phone: 816-373-6565
Fax: 816-478-3100
Email: info@aea.net
Website: http://www.aea.net
Purpose: To support students of avionics and aircraft repair.
Eligibility: Applicants must be high school seniors or college students who plan to or are attending an accredited school in an avionics or aircraft repair program.
Target applicant:
  High school students
  College students
  Adult students
Minimum GPA: None.
Amount: $1,000.
Number of awards: 1.
Deadline: February 15.
How to apply: Applications are available by contacting the organization for more information.

(938) · LTK Engineering Services Scholarship

Conference of Minority Transportation Officials
818 18th Street NW, Suite 850
Washington, DC 20006
Phone: 202-530-0551
Fax: 202-530-0617
Email: comto@comto.org
Website: http://www.comto.org
Purpose: To support students who are majoring in engineering or other technical fields related to transportation.
Eligibility: Applicants must either be current COMTO members or be willing to join within 30 days of receiving the scholarship. Students must be at least in their junior year of college or in graduate school, and they must have at least a 3.0 GPA. Applicants must be enrolled in at least twelve credits per semester. Students must submit a short essay and two letters of recommendation.
Target applicant:
  College students
  Graduate school students
  Adult students
Minimum GPA: 3.0
Amount: $6,000.
Number of awards: Varies.
Deadline: April 4.
How to apply: Applications are available online.

(939) · LULAC GM Fund

League of United Latin American Citizens
2000 L Street NW
Suite 610
Washington, DC 20036
Phone: 202-835-9646
Fax: 202-835-9685
Email: scholarships@lnesc.org
Website: http://www.lnesc.org
Purpose: To aid minority engineering students with completing college.
Eligibility: Applicants must be minority full-time college students and must major or plan to major in courses leading to an engineering career. Selection is based on academics, engineering skills, writing ability, extracurricular activities and community service. Applicants must have a college grade point average of at least 3.2, or for entering freshman, must have a high school grade point average of at least 3.5. Entering freshman must have also scored at least 23 on the ACT test (composite) or at least 970 on the SAT test (verbal & math).
Target applicant:
  College students
  Adult students
Minimum GPA: 3.2 college GPA or 3.5 high school GPA
Amount: $2,000.
Number of awards: 20.
Scholarship may be renewable.
Deadline: July 15.
How to apply: Applications are available online.

(940) · Lydia's Professional Uniform/AACN Excellence in Academics Nursing Scholarship

American Association of Colleges of Nursing
One Dupont Circle NW
Suite 350
Washington, DC 20036
Phone: 202-463-6930
Fax: 202-785-8320
Email: anniea@aacn.nche.edu
Website: http://www.aacn.nche.edu
Purpose: To support undergraduate nursing students.
Eligibility: Applicants must be full-time nursing students in their junior year of a bachelor of science (BSN) program with a minimum 3.5 GPA. The application form and an essay about their career aspirations and financial need are required.
Target applicant:
  College students
  Adult students
Minimum GPA: 3.5
Amount: $2,500.
Number of awards: 2.
Deadline: August 1 and November 1.
How to apply: Applications are available online and may be returned by fax or email.

(941) · Madeline Pickett (Halbert) Cogswell Nursing Scholarship

National Society Daughters of the American Revolution
1776 D Street NW
Washington, DC 20006-5303
Phone: 202-628-1776
Website: http://www.dar.org
Purpose: To support nursing students.
Eligibility: Applicants must desire to attend or be attending an accredited school of nursing. Applicants must be members, descendents of members or eligible for membership in NSDAR. Applicants must put their DAR Member Number on the Application.

Target applicant:
  High school students
  College students
  Adult students
Minimum GPA: None.
Amount: $500.
Number of awards: 1.
Deadline: February 15 and August 15.
How to apply: Applications are available by written request.

(942) · Margaret E. Swanson Scholarship

American Dental Hygienists' Association (ADHA) Institute for Oral Health
444 N. Michigan Avenue
Suite 3400
Chicago, IL 60611
Phone: 800-735-4916
Email: institute@adha.net
Website: http://www.adha.org/institute
Purpose: To provide support to dental hygiene students who show leadership potential.
Eligibility: Applicants must have completed one year of an accredited dental hygiene program, pursuing a certificate or associates degree in the field. They must show evidence of organizational leadership potential. Applicants must also demonstrate financial need of at least $1,500, be active members of SADHA or ADHA and submit a goals statement.
Target applicant:
  College students
  Adult students
Minimum GPA: None.
Amount: $1,500.
Number of awards: 1.
Deadline: May 1.
How to apply: Applications are available online.

(943) · Marliave Fund

Association of Engineering Geologists Foundation Marliave Fund
Paul Santi, Department of Geology and Geological Engineering
Colorado School of Mines
Berthoud Hall
Golden, CO 80401
Phone: 303-273-3108
Email: psanti@mines.edu
Website: http://www.aegfoundation.org
Purpose: To reward outstanding students in engineering geology and geological engineering.
Eligibility: Applicants must be seniors or graduate students in a college or university program directly applicable to geological engineering and be members of the Association of Engineering Geologists.
Target applicant:
  College students
  Graduate school students
  Adult students
Minimum GPA: None.
Amount: Varies.
Number of awards: Varies.
Deadline: April 15.
How to apply: Applications are available online or by written request.

(944) · Marsh Affinity Group Services Scholarships

American Dental Hygienists' Association (ADHA) Institute for Oral Health
444 N. Michigan Avenue
Suite 3400
Chicago, IL 60611
Phone: 800-735-4916
Email: institute@adha.net
Website: http://www.adha.org/institute
Purpose: To provide support to successful dental hygiene students.
Eligibility: Applicants must have completed one year of an accredited dental hygiene program and have a GPA between 3.0 and 3.5. They must demonstrate financial need of at least $1,500, submit a goals statement and be active members of SADHA or ADHA.
Target applicant:
  College students
  Adult students
Minimum GPA: 3.0
Amount: $1,000.
Number of awards: Varies.
Deadline: May 1.
How to apply: Applications are available online.

(945) · Marshall E. McCullough Scholarship

National Dairy Shrine
1224 Alton Darby Creek Road
Columbus, OH 43228-9792
Phone: 614-878-5333
Fax: 614-870-2622
Email: shrine@cobaselect.com
Website: http://www.dairyshrine.org
Purpose: To support students who plan careers in agricultural-related communications.
Eligibility: Applicants must be high school seniors planning to enter a four-year university with intent to major in the dairy or animal sciences with a communications emphasis or agricultural journalism with a dairy or animal science emphasis, and they must intend to work in the dairy industry following graduation.
Target applicant:
  High school students
Minimum GPA: None.
Amount: $1,000-$2,500.
Number of awards: 2.
Deadline: March 15.
How to apply: Applications are available online.

(946) · Marvin Mundel Memorial Scholarship

Institute of Industrial Engineers (IIE)
3577 Parkway Lane
Suite 200
Norcross, GA 30092
Phone: 800-494-0460
Fax: 770-441-3295
Email: bcameron@iienet.org
Website: http://www.iienet.org/studentcenter
Purpose: To assist undergraduate engineering students with an interest in work measurement and methods engineering.
Eligibility: Applicants must be full-time undergraduate students enrolled in a college in the United States, Canada or Mexico with an accredited industrial engineering program, major in industrial engineering and be active members. Students may not apply directly for this scholarship and

must be nominated. The award is based on academic ability, character, leadership, potential service to the industrial engineering profession and financial need. Preference is given to students with a demonstrated interest in work measurement and methods engineering.

Target applicant:
    College students
    Adult students
Minimum GPA: 3.4
Amount: $600.
Number of awards: 1.
Deadline: February 15.
How to apply: Nomination forms are available online.

(947) · Mary Gibbon Scholarship

American Society of Extra-Corporeal Technology (AmSECT)
2209 Dickens Road
P.O. Box 11086
Richmond, VA 23230-1086
Phone: 804-565-6363
Fax: 804-282-0090
Email: patelpump@sbcglobal.net
Website: http://www.amsect.org
Purpose: To support perfusion education.
Eligibility: Applicants must be current student members of AmSECT, be in a CAAHEP accredited perfusion education program, have finished 50 percent of the coursework, have a minimum 2.5 GPA and submit an application, essay and transcript.
Target applicant:
    College students
    Graduate school students
    Adult students
Minimum GPA: 2.5
Amount: $2,500.
Number of awards: Varies.
Deadline: December 15.
How to apply: Applications are available online.

(948) · Mary Opal Wolanin Scholarship

National Gerontological Nursing Association (NGNA)
7794 Grow Drive
Pensacola, FL 32514
Phone: 800-723-0560
Fax: 850-484-8762
Email: ngna@puetzamc.com
Website: http://www.ngna.org
Purpose: To award gerontology and geriatric nursing undergraduate and graduate students.
Eligibility: For the undergraduate scholarship, applicants must be full- or part-time nursing students in an accredited U.S. school of nursing and must plan to work in a gerontology or geriatric setting. For the graduate scholarship, applicants must be nursing students with a major in gerontology or geriatric nursing at an accredited U.S. nursing program and carry a minimum of six credits. Applicants must submit two recommendation letters, transcripts, professional/educational statements and financial statements.
Target applicant:
    College students
    Graduate school students
    Adult students
Minimum GPA: 3.0
Amount: $1,500.

Number of awards: 2.
Deadline: June 1.
How to apply: Applications are available online.

(949) · Masonic-Range Science Scholarship

Society for Range Management (SRM)
10030 W. 27th Avenue
Wheat Ridge, CO 80215-6601
Phone: 303-986-3309
Fax: 303-986-3892
Email: vskiff@rangelands.org
Website: http://www.rangelands.org
Purpose: To help a high school senior, college freshman or college sophomore majoring in range science or a closely related field.
Eligibility: Applicants must be sponsored by a member of the Society for Range Management (SRM), the National Association of Conservation Districts (NACD) or the Soil and Water Conservation Society (SWCS). Applicants must also submit an application form, transcript, SAT or ACT scores and two letters of reference.
Target applicant:
    High school students
    College students
    Adult students
Minimum GPA: None.
Amount: Varies.
Number of awards: Varies.
Deadline: January 15.
How to apply: Applications are available online.

(950) · McAllister Memorial Scholarship

AOPA Air Safety Foundation
421 Aviation Way
Frederick, MD 21701
Phone: 301-695-2000
Fax: 301-695-2375
Email: aopahq@aopa.org
Website: http://www.aopa.org
Purpose: To assist students in non-engineering aviation programs.
Eligibility: Applicants must be college juniors or seniors and have at least one semester or quarter to be completed, have a minimum 3.25 GPA and be enrolled in a baccalaureate level, non-engineering aviation degree program at a four-year institution. Applicants must also submit an essay on a topic posted on the website.
Target applicant:
    College students
    Adult students
Minimum GPA: 3.25
Amount: $1,000.
Number of awards: 1.
Deadline: March 31.
How to apply: Applications are available online.

(951) · McConnell Family Scholarship

Epsilon Sigma Alpha Foundation
P.O. Box 270517
Fort Collins, CO 80527
Phone: 970-223-2824
Fax: 970-223-4456
Email: kloyd@knoxy.net
Website: http://www.esaintl.com/esaf

Purpose: To provide financial assistance for veterinary medicine majors.

Eligibility: Applicants must be female and may study at any college or university in any state. Selection is based on scholastic ability (30 percent), financial need (30 percent), leadership (20 percent), character (10 percent) and service (10 percent).

Target applicant:
High school students
College students
Adult students

Minimum GPA: None.

Amount: $1,000.

Number of awards: 2.

Deadline: February 1.

How to apply: Applications are available online.

---

(952) · McNeil Rural Health Scholarship

National Association of Pediatric Nurse Practitioners (NAPNAP)
20 Brace Road
Suite 200
Cherry Hill, NJ 08034-2634
Phone: 856-857-9700
Fax: 856-857-1600
Email: info@napnap.org
Website: http://www.napnap.org

Purpose: To improve pediatric health care provided by pediatric nurse practitioners.

Eligibility: Applicants must be enrolled in a full-time master's degree PNP program, plan to work in a rural area for two years after graduating, be a registered nurse with one year of pediatrics experience (other experience may be considered), have financial need and be a NAPNAP member. An application and RN license are required.

Target applicant:
Graduate school students
Adult students

Minimum GPA: 3.0

Amount: $20,000.

Number of awards: Varies.

Deadline: June 30.

How to apply: Applications are available online.

---

(953) · Medical Student Summer Research Training in Aging Program

American Federation for Aging Research (AFAR)
70 West 40th Street, 11th Floor
New York, NY 10018
Phone: 212-703-9977
Fax: 212-997-0330
Email: grants@afar.org
Website: http://www.afar.org

Purpose: To support early medical students who demonstrate an interest in geriatric medicine or age-related research with an opportunity to serve under top experts in the field.

Eligibility: Applicants must be osteopathic or allopathic students who have completed at least one year of medical school at a U.S. institution. Students must have a faculty sponsor from their home institution. The program lasts 8 to 12 weeks, and monthly stipends are provided.

Target applicant:
Graduate school students
Adult students

Minimum GPA: None.

Amount: Up to $5,193.

Number of awards: 120.

Deadline: February 7.

How to apply: Applications are available online.

---

(954) · Medtronic Physio-Control Advanced Nursing Practice Scholarship

Emergency Nurses Association
915 Lee Street
Des Plaines, IL 60016
Phone: 847-460-4100
Fax: 847-460-4004
Email: foundation@ena.org
Website: http://www.ena.org

Purpose: Monetary assistance for an advanced degree is awarded to an emergency nurse. Priority is given to those pursuing careers in cardiac nursing.

Eligibility: Applicants must be nurses pursuing advanced clinical practice degrees to become clinical nurse specialists or nurse practitioners. Preference is given to applicants focusing on cardiac nursing. Applicants must have been ENA members for at least 12 months before applying.

Target applicant:
Graduate school students
Adult students

Minimum GPA: None.

Amount: $3,000.

Number of awards: 1.

Deadline: June 1.

How to apply: Applications are available online.

---

(955) · Melvin R. Green Scholarships

American Society of Mechanical Engineers
Three Park Avenue
New York, NY 10016
Phone: 800-843-2763
Fax: 973-882-1717
Email: infocentral@asme.org
Website: http://www.asme.org

Purpose: To support mechanical engineering students.

Eligibility: Applicants must have outstanding character and integrity, be ASME student members, be enrolled in an eligible accredited mechanical engineering baccalaureate program, be college juniors or seniors and have strong academic performance.

Target applicant:
College students
Adult students

Minimum GPA: None.

Amount: $3,500.

Number of awards: 3.

Deadline: March 15.

How to apply: Applications are available online.

---

(956) · Members-at-Large Reentry Award

Iota Sigma Pi (ISP)
Dr. Joanne Bedlek-Anslow, MAL Coordinator
Camden High School, Science
1022 Ehrenclou Drive
Camden, SC 29020
Website: http://www.iotasigmapi.info

Purpose: To recognize potential achievement in chemistry and related fields for a woman undergraduate or graduate student who has been absent from academia for at least three years.

Eligibility: Applicants must be female undergraduate or graduate students at an accredited four-year institution and be nominated by a faculty member or an Iota Sigma Pi member.

Target applicant:
College students
Graduate school students
Adult students

Minimum GPA: None.
Amount: $1,000.
Number of awards: 1.
Deadline: March 20.
How to apply: Application information is available online.

(957) · Merit Scholarships and Educational Loans

American Health Information Management Association
Foundation of Research and Education in Health Information Management
233 N. Michigan Avenue, 21st Floor
Chicago, IL 60601-5800
Phone: 312-233-1168
Fax: 312-233-1090
Email: fore@ahima.org
Website: http://www.ahima.org

Purpose: To provide merit scholarships to undergraduate students pursuing degrees in health information administration or health information technology.

Eligibility: Applicants must be members of AHIMA, have at least one semester remaining in their course of study and be taking at least six hours per semester in pursuit of the degree. Scholarships are also available for HIM professionals pursuing graduate degrees in the health information field, and loans are also available.

Target applicant:
College students
Graduate school students
Adult students

Minimum GPA: 3.0
Amount: Up to $5,000.
Number of awards: Varies.
Deadline: April 28.
How to apply: Applications are available online.

(958) · Michael Dunaway Scholarship

American Society of Extra-Corporeal Technology (AmSECT)
2209 Dickens Road
P.O. Box 11086
Richmond, VA 23230-1086
Phone: 804-565-6363
Fax: 804-282-0090
Email: patelpump@sbcglobal.net
Website: http://www.amsect.org

Purpose: To support those studying perfusion.

Eligibility: Applicants must be current student members of AmSECT, be in a CAAHEP accredited perfusion education program, have finished 25 percent of the coursework, have a minimum 2.75 GPA and submit an application, essay and a transcript.

Target applicant:
College students
Graduate school students
Adult students

Minimum GPA: 2.75
Amount: $1,000.
Number of awards: Varies.
Deadline: December 15.
How to apply: Applications are available online.

(959) · Michael Kidger Memorial Scholarship

International Society for Optical Engineering
P.O. Box 10
Bellingham, WA 98227-0010
Phone: 360-685-5452
Fax: 360-647-1445
Email: scholarships@spie.org
Website: http://www.spie.org

Purpose: To support students in the optical design field.

Eligibility: Applicants must be in the optical design field and must have one year remaining of their studies. Students must submit a summary of their academic background and interest in optical design and two letters of recommendation.

Target applicant:
College students
Adult students

Minimum GPA: None.
Amount: $5,000.
Number of awards: 1.
Deadline: March 31.
How to apply: Applications are available online.

(960) · Microsoft Tuition Scholarships

Microsoft Corporation
One Microsoft Way
Redmond, WA 98052-8303
Phone: 800-642-7676
Fax: 425-936-7329
Email: scholars@microsoft.com
Website: http://www.microsoft.com/college/

Purpose: Offering more than a half-million dollars in scholarships, Microsoft is looking for undergraduates who display an interest in the software industry and are committed to leadership.

Eligibility: Applicants must be in a full-time undergraduate program related to computer science. Recipients will have to complete salaried internships in Redmond, Washington. There are special scholarships for women, minorities and disabled students.

Target applicant:
College students
Adult students

Minimum GPA: 3.0
Amount: Varies.
Number of awards: Varies.
Deadline: January 15.
How to apply: Application requirements are online.

(961) · Mid-Continent Instrument Scholarship

Aircraft Electronics Association
4217 South Hocker
Independence, MO 64055
Phone: 816-373-6565
Fax: 816-478-3100
Email: info@aea.net
Website: http://www.aea.net

Purpose: To support students who wish to pursue a career in avionics or aircraft repair.

Eligibility: Applicants must be high school seniors or college students who plan to or are attending an accredited school in an avionics or aircraft repair program.

Target applicant:
High school students
College students
Adult students

Minimum GPA: None.

Amount: $1,000.

Number of awards: 1.

Deadline: February 15.

How to apply: Applications are available by contacting the organization for more information.

(962) · Mildred Nutting Nursing Scholarship

National Society Daughters of the American Revolution
1776 D Street NW
Washington, DC 20006-5303
Phone: 202-628-1776
Website: http://www.dar.org

Purpose: To support students who are studying to become nurses.

Eligibility: Applicants must have been accepted or are currently enrolled in an accredited school of nursing. Preference will be given to candidates from the greater Lowell, MA area.

Target applicant:
High school students
College students
Adult students

Minimum GPA: None.

Amount: $500.

Number of awards: 1.

Deadline: February 15 and August 15.

How to apply: Applications are available by written request.

(963) · Milk Marketing Scholarship

National Dairy Shrine
1224 Alton Darby Creek Road
Columbus, OH 43228-9792
Phone: 614-878-5333
Fax: 614-870-2622
Email: shrine@cobaselect.com
Website: http://www.dairyshrine.org

Purpose: To encourage students to pursue careers in the marketing of dairy goods.

Eligibility: Applicants must be second, third or fourth year college students at two- or four-year universities, have a minimum 2.5 GPA and major in dairy science, animal science, agricultural communications, agricultural education, general agriculture or food and nutrition.

Target applicant:
College students
Adult students

Minimum GPA: 2.5

Amount: $1000-$1,500.

Number of awards: 7.

Deadline: March 15.

How to apply: Applications are available online.

(964) · Milton F. Lunch Research Fellowship

National Society of Professional Engineers
1420 King Street
Alexandria, VA 22314-2794
Phone: 703-684-2885
Fax: 703-836-4875
Email: memserv@nspe.org
Website: http://www.nspe.org

Purpose: To honor the memory of Milton F. Lunch, who was the NSPE's general counsel for 40 years.

Eligibility: Students must be U.S. citizens and be pursuing a career in engineering, architecture, construction or law and be enrolled in an undergraduate or graduate program in one of those fields. Undergraduate students must be rising seniors and have a minimum GPA of 3.0 on a 4.0 scale.

Target applicant:
College students
Graduate school students
Adult students

Minimum GPA: 3.0

Amount: $7,000.

Number of awards: 1.

Deadline: January 30.

How to apply: Applications are available online.

(965) · Minority Dental Student Scholarship

American Dental Association Foundation
211 East Chicago Avenue
Chicago, IL 60611
Phone: 312-440-2763
Fax: 312-440-3526
Email: famularor@ada.org
Website: http://www.ada.org

Purpose: To encourage minority students to pursue careers in dental hygiene, dental assisting, dentistry and dental laboratory technology.

Eligibility: Applicants must be African American, Hispanic or Native American full-time students entering their second year in an accredited dental program and must demonstrate a minimum financial need of $2,500. Applicants must submit applications, two reference forms, enrollment letters and biographies. Selection is based on financial need, academic achievement, biographical sketch and references. A minimum 3.0 GPA is required. Only two scholarship applications per school are allowed, so schools may set their own in-school application deadlines that are earlier.

Target applicant:
College students
Adult students

Minimum GPA: 3.0

Amount: Up to $2,500.

Number of awards: 25.

Deadline: October 16.

How to apply: Applications are available from dental school officials.

(966) · Minority Student Scholarship

American Speech-Language-Hearing Foundation
2200 Research Boulevard
Rockville, MD 20850
Phone: 301-296-8700
Email: foundation@asha.org
Website: http://www.ashfoundation.org

Purpose: To support a minority graduate student in communication sciences and disorders.

Eligibility: Applicants should be full-time minority graduate students. Master's degree candidates must be in programs accredited by the Council on Academic Accreditation for Audiology and Speech Pathology, but doctoral programs do not have to be accredited. Transcripts, an essay and a reference form are required.

Target applicant:
Graduate school students
Adult students

Minimum GPA: None.

Amount: $4,000.

Number of awards: 1.

Deadline: January 13.

How to apply: Applications are available online.

(967) · Monsanto Company/The National Association of Farm Broadcasters Commitment to Agriculture Scholarship

National FFA Organization
P.O. Box 68960
6060 FFA Drive
Indianapolis, IN 46268-0960
Phone: 317-802-6060
Fax: 317-802-6051
Email: scholarships@ffa.org
Website: http://www.ffa.org

Purpose: To support students whose families are involved in production agriculture.

Eligibility: Applicants must be high school seniors or college students planning to enroll or currently enrolled full-time. Students must have a minimum SAT score of 1320 or ACT score of 18, and they must be pursuing degrees in areas related to agriculture. Students only need to complete the online application one time to be considered for all FFA-administered scholarships. The application requires information about the students' activities and a 1,000-word essay. Awards may be used for books, supplies, tuition, fees and room and board. Applicants may be members or non-members of the FFA.

Target applicant:
High school students
College students
Adult students

Minimum GPA: None.

Amount: $1,500.

Number of awards: 100.

Deadline: February 15.

How to apply: Applications are available online.

(968) · Morton B. Duggan, Jr. Memorial Education Recognition Award

American Association for Respiratory Care
9425 North MacArthur Boulevard
Suite 100
Irving, TX 75063-4706
Phone: 972-243-2272
Fax: 972-484-2720
Email: info@aarc.org
Website: http://www.aarc.org

Purpose: To recognize outstanding students in respiratory care education programs.

Eligibility: Applicants must be enrolled in an accredited respiratory care education program and have a minimum 3.0 GPA. Students must submit an original paper on respiratory care. Preference is given to residents of Georgia and South Carolina.

Target applicant:
College students
Graduate school students
Adult students

Minimum GPA: 3.0

Amount: Up to $1,000.

Number of awards: 1.

Deadline: June 15.

How to apply: Applications are available online.

(969) · NAMEPA Scholarship Program

National Association of Minority Engineering Program Administrators
1133 W. Morse Boulevard
Suite 201
Winter Park, FL 32789
Phone: 407-647-8839
Fax: 407-629-2502
Email: namepa@namepa.org
Website: http://www.namepa.org

Purpose: To support minority students to become engineers.

Eligibility: Applicants must be African American, Latino, and American Indian students admitted at a college or university as an engineering major with a minimum 2.7 GPA and minimum ACT score of 25 or minimum SAT score of 1000. Applicants must attend a NAMEPA member institution. Transfer students are also eligible. Selection is based on coursework in high school, course distribution, activities, a one-page narrative and recommendations.

Target applicant:
High school students
College students
Adult students

Minimum GPA: 2.7

Amount: $1,000.

Number of awards: Varies.

Deadline: May 15.

How to apply: Applications are available online.

(970) · Nancy Goodhue Lynch Scholarship

Datatel
4375 Fair Lakes Court
Fairfax, VA 22033
Phone: 800-486-4332
Email: scholars@datatel.com
Website: http://www.datatelscholars.org

Purpose: To support Information Technology students at Datatel client institutions.

Eligibility: Applicants must be undergraduate students majoring in an information technology field and attending a Datatel Client college or university. Students must include a personal statement about why they have chosen to study an information technology field, the impact of technology on their futures and the importance of the scholarship.

Target applicant:
College students
Adult students

Minimum GPA: None.

Amount: $2,500.

Number of awards: 2.
Deadline: January 31.
How to apply: Applications are available online.

(971) · National Aviation Explorer Scholarships

Explorers Learning for Life
P.O. Box 152079
Irving, TX 75015
Phone: 972-580-2433
Fax: 972-580-2137
Email: pchestnu@lflmail.org
Website: http://www.learningforlife.org/exploring
Purpose: To support students who are pursuing careers in the aviation industry.
Eligibility: Students must be active members of an Aviation Explorer post. Applicants must submit an essay and three letters of recommendation.
Target applicant:
    Junior high students or younger
    High school students
    College students
    Adult students
Minimum GPA: None.
Amount: $3,000-$10,000.
Number of awards: 10.
Deadline: March 31.
How to apply: Applications are available online.

(972) · National FFA College and Vocational/ Technical School Scholarship Program

National FFA Organization
P.O. Box 68960
6060 FFA Drive
Indianapolis, IN 46268-0960
Phone: 317-802-6060
Fax: 317-802-6051
Email: scholarships@ffa.org
Website: http://www.ffa.org
Purpose: The scholarship program supports FFA members and agriculture.
Eligibility: FFA awards more than $2 million in scholarships. The programs have various eligibility requirements and award amounts. Applicants must be U.S. citizens and high school seniors or current college students. For some awards, students must be FFA members.
Target applicant:
    High school students
    College students
    Adult students
Minimum GPA: None.
Amount: Varies.
Number of awards: Varies.
Scholarship may be renewable.
Deadline: February 15.
How to apply: Applications are available online or from your local FFA advisor.

(973) · National Garden Clubs Scholarship

National Garden Clubs Inc.
4401 Magnolia Avenue
St. Louis, MO 63110

Phone: 314-776-7574
Fax: 314-776-5108
Email: headquarters@gardenclub.org
Website: http://www.gardenclub.org
Purpose: To promote the study of horticulture and related fields.
Eligibility: Applicants must be full-time juniors, seniors, graduate students or sophomores applying for the junior year and major in one of the following fields: agriculture education, horticulture, floriculture, landscape design, botany, biology, plant pathology/science, forestry, agronomy, environmental concerns, economics, environmental conservation, city planning, wildlife science, habitat or forest/systems ecology, land management or related areas.
Target applicant:
    College students
    Graduate school students
    Adult students
Minimum GPA: 3.25
Amount: $3,500.
Number of awards: 34.
Deadline: March 1.
How to apply: Applications are available online and must be mailed to the applicants' state Garden Club scholarship chairman.

(974) · National Network for Environmental Management Studies Fellowship Program

Environmental Protection Agency
NNEMS Fellowship Program
Tetra Tech EM Inc.
1881 Campus Commons Drive, Suite 200
Reston, VA 20191
Phone: 800-358-8769
Email: steve.michener@ttemi.com
Website: http://www.epa.gov/enviroed/students.html
Purpose: To provide students with research opportunities, to increase public awareness of environmental issues and to encourage students to pursue careers in environmental protection.
Eligibility: Applicants must be undergraduate or graduate students, be U.S. citizens or legal residents, be enrolled in an academic program directly related to pollution control, have a minimum 3.0 GPA, have completed four courses relating to the environmental field and submit a research project proposal.
Target applicant:
    College students
    Graduate school students
    Adult students
Minimum GPA: 3.0
Amount: Stipend during research.
Number of awards: Varies.
Deadline: January.
How to apply: Applications are available online.

(975) · National Nursing Scholarship - College

Common Knowledge Scholarship Foundation
P.O. Box 290361
Davie, FL 33329-0361
Phone: 954-262-8553
Email: info@cksf.org
Website: http://www.cksf.org
Purpose: To reward nursing students based on their knowledge.
Eligibility: Applicants must complete the free online registration and compete by taking a series of short multiple-choice online quizzes

about nursing. Each week, the quiz will have 15 to 25 questions. The winner is determined through a combination of time and accuracy in answering the questions.

Target applicant:
  College students
  Graduate school students
  Adult students
Minimum GPA: None.
Amount: $500.
Number of awards: 1.
Deadline: March 11.
How to apply: Applicants must complete the free online registration and then answer questions.

(976) · National Nursing Scholarship - High School

Common Knowledge Scholarship Foundation
P.O. Box 290361
Davie, FL 33329-0361
Phone: 954-262-8553
Email: info@cksf.org
Website: http://www.cksf.org
Purpose: To reward high school students interested in a career in nursing.
Eligibility: Applicants must compete by taking a series of short multiple-choice online quizzes about nursing. Each week, the quiz will consist of 15 to 25 questions. The winner is determined through a combination of time and accuracy in answering the questions.
Target applicant:
  High school students
Minimum GPA: None.
Amount: $500.
Number of awards: 1.
Deadline: February 11.
How to apply: Applicants must complete the free online registration and then answer questions.

(977) · National Science & Mathematics Access to Retain Talent Grant

Federal Student Aid
U.S. Department of Education
400 Maryland Avenue, SW
Washington, DC 20202
Phone: 800-433-3243
Website: http://studentaid.ed.gov
Purpose: To assist students who are majoring in physical, life or computer sciences, mathematics, technology, engineering or a foreign language that is critical to national security in continuing their educations.
Eligibility: Applicants must be U.S. citizens who are Pell Grant recipients, enrolled full-time in a physical, life or computer science, engineering, mathematics, technology or critical foreign language program at a four-year institution and have a college GPA of 3.0 or higher in the coursework required for the major. Students must be at least college sophomores, and the award may be used for the third and fourth year of undergraduate study.
Target applicant:
  College students
  Adult students
Minimum GPA: 3.0
Amount: Up to $4,000.

Number of awards: Varies.
Deadline: Varies.
How to apply: Applications are available from your financial aid office.

(978) · National Student Design Competition

American Institute of Chemical Engineers - (AIChE)
3 Park Avenue
New York, NY 10016
Phone: 212-591-7634
Fax: 212-591-8890
Email: awards@aiche.org
Website: http://www.aiche.org
Purpose: To test chemical engineering students' skills in calculation and evaluation of technical data and economic factors.
Eligibility: Applicants must be members of an AIChE student chapter.
Target applicant:
  College students
  Graduate school students
  Adult students
Minimum GPA: None.
Amount: $200-$500.
Number of awards: 3.
Deadline: June 4.
How to apply: Applications are available online.

(979) · National Student Nurses' Association Scholarship

National Student Nurses' Association
45 Main Street
Suite 606
Brooklyn, NY 11201
Phone: 718-210-0705
Fax: 718-210-0710
Email: nsna@nsna.org
Website: http://www.nsna.org
Purpose: To promote interest in the nursing field.
Eligibility: Applicants must be currently enrolled in a state-approved school of nursing or pre-nursing in associate degree, baccalaureate, diploma, doctorate or master's programs.
Target applicant:
  College students
  Graduate school students
  Adult students
Minimum GPA: None.
Amount: $1,000-$2,000.
Number of awards: Varies.
Deadline: January 20.
How to apply: Applications are available online.

(980) · National Wildlife Federation Ecology Fellowship

National Wildlife Federation
11100 Wildlife Center Drive
Reston, VA 20190-5362
Phone: 800-822-9919
Website: http://www.nwf.org

Purpose: The fellowship program provides funding for campus ecology projects.
Eligibility: Applicants must create a plan for a campus ecology program, working with a project advisor and verifier. All Campus Ecology fellows are required to attend a training program.
Target applicant:
   College students
   Graduate school students
   Adult students
Minimum GPA: None.
Amount: Up to $1,200.
Number of awards: Varies.
Deadline: December 19.
How to apply: Applications are available online.

(981) · National Young Astronomer Award

Astronomical League
7241 Jarboe
Kansas City, MO 64114
Phone: 816-444-4878
Email: carroll-iorg@kc.rr.com
Website: http://www.astroleague.org
Purpose: To support young astronomers.
Eligibility: Applicants must be 14 to 19 years old, not yet enrolled in college at the award deadline and do not have to be members of an astronomy club or of the Astronomical League. International students of the same age are eligible if they are enrolled in a U.S. secondary school on the application deadline. The application consists of the application form, summary of astronomy related activities and optional exhibits.
Target applicant:
   Junior high students or younger
   High school students
Minimum GPA: None.
Amount: Varies.
Number of awards: 3.
Deadline: January 31.
How to apply: Applications are available online.

(982) · NBRC/AMP Gareth B. Gish, MS, RRT Memorial and William F. Miller, MD Postgraduate Education Recognition Awards

American Association for Respiratory Care
9425 North MacArthur Boulevard
Suite 100
Irving, TX 75063-4706
Phone: 972-243-2272
Fax: 972-484-2720
Email: info@aarc.org
Website: http://www.aarc.org
Purpose: To aid qualified respiratory therapists in pursuing advanced degrees.
Eligibility: Applicants must be respiratory therapists who have been accepted into an advanced degree program of a fully accredited school. Application must be accompanied by an original essay describing how the award will aid in achieving an advanced degree and future goals in health care. A minimum 3.0 GPA is required.
Target applicant:
   College students
   Graduate school students
   Adult students

Minimum GPA: 3.0
Amount: Up to $1,500.
Number of awards: 2.
Deadline: June 15.
How to apply: Applications are available online.

(983) · NBRC/AMP William W. Burgin, Jr. MD and Robert M. Lawrence, MD Education Recognition Awards

American Association for Respiratory Care
9425 North MacArthur Boulevard
Suite 100
Irving, TX 75063-4706
Phone: 972-243-2272
Fax: 972-484-2720
Email: info@aarc.org
Website: http://www.aarc.org
Purpose: To recognize outstanding students in respiratory care education programs.
Eligibility: Applicants must be enrolled in an accredited respiratory care education program as a second-year student pursuing an associate's degree or as a junior or senior pursuing a bachelor's degree. In addition to an original paper dealing with respiratory care, applicants must submit an original essay describing how this award will help them reach their degrees and their future goals in the field of health care.
Target applicant:
   College students
   Adult students
Minimum GPA: None.
Amount: Up to $2,500.
Number of awards: 2.
Deadline: June 15.
How to apply: Applications are available online.

(984) · NCPA Foundation Presidential Scholarship

National Community Pharmacists Association
NCPA Foundation
100 Daingerfield Road
Alexandria, VA 22314
Phone: 703-683-8200
Fax: 703-683-3619
Email: info@ncpanet.org
Website: http://www.ncpanet.org
Purpose: To support students who plan to enter the pharmaceutical field.
Eligibility: Applicants must be student members of NCPA and enrolled in a U.S. school or college of pharmacy full-time. Selection is based on academic achievement and leadership.
Target applicant:
   College students
   Graduate school students
   Adult students
Minimum GPA: None.
Amount: $2,000.
Number of awards: Varies.
Deadline: March 1.
How to apply: Applications are available online.

(985) · NDSEG Fellowship Program

Department of Defense, American Society for Engineering Education
1818 N Street NW
Suite 600
Washington, DC 20036
Phone: 202-331-3516
Fax: 202-265-8504
Email: ndseg@asee.org
Website: http://www.asee.org
Purpose: To award fellowships to those in science and engineering.
Eligibility: Applicants must pursue a doctoral degree in an area of Department of Defense interest: aeronautical and astronautical engineering, biosciences, chemical engineering, chemistry, civil engineering, cognitive, neural, and behavioral sciences, computer and computational sciences, electrical engineering, geosciences, materials science and engineering, mathematics, mechanical engineering, naval architecture and ocean engineering, oceanography and physics. Applicants must have completed no more than one academic year of graduate study as a part-time or full-time student or be in their final year of undergraduate studies. The award is based on academic achievement, personal statements, recommendations and Graduate Record Examination scores. Fellowships may be used only at U.S. institutions of higher education offering doctoral degrees.
Target applicant:
 College students
 Graduate school students
 Adult students
Minimum GPA: None.
Amount: $31,500.
Number of awards: 200.
Scholarship may be renewable.
Deadline: January 6.
How to apply: Applications are available online.

(986) · Need-Based Scholarship Program

National Medical Fellowships Inc.
5 Hanover Square
15th Floor
New York, NY 10004
Phone: 212-483-8880
Email: info@nmfonline.org
Website: http://www.nmfonline.org
Purpose: To help first- and second-year minority medical students.
Eligibility: Applicants must be African American, Mexican American, Native American, Alaska Native, Native Hawaiian or mainland Puerto Rican students accepted by accredited U.S. medical schools for M.D. or D.O. degrees. Select programs are open to third-year students. Applications, transcripts, recommendation letters and financial documents are required.
Target applicant:
 Graduate school students
 Adult students
Minimum GPA: None.
Amount: $10,000.
Number of awards: Varies.
Deadline: June 30.
How to apply: Applications are available online, by mail and from the medical schools.

(987) · NEHA/AAS Scholarship Awards

National Environmental Health Association and the American Academy of Sanitarians
NEHA/AAS Scholarship
Scholarship Coordinator
720 S. Colorado Boulevard, Suite 970
Denver, CO 80246
Phone: 303-756-9090
Fax: 303-691-9490
Email: cdimmitt@neha.org
Website: http://www.neha.org
Purpose: To support students planning careers in environmental health.
Eligibility: Applicants must be either undergraduate or graduate students. The undergraduate scholarships are to be used during the junior or senior year at an Environmental Health Accreditation Council (EHAC) or NEHA member school. The graduate scholarship is available to applicants who are enrolled in a graduate program of studies in environmental health sciences and/or public health.
Target applicant:
 College students
 Graduate school students
 Adult students
Minimum GPA: None.
Amount: Varies.
Number of awards: Varies.
Scholarship may be renewable.
Deadline: February 1.
How to apply: Applications are available online.

(988) · Nellie Yeoh Whetten Award

American Vacuum Society
120 Wall Street, 32nd Floor
New York, NY 10005-3993
Phone: 212-248-0200
Fax: 212-248-0245
Email: angela@avs.org
Website: http://www.avs.org
Purpose: To support women in graduate studies in the sciences and technologies related to AVS.
Eligibility: Applicants must be female graduate students in an accredited academic institution and must send an application, report on candidate form, two letters of recommendation and college and graduate school transcripts.
Target applicant:
 Graduate school students
 Adult students
Minimum GPA: None.
Amount: $1,500.
Number of awards: 3.
Deadline: March 31.
How to apply: Applications are available online.

(989) · NFMC Dorothy Dann Bullock Music Therapy Award and the NFMC Ruth B. Robertson Music Therapy Award

National Federation of Music Clubs Bullock and Robertson Awards
Anita Louise Steele
Gilden School of Music

Ohio University
Athens, OH 45701
Phone: 740-593-4249
Fax: 317-638-0503
Email: steelea@ohio.edu
Website: http://www.nfmc-music.org
Purpose: To assist students who plan to enter careers in music therapy.
Eligibility: Applicants must be college students majoring in music therapy in schools approved by the National Association of Music Therapists and AMTA. Selection is based on musical talent, skills and training with an emphasis on piano ability in accompanying and sight reading. Other selection criteria are self-reliance, leadership, ability to work with groups and dedication to music therapy as a career. Applicants must be members of the National Federation of Music Clubs.
Target applicant:
   College students
   Graduate school students
   Adult students
Minimum GPA: None.
Amount: $400-$1,250.
Number of awards: Varics.
Deadline: March 1.
How to apply: Applications are available online.

---

(990) · NHSC Scholarship
National Health Service Corps
U.S. Department of Health and Human Services
200 Independence Avenue SW
Washington, DC 20201
Phone: 800-221-9393
Email: callcenter@hrsa.gov
Website: http://nhsc.bhpr.hrsa.gov
Purpose: To aid students committed to providing health care in communities of great need.
Eligibility: Applicants must be enrolled or accepted into allopathic or osteopathic medical schools, family nurse practitioner programs, nurse-midwifery programs, physician assistant programs or dental school. Upon completion of training, scholars must choose practice sites in federally designated health professional shortage areas for one year for each year of support received.
Target applicant:
   College students
   Graduate school students
   Adult students
Minimum GPA: None.
Amount: Award covers tuition and fees.
Number of awards: Varies.
Scholarship may be renewable.
Deadline: March 30.
How to apply: Applications are available by telephone request.

---

(991) · Nicholas J. Grant Scholarship
ASM International Foundation
9639 Kinsman Road
Materials Park, OH 44073-0002
Phone: 440-338-5151
Fax: 440-338-4634
Email: crhayes@asminternational.org
Website: http://www.asminternational.org
Purpose: To recognize students who have excelled in scholarship, leadership and service.
Eligibility: Applicants must be student members of ASM International, major in metallurgy or materials science engineering and be juniors or seniors at a North American university that has a bachelor's degree program in science and engineering. Applications, personal statements, transcripts, two recommendation forms, photographs and financial aid officers' contact information are required. The award is based on academics, interest in the metallurgy/materials engineering field, character and financial need. The scholarship provides one year of full tuition.
Target applicant:
   College students
   Adult students
Minimum GPA: None.
Amount: Varies.
Number of awards: Varies.
Deadline: May 1.
How to apply: Applications are available online.

---

(992) · NIH Undergraduate Scholarship Program
U.S. Department of Health and Human Services National Institutes of Health
2 Center Drive
Room 2E30
MSC 0230
Bethesda, MD 20892
Phone: 800-528-7689
Fax: 301-480-3123
Email: ugsp@nih.gov
Website: http://www.ugsp.nih.gov
Purpose: To offer competitive scholarships to students who are committed to careers in biomedical, behavioral and social science health-related research.
Eligibility: Applicants must be enrolled or accepted for enrollment as full-time students at an accredited undergraduate institution, have an underprivileged background and have a minimum 3.5 GPA or be within the top 5 percent of their class. Applicants must also show a commitment to pursuing careers in biomedical, behavioral and social science research at the NIH.
Target applicant:
   College students
   Adult students
Minimum GPA: 3.5
Amount: $20,000.
Number of awards: 15.
Scholarship may be renewable.
Deadline: February 28.
How to apply: Applications are available online.

---

(993) · NIH Undergraduate Scholarship Program for Students from Disadvantaged Backgrounds
National Institutes of Health
Office of Loan Repayment and Scholarship
2 Center Drive
MSC 0230
Bethesda, MD 20892-0230
Phone: 800-528-7689
Fax: 301-480-3123
Email: ugsp@nih.gov
Website: http://www.ugsp.nih.gov

Purpose: To develop new health-related researchers and to give disadvantaged students research opportunities that they might not have otherwise.

Eligibility: Applicants must be planning a career in biomedical, behavioral or social science health-related research, have financial need, have a minimum 3.5 GPA or be within the top 5 percent of their class and attend an accredited school. For every year that students receive the scholarship, they must attend a summer training program and work for one year at the NIH.

Target applicant:
  High school students
  College students
  Adult students
Minimum GPA: 3.5
Amount: Up to $20,000.
Number of awards: Up to 15.
Scholarship may be renewable.
Deadline: February 28.
How to apply: Applications are available online.

---

(994) · NNF Scholarship Program

Neuroscience Nursing Foundation (NNF)
4700 W. Lake Avenue
Glenview, IL 60025
Phone: 888-557-2266
Email: info@aann.org
Website: http://www.aann.org
Purpose: To promote excellence in neuroscience nursing.
Eligibility: Applicants must be registered nurses pursuing undergraduate or graduate studies to enter a career in neuroscience nursing. In addition to the application, applicants must submit resumes, transcripts and RN license.
Target applicant:
  College students
  Graduate school students
  Adult students
Minimum GPA: 3.0
Amount: $1,500.
Number of awards: Varies.
Deadline: January 15.
How to apply: Applications are available online.

---

(995) · Normand R. Dubois Memorial Scholarship

Entomological Society of America
10001 Derekwood Lane
Suite 100
Lanham, MD 20706
Phone: 301-731-4535
Fax: 301-731-4538
Email: esa@entsoc.org
Website: http://www.entsoc.org
Purpose: To encourage research by graduate students on the use of biologically based technologies to protect and preserve forests.
Eligibility: Applicants must be pursuing a master's or doctorate at an accredited university and propose research to advance knowledge of the best way to preserve forests using environmentally friendly and biologically based technologies.
Target applicant:
  Graduate school students
  Adult students
Minimum GPA: None.

Amount: $1,500.
Number of awards: Varies.
Deadline: July 1.
How to apply: Applications are available online.

---

(996) · Nursing Scholarship

CampusRN
2464 Massachusetts Avenue
Suite 210
Cambridge, MA 02140
Phone: 617-661-2613
Fax: 617-661-2620
Email: scholarships@campuscareercenter.com
Website: http://www.campusrn.com/scholarships/scholarships.asp
Purpose: To provide financial assistance for nursing students from all fifty states.
Eligibility: Applicants must be nursing students at schools that have registered in the scholarship program by linking to the CampusRN website. An essay is required. Finalists may be asked to submit awards, letters of recommendation and other materials upon selection. Deadlines are November 15, December 1 or December 15 depending on state.
Target applicant:
  College students
  Graduate school students
  Adult students
Minimum GPA: None.
Amount: $1,000.
Number of awards: 50.
Deadline: Varies.
How to apply: Applications are available online.

---

(997) · Occupational/Physical Therapy Scholarship

National Society Daughters of the American Revolution
1776 D Street NW
Washington, DC 20006-5303
Phone: 202-628-1776
Website: http://www.dar.org
Purpose: To support students who are studying occupational or physical therapy.
Eligibility: Applicants must have financial need and have been accepted or are attending an accredited school of occupational or physical therapy (including art or music therapy).
Target applicant:
  High school students
  College students
  Adult students
Minimum GPA: None.
Amount: $500.
Number of awards: 1.
Deadline: February 15 and August 15.
How to apply: Applications are available by written request.

---

(998) · Oral-B Laboratories Dental Hygiene Scholarships

American Dental Hygienists' Association (ADHA) Institute for Oral Health
444 N. Michigan Avenue
Suite 3400
Chicago, IL 60611
Phone: 800-735-4916

Email: institute@adha.net
Website: http://www.adha.org/institute
Purpose: To provide support to dental hygiene students who are committed to academic excellence, research and education.
Eligibility: Applicants must be pursuing a baccalaureate degree in dental hygiene with a GPA of at least 3.5 and show dedication to professional excellence, scholarship, quality research and dental hygiene education. They must demonstrate financial need of at least $1,500, be active members of SADHA or ADHA and submit a goals statement.
Target applicant:
　　College students
　　Adult students
Minimum GPA: 3.5
Amount: $1,000.
Number of awards: Varies.
Deadline: May 1.
How to apply: Applications are available online.

---

(999) · Parsons Brinckerhoff – Engineering Scholarship
Conference of Minority Transportation Officials
818 18th Street NW, Suite 850
Washington, DC 20006
Phone: 202-530-0551
Fax: 202-530-0617
Email: comto@comto.org
Website: http://www.comto.org
Purpose: To support COMTO members who are studying engineering.
Eligibility: Applicants must be undergraduate students who have been COMTO members for at least one year. They must have at least a 3.0 GPA.
Target applicant:
　　College students
　　Adult students
Minimum GPA: 3.0
Amount: $5,000.
Number of awards: Varies.
Deadline: April 4.
How to apply: Applications are available online.

(1000) · Paul A. Stewart Awards
Wilson Ornithological Society
Dr. Robert B. Payne
Museum of Zoology, University of Michigan
1109 Gedes Avenue
Ann Arbor, MI 48109
Email: rbpayne@umich.edu
Website: http://www.wilsonsociety.org
Purpose: To promote bird research.
Eligibility: Applicants' proposals should, but are not required to, cover the area of the study of bird movements based on banding, using the analysis and recovery of banded birds, with an emphasis on economic ornithology. Applicants must be willing to present their research results at an annual meeting of the Wilson Ornithological Society.
Target applicant:
　　Junior high students or younger
　　High school students
　　College students
　　Graduate school students
　　Adult students
Minimum GPA: None.

Amount: $500.
Number of awards: Up to 4.
Deadline: February 1.
How to apply: Applications are available online.

(1001) · Paul Cole Scholarship Award
Society of Nuclear Medicine
Development Office
1850 Samuel Morse Drive
Reston, VA 20190
Phone: 703-708-9000
Fax: 703-708-9020
Email: grantinfo@snm.org
Website: http://www.snm.org
Purpose: To promote excellence in healthcare through the support of education and research in nuclear medicine technology.
Eligibility: Applicants must have a minimum 2.5 GPA and be high school seniors or college undergraduates enrolled in or accepted by accredited institutions and be in the nuclear medicine technology field.
Target applicant:
　　High school students
　　College students
　　Adult students
Minimum GPA: 2.5
Amount: $1,000.
Number of awards: 32.
Deadline: January 15.
How to apply: Applications are available online.

(1002) · Paul H. Robbins, P.E., Honorary Scholarship
National Society of Professional Engineers
1420 King Street
Alexandria, VA 22314-2794
Phone: 703-684-2885
Fax: 703-836-4875
Email: memserv@nspe.org
Website: http://www.nspe.org
Purpose: To aid students in engineering.
Eligibility: Applicants must be members of NSPE, current engineering undergraduate students (junior year only) and enrolled in ABET-accredited engineering programs that participate in the NSPE Professional Engineers in Education (PEE) Sustaining University Program (SUP).
Target applicant:
　　High school students
Minimum GPA: None.
Amount: $10,000.
Number of awards: 1.
Scholarship may be renewable.
Deadline: May 16.
How to apply: Applications are available online.

(1003) · Payzer Scholarship
EAA Aviation Center
P.O. Box 2683
Oshkosh, WI 54903
Phone: 877-806-8902
Fax: 920-426-6865
Email: scholarships@eaa.org

Website: http://www.youngeagles.org
Purpose: To support students interested in technical careers.
Eligibility: Applicants must be accepted or enrolled in an accredited college or university with an emphasis on technical information and must intend to pursue a career in engineering, mathematics or the physical or biological sciences. Applicants must also be involved in school and community activities as well as aviation and be members of EAA or recommended by an EAA member.
Target applicant:
    High school students
    College students
    Graduate school students
    Adult students
Minimum GPA: None.
Amount: $5,000.
Number of awards: 1.
Deadline: March 1.
How to apply: Applications are available online.

(1004) · Peggy Dixon Two-Year Scholarship

Society of Physics Students
One Physics Ellipse
College Park, MD 20740
Phone: 301-209-3007
Fax: 301-209-0839
Email: sps@aip.org
Website: http://www.spsnational.org
Purpose: To help students seeking a bachelor's degree in physics to transition from a two-year to a four-year program.
Eligibility: Applicants must be members of SPS. Students must have finished at least one semester or quarter of the introductory physics sequence and must be registered in the appropriate subsequent physics classes.
Target applicant:
    College students
    Adult students
Minimum GPA: None.
Amount: $2,000.
Number of awards: 1.
Deadline: February 15.
How to apply: Applications are available online or from chapter advisors.

(1005) · Perfusion Student Scholarship

American Society of Extra-Corporeal Technology (AmSECT)
2209 Dickens Road
P.O. Box 11086
Richmond, VA 23230-1086
Phone: 804-565-6363
Fax: 804-282-0090
Email: patelpump@sbcglobal.net
Website: http://www.amsect.org
Purpose: To support perfusion education.
Eligibility: Applicants must be current student members of AmSECT, be in a CAAHEP accredited perfusion education program, have finished 25 percent of the coursework, have a minimum 2.75 GPA and submit an application, essay and transcript.
Target applicant:
    College students
    Graduate school students
    Adult students

Minimum GPA: 2.75
Amount: $1,000.
Number of awards: Varies.
Deadline: December 15.
How to apply: Applications are available online.

(1006) · Pfizer Inc. Scholarships

American Dental Hygienists' Association (ADHA) Institute for Oral Health
444 N. Michigan Avenue
Suite 3400
Chicago, IL 60611
Phone: 800-735-4916
Email: institute@adha.net
Website: http://www.adha.org/institute
Purpose: To support excellent dental hygiene students.
Eligibility: Applicants must have completed one year in an accredited dental hygiene program with a GPA of 3.5 or higher. They must also demonstrate financial need of at least $1,500, submit a goals statement and be active members of SADHA or ADHA.
Target applicant:
    College students
    Adult students
Minimum GPA: 3.5
Amount: $1,500.
Number of awards: Varies.
Deadline: May 1.
How to apply: Applications are available online.

(1007) · PHCC Educational Foundation Scholarship

Plumbing-Heating-Cooling Contractors–National Association
P.O. Box 6808
180 South Washington Street
Falls Church, VA 22046
Phone: 800-533-7694
Fax: 703-237-7442
Email: scholarships@naphcc.org
Website: http://www.phccweb.org
Purpose: To elevate the technical and business competence of the plumbing-heating-cooling (p-h-c) industry by awarding scholarships to students who are enrolled in a p-h-c-related major.
Eligibility: Applicants must be currently enrolled or plan to enroll in a p-h-c-related major at an accredited four-year college or university or two-year technical college, community college or trade school. Students enrolled in an approved apprentice program must also be working full-time for a licensed plumbing or HVACR contractor who is a member of the PHCC. Two $3,000 scholarships will be awarded to students who are enrolled in either a PHCC-approved apprentice program or a full-time certificate or degree program at an accredited two-year community college, technical college or trade school. Three $12,000 scholarships are awarded to students who are enrolled in an undergraduate degree program at an accredited four-year college or university.
Target applicant:
    High school students
    College students
    Adult students
Minimum GPA: None.
Amount: $3,000-$12,000.
Number of awards: 5.
Deadline: May 1.
How to apply: Applications are available online or by email.

(1008) · Physician Assistant Foundation Scholarship

Physician Assistant Foundation
PA Foundation Scholarship Committee
950 North Washington Street
Alexandria, VA 22314-1552
Phone: 703-519-5686
Fax: 703-684-1924
Email: aapa@aapa.org
Website: http://www.aapa.org
Purpose: To support physician assistants.
Eligibility: Applicants must be American Academy of Physician Assistants (AAPA) members and currently enrolled in the professional phase of a PA training program at an ARC-PA-accredited physician assistant program. Students are judged on the basis of financial need, community and professional involvement, goals and academic performance.
Target applicant:
    College students
    Adult students
Minimum GPA: None.
Amount: Varies.
Number of awards: Varies.
Deadline: January 15.
How to apply: Applications are available online.

(1009) · Pioneer in Perfusion Scholarship

American Society of Extra-Corporeal Technology (AmSECT)
2209 Dickens Road
P.O. Box 11086
Richmond, VA 23230-1086
Phone: 804-565-6363
Fax: 804-282-0090
Email: patelpump@sbcglobal.net
Website: http://www.amsect.org
Purpose: To support perfusion education.
Eligibility: Applicants must be current student members of AmSECT, be in a CAAHEP accredited perfusion education program, have finished 25 percent of the coursework, have a minimum 2.75 GPA and submit an application, essay and transcript.
Target applicant:
    College students
    Graduate school students
    Adult students
Minimum GPA: 2.75
Amount: $1,500.
Number of awards: Varies.
Deadline: December 15.
How to apply: Applications are available online.

(1010) · Pioneers of Flight

National Air Transportation Foundation
Pioneers of Flight Scholarship Program, Attn.: Professor Gregory Schwab, Chair
Department of Aerospace Technology, TC 216
Indiana State University
Terre Haute, IN 47809
Email: aeschwab@isugw.indstate.edu
Website: http://www.nata.aero
Purpose: To assist students pursuing general aviation as a career.

Eligibility: Applicants must be full-time students at an accredited four-year institution, be sophomores or juniors at the time of application and plan to pursue a career in aviation.
Target applicant:
    College students
    Adult students
Minimum GPA: 3.0
Amount: $1,000.
Number of awards: 2.
Deadline: Last Friday in December.
How to apply: Applications are available online.

(1011) · Polymer Modifiers and Additives Division Scholarships

Society of Plastics Engineers
14 Fairfield Drive
Brookfield, CT 06804
Phone: 203-740-5447
Fax: 203-775-1157
Email: foundation@4spe.org
Website: http://www.4spe.org
Purpose: To aid students who have an interest in the plastics industry.
Eligibility: Applicants must have an interest in the plastics industry, major in or take courses leading to a career in the plastics industry and be in good academic standing. Financial need is considered.
Target applicant:
    College students
    Adult students
Minimum GPA: None.
Amount: $4,000.
Number of awards: 4.
Deadline: January 15.
How to apply: Applications are available online.

(1012) · Predoctoral Research Training Fellowship

Epilepsy Foundation
8301 Professional Place
Landover , MD 20785
Phone: 301-459-3700
Email: researchwebsupport@efa.org
Website: http://www.epilepsyfoundation.org
Purpose: To support pre-doctoral students with dissertation research relating to epilepsy.
Eligibility: Applicants must be full-time graduate students pursuing a Ph.D. degree in neuroscience, physiology, pharmacology, psychology, biochemistry, genetics, nursing, pharmacy or other related areas; have a dissertation research project; have a qualified mentor who can supervise the project and have access to resources to conduct the project. The project must be in the U.S. and its territories. The award is based on the quality of the dissertation project, relevance to epilepsy, the applicant's qualifications, the mentor's qualifications and the quality of the proposed environment.
Target applicant:
    Graduate school students
    Adult students
Minimum GPA: None.
Amount: $20,000.
Number of awards: Varies.
Deadline: September 1.
How to apply: Applicants must submit three recommendation letters including one from the mentor, a statement of intent, a biographical

sketch, a cover sheet form, a lay summary, transcripts and a research plan.

(1013) · Presidential Scholarship

American Society of Extra-Corporeal Technology (AmSECT)
2209 Dickens Road
P.O. Box 11086
Richmond, VA 23230-1086
Phone: 804-565-6363
Fax: 804-282-0090
Email: patelpump@sbcglobal.net
Website: http://www.amsect.org
Purpose: To support students in studying perfusion.
Eligibility: Applicants must be current student members of AmSECT, be in a CAAHEP accredited perfusion education program, have finished 25 percent of the coursework, have a minimum 2.75 GPA and submit an application, essay and transcript.
Target applicant:
    College students
    Graduate school students
    Adult students
Minimum GPA: 2.75
Amount: $1,000.
Number of awards: Varies.
Deadline: December 15.
How to apply: Applications are available online.

(1014) · Professional Engineers In Government (PEG)

National Society of Professional Engineers
1420 King Street
Alexandria, VA 22314-2794
Phone: 703-684-2885
Fax: 703-836-4875
Email: memserv@nspe.org
Website: http://www.nspe.org
Purpose: To aid students in engineering.
Eligibility: Applicants must be graduate students pursuing an MBA, master's degree in public administration or master's degree in engineering management and must also be engineering interns or licensed professional engineers. Selection is based on undergraduate GPA, GRE or GMAT score, professional activities, community activities, two recommendation letters, essay and membership. Preference is given to government employees.
Target applicant:
    Graduate school students
    Adult students
Minimum GPA: None.
Amount: $2,500.
Number of awards: 1.
Deadline: March 15.
How to apply: Applications are available online.

(1015) · Professional Engineers In Industry (PEI) Scholarship

National Society of Professional Engineers
1420 King Street
Alexandria, VA 22314-2794
Phone: 703-684-2885
Fax: 703-836-4875
Email: memserv@nspe.org
Website: http://www.nspe.org
Purpose: To aid students in engineering.
Eligibility: Applicants must be undergraduate sophomores, juniors or seniors or graduate students with a minimum 2.5 GPA who are sponsored by a NSPE/PEI member and enrolled in an accredited engineering program. Preference is given to relatives or dependents of NSPE members.
Target applicant:
    College students
    Graduate school students
    Adult students
Minimum GPA: 2.5
Amount: $2,500.
Number of awards: 1.
Deadline: April 1.
How to apply: Applications are available online.

(1016) · Rain Bird Scholarship

Landscape Architecture Foundation
818 18th Street NW
Suite 810
Washington, DC 20006
Phone: 202-331-7070
Fax: 202-331-7079
Email: scholarships@lafoundation.org
Website: http://www.laprofession.org
Purpose: To recognize outstanding landscape architecture students.
Eligibility: Applicants must be college juniors or fourth- or fifth-year seniors who are landscape architecture, horticulture or irrigation science students who have a demonstrated commitment to the landscape architecture profession and exhibit financial need. Applications can only be sent by email.
Target applicant:
    College students
    Adult students
Minimum GPA: None.
Amount: $2,500.
Number of awards: 1.
Deadline: February 15.
How to apply: Applicants should follow the guidelines.

(1017) · Raney Fund Award

American Society of Ichthyologists and Herpetologists
Maureen Donnelly, Secretary
Department of Biological Sciences, Florida International University
11200 SW 8th Street
Miami, FL 33199
Phone: 305-348-1235
Fax: 305-348-1986
Email: asih@fiu.edu
Website: http://www.asih.org
Purpose: To support young ichthyologists.
Eligibility: Applicants should be members of ASIH and should be enrolled for an advanced degree, although those with developing careers may receive the award under exceptional circumstances. Awards may be used for museums or laboratory study, travel, fieldwork or other activities that will enhance their professional careers and their contributions to the science of ichthyology. Scholarships are awarded on the basis of merit and need.
Target applicant:
    Graduate school students
    Adult students

Minimum GPA: None.
Amount: $400-$1,000.
Number of awards: Varies.
Deadline: March 1.
How to apply: Applications are available by email or written request.

(1018) · Raymond Davis Scholarship

Society for Imaging Science and Technology
7003 Kilworth Lane
Springfield, VA 22151
Phone: 703-642-9090
Fax: 703-642-9094
Email: info@imaging.org
Website: http://www.imaging.org
Purpose: To support students who are studying imaging science and technology.
Eligibility: Applicants must be full-time graduate or undergraduate students studying photographic or imaging engineering or science who have completed or will complete two academic years of college before the term of the scholarship.
Target applicant:
    College students
    Graduate school students
    Adult students
Minimum GPA: None.
Amount: $1,000.
Number of awards: Varies.
Deadline: December 15.
How to apply: Applications are available online.

(1019) · Raymond E. Page Scholarship

Landscape Architecture Foundation
818 18th Street NW
Suite 810
Washington, DC 20006
Phone: 202-331-7070
Fax: 202-331-7079
Email: scholarships@lafoundation.org
Website: http://www.laprofession.org
Purpose: To support landscape architecture students.
Eligibility: Applicants must study landscape architecture and submit a two-page essay describing their financial need and how they plan to use to award. Selection is based on essay and a letter of recommendation from a current professor.
Target applicant:
    College students
    Adult students
Minimum GPA: None.
Amount: $1,000.
Number of awards: 1.
Deadline: April.
How to apply: Applications are available by written request.

(1020) · Research Award

American Ornithologists' Union
Avian Ecology Lab
Archbold Biological Station
123 Main Drive
Venus, FL 33960
Phone: 863-465-2571
Email: rbowman@archbold-station.org
Website: http://www.aou.org
Purpose: To provide research funding for members of the American Ornithologists Union.
Eligibility: Applicants must be members of the AOU and must submit proposals for research projects on avian biology, avian systematics, paleo-ornithology, biogeography, neotropical biology or ornithology.
Target applicant:
    College students
    Graduate school students
    Adult students
Minimum GPA: None.
Amount: $1,800.
Number of awards: 30.
Deadline: February 1.
How to apply: The submission procedure and tips for writing a proposal are described on the website.

(1021) · Research Training Fellowships for Medical Students (Medical Fellows Program)

Howard Hughes Medical Institute
4000 Jones Bridge Road
Chevy Chase, MD 20815-6789
Phone: 800-448-4882
Fax: 301-215-8888
Email: fellows@hhmi.org
Website: http://www.hhmi.org
Purpose: To support a year of full-time biomedical research training for medical and dental students.
Eligibility: Applicants must be enrolled in a U.S. medical school or dental school, and the fellowship research may be conducted at an academic or nonprofit institution in the United States or abroad if the fellow's mentor is affiliated with a U.S. institution. The research should focus on biological processes or disease mechanisms. The fellowship is based on the applicant's ability, potential research career as a physician/scientist and training. Applicants must submit research plans, personal statements, letters of reference, transcripts and MCAT or DAT scores.
Target applicant:
    Graduate school students
    Adult students
Minimum GPA: None.
Amount: $25,000.
Number of awards: Up to 60.
Deadline: January 11.
How to apply: Applications are available online.

(1022) · Robert B. Oliver ASNT Scholarship

American Society for Nondestructive Testing
1711 Arlingate Lane
P.O. Box 28518
Columbus, OH 43228
Phone: 800-222-2768
Fax: 614-274-6899
Email: sthomas@asnt.org
Website: http://www.asnt.org
Purpose: To support students in nondestructive testing.
Eligibility: Applicants must be undergraduate students enrolled in an engineering program of an accredited university and specialize in nondestructive testing (NDT). A nominating letter, transcript, three letters of recommendation and an essay describing the role of NDT/NDE in their career are required. The award is based on creativity,

content, format and readability and the student's involvement in a research project.
Target applicant:
  College students
  Adult students
Minimum GPA: None.
Amount: $2,500.
Number of awards: Varies.
Deadline: February 15.
How to apply: Applications are available online.

(1023) · Robert E. Altenhofen Memorial Scholarship
American Society for Photogrammetry and Remote Sensing
5410 Grosvenor Lane
Suite 210
Bethesda, MD 20814
Phone: 301-493-0290 x101
Fax: 301-493-0208
Email: scholarships@asprs.org
Website: http://www.asprs.org
Purpose: To encourage and commend college students who display ability in the theoretical aspects of photogrammetry.
Eligibility: Applicants must be undergraduate or graduate students and submit several pieces with their applications including: a two-page statement regarding plans for continuing studies in theoretical photogrammetry, papers, research reports or other items written by the applicants and academic transcripts. Recipients are required to submit a report on the work they accomplish during the award period.
Target applicant:
  College students
  Graduate school students
  Adult students
Minimum GPA: None.
Amount: $2,000.
Number of awards: 1.
Deadline: December 3.
How to apply: Applications are available online.

(1024) · Robert E. Thunen Memorial Scholarships
Illuminating Engineering Society of North America
1514 Gibbons Drive
Alameda, CA 94501
Phone: 510-864-0204
Fax: 510-864-8511
Email: mrcatisbac@aol.com
Website: http://www.iesna.org
Purpose: To help students who plan to pursue illumination as a career.
Eligibility: Applicants must be full-time junior, senior or graduate students in an accredited four-year college in Northern California, Nevada, Oregon or Washington who plan to pursue illumination as a career. The application, statement of purpose and at least three letters of recommendation are required. Students should review the IESNA Lighting Handbook to see the available fields of study.
Target applicant:
  College students
  Graduate school students
  Adult students
Minimum GPA: None.
Amount: $2,500.
Number of awards: 2.

Deadline: April 1.
How to apply: Applications are available by mail and email.

(1025) · Robert F. Sammataro Pressure Vessel Piping Division Scholarship
American Society of Mechanical Engineers
Three Park Avenue
New York, NY 10016
Phone: 800-843-2763
Fax: 973-882-1717
Email: infocentral@asme.org
Website: http://www.asme.org
Purpose: To support mechanical engineering students.
Eligibility: Applicants must be ASME student members and be enrolled in an eligible accredited mechanical engineering baccalaureate program. Applicants must demonstrate a special interest in pressure vessels and piping.
Target applicant:
  College students
  Adult students
Minimum GPA: None.
Amount: $1,000.
Number of awards: 1.
Deadline: March 15.
How to apply: Applications are available online.

(1026) · Robert Felix Memorial Scholarship
Tree Research and Education Endowment Fund
711 E. Roosevelt Road
Wheaton, IL 60172
Phone: 630-221-8127
Fax: 630-690-0702
Email: treefund@treefund.org
Website: http://www.treefund.org
Purpose: To help undergraduate and technical college students pursuing careers in commercial arboriculture.
Eligibility: Applicants should be undergraduate or technical college students entering the second year of a two-year program or entering the third or fourth year of a four-year program, plan to pursue a career in commercial arboriculture and be student members of the International Society of Arboriculture. An advisor referral, two letters of recommendation, letter of intent from applicant and application forms are required.
Target applicant:
  College students
  Adult students
Minimum GPA: 3.0.
Amount: $3,000.
Number of awards: 4.
Deadline: May 1.
How to apply: Applications are available online.

(1027) · RTKL Traveling Fellowship
American Architectural Foundation
1799 New York Avenue NW
Washington, DC 20006
Phone: 202-626-7318
Fax: 202-626-7420
Email: info@archfoundation.org
Website: http://www.archfoundation.org

Purpose: To encourage travel outside the United States for students in pursuit of a professional architecture degree.
Eligibility: Applicants must be in the second-to-last year of a BArch or MArch program and must complete travels before graduating. Travel pursuits should further the student's education.
Target applicant:
  College students
  Graduate school students
  Adult students
Minimum GPA: None.
Amount: $2,500.
Number of awards: 1.
Deadline: February 15.
How to apply: Applications are available online.

(1028) · Russell and Sigurd Varian Award

American Vacuum Society
120 Wall Street, 32nd Floor
New York, NY 10005-3993
Phone: 212-248-0200
Fax: 212-248-0245
Email: angela@avs.org
Website: http://www.avs.org
Purpose: To support continuing graduate studies in the sciences and technologies related to AVS.
Eligibility: Applicants must be graduate students in an accredited academic institution. Five finalists are invited to present talks on their research to the trustees at the international symposium. The trustees then select one student to receive the award, which also covers travel expenses. Applicants should submit applications, research summaries, letters of recommendations and transcripts.
Target applicant:
  Graduate school students
  Adult students
Minimum GPA: None.
Amount: $1,500.
Number of awards: 1.
Deadline: March 31.
How to apply: Applications are available online.

(1029) · Ruth Abernathy Presidential Scholarship

American Alliance for Health, Physical Education, Recreation and Dance
1900 Association Drive
Reston, VA 20191
Phone: 800-213-7193
Email: dcallis@aahperd.org
Website: http://www.aahperd.org
Purpose: To honor deserving students in the areas of health, physical education, recreation and dance.
Eligibility: Applicants must be members of the American Alliance for Health, Physical Education, Recreation and Dance (AAHPERD), but they may join when applying and must major in health, physical education, recreation or dance. Undergraduate applicants must have a minimum 3.5 GPA and have junior or senior status when applying. Graduate applicants must have a minimum 3.5 GPA and have completed one semester of full-time study. Selection is based on scholastic achievement, leadership, community service and character.

Target applicant:
  College students
  Graduate school students
  Adult students
Minimum GPA: 3.5
Amount: $1,000-$1,500.
Number of awards: 5.
Deadline: October 15.
How to apply: Applications are available online.

(1030) · SAE Engineering Scholarships

Society of Automotive Engineers (SAE)
400 Commonwealth Drive
Warrendale, PA 15096-0001
Phone: 724-776-4841
Fax: 724-776-0790
Email: customerservice@sae.org
Website: http://www.sae.org
Purpose: To offer a number of scholarships to qualified students who are interested in the study of engineering and related sciences.
Eligibility: Applicants must be high school seniors and intend to enroll in an engineering or related science program and meet minimum grade point averages and SAT/ACT scores. There are several corporate sponsored scholarships available. There is a $5 fee. It is highly recommended that you research the scholarship and awarding organization before applying for a scholarship with a fee. There are many scholarships that do not require a fee.
Target applicant:
  High school students
Minimum GPA: None.
Amount: $1,000-$10,000.
Number of awards: Varies.
Scholarship may be renewable.
Deadline: December 1.
How to apply: Applications are available online.

(1031) · Sandra R. Spaulding Memorial Scholarship

California Nurses Association
2000 Franklin Street
Oakland, CA 94612
Phone: 510-273-2200
Email: execoffice@calnurses.org
Website: http://www.calnurse.org
Purpose: To support diversity in nursing both in terms of ethnicity and socio-economic background.
Eligibility: Students must be accepted to an accredited second-year ADN degree program at least half-time and plan to complete the program within two years. References, financial need, professional vision and direction and participation in nursing and health-related organizations are considered.
Target applicant:
  College students
  Adult students
Minimum GPA: None.
Amount: Varies.
Number of awards: Varies.
Deadline: July 1.
How to apply: Applications are available online.

(1032) · Science and Technology Scholars Program

Micron
c/o Scholarship Management Services
One Scholarship Way
P.O. Box 297
St. Peter, MN 56082
Phone: 800-537-4180
Website: http://www.micron.com
Purpose: To reward academic excellence and leadership while encouraging careers in engineering, science and computer science.
Eligibility: Applicants must be high school seniors from Idaho, Utah, Texas, Colorado or Virginia planning to major in engineering, computer science, physics, chemistry or material sciences. They must have at least a 3.5 GPA and an SAT combined score of 1350 or an ACT composite score of 30. Applicants must also demonstrate leadership in school, work or extracurricular activities.
Target applicant:
  High school students
Minimum GPA: 3.5
Amount: $16,500-$55,000.
Number of awards: Up to 13.
Deadline: January 19.
How to apply: Applications are distributed to eligible students in November and are also available online.

(1033) · Scotts Company Scholars Program

Golf Course Superintendents Association of America Foundation
GCSAA Career Development Department
GCSAA Scholars Competition
1421 Research Park Drive
Lawrence, KS 66049
Phone: 800-472-7878
Email: infobox@gcsaa.org
Website: http://www.gcsaa.org
Purpose: To offer monetary assistance for postsecondary education to a students from diverse cultural and socioeconomic backgrounds.
Eligibility: Applicants must be graduating high school seniors or college freshmen, sophomores or juniors who have been accepted at a two-year or longer program and must be pursuing a career in the green industry.
Target applicant:
  High school students
  College students
  Adult students
Minimum GPA: None.
Amount: $500-$2,500.
Number of awards: 7.
Deadline: March 1.
How to apply: Applications are available by contacting Pam Smith, 800-472-7878 x3678.

(1034) · SEA Scholarship Contest

Scientists and Engineers for America
1725 DeSales Street NW
Sixth Floor
Washington, DC 20036
Phone: 202-223-6444
Fax: 888-747-5677
Website: http://sharp.sefora.org
Purpose: To encourage students to learn more about current science policy issues.
Eligibility: Applicants must be high school, undergraduate or graduate students in the United States. They must add factual, non-partisan information to the SHARP wiki in order to participate. Prizes are given for the top two contributors as well as a prize for the most interesting information added.
Target applicant:
  High school students
  College students
  Graduate school students
  Adult students
Minimum GPA: None.
Amount: $250.
Number of awards: 3.
Deadline: December 15.
How to apply: Applicants must send an email with their name and SHARP user name to the SHARP Network via their contact page at http://sharp.sefora.org/contact/.

(1035) · SemiZone E-Learning Fellowships

Electrochemical Society
65 South Main Street, Building D
Pennington, NJ 08534-2839
Phone: 609-737-1902
Fax: 609-737-2743
Email: awards@electrochem.org
Website: http://www.electrochem.org
Purpose: To provide training for ECS members.
Eligibility: Applicants should be Electrochemical Society (ECS) student members, ECS members who are currently unemployed or in job transition, ECS members who are full-time employees of academic and other non-profit institutions, retired professionals or industry members under the age of 30 and interested in SemiZone distance-learning courses.
Target applicant:
  College students
  Graduate school students
  Adult students
Minimum GPA: None.
Amount: $1,000.
Number of awards: 3.
Deadline: Varies.
How to apply: Contact the organization for application information.

(1036) · Sertoma Communicative Disorders Scholarship

Sertoma International
1912 E. Meyer Boulevard
Kansas City, MO 64132
Phone: 816-333-8300
Fax: 816-333-4320
Email: infosertoma@sertomahq.org
Website: http://www.sertoma.org
Purpose: To fund graduate students of audiology and speech-language pathology.
Eligibility: Applicants must be citizens of the U.S. Applicants must also be accepted into a graduate level program in speech language pathology and/or audiology at a college in the U.S. recognized by ASHA's Council and have a minimum 3.2 overall GPA in all undergraduate and graduate-level courses.

Target applicant:
    College students
    Graduate school students
    Adult students
Minimum GPA: 3.2
Amount: $1,000.
Number of awards: Varies.
Deadline: March 30.
How to apply: Applications are available online.

(1037) · Shaw-Worth Memorial Scholarship

Humane Society of the United States
New England Regional Office
P.O. Box 619
Jacksonville, VT 05342
Phone: 802-368-2790
Fax: 802-368-2756
Email: nero@hsus.org
Website: http://www.hsus.org
Purpose: To recognize a New England high school senior who has made a meaningful contribution to animal protection over a significant period of time.
Eligibility: Applicants must be high school seniors in a New England public, private, parochial or vocational school. Awards are based on the work the applicants have done on behalf of animals, such as inspiring leadership in animal protection organizations or presentations on humane topics. Neither scholastic standing nor financial need are considered. No application is required, only a narrative about the applicants' achievements in animal protection.
Target applicant:
    High school students
Minimum GPA: None.
Amount: $1,500.
Number of awards: 1.
Deadline: March 15.
How to apply: Submit materials to the address listed.

(1038) · Shlemon Awards

Geological Society of America
Program Officer
Grants, Awards and Recognition
P.O. Box 9140
Boulder, CO 80301-9140
Phone: 303-357-1028
Fax: 303-357-1070
Email: awards@geosociety.org
Website: http://www.geosociety.org
Purpose: To assist graduate students in conducting research in engineering geology.
Eligibility: Applicants must be members of the Geological Society of America's Engineering Geology Division, and they must be conducting research at the master's or doctoral level.
Target applicant:
    Graduate school students
    Adult students
Minimum GPA: None.
Amount: $500-$1,000.
Number of awards: 4.
Deadline: March 15.
How to apply: Applications are available online.

(1039) · Siemens Westinghouse Competition in Math, Science and Technology

Siemens Foundation
170 Wood Avenue South
Iselin, NJ 08330
Phone: 877-822-5233
Fax: 732-603-5890
Email: foundation.us@siemens.com
Website: http://www.siemens-foundation.org
Purpose: To provide high school students with an opportunity to meet other students interested in math, science and technology and to provide monetary assistance with college expenses.
Eligibility: Students must submit research reports either individually or in teams of two or three members. Individual applicants must be high school seniors. Team project applicants must be high school students but do not need to be seniors. Projects may be scientific research, technological inventions or mathematical theories.
Target applicant:
    High school students
Minimum GPA: None.
Amount: $1,000-$100,000.
Number of awards: Varies.
Deadline: October 1.
How to apply: Applications are available online.

(1040) · Small Cash Grant Program

American Society of Certified Engineering Technicians (ASCET)
P.O. Box 1536
Brandon, MS 39043
Phone: 601-824-8991
Email: general-manager@ascet.org
Website: http://www.ascet.org
Purpose: To help engineering technology students.
Eligibility: Applicants must be a student, certified, regular, registered or associate member of the American Society of Certified Engineering Technicians (ASCET) or be high school seniors in the last five months of the academic year who will be enrolled in an engineering technology curriculum no later than six months following the selection for the award. Students must have passing grades in their present curriculum and submit transcripts and a recommendation letter.
Target applicant:
    High school students
    College students
    Adult students
Minimum GPA: None.
Amount: $100.
Number of awards: Varies.
Deadline: April 1.
How to apply: Applications are available online.

(1041) · Society of Exploration Geophysicists (SEG) Scholarship

Society of Exploration Geophysicists
Scholarship Committee
SEG Foundation
P.O. Box 702740
Tulsa, OK 74170-2740
Phone: 918-497-5500
Fax: 918-497-5560
Email: scholarships@seg.org

Website: http://www.seg.org

Purpose: To fund individuals who are involved or interested in the field of geophysics.

Eligibility: Applicants must intend to pursue a career in exploration geophysics. Applicants must also be one of the following: A high school student with above average grades planning to enter college the next fall term, an undergraduate whose grades are above average or a graduate student pursuing a career in exploration geophysics in operations, teaching or research.

Target applicant:
High school students
College students
Graduate school students
Adult students

Minimum GPA: None.

Amount: $500-$14,000.

Number of awards: Varies.

Scholarship may be renewable.

Deadline: February 1.

How to apply: Applications are available online or by written request.

(1042) · Society of Naval Architects and Marine Engineers Undergraduate Scholarships

Society of Naval Architects and Marine Engineers
601 Pavonia Avenue
Jersey City, NJ 07306
Phone: 201-798-4800
Fax: 201-798-4975
Email: efaustino@sname.org
Website: http://www.sname.org

Purpose: To assist college juniors and seniors who are studying marine industry fields.

Eligibility: Applicants must be U.S. or Canadian college juniors and seniors who are members of the SNAME and are working towards degrees in naval architecture, marine engineering, ocean engineering or marine industry related areas fields.

Target applicant:
College students
Adult students

Minimum GPA: None.

Amount: $2,000.

Number of awards: Varies.

Scholarship may be renewable.

Deadline: Varies.

How to apply: Applications are available by email.

(1043) · Society of Plastics Engineers (SPE) General Scholarships

Society of Plastics Engineers
14 Fairfield Drive
Brookfield, CT 06804
Phone: 203-740-5447
Fax: 203-775-1157
Email: foundation@4spe.org
Website: http://www.4spe.org

Purpose: To aid students who have demonstrated or expressed an interest in the plastics industry.

Eligibility: Applicants must have a demonstrated or expressed interest in the plastics industry and be majoring in or taking courses that would lead to a career in the plastics industry. Applicants must be in good academic standing. Financial need is considered for most scholarships.

Target applicant:
College students
Adult students

Minimum GPA: None.

Amount: Up to $4,000.

Number of awards: Varies.

Scholarship may be renewable.

Deadline: January 15.

How to apply: Applications are available online.

(1044) · SPIE Student Scholarships

International Society for Optical Engineering
P.O. Box 10
Bellingham, WA 98227-0010
Phone: 360-685-5452
Fax: 360-647-1445
Email: scholarships@spie.org
Website: http://www.spie.org

Purpose: To promote students who have the potential to contribute to the field of optics.

Eligibility: Applicants must be high school, undergraduate or graduate students enrolled full-time in programs in the field of optics, optical science and engineering. Students must be members of SPIE, although they may submit a membership application along with the scholarship application. Applicants must also submit two sealed letters of reference.

Target applicant:
High school students
College students
Adult students

Minimum GPA: None.

Amount: Varies.

Number of awards: Varies.

Deadline: January 11.

How to apply: Applications are available online.

(1045) · Spring Meadow Nursery Scholarship

American Nursery and Landscape Association
Horticultural Research Institute
1000 Vermont Avenue NW
Suite 300
Washington, DC 20005
Phone: 202-789-5980 x3014
Fax: 202-789-1893
Email: tjodon@anla.org
Website: http://www.anla.org

Purpose: To help students obtain a degree in horticulture.

Eligibility: Applicants must be enrolled full-time in an undergraduate or graduate landscape horticultural or related program at a two- or four-year accredited institution. Preference is given to those who plan to pursue a career in horticulture.

Target applicant:
College students
Graduate school students
Adult students

Minimum GPA: 2.25

Amount: Varies.

Number of awards: Varies.

Scholarship may be renewable.

Deadline: April 1.
How to apply: Applications are available online.

(1046) · SPS Leadership Scholarships

Society of Physics Students
One Physics Ellipse
College Park, MD 20740
Phone: 301-209-3007
Fax: 301-209-0839
Email: sps@aip.org
Website: http://www.spsnational.org
Purpose: To further the study of physics.
Eligibility: Applicants must be undergraduates at least in their junior year, physics majors and active members of SPS.
Target applicant:
　　College students
　　Adult students
Minimum GPA: None.
Amount: $2,000-$5,000.
Number of awards: 21.
Deadline: February 15.
How to apply: Applications are available online and from SPS Chapter Advisors.

(1047) · Stan Beck Fellowship

Entomological Society of America
10001 Derekwood Lane
Suite 100
Lanham, MD 20706
Phone: 301-731-4535
Fax: 301-731-4538
Email: esa@entsoc.org
Website: http://www.entsoc.org
Purpose: To support college or graduate students in entomology.
Eligibility: Applicants must be undergraduate or graduate students in entomology who demonstrate need based on physical limitations, or economic, minority or environmental conditions.
Target applicant:
　　College students
　　Graduate school students
　　Adult students
Minimum GPA: None.
Amount: Varies.
Number of awards: 1.
Deadline: July 1.
How to apply: Applications are available online.

(1048) · STEEL Engineering Education Link Initiative

Iron and Steel Society
Attn.: Lori Wharrey
AIST Foundation
186 Thorn Hill Road
Warrendale, PA 15086
Phone: 724-776-6040 x621
Fax: 724-776-1880
Email: lwharrey@aist.org
Website: http://www.aistfoundation.org
Purpose: To increase the number of students studying engineering and pursuing careers in the iron and steel industry.

Eligibility: Applicants must be juniors in an accredited North American university with a minimum GPA of 3.0, and they must demonstrate interest in the iron and steel industry. They must also be eligible for and commit to a summer internship at a steel company in the country in which they are studying.
Target applicant:
　　College students
　　Adult students
Minimum GPA: 3.0
Amount: $5,000.
Number of awards: 10.
Scholarship may be renewable.
Deadline: March 2.
How to apply: Applications are available online. Questions about this specific scholarship may be directed to blakshmi@steel.org or 202-452-7143.

(1049) · Stoye and Storer Awards

American Society of Ichthyologists and Herpetologists
Maureen Donnelly, Secretary
Department of Biological Sciences, Florida International University
11200 SW 8th Street
Miami, FL 33199
Phone: 305-348-1235
Fax: 305-348-1986
Email: asih@fiu.edu
Website: http://www.asih.org
Purpose: To recognize the best oral and poster presentations in categories related to ichthyology and herpetology.
Eligibility: Applicants must be the sole authors and presenters of their projects, be members of ASIH, be full-time students or have completed a thesis or dissertation defense during the previous 12 months. Presentations are judged by introduction, methods, data analysis and interpretation, conclusions, presentation and visual aids.
Target applicant:
　　College students
　　Graduate school students
　　Adult students
Minimum GPA: None.
Amount: Varies.
Number of awards: Varies.
Deadline: July.
How to apply: Applications are available by request.

(1050) · Student Design Competition

Society of American Registered Architects
P.O. Box 280
Newport, TN 37822
Phone: 888-385-7272
Fax: 423-487-0365
Email: cathiemoscato@sara-national.org
Website: http://www.sara-national.org
Purpose: To support architecture students.
Eligibility: Applicants may be attending accredited architectural schools, be undergraduate students in a Bachelor of Arts or a Bachelor of Science in an architecture program or be graduate students in a Master of Architecture program in pursuit of a first professional degree. Students must secure the sponsorship of a faculty member.
Target applicant:
　　College students
　　Graduate school students
　　Adult students

Minimum GPA: None.
Amount: $500-$6,000.
Number of awards: 3.
Deadline: September 1 for registration form.
How to apply: Applications are available online or by written request.

(1051) · Student Poster Session Awards

Electrochemical Society
65 South Main Street, Building D
Pennington, NJ 08534-2839
Phone: 609-737-1902
Fax: 609-737-2743
Email: awards@electrochem.org
Website: http://www.electrochem.org
Purpose: To award students for work related to fields of interest to ECS.
Eligibility: Applicants must be pursuing degrees at any college or university and prepare an abstract on work performed. The applicants must also prepare a poster to present at the society meeting where they will be judged. Two awards are in the categories of electrochemical science and technology and solid-state science and technology.
Target applicant:
    College students
    Graduate school students
    Adult students
Minimum GPA: None.
Amount: $250.
Number of awards: 2.
Deadline: Varies.
How to apply: Application materials are described online.

(1052) · Student Research Fellowship Award

Crohn's and Colitis Foundation of America Inc.
386 Park Avenue South
17th floor
New York, NY 10016
Phone: 800-932-2423
Email: info@ccfa.org
Website: http://www.ccfa.org
Purpose: To stimulate interest in research careers in inflammatory bowel disease by providing salary support for research projects.
Eligibility: Applicants must be undergraduate, graduate or medical students not yet engaged in thesis research. Students must attend an accredited North American school and conduct their research with a mentor. The planned research project must last at least 10 weeks and must be relevant to IBD.
Target applicant:
    College students
    Graduate school students
    Adult students
Minimum GPA: None.
Amount: $2,500.
Number of awards: Up to 16.
Deadline: March 15.
How to apply: Applications are available online.

(1053) · Student Research Scholarships

Bat Conservation International
Scholarship Program
P.O. Box 162603
Austin, TX 78716
Phone: 512-327-9721
Fax: 512-327-9724
Email: grants@batcon.org
Website: http://www.batcon.org
Purpose: To support students who will contribute to our knowledge about bats.
Eligibility: Applicants must be graduate students and submit a research proposal that addresses a specific area of bat conservation. The application form provides several potential research topics.
Target applicant:
    Graduate school students
    Adult students
Minimum GPA: None.
Amount: $1,000-$5,000.
Number of awards: Varies.
Deadline: December 15.
How to apply: Applications are available online.

(1054) · Student Scholarships

American Association of Women Dentists
216 W. Jackson Boulevard
Suite 625
Chicago, IL 60606
Phone: 800-920-2293
Email: nfo@womendentists.org
Website: http://www.aawd.org
Purpose: To support women in dentistry.
Eligibility: Applicants must be sophomore or juniors in dental school, demonstrate financial need and be members of the American Association of Women Dentists.
Target applicant:
    Graduate school students
    Adult students
Minimum GPA: None.
Amount: $2,000.
Number of awards: Varies.
Deadline: August 1.
How to apply: Applications are online.

(1055) · Student Travel Contingency Grants

International Society for Optical Engineering
P.O. Box 10
Bellingham, WA 98227-0010
Phone: 360-685-5452
Fax: 360-647-1445
Email: scholarships@spie.org
Website: http://www.spie.org
Purpose: To assist students who need support to travel to present at a SPIE meeting.
Eligibility: Applicants must be presenting an accepted paper at a SPIE-sponsored meeting and not have any other way of supporting their travel. Applicants must be full-time students who are not full-time employees in industry, government or academia. The students must also submit a letter of recommendation and a written statement of support from the chair of the SPIE-sponsored meeting.
Target applicant:
    College students
    Graduate school students
    Adult students

Minimum GPA: None.
Amount: $500-$750.
Number of awards: Varies.
Deadline: 10 weeks prior to the start of meeting.
How to apply: Applications are available online.

(1056) · Surgical Technology Scholarships

Foundation for Surgical Technology
6 West Dry Creek Circle
Suite 200
Littleton, CO 80120
Phone: 800-637-7433
Fax: 888-627-8018
Website: http://www.ffst.org
Purpose: To offer assistance to those who seek a career in surgical technology.
Eligibility: Applicants must be currently enrolled in a surgical technology program accredited by the Commission of Accreditation of Allied Health Education Programs. Both academic ability and financial need must be demonstrated.
Target applicant:
   College students
   Adult students
Minimum GPA: None.
Amount: Varies.
Number of awards: Varies.
Deadline: April 1.
How to apply: Applications are available online.

(1057) · Ted Neward Scholarship

Society of Plastics Engineers
14 Fairfield Drive
Brookfield, CT 06804
Phone: 203-740-5447
Fax: 203-775-1157
Email: foundation@4spe.org
Website: http://www.4spe.org
Purpose: To aid students who have an interest in the plastics industry.
Eligibility: Applicants must be U.S. citizens, have an interest in the plastics industry, major in or take courses leading to a career in the plastics industry and be in good academic standing. Financial need is considered.
Target applicant:
   College students
   Graduate school students
   Adult students
Minimum GPA: None.
Amount: $3,000.
Number of awards: 2.
Deadline: January 15.
How to apply: Applications are available online.

(1058) · The Father James B. Macelwane Annual Awards in Meteorology

American Meteorological Society
Macelwane Award
45 Beacon Street
Boston, MA 02108-3693
Phone: 617-227-2426 x246
Fax: 617-742-8718
Email: dfernand@ametsoc.org
Website: http://www.ametsoc.org/AMS/
Purpose: To encourage interest in meteorology among college students.
Eligibility: Applicants must be enrolled as undergraduates and submit an original student paper on an aspect of atmospheric science. No more than two students from any one institution may enter papers in any one contest, and there is no application form needed.
Target applicant:
   College students
   Adult students
Minimum GPA: None.
Amount: $1,000.
Number of awards: 1.
Deadline: July 31.
How to apply: Submit materials to address listed.

(1059) · The SCTE Cascade Range Chapter - Telecommunications Scholarship

Common Knowledge Scholarship Foundation
P.O. Box 290361
Davie, FL 33329-0361
Phone: 954-262-8553
Email: info@cksf.org
Website: http://www.cksf.org
Purpose: To support students who are pursuing careers in telecommunications.
Eligibility: Applicants must register online with CKSF. Students must take online quizzes featuring questions on common knowledge. The student with the most points from correct answers and the shortest time that it takes to answer the questions wins the scholarship.
Target applicant:
   High school students
   College students
   Adult students
Minimum GPA: None.
Amount: $500.
Number of awards: 1.
Deadline: February 22.
How to apply: Applications are available online.

(1060) · Thermoforming Division Memorial Scholarships

Society of Plastics Engineers
14 Fairfield Drive
Brookfield, CT 06804
Phone: 203-740-5447
Fax: 203-775-1157
Email: foundation@4spe.org
Website: http://www.4spe.org
Purpose: To aid students who have an interest in the plastics industry.
Eligibility: Applicants must have a 3.0 GPA and an interest in the plastics industry, major in or take courses leading to a career in the plastics industry and be in good academic standing. Applicants must have experience in the thermoforming industry, such as courses taken, research conducted or jobs held.
Target applicant:
   College students
   Graduate school students
   Adult students
Minimum GPA: 3.0

Amount: $5,000.
Number of awards: 2.
Deadline: January 15.
How to apply: Applications are available online.

(1061) · Thermoset Division/James I. MacKenzie Memorial Scholarship

Society of Plastics Engineers
14 Fairfield Drive
Brookfield, CT 06804
Phone: 203-740-5447
Fax: 203-775-1157
Email: foundation@4spe.org
Website: http://www.4spe.org
Purpose: To aid students who have an interest in the plastics industry and have experience in the thermoset industry.
Eligibility: Applicants must have an interest in the plastics industry and major in or take courses leading to a career in the plastics industry. Applicants must also have experience in the thermoset industry, such as courses taken, research conducted or jobs held.
Target applicant:
    College students
    Adult students
Minimum GPA: None.
Amount: $2,000.
Number of awards: 1-2.
Deadline: January 15.
How to apply: Applications are available online.

(1062) · Thomas M. Stetson Scholarship

American Ground Water Trust
16 Centre Street
Concord, NH 03301
Phone: 603-228-5444
Fax: 603-228-6557
Website: http://www.agwt.org
Purpose: To provide scholarships for high school seniors pursuing careers in a ground water-related field.
Eligibility: Applicants must be high school seniors with intentions to pursue a career in ground water-related field. Applicants must attend a college or university located west of the Mississippi River.
Target applicant:
    High school students
Minimum GPA: 3.0
Amount: $1,000.
Number of awards: 1.
Deadline: June 1.
How to apply: Applications are available online.

(1063) · Thomas R. Camp Scholarship

American Water Works Association
6666 W. Quincy Avenue
Denver, CO 80235-3098
Phone: 303-347-6201
Fax: 303-795-7603
Email: swheeler@awwa.org
Website: http://www.awwa.org
Purpose: To support students conducting applied research in the drinking water field.

Eligibility: Applicants must pursue graduate degrees at an institution of higher education in Canada, Guam, Puerto Rico, Mexico or the U.S. This is awarded to doctoral students in even years and master's students in odd years. Applicants must submit applications, resumes, transcripts, GRE scores, three recommendation letters, statements and research plans. The award is based on academics and leadership.
Target applicant:
    Graduate school students
    Adult students
Minimum GPA: None.
Amount: $5,000.
Number of awards: 1.
Deadline: January 15.
How to apply: Applications are available online.

(1064) · Thompson Delmar Learning Student Scholarship

Association of Surgical Technologists
6 W. Dry Creek Circle
Littleton, CO 80120
Phone: 800-637-7433
Fax: 303-694-9169
Email: kfrey@ast.org
Website: http://www.ast.org
Purpose: To support surgical technology students.
Eligibility: The award is based on academic achievement and writing skills. Applicants must plan to attend or currently attend a CAAHEP-accredited program. Applications and progress reports are required.
Target applicant:
    College students
    Adult students
Minimum GPA: 2.5
Amount: $1,000.
Number of awards: 1.
Deadline: April 1.
How to apply: Applications are available online.

(1065) · Tilford Fund

Association of Engineering Geologists Foundation Tilford Fund
NRT Scholarship Committee
70 Forest Lane
Placitas, NM 87043
Website: http://www.aegfoundation.org
Purpose: To provide financial assistance for field studies in engineering geology.
Eligibility: Applicants must be members of the Association of Engineering Geologists who are college or graduate students. Applicants are chosen on the basis of scholarship, ability, participation and potential for contributions to the profession.
Target applicant:
    College students
    Graduate school students
    Adult students
Minimum GPA: None.
Amount: Varies.
Number of awards: Varies.
Deadline: February 16.
How to apply: Applications are available online.

(1066) · Timothy Bigelow and Palmer W. Bigelow, Jr. Scholarship

American Nursery and Landscape Association
Horticultural Research Institute
1000 Vermont Avenue NW
Suite 300
Washington, DC 20005
Phone: 202-789-5980 x3014
Fax: 202-789-1893
Email: tjodon@anla.org
Website: http://www.anla.org
Purpose: To help students from New England who want to pursue a career in horticulture.
Eligibility: Applicants must be seniors in a two-year course and have finished the first year, juniors in a four-year course and have finished the first two years or be graduate students. Undergraduates must have a minimum 2.25 GPA and graduate students a minimum 3.0 GPA. Students must be from Connecticut, Maine, Massachusetts, New Hampshire, Rhode Island or Vermont. Preference will be given to applicants who have financial need and who plan to work in the nursery industry after graduation, including starting a business.
Target applicant:
  College students
  Graduate school students
  Adult students
Minimum GPA: 2.25 for undergraduate students; 3.0 for graduate students
Amount: $2,500.
Number of awards: 3.
Deadline: April 1.
How to apply: Applications are available online or by mail.

(1067) · Travel Grants

Geological Society of America
Program Officer
Grants, Awards and Recognition
P.O. Box 9140
Boulder, CO 80301-9140
Phone: 303-357-1028
Fax: 303-357-1070
Email: awards@geosociety.org
Website: http://www.geosociety.org
Purpose: To provide undergraduate and graduate students with grants to travel to GSA section meetings and to the GSA annual meeting.
Eligibility: Applicants must be members of GSA. Each regional section has its own application process.
Target applicant:
  College students
  Graduate school students
  Adult students
Minimum GPA: None.
Amount: Varies.
Number of awards: Varies.
Deadline: Varies.
How to apply: Application information for each region is available online.

(1068) · Trimmer Foundation Student Scholarships

Associated Builders and Contractors
Trimmer Education Foundation
4250 N. Fairfax Drive
9th Floor
Arlington, VA 22203
Phone: 703-812-2000
Email: studentchapters@abc.org
Website: http://www.abc.org
Purpose: To assist students in construction-related degree programs.
Eligibility: Applicants must be enrolled in a construction-related program and must be current active members in the student chapter program or be employed by an ABC firm.
Target applicant:
  College students
  Adult students
Minimum GPA: 2.85
Amount: Up to $1,000.
Number of awards: Varies.
Deadline: Late May/early June.
How to apply: Applications are available by email request.

(1069) · Tylenol Scholarship

Tylenol
Phone: 877-895-3665
Website: http://www.tylenolscholarship.com
Purpose: Each year Tylenol gives away $250,000 in scholarships to college and graduate students pursuing careers in healthcare.
Eligibility: Applicants must major or intend to major in a health care-related area.
Target applicant:
  College students
  Graduate school students
  Adult students
Minimum GPA: None.
Amount: $1,000-$5,000.
Number of awards: 120.
Deadline: May 15.
How to apply: Applications are available online.

(1070) · Undergraduate Award for Excellence in Chemistry

Iota Sigma Pi (ISP) ND
Professor Kathryn A. Thomasson, Iota Sigma Pi Director for Student Awards
University of North Dakota, Department of Chemistry
P.O. Box 9024
Grand Forks, ND 58202-9024
Phone: 701-777-3199
Fax: 701-777-2331
Email: kthomasson@chem.und.edu
Website: http://www.iotasigmapi.info
Purpose: To award female undergraduate students for excellence in the field of chemistry study.
Eligibility: Applicants must be female senior chemistry students at an accredited four-year college or university and be nominated by a member of the faculty.
Target applicant:
  College students
  Adult students
Minimum GPA: None.
Amount: $500.
Number of awards: 1.
Deadline: February 15.
How to apply: Applications are available online.

(1071) · Undergraduate Scholarship

Entomological Society of America
10001 Derekwood Lane
Suite 100
Lanham, MD 20706
Phone: 301-731-4535
Fax: 301-731-4538
Email: esa@entsoc.org
Website: http://www.entsoc.org
Purpose: To help students enter the field of entomology.
Eligibility: Applicants must have been enrolled in the previous fall as undergraduate students in entomology, zoology, biology or a related science at a college or university and must have accumulated a minimum of 30 credits at the time the award is presented in August. Students must have completed at least one course in entomology or a project in entomology.
Target applicant:
    College students
    Adult students
Minimum GPA: None.
Amount: Varies.
Number of awards: 4.
Deadline: June 1.
How to apply: Applications are available online.

(1072) · Undergraduate Scholarship and Construction Crafts Scholarship

National Association of Women in Construction Founders' Scholarship Foundation
327 S. Adams Street
Fort Worth, TX 76104
Phone: 800-552-3506
Fax: 817-877-0324
Email: theresap@nawic.org
Website: http://www.nawic.org
Purpose: To offer financial aid to women pursuing construction-related degrees.
Eligibility: Applicants must be currently enrolled in a construction-related degree program as full-time students, have at least one term of study remaining in a course of study leading to a degree or an associate degree in a construction-related field, desire a career in a construction-related field and have a minimum 3.0 GPA.
Target applicant:
    College students
    Adult students
Minimum GPA: 3.0
Amount: $1,000-$2,000.
Number of awards: Varies.
Deadline: March 15.
How to apply: Applications are available online.

(1073) · Undergraduate Student Research Grants

Geological Society of America
Program Officer
Grants, Awards and Recognition
P.O. Box 9140
Boulder, CO 80301-9140
Phone: 303-357-1028
Fax: 303-357-1070
Email: awards@geosociety.org
Website: http://www.geosociety.org
Purpose: To provide research grants to undergraduate students studying geology who are members of GSA.
Eligibility: Applicants must be members of GSA and attend school in one of the following GSA sections: Northeastern, North-Central or Southeastern. Each section has a separate application process.
Target applicant:
    High school students
    College students
    Adult students
Minimum GPA: None.
Amount: Varies.
Number of awards: Varies.
Deadline: Varies.
How to apply: Application instructions for each region are available online.

(1074) · Undergraduate Student Summer Research Fellowships

American Physiological Society
Education Office
9650 Rockville Pike
Bethesda, MD 20814-3991
Phone: 301-634-7787
Fax: 301-634-7241
Email: education@the-aps.org
Website: http://www.the-aps.org
Purpose: To support full-time summer study for undergraduate students in the laboratory of an established researcher.
Eligibility: Applicants must be enrolled in an undergraduate program, and faculty sponsor must be an active member of APS. Fellowships are awarded to students pursuing a career as a basic research scientist.
Target applicant:
    College students
    Adult students
Minimum GPA: None.
Amount: $3,000.
Number of awards: Up to 12.
Deadline: February 3.
How to apply: Applications are available online.

(1075) · Undergraduate Summer Student Research Assistantship

National Radio Astronomy Observatory (NRAO)
NRAO Headquarters
520 Edgemont Road
Charlottesville, VA 22903
Phone: 434-296-0211
Fax: 434-296-0278
Email: info@nrao.edu
Website: http://www.nrao.edu
Purpose: To allow students to perform astronomical research at National Radio Astronomy Observatory (NRAO) sites.
Eligibility: Depending on the specific program, applicants must be either undergraduates or graduating college seniors. Recipients work on-site for 10 to 12 weeks, beginning in late May or early June.
Target applicant:
    College students
    Adult students
Minimum GPA: None.
Amount: $425 per week stipend.

Number of awards: Varies.
Deadline: January 23.
How to apply: Applications are available online.

(1076) · United Parcel Service Scholarship for Female Students

Institute of Industrial Engineers (IIE)
3577 Parkway Lane
Suite 200
Norcross, GA 30092
Phone: 800-494-0460
Fax: 770-441-3295
Email: bcameron@iienet.org
Website: http://www.iienet.org/studentcenter
Purpose: To help female undergraduate engineering students.
Eligibility: Applicants must be full-time female students at an institution in the United States, Canada or Mexico with an accredited industrial engineering program, majoring in industrial engineering or its equivalent and active members. Students may not apply directly for this scholarship and must be nominated. The award is based on academic ability, character, leadership, potential service to the industrial engineering profession and financial need.
Target applicant:
 College students
 Adult students
Minimum GPA: 3.4
Amount: $4,000.
Number of awards: 1.
Deadline: February 15.
How to apply: Nomination forms are available online.

(1077) · Usrey Family Scholarship

American Nursery and Landscape Association
Horticultural Research Institute
1000 Vermont Avenue NW
Suite 300
Washington, DC 20005
Phone: 202-789-5980 x3014
Fax: 202-789-1893
Email: tjodon@anla.org
Website: http://www.anla.org
Purpose: To help students who are seeking careers in horticulture.
Eligibility: Applicants must be in an undergraduate or graduate landscape horticulture program or related field at a two or four-year California state university or college. Applicants must also be current, full-time students, academically competitive and have a minimum 2.25 GPA and a minimum 2.7 GPA in the major. Preference is given to applicants who plan to work in the nursery industry after graduation. Applicants must submit applications, cover letters, resumes, transcripts and two recommendation letters.
Target applicant:
 College students
 Graduate school students
 Adult students
Minimum GPA: 2.25
Amount: Varies.
Number of awards: Varies.
Deadline: April 1.
How to apply: Applications are available online.

(1078) · Vertical Flight Foundation Engineering Scholarships

Vertical Flight Foundation
217 N. Washington Street
Alexandria, VA 22314
Phone: 703-684-6777
Fax: 703-739-9279
Email: staff@vtol.org
Website: http://www.vtol.org
Purpose: The Vertical Flight Foundation was founded to support the education in rotorcraft and vertical-takeoff-and-landing aircraft engineering.
Eligibility: Applicants must be full-time students at accredited schools of engineering and submit a transcript with an academic endorsement from a professor or dean. Applicants need not be members of AHS.
Target applicant:
 College students
 Graduate school students
 Adult students
Minimum GPA: None.
Amount: $2,000-$4,000.
Number of awards: Varies.
Deadline: February 1.
How to apply: Applications are available online.

(1079) · Vinyl Plastics Division Scholarship

Society of Plastics Engineers
14 Fairfield Drive
Brookfield, CT 06804
Phone: 203-740-5447
Fax: 203-775-1157
Email: foundation@4spe.org
Website: http://www.4spe.org
Purpose: To aid students who plan to enter the vinyl plastics industry.
Eligibility: Applicants must be undergraduate students pursuing a career in the plastics industry and be in good academic standing. Preference is given to applicants with experience in the vinyl industry. Financial need is considered.
Target applicant:
 College students
 Adult students
Minimum GPA: None.
Amount: $1,000.
Number of awards: 1.
Deadline: January 15.
How to apply: Applications are available online.

(1080) · W. Malcolm Harding Scholarship, Philip F. French Scholarship and Owen Hallberg Scholarship

National Council of Farmer Cooperatives
50 F Street NW
Suite 900
Washington, DC 20001
Phone: 202-626-8700
Fax: 202-626-8722
Website: http://www.ncfc.org
Purpose: To aid students in the pursuit of education on farmer cooperative topics.

Eligibility: Applicants must be nominated by their college or university department or local cooperative, and have an interest in the cooperative form of business. In addition, four undergraduate awards of $200 each will be awarded to junior and senior students of a college or university, or second year students of junior colleges or technical institute. Papers must be submitted through a college or university instructor.

Target applicant:
    College students
    Adult students
Minimum GPA: None.
Amount: $200-$1,000.
Number of awards: 7.
Deadline: April 1 and June 1.
How to apply: Applications will be mailed upon receipt of nomination forms.

(1081) · Wilhelm-Frankowski Scholarship

American Medical Women's Association
211 N. Union Street, Suite 100
Alexandria, VA 22314
Website: http://www.amwa-doc.org
Purpose: To recognize women in the medical community and to encourage medical pursuits for young women.
Eligibility: The award is meant to support students who contribute to their medical communities.
Target applicant:
    College students
    Adult students
Minimum GPA: None.
Amount: Varies.
Number of awards: Varies.
Deadline: Varies.
How to apply: Contact the organization for more information.

(1082) · William A. Fischer Memorial Scholarship

American Society for Photogrammetry and Remote Sensing
5410 Grosvenor Lane
Suite 210
Bethesda, MD 20814
Phone: 301-493-0290 x101
Fax: 301-493-0208
Email: scholarships@asprs.org
Website: http://www.asprs.org
Purpose: To support graduate study in new uses of remote sensing data or techniques that relate to the natural, cultural or agricultural resources of the Earth.
Eligibility: Applicants must be prospective or current graduate students and submit letters of recommendation, a two-page statement detailing educational and career plans for continuing studies in remote sensing applications and transcripts. It is also recommended that applicants submit technical papers, research reports or other items that indicate their capabilities. Recipients must submit a report of their work during the award period.
Target applicant:
    College students
    Graduate school students
    Adult students
Minimum GPA: None.
Amount: $2,000.
Number of awards: 1.
Deadline: December 3.
How to apply: Applications are available online.

(1083) · William J. Locklin Scholarship

Landscape Architecture Foundation
818 18th Street NW
Suite 810
Washington, DC 20006
Phone: 202-331-7070
Fax: 202-331-7079
Email: scholarships@lafoundation.org
Website: http://www.laprofession.org
Purpose: To recognize the importance of 24-hour lighting in landscape design.
Eligibility: Applicants must submit an essay describing their design project as well as visual samples and a letter of recommendation from a professor.
Target applicant:
    High school students
    College students
    Graduate school students
    Adult students
Minimum GPA: None.
Amount: $1,000.
Number of awards: Varies.
Deadline: Varies.
How to apply: Applications are available by written request.

(1084) · William Park Woodside Founder's Scholarship

ASM International Foundation
9639 Kinsman Road
Materials Park, OH 44073-0002
Phone: 440-338-5151
Fax: 440-338-4634
Email: crhayes@asminternational.org
Website: http://www.asminternational.org
Purpose: To support students who follow the spirit of ASM International.
Eligibility: Applicants must be student members of ASM International, major in metallurgy or materials science engineering and be juniors or seniors at a North American university that has a bachelor's degree program in science and engineering. Applications, personal statements, transcripts, two recommendation forms, photographs and financial aid officers' contact information are required. The award is based on academics, interest in the metallurgy/materials engineering field, character and financial need. The award is for one year of full tuition up to $10,000.
Target applicant:
    College students
    Adult students
Minimum GPA: None.
Amount: Up to $10,000.
Number of awards: Varies.
Deadline: May 1.
How to apply: Applications are available online.

(1085) · William R. Kimel, P.E., Engineering Scholarship

National Society of Professional Engineers
1420 King Street
Alexandria, VA 22314-2794
Phone: 703-684-2885
Fax: 703-836-4875

Email: memserv@nspe.org
Website: http://www.nspe.org
Purpose: To assist engineering students from Kansas and Missouri in paying for their education.
Eligibility: Applicants must be permanent residents of and enrolled in an accredited undergraduate engineering program in Kansas or Missouri. Applications are only considered from students in their junior year.
Target applicant:
  College students
  Adult students
Minimum GPA: None.
Amount: $2,500.
Number of awards: 1.
Deadline: March 1.
How to apply: Applications are available online.

(1086) · Women's Scholarship

National Strength and Conditioning Association (NSCA) Foundation
1885 Bob Johnson Drive
Colorado Springs, CO 80906
Phone: 800-815-6826
Fax: 719-632-6367
Email: nsca@nsca-lift.org
Website: http://www.nsca-lift.org
Purpose: To encourage women to enter the field of strength and conditioning.
Eligibility: Applicants should be women age 17 and older who have been accepted by an accredited institution for a graduate degree in strength and conditioning. Applicants must be NSCA members and plan to pursue careers in strength and conditioning. A cover letter of application, application form, resume, transcript, three letters of recommendation and essay are required. The award is based on grades, strength and conditioning experience, NSCA involvement, awards, community involvement, essay and recommendations.
Target applicant:
  Graduate school students
  Adult students
Minimum GPA: None.
Amount: $1,000.
Number of awards: 2.
Deadline: March 15.
How to apply: Application materials are described online.

(1087) · Yanmar/SAE Scholarship

Society of Automotive Engineers (SAE)
400 Commonwealth Drive
Warrendale, PA 15096-0001
Phone: 724-776-4841
Fax: 724-776-0790
Email: customerservice@sae.org
Website: http://www.sae.org
Purpose: This scholarship is sponsored by the SAE Foundation and the Yanmar Diesel America Corporation.
Eligibility: Applicants must be entering their senior year of undergraduate engineering or enrolled in a postgraduate engineering or related science program. Applicants must also pursue a course of study or research related to the conservation of energy in transportation, agriculture and construction and power generation.

Target applicant:
  College students
  Graduate school students
  Adult students
Minimum GPA: None.
Amount: $1,000.
Number of awards: 1.
Scholarship may be renewable.
Deadline: April 1.
How to apply: Applications are available online.

(1088) · Young Naturalist Awards

American Museum of Natural History
Central Park West at 79th Street
New York, NY 10024
Phone: 212-533-0222
Email: yna@amnh.org
Website: http://www.amnh.org
Purpose: To reward students for their research-based essays to promote participation and communication in science.
Eligibility: Applicants must be students in grade 7 through 12 who are currently enrolled in a public, private, parochial or home school in the United States, Canada, U.S. territories or in a U.S.-sponsored school abroad. The essays must be based on studies in school or an educational program and the theme that is the same every year: "Scientific Discovery Begins with Expeditions!" Students may choose a topic in biology, earth science or astronomy and take an expedition to an area where they can explore their topic. The expedition does not have to be complicated. Each essay must include a list of references. Essays are judged primarily on scientific merit.
Target applicant:
  Junior high students or younger
  High school students
Minimum GPA: None.
Amount: $2,500.
Number of awards: 12.
Deadline: March 1.
How to apply: Applications are available online, by mail, by phone or by email.

(1089) · Youth Activity Grant

Explorers Club
46 E. 70th Street
New York, NY 10021
Phone: 212-628-8383
Fax: 212-288-4449
Email: youth@explorers.org
Website: http://www.explorers.org
Purpose: To provide grants for high school and college students to research the natural sciences through field research.
Eligibility: Applicants must provide a three-page explanation of their project, be high school or college students and be U.S. residents. The grants allow students to conduct field research in the natural sciences under the supervision of a qualified scientist or institution.
Target applicant:
  High school students
  College students
  Adult students
Minimum GPA: None.
Amount: $500-$1,500.
Number of awards: Varies.

Deadline: Varies.
How to apply: Applications are available online.

(1090) · Youth Incentive Award

Coleopterists Society
Dr. David G. Furth, Entomology, NHB, MRC 165
P.O. Box 37012
Smithsonian institution
Washington, DC 20013-7012
Phone: 202-633-0990
Fax: 202-786-2894
Email: furthd@si.edu
Website: http://www.coleopsoc.org
Purpose: To recognize young people studying beetles.
Eligibility: Applicants should be coleopterists in grades 7-12 and submit individual proposals such as field collecting trips to conduct beetle species inventories or diversity studies, attending workshops or visiting entomology or natural history museums for training and projects on beetles, studying beetle biology, etc. Students are strongly encouraged to find an adult advisor (i.e., teacher, youth group leader, parent) to provide guidance in the proposal development, but the proposal must be written by the applicant. The Coleopterists Society can help establish contacts between applicants and professional colcopterists. The award is based on creativity, educational benefit to the applicant, scientific merit, feasibility and budget. There are two winners: one for grades 7-9 and one for grades 10-12.
Target applicant:
Junior high students or younger
High school students
Minimum GPA: None.
Amount: Varies.
Number of awards: 2.
Deadline: November 15.
How to apply: Applications are available online.

(1091) · Youth Program

Appaloosa Horse Club
Appaloosa Youth Foundation Scholarship Committee
2720 W. Pullman Road
Moscow, ID 83843
Phone: 208-882-5578
Fax: 208-882-8150
Email: acaap@appaloosa.com
Website: http://www.appaloosa.com
Purpose: To reward student members of the Appaloosa Youth Association or the Appaloosa Horse Club who are pursuing higher education.
Eligibility: Applicants must be members of the Appaloosa Youth Association or the Appaloosa Horse Club and must attend or plan to attend an institute of higher learning.
Target applicant:
High school students
College students
Graduate school students
Adult students
Minimum GPA: 2.5
Amount: $1,000-$2,000.
Number of awards: 9.
Scholarship may be renewable.
Deadline: June 10.
How to apply: Applications are available online.

STATE

(1092) · 3 Percent Scholarships

New Mexico Higher Education Department
1068 Cerrillos Road
Santa Fe, NM 87505
Phone: 800-279-9777
Fax: 505-476-6511
Email: heather.romero@state.nm.us
Website: http://hed.state.nm.us
Purpose: To support New Mexico undergraduate and graduate students to attend postsecondary institutions in New Mexico.
Eligibility: Applicants must be undergraduate or graduate students who attend public postsecondary institutions in New Mexico. Each participating college or university has its own eligibility requirements.
Target applicant:
College students
Graduate school students
Adult students
Minimum GPA: None.
Amount: Up to full tuition and fees.
Number of awards: Varies.
Deadline: Varies.
How to apply: Contact your financial aid office.

(1093) · ABC Stores Jumpstart Scholarship

Hawaii Community Foundation - Scholarships
1164 Bishop Street, Suite 800
Honolulu, HI 96813
Phone: 888-731-3863
Fax: 808-521-6286
Email: scholarships@hcf-hawaii.org
Website: http://www.hawaiicommunityfoundation.org
Purpose: To support employees of ABC Stores and their dependents.
Eligibility: Applicants must reside in Nevada, Hawaii, Guam or Saipan. Students must have at least a 2.7 GPA.
Target applicant:
High school students
College students
Adult students
Minimum GPA: 2.7
Amount: Varies.
Number of awards: Varies.
Deadline: March 1.
How to apply: To apply, register online, complete the online application and select the scholarships to which you wish to apply. In addition, mail the supporting materials: printed confirmation page from the online application, personal statement, copy of Student Aid Report (SAR) available at www.fafsa.ed.gov and official transcript.

(1094) · Academic Challenge Scholarship

Arkansas Department of Higher Education
114 East Capitol
Little Rock, AR 72201-3818
Phone: 501-371-2050
Fax: 501-371-2001
Email: finaid@adhe.arknet.edu
Website: http://www.arkansashighered.com
Purpose: To encourage Arkansas high school graduates to enroll in Arkansas colleges and universities.

Eligibility: Applicants must be graduating Arkansas high school seniors who meet academic minimum standards and income requirements.

Target applicant:

High school students

Minimum GPA: 2.25

Amount: Up to $3,500.

Number of awards: Varies.

Scholarship may be renewable.

Deadline: June 1.

How to apply: Applications are available through your high school counselor.

(1095) · Academic Excellence Scholarship

State of Wisconsin Higher Educational Aids Board

P.O. Box 7885

Madison, WI 53707

Phone: 608-267-2206

Fax: 608-267-2808

Email: heabmail@heab.state.wi.us

Website: http://heab.state.wi.us

Purpose: To assist outstanding Wisconsin students.

Eligibility: Applicants must be Wisconsin high school seniors who plan to enroll full-time at an eligible Wisconsin college or university. The award is given to the student with the highest GPA in each public and private Wisconsin high school.

Target applicant:

High school students

Minimum GPA: None.

Amount: $2,250-Full tuition.

Number of awards: Varies.

Deadline: Varies.

How to apply: Contact your high school guidance counselor.

(1096) · Academic Scholars Program

Oklahoma State Regents for Higher Education

655 Research Parkway, Suite 200

Oklahoma City, OK 73104

Phone: 800-858-1840

Fax: 405-225-9230

Email: studentinfo@osrhe.edu

Website: http://www.okhighered.org

Purpose: To assist students in attending Oklahoma colleges and universities.

Eligibility: Applicants can qualify for the program by being Oklahoma or out-of-state students who are named National Merit Scholars, National Merit Finalists or U.S. Presidential Scholars, by being Oklahoma residents who score above the 99.5 percentile on the SAT or ACT or by being nominated by a public college or institution. Applicants must attend an Oklahoma college or university.

Target applicant:

High school students

Minimum GPA: None.

Amount: Full tuition.

Number of awards: Varies.

Deadline: Varies.

How to apply: Applications are available from your high school guidance counselor, by telephone request and online.

(1097) · Academic Scholarship Program

Ohio Board of Regents

State Grants and Scholarships Department

P.O. Box 182452

Columbus, OH 43218-2452

Phone: 888-833-1133

Fax: 614-752-5903

Website: http://www.regents.ohio.gov

Purpose: To assist outstanding Ohio high school students.

Eligibility: Applicants must be Ohio high school seniors who plan to attend full-time an Ohio undergraduate institution and who meet academic requirements. The award is given to at least one student from each participating high school.

Target applicant:

High school students

Minimum GPA: None.

Amount: Varies.

Number of awards: Varies.

Deadline: February 23.

How to apply: Contact your high school guidance counselor.

(1098) · Access College Early Scholarship

Nebraska Coordinating Commission for Postsecondary Education

P.O. Box 95005

Lincoln, NE 68509

Phone: 402-471-2847

Fax: 402-471-2886

Email: ritchie.morrow@ccpe.ne.gov

Website: http://www.ccpe.state.ne.us

Purpose: To support Nebraska high school students who are enrolled in early college courses.

Eligibility: Applicants must demonstrate financial need through proof of participation in government aid programs or documentation of recent family hardships.

Target applicant:

High school students

Minimum GPA: None.

Amount: Varies.

Number of awards: Varies.

Scholarship may be renewable.

Deadline: Varies.

How to apply: Applications are available online.

(1099) · Access to Better Learning and Education Grant Program

Florida Department of Education

Office of Student Financial Assistance

1940 N. Monroe Street

Suite 70

Tallahassee, FL 32303-4759

Phone: 888-827-2004

Fax: 850-245-9667

Email: osfa@fldoe.org

Website: http://www.floridastudentfinancialaid.org

Purpose: To help undergraduate students from Florida who want to attend Florida private colleges or universities.

Eligibility: Applicants must be Florida residents for at least a year and first-time undergraduate students enrolled in degree programs (except theology or divinity degrees). Applicants must meet Florida's general state aid eligibility requirements. Participating institutions determine application procedures, deadlines and student eligibility.

Target applicant:
High school students
College students
Adult students
Minimum GPA: None.
Amount: Varies.
Number of awards: Varies.
Scholarship may be renewable.
Deadline: Varies.
How to apply: Contact the financial aid office at eligible Florida colleges and universities.

(1100) · Ada Mucklestone Memorial Scholarship

American Legion Auxiliary, Department of Illinois
2720 E. Lincoln
Bloomington, IL 61704
Phone: 309-663-9366
Email: webmaster@illegion.org
Website: http://www.illegion.org/auxiliary/mem_Education.html
Purpose: To provide financial aid to students who are children, grandchildren or great-grandchildren of veterans who are eligible for membership in the American Legion.
Eligibility: Students must be residents of Illinois who are in their senior year of high school or who have graduated but have not previously attended college. They must be children, grandchildren, or great-grandchildren of Armed Forces veterans who served during American Legion eligibility dates.
Target applicant:
High school students
Minimum GPA: None.
Amount: $800-$1,200.
Number of awards: Varies.
Deadline: March 15.
How to apply: Applications are available by mail.

(1101) · Adult Part-Time Grant

Office of Scholarships and Grants, Bureau of Student Financial Assistance
P.O. Box 30462
Lansing, MI 48909
Phone: 888-4-GRANTS
Email: treasscholgrant@michigan.gov
Website: http://www.michigan.gov/mistudentaid
Purpose: To assist financially needy, independent undergraduates who have been out of high school for at least two years.
Eligibility: Applicants must be Michigan residents enrolled at a participating public or independent degree-granting Michigan college or university on a part-time basis. Applicants must be able to show financial need and not be in default on an educational loan. This award is distributed through each participating college.
Target applicant:
College students
Adult students
Minimum GPA: None.
Amount: Varies.
Number of awards: Varies.
Scholarship may be renewable.
Deadline: Varies.
How to apply: For detailed information and application procedures contact the college or university financial aid office.

(1102) · Agenda for Delaware Women Trailblazer Scholarship

Delaware Higher Education Commission
Carvel State Office Building, 5th Floor
820 N. French Street
Wilmington, DE 19801-3509
Phone: 800-292-7935
Fax: 302-577-6765
Email: dhec@doe.k12.de.us
Website: http://www.doe.k12.de.us/infosuites/students_family/dhec/
Purpose: To support female Delaware undergraduate students.
Eligibility: Applicants must be legal residents of Delaware who will enroll in a public or private nonprofit college in Delaware as an undergraduate with a minimum 2.5 GPA. Based 50 percent on financial need and 50 percent on community and school activities, vision, participation and leadership.
Target applicant:
High school students
College students
Adult students
Minimum GPA: 2.5
Amount: $2,500.
Number of awards: 2.
Deadline: April 12.
How to apply: Applications are available online.

(1103) · Agnes M. Lindsay Scholarship

Massachusetts Office of Student Financial Assistance
454 Broadway
Suite 200
Revere, MA 02151
Phone: 617-727-9420
Fax: 617-727-0667
Email: osfa@osfa.mass.edu
Website: http://www.osfa.mass.edu
Purpose: To provide assistance to Massachusetts students who are from rural parts of the state, demonstrate financial need and attend a Massachusetts public institution of higher education.
Eligibility: Applicants must be permanent Massachusetts residents for at least one year before the beginning of the academic year. Applicants must also be enrolled full-time in an undergraduate program and maintain satisfactory academic progress.
Target applicant:
College students
Adult students
Minimum GPA: None.
Amount: Varies.
Number of awards: Varies.
Deadline: Varies.
How to apply: Applications are available by phone.

(1104) · Aid for Part-Time Study

New York State Higher Education Services Corporation (HESC)
99 Washington Avenue
Albany, NY 12255
Phone: 888-697-4372
Email: hescwebmail@hesc.org
Website: http://www.hesc.com
Purpose: To assist part-time undergraduate students at New York State institutions.

Eligibility: Applicants must meet income eligibility requirements, be enrolled for at least 3 but less than 12 semester hours per semester or at least 4 but less than 8 semester hours per quarter in an eligible undergraduate program, be New York State residents and be U.S. citizens or eligible noncitizens. Tuition charges must exceed $100 per year, and once payments begin students must maintain a C average.

Target applicant:
    High school students
    College students
    Adult students
Minimum GPA: None.
Amount: Up to $2,000.
Number of awards: Varies.
Scholarship may be renewable.
Deadline: Varies.
How to apply: Contact the financial aid office to receive an APTS application.

(1105) · Alabama Past President's Memorial Scholarship

Epsilon Sigma Alpha Foundation
P.O. Box 270517
Fort Collins, CO 80527
Phone: 970-223-2824
Fax: 970-223-4456
Email: kloyd@knoxy.net
Website: http://www.esaintl.com/esaf
Purpose: To provide educational assistance to Alabama residents.
Eligibility: Applicants may pursue any major at any school. They must demonstrate financial need and scholastic achievement. Selection is based on character (10 percent), leadership (20 percent), service (10 percent), financial need (30 percent) and scholastic ability (30 percent).
Target applicant:
    High school students
    College students
    Adult students
Minimum GPA: None.
Amount: $500.
Number of awards: 2.
Deadline: February 1.
How to apply: Applications are available online.

(1106) · Alabama Student Grant Program

State of Alabama
Commission on Higher Education
100 N. Union Street
P.O. Box 302000
Montgomery, AL 36130-2000
Phone: 334-242-1998
Fax: 334-242-0268
Website: http://www.ache.state.al.us
Purpose: To assist Alabama residents planning to attend colleges in the state.
Eligibility: Applicants must be Alabama residents attending or planning to attend Birmingham-Southern College, Concordia College, Faulkner University, Huntingdon College, Judson College, Miles College, Oakwood College, Samford University, Selma University, Southeastern Bible College, Southern Vocational College, Spring Hill College, Stillman College or the University of Mobile.

Target applicant:
    High school students
    College students
    Adult students
Minimum GPA: None.
Amount: Up to $1,200.
Number of awards: Varies.
Deadline: Varies.
How to apply: Contact the college financial aid office.

(1107) · Alan Johnston Memorial Scholarship

Los Alamos National Laboratory Foundation
1302 Calle de la Merced
Suite A
Espanola, NM 87532
Phone: 505-753-8890
Fax: 505-753-8915
Email: info@lanlfoundation.org
Website: http://www.lanlfoundation.org
Purpose: To support undergraduate students from Northern New Mexico.
Eligibility: Students must have at least a 3.25 GPA, and they must have either an SAT score of at least 1350 or an ACT score of at least 19. Applicants must submit an essay and two letters of recommendation.
Target applicant:
    High school students
    College students
    Adult students
Minimum GPA: 3.25
Amount: $1,000.
Number of awards: Varies.
Deadline: January 22.
How to apply: Applications are available online.

(1108) · Alaska State Council Endowment

Epsilon Sigma Alpha Foundation
P.O. Box 270517
Fort Collins, CO 80527
Phone: 970-223-2824
Fax: 970-223-4456
Email: kloyd@knoxy.net
Website: http://www.esaintl.com/esaf
Purpose: To provide financial assistance for Alaska students.
Eligibility: Applicants must have a GPA between 2.0 and 3.2. They may attend any school and pursue any major. Applicants are judged on character (25 percent), leadership (25 percent), service (20 percent), financial need (15 percent) and scholastic ability (15 percent).
Target applicant:
    High school students
    College students
    Adult students
Minimum GPA: 2.0
Amount: $500.
Number of awards: 1.
Deadline: February 1.
How to apply: Applications are available online.

(1109) · Albert H. Hix. W8AH Memorial Scholarship

American Radio Relay League Foundation
225 Main Street
Newington, CT 06111

Phone: 860-594-0397
Fax: 860-594-0259
Email: foundation@arrl.org
Website: http://www.arrl.org
Purpose: To provide scholarship assistance to amateur radio operators who are from the West Virginia Section or Roanoke Division or who are attending school in the West Virginia section.
Eligibility: Applicants must hold a General Class or higher Amateur Radio License and have a GPA of 3.0 or higher.
Target applicant:
 High school students
 College students
 Adult students
Minimum GPA: 3.0
Amount: $500.
Number of awards: 1.
Deadline: February 1.
How to apply: Applications are available online.

(1110) · Albert M. Lappin Scholarship
American Legion, Department of Kansas
1314 SW Topeka Boulevard
Topeka, KS 66612
Phone: 785-232-9315
Fax: 785-232-1399
Website: http://www.ksamlegion.org
Purpose: To assist the education of needy and worthy children of American Legion and American Legion Auxiliary members.
Eligibility: Applicants must be high school seniors or college freshmen or sophomores who are average or better students. They must be the son or daughter of a veteran and enrolling or enrolled in a post-secondary school in Kansas. A parent must have been a member of the Kansas American Legion or American Legion Auxiliary for the previous three years. In addition, the children of deceased parents are eligible if the parent was a paid member at the time of death. Applicants must submit a 1040 income statement, documentation of parent's veteran status, three letters of recommendation with only one from a teacher, an essay on the topic of "Why I Want to Go to College" and a high school transcript. Applicants must maintain a C average in college and verify enrollment at the start of each semester.
Target applicant:
 High school students
 College students
 Adult students
Minimum GPA: None.
Amount: $1,000.
Number of awards: 1.
Deadline: February 15.
How to apply: Applications are available online.

(1111) · Albert Yanni Scholarship Program
West Virginia Department of Education
Building 6, Room 243
1900 Kanawha Boulevard E.
Charleston, WV 25305
Phone: 304-558-3897
Email: gcoulson@access.k12.wv.us
Website: http://wvde.state.wv.us
Purpose: To provide incentives and encouragement for career and technical students to pursue higher education.
Eligibility: Applicants must be public high school seniors in West Virginia who rank in the top quarter of their class or have an unweighted

GPA of 3.0 or higher. They must have completed four or more units in a single technical concentration, have no final semester grades below a C and plan to pursue higher education in a career field related to their technical concentration.
Target applicant:
 High school students
Minimum GPA: 3.0
Amount: $2,000.
Number of awards: Up to 20.
Deadline: March 31.
How to apply: Applications are available online.

(1112) · Albuquerque ARC/Toby Cross Scholarship
American Radio Relay League Foundation
225 Main Street
Newington, CT 06111
Phone: 860-594-0397
Fax: 860-594-0259
Email: foundation@arrl.org
Website: http://www.arrl.org
Purpose: To provide financial assistance to amateur radio operators.
Eligibility: Applicants must be New Mexico residents who hold an amateur radio license. They should be candidates for undergraduate degrees.
Target applicant:
 High school students
 College students
 Adult students
Minimum GPA: None.
Amount: $500.
Number of awards: 1.
Deadline: February 1.
How to apply: Applications are available online.

(1113) · Alert Scholarship
Alert Magazine
P.O. Box 4833
Boise, ID 83711
Phone: 208-375-7911
Fax: 208-376-0770
Website: http://www.alertmagazine.org
Purpose: To promote the prevention of drug and alcohol abuse.
Eligibility: Scholarships are awarded for the best editorials on the prevention of drug and alcohol abuse. Winning editorials will be published in Alert Magazine. Applicants must be high school students between the ages of 18 and 19 and residents of Colorado, Idaho, Montana, North Dakota, South Dakota, Washington or Wyoming.
Target applicant:
 High school students
Minimum GPA: 2.5
Amount: $500.
Number of awards: Varies.
Deadline: Ongoing.
How to apply: No application necessary.

(1114) · Allan Eldin and Agnes Sutorik Geiger Scholarship Fund
Hawaii Community Foundation - Scholarships
1164 Bishop Street, Suite 800
Honolulu, HI 96813

Phone: 888-731-3863
Fax: 808-521-6286
Email: scholarships@hcf-hawaii.org
Website: http://www.hawaiicommunityfoundation.org
Purpose: To support Hawaii students who are pursuing degrees in veterinary science.
Eligibility: Students must have at least a 3.0 GPA.
Target applicant:
> High school students
> College students
> Adult students

Minimum GPA: 3.0
Amount: Varies.
Number of awards: Varies.
Deadline: March 1.
How to apply: To apply, register online, complete the online application and select the scholarships to which you wish to apply. In addition, mail the supporting materials: printed confirmation page from the online application, personal statement, copy of Student Aid Report (SAR) available at www.fafsa.ed.gov and official transcript.

(1115) · Allied Health Care Professional Scholarship Program

Illinois Department of Public Health
535 W. Jefferson Street
Springfield, IL 62761
Phone: 217-782-4977
Fax: 217-782-3987
Email: dph.mailus@illinois.gov
Website: http://www.idph.state.il.us
Purpose: To encourage more nurse practitioners, physician assistants and certified nurse midwives to set up practices in rural areas of Illinois.
Eligibility: Applicants must be accepted to or currently enrolled in an accredited Illinois school to become a nurse practitioner, physician assistant or certified nurse midwife. Students must demonstrate financial need, and they may be full-time or part-time students as long as part-time students are enrolled for at least a third of the hours required to be a full-time student. Scholarship recipients agree to set up their practice in designated shortage areas after graduation.
Target applicant:
> High school students
> College students
> Graduate school students
> Adult students

Minimum GPA: None.
Amount: $7,500.
Number of awards: Varies.
Scholarship may be renewable.
Deadline: June 30.
How to apply: Applications are available online.

(1116) · Allied Healthcare Scholarship Program

California Health and Welfare Agency - Office of Statewide Health Planning and Development
Health Professions Education Foundation
818 K Street, Room 210
Sacramento, CA 95814
Phone: 916-324-6500
Fax: 916-324-6585
Email: hpef@oshpd.state.ca.us
Website: http://www.healthprofessions.ca.gov

Purpose: To increase the number of allied healthcare professional working in medically underserved areas of California.
Eligibility: Applicants must be enrolled in a California community college or university and be studying one of the following programs: medical imaging, occupational therapy, physical therapy, respiratory care, social work, pharmacy and diagnostic medical sonography, pharmacy technician, medical laboratory technologist, surgical technician or ultrasound technician. Those selected will complete a one-year service contract or work volunteer hours in a medically underserved area of California. Financial need, work experience, academic achievement and community involvement are considered. Preference is given to those who expect to graduate within two years of application.
Target applicant:
> College students
> Graduate school students
> Adult students

Minimum GPA: None.
Amount: Up to $4,000.
Number of awards: Varies.
Scholarship may be renewable.
Deadline: March, September.
How to apply: Applications are available online.

(1117) · Alma White - Delta Kappa Gamma Scholarship

Hawaii Community Foundation - Scholarships
1164 Bishop Street, Suite 800
Honolulu, HI 96813
Phone: 888-731-3863
Fax: 808-521-6286
Email: scholarships@hcf-hawaii.org
Website: http://www.hawaiicommunityfoundation.org
Purpose: To support students in Hawaii who are planning careers in teaching.
Eligibility: Applicants must be majoring in education. Students must be a college junior, college senior or graduate student.
Target applicant:
> College students
> Graduate school students
> Adult students

Minimum GPA: None.
Amount: Varies.
Number of awards: Varies.
Deadline: March 1.
How to apply: To apply, register online, complete the online application and select the scholarships to which you wish to apply. In addition, mail the supporting materials: printed confirmation page from the online application, personal statement, copy of Student Aid Report (SAR) available at www.fafsa.ed.gov and official transcript.

(1118) · Alpha Chi #2055 ESA Endowment

Epsilon Sigma Alpha Foundation
P.O. Box 270517
Fort Collins, CO 80527
Phone: 970-223-2824
Fax: 970-223-4456
Email: kloyd@knoxy.net
Website: http://www.esaintl.com/esaf
Purpose: To provide education opportunities for Virginia residents.
Eligibility: Applicants must be residents of Augusta, Staunton or Waynesboro County, Virginia. They may choose any major, but must

attend a school in Virginia. Applicants are selected based on character (10 percent), leadership (20 percent), service (10 percent), financial need (30 percent) and scholastic ability (30 percent).

Target applicant:
High school students
College students
Adult students

Minimum GPA: None.

Amount: $500.

Number of awards: 1.

Deadline: February 1.

How to apply: Applications are available online.

(1119) · Alpha Omichrom - Arizona Endowment

Epsilon Sigma Alpha Foundation
P.O. Box 270517
Fort Collins, CO 80527
Phone: 970-223-2824
Fax: 970-223-4456
Email: kloyd@knoxy.net
Website: http://www.esaintl.com/esaf

Purpose: To provide financial assistance for Arizona students.

Eligibility: Applicants may attend any school and pursue any major. Selection of applicants is based on scholastic ability (50 percent), financial need (25 percent), character (10 percent), leadership (10 percent) and service (5 percent).

Target applicant:
High school students
College students
Adult students

Minimum GPA: None.

Amount: $1,000.

Number of awards: 1.

Deadline: February 1.

How to apply: Applications are available online.

(1120) · Alyce J. Corbin Scholarship Endowment

Epsilon Sigma Alpha Foundation
P.O. Box 270517
Fort Collins, CO 80527
Phone: 970-223-2824
Fax: 970-223-4456
Email: kloyd@knoxy.net
Website: http://www.esaintl.com/esaf

Purpose: To provide assistance to Michigan residents pursuing higher education.

Eligibility: Applicants may attend any college or university and major in any field. Selection is based on the following criteria: scholastic ability (30 percent), financial need (30 percent), leadership (20 percent), service (10 percent) and character (10 percent).

Target applicant:
High school students
College students
Adult students

Minimum GPA: None.

Amount: $500.

Number of awards: 1.

Deadline: February 1.

How to apply: Applications are available online.

(1121) · Ambassador Minerva Jean Falcon Hawaii Scholarship

Hawaii Community Foundation - Scholarships
1164 Bishop Street, Suite 800
Honolulu, HI 96813
Phone: 888-731-3863
Fax: 808-521-6286
Email: scholarships@hcf-hawaii.org
Website: http://www.hawaiicommunityfoundation.org

Purpose: To support students of Filipino ancestry.

Eligibility: Students must be starting their freshman year of college, and they must attend school in Hawaii.

Target applicant:
High school students
College students
Adult students

Minimum GPA: None.

Amount: Varies.

Number of awards: Varies.

Deadline: March 1.

How to apply: To apply, register online, complete the online application and select the scholarships to which you wish to apply. In addition, mail the supporting materials: printed confirmation page from the online application, personal statement, copy of Student Aid Report (SAR) available at www.fafsa.ed.gov and official transcript.

(1122) · Amelia Tucker Capehart Foundation Scholarship

Center for Scholarship Administration
Wachovia Accounts
4320-G Wade Hampton Boulevard
Taylors, SC 29687
Phone: 866-608-0001
Email: wachoviascholars@bellsouth.net
Website: http://www.wachoviascholars.com

Purpose: To provide financial assistance to North Carolina graduates.

Eligibility: Applicants must be graduates of an accredited North Carolina high school and demonstrate high personal character, financial need and academic ability and achievement.

Target applicant:
High school students

Minimum GPA: None.

Amount: Varies.

Number of awards: Varies.

Deadline: March 3.

How to apply: Applications are available online.

(1123) · American Association of Japanese University Women Scholarship Program

American Association of Japanese University Women
Sumiko Takase
5110 Llano Drive
Woodland Hills, CA 91364
Phone: 818-703-0208
Email: scholarship@aajuw.org
Website: http://www.aajuw.org/Scholarship.htm

Purpose: To support female students who demonstrate leadership and facilitate cultural relationships.

Eligibility: Applicants must be starting their junior year or higher at a California school. They must be able to attend the awards ceremony in Los Angeles at their own expense. Students must also submit an essay showing how their studies will contribute to leadership or to the relationship between the United States and Japan.

Target applicant:
  College students
  Adult students
Minimum GPA: None.
Amount: $1,500.
Number of awards: 3.
Deadline: September 30.
How to apply: Applications are available online.

(1124) · American Essay Contest Scholarship

American Legion Auxiliary, Department of Illinois
2720 E. Lincoln
Bloomington, IL 61704
Phone: 309-663-9366
Email: webmaster@illegion.org
Website: http://www.illegion.org/auxiliary/mem_Education.html
Purpose: To award outstanding 500-word essays written on assigned topics.
Eligibility: Applicants must be enrolled in an Illinois school in grades eight to twelve.
Target applicant:
  Junior high students or younger
  High school students
Minimum GPA: None.
Amount: Up to $75.
Number of awards: Varies.
Deadline: February 2.
How to apply: Application information is available by contacting the local American Legion Unit or Auxiliary.

(1125) · American Indian Endowed Scholarship

Washington Higher Education Coordinating Board
917 Lakeridge Way
P.O. Box 43430
Olympia, WA 98504
Phone: 360-753-7850
Fax: 360-753-6243
Email: info@hecb.wa.gov
Website: http://www.hecb.wa.gov
Purpose: To help students who have ties to the Native American community and have financial need pay for higher education.
Eligibility: Applicants must have financial need according to a completed Free Application for Federal Student Aid (FAFSA), be residents of Washington state and enroll full-time as an undergraduate or graduate in an eligible program.
Target applicant:
  High school students
  College students
  Graduate school students
  Adult students
Minimum GPA: None.
Amount: Up to $2,000.
Number of awards: Approximately 15.
Scholarship may be renewable.
Deadline: February 1.
How to apply: Applications are available online.

(1126) · American Institute of Graphic Arts (AIGA) Honolulu Chapter Scholarship Fund

Hawaii Community Foundation - Scholarships
1164 Bishop Street, Suite 800
Honolulu, HI 96813
Phone: 888-731-3863
Fax: 808-521-6286
Email: scholarships@hcf-hawaii.org
Website: http://www.hawaiicommunityfoundation.org
Purpose: To support students who are majoring in graphic design, visual communication or commercial arts.
Eligibility: Students must be residents of Hawaii.
Target applicant:
  High school students
  College students
  Adult students
Minimum GPA: None.
Amount: Varies.
Number of awards: Varies.
Deadline: March 1.
How to apply: To apply, register online, complete the online application and select the scholarships to which you wish to apply. In addition, mail the supporting materials: printed confirmation page from the online application, personal statement, copy of Student Aid Report (SAR) available at www.fafsa.ed.gov and official transcript.

(1127) · American Justice Essay Scholarship

Washington State Trial Lawyers Association
1809 7th Avenue #1500
Seattle, WA 98101-1328
Phone: 206-464-1011
Fax: 206-464-0703
Email: wstla@wstla.org
Website: http://www.wstla.org
Purpose: To promote awareness of the role that the civil justice system plays in society through an essay contest.
Eligibility: Applicants must be attending high school in the state of Washington and must subsequently attend college in order to receive the scholarship. Essays must be four to five pages and be on the given topic on advocacy in the American justice system.
Target applicant:
  High school students
Minimum GPA: None.
Amount: $2,000-$3,000.
Number of awards: 3.
Deadline: March 21.
How to apply: Applications are available online.

(1128) · American Legion Auxiliary, Department of California $1,000 Scholarships

American Legion Auxiliary, Department of California
401 Van Ness Avenue
Room 113
San Francisco, CA 94102
Phone: 415-861-5092
Fax: 415-861-8365
Email: calegionaux@calegionaux.org
Website: http://www.calegionaux.org
Purpose: To provide support to the children of U.S. Armed Forces members.

Eligibility: One of applicants' parents must have served in the U.S. Armed Forces during an eligible period. Applicants must be California resident high school seniors or graduates who have had to postpone school due to health or financial reasons and plan to attend a California college or university. Applicants must also demonstrate financial need.

Target applicant:
High school students
College students
Adult students

Minimum GPA: None.

Amount: $1,000.

Number of awards: 5.

Deadline: March 15.

How to apply: Applications are available online.

(1129) · American Legion Auxiliary, Department of California $2,000 Scholarships

American Legion Auxiliary, Department of California
401 Van Ness Avenue
Room 113
San Francisco, CA 94102
Phone: 415-861-5092
Fax: 415-861-8365
Email: calegionaux@calegionaux.org
Website: http://www.calegionaux.org
Purpose: To provide support to children of U.S. Armed Forces members.
Eligibility: One of applicants' parents must have served in the U.S. Armed Forces during an eligible period. Applicants must attend a California college or university, be California resident high school seniors or graduates who have not begun college because of illness or need and demonstrate need.

Target applicant:
High school students
College students
Adult students

Minimum GPA: None.

Amount: $2,000.

Number of awards: 1.

Deadline: March 15.

How to apply: Applications are available online.

(1130) · American Legion Auxiliary, Department of California $500 Scholarships

American Legion Auxiliary, Department of California
401 Van Ness Avenue
Room 113
San Francisco, CA 94102
Phone: 415-861-5092
Fax: 415-861-8365
Email: calegionaux@calegionaux.org
Website: http://www.calegionaux.org
Purpose: To provide support to the children of U.S. Armed Forces members.
Eligibility: One of applicant's parents must have served in the U.S. Armed Forces during an eligible period. Applicants must be California resident high school seniors or graduates who have had to postpone school due to health or financial reasons and plan to attend a California college or university. Applicants must also demonstrate financial need.

Target applicant:
High school students
College students
Adult students

Minimum GPA: None.

Amount: $500.

Number of awards: 5.

Deadline: March 15.

How to apply: Applications are available online.

(1131) · American Savings Bank Scholarship Program

Hawaii Community Foundation - Scholarships
1164 Bishop Street, Suite 800
Honolulu, HI 96813
Phone: 888-731-3863
Fax: 808-521-6286
Email: scholarships@hcf-hawaii.org
Website: http://www.hawaiicommunityfoundation.org
Purpose: To assist Hawaii high school graduates with college expenses at state schools.
Eligibility: Applicants must be entering college freshmen and demonstrate scholastic aptitude, leadership, financial need and character. Four scholarships are awarded, one for the University of Hawaii College System, one for Chaminade University of Honolulu, one for Brigham Young University-Hawaii Campus and one for Hawaii Pacific University. Applicants must be full-time students and must have a minimum 3.0 GPA. The award is renewable and includes an offer of a paid internship.

Target applicant:
High school students

Minimum GPA: 3.0

Amount: $5,000.

Number of awards: 4.

Scholarship may be renewable.

Deadline: March 1.

How to apply: Applications are available at any American Savings Branch.

(1132) · Americanism and Government Test Program

American Legion, Department of Wisconsin
2930 American Legion Drive
P.O. Box 388
Portage, WI 53901
Phone: 608-745-1090
Fax: 608-745-0179
Email: info@wilegion.org
Website: http://www.wilegion.org
Purpose: To award outstanding performance on the Americanism and Government Test, a 50-question examination based on state and federal government and history.
Eligibility: Participants must be enrolled in a Wisconsin high school and in their sophomore, junior or senior year.

Target applicant:
High school students

Minimum GPA: None.

Amount: Up to $500.

Number of awards: 32.

Deadline: Varies.

How to apply: Application information is available by contacting your local principal, teacher or guidance counselor.

(1133) · Angie M. Houtz Memorial Fund Scholarship

Angie M. Houtz Memorial Fund
P.O. Box 634
Olney, MD 20830-0634
Email: angiefund@yahoo.com
Website: http://www.angiemhoutzmemorialfund.com
Purpose: To honor the memory of Angie Houtz, victim of the September 11, 2001 attack on the Pentagon.
Eligibility: Applicants must attend or be accepted to attend a public college in Maryland full-time. They must have an unweighted GPA of 3.0 or higher and have participated in at least 200 hours of community service. They cannot be related to a member of the scholarship fund's board of directors.
Target applicant:
    High school students
    College students
    Adult students
Minimum GPA: 3.0
Amount: $3,000.
Number of awards: Varies.
Deadline: April 30.
How to apply: Applications are available online.

(1134) · Antonio Cirino Memorial Art Education Fellowship

Rhode Island Foundation
One Union Station
Providence, RI 02903
Phone: 401-274-4564
Fax: 401-331-8085
Email: libbym@rifoundation.org
Website: http://www.rifoundation.org
Purpose: To support Rhode Island students who are pursuing careers in art education.
Eligibility: Applicants must demonstrate an interest in learning about and practicing art. Preference will be given to visual artists. Students must be enrolled or planning to enroll in a master's or doctoral program that will lead to a career in art education.
Target applicant:
    Graduate school students
    Adult students
Minimum GPA: None.
Amount: $2,000-$10,000.
Number of awards: 8-10.
Scholarship may be renewable.
Deadline: May 16.
How to apply: Applications are available online.

(1135) · Arizona BPW Foundation Annual Scholarships

Arizona Business and Professional Women's Foundation
P.O. Box 32596
Phoenix, AZ 85064
Website: http://www.arizonabpwfoundation.com/scholarships.html
Purpose: To provide education assistance to women.
Eligibility: Applicants must be women who are returning to school to broaden their job prospects at a community college in Arizona. They must provide a career goal statement, financial need statement, most recent transcript, most recent income tax return and two letters of recommendation.

Target applicant:
    College students
    Adult students
Minimum GPA: None.
Amount: Varies.
Number of awards: Varies.
Deadline: March 1.
How to apply: Applications are available online.

(1136) · Arizona Chapter MOAA Educational Scholarships

Military Officers Association of American-Arizona Chapter
4333 W. Echo Lane
Glendale, AZ 85302
Phone: 623-931-1546
Email: terrytassin@cox.net
Website: http://www.azchaptermoaa.org
Purpose: To provide educational assistance to JROTC graduates.
Eligibility: Applicants must be in the next-to-last year of a JROTC program. They must be in good academic standing and demonstrate loyalty and potential for military leadership. They must attend a high school sponsored by the Arizona Chapter of MOAA.
Target applicant:
    High school students
Minimum GPA: None.
Amount: Varies.
Number of awards: Varies.
Deadline: Varies.
How to apply: Applications are available online.

(1137) · Arizona Council Endowment Scholarship

Epsilon Sigma Alpha Foundation
P.O. Box 270517
Fort Collins, CO 80527
Phone: 970-223-2824
Fax: 970-223-4456
Email: kloyd@knoxy.net
Website: http://www.esaintl.com/esaf
Purpose: To provide financial assistance for Arizona students.
Eligibility: Applicants must attend or plan to attend an Arizona institution of higher learning. Any major is acceptable. Selection is based on character (10 percent), leadership (20 percent), service (10 percent), financial need (30 percent) and scholastic ability (30 percent).
Target applicant:
    High school students
    College students
    Adult students
Minimum GPA: None.
Amount: $500.
Number of awards: 1.
Deadline: February 1.
How to apply: Applications are available online.

(1138) · Arizona Non-Traditional Education for Women Scholarships

Arizona Business and Professional Women's Foundation
P.O. Box 32596
Phoenix, AZ 85064
Website: http://www.arizonabpwfoundation.com/scholarships.html

Purpose: To provide assistance for women pursuing male-dominated career paths.
Eligibility: Applicants must be returning to school to pursue a career in an occupation in which 25 percent or fewer of the jobs are held by women. They must attend an institution of higher learning in the state of Arizona and be 20 years of age or older.
Target applicant:
  College students
  Adult students
Minimum GPA: None.
Amount: Varies.
Number of awards: Varies.
Deadline: March 1.
How to apply: Applications are available online.

(1139) · Arizona Private Postsecondary Education Student Financial Assistance Program (PFAP)

Arizona Commission for Postsecondary Education
2020 N. Central Avenue, Suite 550
Phoenix, AZ 85004
Phone: 602-258-2435
Fax: 602-258-2483
Email: judi@azhighered.org
Website: http://www.azhighered.org
Purpose: To assist Arizona students earning baccalaureate degrees at private postsecondary schools.
Eligibility: Applicants must be residents of Arizona attending a licensed and accredited private postsecondary institution.
Target applicant:
  College students
  Adult students
Minimum GPA: None.
Amount: Varies.
Number of awards: Varies.
Scholarship may be renewable.
Deadline: Ongoing.
How to apply: Applications are available through your school's financial aid office.

(1140) · Arkansas Oratorical Contest

American Legion, Department of Arkansas
Department Oratorical Chairman, Roger Lacy
P.O. Box 3280
Little Rock, AR 72203
Phone: 501-375-1104
Fax: 501-375-4236
Email: alegion@swbell.net
Website: http://www.arlegion.org/Oratorical.html
Purpose: To enhance high school students' experience with and understanding of the U.S. Constitution. The contest will help develop students' leadership skills and civic appreciation, as well as the ability to deliver thoughtful, insightful orations regarding U.S. citizenship and its inherent responsibilities.
Eligibility: Applicants must be high school students under the age of 20 who are U.S. citizens or legal residents and residents of the state. Students first give an oration within their state and winners compete at the national level. The oration must be related to the Constitution of the United States focusing on the duties and obligations citizens have to the government. It must be in English and be between eight and ten minutes. There is also an assigned topic which is posted on the website, and it should be between three and five minutes.

Target applicant:
  High school students
Minimum GPA: None.
Amount: $3,500.
Number of awards: Varies.
Deadline: December 15.
How to apply: Applications are available online.

(1141) · Arkansas Service Memorial Fund

Arkansas Community Foundation
1400 W. Markham
Suite 206
Little Rock, AR 72201
Phone: 888-220-2723
Fax: 501-372-1166
Email: arcf@arcf.org
Website: http://www.arcf.org
Purpose: To provide financial assistance for students with a parent who died in service to his or her community, state or nation.
Eligibility: Applicants must be Arkansas residents who plan to attend an institution of higher learning in the state. Scholarships are awarded by local Arkansas Community Foundation chapters.
Target applicant:
  High school students
  College students
  Adult students
Minimum GPA: None.
Amount: Varies.
Number of awards: Varies.
Deadline: Varies.
How to apply: Applications are available online.

(1142) · Arkansas State Council Endowment

Epsilon Sigma Alpha Foundation
P.O. Box 270517
Fort Collins, CO 80527
Phone: 970-223-2824
Fax: 970-223-4456
Email: kloyd@knoxy.net
Website: http://www.esaintl.com/esaf
Purpose: To provide funds for the education of Arkansas students.
Eligibility: Applicants may attend any institution of higher learning and pursue any major. Selection is based on the following criteria: character (10 percent), leadership (20 percent), service (10 percent), financial need (30 percent) and scholastic ability (30 percent).
Target applicant:
  High school students
  College students
  Adult students
Minimum GPA: None.
Amount: $500.
Number of awards: 2.
Deadline: February 1.
How to apply: Applications are available online.

(1143) · Arkansas Student Assistance Grant Program

Arkansas Department of Higher Education
114 East Capitol
Little Rock, AR 72201-3818
Phone: 501-371-2050

Fax: 501-371-2001
Email: finaid@adhe.arknet.edu
Website: http://www.arkansashighered.com
Purpose: To help Arkansas students in need.
Eligibility: Applicants must complete the Free Application for Federal Student Aid (FAFSA) as a paper application, a renewal application or an electronic application. They must be eligible for a Pell Grant and meet the other general eligibility requirements for federal financial aid programs. They also must be attending a college within the state full-time. Awards are made on a first come, first served basis.
Target applicant:
    High school students
    College students
    Adult students
Minimum GPA: None.
Amount: $600.
Number of awards: Varies.
Deadline: April 1.
How to apply: The FAFSA is available online at http://www.fafsa.ed.gov or by mail.

(1144) · Art Scholarship

Liberty Graphics
P.O. Box 5
44 Main Street
Liberty, ME 04949
Phone: 207-589-4596
Fax: 207-589-4415
Email: jay@lgtees.com
Website: http://www.lgtees.com
Purpose: To encourage exploration and expression through traditional visual mediums.
Eligibility: Applicants must be seniors at a Maine high school, be legal residents of Maine and major in art. Students must submit artwork, usually with a theme of Maine and the outdoors.
Target applicant:
    High school students
Minimum GPA: None.
Amount: $1,000.
Number of awards: 1.
Deadline: April 15.
How to apply: Applications are available from your high school guidance counselor or on the Liberty Graphics website beginning in late February or early March of each year.

(1145) · Aspire Award

Tennessee Student Assistance Corporation
404 James Robertson Parkway
Suite 1510, Parkway Towers
Nashville, TN 37243
Phone: 800-342-1663
Fax: 615-741-6101
Email: tsac.aidinfo@state.tn.us
Website: http://www.collegepaystn.com
Purpose: To provide supplemental support to recipients of the Tennessee HOPE Scholarship.
Eligibility: Applicants must be entering freshmen with a minimum ACT score of 21, minimum SAT score of 980 or minimum 3.0 GPA. Home-schooled applicants must have a minimum ACT score of 21 or SAT score of 980. GED applicants must have a minimum GED score of

525 and minimum ACT score of 21 or SAT score of 980. Independent students or the parents of dependent students must have an adjusted gross income under $36,000.
Target applicant:
    High school students
Minimum GPA: 3.0
Amount: $1,500.
Number of awards: Varies.
Deadline: September 1.
How to apply: Applications are available through completion of the FAFSA.

(1146) · Associate Degree Nursing Scholarship Program

California Health and Welfare Agency - Office of Statewide Health Planning and Development
Health Professions Education Foundation
818 K Street, Room 210
Sacramento, CA 95814
Phone: 916-324-6500
Fax: 916-324-6585
Email: hpef@oshpd.state.ca.us
Website: http://www.healthprofessions.ca.gov
Purpose: To increase the number of registered nurses working in medically underserved areas of California.
Eligibility: Applicants must be California residents enrolled in an associate degree nursing program at a California school, agree to pursue a bachelor's degree in nursing within five years and be fluent in a language other than English. Financial need, work experience, community involvement and academic achievement are considered. Preference is given to those who will graduate within two years and to those who plan to remain in a medically underserved area past the service time required. Recipients must sign a two-year service contract to work in a medically underserved area as an RN.
Target applicant:
    College students
    Adult students
Minimum GPA: None.
Amount: $8,000.
Number of awards: Varies.
Scholarship may be renewable.
Deadline: March, September.
How to apply: Applications are available online.

(1147) · Atsuhiko Tateuchi Memorial Scholarship

Seattle Foundation
1200 Fifth Avenue
Suite 1300
Seattle, WA 98101-3151
Phone: 206-622-2294
Fax: 206-622-7673
Email: info@seattlefoundation.org
Website: http://www.seattlefoundation.org
Purpose: To provide financial assistance for hard-working students from the Pacific Rim states.
Eligibility: Applicants must be high school seniors or undergraduate students from Washington, Oregon, California, Hawaii or Alaska with demonstrated financial need. They must have a GPA of 3.0 or higher. Preference is given to students with Japanese or other Asian ancestry.

Target applicant:
High school students
College students
Adult students
Minimum GPA: 3.0
Amount: $5,000.
Number of awards: Up to 10.
Deadline: March 31.
How to apply: Applications are available online.

(1148) · AWA Scholarships

Association for Women in Architecture
22815 Frampton Avenue
Torrance, CA 90501-5304
Phone: 310-534-8466
Fax: 310-257-6885
Email: scholarship@awa-la.org
Website: http://www.awa-la.org
Purpose: To support women studying architecture.
Eligibility: Applicants must be female residents of California or attend a California school and must be enrolled in one of the following majors: architecture, landscape architecture, urban and/or land planning, interior design, environmental design, architectural rendering and illustrating, civil, electrical, mechanical or structural engineering. Applicants must also have completed a minimum of 18 units in their major by the application due date. The award is based on grades, personal statement, financial need, recommendations and submitted materials. Applicants must be able to go to Los Angeles for interviews. Applications, two recommendation letters, transcripts, financial statements, personal statements and self-addressed stamped envelopes are required.
Target applicant:
College students
Graduate school students
Adult students
Minimum GPA: None.
Amount: $2,500.
Number of awards: Varies.
Deadline: April 27.
How to apply: Applications are available online.

(1149) · Baccalaureate Scholarship

Texas 4-H Youth Development Foundation
7607 Eastmark Drive, Suite 101
College Station, TX 77840
Phone: 979-845-1213
Fax: 979-845-6495
Email: texas4hfoundation@ag.tamu.edu
Website: http://www.texas4hfoundation.org
Purpose: To support Texas 4-H members who are planning to pursue a bachelor's degree.
Eligibility: Students must be high school seniors who have actively participated in a Texas 4-H program during at least part of the year. They must have formally applied to a Texas college or university, and they must meet the school's admission requirements. Applicants must have a score of at least 1350 on the SAT or 19 on the ACT. Students must provide information about their 4-H achievements, financial need, community service participation and leadership skills.
Target applicant:
High school students
Minimum GPA: None.
Amount: $1,500-$15,000.

Number of awards: Varies.
Deadline: February 15.
How to apply: Applications are available online.

(1150) · Bach Organ and Keyboard Music Scholarship

Rhode Island Foundation
One Union Station
Providence, RI 02903
Phone: 401-274-4564
Fax: 401-331-8085
Email: libbym@rifoundation.org
Website: http://www.rifoundation.org
Purpose: To support music majors who are studying keyboard instruments.
Eligibility: Applicants must be residents of the state of Rhode Island. Students must be currently enrolled in a college music program, and they must show financial need.
Target applicant:
High school students
College students
Graduate school students
Adult students
Minimum GPA: None.
Amount: Up to $1,000.
Number of awards: 3.
Deadline: June 9.
How to apply: Applications are available online.

(1151) · Bachelor of Science Nursing Scholarship Program

California Health and Welfare Agency - Office of Statewide Health Planning and Development
Health Professions Education Foundation
818 K Street, Room 210
Sacramento, CA 95814
Phone: 916-324-6500
Fax: 916-324-6585
Email: hpef@oshpd.state.ca.us
Website: http://www.healthprofessions.ca.gov
Purpose: To increase the number of professional nurses practicing in medically underserved areas of California by assisting nursing students attending California schools.
Eligibility: Applicants must be attending a California undergraduate nursing program and be fluent in a language other than English. Financial need, work experience, academic achievement and community involvement are considered. A two-year service agreement to work in a medically underserved area of California is required. Preference is given to those who expect to graduate within two years and to those who plan to remain in a medically underserved area after the service agreement has expired.
Target applicant:
College students
Adult students
Minimum GPA: None.
Amount: $10,000.
Number of awards: Varies.
Scholarship may be renewable.
Deadline: March, September.
How to apply: Applications are available online.

(1152) · Banatao Filipino American Education Fund

Asian Pacific Fund
225 Bush Street
Suite 590
San Francisco, CA 94104
Phone: 415-433-6859
Fax: 415-433-2425
Email: scholarship@asianpacificfund.org
Website: http://www.asianpacificfund.org
Purpose: To help school students of Filipino heritage in pursuing a college education.
Eligibility: Applicants for the college scholarship should be high school seniors of at least half Filipino heritage with a GPA of at least a "B" who will enroll at four-year colleges or universities and plan to major in engineering, computer science or physical sciences (health professionals, such as doctors and nurses not included). Each scholarship is renewable up to three years based on satisfactory academic performance in a full-time undergraduate program. Awards are for undergraduate study only and are based on potential, motivation and financial need. Applicants must be residents of one of the following counties: Alameda, Contra Costa, Marin, Merced, Monterey, Napa, Sacramento, San Francisco, San Joaquin, San Mateo, Santa Clara, Santa Cruz, Solano, Sonoma or Stanislaus. Applicants for the college prep scholarship must be high school juniors of at least half Filipino heritage with a GPA of 2.7 who plan to attend four-year colleges or universities and are interested in SAT preparation and college admissions counseling. Students should have an interest in engineering, math or science and be residents of one of the the following counties: Alameda, Contra Costa, Marin, Napa, San Francisco, San Joaquin, San Mateo, Santa Clara, Solano or Sonoma.
Target applicant:
    High school students
Minimum GPA: 2.7
Amount: Varies.
Number of awards: Varies.
Scholarship may be renewable.
Deadline: February 10.
How to apply: Application are available online.

(1153) · Bank of America Achievement Awards

Bank of America Foundation
Department 3246
P.O. Box 37000
San Francisco, CA 94137
Phone: 800-218-9946
Website: http://www.bankofamerica.com/foundation/index.
cfm?template=fd_ca
Purpose: To provide educational assistance to California students.
Eligibility: Applicants must be high school seniors from the state of California. A committee at each high school nominates outstanding students in the categories of applied arts and trades, fine arts, liberal arts and science and mathematics. Scholastic ability, awards and participation in school and community activities are considered.
Target applicant:
    High school students
Minimum GPA: None.
Amount: Up to $2,000.
Number of awards: Varies.
Deadline: Varies.
How to apply: Participants must be nominated by their schools.

(1154) · Barking Foundation Grants and Scholarships

Barking Foundation
P.O. Box 855
Bangor, ME 04401
Phone: 207-990-2910
Fax: 207-990-2975
Email: info@barkingfoundation.org
Website: http://www.barkingfoundation.org
Purpose: To financially assist residents of Maine with their post-secondary education goals.
Eligibility: Applicants must be residents of Maine and have demonstrated financial need. There is no minimum GPA requirement for first-time applicants, but to reapply, recipients must have a minimum 3.0 GPA.
Target applicant:
    College students
    Adult students
Minimum GPA: None.
Amount: $3,000.
Number of awards: 50.
Scholarship may be renewable.
Deadline: February 15.
How to apply: Printable applications are available online, but applications must be mailed.

(1155) · Bego Fund Scholarships

Community Foundation of New Jersey
P.O. Box 338
Morristown, NJ 07963-0338
Phone: 973-267-5533
Fax: 973-267-2903
Email: fkrueger@cfnj.org
Website: http://www.cfnj.org
Purpose: To provide education assistance to New Jersey, New York and Pennsylvania residents.
Eligibility: Applicants must be high school seniors or current college students. Preference is given to students from immigrant families who are U.S. residents, naturalized citizens or first generation U.S. citizens. A resume, statement of career goals, character reference and transcripts are required.
Target applicant:
    High school students
    College students
    Adult students
Minimum GPA: None.
Amount: $1,000-$4,000.
Number of awards: 2.
Scholarship may be renewable.
Deadline: May.
How to apply: Applications are available online.

(1156) · Benjamin Franklin/Edith Green Scholarship

Oregon Student Assistance Commission
1500 Valley River Drive
Suite 100
Eugene, OR 97401
Phone: 541-687-7400
Fax: 541-687-7414
Email: awardinfo@mercury.osac.state.or.us
Website: http://www.osac.state.or.us
Purpose: To assist Oregon high school students.

Eligibility: Applicants must be graduating Oregon high school seniors who plan to attend a four-year public Oregon college.
Target applicant:
    High school students
Minimum GPA: None.
Amount: Varies.
Number of awards: Varies.
Deadline: March 1.
How to apply: Applications are available online.

(1157) · Beta Zeta OKC/Robert Glenn Rapp Foundation

Epsilon Sigma Alpha Foundation
P.O. Box 270517
Fort Collins, CO 80527
Phone: 970-223-2824
Fax: 970-223-4456
Email: kloyd@knoxy.net
Website: http://www.esaintl.com/esaf
Purpose: To provide financial assistance to Oklahoma students.
Eligibility: Applicants may attend any school in Oklahoma and major in any field. Selection is based on financial need (50 percent), scholastic ability (25 percent), character (10 percent), leadership (10 percent) and service (5 percent).
Target applicant:
    High school students
    College students
    Adult students
Minimum GPA: None.
Amount: $1,000.
Number of awards: 3.
Deadline: February 1.
How to apply: Applications are available online.

(1158) · Betty Sanders Scholarship Endowment

Epsilon Sigma Alpha Foundation
P.O. Box 270517
Fort Collins, CO 80527
Phone: 970-223-2824
Fax: 970-223-4456
Email: kloyd@knoxy.net
Website: http://www.esaintl.com/esaf
Purpose: To provide financial assistance for Florida residents.
Eligibility: Applicants may pursue any major at any college or university. Selection is based on scholastic ability (30 percent), financial need (30 percent), leadership (20 percent), character (10 percent) and service (10 percent).
Target applicant:
    High school students
    College students
    Adult students
Minimum GPA: None.
Amount: $500.
Number of awards: 1.
Deadline: February 1.
How to apply: Applications are available online.

(1159) · BI-LO Minority Scholarship Program

BI-LO Corporation
P.O. Box 1465
Taylors, SC 29687
Website: http://www.scholarshipprograms.org
Purpose: To support minority high school students who might be interested in a career at the BI-LO company.
Eligibility: Applicants must be minority high school seniors who plan to enroll as freshmen at Benedict College, Claflin University, Morris College, North Carolina A&T State University and South Carolina State University. Applicants must agree to participate in the BI-LO Cooperative Education Program for one semester in the summer following their sophomore year. Applicants must have a minimum 3.0 GPA, minimum SAT score of 900 and be interested in pursuing a career in the food retail industry, which may include accounting, business management, marketing, distribution management, communications, pharmacy, human resources, information systems, advertising and finance.
Target applicant:
    High school students
Minimum GPA: 3.0
Amount: Varies.
Number of awards: Varies.
Deadline: February 15.
How to apply: Applications are available online.

(1160) · Big 33 Scholarship Foundation Scholarships

Big 33 Scholarship Foundation
P.O. Box 213
511 Bridge Street
New Cumberland, PA 17070
Phone: 717-774-3303
Fax: 717-774-1749
Email: info@big33.org
Website: http://www.big33.org
Purpose: To provide need-based scholarships to high school seniors with well-rounded educational and extracurricular success.
Eligibility: Applicants must be high school seniors enrolled in a public or accredited private school in Ohio or Pennsylvania. Students must have at least a 2.0 grade point average from their sophomore and junior year and be planning to continue education beyond high school at a technical school or accredited higher education institution.
Target applicant:
    High school students
Minimum GPA: 2.0
Amount: Varies.
Number of awards: Varies.
Deadline: February 1.
How to apply: Applications are available online.

(1161) · Big Y Scholarships

Big Y
Scholarship Committee
P.O. Box 7840
Springfield, MA 01102-7840
Phone: 413-504-4047
Website: http://www.bigy.com
Purpose: To reward students in the Big Y market area and those affiliated with Big Y.

Eligibility: Applicants must either be Big Y employees or their dependents or must reside or attend school in Western or Central Massachusetts, Norfolk County, Massachusetts or Connecticut. The scholarships are available to high school seniors, undergraduates, graduates, community college students and adult students. Applicants should submit transcripts, college entrance exams scores and two recommendation letters. Big Y employees must submit one recommendation from their supervisor. Selection is based on achievements, awards, community involvement, leadership positions and class rank. Eight scholarships are available specifically for dependents of law enforcement officers and firefighters.

Target applicant:
  High school students
  College students
  Graduate school students
  Adult students
Minimum GPA: None.
Amount: Varies.
Number of awards: 300.
Deadline: February 1.
How to apply: Applications are available at any Big Y location from October through January each year. Applications are also available at guidance offices of schools within Big Y's market area.

(1162) · Blossom Kalama Evans Memorial Scholarship Fund

Hawaii Community Foundation - Scholarships
1164 Bishop Street, Suite 800
Honolulu, HI 96813
Phone: 888-731-3863
Fax: 808-521-6286
Email: scholarships@hcf-hawaii.org
Website: http://www.hawaiicommunityfoundation.org
Purpose: To support students who are dedicated to serving the native Hawaiian community.
Eligibility: Applicants must be of Hawaiian ancestry, and they must be a college junior, college senior or graduate student.
Target applicant:
  College students
  Graduate school students
  Adult students
Minimum GPA: None.
Amount: Varies.
Number of awards: Varies.
Deadline: March 1.
How to apply: To apply, register online, complete the online application and select the scholarships to which you wish to apply. In addition, mail the supporting materials: printed confirmation page from the online application, personal statement, copy of Student Aid Report (SAR) available at www.fafsa.ed.gov and official transcript.

(1163) · Board of Governors' Medical Scholarship-Loan Program

College Foundation of North Carolina
P.O. Box 41966
Raleigh, NC 27629-1966
Phone: 866-234-6400
Fax: 919-821-3139
Email: programinformation@cfnc.org
Website: http://www.cfnc.org
Purpose: To assist medical students at North Carolina institutions who have financial need and want to practice medicine in the state.
Eligibility: Applicants must be accepted to the Duke University School of Medicine, Brody School of Medicine at East Carolina University, The University of North Carolina at Chapel Hill School of Medicine or the Wake Forest University School of Medicine. They must be residents of North Carolina.
Target applicant:
  Graduate school students
  Adult students
Minimum GPA: None.
Amount: Up to full tuition plus $5,000.
Number of awards: Up to 20.
Scholarship may be renewable.
Deadline: May 15.
How to apply: Applications are available from your school's financial aid office.

(1164) · Boettcher Foundation Scholarship

Boettcher Foundation
600 Seventeenth Street
Suite 2210 South
Denver, CO 80202-5422
Phone: 800-323-9640
Email: scholarships@boettcherfoundation.org
Website: http://www.boettcherfoundation.org
Purpose: To recognize high school seniors who plan to make contributions to the people in the state of Colorado.
Eligibility: Applicants must be high school seniors and current, legal residents of the state of Colorado who will graduate in the top 5 percent of their class. Applicants must have a composite score of 27 on the ACT or 1200 on the SAT. They should submit applications, essays, transcripts and standardized test scores. Selection is based on academic merit, demonstration of leadership skills, community service and character.
Target applicant:
  High school students
Minimum GPA: None.
Amount: Varies.
Number of awards: Varies.
Scholarship may be renewable.
Deadline: November 1.
How to apply: Contact high school counselors for more information.

(1165) · Booz Allen Hawaii Scholarship Fund

Hawaii Community Foundation - Scholarships
1164 Bishop Street, Suite 800
Honolulu, HI 96813
Phone: 888-731-3863
Fax: 808-521-6286
Email: scholarships@hcf-hawaii.org
Website: http://www.hawaiicommunityfoundation.org
Purpose: To support undergraduate students in Hawaii.
Eligibility: Students must be residents of Hawaii or dependents of military members stationed there. Applicants must be attending or planning to attend a four-year college or university. Students must have at least a 3.0 GPA.
Target applicant:
  High school students
  College students
  Adult students
Minimum GPA: 3.0

Amount: Varies.
Number of awards: Varies.
Deadline: March 1.
How to apply: To apply, register online, complete the online application and select the scholarships to which you wish to apply. In addition, mail the supporting materials: printed confirmation page from the online application, personal statement, copy of Student Aid Report (SAR) available at www.fafsa.ed.gov and official transcript.

(1166) · Boy Scout Scholarship

American Legion, Department of Illinois
P.O. Box 2910
Bloomington, IL 61702
Phone: 309-663-0361
Fax: 309-663-5783
Website: http://www.illegion.org
Purpose: To award a member of the Boy Scouts with a one-year scholarship.
Eligibility: Applicants must be graduating seniors in high school, Senior Boy Scouts or Explorers and residents of Illinois. Students must write an essay on Americanism and/or Boy Scout programs.
Target applicant:
    High school students
Minimum GPA: None.
Amount: Up to $1,000.
Number of awards: 5.
Deadline: April 30.
How to apply: Application information is available by contacting your local Boy Scout office or American Legion Scout Chairman.

(1167) · Buena M. Chesshir Memorial Women's Educational Scholarship

Business and Professional Women of Virginia
P.O. Box 4842
McLean, VA 22103-4842
Website: www.bpwva.org/scholarships.shtml
Purpose: To provide financial assistance for mature women seeking higher education.
Eligibility: Applicants must be women who are 25 years of age or older, U.S. citizens and residents of Virginia. They must be accepted into an accredited program at a Virginia institution of higher learning. Financial need is required.
Target applicant:
    College students
    Adult students
Minimum GPA: None.
Amount: Up to $1,000.
Number of awards: Varies.
Deadline: April 1.
How to apply: Applications are available online.

(1168) · Buena M. Chesshir Scholarship

Virginia Business and Professional Women's Foundation
P.O. Box 4842
McLean, VA 22103-4842
Phone: 800-525-3729
Email: bpwfoundation@act.org
Website: http://www.vabpwfoundation.org
Purpose: To support adult women in Virginia who are planning to continue their education.

Eligibility: Applicants must be at least 25 years of age, and they must have a definite plan to use their education for advancement in the workplace. Students must be officially accepted at a Virginia college, and they must complete a bachelor's or master's degree within two years. Applicants must provide three letters of recommendation. Awards are based on financial need, educational goals and academic achievement.
Target applicant:
    College students
    Graduate school students
    Adult students
Minimum GPA: None.
Amount: $500-$1,000.
Number of awards: Varies.
Scholarship may be renewable.
Deadline: April 1.
How to apply: Applications are available online.

(1169) · Business and Professional Women of Kentucky Foundation Grant

Kentucky Federation of Business and Professional Women
200 Compton Drive
Frankfort, KY 40601
Phone: 606-451-6654
Email: joanne.story@kctcs.edu
Website: www.bpw-ky.org/foundation.shtml
Purpose: To promote economic self-sufficiency for Kentucky women.
Eligibility: Applicants must be Kentucky residents who are at least 18 years of age. They must be employed or planning a career in the Kentucky workforce and attending an institution of higher learning. Individuals may receive a grant no more than once every 24 months. Deadlines are April 30 and October 31 of each year.
Target applicant:
    High school students
    College students
    Adult students
Minimum GPA: None.
Amount: Varies.
Number of awards: Varies.
Deadline: April 30.
How to apply: Applications are available online.

(1170) · Business and Professional Women Utah Foundation Scholarship

Utah State Business and Professional Women
P.O. Box 561
Salt Lake City, UT 84110-0561
Email: savvychef@aol.com
Website: http://www.bpwut.org
Purpose: To provide financial assistance to help Utah residents seeking higher education.
Eligibility: Applicants must be U.S. citizens and Utah residents who are 21 years of age or older. They must be accepted into a program of study at an approved Utah institution of higher learning, and they must be entering or reentering the workforce or obtaining skills that will help them advance in current employment. Financial need is required.
Target applicant:
    College students
    Adult students
Minimum GPA: None.
Amount: Up to $3,000.

Number of awards: Varies.
Deadline: Varies.
How to apply: Applications are available online.

(1171) · Business and Professional Women/Maine Continuing Education Scholarship

Business and Professional Women/Maine Futurama Foundation
103 County Road
Oakland, ME 04963
Email: webmaster@bpwmaine.org
Website: http://www.bpwmaine.org/files/index.php?id=10
Purpose: To provide financial assistance to female students.
Eligibility: Applicants must be Maine residents who have completed at least one year of college or will have done so by the end of the spring semester following application. They must be in good standing or on an approved leave of absence of one year or less at their educational institution. Financial need is required, and the student must have a definite plan to complete the program in which she is enrolled.
Target applicant:
    College students
    Adult students
Minimum GPA: None.
Amount: Varies.
Number of awards: Varies.
Deadline: April 20.
How to apply: Applications are available online.

(1172) · Cal Grant Entitlement Award

California Student Aid Commission
P.O. Box 419026
Rancho Cordova, CA 95741-9026
Phone: 888-224-7268
Fax: 916-464-8002
Email: studentsupport@csac.ca.gov
Website: http://www.csac.ca.gov
Purpose: To support California resident students.
Eligibility: Applicants must complete the Free Application for Federal Student Aid (FAFSA) and file a verified grade point average with the California Student Aid Commission. Students must be California residents, be U.S. citizens or eligible noncitizens, meet U.S. Selective Service requirements, attend an eligible California postsecondary institution, be enrolled at least half-time, maintain satisfactory academic progress and not be in default on any student loan. Cal Grant A Entitlement Awards are for undergraduate institutions of not less than two academic years. Cal Grant B Entitlement Awards are for low-income students for living and transportation expenses, supplies and books at institutions of not less than one year. Cal Grant C Awards are for occupational or vocational programs. Cal Grant T Awards are for teacher credential candidates.
Target applicant:
    High school students
    College students
    Adult students
Minimum GPA: None.
Amount: Varies.
Number of awards: Varies.
Deadline: March 2.
How to apply: Applications are available by request.

(1173) · California - Hawaii Elks Major Project Undergraduate Scholarship Program for Students with Disabilities

California-Hawaii Elks Association
5450 E. Lamona Avenue
Fresno, CA 93727-2224
Phone: 559-222-8071
Fax: 559-222-8073
Website: http://www.chea-elks.org
Purpose: To provide education assistance for students with disabilities.
Eligibility: Applicants must be U.S. citizens and California or Hawaii residents who have a physical, neurological, visual or hearing impairment or a speech/language disorder. They must be high school seniors or graduates or have passed the GED or California High School Proficiency Examination.
Target applicant:
    High school students
Minimum GPA: None.
Amount: $1,000-$2,000.
Number of awards: 20-30.
Scholarship may be renewable.
Deadline: March 15.
How to apply: Applications are available online.

(1174) · California Community Foundation Scholarships

California Community Foundation
445 S. Figueroa Street, Suite 3400
Los Angeles, CA 90071-1638
Phone: 213-413-4130
Fax: 213-622-2979
Email: csalazar@ccf-la.org
Website: http://www.calfund.org
Purpose: To assist California residents attending college or graduate school.
Eligibility: The fund has about $2 million which is disbursed through a variety of scholarships for California residents pursuing higher education through undergraduate or graduate work in or out of state. There are scholarships for students pursuing specific majors, with specific personal, academic or leadership qualities and that honor family members or colleagues.
Target applicant:
    High school students
    College students
    Graduate school students
    Adult students
Minimum GPA: None.
Amount: Varies.
Number of awards: 150.
Scholarship may be renewable.
Deadline: Varies.
How to apply: Please contact your financial aid office for more information.

(1175) · California Community Service Scholarship Program

National Medical Fellowships Inc. California Community Service Scholarship
The Chancery Building

564 Market Street
Suite 209
San Francisco, CA 94104
Phone: 415-397-2526
Fax: 415-397-2556
Email: info@nmfonline.org
Website: http://www.nmfonline.org
Purpose: To allow minority students to participate in research or community-based clinical training to promote health issues of medically underserved communities in California.
Eligibility: Applicants must be African American, mainland Puerto Rican, Mexican American, Native Hawaiian, Alaska Native or American Indian second- or third-year students at California medical schools. The award is for the third or fourth year of medical school and is based on commitment to practice in California, interest in community-based primary care, academic performance, leadership and financial need. Recommendation letters, applications, statements, transcripts, financial aid documents and essays are required.
Target applicant:
   Graduate school students
   Adult students
Minimum GPA: None.
Amount: $7,500.
Number of awards: Varies.
Deadline: January 15.
How to apply: Applications are available online.

(1176) · California Council of the Blind Scholarships

California Council of the Blind
578 B Street
Hayward, CA 94541
Phone: 510-537-7877
Fax: 510-537-7830
Email: ccotb@earthlink.net
Website: http://www.ccbnet.org
Purpose: To assist blind California residents for college, graduate or vocational studies.
Eligibility: Applicants must be legally blind residents of California attending an accredited college, university or vocational school full-time or with at least 12 units per term. The school does not have to be in California. Proof of blindness is required. A letter from the local chapter's president or member recommending the applicant is helpful. Award money can't be spent on food, clothing or shelter.
Target applicant:
   College students
   Graduate school students
   Adult students
Minimum GPA: None.
Amount: Varies.
Number of awards: Varies.
Scholarship may be renewable.
Deadline: June 15.
How to apply: Applications are available online.

(1177) · California Fee Waiver Program for Children of Veterans

California Department of Veterans Affairs
1227 O Street
Sacramento, CA 95814
Phone: 800-952-5626

Website: http://www.cdva.ca.gov
Purpose: To provide educational assistance for dependents of veterans.
Eligibility: Applicants must be the children, spouses, unmarried surviving spouses or registered domestic partners of veterans who are deceased or totally disabled due to service-related causes. The veteran must have served during a qualifying war period, and the child must be under 27 years of age (30 if the child is a veteran). There is no age limit for spouses or domestic partners. Children of veterans who have a service-connected disability, had one at the time of death or died of service-related causes may qualify if their income is at or below the national poverty level. In this case, there is no age limit.
Target applicant:
   High school students
   College students
   Adult students
Minimum GPA: None.
Amount: Tuition.
Number of awards: Varies.
Scholarship may be renewable.
Deadline: Varies.
How to apply: Applications are available online.

(1178) · California Fee Waiver Program for Dependents of Deceased or Disabled National Guard Members

California Department of Veterans Affairs
1227 O Street
Sacramento, CA 95814
Phone: 800-952-5626
Website: http://www.cdva.ca.gov
Purpose: To provide education assistance to dependents of deceased or disabled National Guard members.
Eligibility: Applicants must be dependents or surviving spouses or domestic partners of California National Guard members who were killed or permanently disabled during active duty in service to the state. Spouses or domestic partners must not have remarried or terminated the relationship.
Target applicant:
   High school students
   College students
   Adult students
Minimum GPA: None.
Amount: Tuition.
Number of awards: Varies.
Scholarship may be renewable.
Deadline: Varies.
How to apply: Applications are available online.

(1179) · California Fee Waiver Program for Recipients of the Medal of Honor and Their Children

California Department of Veterans Affairs
1227 O Street
Sacramento, CA 95814
Phone: 800-952-5626
Website: http://www.cdva.ca.gov
Purpose: To provide financial assistance for Medal of Honor recipients and their families.
Eligibility: Applicants must be Medal of Honor recipients, their children or dependents of a Registered Domestic Partner. Children must meet

age, income and residency requirements. This award is only applicable toward undergraduate studies.

Target applicant:
   High school students
   College students
   Adult students
Minimum GPA: None.
Amount: Tuition.
Number of awards: Varies.
Scholarship may be renewable.
Deadline: Varies.
How to apply: Applications are available online.

(1180) · California Interscholastic Federation (CIF) Scholar-Athlete of the Year

California Interscholastic Federation (CIF)
CIF State Office
Attn.: CIF Scholar-Athlete of the Year
1320 Harbor Bay Parkway, Suite 140
Alameda, CA 94502
Phone: 510-521-4447
Fax: 510-521-4449
Email: info@cifstate.org
Website: http://www.cifstate.org
Purpose: To recognize high school student-athletes with exemplary academic and athletic careers and personal standards.
Eligibility: Applicants must be high school seniors with a minimum 3.7 GPA, demonstrate outstanding athletic performance in a minimum of two years of varsity play in California and exhibit character, trustworthiness, respect, responsibility, fairness, caring and citizenship.
Target applicant:
   High school students
Minimum GPA: 3.7
Amount: Varies.
Number of awards: 2.
Deadline: February 27.
How to apply: Applications are available by request.

(1181) · California Masonic Foundation Scholarship

California Masonic Foundation
1111 California Street
San Francisco, CA 94108-2284
Phone: 415-776-7000
Email: foundation@californiamasons.org
Website: http://www.freemason.org
Purpose: To aid students in pursuit of a higher education.
Eligibility: Applicants must be U.S. citizens, be California residents for at least one year, be current high school seniors with a minimum 3.0 GPA, plan to attend an accredited two- or four-year college or university full-time and demonstrate financial need. There are a number of awards based on residence, career goals and general selection criteria.
Target applicant:
   High school students
Minimum GPA: 3.0
Amount: $500-$45,000.
Number of awards: Varies.
Scholarship may be renewable.
Deadline: February 15.
How to apply: Applications are available online.

(1182) · California Oratorical Contest

American Legion, Department of California
401 Van Ness Avenue, Room 117
San Francisco, CA 94102
Phone: 415-431-2400
Fax: 415-255-1571
Email: calegion@pacific.net
Website: http://www.calegion.org
Purpose: To enhance high school students' experience with and understanding of the U.S. Constitution. The contest will help develop students' leadership skills and civic appreciation, as well as the ability to deliver thoughtful, insightful orations regarding U.S. citizenship and its inherent responsibilities.
Eligibility: Applicants must be high school students under the age of 20 who are U.S. citizens or legal residents and residents of the state. Students first give an oration within their state and winners compete at the national level. The oration must be related to the Constitution of the United States focusing on the duties and obligations citizens have to the government. It must be in English and be between eight and ten minutes. There is also an assigned topic which is posted on the website, and it should be between three and five minutes.
Target applicant:
   Junior high students or younger
   High school students
Minimum GPA: None.
Amount: Up to $2,700.
Number of awards: Varies.
Deadline: February 25.
How to apply: Applications are available by email.

(1183) · California State Council Past President's Auxillary

Epsilon Sigma Alpha Foundation
P.O. Box 270517
Fort Collins, CO 80527
Phone: 970-223-2824
Fax: 970-223-4456
Email: kloyd@knoxy.net
Website: http://www.esaintl.com/esaf
Purpose: To provide financial assistance to California students.
Eligibility: Applicants may attend any college or university and pursue any major. Selection criteria are as follows: scholastic ability (30 percent), financial need (30 percent), leadership (20 percent), character (10 percent) and service (10 percent).
Target applicant:
   High school students
   College students
   Adult students
Minimum GPA: None.
Amount: $500.
Number of awards: 2.
Deadline: February 1.
How to apply: Applications are available online.

(1184) · California State Fair Academic Achievers Scholarships

California State Fair
P.O. Box 15649
Sacramento, CA 95852
Phone: 916-263-3636

Email: koneil@calexpo.com
Website: http://www.bigfun.org
Purpose: To reward and motivate well-rounded, high-achieving California students.
Eligibility: Applicants must be enrolled or plan to enroll in a four-year accredited California institution of higher learning. They must have a GPA of 3.0 or higher and have a valid California ID.
Target applicant:
    High school students
    College students
    Adult students
Minimum GPA: None.
Amount: Up to $5.000.
Number of awards: 32.
Deadline: March 21.
How to apply: Applications are available online.

(1185) · California State PTA Scholarship

California State PTA
930 Georgia Street
Los Angeles, CA 90015-1322
Phone: 213-620-1100
Fax: 213-620-1411
Website: http://www.capta.org
Purpose: To support high school seniors who have contributed to the community.
Eligibility: Applicants must attend a public California high school, be high school seniors who have served their school and community and be members of the PTA.
Target applicant:
    High school students
Minimum GPA: None.
Amount: Varies.
Number of awards: Varies.
Deadline: February 1.
How to apply: Applications are available online.

(1186) · California/Em Bullock Memorial Endowment

Epsilon Sigma Alpha Foundation
P.O. Box 270517
Fort Collins, CO 80527
Phone: 970-223-2824
Fax: 970-223-4456
Email: kloyd@knoxy.net
Website: http://www.esaintl.com/esaf
Purpose: To provide financial assistance to California students.
Eligibility: Applicants may attend any institution of higher learning and pursue any major. Selection is based on scholastic ability (30 percent), financial need (30 percent), leadership (20 percent), character (10 percent) and service (10 percent).
Target applicant:
    High school students
    College students
    Adult students
Minimum GPA: None.
Amount: $500.
Number of awards: 2.
Deadline: February 1.
How to apply: Applications are available online.

(1187) · Candon, Todd and Seabolt Scholarship Fund

Hawaii Community Foundation - Scholarships
1164 Bishop Street, Suite 800
Honolulu, HI 96813
Phone: 888-731-3863
Fax: 808-521-6286
Email: scholarships@hcf-hawaii.org
Website: http://www.hawaiicommunityfoundation.org
Purpose: To support Hawaii students who are majoring in accounting or finance.
Eligibility: Students must be in their junior or senior year of college with at least a 2.7 GPA.
Target applicant:
    College students
    Adult students
Minimum GPA: 2.7
Amount: Varies.
Number of awards: Varies.
Deadline: March 1.
How to apply: To apply, register online, complete the online application and select the scholarships to which you wish to apply. In addition, mail the supporting materials: printed confirmation page from the online application, personal statement, copy of Student Aid Report (SAR) available at www.fafsa.ed.gov and official transcript.

(1188) · Caped General Excellence Scholarship

California Association for Postsecondary Education and Disability
71423 Biskra Road
Rancho Mirage, CA 92270
Phone: 909-537-5238
Fax: 760-340-5275
Email: bjaworski@csub.edu
Website: http://www.caped.net
Purpose: To provide financial assistance to high achievers in academics, community and campus life.
Eligibility: Applicants must have a verifiable disability and demonstrate financial need. A minimum GPA of 2.5 is required for undergraduates, and a minimum GPA of 3.0 for graduate students. Applicants must be taking at least six semester units or four quarter units at a public or private California institution of higher learning.
Target applicant:
    College students
    Graduate school students
    Adult students
Minimum GPA: 2.5 for undergraduate students; 3.0 for graduate students
Amount: $1,500.
Number of awards: 1.
Deadline: September 19.
How to apply: Applications are available online.

(1189) · Capitol Scholarship

Connecticut Department of Higher Education
61 Woodland Street
Hartford, CT 06105-2326
Phone: 860-947-1855
Fax: 860-947-1838
Email: byrd@ctdhe.org
Website: http://www.ctdhe.org
Purpose: To assist Connecticut student residents.

The Ultimate Scholarship Book 2010
Scholarship Directory (State of Residence)

Eligibility: Applicants must be Connecticut residents who are U.S. citizens or permanent resident aliens and high school seniors or graduates in the top 20 percent of their class or with a minimum SAT score of 1800. The award must be used at a Connecticut college or at colleges in states that have reciprocity agreements and is based on financial need.

Target applicant:
High school students
College students
Adult students

Minimum GPA: None.
Amount: Up to $3,000.
Number of awards: Varies.
Deadline: February 15.
How to apply: Applications are available online.

(1190) · CAPPS Scholarship Program

California Association of Private Postsecondary Schools
400 Capitol Mall
Suite 1560
Sacramento, CA 95814
Phone: 916-447-5500
Email: info@cappsonline.org
Website: http://www.cappsonline.org
Purpose: To allow private postsecondary schools to offer tuition scholarships to students.
Eligibility: Applicants must be legal California residents who have fulfilled the admission requirements for the school that is pledging their CAPPS scholarship. Application is restricted to high school and adult students only. Recipients are chosen on the basis of application date and each individual school's judging standards.

Target applicant:
High school students
Adult students

Minimum GPA: None.
Amount: Varies.
Number of awards: Varies.
Deadline: July 21.
How to apply: Applications are available online.

(1191) · Career Advancement Program Tuition Waiver

Massachusetts Office of Student Financial Assistance
454 Broadway
Suite 200
Revere, MA 02151
Phone: 617-727-9420
Fax: 617-727-0667
Email: osfa@osfa.mass.edu
Website: http://www.osfa.mass.edu
Purpose: To support Massachusetts public school teachers in the first three years of teaching.
Eligibility: Applicants must pass all three parts of the Massachusetts Teachers Test. They must be teaching at a Massachusetts public school in the same year that the award is used and they must be residents of the state. Applicants must also enroll in graduate courses at one of the nine Massachusetts State College campuses or the University of Massachusetts.

Target applicant:
Graduate school students
Adult students

Minimum GPA: None.

Amount: Varies.
Number of awards: Varies.
Scholarship may be renewable.
Deadline: Varies.
How to apply: Applications are available at college financial aid offices.

(1192) · Career Colleges and Schools of Texas Scholarship Program

Career Colleges and Schools of Texas
P.O. Box 11539
Austin, TX 78711
Phone: 866-909-2278
Email: scholars@careerscholarships.org
Website: http://www.colleges-schools.org
Purpose: To help Texas high school seniors who want to attend trade or technical schools in the state.
Eligibility: Participating institutions, which are listed on the website, provide scholarships to students who choose to enroll at their schools. Since each school has its own guidelines, applicants should contact a particular school for more information.

Target applicant:
High school students

Minimum GPA: None.
Amount: $1,000.
Number of awards: Varies.
Deadline: Varies.
How to apply: Applicants should contact their high school counselors or participating schools.

(1193) · Cargill Community Scholarship Program

National FFA Organization
P.O. Box 68960
6060 FFA Drive
Indianapolis, IN 46268-0960
Phone: 317-802-6060
Fax: 317-802-6051
Email: scholarships@ffa.org
Website: http://www.ffa.org
Purpose: To provide financial assistance for well-rounded high school students.
Eligibility: Applicants must be pursuing a two- or four-year degree. They must live near a Cargill or Cargill joint venture facility, and their applications must be signed by a local Cargill employee. Academic achievement, leadership and community service are required. Cargill has locations in Arkansas; Colorado; the Gulf Area communities of Alabama, Louisiana and Texas; Illinois; Indiana; Iowa; Kansas; Minnesota; Missouri; Nebraska; North Dakota; Ohio; South Dakota; Texas and Wisconsin.

Target applicant:
High school students

Minimum GPA: None.
Amount: $1,000.
Number of awards: 350.
Deadline: February 17.
How to apply: Applications are available online.

(1194) · Carl W. Christiansen Scholarship

Rhode Island Society of Certified Public Accountants
45 Royal Little Drive
Providence, RI 02904

Phone: 401-331-5720
Fax: 401-454-5780
Email: rmancini@riscpa.org
Website: http://www.riscpa.org
Purpose: To support Rhode Island students who are pursuing careers in public accounting.
Eligibility: Students must have at least a 3.0 GPA. Applicants must submit a short essay and a letter of recommendation.
Target applicant:
    College students
    Adult students
Minimum GPA: 3.0
Amount: Varies.
Number of awards: Varies.
Deadline: January 15.
How to apply: Applications are available online.

(1195) · Carol Haas Scholarship

Epsilon Sigma Alpha Foundation
P.O. Box 270517
Fort Collins, CO 80527
Phone: 970-223-2824
Fax: 970-223-4456
Email: kloyd@knoxy.net
Website: http://www.esaintl.com/esaf
Purpose: To provide funds for the education of Ohio residents.
Eligibility: Applicants may pursue any major at any school. Selection is based equally on character, leadership, service, financial need and scholastic ability.
Target applicant:
    High school students
    College students
    Adult students
Minimum GPA: None.
Amount: $500.
Number of awards: 1.
Deadline: February 1.
How to apply: Applications are available online.

(1196) · Carol Nigus Leadership Scholarship

Kansas Federation of Business and Professional Women's Club
P.O. Box 53
Manhattan, KS 66505-0053
Phone: 785-539-1369
Email: bgjhawk80@yahoo.com
Website: http://www.bpwkansas.org/scholarships_and_loans.htm
Purpose: To provide financial assistance to students with leadership potential.
Eligibility: Applicants may be college students, or high school students who are concurrently enrolled in college classes, at an institution of higher learning in Kansas. They must have an extensive record of public and community service. A written summary of the applicant's involvement in community affairs is required.
Target applicant:
    High school students
    College students
    Adult students
Minimum GPA: None.
Amount: Varies.
Number of awards: Varies.
Deadline: February 1.
How to apply: Applications are available online.

(1197) · Carolina Rice Scholarship Program

Carolina Rice
c/o Riviana Foods Inc.
P.O. Box 2636
Houston, TX 77252
Phone: 808-226-9522
Fax: 713-942-1826
Website: http://www.carolinarice.com/scholarship
Purpose: To assist students in metropolitan areas in obtaining higher education.
Eligibility: Applicants must be high school seniors in New York/New Jersey, Chicago, Miami Dade and Broward Counties, Los Angeles and Orange County or San Francisco/San Jose. They must submit essays on how a college education will help them achieve their goals.
Target applicant:
    High school students
Minimum GPA: None.
Amount: $2,000.
Number of awards: 5.
Deadline: February 16.
How to apply: Applications are available online.

(1198) · Carpenter Scholarship

Club Zion
221 Chester Avenue
Bakersfield, CA 93301
Phone: 661-631-2582
Email: contact@clubzion.com
Website: http://www.clubzion.com
Purpose: To assist Christian students who are interested in a trade career.
Eligibility: Applicants must live in the Kern County, California area and have dedicated their lives to Christ. They must have a GPA of 3.0 or higher and be involved in a local church. Two letters of recommendation, SAT scores and high school transcripts are required. Winners must complete one hour of ministry service or volunteer work each week.
Target applicant:
    High school students
Minimum GPA: 3.0
Amount: Varies.
Number of awards: Varies.
Deadline: March 31.
How to apply: Applications are available from Club Zion.

(1199) · Cash Grant Program

Massachusetts Office of Student Financial Assistance
454 Broadway
Suite 200
Revere, MA 02151
Phone: 617-727-9420
Fax: 617-727-0667
Email: osfa@osfa.mass.edu
Website: http://www.osfa.mass.edu
Purpose: To help needy students pay college or university fees and non-state-supported tuition.
Eligibility: Students must be permanent residents of Massachusetts for at least one year before the academic year for which the grant is awarded. Students must also demonstrate financial need, be enrolled in at least three credits per semester in an eligible undergraduate program and not have previously earned a bachelor's degree or higher.

Target applicant:
- High school students
- College students
- Adult students

Minimum GPA: None.
Amount: Varies.
Number of awards: Varies.
Scholarship may be renewable.
Deadline: Varies.
How to apply: Applications are available from your financial aid office.

(1200) · Castle & Cooke George W.Y. Yim Scholarship Fund

Hawaii Community Foundation - Scholarships
1164 Bishop Street, Suite 800
Honolulu, HI 96813
Phone: 888-731-3863
Fax: 808-521-6286
Email: scholarships@hcf-hawaii.org
Website: http://www.hawaiicommunityfoundation.org
Purpose: To support the dependents of Castle and Cooke employees.
Eligibility: Employees must have had at least one year of service with an affiliated company of Castle and Cooke Hawaii. Students must have at least a 3.0 GPA.
Target applicant:
- High school students
- College students
- Adult students

Minimum GPA: 3.0
Amount: Varies.
Number of awards: Varies.
Deadline: March 1.
How to apply: To apply, register online, complete the online application and select the scholarships to which you wish to apply. In addition, mail the supporting materials: printed confirmation page from the online application, personal statement, copy of Student Aid Report (SAR) available at www.fafsa.ed.gov and official transcript.

(1201) · Cayetano Foundation Scholarship

Hawaii Community Foundation - Scholarships
1164 Bishop Street, Suite 800
Honolulu, HI 96813
Phone: 888-731-3863
Fax: 808-521-6286
Email: scholarships@hcf-hawaii.org
Website: http://www.hawaiicommunityfoundation.org
Purpose: To support graduating high school seniors in Hawaii who have faced financial or personal obstacles.
Eligibility: Students must have community service experience, and they must have at least a 3.5 GPA.
Target applicant:
- High school students

Minimum GPA: 3.5
Amount: Varies.
Number of awards: Varies.
Deadline: March 1.
How to apply: To apply, register online, complete the online application and select the scholarships to which you wish to apply. In addition, mail the supporting materials: printed confirmation page from the online application, personal statement, copy of Student Aid Report (SAR)

available at www.fafsa.ed.gov, essay, two letters of recommendation and official transcript.

(1202) · CCNMA Scholarships

California Chicano News Media Association
USC Annenberg School of Journalism
One California Plaza
300 S. Grand Avenue, Suite 3950
Los Angeles, CA 90071-3175
Phone: 213-437-4408
Fax: 213-437-4423
Email: ccmainfo@ccnma.org
Website: http://www.ccnma.org
Purpose: To support Latino students with career goals in journalism.
Eligibility: Applicants must be Latino and either California residents or be attending California schools. While the student's degree does not have to be in journalism, they must demonstrate plans to pursue a career in journalism. An interview and autobiographical essay are required. Awards are based also on financial need, academic achievement and a civic responsibility.
Target applicant:
- High school students
- College students
- Adult students

Minimum GPA: None.
Amount: $500-$2,000.
Number of awards: Varies.
Deadline: April 3.
How to apply: Applications are available online.

(1203) · Central Arizona DX Association Scholarship

American Radio Relay League Foundation
225 Main Street
Newington, CT 06111
Phone: 860-594-0397
Fax: 860-594-0259
Email: foundation@arrl.org
Website: http://www.arrl.org
Purpose: To provide scholarship assistance to amateur radio operators from Arizona.
Eligibility: Applicants must be Arizona residents with a Technician Class or higher Amateur Radio License. They must have a GPA of 3.2 or higher. Graduating high school seniors receive preference over current college students.
Target applicant:
- High school students
- College students
- Adult students

Minimum GPA: 3.2
Amount: $500.
Number of awards: 1.
Deadline: February 1.
How to apply: Applications are available online.

(1204) · CESDA Diversity Scholarship

Colorado Educational Services and Development Association
P.O. Box 40214
Denver, CO 80204
Phone: 303-352-3231
Email: melissa.quinteros@ccd.edu

Website: http://www.cesda.org

Purpose: To provide financial assistance for disadvantaged students.

Eligibility: Applicants must be either first generation college students, members of underrepresented ethnic or racial minorities or show financial need. They must be Colorado residents who are high school seniors at the time of application. Students must have a GPA of 2.8 or higher and enroll in a two- or four-year Colorado college or university in the fall following graduation. They must take at least six credit hours to qualify.

Target applicant:
   High school students

Minimum GPA: 2.8

Amount: $1,000.

Number of awards: Varies.

Deadline: March 1.

How to apply: Applications are available online.

(1205) · CEW Scholarships

Center for the Education of Women
330 E. Liberty
Ann Arbor, MI 48104-2289
Phone: 734-998-7080
Fax: 734-998-6203
Website: http://www.umich.edu/~cew

Purpose: To support women who are returning to college after an interruption.

Eligibility: Applicants must be women who are returning to school after an interruption of at least 48 consecutive months or a total of 50 months excluding interruptions of less than 8 months. Candidates must be working toward a clear educational goal at any University of Michigan campus. Preference is given to women wishing to study in non-traditional fields such as mathematics, physical sciences and engineering.

Target applicant:
   Graduate school students
   Adult students

Minimum GPA: None.

Amount: $1,500-$8,000.

Number of awards: Approximately 38.

Deadline: January 9.

How to apply: Applications are available online.

(1206) · Charles B. Atchison, Jr. Endowment

Epsilon Sigma Alpha Foundation
P.O. Box 270517
Fort Collins, CO 80527
Phone: 970-223-2824
Fax: 970-223-4456
Email: kloyd@knoxy.net
Website: http://www.esaintl.com/esaf

Purpose: To provide financial assistance to Illinois students.

Eligibility: Applicants must major in business or computer programming and may attend any college or university. Selection of applicants is based on character (10 percent), leadership (20 percent), service (10 percent), financial need (30 percent) and scholastic ability (30 percent).

Target applicant:
   High school students
   College students
   Adult students

Minimum GPA: None.

Amount: $600.

Number of awards: 1.

Deadline: February 1.

How to apply: Applications are available online.

(1207) · Charles B. Washington Scholarship

Urban League of Nebraska Inc.
3040 Lake Street
Omaha, NE 68111
Phone: 402-451-1066
Fax: 402-453-1342
Website: http://www.urbanleagueneb.org

Purpose: To provide financial assistance for students with outstanding achievements.

Eligibility: Applicants must be U.S. citizens and Nebraska residents with financial need. They may be undergraduate, graduate or professional school students. A minimum ACT score of 14 is required for high school seniors and a GED score of 45 for those who did not receive a diploma. Undergraduate students must have a GPA of 2.5 or higher, and graduate students must have a GPA of 3.0 or higher. Professional school students must demonstrate satisfactory progress in their studies. Talents, skills, potential and commitment to the community are considered.

Target applicant:
   High school students
   College students
   Graduate school students
   Adult students

Minimum GPA: 2.5 for undergraduate students; 3.0 for graduate students

Amount: Varies.

Number of awards: Varies.

Deadline: March 11.

How to apply: Applications are available from your school's financial aid office.

(1208) · Charles Gallagher Student Financial Assistance Program

Missouri Student Assistance Resource Services (MOSTARS)
Missouri Department of Higher Education
3515 Amazonas Drive
Jefferson City, MO 65109
Phone: 800-473-6757
Fax: 573-751-6635
Website: http://www.dhe.mo.gov

Purpose: To provide need-based grants for Missouri citizens to access Missouri postsecondary education.

Eligibility: Applicants must be U.S. citizens or eligible noncitizens, Missouri residents who are full-time undergraduates at an approved Missouri postsecondary schools and working toward their first baccalaureate degree. Applicants must demonstrate financial need.

Target applicant:
   High school students
   College students
   Adult students

Minimum GPA: None.

Amount: Varies.

Number of awards: Varies.

Scholarship may be renewable.

Deadline: April 1.

How to apply: Complete the Free Application for Federal Student Aid (FAFSA) by April 1 of the upcoming academic year.

(1209) · Charles McDaniel Teacher Scholarship

Georgia Student Finance Commission
2082 East Exchange Place
Tucker, GA 30084
Phone: 800-505-4732
Fax: 770-724-9089
Email: support@gacollege411.org
Website: http://www.gacollege411.org
Purpose: To support students in Georgia pursuing a degree in teaching.
Eligibility: Applicants must be full-time juniors or seniors at a public Georgia college or university. They must be admitted to their school's college or department of education and have a GPA of 3.25 or higher. Applicants must be legal residents of Georgia, have graduated from a Georgia high school, be U.S. citizens or permanent resident aliens, be in compliance with Selective Service requirements and not be in default on student financial aid. Eligible colleges and universities can nominate one student each year.
Target applicant:
  College students
  Adult students
Minimum GPA: 3.25
Amount: $1,000.
Number of awards: 3.
Deadline: July 15.
How to apply: Applications are available online and from college education departments.

(1210) · Charles R. Hemenway Memorial Scholarship

University of Hawaii
Student Services Center Room 413
2600 Campus Road
Honolulu, HI 96822
Phone: 808-956-4642
Email: seed@hawaii.edu
Website: http://www.hawaii.edu/diversity
Purpose: To assist residents of Hawaii with college education expenses.
Eligibility: Applicants must demonstrate financial need and be Hawaii residents. Applicants must also be enrolled at least half-time at any of the campuses of the University of Hawaii. Selection is based on character and "qualities of good citizenship."
Target applicant:
  High school students
  College students
  Adult students
Minimum GPA: 2.0
Amount: $2,000.
Number of awards: Varies.
Scholarship may be renewable.
Deadline: Varies.
How to apply: Contact your financial aid office.

(1211) · Charles W. and Annette Hill Scholarship

American Legion, Department of Kansas
1314 SW Topeka Boulevard
Topeka, KS 66612
Phone: 785-232-9315
Fax: 785-232-1399
Website: http://www.ksamlegion.org
Purpose: To provide financial assistance to needy and worthy children of members of the American Legion.
Eligibility: Applicants must be descendents of an American Legion member with a GPA of at least 3.0. Special consideration will be given to students studying science, engineering or business administration. Applicants must submit three letters of recommendation with only one from a teacher, an essay on "Why I Want to Go to College," a high school transcript, documentation of parent's veteran status and a 1040 income statement. Applicants must maintain a 3.0 GPA in college and verify enrollment at the start of each semester.
Target applicant:
  High school students
  College students
  Adult students
Minimum GPA: 3.0
Amount: $1,000.
Number of awards: 1.
Deadline: February 15.
How to apply: Applications are available online.

(1212) · Charles W. Riley Fire and Emergency Medical Services Tuition Reimbursement Program

Maryland Higher Education Commission
Office of Student Financial Assistance
839 Bestgate Road, Suite 400
Annapolis, MD 21401
Phone: 800-974-1024
Fax: 410-260-3200
Email: osfamail@mhec.state.md.us
Website: http://www.mhec.state.md.us
Purpose: To support Maryland students who are majoring and working in firefighting or emergency medical services fields.
Eligibility: Applicants must be active firefighters, ambulance or rescue squad members living and serving in the state of Maryland. Students must attend a Maryland college majoring in fire service technology or emergency medical technology. They must continue to serve throughout college and for one year after graduating.
Target applicant:
  College students
  Graduate school students
  Adult students
Minimum GPA: None.
Amount: Varies.
Number of awards: Varies.
Scholarship may be renewable.
Deadline: July 1.
How to apply: Applications are available online.

(1213) · Charline E. McCue Memorial Endowment

Epsilon Sigma Alpha Foundation
P.O. Box 270517
Fort Collins, CO 80527
Phone: 970-223-2824
Fax: 970-223-4456
Email: kloyd@knoxy.net
Website: http://www.esaintl.com/esaf
Purpose: To provide financial assistance to those pursuing majors in the arts.
Eligibility: Applicants must be California residents who are majoring in drama, dance or painting at any school. They must have a GPA of 3.0 to 3.5. Selection is based on financial need (50 percent), scholastic

ability (25 percent), character (10 percent), leadership (10 percent) and service (5 percent).

Target applicant:
   High school students
   College students
   Adult students
Minimum GPA: 3.0
Amount: $500.
Number of awards: 1.
Deadline: February 1.
How to apply: Applications are available online.

(1214) · Cheryl A. Ruggiero Scholarship

Rhode Island Society of Certified Public Accountants
45 Royal Little Drive
Providence, RI 02904
Phone: 401-331-5720
Fax: 401-454-5780
Email: rmancini@riscpa.org
Website: http://www.riscpa.org
Purpose: To support female students who are pursuing careers in public accounting.
Eligibility: Students must be residents of the state of Rhode Island, and they must have at least a 3.0 GPA. Applicants must submit a short essay and a letter of recommendation.
Target applicant:
   College students
   Adult students
Minimum GPA: 3.0
Amount: Varies.
Number of awards: Varies.
Deadline: January 15.
How to apply: Applications are available online.

(1215) · Chesapeake Urology Associates Scholarship

Central Scholarship Bureau
1700 Reisterstown Road
Suite 220
Baltimore, MD 21208-2903
Phone: 410-415-5558
Fax: 410-415-5501
Email: info@centralsb.org
Website: http://www.centralsb.org
Purpose: To assist full-time Maryland undergraduate students pursuing a degree in pre-medicine, pre-nursing and ancillary health fields.
Eligibility: Applicants must be U.S. citizens or permanent residents, have a minimum 2.0 GPA and meet specified income requirements. The awards are based on commitment to the medical field, financial need and academic excellence. An application form, budget form, school bill, transcript, Student Aid Report, school financial aid award letter and essay are required.
Target applicant:
   High school students
   College students
   Adult students
Minimum GPA: None.
Amount: $5,000.
Number of awards: 3.
Deadline: May 31.
How to apply: Applications are available online.

(1216) · Chicago Scholars Award

Chicago Scholars Foundation
333 W. Wacker Drive, 33rd Floor
Chicago, IL 60606
Phone: 312-917-6868
Fax: 312-917-7806
Email: chischolars@nuveen.com
Website: http://www.chicagoscholars.org
Purpose: To recognize high school seniors in the Chicago area who have overcome considerable obstacles to succeed in high school and attend college.
Eligibility: One award is presented to one senior from each Chicago high school graduating class. Applicants must be nominated by their high school and be Chicago residents or attend a Chicago high school and have a minimum 3.5 GPA. Applicants' financial need is also a consideration.
Target applicant:
   High school students
Minimum GPA: 3.5
Amount: $1,000.
Number of awards: Varies.
Deadline: Varies.
How to apply: Applicants must be nominated by their high schools.

(1217) · Chicana/Latina Foundation Scholarship

Chicana/Latina Foundation Scholarship Program
1419 Burlingame Avenue, Suite N
Burlingame, CA 94010
Phone: 650-373-1084
Fax: 650-373-1090
Email: info@chicanalatina.org
Website: http://www.chicanalatina.org
Purpose: To assist Latina students in completing their educations.
Eligibility: Applicants must be Chicana/Latina women who have lived in the Northern California counties for at least two years and are attending school at an accredited institution in the same region. Undergraduate applicants must be full-time students who have completed at least 15 semester units and earned a 2.5 GPA. Applicants must demonstrate leadership and community involvement and agree to volunteer at least five years in support of the Chicana/Latina Foundation if they receive the scholarship.
Target applicant:
   College students
   Graduate school students
   Adult students
Minimum GPA: 2.5
Amount: $1,500.
Number of awards: Varies.
Deadline: March 20.
How to apply: Applications are available online.

(1218) · Child Care Provider Scholarship

Maryland Higher Education Commission
Office of Student Financial Assistance
839 Bestgate Road, Suite 400
Annapolis, MD 21401
Phone: 800-974-1024
Fax: 410-260-3200
Email: osfamail@mhec.state.md.us
Website: http://www.mhec.state.md.us

Purpose: To encourage and support students to enter the field of childhood development or early childhood education.

Eligibility: Applicants and their parents must be legal residents of the state of Maryland. Applicants must enroll at a two- or four-year Maryland college or university as a full-time or part-time degree-seeking undergraduate. Applicants must enter a child development program or an early childhood education program. Applicants must also sign a promissory note agreeing to provide child care services in Maryland at the rate of one year for each year of the award.

Target applicant:
  High school students
  College students
  Adult students

Minimum GPA: None.

Amount: $1,000-$2,000.

Number of awards: Varies.

Scholarship may be renewable.

Deadline: June 15.

How to apply: Complete and file a Child Care Provider Scholarship application.

(1219) · Children and Youth Scholarships

American Legion, Department of Maine
21 College Avenue
Waterville, ME 04901
Phone: 207-873-3229
Email: legionme@me.acadia.net
Website: http://www.mainelegion.org

Purpose: To provide financial support to Maine students.

Eligibility: Applicants must be high school seniors or college students attending or planning to attend an accredited college or vocational school. Applicants must also demonstrate financial need and include two letters of recommendation and a personal statement.

Target applicant:
  High school students
  College students
  Adult students

Minimum GPA: None.

Amount: $500.

Number of awards: 7.

Deadline: May 1.

How to apply: Applications are available online.

(1220) · Chiropractic Education Assistance Scholarship

Oklahoma State Regents for Higher Education
655 Research Parkway, Suite 200
Oklahoma City, OK 73104
Phone: 800-858-1840
Fax: 405-225-9230
Email: studentinfo@osrhe.edu
Website: http://www.okhighered.org

Purpose: To provide financial assistance to Oklahoma students who are studying chiropractic at out-of-state institutions.

Eligibility: Applicants must have been Oklahoma residents for at least five years and be enrolled in or accepted to an accredited chiropractic school. They must maintain a minimum GPA of 3.0.

Target applicant:
  High school students
  College students

Graduate school students
  Adult students

Minimum GPA: 3.0.

Amount: Up to $6,000.

Number of awards: Varies.

Scholarship may be renewable.

Deadline: Varies.

How to apply: Applications are available from your institution.

(1221) · Chittenden Bank Scholarship

Vermont Student Assistance Corporation
10 E. Allen Street
P.O. Box 2000
Winooski, VT 05404
Phone: 888-253-4819
Fax: 802-654-3765
Email: info@vsac.org
Website: http://www.vsac.org

Purpose: To provide financial assistance to Vermont students.

Eligibility: Applicants must be high school or college students attending or planning to attend an accredited Vermont college or university that is approved for Title IV funding. They must demonstrate academic achievement, financial need and school or community involvement.

Target applicant:
  High school students
  College students
  Adult students

Minimum GPA: None.

Amount: $2,500.

Number of awards: 2.

Deadline: March 1.

How to apply: Applications are available online.

(1222) · Christa McAuliffe Scholarship

Tennessee Student Assistance Corporation
404 James Robertson Parkway
Suite 1510, Parkway Towers
Nashville, TN 37243
Phone: 800-342-1663
Fax: 615-741-6101
Email: tsac.aidinfo@state.tn.us
Website: http://www.collegepaystn.com

Purpose: To support Tennessee students who are pursuing careers in teaching.

Eligibility: Applicants must be in the second semester of their junior year in a teaching program at a Tennessee college, and they must be enrolled full-time. Students must have at least a 3.5 GPA and an SAT or ACT score that is at least as high as the national average. They must not have any defaulted state or federal student loans. Recipients must agree to teach in a Tennessee elementary or secondary school for a period of time upon graduation.

Target applicant:
  College students
  Adult students

Minimum GPA: 3.5

Amount: Up to $1000.

Number of awards: Varies.

Deadline: April 1.

How to apply: Applications are available online.

(1223) · Christian A. Herter Memorial Scholarship Program

Massachusetts Office of Student Financial Assistance
454 Broadway
Suite 200
Revere, MA 02151
Phone: 617-727-9420
Fax: 617-727-0667
Email: osfa@osfa.mass.edu
Website: http://www.osfa.mass.edu
Purpose: To provide educational opportunities to Massachusetts students who demonstrate academic promise and a desire to attend post-secondary institutions.
Eligibility: Applicants must be enrolled in a public or private secondary school in the Commonwealth of Massachusetts and be legal residents of the state. Applicants must have a cumulative grade point average of 2.5 and exhibit difficult personal circumstances, high financial need and strong academic promise to continue education beyond the secondary level.
Target applicant:
    High school students
Minimum GPA: None.
Amount: Varies.
Number of awards: Varies.
Scholarship may be renewable.
Deadline: April 1.
How to apply: Applications are available online.

(1224) · Churchill Family Scholarship

Maine Community Foundation
245 Main Street
Ellsworth, ME 04605
Phone: 207-667-9735
Fax: 207-667-0447
Email: jwarren@mainecf.org
Website: http://www.mainecf.org
Purpose: To support students in vocal music education or performance.
Eligibility: Students must be female high school seniors in Maine and planning to major in vocal music education or performance.
Target applicant:
    High school students
Minimum GPA: None.
Amount: Varies.
Number of awards: Varies.
Deadline: April 30.
How to apply: Applications are available in January on the Maine Community Foundation website or by contacting Musica de Filia.

(1225) · Cindy Kolb Memorial Scholarship

California Association for Postsecondary Education and Disability
71423 Biskra Road
Rancho Mirage, CA 92270
Phone: 909-537-5238
Fax: 760-340-5275
Email: bjaworski@csub.edu
Website: http://www.caped.net
Purpose: To provide financial assistance for students with disabilities.
Eligibility: Applicants must have a verifiable disability. They must be students at a four-year institution of higher learning in California with a GPA of at least 2.5 if an undergraduate or 3.0 if a graduate student. A letter of recommendation, a letter of application and documentation of the student's disability is required.
Target applicant:
    College students
    Graduate school students
    Adult students
Minimum GPA: 2.5
Amount: $1,000.
Number of awards: 1.
Deadline: September 19.
How to apply: Applications are available online.

(1226) · City of Fountains - Missouri

Epsilon Sigma Alpha Foundation
P.O. Box 270517
Fort Collins, CO 80527
Phone: 970-223-2824
Fax: 970-223-4456
Email: kloyd@knoxy.net
Website: http://www.esaintl.com/esaf
Purpose: To provide financial assistance for Missouri students.
Eligibility: Applicants may study any major at any school. Selection is based on service (35 percent), financial need (35 percent), character (10 percent), leadership (10 percent) and scholastic ability (10 percent).
Target applicant:
    High school students
    College students
    Adult students
Minimum GPA: None.
Amount: $500.
Number of awards: 1.
Deadline: February 1.
How to apply: Applications are available online.

(1227) · Clanseer and Anna Johnson Scholarships

Community Foundation of New Jersey
P.O. Box 338
Morristown, NJ 07963-0338
Phone: 973-267-5533
Fax: 973-267-2903
Email: fkrueger@cfnj.org
Website: http://www.cfnj.org
Purpose: To provide education assistance for disadvantaged African American students.
Eligibility: Applicants must have been born in the United States and be New Jersey residents. They must have an A or B average in science and math-related subjects and maintain above average grades overall. Financial need and merit are considered. Scholarship winners are asked to perform at least ten hours of community service each week for a year following graduation.
Target applicant:
    High school students
Minimum GPA: None.
Amount: $6,500.
Number of awards: 4.
Deadline: April 21.
How to apply: Applications are available online.

(1228) · Clem Judd, Jr., Memorial Scholarship

Hawaii Hotel and Lodging Association
2250 Kalakaua Avenue
Suite 404-4
Honolulu, HI 96815
Website: http://www.hawaiihotels.org
Purpose: To help Hawaiian residents majoring in hotel management.
Eligibility: Applicants must have a minimum 3.0 GPA, be able to prove Hawaiian ancestry and be enrolled full-time at a U.S. university or college.
Target applicant:
  High school students
  College students
  Adult students
Minimum GPA: 3.0
Amount: $2,500.
Number of awards: 1.
Deadline: July 1.
How to apply: Applications are available by written request beginning February 1.

(1229) · Collaborative Teachers Tuition Waiver

Massachusetts Office of Student Financial Assistance
454 Broadway
Suite 200
Revere, MA 02151
Phone: 617-727-9420
Fax: 617-727-0667
Email: osfa@osfa.mass.edu
Website: http://www.osfa.mass.edu
Purpose: To provide graduate school tuition waivers for Massachusetts teachers who become student teacher mentors.
Eligibility: Applicants must be public school teachers living and working in the state of Massachusetts. They must also agree to mentor a student teacher from a state college or university in their own classroom, and they must be planning to attend graduate school at one of the nine campuses of Massachusetts State College or the University of Massachusetts.
Target applicant:
  Graduate school students
  Adult students
Minimum GPA: None.
Amount: Varies.
Number of awards: Varies.
Scholarship may be renewable.
Deadline: Varies.
How to apply: Applications are available at college financial aid offices.

(1230) · College Access Program

Kentucky Higher Education Assistance Authority
P.O. Box 798
Frankfort, KY 40602
Phone: 800-928-8926
Email: blane@kheaa.com
Website: http://www.kheaa.com
Purpose: To aid Kentucky students with financial need.
Eligibility: Applicants must be Kentucky residents, be enrolled at least half-time in undergraduate academic programs and have an Expected Family Contribution (EFC) based on the FAFSA of lower than approximately $3,850.

Target applicant:
  College students
  Adult students
Minimum GPA: None.
Amount: $1,400.
Number of awards: Varies.
Deadline: Varies.
How to apply: Complete the Free Application for Federal Student Aid (FAFSA).

(1231) · College Affordability Grant

New Mexico Higher Education Department
1068 Cerrillos Road
Santa Fe, NM 87505
Phone: 800-279-9777
Fax: 505-476-6511
Email: heather.romero@state.nm.us
Website: http://hed.state.nm.us
Purpose: To support New Mexico residents who are attending public colleges in the state.
Eligibility: Applicants must demonstrate financial need, and they cannot have any other state grants or scholarships. Students must be enrolled in at least six credit hours per semester.
Target applicant:
  High school students
  College students
  Adult students
Minimum GPA: None.
Amount: Up to $1000.
Number of awards: Varies.
Scholarship may be renewable.
Deadline: Varies.
How to apply: Applications are available at college financial aid offices.

(1232) · College Scholarship Assistance Program

State Council of Higher Education for Virginia
101 N. 14th Street
James Monroe Building
Richmond, VA 23219
Phone: 804-225-2600
Fax: 804-225-2604
Email: communications@schev.edu
Website: http://www.schev.edu
Purpose: To assist Virginia students with extreme financial need.
Eligibility: Applicants must be U.S. citizens or eligible noncitizens, enrolled or planning to enroll at least half-time in a Virginia public or eligible private nonprofit two- or four-year college or university and be residents of Virginia.
Target applicant:
  High school students
  College students
  Adult students
Minimum GPA: None.
Amount: $400-$5,000.
Number of awards: Varies.
Deadline: Varies.
How to apply: Complete the Free Application for Federal Student Aid (FAFSA).

(1233) · CollegeBoundfund Academic Promise Scholarship

Rhode Island Higher Education Assistance Authority
560 Jefferson Boulevard
Warwick, RI 02886
Phone: 401-736-1100
Fax: 401-732-3541
Email: scholarships@riheaa.org
Website: http://www.riheaa.org
Purpose: To assist outstanding Rhode Island high school students.
Eligibility: Applicants must be graduating Rhode Island high school seniors who plan to attend a postsecondary institution full-time and demonstrate academic achievement and financial need.
Target applicant:
   High school students
Minimum GPA: None.
Amount: Up to $10,000.
Number of awards: Varies.
Scholarship may be renewable.
Deadline: March 1.
How to apply: Complete the Free Application for Federal Student Aid (FAFSA).

(1234) · Collegiate Scholarship

Texas 4-H Youth Development Foundation
7607 Eastmark Drive, Suite 101
College Station, TX 77840
Phone: 979-845-1213
Fax: 979-845-6495
Email: texas4hfoundation@ag.tamu.edu
Website: http://www.texas4hfoundation.org
Purpose: To support undergraduate students in Texas.
Eligibility: Applicants must have actively participated in a 4-H program during their high school years. They must be currently enrolled full-time with at least a 2.7 GPA. Recipients must have completed at least 30 credit hours by the time scholarship payments begin. Awards are based on financial need, academic achievement and 4-H experience.
Target applicant:
   College students
   Adult students
Minimum GPA: 2.7
Amount: $1,500-$2,000.
Number of awards: Varies.
Deadline: March 1.
How to apply: Applications are available online.

(1235) · Colorado Business and Professional Women Education Foundation

Colorado Federation of Business and Professional Women
P.O. Box 1189
Boulder, CO 80306-1189
Phone: 303-443-2573
Email: office@cbpwef.org
Website: http://www.cbpwef.org/Scholarships.aspx
Purpose: To provide education assistance for adult women.
Eligibility: Applicants must be women who are 25 years of age or older, United States citizens and Colorado residents for at least 12 months prior to the application deadline. They must be enrolled in or attending an accredited Colorado college, university or vocational training institution. Deadlines for application are May 31 for the fall semester and October 31 for the spring semester.
Target applicant:
   College students
   Adult students
Minimum GPA: None.
Amount: Varies.
Number of awards: Varies.
Deadline: May 31 and October 31.
How to apply: Applications are available online.

(1236) · Colorado Masons Benevolent Fund Scholarships

Colorado Masons Benevolent Fund Association
1130 Panorama Drive
Colorado Springs, CO 80904
Email: scholarships@coloradomasons.org
Website: http://www.coloradomasons.org
Purpose: To help Colorado students.
Eligibility: Applicants must be graduating seniors from a Colorado public high school planning to attend a Colorado postsecondary institution. Selection is based on leadership, maturity, need and scholastic ability without reference to race, creed, color, sex or Masonic relationship.
Target applicant:
   High school students
Minimum GPA: None.
Amount: $7,000.
Number of awards: Varies.
Scholarship may be renewable.
Deadline: March 7.
How to apply: Contact your high school counselor.

(1237) · Colorado Oratorical Contest

American Legion, Department of Colorado
7465 E. 1st Avenue, Suite D
Denver, CO 80230
Phone: 303-366-5201
Fax: 303-366-7618
Email: garylbarnett@comcast.net
Website: http://www.coloradolegion.org
Purpose: To enhance high school students' experience with and understanding of the U.S. Constitution. The contest will help develop students' leadership skills and civic appreciation, as well as the ability to deliver thoughtful, insightful orations regarding U.S. citizenship and its inherent responsibilities.
Eligibility: Applicants must be high school students under the age of 20 who are U.S. citizens or legal residents and residents of the state. Students first give an oration within their state and winners compete at the national level. The oration must be related to the Constitution of the United States focusing on the duties and obligations citizens have to the government. It must be in English and be between eight and ten minutes. There is also an assigned topic which is posted on the website, and it should be between three and five minutes.
Target applicant:
   Junior high students or younger
   High school students
Minimum GPA: None.
Amount: Up to $4,000.
Number of awards: Varies.
Deadline: March 10.
How to apply: Applications are available online.

(1238) · Colorado Student Aid Program

Colorado Commission on Higher Education
1380 Lawrence Street
Suite 1200
Denver, CO 80204
Phone: 303-866-2723
Fax: 303-866-4266
Email: cche@state.co.us
Website: http://www.state.co.us/cche
Purpose: To assist Colorado student residents.
Eligibility: Applicants must be Colorado residents who plan to enroll or are enrolled in eligible programs at eligible Colorado postsecondary institutions. Applicants must make satisfactory academic progress and have not defaulted in educational loans or grants. Awards are need-based and merit-based and are made by institutions to students.
Target applicant:
    High school students
    College students
    Adult students
Minimum GPA: None.
Amount: Varies.
Number of awards: Varies.
Deadline: Varies.
How to apply: Contact your financial aid office.

(1239) · Colorado Undergraduate Merit Scholarships

Colorado Commission on Higher Education
1380 Lawrence Street
Suite 1200
Denver, CO 80204
Phone: 303-866-2723
Fax: 303-866-4266
Email: cche@state.co.us
Website: http://www.state.co.us/cche
Purpose: To help students attending Colorado state-supported institutions at the undergraduate level.
Eligibility: Applicants must be Colorado residents, demonstrate academic achievement and have not defaulted on any student loans. A transcript, test scores and application form are required. The award may be used for tuition, fees, room, board, books, supplies or other expenses related to attendance at participating Colorado institutions. A list of these institutions is available on the website.
Target applicant:
    High school students
    College students
    Adult students
Minimum GPA: 3.0
Amount: Varies.
Number of awards: Varies.
Scholarship may be renewable.
Deadline: Varies.
How to apply: Contact the financial aid office at participating institutions.

(1240) · Commonwealth "Good Citizen" Scholarships

Association of Independent Colleges and Universities of Pennsylvania
101 N. Front Street
Harrisburg, PA 17101
Phone: 717-232-8649
Fax: 717-233-8574
Email: duck@aicup.org
Website: http://www.aicup.org
Purpose: To provide financial assistance for students who have demonstrated good citizenship.
Eligibility: Applicants must have demonstrated a commitment to community service and creativity in shaping volunteer activities. They must be full-time current or upcoming undergraduate students at an AICUP member college or university. A two-page essay is required.
Target applicant:
    High school students
    College students
    Adult students
Minimum GPA: None.
Amount: $1,000.
Number of awards: 6.
Deadline: April 15.
How to apply: Applications are available from financial aid offices of qualifying institutions.

(1241) · Community Banker Association of Illinois Annual Scholarship Program

Community Banker Association of Illinois
901 Community Drive
Springfield, IL 62703-5184
Phone: 800-736-2224
Email: bobbiw@cbai.com
Website: http://www.cbai.com
Purpose: To assist Illinois high school seniors.
Eligibility: Applicants must write essays and be sponsored by a participating CBAI member bank. There is an essay topic related to community banking, and the short essays are judged on understanding of community banking philosophy, accurate information, clear and concise sentences, logical organization, proper grammar, correct punctuation and spelling and conclusion/summary.
Target applicant:
    High school students
Minimum GPA: None.
Amount: $4,000.
Number of awards: 13.
Deadline: February 13.
How to apply: A list of participating banks and more information is available by email.

(1242) · Community College Grant and Loan Program

College Foundation of North Carolina
P.O. Box 41966
Raleigh, NC 27629-1966
Phone: 866-234-6400
Fax: 919-821-3139
Email: programinformation@cfnc.org
Website: http://www.cfnc.org
Purpose: To assist North Carolina community college students.
Eligibility: Applicants must be North Carolina residents, demonstrate financial need and attend North Carolina community colleges for at least six credit hours per semester. Eligibility is based on the same criteria as for the Federal Pell Grants.
Target applicant:
    College students
    Adult students

Minimum GPA: None.
Amount: Varies.
Number of awards: Varies.
Deadline: Varies.
How to apply: Complete the Free Application for Federal Student Aid (FAFSA).

(1243) · Community Scholarship Fund

Hawaii Community Foundation - Scholarships
1164 Bishop Street, Suite 800
Honolulu, HI 96813
Phone: 888-731-3863
Fax: 808-521-6286
Email: scholarships@hcf-hawaii.org
Website: http://www.hawaiicommunityfoundation.org
Purpose: To assist college and graduate students majoring in arts, education, humanities or social science.
Eligibility: Applicants must demonstrate accomplishment, motivation, initiative, vision and intention to work in Hawaii and major in the arts, architecture, education, humanities or social science.
Target applicant:
   High school students
   College students
   Graduate school students
   Adult students
Minimum GPA: None.
Amount: Varies.
Number of awards: Varies.
Deadline: March 1.
How to apply: To apply, register online, complete the online application and select the scholarships to which you wish to apply. In addition, mail the supporting materials: printed confirmation page from the online application, personal statement, copy of Student Aid Report (SAR) available at www.fafsa.ed.gov and official transcript.

(1244) · Competitive Scholarships

New Mexico Higher Education Department
1068 Cerrillos Road
Santa Fe, NM 87505
Phone: 800-279-9777
Fax: 505-476-6511
Email: heather.romero@state.nm.us
Website: http://hed.state.nm.us
Purpose: To provide a financial incentive for exceptional out-of-state students to attend college in New Mexico.
Eligibility: Applicants must be non-residents of the state of New Mexico, and they must be willing to enroll full-time in a public four-year university in New Mexico. Students applying to Eastern New Mexico University, New Mexico Highlands University, New Mexico Institute of Mining and Technology or Western New Mexico University must have one of the following combinations: a GPA of at least 3.0 and an ACT score of at least 23 or a GPA of at least 3.5 and an ACT of at least 20. Students applying to the University of New Mexico or New Mexico State University must have either an ACT score of 26 and a GPA of 3.0 or an ACT score of 23 and a GPA of 3.5.
Target applicant:
   High school students
   College students
   Adult students
Minimum GPA: 3.0
Amount: $100.

Number of awards: Varies.
Scholarship may be renewable.
Deadline: Varies.
How to apply: Applications are available at college financial aid offices.

(1245) · Connecticut Aid for Public College Students

Connecticut Department of Higher Education
61 Woodland Street
Hartford, CT 06105-2326
Phone: 860-947-1855
Fax: 860-947-1838
Email: byrd@ctdhe.org
Website: http://www.ctdhe.org
Purpose: To assist Connecticut student residents.
Eligibility: Applicants must be Connecticut residents attending a public Connecticut college or university. The award is based on financial need.
Target applicant:
   High school students
   College students
   Adult students
Minimum GPA: None.
Amount: Up to amount of unmet financial need.
Number of awards: Varies.
Deadline: Varies.
How to apply: Apply through your college financial aid office.

(1246) · Connecticut Independent College Student Grant Program

Connecticut Department of Higher Education
61 Woodland Street
Hartford, CT 06105-2326
Phone: 860-947-1855
Fax: 860-947-1838
Email: byrd@ctdhe.org
Website: http://www.ctdhe.org
Purpose: To assist Connecticut student residents.
Eligibility: Applicants must be Connecticut residents attending an independent Connecticut college or university. Awards are based on financial need.
Target applicant:
   High school students
   College students
   Adult students
Minimum GPA: None.
Amount: Up to $8,500.
Number of awards: Varies.
Deadline: Varies.
How to apply: Apply through your college financial aid office.

(1247) · Continuing/Re-entry Students Scholarship

American Legion Auxiliary, Department of California
401 Van Ness Avenue
Room 113
San Francisco, CA 94102
Phone: 415-861-5092
Fax: 415-861-8365
Email: calegionaux@calegionaux.org
Website: http://www.calegionaux.org

The Ultimate Scholarship Book 2010
Scholarship Directory (State of Residence)

Purpose: To provide support to children of U.S. Armed Forces members.
Eligibility: One of applicant's parents must have served in the U.S. Armed Forces during an eligible period. Applicants must be California residents planning to attend a California college or university and must be continuing or re-entry college students.
Target applicant:
    College students
    Adult students
Minimum GPA: None.
Amount: $1,000.
Number of awards: 2.
Deadline: March 15.
How to apply: Applications are available online.

(1248) · Cora Aguda Manayan Fund

Hawaii Community Foundation - Scholarships
1164 Bishop Street, Suite 800
Honolulu, HI 96813
Phone: 888-731-3863
Fax: 808-521-6286
Email: scholarships@hcf-hawaii.org
Website: http://www.hawaiicommunityfoundation.org
Purpose: To support Hawaii students of Filipino ancestry who are dedicated to helping others.
Eligibility: Students must be majoring in a health-related field. Preference may be given to students who are attending school in Hawaii.
Target applicant:
    High school students
    College students
    Adult students
Minimum GPA: None.
Amount: Varies.
Number of awards: Varies.
Deadline: March 1.
How to apply: To apply, register online, complete the online application and select the scholarships to which you wish to apply. In addition, mail the supporting materials: printed confirmation page from the online application, personal statement, copy of Student Aid Report (SAR) available at www.fafsa.ed.gov and official transcript.

(1249) · Cora E. and Royal L. Scott Family Endowment

Epsilon Sigma Alpha Foundation
P.O. Box 270517
Fort Collins, CO 80527
Phone: 970-223-2824
Fax: 970-223-4456
Email: kloyd@knoxy.net
Website: http://www.esaintl.com/esaf
Purpose: To provide financial assistance for South Dakota residents.
Eligibility: Applicants may purse any major at any South Dakota college or university. Selection is based on character (25 percent), leadership (25 percent), service (20 percent), financial need (15 percent) and scholastic ability (15 percent).
Target applicant:
    High school students
    College students
    Adult students
Minimum GPA: None.
Amount: $750.
Number of awards: 1.

Deadline: February 1.
How to apply: Applications are available online.

(1250) · Costco Wholesale Scholarships

Independent Colleges of Washington
600 Stewart Street, Suite 600
Seattle, WA 98101
Phone: 206-623-4494
Fax: 206-625-9621
Email: info@icwashington.org
Website: http://www.icwashington.org
Purpose: To assist minority students with financial need who are attending an independent college of Washington.
Eligibility: Applicants must demonstrate financial need and be a member of an underrepresented minority population. Students at Pacific Lutheran University, Seattle Pacific University, St. Martin's University, University of Puget Sound, Walla Walla University, Whitman College and Whitworth University are eligible.
Target applicant:
    College students
    Adult students
Minimum GPA: None.
Amount: Varies.
Number of awards: Varies.
Deadline: Varies.
How to apply: No application is necessary. Each college or university selects recipients from eligible students.

(1251) · Courageous Heart Scholarship

Texas 4-H Youth Development Foundation
7607 Eastmark Drive, Suite 101
College Station, TX 77840
Phone: 979-845-1213
Fax: 979-845-6495
Email: texas4hfoundation@ag.tamu.edu
Website: http://www.texas4hfoundation.org
Purpose: To support Texas high school students who have overcome serious obstacles related to health, family or education.
Eligibility: Applicants must have actively participated in a 4-H program for at least part of the year. They must have formally applied to a Texas college or university, and they must meet all requirements for admission. Students must provide documentation of the obstacles they have faced.
Target applicant:
    High school students
Minimum GPA: None.
Amount: $1,500-$15,000.
Number of awards: Varies.
Deadline: February 15.
How to apply: Applications are available online.

(1252) · Critical Needs Teacher Program

Mississippi Office of Student Financial Aid
3825 Ridgewood Road
Jackson, MS 39211
Phone: 800-327-2980
Fax: 601-432-6527
Email: sfa@ihl.state.ms.us
Website: http://www.ihl.state.ms.us
Purpose: To increase the supply of teachers for public schools in Mississippi.

354

Eligibility: Applicants must be enrolled as full-time students in programs leading to an 'A' level teaching license and must have a college GPA of 2.5 or higher. Applicants must be admitted to an eligible Mississippi institution at the time of application. Applicants must also agree to the service obligation, which calls for one year of service in a Mississippi public school district located in a critical teacher shortage area for each year the scholarship is received.

Target applicant:
   College students
   Graduate school students
   Adult students
Minimum GPA: None.
Amount: Full tuition.
Number of awards: Varies.
Scholarship may be renewable.
Deadline: March 31.
How to apply: Contact the Mississippi Office of Student Financial Aid for an application.

(1253) · Critical Teacher Shortage Loan Forgiveness Program

Florida Department of Education
Office of Student Financial Assistance
1940 N. Monroe Street
Suite 70
Tallahassee, FL 32303-4759
Phone: 888-827-2004
Fax: 850-245-9667
Email: osfa@fldoe.org
Website: http://www.floridastudentfinancialaid.org
Purpose: To help Florida public school teachers with loans.
Eligibility: Applicants should be teaching in the critical shortage area full-time at least 90 days of the school year under contract at a publicly funded Florida school, and they should have valid Florida teacher's certificates (temporary or professional) or Florida Department of Health licenses (temporary or permanent) in the same critical shortage area as teaching. Applicants must apply by the end of the first year of having both the critical shortage position and the critical shortage certificate or license. This program helps repay undergraduate and graduate educational loans that led to certification in a critical teacher shortage subject area, and the loans must have paid for courses before becoming a certified teacher. Applicants should submit applications and transcripts. A list of critical teacher shortage areas is listed online.

Target applicant:
   College students
   Graduate school students
   Adult students
Minimum GPA: None.
Amount: Varies.
Number of awards: Varies.
Scholarship may be renewable.
Deadline: July 15.
How to apply: Applications are available online.

(1254) · Critical Teacher Shortage Tuition Reimbursement Program

Florida Department of Education
Office of Student Financial Assistance
1940 N. Monroe Street
Suite 70
Tallahassee, FL 32303-4759
Phone: 888-827-2004

Fax: 850-245-9667
Email: osfa@fldoe.org
Website: http://www.floridastudentfinancialaid.org
Purpose: To help Florida full-time publicly-funded school employees get teacher's certification at a grade level and in a subject area designated as a critical teacher shortage subject area.
Eligibility: Applicants must have valid Florida Teacher's Certificates (temporary or professional) or Florida Department of Health Licenses (temporary or permanent) and be enrolled in undergraduate or graduate courses.
Target applicant:
   College students
   Graduate school students
   Adult students
Minimum GPA: 3.0
Amount: Varies.
Number of awards: Varies.
Deadline: September 15.
How to apply: Applications are available online.

(1255) · Crumley and Associates - Crib to College Scholarship

Crumley and Associates
Attn.: Stephen M. Keaney, Community Relations and Business Development Manager
2400 Freeman Mill Road
Suite 300
Greensboro, NC 27406
Email: smkeaney@crumleyandassociates.com
Website: http://www.crumleyandassociates.com
Purpose: To help North Carolina high school seniors who have performed community service.
Eligibility: Applicants must plan to attend four-year colleges or universities. Transcripts, three recommendation letters, applications and essays are required. Winners also receive laptop computers. No phone calls, please.
Target applicant:
   High school students
Minimum GPA: 3.0
Amount: $1,000.
Number of awards: 5.
Deadline: March 15.
How to apply: Applications are available online.

(1256) · CTA César E. Chávez Memorial Education Awards Program

California Teachers Association (CTA)
CTA Human Rights Department
P.O. Box 921
Burlingame, CA 94011-0921
Phone: 650-697-1400
Fax: 650-552-5001
Website: http://www.cta.org
Purpose: To honor César Chávez by rewarding students and teachers who follow his vision and guiding principles.
Eligibility: A student or group of up to five students must submit an essay or visual piece under the supervision of a teacher or professor who is a member of the CTA. Students may be in kindergarten through high school or in community college. All works must focus on topics such as non-violence and their relationship to Chávez's legacy. Visit the

website for a complete list of topics and specific essay and visual arts submission requirements.

Target applicant:
Junior high students or younger
High school students
College students
Adult students

Minimum GPA: None.
Amount: Varies.
Number of awards: Varies.
Deadline: March 24.
How to apply: Applications are available online.

(1257) · DC Tuition Assistance Grant Program

Government of the District of Columbia
DC Tuition Assistance Grant Program
441 4th Street NW, Suite 350 North
Washington, DC 20001
Phone: 877-485-6751
Website: http://www.tuitiongrant.washingtondc.gov
Purpose: To provide financial assistance to students in the District of Columbia who wish to attend either a public university in a different state or a historically Black college or university.
Eligibility: Applicants must be residents who have lived in the District of Columbia for at least 12 months prior to the beginning of their freshman year of college. Applicants must also either plan to or be currently enrolled at least half-time in an undergraduate or certificate program.
Target applicant:
High school students
College students

Minimum GPA: None.
Amount: Up to $10,000.
Number of awards: Varies.
Scholarship may be renewable.
Deadline: June 30.
How to apply: Applications are available online.

(1258) · Dallas Morning News Annual Teenage Citizenship Tribute

Dallas Morning News
TACT/Community Services
P.O. Box 655237
Dallas, TX 75265
Phone: 214-977-7256
Website: http://tact.dallasnews.com
Purpose: To recognize Dallas-area students for exemplary performance in school and the community.
Eligibility: Applicants must be high school seniors from Collin, Dallas, Denton, Ellis, Hunt, Kaufman, Rockwell, Parker or Tarrant counties. Applicants are individually interviewed by judges and evaluated in terms of academics, extracurricular activities, leadership skills, volunteer activities, community involvement and commitment.
Target applicant:
High school students

Minimum GPA: None.
Amount: $500-$2,000.
Number of awards: 20.
Scholarship may be renewable.
Deadline: February 13.
How to apply: Applications are available online.

(1259) · Dana Christmas Scholarship for Heroism

New Jersey Higher Education Student Assistance Authority
P.O. Box 540
Trenton, NJ 08625
Phone: 800-792-8670
Email: clientservices@hesaa.org
Website: http://www.hesaa.org
Purpose: To support New Jersey students who have carried out heroic acts.
Eligibility: Applicants must have been 21 years old or younger and residents of the state of New Jersey during the time of their heroic act.
Target applicant:
Junior high students or younger
High school students
College students
Adult students

Minimum GPA: None.
Amount: $10,000.
Number of awards: Up to 5.
Deadline: October 12.
How to apply: Applications are available online.

(1260) · Daniel Cardillo Charitable Fund

Maine Community Foundation
245 Main Street
Ellsworth, ME 04605
Phone: 207-667-9735
Fax: 207-667-0447
Email: jwarren@mainecf.org
Website: http://www.mainecf.org
Purpose: To provide financial support for young people to pursue their extracurricular interests.
Eligibility: Students must be passionately committed to an activity outside of school, and they must show financial need for further pursuit of that activity. Applicants should also be able to show that they care deeply about other people.
Target applicant:
High school students

Minimum GPA: None.
Amount: Varies.
Number of awards: Varies.
Deadline: May 1.
How to apply: Applications are available online.

(1261) · Daniel E. Lambert Memorial Scholarship

American Legion, Department of Maine
21 College Avenue
Waterville, ME 04901
Phone: 207-873-3229
Email: legionme@me.acadia.net
Website: http://www.mainelegion.org
Purpose: To support the descendents of veterans who demonstrate financial need and who are residents of Maine.
Eligibility: Applicants must be enrolled in an accredited college or vocational technical school and be U.S. citizens. A parent or grandparent must be a veteran, verified by a copy of military discharge papers with the application. Applicants must have good character and believe in the American way of life.
Target applicant:
College students
Adult students

Minimum GPA: None.
Amount: $1,000.
Number of awards: Up to 2.
Deadline: May 1.
How to apply: Applications are available online.

(1262) · David M. Irwin Friend of Higher Education Award

Independent Colleges of Washington
600 Stewart Street, Suite 600
Seattle, WA 98101
Phone: 206-623-4494
Fax: 206-625-9621
Email: info@icwashington.org
Website: http://www.icwashington.org
Purpose: To assist promising students in attending an independent college of Washington.
Eligibility: Applicants must be juniors or seniors in college. Preference is given to those with a GPA between 2.5 and 3.0. Students attending Gonzaga University, Heritage University, Pacific Lutheran University, Saint Martin's University, Seattle Pacific University, Seattle University, University of Puget Sound, Walla Walla University, Whitman College or Whitworth University are eligible.
Target applicant:
    College students
    Adult students
Minimum GPA: None.
Amount: Up to $3,000.
Number of awards: Varies.
Deadline: March 14.
How to apply: Applications are available online or from your school's financial aid office.

(1263) · David W. Misek, N8NPX Memorial Scholarship

American Radio Relay League Foundation
225 Main Street
Newington, CT 06111
Phone: 860-594-0397
Fax: 860-594-0259
Email: foundation@arrl.org
Website: http://www.arrl.org
Purpose: To provide financial assistance to amateur radio operators from Ohio.
Eligibility: Applicants must hold a Technician Class or higher Amateur Radio License and attend or plan to attend a four-year college or university. They must be current residents of Greene, Montgomery, Champaign, Darke, Preble, Miami, Clark, Butler or Warren County, Ohio.
Target applicant:
    High school students
    College students
    Adult students
Minimum GPA: None.
Amount: $1,500.
Number of awards: Up to 3.
Deadline: February 1.
How to apply: Applications are available online.

(1264) · Deborah Humphrey Scholarship

Epsilon Sigma Alpha Foundation
P.O. Box 270517
Fort Collins, CO 80527
Phone: 970-223-2824
Fax: 970-223-4456
Email: kloyd@knoxy.net
Website: http://www.esaintl.com/esaf
Purpose: To provide financial assistance for New Mexico residents.
Eligibility: Applicants must attend a college or university in New Mexico. They may major in any field. Financial need is required. Selection is based on character (10 percent), leadership (10 percent), service (5 percent), scholastic ability (25 percent) and financial need (50 percent).
Target applicant:
    High school students
    College students
    Adult students
Minimum GPA: None.
Amount: $1,000.
Number of awards: 1.
Deadline: February 1.
How to apply: Applications are available online.

(1265) · Delaware Diamond State Scholarship

Delaware Higher Education Commission
Carvel State Office Building, 5th Floor
820 N. French Street
Wilmington, DE 19801-3509
Phone: 800-292-7935
Fax: 302-577-6765
Email: dhec@doe.k12.de.us
Website: http://www.doe.k12.de.us/infosuites/students_family/dhec/
Purpose: To support academically-talented Delaware student residents.
Eligibility: Applicants must be residents of Delaware, U.S. citizens or eligible non-citizens, high school seniors who rank in the upper quarter of their class and score a minimum of 1200 on the SAT and enroll as full-time students in a degree program at a regionally accredited college.
Target applicant:
    High school students
Minimum GPA: None.
Amount: $1,250.
Number of awards: 50.
Scholarship may be renewable.
Deadline: March 28.
How to apply: Applications are available online.

(1266) · Delaware Governor's Workforce Development Grant

Delaware Higher Education Commission
Carvel State Office Building, 5th Floor
820 N. French Street
Wilmington, DE 19801-3509
Phone: 800-292-7935
Fax: 302-577-6765
Email: dhec@doe.k12.de.us
Website: http://www.doe.k12.de.us/infosuites/students_family/dhec/
Purpose: To assist students who are also working in Delaware.

Eligibility: Applicants must be residents of Delaware and U.S. citizens or eligible non-citizens who are 18 or older. Applicants must meet income requirements. Students must attend a participating school in Delaware on a part-time basis and be employed in Delaware full-time with a small employer, part-time, or through temporary employment. Applicants must be employed by an eligible employer who contributes to the Blue Collar Training Fund Program. Academic progress is monitored.

Target applicant:
    College students
    Adult students
Minimum GPA: None.
Amount: Up to $2,000.
Number of awards: Varies.
Scholarship may be renewable.
Deadline: End of free drop/add period each semester.
How to apply: Applications are available online.

(1267) · Delaware Scholarship Incentive Program

Delaware Higher Education Commission
Carvel State Office Building, 5th Floor
820 N. French Street
Wilmington, DE 19801-3509
Phone: 800-292-7935
Fax: 302-577-6765
Email: dhec@doe.k12.de.us
Website: http://www.doe.k12.de.us/infosuites/students_family/dhec/
Purpose: To assist Delaware student residents.
Eligibility: Applicants must be legal residents of Delaware and U.S. citizens or eligible non-citizens who are enrolled full-time at a regionally-accredited undergraduate institution in Delaware or Pennsylvania. Other undergraduate and graduate students will be considered if their major is not available at a public college in Delaware. Students must demonstrate substantial financial need and have a minimum 2.5 GPA. Applicants must also submit the Free Application for Federal Student Aid (FAFSA).

Target applicant:
    High school students
    College students
    Graduate school students
    Adult students
Minimum GPA: 2.5
Amount: $700-$2,220.
Number of awards: Varies.
Deadline: April 15.
How to apply: Delaware residents are automatically considered for the scholarship when their FAFSA form is received.

(1268) · Delegate Scholarship

Maryland Higher Education Commission
Office of Student Financial Assistance
839 Bestgate Road, Suite 400
Annapolis, MD 21401
Phone: 800-974-1024
Fax: 410-260-3200
Email: osfamail@mhec.state.md.us
Website: http://www.mhec.state.md.us
Purpose: To assist Maryland undergraduate and graduate students who can demonstrate financial need.
Eligibility: Applicants must be legal residents of the state of Maryland and complete the Free Application for Federal Student Aid (FAFSA).

Some delegates have supplementary forms. Contact your delegate's office for complete details. Applicants must show financial need.
Target applicant:
    High school students
    College students
    Graduate school students
    Adult students
Minimum GPA: None.
Amount: $200-$2,000.
Number of awards: Varies.
Scholarship may be renewable.
Deadline: Varies.
How to apply: Complete and file the Free Application for Federal Student Aid (FAFSA). Contact delegate's office for specific application forms. The Office of Student Financial Assistance (OSFA) can provide a list of all State legislators.

(1269) · Diana and Leon Feffer Scholarship Fund

Community Foundation of Western Massachusetts
1500 Main Street
P.O. Box 15769
Springfield, MA 01115
Phone: 413-732-2858
Fax: 413-733-8565
Email: scholar@communityfoundation.org
Website: http://www.communityfoundation.org
Purpose: To help residents of western Massachusetts to attend college or graduate school.
Eligibility: Applicants must attend a U.S. college or university part-time or full-time. Application forms, transcripts and Student Aid Reports are required. Selection is based on financial need and academic merit.
Target applicant:
    High school students
    College students
    Graduate school students
    Adult students
Minimum GPA: None.
Amount: Varies.
Number of awards: Varies.
Deadline: March 31.
How to apply: Applications are available online and by phone.

(1270) · Discovery Fund

Maine Community Foundation
245 Main Street
Ellsworth, ME 04605
Phone: 207-667-9735
Fax: 207-667-0447
Email: jwarren@mainecf.org
Website: http://www.mainecf.org
Purpose: To provide Maine students with financial support towards the pursuit of their extracurricular interests.
Eligibility: Applicants must be currently attending a public, private or parochial high school in Maine. Students born in Maine will be given preference over others.
Target applicant:
    High school students
Minimum GPA: None.
Amount: Varies.
Number of awards: Varies.

Deadline: April 1.
How to apply: Applications are available at high school guidance offices or online.

(1271) · Distinguished Scholar Award

Maryland Higher Education Commission
Office of Student Financial Assistance
839 Bestgate Road, Suite 400
Annapolis, MD 21401
Phone: 800-974-1024
Fax: 410-260-3200
Email: osfamail@mhec.state.md.us
Website: http://www.mhec.state.md.us
Purpose: To recognize high academic performing Maryland students.
Eligibility: Applicants must be high school juniors and U.S. citizens or eligible noncitizens. Finalists in the National Merit Scholarship and National Achievement Scholarship programs will automatically receive the award if they attend a Maryland institution. Applications must be submitted directly to your high school guidance counselor.
Target applicant:
    High school students
Minimum GPA: None.
Amount: Varies.
Number of awards: Varies.
Scholarship may be renewable.
Deadline: February.
How to apply: Applications may be obtained from the high school guidance counselor.

(1272) · Distinguished Scholar Community College Transfer Program

Maryland Higher Education Commission
Office of Student Financial Assistance
839 Bestgate Road, Suite 400
Annapolis, MD 21401
Phone: 800-974-1024
Fax: 410-260-3200
Email: osfamail@mhec.state.md.us
Website: http://www.mhec.state.md.us
Purpose: To provide financial support for Maryland community college students transferring to four-year Maryland colleges.
Eligibility: Applicants must have 60 credit hours completed at a Maryland community college with a grade point average of at least 3.0. Students must apply for the scholarship within one year of graduating from community college, and afterwards they must attend a Maryland four-year college as a full-time student.
Target applicant:
    College students
    Adult students
Minimum GPA: 3.0
Amount: $3,000.
Number of awards: Varies.
Scholarship may be renewable.
Deadline: March 1.
How to apply: Applications are available online.

(1273) · District of Columbia Tuition Assistance Grant

DC Tuition Assistance Grant Office
441 4th Street NW
Suite 450 North
Washington, DC 20001
Phone: 202-727-2824
Website: http://www.tuitiongrant.dc.gov
Purpose: To make attending out-of-state, private and Historically Black schools more affordable for DC residents.
Eligibility: Applicants must be residents of Washington, DC for at least 12 months before the start of their freshman year of college, high school graduates or GED recipients, enrolled at least half-time at an eligible institution, and be 24 years of age or younger. Applicants must maintain satisfactory academic progress, not have defaulted on student loans, have registered with the Selective Service, be U.S. citizens or permanent residents, have not already received a B.A. or B.S. and have not been incarcerated.
Target applicant:
    High school students
    College students
Minimum GPA: None.
Amount: Up to $10,000 per year for students attending U.S. public colleges or universities.
Number of awards: Varies.
Scholarship may be renewable.
Deadline: June 30.
How to apply: Applications are available online.

(1274) · Doc and Cathy Holsted Honorarium

Epsilon Sigma Alpha Foundation
P.O. Box 270517
Fort Collins, CO 80527
Phone: 970-223-2824
Fax: 970-223-4456
Email: kloyd@knoxy.net
Website: http://www.esaintl.com/esaf
Purpose: To provide financial assistance to Oklahoma residents who wish to attend college.
Eligibility: Applicants may attend any college or university and pursue any major. Selection is based on scholastic ability (30 percent), financial need (30 percent), leadership (20 percent), character (10 percent) and service (10 percent).
Target applicant:
    High school students
    College students
    Adult students
Minimum GPA: None.
Amount: $1,000.
Number of awards: 1.
Deadline: February 1.
How to apply: Applications are available online.

(1275) · Dominique Lisa Pandolfo Scholarship

Community Foundation of New Jersey
P.O. Box 338
Morristown, NJ 07963-0338
Phone: 973-267-5533
Fax: 973-267-2903
Email: fkrueger@cfnj.org
Website: http://www.cfnj.org
Purpose: To help young women achieve their goals and be successful.
Eligibility: Applicants must be females who have been nominated by the Dominique Lisa Pandolfo Scholarship Committee. They must exhibit outstanding character, potential, merit, personality and leadership qualities, and they must demonstrate financial need. Applicants must be New Jersey residents.

Target applicant:
High school students
Minimum GPA: None.
Amount: $5,000.
Number of awards: 1.
Deadline: April 21.
How to apply: Applications are available online.

(1276) · Don't Mess with Texas Scholarship

Don't Mess with Texas
c/o EnviroMedia
1717 West 6th Street, Suite 400
Austin, TX 78703
Phone: 512-476-4368
Email: scholarship@dontmesswithtexas.org
Website: http://www.dontmesswithtexas.org
Purpose: To support students concerned about litter.
Eligibility: Student must be a Texas high school senior who wants to attend a two- or four-year college or university in Texas. To apply for the scholarship, students must complete the application and one or two essays and submit two letters of recommendation (one from a school-related source and the other from a non-school related source).
Target applicant:
High school students
Minimum GPA: None.
Amount: $1,000-$3,000.
Number of awards: 3.
Deadline: April 4.
How to apply: Applications are available online.

(1277) · Doris and Clarence Glick Classical Music Scholarship

Hawaii Community Foundation - Scholarships
1164 Bishop Street, Suite 800
Honolulu, HI 96813
Phone: 888-731-3863
Fax: 808-521-6286
Email: scholarships@hcf-hawaii.org
Website: http://www.hawaiicommunityfoundation.org
Purpose: To provide financial assistance for Hawaii students of classical music.
Eligibility: Applicants must be majoring in music with an emphasis on classical music. They must have a GPA of 2.7 or higher, and they must describe their program of study as it relates to classical music in their personal statement.
Target applicant:
High school students
College students
Adult students
Minimum GPA: 2.7
Amount: Varies.
Number of awards: Varies.
Deadline: March 1.
How to apply: To apply, register online, complete the online application and select the scholarships to which you wish to apply. In addition, mail the supporting materials: printed confirmation page from the online application, personal statement, copy of Student Aid Report (SAR) available at www.fafsa.ed.gov and official transcript.

(1278) · Doris Morris Scholarship Endowment

Epsilon Sigma Alpha Foundation
P.O. Box 270517
Fort Collins, CO 80527
Phone: 970-223-2824
Fax: 970-223-4456
Email: kloyd@knoxy.net
Website: http://www.esaintl.com/esaf
Purpose: To provide financial assistance for students from Florida.
Eligibility: Applicants may major in any field at any college or university. Selection is based equally on character, leadership, service, financial need and scholastic ability.
Target applicant:
High school students
College students
Adult students
Minimum GPA: None.
Amount: $500.
Number of awards: 1.
Deadline: February 1.
How to apply: Applications are available online.

(1279) · Dorothy and Jim Meade Memorial Endowment

Epsilon Sigma Alpha Foundation
P.O. Box 270517
Fort Collins, CO 80527
Phone: 970-223-2824
Fax: 970-223-4456
Email: kloyd@knoxy.net
Website: http://www.esaintl.com/esaf
Purpose: To provide financial assistance to Washington State students.
Eligibility: Applicants may pursue any major at any school. Selection is based on scholastic ability (30 percent), financial need (30 percent), leadership (20 percent), character (10 percent) and service (10 percent).
Target applicant:
High school students
College students
Adult students
Minimum GPA: None.
Amount: $700.
Number of awards: 1.
Deadline: February 1.
How to apply: Applications are available online.

(1280) · Dorothy Campbell Memorial Scholarship

Oregon Student Assistance Commission
1500 Valley River Drive
Suite 100
Eugene, OR 97401
Phone: 541-687-7400
Fax: 541-687-7414
Email: awardinfo@mercury.osac.state.or.us
Website: http://www.osac.state.or.us
Purpose: To assist female Oregon high school students.
Eligibility: Applicants must be female graduates of an Oregon high school, have a minimum 2.75 GPA and attend a four-year Oregon college.

Target applicant:
High school students
Minimum GPA: 2.75
Amount: Varies.
Number of awards: Varies.
Scholarship may be renewable.
Deadline: March 1.
How to apply: Applications are available online.

(1281) · Dottie Martin Teachers Scholarship

North Carolina Federation of Republican Women
Joyce Glass, Chairman
4413 Driftwood Drive
Clemmons, NC 27012
Phone: 336-766-0067
Email: fglass@triad.rr.com
Website: http;//www.ncfederationofrepublicanwomen.org
Purpose: To support education students.
Eligibility: Applicants must be current college students planning to enter the field of education. The scholarship committee is especially interested in students who want to go into the fields of child guidance and counseling to make a difference in the lives of North Carolina children. Applicants must include an essay addressing their reasons for applying, career goals, plans for teaching in North Carolina, a description of their financial situation, why they should receive the scholarship and information on their personal values.
Target applicant:
College students
Graduate school students
Adult students
Minimum GPA: None.
Amount: $500.
Number of awards: 1.
Deadline: June 1.
How to apply: Applications are available online.

(1282) · Douvas Memorial Scholarship

Wyoming Department of Education
2300 Capitol Avenue
Hathaway Building, 2nd Floor
Cheyenne, WY 82002
Phone: 307-777-7673
Fax: 307-777-6234
Email: webmaster@educ.state.ky.us
Website: http://www.k12.wy.us
Purpose: To assist first generation Americans in obtaining higher education.
Eligibility: Applicants must have been born in the United States but have parents who were born outside the country. They must be high school seniors or between the ages of 18 and 22, and they must be Wyoming residents. They must attend a Wyoming community college or the University of Wyoming.
Target applicant:
High school students
College students
Minimum GPA: None.
Amount: $500.
Number of awards: 1.
Deadline: April 20.
How to apply: Applications are available online.

(1283) · Downeast Feline Fund

Maine Community Foundation
245 Main Street
Ellsworth, ME 04605
Phone: 207-667-9735
Fax: 207-667-0447
Email: jwarren@mainecf.org
Website: http://www.mainecf.org
Purpose: To provide support to students from Maine who are pursuing veterinary education.
Eligibility: Applicants must be graduates of Maine high schools. They must be currently enrolled in a school of veterinary medicine. Preference will be given to students who are in their third or fourth year of school.
Target applicant:
College students
Adult students
Minimum GPA: None.
Amount: Varies.
Number of awards: Varies.
Deadline: June 1.
How to apply: Applications are available online.

(1284) · Dr. Alvin and Monica Saake Foundation Scholarship

Hawaii Community Foundation - Scholarships
1164 Bishop Street, Suite 800
Honolulu, HI 96813
Phone: 888-731-3863
Fax: 808-521-6286
Email: scholarships@hcf-hawaii.org
Website: http://www.hawaiicommunityfoundation.org
Purpose: To provide assistance for Hawaii students who are majoring in sports medicine and related fields.
Eligibility: Applicants must plan to attend an accredited college or university full-time, major in kinesiology, sports medicine, physical therapy, occupational therapy or a related field. They must have a minimum GPA of 2.7 and be college juniors, college seniors or graduate students.
Target applicant:
College students
Graduate school students
Adult students
Minimum GPA: 2.7
Amount: Varies.
Number of awards: Varies.
Deadline: March 1.
How to apply: To apply, register online, complete the online application and select the scholarships to which you wish to apply. In addition, mail the supporting materials: printed confirmation page from the online application, personal statement, copy of Student Aid Report (SAR) available at www.fafsa.ed.gov and official transcript.

(1285) · Dr. and Mrs. Arthur F. Sullivan Fund

Connecticut Community Foundation Center for Philanthropy
43 Field Street
Waterbury, CT 06702
Phone: 203-753-1315
Fax: 203-756-3054
Email: info@conncf.org

Website: http://www.conncf.org

Purpose: To provide financial assistance to students who are entering or enrolled in medical school.

Eligibility: Applicants must be accepted to or enrolled in medical school. They must reside in the Connecticut Community Foundation's service area and demonstrate exemplary academic achievement.

Target applicant:

   College students

   Graduate school students

   Adult students

Minimum GPA: None.

Amount: Approximately $500.

Number of awards: Varies.

Deadline: March 1.

How to apply: Applications are available online.

(1286) · Dr. Donald L. Moak Scholarship

Alabama Bankers Association

534 Adams Avenue

Montgomery, AL 36104

Phone: 334-834-1890

Fax: 334-834-4443

Email: info@alabamabankers.org

Website: http://www.alabamabankers.org

Purpose: To provide educational assistance for the children of bankers.

Eligibility: Applicants must be Alabama residents with a parent who is employed full-time at an Alabama bank. They must be high school seniors at the time of application and plan to enroll in a college or university full-time. SAT or ACT scores are required, but there is no minimum score to be considered.

Target applicant:

   High school students

Minimum GPA: None.

Amount: $1,000.

Number of awards: 1.

Deadline: April 1.

How to apply: Applications are available online.

(1287) · Dr. Edison and Sallie Miyawaki Scholarship Fund

Hawaii Community Foundation - Scholarships

1164 Bishop Street, Suite 800

Honolulu, HI 96813

Phone: 888-731-3863

Fax: 808-521-6286

Email: scholarships@hcf-hawaii.org

Website: http://www.hawaiicommunityfoundation.org

Purpose: To reward students with outstanding achievement in extracurricular activities.

Eligibility: Applicants must be Hawaii residents who plan to attend an accredited institution of higher learning. They must have a GPA of 3.3 or higher, demonstrate financial need and have outstanding achievement in extracurricular activities.

Target applicant:

   High school students

   College students

   Adult students

Minimum GPA: 3.3

Amount: Varies.

Number of awards: Varies.

Deadline: March 1.

How to apply: To apply, register online, complete the online application and select the scholarships to which you wish to apply. In addition, mail the supporting materials: printed confirmation page from the online application, personal statement, copy of Student Aid Report (SAR) available at www.fafsa.ed.gov and official transcript.

(1288) · Dr. Hans and Clara Zimmerman Foundation Education Scholarship

Hawaii Community Foundation - Scholarships

1164 Bishop Street, Suite 800

Honolulu, HI 96813

Phone: 888-731-3863

Fax: 808-521-6286

Email: scholarships@hcf-hawaii.org

Website: http://www.hawaiicommunityfoundation.org

Purpose: To provide financial assistance to Hawaii students who want to study education.

Eligibility: Applicants major in education with an emphasis in teaching. They must have a GPA of 2.8 or higher, demonstrate good character and be full-time students. Preference is given to students of Hawaiian ethnicity and to students with at least two years of teaching experience. Applicants must discuss their teaching philosophies in their personal statement.

Target applicant:

   High school students

   College students

   Graduate school students

   Adult students

Minimum GPA: 2.8

Amount: Varies.

Number of awards: Varies.

Deadline: March 1.

How to apply: To apply, register online, complete the online application and select the scholarships to which you wish to apply. In addition, mail the supporting materials: printed confirmation page from the online application, personal statement, copy of Student Aid Report (SAR) available at www.fafsa.ed.gov and official transcript.

(1289) · Dr. Hans and Clara Zimmerman Foundation Health Scholarships

Hawaii Community Foundation - Scholarships

1164 Bishop Street, Suite 800

Honolulu, HI 96813

Phone: 888-731-3863

Fax: 808-521-6286

Email: scholarships@hcf-hawaii.org

Website: http://www.hawaiicommunityfoundation.org

Purpose: To provide financial assistance to Hawaii students who want to study in health fields.

Eligibility: Applicants must plan to major in a health-related field other than sports medicine, non-clinical psychology or social work at a U.S. college or university. They must be full-time college juniors, college seniors or graduate students, and they must have a GPA of 3.0 or higher.

Target applicant:

   College students

   Graduate school students

   Adult students

Minimum GPA: 3.0
Amount: Varies.
Number of awards: Varies.
Deadline: March 1.
How to apply: To apply, register online, complete the online application and select the scholarships to which you wish to apply. In addition, mail the supporting materials: printed confirmation page from the online application, personal statement, copy of Student Aid Report (SAR) available at www.fafsa.ed.gov and official transcript.

(1290) · Dr. Sidney E. Milburn Memorial Scholarship

Epsilon Sigma Alpha Foundation
P.O. Box 270517
Fort Collins, CO 80527
Phone: 970-223-2824
Fax: 970-223-4456
Email: kloyd@knoxy.net
Website: http://www.esaintl.com/esaf
Purpose: To provide education assistance to South Dakota students.
Eligibility: Applicants may attend any college or university and major in any field. Selection criteria include character (25 percent), leadership (25 percent), service (20 percent), financial need (15 percent) and scholastic ability (15 percent).
Target applicant:
    High school students
    College students
    Adult students
Minimum GPA: None.
Amount: $750.
Number of awards: 1.
Deadline: February 1.
How to apply: Applications are available online.

(1291) · DSS Adopted Children Tuition Waiver

Massachusetts Office of Student Financial Assistance
454 Broadway
Suite 200
Revere, MA 02151
Phone: 617-727-9420
Fax: 617-727-0667
Email: osfa@osfa.mass.edu
Website: http://www.osfa.mass.edu
Purpose: To lessen the financial burden on adopting parents in Massachusetts by extending tuition waivers at eligible schools.
Eligibility: Applicants must be under the age of twenty-four and adopted through the Department of Social Services by eligible Massachusetts residents. The tuition waiver encompasses 100 percent of tuition for state-supported courses at all of the Massachusetts public institutions of higher education, excluding graduate courses.
Target applicant:
    High school students
    College students
Minimum GPA: None.
Amount: Tuition waiver.
Number of awards: Varies.
Scholarship may be renewable.
Deadline: Varies.
How to apply: Contact the financial aid office at the institution attending or planning to attend for application forms and deadlines.

(1292) · DSS Tuition Waiver For Foster Care Children

Massachusetts Office of Student Financial Assistance
454 Broadway
Suite 200
Revere, MA 02151
Phone: 617-727-9420
Fax: 617-727-0667
Email: osfa@osfa.mass.edu
Website: http://www.osfa.mass.edu
Purpose: To provide financial support to Massachusetts foster children who are pursuing higher education.
Eligibility: Applicants must be current or former foster children who were placed in Massachusetts state custody for at least 12 months due to a Care and Protection Petition. They must not have been adopted or returned home, and they must be 24 years old or younger. Students must be enrolled as full-time undergraduates at a state-supported school.
Target applicant:
    High school students
    College students
    Adult students
Minimum GPA: None.
Amount: Varies.
Number of awards: Varies.
Deadline: Varies.
How to apply: Applications are available at college financial aid offices.

(1293) · Duke Kahanamoku Outrigger Scholarship

Outrigger Duke Kahanamoku Foundation
Scholarship Committee
P.O. Box 2498
Honolulu, HI 96804
Phone: 808-545-4880
Fax: 808-532-0560
Email: info@dukefoundation.org
Website: http://www.dukefoundation.org
Purpose: To support Hawaii students who are involved in water sports.
Eligibility: Applicants must be Hawaii residents and demonstrate financial need and athletic involvement. Preference is given to the water sports.
Target applicant:
    High school students
    College students
    Adult students
Minimum GPA: None.
Amount: Varies.
Number of awards: Varies.
Deadline: March 15.
How to apply: Applications are available online.

(1294) · Dunn Fellowship Program and Marzullo Internship Program

Governor's Office of the State of Illinois
Dunn Fellowship Program and Marzullo Internship Program
503 William G. Stratton Building
Springfield, IL 62706
Phone: 217-524-1381
Website: http://www.dunnfellow.com

Purpose: To provide college graduates with an opportunity to experience daily operations in state government for one year.

Eligibility: Fellows must possess a bachelor's degree, and Vito Marzullo interns must be Illinois residents. Fellows will be assigned to various posts in the Governor's office or in an office under the Governor's jurisdiction.

Target applicant:
    College students
    Adult students

Minimum GPA: None.

Amount: $20,028.

Number of awards: Varies.

Deadline: January 31.

How to apply: Applications are available online or by mail.

(1295) · E.E. Black Scholarship Fund

Hawaii Community Foundation - Scholarships
1164 Bishop Street, Suite 800
Honolulu, HI 96813
Phone: 888-731-3863
Fax: 808-521-6286
Email: scholarships@hcf-hawaii.org
Website: http://www.hawaiicommunityfoundation.org

Purpose: To provide financial assistance to dependents of Tesoro Hawaii employees.

Eligibility: Applicants must be dependents of Tesoro Hawaii employees or the company's subsidiaries. They must be full-time undergraduate students, and they must maintain a GPA of 3.0 or higher.

Target applicant:
    High school students
    College students
    Adult students

Minimum GPA: 3.0

Amount: Varies.

Number of awards: Varies.

Deadline: March 1.

How to apply: To apply, register online, complete the online application and select the scholarships to which you wish to apply. In addition, mail the supporting materials: printed confirmation page from the online application, personal statement, copy of Student Aid Report (SAR) available at www.fafsa.ed.gov and official transcript.

(1296) · Eagle Scout of the Year

American Legion, Department of Wisconsin
2930 American Legion Drive
P.O. Box 388
Portage, WI 53901
Phone: 608-745-1090
Fax: 608-745-0179
Email: info@wilegion.org
Website: http://www.wilegion.org

Purpose: To award outstanding service as an Eagle Scout at the state level.

Eligibility: Applicants must demonstrate outstanding service in community, church and school and must be at least 15 years of age, in high school and either members of a troop chartered by the American Legion/Auxiliary or sons or grandsons of members of the American Legion/Auxiliary. Students must have received the Eagle Scout Award as well as the Boy Scout religious emblem. Scholarships may be used to attend a state-accredited college, university or other school above the high school level.

Target applicant:
    High school students

Minimum GPA: None.

Amount: $1,000.

Number of awards: 1.

Deadline: Varies.

How to apply: Applications are available from the local Legion Post or from the Wisconsin American Legion Headquarters.

(1297) · Early Childhood Educators Scholarship

Massachusetts Office of Student Financial Assistance
454 Broadway
Suite 200
Revere, MA 02151
Phone: 617-727-9420
Fax: 617-727-0667
Email: osfa@osfa.mass.edu
Website: http://www.osfa.mass.edu

Purpose: To support the education of Massachusetts teachers employed in early childhood settings.

Eligibility: Applicants must be legal residents of Massachusetts who have worked as early childhood educators in the state for at least one year prior to receiving the scholarship. They must continue working in the profession while enrolled in school and upon completion of the degree. Students must be enrolled in Early Childhood Education or a related undergraduate program, and they cannot have any previously earned bachelor's degrees.

Target applicant:
    College students
    Adult students

Minimum GPA: None.

Amount: Varies.

Number of awards: Varies.

Scholarship may be renewable.

Deadline: July 1.

How to apply: Applications are available online.

(1298) · Early College for ME

Early College for ME
Maine Community College System
323 State Street
Augusta, ME 04330-7131
Phone: 207-767-5210 x4115
Email: info@mccs.me.edu
Website: http://www.earlycollege.me.edu

Purpose: To help high school students who are undecided about college.

Eligibility: Applicants must be in their junior year of high school at one of the 74 Maine high schools that are participating in the program. Students must be Maine residents for at least one year prior to entering the first year of college and must have not yet made plans for college and yet be capable of succeeding at a community college. High schools may also take financial need into consideration when selecting students for the program as well as whether or not the student is the first one to attend college in their family. The program provides community college courses in the senior year of high school as well as financial aid for a one-year or two-year degree program at a Maine community college.

Target applicant:
    High school students

Minimum GPA: None.

Amount: Up to $2000.

Number of awards: Varies.
Deadline: Unknown.
How to apply: Speak with your guidance counselor at your high school about entering the program.

(1299) · Edmund F. Maxwell Foundation Scholarship

Edmund F. Maxwell Foundation
P.O. Box 22537
Seattle, WA 98122-0537
Email: admin@maxwell.org
Website: http://www.maxwell.org
Purpose: The scholarship is intended to assist high-achieving students who follow the ideals of Edmund F. Maxwell: ability, aptitude and citizenship.
Eligibility: Applicants must be from Western Washington and plan to attend an accredited independent school that is primarily not tax-funded. Students must submit a FAFSA form and demonstrate financial need.
Target applicant:
    High school students
Minimum GPA: None.
Amount: $3,500.
Number of awards: Varies.
Scholarship may be renewable.
Deadline: April 30.
How to apply: Applications are available online at http://www.maxwell.org/app.html.

(1300) · Education Access Rewards North Carolina Scholars Fund

College Foundation of North Carolina
P.O. Box 41966
Raleigh, NC 27629-1966
Phone: 866-234-6400
Fax: 919-821-3139
Email: programinformation@cfnc.org
Website: http://www.cfnc.org
Purpose: To provide financial assistance to students of North Carolina community colleges and universities.
Eligibility: Applicants must be legal residents of North Carolina and the United States who are enrolling full-time in a North Carolina public university or community college for the first time. Applicants must be dependents of families who are at or below 200 percent of the poverty line and meet all other requirements for the federal Pell Grant.
Target applicant:
    High school students
Minimum GPA: None.
Amount: $4,000.
Number of awards: Varies.
Scholarship may be renewable.
Deadline: Varies.
How to apply: All students who meet the requirements and file a Free Application for Federal Student Aid and list at least one North Carolina public college or university will be considered.

(1301) · Educational Assistance (EA) Grant

Maryland Higher Education Commission
Office of Student Financial Assistance
839 Bestgate Road, Suite 400
Annapolis, MD 21401
Phone: 800-974-1024
Fax: 410-260-3200
Email: osfamail@mhec.state.md.us
Website: http://www.mhec.state.md.us
Purpose: To help Maryland students with financial need afford college.
Eligibility: Applicants and their parents must both be legal residents of the state of Maryland, U.S. citizens or eligible noncitizens and complete the Free Application for Federal Student Aid (FAFSA).
Target applicant:
    High school students
    College students
    Adult students
Minimum GPA: None.
Amount: $400-$2,700.
Number of awards: Varies.
Scholarship may be renewable.
Deadline: March 1.
How to apply: Complete the FAFSA.

(1302) · Educational Excellence Scholarship

Kentucky Higher Education Assistance Authority
P.O. Box 798
Frankfort, KY 40602
Phone: 800-928-8926
Email: blane@kheaa.com
Website: http://www.kheaa.com
Purpose: To reward outstanding Kentucky high school students.
Eligibility: Applicants must have a minimum 2.5 GPA, be graduating from eligible Kentucky high schools and meet high school graduation requirements. The scholarship amount is based on high school GPA and ACT composite score.
Target applicant:
    High school students
Minimum GPA: 2.5
Amount: Varies.
Number of awards: Varies.
Scholarship may be renewable.
Deadline: Varies.
How to apply: High schools send eligible students' GPAs to the Kentucky Department of Education.

(1303) · Educational Opportunity Fund

New Jersey Commission on Higher Education
20 W. State Street, 7th Floor
P.O. Box 542
Trenton, NJ 08625
Phone: 609-984-2709
Fax: 609-292-7225
Email: glang@che.state.nj.us
Website: http://www.state.nj.us/highereducation
Purpose: To assist students from disadvantaged backgrounds to attend higher education institutions in New Jersey.
Eligibility: Applicants must be New Jersey residents who attend a school in the state and have poverty level incomes. Awards are available for undergraduate students and graduate students through the Graduate Grants, Martin Luther King Physician-Dentist Scholarship and C. Clyde Ferguson Law Scholarship.
Target applicant:
    High school students
    College students
    Graduate school students
    Adult students

Minimum GPA: None.
Amount: $2,100-$4,150.
Number of awards: Varies.
Deadline: Varies.
How to apply: Contact your financial aid office.

(1304) · Educational Opportunity Fund (EOF) Grant

New Jersey Higher Education Student Assistance Authority
P.O. Box 540
Trenton, NJ 08625
Phone: 800-792-8670
Email: clientservices@hesaa.org
Website: http://www.hesaa.org
Purpose: To support underprivileged students in New Jersey.
Eligibility: Applicants must be able to show financial need and a background of family poverty, and they cannot exceed the established maximum income. They must be enrolled full-time in one of the participating public or private colleges in New Jersey, and they must have been residents of the state for at least 12 months prior to enrollment. Students pursuing a bachelor's degree cannot have any prior baccalaureate degrees, and students pursuing a two-year degree cannot have any previous associate's degrees. Applicants must not major in theology or divinity.
Target applicant:
  High school students
  College students
  Adult students
Minimum GPA: None.
Amount: $200-$4,350.
Number of awards: Varies.
Scholarship may be renewable.
Deadline: Varies.
How to apply: Applications are available from campus EOF directors.

(1305) · Educational Opportunity Grant

Washington Higher Education Coordinating Board
917 Lakeridge Way
P.O. Box 43430
Olympia, WA 98504
Phone: 360-753-7850
Fax: 360-753-6243
Email: info@hecb.wa.gov
Website: http://www.hecb.wa.gov
Purpose: To assist students with financial need and who are unable to relocate in completing their bachelor's degrees.
Eligibility: Applicants must be Washington residents who have personal barriers or other factors that prohibit them from relocating to attend college. They must have already reached junior standing before enrolling for the first time in an eligible four-year college, and they must have financial need.
Target applicant:
  College students
  Adult students
Minimum GPA: None.
Amount: Up to $2,500.
Number of awards: Varies.
Scholarship may be renewable.
Deadline: Varies.
How to apply: Applications are available online.

(1306) · Educational Rewards Grant

Massachusetts Office of Student Financial Assistance
454 Broadway
Suite 200
Revere, MA 02151
Phone: 617-727-9420
Fax: 617-727-0667
Email: osfa@osfa.mass.edu
Website: http://www.osfa.mass.edu
Purpose: To assist dislocated or incumbent workers in getting the education they need to gain employment in high-demand occupations.
Eligibility: Students must be dislocated workers, or their income must be at or below 200 percent of poverty level. Students must also be enrolled in an eligible program at an eligible institution, and they must be U.S. citizens and Massachusetts residents.
Target applicant:
  College students
  Adult students
Minimum GPA: None.
Amount: Up to $3,000.
Number of awards: Varies.
Deadline: Varies.
How to apply: Applications are available online. Applicants must also complete the Free Application for Federal Student Aid.

(1307) · Edward J. Bloustein Distinguished Scholars

New Jersey Higher Education Student Assistance Authority
P.O. Box 540
Trenton, NJ 08625
Phone: 800-792-8670
Email: clientservices@hesaa.org
Website: http://www.hesaa.org
Purpose: To support the highest achieving New Jersey students.
Eligibility: Applicants must be high school seniors who are New Jersey residents, be ranked in the top 10 percent of their classes, have a minimum SAT score of 1260 and plan to attend an institution of higher education. Juniors who are ranked first, second or third in their class at the end of the year may also apply. Applicants who attend high schools in the state's urban and economically distressed areas, who rank in the top 10 percent of their class and who have a minimum 3.0 GPA may also be selected through funding from the Urban Scholars Program.
Target applicant:
  High school students
Minimum GPA: None.
Amount: $1,000.
Number of awards: Varies.
Scholarship may be renewable.
Deadline: October 1.
How to apply: Applicants are nominated by their high schools and must complete and submit the Free Application for Federal Student Aid (FAFSA).

(1308) · Edward Payson and Bernice Piilani Irwin Scholarship

Hawaii Community Foundation - Scholarships
1164 Bishop Street, Suite 800
Honolulu, HI 96813
Phone: 888-731-3863

Fax: 808-521-6286
Email: scholarships@hcf-hawaii.org
Website: http://www.hawaiicommunityfoundation.org
Purpose: To provide financial assistance to Hawaii students who are pursuing careers in journalism.
Eligibility: Applicants must be college juniors, college seniors or graduate students majoring in journalism or communications. They must have a GPA of 2.7 or higher.
Target applicant:
   College students
   Graduate school students
   Adult students
Minimum GPA: 2.7
Amount: Varies.
Number of awards: Varies.
Deadline: March 1.
How to apply: To apply, register online, complete the online application and select the scholarships to which you wish to apply. In addition, mail the supporting materials: printed confirmation page from the online application, personal statement, copy of Student Aid Report (SAR) available at www.fafsa.ed.gov and official transcript.

(1309) · Eizo and Toyo Sakumoto Trust Scholarship

Hawaii Community Foundation - Scholarships
1164 Bishop Street, Suite 800
Honolulu, HI 96813
Phone: 888-731-3863
Fax: 808-521-6286
Email: scholarships@hcf-hawaii.org
Website: http://www.hawaiicommunityfoundation.org
Purpose: To assist Hawaiian students of Japanese ancestry.
Eligibility: Applicants must be Hawaii residents of primarily Japanese ancestry who were born in the state and plan to attend a college or university in Hawaii. They must have a GPA of 3.5 or higher.
Target applicant:
   High school students
   College students
   Adult students
Minimum GPA: 3.5
Amount: Varies.
Number of awards: Varies.
Deadline: March 1.
How to apply: To apply, register online, complete the online application and select the scholarships to which you wish to apply. In addition, mail the supporting materials: printed confirmation page from the online application, personal statement, copy of Student Aid Report (SAR) available at www.fafsa.ed.gov and official transcript.

(1310) · Elizabeth Ware Scholarship

Arkansas Business and Professional Women
P.O. Box 3499
Camden, AR 71711
Phone: 870-574-4560
Email: datchiso@sautech.edu
Website: http://www.arkansasbpw.org/scholarships.htm
Purpose: To provide financial assistance to women who are pursuing undergraduate education.
Eligibility: Applicants must be Arkansas residents who attend an accredited college or university. They must make a statement of goals, major choice and reason that funds are needed.

Target applicant:
   College students
   Adult students
Minimum GPA: None.
Amount: $500.
Number of awards: Varies.
Deadline: April 16.
How to apply: Applications are available online.

(1311) · Ellen R. Clayton Scholarship for Nursing Students

Central Scholarship Bureau
1700 Reisterstown Road
Suite 220
Baltimore, MD 21208-2903
Phone: 410-415-5558
Fax: 410-415-5501
Email: info@centralsb.org
Website: http://www.centralsb.org
Purpose: To assist full-time undergraduate or graduate students who are pursuing a degree in nursing.
Eligibility: Applicants must be Maryland residents, be U.S. citizens or permanent residents, meet specified income requirements and have a minimum 2.0 GPA. An application form, budget form, school bill, transcript, Student Aid Report, school financial aid award letter and essay are required.
Target applicant:
   High school students
   College students
   Graduate school students
   Adult students
Minimum GPA: 2.0
Amount: $2,500.
Number of awards: 2.
Deadline: May 31.
How to apply: Applications are available online.

(1312) · Ellison Onizuka Memorial Scholarship Fund

Hawaii Community Foundation - Scholarships
1164 Bishop Street, Suite 800
Honolulu, HI 96813
Phone: 888-731-3863
Fax: 808-521-6286
Email: scholarships@hcf-hawaii.org
Website: http://www.hawaiicommunityfoundation.org
Purpose: To provide financial assistance to Hawaii students who plan to major in aerospace engineering.
Eligibility: Applicants must be graduating high school in the year of application and plan to pursue a degree in aerospace engineering or a related field. Students must have a GPA of 2.7, and their transcripts must list their SAT scores.
Target applicant:
   High school students
Minimum GPA: 2.7
Amount: Varies.
Number of awards: Varies.
Deadline: March 1.
How to apply: To apply, register online, complete the online application and select the scholarships to which you wish to apply. In addition, mail the supporting materials: printed confirmation page from the online application, two letters of recommendation, personal statement,

copy of Student Aid Report (SAR) available at www.fafsa.ed.gov and official transcript. The personal statement must describe participation in extracurricular activities, clubs and community service.

(1313) · Eloise Collins Endowment

Epsilon Sigma Alpha Foundation
P.O. Box 270517
Fort Collins, CO 80527
Phone: 970-223-2824
Fax: 970-223-4456
Email: kloyd@knoxy.net
Website: http://www.esaintl.com/esaf
Purpose: To provide financial assistance to women studying medicine.
Eligibility: Applicants must be Louisiana residents majoring in a medical field at any school. They must demonstrate financial need. Selection is based on service (5 percent), character (10 percent), leadership (10 percent), scholastic ability (25 percent) and financial need (50 percent).
Target applicant:
  High school students
  College students
  Adult students
Minimum GPA: None.
Amount: $500.
Number of awards: 1.
Deadline: February 1.
How to apply: Applications are available online.

(1314) · Elsie M. Vogler / Lois E. Carter Memorial Teaching

Epsilon Sigma Alpha Foundation
P.O. Box 270517
Fort Collins, CO 80527
Phone: 970-223-2824
Fax: 970-223-4456
Email: kloyd@knoxy.net
Website: http://www.esaintl.com/esaf
Purpose: To provide financial assistance to teaching majors.
Eligibility: Applicants must be residents of Arizona or Michigan. They may study teaching at any college or university. Selection is based equally on character, leadership, service, financial need and scholastic ability.
Target applicant:
  High school students
  College students
  Adult students
Minimum GPA: None.
Amount: $1,000.
Number of awards: 1.
Deadline: February 1.
How to apply: Applications are available online.

(1315) · Emily M. Hewitt Memorial Scholarship

Calaveras Big Trees Association
P.O. Box 1196
Arnold, CA 95223
Phone: 209-795-3840
Fax: 209-795-6680
Email: info@bigtrees.org
Website: http://www.bigtrees.org

Purpose: To support students who are commited to communicate a love of nature and an understanding of need to practice conservation.
Eligibility: Applicants must be enrolled full-time in an accredited California post-secondary educational institution and must have career goals that are related to communicating and interpreting nature's wonder. Students pursuing degrees in environmental protection, forestry, wildlife and fisheries biology, parks and recreation, park management, environmental law and public policy, environmental art and California history are encouraged to apply. Selection is based on dedication to the ideals of the scholarship and financial need.
Target applicant:
  College students
  Adult students
Minimum GPA: None.
Amount: $1,000.
Number of awards: 1.
Deadline: April 15.
How to apply: Student must submit a statement of personal and career goals, a resume (and portfolio if applicable) and transcripts of all college work completed to date. On the cover page, include your name, address, phone number and college major.

(1316) · Engineering and Land Surveying Scholarships

Consulting Engineers and Land Surveyors of California
1303 J Street
Suite 450
Sacramento, CA 95814
Phone: 916-441-7991
Fax: 916-441-6312
Website: http://www.celsoc.org
Purpose: To help undergraduate and graduate students studying engineering or land surveying at California schools.
Eligibility: Applicants must be entering their third or fourth year (or fifth year of a five-year program) of undergraduate study for the upper division scholarships or be entering or continuing graduate study for the graduate scholarships. Undergraduate students must be enrolled full-time and working toward a degree at an accredited engineering or land surveying program. Graduate students must be enrolled at least half time and working toward a degree at an accredited engineering or land surveying program. Students must submit application folders, including 500-word essays, transcripts and recommendation forms.
Target applicant:
  College students
  Graduate school students
  Adult students
Minimum GPA: 3.2
Amount: $7,500.
Number of awards: Varies.
Deadline: April 28.
How to apply: Applications are available online.

(1317) · Epsilon Sigma Alpha

College Foundation of North Carolina
P.O. Box 41966
Raleigh, NC 27629-1966
Phone: 866-234-6400
Fax: 919-821-3139
Email: programinformation@cfnc.org
Website: http://www.cfnc.org
Purpose: To provide financial assistance to students who want to work with exceptional children.

Eligibility: Applicants must be enrolled in an accredited college or university, either at the undergraduate level or as a North Carolina teacher seeking training and must be training to work with special needs children up to the age of 21 in an educational setting. They must agree to teach at a North Carolina public school for at least one year after graduation.
Target applicant:
College students
Graduate school students
Adult students
Minimum GPA: None.
Amount: Varies.
Number of awards: Varies.
Deadline: April 1.
How to apply: Applications are available online.

(1318) · Esther Kanagawa Memorial Art Scholarship
Hawaii Community Foundation - Scholarships
1164 Bishop Street, Suite 800
Honolulu, HI 96813
Phone: 888-731-3863
Fax: 808-521-6286
Email: scholarships@hcf-hawaii.org
Website: http://www.hawaiicommunityfoundation.org
Purpose: To provide financial assistance to Hawaii students who are majoring in fine arts.
Eligibility: Applicants must majoring in fine arts at an accredited college or university. They must have a GPA of 2.7 or higher and demonstrate financial need and good character.
Target applicant:
High school students
College students
Adult students
Minimum GPA: 2.7
Amount: Varies.
Number of awards: Varies.
Deadline: March 1.
How to apply: To apply, register online, complete the online application and select the scholarships to which you wish to apply. In addition, mail the supporting materials: printed confirmation page from the online application, personal statement, copy of Student Aid Report (SAR) available at www.fafsa.ed.gov and official transcript.

(1319) · Ethics in Business Scholarship Program
Florida Department of Education
Office of Student Financial Assistance
1940 N. Monroe Street
Suite 70
Tallahassee, FL 32303-4759
Phone: 888-827-2004
Fax: 850-245-9667
Email: osfa@fldoe.org
Website: http://www.floridastudentfinancialaid.org
Purpose: To help undergraduate college students who enroll at community colleges and eligible private Florida colleges or universities.
Eligibility: Applicants should contact financial aid offices at participating institutions for more information. Participating institutions determine deadlines, award amounts and eligibility.
Target applicant:
High school students
College students
Adult students

Minimum GPA: None.
Amount: Varies.
Number of awards: Varies.
Deadline: Varies.
How to apply: Contact financial aid offices at participating institutions.

(1320) · Excel Awards
Indiana Farm Bureau
P.O. Box 1250
Indianapolis, IN 46206-1250
Phone: 800-723-3276
Website: http://www.infarmbureau.com
Purpose: To reward and promote the self-expression of high school authors, poets, artist, songwriters, filmmakers and performers.
Eligibility: Students must be enrolled in an Indiana high school or affiliated career center and must create a project based on the provided topic. There are six categories: 2-D art, 3-D art, music, performance art, video art and writing. Home school students may also enter if they work closely on their project with a high school teacher.
Target applicant:
High school students
Minimum GPA: None.
Amount: $2,000-$3,000.
Number of awards: 18.
Deadline: January 25.
How to apply: Applications are available online.

(1321) · Excel Staffing Companies Scholarships for Excellence in Continuing Education
Albuquerque Community Foundation (ACF)
P.O. Box 36960
Albuquerque, NM 87176
Phone: 505-883-6240
Fax: 505-883-3629
Email: foundation@albuquerquefoundation.org
Website: http://www.albuquerquefoundation.org
Purpose: To assist individuals who demonstrate a commitment to achieving a career goal.
Eligibility: Applicants must be at least 21 years old and be Albuquerque area residents. Applicants must also work a minimum of 30 hours a week, have a 3.0 minimum GPA and be in need of financial assistance to obtain a goal.
Target applicant:
College students
Graduate school students
Adult students
Minimum GPA: 3.0
Amount: Up to $1,000.
Number of awards: Varies.
Scholarship may be renewable.
Deadline: July 2.
How to apply: Applications are available online.

(1322) · Excellence in Service Award
Florida's Office of Campus Volunteers
Florida Campus Compact
325 John Knox Road
Building F, Suite 210
Tallahassee, FL 32303

369

Phone: 850-488-7782
Fax: 850-922-2928
Email: info@floridacompact.org
Website: http://www.floridacompact.org
Purpose: To reward students who perform outstanding acts of service in their communities.
Eligibility: Applicants must be full-time undergraduate students at an accredited public or private institution of higher education within the state of Florida.
Target applicant:
    College students
    Adult students
Minimum GPA: None.
Amount: $1,000.
Number of awards: 3.
Deadline: April 30.
How to apply: Applications are available online.

(1323) · Exceptional Circumstances Scholarships

Workforce Safety and Insurance
P.O. Box 5585
Bismarck, ND 58506-5585
Phone: 701-328-3828
Fax: 701-328-3820
Email: ndwsi@nd.gov
Website: http://www.workforcesafety.com/workers/typesofbenefits.asp
Purpose: To provide financial assistance to injured North Dakota workers.
Eligibility: Applicants must be workers who have been injured on the job and would benefit from the funds due to exceptional circumstances. They must have completed the WSI rehabilitation process, and there must be no outstanding litigation on a rehabilitation plan. Applicants must reapply each year and maintain a satisfactory GPA in order to continue to receive funds.
Target applicant:
    High school students
    College students
    Adult students
Minimum GPA: None.
Amount: Tuition.
Number of awards: Varies.
Scholarship may be renewable.
Deadline: Varies.
How to apply: Applications are available by phone.

(1324) · Family District 1 Scholarships

American Hellenic Education Progressive Association
1909 Q Street NW
Suite 500
Washington, DC 20009
Phone: 202-232-6300
Fax: 202-232-2140
Email: ahepa@ahepa.org
Website: http://www.ahepa.org
Purpose: To provide financial assistance for those pursuing higher education.
Eligibility: Applicants must be graduating seniors, high school graduates or current undergraduate or graduate students who plan to attend a college or university full-time during the calendar year of application. They must be residents of Alabama, Georgia, Mississippi, South Carolina, Tennessee or Florida.

Target applicant:
    High school students
    College students
    Graduate school students
    Adult students
Minimum GPA: None.
Amount: Varies.
Number of awards: varies.
Deadline: January 10.
How to apply: Applications are available online. The current application must be used and must be sent by certified mail and return receipt requested.

(1325) · Federal Chafee Educational and Training Grant

Oregon Student Assistance Commission
1500 Valley River Drive
Suite 100
Eugene, OR 97401
Phone: 541-687-7400
Fax: 541-687-7414
Email: awardinfo@mercury.osac.state.or.us
Website: http://www.osac.state.or.us
Purpose: To provide financial assistance to students who have been in foster care.
Eligibility: Applicants must be in foster care or have been in foster care for at least six months after their 14th birthday or be adopted from the foster care system after age 16. Funding is provided on a first come, first served basis. The deadlines are: August 1 for the fall term, November 1 for the winter term, February 1 for the spring term and May 1 for the summer term.
Target applicant:
    High school students
    College students
    Graduate school students
Minimum GPA: None.
Amount: Up to $5,000.
Number of awards: Varies.
Scholarship may be renewable.
Deadline: Varies.
How to apply: Applications are available online.

(1326) · Fellowship on Women and Public Policy

Center for Women in Government and Civil Society
University at Albany, SUNY
135 Western Avenue
Draper Hall 302
Albany, NY 12222
Phone: 518-442-3900
Fax: 518-442-3877
Website: http://www.cwig.albany.edu
Purpose: To encourage New York state graduate students to pursue jobs in public policy.
Eligibility: Students must be enrolled in a graduate program at an accredited college or university in New York and have completed at least 12 credits before applying but not be scheduled to graduate before the internship. Applicants must demonstrate an interest in improving the status of women and underrepresented populations.
Target applicant:
    Graduate school students
    Adult students

Minimum GPA: None.

Amount: $9,000 stipend and tuition assistance.

Number of awards: Varies.

Deadline: May 15, although applications will be considered throughout the fall.

How to apply: Applications are available online.

(1327) · Filipino Nurses' Organization of Hawaii Scholarship

Hawaii Community Foundation - Scholarships
1164 Bishop Street, Suite 800
Honolulu, HI 96813
Phone: 888-731-3863
Fax: 808-521-6286
Email: scholarships@hcf-hawaii.org
Website: http://www.hawaiicommunityfoundation.org
Purpose: To assist Filipino students who are seeking degrees in nursing.
Eligibility: Applicants must be Hawaii residents who are of Filipino descent. They must be full-time students with a minimum GPA of 2.7.
Target applicant:
   High school students
   College students
   Adult students
Minimum GPA: 2.7
Amount: Varies.
Number of awards: Varies.
Deadline: March 1.
How to apply: To apply, register online, complete the online application and select the scholarships to which you wish to apply. In addition, mail the supporting materials: printed confirmation page from the online application, personal statement, copy of Student Aid Report (SAR) available at www.fafsa.ed.gov and official transcript.

(1328) · Financial Women International Scholarship

Hawaii Community Foundation - Scholarships
1164 Bishop Street, Suite 800
Honolulu, HI 96813
Phone: 888-731-3863
Fax: 808-521-6286
Email: scholarships@hcf-hawaii.org
Website: http://www.hawaiicommunityfoundation.org
Purpose: To provide financial assistance to female business majors in Hawaii.
Eligibility: Applicants must be college juniors, college seniors or graduate students. They must have a minimum GPA of 3.5.
Target applicant:
   College students
   Graduate school students
   Adult students
Minimum GPA: 3.5
Amount: Varies.
Number of awards: Varies.
Deadline: March 1.
How to apply: To apply, register online, complete the online application and select the scholarships to which you wish to apply. In addition, mail the supporting materials: printed confirmation page from the online application, personal statement, copy of Student Aid Report (SAR) available at www.fafsa.ed.gov and official transcript.

(1329) · First Generation Matching Grant Program

Florida Department of Education
Office of Student Financial Assistance
1940 N. Monroe Street
Suite 70
Tallahassee, FL 32303-4759
Phone: 888-827-2004
Fax: 850-245-9667
Email: osfa@fldoe.org
Website: http://www.floridastudentfinancialaid.org
Purpose: To help Florida undergraduate students with financial need who are enrolled in state universities and whose parents have not earned bachelor's degrees.
Eligibility: Applicants must submit applications and the Free Application for Federal Student Aid (FAFSA). Each university determines its own deadline.
Target applicant:
   High school students
   College students
   Adult students
Minimum GPA: None.
Amount: Varies.
Number of awards: Varies.
Deadline: Varies.
How to apply: Applications are at the financial aid offices of state universities.

(1330) · First in Family Scholarship

J. Craig and Page T. Smith Scholarship Foundation
505 20th Street N
Suite 1800
Birmingham, AL 35203
Phone: 205-250-6669
Email: scholarships@jcraigsmithfoundation.org
Website: http://jcraigsmithfoundation.org
Purpose: To provide assistance for students who face financial, physical or emotional challenges and who have participated in volunteer work or assisted their families.
Eligibility: Applicants must be seniors at an Alabama high school and plan to attend an Alabama four-year college the following fall. Students must also write two essays about their future plans and their community service or family assistance endeavors and provide three letters of recommendation.
Target applicant:
   High school students
Minimum GPA: None.
Amount: Varies.
Number of awards: Varies.
Deadline: January 15.
How to apply: Applications are available online or by mail.

(1331) · Flora Burns/Virginia State Council Endowment

Epsilon Sigma Alpha Foundation
P.O. Box 270517
Fort Collins, CO 80527
Phone: 970-223-2824
Fax: 970-223-4456
Email: kloyd@knoxy.net
Website: http://www.esaintl.com/esaf

Purpose: To provide education opportunities for Virginia students.
Eligibility: Applicants may pursue any major at any college or university. Selection is based on the following criteria: character (10 percent), leadership (10 percent), service (5 percent), financial need (50 percent) and scholastic ability (25 percent).
Target applicant:
   High school students
   College students
   Adult students
Minimum GPA: None.
Amount: $1,000.
Number of awards: 2.
Deadline: February 1.
How to apply: Applications are available online.

(1332) · Florence Allen Scholarship for Ohio Women

Ohio Federation of Business and Professional Women
3500 Granger Road
Medina, OH 44256
Phone: 866-642-7948
Email: bpwohiofaef@aol.com
Website: http://www.bpwohio.org
Purpose: To provide financial assistance for Ohio women.
Eligibility: Applicants must be U.S. citizens and undergraduates enrolled at an accredited degree-granting institution recognized by a state Board of Regents. Awards are given to traditional students and to non-traditional students who are 30 years of age or older. Traditional students must be enrolled full-time to be eligible.
Target applicant:
   High school students
   College students
   Adult students
Minimum GPA: None.
Amount: Varies.
Number of awards: Varies.
Deadline: April 1.
How to apply: Applications are available by mail or email.

(1333) · Florida Association of Postsecondary Schools and Colleges Scholarship Program

Florida Association of Postsecondary Schools and Colleges
150 S. Monroe Street, Suite 303
Tallahassee, FL 32301
Phone: 850-577-3139
Fax: 850-577-3133
Email: mail@fapsc.org
Website: http://www.fapsc.org
Purpose: To provide full and partial-tuition scholarships to Florida students.
Eligibility: Applicants must either be graduating from high school or receiving a GED in Florida.
Target applicant:
   High school students
Minimum GPA: None.
Amount: Varies.
Number of awards: Varies.
Deadline: March 1.
How to apply: Applications are available from guidance counselors and participating FAPSC schools.

(1334) · Florida Bright Futures Scholarship Program

Florida Department of Education
Office of Student Financial Assistance
1940 N. Monroe Street
Suite 70
Tallahassee, FL 32303-4759
Phone: 888-827-2004
Fax: 850-245-9667
Email: osfa@fldoe.org
Website: http://www.floridastudentfinancialaid.org
Purpose: Lottery-funded scholarships are awarded to Florida high school seniors as reward for academic achievements and to assist with postsecondary education.
Eligibility: Applicants must earn a Florida high school diploma or equivalent, have not been found guilty or pled no contest to a felony charge and meet the award's academic requirements. Applicants must also be Florida residents, U.S. citizens or eligible noncitizens and be accepted by and enrolled in an eligible Florida public or private college or vocational school at least quarter time. Application must be completed during the senior year of high school.
Target applicant:
   High school students
Minimum GPA: None.
Amount: Tuition and fees.
Number of awards: Varies.
Deadline: May 30.
How to apply: Apply by completing the Florida Financial Aid Application. The application is available online at www.floridastudentfinancialaid.org or from your high school guidance counselor.

(1335) · Florida Oratorical Contest

American Legion, Department of Florida
P.O. Box 547859
Orlando, FL 32854
Phone: 407-295-2631
Fax: 407-299-0901
Website: http://www.floridalegion.org
Purpose: To enhance high school students' experience with and understanding of the U.S. Constitution. The contest will help develop students' leadership skills and civic appreciation, as well as the ability to deliver thoughtful, insightful orations regarding U.S. citizenship and its inherent responsibilities.
Eligibility: Applicants must be high school students under the age of 20 who are U.S. citizens or legal residents and residents of the state. Students first give an oration within their state and winners compete at the national level. The oration must be related to the Constitution of the United States focusing on the duties and obligations citizens have to the government. It must be in English and be between eight and ten minutes. There is also an assigned topic which is posted on the website, and it should be between three and five minutes.
Target applicant:
   Junior high students or younger
   High school students
Minimum GPA: None.
Amount: Up to $4,000.
Number of awards: Varies.
Deadline: Varies.
How to apply: Applications are available by contacting the local American Legion Post.

(1336) · Florida Student Assistance Grant Program

Florida Department of Education
Office of Student Financial Assistance
1940 N. Monroe Street
Suite 70
Tallahassee, FL 32303-4759
Phone: 888-827-2004
Fax: 850-245-9667
Email: osfa@fldoe.org
Website: http://www.floridastudentfinancialaid.org
Purpose: To help degree-seeking, Florida resident, undergraduate students who have financial need and who are enrolled in participating postsecondary institutions.
Eligibility: There are three student financial aid programs: The Florida Public Student Assistance Grant is for students who attend state universities and public community colleges. The Florida Private Student Assistance Grant is for students who attend eligible private, non-profit, four-year colleges and universities. The Florida Postsecondary Student Assistance Grant is for students who attend eligible degree-granting private colleges and universities that are ineligible under the Florida Private Student Assistance Grant. High school students in the top 20 percent of their classes receive priority funding.
Target applicant:
    High school students
    College students
    Adult students
Minimum GPA: None.
Amount: $1,722.
Number of awards: Varies.
Scholarship may be renewable.
Deadline: Each school determines its own deadline.
How to apply: Applicants must submit the Free Application for Federal Student Aid (FAFSA).

(1337) · Ford Opportunity Program Scholarship

Oregon Student Assistance Commission
1500 Valley River Drive
Suite 100
Eugene, OR 97401
Phone: 541-687-7400
Fax: 541-687-7414
Email: awardinfo@mercury.osac.state.or.us
Website: http://www.osac.state.or.us
Purpose: To assist Oregon residents who are single heads of households.
Eligibility: Applicants must be Oregon single heads of household with custody of dependent children, have a minimum 3.0 GPA or 2900 GED score and attend a four-year Oregon college or community college.
Target applicant:
    High school students
    College students
    Adult students
Minimum GPA: 3.0
Amount: Varies.
Number of awards: Varies.
Deadline: March 1.
How to apply: Applications are available online.

(1338) · Ford Scholars Scholarship

Oregon Student Assistance Commission
1500 Valley River Drive
Suite 100
Eugene, OR 97401
Phone: 541-687-7400
Fax: 541-687-7414
Email: awardinfo@mercury.osac.state.or.us
Website: http://www.osac.state.or.us
Purpose: To assist Oregon students.
Eligibility: Applicants must be graduating high school seniors, high school graduates who have not been full-time undergraduates or community college students who are entering their junior year at an Oregon four-year college. Applicants must also have a minimum 3.0 GPA or GED score of 2900.
Target applicant:
    High school students
    College students
    Adult students
Minimum GPA: 3.0
Amount: Varies.
Number of awards: Varies.
Deadline: March 1.
How to apply: Applications are available online.

(1339) · Foster Child Grant Program

Massachusetts Office of Student Financial Assistance
454 Broadway
Suite 200
Revere, MA 02151
Phone: 617-727-9420
Fax: 617-727-0667
Email: osfa@osfa.mass.edu
Website: http://www.osfa.mass.edu
Purpose: To assist children who have lived in foster homes in obtaining higher education.
Eligibility: Applicants must be placed in the custody of the Department of Social Services and be permanent residents of the state of Massachusetts. Students must also be 24 years of age or younger and apply for financial aid.
Target applicant:
    High school students
    College students
    Graduate school students
Minimum GPA: None.
Amount: Up to $6,000.
Number of awards: Varies.
Scholarship may be renewable.
Deadline: Varies.
How to apply: Applications are available by phone from the Massachusetts Office of Student Financial Assistance or from your social worker.

(1340) · Frank del Olmo Memorial Scholarship

California Chicano News Media Association
USC Annenberg School of Journalism
One California Plaza
300 S. Grand Avenue, Suite 3950
Los Angeles, CA 90071-3175
Phone: 213-437-4408

Fax: 213-437-4423
Email: ccmainfo@ccnma.org
Website: http://www.ccnma.org
Purpose: To assist California Latino college students who demonstrate a desire to pursue a career in journalism.
Eligibility: Applicants must be Latino, be either California residents or attending California schools and have an interest in pursuing a journalism career. An interview is required. Financial need, academic achievement and community involvement are also considered.
Target applicant:
  High school students
  College students
  Adult students
Minimum GPA: None.
Amount: $500-$2,000.
Number of awards: Varies.
Deadline: April 3.
How to apply: Applications are available online.

(1341) · Frank O'Bannon Grant Program

State Student Assistance Commission of Indiana
150 W. Market Street
Suite 500
Indianapolis, IN 46204
Phone: 888-528-4719
Fax: 317-232-3260
Email: grants@ssaci.state.in.us
Website: http://www.in.gov/ssaci
Purpose: To aid Indiana students in attending eligible postsecondary schools.
Eligibility: Applicants must be high school graduates and attend or plan to attend eligible Indiana colleges or universities full-time.
Target applicant:
  High school students
  College students
  Adult students
Minimum GPA: None.
Amount: Varies.
Number of awards: Varies.
Deadline: March 10.
How to apply: Complete the Free Application for Federal Student Aid (FAFSA).

(1342) · Freehold Soil Conservation District Scholarship

Freehold Soil Conservation District
4000 Kozloski Road
P.O. Box 5033
Freehold, NJ 07728
Phone: 732-683-8500
Fax: 732-683-9140
Email: info@freeholdscd.org
Website: http://www.freeholdscd.org
Purpose: To support college juniors and seniors majoring in the conservation of natural resources.
Eligibility: Applicants must be residents of Middlesex or Monmouth County, New Jersey, entering the junior or senior year in the fall. Students must major in an area related to conservation of natural resources such as agriculture; forestry; conservation; environmental or soil science;

environmental studies, education or policy; resource management or geology.
Target applicant:
  College students
  Adult students
Minimum GPA: None.
Amount: $1,000.
Number of awards: 3.
Deadline: April 7.
How to apply: Applications are available online.

(1343) · Fresh Start Scholarship

Fresh Start Scholarship Foundation
P.O. Box 7784
Wilmington, DE 19803
Phone: 302-656-4411
Fax: 610-347-0438
Email: fsscholar@comcast.net
Website: http://www.wwb.org/freshstart.html
Purpose: To help women who are returning to school.
Eligibility: Applicants should be women at least 20 years old with financial need who have a high school diploma or G.E.D., have had at least a two year break in education either after finishing high school or during college studies and are enrolled in a Delaware college in a two- or four-year degree program at the undergraduate level. Applicants should have at least a C average if already in college.
Target applicant:
  College students
  Adult students
Minimum GPA: None.
Amount: Varies.
Number of awards: Varies.
Deadline: May 31.
How to apply: Applications are available online or by mail and include a personal statement. A social service agency or college representative should recommend applicants.

(1344) · Futurama Foundation Career Advancement Scholarship

Business and Professional Women/Maine Futurama Foundation
103 County Road
Oakland, ME 04963
Email: webmaster@bpwmaine.org
Website: http://www.bpwmaine.org/files/index.php?id=10
Purpose: To provide financial assistance for women who want to advance their careers.
Eligibility: Applicants must be female Maine residents who are age 30 or older. They must need financial assistance to improve their skills or complete education for career advancement. They must have a definite plan to use their training to improve their chances of advancement, train for a new career or to enter or reenter the job market.
Target applicant:
  College students
  Adult students
Minimum GPA: None.
Amount: $1,200.
Number of awards: 1.
Deadline: April 20.
How to apply: Applications are available from your local BPW chapter or your financial aid office.

(1345) · Future Educators Academy

New Hampshire Postsecondary Education Commission
3 Barrell Court
Suite 300
Concord, NH 03301
Phone: 603-271-2555 x352
Fax: 603-271-2696
Email: jknapp@pec.state.nh.us
Website: http://www.state.nh.us/postsecondary
Purpose: To support graduating high school seniors in New Hampshire who will be majoring in education.
Eligibility: Students must have completed or be currently enrolled in the FEA "Exploring the Art of Teaching" program at their high school. Applicants must plan to enroll in a teacher preparation program at a two-year or four-year college in New Hampshire, and they must plan to teach in New Hampshire for a period of time after graduation.
Target applicant:
  High school students
Minimum GPA: None.
Amount: $5,000-$10,000.
Number of awards: Varies.
Deadline: March 1.
How to apply: Applications are available from FEA teachers.

(1346) · Future Teachers Conditional Scholarship

Washington Higher Education Coordinating Board
917 Lakeridge Way
P.O. Box 43430
Olympia, WA 98504
Phone: 360-753-7850
Fax: 360-753-6243
Email: info@hecb.wa.gov
Website: http://www.hecb.wa.gov
Purpose: To encourage outstanding students to pursue teaching careers and to encourage current teachers to get endorsements in shortage areas.
Eligibility: Applicants must be Washington residents who plan to earn a residency teacher certificate or a shortage subject endorsement, intend to become employed as a classroom teacher in a Washington public primary or secondary school, plan to attend college half-time or more and are not planning to pursue degrees in theology. Selection is based on academic ability, bilingual ability, contributions to schools, length of time until education is completed and commitment to work as a Washington public school teacher.
Target applicant:
  College students
  Graduate school students
  Adult students
Minimum GPA: None.
Amount: Varies.
Number of awards: Varies.
Deadline: October 10.
How to apply: Applications are available online.

(1347) · Future Teachers Scholarship

Oklahoma State Regents for Higher Education
655 Research Parkway, Suite 200
Oklahoma City, OK 73104
Phone: 800-858-1840
Fax: 405-225-9230
Email: studentinfo@osrhe.edu
Website: http://www.okhighered.org
Purpose: To encourage students to become teachers in critical teacher shortage areas in Oklahoma public schools.
Eligibility: Applicants must be residents of Oklahoma who have been nominated by their institution on the basis of rank in the top 15 percent of high school class, rank in the top 15 percent of students in SAT or ACT scores and be admitted to an education program at an accredited Oklahoma institution or have high academic achievement in undergraduate coursework. Applicants must maintain a GPA of 2.5 or higher and agree to teach in a shortage area in an Oklahoma public school for at least three years after graduation and licensure.
Target applicant:
  High school students
  College students
  Adult students
Minimum GPA: 2.5
Amount: Up to $1,500.
Number of awards: Varies.
Deadline: Varies.
How to apply: Applications are submitted by the nominating institution.

(1348) · Gallo Blue Chip Scholarship

Harness Horse Youth Foundation
16575 Carey Road
Westfield, IN 46074
Phone: 317-867-5877
Fax: 317-867-5896
Email: ellen@hhyf.org
Website: http://www.hhyf.org
Purpose: To support the children of horse trainers and caretakers.
Eligibility: Applicants must have been raised or currently reside in New Jersey or New York. Students must be at least in their senior year of high school, and they cannot be pursuing a graduate degree. Selection is based on financial need and academic achievements.
Target applicant:
  High school students
  College students
  Adult students
Minimum GPA: None.
Amount: Varies.
Number of awards: Varies.
Deadline: April 30.
How to apply: Applications are available online.

(1349) · GEAR UP ALASKA Scholarship Program

Alaska Commission on Postsecondary Education
3030 Vintage Boulevard
Juneau, AK 99801
Phone: 800-441-2962
Fax: 907-465-5316
Email: customer_service@acpe.state.ak.us
Website: http://alaskadvantage.state.ak.us
Purpose: To provide financial aid to students in Alaska.
Eligibility: Applicants must be students under the age of 22 who have participated in GEAR UP Programs in 6th, 7th and 8th grade and who have met GEAR UP academic requirements. Students must be seniors at an Alaskan high school or have received a diploma or GED from an Alaskan high school. Applicants must complete the Free Application for Federal Student Aid (FAFSA) and then submit the Student Aid Report (SAR) and federal income tax forms with their application. The award is based on financial need.

Target applicant:
   High school students
   College students
Minimum GPA: None.
Amount: $7,000 for full-time and $3,500 for part-time students.
Number of awards: Varies.
Scholarship may be renewable.
Deadline: May 31.
How to apply: Applications are available by contacting the scholarship coordinator.

(1350) · GEAR UP Summer Scholarship

State Student Assistance Commission of Indiana
150 W. Market Street
Suite 500
Indianapolis, IN 46204
Phone: 888-528-4719
Fax: 317-232-3260
Email: grants@ssaci.state.in.us
Website: http://www.in.gov/ssaci
Purpose: To support Indiana students who are planning to enroll in summer courses.
Eligibility: Applicants must be high school seniors or college freshmen, and they must be enrolled or planning to enroll full-time at an Indiana college. Students must be eligible for the 21st Century Scholars Program. Scholarship funds may be used for college preparatory courses, prerequisites or degree requirements.
Target applicant:
   High school students
   College students
   Adult students
Minimum GPA: None.
Amount: $1,500.
Number of awards: Varies.
Deadline: Varies.
How to apply: Applications are available by mail.

(1351) · General Assembly Merit Scholarship

Tennessee Student Assistance Corporation
404 James Robertson Parkway
Suite 1510, Parkway Towers
Nashville, TN 37243
Phone: 800-342-1663
Fax: 615-741-6101
Email: tsac.aidinfo@state.tn.us
Website: http://www.collegepaystn.com
Purpose: To provide supplemental support to recipients of the Tennessee HOPE Scholarship.
Eligibility: Students graduating from public schools or category 1, 2 and 3 private schools must have at least a 3.75 GPA and either a 29 on the ACT or a 1280 on the SAT. Home-schooled or non-category 1, 2 or 3 private school students must complete at least 12 college credit hours while in high school, and they must have at least a 3.0 GPA in those courses. Recipients of the Aspire Award are not eligible.
Target applicant:
   High school students
   College students
   Adult students
Minimum GPA: 3.75
Amount: $1,000.
Number of awards: Varies.

Deadline: September 1.
How to apply: Applications are available through completion of the FAFSA.

(1352) · General Assembly Scholarship

Illinois Student Assistance Commission
1755 Lake Cook Road
Deerfield, IL 60015
Phone: 800-899-4722
Fax: 847-831-8549
Email: collegezone@isac.org
Website: http://www.collegezone.com
Purpose: To assist Illinois students.
Eligibility: Applicants must be Illinois high school students planning to attend a state-supported university. They must contact their State Senator and State Representative to be considered for the award, and they must live within the legislative district of that Senator or Representative.
Target applicant:
   High school students
Minimum GPA: None.
Amount: Full tuition for one to four years.
Number of awards: 1-4 per district.
Scholarship may be renewable.
Deadline: Varies.
How to apply: Applications are available from your State Senator and State Representative.

(1353) · George Mason Business Scholarship Fund

Hawaii Community Foundation - Scholarships
1164 Bishop Street, Suite 800
Honolulu, HI 96813
Phone: 888-731-3863
Fax: 808-521-6286
Email: scholarships@hcf-hawaii.org
Website: http://www.hawaiicommunityfoundation.org
Purpose: To assist Hawaii students who are majoring in business administration.
Eligibility: Applicants must be seniors at a Hawaiian college or university and have a GPA of 3.0 or higher. They must discuss why they have chosen to pursue a business career and how they expect to make a difference in the business world in their personal statement.
Target applicant:
   College students
   Adult students
Minimum GPA: 3.0
Amount: Varies.
Number of awards: Varies.
Deadline: March 1.
How to apply: To apply, register online, complete the online application and select the scholarships to which you wish to apply. In addition, mail the supporting materials: printed confirmation page from the online application, personal statement, copy of Student Aid Report (SAR) available at www.fafsa.ed.gov and official transcript.

(1354) · Georgia Men of ESA Endowment

Epsilon Sigma Alpha Foundation
P.O. Box 270517
Fort Collins, CO 80527
Phone: 970-223-2824
Fax: 970-223-4456
Email: kloyd@knoxy.net

Website: http://www.esaintl.com/esaf
Purpose: To provide financial assistance to Georgia residents.
Eligibility: Applicants may pursue any major at any college or university. Criteria for selection include scholastic ability (30 percent), financial need (30 percent), leadership (20 percent), service (10 percent) and character (10 percent).
Target applicant:
  High school students
  College students
  Adult students
Minimum GPA: None.
Amount: $500.
Number of awards: 1.
Deadline: February 1.
How to apply: Applications are available online.

(1355) · Georgia Oratorical Contest

American Legion, Department of Georgia
3035 Mt. Zion Road
Stockbridge, GA 30281
Phone: 678-289-8883
Fax: 678-289-8885
Email: amerlegga@bellsouth.net
Website: http://www.galegion.org
Purpose: To enhance high school students' experience with and understanding of the U.S. Constitution. The contest will help develop students' leadership skills and civic appreciation, as well as the ability to deliver thoughtful, insightful orations regarding U.S. citizenship and its inherent responsibilities.
Eligibility: Applicants must be high school students under the age of 20 who are U.S. citizens or legal residents and residents of the state. Students first give an oration within their state and winners compete at the national level. The oration must be related to the Constitution of the United States focusing on the duties and obligations citizens have to the government. It must be in English and be between eight and ten minutes. There is also an assigned topic which is posted on the website, and it should be between three and five minutes.
Target applicant:
  Junior high students or younger
  High school students
Minimum GPA: None.
Amount: Up to $2,800.
Number of awards: Varies.
Deadline: March 3.
How to apply: Applications are available by contacting the local American Legion Post.

(1356) · Georgia Tuition Equalization Grant

Georgia Student Finance Commission
2082 East Exchange Place
Tucker, GA 30084
Phone: 800-505-4732
Fax: 770-724-9089
Email: support@gacollege411.org
Website: http://www.gacollege411.org
Purpose: To support Georgia resident students.
Eligibility: Applicants must be full-time students at eligible private colleges or universities in Georgia or in out-of-state four-year public colleges within 50 miles of students' residences and be U.S. citizens.
Target applicant:
  College students
  Adult students

Minimum GPA: None.
Amount: Varies.
Number of awards: Varies.
Scholarship may be renewable.
Deadline: Varies.
How to apply: Applications are available online.

(1357) · Get Ready for Math and Science Conditional Scholarship Program

Washington Higher Education Coordinating Board
917 Lakeridge Way
P.O. Box 43430
Olympia, WA 98504
Phone: 360-753-7850
Fax: 360-753-6243
Email: info@hecb.wa.gov
Website: http://www.hecb.wa.gov
Purpose: To assist high achievers in math and science in obtaining a degree in a qualified math or science program.
Eligibility: Applicants must be Washington students who achieve a level 4 on the math or science section of the tenth grade WASL or score above the 95th percentile in math on the SAT or ACT and come from a family with income at or below 125 percent of the state's median family income for two years prior to application. They must begin college within one year of high school graduation, make satisfactory academic progress and enter in a qualifying math or science program by the end of the first term of their junior year. They must also make a commitment to work in a qualifying math or science occupation within the state for at least three years.
Target applicant:
  High school students
Minimum GPA: None.
Amount: Varies.
Number of awards: Varies.
Scholarship may be renewable.
Deadline: Varies.
How to apply: Applications are available from the College Success Foundation by phone at 877-655-4097.

(1358) · Gilbert Matching Student Grant

Massachusetts Office of Student Financial Assistance
454 Broadway
Suite 200
Revere, MA 02151
Phone: 617-727-9420
Fax: 617-727-0667
Email: osfa@osfa.mass.edu
Website: http://www.osfa.mass.edu
Purpose: To assist needy students in attending private institutions of higher education or nursing schools.
Eligibility: Students must be permanent residents of Massachusetts, demonstrate financial need, maintain satisfactory academic progress and attend an eligible Massachusetts institution. Applicants must not have earned a bachelor's or professional degree, nor a first diploma from a hospital or professional nursing program.
Target applicant:
  High school students
  College students
  Adult students
Minimum GPA: None.
Amount: Up to $2,500.

Number of awards: Varies.
Scholarship may be renewable.
Deadline: Varies.
How to apply: Applications are available from your school's financial aid office.

(1359) · GlaxoSmithKlein Opportunity Scholarships

Triangle Community Foundation
Scholarship Programs
P.O. Box 12834
Research Triangle Park, NC 27709
Phone: 919-474-8370
Fax: 919-941-9208
Email: info@trianglecf.org
Website: http://www.trianglecf.org
Purpose: To assist North Carolina students who have overcome significant adversity.
Eligibility: Applicants must have been residents of Chatham, Durham, Orange or Wake County for the past six months and must be legal residents of the U.S. Only those who have overcome significant adversity should apply. There are no age or income limitations, and the award may be used at technical or community colleges, four-year colleges or universities or vocational or trade programs.
Target applicant:
　　High school students
　　College students
　　Adult students
Minimum GPA: None.
Amount: Up to $5,000.
Number of awards: Varies.
Scholarship may be renewable.
Deadline: April 1.
How to apply: Applications are available online.

(1360) · Golden Apple Scholars of Illinois (Illinois Scholars Program)

Illinois Department of Public Health
535 W. Jefferson Street
Springfield, IL 62761
Phone: 217-782-4977
Fax: 217-782-3987
Email: dph.mailus@illinois.gov
Website: http://www.idph.state.il.us
Purpose: To offer scholarships to promising students pursuing teaching degrees.
Eligibility: Applicants must be Illinois high school seniors or college sophomores at one of the 53 partner universities in Illinois who are interested in teaching. There are a limited number of spots for college sophomores, and all college students must be nominated by a university liaison. Students must commit to teaching in an Illinois school of need for five years after graduation.
Target applicant:
　　High school students
　　College students
　　Adult students
Minimum GPA: None.
Amount: Financial assistance for four years at one of 53 colleges in Illinois.
Number of awards: Varies.
Scholarship may be renewable.
Deadline: November 30.

How to apply: Applications are available by calling 312-407-0433, extension 105.

(1361) · Golden LEAF Scholars Program - Two-Year Colleges

College Foundation of North Carolina
P.O. Box 41966
Raleigh, NC 27629-1966
Phone: 866-234-6400
Fax: 919-821-3139
Email: programinformation@cfnc.org
Website: http://www.cfnc.org
Purpose: To provide need-based financial assistance to North Carolina community college students.
Eligibility: Applicants must be residents of one of the 73 eligible counties and meet specific income requirements as evidenced by FAFSA information (for curriculum students) or the federal TRIO formula (for occupational education students). Degree-seeking students must be enrolled at least half-time.
Target applicant:
　　High school students
　　College students
　　Adult students
Minimum GPA: None.
Amount: Up to $750.
Number of awards: Varies.
Scholarship may be renewable.
Deadline: Varies.
How to apply: Applications are available online.

(1362) · Good Eats Scholarship Fund

Hawaii Community Foundation - Scholarships
1164 Bishop Street, Suite 800
Honolulu, HI 96813
Phone: 888-731-3863
Fax: 808-521-6286
Email: scholarships@hcf-hawaii.org
Website: http://www.hawaiicommunityfoundation.org
Purpose: To provide financial assistance to Hawaii students pursuing degrees in agriculture and culinary arts, and to encourage them to return to Hawaii upon graduation.
Eligibility: Applicants must be Hawaii residents who plan to study culinary arts or agriculture at a college or university in the continental United States. They must have a GPA of 2.7 or higher and demonstrate interest in food production and preparation through their school or community activities.
Target applicant:
　　High school students
　　College students
　　Adult students
Minimum GPA: 2.7
Amount: Varies.
Number of awards: Varies.
Deadline: March 1.
How to apply: To apply, register online, complete the online application and select the scholarships to which you wish to apply. In addition, mail the supporting materials: printed confirmation page from the online application, personal statement, copy of Student Aid Report (SAR) available at www.fafsa.ed.gov and official transcript.

(1363) · Gordon and Betty Cape Endowment for Continuing Education

Epsilon Sigma Alpha Foundation
P.O. Box 270517
Fort Collins, CO 80527
Phone: 970-223-2824
Fax: 970-223-4456
Email: kloyd@knoxy.net
Website: http://www.esaintl.com/esaf
Purpose: To provide assistance to non-traditional Kansas students.
Eligibility: Applicants must be returning to school for a degree or career enhancement and must enroll for at least six semester hours. They may pursue any major at any school. Selection is based equally on character, leadership, service, financial need and scholastic ability.
Target applicant:
  High school students
  College students
  Adult students
Minimum GPA: None.
Amount: $800.
Number of awards: 1.
Deadline: February 1.
How to apply: Applications are available online.

(1364) · Governor James B. Hunt College Scholarships and Governor James G. Martin College Scholarships

College Foundation of North Carolina
P.O. Box 41966
Raleigh, NC 27629-1966
Phone: 866-234-6400
Fax: 919-821-3139
Email: programinformation@cfnc.org
Website: http://www.cfnc.org
Purpose: To assist outstanding North Carolina high school students.
Eligibility: Applicants must be high school seniors who reside in North Carolina and who plan to attend full-time a public or private four-year college or university in North Carolina.
Target applicant:
  High school students
Minimum GPA: None.
Amount: Varies.
Number of awards: Varies.
Scholarship may be renewable.
Deadline: March 15.
How to apply: Each postsecondary institution may nominate two students.

(1365) · Governor's Challenge Scholarship

Idaho State Board of Education
P.O. Box 83720
Boise, ID 83720
Phone: 208-334-2270
Fax: 208-334-2632
Email: dkelly@osbe.state.id.us
Website: http://www.boardofed.idaho.gov
Purpose: Monetary assistance is provided to Idaho resident high school seniors planning to attend state colleges.
Eligibility: Applicants must be Idaho high school seniors planning to attend Idaho colleges or universities full-time and have a minimum 2.8 GPA. Public service is a significant factor.

Target applicant:
  High school students
Minimum GPA: 2.8
Amount: $3,000.
Number of awards: 12.
Scholarship may be renewable.
Deadline: December 15.
How to apply: Applications are available online.

(1366) · Governor's Opportunity Scholarship

Colorado Commission on Higher Education
1380 Lawrence Street
Suite 1200
Denver, CO 80204
Phone: 303-866-2723
Fax: 303-866-4266
Email: cche@state.co.us
Website: http://www.state.co.us/cche
Purpose: To help Colorado college freshmen with financial need attend colleges in the state.
Eligibility: Applicants must be U.S. citizens or permanent residents, plan to attend college full-time and have an Expected Family Contribution or parental contribution of "0" on the Free Application for Federal Student Aid (FAFSA). Students should apply to their desired college and submit the FAFSA. Then, nominators and students must submit the Governor's Opportunity Scholarship nomination form to each institution to which the student is applying. A copy should also be sent to the Colorado Commission on Higher Education.
Target applicant:
  High school students
Minimum GPA: None.
Amount: Varies.
Number of awards: 250.
Scholarship may be renewable.
Deadline: Varies.
How to apply: Nomination forms are available online.

(1367) · Governor's Postsecondary Merit Scholarship

Montana Guaranteed Student Loan Program
P.O. Box 203101
Helena, MT 59620
Phone: 800-537-7508
Fax: 406-444-1869
Website: http://www.mgslp.state.mt.us
Purpose: To assist Montana residents in getting a college education in the state and to reduce the amount of student debt so that more students can remain in the state after graduation.
Eligibility: Students must be residents of Montana who have been accepted to an eligible institution of higher learning in the state. Students must also have a minimum GPA of 3.0, SAT score of 20 or higher or SAT score of 1380 and be enrolled in a certificate, associate or bachelor's degree program.
Target applicant:
  High school students
Minimum GPA: 3.0
Amount: $2,000.
Number of awards: Varies.
Deadline: February 15.
How to apply: Applications are available online.

(1368) · Governor's Postsecondary Merit-At-Large Scholarship

Montana Guaranteed Student Loan Program
P.O. Box 203101
Helena, MT 59620
Phone: 800-537-7508
Fax: 406-444-1869
Website: http://www.mgslp.state.mt.us
Purpose: To assist students in obtaining higher education. Home schooled and other non-traditional students are encouraged to apply.
Eligibility: Applicants must be residents of Montana who are entering college as freshmen and seeking their first certificate or undergraduate degree.
Target applicant:
    High school students
Minimum GPA: None.
Amount: $2,000.
Number of awards: Varies.
Scholarship may be renewable.
Deadline: March 31.
How to apply: Applications are available online.

(1369) · Governor's Scholars Program

Arkansas Department of Higher Education
114 East Capitol
Little Rock, AR 72201-3818
Phone: 501-371-2050
Fax: 501-371-2001
Email: finaid@adhe.arknet.edu
Website: http://www.arkansashighered.com
Purpose: To assist outstanding Arkansas high school graduates to encourage them to attend postsecondary schools in Arkansas.
Eligibility: Applicants must be Arkansas graduating high school seniors who will attend an Arkansas college or university. Selection is based on academic achievement, test scores and leadership. A minimum ACT score of 27, SAT score of 1220 or 3.5 GPA in academic courses is required.
Target applicant:
    High school students
Minimum GPA: 3.5
Amount: $4,000.
Number of awards: At least 75.
Scholarship may be renewable.
Deadline: February 1.
How to apply: Applications are available through your high school counselor and online.

(1370) · Governor's Scholarship Program

Georgia Student Finance Commission
2082 East Exchange Place
Tucker, GA 30084
Phone: 800-505-4732
Fax: 770-724-9089
Email: support@gacollege411.org
Website: http://www.gacollege411.org
Purpose: To aid graduating Georgia high school seniors attend Georgia colleges or universities.
Eligibility: Applicants must be selected by the Georgia Department of Education or be a valedictorian, salutatorian or STAR student and enroll full-time as an undergraduate at a Georgia institution. A minimum 3.0 GPA is required for renewal.
Target applicant:
    High school students
Minimum GPA: None.
Amount: Varies.
Number of awards: Varies.
Scholarship may be renewable.
Deadline: Varies.
How to apply: Applications are available online.

(1371) · Graduate and Professional Scholarship Program

Maryland Higher Education Commission
Office of Student Financial Assistance
839 Bestgate Road, Suite 400
Annapolis, MD 21401
Phone: 800-974-1024
Fax: 410-260-3200
Email: osfamail@mhec.state.md.us
Website: http://www.mhec.state.md.us
Purpose: To assist graduate and professional students who can demonstrate financial need.
Eligibility: Applicants must be U.S. citizens or eligible noncitizens, legal residents of the state of Maryland and complete the Free Application for Federal Student Aid (FAFSA). Applicants must contact the financial aid office of the institution they are attending and request to be considered for a Graduate and Professional Scholarship. Grants can only be used at the following schools: University of Maryland, Baltimore (UMB) Schools of Medicine, Dentistry, Law, Pharmacy, or Social Work; University of Baltimore School of Law; The Johns Hopkins University School of Medicine; The Virginia-Maryland Regional College of Veterinary Medicine or certain Maryland institutions offering a master's degree in nursing or social work.
Target applicant:
    Graduate school students
    Adult students
Minimum GPA: None.
Amount: $1,000-$5,000.
Number of awards: Varies.
Scholarship may be renewable.
Deadline: Varies.
How to apply: Complete the FAFSA and contact the financial aid office.

(1372) · Graduate and Undergraduate Assistance Program

State Council of Higher Education for Virginia
101 N. 14th Street
James Monroe Building
Richmond, VA 23219
Phone: 804-225-2600
Fax: 804-225-2604
Email: communications@schev.edu
Website: http://www.schev.edu
Purpose: To assist students in attending Virginia schools.
Eligibility: Applicants must be admitted to an eligible Virginia college or university and demonstrate academic excellence. Applicants do not need to be Virginia residents.

Target applicant:
    High school students
    College students
    Graduate school students
    Adult students
Minimum GPA: None.
Amount: Varies.
Number of awards: Varies.
Deadline: Varies.
How to apply: Contact your financial aid office.

(1373) · Graduate Tuition Waiver

Massachusetts Office of Student Financial Assistance
454 Broadway
Suite 200
Revere, MA 02151
Phone: 617-727-9420
Fax: 617-727-0667
Email: osfa@osfa.mass.edu
Website: http://www.osfa.mass.edu
Purpose: To provide financial support to Massachusetts graduate students.
Eligibility: Students must be enrolled in graduate level courses at a Massachusetts public school that is not a community college. Applicants must not owe any refunds on previously received financial aid, and they must not have defaulted on any government loans.
Target applicant:
    Graduate school students
    Adult students
Minimum GPA: None.
Amount: Varies.
Number of awards: Varies.
Deadline: Varies.
How to apply: Applications are available at college financial aid offices.

(1374) · Granite State Scholars Program

New Hampshire Postsecondary Education Commission
3 Barrell Court
Suite 300
Concord, NH 03301
Phone: 603-271-2555 x352
Fax: 603-271-2696
Email: jknapp@pec.state.nh.us
Website: http://www.state.nh.us/postsecondary
Purpose: To support Granite State Scholars in New Hampshire.
Eligibility: Students must have been designated as Granite State Scholars in high school. Students become Scholars by being ranked in the top 10 percent of their class and having a combined SAT I score of 1200 or more (math and reading comprehension) or an equivalent ACT score. They must be pursuing an undergraduate degree at a public school in New Hampshire, and they must have no previous bachelor's degrees. Applicants must also show financial need.
Target applicant:
    High school students
    College students
    Adult students
Minimum GPA: None.
Amount: Varies.
Number of awards: Varies.
Deadline: Varies.

How to apply: Applications are available at college financial aid offices.

(1375) · Granville P. Meade Scholarship

Virginia Department of Education
P.O. Box 2120
Richmond, VA 23218
Phone: 804-225-3349
Fax: 804-371-2456
Email: joseph.wharff@doe.virginia.gov
Website: http://www.pen.k12.va.us
Purpose: To support graduating high school seniors in Virginia.
Eligibility: Students must have been born in Virginia, and they must plan to attend a public or private Virginia school. They must demonstrate financial need, academic achievement, extracurricular activities and good character. Recipients must maintain a 2.5 GPA.
Target applicant:
    High school students
Minimum GPA: 2.5
Amount: $2,000.
Number of awards: Varies.
Scholarship may be renewable.
Deadline: March 7.
How to apply: Applications are available online.

(1376) · Greater Kanawha Valley Foundation Scholarship Program

Greater Kanawha Valley Foundation
1600 Huntington Square
900 Lee Street, East
Charleston, WV 25301
Phone: 304-346-3620
Fax: 304-346-3640
Email: tgkvf@tgkvf.org
Website: http://www.tgkvf.org
Purpose: To provide financial assistance to prospective college students from the state of West Virginia.
Eligibility: Applicants must be residents of West Virginia, be full-time students (12 hours) and demonstrate good moral character. Many awards are available, and each individual award may have additional eligibility requirements.
Target applicant:
    High school students
    College students
    Adult students
Minimum GPA: 2.5
Amount: Varies.
Number of awards: 70.
Scholarship may be renewable.
Deadline: February 17.
How to apply: Applications are available online at http://www.tgkvf.org/scholar.htm.

(1377) · Greenhouse Scholars Scholarship

Greenhouse Scholars
Attn: Amy Vreeland
1011 Walnut Street
2nd Floor
Boulder, CO 80302
Phone: 303-460-1735

Fax: 303-464-7796
Email: avreeland@greenhousescholars.org
Website: http://www.greenhousescholars.org
Purpose: To provide financial assistance to high-performing, under-resourced students who are leaders and contributors to their communities.
Eligibility: Applicants must be high school seniors who plan to attend a four-year college or university. They must be U.S. citizens who reside and attend school in Colorado. They must have an unweighted GPA of 3.5 or higher, and they must demonstrate leadership, perseverance and financial need. Their household income must be $70,000 a year or less. Winners must participate in an internship and the company's Whole Person program.
Target applicant:
    High school students
Minimum GPA: 3.0
Amount: Up to $5,000.
Number of awards: Varies.
Scholarship may be renewable.
Deadline: January 20.
How to apply: Applications are available online.

(1378) · Growing Up Asian in America

Asian Pacific Fund
225 Bush Street
Suite 590
San Francisco, CA 94104
Phone: 415-433-6859
Fax: 415-433-2425
Email: scholarship@asianpacificfund.org
Website: http://www.asianpacificfund.org
Purpose: To celebrate Asian heritage.
Eligibility: Applicants do NOT need to be Asian American. Students must be K-12 students in the nine counties of the San Francisco Bay Area and must submit entries in the art and essay categories. There is a theme for each year's competition.
Target applicant:
    Junior high students or younger
    High school students
Minimum GPA: None.
Amount: Total of $27,000.
Number of awards: Varies.
Deadline: March 2.
How to apply: Applications are available at schools and libraries.

(1379) · Guardian Scholarships

Workforce Safety and Insurance
P.O. Box 5585
Bismarck, ND 58506-5585
Phone: 701-328-3828
Fax: 701-328-3820
Email: ndwsi@nd.gov
Website: http://www.workforcesafety.com/workers/typesofbenefits.asp
Purpose: To provide financial assistance to the families of North Dakota workers who lost their lives due to work-related injuries.
Eligibility: Applicants must be spouses or dependent children of workers who died as a result of work-related injuries. Upon approval, they may receive funds for up to five years if they reapply each year and maintain a satisfactory GPA.

Target applicant:
    High school students
    College students
    Adult students
Minimum GPA: None.
Amount: Up to $4,000.
Number of awards: Varies.
Scholarship may be renewable.
Deadline: Varies.
How to apply: Applications are available by phone.

(1380) · Guy M. Wilson Scholarship

American Legion, Department of Michigan
212 N. Verlinden Avenue
Lansing, MI 48915
Phone: 517-371-4720 x25
Fax: 517-371-2401
Email: programs@michiganlegion.org
Website: http://www.michiganlegion.org
Purpose: To aid students who are the sons or daughters of veterans who plan to attend a Michigan college.
Eligibility: Applicants must be residents of Michigan who are planning to attend a Michigan college or university and who are the sons or daughters of veterans. Students must have a minimum GPA of 2.5 and must have demonstrated financial need. Applicants must provide proof of a parent's military service record and an indication of their abilities to fulfill their goals and intentions. They should send scholarship information to their county district committee person.
Target applicant:
    High school students
Minimum GPA: 2.5
Amount: $500.
Number of awards: Varies.
Deadline: January 5.
How to apply: Applications are available online.

(1381) · Guy P. Gannett Scholarship

Maine Community Foundation
245 Main Street
Ellsworth, ME 04605
Phone: 207-667-9735
Fax: 207-667-0447
Email: jwarren@mainecf.org
Website: http://www.mainecf.org
Purpose: To provide renewable financial support to students in Maine who are majoring in journalism or a related field.
Eligibility: Students must be graduates of Maine high schools or home-schooled in Maine. Applicants are considered for the award based on their interest in journalism, financial need and academic achievement. They must also continue to demonstrate an interest in journalism in college.
Target applicant:
    High school students
    College students
    Graduate school students
    Adult students
Minimum GPA: None.
Amount: Varies.
Number of awards: Varies.
Scholarship may be renewable.
Deadline: May 1.

How to apply: Applications are available online in January or by contacting the Maine Community Foundation.

(1382) · Hawaii Community Foundation Scholarships

Hawaii Community Foundation - Scholarships
1164 Bishop Street, Suite 800
Honolulu, HI 96813
Phone: 888-731-3863
Fax: 808-521-6286
Email: scholarships@hcf-hawaii.org
Website: http://www.hawaiicommunityfoundation.org
Purpose: To help Hawaii residents who show financial need.
Eligibility: The Hawaii Community Foundation Scholarship Program has over 120 different scholarship funds covering areas such as vocational education, those in foster care, ethnicity, religion and major. Applicants must be Hawaii residents who plan to attend nonprofit two- or four-year colleges as either full-time undergraduate or graduate students. Applicants must also have academic achievement and good moral character. A personal statement, Student Aid Report, transcript, recommendation letter and essay may be required depending on the specific scholarship.
Target applicant:
    High school students
    College students
    Graduate school students
    Adult students
Minimum GPA: 2.7
Amount: $1,800.
Number of awards: Varies.
Deadline: March 1.
How to apply: Applications are available online.

(1383) · Hawaii Society of Certified Public Accountants Scholarship Fund

Hawaii Community Foundation - Scholarships
1164 Bishop Street, Suite 800
Honolulu, HI 96813
Phone: 888-731-3863
Fax: 808-521-6286
Email: scholarships@hcf-hawaii.org
Website: http://www.hawaiicommunityfoundation.org
Purpose: To provide financial assistance for those pursuing degrees in accounting.
Eligibility: Applicants must be college juniors, college seniors or graduate students attending an accredited four-year Hawaii institution of higher learning with a major or concentration in accounting. They must have a minimum GPA of 3.0.
Target applicant:
    College students
    Graduate school students
    Adult students
Minimum GPA: 3.0
Amount: Varies.
Number of awards: Varies.
Deadline: March 1.
How to apply: To apply, register online, complete the online application and select the scholarships to which you wish to apply. In addition, mail the supporting materials: printed confirmation page from the online application, personal statement, copy of Student Aid Report (SAR) available at www.fafsa.ed.gov and official transcript.

(1384) · Hawaii Veterans Memorial Fund Scholarship

Hawaii Community Foundation - Scholarships
1164 Bishop Street, Suite 800
Honolulu, HI 96813
Phone: 888-731-3863
Fax: 808-521-6286
Email: scholarships@hcf-hawaii.org
Website: http://www.hawaiicommunityfoundation.org
Purpose: To provide financial assistance for Hawaii graduate students.
Eligibility: Applicants must be pursuing graduate studies at a U.S. college or university. They must have a GPA of 3.5 or higher. An additional award is available for students with high academic achievement, excellent character and an interest in contributing to professional and community service activities in Hawaii. Applicants do not need to be veterans or the children of veterans.
Target applicant:
    College students
    Graduate school students
    Adult students
Minimum GPA: 3.5
Amount: Varies.
Number of awards: Varies.
Deadline: March 1.
How to apply: To apply, register online, complete the online application and select the scholarships to which you wish to apply. In addition, mail the supporting materials: printed confirmation page from the online application, personal statement, copy of Student Aid Report (SAR) available at www.fafsa.ed.gov and official transcript.

(1385) · Hawkins-Tuma Memorial

Epsilon Sigma Alpha Foundation
P.O. Box 270517
Fort Collins, CO 80527
Phone: 970-223-2824
Fax: 970-223-4456
Email: kloyd@knoxy.net
Website: http://www.esaintl.com/esaf
Purpose: To provide financial assistance to graduating Oklahoma seniors who wish to obtain higher education.
Eligibility: Applicants may pursue any major at any school. Selection is based on the following criteria: scholastic ability (30 percent), financial need (30 percent), leadership (20 percent), service (10 percent) and character (10 percent).
Target applicant:
    High school students
Minimum GPA: None.
Amount: $500.
Number of awards: 1.
Deadline: February 1.
How to apply: Applications are available online.

(1386) · Hazel Knapp Endowment

Epsilon Sigma Alpha Foundation
P.O. Box 270517
Fort Collins, CO 80527
Phone: 970-223-2824
Fax: 970-223-4456
Email: kloyd@knoxy.net

Website: http://www.esaintl.com/esaf
Purpose: To provide financial assistance to Oregon residents.
Eligibility: Applicants may pursue any major at any college or university. Selection is based equally on character, leadership, service, financial need and scholastic ability.
Target applicant:
  High school students
  College students
  Adult students
Minimum GPA: None.
Amount: $1,000.
Number of awards: 1.
Deadline: February 1.
How to apply: Applications are available online.

(1387) · Health Professional Loan Repayment

Washington Higher Education Coordinating Board
917 Lakeridge Way
P.O. Box 43430
Olympia, WA 98504
Phone: 360-753-7850
Fax: 360-753-6243
Email: info@hecb.wa.gov
Website: http://www.hecb.wa.gov
Purpose: To attract health professionals to work in shortage areas in Washington state.
Eligibility: Applicants must be employed, or be under contract to be employed, at an eligible site, provide proof of eligible student debt, provide primary care and sign a contract to serve for at least three years. Eligible professions are physician, physician assistant or nurse practitioner, licensed nurse, midwife, pharmacist, dentist or dental hygienist.
Target applicant:
  College students
  Graduate school students
  Adult students
Minimum GPA: None.
Amount: Up to $35,000.
Number of awards: Varies.
Scholarship may be renewable.
Deadline: Varies.
How to apply: Applications are available online.

(1388) · Health Professional Scholarship

Washington Higher Education Coordinating Board
917 Lakeridge Way
P.O. Box 43430
Olympia, WA 98504
Phone: 360-753-7850
Fax: 360-753-6243
Email: info@hecb.wa.gov
Website: http://www.hecb.wa.gov
Purpose: To attract health professionals to work in shortage areas in Washington state.
Eligibility: Applicants must be training for primary care health professions, be U.S. citizens, have completed all applicable prerequisite coursework and sign a Promissory Note that states that they will serve for at least three years in a shortage area in Washington state. They must not be in default on a student loan.

Target applicant:
  College students
  Graduate school students
  Adult students
Minimum GPA: None.
Amount: Varies.
Number of awards: Varies.
Scholarship may be renewable.
Deadline: April 30.
How to apply: Applications are available online.

(1389) · Health Professions Education Scholarship Program

California Health and Welfare Agency - Office of Statewide Health Planning and Development
Health Professions Education Foundation
818 K Street, Room 210
Sacramento, CA 95814
Phone: 916-324-6500
Fax: 916-324-6585
Email: hpef@oshpd.state.ca.us
Website: http://www.healthprofessions.ca.gov
Purpose: To increase medical care to underserved areas of California by assisting residents who are studying to become dentists, dental hygienists, nurse practitioners, certified midwives and physician assistants.
Eligibility: Applicants must be California residents who have been accepted by or are enrolled in an accredited California program. Financial need, work experience and career goals are considered, and preference is given to applicants who plan to remain in a medically underserved area past the service time. Those selected must sign a two-year service agreement to work in a medically underserved area of California.
Target applicant:
  College students
  Graduate school students
  Adult students
Minimum GPA: None.
Amount: $10,000.
Number of awards: Varies.
Scholarship may be renewable.
Deadline: March.
How to apply: Applications are available online.

(1390) · Helen McSpadden Memorial Endowment

Epsilon Sigma Alpha Foundation
P.O. Box 270517
Fort Collins, CO 80527
Phone: 970-223-2824
Fax: 970-223-4456
Email: kloyd@knoxy.net
Website: http://www.esaintl.com/esaf
Purpose: To provide financial assistance for students pursuing continuing education.
Eligibility: Applicants must be Colorado residents. They may pursue any major at any college or university. Selection is based on scholastic ability (30 percent), financial need (30 percent), leadership (20 percent), character (10 percent) and service (10 percent).
Target applicant:
  High school students
  College students
  Adult students
Minimum GPA: None.

Amount: $500.
Number of awards: 1.
Deadline: February 1.
How to apply: Applications are available online.

(1391) · Henry A. Zuberano Scholarship

Hawaii Community Foundation - Scholarships
1164 Bishop Street, Suite 800
Honolulu, HI 96813
Phone: 888-731-3863
Fax: 808-521-6286
Email: scholarships@hcf-hawaii.org
Website: http://www.hawaiicommunityfoundation.org
Purpose: To assist Hawaii students who are majoring in political science, international relations, international business or public administration.
Eligibility: Applicants must have a GPA of 2.7 or higher.
Target applicant:
 High school students
 College students
 Adult students
Minimum GPA: 2.7
Amount: Varies.
Number of awards: Varies.
Deadline: March 1.
How to apply: To apply, register online, complete the online application and select the scholarships to which you wish to apply. In addition, mail the supporting materials: printed confirmation page from the online application, personal statement, copy of Student Aid Report (SAR) available at www.fafsa.ed.gov and official transcript.

(1392) · Henry Sachs Foundation Scholarship

Henry Sachs Foundation
90 S. Cascade Avenue
Suite 1410
Colorado Springs, CO 80903
Phone: 719-633-2353
Email: info@sachsfoundation.org
Website: http://www.sachsfoundation.org
Purpose: To aid African American high school students in Colorado to obtain a college education.
Eligibility: Applicants must be African-American residents of Colorado for at least five years. Applicants must be either seniors in high school or have graduated in the last three years but are not currently attending college. Awards are based on high school grade point average and financial need. If selected, applicants must attend a personal interview in order to receive the grant money.
Target applicant:
 High school students
Minimum GPA: None.
Amount: $4,000.
Number of awards: 50.
Scholarship may be renewable.
Deadline: March 1.
How to apply: Applications are available online.

(1393) · Herbert Hoover Uncommon Student Award

Herbert Hoover Presidential Library Association
P.O. Box 696
West Branch, IA 52358
Phone: 800-828-0475
Fax: 319-643-2391
Email: scholarship@hooverassociation.org
Website: http://www.hooverassociation.org
Purpose: To honor Herbert Hoover by rewarding students who live up to his ideal of the "uncommon man."
Eligibility: Applicants must be juniors in an Iowa high school or homeschool. Students must submit a project proposal and two letters of recommendation. Recipients must attend a weekend program during the summer and are expected to complete the proposed project. Grades, essays and test scores are not considered.
Target applicant:
 High school students
Minimum GPA: None.
Amount: $750-$5,000.
Number of awards: Approximately 15.
Deadline: March 31.
How to apply: Applications are available online.

(1394) · Hideko and Zenzo Matsuyama Scholarship Fund

Hawaii Community Foundation - Scholarships
1164 Bishop Street, Suite 800
Honolulu, HI 96813
Phone: 888-731-3863
Fax: 808-521-6286
Email: scholarships@hcf-hawaii.org
Website: http://www.hawaiicommunityfoundation.org
Purpose: To provide financial assistance for high school graduates who are seeking higher education.
Eligibility: Applicants must be graduates of Hawaiian high schools or GED recipients who plan to attend a college or university in Hawaii or the continental U.S. full-time. They must have a GPA of 3.0 or higher. Preference may be given to individuals of Japanese descent who were born in Hawaii.
Target applicant:
 College students
 Adult students
Minimum GPA: 3.0
Amount: Varies.
Number of awards: Varies.
Deadline: March 1.
How to apply: To apply, register online, complete the online application and select the scholarships to which you wish to apply. In addition, mail the supporting materials: printed confirmation page from the online application, personal statement, copy of Student Aid Report (SAR) available at www.fafsa.ed.gov and official transcript.

(1395) · High Technology Scholar/Intern Tuition Waiver

Massachusetts Office of Student Financial Assistance
454 Broadway
Suite 200
Revere, MA 02151
Phone: 617-727-9420
Fax: 617-727-0667
Email: osfa@osfa.mass.edu
Website: http://www.osfa.mass.edu
Purpose: To provide financial aid and internship connections to computer technology and engineering students in Massachusetts.

Eligibility: Students must be enrolled in an undergraduate program at a Massachusetts public college and must not have previously earned a bachelor's degree. Applicants must have approval from the company or organization that is funding the scholarship. Students must not owe refunds on any previous financial aid or have any defaulted government loans.

Target applicant:
   High school students
   College students
   Adult students
Minimum GPA: None.
Amount: Varies.
Number of awards: Varies.
Deadline: Varies.
How to apply: Applications are available at college financial aid offices.

(1396) · Higher Education Academic Scholarship Program (Bright Flight)

Missouri Student Assistance Resource Services (MOSTARS)
Missouri Department of Higher Education
3515 Amazonas Drive
Jefferson City, MO 65109
Phone: 800-473-6757
Fax: 573-751-6635
Website: http://www.dhe.mo.gov
Purpose: This merit-based program encourages top-ranked high school seniors to attend approved Missouri postsecondary schools.
Eligibility: Applicants must be U.S. citizens or eligible noncitizens, Missouri residents and have an ACT or SAT score within the top 3 percent of all Missouri students taking those tests. Applicants must be high school seniors who enroll as first-time, full-time students at an approved Missouri postsecondary school.
Target applicant:
   High school students
Minimum GPA: None.
Amount: Varies.
Number of awards: Varies.
Scholarship may be renewable.
Deadline: July 31.
How to apply: For an application contact your high school counselor or MOSTARS.

(1397) · Higher Education Adult Part-Time Student (HEAPS) Grant Program

West Virginia Higher Education Policy Commission
1018 Kanawha Boulevard, East
Fifth Floor
Charleston, WV 25301
Phone: 304-558-2101
Fax: 304-558-5719
Website: http://www.hepc.wvnet.edu
Purpose: To assist adult West Virginia students.
Eligibility: Applicants must be West Virginia residents, be U.S. citizens or permanent residents, be enrolled or accepted for enrollment in an undergraduate institution on a part-time basis and demonstrate financial need.
Target applicant:
   College students
   Adult students
Minimum GPA: None.

Amount: Varies.
Number of awards: Varies.
Scholarship may be renewable.
Deadline: Deadline of individual institution.
How to apply: Complete the Free Application for Federal Student Aid (FAFSA).

(1398) · Higher Education Grant

State of Wisconsin Higher Educational Aids Board
P.O. Box 7885
Madison, WI 53707
Phone: 608-267-2206
Fax: 608-267-2808
Email: heabmail@heab.state.wi.us
Website: http://heab.state.wi.us
Purpose: To assist Wisconsin students with financial need.
Eligibility: Applicants must be Wisconsin undergraduate students with financial need who attend Wisconsin colleges or universities at least half-time. Based on financial need.
Target applicant:
   College students
   Adult students
Minimum GPA: None.
Amount: Up to $1,800.
Number of awards: Varies.
Scholarship may be renewable.
Deadline: Varies.
How to apply: Complete the Free Application for Federal Student Aid (FAFSA).

(1399) · Higher Education Grant Program

West Virginia Higher Education Policy Commission
1018 Kanawha Boulevard, East
Fifth Floor
Charleston, WV 25301
Phone: 304-558-2101
Fax: 304-558-5719
Website: http://www.hepc.wvnet.edu
Purpose: To assist West Virginia students with financial need.
Eligibility: Applicants must be West Virginia residents, be U.S. citizens, demonstrate financial need and enroll full-time at an eligible undergraduate college or university in West Virginia or Pennsylvania.
Target applicant:
   College students
   Adult students
Minimum GPA: None.
Amount: Up to $2,700.
Number of awards: Varies.
Deadline: March 1.
How to apply: Complete the Free Application for Federal Student Aid (FAFSA) and the Common Application for State-Level Financial Aid Programs available online.

(1400) · Higher Education Legislative Plan (HELP)

Mississippi Office of Student Financial Aid
3825 Ridgewood Road
Jackson, MS 39211
Phone: 800-327-2980
Fax: 601-432-6527
Email: sfa@ihl.state.ms.us

Website: http://www.ihl.state.ms.us

Purpose: To assist financially needy Mississippi students afford tuition.

Eligibility: Applicants must be U.S. citizens or eligible noncitizens, Mississippi residents and have a minimum college GPA of 2.5 and have graduated from high school within the past two years. Applicants must be attending an eligible Mississippi institution, must have a minimum ACT score of 20 and must document an average gross income of $36,000 or less over the prior two years, and must have the results of a processed Student Aid Report (SAR). Students who file the Free Application for Federal Student Aid (FAFSA) will receive a SAR report.

Target applicant:
  High school students
  College students
  Adult students

Minimum GPA: None.

Amount: Varies.

Number of awards: Varies.

Scholarship may be renewable.

Deadline: March 31.

How to apply: Contact the Mississippi Office of Student Financial Aid for an application.

(1401) · Hobble (LPN) Nursing Scholarship

American Legion, Department of Kansas
1314 SW Topeka Boulevard
Topeka, KS 66612
Phone: 785-232-9315
Fax: 785-232-1399
Website: http://www.ksamlegion.org

Purpose: To assist future Kansas nurses.

Eligibility: Applicants must be Kansas residents attending an accredited Kansas school to receive a degree in Licensed Practical Nursing (LPN) and planning to practice their career in Kansas. Applicants must also demonstrate financial need and be 18 before taking the Kansas State Board examination.

Target applicant:
  High school students
  College students
  Adult students

Minimum GPA: None.

Amount: $300.

Number of awards: 1.

Deadline: February 15.

How to apply: Applications are available online and may be requested from Department Headquarters.

(1402) · Hoku Scholarship Fund

Hawaii Community Foundation - Scholarships
1164 Bishop Street, Suite 800
Honolulu, HI 96813
Phone: 888-731-3863
Fax: 808-521-6286
Email: scholarships@hcf-hawaii.org
Website: http://www.hawaiicommunityfoundation.org

Purpose: To provide financial assistance to students interested in pursuing observatory careers in math or science.

Eligibility: Applicants must be Hawaii residents who are pursuing observatory careers with majors in physics, astronomy, mathematics, engineering, technology or computer science. They must be full-time students, demonstrate financial need and have a GPA of 3.0 or higher.

Target applicant:
  High school students
  College students
  Adult students

Minimum GPA: 3.0.

Amount: Varies.

Number of awards: Varies.

Deadline: March 1.

How to apply: To apply, register online, complete the online application and select the scholarships to which you wish to apply. In addition, mail the supporting materials: printed confirmation page from the online application, personal statement, copy of Student Aid Report (SAR) available at www.fafsa.ed.gov and official transcript.

(1403) · HomeStreet Bank Scholarships

Independent Colleges of Washington
600 Stewart Street, Suite 600
Seattle, WA 98101
Phone: 206-623-4494
Fax: 206-625-9621
Email: info@icwashington.org
Website: http://www.icwashington.org

Purpose: To provide assistance to students with financial need and who are attending an independent college of Washington.

Eligibility: Recipients should have low or moderate income and be in good academic standing with their college or university. Students attending Gonzaga University, Heritage University, Pacific Lutheran University, Saint Martin's University, Seattle Pacific University, Seattle University, University of Puget Sound, Walla Walla University, Whitman College or Whitworth University are eligible.

Target applicant:
  College students
  Adult students

Minimum GPA: None.

Amount: $1,000.

Number of awards: 10.

Deadline: Varies.

How to apply: No application is required. Recipients are selected by their school's financial aid office.

(1404) · Honors Award

Louisiana Office of Student Financial Assistance
P.O. Box 91202
Baton Rouge, LA 70821-9202
Phone: 800-259-5626 x1012
Fax: 225-922-0790
Email: custserv@osfa.la.gov
Website: http://www.osfa.state.la.us

Purpose: To aid Louisiana student residents.

Eligibility: Applicants must be Louisiana residents and U.S. citizens, apply during their senior year in high school, use the award at a Louisiana college or university, have a minimum 3.0 GPA and have a minimum ACT score of 27 or equivalent SAT I score.

Target applicant:
  High school students

Minimum GPA: 3.0.

Amount: Tuition plus $800.

Number of awards: Varies.

Scholarship may be renewable.

Deadline: July 1.
How to apply: The application is the Free Application for Federal Student Aid (FAFSA). ACT or SAT I scores must also be reported.

(1405) · Hoosier Scholar Award

State Student Assistance Commission of Indiana
150 W. Market Street
Suite 500
Indianapolis, IN 46204
Phone: 888-528-4719
Fax: 317-232-3260
Email: grants@ssaci.state.in.us
Website: http://www.in.gov/ssaci
Purpose: Monetary assistance is provided to Indiana resident high school seniors with freshman expenses at state schools.
Eligibility: Applicants must be graduating Indiana high school seniors, rank in the top 20 percent of their graduating class and plan to attend an Indiana institution of higher education full-time. Scholars are chosen by high school guidance counselors. Selection is based on educational merit.
Target applicant:
  High school students
Minimum GPA: None.
Amount: $500.
Number of awards: Varies.
Deadline: Varies.
How to apply: Winners are selected by their high school.

(1406) · Hope Baney Memorial Endowment

Epsilon Sigma Alpha Foundation
P.O. Box 270517
Fort Collins, CO 80527
Phone: 970-223-2824
Fax: 970-223-4456
Email: kloyd@knoxy.net
Website: http://www.esaintl.com/esaf
Purpose: To provide financial assistance to Oregon students who study teaching.
Eligibility: Applicants may attend any institution of higher learning in the state of Oregon. Selection is based equally on the following factors: character, leadership, service, financial need and scholastic ability.
Target applicant:
  High school students
  College students
  Adult students
Minimum GPA: None.
Amount: $500.
Number of awards: 1.
Deadline: February 1.
How to apply: Applications are available online.

(1407) · Hope Community College Transfer Scholarship

Maryland Higher Education Commission
Office of Student Financial Assistance
839 Bestgate Road, Suite 400
Annapolis, MD 21401
Phone: 800-974-1024
Fax: 410-260-3200

Email: osfamail@mhec.state.md.us
Website: http://www.mhec.state.md.us
Purpose: To help Maryland community college students who want to transfer into a four-year Maryland college or university.
Eligibility: Applicants must be U.S. citizens or eligible noncitizens and current Maryland community college students who will have completed at least 60 credits or who will have earned an associate's degree by the end of the semester in which they will transfer to a Maryland four-year institution.
Target applicant:
  College students
  Adult students
Minimum GPA: None.
Amount: Varies.
Number of awards: Varies.
Scholarship may be renewable.
Deadline: January 1-March 1.
How to apply: Complete and file the Free Application for Federal Student Aid (FAFSA), and complete and file the HOPE Community College Transfer Scholarship application.

(1408) · HOPE General Scholarship

Maryland Higher Education Commission
Office of Student Financial Assistance
839 Bestgate Road, Suite 400
Annapolis, MD 21401
Phone: 800-974-1024
Fax: 410-260-3200
Email: osfamail@mhec.state.md.us
Website: http://www.mhec.state.md.us
Purpose: To help Maryland students who major in certain fields at Maryland colleges.
Eligibility: Applicants and their parents must be Maryland residents. All applicants must have an unweighted cumulative high school GPA of 3.0 or higher. Applicant's family income may not exceed $95,000 annually. Applicants must enroll at a two- or four-year Maryland college or university as a full-time, degree-seeking undergraduate student and major in an eligible program. Eligible programs include: agriculture and natural resources, area studies, business and management, communications, fine arts and applied arts, foreign languages, health professions, home economics, interdisciplinary, law, letters (English), psychology, public affairs, social sciences and theology. All applicants are ranked by cumulative grade point average.
Target applicant:
  High school students
  College students
  Adult students
Minimum GPA: 3.0
Amount: $1,000-$3,000.
Number of awards: Varies.
Scholarship may be renewable.
Deadline: January 1-March 1.
How to apply: Complete and file the Free Application for Federal Student Aid (FAFSA), and complete and file the HOPE Scholarship application.

(1409) · HOPE Scholarship Program

Georgia Student Finance Commission
2082 East Exchange Place
Tucker, GA 30084
Phone: 800-505-4732

Fax: 770-724-9089
Email: support@gacollege411.org
Website: http://www.gacollege411.org
Purpose: To support students attending Georgia institutions.
Eligibility: Applicants must have graduated from high school and be attending or planning to attend college in Georgia.
Target applicant:
   High school students
   College students
   Adult students
Minimum GPA: None.
Amount: Varies.
Number of awards: Varies.
Scholarship may be renewable.
Deadline: Varies.
How to apply: Applications are available online.

(1410) · Howard P. Rawlings Guaranteed Access (GA) Grant

Maryland Higher Education Commission
Office of Student Financial Assistance
839 Bestgate Road, Suite 400
Annapolis, MD 21401
Phone: 800-974-1024
Fax: 410-260-3200
Email: osfamail@mhec.state.md.us
Website: http://www.mhec.state.md.us
Purpose: To help Maryland students with financial need afford college.
Eligibility: Applicants and their parents must both be legal residents of the state of Maryland. Applicants must be U.S. citizens or eligible noncitizens, complete the Free Application for Federal Student Aid (FAFSA) and the Guaranteed Access (GA) Grant application. Applicants and families must also meet the established income limits to qualify.
Target applicant:
   High school students
Minimum GPA: None.
Amount: $400-$10,200.
Number of awards: Varies.
Scholarship may be renewable.
Deadline: March 1.
How to apply: Complete the FAFSA.

(1411) · Hugh A. Smith Scholarship Fund

American Legion, Department of Kansas
1314 SW Topeka Boulevard
Topeka, KS 66612
Phone: 785-232-9315
Fax: 785-232-1399
Website: http://www.ksamlegion.org
Purpose: To provide assistance to needy and worthy children of American Legion and American Legion Auxiliary members.
Eligibility: Applicants must be average or better students who are high school seniors or college freshmen or sophomores enrolling or enrolled in a post-secondary school in Kansas. They must be the son or daughter of a veteran, and a parent must have been a member of the Kansas American Legion or American Legion Auxiliary for the past three years. The children of deceased parents are also eligible if the parent was a paid member at the time of death. Applicants must submit three letters of recommendation, including one from a teacher, an essay on "Why I

Want to Go to College," high school transcript, a 1040 income statement and documentation of parent's veteran status.
Target applicant:
   High school students
   College students
   Adult students
Minimum GPA: None.
Amount: $500.
Number of awards: 1.
Deadline: February 15.
How to apply: Applications are available online.

(1412) · Ichiro and Masako Hirata Scholarship

Hawaii Community Foundation - Scholarships
1164 Bishop Street, Suite 800
Honolulu, HI 96813
Phone: 888-731-3863
Fax: 808-521-6286
Email: scholarships@hcf-hawaii.org
Website: http://www.hawaiicommunityfoundation.org
Purpose: To provide financial assistance to Hawaii students who are pursuing degrees in education.
Eligibility: Applicants must be majoring or concentrating in education. They must be college juniors, college seniors or graduate students and have a GPA of 3.0 or higher.
Target applicant:
   College students
   Graduate school students
   Adult students
Minimum GPA: 3.0
Amount: Varies.
Number of awards: Varies.
Deadline: March 1.
How to apply: To apply, register online, complete the online application and select the scholarships to which you wish to apply. In addition, mail the supporting materials: printed confirmation page from the online application, personal statement, copy of Student Aid Report (SAR) available at www.fafsa.ed.gov and official transcript.

(1413) · Idaho Promise Category A Scholarship

Idaho State Board of Education
P.O. Box 83720
Boise, ID 83720
Phone: 208-334-2270
Fax: 208-334-2632
Email: dkelly@osbe.state.id.us
Website: http://www.boardofed.idaho.gov
Purpose: To support outstanding Idaho high school seniors.
Eligibility: Applicants must be Idaho residents, be graduating seniors of Idaho high schools and enroll full-time at an eligible Idaho college or university. Academic applicants must also be in the top 10 percent of their graduating class, have a minimum 3.5 GPA and a minimum ACT score of 28. Professional-technical applicants must have a minimum 2.8 GPA and take the COMPASS test.
Target applicant:
   High school students
Minimum GPA: Varies
Amount: $3,000.
Number of awards: 25.
Scholarship may be renewable.

Deadline: Varies.
How to apply: Contact your high school guidance counselor.

(1414) · Idaho Promise Category B Scholarship

Idaho State Board of Education
P.O. Box 83720
Boise, ID 83720
Phone: 208-334-2270
Fax: 208-334-2632
Email: dkelly@osbe.state.id.us
Website: http://www.boardofed.idaho.gov
Purpose: Monetary assistance is provided to Idaho resident high school students with their freshman expenses at Idaho colleges or universities.
Eligibility: Applicants must have graduated from an Idaho high school, be entering freshmen at an eligible Idaho college or university, be residents of Idaho and have a minimum 3.0 GPA or minimum ACT score of 20. Applicants must also be younger than 22 years old and complete at least 12 credits per semester with a minimum 2.5 GPA to remain eligible for renewal.
Target applicant:
  High school students
  College students
Minimum GPA: 3.0
Amount: $250.
Number of awards: Varies.
Scholarship may be renewable.
Deadline: Varies.
How to apply: Contact eligible college or university financial aid office.

(1415) · Illinois American Legion Scholarship Program

American Legion Auxiliary, Department of Illinois
2720 E. Lincoln
Bloomington, IL 61704
Phone: 309-663-9366
Email: webmaster@illegion.org
Website: http://www.illegion.org/auxiliary/mem_Education.html
Purpose: To award scholarships to graduating students enrolled in Illinois high schools.
Eligibility: Applicants must be children or grandchildren of American Legion Illinois members and must be in their senior year of high school. Awards may be used to further education at an accredited college, university or technical school.
Target applicant:
  High school students
Minimum GPA: None.
Amount: $1,000.
Number of awards: 20.
Deadline: March 15.
How to apply: Application information is available by contacting the American Legion, Department of Illinois.

(1416) · Illinois AMVETS Junior ROTC Scholarship

Illinois AMVETS Service Foundation
AMVETS Department of Illinois
2200 South Sixth Street
Springfield, IL 62703
Phone: 217-528-4713
Fax: 217-528-9896

Email: crystal@ilamvets.org
Website: http://www.ilamvets.org
Purpose: To provide financial assistance for college to high school ROTC members.
Eligibility: Applicants must be Illinois high school seniors who are participating in a Junior ROTC program and have taken the SAT or ACT.
Target applicant:
  High school students
Minimum GPA: None.
Amount: $3,000.
Number of awards: Varies.
Deadline: March 1.
How to apply: Applications are available online.

(1417) · Illinois AMVETS Ladies Auxiliary Memorial Scholarship

Illinois AMVETS Service Foundation
AMVETS Department of Illinois
2200 South Sixth Street
Springfield, IL 62703
Phone: 217-528-4713
Fax: 217-528-9896
Email: crystal@ilamvets.org
Website: http://www.ilamvets.org
Purpose: To provide financial assistance to children and grandchildren of U.S. veterans and members of the military.
Eligibility: Applicants must be Illinois high school seniors who have taken the SAT or ACT, and they must be the children or grandchildren of veterans who were honorably discharged after September 15, 1940 or who are currently serving in the military.
Target applicant:
  High school students
Minimum GPA: None.
Amount: $500.
Number of awards: Varies.
Deadline: March 1.
How to apply: Applications are available online.

(1418) · Illinois AMVETS Ladies Auxiliary Worchid Scholarship

Illinois AMVETS Service Foundation
AMVETS Department of Illinois
2200 South Sixth Street
Springfield, IL 62703
Phone: 217-528-4713
Fax: 217-528-9896
Email: crystal@ilamvets.org
Website: http://www.ilamvets.org
Purpose: To provide financial assistance for students whose parents are U.S. veterans.
Eligibility: Applicants must be Illinois high school seniors whose mother or father is a U.S. veteran who was honorably discharged after September 15, 1940. They must also have taken the SAT or ACT.
Target applicant:
  High school students
Minimum GPA: None.
Amount: $500.
Number of awards: Varies.
Deadline: March 1.
How to apply: Applications are available online.

(1419) · Illinois AMVETS Sad Sacks Nursing Scholarship

Illinois AMVETS Service Foundation
AMVETS Department of Illinois
2200 South Sixth Street
Springfield, IL 62703
Phone: 217-528-4713
Fax: 217-528-9896
Email: crystal@ilamvets.org
Website: http://www.ilamvets.org
Purpose: To assist Illinois students who are pursuing a career in nursing.
Eligibility: Applicants must be Illinois high school seniors who have been accepted into a nursing program or students who are already attending nursing school in Illinois. They must have financial need and a satisfactory academic record, character and activity record. Dependents of deceased or disabled veterans receive priority.
Target applicant:
    High school students
    College students
    Adult students
Minimum GPA: None.
Amount: Varies.
Number of awards: Varies.
Deadline: March 1.
How to apply: Applications are available online.

(1420) · Illinois AMVETS Service Foundation Scholarship

Illinois AMVETS Service Foundation
AMVETS Department of Illinois
2200 South Sixth Street
Springfield, IL 62703
Phone: 217-528-4713
Fax: 217-528-9896
Email: crystal@ilamvets.org
Website: http://www.ilamvets.org
Purpose: To help Illinois students pay for college.
Eligibility: Applicants musts be Illinois high school seniors who have taken the SAT or ACT. Preference is given to students who are the children or grandchildren of Illinois veterans.
Target applicant:
    High school students
Minimum GPA: None.
Amount: $3,000.
Number of awards: Varies.
Deadline: March 1.
How to apply: Applications are available online.

(1421) · Illinois AMVETS Trade School Scholarship

Illinois AMVETS Service Foundation
AMVETS Department of Illinois
2200 South Sixth Street
Springfield, IL 62703
Phone: 217-528-4713
Fax: 217-528-9896
Email: crystal@ilamvets.org
Website: http://www.ilamvets.org
Purpose: To provide financial assistance to Illinois students who plan to attend a trade school.

Eligibility: Applicants must be seniors at an Illinois high school who have been accepted into a trade school program. Students must submit a copy of their acceptance letter with the application form. Preference is given to students who are the children or grandchildren of veterans.
Target applicant:
    High school students
Minimum GPA: None.
Amount: $3,000.
Number of awards: Varies.
Deadline: March 1.
How to apply: Applications are available online.

(1422) · Illinois Future Teacher Corps (IFTC) Program

Illinois Student Assistance Commission
1755 Lake Cook Road
Deerfield, IL 60015
Phone: 800-899-4722
Fax: 847-831-8549
Email: collegezone@isac.org
Website: http://www.collegezone.com
Purpose: To assist talented and financially needy students who are interested in pursuing a career in education.
Eligibility: Applicants must be Illinois residents who are U.S. citizens or eligible non-citizens. They must be enrolled as a junior or above in an approved teacher education program and maintain at least a 2.5 GPA. Applicants must submit a FAFSA form, comply with Selective Service requirements and not be in default on any student loans. Applicants are not eligible to receive the scholarship in the same year as receiving a Minority Teachers of Illinois (MTI) Scholarship or Illinois Special Education Teacher Tuition Waiver (SETTW). Scholarship recipients agree to teach in Illinois after graduating.
Target applicant:
    College students
    Graduate school students
    Adult students
Minimum GPA: 2.5
Amount: $5,000-$15,000.
Number of awards: Varies.
Scholarship may be renewable.
Deadline: March 1, but applications received after this date will be considered as funding allows.
How to apply: Applications are available online.

(1423) · Illinois Incentive for Access (IIA) Program

Illinois Department of Public Health
535 W. Jefferson Street
Springfield, IL 62761
Phone: 217-782-4977
Fax: 217-782-3987
Email: dph.mailus@illinois.gov
Website: http://www.idph.state.il.us
Purpose: To aid Illinois students who have extreme financial need.
Eligibility: Applicants must be Illinois residents, be enrolled at least half-time as freshmen at a participating Illinois school and have an Expected Family Contribution (EFC) of zero.
Target applicant:
    College students
    Adult students
Minimum GPA: None.
Amount: $500.
Number of awards: Varies.

Deadline: As soon as possible after January 1.
How to apply: Complete the Free Application for Federal Student Aid (FAFSA).

(1424) · Illinois Oratorical Contest

American Legion Auxiliary, Department of Illinois
2720 E. Lincoln
Bloomington, IL 61704
Phone: 309-663-9366
Email: webmaster@illegion.org
Website: http://www.illegion.org/auxiliary/mem_Education.html
Purpose: To enhance high school students' experience with and understanding of the U.S. Constitution. The contest will help develop students' leadership skills and civic appreciation, as well as the ability to deliver thoughtful, insightful orations regarding U.S. citizenship and its inherent responsibilities.
Eligibility: Applicants must be high school students under the age of 20 who are U.S. citizens or legal residents and residents of the state. Students first give an oration within their state and winners compete at the national level. The oration must be related to the Constitution of the United States focusing on the duties and obligations citizens have to the government. It must be in English and be between eight and ten minutes. There is also an assigned topic which is posted on the website, and it should be between three and five minutes.
Target applicant:
High school students
Minimum GPA: None.
Amount: Up to $1,600.
Number of awards: Varies.
Deadline: February.
How to apply: Application information is available by contacting the local American Legion Post or Illinois Department Headquarters.

(1425) · Illinois State Endowment

Epsilon Sigma Alpha Foundation
P.O. Box 270517
Fort Collins, CO 80527
Phone: 970-223-2824
Fax: 970-223-4456
Email: kloyd@knoxy.net
Website: http://www.esaintl.com/esaf
Purpose: To provide financial assistance for Illinois residents.
Eligibility: Applicants may pursue any major at any institution of higher learning. Selection is based on scholastic ability (30 percent), financial need (30 percent), leadership (20 percent), character (10 percent) and service (10 percent).
Target applicant:
High school students
College students
Adult students
Minimum GPA: None.
Amount: $500.
Number of awards: 2.
Deadline: February 1.
How to apply: Applications are available online.

(1426) · Incentive Grants

Vermont Student Assistance Corporation
10 E. Allen Street
P.O. Box 2000

Winooski, VT 05404
Phone: 888-253-4819
Fax: 802-654-3765
Email: info@vsac.org
Website: http://www.vsac.org
Purpose: To assist Vermont students.
Eligibility: Applicants must be Vermont residents who demonstrate financial need and plan to attend college full-time.
Target applicant:
High school students
College students
Adult students
Minimum GPA: None.
Amount: Up to $8,700.
Number of awards: Varies.
Deadline: Varies.
How to apply: Applications are available online.

(1427) · Incentive Program for Aspiring Teachers

Massachusetts Office of Student Financial Assistance
454 Broadway
Suite 200
Revere, MA 02151
Phone: 617-727-9420
Fax: 617-727-0667
Email: osfa@osfa.mass.edu
Website: http://www.osfa.mass.edu
Purpose: To provide financial support for Massachusetts college students who are studying to become teachers.
Eligibility: Applicants must be in their third or fourth year at a public college in the state of Massachusetts, and they must be enrolled in a field with teacher shortages. They must have a 3.0 GPA in general education courses, and they must remain in satisfactory academic standing while receiving the scholarship. Students must agree to work in a public school in Massachusetts for two years after earning a bachelor's degree.
Target applicant:
College students
Adult students
Minimum GPA: 3.0
Amount: Varies.
Number of awards: Varies.
Scholarship may be renewable.
Deadline: Varies.
How to apply: Applications are available at college financial aid offices.

(1428) · Independent Living Act (Foster Care Tuition Waiver)

Oklahoma State Regents for Higher Education
655 Research Parkway, Suite 200
Oklahoma City, OK 73104
Phone: 800-858-1840
Fax: 405-225-9230
Email: studentinfo@osrhe.edu
Website: http://www.okhighered.org
Purpose: To assist students who have been in foster care in obtaining higher education.
Eligibility: Applicants must be residents of Oklahoma who have graduated within the past three years from an accredited high school in or bordering Oklahoma or have received their GED. They must be 21 years of age or younger and have been in DHS custody for at least

nine months between ages 16 and 18. They must be enrolled in a public institution or in certain programs at technology centers.

Target applicant:
High school students
College students
Minimum GPA: None.
Amount: Tuition.
Number of awards: Varies.
Scholarship may be renewable.
Deadline: Varies.
How to apply: Contact by phone or email for more information on how to apply.

(1429) · Indiana BPW Women in Transition Scholarship

Indiana Business and Professional Women's Foundation Inc.
P.O. Box 33
Knightstown, IN 46168
Phone: 765-345-9812
Email: bpwin@msn.com
Website: http://www.indianabpwfoundation.org/scholarships.htm
Purpose: To support women who are re-entering the workforce or changing careers.
Eligibility: Applicants must be Indiana residents for at least one year prior to the date of application. Students must be at least 30 years old, show financial need and have applied to attend a post-secondary institution at least part-time.
Target applicant:
College students
Adult students
Minimum GPA: None.
Amount: Varies.
Number of awards: Varies.
Scholarship may be renewable.
Deadline: February 15.
How to apply: Applications are available online.

(1430) · Indiana BPW Working Women Scholarship

Indiana Business and Professional Women's Foundation Inc.
P.O. Box 33
Knightstown, IN 46168
Phone: 765-345-9812
Email: bpwin@msn.com
Website: http://www.indianabpwfoundation.org/scholarships.htm
Purpose: To support women who are working while attending school.
Eligibility: Applicants must work at least 20 hours per week, and they must attend school at least part-time. Students must be 25 years of age or older. They must have been Indiana residents for at least one year prior to the date of application. Applicants must show financial need.
Target applicant:
College students
Adult students
Minimum GPA: None.
Amount: Varies.
Number of awards: Varies.
Scholarship may be renewable.
Deadline: February 15.
How to apply: Applications are available online.

(1431) · Indiana Oratorical Contest

American Legion, Department of Indiana
777 N. Meridian Street
Indianapolis, IN 46204
Phone: 317-630-1300
Website: http://www.indlegion.org
Purpose: To enhance high school students' experience with and understanding of the U.S. Constitution. The contest will help develop students' leadership skills and civic appreciation, as well as the ability to deliver thoughtful, insightful orations regarding U.S. citizenship and its inherent responsibilities.
Eligibility: Applicants must be high school students under the age of 20 who are U.S. citizens or legal residents and residents of the state. Students first give an oration within their state and winners compete at the national level. The oration must be related to the Constitution of the United States focusing on the duties and obligations citizens have to the government. It must be in English and be between eight and ten minutes. There is also an assigned topic which is posted on the website, and it should be between three and five minutes.
Target applicant:
High school students
Minimum GPA: None.
Amount: Up to $3,200.
Number of awards: Varies.
Deadline: December 8.
How to apply: Application information is available from the local American Legion Post and online.

(1432) · Instructional Grant

Ohio Board of Regents
State Grants and Scholarships Department
P.O. Box 182452
Columbus, OH 43218-2452
Phone: 888-833-1133
Fax: 614-752-5903
Website: http://www.regents.ohio.gov
Purpose: To assist Ohio undergraduate students with financial need.
Eligibility: Applicants must be Ohio residents, full-time undergraduate students and come from low or moderate income families.
Target applicant:
College students
Adult students
Minimum GPA: None.
Amount: Up to approximately $5,500.
Number of awards: Varies.
Deadline: October 1.
How to apply: Complete the Free Application for Federal Student Aid (FAFSA).

(1433) · Ione M. Allen Music Scholarship

Center for Scholarship Administration
Wachovia Accounts
4320-G Wade Hampton Boulevard
Taylors, SC 29687
Phone: 866-608-0001
Email: wachoviascholars@bellsouth.net
Website: http://www.wachoviascholars.com
Purpose: To provide financial assistance to Western North Carolina students who are interested in music.

Eligibility: Applicants must be residents of Buncombe, Cherokee, Clay, Graham, Haywood, Henderson, Jackson, Macon, Madison, Polk, Swain or Transylvania County, North Carolina. They must possess musical talent and attend an accredited conservatory or other institution with a recognized music department. All applicants must be interviewed and present a performance.
Target applicant:
    High school students
Minimum GPA: None.
Amount: Varies.
Number of awards: Varies.
Scholarship may be renewable.
Deadline: February 1.
How to apply: Applications are available online.

(1434) · Iowa Grants

Iowa College Student Aid Commission
200 10th Street, 4th Floor
Des Moines, IA 50309
Phone: 515-242-3344
Fax: 515-242-3388
Email: info@iowacollegeaid.org
Website: http://www.iowacollegeaid.org
Purpose: To assist needy Iowa students.
Eligibility: Applicants must be enrolled in or planning to enroll at least part-time in an undergraduate program at eligible Iowa colleges, universities and community colleges and be U.S. citizens. Selection is based on need, with priority given to the neediest applicants.
Target applicant:
    High school students
    College students
    Adult students
Minimum GPA: None.
Amount: $1,000.
Number of awards: Varies.
Scholarship may be renewable.
Deadline: As soon as possible after January 1.
How to apply: Complete the Free Application for Federal Student Aid (FAFSA).

(1435) · Iowa Oratorical Contest

American Legion, Department of Iowa
720 Lyon Street
Des Moines, IA 50309
Phone: 800-365-8387
Fax: 515-282-7583
Email: programs@ialegion.org
Website: http://www.ialegion.org
Purpose: To enhance high school students' experience with and understanding of the U.S. Constitution. The contest will help develop students' leadership skills and civic appreciation, as well as the ability to deliver thoughtful, insightful orations regarding U.S. citizenship and its inherent responsibilities.
Eligibility: Applicants must be high school students under the age of 20 who are U.S. citizens or legal residents and residents of the state. Students first give an oration within their state and winners compete at the national level. The oration must be related to the Constitution of the United States focusing on the duties and obligations citizens have to the government. It must be in English and be between eight and ten minutes. There is also an assigned topic which is posted on the website, and it should be between three and five minutes.

Target applicant:
    High school students
Minimum GPA: None.
Amount: Up to $3,500.
Number of awards: Varies.
Deadline: February 18.
How to apply: Applications are available online.

(1436) · Iowa Tuition Grants

Iowa College Student Aid Commission
200 10th Street, 4th Floor
Des Moines, IA 50309
Phone: 515-242-3344
Fax: 515-242-3388
Email: info@iowacollegeaid.org
Website: http://www.iowacollegeaid.org
Purpose: To help students attend Iowa's independent colleges and universities.
Eligibility: Applicants must be enrolled in or planning to enroll at least part-time in an eligible Iowa college or university and demonstrate financial need. Priority is given to the neediest applicants.
Target applicant:
    High school students
    College students
    Adult students
Minimum GPA: None.
Amount: $4,000.
Number of awards: Varies.
Scholarship may be renewable.
Deadline: July 1.
How to apply: Complete the Free Application for Federal Student Aid (FAFSA).

(1437) · Iowa Vocational-Technical Tuition Grants

Iowa College Student Aid Commission
200 10th Street, 4th Floor
Des Moines, IA 50309
Phone: 515-242-3344
Fax: 515-242-3388
Email: info@iowacollegeaid.org
Website: http://www.iowacollegeaid.org
Purpose: To aid those Iowa residents enrolled in vocational-technical programs at community colleges.
Eligibility: Applicants must be enrolled in or planning to enroll in a career education or option course of at least 12 weeks duration at an Iowa area community college and be U.S. citizens or permanent residents.
Target applicant:
    High school students
    College students
    Adult students
Minimum GPA: None.
Amount: $1,200.
Number of awards: Varies.
Scholarship may be renewable.
Deadline: July 1.
How to apply: Complete the Free Application for Federal Student Aid (FAFSA).

(1438) · Irvine W. Cook WA0CGS Scholarship

American Radio Relay League Foundation
225 Main Street
Newington, CT 06111
Phone: 860-594-0397
Fax: 860-594-0259
Email: foundation@arrl.org
Website: http://www.arrl.org
Purpose: To provide scholarship assistance to Kansas residents who are amateur radio operators.
Eligibility: Applicants must be residents of Kansas and holders of an active amateur radio license of any class. Preference is given to students who are studying electronics, communications or a related subject at the baccalaureate level or higher.
Target applicant:
   College students
   Graduate school students
   Adult students
Minimum GPA: None.
Amount: $1,000.
Number of awards: 1.
Deadline: February 1.
How to apply: Applications are available online.

(1439) · J.A. Knowles Memorial Scholarship

United Methodist Church
Office of Loans and Scholarships
P.O. BOX 340007
Nashville, TN 37203-0007
Phone: 615-340-7344
Fax: 615-340-7367
Email: umscholar@gbhem.org
Website: http://www.gbhem.org
Purpose: To support Texas Methodist college students.
Eligibility: Applicants must be enrolled full-time at any accredited college or graduate school in Texas and active members of the Methodist church in Texas for at least one year before applying for the scholarship. Students must have at least a 2.5 GPA and be U.S. citizens or permanent residents.
Target applicant:
   High school students
   College students
   Graduate school students
   Adult students
Minimum GPA: 2.5
Amount: Varies.
Number of awards: Varies.
Deadline: Varies.
How to apply: Applications are available online in January.

(1440) · J.D. Edsal Advertising Scholarship/Women's Advertising Club Scholarship

Rhode Island Foundation
One Union Station
Providence, RI 02903
Phone: 401-274-4564
Fax: 401-331-8085
Email: libbym@rifoundation.org
Website: http://www.rifoundation.org
Purpose: To support undergraduate students who are planning to work in advertising.

Eligibility: Applicants must be residents of Rhode Island. They must be majoring in advertising, public relations, graphic design, marketing, film, television or broadcast production. Students must be at least in their sophomore year of college, and they must be attending school full-time. Applicants must show financial need and a commitment to an advertising career.
Target applicant:
   College students
   Adult students
Minimum GPA: None.
Amount: $1,500.
Number of awards: 1.
Deadline: April 30.
How to apply: Applications are available online.

(1441) · Jack and Lucille Crossno Memorial Endowment

Epsilon Sigma Alpha Foundation
P.O. Box 270517
Fort Collins, CO 80527
Phone: 970-223-2824
Fax: 970-223-4456
Email: kloyd@knoxy.net
Website: http://www.esaintl.com/esaf
Purpose: To provide financial assistance to Kansas residents.
Eligibility: Applicants must attend a Kansas institution of higher learning. Any major is allowed. Selection is based equally on character, leadership, service, financial need and scholastic ability.
Target applicant:
   High school students
   College students
   Adult students
Minimum GPA: None.
Amount: $600.
Number of awards: 2.
Deadline: February 1.
How to apply: Applications are available online.

(1442) · Jack F. Tolbert Memorial Student Grant Program

Maryland Higher Education Commission
Office of Student Financial Assistance
839 Bestgate Road, Suite 400
Annapolis, MD 21401
Phone: 800-974-1024
Fax: 410-260-3200
Email: osfamail@mhec.state.md.us
Website: http://www.mhec.state.md.us
Purpose: To assist students who are attending or planning to attend a private career school.
Eligibility: Students and their parents if they are dependents must be residents of Maryland. Applicants must also enroll at an approved private career school in the state for at least 18 hours per week.
Target applicant:
   High school students
   College students
   Adult students
Minimum GPA: None.
Amount: Up to $500.
Number of awards: Varies.
Scholarship may be renewable.

Deadline: March 1.

How to apply: Students apply by completing the Free Application for Federal Student Aid (FAFSA) and turning it in to the financial aid office of the career school they will attend.

(1443) · James J. Burns and C.A. Haynes Scholarship

Rhode Island Foundation
One Union Station
Providence, RI 02903
Phone: 401-274-4564
Fax: 401-331-8085
Email: libbym@rifoundation.org
Website: http://www.rifoundation.org
Purpose: To support students who are planning to work in the textile industry.
Eligibility: Students must be currently enrolled in a textile program. They must demonstrate financial need or academic excellence. Preference will be given to students whose parents are members of the National Association of Textile Supervisors.
Target applicant:
  High school students
  College students
  Graduate school students
  Adult students
Minimum GPA: None.
Amount: $1,000.
Number of awards: 2.
Deadline: April 30.
How to apply: Applications are available online.

(1444) · James L. Shriver Scholarship

Community Foundation of Western Massachusetts
1500 Main Street
P.O. Box 15769
Springfield, MA 01115
Phone: 413-732-2858
Fax: 413-733-8565
Email: scholar@communityfoundation.org
Website: http://www.communityfoundation.org
Purpose: To help students from western Massachusetts to pursue technical careers.
Eligibility: Applicants must attend a U.S. college or university part-time or full-time. Application forms, transcripts and Student Aid Reports are required. Selection is based on financial need and academic merit.
Target applicant:
  High school students
  College students
  Graduate school students
  Adult students
Minimum GPA: None.
Amount: $500.
Number of awards: 1.
Deadline: March 31.
How to apply: Applications are available online and by phone.

(1445) · James V. Day Scholarship

American Legion, Department of Maine
21 College Avenue
Waterville, ME 04901
Phone: 207-873-3229
Email: legionme@me.acadia.net
Website: http://www.mainelegion.org
Purpose: To provide financial assistance to the children or grandchildren of American Legion, Department of Maine members.
Eligibility: Applicants must be U.S. citizens, residents of Maine and graduating high school seniors. They must be enrolled in an accredited college or vocational technical school and provide evidence of financial need. Applicants must demonstrate good character and a belief in the American way of life.
Target applicant:
  High school students
Minimum GPA: None.
Amount: $500.
Number of awards: 1.
Deadline: May 1.
How to apply: Applications are available online.

(1446) · James W. Colgan Loan

Community Foundation of Western Massachusetts
1500 Main Street
P.O. Box 15769
Springfield, MA 01115
Phone: 413-732-2858
Fax: 413-733-8565
Email: scholar@communityfoundation.org
Website: http://www.communityfoundation.org
Purpose: To provide interest-free educational loans for students who have lived in Massachusetts for the past five years.
Eligibility: Applicants must be part-time or full-time undergraduate or graduate students. Students should provide application forms, transcripts and Student Aid Reports. Recipients will begin repaying the loan three months after graduation, and no interest is charged as long as the monthly payments are made on time.
Target applicant:
  High school students
  College students
  Graduate school students
  Adult students
Minimum GPA: None.
Amount: Varies.
Number of awards: Varies.
Deadline: March 31.
How to apply: Applications are available online and by phone.

(1447) · James. F. Byrnes Scholarships

James F. Byrnes Foundation
P.O. Box 6781
Columbia, SC 29260-6781
Phone: 803-254-9325
Fax: 803-254-9354
Email: Info@byrnesscholars.org
Website: http://www.byrnesscholars.org
Purpose: To support South Carolina students with deceased parents.
Eligibility: Applicants must be residents of South Carolina whose parent or parents are deceased and must attend or plan to attend a four-year college or university.
Target applicant:
  High school students
  College students
  Adult students

Minimum GPA: 2.5
Amount: Up to $11,000.
Number of awards: Varies.
Scholarship may be renewable.
Deadline: February 15.
How to apply: Applications are available online.

(1448) · Jan Reppentine / Arkansas State Council Endowment

Epsilon Sigma Alpha Foundation
P.O. Box 270517
Fort Collins, CO 80527
Phone: 970-223-2824
Fax: 970-223-4456
Email: kloyd@knoxy.net
Website: http://www.esaintl.com/esaf
Purpose: To provide financial assistance for Arkansas students.
Eligibility: Applicants may pursue any major at any institution of higher learning. Selection is based on service (5 percent), character (10 percent), leadership (10 percent), scholastic ability (25 percent) and financial need (50 percent).
Target applicant:
  High school students
  College students
  Adult students
Minimum GPA: None.
Amount: $500.
Number of awards: 1.
Deadline: February 1.
How to apply: Applications are available online.

(1449) · Jane Matthews Memorial Scholarship Endowment

Epsilon Sigma Alpha Foundation
P.O. Box 270517
Fort Collins, CO 80527
Phone: 970-223-2824
Fax: 970-223-4456
Email: kloyd@knoxy.net
Website: http://www.esaintl.com/esaf
Purpose: To assist music majors.
Eligibility: Applicants must be residents of Oklahoma. They may study music at any institution of higher learning. Selection is based on scholastic ability (30 percent), financial need (30 percent), leadership (20 percent), character (10 percent) and service (10 percent).
Target applicant:
  High school students
  College students
  Adult students
Minimum GPA: None.
Amount: $1,000.
Number of awards: 1.
Deadline: February 1.
How to apply: Applications are available online.

(1450) · Jennings and Beulah Haggerty Scholarship

Lincoln Community Foundation
215 Centennial Mall South, Suite 100
Lincoln, NE 68508
Phone: 402-474-2345
Fax: 402-476-8532
Email: lcf@lcf.org
Website: http://www.lcf.org
Purpose: To support high school seniors in Lincoln, Nebraska.
Eligibility: Students must rank in the top 1/3 of their high school class. Applicants must have financial need, and they must apply for financial aid at their chosen school before contacting the Lincoln Community Foundation.
Target applicant:
  High school students
Minimum GPA: None.
Amount: $500-$2,000.
Number of awards: Varies.
Deadline: July 1.
How to apply: Applications are available online.

(1451) · Jerome B. Steinbach Scholarship

Oregon Student Assistance Commission
1500 Valley River Drive
Suite 100
Eugene, OR 97401
Phone: 541-687-7400
Fax: 541-687-7414
Email: awardinfo@mercury.osac.state.or.us
Website: http://www.osac.state.or.us
Purpose: To assist Oregon undergraduate students.
Eligibility: Applicants must be Oregon residents entering their sophomore year or higher in college and have a minimum 3.5 college GPA.
Target applicant:
  College students
  Adult students
Minimum GPA: None.
Amount: Varies.
Number of awards: Varies.
Deadline: March 1.
How to apply: Applications are available online.

(1452) · Jewel Gardiner Memorial Scholarship

California School Library Association Jewel Gardiner Memorial Scholarship Chair
717 K Street
Suite 515
Sacramento, CA 95814
Email: ebell@pleasanton.k12.ca.us
Website: http://www.schoolibrary.org
Purpose: To encourage students in library media teacher programs.
Eligibility: Applicants must be currently enrolled in a library media teacher program or have been enrolled at any time during the previous year. Preference is given to first-time award recipients, current California School Library Association members and candidates with teaching experience. Applicants may win the award twice.
Target applicant:
  College students
  Graduate school students
  Adult students
Minimum GPA: None.
Amount: $1,000.
Number of awards: 2 (1 for each semester).

Deadline: August 1 and November 1.
How to apply: Applications are available online.

(1453) · Jimmy Rane Foundation Scholarships

Jimmy Rane Foundation
P.O. Box 40
Abbeville, AL 36310
Phone: 866-763-4228
Email: jimmyrane@act.org
Website: http://www.jimmyranefoundation.org
Purpose: To support students who are planning to pursue undergraduate degrees.
Eligibility: Applicants must be high school seniors who are residents of North Carolina, South Carolina, Georgia, Alabama, Oklahoma, Missouri, Nebraska, Arkansas, Tennessee, Louisiana, Mississippi, Florida or Texas.
Target applicant:
   High school students
Minimum GPA: None.
Amount: Varies.
Number of awards: Varies.
Deadline: February 20.
How to apply: Applications are available online.

(1454) · Joe Foss, An American Hero Scholarship

Sioux Falls Area Community Foundation
300 N. Phillips Avenue, Suite 102
Sioux Falls, SD 57104
Phone: 605-336-7055
Email: pgale@sfacf.org
Website: http://www.sfacf.org
Purpose: To support high school seniors who have strong values, courage and patriotism.
Eligibility: Applicants must have at least a 3.5 GPA and an ACT score of 21 or above. Students must reside in South Dakota.
Target applicant:
   High school students
Minimum GPA: 3.5
Amount: $1,000.
Number of awards: Varies.
Deadline: March 15.
How to apply: Applications are available online.

(1455) · Joel Abromson Memorial Scholarship

EqualityMaine
P.O. Box 1951
1 Pleasant Street, 2nd Floor
Portland, ME 04104
Phone: 207-761-3732
Fax: 207-761-3752
Email: info@equalitymaine.org
Website: http://www.equalitymaine.org
Purpose: To promote equality for students regardless of their sexual orientation and gender expression through an essay contest.
Eligibility: Applicants must be Maine high school seniors, and they must be accepted to an institution of higher learning.
Target applicant:
   High school students
Minimum GPA: None.

Amount: Up to $1,000.
Number of awards: Varies.
Deadline: April 15.
How to apply: Students may apply by sending a cover letter, essay, two letters of recommendation and a copy of their college acceptance letter to EqualityMaine.

(1456) · Joel Garcia Memorial Scholarship

California Chicano News Media Association
USC Annenberg School of Journalism
One California Plaza
300 S. Grand Avenue, Suite 3950
Los Angeles, CA 90071-3175
Phone: 213-437-4408
Fax: 213-437-4423
Email: ccmainfo@ccnma.org
Website: http://www.ccnma.org
Purpose: To support Latino students studying journalism who are California residents or are attending California schools.
Eligibility: Applicants must be Latino and either attending California schools or be California residents attending out-of-state schools. Students must show an interest in journalism (broadcast, print, photo or online) and demonstrate financial need and academic achievement.
Target applicant:
   High school students
   College students
   Adult students
Minimum GPA: None.
Amount: $500-$2,000.
Number of awards: Varies.
Deadline: April.
How to apply: Applications are available online, by email, by mail or by phone.

(1457) · John and Abigail Adams Scholarship

Massachusetts Office of Student Financial Assistance
454 Broadway
Suite 200
Revere, MA 02151
Phone: 617-727-9420
Fax: 617-727-0667
Email: osfa@osfa.mass.edu
Website: http://www.osfa.mass.edu
Purpose: To attract high-performing high school seniors to Massachusetts public institutions of higher education and to reward previous achievements.
Eligibility: Applicants must be permanent residents of Massachusetts, score in the Advanced category in one category of the 10th grade MCAS test and in the Proficient or Advanced category in the other and have a combined MCAS score in the top 25 percent of their school district. Scholarship winners must maintain a 3.0 or higher GPA for continued eligibility.
Target applicant:
   High school students
Minimum GPA: None.
Amount: Full Tuition.
Number of awards: Varies.
Scholarship may be renewable.
Deadline: Varies.
How to apply: No application is necessary, but students must complete the Free Application for Federal Student Aid.

(1458) · John and Anne Clifton Scholarship

Hawaii Community Foundation - Scholarships
1164 Bishop Street, Suite 800
Honolulu, HI 96813
Phone: 888-731-3863
Fax: 808-521-6286
Email: scholarships@hcf-hawaii.org
Website: http://www.hawaiicommunityfoundation.org
Purpose: To assist students pursuing vocational degrees.
Eligibility: Applicants must be enrolled in a vocational program at a University of Hawaii school.
Target applicant:
  High school students
  College students
  Adult students
Minimum GPA: None.
Amount: Varies.
Number of awards: Varies.
Deadline: July 1.
How to apply: Applications are available online beginning in early March.

(1459) · John Blanchard Memorial Scholarship

California School Library Association
1001 26th Street
Sacramento, CA 95816
Phone: 916-447-2684
Fax: 916-447-2695
Email: csla@pacbell.net
Website: http://www.schoolibrary.org
Purpose: To assist a school library paraprofessional in becoming a certified school library media teacher.
Eligibility: Applicants must be members of the California School Library Association who are currently working or have worked in the last three years in a classified library position. Candidates must be currently enrolled in a degree program for certification as a library media teacher and California residents planning to work in California after completing their programs. Three letters of recommendation are required.
Target applicant:
  College students
  Graduate school students
  Adult students
Minimum GPA: None.
Amount: $2,000.
Number of awards: 1.
Deadline: June 30.
How to apply: Applications are available online.

(1460) · John Dawe Dental Education Fund

Hawaii Community Foundation - Scholarships
1164 Bishop Street, Suite 800
Honolulu, HI 96813
Phone: 888-731-3863
Fax: 808-521-6286
Email: scholarships@hcf-hawaii.org
Website: http://www.hawaiicommunityfoundation.org
Purpose: To provide financial assistance to Hawaii students pursuing careers in dental professions.
Eligibility: Applicants must be enrolled full-time in a school of dentistry, dental hygiene or dental assisting. They must have a GPA of 2.7 or higher. Two letters of recommendation and a letter from the applicant's school confirming enrollment in the dentistry or dental hygiene program are required.
Target applicant:
  High school students
  College students
  Graduate school students
  Adult students
Minimum GPA: 2.7
Amount: Varies.
Number of awards: Varies.
Deadline: March 1.
How to apply: To apply, register online, complete the online application and select the scholarships to which you wish to apply. In addition, mail the supporting materials: printed confirmation page from the online application, personal statement, copy of Student Aid Report (SAR) available at www.fafsa.ed.gov and official transcript.

(1461) · John M. Ross Foundation Scholarships

Hawaii Community Foundation - Scholarships
1164 Bishop Street, Suite 800
Honolulu, HI 96813
Phone: 888-731-3863
Fax: 808-521-6286
Email: scholarships@hcf-hawaii.org
Website: http://www.hawaiicommunityfoundation.org
Purpose: To assist Hawaii resident students with preference given to those with Big Island ancestry.
Eligibility: Applicants must be residents of Hawaii and entering freshman or undergraduate students. Preference is given to applicants with roots on the Big Island who plan to remain on or return to it.
Target applicant:
  High school students
  College students
  Adult students
Minimum GPA: None.
Amount: Varies.
Number of awards: Varies.
Deadline: March 1.
How to apply: Applications are available by written request.

(1462) · Johnnie and Tom Moseley Memorial Endowment

Epsilon Sigma Alpha Foundation
P.O. Box 270517
Fort Collins, CO 80527
Phone: 970-223-2824
Fax: 970-223-4456
Email: kloyd@knoxy.net
Website: http://www.esaintl.com/esaf
Purpose: To provide financial assistance to Texas residents pursuing higher learning.
Eligibility: Applicants may pursue any major at any Texas college or university. Selection is based on scholastic ability (30 percent), financial need (30 percent), leadership (20 percent), character (10 percent) and service (10 percent).
Target applicant:
  High school students
  College students
  Adult students

Minimum GPA: None.
Amount: $500.
Number of awards: 1.
Deadline: February 1.
How to apply: Applications are available online.

(1463) · Joint Admissions Tuition Advantage Program Waiver

Massachusetts Office of Student Financial Assistance
454 Broadway
Suite 200
Revere, MA 02151
Phone: 617-727-9420
Fax: 617-727-0667
Email: osfa@osfa.mass.edu
Website: http://www.osfa.mass.edu
Purpose: To encourage community college graduates to enter into a four-year program by awarding a tuition waiver equal to 33 percent of the resident tuition rate at a state college or participating university.
Eligibility: Applicants must be enrolled in a state college or university and have completed an associate degree at a public community college within the prior calendar year as a participant in the Joint Admissions Program with a minimum GPA of 3.0.
Target applicant:
  College students
  Adult students
Minimum GPA: 3.0
Amount: Up to 33 percent of state tuition.
Number of awards: Varies.
Scholarship may be renewable.
Deadline: Varies.
How to apply: Contact the financial aid office at the institution attending or planning to attend for application forms and deadlines.

(1464) · Jose Marti Scholarship Challenge Grant

Florida Department of Education
Office of Student Financial Assistance
1940 N. Monroe Street
Suite 70
Tallahassee, FL 32303-4759
Phone: 888-827-2004
Fax: 850-245-9667
Email: osfa@fldoe.org
Website: http://www.floridastudentfinancialaid.org
Purpose: To help Florida students in need who are of Hispanic origin.
Eligibility: Applicants must have been born in or have a natural parent who was born in either Mexico or Spain, or a Hispanic country of the Caribbean, Central or South America, regardless of race. Students must plan to attend Florida public or eligible private institutions as undergraduate or graduate students, but graduating high school seniors get preference.
Target applicant:
  High school students
  College students
  Graduate school students
  Adult students
Minimum GPA: 3.0
Amount: $2,000.

Number of awards: Varies.
Scholarship may be renewable.
Deadline: April 1.
How to apply: Applicants must submit the initial student Florida Financial Aid Application by April 1 and the Free Application for Federal Student Aid (FAFSA) by May 15.

(1465) · Joseph W. Mayo ALS Scholarship

Maine Community Foundation
245 Main Street
Ellsworth, ME 04605
Phone: 207-667-9735
Fax: 207-667-0447
Email: jwarren@mainecf.org
Website: http://www.mainecf.org
Purpose: To support students who are related to or caring for Amyotrophic Lateral Sclerosis (ALS)/Lou Gehrig's Disease patients.
Eligibility: Students must currently be attending a post-secondary school. While their current school may be in any state, they must have graduated from a Maine high school or received a GED in Maine. Applicants should also be related to an ALS patient in one of the following ways: children, stepchildren, grandchildren, spouses, domestic partners or primary caregivers.
Target applicant:
  College students
  Adult students
Minimum GPA: None.
Amount: Varies.
Number of awards: Varies.
Deadline: May 1.
How to apply: Applications are available online.

(1466) · Juanita Carter Adams/Florida State Council Endowment

Epsilon Sigma Alpha Foundation
P.O. Box 270517
Fort Collins, CO 80527
Phone: 970-223-2824
Fax: 970-223-4456
Email: kloyd@knoxy.net
Website: http://www.esaintl.com/esaf
Purpose: To provide financial assistance to students from North Carolina and Florida.
Eligibility: Applicants may major in any subject at any institution of higher learning. They must demonstrate financial need and scholastic achievement. Selection is based on character (10 percent), leadership (20 percent), service (10 percent), financial need (30 percent) and scholastic ability (30 percent). The award alternates each year between a Greensboro, North Carolina student and a Florida student.
Target applicant:
  High school students
  College students
  Adult students
Minimum GPA: None.
Amount: $466.
Number of awards: 1.
Deadline: February 1.
How to apply: Applications are available online.

(1467) · Judge William F. Cooper Scholarship

Center for Scholarship Administration
Wachovia Accounts
4320-G Wade Hampton Boulevard
Taylors, SC 29687
Phone: 866-608-0001
Email: wachoviascholars@bellsouth.net
Website: http://www.wachoviascholars.com
Purpose: To provide financial assistance to female students from Georgia who plan to attend college in South Carolina.
Eligibility: Applicants must be high school seniors who have financial need. Students must have an acceptable GPA and plan to study in any field except law, theology or medicine. Nursing is acceptable.
Target applicant:
    High school students
Minimum GPA: None.
Amount: Varies.
Number of awards: Varies.
Scholarship may be renewable.
Deadline: April.
How to apply: Applications are available online.

(1468) · Juliette M. Atherton Scholarship - Seminary Studies

Hawaii Community Foundation - Scholarships
1164 Bishop Street, Suite 800
Honolulu, HI 96813
Phone: 888-731-3863
Fax: 808-521-6286
Email: scholarships@hcf-hawaii.org
Website: http://www.hawaiicommunityfoundation.org
Purpose: To support Hawaii students who plan to be ordained in the Protestant faith.
Eligibility: Students must be attending a graduate school of theology.
Target applicant:
    Graduate school students
    Adult students
Minimum GPA: None.
Amount: Varies.
Number of awards: Varies.
Deadline: March 1.
How to apply: To apply, register online, complete the online application and select the scholarships to which you wish to apply. In addition, mail the supporting materials: printed confirmation page from the online application, personal statement, copy of Student Aid Report (SAR) available at www.fafsa.ed.gov and official transcript.

(1469) · Just Enterprises (Judi & Steve York) Endowment

Epsilon Sigma Alpha Foundation
P.O. Box 270517
Fort Collins, CO 80527
Phone: 970-223-2824
Fax: 970-223-4456
Email: kloyd@knoxy.net
Website: http://www.esaintl.com/esaf

Purpose: To provide funds for Oklahoma students who are seeking higher education.
Eligibility: Applicants may attend any college or university and pursue any major. Selection is based on scholastic ability (30 percent), financial need (30 percent), leadership (20 percent), service (10 percent) and character (10 percent).
Target applicant:
    High school students
    College students
    Adult students
Minimum GPA: None.
Amount: $1,000.
Number of awards: 1.
Deadline: February 1.
How to apply: Applications are available online.

(1470) · Kansas BPW Educational Foundation Career Development Scholarship

Kansas Business and Professional Women's Educational Foundation
1620 Eye Street NW
Suite 210
Washington, DC 20006
Phone: 202-293-1100
Email: desmith@fcbankonline.com
Website: http://www.bpwkansas.org/scholarships_and_loans.htm
Purpose: To provide financial assistance to individuals who want to broaden their education or increase their earning potential.
Eligibility: Applicants must be Kansas residents who are high school graduates. They must be in the work force and wish to obtain higher education for career advancement purposes.
Target applicant:
    College students
    Graduate school students
    Adult students
Minimum GPA: None.
Amount: Varies.
Number of awards: Varies.
Deadline: December 31.
How to apply: Applications are available online or from your local BPW chapter.

(1471) · Kansas BPW Educational Foundation Career Preparatory Scholarship

Kansas Business and Professional Women's Educational Foundation
1620 Eye Street NW
Suite 210
Washington, DC 20006
Phone: 202-293-1100
Email: desmith@fcbankonline.com
Website: http://www.bpwkansas.org/scholarships_and_loans.htm
Purpose: To provide financial assistance to students who are enrolled in one- or two-year academic, career, vocational or technical programs.
Eligibility: Applicants must residents of Kansas who are enrolled in a one- or two-year academic, career, vocational or technical program that they can use to gain employment or transfer to a four-year program upon graduation.
Target applicant:
    High school students
    College students
    Adult students
Minimum GPA: None.

Amount: Varies.
Number of awards: Varies.
Deadline: December 31.
How to apply: Applications are available online or from your local BPW chapter.

(1472) · Kansas BPW Educational Foundation Undergraduate Scholarship

Kansas Business and Professional Women's Educational Foundation
1620 Eye Street NW
Suite 210
Washington, DC 20006
Phone: 202-293-1100
Email: desmith@fcbankonline.com
Website: http://www.bpwkansas.org/scholarships_and_loans.htm
Purpose: To provide assistance to Kansas students.
Eligibility: Applicants must be Kansas residents who are enrolled in their sophomore, junior or senior year of an undergraduate program at an accredited college or university. Students must also be high school graduates at the time of applying.
Target applicant:
   College students
   Adult students
Minimum GPA: None.
Amount: Varies.
Number of awards: Varies.
Deadline: December 31.
How to apply: Applications are available online or from your local BPW chapter.

(1473) · Kansas Comprehensive Grants

Kansas Board of Regents
Curtis State Office Building
Suite 520
1000 SW Jackson Street
Topeka, KS 66612
Phone: 785-296-3421
Fax: 785-296-0983
Email: dlindeman@ksbor.org
Website: http://www.kansasregents.org
Purpose: To help needy Kansas students attend Kansas colleges and universities.
Eligibility: Applicants must be enrolled full-time at an eligible Kansas institution. Selection is based on financial need.
Target applicant:
   College students
   Adult students
Minimum GPA: None.
Amount: $100-$3,000.
Number of awards: Varies.
Deadline: April 1.
How to apply: Complete the Free Application for Federal Student Aid (FAFSA).

(1474) · Kansas Ethnic Minority Scholarship

Kansas Board of Regents
Curtis State Office Building
Suite 520
1000 SW Jackson Street
Topeka, KS 66612

Phone: 785-296-3421
Fax: 785-296-0983
Email: dlindeman@ksbor.org
Website: http://www.kansasregents.org
Purpose: To aid outstanding Kansas minority students with financial need.
Eligibility: Applicants must be African American, Native Indian or Alaskan Native, Asian or Pacific Islander or Hispanic. Priority is given to graduating high school seniors. Applicants must have one of the following: a minimum ACT score of 21 or SAT score of 816, a minimum 3.0 GPA, a top 33 percent ranking in their high school class, completion of Kansas Scholars Curriculum, selection by National Merit Corporation or selection by College Board as a Hispanic Scholar.
Target applicant:
   High school students
   College students
   Adult students
Minimum GPA: 3.0
Amount: $1,850.
Number of awards: Varies.
Scholarship may be renewable.
Deadline: April.
How to apply: Applications are available online.

(1475) · Kansas Lamplighter Memorial Endowment

Epsilon Sigma Alpha Foundation
P.O. Box 270517
Fort Collins, CO 80527
Phone: 970-223-2824
Fax: 970-223-4456
Email: kloyd@knoxy.net
Website: http://www.esaintl.com/esaf
Purpose: To provide financial assistance for Kansas residents.
Eligibility: Applicants must attend a college or university in Kansas. They may major in any field. Selection is based on financial need (50 percent), scholastic ability (25 percent), character (10 percent), leadership (10 percent) and service (5 percent).
Target applicant:
   High school students
   College students
   Adult students
Minimum GPA: None.
Amount: $1,000.
Number of awards: 1.
Deadline: February 1.
How to apply: Applications are available online.

(1476) · Kansas Oratorical Contest

American Legion, Department of Kansas
1314 SW Topeka Boulevard
Topeka, KS 66612
Phone: 785-232-9315
Fax: 785-232-1399
Website: http://www.ksamlegion.org
Purpose: To enhance high school students' experience with and understanding of the U.S. Constitution. The contest will help develop students' leadership skills and civic appreciation, as well as the ability to deliver thoughtful, insightful orations regarding U.S. citizenship and its inherent responsibilities.
Eligibility: Applicants must be high school students under the age of 20 who are U.S. citizens or legal residents and residents of the state.

Students first give an oration within their state and winners compete at the national level. The oration must be related to the Constitution of the United States focusing on the duties and obligations citizens have to the government. It must be in English and be between eight and ten minutes. There is also an assigned topic which is posted on the website, and it should be between three and five minutes.
Target applicant:
  High school students
Minimum GPA: None.
Amount: $150-$1,500.
Number of awards: 4+local scholarships.
Deadline: January 15.
How to apply: Applications are available from schools and local American Legion Posts.

(1477) · Kansas State Council Endowment

Epsilon Sigma Alpha Foundation
P.O. Box 270517
Fort Collins, CO 80527
Phone: 970-223-2824
Fax: 970-223-4456
Email: kloyd@knoxy.net
Website: http://www.esaintl.com/esaf
Purpose: To provide funds for the education of Kansas residents.
Eligibility: Applicants may attend any college or university and pursue any major. Selection is based on the following criteria: scholastic ability (30 percent), financial need (30 percent), leadership (20 percent), service (10 percent) and character (10 percent).
Target applicant:
  High school students
  College students
  Adult students
Minimum GPA: None.
Amount: $1,500.
Number of awards: 1.
Deadline: February 1.
How to apply: Applications are available online.

(1478) · Karen B. Lewis Career Education Scholarship

Virginia Business and Professional Women's Foundation
P.O. Box 4842
McLean, VA 22103-4842
Phone: 800-525-3729
Email: bpwfoundation@act.org
Website: http://www.vabpwfoundation.org
Purpose: To support female students who are enrolled in technical schools or career training programs.
Eligibility: Applicants must be at least 18 years of age and be accepted into an accredited training program in the state of Virginia. Students must complete their course of study within two years. Applicants must show financial need and have concrete plans to use their training for advancement in business, industry or trade occupations.
Target applicant:
  High school students
  College students
  Adult students
Minimum GPA: None.
Amount: $500-$1,000.
Number of awards: Varies.
Deadline: April 1.
How to apply: Applications are available online.

(1479) · Kay Mills Memorial Scholarship

Epsilon Sigma Alpha Foundation
P.O. Box 270517
Fort Collins, CO 80527
Phone: 970-223-2824
Fax: 970-223-4456
Email: kloyd@knoxy.net
Website: http://www.esaintl.com/esaf
Purpose: To provide financial assistance for teaching majors.
Eligibility: Applicants must be Texas residents and may study teaching at any college or university. Selection is based on scholastic ability (30 percent), financial need (30 percent), leadership (20 percent), character (10 percent) and service (10 percent).
Target applicant:
  High school students
  College students
  Adult students
Minimum GPA: None.
Amount: $500.
Number of awards: 1.
Deadline: February 1.
How to apply: Applications are available online.

(1480) · Kentucky State Council Endowment Scholarship

Epsilon Sigma Alpha Foundation
P.O. Box 270517
Fort Collins, CO 80527
Phone: 970-223-2824
Fax: 970-223-4456
Email: kloyd@knoxy.net
Website: http://www.esaintl.com/esaf
Purpose: To provide financial assistance for Kentucky residents.
Eligibility: Applicants may attend any institution of higher learning and major in any field. Selection is based on financial need (50 percent), scholastic ability (25 percent), character (10 percent), leadership (10 percent) and service (5 percent).
Target applicant:
  High school students
  College students
  Adult students
Minimum GPA: None.
Amount: $1,500.
Number of awards: 1.
Deadline: February 1.
How to apply: Applications are available online.

(1481) · Kentucky Tuition Grant

Kentucky Higher Education Assistance Authority
P.O. Box 798
Frankfort, KY 40602
Phone: 800-928-8926
Email: blane@kheaa.com
Website: http://www.kheaa.com
Purpose: To provide grants to Kentucky residents to attend the Commonwealth's independent colleges.
Eligibility: Applicants must be full-time students enrolled at eligible private institutions. Students must not be enrolled in divinity, theology or religious education degree programs. This is a need-based program.

Target applicant:
   College students
   Adult students
Minimum GPA: None.
Amount: $200-$2,600.
Number of awards: Varies.
Deadline: Varies.
How to apply: Complete the Free Application for Federal Student Aid (FAFSA).

(1482) · Kids' Chance of Louisiana Scholarships

Louisiana Bar Foundation
601 St. Charles Avenue
Third Floor
New Orleans, LA 70130
Phone: 504-561-1046
Fax: 504-566-1926
Email: kidschance@raisingthebar.org
Website: http://www.raisingthebar.org
Purpose: To assist students whose parents were killed or injured on the job.
Eligibility: Applicants must be dependents of workers who died or were permanently disabled in a compensable work-related accident in Louisiana. They must be Louisiana residents 16 to 25 years of age, maintain a C average or higher and demonstrate financial need. Applicants must plan to work toward an associate's or bachelor's degree, certificate or license at an accredited Louisiana institution of higher learning.
Target applicant:
   High school students
   College students
Minimum GPA: None.
Amount: Varies.
Number of awards: Varies.
Deadline: February 28.
How to apply: Applications are available online.

(1483) · Kids' Chance of Washington Scholarships

Kids' Chance of Washington
P.O. Box 185
Olympia, WA 98507-0185
Phone: 800-572-5762
Fax: 360-943-2333
Email: debbie@wscff.org
Website: http://www.kidschancewa.com
Purpose: To provide financial assistance to children and spouses of Washington workers who have been killed or injured on the job.
Eligibility: Applicants must be children or spouses of Washington workers who have died or been seriously injured due to a work-related injury. They must also have financial need.
Target applicant:
   High school students
   College students
   Adult students
Minimum GPA: None.
Amount: Varies.
Number of awards: Varies.
Deadline: Varies.
How to apply: Applications are available online.

(1484) · Kids' Chance of West Virginia Scholarships

Greater Kanawha Valley Foundation
1600 Huntington Square
900 Lee Street, East
Charleston, WV 25301
Phone: 304-346-3620
Fax: 304-346-3640
Email: tgkvf@tgkvf.org
Website: http://www.tgkvf.org
Purpose: To provide financial assistance to children of workers who were disabled or fatally injured on the job.
Eligibility: Applicants must be children between the ages of 16 and 25 whose parent was permanently and totally disabled or fatally injured in a compensable work-related accident in West Virginia. Academic performance, leadership and contributions to school and community are considered.
Target applicant:
   High school students
   College students
Minimum GPA: None.
Amount: Varies.
Number of awards: 2.
Deadline: Varies.
How to apply: Applications are available online.

(1485) · Kimber Richter Family Scholarship

Community Foundation of Western Massachusetts
1500 Main Street
P.O. Box 15769
Springfield, MA 01115
Phone: 413-732-2858
Fax: 413-733-8565
Email: scholar@communityfoundation.org
Website: http://www.communityfoundation.org
Purpose: To help students of the Baha'i faith from western Massachusetts.
Eligibility: Applicants must attend a U.S. college or university part-time or full-time. Application forms, transcripts and Student Aid Reports are required. Selection is based on financial need and academic merit.
Target applicant:
   High school students
   College students
   Graduate school students
   Adult students
Minimum GPA: None.
Amount: $500.
Number of awards: 1.
Deadline: March 31.
How to apply: Applications are available online and by phone.

(1486) · Kittie M. Fairey Educational Fund Scholarships

Kittie M. Fairey Educational Fund Scholarship Program
4320-G Wade Hampton Boulevard
Taylors, SC 29687
Phone: 866-608-0001
Email: sandralee41@bellsouth.net
Website: http://www.scholarshipprograms.org
Purpose: To help South Carolina high school seniors who want to attend colleges or universities in the state.

Eligibility: Applicants must be high school seniors with a minimum combined SAT score of 900 who plan to be full-time students pursuing a bachelor's of arts or bachelor's of science degree. Selection is based on academic merit and financial need, and the applicants' parents' adjusted gross income must not exceed $40,000. A transcript, recommendation letter, essay and parents' tax documents are required. Employees of Wachovia Bank are not eligible.
Target applicant:
    High school students
Minimum GPA: 3.0
Amount: Varies.
Number of awards: Varies.
Scholarship may be renewable.
Deadline: January 30.
How to apply: Applications are available online.

(1487) · Kohl Excellence Scholarships

Herb Kohl Educational Foundation Inc.
P.O. Box 7841
Madison, WI 53707
Phone: 608-266-1098
Email: john.johnson@dpi.state.wi.us
Website: http://www.kohleducation.org/students
Purpose: To assist Wisconsin students in obtaining higher education.
Eligibility: Applicants must be Wisconsin residents who are graduating high school in the year of application. They must be in good standing with their schools and demonstrate the potential for success in postsecondary education.
Target applicant:
    High school students
Minimum GPA: None.
Amount: $1,000.
Number of awards: 100.
Deadline: November.
How to apply: Applications are available online starting in October of each year and from Wisconsin high schools in mid-September.

(1488) · La Plaza Scholarship Fund

Central Indiana Community Foundation
615 North Alabama Street
Suite 119
Indianapolis, IN 46204-1498
Phone: 317-634-2423
Fax: 317-684-0943
Website: http://www.cicf.org
Purpose: To provide financial assistance to Indiana residents who are self-motivated and have financial need.
Eligibility: Applicants must be high school seniors who have demonstrated financial need and self-motivation. They must have a GPA of 2.7 or higher and plan to attend an Indiana college or university. Preference is given to Hispanic students and to those attending four-year degree programs.
Target applicant:
    High school students
Minimum GPA: 2.7
Amount: Varies.
Number of awards: Varies.
Deadline: March 7.
How to apply: Applications are available online.

(1489) · Laheenae Rebecca Hart Gay Scholarship

Hawaii Community Foundation - Scholarships
1164 Bishop Street, Suite 800
Honolulu, HI 96813
Phone: 888-731-3863
Fax: 808-521-6286
Email: scholarships@hcf-hawaii.org
Website: http://www.hawaiicommunityfoundation.org
Purpose: To support Hawaii students who are pursuing degrees in art.
Eligibility: Students may major in any art field except performing arts, film arts or culinary arts.
Target applicant:
    High school students
    College students
    Adult students
Minimum GPA: None.
Amount: $1,000.
Number of awards: 1.
Deadline: March 1.
How to apply: To apply, register online, complete the online application and select the scholarships to which you wish to apply. In addition, mail the supporting materials: printed confirmation page from the online application, personal statement, copy of Student Aid Report (SAR) available at www.fafsa.ed.gov and official transcript.

(1490) · Lapiz Family Scholarship

Asian Pacific Fund
225 Bush Street
Suite 590
San Francisco, CA 94104
Phone: 415-433-6859
Fax: 415-433-2425
Email: scholarship@asianpacificfund.org
Website: http://www.asianpacificfund.org
Purpose: To support students from farm working backgrounds who attend the University of California.
Eligibility: Applicants must be full-time undergraduate students at University of California (preference given to students at UC Davis and UC Santa Cruz), be farm workers or the children of farm or migrant workers and have a minimum 3.0 GPA. The award is based on merit and financial need. Applicants should submit applications, transcripts, essays, resumes and Student Aid Reports.
Target applicant:
    College students
    Adult students
Minimum GPA: 3.0
Amount: $1,000.
Number of awards: 2.
Deadline: March 31.
How to apply: Applications are available online.

(1491) · Last Dollar Grant

CollegeBound Foundation
Scholarship, Research and Retention Services
300 Water Street
Suite 300
Baltimore, MD 21202
Phone: 410-783-2905
Fax: 410-727-5786

Email: info@collegeboundfoundation.org
Website: http://www.collegeboundfoundation.org
Purpose: To help Baltimore City public high school graduates who will attend Maryland colleges.
Eligibility: Applicants must be new graduates of Baltimore City public high schools, have family income of no more than $75,000 per year and contribute at least 15 percent of their college costs through self-help. Students must attend Bowie State University, Coppin State University, Frostburg State University, Morgan State University, St. Mary's College of Maryland, Towson University, University of Maryland College Park, University of Maryland Eastern Shore or Villa Julie College. Applicants must also attend the Transition to College Workshop and the Annual Scholars' Luncheon and other program events scheduled throughout the year. The Student Aid Report, college acceptance letters, financial aid award letter and transcript are required. The grant is given to students whose Expected Family Contribution and financial aid package are less than the cost to attend college. The award is renewable up to five years.
Target applicant:
    High school students
Minimum GPA: None.
Amount: $3,000.
Number of awards: Varies.
Scholarship may be renewable.
Deadline: March 19.
How to apply: Applications are available online.

(1492) · Laura N. Dowsett Fund
Hawaii Community Foundation - Scholarships
1164 Bishop Street, Suite 800
Honolulu, HI 96813
Phone: 888-731-3863
Fax: 808-521-6286
Email: scholarships@hcf-hawaii.org
Website: http://www.hawaiicommunityfoundation.org
Purpose: To support Hawaii students who are majoring in occupational therapy.
Eligibility: Applicants must be college juniors, college seniors or graduate students.
Target applicant:
    College students
    Graduate school students
    Adult students
Minimum GPA: None.
Amount: Varies.
Number of awards: Varies.
Deadline: March 1.
How to apply: To apply, register online, complete the online application and select the scholarships to which you wish to apply. In addition, mail the supporting materials: printed confirmation page from the online application, personal statement, copy of Student Aid Report (SAR) available at www.fafsa.ed.gov and official transcript.

(1493) · Leadership for Diversity Scholarship
California School Library Association
1001 26th Street
Sacramento, CA 95816
Phone: 916-447-2684
Fax: 916-447-2695
Email: csla@pacbell.net
Website: http://www.schoollibrary.org

Purpose: To encourage diversity in the library media teacher profession.
Eligibility: Applicants must be members of a traditionally underrepresented group attending or planning to attend an accredited library media teacher credential program and plan to work in California for three years after completing the program. Applicants must provide a 250-word statement about their qualifications, career goals, financial situation and commitment to supporting multicultural students and two letters of reference.
Target applicant:
    High school students
    College students
    Graduate school students
    Adult students
Minimum GPA: None.
Amount: $1,500.
Number of awards: 1.
Deadline: June 30.
How to apply: Applications are available online.

(1494) · Leadership Scholarship
Los Alamos National Laboratory Foundation
1302 Calle de la Merced
Suite A
Espanola, NM 87532
Phone: 505-753-8890
Fax: 505-753-8915
Email: info@lanlfoundation.org
Website: http://www.lanlfoundation.org
Purpose: To support students from Northern New Mexico who have demonstrated leadership skills in their homes, schools and communities.
Eligibility: Students must have at least a 3.25 GPA, and they must have either an SAT score of at least 1350 or an ACT score of at least 19. Applicants must submit an essay and two letters of recommendation.
Target applicant:
    High school students
    College students
    Adult students
Minimum GPA: 3.25
Amount: $1,000.
Number of awards: Varies.
Scholarship may be renewable.
Deadline: January 22.
How to apply: Applications are available online.

(1495) · Lebanese American Heritage Club Scholarships
Lebanese American Heritage Club
4337 Maple Road
Dearborn, MI 48126
Phone: 313-846-8480
Fax: 313-846-2710
Email: lahc@lahc.org
Website: http://www.lahc.org/scholarship/eligibility

Purpose: To encourage members of the Lebanese American community to become involved with regional and national media.

Eligibility: Applicants must U.S. citizens and Michigan residents, be of Arab descent and have a GPA of 3.0 or higher (3.5 for graduate students). They must maintain full-time status. Special consideration is given to students majoring in mass communications, political science and related fields, those enrolled or planning to attend institutions that contribute to the Arab American Scholarship Fund and those who did not receive the scholarship in the preceding year.

Target applicant:
  High school students
  College students
  Graduate school students
  Adult students
Minimum GPA: 3.0-3.5
Amount: $1,000.
Number of awards: Varies.
Deadline: April 6.
How to apply: Applications are available online.

(1496) · Lee-Jackson Foundation Scholarship

Lee-Jackson Foundation
P.O. Box 8121
Charlottesville, VA 22906
Phone: 434-977-1861
Website: http://www.lee-jackson.org
Purpose: To honor the memories of Robert E. Lee and Thomas J. "Stonewall" Jackson and provide scholarships to Virginia students.
Eligibility: Applicants must be juniors, seniors or the equivalent in a Virginia public high school, private high school or homeschooling program and be residents of Virginia who plan to attend an accredited four-year college or university in the U.S. as full-time students. Financial need is not a basis for selection. Applicants must write an essay that demonstrates an appreciation for the character and virtues of Generals Robert E. Lee and Thomas "Stonewall" Jackson.
Target applicant:
  High school students
Minimum GPA: None.
Amount: $1,000-$10,000.
Number of awards: Varies.
Deadline: Mid-December.
How to apply: Applications are available online and must be submitted to your school principal or guidance counselor by your school's deadline, which is typically mid-December.

(1497) · Legacy of Learning Scholarships

Workers Compensation Fund
392 East 6400 South
Murray, UT 84107
Phone: 801-288-8060
Fax: 801-284-8983
Email: pjones@wcfgroup.com
Website: http://www.wcfgroup.com
Purpose: To provide financial assistance to dependents of Utah workers killed in on-the-job accidents.
Eligibility: Applicants must be the spouse or child of a worker who died in an industrial accident that is compensable through the Workers Compensation Fund. Transcript with SAT or ACT scores and two letters of recommendation are required.

Target applicant:
  High school students
  College students
  Adult students
Minimum GPA: None.
Amount: Up to $1,500.
Number of awards: Varies.
Deadline: July 1.
How to apply: Applications are available online.

(1498) · Legislative Endowment Scholarships

New Mexico Higher Education Department
1068 Cerrillos Road
Santa Fe, NM 87505
Phone: 800-279-9777
Fax: 505-476-6511
Email: heather.romero@state.nm.us
Website: http://hed.state.nm.us
Purpose: To support New Mexico undergraduate students with financial need attend postsecondary institutions in New Mexico.
Eligibility: Applicants must be undergraduate students who are New Mexico residents and attending public postsecondary institutions at least half-time in the state. Preference is given to adult students and transfer students from two-year New Mexico public postsecondary institutions to four-year institutions.
Target applicant:
  College students
  Adult students
Minimum GPA: None.
Amount: $1,000-$2,500.
Number of awards: Varies.
Deadline: Varies.
How to apply: Contact your financial aid office and complete the Free Application for Federal Student Aid (FAFSA).

(1499) · Legislative Essay Scholarship

Delaware Higher Education Commission
Carvel State Office Building, 5th Floor
820 N. French Street
Wilmington, DE 19801-3509
Phone: 800-292-7935
Fax: 302-577-6765
Email: dhec@doe.k12.de.us
Website: http://www.doe.k12.de.us/infosuites/students_family/dhec/
Purpose: To reward Delaware high school seniors who submit winning essays.
Eligibility: Applicants must be seniors in public or private schools or in home school programs who plan to enroll full-time at nonprofit, regionally accredited colleges. Applicants should submit essays on a topic listed on the website.
Target applicant:
  High school students
Minimum GPA: None.
Amount: $1,000.
Number of awards: Up to 62.
Deadline: November 30.
How to apply: Applications are available online.

(1500) · Legislative for Future Excellence (LIFE) Scholarship Program

South Carolina Commission on Higher Education
1333 Main Street
Suite 200
Columbia, SC 29201
Phone: 803-737-2260
Fax: 803-737-2297
Email: shubbard@che.sc.gov
Website: http://www.che400.state.sc.us
Purpose: Monetary assistance is provided to South Carolina resident students pursuing higher education.
Eligibility: Applicants must graduate from a high school in South Carolina or outside of South Carolina if parent is a legal resident of South Carolina, attend an eligible South Carolina public or private college full-time and be a resident of South Carolina. Entering freshmen must meet two of the following: have a minimum 3.0 GPA, a minimum SAT score of 1100 or ACT score of 24 or graduate in the top 30 percent of their class.
Target applicant:
    High school students
    College students
    Adult students
Minimum GPA: 3.0
Amount: $4,700.
Number of awards: Varies.
Scholarship may be renewable.
Deadline: Varies.
How to apply: Your college will determine your eligibility based on your high school transcript. There is no application form.

(1501) · Legislative Lottery Scholarships

New Mexico Higher Education Department
1068 Cerrillos Road
Santa Fe, NM 87505
Phone: 800-279-9777
Fax: 505-476-6511
Email: heather.romero@state.nm.us
Website: http://hed.state.nm.us
Purpose: To support graduating New Mexico high school seniors with financial need.
Eligibility: Applicants must be graduating high school seniors in New Mexico, enroll full-time at an eligible New Mexico public college or university and maintain a minimum 2.5 GPA during the first college semester.
Target applicant:
    High school students
Minimum GPA: None.
Amount: Up to full tuition.
Number of awards: Varies.
Scholarship may be renewable.
Deadline: Varies.
How to apply: Contact your financial aid office.

(1502) · Leo Bourassa Scholarship

Virginia Lakes and Watersheds Association
4229 Lafayette Center Drive
Suite 1850
Chantilly, VA 20151
Phone: 757-671-6222

Email: shelly.frie@ch2m.com
Website: http://www.vlwa.org/leo.html
Purpose: To acknowledge students for their accomplishments in the field of water resources.
Eligibility: Applicants must be Virginia residents and students in good standing at an accredited college or university in the state. They must complete at least two semesters of undergraduate study by the award date. They must also be full-time undergraduate or full- or part-time graduate students enrolled in curricula related to water resources.
Target applicant:
    College students
    Graduate school students
    Adult students
Minimum GPA: None.
Amount: $2.50.
Number of awards: 2.
Deadline: May 31.
How to apply: Applications are available online.

(1503) · Leslie Moore - Baltimore and Howard County Scholarship

CollegeBound Foundation
Scholarship, Research and Retention Services
300 Water Street
Suite 300
Baltimore, MD 21202
Phone: 410-783-2905
Fax: 410-727-5786
Email: info@collegeboundfoundation.org
Website: http://www.collegeboundfoundation.org
Purpose: To help Baltimore and Howard County public high school seniors who have performed community service.
Eligibility: Applicants must be accepted to community colleges, universities or technical schools. A transcript, essay, two recommendation letters and college acceptance letters are required, and finalists should be available for interviews. One award is for a Baltimore county public high school senior, and the other award is for a Howard county public high school senior.
Target applicant:
    High school students
Minimum GPA: 2.0
Amount: $2,500.
Number of awards: 2.
Scholarship may be renewable.
Deadline: March 19.
How to apply: Applications are available online.

(1504) · Lessans Family Scholarship

Central Scholarship Bureau
1700 Reisterstown Road
Suite 220
Baltimore, MD 21208-2903
Phone: 410-415-5558
Fax: 410-415-5501
Email: info@centralsb.org
Website: http://www.centralsb.org
Purpose: To assist undergraduate Jewish students in Maryland.
Eligibility: Applicants must have already applied for a Central Scholarship Bureau interest-free loan for the current year, be enrolled at an accredited college, university or vocational school, have a certain income level and apply for financial aid and, if offered, accept a

subsidized Stafford loan. An application form, budget form, copy of school bills, transcript, Student Aid Report, school financial aid award letter and essay are required. Selection is based on need and merit.

Target applicant:
  High school students
  College students
  Adult students
Minimum GPA: 3.0
Amount: Varies.
Number of awards: Varies.
Scholarship may be renewable.
Deadline: May 31.
How to apply: Applications are available online.

(1505) · Lest We Forget POW/MIA/KIA Scholarship Fund

Maine Community Foundation
245 Main Street
Ellsworth, ME 04605
Phone: 207-667-9735
Fax: 207-667-0447
Email: jwarren@mainecf.org
Website: http://www.mainecf.org
Purpose: To assist Vietnam veterans and other veterans and their descendants in obtaining a college education.
Eligibility: Applicants must be veterans of the United States Armed Services or their descendants. Priority is given to veterans of Vietnam and their descendants. Graduating high school seniors, non-traditional students and college students may apply.
Target applicant:
  High school students
  College students
  Adult students
Minimum GPA: None.
Amount: Varies.
Number of awards: Varies.
Deadline: May 1.
How to apply: Applications are available from high school guidance offices or the Maine Community Foundation.

(1506) · Leveraged Incentive Grant Program

New Hampshire Postsecondary Education Commission
3 Barrell Court
Suite 300
Concord, NH 03301
Phone: 603-271-2555 x352
Fax: 603-271-2696
Email: jknapp@pec.state.nh.us
Website: http://www.state.nh.us/postsecondary
Purpose: To provide financial assistance based on merit and need to undergraduate students at New Hampshire institutions of higher learning.
Eligibility: Applicants must be residents of New Hampshire, demonstrate financial need and merit and be full-time sophomore, junior or senior students at an accredited undergraduate institution.
Target applicant:
  College students
  Adult students
Minimum GPA: None.
Amount: Up to $7,500.
Number of awards: Varies.

Deadline: Varies.
How to apply: Applications are available from your financial aid office.

(1507) · Leveraging Educational Assistance Partnership (LEAP)

Louisiana Office of Student Financial Assistance
P.O. Box 91202
Baton Rouge, LA 70821-9202
Phone: 800-259-5626 x1012
Fax: 225-922-0790
Email: custserv@osfa.la.gov
Website: http://www.osfa.state.la.us
Purpose: To provide need-based grants to academically qualified Louisiana students.
Eligibility: Students must be U.S. citizens or eligible noncitizens and residents of Louisiana, earn a high school diploma with a minimum 2.0 GPA or GED score minimum and meet the selection criteria of their particular college. All applicants must have substantial financial need as demonstrated on the Free Application for Federal Student Aid (FAFSA) form.
Target applicant:
  High school students
  College students
  Adult students
Minimum GPA: 2.0
Amount: $200-$2,000.
Number of awards: Varies.
Scholarship may be renewable.
Deadline: July 1.
How to apply: Contact your school's financial aid office for specific information about their LEAP program.

(1508) · Leveraging Educational Assistance Partnership (LEAP)

Arizona Commission for Postsecondary Education
2020 N. Central Avenue, Suite 550
Phoenix, AZ 85004
Phone: 602-258-2435
Fax: 602-258-2483
Email: judi@azhighered.org
Website: http://www.azhighered.org
Purpose: State and federal agencies have partnered together to provide awards to Arizona college and graduate students attending Arizona schools.
Eligibility: Applicants must be Arizona residents attending participating Arizona postsecondary institutions full-time or half-time as undergraduate or graduate students. The award is based on financial need.
Target applicant:
  High school students
  College students
  Graduate school students
  Adult students
Minimum GPA: None.
Amount: Varies.
Number of awards: Varies.
Deadline: Varies.
How to apply: Apply through your financial aid office.

(1509) · Leveraging Educational Assistance Partnership (LEAP) Grant

Georgia Student Finance Commission
2082 East Exchange Place
Tucker, GA 30084
Phone: 800-505-4732
Fax: 770-724-9089
Email: support@gacollege411.org
Website: http://www.gacollege411.org
Purpose: To aid residents of Georgia with substantial financial need in attending postsecondary institutions in Georgia.
Eligibility: Applicants must demonstrate substantial financial need, be eligible to receive the Pell Grant and be enrolled at a Georgia college, university or technical college at least half-time. Applicants must also complete and submit the Free Application for Federal Student Aid (FAFSA) and for renewal must maintain satisfactory academic progress.
Target applicant:
    College students
    Adult students
Minimum GPA: None.
Amount: Varies.
Number of awards: Varies.
Scholarship may be renewable.
Deadline: Varies.
How to apply: Applications are available by telephone request.

(1510) · Leveraging Educational Assistance Partnership (LEAP) Grants

Utah Higher Education Assistance Authority
Board of Regents Building, The Gateway
60 South 400 West
Salt Lake City, UT 84101
Phone: 801-321-7200
Fax: 801-321-7299
Email: uheaa@utahsbr.edu
Website: http://www.uheaa.org
Purpose: To assist students in attending Utah colleges.
Eligibility: Applicants must demonstrate need according to the federal guidelines. Eligibility requirements differ by campus. It is recommended that students apply early because there are limited funds.
Target applicant:
    High school students
    College students
    Adult students
Minimum GPA: None.
Amount: Up to $2,500.
Number of awards: Varies.
Deadline: Varies.
How to apply: Complete the Free Application for Federal Student Aid (FAFSA).

(1511) · Leveraging Educational Assistance State Partnership Program (LEAP)

Idaho State Board of Education
P.O. Box 83720
Boise, ID 83720
Phone: 208-334-2270
Fax: 208-334-2632
Email: dkelly@osbe.state.id.us
Website: http://www.boardofed.idaho.gov
Purpose: To aid students attending Idaho colleges or universities regardless of their states of residence.
Eligibility: Applicants must demonstrate financial need, attend eligible public or private colleges or universities in Idaho and take a minimum of six credits. Applicants may be residents of any state.
Target applicant:
    College students
    Adult students
Minimum GPA: None.
Amount: $5,000.
Number of awards: Varies.
Scholarship may be renewable.
Deadline: Varies.
How to apply: Contact your financial aid office.

(1512) · Library Media Teacher Scholarship

California School Library Association Paraprofessional Scholarship
1001 26th Street
Sacramento, CA 95816
Phone: 916-447-2684
Fax: 916-447-2695
Email: csla@pacbell.net
Website: http://www.schoollibrary.org
Purpose: To encourage students who plan to become library media teachers.
Eligibility: Applicants must be currently enrolled in a school library media credential program or master's degree program. Candidates must be residents of the California School Library Association Southern Section region and must provide three letters of recommendation.
Target applicant:
    College students
    Graduate school students
    Adult students
Minimum GPA: None.
Amount: $1,500.
Number of awards: 1.
Deadline: March 11.
How to apply: Applications are available online.

(1513) · License Plate Insignia Scholarship

Texas Higher Education Coordinating Board
P.O. Box 12788
Austin, TX 78711
Phone: 512-427-6101
Fax: 512-427-6127
Website: http://www.collegefortexans.com
Purpose: To assist Texas students with financial need.
Eligibility: Applicants must be Texas residents who are enrolled at least half-time at eligible public or private nonprofit colleges or universities in Texas and must demonstrate financial need.
Target applicant:
    College students
    Adult students
Minimum GPA: None.
Amount: Varies.
Number of awards: Varies.
Deadline: Varies.
How to apply: Complete the Free Application for Federal Student Aid (FAFSA).

(1514) · Lilly Endowment Community Scholarship Program

Independent Colleges of Indiana
3135 N. Meridian Street
Indianapolis, IN 46208-4717
Phone: 317-236-6090
Fax: 317-236-6086
Email: info@icindiana.org
Website: http://www.icindiana.org/lecsp/lilly.asp
Purpose: To raise the level of education in Indiana.
Eligibility: Applicants must be Indiana high school seniors who have been accepted into a full-time bachelor's degree program at an accredited public or private institution of higher learning in Indiana.
Target applicant:
High school students
Minimum GPA: None.
Amount: Full Tuition.
Number of awards: 92.
Scholarship may be renewable.
Deadline: January 11.
How to apply: Applications are available online and from local Indiana Community Foundations.

(1515) · Lilly Lorénzen Scholarship

American Swedish Institute
2600 Park Avenue
Minneapolis, MN 55407
Phone: 612-870-3374
Fax: 612-871-8682
Email: ninac@americanswedishinst.org
Website: http://www.americanswedishinst.org
Purpose: To assist Minnesota residents who wish to carry out scholarly or creative studies in Sweden.
Eligibility: Applicants must speak Swedish and have a desire to contribute to American-Swedish cultural exchange. They must plan to carry out studies in Sweden and have demonstrable achievement in their chosen field of study. Students must provide a college transcript or statement of professional and community achievement.
Target applicant:
College students
Graduate school students
Adult students
Minimum GPA: None.
Amount: $2,500.
Number of awards: 1.
Deadline: May 1.
How to apply: Applications are available online.

(1516) · Lily and Catello Sorrentino Memorial Scholarship

Rhode Island Foundation
One Union Station
Providence, RI 02903
Phone: 401-274-4564
Fax: 401-331-8085
Email: libbym@rifoundation.org
Website: http://www.rifoundation.org
Purpose: To assist adult students who are continuing their undergraduate studies at colleges or universities in Rhode Island.

Eligibility: Applicants must be residents of Rhode Island, be over 45 years of age and attend a non-parochial college or university in the state.
Target applicant:
College students
Adult students
Minimum GPA: None.
Amount: $350-$1,000.
Number of awards: Varies.
Deadline: May 14.
How to apply: Applications are available online.

(1517) · Lisa Sechrist Memorial Foundation Scholarship

Lisa Sechrist Memorial Foundation
8500 Executive Park Avenue
Suite 300
Fairfax, VA 22031
Website: http://www.lisasechrist.com/scholarship.html
Purpose: To honor the memory of Lisa Sechrist by assisting young women in obtaining a college education.
Eligibility: Applicants must be Virginia high school seniors in the process of applying to an accredited college, university or technical school or who have already been accepted. Members of honor societies and those who participate in sports or other extracurricular activities will receive special consideration. Selection is based on need, integrity, merit and academic potential.
Target applicant:
High school students
Minimum GPA: None.
Amount: Up to $10,000.
Number of awards: 1.
Deadline: March 31.
How to apply: Applications are available online.

(1518) · Loan Assistance Repayment Program Primary Care Services

Maryland Higher Education Commission
Office of Student Financial Assistance
839 Bestgate Road, Suite 400
Annapolis, MD 21401
Phone: 800-974-1024
Fax: 410-260-3200
Email: osfamail@mhec.state.md.us
Website: http://www.mhec.state.md.us
Purpose: To support primary care physicians and medical residents.
Eligibility: Medical resident applicants must be graduates of a Maryland college, and they must have at least one year remaining in a primary care residency program. Physician applicants must have a valid primary care license and currently work in an underserved area of Maryland. All applicants must have outstanding loans on which they have not defaulted. Specialization in one of the following fields is required: general internal medicine, family practice medicine, general pediatrics, obstetrics/gynecology or gynecology. Applicants must agree to work in an underserved area of Maryland for two to four years after winning the scholarship and completing their residency.
Target applicant:
Graduate school students
Adult students
Minimum GPA: None.
Amount: $25,000-$30,000.

Number of awards: Varies.
Scholarship may be renewable.
Deadline: Rolling.
How to apply: Applications are available from the Department of Health and Mental Hygiene.

(1519) · Lois Livingston McMillen Memorial Fund

Connecticut Community Foundation Center for Philanthropy
43 Field Street
Waterbury, CT 06702
Phone: 203-753-1315
Fax: 203-756-3054
Email: info@conncf.org
Website: http://www.conncf.org
Purpose: To provide financial assistance to women who are studying or plan to study art, especially painting or design.
Eligibility: Applicants must be women who plan to study art at an accredited college or university or in an artist-in-residence program. They must also live in the Connecticut Community Foundation's service area.
Target applicant:
    High school students
    College students
    Adult students
Minimum GPA: None.
Amount: Up to $4,000.
Number of awards: Varies.
Deadline: March 1.
How to apply: Applications are available online.

(1520) · Lori Rhett Memorial Scholarship

National Association for Campus Activities
13 Harbison Way
Columbia, SC 29212
Phone: 803-732-6222
Fax: 803-749-1047
Email: info@naca.org
Website: http://www.naca.org
Purpose: The scholarship recognizes the achievements of student leaders.
Eligibility: Applicants must hold a significant campus leadership position and demonstrate significant leadership skills and abilities. Students must also be making significant contributions through on- or off-campus volunteering and must attend school in Alaska, Idaho, Montana, Oregon or Washington.
Target applicant:
    College students
    Adult students
Minimum GPA: 2.5
Amount: Varies.
Number of awards: 1.
Deadline: June 30.
How to apply: Applications are available online.

(1521) · Los Alamos Employees' Scholarship

Los Alamos National Laboratory Foundation
1302 Calle de la Merced
Suite A
Espanola, NM 87532
Phone: 505-753-8890

Fax: 505-753-8915
Email: info@lanlfoundation.org
Website: http://www.lanlfoundation.org
Purpose: To provide financial assistance for students in northern New Mexico who plan to pursue undergraduate degrees in fields of study that will benefit the community.
Eligibility: Selection is based on academic performance, including the pursuit in high school of a rigorous course of study, GPA and standardized test scores, varied extracurricular and community service activities, strong critical thinking skills and career goals that are relevant to the needs of the northern New Mexico community. Some consideration is also given to financial need, ethnic diversity and equally representing all the regions of northern New Mexico. Applicants must have a minimum 3.25 GPA and either minimum score of 19 on the ACT or 930 on the SAT (Math and Critical Reading).
Target applicant:
    College students
    Adult students
Minimum GPA: 3.25
Amount: Varies.
Number of awards: Varies.
Scholarship may be renewable.
Deadline: January 22.
How to apply: Applications are available online.

(1522) · Los Alamos National Laboratory Foundation

Los Alamos National Laboratory Foundation
1302 Calle de la Merced
Suite A
Espanola, NM 87532
Phone: 505-753-8890
Fax: 505-753-8915
Email: info@lanlfoundation.org
Website: http://www.lanlfoundation.org
Purpose: To assist Northern New Mexico students in obtaining higher education.
Eligibility: Applicants must be permanent residents of the counties of Los Alamos, Mora, Rio Arriba, San Miguel, Sandoval, Santa Fe or Taos, New Mexico. Several scholarships are available, some open to all and some based on area of study.
Target applicant:
    High school students
    College students
    Adult students
Minimum GPA: None.
Amount: Up to $7,500.
Number of awards: Varies.
Scholarship may be renewable.
Deadline: January 22.
How to apply: Applications are available online.

(1523) · Lottery Tuition Assistance Program

South Carolina Board for Technical and Comprehensive Education
1333 Main Street
Suite 200
Columbia, SC 29201
Phone: 803-737-2260
Fax: 803-737-2297
Email: mmdowell@che.sc.gov
Website: http://www.che400.state.sc.us

Purpose: To assist South Carolina residents attending a two-year public or independent institution of higher learning.

Eligibility: Applicants must complete the Free Application for Federal Student Aid (FAFSA), be residents of South Carolina and be enrolled a minimum of six credit hours at a technical college.

Target applicant:
  High school students
  College students
  Adult students

Minimum GPA: None.

Amount: Varies.

Number of awards: Varies.

Deadline: Varies.

How to apply: Applications are available by telephone request.

(1524) · Louis B. Russell, Jr. Memorial Scholarship

Indiana State Teachers Association
150 W. Market Street
Indianapolis, IN 46204
Phone: 800-382-4037
Email: dboyd@ista-in.org
Website: http://www.ista-in.org/dynamic.aspx?id=162

Purpose: To provide financial assistance to ethnic minorities who are seeking vocational or technical education.

Eligibility: Applicants must be ethnic minority high school seniors who plan to pursue education in the area of industrial arts, vocational education or technical education at an accredited college or university.

Target applicant:
  High school students

Minimum GPA: None.

Amount: $1,000.

Number of awards: 1.

Scholarship may be renewable.

Deadline: March.

How to apply: Applications are available online.

(1525) · Louisiana Go Grant

Louisiana Office of Student Financial Assistance
P.O. Box 91202
Baton Rouge, LA 70821-9202
Phone: 800-259-5626 x1012
Fax: 225-922-0790
Email: custserv@osfa.la.gov
Website: http://www.osfa.state.la.us

Purpose: To help students from moderate and low income families afford a college education.

Eligibility: Applicants must be Louisiana residents who have been admitted and enrolled in an undergraduate program at a Louisiana public or private college or university. They must be first time freshmen or adult students who have not been enrolled in credit bearing courses for at least one academic year. Financial need is required.

Target applicant:
  High school students
  College students
  Adult students

Minimum GPA: None.

Amount: Up to $2,000.

Number of awards: Varies.

Deadline: Varies.

How to apply: All eligible students who have filed a Free Application for Federal Student Aid are considered for this grant.

(1526) · Louisiana Memorial Scholarship

American Radio Relay League Foundation
225 Main Street
Newington, CT 06111
Phone: 860-594-0397
Fax: 860-594-0259
Email: foundation@arrl.org
Website: http://www.arrl.org

Purpose: To provide financial assistance to Louisiana students who are amateur radio operators.

Eligibility: Applicants must hold a Technician Class or higher Amateur Radio License and either be Louisiana residents or attend school in Louisiana. They must have a GPA of 3.0 or higher. Only students who are accepted to or enrolled in a four-year college or university are eligible.

Target applicant:
  High school students
  College students
  Adult students

Minimum GPA: 3.0.

Amount: $500.

Number of awards: 1.

Deadline: February 1.

How to apply: Applications are available online.

(1527) · Louisiana Veterans State Aid Program

Louisiana Department of Veterans Affairs
1885 Wooddale Boulevard
P.O. Box 94095
Baton Rouge, LA 70804-9095
Phone: 225-922-0500
Fax: 225-922-0511
Email: wdixon@vetaffairs.com
Website: http://www.vetaffairs.com

Purpose: To provide financial aid for children and spouses of dead or disabled veterans.

Eligibility: Applicants must be children or surviving spouses of United States Armed Forces veterans who died or became at least 90 percent disabled in service or from a service-connected disability incurred during wartime. Deceased veterans must have been a Louisiana resident for at least 12 months before entering the service, and disabled veterans must have lived in the state at least 24 months prior to the dependent's admission into the program. Spouses must use the program within 10 years of establishing eligibility, and children must be between 16 and 25 years of age.

Target applicant:
  High school students
  College students
  Adult students

Minimum GPA: None.

Amount: Tuition.

Number of awards: Varies.

Scholarship may be renewable.

Deadline: Varies.

How to apply: Applications are available from your Parish Veterans Service Office.

(1528) · Lucille Eastin Memorial Scholarship

Epsilon Sigma Alpha Foundation
P.O. Box 270517
Fort Collins, CO 80527

Phone: 970-223-2824
Fax: 970-223-4456
Email: kloyd@knoxy.net
Website: http://www.esaintl.com/esaf
Purpose: To provide funds for the education of Colorado residents.
Eligibility: Applicants may attend any college or university and pursue any major. Selection is based on scholastic ability (30 percent), financial need (30 percent), leadership (20 percent), character (10 percent) and service (10 percent).
Target applicant:
  High school students
  College students
  Adult students
Minimum GPA: None.
Amount: $500.
Number of awards: 1.
Deadline: February 1.
How to apply: Applications are available online.

(1529) · Luso-American Education Foundation General Fund Scholarship

Luso-American Education Foundation
P.O. Box 2967
Dublin, CA 94568
Phone: 925-828-3883
Fax: 925-828-3883
Email: odom@luso-american.org
Website: http://www.luso-american.org/laef/html/scholarshipofferings.htm
Purpose: To provide educational opportunities for Portuguese students.
Eligibility: Applicants must be residents of California and high school students who are of Portuguese descent with a GPA of 3.5 or higher, or who are taking classes in the Portuguese language with a GPA of 3.0 or higher. They must be enrolled in a college, university, trade or business school and have taken the SAT or ACT. Two letters of recommendation are required.
Target applicant:
  High school students
Minimum GPA: 3.0
Amount: $500-$1,500.
Number of awards: 13-17.
Deadline: March 1.
How to apply: Applications are available by phone, fax, mail or email.

(1530) · Luterman Scholarship

American Legion, Department of New Jersey
135 W. Hanover Street
Trenton, NJ 08618
Phone: 609-695-5418
Fax: 609-394-1532
Email: adjutant@njamericanlegion.org
Website: http://www.njamericanlegion.org
Purpose: To award descendants of American Legion members with scholarships.
Eligibility: Applicants must be direct descendants of American Legion, Department of New Jersey members. Applicants must be high school seniors and use the award in the year it is received.
Target applicant:
  High school students

Minimum GPA: None.
Amount: Up to $4,000.
Number of awards: Varies.
Deadline: February 15.
How to apply: Applications are available by contacting the local Post or Department Headquarters.

(1531) · Lynn M. Smith Memorial Scholarship

California Association for Postsecondary Education and Disability
71423 Biskra Road
Rancho Mirage, CA 92270
Phone: 909-537-5238
Fax: 760-340-5275
Email: bjaworski@csub.edu
Website: http://www.caped.net
Purpose: To provide financial assistance to community college students with disabilities in California.
Eligibility: Applicants must have a verifiable disability and demonstrate financial need. They must be currently enrolled in a community college and pursuing a vocational career path.
Target applicant:
  College students
  Adult students
Minimum GPA: None.
Amount: $1,000.
Number of awards: 1.
Deadline: September 14.
How to apply: Applications are available online.

(1532) · Maine BPW Continuing Education Scholarship

Business and Professional Women/Maine Futurama Foundation
103 County Road
Oakland, ME 04963
Email: webmaster@bpwmaine.org
Website: http://www.bpwmaine.org/files/index.php?id=10
Purpose: To provide financial assistance to Maine women who are already attending an institution of higher learning.
Eligibility: Applicants must be female Maine residents who are currently attending a college or training program.
Target applicant:
  College students
  Graduate school students
  Adult students
Minimum GPA: None.
Amount: $1,200.
Number of awards: Varies.
Deadline: April 30.
How to apply: Applications are available from your local BPW chapter.

(1533) · Maine Community Foundation Scholarship Program

Maine Community Foundation
245 Main Street
Ellsworth, ME 04605
Phone: 207-667-9735
Fax: 207-667-0447
Email: jwarren@mainecf.org

Website: http://www.mainecf.org
Purpose: To provide financial assistance to Maine students.
Eligibility: There are a number of scholarships in this program for Maine traditional and adult students to attend private high schools, undergraduate colleges or graduate schools. Many are limited to residents of a specific county or graduates of a certain high school.
Target applicant:
High school students
College students
Graduate school students
Adult students
Minimum GPA: None.
Amount: Varies.
Number of awards: Varies.
Deadline: April.
How to apply: Applications are available online.

(1534) · Maine Demolay and Pine Tree Youth Foundation Scholarships

Maine Demolay and Pine Tree Youth Foundation
P.O. Box 816
Bangor, ME 04402
Phone: 207-773-5184
Email: grandlodge@mainemason.org
Website: http://www.pinetreeyouth.org
Purpose: To support Maine high school seniors.
Eligibility: Applicants must submit a short essay. Students must demonstrate financial need.
Target applicant:
High school students
Minimum GPA: None.
Amount: Varies.
Number of awards: Varies.
Deadline: March 23.
How to apply: Applications are available online.

(1535) · Maine Legislative Memorial Scholarship Fund

Maine Education Services
131 Presumpscot Street
Portland, ME 04103
Phone: 800-922-6352
Fax: 207-791-3616
Email: info@mesfoundation.com
Website: http://www.mesfoundation.com
Purpose: To support Maine students who are planning to attend or currently attend college in Maine.
Eligibility: Students must be accepted to or enrolled in a Maine college, technical school or graduate school. Applicants must be able to show academic excellence, community service or employment and financial need.
Target applicant:
High school students
College students
Graduate school students
Adult students
Minimum GPA: None.
Amount: $1000.
Number of awards: 16.
Deadline: April 16.
How to apply: Applications are available online.

(1536) · Maine Masonic Aid for Continuing Education

Maine Education Services
131 Presumpscot Street
Portland, ME 04103
Phone: 800-922-6352
Fax: 207-791-3616
Email: info@mesfoundation.com
Website: http://www.mesfoundation.com
Purpose: To assist adults who are pursuing higher education in Maine.
Eligibility: Applicants must qualify for independent student status for the purposes of federal financial aid. They must demonstrate financial need as well as a commitment to community service and intent to complete their educational plans.
Target applicant:
College students
Adult students
Minimum GPA: None.
Amount: Up to $1,000.
Number of awards: 12.
Deadline: April 18.
How to apply: Applications are available online.

(1537) · Maine Metal Products Association Scholarship

Maine Education Services
131 Presumpscot Street
Portland, ME 04103
Phone: 800-922-6352
Fax: 207-791-3616
Email: info@mesfoundation.com
Website: http://www.mesfoundation.com
Purpose: To support outstanding students who are planning to study metal working trades in college or technical school.
Eligibility: Students must be residents of the state of Maine, and they must be accepted or enrolled in a Maine post secondary school. They must be in school full-time with a C average. Applicants should also have plans to study one of the following metal working fields: mechanical engineering, machine tool technology, sheet metal fabrication, welding or metals industry CADCAM.
Target applicant:
High school students
College students
Adult students
Minimum GPA: 2.0
Amount: Varies.
Number of awards: Varies.
Deadline: June 1.
How to apply: Applications are available online.

(1538) · Maine Oratorical Contest

American Legion, Department of Maine
21 College Avenue
Waterville, ME 04901
Phone: 207-873-3229
Email: legionme@me.acadia.net
Website: http://www.mainelegion.org
Purpose: To enhance high school students' experience with and understanding of the U.S. Constitution. The contest will help develop students' leadership skills and civic appreciation, as well as the ability

to deliver thoughtful, insightful orations regarding U.S. citizenship and its inherent responsibilities.

Eligibility: Applicants must be high school students under the age of 20 who are U.S. citizens or legal residents and residents of the state. Students first give an oration within their state and winners compete at the national level. The oration must be related to the Constitution of the United States focusing on the duties and obligations citizens have to the government. It must be in English and be between eight and ten minutes. There is also an assigned topic which is posted on the website, and it should be between three and five minutes.

Target applicant:
 High school students
Minimum GPA: None.
Amount: Varies.
Number of awards: Varies.
Deadline: Varies.
How to apply: Application information is available by contacting the local American Legion Post.

(1539) · Maine State Chamber of Commerce Scholarship

Maine Education Services
131 Presumpscot Street
Portland, ME 04103
Phone: 800-922-6352
Fax: 207-791-3616
Email: info@mesfoundation.com
Website: http://www.mesfoundation.com
Purpose: To provide support to high school seniors who plan to study education or business and to adult students who are currently studying education.
Eligibility: Applicants must be currently attending a Maine high school in order to be eligible for the high school award, and preference may be given to students who are planning to attend Maine colleges. Preference will also be given to students who are planning to major in fields related to education or business. Students applying for the adult award must have independent status and must be studying education at a two-year college.
Target applicant:
 High school students
 College students
 Adult students
Minimum GPA: None.
Amount: $1500.
Number of awards: 3.
Deadline: April 16.
How to apply: Applications are available online.

(1540) · Maine State Grant Program

Maine Education Assistance Division
Finance Authority of Maine (FAME)
5 Community Drive
P.O. Box 949
Augusta, ME 04332
Phone: 800-228-3734
Fax: 207-623-0095
Email: education@famemaine.com
Website: http://www.famemaine.com
Purpose: To support Maine undergraduate students who have financial need.

Eligibility: Applicants must be U.S. citizens or eligible noncitizens, be Maine residents and submit the Free Application for Federal Student Aid (FAFSA) by May 1. If eligible, applicants will receive a notice of award in August.
Target applicant:
 High school students
 College students
 Graduate school students
 Adult students
Minimum GPA: None.
Amount: $500-$1,250.
Number of awards: Varies.
Scholarship may be renewable.
Deadline: May 1.
How to apply: Complete the FAFSA.

(1541) · Maine State Society Foundation Scholarship

Maine State Society Foundation of Washington, DC
3678 Bay Drive
Edgewater, MD 21037
Phone: 703-237-1031
Email: joanmbeach@aol.com
Website: http://www.mainestatesociety.org
Purpose: To provide financial assistance to Maine students.
Eligibility: Applicants must be full-time students who are at least sophomores and must attend an accredited, non-profit college or university located in Maine.
Target applicant:
 College students
Minimum GPA: 3.0
Amount: $1,000.
Number of awards: Varies.
Deadline: April 1.
How to apply: Applications are available by mail and online.

(1542) · Maine Veterans Dependents Educational Benefits

Bureau of Veterans' Services
117 State House Station
Augusta, ME 04333-0117
Phone: 207-626-4464
Fax: 207-626-4471
Email: mainebvs@maine.gov
Website: http://www.maine.gov/dvem/bvs/educational_benefits.htm
Purpose: To provide the opportunity for dependents of veterans to obtain higher education.
Eligibility: Applicants must be children whose mother or father is or was a veteran in the state of Maine. They must be at least 16 years old and be high school graduates. They must be pursuing a college degree. Benefits must be awarded prior to the dependent's 22nd birthday, unless he or she is serving in the U.S. Armed Forces, in which case they may be awarded until his or her 26th birthday.
Target applicant:
 High school students
 College students
 Adult students
Minimum GPA: None.
Amount: Tuition.
Number of awards: Varies.
Scholarship may be renewable.

Deadline: Varies.
How to apply: Applications are available online.

(1543) · Maine Vietnam Veterans Scholarship

Maine Community Foundation
245 Main Street
Ellsworth, ME 04605
Phone: 207-667-9735
Fax: 207-667-0447
Email: jwarren@mainecf.org
Website: http://www.mainecf.org
Purpose: To support Vietnam veterans from Maine and their descendants.
Eligibility: Applicants must either have served in the United States Armed Forces in Vietnam or be descendants of someone who served in Vietnam. In some cases, children of U.S. Armed Forces veterans in general may qualify.
Target applicant:
    High school students
    College students
    Graduate school students
    Adult students
Minimum GPA: None.
Amount: Varies.
Number of awards: Varies.
Deadline: May 1.
How to apply: Applications are available at high school guidance offices or online.

(1544) · Mainely Character Scholarship

Mainely Character
P.O. Box 11131
Portland, ME 04103
Email: info@mainelycharacter.org
Website: http://www.mainelycharacter.org
Purpose: To reward Maine students who demonstrate good character and positive self-development.
Eligibility: Applicants must be Maine residents who plan to attend a Title IV eligible institution of higher learning for the first time in the fall following application. They should display the characteristics of courage, integrity, responsibility and concern. A 500-word essay is required.
Target applicant:
    High school students
Minimum GPA: None.
Amount: $5,000.
Number of awards: 1.
Deadline: March 1.
How to apply: Applications are available online.

(1545) · Malcolm Baldrige Scholarship

Connecticut Community Foundation Center for Philanthropy
43 Field Street
Waterbury, CT 06702
Phone: 203-753-1315
Fax: 203-756-3054
Email: info@conncf.org
Website: http://www.conncf.org
Purpose: To provide financial assistance to students in international business, trade or manufacturing.
Eligibility: Applicants must be Connecticut students who are entering or currently attending a Connecticut college or university, and they must demonstrate exemplary academic achievement. International business students must be fluent in or be formally studying a foreign language.
Target applicant:
    High school students
    College students
    Adult students
Minimum GPA: None.
Amount: $2,000-$4,000.
Number of awards: Varies.
Deadline: March 1.
How to apply: Applications are available online.

(1546) · Mamoru and Aiko Takitani Foundation Scholarship

Mamoru and Aiko Takitani Foundation
P.O. Box 10687
Honolulu, HI 96816
Email: info@takitanifoundation.org
Website: http://www.takitani.org
Purpose: To assist Hawaii resident students with business school, technical school, community college or four-year college expenses.
Eligibility: Applicants must be graduating high school seniors and Hawaii residents. Applicants must also demonstrate scholastic achievement, participation in activities and have been accepted into an accredited institution. Community service and financial need are also considered.
Target applicant:
    High school students
Minimum GPA: None.
Amount: $1,000-$10,000.
Number of awards: Varies.
Deadline: March 1.
How to apply: Contact your high school guidance counselor.

(1547) · Mara Crawford Personal Development Scholarship

Kansas Business and Professional Women's Educational Foundation
1620 Eye Street NW
Suite 210
Washington, DC 20006
Phone: 202-293-1100
Email: desmith@fcbankonline.com
Website: http://www.bpwkansas.org/scholarships_and_loans.htm
Purpose: To provide scholarship assistance to women in the work force who want to better themselves and their families.
Eligibility: Applicants must be women who graduated from high school at least five years ago. They must have completed a BPW Young Careerist or Individual Development program. Preference is given to those with serious family obligations.
Target applicant:
    College students
    Adult students
Minimum GPA: None.
Amount: Varies.
Number of awards: Varies.
Deadline: December 31.
How to apply: Applications are available online or from your local BPW chapter.

(1548) · MARC Endowment

Epsilon Sigma Alpha Foundation
P.O. Box 270517
Fort Collins, CO 80527
Phone: 970-223-2824
Fax: 970-223-4456
Email: kloyd@knoxy.net
Website: http://www.esaintl.com/esaf
Purpose: To provide financial assistance to Midwest students.
Eligibility: Applicants must be residents of Illinois, Indiana, Iowa, Michigan, Minnesota, Missouri, Nebraska, Ohio, South Dakota or Wisconsin. They may pursue any major at any institution of higher learning. Selection is based on scholastic ability (30 percent), financial need (30 percent), leadership (20 percent), character (10 percent) and service (10 percent).
Target applicant:
    High school students
    College students
    Adult students
Minimum GPA: None.
Amount: $1,000.
Number of awards: 1.
Deadline: February 1.
How to apply: Applications are available online.

(1549) · Marguerite Ross Barnett Memorial Scholarship

Missouri Student Assistance Resource Services (MOSTARS)
Missouri Department of Higher Education
3515 Amazonas Drive
Jefferson City, MO 65109
Phone: 800-473-6757
Fax: 573-751-6635
Website: http://www.dhe.mo.gov
Purpose: This scholarship was established for students who are employed while attending school part-time.
Eligibility: Applicants must be U.S. citizens or eligible noncitizens, Missouri residents and enrolled at least half-time but less than full-time at a participating Missouri college or university. Applicants must also be employed for at least 20 hours per week and be able to demonstrate financial need.
Target applicant:
    High school students
    College students
    Adult students
Minimum GPA: None.
Amount: Varies.
Number of awards: Varies.
Scholarship may be renewable.
Deadline: April 1.
How to apply: Applications are available online.

(1550) · Marion Maccarrell Scott Scholarship

Hawaii Community Foundation - Scholarships
1164 Bishop Street, Suite 800
Honolulu, HI 96813
Phone: 888-731-3863
Fax: 808-521-6286
Email: scholarships@hcf-hawaii.org
Website: http://www.hawaiicommunityfoundation.org
Purpose: To support graduating high school students in Hawaii who are committed to world peace.
Eligibility: Applicants must have attended a public high school in Hawaii, and they must plan to attend college on the U.S. mainland. Students must have at least a 2.8 GPA.
Target applicant:
    High school students
Minimum GPA: 2.8
Amount: Varies.
Number of awards: Varies.
Deadline: March 1.
How to apply: To apply, register online, complete the online application and select the scholarships to which you wish to apply. In addition, mail the supporting materials: printed confirmation page from the online application, personal statement, essay, copy of Student Aid Report (SAR) available at www.fafsa.ed.gov and official transcript.

(1551) · Marjorie J. Hamrick Memorial Endowment

Epsilon Sigma Alpha Foundation
P.O. Box 270517
Fort Collins, CO 80527
Phone: 970-223-2824
Fax: 970-223-4456
Email: kloyd@knoxy.net
Website: http://www.esaintl.com/esaf
Purpose: To support students who are physical, occupational or speech therapy majors.
Eligibility: Applicants must be Washington residents and may attend any college or university. Selection criteria include scholastic ability (30 percent), financial need (30 percent), leadership (20 percent), character (10 percent) and service (10 percent).
Target applicant:
    High school students
    College students
    Adult students
Minimum GPA: None.
Amount: $500.
Number of awards: 1.
Deadline: February 1.
How to apply: Applications are available online.

(1552) · Marlin R. Scarborough Memorial Scholarship

South Dakota Board of Regents
306 East Capitol Ave, Suite 200
Pierre, SD 57501-2545
Phone: 605-773-3455
Fax: 605-773-5320
Email: info@sdbor.edu
Website: http://www.sdbor.edu
Purpose: To support undergraduate students in South Dakota.
Eligibility: Applicants must submit an essay detailing their leadership qualities, academic achievements and community service. Students must attend a public South Dakota university with at least a 3.5 GPA, and they must be in their junior year at the time they receive the scholarship funding.
Target applicant:
    College students
    Adult students
Minimum GPA: 3.5
Amount: $1,000.
Number of awards: 6.

Deadline: Varies.
How to apply: Applications are available online.

(1553) · Martha Strickland Scholarship

Epsilon Sigma Alpha Foundation
P.O. Box 270517
Fort Collins, CO 80527
Phone: 970-223-2824
Fax: 970-223-4456
Email: kloyd@knoxy.net
Website: http://www.esaintl.com/esaf
Purpose: To provide financial assistance for female Florida residents.
Eligibility: Students may pursue any major at any college or university. Selection is based on the following characteristics: character (10 percent), leadership (20 percent), service (10 percent), financial need (30 percent) and scholastic ability (30 percent).
Target applicant:
  High school students
  College students
  Adult students
Minimum GPA: None.
Amount: $500.
Number of awards: 1.
Deadline: February 1.
How to apply: Applications are available online.

(1554) · Mary Karele Milligan Scholarship

Czech Cultural Center
4920 San Jacinto
Houston, TX 77004
Phone: 713-528-2060
Fax: 713-528-2017
Email: czech@czechcenter.org
Website: http://www.czechcenter.org
Purpose: To provide financial assistance to children of Czech descent.
Eligibility: Applicants must have at least one Czech parent and be full-time undergraduate degree candidates to a four-year college or university. They must either be Texas residents or sons or daughters of members of the Czech Cultural Center Houston.
Target applicant:
  High school students
Minimum GPA: None.
Amount: $1,000.
Number of awards: 3.
Scholarship may be renewable.
Deadline: March 12.
How to apply: Applications are available online.

(1555) · Mary Macon McGuire Educational Grant

Virginia Federation of Women's Clubs
P.O. Box 8750
Richmond, VA 23226
Phone: 800-699-8392
Fax: 804-288-0341
Email: headquarters@gfwcvirginia.org
Website: http://www.gfwcvirginia.org
Purpose: To support Virginia women who are returning to school in order to better support their families.
Eligibility: Students must submit an essay and three letters of recommendation. Applicants must show financial need.

Target applicant:
  College students
  Adult students
Minimum GPA: None.
Amount: $2,500.
Number of awards: 2.
Deadline: March 15.
How to apply: Applications are available online.

(1556) · Mary McLeod Bethune Scholarship Program

Florida Department of Education
Office of Student Financial Assistance
1940 N. Monroe Street
Suite 70
Tallahassee, FL 32303-4759
Phone: 888-827-2004
Fax: 850-245-9667
Email: osfa@fldoe.org
Website: http://www.floridastudentfinancialaid.org
Purpose: To help Florida-resident undergraduate students who attend or plan to attend Bethune-Coleman College, Edward Waters College, Florida A&M University or Florida Memorial University.
Eligibility: Applicants must show financial need as determined by the school and meet the application procedures and deadlines of the participating schools.
Target applicant:
  High school students
  College students
  Adult students
Minimum GPA: 3.0
Amount: $3,000.
Number of awards: Varies.
Scholarship may be renewable.
Deadline: Varies.
How to apply: Applications may be obtained from the participating schools' financial aid offices.

(1557) · Mary Rubin and Benjamin M. Rubin Scholarship Fund

Central Scholarship Bureau
1700 Reisterstown Road
Suite 220
Baltimore, MD 21208-2903
Phone: 410-415-5558
Fax: 410-415-5501
Email: info@centralsb.org
Website: http://www.centralsb.org
Purpose: To help women from Maryland who plan to attend an accredited school.
Eligibility: Applicants must have been out of high school for at least a year and be permanent residents of Maryland. Selection is based on academic achievement, extracurricular activities and financial need. A transcript, recommendation, Student Aid Report (SAR), school financial aid letter, budget form and essay are required.
Target applicant:
  College students
  Graduate school students
  Adult students
Minimum GPA: 3.0
Amount: $2,500.
Number of awards: Varies.

Deadline: March 1.
How to apply: Applications are available online.

(1558) · Maryann K. Murtha Memorial Scholarship

American Legion Auxiliary, Department of New York
112 State Street
Suite 1310
Albany, NY 12207
Phone: 518-463-1162
Fax: 518-449-5406
Email: alanyterry@nycap.rr.com
Website: http://www.deptny.org/Scholarships.htm
Purpose: To provide financial assistance to students whose parents, grandparents or great-grandparents served in the Armed Forces during wartime.
Eligibility: Applicants must be children, grandchildren or great-grandchildren of Armed Forces veterans who served during World War I, World War II, the Korean Conflict, the Vietnam War, Grenada/Lebanon, Panama or the Persian Gulf. Students must be high school seniors, U.S. citizens and New York State residents.
Target applicant:
   High school students
Minimum GPA: None.
Amount: $1,000.
Number of awards: 1.
Deadline: March 1.
How to apply: Applications are available online.

(1559) · Maryland Community Cancer Scholarship

Ulman Cancer Fund for Young Adults
4725 Dorsey Hall Drive, Suite A
Ellicott City, MD 21042
Phone: 410-964-0202
Email: scholarship@ulmanfund.org
Website: http://www.ulmanfund.org
Purpose: To support Maryland students who are cancer survivors.
Eligibility: Students must show financial need, community service participation, medical hardship, commitment to education and career goals and how they have used their experience to help others.
Target applicant:
   High school students
   College students
   Adult students
Minimum GPA: None.
Amount: $2,500.
Number of awards: Varies.
Deadline: May 10.
How to apply: Applications are available online.

(1560) · Masonic Scholarship Program

Grand Lodge of Iowa, A.F. and A.M.
Scholarship Selection Committee
P.O. Box 279
Cedar Rapids, Iowa 52406-0279
Phone: 319-365-1438
Fax: 319-365-1439
Email: scholarships@gl-iowa.org
Website: http://www.gl-iowa.org
Purpose: To reward high school seniors from Iowa public high schools for academics and leadership skills.

Eligibility: Applicants must be pursuing a post-secondary education in any state at an institution which provides a two-year or four-year college program or vocational training. They do not need to have a Masonic connection. Selection is based on academic record, communication skills and financial need, but the most important is service to school and community with an emphasis on leadership roles. Finalists will be asked to appear before the committee for personal interviews.
Target applicant:
   High school students
Minimum GPA: None.
Amount: $2,000.
Number of awards: 60.
Deadline: February 1.
How to apply: Applications are available online or from guidance departments at Iowa public high schools.

(1561) · Massachusetts Community Colleges Access Grant

Massachusetts Community Colleges
Old South Building
294 Washington Street
Mezzanine #18
Boston, MA 02108
Phone: 617-542-2911
Email: jshamon@mcceo.mass.edu
Website: http://www.masscc.org/student_tuition.asp
Purpose: To make a Massachusetts community college education accessible for all.
Eligibility: Applicants must be pursuing an associate degree at a Massachusetts community college. Students whose household income is $36,000 per year or less are eligible to receive funds to cover full tuition and fees.
Target applicant:
   High school students
   College students
   Adult students
Minimum GPA: None.
Amount: Up to full tuition.
Number of awards: Varies.
Deadline: Varies.
How to apply: Applications are available from Massachusetts community college financial aid offices.

(1562) · MASSGrant

Massachusetts Office of Student Financial Assistance
454 Broadway
Suite 200
Revere, MA 02151
Phone: 617-727-9420
Fax: 617-727-0667
Email: osfa@osfa.mass.edu
Website: http://www.osfa.mass.edu
Purpose: To provide need-based financial assistance to undergraduate students who reside in Massachusetts and who are enrolled in and pursuing a program of higher education.
Eligibility: Applicants must be permanent legal residents of Massachusetts and have an Expected Family Contribution (EFC) between $0 and $3,800. Applicants must be enrolled as full-time students in a certificate, associate or bachelor's degree program and not have received a prior bachelor's degree or its equivalent.

Target applicant:
High school students
College students
Adult students
Minimum GPA: None.
Amount: $300-$2,000.
Number of awards: Varies.
Scholarship may be renewable.
Deadline: May 1.
How to apply: Complete and submit the Free Application for Federal Student Aid (FAFSA).

(1563) · Math and Science Teaching Incentive Scholarships

New York State Higher Education Services Corporation (HESC)
99 Washington Avenue
Albany, NY 12255
Phone: 888-697-4372
Email: hescwebmail@hesc.org
Website: http://www.hesc.com
Purpose: To support students in New York who are planning careers in math or science secondary education.
Eligibility: Applicants must have at least a 2.5 GPA. Recipients must agree to work for at least five years after graduation as a secondary school science or math teacher in the state of New York.
Target applicant:
College students
Adult students
Minimum GPA: 2.5
Amount: Up to $4,375.
Number of awards: Varies.
Scholarship may be renewable.
Deadline: Varies.
How to apply: Applications are available online.

(1564) · Mathematics and Science Teachers Scholarship Program

Massachusetts Office of Student Financial Assistance
454 Broadway
Suite 200
Revere, MA 02151
Phone: 617-727-9420
Fax: 617-727-0667
Email: osfa@osfa.mass.edu
Website: http://www.osfa.mass.edu
Purpose: To provide support to Massachusetts teachers who are currently teaching math or science and need required schooling to satisfy certification requirements.
Eligibility: Applicants must be currently teaching math or science at a Massachusetts public K-12 school, and they must continue to be employed in that capacity throughout the completion of the degree. Students must be enrolled in an undergraduate or graduate degree program for certification in math or science. They must sign an agreement to continue teaching one of these subjects in Massachusetts for a specified length of time after completion of the degree program.
Target applicant:
College students
Graduate school students
Adult students
Minimum GPA: None.
Amount: Varies.

Number of awards: Varies.
Scholarship may be renewable.
Deadline: October 15.
How to apply: Applications are available online.

(1565) · Matters of Life and Death Writing Contest

Compassion and Choices of Northern California
3701 Sacramento Street, #439
San Francisco, CA 94118
Phone: 866-825-8967
Email: admin@compassionandchoicesnca.org
Website: http://www.compassionandchoicesnca.org/essay.php
Purpose: To provide financial assistance to college-bound youth and to expose them to aid-in-dying issues.
Eligibility: Applicants must be high school juniors or seniors in the state of California in the year of application. They must plan to attend an institution of higher learning upon graduation. A 1,000 to 1,500 word essay is required on a topic related to aid-in-dying.
Target applicant:
High school students
Minimum GPA: None.
Amount: Up to $1,000.
Number of awards: 3.
Deadline: April 15.
How to apply: No application form is required. Applicants must send an essay with a cover letter that includes their name, address, phone number, email address, school name and grade level.

(1566) · McCurry Foundation Scholarship

McCurry Foundation Inc.
Scholarship Selection Committee
11645 Beach Boulevard, Suite 200
Jacksonville, FL 32246
Website: http://www.mccurryfoundation.org
Purpose: To provide assistance to college students who have demonstrated leadership, a responsible work ethic and academic excellence.
Eligibility: Applicants must be public high school seniors who have demonstrated leadership, a responsible work ethic, community involvement, service and academic excellence with a GPA of at least 3.0. Students must demonstrate financial need with a maximum family income of $75,000. Preference is given to students from Clay, Duval, Nassau and St. Johns Counties in Florida and from Glynn County in Georgia.
Target applicant:
High school students
Minimum GPA: 3.0
Amount: Varies.
Number of awards: Varies.
Scholarship may be renewable.
Deadline: February 15.
How to apply: Applications are available online.

(1567) · Medallion Fund

New Hampshire Charitable Foundation
37 Pleasant Street
Concord, NH 03301-4005
Phone: 603-225-6641
Fax: 603-225-1700
Email: info@nhcf.org
Website: http://www.nhcf.org/page16960.cfm

Purpose: To improve the skilled workforce in areas of need in New Hampshire.

Eligibility: Applicants must be enrolling in an accredited vocational or technical program that does not lead to a bachelor's or advanced degree. They must be legal residents of New Hampshire and intend to work in a vocational or technical career when their schooling is complete. Preference is given to those who plan to go into the manufacturing trade sector or have little or no other opportunities for training or education.

Target applicant:
　　High school students
　　College students
　　Adult students

Minimum GPA: None.

Amount: Varies.

Number of awards: Varies.

Deadline: Varies.

How to apply: Applications are available online.

(1568) · Medical Student Scholarship Program

Illinois Department of Public Health
535 W. Jefferson Street
Springfield, IL 62761
Phone: 217-782-4977
Fax: 217-782-3987
Email: dph.mailus@illinois.gov
Website: http://www.idph.state.il.us

Purpose: To increase the number of medical professionals in rural areas of Illinois.

Eligibility: Applicants must be Illinois residents enrolled in an Illinois allopathic or osteopathic medical school. Students must be planning to practice in one or more of the following medical fields: family practice, general internal medicine, general pediatrics or obstetrics/gynecology. Applicants must show evidence of financial need. Scholarship recipients agree to set up practice in an area designated as having a shortage of primary care providers.

Target applicant:
　　Graduate school students
　　Adult students

Minimum GPA: None.

Amount: Tuition, fees and living expenses.

Number of awards: Varies.

Scholarship may be renewable.

Deadline: May 15.

How to apply: Applications are available online.

(1569) · MEFA UPlan Prepaid Tuition Waiver Program

Massachusetts Educational Financing Authority
125 Summer Street
Suite 300
Boston, MA 02110
Phone: 800-449-6332
Fax: 617-261-9765
Email: info@mefa.org
Website: http://www.mefa.org

Purpose: To provide financial aid in the form of tuition waivers to Massachusetts students who prepay their tuition at lower rates.

Eligibility: Applicants must be planning to attend a school in the state of Massachusetts which participates in the UPlan program.

Target applicant:
　　Junior high students or younger
　　High school students
　　College students
　　Adult students

Minimum GPA: None.

Amount: Varies.

Number of awards: Varies.

Scholarship may be renewable.

Deadline: Varies.

How to apply: Applications are available online.

(1570) · Mellinger Scholarships

Edward Arthur Mellinger Educational Foundation Inc.
1025 E. Broadway
P.O. Box 770
Monmouth, IL 61462
Phone: 309-734-2419
Fax: 309-734-4435
Email: info@mellinger.org
Website: http://www.mellinger.org

Purpose: The E. A. Mellinger Foundation supports education as a memorial to its namesake.

Eligibility: Applicants must live in Western Illinois or Eastern Iowa, submit the FAFSA form and demonstrate financial need and attend an accredited university. Awards are based on academic achievement. Part-time students are also eligible for scholarships, and loans are also available to graduate students.

Target applicant:
　　High school students
　　College students
　　Adult students

Minimum GPA: None.

Amount: $300-$1,200.

Number of awards: Varies.

Scholarship may be renewable.

Deadline: May 1.

How to apply: Applications are available by mail or online. Application forms are only available from February 1 to May 1 each year.

(1571) · Memorial Scholarships

New York State Higher Education Services Corporation (HESC)
99 Washington Avenue
Albany, NY 12255
Phone: 888-697-4372
Email: hescwebmail@hesc.org
Website: http://www.hesc.com

Purpose: To support the spouses and dependents of deceased firefighters, volunteer firefighters, police officers, peace officers and EMS workers from the state of New York.

Eligibility: Applicants must be full-time undergraduate students, and they may attend any public or private school in the state of New York.

Target applicant:
　　College students
　　Adult students

Minimum GPA: None.

Amount: Varies.

Number of awards: Varies.

Scholarship may be renewable.

Deadline: Varies.

How to apply: Applications are available online.

(1572) · Merit Recognition Scholarship (MRS) Program

Illinois Department of Public Health
535 W. Jefferson Street
Springfield, IL 62761
Phone: 217-782-4977
Fax: 217-782-3987
Email: dph.mailus@illinois.gov
Website: http://www.idph.state.il.us
Purpose: To aid Illinois high school students.
Eligibility: Applicants must be graduating seniors or have graduated within a year of application from an Illinois high school, be ranked in the top 5 percent of their class OR received a ACT, SAT I or Prairie State Achievement Exam test score in the top 5 percent of all Illinois students who took the exam at the same time and attend a MAP-approved Illinois institution as an undergraduate at least half-time.
Target applicant:
  High school students
  College students
  Adult students
Minimum GPA: None.
Amount: Varies.
Number of awards: Varies.
Deadline: Varies.
How to apply: Qualifying students are automatically sent applications.

(1573) · Mexican Scholarship Fund

Central Indiana Community Foundation
615 North Alabama Street
Suite 119
Indianapolis, IN 46204-1498
Phone: 317-634-2423
Fax: 317-684-0943
Website: http://www.cicf.org
Purpose: To provide financial assistance to Indiana residents of Mexican descent.
Eligibility: Applicants must have a minimum GPA of 3.3, demonstrate academic promise and demonstrate financial need. Preference is given to students of Mexican descent. Awards may be used for tuition, required fees or room and board.
Target applicant:
  High school students
Minimum GPA: 3.3
Amount: Varies.
Number of awards: Varies.
Deadline: March 7.
How to apply: Applications are available online.

(1574) · MHEG- Montana Higher Education Grant

Student Assistance Foundation of Montana
2500 Broadway
Helena, MT 59601
Phone: 406-495-7800
Fax: 406-495-7880
Email: vsteiner@safmt.org
Website: http://www.safmt.org
Purpose: To assist Montana students with financial need pay for college.
Eligibility: Applicants must be U.S. citizens or eligible noncitizens, Montana residents and have exceptional financial need. Grants are awarded through individual colleges and universities.

Target applicant:
  High school students
  College students
  Adult students
Minimum GPA: None.
Amount: Varies.
Number of awards: Varies.
Scholarship may be renewable.
Deadline: Varies.
How to apply: Complete the Free Application for Federal Student Aid (FAFSA). Contact your college's financial aid office for details.

(1575) · Michael Curry Summer Internship Program

Governor's Office of the State of Illinois Michael Curry Summer Internship Program
107 William G. Stratton Building
Springfield, IL 62706
Phone: 217-782-5189
Website: http://www.illinois.gov/GOV/internships.htm
Purpose: To provide internships for college juniors, seniors or graduate students.
Eligibility: Applicants must be Illinois residents. Recipients work full-time in an agency under the jurisdiction of the Governor for 10 weeks during the summer.
Target applicant:
  College students
  Graduate school students
  Adult students
Minimum GPA: None.
Amount: Varies.
Number of awards: Varies.
Deadline: January 31.
How to apply: Applications are available online or by mail.

(1576) · Michigan Competitive Scholarship

Office of Scholarships and Grants, Bureau of Student Financial Assistance
P.O. Box 30462
Lansing, MI 48909
Phone: 888-4-GRANTS
Email: treasscholgrant@michigan.gov
Website: http://www.michigan.gov/mistudentaid
Purpose: To assist students who plan to attend a Michigan public or private college.
Eligibility: Applicants must be Michigan residents since July 1 of the previous calendar year and have received a qualifying score on the ACT and a minimum 2.0 GPA. Applicants must also demonstrate financial need and be enrolled in an approved Michigan college or university. Applicants cannot be pursuing a degree in theology, divinity or religious education. This award is based on both financial need and academic merit.
Target applicant:
  High school students
  College students
  Adult students
Minimum GPA: None.
Amount: Varies.
Number of awards: Varies.
Scholarship may be renewable.

Deadline: February 21 or March 21.
How to apply: File a Free Application for Federal Student Aid (FAFSA).

(1577) · Michigan Department of Treasury

Michigan Department of Treasury
P.O. Box 30462
Lansing, MI 48909
Phone: 888-447-2687
Email: osg@michigan.gov
Website: http://www.michigan.gov
Purpose: To remind Michigan families of the importance of saving for higher education.
Eligibility: Applicants must be Michigan residents who are in the 12th grade or below and do not already have four years paid of the Michigan Education Trust prepaid tuition plan. An adult must enter on the student's behalf. The award pays for one semester of free tuition.
Target applicant:
  Junior high students or younger
  High school students
Minimum GPA: None.
Amount: One semester of tuition.
Number of awards: 1.
Deadline: August 31.
How to apply: Applications are available online.

(1578) · Michigan Educational Opportunity Grant

Office of Scholarships and Grants, Bureau of Student Financial Assistance
P.O. Box 30462
Lansing, MI 48909
Phone: 888-4-GRANTS
Email: treasscholgrant@michigan.gov
Website: http://www.michigan.gov/mistudentaid
Purpose: To assist needy undergraduate students who enroll on at least a half-time basis at a Michigan public community college or university.
Eligibility: Applicants must be residents of Michigan and enrolled at least half-time in eligible undergraduate programs. Applicants must be able to demonstrate financial need and not be in default on an educational loan.
Target applicant:
  College students
  Adult students
Minimum GPA: None.
Amount: Varies.
Number of awards: Varies.
Scholarship may be renewable.
Deadline: Varies.
How to apply: The college awards the funds. Qualifying students apply for this need-based aid by filing a Free Application for Federal Student Aid (FAFSA). The college's financial aid award letter is the means by which students are notified regarding eligibility.

(1579) · Michigan Oratorical Contest

American Legion, Department of Michigan
212 N. Verlinden Avenue
Lansing, MI 48915
Phone: 517-371-4720 x25
Fax: 517-371-2401

Email: programs@michiganlegion.org
Website: http://www.michiganlegion.org
Purpose: To enhance high school students' experience with and understanding of the U.S. Constitution. The contest will help develop students' leadership skills and civic appreciation, as well as the ability to deliver thoughtful, insightful orations regarding U.S. citizenship and its inherent responsibilities.
Eligibility: Applicants must be high school students under the age of 20 who are U.S. citizens or legal residents and residents of the state. Students first give an oration within their state and winners compete at the national level. The oration must be related to the Constitution of the United States focusing on the duties and obligations citizens have to the government. It must be in English and be between eight and ten minutes. There is also an assigned topic which is posted on the website, and it should be between three and five minutes.
Target applicant:
  High school students
Minimum GPA: None.
Amount: Up to $1,000.
Number of awards: Varies.
Deadline: January 5.
How to apply: Application information is available by contacting the appropriate American Legion Oratorical Zone Chairman.

(1580) · Michigan Tuition Grant

Office of Scholarships and Grants, Bureau of Student Financial Assistance
P.O. Box 30462
Lansing, MI 48909
Phone: 888-4-GRANTS
Email: treasscholgrant@michigan.gov
Website: http://www.michigan.gov/mistudentaid
Purpose: To assist undergraduate and graduate students with financial need pay for tuition at Michigan colleges and universities.
Eligibility: Applicants must be Michigan residents and attend an approved Michigan college or university. Applicants must also demonstrate financial need and not be in default on an educational loan.
Target applicant:
  College students
  Graduate school students
  Adult students
Minimum GPA: None.
Amount: Varies.
Number of awards: Varies.
Scholarship may be renewable.
Deadline: September 1.
How to apply: File a Free Application for Federal Student Aid (FAFSA). Priority will be given to students who apply before September 1.

(1581) · Middle School Essay Contest

American Legion, Department of Virginia
1708 Commonwealth Avenue
Richmond, VA 23230
Phone: 804-353-6606
Fax: 804-358-1940
Website: http://www.valegion.org
Purpose: To promote citizenship in young Virginia students.
Eligibility: Applicants must write an essay on an assigned topic. The essay should be written at the student's desk during school time and

will be evaluated based on originality, sincerity and the student's ability to communicate meaning.
Target applicant:
Junior high students or younger
Minimum GPA: None.
Amount: $100-$500.
Number of awards: 3+local awards.
Deadline: Varies.
How to apply: Applications are available online and from sponsoring Posts.

(1582) · Midwest Student Exchange Program

Midwest Higher Education Commission
1300 S. Second Street
Suite 130
Minneapolis, MN 55454-1079
Phone: 612-626-8288
Fax: 612-626-8290
Email: mhec@mhec.org
Website: http://www.mhec.org
Purpose: The program aims to make attending out-of-state schools more affordable for students in member states.
Eligibility: Applicants must currently live in Kansas, Michigan, Minnesota, Missouri, Nebraska or North Dakota and wish to attend a participating school in one of these states outside their own. Other eligibility requirements vary depending on the state and school.
Target applicant:
High school students
College students
Graduate school students
Adult students
Minimum GPA: None.
Amount: $500-$3,000.
Number of awards: Varies.
Scholarship may be renewable.
Deadline: Varies.
How to apply: Students must clearly mark that they are an MSEP student when applying to the school of their choice.

(1583) · Mildred R. Knoles Opportunity Scholarship

American Legion Auxiliary, Department of Illinois
2720 E. Lincoln
Bloomington, IL 61704
Phone: 309-663-9366
Email: webmaster@illegion.org
Website: http://www.illegion.org/auxiliary/mem_Education.html
Purpose: To provide financial assistance to Illinois veterans and their descendants.
Eligibility: Applicants must be veterans who served during eligibility dates or their children, grandchildren or great-grandchildren. They must be residents of Illinois and be in need of financial assistance.
Target applicant:
High school students
College students
Adult students
Minimum GPA: None.
Amount: Up to $1,000.
Number of awards: Varies.
Deadline: Varies.
How to apply: Applications are available from your local American Legion Auxiliary.

(1584) · Mildred Towle Scholarship - Study Abroad

Hawaii Community Foundation - Scholarships
1164 Bishop Street, Suite 800
Honolulu, HI 96813
Phone: 888-731-3863
Fax: 808-521-6286
Email: scholarships@hcf-hawaii.org
Website: http://www.hawaiicommunityfoundation.org
Purpose: To support Hawaii students who plan to study abroad.
Eligibility: Applicants must study abroad as a junior, senior or graduate student. Students must have at least a 3.0 GPA.
Target applicant:
College students
Graduate school students
Adult students
Minimum GPA: 3.0
Amount: Varies.
Number of awards: Varies.
Deadline: March 1.
How to apply: To apply, register online, complete the online application and select the scholarships to which you wish to apply. In addition, mail the supporting materials: printed confirmation page from the online application, personal statement, copy of Student Aid Report (SAR) available at www.fafsa.ed.gov and official transcript.

(1585) · Mildred Towle Scholarship for African-Americans

Hawaii Community Foundation - Scholarships
1164 Bishop Street, Suite 800
Honolulu, HI 96813
Phone: 888-731-3863
Fax: 808-521-6286
Email: scholarships@hcf-hawaii.org
Website: http://www.hawaiicommunityfoundation.org
Purpose: To support African American students who are attending colleges in Hawaii.
Eligibility: Students must have at least a 3.0 GPA.
Target applicant:
High school students
College students
Adult students
Minimum GPA: 3.0
Amount: Varies.
Number of awards: Varies.
Deadline: March 1.
How to apply: To apply, register online, complete the online application and select the scholarships to which you wish to apply. In addition, mail the supporting materials: printed confirmation page from the online application, personal statement, copy of Student Aid Report (SAR) available at www.fafsa.ed.gov and official transcript.

(1586) · Military Service Recognition Scholarship

New York State Higher Education Services Corporation (HESC)
99 Washington Avenue
Albany, NY 12255
Phone: 888-697-4372
Email: hescwebmail@hesc.org
Website: http://www.hesc.com
Purpose: To support the dependents and spouses of injured or deceased military personnel from the state of New York.

Eligibility: Military personnel must have been injured on or after August 2, 1990, and they must have been New York state residents at the time of the injury.
Target applicant:
  High school students
  College students
  Adult students
Minimum GPA: None.
Amount: Varies.
Number of awards: Varies.
Scholarship may be renewable.
Deadline: Varies.
How to apply: Applications are available online.

(1587) · Milton Fisher Scholarship for Innovation and Creativity

Community Foundation for Greater New Haven
70 Audubon Street
New Haven, CT 06510-9755
Phone: 203-777-2386
Fax: 203-787-6584
Email: contactus@cfgnh.org
Website: http://www.cfgnh.org
Purpose: To reward and encourage innovative problem solving.
Eligibility: Applicants must be high school juniors or seniors or must be entering or in the first year of an undergraduate degree program. They must be Connecticut or New York City residents or students who attend or plan to attend a Connecticut or New York City institution of higher learning.
Target applicant:
  High school students
  College students
  Adult students
Minimum GPA: None.
Amount: Up to $5,000.
Number of awards: 4-6.
Deadline: June 18.
How to apply: Applications are available online.

(1588) · Minnesota Academic Excellence Scholarship

Minnesota Higher Education Services Office
1450 Energy Park Drive
Suite 350
Saint Paul, MN 55108
Phone: 651-642-0567
Fax: 651-642-0675
Email: info@heso.state.mn.us
Website: http://www.mheso.state.mn.us
Purpose: To help students who have demonstrated outstanding ability, achievement and potential in selected areas of study.
Eligibility: Applicants must be Minnesota residents who have been admitted to a full-time program in an approved Minnesota college or university. Applicants must have demonstrated achievement in one of the following subjects: English or creative writing, fine arts, foreign language, math, science or social science.
Target applicant:
  High school students
  College students
  Adult students
Minimum GPA: None.

Amount: Varies.
Number of awards: Varies.
Scholarship may be renewable.
Deadline: Varies.
How to apply: For information about the status of this program, applicants should contact the schools they wish to attend.

(1589) · Minnesota Indian Scholarship Program

Minnesota Higher Education Services Office
1450 Energy Park Drive
Suite 350
Saint Paul, MN 55108
Phone: 651-642-0567
Fax: 651-642-0675
Email: info@heso.state.mn.us
Website: http://www.mheso.state.mn.us
Purpose: To provide money to help Native American students pay for higher education.
Eligibility: Applicants must be at least one-fourth Native American, Minnesota residents and members of a federally recognized Indian tribe. Applicants must be a high school graduate or posses a GED and have been accepted by an approved college, university or vocational school in Minnesota.
Target applicant:
  College students
  Graduate school students
  Adult students
Minimum GPA: None.
Amount: Varies.
Number of awards: Varies.
Scholarship may be renewable.
Deadline: Varies.
How to apply: This award is administered by the Minnesota Department of Children, Families, and Learning (CFL) and must be approved by the Minnesota Indian Scholarship Committee. To receive an application, contact your local tribal education office.

(1590) · Minnesota Oratorical Contest

American Legion, Department of Minnesota
Third Floor, Veterans Service Building
20 W. 12th Street, Room 300A
St. Paul, MN 55155
Phone: 651-291-1800
Fax: 651-291-1057
Email: department@mnlegion.org
Website: http://www.mnlegion.org
Purpose: To enhance high school students' experience with and understanding of the U.S. Constitution. The contest will help develop students' leadership skills and civic appreciation, as well as the ability to deliver thoughtful, insightful orations regarding U.S. citizenship and its inherent responsibilities.
Eligibility: Applicants must be high school students under the age of 20 who are U.S. citizens or legal residents and residents of the state. Students first give an oration within their state and winners compete at the national level. The oration must be related to the Constitution of the United States focusing on the duties and obligations citizens have to the government. It must be in English and be between eight and ten minutes. There is also an assigned topic which is posted on the website, and it should be between three and five minutes.
Target applicant:
  High school students

Minimum GPA: None.
Amount: Up to $1,200.
Number of awards: 4.
Deadline: January 31.
How to apply: Application information is available by email.

(1591) · Minnesota State Grant

Minnesota Higher Education Services Office
1450 Energy Park Drive
Suite 350
Saint Paul, MN 55108
Phone: 651-642-0567
Fax: 651-642-0675
Email: info@heso.state.mn.us
Website: http://www.mheso.state.mn.us
Purpose: To help students from low and moderate income families pay for colleges or universities.
Eligibility: Applicants must be Minnesota residents who are high school graduates and will be 17 years of age or over by the end of the academic year. Applicants must be enrolled as undergraduates for at least three credits at one of more than 160 eligible schools in Minnesota.
Target applicant:
  College students
  Adult students
Minimum GPA: None.
Amount: Varies.
Number of awards: Varies.
Scholarship may be renewable.
Deadline: Varies.
How to apply: Use the Free Application for Federal Student Aid (FAFSA) to apply for the Minnesota State Grant.

(1592) · Minnesota State Memorial Endowment

Epsilon Sigma Alpha Foundation
P.O. Box 270517
Fort Collins, CO 80527
Phone: 970-223-2824
Fax: 970-223-4456
Email: kloyd@knoxy.net
Website: http://www.esaintl.com/esaf
Purpose: To assist Minnesota residents in obtaining higher education.
Eligibility: Applicants may pursue any major at any college or university. Criteria for selection include scholastic ability (30 percent), financial need (30 percent), leadership (20 percent), character (10 percent) and service (10 percent).
Target applicant:
  High school students
  College students
  Adult students
Minimum GPA: None.
Amount: $2,500.
Number of awards: 4.
Deadline: February 1.
How to apply: Applications are available online.

(1593) · Minority and At-Risk Scholarship

Idaho State Board of Education
P.O. Box 83720
Boise, ID 83720
Phone: 208-334-2270

Fax: 208-334-2632
Email: dkelly@osbe.state.id.us
Website: http://www.boardofed.idaho.gov
Purpose: To aid students who are "at-risk" of not being able to be college educated due to cultural, economic or physical circumstances.
Eligibility: Applicants must have graduated from an Idaho high school, and meet three of the following criteria: be a first-generation college student, be disabled, be a migrant farm worker or the dependent of one, demonstrate significant financial need or be a member of an ethnic minority underrepresented in Idaho higher education. Applicants must also attend an eligible Idaho college or university.
Target applicant:
  College students
  Adult students
Minimum GPA: None.
Amount: $3,000.
Number of awards: Varies.
Scholarship may be renewable.
Deadline: Varies.
How to apply: Applications are available by telephone request.

(1594) · Minority Teacher/Special Education Services Scholarship

State Student Assistance Commission of Indiana
150 W. Market Street
Suite 500
Indianapolis, IN 46204
Phone: 888-528-4719
Fax: 317-232-3260
Email: grants@ssaci.state.in.us
Website: http://www.in.gov/ssaci
Purpose: To support students in Indiana who are pursuing degrees in teaching, special education, physical therapy or occupational therapy.
Eligibility: Applicants must be enrolled or planning to enroll in college full-time. Students must have at least a 2.0 GPA, and financial need may be considered. Preference will be given to black and Hispanic students. Students must agree to work in the state of Indiana for a period of time after graduation.
Target applicant:
  High school students
  College students
  Adult students
Minimum GPA: 2.0
Amount: $1,000.
Number of awards: Varies.
Scholarship may be renewable.
Deadline: Varies.
How to apply: Applications are available online.

(1595) · Mississippi Educational Assistance for MIA/POW Dependents

Mississippi State Veterans Affairs Board
P.O. Box 5947
Pearl, MS 39288-5947
Phone: 601-576-4850
Fax: 601-576-4868
Email: grice@vab.state.ms.us
Website: http://www.vab.state.ms.us
Purpose: To provide educational assistance to children of veterans reported as POW or MIA.

Eligibility: Applicants must be dependents of armed service members from or stationed in Mississippi who have been prisoners of war or missing in action. The scholarship will pay tuition for up to eight semesters at an accredited institution of higher learning.

Target applicant:
High school students
College students
Adult students

Minimum GPA: None.

Amount: Tuition.

Number of awards: Varies.

Deadline: Varies.

How to apply: Applications are available from Mississippi Veterans Affairs offices.

(1596) · Mississippi Eminent Scholars Grant (MESG)

Mississippi Office of Student Financial Aid
3825 Ridgewood Road
Jackson, MS 39211
Phone: 800-327-2980
Fax: 601-432-6527
Email: sfa@ihl.state.ms.us
Website: http://www.ihl.state.ms.us

Purpose: To recognize academically high performing Mississippi students.

Eligibility: Applicants must be U.S. citizens or eligible noncitizens and current legal residents of Mississippi who are enrolled as full-time, 'first-time-in-college' undergraduates. Applicants must have a high school GPA of 3.5 and a minimum ACT of 29. National Merit/National Achievement semifinalists with a 3.5 GPA qualify without the test score.

Target applicant:
High school students

Minimum GPA: None.

Amount: 3.5

Number of awards: Varies.
Scholarship may be renewable.

Deadline: September.

How to apply: Applicants must complete an MTAG/MESG application and either a FAFSA or a Statement of Certification (a waiver for completing the FAFSA).

(1597) · Mississippi Scholarship

American Radio Relay League Foundation
225 Main Street
Newington, CT 06111
Phone: 860-594-0397
Fax: 860-594-0259
Email: foundation@arrl.org
Website: http://www.arrl.org

Purpose: To provide financial assistance to Mississippi students who are amateur radio operators and are studying electronics or communications.

Eligibility: Applicants must be licensed amateur radio operators and residents of Mississippi who attend an institution of higher learning in Mississippi. They must be seeking a bachelor's degree or higher in electronics, communication or a related field, and they must be under 30 years old.

Target applicant:
High school students
College students

Graduate school students
Adult students

Minimum GPA: None.

Amount: $500.

Number of awards: 1.

Deadline: February 1.

How to apply: Applications are available online.

(1598) · Mississippi Tuition Assistance Grant (MTAG)

Mississippi Office of Student Financial Aid
3825 Ridgewood Road
Jackson, MS 39211
Phone: 800-327-2980
Fax: 601-432-6527
Email: sfa@ihl.state.ms.us
Website: http://www.ihl.state.ms.us

Purpose: To assist financially needy Mississippi students afford tuition.

Eligibility: Applicants must be current legal residents of Mississippi who are enrolled as full-time undergraduates. Applicants must have a high school grade-point average of 2.5 and a minimum ACT of 15.

Target applicant:
High school students
College students
Adult students

Minimum GPA: None.

Amount: Varies.

Number of awards: Varies.
Scholarship may be renewable.

Deadline: September.

How to apply: Applicants must complete an MTAG/MESG application and either a FAFSA or a Statement of Certification (a waiver for completing the FAFSA).

(1599) · Missouri College Guarantee Program

Missouri Student Assistance Resource Services (MOSTARS)
Missouri Department of Higher Education
3515 Amazonas Drive
Jefferson City, MO 65109
Phone: 800-473-6757
Fax: 573-751-6635
Website: http://www.dhe.mo.gov

Purpose: To assist Missouri students who have demonstrated financial need and high school or college academic achievement.

Eligibility: Applicants must be U.S. citizens or eligible noncitizens, Missouri residents and have a high school GPA of 2.5 and an ACT score of 20 or an SAT I score of 950. Applicants must have participated in high school extracurricular activities and be enrolled full-time at a participating Missouri college or university.

Target applicant:
High school students
College students
Adult students

Minimum GPA: 2.5

Amount: Varies.

Number of awards: Varies.
Scholarship may be renewable.

Deadline: April 1.

How to apply: Complete the Free Application for Federal Student Aid (FAFSA) and have achieved the required ACT or SAT score and the other high school eligibility requirements by April 1.

(1600) · Missouri General BPW Scholarship

Missouri Business and Professional Women's Foundation Inc.
Attn: Mary Kay Pace
1503 Paradise Valley Drive
High Ridge, MO 63049
Phone: 636-677-2951
Email: bpwmo@yahoo.com
Website: http://www.bpwmo.org/files/index.php?id=14
Purpose: To provide financial assistance to female Missouri residents who have been accepted into a course of study at an accredited institution of higher learning.
Eligibility: Applicants must be U.S. citizens and have demonstrated financial need. Students do not need to be members of the organization.
Target applicant:
    High school students
Minimum GPA: None.
Amount: Varies.
Number of awards: Varies.
Deadline: January 15.
How to apply: Applications are available online. An application form, financial information, three letters of recommendation and a personal statement are required.

(1601) · Missouri Oratorical Contest

American Legion, Department of Missouri
P.O. Box 179
Jefferson City, MO 65102
Phone: 800-846-9023
Fax: 573-893-2980
Email: bmayberry@missourilegion.org
Website: http://www.missourilegion.org/programs/oratorical.htm
Purpose: To enhance high school students' experience with and understanding of the U.S. Constitution. The contest will help develop students' leadership skills and civic appreciation, as well as the ability to deliver thoughtful, insightful orations regarding U.S. citizenship and its inherent responsibilities.
Eligibility: Applicants must be high school students under the age of 20 who are U.S. citizens or legal residents and residents of the state. Students first give an oration within their state and winners compete at the national level. The oration must be related to the Constitution of the United States focusing on the duties and obligations citizens have to the government. It must be in English and be between eight and ten minutes. There is also an assigned topic which is posted on the website, and it should be between three and five minutes.
Target applicant:
    High school students
Minimum GPA: None.
Amount: Up to $3,500.
Number of awards: Varies.
Deadline: November 30.
How to apply: Application information is available by email.

(1602) · Missouri State Council Endowment

Epsilon Sigma Alpha Foundation
P.O. Box 270517
Fort Collins, CO 80527
Phone: 970-223-2824
Fax: 970-223-4456
Email: kloyd@knoxy.net
Website: http://www.esaintl.com/esaf

Purpose: To provide financial assistance for Missouri residents.
Eligibility: Applicants may pursue any major at any school. Selection is based on scholastic ability (30 percent), financial need (30 percent), leadership (20 percent), character (10 percent) and service (10 percent).
Target applicant:
    High school students
    College students
    Adult students
Minimum GPA: None.
Amount: $900.
Number of awards: 1.
Deadline: February 1.
How to apply: Applications are available online.

(1603) · Missouri Torchbearers Scholarship Endowment

Epsilon Sigma Alpha Foundation
P.O. Box 270517
Fort Collins, CO 80527
Phone: 970-223-2824
Fax: 970-223-4456
Email: kloyd@knoxy.net
Website: http://www.esaintl.com/esaf
Purpose: To provide financial assistance for Missouri residents.
Eligibility: Applicants must may pursue any major at any school. A GPA of 3.0 or higher is required. Selection is based on character (25 percent), leadership (25 percent), service (20 percent), financial need (15 percent) and scholastic ability (15 percent).
Target applicant:
    High school students
    College students
    Adult students
Minimum GPA: 3.0
Amount: $1,000.
Number of awards: 1.
Deadline: February 1.
How to apply: Applications are available online.

(1604) · Monetary Award Program (MAP)

Illinois Department of Public Health
535 W. Jefferson Street
Springfield, IL 62761
Phone: 217-782-4977
Fax: 217-782-3987
Email: dph.mailus@illinois.gov
Website: http://www.idph.state.il.us
Purpose: To provide grants to eligible Illinois undergraduate students.
Eligibility: Applicants must be residents of Illinois, enrolled at a MAP-approved Illinois institution and carry a minimum of three hours per term. Applicants must also demonstrate financial need and maintain satisfactory academic progress.
Target applicant:
    High school students
    College students
    Adult students
Minimum GPA: None.
Amount: Varies.
Number of awards: Varies.
Scholarship may be renewable.

Deadline: As soon as possible after January 1.
How to apply: Complete the Free Application for Federal Student Aid (FAFSA).

(1605) · Money to Learn Scholarship

Union Bank and Trust
18 W. 23rd Street
Attn.: Franny Madsen
Kearney, NE 68847
Phone: 308-237-7593
Website: http://www.asapubt.com
Purpose: To help Nebraska high school students.
Eligibility: Applicants must be Nebraska high schools seniors in the upper 1/3 of their graduating class or have a minimum ACT score of 20 and must plan to attend post-secondary institutions full-time in the state. Applicants should submit scholarship applications, proof of class rank and/or test scores and non-returnable photos for publicity purposes. Selection is based on meeting the minimum requirements and the quality of the essay.
Target applicant:
    High school students
Minimum GPA: None.
Amount: $500.
Number of awards: 24.
Deadline: March 15.
How to apply: Applications are available online.

(1606) · Montana State ESA Council Scholarship

Epsilon Sigma Alpha Foundation
P.O. Box 270517
Fort Collins, CO 80527
Phone: 970-223-2824
Fax: 970-223-4456
Email: kloyd@knoxy.net
Website: http://www.esaintl.com/esaf
Purpose: To provide funds for the education of Montana residents.
Eligibility: Applicants may pursue any major at any Montana college or university. Selection is based on the following criteria: scholastic ability (30 percent), financial need (30 percent), leadership (20 percent), character (10 percent) and service (10 percent).
Target applicant:
    High school students
    College students
    Adult students
Minimum GPA: None.
Amount: $1,000.
Number of awards: 1.
Deadline: February 1.
How to apply: Applications are available online.

(1607) · Montana University System Honor Scholarship

Montana Guaranteed Student Loan Program
P.O. Box 203101
Helena, MT 59620
Phone: 800-537-7508
Fax: 406-444-1869
Website: http://www.mgslp.state.mt.us
Purpose: To reward Montana high school seniors with outstanding academic achievement.

Eligibility: Applicants must have a 3.4 or higher GPA, meet specific college preparatory requirements and have been enrolled in an accredited Montana high school for at least three years prior to graduation, including their senior year. Applicants must also be accepted to and attend a Montana public university or community college.
Target applicant:
    High school students
Minimum GPA: 3.4
Amount: Varies.
Number of awards: Up to 200.
Scholarship may be renewable.
Deadline: February 15.
How to apply: Applications are available from your high school guidance counselor.

(1608) · MTAP - Montana Tuition Assistance Program/ Baker Grant

Student Assistance Foundation of Montana
2500 Broadway
Helena, MT 59601
Phone: 406-495-7800
Fax: 406-495-7880
Email: vsteiner@safmt.org
Website: http://www.safmt.org
Purpose: To assist Montana students with financial need to pay for college.
Eligibility: Applicants must be U.S. citizens or eligible noncitizens and residents of Montana who have earnings greater than $2,575 and an EFC of between $0 and $6,500.
Target applicant:
    High school students
    College students
    Adult students
Minimum GPA: None.
Amount: $100-$1,000.
Number of awards: Varies.
Scholarship may be renewable.
Deadline: Varies.
How to apply: Contact your college's financial aid office for details.

(1609) · Multicultural Association Scholarship

Urban League of Nebraska Inc.
3040 Lake Street
Omaha, NE 68111
Phone: 402-451-1066
Fax: 402-453-1342
Website: http://www.urbanleagueneb.org
Purpose: To assist graduating high school seniors and current college students in paying for higher education.
Eligibility: Applicants must be Nebraska residents. College students must have a GPA of 2.5 or higher. Two letters of recommendation are required, and an interview may be requested.
Target applicant:
    High school students
    College students
    Adult students
Minimum GPA: 2.5
Amount: Varies.
Number of awards: Varies.
Deadline: May 15.
How to apply: Applications are available online.

(1610) · Music Committee Scholarship

American Legion, Department of Kansas
1314 SW Topeka Boulevard
Topeka, KS 66612
Phone: 785-232-9315
Fax: 785-232-1399
Website: http://www.ksamlegion.org
Purpose: To support Kansas students who have distinguished themselves in the field of music.
Eligibility: Applicants must be Kansas residents who are currently high school seniors or college freshmen or sophomores. They must have a proven talent and background in music and be planning to major or minor in music at an approved Kansas post-secondary institution. Applicants must also be average or better students. Three letters of recommendation, with only one from a music teacher, a 1040 income statement, a high school transcript and a statement describing why they are applying for the scholarship are required. The scholarship will be awarded in two installments; recipients must maintain a C average to receive the second installment.
Target applicant:
    High school students
    College students
    Adult students
Minimum GPA: None.
Amount: $1,000.
Number of awards: 1.
Deadline: February 15.
How to apply: Applications are available online.

(1611) · Myre Starr Honorarium Endowment

Epsilon Sigma Alpha Foundation
P.O. Box 270517
Fort Collins, CO 80527
Phone: 970-223-2824
Fax: 970-223-4456
Email: kloyd@knoxy.net
Website: http://www.esaintl.com/esaf
Purpose: To provide educational opportunities for Oklahoma students.
Eligibility: Applicants may pursue any major at any school. Selection is based on the following characteristics: character (10 percent), leadership (20 percent), service (10 percent), financial need (30 percent) and scholastic ability (30 percent).
Target applicant:
    High school students
    College students
    Adult students
Minimum GPA: None.
Amount: $500.
Number of awards: 1.
Deadline: February 1.
How to apply: Applications are available online.

(1612) · NACA East Coast Undergraduate Scholarship for Student Leaders

National Association for Campus Activities
13 Harbison Way
Columbia, SC 29212
Phone: 803-732-6222
Fax: 803-749-1047
Email: info@naca.org
Website: http://www.naca.org
Purpose: To provide financial assistance to East Coast student leaders.
Eligibility: Students must hold a significant campus leadership position, demonstrate significant leadership skills and abilities and make significant contributions through on- or off-campus volunteering. Students must attend school in Delaware, New Jersey, Maryland, New York, Eastern Pennsylvania or Washington, DC.
Target applicant:
    College students
    Adult students
Minimum GPA: 2.5
Amount: Varies.
Number of awards: 2.
Deadline: March 31.
How to apply: Applications are available online.

(1613) · NACA Southeast Region Student Leader Scholarship

National Association for Campus Activities
13 Harbison Way
Columbia, SC 29212
Phone: 803-732-6222
Fax: 803-749-1047
Email: info@naca.org
Website: http://www.naca.org
Purpose: To provide financial assistance to Southeast student leaders.
Eligibility: Students must hold a significant campus leadership position, demonstrate significant leadership skills and abilities and make significant contributions through on- or off-campus volunteering. Students must attend school in Alabama, Florida, Georgia, Mississippi, North Carolina, South Carolina, Tennessee, Virginia or Puerto Rico.
Target applicant:
    College students
    Adult students
Minimum GPA: None.
Amount: Varies.
Number of awards: Up to 4.
Deadline: March 31.
How to apply: Applications are available online.

(1614) · Nancy Penn Lyons Scholarship Fund

Community Foundation for Greater Atlanta Inc.
50 Hurt Plaza
Suite 449
Atlanta, GA 30303
Phone: 404-688-5525
Email: info@atlcf.org
Website: http://www.atlcf.org/GrantsScholarships/Scholarships/NancyPennLyons.aspx
Purpose: To provide assistance to needy students who have been accepted to prestigious or out-of-state universities.
Eligibility: Applicants must be graduating high school seniors who have been Georgia residents for at least one year. They must have an ACT score of 22 or higher or an SAT composite score of 1000 or higher and a GPA of 3.0 or greater. They must have participated in community service and have financial need, and they must not be attending a public institution in the state of Georgia.
Target applicant:
    High school students

Minimum GPA: 3.0
Amount: $5,000.
Number of awards: 5.
Scholarship may be renewable.
Deadline: April 19.
How to apply: Applications are available online.

(1615) · NC Student Loan Program for Health, Science and Mathematics

College Foundation of North Carolina
P.O. Box 41966
Raleigh, NC 27629-1966
Phone: 866-234-6400
Fax: 919-821-3139
Email: programinformation@cfnc.org
Website: http://www.cfnc.org
Purpose: To provide financial assistance to students in health, science and mathematics in North Carolina.
Eligibility: Applicants must be North Carolina residents who have been accepted into associate, bachelor's, master's or doctoral degree programs that lead to degrees in qualifying health, science or mathematics majors. Recipients must enroll full-time for fall and spring semesters. Recipients must repay the loans either through service or in cash.
Target applicant:
　　High school students
　　College students
　　Graduate school students
　　Adult students
Minimum GPA: None.
Amount: Up to $8,500.
Number of awards: Varies.
Loan may be renewable.
Deadline: May 1.
How to apply: Applications are available online.

(1616) · Nebraska ESA Endowed Scholarship

Epsilon Sigma Alpha Foundation
P.O. Box 270517
Fort Collins, CO 80527
Phone: 970-223-2824
Fax: 970-223-4456
Email: kloyd@knoxy.net
Website: http://www.esaintl.com/esaf
Purpose: To provide financial assistance for Nebraska residents.
Eligibility: Applicants may attend any college or university and major in any field. Selection is based equally on the following criteria: character, leadership, service, financial need and scholastic ability.
Target applicant:
　　High school students
　　College students
　　Adult students
Minimum GPA: None.
Amount: $500.
Number of awards: 1.
Deadline: February 1.
How to apply: Applications are available online.

(1617) · Nebraska State Grant

Nebraska Coordinating Commission for Postsecondary Education
P.O. Box 95005
Lincoln, NE 68509
Phone: 402-471-2847
Fax: 402-471-2886
Email: ritchie.morrow@ccpe.ne.gov
Website: http://www.ccpe.state.ne.us
Purpose: To support Nebraska college students.
Eligibility: Students must be eligible for the Federal Pell Grant and attend a Nebraska postsecondary institution.
Target applicant:
　　High school students
　　College students
　　Adult students
Minimum GPA: None.
Amount: Varies.
Number of awards: Varies.
Deadline: Varies.
How to apply: Applications are available at college financial aid offices, and students apply through their colleges. Students must complete the Free Application for Federal Student Aid (FAFSA).

(1618) · Nebraska Veterans' Aid Fund Waiver of Tuition

Nebraska Department of Veterans' Affairs
State Service Office
5631 S. 48 Street
Lincoln, NE 68516
Phone: 402-420-4021
Fax: 402-471-7070
Website: http://www.vets.state.ne.us/index_html?page=content/benefits.html
Purpose: To provide assistance to children and spouses of Nebraska veterans.
Eligibility: Applicants must be the children, stepchildren, spouses or widows of veterans who died of a service-connected injury or illness, became totally and permanently disabled as a result of military service or was classified as MIA or POW during armed conflict after August 4th, 1964. They must be Nebraska residents and attend a state college, university or community college.
Target applicant:
　　High school students
　　College students
　　Adult students
Minimum GPA: None.
Amount: Tuition.
Number of awards: Varies.
Scholarship may be renewable.
Deadline: Varies.
How to apply: Applications are available from your County Veterans Service Officer.

(1619) · Nebraskans of World War II Scholarships

Nebraska State Historical Society Foundation
P.O. Box 82554
1500 R Street
Lincoln, NE 68501
Phone: 888-515-3535

Email: web@nebraskahistory.org

Website: http://www.nebraskahistory.org

Purpose: To honor the memory of Edward J. Clough and Adrian B. DePutron, two World War II servicemen from Lincoln, Nebraska.

Eligibility: Applicants must be high school seniors in one of the following Nebraska towns: Alda, Broken Bow, Brule, Central City, Cozad, Nelson, Gothenburg, Kearney, Lincoln, Madison, Mitchell, Ravenna, Newark, North Bend, Omaha, Palisade, Potter or St. Michael. They must have a GPA of 3.75 or higher. An essay, resume and two letters of reference are required.

Target applicant:
High school students

Minimum GPA: 3.75

Amount: $1,000.

Number of awards: 7.

Deadline: January 15.

How to apply: Applications are available from school counselors or the Nebraska State Historical Society Foundation.

(1620) · Ned McWherter Scholars Program

Tennessee Student Assistance Corporation

404 James Robertson Parkway

Suite 1510, Parkway Towers

Nashville, TN 37243

Phone: 800-342-1663

Fax: 615-741-6101

Email: tsac.aidinfo@state.tn.us

Website: http://www.collegepaystn.com

Purpose: To assist Tennessee students with financial need.

Eligibility: Applicants must be Tennessee residents, high school seniors or recent graduates who plan to attend an eligible Tennessee undergraduate institution full-time, U.S. citizens and have a minimum 3.5 GPA and SAT or ACT scores in the top 5 percent nationally.

Target applicant:
High school students

Minimum GPA: 3.5

Amount: Up to $6,000.

Number of awards: Varies.

Deadline: February 15.

How to apply: Applications are available from your high school guidance counselor and online.

(1621) · Need Based Tuition Waiver Program

Massachusetts Office of Student Financial Assistance

454 Broadway

Suite 200

Revere, MA 02151

Phone: 617-727-9420

Fax: 617-727-0667

Email: osfa@osfa.mass.edu

Website: http://www.osfa.mass.edu

Purpose: To support Massachusetts students who are in need of supplemental financial aid.

Eligibility: Applicants must live in the state of Massachusetts for at least one year prior to the beginning of the school year, and they must be enrolled in a state funded college. They must be in an undergraduate program with at least three credits per semester. Students must not owe any refunds on prior scholarships and cannot have any defaulted government loans. They must also be able to show proof of financial need.

Target applicant:
High school students
College students
Adult students

Minimum GPA: None.

Amount: Varies.

Number of awards: Varies.

Deadline: Varies.

How to apply: Applications are available at college financial aid offices.

(1622) · Nettie Tucker Yowell Scholarship

Virginia Business and Professional Women's Foundation

P.O. Box 4842

McLean, VA 22103-4842

Phone: 800-525-3729

Email: bpwfoundation@act.org

Website: http://www.vabpwfoundation.org

Purpose: To support Virginia residents who are pursuing bachelor's degrees.

Eligibility: Applicants must be high school seniors with at least a 3.0 GPA. They must pass all SOL tests and score at least 1000 on the SAT. Students must obtain a letter of recommendation from a guidance counselor or principal. Awards are based on financial need, academic achievements, educational goals and commitment to the Virginia BPW mission.

Target applicant:
High school students

Minimum GPA: 3.0

Amount: $500-$1,000.

Number of awards: Varies.

Deadline: April 1.

How to apply: Applications are available online.

(1623) · Nevada Millennium Scholarship

Nevada Office of the State Treasurer

555 E. Washington Avenue

Suite 4600

Las Vegas, NV 89101

Phone: 888-477-2667

Fax: 702-486-3246

Email: millenniumscholarshi@nevadatreasurer.gov

Website: https://nevadatreasurer.gov

Purpose: To assist students who have attained high academic achievement in a Nevada high school.

Eligibility: Applicants must graduate from a Nevada public or private high school with a GPA of 3.25 or higher, pass all areas of the Nevada High School Proficiency Exam and have been a resident of Nevada for at least two years in high school.

Target applicant:
High school students

Minimum GPA: 3.25

Amount: Varies.

Number of awards: Varies.

Scholarship may be renewable.

Deadline: Varies.

How to apply: Applications are not required. Your school district will submit your name to the State Treasurer's office if you are eligible.

(1624) · Nevada Women's Fund Scholarships

Nevada Women's Fund
770 Smithridge Drive
Suite 300
Reno, NV 89502
Phone: 775-786-2335
Fax: 775-786-8152
Email: info@nevadawomensfund.org
Website: http://www.nevadawomensfund.org
Purpose: To improve the lives of women and children in northern Nevada.
Eligibility: Northern Nevada residents and those attending northern Nevada schools receive preference.
Target applicant:
    High school students
    College students
    Graduate school students
    Adult students
Minimum GPA: None.
Amount: $500 and up.
Number of awards: Varies.
Deadline: February 27.
How to apply: Applications are available online or from several offices listed on the website.

(1625) · New Century Scholarship

Utah State Board of Regents
Board of Regents Building, The Gateway
60 South 400 West
Salt Lake City, UT 84101
Phone: 801-321-7107
Website: http://www.utahsbr.edu
Purpose: To assist Utah high school students.
Eligibility: Applicants must be high school students who have completed the equivalent of an associate's degree at a Utah state institution of higher education by September 1 of their high school graduation year. The award provides assistance for the bachelor's degree at a state college.
Target applicant:
    High school students
Minimum GPA: None.
Amount: Varies.
Number of awards: Varies.
Scholarship may be renewable.
Deadline: Varies.
How to apply: Applications are available online.

(1626) · New England Regional Student Program

New England Board of Higher Education
45 Temple Place
Boston, MA 02111
Phone: 617-357-9620
Fax: 617-338-1577
Email: rsp@nebhe.org
Website: http://www.nebhe.org
Purpose: The program lowers tuition rates for New England students who must travel out of state for their desired major.
Eligibility: Students must be residents of Connecticut, Maine, Massachusetts, New Hampshire, Rhode Island or Vermont and attend a school in another of those states that offers an RSP program in their major. The major must not be available at an in-school state.

Target applicant:
    High school students
    College students
    Graduate school students
    Adult students
Minimum GPA: None.
Amount: Varies.
Number of awards: Varies.
Scholarship may be renewable.
Deadline: Varies.
How to apply: Students should note that they are interested in the RSP program on their regular college application.

(1627) · New Hampshire Charitable Foundation Adult Student Aid Program

New Hampshire Charitable Foundation
37 Pleasant Street
Concord, NH 03301-4005
Phone: 603-225-6641
Fax: 603-225-1700
Email: info@nhcf.org
Website: http://www.nhcf.org/page16960.cfm
Purpose: To provide financial assistance to adults who are pursuing undergraduate degrees or training.
Eligibility: Applicants must be independent students and legal New Hampshire residents. They must have applied for financial aid and still have unmet financial need. Applicants may be enrolled in a degree or non-degree program, but courses do not have to be taken for credit. Preference is given to single parents, students who have previously received funding through the program and successfully completed coursework and students with little education beyond high school.
Target applicant:
    College students
    Adult students
Minimum GPA: None.
Amount: Up to $500.
Number of awards: Varies.
Scholarship may be renewable.
Deadline: Varies.
How to apply: Applications are available online.

(1628) · New Hampshire Charitable Foundation Statewide Student Aid Program

New Hampshire Charitable Foundation
37 Pleasant Street
Concord, NH 03301-4005
Phone: 603-225-6641
Fax: 603-225-1700
Email: info@nhcf.org
Website: http://www.nhcf.org/page16960.cfm
Purpose: To allow New Hampshire students to access over 50 scholarship and loan opportunities through a single application.
Eligibility: Applicants must be New Hampshire residents between the ages of 17 and 23 who plan to pursue a bachelor's degree or graduate students of any age. They must enroll at least half-time to qualify.
Target applicant:
    High school students
    College students
    Graduate school students
    Adult students

Minimum GPA: None.
Amount: Varies.
Number of awards: Varies.
Deadline: April 13.
How to apply: Applications are available online.

(1629) · New Hampshire Incentive Program

New Hampshire Postsecondary Education Commission
3 Barrell Court
Suite 300
Concord, NH 03301
Phone: 603-271-2555 x352
Fax: 603-271-2696
Email: jknapp@pec.state.nh.us
Website: http://www.state.nh.us/postsecondary
Purpose: To assist New Hampshire students attending eligible New England institutions.
Eligibility: Applicants must be New Hampshire residents, demonstrate financial need and be working towards their first bachelor's degree at an eligible New England institution.
Target applicant:
  College students
  Adult students
Minimum GPA: None.
Amount: $125-$1,000.
Number of awards: Varies.
Deadline: May 1.
How to apply: Applicants must complete the Free Application for Federal Student Aid (FAFSA).

(1630) · New Jersey Oratorical Contest

American Legion, Department of New Jersey
135 W. Hanover Street
Trenton, NJ 08618
Phone: 609-695-5418
Fax: 609-394-1532
Email: adjudant@njamericanlegion.org
Website: http://www.njamericanlegion.org
Purpose: To enhance high school students' experience with and understanding of the U.S. Constitution. The contest will help develop students' leadership skills and civic appreciation, as well as the ability to deliver thoughtful, insightful orations regarding U.S. citizenship and its inherent responsibilities.
Eligibility: Applicants must be high school students under the age of 20 who are U.S. citizens or legal residents and residents of the state. Students first give an oration within their state and winners compete at the national level. The oration must be related to the Constitution of the United States focusing on the duties and obligations citizens have to the government. It must be in English and be between eight and ten minutes. There is also an assigned topic which is posted on the website, and it should be between three and five minutes.
Target applicant:
  High school students
Minimum GPA: None.
Amount: Up to $5,500.
Number of awards: 5.
Deadline: March 18.
How to apply: Application information is available by email: ray@njamericanlegion.org.

(1631) · New Jersey School Counselor Association Scholarships

New Jersey School Counselor Association Inc.
5 Split Rock Place
Moorestown, NJ 08057
Phone: 856-234-8884
Email: jimlukach@msn.com
Website: http://www.njsca.org
Purpose: To spread awareness of the importance of the role of school counselors.
Eligibility: Applicants must be New Jersey residents who will be graduating in the year of application. They must have been accepted to and plan to enroll in an institution of higher learning. A 300-500 word essay is required.
Target applicant:
  High school students
Minimum GPA: None.
Amount: $1,000.
Number of awards: 3.
Deadline: April 8.
How to apply: Applications are available online.

(1632) · New Jersey State Elks Handicapped Children's Scholarship

New Jersey State Elks
665 Rahway Avenue
P.O. Box 1596
Woodbridge, NJ 07095
Phone: 732-326-1300
Website: http://www.njelks.org
Purpose: To assist students with physical handicaps in obtaining higher education.
Eligibility: Applicants must be New Jersey residents and high school seniors with physical handicaps. They must demonstrate financial need and excellent academic standing.
Target applicant:
  High school students
Minimum GPA: None.
Amount: $2,500.
Number of awards: 2.
Scholarship may be renewable.
Deadline: April 16.
How to apply: Applications are available online or by phone.

(1633) · New Mexico Children of Deceased Veterans Scholarships

New Mexico Department of Veterans' Services
P.O. Box 2324
Santa Fe, NM 87504
Phone: 505-827-6300
Website: http://www.dvs.state.nm.us
Purpose: To provide higher education opportunities for children of deceased veterans.
Eligibility: Applicants must be children between the ages of 16 and 26 whose parent was a veteran who was killed in action or who died of a battle-related injury. The waiver covers tuition at any state funded college or university as well as a $150 per semester stipend to help cover books or fees.
Target applicant:
  High school students

College students
Adult students
Minimum GPA: None.
Amount: Tuition.
Number of awards: Varies.
Scholarship may be renewable.
Deadline: Varies.
How to apply: Applications are available online.

(1634) · New Mexico Scholars

New Mexico Higher Education Department
1068 Cerrillos Road
Santa Fe, NM 87505
Phone: 800-279-9777
Fax: 505-476-6511
Email: heather.romero@state.nm.us
Website: http://hed.state.nm.us
Purpose: To support New Mexico undergraduate students with financial need attend postsecondary institutions in New Mexico.
Eligibility: Applicants must be undergraduate students attending selected New Mexico public institutions or designated private non-profit colleges, meet family income requirements, be under the age of 22 and have graduated in the top 5 percent of their high school class or have a minimum ACT score of 25.
Target applicant:
College students
Minimum GPA: None.
Amount: Up to full tuition.
Number of awards: Varies.
Deadline: Varies.
How to apply: Contact your financial aid office.

(1635) · New Mexico State Council Road Runner Endowment

Epsilon Sigma Alpha Foundation
P.O. Box 270517
Fort Collins, CO 80527
Phone: 970-223-2824
Fax: 970-223-4456
Email: kloyd@knoxy.net
Website: http://www.esaintl.com/esaf
Purpose: To provide financial assistance for New Mexico students.
Eligibility: Applicants must be from the state of New Mexico or from Farwell or El Paso, Texas. They may pursue any major at any college or university. Selection is based on the following criteria: character (10 percent), leadership (10 percent), scholastic ability (10 percent), service 35 percent) and financial need (35 percent).
Target applicant:
High school students
College students
Adult students
Minimum GPA: None.
Amount: $1,000.
Number of awards: 1.
Deadline: February 1.
How to apply: Applications are available online.

(1636) · New York Legion Auxilliary Department Scholarship

American Legion Auxiliary, Department of New York
112 State Street
Suite 1310
Albany, NY 12207
Phone: 518-463-1162
Fax: 518-449-5406
Email: alanyterry@nycap.rr.com
Website: http://www.deptny.org/Scholarships.htm
Purpose: To assist students whose parents, grandparents or great-grandparents served in the Armed Forces during wartime.
Eligibility: Applicants must be children, grandchildren or great-grandchildren of veterans who served in the Armed Forces during World War I, World War II, the Korean Conflict, the Vietnam War, Grenada/Lebanon, Panama or the Persian Gulf. Students must be high school seniors and be New York State residents and U.S. citizens.
Target applicant:
High school students
Minimum GPA: None.
Amount: $1,000.
Number of awards: 1.
Deadline: March 1.
How to apply: Applications are available online.

(1637) · New York Legion Auxilliary District Scholarships

American Legion Auxiliary, Department of New York
112 State Street
Suite 1310
Albany, NY 12207
Phone: 518-463-1162
Fax: 518-449-5406
Email: alanyterry@nycap.rr.com
Website: http://www.deptny.org/Scholarships.htm
Purpose: To provide financial assistance to children, grandchildren and great-grandchildren of war veterans.
Eligibility: Applicants must be children, grandchildren or great-grandchildren of Armed Forces veterans of World War I, World War II, the Korean Conflict, the Vietnam War, Grenada/Lebanon, Panama or the Persian Gulf. Students must be high school seniors and must be U.S. citizens and New York State residents.
Target applicant:
High school students
Minimum GPA: None.
Amount: $1,000.
Number of awards: 1.
Deadline: March 1.
How to apply: Applications are available online.

(1638) · New York Lottery Leaders of Tomorrow Scholarship

New York Lottery LOT Scholarships
One Broadway Center
P.O. Box 7540
Schenectady, NY 12301-7540
Phone: 518-388-3415
Fax: 518-388-3423
Email: lotscholar@lottery.state.ny.us
Website: http://www.nylottery.org/lot

Purpose: To help New York State high school seniors who plan to attend colleges in the state.

Eligibility: Applicants must have demonstrated leadership skills in their extracurricular activities and community service, have B averages and plan to be full-time students at New York State colleges, universities, community colleges or trade schools and maintain B averages there.

Target applicant:
    High school students

Minimum GPA: None.

Amount: $4,000.

Number of awards: Varies.

Scholarship may be renewable.

Deadline: March 9.

How to apply: Applications are available from high school guidance counselors.

(1639) · New York Oratorical Contest

American Legion, Department of New York
112 State Street, Suite 1300
Albany, NY 12207
Email: info@nylegion.org
Website: http://www.ny.legion.org

Purpose: To enhance high school students' experience with and understanding of the U.S. Constitution. The contest will help develop students' leadership skills and civic appreciation, as well as the ability to deliver thoughtful, insightful orations regarding U.S. citizenship and its inherent responsibilities.

Eligibility: Applicants must be high school students under the age of 20 who are U.S. citizens or legal residents and residents of the state. Students first give an oration within their state and winners compete at the national level. The oration must be related to the Constitution of the United States focusing on the duties and obligations citizens have to the government. It must be in English and be between eight and ten minutes. There is also an assigned topic which is posted on the website, and it should be between three and five minutes.

Target applicant:
    High school students

Minimum GPA: None.

Amount: Varies.

Number of awards: Varies.

Deadline: March 10.

How to apply: Application information is available by contacting the local American Legion Post.

(1640) · Nissan Hawaii High School Hall of Honor

High School Athletic Association
P.O. Box 62029
Honolulu, HI 96839
Website: http://www.sportshigh.com

Purpose: To support Hawaii high school seniors who are athletes.

Eligibility: Applicants must be graduating high school seniors and athletes in any organized sport in Hawaii. Selection is based primarily on sports achievements. Factors considered include contributions to the team, sportsmanship, character, participation in school activities and community involvement.

Target applicant:
    High school students

Minimum GPA: None.

Amount: $2,000.

Number of awards: 12.

Deadline: May 2.

How to apply: Applications are available by written request.

(1641) · Nissan Scholarship

Nissan North America
P.O. Box 685003
Franklin, TN 37068
Phone: 800-647-7261
Email: webmaster@nissanusa.com
Website: http://www.nissanusa.com

Purpose: To assist Mississippi high school seniors in attending public two-year or four-year colleges.

Eligibility: Applicants must have a minimum GPA of 2.5 and a minimum ACT score of 20 or SAT score of 820, have demonstrated financial need and be accepted as a full-time student at a Mississippi public college or university.

Target applicant:
    High school students

Minimum GPA: 2.5

Amount: Full tuition.

Number of awards: Varies.

Deadline: March 1.

How to apply: No application is necessary. However, students must mail an essay, resume, high school transcript with ACT or SAT score and FAFSA results to Mississippi Office of Student Financial Aid, 3825 Ridgewood Road, Jackson, MS 39211-6453.

(1642) · NJ Student Tuition Assistance Reward Scholarship

New Jersey Higher Education Student Assistance Authority
P.O. Box 540
Trenton, NJ 08625
Phone: 800-792-8670
Email: clientservices@hesaa.org
Website: http://www.hesaa.org

Purpose: To support community college students in New Jersey who graduated from high school with excellent academic standing.

Eligibility: Applicants must have graduated from a New Jersey high school in the top 20 percent of their class, and they must have been state residents for at least 12 months prior to graduation. Students must enroll full-time in their home county college by the fifth semester after graduating from high school.

Target applicant:
    High school students
    College students
    Adult students

Minimum GPA: None.

Amount: Varies.

Number of awards: Varies.

Scholarship may be renewable.

Deadline: October 1.

How to apply: Applications are available at college financial aid offices.

(1643) · NJ Student Tuition Assistance Reward Scholarship II

New Jersey Higher Education Student Assistance Authority
P.O. Box 540
Trenton, NJ 08625
Phone: 800-792-8670
Email: clientservices@hesaa.org
Website: http://www.hesaa.org

Purpose: To support NJ STARS students who are transferring to four-year colleges.

Eligibility: Applicants must be county college graduates with an associate's degree, and they must have a GPA of at least 3.0. They must either be NJ STARS recipients or have other full state or federal aid during the semester in which they graduate. Students must be enrolled full-time at a New Jersey four-year college within two semesters of graduation.

Target applicant:
  College students
  Adult students
Minimum GPA: 3.0
Amount: Varies.
Number of awards: Varies.
Scholarship may be renewable.
Deadline: October 1.
How to apply: Applications are available at college financial aid offices.

(1644) · NJVVM Scholarship Program

New Jersey Vietnam Veterans' Memorial Foundation
1 Memorial Lane
P.O. Box 648
Holmdel, NJ 07733
Phone: 800-648-8387
Fax: 732-335-1107
Email: sjsmith2@njvvmf.org
Website: http://www.njvvmf.org
Purpose: To support high school seniors in New Jersey who have visited the New Jersey Vietnam Veterans' Memorial.

Eligibility: Applicants must submit an essay on their experience visiting the New Jersey Vietnam Veterans Memorial.

Target applicant:
  High school students
Minimum GPA: None.
Amount: $2,500.
Number of awards: 2.
Deadline: April 18.
How to apply: Applications are available online.

(1645) · NMASBO Scholarship

New Mexico Association of School Business Officials
P.O. Box 7535
Albuquerque, NM 87194-7535
Phone: 505-923-3283
Fax: 505-923-3114
Email: info@nmasbo.org
Website: http://www.nmasbo.org
Purpose: To support graduating high school seniors in New Mexico.

Eligibility: Students must have at least a 3.0 GPA. Applicants must submit an essay and two letters of recommendation. Students must plan to attend a New Mexico college or university on a full-time basis.

Target applicant:
  High school students
Minimum GPA: 3.0
Amount: $1500.
Number of awards: 7-10.
Deadline: April 15.
How to apply: Applications are available online.

(1646) · NMPRSA Scholarship

New Mexico Chapter of the Public Relations Society of America
5620 Wyoming NE
Suite A
Albuquerque, NM 87109
Phone: 505-856-9933
Fax: 505-856-9935
Email: oliver@squirescompany.com
Website: http://www.nmprsa.org
Purpose: To support New Mexico students who are majoring in communications fields.

Eligibility: Applicants must be pursuing undergraduate degrees in public relations, mass communications, journalism or visual communications. Preference is given to students who are majoring in public relations.

Target applicant:
  College students
  Adult students
Minimum GPA: None.
Amount: $500.
Number of awards: Varies.
Deadline: November 9.
How to apply: Applications are available online.

(1647) · NNM American Society of Mechanical Engineers Scholarship

Los Alamos National Laboratory Foundation
1302 Calle de la Merced
Suite A
Espanola, NM 87532
Phone: 505-753-8890
Fax: 505-753-8915
Email: info@lanlfoundation.org
Website: http://www.lanlfoundation.org
Purpose: To support undergraduate students from Northern New Mexico who are majoring in mechanical engineering.

Eligibility: Students must have at least a 3.25 GPA, and they must have either an SAT score of at least 1350 or an ACT score of at least 19. Applicants must submit an essay and two letters of recommendation.

Target applicant:
  High school students
  College students
  Adult students
Minimum GPA: 3.25
Amount: $1,000.
Number of awards: Varies.
Deadline: January 22.
How to apply: Applications are available online.

(1648) · Norma L. Moore Endowment

Epsilon Sigma Alpha Foundation
P.O. Box 270517
Fort Collins, CO 80527
Phone: 970-223-2824
Fax: 970-223-4456
Email: kloyd@knoxy.net
Website: http://www.esaintl.com/esaf
Purpose: To provide financial assistance for female Oklahoma residents.

Eligibility: Applicants may pursue any major at any institution of higher learning. Selection is based on the following criteria: service (5 percent), character (10 percent), leadership (10 percent), scholastic ability (25 percent) and financial need (50 percent).

Target applicant:
- High school students
- College students
- Adult students

Minimum GPA: None.
Amount: $500.
Number of awards: 1.
Deadline: February 1.
How to apply: Applications are available online.

(1649) · Norman & Ruth Good Educational Endowment

Lincoln Community Foundation
215 Centennial Mall South, Suite 100
Lincoln, NE 68508
Phone: 402-474-2345
Fax: 402-476-8532
Email: lcf@lcf.org
Website: http://www.lcf.org
Purpose: To assist Nebraska students.
Eligibility: Applicants must be attending a private college in Nebraska and must be in their junior or senior year. Applicants may not apply if the scholarship money is to be used for summer programs or schools that are not valid degree-granting institutions.

Target applicant:
- College students
- Adult students

Minimum GPA: 3.5
Amount: Varies.
Number of awards: Varies.
Scholarship may be renewable.
Deadline: April 15.
How to apply: Applications are available online.

(1650) · Norman E. Strohmeier, W2VRS Memorial Scholarship

American Radio Relay League Foundation
225 Main Street
Newington, CT 06111
Phone: 860-594-0397
Fax: 860-594-0259
Email: foundation@arrl.org
Website: http://www.arrl.org
Purpose: To support students from western New York who are involved in amateur radio.
Eligibility: Applicants must have an amateur radio license of Technician Class or higher. Students must have at least a 3.2 GPA, and preference will be given to graduating high school seniors.

Target applicant:
- High school students

Minimum GPA: 3.2
Amount: $500.
Number of awards: 1.
Deadline: February 1.
How to apply: Applications are available online.

(1651) · Norman S. and Betty M. Fitzhugh Fund

Greater Kanawha Valley Foundation
1600 Huntington Square
900 Lee Street, East
Charleston, WV 25301
Phone: 304-346-3620
Fax: 304-346-3640
Email: tgkvf@tgkvf.org
Website: http://www.tgkvf.org
Purpose: To provide financial assistance to West Virginia residents wishing to earn a college education.
Eligibility: Applicants must be full-time students (12 hours) and demonstrate good moral character and academic excellence.

Target applicant:
- High school students
- College students
- Adult students

Minimum GPA: 2.5
Amount: $500.
Number of awards: 1.
Scholarship may be renewable.
Deadline: February 17.
How to apply: Applications are available online at http://www.tgkvf.org/scholar.htm or by email at shoover@tgkvf.org.

(1652) · North Carolina Bar Association Scholarship

College Foundation of North Carolina
P.O. Box 41966
Raleigh, NC 27629-1966
Phone: 866-234-6400
Fax: 919-821-3139
Email: programinformation@cfnc.org
Website: http://www.cfnc.org
Purpose: To provide financial assistance to students whose parents are North Carolina law enforcement officers who were killed or permanently disabled in the line of duty.
Eligibility: Applicants must be children of a North Carolina police officer who was killed or permanently disabled while on duty and must be enrolled or accepted to an institution approved by the scholarship committee. They must also apply before their 27th birthday and demonstrate financial need and merit.

Target applicant:
- High school students
- College students
- Adult students

Minimum GPA: None.
Amount: Varies.
Number of awards: Varies.
Deadline: April 1.
How to apply: Applications are available online.

(1653) · North Carolina Education Lottery Scholarship

College Foundation of North Carolina
P.O. Box 41966
Raleigh, NC 27629-1966
Phone: 866-234-6400
Fax: 919-821-3139
Email: programinformation@cfnc.org
Website: http://www.cfnc.org

Purpose: To provide financial assistance to North Carolina residents with financial need who are attending North Carolina colleges and universities.

Eligibility: Applicants must be enrolled for at least six credit hours per semester in an undergraduate degree-seeking program at an eligible North Carolina institution and meet satisfactory academic progress requirements. Students who meet the same criteria as the Federal Pell Grant and those with an Estimated Family Contribution of $5,000 or less are eligible for the scholarship.

Target applicant:
College students
Adult students

Minimum GPA: None.
Amount: Up to $2,500.
Number of awards: 30,000.
Deadline: Varies.
How to apply: Qualified students who submit the Free Application for Federal Student Aid (FAFSA) will be considered.

(1654) · North Carolina Oratorical Contest

American Legion, Department of North Carolina
4 N. Blount Street
P.O. Box 26657
Raleigh, NC 27611
Phone: 919-832-7506
Fax: 919-832-6428
Email: nclegion@nc.rr.com
Website: http://nclegion.org/orate.htm

Purpose: To enhance high school students' experience with and understanding of the U.S. Constitution. The contest will help develop students' leadership skills and civic appreciation, as well as the ability to deliver thoughtful, insightful orations regarding U.S. citizenship and its inherent responsibilities.

Eligibility: Applicants must be high school students under the age of 20 who are U.S. citizens or legal residents and residents of the state. Students first give an oration within their state and winners compete at the national level. The oration must be related to the Constitution of the United States focusing on the duties and obligations citizens have to the government. It must be in English and be between eight and ten minutes. There is also an assigned topic which is posted on the website, and it should be between three and five minutes.

Target applicant:
High school students

Minimum GPA: None.
Amount: Varies.
Number of awards: Varies.
Deadline: Varies.
How to apply: Application information is available by contacting the local post by email.

(1655) · North Carolina PTA Scholarship

North Carolina PTA
3501 Glenwood Avenue
Raleigh, NC 27612
Email: office@ncpta.org
Website: http://www.ncpta.org

Purpose: To recognize outstanding high school students who are members of their PTA.

Eligibility: Applicants must be North Carolina graduating high school seniors who are members of their high school PTA or PTSA.

Target applicant:
High school students

Minimum GPA: None.
Amount: Varies.
Number of awards: Varies.
Deadline: January 15.
How to apply: Applications are available online or through your PTA.

(1656) · North Carolina Veterans Scholarships

College Foundation of North Carolina
P.O. Box 41966
Raleigh, NC 27629-1966
Phone: 866-234-6400
Fax: 919-821-3139
Email: programinformation@cfnc.org
Website: http://www.cfnc.org

Purpose: To provide financial assistance to children of deceased, disabled and POW/MIA veterans.

Eligibility: Applicants must be children of deceased, disabled, POW or MIA veterans who were legal residents of North Carolina when they entered into service or must have been born and continuously resided within the state.

Target applicant:
High school students
College students
Adult students

Minimum GPA: None.
Amount: Up to full tuition.
Number of awards: Varies.
Scholarship may be renewable.
Deadline: February 28.
How to apply: Applications are available online or by mail.

(1657) · North Dakota Educational Assistance for Dependents of Veterans

Department of Veterans Affairs
Veterans Benefits Administration
810 Vermont Avenue NW
Washington, DC 20420
Phone: 888-442-4551
Website: http://www.gibill.va.gov

Purpose: To assist dependents of deceased or disabled veterans in obtaining higher education.

Eligibility: Applicants must be dependents of a North Dakota veteran who was killed in action, died or became disabled because of a service-connected injury, was a prisoner of war or was declared missing in action. Students must enroll in a North Dakota public institution of higher learning and earn their degree or certificate within 45 months or ten semesters.

Target applicant:
High school students
College students
Adult students

Minimum GPA: None.
Amount: Tuition.
Number of awards: Varies.
Scholarship may be renewable.
Deadline: Varies.
How to apply: Applications are available from your financial aid office.

(1658) · Nurse Education Scholarship Loan Program

College Foundation of North Carolina
P.O. Box 41966
Raleigh, NC 27629-1966
Phone: 866-234-6400
Fax: 919-821-3139
Email: programinformation@cfnc.org
Website: http://www.cfnc.org
Purpose: To reduce the shortage of nurses in the state of North Carolina.
Eligibility: Applicants must be enrolled in an LPN or RN licensure program at a North Carolina college or university. They must demonstrate financial need and adequate academic performance, and they must be U.S. citizens and North Carolina residents. The funds must be paid back after graduation, either through service as a full-time licensed nurse in the state or in cash.
Target applicant:
  High school students
  College students
  Adult students
Minimum GPA: None.
Amount: Up to $5,000.
Number of awards: Varies.
Scholarship may be renewable.
Deadline: Varies.
How to apply: Applications are available from your financial aid office.

(1659) · Nurse Educator Scholarship Program (NESP)

Illinois Student Assistance Commission
1755 Lake Cook Road
Deerfield, IL 60015
Phone: 800-899-4722
Fax: 847-831-8549
Email: collegezone@isac.org
Website: http://www.collegezone.com
Purpose: To increase the number of nurse educators in Illinois.
Eligibility: Applicants must be Illinois residents and U.S. citizens or permanent residents who have earned a bachelor's degree and plan to pursue a graduate degree in nursing education at an approved college. Applicants must apply for federal financial aid, comply with all Selective Service requirements and not be in default on any student loans. Scholarship recipients agree to teach in the field of nursing education in Illinois after graduation.
Target applicant:
  College students
  Graduate school students
  Adult students
Minimum GPA: None.
Amount: Tuition, fees and living stipend.
Number of awards: Varies.
Scholarship may be renewable.
Deadline: March 1, but applications received after that date will be considered if funding remains.
How to apply: Applications are available online.

(1660) · Nurse Support Program II - Graduate Nursing Faculty Scholarship

Maryland Higher Education Commission
Office of Student Financial Assistance
839 Bestgate Road, Suite 400
Annapolis, MD 21401
Phone: 800-974-1024
Fax: 410-260-3200
Email: osfamail@mhec.state.md.us
Website: http://www.mhec.state.md.us
Purpose: To support graduate nursing students who are planning to join the faculty at a Maryland college.
Eligibility: Applicants must be Maryland residents, and they must be enrolled full-time or part-time at a Maryland school as graduate nursing students. Full-time students must agree to complete their graduate program within two years. All students must agree to work in the nursing faculty of a Maryland college within six months of graduation.
Target applicant:
  College students
  Graduate school students
  Adult students
Minimum GPA: None.
Amount: Up to $26,000.
Number of awards: Varies.
Scholarship may be renewable.
Deadline: Varies.
How to apply: Applications are available online.

(1661) · Nursing Education Scholarship Program

Illinois Department of Public Health
535 W. Jefferson Street
Springfield, IL 62761
Phone: 217-782-4977
Fax: 217-782-3987
Email: dph.mailus@illinois.gov
Website: http://www.idph.state.il.us
Purpose: To increase the number of nurses in Illinois.
Eligibility: Applicants must be Illinois residents, having lived in the state for one year prior to applying and be U.S. citizens or permanent residents. Applicants must be accepted to or enrolled in an approved nursing program and demonstrate financial need. Scholarship recipients must agree to work as a nurse in Illinois after graduation.
Target applicant:
  High school students
  College students
  Graduate school students
  Adult students
Minimum GPA: None.
Amount: Tuition and fees for nursing program.
Number of awards: Varies.
Scholarship may be renewable.
Deadline: May 31.
How to apply: Applications are available online.

(1662) · Nursing Scholarship Fund

State Student Assistance Commission of Indiana
150 W. Market Street
Suite 500
Indianapolis, IN 46204
Phone: 888-528-4719
Fax: 317-232-3260
Email: grants@ssaci.state.in.us
Website: http://www.in.gov/ssaci

Purpose: To support Indiana residents who are pursuing nursing careers.

Eligibility: Applicants must be enrolled full-time or part-time in an Indiana college nursing program. They must demonstrate financial need and have at least a 2.0 GPA. Students must agree to work as nurses in the state of Indiana for at least two years after graduation.

Target applicant:
High school students
College students
Adult students

Minimum GPA: 2.0

Amount: Up to $5,000.

Number of awards: Varies.

Scholarship may be renewable.

Deadline: Varies.

How to apply: Applications are available online.

(1663) · Ohio Legion Scholarships

American Legion, Department of Ohio
P.O. Box 8007
Delaware, OH 43015
Phone: 740-362-7478
Fax: 740-362-1429
Email: ohlegion@iwaynet.net
Website: http://www.ohiolegion.com/scholarships/info.htm

Purpose: To provide financial assistance to deserving Ohio students.

Eligibility: Applicants must be high school seniors, Legionnaires or their descendants or spouses or surviving spouses or children of members of the U.S. military who died on active duty or from injuries incurred on active duty.

Target applicant:
High school students
College students
Adult students

Minimum GPA: None.

Amount: Varies.

Deadline: April 15.

How to apply: Applications are available online, by mail or by phone.

(1664) · Ohio State Council / Nancy Waymire Memorial

Epsilon Sigma Alpha Foundation
P.O. Box 270517
Fort Collins, CO 80527
Phone: 970-223-2824
Fax: 970-223-4456
Email: kloyd@knoxy.net
Website: http://www.esaintl.com/esaf

Purpose: To provide financial assistance for Ohio residents.

Eligibility: Applicants may attend any college or university and pursue any major. Financial need is required. Selection is based on the following criteria: service (5 percent), character (10 percent), leadership (10 percent), scholastic ability (25 percent) and financial need (50 percent).

Target applicant:
High school students
College students
Adult students

Minimum GPA: None.

Amount: $1,000.

Number of awards: 1.

Deadline: February 1.

How to apply: Applications are available online.

(1665) · Ohio War Orphans Scholarship

Ohio Board of Regents
State Grants and Scholarships Department
P.O. Box 182452
Columbus, OH 43218-2452
Phone: 888-833-1133
Fax: 614-752-5903
Website: http://www.regents.ohio.gov

Purpose: To provide tuition assistance to war orphans.

Eligibility: Applicants must be children of deceased or severely disabled Ohio war veterans. They must be Ohio residents under the age of 25 and be enrolled full-time in an undergraduate program at an eligible Ohio institution of higher learning. The award covers all instructional charges and general fees at public institutions and a portion of them at private institutions.

Target applicant:
High school students
College students

Minimum GPA: None.

Amount: Varies.

Number of awards: Varies.

Scholarship may be renewable.

Deadline: Varies.

How to apply: Applications are available from the Ohio Board of Regents, high school guidance offices, college financial aid offices and veterans service offices.

(1666) · Oklahoma Council - District IV

Epsilon Sigma Alpha Foundation
P.O. Box 270517
Fort Collins, CO 80527
Phone: 970-223-2824
Fax: 970-223-4456
Email: kloyd@knoxy.net
Website: http://www.esaintl.com/esaf

Purpose: To provide financial assistance for Oklahoma residents.

Eligibility: Applicants may pursue any major at any institution of higher learning. Selection is based on the following criteria: service (5 percent), character (10 percent), leadership (10 percent), scholastic ability (25 percent) and financial need (50 percent).

Target applicant:
High school students
College students
Adult students

Minimum GPA: None.

Amount: $1,000.

Number of awards: 1.

Deadline: February 1.

How to apply: Applications are available online.

(1667) · Oklahoma Council / District II

Epsilon Sigma Alpha Foundation
P.O. Box 270517
Fort Collins, CO 80527
Phone: 970-223-2824
Fax: 970-223-4456

Email: kloyd@knoxy.net

Website: http://www.esaintl.com/esaf

Purpose: To provide financial assistance for Oklahoma residents.

Eligibility: Applicants may attend any institution of higher learning and major in any field. Selection is based on service (5 percent), character (10 percent), leadership (10 percent), scholastic ability (25 percent) and financial need (50 percent).

Target applicant:
  High school students
  College students
  Adult students

Minimum GPA: None.

Amount: $500.

Number of awards: 1.

Deadline: February 1.

How to apply: Applications are available online.

(1668) · Oklahoma Foundation for Excellence Academic All-State Scholarships

Oklahoma Foundation for Excellence

120 N. Robinson Avenue #1420-W

Oklahoma City, OK 73102

Phone: 405-236-0006

Fax: 405-236-8690

Email: info@ofe.org

Website: http://www.ofe.org/awards

Purpose: To reward Oklahoma students with high academic achievement.

Eligibility: Applicants must be high school seniors who are nominated by their school principals or superintendents. They must have an ACT score of 30 or higher or an SAT score of 1350 or higher or be a semi-finalist for a National Merit, National Achievement or National Hispanic Scholarship. An essay is required.

Target applicant:
  High school students

Minimum GPA: None.

Amount: $2,000.

Number of awards: 100.

Deadline: Varies.

How to apply: Applications are available from your school.

(1669) · Oklahoma Tuition Aid Grant Program (OTAG)

Oklahoma State Regents for Higher Education (OTAG)

Oklahoma Tuition Aid Grant Program (OTAG)

P.O. Box 108850

Oklahoma City, OK 73101

Phone: 877-662-6231

Email: otaginfo@otag.org

Website: http://www.okhighered.org

Purpose: To assist Oklahoma students with financial need.

Eligibility: Applicants must be Oklahoma residents who attend eligible undergraduate or graduate institutions in Oklahoma and have financial need.

Target applicant:
  High school students
  College students
  Graduate school students
  Adult students

Minimum GPA: None.

Amount: $1,000-$1,300.

Number of awards: Varies.

Deadline: April 30-June 30.

How to apply: Complete the Free Application for Federal Student Aid (FAFSA).

(1670) · Oklahoma Tuition Equalization Grant Program (OTEG)

Oklahoma State Regents for Higher Education (OTEG)

655 Research Parkway, Suite 200

Oklahoma City, OK 73104

Phone: 877-622-6231

Fax: 405-225-9230

Email: rrichardson@osrhe.edu

Website: http://www.okhighered.org

Purpose: To provide financial assistance for Oklahoma residents who are attending private institutions in the state.

Eligibility: Applicants must be enrolled in an undergraduate program at a private institution of higher learning full-time. They must have a family income of no more than $50,000, make satisfactory academic progress and not have already earned a bachelor's degree.

Target applicant:
  High school students
  College students
  Adult students

Minimum GPA: None.

Amount: $2,000.

Number of awards: Varies.

Deadline: Varies.

How to apply: Eligible students who file a Free Application for Federal Student Aid (FAFSA) will be considered.

(1671) · Oklahoma Youth with Promise Scholarship Fund

Oklahoma City Community Foundation

P.O. Box 1146

Oklahoma City, OK 73101-1146

Phone: 405-235-5603

Fax: 405-235-5612

Email: info@occf.org

Website: http://www.occf.org/scholarshipcenter.html

Purpose: To provide educational assistance to students who graduated while in foster care.

Eligibility: Applicants must be graduates of Oklahoma high schools who were in the custody of the Oklahoma Department of Human Services at the time of graduation. They must have a minimum GPA of 2.0. Financial need is considered.

Target applicant:
  High school students
  College students
  Adult students

Minimum GPA: 2.0

Amount: $800-$1,200.

Number of awards: Varies.

Deadline: Varies.

How to apply: Applications are available online.

(1672) · Oklahoma's Promise

Oklahoma State Regents for Higher Education

655 Research Parkway, Suite 200

Oklahoma City, OK 73104

Phone: 800-858-1840

Fax: 405-225-9230
Email: studentinfo@osrhe.edu
Website: http://www.okhighered.org
Purpose: To assist children of families with income below $50,000 in preparing for and paying for college.
Eligibility: Applicants must be Oklahoma residents who are enrolled in the eighth, ninth or tenth grade at an Oklahoma high school (or are homeschool students between the ages of 13 and 15) and whose parents' income is less than $50,000 per year. They must take certain college preparatory courses in high school, maintain a GPA of 2.5 or higher and "stay out of trouble" such as gangs, drugs or alcohol.
Target applicant:
    Junior high students or younger
    High school students
Minimum GPA: 2.5
Amount: Tuition.
Number of awards: Varies.
Scholarship may be renewable.
Deadline: Varies.
How to apply: Applications are available online.

(1673) · Olive Griffith Memorial Scholarship

Epsilon Sigma Alpha Foundation
P.O. Box 270517
Fort Collins, CO 80527
Phone: 970-223-2824
Fax: 970-223-4456
Email: kloyd@knoxy.net
Website: http://www.esaintl.com/esaf
Purpose: To provide financial assistance to students majoring in teaching from Montana.
Eligibility: Applicants must major in elementary or secondary education. They may attend any college or university. Selection criteria include financial need (35 percent), service (35 percent), scholastic ability (10 percent), character (10 percent) and leadership (10 percent).
Target applicant:
    High school students
    College students
    Adult students
Minimum GPA: None.
Amount: $1,000.
Number of awards: 1.
Deadline: February 1.
How to apply: Applications are available online.

(1674) · Opportunity Award

Louisiana Office of Student Financial Assistance
P.O. Box 91202
Baton Rouge, LA 70821-9202
Phone: 800-259-5626 x1012
Fax: 225-922-0790
Email: custserv@osfa.la.gov
Website: http://www.osfa.state.la.us
Purpose: To aid Louisiana student residents.
Eligibility: Applicants must be Louisiana residents, U.S. citizens, have a minimum 2.5 GPA, have a minimum ACT score of 20 or equivalent SAT I score and apply during their senior year in high school. Applicants must use the award at a Louisiana college or university.
Target applicant:
    High school students

Minimum GPA: 2.5
Amount: Varies.
Number of awards: Varies.
Scholarship may be renewable.
Deadline: July 1.
How to apply: The application is the Free Application for Federal Student Aid (FAFSA). ACT or SAT I scores must also be reported.

(1675) · Opportunity Grant

Washington State Board for Community and Technical Colleges
P.O. Box 42495
1300 Quince Street SE
Olympia, WA 98504-2495
Phone: 360-704-4400
Fax: 360-704-4415
Email: webmaster@sbctc.ctc.edu
Website: http://www.sbctc.ctc.edu
Purpose: To assist Washington adult students.
Eligibility: Applicants must be adult students with financial need who are attending a community or technical college. The grant provides funding for up to 45 credits over a maximum of three years and up to $1,000 for books and supplies per year. In addition, there are support services such as tutoring, career advising, emergency transportation and emergency child care.
Target applicant:
    College students
    Adult students
Minimum GPA: None.
Amount: Tuition.
Number of awards: 4,000.
Scholarship may be renewable.
Deadline: Varies.
How to apply: Applicants must complete the Free Application for Federal Student Aid (FAFSA). Contact your college for more information.

(1676) · ORCA Bob Hasson Memorial Scholarship Fund

Oregon Collectors Association
ORCA Scholarship Fund
3012 NE 111th Circle
Vancouver, WA 98686
Phone: 503-201-0858
Email: dcj@pandhbilling.com
Website: http://units.acainternational.org/oregon
Purpose: To provide financial assistance to Oregon students who are attending a college or university in Oregon.
Eligibility: Applicants must be high school seniors in the state of Oregon who are not children or grandchildren of owners or officers of Oregon collection agencies. Students must write an essay on a specific topic and if selected as finalists must attend the Oregon Collectors Association Spring Convention and read their essays.
Target applicant:
    High school students
Minimum GPA: None.
Amount: $1,500-$3,000.
Number of awards: 3.
Deadline: March 1.
How to apply: Students must send an essay via mail or email to apply.

(1677) · Oregon Association of Student Councils Scholarships

Confederation of Oregon School Administrators
707 13th Street SE
Suite 100
Salem, OR 97301
Phone: 503-581-3141
Fax: 503-581-9840
Email: carmy@cosa.k12.or.us
Website: http://www.cosa.k12.or.us
Purpose: To provide financial assistance to Oregon students who plan to attend Oregon colleges or universities.
Eligibility: Applicants must be graduating seniors at an Oregon public high school who plan to attend a public or private institution of higher learning in the state. They must have a 3.5 or higher GPA, be active in school and community activities and be endorsed by a COSA member.
Target applicant:
　High school students
Minimum GPA: 3.5
Amount: $1,000.
Number of awards: 12.
Deadline: February 22.
How to apply: Applications are available online.

(1678) · Oregon National Guard State Tuition Program

Oregon Student Assistance Commission
1500 Valley River Drive
Suite 100
Eugene, OR 97401
Phone: 541-687-7400
Fax: 541-687-7414
Email: awardinfo@mercury.osac.state.or.us
Website: http://www.osac.state.or.us
Purpose: To support students from Oregon who are in the National Guard.
Eligibility: Students must be new recruits or reenlistments in the National Guard. They must have been residents of Oregon for at least 12 months prior to college enrollment.
Target applicant:
　High school students
　College students
　Graduate school students
　Adult students
Minimum GPA: None.
Amount: Varies.
Number of awards: Varies.
Scholarship may be renewable.
Deadline: March 1.
How to apply: Applications are available online.

(1679) · Oregon Nursing Services Program

Oregon Student Assistance Commission
1500 Valley River Drive
Suite 100
Eugene, OR 97401
Phone: 541-687-7400
Fax: 541-687-7414
Email: awardinfo@mercury.osac.state.or.us
Website: http://www.osac.state.or.us
Purpose: To support Oregon nurses through loan repayment.
Eligibility: Applicants must either be students in their final year of an RN program, recent graduates of RN programs or practicing registered nurses. They must agree to work full-time for at least two years in areas of Oregon with nursing shortages.
Target applicant:
　College students
　Adult students
Minimum GPA: None.
Amount: Varies.
Number of awards: Varies.
Scholarship may be renewable.
Deadline: Varies.
How to apply: Applications are available online.

(1680) · Oregon Opportunity Grant

Oregon Student Assistance Commission
1500 Valley River Drive
Suite 100
Eugene, OR 97401
Phone: 541-687-7400
Fax: 541-687-7414
Email: awardinfo@mercury.osac.state.or.us
Website: http://www.osac.state.or.us
Purpose: To provide financial assistance to Oregon residents in need.
Eligibility: Applicants must have financial need and be enrolled at least half-time in an undergraduate program at a participating Oregon college or university. They must be Oregon residents and U.S. citizens or eligible noncitizens, and they must be eligible for a Federal Pell Grant.
Target applicant:
　College students
　Graduate school students
　Adult students
Minimum GPA: None.
Amount: Varies.
Number of awards: Varies.
Deadline: Varies.
How to apply: Qualified students who submit a Free Application for Federal Student Aid (FAFSA) will be considered.

(1681) · Oregon Scholarship Fund Community College Student Award

Oregon Student Assistance Commission
1500 Valley River Drive
Suite 100
Eugene, OR 97401
Phone: 541-687-7400
Fax: 541-687-7414
Email: awardinfo@mercury.osac.state.or.us
Website: http://www.osac.state.or.us
Purpose: To assist Oregon community college students.
Eligibility: Applicants must be Oregon residents enrolled or planning to enroll in a community college in Oregon.
Target applicant:
　High school students
　College students
　Adult students
Minimum GPA: None.
Amount: Varies.
Number of awards: Varies.
Deadline: March 1.
How to apply: Applications are available online.

(1682) · Oregon State Council Endowment

Epsilon Sigma Alpha Foundation
P.O. Box 270517
Fort Collins, CO 80527
Phone: 970-223-2824
Fax: 970-223-4456
Email: kloyd@knoxy.net
Website: http://www.esaintl.com/esaf
Purpose: To provide education opportunities for Oregon residents.
Eligibility: Applicants may attend any college or university and pursue any major. Selection is based equally on character, leadership, service, financial need and scholastic ability.
Target applicant:
    High school students
    College students
    Adult students
Minimum GPA: None.
Amount: $1,000.
Number of awards: 1.
Deadline: February 1.
How to apply: Applications are available online.

(1683) · Oscar and Joyce Whitewing Honorarium Endowment

Epsilon Sigma Alpha Foundation
P.O. Box 270517
Fort Collins, CO 80527
Phone: 970-223-2824
Fax: 970-223-4456
Email: kloyd@knoxy.net
Website: http://www.esaintl.com/esaf
Purpose: To provide financial assistance for Oklahoma students.
Eligibility: Applicants may pursue any major at any school. Selection is based equally on character, leadership, service, financial need and scholastic ability.
Target applicant:
    High school students
    College students
    Adult students
Minimum GPA: None.
Amount: $500.
Number of awards: 1.
Deadline: February 1.
How to apply: Applications are available online.

(1684) · Osher Scholarship

Maine Community College System
323 State Street
Augusta, ME 04330-7131
Phone: 207-629-4000
Fax: 207-629-4048
Email: info@mccs.me.edu
Website: http://www.mccs.me.edu
Purpose: To aid liberal arts students at Maine community colleges.
Eligibility: Students must be Maine residents who are not currently enrolled in any college or university program and who have completed no more than 24 college credits. They must also qualify for and be accepted into the associate of arts degree program in liberal/general studies at a Maine community college.

Target applicant:
    High school students
    College students
    Adult students
Minimum GPA: None.
Amount: $468.
Number of awards: Varies.
Deadline: Unknown.
How to apply: Applications are available from community colleges.

(1685) · Pacers TeamUp Scholarship

Pacers Foundation
125 S. Pennsylvania Street
Indianapolis, IN 46204
Phone: 317-917-2864
Fax: 317-917-2599
Email: foundation@pacers.com
Website: http://www.nba.com/pacers/news/Foundation_Index.html
Purpose: The Pacers TeamUp Scholarship rewards students for community service.
Eligibility: Applicants must be Indiana residents in their senior year of high school planning to attend an accredited four-year college or two-year community or junior college.
Target applicant:
    High school students
Minimum GPA: None.
Amount: $2,000.
Number of awards: 5.
Deadline: March 1.
How to apply: Application information is available by email at foundation@pacers.com, by phone at 317-917-2864 or online.

(1686) · Pacific National Bank Scholarship

Pacific National Bank
345 California Street, 7th Floor
San Francisco, CA 94104
Phone: 415-774-2203
Email: calmojuela@pacificnational.com
Website: http://www.pacificnational.com
Purpose: To assist students from low to moderate income families in the Bay Area.
Eligibility: Applicants must attend a college or university on a full-time basis, have a minimum 3.0 GPA and reside in San Francisco, Marin, San Mateo, Alameda, Contra Costa, San Benito, Santa Clara or Napa county.
Target applicant:
    High school students
    College students
    Adult students
Minimum GPA: 3.0
Amount: $500-$1,500.
Number of awards: Varies.
Deadline: April 30.
How to apply: Applications are available online.

(1687) · Palmetto Fellows Scholarship Program

South Carolina Commission on Higher Education
1333 Main Street
Suite 200
Columbia, SC 29201

Phone: 803-737-2260
Fax: 803-737-2297
Email: shubbard@che.sc.gov
Website: http://www.che400.state.sc.us
Purpose: Monetary assistance is awarded to academically talented South Carolina high school seniors in an effort to encourage them to go to South Carolina colleges.
Eligibility: Applicants must have a minimum SAT score of 1200 or ACT score of 27, have a minimum 3.5 GPA, rank in the top 5 percent of their class, be residents of South Carolina, be enrolled in a public or private high school, be U.S. citizens or permanent residents and plan to attend a college in South Carolina.
Target applicant:
　High school students
Minimum GPA: 3.5
Amount: $6,700.
Number of awards: Varies.
Scholarship may be renewable.
Deadline: Varies.
How to apply: Applications are available through your high school guidance office.

(1688) · Paraprofessional Scholarship

California School Library Association Paraprofessional Scholarship
1001 26th Street
Sacramento, CA 95816
Phone: 916-447-2684
Fax: 916-447-2695
Email: csla@pacbell.net
Website: http://www.schoolibrary.org
Purpose: To increase the number of trained and qualified library technicians in Southern California.
Eligibility: Applicants must be classified library media workers currently enrolled in a two-year paraprofessional program to become a certified library technician. Students must be Southern California residents planning to work in California as library media technicians after completing the program and be members of the California School Library Association. Three letters of recommendation are required.
Target applicant:
　College students
　Graduate school students
　Adult students
Minimum GPA: None.
Amount: $250.
Number of awards: 1.
Deadline: February 15.
How to apply: Applications are available online.

(1689) · Paraprofessional Teacher Preparation Grant

Massachusetts Office of Student Financial Assistance
454 Broadway
Suite 200
Revere, MA 02151
Phone: 617-727-9420
Fax: 617-727-0667
Email: osfa@osfa.mass.edu
Website: http://www.osfa.mass.edu
Purpose: To assist Massachusetts public school paraprofessionals who wish to become certified as full-time teachers.
Eligibility: Applicants must be employed for at least two years as a paraprofessional in a Massachusetts public school and enroll in

an undergraduate program leading to teacher certification, or be employed as a paraprofessional for less than two years and enroll in an undergraduate course of study leading to teacher certification in a high need discipline. Applicants must not have previously earned a bachelor's degree.
Target applicant:
　College students
　Adult students
Minimum GPA: None.
Amount: Up to $7,500.
Number of awards: Varies.
Scholarship may be renewable.
Deadline: Varies.
How to apply: Applications are available online.

(1690) · Paraprofessional-to-LMT Scholarship

California School Library Association Paraprofessional Scholarship
1001 26th Street
Sacramento, CA 95816
Phone: 916-447-2684
Fax: 916-447-2695
Email: csla@pacbell.net
Website: http://www.schoolibrary.org
Purpose: To support school library paraprofessionals who plan to become certified library media teachers.
Eligibility: Applicants must be working or have worked within the last three years in a classified library media position and be currently enrolled in a degree program for a Library Media Teacher credential. Candidates must also be Southern California residents planning to work as Library Media Teachers upon finishing the program and be members of the California School Library Association. Three letters of recommendation are required.
Target applicant:
　College students
　Graduate school students
　Adult students
Minimum GPA: None.
Amount: $500.
Number of awards: 1.
Deadline: March 11.
How to apply: Applications are available online.

(1691) · Parr Family Memorial Endowment

Epsilon Sigma Alpha Foundation
P.O. Box 270517
Fort Collins, CO 80527
Phone: 970-223-2824
Fax: 970-223-4456
Email: kloyd@knoxy.net
Website: http://www.esaintl.com/esaf
Purpose: To provide financial assistance for midwest students.
Eligibility: Applicants must be residents of Illinois, Indiana, Iowa, Michigan, Minnesota, Missouri, Ohio, South Dakota or Wisconsin. They may pursue any major at any college or university. They must have a GPA of 2.5 to 3.0. Selection is based equally on the following criteria: character, leadership, service, financial need and scholastic ability.
Target applicant:
　High school students
　College students
　Adult students
Minimum GPA: 2.5

Amount: $2,000.
Number of awards: 2.
Deadline: February 1.
How to apply: Applications are available online.

(1692) · Part Time-Grant program

Massachusetts Office of Student Financial Assistance
454 Broadway
Suite 200
Revere, MA 02151
Phone: 617-727-9420
Fax: 617-727-0667
Email: osfa@osfa.mass.edu
Website: http://www.osfa.mass.edu
Purpose: To provide need-based financial assistance to part-time students seeking an undergraduate degree or certificate.
Eligibility: Applicants must be permanent legal residents of Massachusetts for at least one year prior to the start of the academic year for which the grant is awarded. Applicants must be enrolled for at least six but fewer than twelve undergraduate credits per academic term in an eligible undergraduate degree program or eligible certificate program. Applicant must not have previously earned a baccalaureate or professional degree. Applicants must show financial aid need.
Target applicant:
    College students
    Adult students
Minimum GPA: None.
Amount: $200-full cost of tuition.
Number of awards: Varies.
Scholarship may be renewable.
Deadline: May 1.
How to apply: Complete and submit the Free Application for Federal Student Aid (FAFSA).

(1693) · Part-Time Assistance Program

State Council of Higher Education for Virginia
101 N. 14th Street
James Monroe Building
Richmond, VA 23219
Phone: 804-225-2600
Fax: 804-225-2604
Email: communications@schev.edu
Website: http://www.schev.edu
Purpose: To assist part-time Virginia students with financial need.
Eligibility: Applicants must attend a school in Virginia's Community College System part-time (three to five hours), be Virginia residents and demonstrate financial need.
Target applicant:
    High school students
    College students
    Adult students
Minimum GPA: None.
Amount: Up to the cost of tuition and fees.
Number of awards: Varies.
Deadline: Varies.
How to apply: Contact your financial aid office.

(1694) · Part-Time Grant

Maryland Higher Education Commission
Office of Student Financial Assistance

839 Bestgate Road, Suite 400
Annapolis, MD 21401
Phone: 800-974-1024
Fax: 410-260-3200
Email: osfamail@mhec.state.md.us
Website: http://www.mhec.state.md.us
Purpose: To assist part-time, degree-seeking undergraduates or students who are simultaneously enrolled in a secondary school and an institution of higher education.
Eligibility: All applicants must be U.S. citizens or eligible noncitizens and legal residents of the state of Maryland. Part-time applicants must complete the Free Application for Federal Student Aid (FAFSA) and contact the financial aid office of the college attending and request to be considered for the Part-Time Grant. Dually enrolled students must contact the college financial aid office to determine the specific application process. This award is based on financial need.
Target applicant:
    High school students
    College students
    Adult students
Minimum GPA: None.
Amount: $200-$1,000.
Number of awards: Varies.
Scholarship may be renewable.
Deadline: March 1.
How to apply: Complete the FAFSA and contact the financial aid office.

(1695) · Part-Time Grant Program

State Student Assistance Commission of Indiana
150 W. Market Street
Suite 500
Indianapolis, IN 46204
Phone: 888-528-4719
Fax: 317-232-3260
Email: grants@ssaci.state.in.us
Website: http://www.in.gov/ssaci
Purpose: To help part-time Indiana students pursue higher education.
Eligibility: Applicants must be undergraduates taking at least 6 but not more than 12 credit hours per term at eligible institutions. This is a need-based award.
Target applicant:
    College students
    Adult students
Minimum GPA: None.
Amount: Varies.
Number of awards: Varies.
Scholarship may be renewable.
Deadline: Varies.
How to apply: Complete the Free Application for Federal Student Aid (FAFSA).

(1696) · Part-Time Grants

Vermont Student Assistance Corporation
10 E. Allen Street
P.O. Box 2000
Winooski, VT 05404
Phone: 888-253-4819
Fax: 802-654-3765
Email: info@vsac.org
Website: http://www.vsac.org

Purpose: To assist Vermont part-time students.

Eligibility: Applicants must be Vermont residents enrolled or planning to enroll in an undergraduate degree, diploma or certificate program and take fewer than 12 credits per semester.

Target applicant:
High school students
College students
Adult students

Minimum GPA: None.

Amount: Varies.

Number of awards: Varies.

Deadline: Varies.

How to apply: Contact your financial aid office.

(1697) · Part-Time Student Instructional Grant

Ohio Board of Regents
State Grants and Scholarships Department
P.O. Box 182452
Columbus, OH 43218-2452
Phone: 888-833-1133
Fax: 614-752-5903
Website: http://www.regents.ohio.gov

Purpose: To assist part-time Ohio undergraduate students.

Eligibility: Applicants must be Ohio residents who attend an eligible Ohio public or private university part-time and who have financial need.

Target applicant:
College students
Adult students

Minimum GPA: None.

Amount: Varies.

Number of awards: Varies.

Deadline: Varies.

How to apply: Contact your financial aid office.

(1698) · Part-Time TAP Program

New York State Higher Education Services Corporation (HESC)
99 Washington Avenue
Albany, NY 12255
Phone: 888-697-4372
Email: hescwebmail@hesc.org
Website: http://www.hesc.com

Purpose: To support undergraduate students in the state of New York.

Eligibility: Applicants may attend either the State University of New York, the City University of New York or any other public New York school. Students must be enrolled in 6-12 credits per semester, and they must have at least a 2.0 GPA. Applicants must have earned 12 credits per semester in at least two consecutive prior semesters. Students must demonstrate financial need through the FAFSA.

Target applicant:
College students
Adult students

Minimum GPA: 2.0

Amount: Up to $5,000.

Number of awards: Varies.

Scholarship may be renewable.

Deadline: Varies.

How to apply: Applications are available online.

(1699) · Part-Time Tuition Aid Grant

New Jersey Higher Education Student Assistance Authority
P.O. Box 540
Trenton, NJ 08625
Phone: 800-792-8670
Email: clientservices@hesaa.org
Website: http://www.hesaa.org

Purpose: To support part-time students who are attending county colleges in New Jersey.

Eligibility: Applicants must be residents of New Jersey for at least 12 months prior to college enrollment. They cannot have any previous degrees or defaulted student loans. Students must be enrolled in 6-11 credits per semester at an approved New Jersey county college, and they cannot be majoring in theology or divinity.

Target applicant:
High school students
College students
Adult students

Minimum GPA: None.

Amount: Varies.

Number of awards: Varies.

Scholarship may be renewable.

Deadline: October 1.

How to apply: Applications are available through completion of the FAFSA.

(1700) · Passport to College Promise Scholarship

Washington Higher Education Coordinating Board
917 Lakeridge Way
P.O. Box 43430
Olympia, WA 98504
Phone: 360-753-7850
Fax: 360-753-6243
Email: info@hecb.wa.gov
Website: http://www.hecb.wa.gov

Purpose: To encourage students who have been in foster care to get ready for college.

Eligibility: Applicants must have spent one year or more in foster care since their 16th birthdays, be Washington residents who will enroll at least half-time in an eligible college by their 21st birthdays, not have earned a bachelor's degree and not be seeking a degree in theology.

Target applicant:
High school students
College students

Minimum GPA: None.

Amount: Varies.

Number of awards: Varies.

Scholarship may be renewable.

Deadline: Varies.

How to apply: Applications are available online.

(1701) · Past Department Presidents' Junior Scholarship Award

American Legion Auxiliary, Department of California
401 Van Ness Avenue
Room 113
San Francisco, CA 94102
Phone: 415-861-5092
Fax: 415-861-8365
Email: calegionaux@calegionaux.org
Website: http://www.calegionaux.org

Purpose: To reward American Legion Auxiliary Juniors.
Eligibility: Applicants must be California resident high school students planning to attend a California college or university, be American Legion Auxiliary members with three years as a Junior and be the children, grandchildren or great grandchildren of a veteran.
Target applicant:
    High school students
Minimum GPA: None.
Amount: Varies.
Number of awards: 1.
Deadline: April 15.
How to apply: Applications are available online.

(1702) · Past Presidents' Parley Nursing Scholarships

American Legion Auxiliary, Department of California
401 Van Ness Avenue
Room 113
San Francisco, CA 94102
Phone: 415-861-5092
Fax: 415-861-8365
Email: calegionaux@calegionaux.org
Website: http://www.calegionaux.org
Purpose: To provide support to the U.S. Armed Forces members and their spouses and children.
Eligibility: Applicants must be residents of California, enrolled or planning to enroll in a nursing program and be the wife, husband, widow, widower or child of a veteran or be veterans themselves.
Target applicant:
    High school students
    College students
    Graduate school students
    Adult students
Minimum GPA: None.
Amount: $500-$1,000.
Number of awards: Varies.
Deadline: April 5.
How to apply: Applications are available online.

(1703) · Paul and Betty Honzik Scholarship

Hawaii Community Foundation - Scholarships
1164 Bishop Street, Suite 800
Honolulu, HI 96813
Phone: 888-731-3863
Fax: 808-521-6286
Email: scholarships@hcf-hawaii.org
Website: http://www.hawaiicommunityfoundation.org
Purpose: To support Presbyterian students in Hawaii.
Eligibility: Students must attend a four-year college or university. Applicants must have at least a 3.0 GPA. A letter of reference from a church or paster is required.
Target applicant:
    High school students
    College students
    Adult students
Minimum GPA: 3.0
Amount: Varies.
Number of awards: Varies.
Deadline: March 1.
How to apply: To apply, register online, complete the online application and select the scholarships to which you wish to apply. In addition, mail the supporting materials: printed confirmation page from the online application, personal statement, letter of reference from church or pastor, copy of Student Aid Report (SAR) available at www.fafsa.ed.gov and official transcript.

(1704) · Paul and Grace Rhudy Fund

Greater Kanawha Valley Foundation
1600 Huntington Square
900 Lee Street, East
Charleston, WV 25301
Phone: 304-346-3620
Fax: 304-346-3640
Email: tgkvf@tgkvf.org
Website: http://www.tgkvf.org
Purpose: To provide financial assistance to West Virginia residents who are interested in pursuing a college education.
Eligibility: Applicants must be residents of West Virginia, be full-time students (12 credit hours) and possess good moral character and proven academic achievement.
Target applicant:
    High school students
    College students
    Adult students
Minimum GPA: 2.5
Amount: $500.
Number of awards: 1.
Scholarship may be renewable.
Deadline: February 17.
How to apply: Applications are available online at http://www.tgkvf.org/scholar.htm or by email at shoover@tgkvf.org.

(1705) · Paul Flaherty Athletic Scholarship

American Legion, Department of Kansas
1314 SW Topeka Boulevard
Topeka, KS 66612
Phone: 785-232-9315
Fax: 785-232-1399
Website: http://www.ksamlegion.org
Purpose: To support student athletes.
Eligibility: Applicants must be high school seniors or college freshmen or sophomores and have participated in high school athletics. Students must be average or better students and submit three letters of recommendation, one of which must be from a coach, a high school transcript, a 1040 income statement and an essay on the topic, "Why I Want to Go to College."
Target applicant:
    High school students
    College students
    Adult students
Minimum GPA: None.
Amount: $250.
Number of awards: 1.
Deadline: July 15.
How to apply: Applications are available online.

(1706) · Paulina L. Sorg Scholarship

Hawaii Community Foundation - Scholarships
1164 Bishop Street, Suite 800
Honolulu, HI 96813
Phone: 888-731-3863
Fax: 808-521-6286

Email: scholarships@hcf-hawaii.org
Website: http://www.hawaiicommunityfoundation.org
Purpose: To support nursing or physical therapy students in Hawaii.
Eligibility: Applicants must be college juniors, college seniors or graduate students.
Target applicant:
  College students
  Graduate school students
  Adult students
Minimum GPA: None.
Amount: Varies.
Number of awards: Varies.
Deadline: March 1.
How to apply: To apply, register online, complete the online application and select the scholarships to which you wish to apply. In addition, mail the supporting materials: printed confirmation page from the online application, personal statement, copy of Student Aid Report (SAR) available at www.fafsa.ed.gov and official transcript.

(1707) · Peggy Jacques Memorial Scholarship

Epsilon Sigma Alpha Foundation
P.O. Box 270517
Fort Collins, CO 80527
Phone: 970-223-2824
Fax: 970-223-4456
Email: kloyd@knoxy.net
Website: http://www.esaintl.com/esaf
Purpose: To provide financial assistance for business administration majors.
Eligibility: Applicants must be residents of Michigan. They may attend any school. Selection is based on character (25 percent), leadership (25 percent), service (20 percent), financial need (15 percent) and scholastic ability (15 percent).
Target applicant:
  High school students
  College students
  Adult students
Minimum GPA: None.
Amount: $500.
Number of awards: 1.
Deadline: February 1.
How to apply: Applications are available online.

(1708) · Pennsylvania Educational Gratuity for Veterans' Dependents

Bureau for Veterans Affairs
Building S-0-47
Fort Indiantown Gap
Annville, PA 17003
Phone: 717-861-8719
Fax: 717-861-9457
Email: bfoster@state.pa.us
Website: http://www.milvet.state.pa.us/DMVA/201.htm
Purpose: To provide financial assistance to children of veterans.
Eligibility: Applicants must be dependents of honorably discharged veterans who served during wartime or armed conflict and have service-connected disabilities or who died in service during war or armed conflict. They must be 16 to 23 years of age and have lived in and attended school in Pennsylvania for five years prior to application, and they must demonstrate financial need.

Target applicant:
  High school students
  College students
Minimum GPA: None.
Amount: Up to $1,000.
Number of awards: Varies.
Scholarship may be renewable.
Deadline: Varies.
How to apply: Applications are available from your local Department of Military and Veterans Affairs.

(1709) · Pennsylvania Knights Templar Educational Foundation Scholarships

Pennsylvania Masonic Youth Foundation
1244 Bainbridge Road
Elizabethtown, PA 17022-9423
Phone: 717-367-1536
Fax: 717-367-0616
Email: pmyf@pagrandlodge.com
Website: http://www.pagrandlodge.org/pyf/scholar
Purpose: To assist students in pursuing higher education.
Eligibility: Applicants must be working toward a two- or four-year college degree, graduate degree or trade school education. This award is open to students regardless of financial circumstances, Masonic ties, age, race or religion.
Target applicant:
  High school students
  College students
  Graduate school students
  Adult students
Minimum GPA: None.
Amount: Varies.
Number of awards: Varies.
Deadline: March 31.
How to apply: Applications are available by mail.

(1710) · Pennsylvania Oratorical Contest

American Legion, Department of Pennsylvania
P.O. Box 2324
Harrisburg, PA 17105
Phone: 717-730-9100
Fax: 717-975-2836
Email: hq@pa-legion.com
Website: http://www.pa-legion.com
Purpose: To enhance high school students' experience with and understanding of the U.S. Constitution. The contest will help develop students' leadership skills and civic appreciation, as well as the ability to deliver thoughtful, insightful orations regarding U.S. citizenship and its inherent responsibilities.
Eligibility: Applicants must be high school students under the age of 20 who are U.S. citizens or legal residents and residents of the state. Students first give an oration within their state and winners compete at the national level. The oration must be related to the Constitution of the United States focusing on the duties and obligations citizens have to the government. It must be in English and be between eight and ten minutes. There is also an assigned topic which is posted on the website, and it should be between three and five minutes.
Target applicant:
  High school students
Minimum GPA: None.
Amount: $4,000-$7,500.

Number of awards: 3.
Deadline: January 13.
How to apply: Applications are available from school coordinators and online.

(1711) · Performance Award

Louisiana Office of Student Financial Assistance
P.O. Box 91202
Baton Rouge, LA 70821-9202
Phone: 800-259-5626 x1012
Fax: 225-922-0790
Email: custserv@osfa.la.gov
Website: http://www.osfa.state.la.us
Purpose: To aid Louisiana student residents.
Eligibility: Applicants must be Louisiana residents, U.S. citizens, apply during their senior year in high school, use the award at a Louisiana college or university, have a minimum 3.0 GPA and have a minimum ACT score of 23 or an equivalent SAT I score.
Target applicant:
   High school students
Minimum GPA: 3.0
Amount: Tuition plus $400.
Number of awards: Varies.
Scholarship may be renewable.
Deadline: July 1.
How to apply: The application is the Free Application for Federal Student Aid (FAFSA). ACT or SAT I scores must also be reported.

(1712) · Philip P. Barker Memorial Scholarship

Los Alamos National Laboratory Foundation
1302 Calle de la Merced
Suite A
Espanola, NM 87532
Phone: 505-753-8890
Fax: 505-753-8915
Email: info@lanlfoundation.org
Website: http://www.lanlfoundation.org
Purpose: To support undergraduate students from Northern New Mexico.
Eligibility: Students must have at least a 3.25 GPA, and they must have either an SAT score of at least 1350 or an ACT score of at least 19. Applicants must submit an essay and two letters of recommendation.
Target applicant:
   High school students
   College students
   Adult students
Minimum GPA: 3.25
Amount: $1,000.
Number of awards: Varies.
Deadline: January 22.
How to apply: Applications are available online.

(1713) · Philippine Cultural Foundation of Hawai'i Scholarship Fund

Hawaii Community Foundation - Scholarships
1164 Bishop Street, Suite 800
Honolulu, HI 96813
Phone: 888-731-3863
Fax: 808-521-6286

Email: scholarships@hcf-hawaii.org
Website: http://www.hawaiicommunityfoundation.org
Purpose: To support students of Filipino ancestry.
Eligibility: Applicants must attend school in Hawaii. Students must be majoring in one of the following subjects: art, humanities, Philippine studies, public relations or communications. Applicants must have at least a 3.5 GPA.
Target applicant:
   High school students
   College students
   Adult students
Minimum GPA: 3.5
Amount: Varies.
Number of awards: Varies.
Deadline: March 1.
How to apply: To apply, register online, complete the online application and select the scholarships to which you wish to apply. In addition, mail the supporting materials: printed confirmation page from the online application, personal statement, copy of Student Aid Report (SAR) available at www.fafsa.ed.gov and official transcript.

(1714) · Pinnacol Foundation Scholarship Program

Pinnacol Foundation
7501 E. Lowry Boulevard
Denver, CO 80230
Phone: 303-361-4775
Email: starkey@pinnacol.com
Website: http://www.pinnacol.com/foundation
Purpose: To provide assistance for students whose parent was killed or injured in a work-related accident.
Eligibility: Applicants must be dependents of workers killed or permanently injured in compensable work-related accidents during employment with Colorado-based employers. They must be between the ages of 16 and 25 and have a diploma or GED or be high school seniors in good standing. Letter of recommendation, essay, transcripts and documentation of the parent's injury or death are required.
Target applicant:
   High school students
   College students
Minimum GPA: None.
Amount: Varies.
Number of awards: Varies.
Deadline: March 31.
How to apply: Applications are available online.

(1715) · Pizza Hut Scholarship Fund

Hawaii Community Foundation - Scholarships
1164 Bishop Street, Suite 800
Honolulu, HI 96813
Phone: 888-731-3863
Fax: 808-521-6286
Email: scholarships@hcf-hawaii.org
Website: http://www.hawaiicommunityfoundation.org
Purpose: To support students in Hawaii with financial need.
Eligibility: Applicants must attend a two- or four-year college or university and have a GPA between 2.5 and 3.5.
Target applicant:
   High school students
   College students
   Adult students

Minimum GPA: 2.5
Amount: Varies.
Number of awards: Varies.
Deadline: March 1.
How to apply: To apply, register online, complete the online application and select the scholarships to which you wish to apply. In addition, mail the supporting materials: printed confirmation page from the online application, personal statement, copy of Student Aid Report (SAR) available at www.fafsa.ed.gov and official transcript.

(1716) · Portuguese Foundation Scholarships

Portuguese Foundation of Connecticut
P.O. Box 331441
West Hartford, CT 06133-1441
Phone: 860-236-5514
Website: http://www.pfict.org/scholar.html
Purpose: To provide financial assistance to Portuguese students.
Eligibility: Applicants must be of Portuguese ancestry and demonstrate financial need. They must be U.S. citizens or permanent residents and residents of Connecticut. They must be applying to or already attending college as a full-time undergraduate student or part-time graduate student. Applicants may not have previously received more than four scholarships from the Portuguese Foundation. Applicants must have taken the SAT.
Target applicant:
   High school students
   College students
   Graduate school students
   Adult students
Minimum GPA: None.
Amount: $1,000.
Number of awards: 4.
Deadline: March 1.
How to apply: Applications are available online.

(1717) · Postsecondary Access Student Scholarship (PASS)

Office of Scholarships and Grants, Bureau of Student Financial Assistance
P.O. Box 30462
Lansing, MI 48909
Phone: 888-4-GRANTS
Email: treasscholgrant@michigan.gov
Website: http://www.michigan.gov/mistudentaid
Purpose: To assist Michigan students in meeting the cost of tuition and fees in pursuit of an associate's degree at a Michigan community college, college or university.
Eligibility: Applicants must be Michigan residents and enrolled in a program leading to an associate degree. Applicants must have scored at level 1 or level 2 on the Michigan Education Assessment Program (MEAP) tests in reading, writing, mathematics and science. Applicants must also be eligible for a Federal Pell Grant. Applicants who meet all criteria except for the MEAP test level requirement are eligible for the PASS award for one year and may receive continued aid if satisfactory academic progress is maintained.
Target applicant:
   College students
   Adult students
Minimum GPA: None.

Amount: Varies.
Number of awards: Varies.
Scholarship may be renewable.
Deadline: February 21 or March 21.
How to apply: File a Free Application for Federal Student Aid (FAFSA).

(1718) · Postsecondary Education Award Program (PEAP)

Nebraska Coordinating Commission for Postsecondary Education
P.O. Box 95005
Lincoln, NE 68509
Phone: 402-471-2847
Fax: 402-471-2886
Email: ritchie.morrow@ccpe.ne.gov
Website: http://www.ccpe.state.ne.us
Purpose: To assist students (including out-of-state students) in attending a Nebraska college or university.
Eligibility: Applicants must be enrolled in a Nebraska college and qualify for a federal Pell grant. Applicants apply for the grant through their specific college or university.
Target applicant:
   College students
   Adult students
Minimum GPA: None.
Amount: Varies.
Number of awards: Varies.
Deadline: Varies.
How to apply: Complete the Free Application for Federal Student Aid (FAFSA).

(1719) · Pre-Nursing Scholarship Program

California Health and Welfare Agency - Office of Statewide Health Planning and Development
Health Professions Education Foundation
818 K Street, Room 210
Sacramento, CA 95814
Phone: 916-324-6500
Fax: 916-324-6585
Email: hpef@oshpd.state.ca.us
Website: http://www.healthprofessions.ca.gov
Purpose: To increase the number of registered nurses in medically underserved areas by providing assistance to pre-nursing students in Central Valley counties in California.
Eligibility: Applicants must be pre-nursing students who are fluent in a language other than English and enrolled in schools in the Central Valley counties of Fresno, Kern, Kings, Madera, Merced or Tulare. Financial need, academic achievement, work experience and community involvement are considered. Preference is given to applicants who plan to remain in a medically underserved area after the service term and Associate Degree Nursing candidates.
Target applicant:
   High school students
   College students
   Graduate school students
   Adult students
Minimum GPA: None.
Amount: $4,000.
Number of awards: Varies.
Deadline: March, September.
How to apply: Applications are available online.

(1720) · PROMISE Scholarships

PROMISE Scholarship Program
1018 Kanawha Boulevard, East
Suite 700
Charleston, WV 25301
Phone: 877-WV-PROMISE
Fax: 304-558-3264
Email: morgenstern@hepc.wvnet.edu
Website: http://www.promisescholarships.org
Purpose: To assist outstanding West Virginia high school students.
Eligibility: Applicants must be West Virginia residents planning to attend an eligible West Virginia public or private college or university, graduate with a minimum 3.0 GPA and have a minimum ACT score of 21 or SAT score of 1000.
Target applicant:
    High school students
Minimum GPA: 3.0
Amount: Varies.
Number of awards: Varies.
Scholarship may be renewable.
Deadline: January 31 for PROMISE application and March 1 for FAFSA.
How to apply: Applications are available online. Applicants must also complete the Free Application for Federal Student Aid (FAFSA).

(1721) · PRSA-Hawaii/Roy Leffingwell Public Relations Scholarship

Hawaii Community Foundation - Scholarships
1164 Bishop Street, Suite 800
Honolulu, HI 96813
Phone: 888-731-3863
Fax: 808-521-6286
Email: scholarships@hcf-hawaii.org
Website: http://www.hawaiicommunityfoundation.org
Purpose: To support Hawaii students who are pursuing careers in public relations.
Eligibility: Applicants must be college juniors, college seniors or graduate students. They must be majoring in public relations, journalism or communications.
Target applicant:
    College students
    Graduate school students
    Adult students
Minimum GPA: None.
Amount: $1,000.
Number of awards: 1.
Deadline: March 1.
How to apply: To apply, register online, complete the online application and select the scholarships to which you wish to apply. In addition, mail the supporting materials: printed confirmation page from the online application, personal statement, copy of Student Aid Report (SAR) available at www.fafsa.ed.gov and official transcript.

(1722) · R. Preston Woodruff, Jr. Scholarships

Arkansas Student Loan Authority
3801 Woodland Heights, Suite 200
Little Rock, AR 72212
Phone: 800-443-6030
Email: info@asla.info
Website: http://www.asla.info

Purpose: To support students who live in Arkansas or are planning to attend school there.
Eligibility: Students must be enrolled or planning to enroll in an undergraduate program with at least a half-time schedule. Applicants must be a high school senior or current college student.
Target applicant:
    High school students
    College students
    Adult students
Minimum GPA: None.
Amount: $1,000.
Number of awards: 20.
Scholarship may be renewable.
Deadline: April 1.
How to apply: Applications are available online.

(1723) · R. Ray Singleton Fund

Greater Kanawha Valley Foundation
1600 Huntington Square
900 Lee Street, East
Charleston, WV 25301
Phone: 304-346-3620
Fax: 304-346-3640
Email: tgkvf@tgkvf.org
Website: http://www.tgkvf.org
Purpose: To provide financial assistance to residents of Kanawha, Boone, Clay, Putnam, Lincoln and Fayette counties in West Virginia who are interested in pursuing a college education.
Eligibility: Applicants must be full-time students and possess good moral character as well as proven academic achievement.
Target applicant:
    High school students
    College students
    Graduate school students
    Adult students
Minimum GPA: 2.5
Amount: $1,000.
Number of awards: 5.
Scholarship may be renewable.
Deadline: February 17.
How to apply: Applications are available online at http://www.tgkvf. org/scholar.htm or via email at shoover@tgkvf.org.

(1724) · Rachel E. Lemieux Youth Scholarship

Business and Professional Women/Maine Futurama Foundation
103 County Road
Oakland, ME 04963
Email: webmaster@bpwmaine.org
Website: http://www.bpwmaine.org/files/index.php?id=10
Purpose: To honor the memory of Rachel E. Lemieux and to provide financial assistance to Maine high school seniors and recent graduates.
Eligibility: Applicants must be female Maine residents who are high school seniors or who have recently graduated.
Target applicant:
    High school students
Minimum GPA: None.
Amount: $1,200.
Number of awards: Varies.
Deadline: April 30.
How to apply: Applications are available from your local BPW chapter.

(1725) · Rae Lee Siporin Award

Los Alamos National Laboratory Foundation
1302 Calle de la Merced
Suite A
Espanola, NM 87532
Phone: 505-753-8890
Fax: 505-753-8915
Email: info@lanlfoundation.org
Website: http://www.lanlfoundation.org
Purpose: To support undergraduate students from Northern New Mexico.
Eligibility: Students must have at least a 3.25 GPA, and they must have either an SAT score of at least 1350 or an ACT score of at least 19. Applicants must submit an essay and two letters of recommendation.
Target applicant:
   High school students
   College students
   Adult students
Minimum GPA: 3.25
Amount: $1,000.
Number of awards: Varies.
Deadline: January 22.
How to apply: Applications are available online.

(1726) · Ralph and Ruth Strother Scholarship

Epsilon Sigma Alpha Foundation
P.O. Box 270517
Fort Collins, CO 80527
Phone: 970-223-2824
Fax: 970-223-4456
Email: kloyd@knoxy.net
Website: http://www.esaintl.com/esaf
Purpose: To provide educational opportunities for Mew Mexico students.
Eligibility: Applicants must attend a college or university in New Mexico. They may major in any subject. Selection is based on the following criteria: scholastic ability (50 percent), financial need (25 percent), character (10 percent), leadership (10 percent) and service (5 percent).
Target applicant:
   High school students
   College students
   Adult students
Minimum GPA: None.
Amount: $1,000.
Number of awards: 1.
Deadline: February 1.
How to apply: Applications are available online.

(1727) · Random House Inc. Creative Writing Competition

Random House Inc. Creative Writing Competition
c/o Scholarship America
One Scholarship Way
P.O. Box 297
St. Peter, MN 56082
Phone: 888-369-3434
Fax: 212-940-7590
Email: worldofexpression@randomhouse.com
Website: http://www.worldofexpression.org
Purpose: To recognize students of New York City Public High Schools for creativity in literature.
Eligibility: Applicants must be seniors in a New York City Public High School who are 21 years old or younger and must not have family members employed by Bertelsmann or its subsidiaries. Students must submit a literary composition. Possible formats include poetry/spoken word, fiction/drama or personal essay/memoir. College essays, book reports, myths and legends will not be accepted. Foreign language submissions are not allowed, and all work must not have been previously published or awarded.
Target applicant:
   High school students
Minimum GPA: None.
Amount: $500-$10,000.
Number of awards: 34.
Deadline: February 9.
How to apply: Applications are available online.

(1728) · Rath Distinguished Scholarship

Wisconsin Foundation for Independent Colleges
4425 North Port Washington Road
Suite 402
Glendale, WI 53212
Phone: 414-273-5980
Email: wfic@wficweb.org
Website: http://www.wficweb.org
Purpose: To honor outstanding students who attend Wisconsin independent colleges.
Eligibility: Applicants must be full-time students at a Wisconsin Foundation for Independent Colleges member institution. Member institutions are listed on the organization's website. They must have a GPA of 3.2 or higher, and entering freshmen must have graduated in the top 25 percent of their class. Financial need is required. Preference goes to Wisconsin residents, but residents of any state may apply.
Target applicant:
   High school students
   College students
   Adult students
Minimum GPA: 3.2
Amount: $10,000.
Number of awards: 30.
Deadline: February 26.
How to apply: Applications are available from your school's financial aid office.

(1729) · Raymond & Catherine Brizzolari Memorial

Epsilon Sigma Alpha Foundation
P.O. Box 270517
Fort Collins, CO 80527
Phone: 970-223-2824
Fax: 970-223-4456
Email: kloyd@knoxy.net
Website: http://www.esaintl.com/esaf
Purpose: To honor the memory of Raymond and Catherine Brizzolari.
Eligibility: Applicants must be Alaska residents and may pursue any major at any school. Selection is based on the following criteria: character (10 percent), leadership (20 percent), service (10 percent), financial need (30 percent) and scholastic ability (30 percent).
Target applicant:
   High school students

College students
Adult students
Minimum GPA: None.
Amount: $500.
Number of awards: 1.
Deadline: February 1.
How to apply: Applications are available online.

(1730) · Raymond F. Cain Scholarship Fund

Hawaii Community Foundation - Scholarships
1164 Bishop Street, Suite 800
Honolulu, HI 96813
Phone: 888-731-3863
Fax: 808-521-6286
Email: scholarships@hcf-hawaii.org
Website: http://www.hawaiicommunityfoundation.org
Purpose: To support students in Hawaii who are majoring in fields related to landscape architecture.
Eligibility: Applicants must have at least a 2.7 GPA, and they must have financial need.
Target applicant:
   High school students
   College students
   Adult students
Minimum GPA: 2.7
Amount: $1,500.
Number of awards: 1.
Deadline: March 1.
How to apply: To apply, register online, complete the online application and select the scholarships to which you wish to apply. In addition, mail the supporting materials: printed confirmation page from the online application, personal statement, copy of Student Aid Report (SAR) available at www.fafsa.ed.gov and official transcript.

(1731) · Raymond T. Wellington, Jr. Memorial Scholarship

American Legion Auxiliary, Department of New York
112 State Street
Suite 1310
Albany, NY 12207
Phone: 518-463-1162
Fax: 518-449-5406
Email: alanyterry@nycap.rr.com
Website: http://www.deptny.org/Scholarships.htm
Purpose: To provide financial assistance to students who are children, grandchildren and great-grandchildren of war veterans.
Eligibility: Applicants must be children, grandchildren or great grand-children of Armed Forces veterans who served in World War I, World War II, the Korean Conflict, the Vietnam War, Grenada/Lebanon, Panama or the Persian Gulf. Students must be high school seniors and must be U.S. citizens and New York State residents.
Target applicant:
   High school students
Minimum GPA: None.
Amount: $1,000.
Number of awards: 1.
Deadline: March 1.
How to apply: Applications are available online.

(1732) · RBC Dain Rauscher Colorado Scholarships

Denver Foundation
55 Madison
8th Floor
Denver, CO 80206
Phone: 303-300-1790
Fax: 303-300-6547
Email: information@denverfoundation.org
Website: http://www.denverfoundation.org/page17851.cfm
Purpose: To provide assistance to outstanding Colorado high school seniors who plan to pursue degrees in science or engineering.
Eligibility: Applicants must be graduating seniors at a Colorado high school who have a 3.75 or higher GPA and have completed college preparatory coursework.
Target applicant:
   High school students
Minimum GPA: 3.75
Amount: $5,000.
Number of awards: 5.
Deadline: Varies.
How to apply: Applications are available online.

(1733) · Regents Award for Children of Veterans

New York State Higher Education Services Corporation (HESC)
99 Washington Avenue
Albany, NY 12255
Phone: 888-697-4372
Email: hescwebmail@hesc.org
Website: http://www.hesc.com
Purpose: To assist students whose parents served in the Armed Forces during times of war or national emergency.
Eligibility: Applicants must have a parent who served in the United States Armed Forces during the Persian Gulf, Vietnam or Korean Conflicts, World War I or II or as a Merchant Seaman during World War II. The parent must be or have been a resident of New York State and have died or suffered a disability of 40 percent or more as a result of service, been classified as missing in action or been a prisoner of war. Students with a parent who has received the expeditionary medal for participation in operations in Lebanon, Grenada or Panama and students born with spina bifida whose parent is a Vietnam Veteran are also eligible.
Target applicant:
   Junior high students or younger
   High school students
   College students
   Graduate school students
   Adult students
Minimum GPA: None.
Amount: $450.
Number of awards: Varies.
Scholarship may be renewable.
Deadline: May 1.
How to apply: Applications are available by phone.

(1734) · Regents Health Care Opportunity Scholarships in Medicine and Dentistry

NYS Education Department, Office of K-16 Initiatives and Access Programs
Scholarships and Grants Administration Unit
Room 1078 Education Building Addition

Albany, NY 12234
Phone: 518-486-1319
Website: http://www.hesc.com
Purpose: To assist medical and dental students who are New York residents.
Eligibility: Applicants must be U.S. citizens or eligible noncitizens, be New York State residents and study full-time in an eligible New York State medical or dental school. Priority is given to students who are economically disadvantaged and members of a minority group. Recipients must work one year for each year of payment received, with a minimum of two years, in a physician-shortage area of New York State.
Target applicant:
    Graduate school students
    Adult students
Minimum GPA: None.
Amount: $10,000.
Number of awards: Varies.
Scholarship may be renewable.
Deadline: Varies.
How to apply: Applications are available by written request.

(1735) · Regents Professional Opportunity Scholarships

NYS Education Department, Bureau of HEOP/VATEA/Scholarships
Education Building Addition
Room 1071
Albany, NY 12234
Phone: 518-486-1319
Website: http://www.hesc.com
Purpose: To assist students in professional programs who are New York residents.
Eligibility: Applicants must be U.S. citizens or eligible noncitizens, be New York State residents and study at an eligible professional program in New York State. Priority is given to students who are economically disadvantaged and members of a minority group. Recipients must work as a licensed professional for one year for each year of payment received in New York State.
Target applicant:
    College students
    Graduate school students
    Adult students
Minimum GPA: None.
Amount: $1,000-$5,000.
Number of awards: Varies.
Scholarship may be renewable.
Deadline: Varies.
How to apply: Applications are available by written request.

(1736) · Regional College Scholarship

Los Alamos National Laboratory Foundation
1302 Calle de la Merced
Suite A
Espanola, NM 87532
Phone: 505-753-8890
Fax: 505-753-8915
Email: info@lanlfoundation.org
Website: http://www.lanlfoundation.org
Purpose: To support residents of Northern New Mexico who are attending college in the region.

Eligibility: Students must have at least a 3.25 GPA, and they must have either an SAT score of at least 1350 or an ACT score of at least 19. Applicants must attend one of the following schools: New Mexico Highlands University, Luna Community College, Santa Fe Community College, University of New Mexico Los Alamos, University of New Mexico Taos or Northern New Mexico College.
Target applicant:
    High school students
    College students
    Adult students
Minimum GPA: 3.25
Amount: Varies.
Number of awards: Varies.
Deadline: January 22.
How to apply: Applications are available online.

(1737) · Regional University Baccalaureate Scholarship

Oklahoma State Regents for Higher Education
655 Research Parkway, Suite 200
Oklahoma City, OK 73104
Phone: 800-858-1840
Fax: 405-225-9230
Email: studentinfo@osrhe.edu
Website: http://www.okhighered.org
Purpose: To provide financial assistance to students of regional universities.
Eligibility: Applicants must be Oklahoma residents who are enrolled in a bachelor's degree program at one of the following schools: Cameron University, East Central University, Langston University, Northeastern State University, Northwestern Oklahoma State University, Oklahoma Panhandle State University, Rogers State University, Southeastern Oklahoma State University, Southwestern Oklahoma State University, University of Central Oklahoma or the University of Science and Arts of Oklahoma. They must also either have an ACT score of 30 or higher or be a National Merit Semifinalist or Commended Student.
Target applicant:
    High school students
Minimum GPA: None.
Amount: Tuition plus $3,000.
Number of awards: Up to 165.
Scholarship may be renewable.
Deadline: Varies.
How to apply: Applications are available from your university.

(1738) · Rehabilitation Assistance for the Blind and Visually Impaired

College Foundation of North Carolina
P.O. Box 41966
Raleigh, NC 27629-1966
Phone: 866-234-6400
Fax: 919-821-3139
Email: programinformation@cfnc.org
Website: http://www.cfnc.org
Purpose: To assist North Carolina undergraduate and graduate students who are blind or visually impaired.
Eligibility: Applicants must be North Carolina residents who are enrolled full-time at a North Carolina college or university. They must be legally blind or have a condition that could result in blindness, and they must be in need of vocational rehabilitation services.

Target applicant:
    College students
    Graduate school students
    Adult students
Minimum GPA: None.
Amount: Varies.
Number of awards: Varies.
Deadline: Varies.
How to apply: Applications are available from the State Division of Services for the Blind at http://www.dhhs.state.nc.us/dsb/.

(1739) · Rhode Island Foundation Association of Former Legislators Scholarship

Rhode Island Foundation
One Union Station
Providence, RI 02903
Phone: 401-274-4564
Fax: 401-331-8085
Email: libbym@rifoundation.org
Website: http://www.rifoundation.org
Purpose: To assist Rhode Island high school seniors with an excellent track record of community service.
Eligibility: Applicants must be Rhode Island high school seniors who have been accepted into college, have demonstrated need and have a substantial amount of community service.
Target applicant:
    High school students
Minimum GPA: None.
Amount: $1,500.
Number of awards: 5.
Deadline: June 1.
How to apply: Applications are available online.

(1740) · Richard W. Tyler Principals Scholarship Program

MELMAC Education Foundation
188 Whitten Road
Augusta, ME 04330
Phone: 866-622-3066
Fax: 207-622-3053
Email: info@melmacfoundation.org
Website: http://www.melmacfoundation.org/grants/principal
Purpose: To assist Maine students and encourage them to continue their college education beyond the first year.
Eligibility: Applicants must be Maine high school students nominated by their school's principal. They must be accepted to a college or university and demonstrate exceptional financial need. They must face challenges or obstacles in their pursuit of an education and be committed to public service.
Target applicant:
    High school students
Minimum GPA: None.
Amount: $1,000.
Number of awards: Varies.
Deadline: Varies.
How to apply: Applications are made on the student's behalf by his or her high school principal.

(1741) · Richie Gregory Fund

Hawaii Community Foundation - Scholarships
1164 Bishop Street, Suite 800
Honolulu, HI 96813
Phone: 888-731-3863
Fax: 808-521-6286
Email: scholarships@hcf-hawaii.org
Website: http://www.hawaiicommunityfoundation.org
Purpose: To support students who are majoring in art.
Eligibility: Applicants must be residents of Hawaii.
Target applicant:
    High school students
    College students
    Adult students
Minimum GPA: None.
Amount: $1,142.
Number of awards: 7.
Deadline: March 1.
How to apply: To apply, register online, complete the online application and select the scholarships to which you wish to apply. In addition, mail the supporting materials: printed confirmation page from the online application, personal statement, copy of Student Aid Report (SAR) available at www.fafsa.ed.gov and official transcript.

(1742) · Robanna Fund

Hawaii Community Foundation - Scholarships
1164 Bishop Street, Suite 800
Honolulu, HI 96813
Phone: 888-731-3863
Fax: 808-521-6286
Email: scholarships@hcf-hawaii.org
Website: http://www.hawaiicommunityfoundation.org
Purpose: To support Hawaii students who plan to work in health care.
Eligibility: Applicants must be in an undergraduate health-related program.
Target applicant:
    High school students
    College students
    Adult students
Minimum GPA: None.
Amount: $1,000.
Number of awards: 8.
Deadline: March 1.
How to apply: To apply, register online, complete the online application and select the scholarships to which you wish to apply. In addition, mail the supporting materials: printed confirmation page from the online application, personal statement, copy of Student Aid Report (SAR) available at www.fafsa.ed.gov and official transcript.

(1743) · Robert C. Byrd Honors Scholarship Program - Alaska

Alaska Department of Education and Early Development
801 W. 10th Street, Suite 200
P.O. Box 110500
Juneau, AK 99811
Phone: 907-465-2800
Fax: 907-465-4156
Email: melora_gaber@eed.state.ak.us
Website: http://www.eed.state.ak.us

Purpose: To support Alaskan high school students in their pursuit of higher education.
Eligibility: Applicants must be high school seniors with the promise of future excellence and achievement. They must be residents of Alaska and U.S. citizens accepted into a college, university or technical school as a full-time student. Applicants must not be in default on any federal student loans. They must include an essay on a social issue of importance to them and three letters of recommendation with their application.
Target applicant:
    High school students
Minimum GPA: None.
Amount: $1,500.
Number of awards: 18.
Scholarship may be renewable.
Deadline: April 2.
How to apply: Applications are available online.

(1744) · Robert C. Byrd Honors Scholarship Program - Arizona

Arizona Department of Education
1535 W. Jefferson Street
Phoenix, AZ 85007
Phone: 800-352-4558
Fax: 602-364-1532
Email: byrd@azed.gov
Website: http://www.ade.state.az.us/byrd
Purpose: To reward Arizona high school students who demonstrate academic excellence.
Eligibility: Applicants must be graduating high school seniors or students who have received a GED who have applied to or been accepted at a post-secondary institution as a full-time student. They must be Arizona residents and U.S. citizens or permanent residents.
Target applicant:
    High school students
Minimum GPA: None.
Amount: $1,500.
Number of awards: Varies.
Scholarship may be renewable.
Deadline: March 26.
How to apply: Applicants must be nominated by their high schools.

(1745) · Robert C. Byrd Honors Scholarship Program - Arkansas

Arkansas Department of Education
4 Capitol Mall
Little Rock, AR 72201
Phone: 501-682-4475
Email: ade.communications@arkansas.gov
Website: http://www.arkansased.org
Purpose: To support high-achieving Arkansas high school graduates.
Eligibility: Applicants must be graduating seniors or recipients of the equivalent of a high school diploma. They must be residents of Arkansas admitted to a post-secondary school. Applicants must show current academic achievement with a promise of future achievement. Students with full scholarship awards or who will be attending military academies are not eligible for the scholarship.
Target applicant:
    High school students
Minimum GPA: None.
Amount: $1,500.
Number of awards: 62.
Scholarship may be renewable.

Deadline: February 16.
How to apply: Applications are available online.

(1746) · Robert C. Byrd Honors Scholarship Program - California

California Student Aid Commission (CSAC)
Attn.: Robert C. Byrd Honors Scholarship Program
P.O. Box 419029
Rancho Cordova, CA 95741-9029
Phone: 888-224-7268
Email: studentsupport@csac.ca.gov
Website: http://www.csac.ca.gov
Purpose: To aid outstanding California resident students.
Eligibility: Applicants must be legal residents of California who are U.S. citizens or eligible noncitizens. Applicants must enroll in and attend a U.S. postsecondary institution on a full-time basis as freshmen, have registered with the Selective Service System and submit a certification form attesting that they are not delinquent or in default on a federal scholarship or educational loan. The Commission reviews applicants by grade point average.
Target applicant:
    High school students
Minimum GPA: None.
Amount: $1,500.
Number of awards: Varies.
Scholarship may be renewable.
Deadline: April 27.
How to apply: Students must apply through their high school program coordinator. Students not currently enrolled in a California high school may obtain an application directly from the California Student Aid Commission.

(1747) · Robert C. Byrd Honors Scholarship Program - Colorado

Colorado Department of Education
Competitive Grants and Awards Unit
1560 Broadway, Suite 1450
Denver, CO 80202
Phone: 303-866-6243
Fax: 303-866-6647
Email: hitt_p@cde.state.co.us
Website: http://www.cde.state.co.us/cdeawards/byrd.htm
Purpose: To promote academic excellence in Colorado high school seniors.
Eligibility: Applicants must be Colorado residents graduating from high school or receiving a GED. They must also be U.S. citizens or national or permanent residents of the U.S. Applicants must have an unweighted GPA of at least 3.8 or a weighted GPA of at least 4.0 and have received a score of 31 or above on the ACT or a score of 2040 or above on the SAT. Students receiving a GED must score in the top 5 percent of Colorado GED scores. Applicants must be accepted into an accredited post-secondary institution and provide proof of acceptance with the application.
Target applicant:
    High school students
Minimum GPA: 3.8
Amount: $1,500.
Number of awards: Varies.
Scholarship may be renewable.
Deadline: April 6.
How to apply: Applications are available online.

(1748) · Robert C. Byrd Honors Scholarship Program - Connecticut

Connecticut Department of Higher Education
61 Woodland Street
Hartford, CT 06105-2326
Phone: 860-947-1855
Fax: 860-947-1838
Email: byrd@ctdhe.org
Website: http://www.ctdhe.org
Purpose: To assist Connecticut student residents.
Eligibility: Applicants must be Connecticut residents who are high school seniors ranking in the top 2 percent of their class or with SAT scores of at least 2100. Selection is based on SAT scores and class rank.
Target applicant:
    High school students
Minimum GPA: None.
Amount: $1,500.
Number of awards: Varies.
Deadline: April 1.
How to apply: Applications are available online.

(1749) · Robert C. Byrd Honors Scholarship Program - Delaware

Delaware Higher Education Commission
Carvel State Office Building, 5th Floor
820 N. French Street
Wilmington, DE 19801-3509
Phone: 800-292-7935
Fax: 302-577-6765
Email: dhec@doe.k12.de.us
Website: http://www.doe.k12.de.us/infosuites/students_family/dhec/
Purpose: To support high-achieving Delaware resident students.
Eligibility: Applicants must be residents of Delaware, U.S. citizens or eligible noncitizens, high school seniors who rank in the upper quarter of their class or GED recipients who score at least 300 on the GED examination, score a minimum of 1200 on the SAT and enroll at least half-time at a regionally-accredited institution of higher education. The program is dependent on U.S. Congressional funding.
Target applicant:
    High school students
    College students
    Graduate school students
    Adult students
Minimum GPA: None.
Amount: $1,500.
Number of awards: 20.
Scholarship may be renewable.
Deadline: March 28.
How to apply: Applications are available online.

(1750) · Robert C. Byrd Honors Scholarship Program - Florida

Florida Department of Education
Office of Student Financial Assistance
1940 N. Monroe Street
Suite 70
Tallahassee, FL 32303-4759
Phone: 888-827-2004
Fax: 850-245-9667

Email: osfa@fldoe.org
Website: http://www.floridastudentfinancialaid.org
Purpose: To support Florida high school graduates who show academic promise.
Eligibility: Applicants must meet Florida's residency requirements for receiving state financial aid as determined by the student's postsecondary school and must not be in default on federal or state student loan programs.
Target applicant:
    High school students
    College students
    Adult students
Minimum GPA: None.
Amount: Varies.
Number of awards: Varies.
Scholarship may be renewable.
Deadline: Varies.
How to apply: Applicants must be nominated by their high school principal, adult education director or principal or headmaster and complete the Florida Financial Aid Application.

(1751) · Robert C. Byrd Honors Scholarship Program - Georgia

Georgia Student Finance Commission
2082 East Exchange Place
Tucker, GA 30084
Phone: 800-505-4732
Fax: 770-724-9089
Email: support@gacollege411.org
Website: http://www.gacollege411.org
Purpose: To aid outstanding Georgia high school students.
Eligibility: Applicants must be U.S. citizens, have recently graduated from a Georgia secondary school and be enrolled at a postsecondary institution. Applicants must also demonstrate academic achievement.
Target applicant:
    High school students
Minimum GPA: None.
Amount: Varies.
Number of awards: 664.
Scholarship may be renewable.
Deadline: Varies.
How to apply: Applications are available by telephone request.

(1752) · Robert C. Byrd Honors Scholarship Program - Hawaii

Hawaii Department of Education
Office of Curriculum, Instruction and Student Support
Student Support Section
641 18th Avenue V-201
Honolulu, HI 96816
Phone: 808-586-3230
Fax: 808-586-3234
Website: http://doe.k12.hi.us
Purpose: To promote academic excellence among Hawaii students.
Eligibility: Applicants must be graduating high school seniors or planning to earn a GED. They must have a GPA of 3.3 or higher and have scored above 1270 on the SAT and/or above 29 on the ACT. GED applicants must score at least 60 points. Applicants must be legal Hawaiian residents, but they may attend high schools outside of Hawaii.

Target applicant:
    High school students
Minimum GPA: 3.3
Amount: $1,500.
Number of awards: Varies.
Scholarship may be renewable.
Deadline: March 15.
How to apply: Applications are available online.

(1753) · Robert C. Byrd Honors Scholarship Program - Idaho

Idaho State Board of Education
P.O. Box 83720
Boise, ID 83720
Phone: 208-334-2270
Fax: 208-334-2632
Email: dkelly@osbe.state.id.us
Website: http://www.boardofed.idaho.gov
Purpose: To recognize outstanding Idaho high school seniors.
Eligibility: Applicants must be U.S. citizens who are graduating seniors of Idaho high schools and who demonstrate outstanding academic achievement. Selection is based on merit.
Target applicant:
    High school students
Minimum GPA: None.
Amount: $1,500.
Number of awards: Varies.
Scholarship may be renewable.
Deadline: January 15.
How to apply: Applications are available online.

(1754) · Robert C. Byrd Honors Scholarship Program - Illinois

Illinois Department of Public Health
535 W. Jefferson Street
Springfield, IL 62761
Phone: 217-782-4977
Fax: 217-782-3987
Email: dph.mailus@illinois.gov
Website: http://www.idph.state.il.us
Purpose: To aid outstanding Illinois high school students.
Eligibility: Applicants must be U.S. citizens, be graduating Illinois high school seniors, demonstrate outstanding academic achievement and be enrolled or accepted for enrollment full-time as undergraduate students.
Target applicant:
    High school students
Minimum GPA: None.
Amount: $1,500.
Number of awards: Varies.
Scholarship may be renewable.
Deadline: July 15.
How to apply: Applicants are nominated by their high schools.

(1755) · Robert C. Byrd Honors Scholarship Program - Indiana

State Student Assistance Commission of Indiana
150 W. Market Street
Suite 500
Indianapolis, IN 46204
Phone: 888-528-4719
Fax: 317-232-3260
Email: grants@ssaci.state.in.us
Website: http://www.in.gov/ssaci
Purpose: Monetary assistance is provided to academically worthy Indiana resident high school seniors with their college expenses.
Eligibility: Applicants must be U.S. citizens who are graduating Indiana high school seniors and have a minimum SAT score of 1300 or a minimum ACT score of 29. Applicants must apply to and enroll in a higher education institution full-time.
Target applicant:
    High school students
Minimum GPA: None.
Amount: $1,500.
Number of awards: Varies.
Scholarship may be renewable.
Deadline: April 24.
How to apply: Applications are available online.

(1756) · Robert C. Byrd Honors Scholarship Program - Iowa

Iowa College Student Aid Commission
200 10th Street, 4th Floor
Des Moines, IA 50309
Phone: 515-242-3344
Fax: 515-242-3388
Email: info@iowacollegeaid.org
Website: http://www.iowacollegeaid.org
Purpose: To recognize top Iowa high school seniors.
Eligibility: Applicants must be ranked in the top 10 percent of their graduating Iowa high school class, have taken required academic courses, have a minimum ACT score of 28 or minimum SAT score of 1240 and have a minimum 3.5 GPA.
Target applicant:
    High school students
Minimum GPA: 3.5
Amount: $1,500.
Number of awards: Varies.
Scholarship may be renewable.
Deadline: February 2.
How to apply: Applications are available from your high school guidance counselor and online.

(1757) · Robert C. Byrd Honors Scholarship Program - Kansas

Kansas State Department of Education
120 SE 10th Avenue
Topeka, KS 66612
Phone: 785-296-3201
Fax: 785-296-7933
Email: contact@ksde.org
Website: http://www.ksde.org
Purpose: To provide scholarship funds to high-achieving seniors in Kansas.
Eligibility: Applicants must be graduating high school seniors or have obtained the equivalent of a high school diploma. They must demonstrate academic achievement and show promise of continued academic achievement and be planning to attend a post-secondary school. Applicants must have an unweighted GPA of at least 3.85 and

score of 32 or above on the ACT. Applicants must be U.S. citizens or legal residents.

Target applicant:
  High school students
Minimum GPA: 3.85
Amount: $1,500.
Number of awards: Varies..
Scholarship may be renewable.
Deadline: February 5.
How to apply: Applications are available online. Two letters of reference and an essay are required.

(1758) · Robert C. Byrd Honors Scholarship Program - Kentucky

Kentucky Higher Education Assistance Authority
P.O. Box 798
Frankfort, KY 40602
Phone: 800-928-8926
Email: blane@kheaa.com
Website: http://www.kheaa.com
Purpose: To assist high-achieving high school seniors and GED recipients.
Eligibility: Applicants must be residents of Kentucky and U.S. citizens or nationals. Students must have a GPA of 3.5 or higher and a score of 23 or higher on the ACT or a score of 1060 or higher on the SAT. GED recipients must receive a score of 2700 or higher. Applicants must be nominated by a high school official or GED coordinator, cannot be in default on a federal loan and males must be in compliance with Selective Service requirements.
Target applicant:
  High school students
Minimum GPA: 3.5
Amount: $1,500.
Number of awards: Varies.
Scholarship may be renewable.
Deadline: February 15 for high school and June 30 for GED.
How to apply: Applications are available online.

(1759) · Robert C. Byrd Honors Scholarship Program - Louisiana

Louisiana Department of Education
P.O. Box 94064
Baton Rouge, LA 70804
Phone: 877-453-2721
Fax: 225-342-0193
Website: http://www.doe.state.la.us
Purpose: To provide financial support to students who have demonstrated academic achievement.
Eligibility: Applicants must be high school students or GED recipients who are Louisiana residents and U.S. citizens. They must have a GPA of at least 3.5 and score above 23 on the ACT or above 970 on the SAT. GED recipients should have a score above 620. Applicants must be planning to attend an accredited post-secondary institution.
Target applicant:
  High school students
Minimum GPA: 3.5
Amount: $1,500.
Number of awards: 124.
Scholarship may be renewable.
Deadline: Varies.

How to apply: Applications are available from high school guidance counselors and GED coordinators.

(1760) · Robert C. Byrd Honors Scholarship Program - Maine

Maine Education Assistance Division
Finance Authority of Maine (FAME)
5 Community Drive
P.O. Box 949
Augusta, ME 04332
Phone: 800-228-3734
Fax: 207-623-0095
Email: education@famemaine.com
Website: http://www.famemaine.com
Purpose: To provide support to high-achieving high school seniors.
Eligibility: Applicants must be graduating high school seniors. Home-schooled seniors are eligible if they submit GED scores and high school transcripts, if available. Applicants must be Maine residents who have demonstrated academic achievement and participation in community service activities. They must submit an essay and ACT or SAT scores.
Target applicant:
  High school students
Minimum GPA: None.
Amount: $1,500.
Number of awards: Varies.
Scholarship may be renewable.
Deadline: May 1.
How to apply: Applications are available online.

(1761) · Robert C. Byrd Honors Scholarship Program - Maryland

Maryland State Department of Education
William Cappe
200 W. Baltimore Street
Baltimore, MD 21201
Email: wcappe@msde.state.md.us
Website: http://www.msde.state.md.us
Purpose: To recognize student achievement and scholastic excellence.
Eligibility: Applicants must be high school seniors who are Maryland residents and in the top 1 percent of their class. They must be admitted full-time to a post-secondary school, excluding military academies.
Target applicant:
  High school students
Minimum GPA: None.
Amount: $1,000-$1,500.
Number of awards: 129.
Deadline: Varies.
How to apply: Applicants must be nominated by school officials.

(1762) · Robert C. Byrd Honors Scholarship Program - Massachusetts

Massachusetts Department of Education
350 Main Street
Malden, MA 02148
Phone: 781-338-6304
Email: steixeira@doe.mass.edu
Website: http://www.doe.mass.edu
Purpose: To reward academic achievement in high school seniors.
Eligibility: Applicants must be high school seniors or be earning the equivalent of a high school diploma. They must be Massachusetts

residents, having lived in the state at least one year prior to beginning college. Applicants must apply to or be accepted at an accredited post-secondary institution. They must have a GPA of at least 3.5, and the scholarship committee will consider school activities, leadership, community service, employment, awards and honors.

Target applicant:
High school students
Minimum GPA: 3.5
Amount: $1,500.
Number of awards: Varies.
Deadline: Varies.
How to apply: Applications are sent to schools, and schools must nominate students.

(1763) · Robert C. Byrd Honors Scholarship Program - Michigan

Office of Scholarships and Grants, Bureau of Student Financial Assistance
P.O. Box 30462
Lansing, MI 48909
Phone: 888-4-GRANTS
Email: treasscholgrant@michigan.gov
Website: http://www.michigan.gov/mistudentaid
Purpose: To assist outstanding Michigan high school seniors.
Eligibility: Applicants must be U.S. citizens or eligible noncitizens, Michigan residents, high school seniors and demonstrate academic excellence.
Target applicant:
High school students
Minimum GPA: None.
Amount: Varies.
Number of awards: Varies.
Scholarship may be renewable.
Deadline: Varies.
How to apply: Each Michigan high school principal may nominate one outstanding senior.

(1764) · Robert C. Byrd Honors Scholarship Program - Minnesota

Minnesota Higher Education Services Office
1450 Energy Park Drive
Suite 350
Saint Paul, MN 55108
Phone: 651-642-0567
Fax: 651-642-0675
Email: info@heso.state.mn.us
Website: http://www.mheso.state.mn.us
Purpose: To assist outstanding Minnesota high school seniors.
Eligibility: Applicants must be U.S. citizens or eligible noncitizens, Minnesota residents, high school seniors and demonstrate academic excellence.
Target applicant:
High school students
Minimum GPA: None.
Amount: Varies.
Number of awards: 125.
Scholarship may be renewable.
Deadline: March.
How to apply: Minnesota Department of Children, Families, & Learning, sends out the nomination information in January. Applicants

apply through their high school and should contact their principal or counselor for application forms.

(1765) · Robert C. Byrd Honors Scholarship Program - Mississippi

Mississippi Department of Education
P.O. Box 771
Jackson, MS 39205
Phone: 601-359-3513
Email: webhelp@mde.k12.ms.us
Website: http://www.mde.k12.ms.us
Purpose: To recognize and promote academic excellence and achievement.
Eligibility: Applicants must be residents of Mississippi and U.S. citizens or permanent residents. They must be graduating high school seniors or have earned their GED during the application year and have applied or been accepted to a post-secondary school. Applications must include ACT or SAT scores, high school transcript or GED test results, extracurricular activities, leadership activities, honors and awards and a one-page essay.
Target applicant:
High school students
Minimum GPA: None.
Amount: $1,100-$1,500.
Number of awards: 70-75.
Scholarship may be renewable.
Deadline: March 31.
How to apply: Applications are available online.

(1766) · Robert C. Byrd Honors Scholarship Program - Missouri

Missouri Department of Elementary and Secondary Education
P.O. Box 480
Jefferson City, MO 65102
Phone: 573-751-1668
Fax: 573-751-8613
Email: webreplyqualtrr@dese.mo.gov
Website: http://www.dese.mo.gov
Purpose: To recognize and promote academic excellence and achievement.
Eligibility: Applicants must be Missouri high school graduates or GED recipients. They must be U.S. citizens or permanent residents. Applicants must be in the top 10 percent of their class and score above the 90th percentile on the ACT.
Target applicant:
High school students
Minimum GPA: None.
Amount: $1,500.
Number of awards: Varies.
Scholarship may be renewable.
Deadline: April 15.
How to apply: Applications are available online.

(1767) · Robert C. Byrd Honors Scholarship Program - Montana

Montana Department of Education
The Montana Office of Public Instruction
P.O. Box 202501
Helena, MT 59620
Website: http://www.opi.state.mt.us

Purpose: To assist outstanding Montana high school seniors.
Eligibility: Applicants must be U.S. citizens or eligible noncitizens, Montana residents, high school seniors and have a GPA of at least 3.6 in a college preparatory curriculum and a cumulative score of 1380 on the SAT or 30 on the ACT.
Target applicant:
　　High school students
Minimum GPA: 3.6
Amount: Varies.
Number of awards: Varies.
Scholarship may be renewable.
Deadline: March.
How to apply: Applications are available at your high school counseling office or online.

(1768) · Robert C. Byrd Honors Scholarship Program - Nebraska

Nebraska Department of Education
301 Centennial Mall South
P.O. Box 94987
Lincoln, NE 68509
Phone: 402-471-2295
Email: mardi.north@nde.ne.gov
Website: http://www.nde.state.ne.us
Purpose: To honor academic excellence and potential.
Eligibility: Applicants must be Nebraska residents who are graduating from high school or receiving a GED with a minimum ACT score of 30. They must be U.S. citizens, nationals or permanent residents. Applicants must have applied or been accepted to a post-secondary school, planning to attend full-time. They must fulfill all Selective Service requirements and not be in default on any student loans.
Target applicant:
　　High school students
Minimum GPA: None.
Amount: Up to $1,500.
Number of awards: 40.
Scholarship may be renewable.
Deadline: March 15.
How to apply: Applications are available online.

(1769) · Robert C. Byrd Honors Scholarship Program - Nevada

Nevada Department of Education
700 E. Fifth Street
Carson City, NV 89701
Phone: 775-687-9200
Fax: 775-687-9101
Website: http://www.doe.nv.gov
Purpose: To recognize and promote excellence and achievement among Nevada students.
Eligibility: Applicants must be legal residents of the State of Nevada, be Nevada High School Scholars Program recipients and be accepted into an institution of higher education.
Target applicant:
　　High school students
Minimum GPA: None.
Amount: $1,500.
Number of awards: 60.
Scholarship may be renewable.
Deadline: Varies.
How to apply: Contact your high school guidance counselor.

(1770) · Robert C. Byrd Honors Scholarship Program - New Hampshire

New Hampshire Postsecondary Education Commission
3 Barrell Court
Suite 300
Concord, NH 03301
Phone: 603-271-2555 x352
Fax: 603-271-2696
Email: jknapp@pec.state.nh.us
Website: http://www.state.nh.us/postsecondary
Purpose: To assist exceptional New Hampshire students in postsecondary study.
Eligibility: Applicants must be New Hampshire residents, U.S. citizens or eligible noncitizens and high school seniors who plan to be full-time college students.
Target applicant:
　　High school students
Minimum GPA: None.
Amount: $1,500.
Number of awards: Varies.
Deadline: First Friday in April.
How to apply: Contact the New Hampshire Department of Education for more information and an application.

(1771) · Robert C. Byrd Honors Scholarship Program - New Jersey

State of New Jersey Department of Education
P.O. Box 500
Trenton, NJ 08625
Phone: 609-292-4469
Website: http://www.state.nj.us/education
Purpose: To reward academic achievement in graduating seniors and GED recipients.
Eligibility: Applicants must be New Jersey residents who are U.S. citizens or permanent residents. Scholarships are awarded based on merit and are renewable for four years of undergraduate study.
Target applicant:
　　High school students
Minimum GPA: None.
Amount: Up to $1,500.
Number of awards: Varies.
Scholarship may be renewable.
Deadline: Varies.
How to apply: Applications are available from the department of education and school officials.

(1772) · Robert C. Byrd Honors Scholarship Program - New Mexico

New Mexico Public Education Department
300 Don Gaspar
Santa Fe, NM 87501
Phone: 505-827-5800
Website: http://www.ped.state.nm.us
Purpose: To recognize the educational accomplishments of outstanding students.
Eligibility: Applicants must be New Mexico residents who are graduating high school seniors or who have received a GED. They must have a GPA of at least 3.5 and score higher than 1220 on the SAT or higher than 27 on the ACT.

Target applicant:
    High school students
Minimum GPA: 3.5
Amount: $1,500.
Number of awards: 44.
Scholarship may be renewable.
Deadline: Varies.
How to apply: Applications are available from school officials and the public education department.

(1773) · Robert C. Byrd Honors Scholarship Program - New York

New York State Higher Education Services Corporation (HESC)
99 Washington Avenue
Albany, NY 12255
Phone: 888-697-4372
Email: hescwebmail@hesc.org
Website: http://www.hesc.com
Purpose: To assist outstanding New York State high school graduates.
Eligibility: Applicants must be high school seniors, New York residents, plan to attend an institution of higher education and have a minimum high school average of 95 or GED of 310 and minimum SAT score of 1250.
Target applicant:
    High school students
Minimum GPA: 3.7
Amount: Up to $1,500.
Number of awards: Varies.
Scholarship may be renewable.
Deadline: Varies.
How to apply: Contact your high school guidance counselor.

(1774) · Robert C. Byrd Honors Scholarship Program - North Carolina

North Carolina Department of Public Instruction
Center for Recruitment and Retention
Division of Human Resource Management, Department of Public Instruction
301 N. Wilmington Street
Wilmington, NC 27601
Phone: 919-807-3300
Fax: 919-807-3362
Email: scholars@dpi.state.nc.us
Website: http://www.ncpublicschools.org
Purpose: To assist academically outstanding North Carolina high school students.
Eligibility: Applicants must be legal North Carolina residents, graduate from a North Carolina high school, have a minimum SAT score of 900 and a minimum 3.0 GPA and be accepted to an approved postsecondary institution in the U.S.
Target applicant:
    High school students
Minimum GPA: 3.0
Amount: $1,500.
Number of awards: 160.
Scholarship may be renewable.
Deadline: February.
How to apply: Students must be nominated by their schools. Contact your high school guidance counselor.

(1775) · Robert C. Byrd Honors Scholarship Program - North Dakota

North Dakota Department of Public Instruction
600 E. Boulevard Avenue, Dept. 201
Floors 9, 10, and 11
Bismarck, ND 58505
Phone: 701-328-2260
Fax: 701-328-2461
Website: http://www.dpi.state.nd.us
Purpose: To recognize outstanding academic achievement.
Eligibility: Applicants must be North Dakota residents who are graduating seniors or have earned a GED. Academic achievement, potential for future academic achievement, leadership, extracurricular involvement and community service will all be considered in awarding the scholarship.
Target applicant:
    High school students
Minimum GPA: None.
Amount: $1,500.
Number of awards: At least 8.
Scholarship may be renewable.
Deadline: Late April.
How to apply: Applications are available from school officials and the department of public instruction.

(1776) · Robert C. Byrd Honors Scholarship Program - Ohio

Ohio Department of Education
25 S. Front Street
Columbus, OH 43128
Phone: 614-466-4590
Email: contact.center@ode.state.oh.us
Website: http://www.ode.state.oh.us
Purpose: To assist outstanding Ohio high school students.
Eligibility: Applicants must be Ohio high school seniors who plan to attend an accredited U.S. undergraduate college or university. This award is given to at least one student in each of Ohio's congressional districts. Selection is based on academic achievement and participation in leadership activities.
Target applicant:
    High school students
Minimum GPA: None.
Amount: Varies.
Number of awards: Varies.
Scholarship may be renewable.
Deadline: Second Friday in March.
How to apply: Contact your high school guidance counselor.

(1777) · Robert C. Byrd Honors Scholarship Program - Oklahoma

Oklahoma State Department of Education
Professional Services Division
Oliver Hodge Building
2500 North Lincoln Boulevard
Oklahoma City, OK 73105
Phone: 405-521-2808
Email: studentinfo@osrhe.edu
Website: http://www.okhighered.org
Purpose: To assist outstanding Oklahoma high school students.

Eligibility: Applicants must be high school seniors who are outstanding academically, U.S. citizens or eligible noncitizens, legal residents of Oklahoma, plan to attend full-time an institution of higher education and meet academic requirements.

Target applicant:
High school students

Minimum GPA: None.

Amount: Varies.

Number of awards: Varies.

Scholarship may be renewable.

Deadline: Varies.

How to apply: Contact your high school guidance counselor.

(1778) · Robert C. Byrd Honors Scholarship Program - Oregon

Oregon Student Assistance Commission
1500 Valley River Drive
Suite 100
Eugene, OR 97401
Phone: 541-687-7400
Fax: 541-687-7414
Email: awardinfo@mercury.osac.state.or.us
Website: http://www.osac.state.or.us

Purpose: To assist Oregon high school students.

Eligibility: Applicants must be Oregon high school seniors, have a minimum 3.85 GPA or minimum GED score of 325 and have a minimum SAT score of 1300 or ACT score of 29.

Target applicant:
High school students

Minimum GPA: 3.85

Amount: Varies.

Number of awards: Varies.

Scholarship may be renewable.

Deadline: March 1.

How to apply: Applications are available online.

(1779) · Robert C. Byrd Honors Scholarship Program - Pennsylvania

Pennsylvania Higher Education Assistance Agency
P.O. Box 8114
Harrisburg, PA 17105
Phone: 800-692-7392
Website: http://www.pheaa.org

Purpose: To assist outstanding Pennsylvania high school students.

Eligibility: Applicants must be high school seniors, Pennsylvania residents, accepted for enrollment at an eligible institution of higher education and U.S. citizens or permanent residents. Applicants must also rank in the top 5 percent of their class, have a minimum 3.5 GPA and have a minimum SAT score of 1150, ACT score of 25 or GED score of 355.

Target applicant:
High school students

Minimum GPA: 3.5

Amount: Varies.

Number of awards: Varies.

Deadline: Varies.

How to apply: Applications are available through your high school counselor or by written request.

(1780) · Robert C. Byrd Honors Scholarship Program - Rhode Island

Rhode Island Department of Elementary and Secondary Education
255 Westminster Street
Providence, RI 02903
Phone: 401-222-4600
Website: http://www.ridoe.net

Purpose: To reward high scholastic achievement.

Eligibility: Applicants must be graduating high school seniors or GED recipients who are residents of Rhode Island and U.S. citizens. The scholarship is awarded based on academic achievements and the student's potential for continued achievement in post-secondary education.

Target applicant:
High school students

Minimum GPA: None.

Amount: $1,500.

Number of awards: Varies.

Scholarship may be renewable.

Deadline: Varies.

How to apply: Applications are available from the Department of Elementary and Secondary Education and from school officials.

(1781) · Robert C. Byrd Honors Scholarship Program - South Carolina

South Carolina Department of Education
Beth Cope, Education Associate
Suite 701
1429 Senate Street
Columbia, SC 29201
Phone: 803-734-8116
Fax: 803-734-8701
Email: info@ed.sc.gov
Website: http://www.ed.sc.gov

Purpose: To help outstanding high school seniors pursue higher education.

Eligibility: Applicants must be graduating seniors in a South Carolina high school. Public, private and home-schooled students are eligible. Applicants must have a score of at least 1300 on the SAT or a score of at least 29 on the ACT and a GPA of 3.5 or higher.

Target applicant:
High school students

Minimum GPA: 3.5

Amount: $1,500.

Number of awards: 96.

Scholarship may be renewable.

Deadline: February 1.

How to apply: Schools and home-school associations select applicants.

(1782) · Robert C. Byrd Honors Scholarship Program - South Dakota

South Dakota Department of Education and Cultural Affairs
700 Governors Drive
Pierre, SD 57501
Phone: 605-773-3426
Website: http://doe.sd.gov

Purpose: To assist outstanding South Dakota high school students.

Eligibility: Applicants must be South Dakota high school seniors who plan to attend full-time an eligible institution of higher education, meet course requirements, have a minimum 3.5 GPA and have a minimum ACT score of 24.

Target applicant:
   High school students
Minimum GPA: 3.5
Amount: Varies.
Number of awards: Varies.
Scholarship may be renewable.
Deadline: May 1.
How to apply: Applications are available online.

(1783) · Robert C. Byrd Honors Scholarship Program - Tennessee

Tennessee Student Assistance Corporation
404 James Robertson Parkway
Suite 1510, Parkway Towers
Nashville, TN 37243
Phone: 800-342-1663
Fax: 615-741-6101
Email: tsac.aidinfo@state.tn.us
Website: http://www.collegepaystn.com
Purpose: To assist outstanding Tennessee high school students.
Eligibility: Applicants must be U.S. citizens or permanent residents, be Tennessee residents, be graduating high school seniors or GED recipients and have a minimum 3.5 GPA and minimum ACT score of 24.
Target applicant:
   High school students
Minimum GPA: 3.5
Amount: Varies.
Number of awards: Varies.
Deadline: March 1.
How to apply: Contact your high school guidance counselor.

(1784) · Robert C. Byrd Honors Scholarship Program - Texas

Texas Higher Education Coordinating Board
P.O. Box 12788
Austin, TX 78711
Phone: 512-427-6101
Fax: 512-427-6127
Website: http://www.collegefortexans.com
Purpose: To assist outstanding Texas high school students.
Eligibility: Applicants must be U.S. citizens or permanent residents who are Texas residents, graduating high school seniors or GED recipients and be nominated by their school.
Target applicant:
   High school students
Minimum GPA: None.
Amount: Varies.
Number of awards: Varies.
Scholarship may be renewable.
Deadline: Varies.
How to apply: Contact your high school guidance counselor.

(1785) · Robert C. Byrd Honors Scholarship Program - Utah

Utah State Office of Education
250 East 500 South
P.O. Box 144200
Salt Lake City, UT 84114
Website: http://www.usoe.k12.ut.us

Purpose: To recognize graduating seniors who have demonstrated academic excellence.
Eligibility: Applicants must be graduating high school seniors in Utah or have an equivalent certificate of graduation. They must be accepted at a post-secondary institution and be planning to attend full-time. Applicants must show evidence of outstanding academic achievement, including a GPA of at least 3.7 and an ACT score of 25 or higher. Applicants must be U.S. citizens or permanent residents.
Target applicant:
   High school students
Minimum GPA: 3.7
Amount: $1,500.
Number of awards: Varies.
Scholarship may be renewable.
Deadline: March 30.
How to apply: Applications are available online.

(1786) · Robert C. Byrd Honors Scholarship Program - Vermont

Vermont Student Assistance Corporation
10 E. Allen Street
P.O. Box 2000
Winooski, VT 05404
Phone: 888-253-4819
Fax: 802-654-3765
Email: info@vsac.org
Website: http://www.vsac.org
Purpose: To recognize students who achieve academic excellence.
Eligibility: Applicants must be graduating high school seniors who have demonstrated academic excellence and show promise for future academic achievements. They must attend an accredited post-secondary institution full-time. Applicants must be residents of Vermont and U.S. citizens or permanent residents.
Target applicant:
   High school students
Minimum GPA: None.
Amount: $1,500.
Number of awards: Up to 15.
Scholarship may be renewable.
Deadline: May 1.
How to apply: Applications are available online.

(1787) · Robert C. Byrd Honors Scholarship Program - Virginia

Virginia Department of Education
P.O. Box 2120
Richmond, VA 23218
Phone: 804-225-3349
Fax: 804-371-2456
Email: joseph.wharff@doe.virginia.gov
Website: http://www.pen.k12.va.us
Purpose: To assist Virginia high school students.
Eligibility: Applicants must be U.S. citizens or eligible noncitizens, Virginia residents, high school seniors and demonstrate academic excellence.
Target applicant:
   High school students
Minimum GPA: None.
Amount: Varies.
Number of awards: Varies.
Deadline: Varies.
How to apply: Contact your high school guidance counselor.

(1788) · Robert C. Byrd Honors Scholarship Program - Washington

Office of Superintendent of Public Instruction
Old Capitol Building
P.O. Box 47200
Olympia, WA 98504
Phone: 360-725-6000
Website: http://www.k12.wa.us
Purpose: To assist outstanding Washington high school students.
Eligibility: Applicants must be U.S. citizens or eligible noncitizens, Washington residents, high school seniors and demonstrate academic excellence.
Target applicant:
  High school students
Minimum GPA: None.
Amount: Varies.
Number of awards: Varies.
Deadline: Varies.
How to apply: Contact your high school guidance counselor.

(1789) · Robert C. Byrd Honors Scholarship Program - West Virginia

West Virginia Higher Education Policy Commission
1018 Kanawha Boulevard, East
Fifth Floor
Charleston, WV 25301
Phone: 304-558-2101
Fax: 304-558-5719
Website: http://www.hepc.wvnet.edu
Purpose: To assist outstanding West Virginia high school students.
Eligibility: Applicants must be U.S. citizens or eligible noncitizens, be West Virginia residents, be high school seniors and demonstrate academic excellence.
Target applicant:
  High school students
Minimum GPA: None.
Amount: Varies.
Number of awards: Varies.
Deadline: March 1.
How to apply: Contact your high school guidance counselor.

(1790) · Robert C. Byrd Honors Scholarship Program - Wisconsin

Wisconsin Department of Public Instruction
125 S. Webster Street
P.O. Box 7841
Madison, WI 53707
Phone: 800-441-4563
Website: http://www.dpi.state.wi.us
Purpose: To assist outstanding Wisconsin students.
Eligibility: Applicants must be U.S. citizens or eligible noncitizens, be Wisconsin residents, be high school seniors and demonstrate academic excellence.
Target applicant:
  High school students
Minimum GPA: None.
Amount: Varies.
Number of awards: Varies.
Deadline: Third week in February.
How to apply: Applicants are nominated by their high schools.

(1791) · Robert C. Byrd Honors Scholarship Program - Wyoming

Wyoming Department of Education
2300 Capitol Avenue
Hathaway Building, 2nd Floor
Cheyenne, WY 82002
Phone: 307-777-7673
Fax: 307-777-6234
Email: webmaster@educ.state.ky.us
Website: http://www.k12.wy.us
Purpose: To assist outstanding Wyoming students.
Eligibility: Applicants must be U.S. citizens or eligible noncitizens, be Wyoming residents, be high school seniors and demonstrate academic excellence.
Target applicant:
  High school students
Minimum GPA: None.
Amount: Varies.
Number of awards: Varies.
Scholarship may be renewable.
Deadline: Varies.
How to apply: Individual applications are NOT available from the Wyoming Department of Education. Contact your high school guidance counselor for an application.

(1792) · Robert D. Blue Scholarship

Treasurer of State
Capitol Building
Des Moines, IA 50319
Phone: 515-281-3067
Fax: 515-281-6962
Email: treasurer@tos.state.ia.us
Website: http://www.rdblue.org
Purpose: To provide financial assistance to deserving Iowa students.
Eligibility: Applicants must be Iowa residents who plan to attend an Iowa institution of higher learning the following school year. They may be high school seniors or current college students. An essay and two references are required.
Target applicant:
  High school students
  College students
  Adult students
Minimum GPA: None.
Amount: Varies.
Number of awards: Varies.
Deadline: May 10.
How to apply: Applications are available online.

(1793) · Rockefeller State Wildlife Scholarship

Louisiana Office of Student Financial Assistance
P.O. Box 91202
Baton Rouge, LA 70821-9202
Phone: 800-259-5626 x1012
Fax: 225-922-0790
Email: custserv@osfa.la.gov
Website: http://www.osfa.state.la.us
Purpose: To assist Louisiana students in wildlife, forestry or marine science.
Eligibility: Applicants must be Louisiana residents for at least one year, be enrolled as full-time undergraduate or graduate students in a Louisiana public college or university, earn a degree in wildlife, forestry

or marine science and have a minimum 2.5 GPA. Applicants must also submit the Free Application for Federal Student Aid (FAFSA) and be U.S. citizens.

Target applicant:
High school students
College students
Graduate school students
Adult students
Minimum GPA: 2.5
Amount: $1,000.
Number of awards: Varies.
Scholarship may be renewable.
Deadline: July 31.
How to apply: Applications are available online or by written request.

(1794) · Roger L. Foster Scholarship

Virginia Police Chiefs Foundation
1606 Santa Rosa Road
Suite 134
Richmond, VA 23288
Phone: 804-285-8227
Fax: 804-285-3363
Website: http://www.vapolicefoundation.org/scholarships/scholarships_rf.html
Purpose: To assist children of Virginia police officers in obtaining higher education.
Eligibility: Applicants must be dependents of active Commonwealth of Virginia police officers. Children of sheriff's deputies, federal officers and civilians working in police agencies are not eligible. Applicants must be enrolled in or accepted to a college or university where they will pursue their first undergraduate degree as a full-time student.
Target applicant:
High school students
College students
Adult students
Minimum GPA: None.
Amount: Varies.
Number of awards: Varies.
Deadline: April 4.
How to apply: Applications are available online.

(1795) · Rosa L. Parks Scholarships

Rosa L. Parks Scholarship Foundation
P.O. Box 950
Detroit, MI 48231
Phone: 313-222-2538
Email: rpscholarship@dnps.com
Website: http://www.rosaparksscholarshipfoundation.org
Purpose: To provide education funds for students who hold ideals close to those of Rosa Parks.
Eligibility: Applicants must be Michigan high school seniors who will graduate by August of the application year. They must have a GPA of 2.5 or higher and have taken the SAT or ACT. An essay is required.
Target applicant:
High school students
Minimum GPA: 2.5
Amount: Varies.
Number of awards: Varies.
Deadline: Varies.
How to apply: Applications are available online.

(1796) · Rosedale Post 346 Scholarship

American Legion, Department of Kansas
1314 SW Topeka Boulevard
Topeka, KS 66612
Phone: 785-232-9315
Fax: 785-232-1399
Website: http://www.ksamlegion.org
Purpose: To assist the children of members of the Kansas American Legion or American Legion Auxiliary.
Eligibility: Applicants must be high school seniors or college freshmen or sophomores who are enrolling or enrolled in an approved post-secondary school. They also must be average or better students who are the children of veterans. The children of deceased parents are also eligible if the parent was a paid member at the time of death. Applicants must submit three letters of recommendation, with at least one from a teacher, an essay on "Why I Want to Go to College," a 1040 income statement, documentation of parent's veteran status and a certified high school transcript.
Target applicant:
High school students
College students
Adult students
Minimum GPA: None.
Amount: $1,500.
Number of awards: 2.
Deadline: February 15.
How to apply: Applications are available online.

(1797) · Rosemary and Nellie Ebrie Foundation

Hawaii Department of Education (DOE)
900 Fort Street Mall
Suite 1300
Honolulu, HI 96813
Phone: 808-566-5570
Email: hern@hawaii.edu
Website: http://doe.k12.hi.us
Purpose: To assist college and graduate students who have Hawaiian ancestry or were born or have been a long-time residents of the Island.
Eligibility: Applicants must be residents of the Island of Hawaii and be of Hawaiian or part-Hawaiian ancestry. Applicants must also submit a four-sheet application and financial form, personal statement, recommendations and transcript.
Target applicant:
High school students
College students
Graduate school students
Adult students
Minimum GPA: None.
Amount: Varies.
Number of awards: Varies.
Deadline: March 1.
How to apply: Applications are available by written request.

(1798) · Rosewood Family Scholarship Program

Florida Department of Education
Office of Student Financial Assistance
1940 N. Monroe Street
Suite 70
Tallahassee, FL 32303-4759
Phone: 888-827-2004

Fax: 850-245-9667
Email: osfa@fldoe.org
Website: http://www.floridastudentfinancialaid.org
Purpose: To help Florida minority students especially direct descendants of Rosewood families.
Eligibility: Applicants must be full-time, undergraduate minority students (Black, Hispanic, Asian, Pacific Islander, American Indian or Alaskan native) who attend state universities, public community colleges or public postsecondary vocational-technical schools. Direct descendants of Rosewood families affected by the incidents of January, 1923 receive preference. The descendants must provide family information on the Florida Financial Aid Application.
Target applicant:
    High school students
    College students
    Adult students
Minimum GPA: None.
Amount: Varies.
Number of awards: 25.
Scholarship may be renewable.
Deadline: April 1.
How to apply: Applicants must submit the Initial Student Florida Financial Aid Applications online by April 1. Florida residents must submit the Free Application for Federal Student Aid (FAFSA) online by May 15. Non-residents must submit the FAFSA in time to receive the Student Aid Report (SAR) from the processor and send a copy of the SAR to the Office of Student Financial Assistance by May 15.

(1799) · Ruppert Educational Grant Program

Silicon Valley Community Foundation
2440 W. El Camino Real
Suite 300
Mountain View, CA 94040
Phone: 650-450-5400
Fax: 650-450-5401
Email: scholarships@siliconvalleycf.org
Website: http://www.siliconvalleycf.org
Purpose: To assist California students who are "late bloomers."
Eligibility: Applicants must be U.S. citizens, be high school seniors in San Mateo County or northern Santa Clara County (Daly City through Mountain View) and have a maximum GPA of 3.3. Students must demonstrate financial need; evidence of partial self-support such as savings from summer jobs, part-time work, etc.; community service and academic promise and GPA improvement during high school years.
Target applicant:
    High school students
Minimum GPA: None.
Amount: $2,000.
Number of awards: Up to 30.
Deadline: March 5.
How to apply: Applications are available online.

(1800) · Ruth Ann Johnson Fund

Greater Kanawha Valley Foundation
1600 Huntington Square
900 Lee Street, East
Charleston, WV 25301
Phone: 304-346-3620
Fax: 304-346-3640
Email: tgkvf@tgkvf.org
Website: http://www.tgkvf.org

Purpose: To provide financial assistance to West Virginia residents who are interested in pursuing a college education.
Eligibility: Applicants must be residents of West Virginia, be full-time students (12 credit hours) and possess good moral character and proven academic achievement.
Target applicant:
    High school students
    College students
    Adult students
Minimum GPA: 2.5
Amount: $1,000.
Number of awards: 39.
Scholarship may be renewable.
Deadline: February 17.
How to apply: Applications are available online or by emailing shoover@tgkvf.org.

(1801) · Safety Essay Contest

American Legion, Department of New Jersey
135 W. Hanover Street
Trenton, NJ 08618
Phone: 609-695-5418
Fax: 609-394-1532
Email: adjudant@njamericanlegion.org
Website: http://www.njamericanlegion.org
Purpose: To award students for exceptional essays regarding safety.
Eligibility: Applicants must be in the 6th, 7th or 8th grade and enrolled in a New Jersey school.
Target applicant:
    Junior high students or younger
Minimum GPA: None.
Amount: Varies.
Number of awards: Varies.
Deadline: March 23.
How to apply: Application information is available from the local Department.

(1802) · Sallie Mae Bank Scholarships

Sallie Mae Bank
P.O. Box 9500
Wilkes-Barre, PA 18773-9500
Phone: 703-984-5628
Website: http://www.salliemae.com/content/salliemaebank
Purpose: To provide financial assistance to engineering, nursing and teaching students.
Eligibility: Applicants must be undergraduate students who are majoring in engineering, nursing or teaching. They must provide proof of application and acceptance from an approved, accredited institution of higher learning in Salt Lake County or Utah County, Utah. Students enrolling in an online school must provide proof of residence in one of these counties.
Target applicant:
    High school students
    College students
    Adult students
Minimum GPA: None.
Amount: $5,000.
Number of awards: 15.
Deadline: March 31.
How to apply: Applications are available from financial aid departments of qualifying schools.

(1803) · San Francisco Section Daniel Cubicciotti Student Award

Electrochemical Society
65 South Main Street, Building D
Pennington, NJ 08534-2839
Phone: 609-737-1902
Fax: 609-737-2743
Email: awards@electrochem.org
Website: http://www.electrochem.org
Purpose: To help a deserving student in Northern California to pursue a career in the physical sciences or engineering.
Eligibility: Applicants must be full- or part-time graduate or advanced undergraduate students in good standing at a university or college in Northern California. Students must major in metallurgy, materials science, chemical engineering or chemistry and be involved in thesis research or other academic activities that relate to electrochemistry. Applicants may be nominated by anyone familiar with their qualifications. The applicant does not have to be a member of The Electrochemical Society. The award is based on academic excellence, quality of research activities, a demonstrated interest in the study of electrochemistry and personal characteristics that reflect Dan Cubicciotti's integrity. Community service and participation in other activities will also be considered.
Target applicant:
    College students
    Graduate school students
    Adult students
Minimum GPA: None.
Amount: $2,000.
Number of awards: 1.
Deadline: February 15.
How to apply: Applicants should submit transcripts, a short description of their history and interests and a letter of recommendation from a university or college faculty member from the appropriate department.

(1804) · Sandy Weisenberger Endowment

Epsilon Sigma Alpha Foundation
P.O. Box 270517
Fort Collins, CO 80527
Phone: 970-223-2824
Fax: 970-223-4456
Email: kloyd@knoxy.net
Website: http://www.esaintl.com/esaf
Purpose: To provide financial assistance for Minnesota residents.
Eligibility: Applicants may attend any school and pursue any major. Selection is based equally on character, leadership, service, financial need and scholastic ability.
Target applicant:
    High school students
    College students
    Adult students
Minimum GPA: None.
Amount: $1,000.
Number of awards: 1.
Deadline: February 1.
How to apply: Applications are available online.

(1805) · Sara E. Jenne Scholarship

Montana State Elks Association
P.O. Box 1274
Polson, MT 59860
Phone: 406-849-5276
Email: robert058@centurytel.net
Website: http://www.elksmt.com
Purpose: To support undergraduate students in Montana.
Eligibility: Students must have completed one year of college or technical school with at least 30 semester hours, and they must have at least a 2.0 GPA. Applicants must show financial need and good character.
Target applicant:
    College students
    Adult students
Minimum GPA: 2.0
Amount: Varies.
Number of awards: Varies.
Deadline: June 1.
How to apply: Applications are available online.

(1806) · Scan|Design Foundation by Inger and Jens Bruun Scholarship for Study in Denmark

Northwest Danish Foundation
Meridian Office Building
1833 North 105th Street, Suite 203
Seattle, WA 98133
Phone: 800-564-7736
Fax: 206-729-6997
Email: seattle@nwdanish.org
Website: http://www.northwestdanishfoundation.org
Purpose: To provide funds for students who wish to study in Denmark.
Eligibility: Applicants must be 18 years of age or older and be Washington or Oregon residents or students who wish to study in Denmark. They may pursue academic, vocational, cultural or artistic studies.
Target applicant:
    High school students
    College students
    Adult students
Minimum GPA: None.
Amount: $5,000.
Number of awards: 1.
Deadline: March 31.
How to apply: Applications are available online.

(1807) · Schneider-Emanuel American Legion Scholarship

American Legion, Department of Wisconsin
2930 American Legion Drive
P.O. Box 388
Portage, WI 53901
Phone: 608-745-1090
Fax: 608-745-0179
Email: info@wilegion.org
Website: http://www.wilegion.org
Purpose: To award scholarships to American Legion members and their children or grandchildren and members of the Sons of the American Legion or Auxiliary.

Eligibility: Applicants must have graduated from an accredited Wisconsin high school and plan to earn an undergraduate degree at a U.S. college or university. Applicants must also have participated in one or more American Legion-sponsored activities listed in the eligibility requirements.
Target applicant:
    High school students
    College students
    Adult students
Minimum GPA: 3.0
Amount: $1,000.
Number of awards: 3.
Deadline: March 1.
How to apply: Applications are available online.

(1808) · Scholars Program

North Dakota University System
10th Floor, State Capitol
600 E. Boulevard Avenue, Dept. 215
Bismarck, ND 58505
Phone: 701-328-2960
Fax: 701-328-2961
Email: ndus.office@ndus.nodak.edu
Website: http://www.ndus.edu
Purpose: To assist outstanding North Dakota high school students.
Eligibility: Applicants must be North Dakota high school seniors, score in the top 20 percent of all students in North Dakota who take the ACT, be in the top 20 percent of their class and attend a North Dakota public or tribal college.
Target applicant:
    High school students
Minimum GPA: None.
Amount: Full tuition.
Number of awards: 40-45.
Scholarship may be renewable.
Deadline: Varies.
How to apply: Applications are available by written request.

(1809) · Scholarship Assistance Program (SAP)

Nebraska Coordinating Commission for Postsecondary Education
P.O. Box 95005
Lincoln, NE 68509
Phone: 402-471-2847
Fax: 402-471-2886
Email: ritchie.morrow@ccpe.ne.gov
Website: http://www.ccpe.state.ne.us
Purpose: To assist Nebraska students attend a Nebraska college or university.
Eligibility: Applicants must be residents of the state of Nebraska, qualify for a federal Pell grant and be enrolled in a Nebraska college. Applicants apply for the grant through their specific college or university.
Target applicant:
    College students
    Adult students
Minimum GPA: None.
Amount: Varies.
Number of awards: Varies.
Scholarship may be renewable.
Deadline: Varies.
How to apply: Complete the Free Application for Federal Student Aid (FAFSA).

(1810) · Scholarships for Academic Excellence

New York State Higher Education Services Corporation (HESC)
99 Washington Avenue
Albany, NY 12255
Phone: 888-697-4372
Email: hescwebmail@hesc.org
Website: http://www.hesc.com
Purpose: To assist outstanding New York State high school graduates.
Eligibility: Applicants must be New York residents who are high school seniors, plan to study at an eligible undergraduate program in New York State and are U.S. citizens or eligible noncitizens. Selection is based on grades in Regents exams.
Target applicant:
    High school students
Minimum GPA: None.
Amount: $500-$1,500.
Number of awards: 8,000.
Scholarship may be renewable.
Deadline: Varies.
How to apply: Students are nominated by their high schools.

(1811) · Scholarships for Orphans of Veterans

New Hampshire Postsecondary Education Commission
3 Barrell Court
Suite 300
Concord, NH 03301
Phone: 603-271-2555 x352
Fax: 603-271-2696
Email: jknapp@pec.state.nh.us
Website: http://www.state.nh.us/postsecondary
Purpose: To provide financial assistance to children of veterans of armed conflict who died while on active duty or from a service-related disability.
Eligibility: Applicants must be New Hampshire residents between the ages of 16 and 25, enrolled in college at least half-time at a New Hampshire public institution of higher learning and have a parent or parents who died while on active duty or from service-related disability.
Target applicant:
    College students
Minimum GPA: None.
Amount: Up to $2,500.
Number of awards: Varies.
Scholarship may be renewable.
How to apply: Applications are available by phone.

(1812) · Science and Technology Scholarship

Maryland Higher Education Commission
Office of Student Financial Assistance
839 Bestgate Road, Suite 400
Annapolis, MD 21401
Phone: 800-974-1024
Fax: 410-260-3200
Email: osfamail@mhec.state.md.us
Website: http://www.mhec.state.md.us
Purpose: To assist Maryland students who are earning an undergraduate degree in the sciences.
Eligibility: Applicants and their parents must be Maryland residents. Applicants not currently enrolled in college must have a cumulative high school GPA of 3.0 or higher. All applicants enrolled in college must have a minimum 3.0 GPA. You must intend to enroll, or be

enrolled, at a two- or four-year Maryland college or university as a full-time, degree-seeking undergraduate and major in one of the following degree programs: biological sciences, computer information science, engineering, mathematics or physical sciences.

Target applicant:
    High school students
    College students
    Adult students
Minimum GPA: 3.0
Amount: $1,000-$3,000.
Number of awards: Varies.
Deadline: January 1-March 1.
How to apply: Complete and file the HOPE Scholarship application.

(1813) · Science or Other Studies Scholarship

Los Alamos National Laboratory Foundation
1302 Calle de la Merced
Suite A
Espanola, NM 87532
Phone: 505-753-8890
Fax: 505-753-8915
Email: info@lanlfoundation.org
Website: http://www.lanlfoundation.org
Purpose: To support undergraduate students in Northern New Mexico.
Eligibility: Students must have at least a 3.25 GPA, and they must have either an SAT score of at least 1350 or an ACT score of at least 19. Applicants must submit an essay and two letters of recommendation.
Target applicant:
    High school students
    College students
    Adult students
Minimum GPA: 3.25
Amount: $1,000-$2,000.
Number of awards: Varies.
Scholarship may be renewable.
Deadline: January 22.
How to apply: Applications are available online.

(1814) · Second Chance Endowment

Epsilon Sigma Alpha Foundation
P.O. Box 270517
Fort Collins, CO 80527
Phone: 970-223-2824
Fax: 970-223-4456
Email: kloyd@knoxy.net
Website: http://www.esaintl.com/esaf
Purpose: To provide financial assistance to non-traditional students.
Eligibility: Applicants must be Illinois residents. They must be at least 25 years of age and be pursuing continuing education to obtain new skills or update existing skills. They may major in any field at any college or university. Selection is based on service (5 percent), character (10 percent), leadership (10 percent), scholastic ability (25 percent) and financial need (50 percent).
Target applicant:
    College students
    Adult students
Minimum GPA: None.
Amount: $1,000.
Number of awards: 1.
Deadline: February 1.
How to apply: Applications are available online.

(1815) · Senator George J. Mitchell Scholarship Research Institute Scholarships

Mitchell Institute
22 Monument Square, Suite 200
Portland, ME 04101
Phone: 888-220-7209
Email: info@mitchellinstitute.org
Website: http://www.mitchellinstitute.org
Purpose: To provide educational opportunities to students in Maine.
Eligibility: Applicants must be legal residents of Maine graduating from a public high school in Maine and attending a two- or four-year program at an accredited college. Scholarships are based on academic performance, community service and financial need. One scholarship is given out at every Maine public high school, with one extra scholarship per county intended for first-generation college students. While the deadline for the application is April 1, supporting materials have a deadline of May 1.
Target applicant:
    High school students
Minimum GPA: None.
Amount: $1,250-$1,500.
Number of awards: Varies.
Scholarship may be renewable.
Deadline: April 1.
How to apply: Applications are available online.

(1816) · Senator Patricia K. McGee Nursing Faculty Scholarship

New York State Higher Education Services Corporation (HESC)
99 Washington Avenue
Albany, NY 12255
Phone: 888-697-4372
Email: hescwebmail@hesc.org
Website: http://www.hesc.com
Purpose: To increase the number of nursing educators and clinical faculty members in the State of New York.
Eligibility: Applicants must be U.S. citizens or eligible non-citizens and residents of New York for one year or more. They must be registered nurses who are licensed in New York, and they must be accepted into a graduate nursing program at an approved college or university in New York. Students must also agree to four years of service as nursing faculty in the state.
Target applicant:
    Graduate school students
    Adult students
Minimum GPA: None.
Amount: Up to $20,000.
Number of awards: Varies.
Scholarship may be renewable.
Deadline: Varies.
How to apply: Applications are available online after June of each year.

(1817) · Senatorial Scholarship

Maryland Higher Education Commission
Office of Student Financial Assistance
839 Bestgate Road, Suite 400
Annapolis, MD 21401
Phone: 800-974-1024
Fax: 410-260-3200

Email: osfamail@mhec.state.md.us
Website: http://www.mhec.state.md.us
Purpose: To assist Maryland undergraduate and graduate students who can demonstrate financial need.
Eligibility: Applicants must be U.S. citizens or eligible noncitizens, legal residents of the state of Maryland and complete the Free Application for Federal Student Aid (FAFSA). Some senators have supplementary forms. Contact your area's senator's office for complete details. All applicants must enroll at a two- or four-year Maryland college or university as degree-seeking undergraduate or graduate student or attend certain private career schools. Applicants must show financial need. High school applicants must also take the SAT I or the ACT.
Target applicant:
  High school students
  College students
  Graduate school students
  Adult students
Minimum GPA: None.
Amount: $200-$2,000.
Number of awards: Varies.
Scholarship may be renewable.
Deadline: Varies.
How to apply: Complete and file the Free Application for Federal Student Aid (FAFSA). Contact senator for specific application forms. The Office of Student Financial Assistance (OSFA) can provide a list of all State legislators.

(1818) · SERC Endowment

Epsilon Sigma Alpha Foundation
P.O. Box 270517
Fort Collins, CO 80527
Phone: 970-223-2824
Fax: 970-223-4456
Email: kloyd@knoxy.net
Website: http://www.esaintl.com/esaf
Purpose: To provide financial assistance to students in the Southeast.
Eligibility: Applicants must be residents of Alabama, Arkansas, Florida, Georgia, Kentucky, Louisiana, Maryland, Mississippi, North Carolina, South Carolina, Tennessee or Virginia. They may pursue any major at any school. Selection is based on scholastic ability (30 percent), financial need (30 percent), leadership (20 percent), character (10 percent) and service (10 percent).
Target applicant:
  High school students
  College students
  Adult students
Minimum GPA: None.
Amount: $900.
Number of awards: 1.
Deadline: February 1.
How to apply: Applications are available online.

(1819) · SGT Felix Delgreco Jr. Scholarship

Connecticut National Guard Foundation Inc.
State Armory
360 Broad Street
Hartford, CT 06105
Phone: 860-241-1550
Fax: 860-293-2929
Email: scholarship.committee@ctngfoundation.org
Website: http://www.ctngfoundation.org/Scholarship.asp

Purpose: To provide financial assistance to children of Connecticut National Guard members.
Eligibility: Applicants must be sons or daughters of a member of the Connecticut Army National Guard. They must be enrolled in or plan to attend an accredited degree or technical program.
Target applicant:
  High school students
  College students
  Adult students
Minimum GPA: None.
Amount: $3,000.
Number of awards: 1.
Deadline: March 1.
How to apply: Applications are available online.

(1820) · Sharon Petelle Specific Learning Disability Scholarship

Epsilon Sigma Alpha Foundation
P.O. Box 270517
Fort Collins, CO 80527
Phone: 970-223-2824
Fax: 970-223-4456
Email: kloyd@knoxy.net
Website: http://www.esaintl.com/esaf
Purpose: To provide financial assistance for students with learning disabilities.
Eligibility: Applicants may pursue any major at any institution of higher learning. Selection is based on the following criteria: character (25 percent), leadership (25 percent), service (20 percent), financial need (15 percent) and scholastic ability (15 percent).
Target applicant:
  High school students
  College students
  Adult students
Minimum GPA: None.
Amount: $505.
Number of awards: 1.
Deadline: February 1.
How to apply: Applications are available online.

(1821) · Sherman and Nancy Reece Scholarship

Epsilon Sigma Alpha Foundation
P.O. Box 270517
Fort Collins, CO 80527
Phone: 970-223-2824
Fax: 970-223-4456
Email: kloyd@knoxy.net
Website: http://www.esaintl.com/esaf
Purpose: To provide financial assistance to high school graduates from South Carolina and Virginia.
Eligibility: Applicants may pursue any major at any college or university. Selection is based on the following criteria: service (5 percent), character (10 percent), leadership (10 percent), scholastic ability (25 percent) and financial need (50 percent). Each year one award is presented to a South Carolina graduate and one to a Virginia graduate.
Target applicant:
  High school students
Minimum GPA: None.
Amount: $3,000.
Number of awards: 2.

Deadline: February 1.
How to apply: Applications are available online.

(1822) · Shirely McKown Scholarship Fund

Hawaii Community Foundation - Scholarships
1164 Bishop Street, Suite 800
Honolulu, HI 96813
Phone: 888-731-3863
Fax: 808-521-6286
Email: scholarships@hcf-hawaii.org
Website: http://www.hawaiicommunityfoundation.org
Purpose: To support Hawaii students who are majoring in journalism, advertising or public relations.
Eligibility: Applicants must be attending a four-year college or university with at least a 3.0 GPA. They must be college juniors, college seniors or graduate students.
Target applicant:
 College students
 Graduate school students
 Adult students
Minimum GPA: 3.0
Amount: $1,000.
Number of awards: 1.
Deadline: March 1.
How to apply: To apply, register online, complete the online application and select the scholarships to which you wish to apply. In addition, mail the supporting materials: printed confirmation page from the online application, personal statement, copy of Student Aid Report (SAR) available at www.fafsa.ed.gov and official transcript.

(1823) · Shirley A. Dreyer Memorial Endowment

Epsilon Sigma Alpha Foundation
P.O. Box 270517
Fort Collins, CO 80527
Phone: 970-223-2824
Fax: 970-223-4456
Email: kloyd@knoxy.net
Website: http://www.esaintl.com/esaf
Purpose: To honor the memory of Shirley A. Dreyer.
Eligibility: Applicants must be North Carolina residents and may attend any school and pursue any major. Selection is based on the following criteria: scholastic ability (30 percent), financial need (30 percent), leadership (20 percent), character (10 percent) and service (10 percent).
Target applicant:
 High school students
 College students
 Adult students
Minimum GPA: None.
Amount: $1,000.
Number of awards: 3.
Deadline: February 1.
How to apply: Applications are available online.

(1824) · Shirley C. Titus Scholarship Fund

California Nurses Association
2000 Franklin Street
Oakland, CA 94612
Phone: 510-273-2200
Email: execoffice@calnurses.org
Website: http://www.calnurse.org
Purpose: To assist California nurses to make them better leaders in the nursing profession.
Eligibility: Applicants must submit an essay describing their educational goals and vision for healthcare, two letters of recommendation, curriculum vitae and a copy of current RN license. Applications are based on educational plans, professional vision and participation in CNA, nursing or health-related organizations.
Target applicant:
 Graduate school students
 Adult students
Minimum GPA: None.
Amount: Varies.
Number of awards: Varies.
Deadline: July 1.
How to apply: Applications are available online.

(1825) · Shoe City-WB54/WB50 Scholarship

Central Scholarship Bureau
1700 Reisterstown Road
Suite 220
Baltimore, MD 21208-2903
Phone: 410-415-5558
Fax: 410-415-5501
Email: info@centralsb.org
Website: http://www.centralsb.org
Purpose: To help high school seniors who live in Maryland or Washington, DC.
Eligibility: Applicants must be permanent residents of Maryland or Washington, DC, plan to attend an accredited college or university full-time and demonstrate financial need. An application, budget form, school bill, transcript, school financial aid award letter and essay are required. Selection is based on financial need, teamwork/community service and academic excellence.
Target applicant:
 High school students
Minimum GPA: None.
Amount: $1,500.
Number of awards: 4.
Deadline: May 31.
How to apply: Applications are available online.

(1826) · Show Me State Endowment

Epsilon Sigma Alpha Foundation
P.O. Box 270517
Fort Collins, CO 80527
Phone: 970-223-2824
Fax: 970-223-4456
Email: kloyd@knoxy.net
Website: http://www.esaintl.com/esaf
Purpose: To provide financial assistance for Missouri students.
Eligibility: Applicants must be students from Missouri and may pursue any major at any school. Selection is based on the following characteristics: character (10 percent), leadership (20 percent), service (10 percent), financial need (30 percent) and scholastic ability (30 percent).
Target applicant:
 High school students
 College students
 Adult students

Minimum GPA: None.
Amount: $1,000.
Number of awards: 1.
Deadline: February 1.
How to apply: Applications are available online.

(1827) · Shuichi, Katsu and Itsuyo Suga Scholarship

Hawaii Community Foundation - Scholarships
1164 Bishop Street, Suite 800
Honolulu, HI 96813
Phone: 888-731-3863
Fax: 808-521-6286
Email: scholarships@hcf-hawaii.org
Website: http://www.hawaiicommunityfoundation.org
Purpose: To support Hawaii students who are majoring in math, physics or science and technology.
Eligibility: Applicants must have at least a 3.0 GPA.
Target applicant:
High school students
College students
Adult students
Minimum GPA: 3.0
Amount: $1,000.
Number of awards: 9.
Deadline: March 1.
How to apply: To apply, register online, complete the online application and select the scholarships to which you wish to apply. In addition, mail the supporting materials: printed confirmation page from the online application, personal statement, copy of Student Aid Report (SAR) available at www.fafsa.ed.gov and official transcript.

(1828) · Silver Knight Award

Miami Herald and El Herald Newspapers
One Herald Plaza
Miami, FL 33132
Phone: 305-376-2905
Email: silverknight@herald.com
Website: http://www.silverknightaward.com
Purpose: To recognize students for their academic achievement and contributions to their school and community.
Eligibility: Applicants must be high school seniors in Miami-Dade and Broward counties in Florida and be nominated by their schools.
Target applicant:
High school students
Minimum GPA: None.
Amount: $500-$1,500.
Number of awards: Varies.
Deadline: Last Friday in January.
How to apply: Contact your high school guidance counselor.

(1829) · Six Meter Club of Chicago Scholarship

American Radio Relay League Foundation
225 Main Street
Newington, CT 06111
Phone: 860-594-0397
Fax: 860-594-0259
Email: foundation@arrl.org
Website: http://www.arrl.org
Purpose: To support Illinois residents who are involved in amateur radio.

Eligibility: Applicants must have an active amateur radio license in any class. Students must be enrolled in an Illinois university or technical school for undergraduate study.
Target applicant:
High school students
College students
Adult students
Minimum GPA: None.
Amount: $500.
Number of awards: 1.
Deadline: February 1.
How to apply: Applications are available online.

(1830) · Skandalaris Family Foundation Scholarships

Skandalaris Family Foundation
840 West Long Lake Road
Suite 601
Troy, MI 48098
Phone: 248-220-2004
Fax: 248-220-2038
Email: info@skandalaris.com
Website: http://www.skandalaris.com
Purpose: To recognize students for their special talents, leadership skills, values and commitment to excellence.
Eligibility: Applicants must be U.S. citizens and high school seniors who have a GPA of 3.5 or higher and an ACT score of 27 or higher or an SAT score of 1200 or higher. Involvement in school, sports and community service is also considered. Most scholarships are granted to Michigan residents.
Target applicant:
High school students
Minimum GPA: 3.5
Amount: Varies.
Number of awards: Varies.
Scholarship may be renewable.
Deadline: May 1.
How to apply: Applications are available online.

(1831) · South Carolina Hope Scholarship

South Carolina Commission on Higher Education
1333 Main Street
Suite 200
Columbia, SC 29201
Phone: 803-737-2260
Fax: 803-737-2297
Email: shubbard@che.sc.gov
Website: http://www.che400.state.sc.us
Purpose: Monetary assistance is provided to those freshmen who do not qualify for LIFE or Palmetto Fellows Scholarships.
Eligibility: Applicants must attend an eligible South Carolina public or private college full-time, be South Carolina residents and have a minimum 3.0 GPA. The award is only applicable to the first year of college.
Target applicant:
High school students
Minimum GPA: 3.0
Amount: Varies.
Number of awards: Varies.
Deadline: Varies.
How to apply: Your college will determine your eligibility based on your high school transcript. There is no application form.

(1832) · South Carolina Sheriffs' Association Scholarships

South Carolina Sheriffs' Association
P.O. Box 21428
Columbia, SC 29221-1428
Phone: 803-772-1101
Fax: 803-772-1197
Website: http://www.sheriffsc.com
Purpose: To provide financial assistance to South Carolina students.
Eligibility: Applicants must be graduating high school seniors and residents of South Carolina. They must plan to attend a college or university in South Carolina. A 1,000-word essay, letters of recommendation from the student's principal and a guidance counselor or teacher and a transcript are required.
Target applicant:
   High school students
Minimum GPA: None.
Amount: $1,000-$2,000.
Number of awards: 5.
Deadline: February 22.
How to apply: Applications are available online.

(1833) · South Carolina Tuition Grants Program

South Carolina Tuition Grants Commission
101 Business Park Boulevard
Suite 2100
Columbia, SC 29203
Phone: 803-896-1120
Fax: 803-896-1126
Email: info@sctuitiongrants.org
Website: http://www.sctuitiongrants.com
Purpose: To assist students who wish to attend independent South Carolina colleges.
Eligibility: Students must be legal residents of South Carolina with financial need. High school seniors must graduate in the top 75 percent of their class or score a minimum of 900 on the SAT or 19 on the ACT. College applicants must complete and pass a minimum of 24 semester hours each year.
Target applicant:
   High school students
   College students
   Adult students
Minimum GPA: None.
Amount: Varies.
Number of awards: Varies.
Scholarship may be renewable.
Deadline: June 30.
How to apply: Fill out the FAFSA, which is available online.

(1834) · South Dakota Free Tuition for Veterans and Others Who Perfomed War Service

South Dakota Board of Regents
306 East Capitol Ave, Suite 200
Pierre, SD 57501-2545
Phone: 605-773-3455
Fax: 605-773-5320
Email: info@sdbor.edu
Website: http://www.sdbor.edu
Purpose: To allow veterans and others who served in war the opportunity to receive higher education.

Eligibility: Applicants must be veterans or others who performed active war service. They must South Dakota residents who qualify for resident tuition and not be entitled to have their tuition or expenses paid by the United States.
Target applicant:
   High school students
   College students
   Graduate school students
   Adult students
Minimum GPA: None.
Amount: Tuition.
Number of awards: Varies.
Scholarship may be renewable.
Deadline: Varies.
How to apply: Applications are available from your financial aid office.

(1835) · Southern Scholarship Foundation Scholarship

Southern Scholarship Foundation
322 Stadium Drive
Tallahassee, FL 32304
Phone: 850-222-3833
Fax: 850-222-6750
Email: info@southernscholarship.org
Website: http://www.southernscholarship.org
Purpose: To provide rent-free housing scholarships to students attending Florida State, University of Florida, Florida A&M, Bethune-Cookman or Florida Gulf Coast University.
Eligibility: Applicants must have financial need, have a minimum 3.0 high school GPA or 2.85 college GPA, demonstrate high character and attend or plan to attend Florida State, the University of Florida, Florida Gulf Coast University, Florida A&M or Bethune-Cookman.
Target applicant:
   High school students
   College students
   Adult students
Minimum GPA: 2.85
Amount: Varies.
Number of awards: Varies.
Scholarship may be renewable.
Deadline: March 1.
How to apply: Applications are available online.

(1836) · Southside Tobacco Forgiveness Loan

Southwest Virginia Higher Education Center
P.O. Box 1987
Arlington, VA 24212
Phone: 276-619-4300
Fax: 276-619-4309
Email: educationinfo@swcenter.edu
Website: http://www.swcenter.edu
Purpose: To support students from the Southside region of Virginia.
Eligibility: Applicants must be attending a public or private four-year college. They must be permanent residents of one of the 24 Southside areas, and they must have been residents of Virginia for at least 12 months. Students must agree to work in the Southside region after graduation. Preference will be given to applicants with the highest GPA's.
Target applicant:
   High school students
   College students
   Adult students

Minimum GPA: None.
Amount: $1,500-$3,000.
Number of awards: Varies.
Scholarship may be renewable.
Deadline: January 15.
How to apply: Applications are available online.

(1837) · Stanley O. McNaughton Community Service Award

Independent Colleges of Washington
600 Stewart Street, Suite 600
Seattle, WA 98101
Phone: 206-623-4494
Fax: 206-625-9621
Email: info@icwashington.org
Website: http://www.icwashington.org
Purpose: To reward students who are committed to community service and who attend an independent college of Washington.
Eligibility: Applicants must be juniors or seniors who have participated in community service in high school and college. Students attending Gonzaga University, Heritage University, Pacific Lutheran University, Saint Martin's University, Seattle Pacific University, Seattle University, University of Puget Sound, Walla Walla University, Whitman College or Whitworth University are eligible.
Target applicant:
   College students
   Adult students
Minimum GPA: None.
Amount: $2,500.
Number of awards: Varies.
Deadline: March 14.
How to apply: Applications are available online or from your school's financial aid office.

(1838) · Stanley Z. Koplik Certificate of Mastery Tuition Waiver Program

Massachusetts Office of Student Financial Assistance
454 Broadway
Suite 200
Revere, MA 02151
Phone: 617-727-9420
Fax: 617-727-0667
Email: osfa@osfa.mass.edu
Website: http://www.osfa.mass.edu
Purpose: To support Massachusetts students who have demonstrated academic merit.
Eligibility: Applicants must be currently enrolled in a public high school in the state of Massachusetts. Students must receive an "Advanced" score on at least one part of the 10th grade MCAS test, and they must score "Proficient" on all of the other sections. They must also have good scores on at least two AP exams, two SAT II exams or combinations of one of those tests and other achievements determined by the Koplik program. Students must maintain a 3.3 GPA while participating in the scholarship.
Target applicant:
   High school students
Minimum GPA: 3.3
Amount: Varies.
Number of awards: Varies.
Deadline: Varies.
How to apply: Applications are available from high schools.

(1839) · State Contractual Scholarship Fund Program

College Foundation of North Carolina
P.O. Box 41966
Raleigh, NC 27629-1966
Phone: 866-234-6400
Fax: 919-821-3139
Email: programinformation@cfnc.org
Website: http://www.cfnc.org
Purpose: To provide financial assistance to needy students attending private colleges and universities in North Carolina.
Eligibility: Applicants must be North Carolina residents who are enrolled in an undergraduate program at an approved North Carolina private postsecondary institution and have unmet financial need. They must not be enrolled in a program that is designed primarily to prepare students for religious vocations. Licensure students may also apply if they have a bachelor's degree and are enrolled in undergraduate classes in a licensure program for teachers or nurses.
Target applicant:
   College students
   Adult students
Minimum GPA: None.
Amount: Varies.
Number of awards: Varies.
Deadline: Varies.
How to apply: See your financial aid office for application details.

(1840) · State Employees Association of North Carolina (SEANC) Scholarships

State Employees Association of North Carolina
P.O. Drawer 27727
Raleigh, NC 27611
Phone: 919-833-6436
Email: rvaughan@seanc.org
Website: http://www.seanc.org
Purpose: To provide financial assistance to SEANC members, their spouses and their children who plan to attend college.
Eligibility: Applicants must be the spouses or children of members and demonstrate either financial need or merit, or applicants must be members working full-time and enrolled in six or more semester hours of undergraduate work or three or more hours of graduate work. Students who are spouses or children must be enrolled full-time.
Target applicant:
   High school students
   College students
   Graduate school students
   Adult students
Minimum GPA: None.
Amount: $500-$1,000.
Number of awards: 100.
Deadline: April 15.
How to apply: Applications are available online or from your guidance counselor or financial aid office.

(1841) · State Grant Program

Pennsylvania Higher Education Assistance Agency (PHEAA)
1200 N. 7th Street
Harrisburg, PA 17102
Phone: 800-692-7392
Website: http://www.pheaa.org

Purpose: To assist Pennsylvania undergraduate students with financial need.
Eligibility: Applicants must be Pennsylvania residents, enroll at least half-time at an eligible undergraduate institution and meet financial need criteria.
Target applicant:
High school students
College students
Adult students
Minimum GPA: None.
Amount: Up to $1,650.
Number of awards: Varies.
Deadline: May 1.
How to apply: Complete the Free Application for Federal Student Aid (FAFSA).

(1842) · State Grant Program
Rhode Island Higher Education Assistance Authority
560 Jefferson Boulevard
Warwick, RI 02886
Phone: 401-736-1100
Fax: 401-732-3541
Email: scholarships@riheaa.org
Website: http://www.riheaa.org
Purpose: To assist Rhode Island students with financial need.
Eligibility: Applicants must be U.S. citizens or eligible noncitizens, Rhode Island residents, enrolled or accepted for enrollment in a degree or certificate program and attend the program at least half-time.
Target applicant:
High school students
College students
Adult students
Minimum GPA: None.
Amount: $250-$750.
Number of awards: Varies.
Deadline: March 1.
How to apply: Complete the Free Application for Federal Student Aid (FAFSA).

(1843) · State Need Grant
Washington Higher Education Coordinating Board
917 Lakeridge Way
P.O. Box 43430
Olympia, WA 98504
Phone: 360-753-7850
Fax: 360-753-6243
Email: info@hecb.wa.gov
Website: http://www.hecb.wa.gov
Purpose: To assist low-income students to pursue undergraduate degrees or train for new careers.
Eligibility: Applicants must be Washington residents who have a family income of 70 percent or less of the state median, enroll at least half-time as an undergraduate student in an eligible program and be pursuing a certificate, associate's degree or bachelor's degree.
Target applicant:
High school students
College students
Adult students
Minimum GPA: None.
Amount: Up to $5,584.

Number of awards: Varies.
Deadline: Varies.
How to apply: Eligible students who have filed a Free Application for Federal Student Aid (FAFSA) are considered.

(1844) · State Need-based Grants
South Carolina Commission on Higher Education
1333 Main Street
Suite 200
Columbia, SC 29201
Phone: 803-737-2260
Fax: 803-737-2297
Email: shubbard@che.sc.gov
Website: http://www.che400.state.sc.us
Purpose: Monetary assistance for higher education is provided to South Carolina resident students.
Eligibility: Applicants must be obtaining their first baccalaureate or professional degree, complete the Free Application for Federal Student Aid (FAFSA) and be residents of South Carolina.
Target applicant:
High school students
College students
Adult students
Minimum GPA: None.
Amount: $2,500.
Number of awards: Varies.
Scholarship may be renewable.
Deadline: Varies.
How to apply: Complete the FAFSA and contact your college's financial aid office if you plan to attend a public college or the South Carolina Commission on Higher Education if you plan to attend a private college.

(1845) · State Nursing Scholarship
Maryland Higher Education Commission
Office of Student Financial Assistance
839 Bestgate Road, Suite 400
Annapolis, MD 21401
Phone: 800-974-1024
Fax: 410-260-3200
Email: osfamail@mhec.state.md.us
Website: http://www.mhec.state.md.us
Purpose: To assist Maryland undergraduates and graduate students who are earning a degree in nursing.
Eligibility: Applicants and their parents must be Maryland residents. Applicants must have a minimum cumulative GPA of 3.0 in high school or college. Applicants must enroll at a two- or four-year Maryland college or university as an undergraduate or graduate student in a program leading to a degree in nursing.
Target applicant:
High school students
College students
Graduate school students
Adult students
Minimum GPA: None.
Amount: Varies.
Number of awards: Varies.
Deadline: June 30.
How to apply: Applications are available by request.

(1846) · State of Iowa Scholarships

Iowa College Student Aid Commission
200 10th Street, 4th Floor
Des Moines, IA 50309
Phone: 515-242-3344
Fax: 515-242-3388
Email: info@iowacollegeaid.org
Website: http://www.iowacollegeaid.org
Purpose: To recognize Iowa's top students.
Eligibility: Applicants must be Iowa residents ranked in the top 15 percent of their high school graduating class. Awards may only be used at eligible Iowa institutions. Selection is based on class rank and standardized test scores.
Target applicant:
   High school students
Minimum GPA: None.
Amount: $400.
Number of awards: Varies.
Deadline: November 3.
How to apply: Applications are available online.

(1847) · State Scholarship

Kansas Board of Regents
Curtis State Office Building
Suite 520
1000 SW Jackson Street
Topeka, KS 66612
Phone: 785-296-3421
Fax: 785-296-0983
Email: dlindeman@ksbor.org
Website: http://www.kansasregents.org
Purpose: To aid needy Kansas students designated as state scholars.
Eligibility: Applicants must have taken the ACT, completed the Regents Scholars Curriculum and be graduating seniors. Applicants are ranked by an index combining ACT score and GPA. The top students are chosen.
Target applicant:
   High school students
Minimum GPA: None.
Amount: $1,000.
Number of awards: Varies.
Scholarship may be renewable.
Deadline: May 1.
How to apply: Complete the Free Application for Federal Student Aid (FAFSA).

(1848) · State Scholarship Award Program (SSAP)

Nebraska Coordinating Commission for Postsecondary Education
P.O. Box 95005
Lincoln, NE 68509
Phone: 402-471-2847
Fax: 402-471-2886
Email: ritchie.morrow@ccpe.ne.gov
Website: http://www.ccpe.state.ne.us
Purpose: To assist Nebraska students in attending a Nebraska college or university.
Eligibility: Applicants must be residents of the state of Nebraska, qualify for a federal Pell grant and be enrolled in a Nebraska college. Applicants apply for the grant through their specific college or university.

Target applicant:
   College students
   Adult students
Minimum GPA: None.
Amount: Varies.
Number of awards: Varies.
Scholarship may be renewable.
Deadline: Varies.
How to apply: Complete the Free Application for Federal Student Aid (FAFSA).

(1849) · State Student Incentive Grant Program

North Dakota University System
10th Floor, State Capitol
600 E. Boulevard Avenue, Dept. 215
Bismarck, ND 58505
Phone: 701-328-2960
Fax: 701-328-2961
Email: ndus.office@ndus.nodak.edu
Website: http://www.ndus.edu
Purpose: To assist North Dakota students with financial need.
Eligibility: Applicants must be U.S. citizens or permanent residents, North Dakota residents, high school graduates and attend an eligible college in North Dakota full-time.
Target applicant:
   High school students
   College students
   Adult students
Minimum GPA: None.
Amount: Varies.
Number of awards: 3,800.
Deadline: April 15.
How to apply: Complete the Free Application for Federal Student Aid (FAFSA).

(1850) · State Work Study

Washington Higher Education Coordinating Board
917 Lakeridge Way
P.O. Box 43430
Olympia, WA 98504
Phone: 360-753-7850
Fax: 360-753-6243
Email: info@hecb.wa.gov
Website: http://www.hecb.wa.gov
Purpose: To help low and middle income students earn money for college while gaining work experience.
Eligibility: Applicants must have demonstrated financial need according to the FAFSA, enroll at least half-time in an eligible undergraduate or graduate program and not be seeking a degree in theology.
Target applicant:
   High school students
   College students
   Graduate school students
   Adult students
Minimum GPA: None.
Amount: Varies.
Number of awards: Varies.
Deadline: Varies.
How to apply: Eligible students who have filed a Free Application for Federal Student Aid (FAFSA) will be considered.

(1851) · Sterling Scholar Award Program

Hawaii Department of Education
Office of Curriculum, Instruction and Student Support
Student Support Section
641 18th Avenue V-201
Honolulu, HI 96816
Phone: 808-586-3230
Fax: 808-586-3234
Website: http://doe.k12.hi.us
Purpose: To support outstanding Hawaii high school seniors.
Eligibility: Applicants must be graduating high school seniors and demonstrate leadership and citizenship in English, industrial arts, speech/drama, business education, foreign language, visual arts, mathematics, science, music, social science, Hawaiian studies or computer science and technology.
Target applicant:
　High school students
Minimum GPA: None.
Amount: Varies.
Number of awards: 65.
Deadline: December.
How to apply: Applications are available from the department heads of each high school.

(1852) · Stormy Valley Scholarship Fund

Epsilon Sigma Alpha Foundation
P.O. Box 270517
Fort Collins, CO 80527
Phone: 970-223-2824
Fax: 970-223-4456
Email: kloyd@knoxy.net
Website: http://www.esaintl.com/esaf
Purpose: To provide educational opportunities for Oklahoma students.
Eligibility: Applicants must attend a school in Oklahoma. They may pursue any major. Selection is based equally on character, leadership, service, financial need and scholastic ability.
Target applicant:
　High school students
　College students
　Adult students
Minimum GPA: None.
Amount: $500.
Number of awards: 1.
Deadline: February 1.
How to apply: Applications are available online.

(1853) · Student Assistance Award Program

Tennessee Student Assistance Corporation
404 James Robertson Parkway
Suite 1510, Parkway Towers
Nashville, TN 37243
Phone: 800-342-1663
Fax: 615-741-6101
Email: tsac.aidinfo@state.tn.us
Website: http://www.collegepaystn.com
Purpose: To assist Tennessee students with financial need.
Eligibility: Applicants must attend or be accepted at eligible undergraduate higher education institutions in Tennessee for at least half-time and demonstrate financial need.

Target applicant:
　High school students
　College students
　Adult students
Minimum GPA: None.
Amount: Varies.
Number of awards: Varies.
Deadline: May 1.
How to apply: Complete the Free Application for Federal Student Aid (FAFSA).

(1854) · Student Choice Grant Program

Ohio Board of Regents
State Grants and Scholarships Department
P.O. Box 182452
Columbus, OH 43218-2452
Phone: 888-833-1133
Fax: 614-752-5903
Website: http://www.regents.ohio.gov
Purpose: To assist Ohio students attending private nonprofit colleges and universities in Ohio.
Eligibility: Applicants must be Ohio residents who attend an eligible Ohio private university full-time.
Target applicant:
　High school students
　College students
　Adult students
Minimum GPA: None.
Amount: Varies.
Number of awards: Varies.
Deadline: Varies.
How to apply: Contact your financial aid office.

(1855) · Student Incentive Grant

College Foundation of North Carolina
P.O. Box 41966
Raleigh, NC 27629-1966
Phone: 866-234-6400
Fax: 919-821-3139
Email: programinformation@cfnc.org
Website: http://www.cfnc.org
Purpose: To assist outstanding North Carolina high school graduates.
Eligibility: Successful applicants must be North Carolina residents enrolled full-time at a state college or university. Study programs cannot be in preparation for a religious career. Students must demonstrate financial need and maintain adequate academic progress.
Target applicant:
　High school students
　College students
　Adult students
Minimum GPA: None.
Amount: $750.
Number of awards: Varies.
Scholarship may be renewable.
Deadline: March 15.
How to apply: Contact your financial aid office.

(1856) · Student Incentive Grants

New Mexico Higher Education Department
1068 Cerrillos Road
Santa Fe, NM 87505
Phone: 800-279-9777
Fax: 505-476-6511
Email: heather.romero@state.nm.us
Website: http://hed.state.nm.us
Purpose: To support New Mexico undergraduate students with financial need to attend postsecondary institutions in New Mexico.
Eligibility: Applicants must be New Mexico resident undergraduate students and attend public and selected private nonprofit postsecondary institutions in New Mexico at least half-time.
Target applicant:
    College students
    Adult students
Minimum GPA: None.
Amount: $200-$2,500.
Number of awards: Varies.
Deadline: Varies.
How to apply: Contact your financial aid office.

(1857) · Stutz Scholarship

American Legion, Department of New Jersey
135 W. Hanover Street
Trenton, NJ 08618
Phone: 609-695-5418
Fax: 609-394-1532
Email: adjudant@njamericanlegion.org
Website: http://www.njamericanlegion.org
Purpose: To award children of American Legion members with scholarships.
Eligibility: Applicants must be children of members of the American Legion, Department of New Jersey. Applicants must also be high school seniors and use the award in the year it is received.
Target applicant:
    High school students
Minimum GPA: None.
Amount: $4,000.
Number of awards: 1.
Deadline: February 15.
How to apply: Applications are available by contacting the local Post or Department Headquarters.

(1858) · Sun Student College Scholarship Program

Phoenix Suns Charities
P.O. Box 1369
Phoenix, AZ 85001
Website: http://www.suns.com
Purpose: As part of the series of grants offered by the Phoenix Suns to help children in Arizona, the Student College Scholarship Program assists Arizona high school seniors with their college expenses.
Eligibility: Eligible candidates must be seniors in an Arizona high school.
Target applicant:
    High school students
Minimum GPA: 2.5
Amount: $1,000-$5,000.
Number of awards: Varies.

Deadline: Varies.
How to apply: Contact the Phoenix Suns Charities via their website.

(1859) · Sussman-Miller Educational Assistance Award

Albuquerque Community Foundation (ACF)
P.O. Box 36960
Albuquerque, NM 87176
Phone: 505-883-6240
Fax: 505-883-3629
Email: foundation@albuquerquefoundation.org
Website: http://www.albuquerquefoundation.org
Purpose: To assist New Mexico high school graduates and college undergraduates.
Eligibility: Students must be New Mexico residents for a minimum of one year, have been awarded a financial package that does not satisfy demonstrated need and be accepted by and have chosen to attend a U.S. post-secondary, accredited, nonprofit educational institution full-time. High school applicants need to graduate from an accredited public or private high school and have a 3.0 minimum GPA. Undergraduate applicants must have completed a minimum of one semester of undergraduate study with a 2.5 minimum GPA and cannot be applying for residency in another state.
Target applicant:
    High school students
    College students
    Adult students
Minimum GPA: 2.5 undergraduate; 3.0 high school
Amount: $500-$2,500.
Number of awards: Varies.
Deadline: April 19 or June 28.
How to apply: Applications are available online.

(1860) · Tadeusz Sendzimir Fund

Connecticut Community Foundation Center for Philanthropy
43 Field Street
Waterbury, CT 06702
Phone: 203-753-1315
Fax: 203-756-3054
Email: info@conncf.org
Website: http://www.conncf.org
Purpose: To provide financial assistance to students who are studying Polish language, history or culture.
Eligibility: Applicants must be Connecticut residents who are either in the U.S. during the academic year or in Poland during the summer. Academic year applicants must be taking undergraduate courses in Polish history, culture and language or be graduate students majoring in Slavic studies with an emphasis on Polish culture. Preference is given to students of Polish descent.
Target applicant:
    College students
    Graduate school students
    Adult students
Minimum GPA: None.
Amount: $3,000-$5,000.
Number of awards: 2.
Deadline: March 1.
How to apply: Applications are available online.

(1861) · Talent Incentive Program (TIP) Grant

State of Wisconsin Higher Educational Aids Board
P.O. Box 7885
Madison, WI 53707
Phone: 608-267-2206
Fax: 608-267-2808
Email: heabmail@heab.state.wi.us
Website: http://heab.state.wi.us
Purpose: To assist Wisconsin students with financial need.
Eligibility: Applicants must be Wisconsin first-time college freshmen with financial need who plan to attend Wisconsin colleges or universities at least half-time.
Target applicant:
    High school students
Minimum GPA: None.
Amount: Up to $1,800.
Number of awards: Varies.
Scholarship may be renewable.
Deadline: Varies.
How to apply: Complete the Free Application for Federal Student Aid (FAFSA). Applicants must be nominated by their financial aid office or the Wisconsin Educational Opportunities Program.

(1862) · Technical Award

Louisiana Office of Student Financial Assistance
P.O. Box 91202
Baton Rouge, LA 70821-9202
Phone: 800-259-5626 x1012
Fax: 225-922-0790
Email: custserv@osfa.la.gov
Website: http://www.osfa.state.la.us
Purpose: To assist Louisiana resident students.
Eligibility: Applicants must be Louisiana residents, apply during their junior or senior year in a public high school, and pursue an industry-based occupational or vocational credential in a public college or university that meets certain standards. They must also have a minimum 2.0 GPA Score, at least 15 on the English and Mathematics subsections of the ACT PLAN Assessment, have at least minimum passing scores in English and Mathematics on the GEE and have prepared a 5-year education and career plan.
Target applicant:
    High school students
Minimum GPA: 2.0
Amount: $600.
Number of awards: Varies.
Scholarship may be renewable.
Deadline: July 2.
How to apply: Applications are available online or from guidance counselors.

(1863) · Technical Certification Scholarship

Texas 4-H Youth Development Foundation
7607 Eastmark Drive, Suite 101
College Station, TX 77840
Phone: 979-845-1213
Fax: 979-845-6495
Email: texas4hfoundation@ag.tamu.edu
Website: http://www.texas4hfoundation.org
Purpose: To support Texas high school seniors who plan to pursue a technical program.
Eligibility: Applicants must have actively participated in a 4-H program for at least part of the year. They must have formally applied to a Texas college or university, and they must meet all requirements for admission. Students must not have any plans to continue their college education after completion of a technical program.
Target applicant:
    High school students
Minimum GPA: None.
Amount: $1,500-$15,000.
Number of awards: Varies.
Deadline: February 15.
How to apply: Applications are available online.

(1864) · Ted and Nora Anderson Scholarships

American Legion, Department of Kansas
1314 SW Topeka Boulevard
Topeka, KS 66612
Phone: 785-232-9315
Fax: 785-232-1399
Website: http://www.ksamlegion.org
Purpose: To support worthy and needy children of American Legion and American Legion Auxiliary members as they pursue their educations.
Eligibility: Applicants must be high school seniors or college freshmen or sophomores who are average or better students. They must be enrolling or enrolled in a post-secondary school in Kansas and the son or daughter of a veteran. At least one parent must have been a member of the Kansas American Legion or American Legion Auxiliary for the past three years. The children of deceased parents are also eligible as long as the parent was a paid member at the time of death. Applicants must submit three letters of recommendation, with only one from a teacher, a 1040 income statement, documentation of parent's veteran status, an essay on "Why I Want to Go to College" and a high school transcript.
Target applicant:
    High school students
    College students
    Adult students
Minimum GPA: None.
Amount: $500.
Number of awards: Up to 4.
Deadline: February 15.
How to apply: Applications are available online.

(1865) · Tennessee HOPE Access Grant

Tennessee Student Assistance Corporation
404 James Robertson Parkway
Suite 1510, Parkway Towers
Nashville, TN 37243
Phone: 800-342-1663
Fax: 615-741-6101
Email: tsac.aidinfo@state.tn.us
Website: http://www.collegepaystn.com
Purpose: To support students who do not qualify for the Tennessee HOPE Grant.
Eligibility: Applicants must be entering freshmen who have a GPA between 2.75 and 2.99. They must also have either an ACT score between 18 and 20 or an SAT score between 860 and 970. Independent students or the parents of dependent students must have an adjusted gross income under $36,000.
Target applicant:
    High school students
Minimum GPA: 2.75

Amount: $1,750-$2,750.
Number of awards: Varies.
Deadline: September 1.
How to apply: Applications are available through completion of the FAFSA.

(1866) · Tennessee HOPE Lottery Scholarship

Tennessee Student Assistance Corporation
404 James Robertson Parkway
Suite 1510, Parkway Towers
Nashville, TN 37243
Phone: 800-342-1663
Fax: 615-741-6101
Email: tsac.aidinfo@state.tn.us
Website: http://www.collegepaystn.com
Purpose: To support undergraduate students in Tennessee.
Eligibility: Applicants must be entering freshmen and either have at least a 3.0 GPA, a score of 21 on the ACT or a score of 980 on the SAT. GED students must also score at least a 525 on the GED test. Home-schooled students and some private school students must meet additional requirements. Applicants must be Tennessee residents for at least one year prior to the application deadline.
Target applicant:
   High school students
Minimum GPA: 3.0
Amount: $2,000-$4,000.
Number of awards: Varies.
Scholarship may be renewable.
Deadline: September 1.
How to apply: Applications are available through completion of the FAFSA.

(1867) · Tese Caldarelli Memorial Scholarship

National Association for Campus Activities
13 Harbison Way
Columbia, SC 29212
Phone: 803-732-6222
Fax: 803-749-1047
Email: info@naca.org
Website: http://www.naca.org
Purpose: To provide financial assistance to student leaders.
Eligibility: Students must hold a significant campus leadership position and demonstrate significant leadership skills and abilities. Students must also be making significant contributions through on- or off-campus volunteering. Applicants must also be current undergraduate or graduate students in Kentucky, Michigan, Ohio, Western Pennsylvania or West Virginia.
Target applicant:
   College students
   Graduate school students
   Adult students
Minimum GPA: 3.0
Amount: Varies.
Number of awards: Varies.
Deadline: November 1.
How to apply: Applications are available online.

(1868) · Texas Oratorical Contest

American Legion, Department of Texas
3401 Ed Bluestein Boulevard
Austin, TX 78721
Phone: 512-472-4138
Fax: 512-472-0603
Email: programs@txlegion.org
Website: http://www.txlegion.org
Purpose: To enhance high school students' experience with and understanding of the U.S. Constitution. The contest will help develop students' leadership skills and civic appreciation, as well as the ability to deliver thoughtful, insightful orations regarding U.S. citizenship and its inherent responsibilities.
Eligibility: Applicants must be high school students under the age of 20 who are U.S. citizens or legal residents and residents of the state. Students first give an oration within their state and winners compete at the national level. The oration must be related to the Constitution of the United States focusing on the duties and obligations citizens have to the government. It must be in English and be between eight and ten minutes. There is also an assigned topic which is posted on the website, and it should be between three and five minutes.
Target applicant:
   High school students
Minimum GPA: None.
Amount: Varies.
Number of awards: 4.
Deadline: November.
How to apply: Application information is available online or by contacting the local post.

(1869) · Texas Public Educational Grant

Texas Higher Education Coordinating Board
P.O. Box 12788
Austin, TX 78711
Phone: 512-427-6101
Fax: 512-427-6127
Website: http://www.collegefortexans.com
Purpose: To assist Texas students with financial need.
Eligibility: Applicants must attend public colleges or universities in Texas and demonstrate financial need. Individual institutions determine additional eligibility criteria.
Target applicant:
   High school students
   College students
   Graduate school students
   Adult students
Minimum GPA: None.
Amount: Varies.
Number of awards: Varies.
Deadline: Varies.
How to apply: Complete the Free Application for Federal Student Aid (FAFSA) and contact your financial aid office.

(1870) · The Colorado Lamplighter's Endowment

Epsilon Sigma Alpha Foundation
P.O. Box 270517
Fort Collins, CO 80527
Phone: 970-223-2824
Fax: 970-223-4456
Email: kloyd@knoxy.net
Website: http://www.esaintl.com/esaf

Purpose: To provide financial assistance to Colorado residents.
Eligibility: Applicants may attend any college or university and pursue any major. Selection is based equally on character, leadership, service, financial need and scholastic ability.
Target applicant:
    High school students
    College students
    Adult students
Minimum GPA: None.
Amount: $500.
Number of awards: 1.
Deadline: February 1.
How to apply: Applications are available online.

(1871) · The Francis Ouimet Scholarship Fund

Francis Ouimet Scholarship Fund
300 Arnold Palmer Boulevard
Norton, MA 02766
Phone: 774-430-9090
Fax: 774-430-9091
Email: marionm@ouimet.org
Website: http://www.ouimet.org
Purpose: To provide merit- and need-based scholarships to students who have worked at Massachusetts golf clubs.
Eligibility: Applicants must have served at least two years as golf caddies, as golf pro shop workers or in course superintendent operations. The award is to be used for undergraduate study.
Target applicant:
    High school students
    College students
    Adult students
Minimum GPA: None.
Amount: Up to $20,000.
Number of awards: Varies.
Scholarship may be renewable.
Deadline: December 1.
How to apply: Applications are available by mail or by online request.

(1872) · The Heart of a Marine Foundation Scholarship

Heart of a Marine Foundation
P.O. Box 1732
Elk Grove Village, IL 60007
Phone: 847-621-7324
Email: theheartofamarine@comcast.net
Website: http://www.heartofamarine.org
Purpose: To support students from New Jersey and Illinois who have outstanding character.
Eligibility: Applicants must be graduating high school seniors or discharged military personnel. Students must demonstrate loyalty, patriotism, honor, respect and compassion for others.
Target applicant:
    High school students
    Adult students
Minimum GPA: None.
Amount: Varies.
Number of awards: Varies.
Deadline: Varies.
How to apply: Applications are available online.

(1873) · The SCTE Badger State Chapter - Telecommunications Scholarship

Common Knowledge Scholarship Foundation
P.O. Box 290361
Davie, FL 33329-0361
Phone: 954-262-8553
Email: info@cksf.org
Website: http://www.cksf.org
Purpose: To provide financial assistance to telecommunications students in Wisconsin.
Eligibility: Applicants must be enrolled in or accepted to the telecommunications program at Wisconsin Indianhead Technical College. They must compete for scholarship money via an online quiz.
Target applicant:
    High school students
    College students
    Adult students
Minimum GPA: None.
Amount: $1,000.
Number of awards: 2.
Deadline: February 22.
How to apply: Applications are available online.

(1874) · Theodore Gordon Flyfishers, Inc. Founders Fund Scholarship

Environmental Consortium of Hudson Valley Colleges & Universities
c/o Pace Academy for the Environment
861 Bedford Road
Choate 221N
Pleasantville, NY 10570
Phone: 914-773-3738
Fax: 914-773-3265
Email: envtlconsortium@pace.edu
Website: http://environmentalconsortium.org
Purpose: To support a student who excels in the environmental field at one of the member institutions of the consortium.
Eligibility: Applicants must be U.S. citizens enrolled full-time and at least in the second year of college or in graduate school. Students must major in an area of environmental studies such as, but not limited to, ecology, hydrology, conservation biology, natural resource management, zoology or environmental law and policy. A list of member institutions is online.
Target applicant:
    College students
    Graduate school students
    Adult students
Minimum GPA: 3.0
Amount: $2,000.
Number of awards: 1.
Deadline: April 1.
How to apply: Applications are available online.

(1875) · Toby Wright Scholarship

Workers' Compensation Association of New Mexico
P.O. Box 35757
Station D
Albuquerque, NM 87176
Phone: 800-640-0724
Email: scibrock@qwest.net
Website: http://www.wcaofnm.com

Purpose: To support the children of injured New Mexico workers.
Eligibility: Applicants must have a parent who was badly injured or killed in a work-related accident which resulted in economic hardship and New Mexico worker's compensation. Students must be between the ages of 16 and 25, and they must attend college or technical school in New Mexico.
Target applicant:
    High school students
    College students
Minimum GPA: None.
Amount: Varies.
Number of awards: Varies.
Scholarship may be renewable.
Deadline: Varies.
How to apply: Applications are available online.

(1876) · Tomorrow's Teachers Scholarship Program

Massachusetts Office of Student Financial Assistance
454 Broadway
Suite 200
Revere, MA 02151
Phone: 617-727-9420
Fax: 617-727-0667
Email: osfa@osfa.mass.edu
Website: http://www.osfa.mass.edu
Purpose: To provide scholarships to academically talented high school students who wish to pursue a teaching career.
Eligibility: Applicants must be permanent legal residents of Massachusetts and rank in the top 25 percent of their high school class. Applicants must agree to enroll and complete a four-year bachelor's degree program at an eligible college or university leading to teacher certification and agree to teach for four years in Massachusetts public schools.
Target applicant:
    High school students
Minimum GPA: None.
Amount: Varies.
Number of awards: Varies.
Scholarship may be renewable.
Deadline: Varies.
How to apply: Applications are available online.

(1877) · Tongan Cultural Society Scholarship

Hawaii Community Foundation - Scholarships
1164 Bishop Street, Suite 800
Honolulu, HI 96813
Phone: 888-731-3863
Fax: 808-521-6286
Email: scholarships@hcf-hawaii.org
Website: http://www.hawaiicommunityfoundation.org
Purpose: To support students of Tongan ancestry.
Eligibility: Applicants must attend school in Hawaii.
Target applicant:
    High school students
    College students
    Adult students
Minimum GPA: None.
Amount: $1,750.
Number of awards: 3.
Deadline: March 1.

How to apply: To apply, register online, complete the online application and select the scholarships to which you wish to apply. In addition, mail the supporting materials: printed confirmation page from the online application, personal statement, copy of Student Aid Report (SAR) available at www.fafsa.ed.gov and official transcript.

(1878) · Toward Excellence, Access and Success (TEXAS) Grant II Program (TGII)

Texas Higher Education Coordinating Board
P.O. Box 12788
Austin, TX 78711
Phone: 512-427-6101
Fax: 512-427-6127
Website: http://www.collegefortexans.com
Purpose: To assist Texas two-year college students with financial need.
Eligibility: Applicants must be Texas residents, enrolled at least half-time in a public Texas two-year community college, technical college or public state college and demonstrate financial need.
Target applicant:
    College students
    Adult students
Minimum GPA: None.
Amount: $1,300 per semester.
Number of awards: Varies.
Deadline: Varies.
How to apply: Complete the Free Application for Federal Student Aid (FAFSA).

(1879) · Toward Excellence, Access and Success (TEXAS) Grant Program

Texas Higher Education Coordinating Board
P.O. Box 12788
Austin, TX 78711
Phone: 512-427-6101
Fax: 512-427-6127
Website: http://www.collegefortexans.com
Purpose: To assist Texas students with financial need who have received their associate's degree.
Eligibility: Applicants must be Texas residents, have earned their associate's degree and enroll in a Texas higher level undergraduate program at least 3/4 time and demonstrate financial need.
Target applicant:
    College students
    Adult students
Minimum GPA: None.
Amount: $1,475 per semester.
Number of awards: Varies.
Deadline: Varies.
How to apply: Complete the Free Application for Federal Student Aid (FAFSA).

(1880) · Township Officials of Illinois Scholarship

Township Officials of Illinois
408 S. 5th Street
Springfield, IL 62701
Phone: 217-744-2212
Fax: 217-744-7419
Email: bryantoi@toi.org
Website: http://www.toi.org

Purpose: To promote the ideas of quality local government and civic duty and to recruit young people into the TOI.

Eligibility: Applicants must be high school seniors attending an Illinois college or university in the fall.

Target applicant:
   High school students

Minimum GPA: None.

Amount: Varies.

Number of awards: Varies.

Deadline: March 1.

How to apply: Applications are available online in January.

(1881) · Treacy Company Scholarship

Treacy Company
P.O. Box 1700
Helena, MT 59624
Phone: 406-443-3549

Purpose: To support students in Montana, Idaho, North Dakota and South Dakota.

Eligibility: Applicants must be freshmen or sophomores in college and reside in Montana, Idaho, North Dakota or South Dakota.

Target applicant:
   College students
   Adult students

Minimum GPA: None.

Amount: $400.

Number of awards: Varies.

Scholarship may be renewable.

Deadline: Varies.

How to apply: Applications are available by mail.

(1882) · Tsung Tsin Association Scholarship

Tsung Tsin Association
Chairperson, Scholarship Committee
47-701 Hui Alala Street
Kaneohe, HI 96744
Phone: 808-533-3998

Purpose: To help outstanding Hawaii students pay for college.

Eligibility: Applicants must be high school seniors, college undergraduates or graduate students and must be attending or planning to attend a post-secondary institution. Applicants must provide a transcript, SAT scores, recommendations and autobiographical sketch. Community service and career goals are taken into consideration.

Target applicant:
   High school students
   College students
   Graduate school students
   Adult students

Minimum GPA: None.

Amount: $750.

Number of awards: 1.

Deadline: April 20.

How to apply: Applications are available by written request.

(1883) · Tuition Aid Grant

New Jersey Higher Education Student Assistance Authority
P.O. Box 540
Trenton, NJ 08625
Phone: 800-792-8670

Email: clientservices@hesaa.org
Website: http://www.hesaa.org

Purpose: To support New Jersey students who are unable to pay the full cost of tuition.

Eligibility: Students must be residents of New Jersey for at least 12 months prior to college enrollment, enroll in an approved New Jersey school and remain in school full-time in an undergraduate program. Applicants cannot have any previous degrees, and they cannot be enrolled in theology or divinity programs.

Target applicant:
   High school students
   College students
   Adult students

Minimum GPA: None.

Amount: Varies.

Number of awards: Varies.

Scholarship may be renewable.

Deadline: October 1.

How to apply: Applications are available through completion of the FAFSA.

(1884) · Tuition Assistance Program (TAP)

New York State Higher Education Services Corporation (HESC)
99 Washington Avenue
Albany, NY 12255
Phone: 888-697-4372
Email: hescwebmail@hesc.org
Website: http://www.hesc.com

Purpose: To assist New York resident students in attending in-state postsecondary institutions.

Eligibility: Applicants must be U.S. citizens or eligible noncitizens, be legal residents of New York State, study full-time at an eligible New York State postsecondary institution as undergraduate or graduate students, meet income eligibility requirements and maintain a "C" average in college.

Target applicant:
   High school students
   College students
   Graduate school students
   Adult students

Minimum GPA: None.

Amount: Up to $5,000.

Number of awards: Varies.

Scholarship may be renewable.

Deadline: May 1.

How to apply: Complete the Free Application for Federal Student Aid (FAFSA), including a New York school on the application and then complete the Express TAP Application.

(1885) · Tuition Equalization Grant Program (TEG)

Texas Higher Education Coordinating Board
P.O. Box 12788
Austin, TX 78711
Phone: 512-427-6101
Fax: 512-427-6127
Website: http://www.collegefortexans.com

Purpose: To assist students with financial need in attending private nonprofit colleges or universities in Texas.

Eligibility: Applicants must be Texas residents or nonresident National Merit Finalists, enroll in a Texas institution at least half-time and demonstrate financial need.

Target applicant:
High school students
Minimum GPA: None.
Amount: Varies.
Number of awards: Varies.
Deadline: Varies.
How to apply: Complete the Free Application for Federal Student Aid (FAFSA).

(1886) · Tuition Grant

State of Wisconsin Higher Educational Aids Board
P.O. Box 7885
Madison, WI 53707
Phone: 608-267-2206
Fax: 608-267-2808
Email: heabmail@heab.state.wi.us
Website: http://heab.state.wi.us
Purpose: To assist Wisconsin students with financial need who attend private Wisconsin colleges.
Eligibility: Applicants must be Wisconsin undergraduate students with financial need who attend private Wisconsin colleges or universities at least half-time.
Target applicant:
College students
Adult students
Minimum GPA: None.
Amount: Varies.
Number of awards: Varies.
Deadline: Varies.
How to apply: Complete the Free Application for Federal Student Aid (FAFSA).

(1887) · Tuition Reduction for Non-Resident Nursing Students

Maryland Higher Education Commission
Office of Student Financial Assistance
839 Bestgate Road, Suite 400
Annapolis, MD 21401
Phone: 800-974-1024
Fax: 410-260-3200
Email: osfamail@mhec.state.md.us
Website: http://www.mhec.state.md.us
Purpose: To support non-resident nursing students who are attending college in Maryland.
Eligibility: Applicants cannot be residents of the state of Maryland, but they must be enrolled in a two-year or four-year undergraduate nursing program in Maryland. Students must agree to work full-time at a Maryland hospital after graduation, for a period of four years for full-time students and two years for part-time students.
Target applicant:
High school students
College students
Adult students
Minimum GPA: None.
Amount: Varies.
Number of awards: Varies.
Scholarship may be renewable.
Deadline: Varies.
How to apply: Applications are available online.

(1888) · Tuition Waiver for Foster Care Recipients

Maryland Higher Education Commission
Office of Student Financial Assistance
839 Bestgate Road, Suite 400
Annapolis, MD 21401
Phone: 800-974-1024
Fax: 410-260-3200
Email: osfamail@mhec.state.md.us
Website: http://www.mhec.state.md.us
Purpose: To assist students who have resided in foster care in attending a public college.
Eligibility: Applicants must be under the age of 21 and have lived in foster care in the state of Maryland when they graduated high school or have lived in foster care on their 14th birthday and subsequently been adopted.
Target applicant:
High school students
College students
Minimum GPA: None.
Amount: Varies.
Number of awards: Varies.
Scholarship may be renewable.
Deadline: March 1.
How to apply: Students may apply by filing the FAFSA and contacting the financial aid office at the institution they plan to attend.

(1889) · Tulsa Area Council Endowment

Epsilon Sigma Alpha Foundation
P.O. Box 270517
Fort Collins, CO 80527
Phone: 970-223-2824
Fax: 970-223-4456
Email: kloyd@knoxy.net
Website: http://www.esaintl.com/esaf
Purpose: To provide financial assistance for female Oklahoma students.
Eligibility: Applicants must attend a college or university in Oklahoma. They may pursue any major.
Target applicant:
High school students
College students
Adult students
Minimum GPA: None.
Amount: $500.
Number of awards: 1.
Deadline: February 1.
How to apply: Applications are available online.

(1890) · Twenty-first Century Scholars Program

State Student Assistance Commission of Indiana
150 W. Market Street
Suite 500
Indianapolis, IN 46204
Phone: 888-528-4719
Fax: 317-232-3260
Email: grants@ssaci.state.in.us
Website: http://www.in.gov/ssaci
Purpose: To support Indiana middle school students from families with low to moderate incomes.

Eligibility: Applicants must be in 7th or 8th grade at a school recognized by the Indiana Department of Education. Students must meet the maximum income requirements, be wards of the state or county or be in foster care. Scholarship funds may only be used at eligible Indiana colleges or technical schools.

Target applicant:
Junior high students or younger

Minimum GPA: None.

Amount: Varies.

Number of awards: Varies.

Scholarship may be renewable.

Deadline: June 30.

How to apply: Applications are available at Indiana middle schools.

(1891) · Two-Year College Academic Scholarship Program

State of Alabama
Commission on Higher Education
100 N. Union Street
P.O. Box 302000
Montgomery, AL 36130-2000
Phone: 334-242-1998
Fax: 334-242-0268
Website: http://www.ache.state.al.us

Purpose: To assist students attending two-year colleges in Alabama.

Eligibility: Applicants must be accepted for enrollment at a public two-year postsecondary educational institution in Alabama. Selection is based on academic merit and is not based on financial need.

Target applicant:
High school students

Minimum GPA: None.

Amount: Award will not exceed the in-state tuition and books for a public two-year college.

Number of awards: Varies.

Scholarship may be renewable.

Deadline: Varies.

How to apply: Contact the college financial aid office.

(1892) · UC Nonresident Fee Scholarship

Los Alamos National Laboratory Foundation
1302 Calle de la Merced
Suite A
Espanola, NM 87532
Phone: 505-753-8890
Fax: 505-753-8915
Email: info@lanlfoundation.org
Website: http://www.lanlfoundation.org

Purpose: To support students from Northern New Mexico who are attending or plan to attend the University of California.

Eligibility: Students must have at least a 3.25 GPA, and they must have either an SAT score of at least 1350 or an ACT score of at least 19. Applicants must submit an essay and two letters of recommendation. Preference will be given to students with financial need and those who are the first generation in the family to attend college.

Target applicant:
High school students
College students
Adult students

Minimum GPA: 3.25

Amount: Varies.

Number of awards: Varies.

Scholarship may be renewable.

Deadline: January 22.

How to apply: Applications are available online.

(1893) · University of North Carolina Need Based Grant

College Foundation of North Carolina
P.O. Box 41966
Raleigh, NC 27629-1966
Phone: 866-234-6400
Fax: 919-821-3139
Email: programinformation@cfnc.org
Website: http://www.cfnc.org

Purpose: To provide financial assistance to students attending a campus of the University of North Carolina.

Eligibility: Applicants must be enrolled in six or more credit hours at one of the 16 campuses of the University of North Carolina. They must also demonstrate financial need.

Target applicant:
High school students
College students
Adult students

Minimum GPA: None.

Amount: Varies.

Number of awards: Varies.

Deadline: Varies.

How to apply: Applicants must complete the Free Application for Federal Student Aid and list at least one campus of the University of North Carolina on it.

(1894) · Urban Scholars Award

New Jersey Higher Education Student Assistance Authority
P.O. Box 540
Trenton, NJ 08625
Phone: 800-792-8670
Email: clientservices@hesaa.org
Website: http://www.hesaa.org

Purpose: To support New Jersey high school seniors from urban or economically depressed areas.

Eligibility: Applicants must be New Jersey residents for at least 12 months prior to college enrollment, and they must enroll full-time in an approved state college. Students must show outstanding academic achievement in high school through SAT scores and transcripts.

Target applicant:
High school students

Minimum GPA: None.

Amount: $1,000.

Number of awards: Varies.

Scholarship may be renewable.

Deadline: Varies.

How to apply: Applications are available from high school guidance counselors.

(1895) · Utah Centennial Opportunity Program for Education (UCOPE) Grants

Utah Higher Education Assistance Authority
Board of Regents Building, The Gateway
60 South 400 West

Salt Lake City, UT 84101
Phone: 801-321-7200
Fax: 801-321-7299
Email: uheaa@utahsbr.edu
Website: http://www.uheaa.org
Purpose: To assist Utah students in attending Utah colleges.
Eligibility: Applicants must be residents of Utah attending schools in Utah. Eligibility requirements differ by campus. It is recommended that students apply early because there are limited funds.
Target applicant:
  High school students
  College students
  Adult students
Minimum GPA: None.
Amount: Varies.
Number of awards: Varies.
Deadline: Varies.
How to apply: Complete the Free Application for Federal Student Aid (FAFSA).

(1896) · Valedictorial Program Tuition Waiver

Massachusetts Office of Student Financial Assistance
454 Broadway
Suite 200
Revere, MA 02151
Phone: 617-727-9420
Fax: 617-727-0667
Email: osfa@osfa.mass.edu
Website: http://www.osfa.mass.edu
Purpose: To provide comprehensive financial aid to Massachusetts valedictorians.
Eligibility: Applicants must be designated as a valedictorian by a public or private high school in the state of Massachusetts, and they must be residents of the state for at least one year prior to the beginning of the school year. Students must enroll in a Massachusetts public college and meet individual requirements for the program imposed by the school. They cannot owe refunds on previous financial aid or have any defaulted government loans.
Target applicant:
  High school students
Minimum GPA: None.
Amount: Varies.
Number of awards: Varies.
Scholarship may be renewable.
Deadline: Varies.
How to apply: Applications are available at college financial aid offices.

(1897) · Vermont Oratorical Contest

American Legion, Department of Vermont
P.O. Box 396
126 State Street
Montpelier, VT 05601
Phone: 802-223-7131
Fax: 802-223-0318
Email: alvthq@verizon.net
Website: http://www.legionvthq.com
Purpose: To enhance high school students' experience with and understanding of the U.S. Constitution. The contest will help develop students' leadership skills and civic appreciation, as well as the ability to deliver thoughtful, insightful orations regarding U.S. citizenship and its inherent responsibilities.
Eligibility: Applicants must be high school students under the age of 20 who are U.S. citizens or legal residents and residents of the state. Students first give an oration within their state and winners compete at the national level. The oration must be related to the Constitution of the United States focusing on the duties and obligations citizens have to the government. It must be in English and be between eight and ten minutes. There is also an assigned topic which is posted on the website, and it should be between three and five minutes.
Target applicant:
  High school students
Minimum GPA: None.
Amount: $100-$2,000.
Number of awards: At least 2.
Deadline: Varies.
How to apply: Applications are available from district representatives.

(1898) · Veterans Tuition Awards

New York State Higher Education Services Corporation (HESC)
99 Washington Avenue
Albany, NY 12255
Phone: 888-697-4372
Email: hescwebmail@hesc.org
Website: http://www.hesc.com
Purpose: To assist veterans in obtaining higher education.
Eligibility: Applicants must be veterans from New York State who have been honorably discharged and served in Indochina between December 22, 1961 and May 7, 1975, the Persian Gulf on or after August 2, 1990 or Afghanistan on or after September 11, 2001. Applicants must also have applied for the Tuition Assistant Program if studying full-time, and the Federal Pell Grant whether studying full-time or part-time, unless enrolled in a vocational training program.
Target applicant:
  College students
  Graduate school students
  Adult students
Minimum GPA: None.
Amount: Up to $2,000.
Number of awards: Varies.
Scholarship may be renewable.
Deadline: May 1.
How to apply: Applications are available from your institution's financial aid office or by phone from HESC.

(1899) · Veterinary Education Program

New Hampshire Postsecondary Education Commission
3 Barrell Court
Suite 300
Concord, NH 03301
Phone: 603-271-2555 x352
Fax: 603-271-2696
Email: jknapp@pec.state.nh.us
Website: http://www.state.nh.us/postsecondary
Purpose: To support veterinary medicine students in New Hampshire.
Eligibility: Applicants must have been New Hampshire residents for at least 12 months prior to the beginning of the school year and must have graduated from a New Hampshire high school within the last six years.

Target applicant:
  College students
  Graduate school students
  Adult students
Minimum GPA: None.
Amount: $12,000.
Number of awards: Varies.
Scholarship may be renewable.
Deadline: Varies.
How to apply: Applications are available at the University of New Hampshire College of Life Sciences and Agriculture.

(1900) · Vi Gardner Memorial Endowment

Epsilon Sigma Alpha Foundation
P.O. Box 270517
Fort Collins, CO 80527
Phone: 970-223-2824
Fax: 970-223-4456
Email: kloyd@knoxy.net
Website: http://www.esaintl.com/esaf
Purpose: To provide financial assistance to Oklahoma residents.
Eligibility: Applicants may pursue any major at any school. Selection criteria include scholastic ability (30 percent), financial need (30 percent), leadership (20 percent), character (10 percent) and service (10 percent).
Target applicant:
  High school students
  College students
  Adult students
Minimum GPA: None.
Amount: $500.
Number of awards: 1.
Deadline: February 1.
How to apply: Applications are available online.

(1901) · Victoria S. and Bradley L. Geist Foundation

Hawaii Community Foundation - Scholarships
1164 Bishop Street, Suite 800
Honolulu, HI 96813
Phone: 888-731-3863
Fax: 808-521-6286
Email: scholarships@hcf-hawaii.org
Website: http://www.hawaiicommunityfoundation.org
Purpose: To support students who have been in the Hawaii foster care system.
Eligibility: Applicants must be residents of Hawaii. Students must not have been legally adopted before the age of 18.
Target applicant:
  High school students
  College students
  Adult students
Minimum GPA: None.
Amount: $2,228.
Number of awards: 151.
Scholarship may be renewable.
Deadline: June 1.
How to apply: Applications are available online. In addition, mail the supporting materials: confirmation letter from a case worker, personal statement and official transcript.

(1902) · Vietnam Veterans' Scholarship

New Mexico Higher Education Department
1068 Cerrillos Road
Santa Fe, NM 87505
Phone: 800-279-9777
Fax: 505-476-6511
Email: heather.romero@state.nm.us
Website: http://hed.state.nm.us
Purpose: To support Vietnam veterans who are attending college in New Mexico.
Eligibility: Applicants must have been honorably discharged from the armed forces, and they must have received a Vietnam campaign medal for serving in Vietnam anytime between August 5, 1964 and the official end of the war. Students must be attending either a public school or one of the following private schools in New Mexico: the College of Santa Fe, St. John's College or the College of the Southwest. They must have been New Mexico residents when entering the armed forces or have lived in the state for at least 10 years.
Target applicant:
  College students
  Graduate school students
  Adult students
Minimum GPA: None.
Amount: Varies.
Number of awards: Varies.
Scholarship may be renewable.
Deadline: Varies.
How to apply: Applications are available at college financial aid offices.

(1903) · Vincent L. Hawkinson Scholarship for Peace and Justice

Vincent L. Hawkinson Foundation for Peace and Justice
324 Harvard Street S.E.
Minneapolis, MN 55414
Phone: 612-331-8125
Email: info@graceattheu.org
Website: http://www.graceattheu.org
Purpose: To provide financial assistance to undergraduate and graduate students who share the ideals of the Rev. Vincent L. Hawkinson, a leader of Grace University Lutheran Church for more than 30 years.
Eligibility: Applicants must advocate peace, reside in Iowa, Minnesota, North Dakota, South Dakota or Wisconsin and attend an interview in Minneapolis and the fall awards ceremony.
Target applicant:
  High school students
  College students
  Graduate school students
  Adult students
Minimum GPA: None.
Amount: $1,500.
Number of awards: 1.
Deadline: April 1.
How to apply: Applications are available by sending a self-addressed stamped envelope, by email or online.

(1904) · Virginia Commonwealth Award Program

State Council of Higher Education for Virginia
101 N. 14th Street
James Monroe Building
Richmond, VA 23219

Phone: 804-225-2600
Fax: 804-225-2604
Email: communications@schev.edu
Website: http://www.schev.edu
Purpose: To assist Virginia students with financial need.
Eligibility: Undergraduate applicants must be admitted to a Virginia public two- or four-year college or university, be enrolled at least half-time, be residents of Virginia, be U.S. citizens or eligible noncitizens and demonstrate financial need. Graduate applicants must be enrolled full-time in an eligible Virginia graduate degree program.
Target applicant:
   High school students
   College students
   Graduate school students
   Adult students
Minimum GPA: None.
Amount: Varies.
Number of awards: Varies.
Scholarship may be renewable.
Deadline: Varies.
How to apply: Contact your financial aid office.

(1905) · Virginia Guaranteed Assistance Program

State Council of Higher Education for Virginia
101 N. 14th Street
James Monroe Building
Richmond, VA 23219
Phone: 804-225-2600
Fax: 804-225-2604
Email: communications@schev.edu
Website: http://www.schev.edu
Purpose: To provide a financial incentive for economically disadvantaged students to consider attending college.
Eligibility: Applicants must have graduated from a Virginia high school with at least a 2.5 GPA, and they must be enrolled full-time in a two-year or four-year college in the state. Students must be classified as dependents. Preference will be given to students with the greatest financial need.
Target applicant:
   High school students
   College students
   Adult students
Minimum GPA: 2.5
Amount: Varies.
Number of awards: Varies.
Scholarship may be renewable.
Deadline: Varies.
How to apply: Applications are available at college financial aid offices.

(1906) · Virginia High School League Achievement Award

Virginia High School League Foundation
1642 State Farm Boulevard
Charlottesville, VA 22911
Phone: 434-977-8475
Fax: 434-977-5943
Email: ktilley@vhsl.org
Website: http://www.vhsl.org
Purpose: To support students who have made outstanding achievements in sports, academics or courageousness.

Eligibility: Students must be from a Virginia high school in Group A, AA or AAA. Applicants must show participation in VHSL activities and other school or community activities. They must have at least a 3.0 GPA.
Target applicant:
   High school students
Minimum GPA: 3.0
Amount: $1,000.
Number of awards: 10.
Deadline: March 15.
How to apply: Applications are available online.

(1907) · Virginia High School League Charles E. Savedge Journalism Scholarship

Virginia High School League Foundation
1642 State Farm Boulevard
Charlottesville, VA 22911
Phone: 434-977-8475
Fax: 434-977-5943
Email: ktilley@vhsl.org
Website: http://www.vhsl.org
Purpose: To support student journalists in Virginia.
Eligibility: Applicants must be active members of a high school newspaper, yearbook or other publication. Students must be in their senior year and have plans to study journalism in college.
Target applicant:
   High school students
Minimum GPA: None.
Amount: $500.
Number of awards: Varies.
Deadline: March 1.
How to apply: Applications are available online.

(1908) · Virginia Tuition Assistance Grant Program (VTAG)

State Council of Higher Education for Virginia
101 N. 14th Street
James Monroe Building
Richmond, VA 23219
Phone: 804-225-2600
Fax: 804-225-2604
Email: communications@schev.edu
Website: http://www.schev.edu
Purpose: To assist Virginia students.
Eligibility: Applicants must be Virginia residents and enrolled full-time as undergraduate, graduate or professional students in an eligible private Virginia institution.
Target applicant:
   High school students
   College students
   Graduate school students
   Adult students
Minimum GPA: None.
Amount: $2,000-$2,600.
Number of awards: Varies.
Scholarship may be renewable.
Deadline: July 31.
How to apply: Applications are available online or contact your financial aid office.

(1909) · Vocational Rehabilitation Program

College Foundation of North Carolina
P.O. Box 41966
Raleigh, NC 27629-1966
Phone: 866-234-6400
Fax: 919-821-3139
Email: programinformation@cfnc.org
Website: http://www.cfnc.org
Purpose: To provide financial assistance to students with mental and physical disabilities that hinder their ability to obtain employment.
Eligibility: The program provides assistance with counseling, job placement and some support services that is not based on financial need. Need is considered for assistance with tuition and fees, transportation and books.
Target applicant:
　High school students
　College students
　Graduate school students
　Adult students
Minimum GPA: None.
Amount: Up to $2,428.
Number of awards: Varies.
Deadline: Varies.
How to apply: Applications are available from your local Vocational Rehabilitation Office or by mail or phone. The website for the office is www.dhhs.state.nc.us/docs/divinfo/dvr.htm.

(1910) · Vocational Scholarship

Kansas Board of Regents
Curtis State Office Building
Suite 520
1000 SW Jackson Street
Topeka, KS 66612
Phone: 785-296-3421
Fax: 785-296-0983
Email: dlindeman@ksbor.org
Website: http://www.kansasregents.org
Purpose: To assist Kansas students to attend vocational colleges.
Eligibility: Applicants must be enrolled in approved vocational programs and take the vocational exam. Selection is based on exam scores.
Target applicant:
　High school students
　College students
　Adult students
Minimum GPA: None.
Amount: $500.
Number of awards: 250.
Scholarship may be renewable.
Deadline: Varies.
How to apply: Applications are available online.

(1911) · Volunteer Recruitment Service Scholarship

New York State Higher Education Services Corporation (HESC)
99 Washington Avenue
Albany, NY 12255
Phone: 888-697-4372
Email: hescwebmail@hesc.org
Website: http://www.hesc.com
Purpose: To support volunteer firefighters and ambulance personnel from the state of New York.
Eligibility: Applicants must have been New York state residents for at least one year. Students must be enrolled in at least six credits per term in an undergraduate degree program in the state of New York. Applicants who are 23 or older must have less than six months of volunteer service at the initial time of award, but there are no service requirements for those under 23 years of age. Students must not have any previous baccalaureate degrees. Recipients must maintain a 2.0 GPA and keep an active volunteer status while receiving the scholarship.
Target applicant:
　College students
　Adult students
Minimum GPA: 2.0
Amount: Varies.
Number of awards: Varies.
Scholarship may be renewable.
Deadline: May 1.
How to apply: Applications are available from volunteer company officials.

(1912) · VSAC Board of Directors Bette Matkowski Scholarship

Vermont Student Assistance Corporation
10 E. Allen Street
P.O. Box 2000
Winooski, VT 05404
Phone: 888-253-4819
Fax: 802-654-3765
Email: info@vsac.org
Website: http://www.vsac.org
Purpose: To honor the contributions of board member Bette Matkowski to the VSAC.
Eligibility: Applicants must be adult students who attend a Title IV eligible college or university and demonstrate financial need. An essay is required.
Target applicant:
　College students
　Adult students
Minimum GPA: None.
Amount: $1,000.
Number of awards: 2.
Deadline: March 1.
How to apply: Applications are available online.

(1913) · W.P. Black Scholarship Fund

Greater Kanawha Valley Foundation
1600 Huntington Square
900 Lee Street, East
Charleston, WV 25301
Phone: 304-346-3620
Fax: 304-346-3640
Email: tgkvf@tgkvf.org
Website: http://www.tgkvf.org
Purpose: To aid West Virginia students.
Eligibility: Applicants must be residents of West Virginia who are full-time students, have a minimum 2.5 GPA, have a minimum ACT score of 20, be of good moral character and demonstrate significant financial need.
Target applicant:
　High school students
　College students
　Adult students

Minimum GPA: 2.5
Amount: $1,000.
Number of awards: 114.
Scholarship may be renewable.
Deadline: February 17.
How to apply: Applications are available online.

(1914) · Wachovia Citizenship Scholarship

Virginia Department of Education
P.O. Box 2120
Richmond, VA 23218
Phone: 804-225-3349
Fax: 804-371-2456
Email: joseph.wharff@doe.virginia.gov
Website: http://www.pen.k12.va.us
Purpose: To assist high school seniors in paying for higher education.
Eligibility: Applicants must be graduating high school seniors at Virginia High School League A, AA or AAA schools. Students must demonstrate outstanding citizenship.
Target applicant:
 High school students
Minimum GPA: None.
Amount: $1,000.
Number of awards: 6.
Deadline: Varies.
How to apply: Applications are available by phone at (434) 977-8475.

(1915) · Wachovia Technical Scholarship

College Foundation of North Carolina
P.O. Box 41966
Raleigh, NC 27629-1966
Phone: 866-234-6400
Fax: 919-821-3139
Email: programinformation@cfnc.org
Website: http://www.cfnc.org
Purpose: To assist students with financial need who are enrolled in two-year technical programs in North Carolina community colleges.
Eligibility: Applicants must be enrolled full-time in their second year of a technical program. Financial need and academic merit are required. The award may be used for books, tuition or transportation.
Target applicant:
 College students
 Adult students
Minimum GPA: None.
Amount: $500.
Number of awards: 58.
Deadline: Varies.
How to apply: Recipients are selected by a committee at each individual community college. Contact your college for more information.

(1916) · Walter and Ruby Behlen Memorial Scholarship

National FFA Organization
P.O. Box 68960
6060 FFA Drive
Indianapolis, IN 46268-0960
Phone: 317-802-6060

Fax: 317-802-6051
Email: scholarships@ffa.org
Website: http://www.ffa.org
Purpose: To support Nebraska students who are majoring in agriculture.
Eligibility: Applicants must be current FFA members and high school seniors or college students planning to enroll or currently enrolled full-time. They may be pursuing two-year or four-year degrees in any field of agriculture. Students only need to complete the online application one time to be considered for all FFA-administered scholarships. The application requires information about the students' activities and a 1,000-word essay. Awards may be used for books, supplies, tuition, fees and room and board.
Target applicant:
 High school students
 College students
 Adult students
Minimum GPA: None.
Amount: $1,000.
Number of awards: 1.
Deadline: February 15.
How to apply: Applications are available online.

(1917) · WaMu Future Teachers of Color Scholarships

Independent Colleges of Washington
600 Stewart Street, Suite 600
Seattle, WA 98101
Phone: 206-623-4494
Fax: 206-625-9621
Email: info@icwashington.org
Website: http://www.icwashington.org
Purpose: To assist minority students who are studying to become teachers at an independent college of Washington.
Eligibility: Applicants must have financial need and be members of an underrepresented minority group. They must also be committed to a teaching career. Students attending Gonzaga University, Heritage University, Pacific Lutheran University, Saint Martin's University, Seattle Pacific University, Seattle University, University of Puget Sound, Walla Walla University, Whitman College or Whitworth University are eligible.
Target applicant:
 College students
 Adult students
Minimum GPA: None.
Amount: Up to $3,000.
Number of awards: Varies.
Deadline: March 19.
How to apply: Applications are available online or from your school's financial aid office.

(1918) · Washington Award for Vocational Excellence

Washington Higher Education Coordinating Board
917 Lakeridge Way
P.O. Box 43430
Olympia, WA 98504
Phone: 360-753-7850
Fax: 360-753-6243
Email: info@hecb.wa.gov
Website: http://www.hecb.wa.gov
Purpose: To reward students for outstanding achievement in vocational or technical education.

Eligibility: Applicants must be enrolled in a Washington high school, skills center or public community or technical college, graduate high school with at least 360 hours in an approved vocational program or have completed at least one year in an eligible vocational program by June 30th of the award year and not have previously received a WAVE scholarship.

Target applicant:
    High school students
    College students
    Adult students
Minimum GPA: None.
Amount: Up to $6,290.
Number of awards: Varies.
Scholarship may be renewable.
Deadline: Varies.
How to apply: Students must be nominated by a counselor or administrator.

(1919) · Washington College Bound Scholarship

Washington Higher Education Coordinating Board
917 Lakeridge Way
P.O. Box 43430
Olympia, WA 98504
Phone: 360-753-7850
Fax: 360-753-6243
Email: info@hecb.wa.gov
Website: http://www.hecb.wa.gov
Purpose: To provide an incentive for students and their families who might not consider college due to financial concerns.
Eligibility: Applicants must be Washington students in the seventh or eighth grades who are eligible for free or reduced-price lunch, and they must sign a pledge to participate in the program. The student's family income must be 65 percent or less of the state's median income when he or she graduates high school, and his or her GPA must be 2.0 or higher in order to receive the scholarship.
Target applicant:
    Junior high students or younger
Minimum GPA: 2.0
Amount: Tuition.
Number of awards: Varies.
Scholarship may be renewable.
Deadline: Varies.
How to apply: Applications are available online.

(1920) · Washington Oratorical Contest

American Legion, Department of Washington
P.O. Box 3917
Lacey, WA 98509
Phone: 360-491-4373
Fax: 360-491-7442
Email: americanismchairman@americanism-alwa.org
Website: http://www.americanism-alwa.org
Purpose: To enhance high school students' experience with and understanding of the U.S. Constitution. The contest will help develop students' leadership skills and civic appreciation, as well as the ability to deliver thoughtful, insightful orations regarding U.S. citizenship and its inherent responsibilities.
Eligibility: Applicants must be high school students under the age of 20 who are U.S. citizens or legal residents and residents of the state. Students first give an oration within their state and winners compete at the national level. The oration must be related to the Constitution of the United States focusing on the duties and obligations citizens have to the government. It must be in English and be between eight and ten minutes. There is also an assigned topic which is posted on the website, and it should be between three and five minutes.
Target applicant:
    High school students
Minimum GPA: None.
Amount: Varies.
Number of awards: Varies.
Deadline: January 15.
How to apply: Application information is available online.

(1921) · Washington Scholars Grant Program

Washington Higher Education Coordinating Board
917 Lakeridge Way
P.O. Box 43430
Olympia, WA 98504
Phone: 360-753-7850
Fax: 360-753-6243
Email: info@hecb.wa.gov
Website: http://www.hecb.wa.gov
Purpose: To assist Washington high school students.
Eligibility: Applicants must be Washington high school seniors planning to enroll in an eligible Washington college or university. Selection is based on academic achievements, leadership and community activities.
Target applicant:
    High school students
Minimum GPA: None.
Amount: Varies.
Number of awards: Varies.
Scholarship may be renewable.
Deadline: Varies.
How to apply: Students are nominated by their high schools.

(1922) · Washington State Achievers Program

College Success Foundation
1605 NW Sammamish Road
Suite 100
Issaquah, WA 98027
Phone: 425-416-2000
Fax: 425-416-2001
Email: info@collegesuccessfoundation.org
Website: http://www.collegesuccessfoundation.org
Purpose: To provide financial assistance to students in high schools serving large low-income populations in Washington state, encouraging these high schools to raise efforts to improve academic achievement.
Eligibility: Applicants must be a junior or senior in high school at a foundation-designated Achievers high school in Washington state, have a family income that is in the lowest 35 percent of Washington state's family income level and plan to enroll in a Washington public or independent college for at least two years of their college education.
Target applicant:
    High school students
Minimum GPA: None.
Amount: $5,000.
Number of awards: Varies.
Scholarship may be renewable.
Deadline: October 23.
How to apply: Applications are available at the selected high schools and on the Washington Education Foundation's website at http://www.waedfoundation.org.

(1923) · Washington State Auto Dealers Association Awards

Independent Colleges of Washington
600 Stewart Street, Suite 600
Seattle, WA 98101
Phone: 206-623-4494
Fax: 206-625-9621
Email: info@icwashington.org
Website: http://www.icwashington.org
Purpose: To provide financial assistance for business majors.
Eligibility: Recipients must be Washington state residents who are majoring in business or a related field or graduate students who have received the award as undergraduates. Preference is given to minority students. Students attending Gonzaga University, Heritage University, Pacific Lutheran University, Saint Martin's University, Seattle Pacific University, Seattle University, University of Puget Sound, Walla Walla University, Whitman College or Whitworth University are eligible.
Target applicant:
  College students
  Graduate school students
  Adult students
Minimum GPA: None.
Amount: $500.
Number of awards: 10.
Deadline: Varies.
How to apply: No application is necessary. ICW colleges and universities select recipients from their schools.

(1924) · Washington State Endowment Scholarship

Epsilon Sigma Alpha Foundation
P.O. Box 270517
Fort Collins, CO 80527
Phone: 970-223-2824
Fax: 970-223-4456
Email: kloyd@knoxy.net
Website: http://www.esaintl.com/esaf
Purpose: To provide education opportunities for Washington State residents.
Eligibility: Applicants may pursue any major at any school. Selection is based on the following characteristics: character (10 percent), leadership (20 percent), service (10 percent), financial need (30 percent) and scholastic ability (30 percent).
Target applicant:
  High school students
  College students
  Adult students
Minimum GPA: None.
Amount: $500.
Number of awards: 2.
Deadline: February 1.
How to apply: Applications are available online.

(1925) · Washington State PTA Financial Grant

Washington State PTA
2003 65th Avenue West
Tacoma, WA 98466-6215
Phone: 253-565-2153
Email: wapta@wastatepta.org
Website: http://www.wastatepta.org

Purpose: To provide financial assistance to graduates of Washington public high schools.
Eligibility: Applicants must meet maximum household income requirements and be entering their freshman year of college. Academic performance and community service are also considered.
Target applicant:
  High school students
Minimum GPA: None.
Amount: $1,000-$2,000.
Number of awards: Varies.
Deadline: February 10.
How to apply: Applications are available online.

(1926) · West Virginia Scholarship

Epsilon Sigma Alpha Foundation
P.O. Box 270517
Fort Collins, CO 80527
Phone: 970-223-2824
Fax: 970-223-4456
Email: kloyd@knoxy.net
Website: http://www.esaintl.com/esaf
Purpose: To provide education opportunities for West Virginia residents.
Eligibility: Applicants may pursue any major at any institution of higher learning. Selection is based equally on character, leadership, service, financial need and scholastic ability.
Target applicant:
  High school students
  College students
  Adult students
Minimum GPA: None.
Amount: $1,000.
Number of awards: 1.
Deadline: February 1.
How to apply: Applications are available online.

(1927) · Wilder-Naifeh Technical Skills Grant

Tennessee Student Assistance Corporation
404 James Robertson Parkway
Suite 1510, Parkway Towers
Nashville, TN 37243
Phone: 800-342-1663
Fax: 615-741-6101
Email: tsac.aidinfo@state.tn.us
Website: http://www.collegepaystn.com
Purpose: To support students enrolled in Tennessee Technology Centers.
Eligibility: Applicants cannot be prior recipients of the Wilder-Naifeh Grant or the Tennessee HOPE Scholarship. Students must be Tennessee residents for at least one year prior to the beginning of the school term. A list of Tennessee Technology Centers is available online.
Target applicant:
  High school students
  College students
  Adult students
Minimum GPA: None.
Amount: Up to $2,000.
Number of awards: Varies.
Deadline: September 1.
How to apply: Applications are available through completion of the FAFSA.

(1928) · William A. and Vinnie E. Dexter Scholarship

Community Foundation of Western Massachusetts
1500 Main Street
P.O. Box 15769
Springfield, MA 01115
Phone: 413-732-2858
Fax: 413-733-8565
Email: scholar@communityfoundation.org
Website: http://www.communityfoundation.org
Purpose: To help graduating high school seniors in western Massachusetts.
Eligibility: Applicants must plan to attend college part-time or full-time. Application forms, transcripts and Student Aid Reports (from completing the FAFSA) are required.
Target applicant:
 High school students
Minimum GPA: None.
Amount: Varies.
Number of awards: Varies.
Deadline: March 31.
How to apply: Applications are available online and by phone.

(1929) · William D. and Jewell Brewer Scholarship

American Legion, Department of Michigan
212 N. Verlinden Avenue
Lansing, MI 48915
Phone: 517-371-4720 x25
Fax: 517-371-2401
Email: programs@michiganlegion.org
Website: http://www.michiganlegion.org
Purpose: To support Michigan students who are the sons, daughters or grandchildren of veterans.
Eligibility: Applicants must be sons, daughters or grandchildren of wartime veterans, residents of Michigan, have a minimum 2.5 GPA and plan to attend a college or university. Scholarships are based on financial need, academic standing and applicants' goals. Applicants must also provide proof of a parent's military service record. They should send scholarship information to the county district committee person.
Target applicant:
 High school students
 College students
 Graduate school students
 Adult students
Minimum GPA: 2.5
Amount: $500.
Number of awards: Varies.
Deadline: January 5.
How to apply: Applications are available online.

(1930) · William D. Squires Scholarship

William D. Squires Educational Foundation
P.O. Box 2940
Jupiter, FL 33468-2940
Phone: 561-741-7751
Email: wmdsquires@comcast.net
Website: http://www.wmd-squires-foundation.org
Purpose: To provide financial assistance to needy Ohio students with specific career goals.
Eligibility: Applicants must be Ohio high school seniors with demonstrated financial need who have specific career goals and are highly motivated. They must plan to enroll in a degree, diploma or certificate program at an accredited college or university, and they must have a minimum GPA of 3.2.
Target applicant:
 High school students
Minimum GPA: 3.2
Amount: $3,000.
Number of awards: 12.
Scholarship may be renewable.
Deadline: April 5.
How to apply: Applications are available online.

(1931) · William G. Saletic Scholarship

Independent Colleges of Washington
600 Stewart Street, Suite 600
Seattle, WA 98101
Phone: 206-623-4494
Fax: 206-625-9621
Email: info@icwashington.org
Website: http://www.icwashington.org
Purpose: To provide financial assistance to students who are studying politics or history at an independent college of Washington.
Eligibility: Applicants must be juniors or seniors who are studying or majoring in politics or history. Students attending Gonzaga University, Heritage University, Pacific Lutheran University, Saint Martin's University, Seattle Pacific University, Seattle University, University of Puget Sound, Walla Walla University, Whitman College or Whitworth University are eligible.
Target applicant:
 College students
 Adult students
Minimum GPA: None.
Amount: $1,000.
Number of awards: Varies.
Deadline: March 14.
How to apply: Applications are available online or from your school's financial aid office.

(1932) · William James and Dorothy Bading Lanquist Fund

Hawaii Community Foundation - Scholarships
1164 Bishop Street, Suite 800
Honolulu, HI 96813
Phone: 888-731-3863
Fax: 808-521-6286
Email: scholarships@hcf-hawaii.org
Website: http://www.hawaiicommunityfoundation.org
Purpose: To support students who are majoring in physical sciences and related fields.
Eligibility: Applicants must be residents of Hawaii.
Target applicant:
 High school students
 College students
 Adult students
Minimum GPA: None.
Amount: $1,000.
Number of awards: 8.
Deadline: March 1.
How to apply: To apply, register online, complete the online application and select the scholarships to which you wish to apply. In addition, mail the supporting materials: printed confirmation page from the online

application, personal statement, copy of Student Aid Report (SAR) available at www.fafsa.ed.gov and official transcript.

(1933) · William L. Boyd, IV, Florida Resident Access Grant

Florida Department of Education
Office of Student Financial Assistance
1940 N. Monroe Street
Suite 70
Tallahassee, FL 32303-4759
Phone: 888-827-2004
Fax: 850-245-9667
Email: osfa@fldoe.org
Website: http://www.floridastudentfinancialaid.org
Purpose: Provides monetary assistance to Florida undergraduate college students enrolled at eligible, private, non-profit Florida schools.
Eligibility: Applicants must attend an eligible private, nonprofit Florida college or university, be Florida residents and not be in default on any state or federal grant, loan or scholarship. Requirements vary by institution.
Target applicant:
    High school students
    College students
    Adult students
Minimum GPA: None.
Amount: Varies.
Number of awards: Varies.
Scholarship may be renewable.
Deadline: Varies.
How to apply: Contact your financial aid office.

(1934) · William P. Willis Scholarship Program

Oklahoma State Regents for Higher Education
655 Research Parkway, Suite 200
Oklahoma City, OK 73104
Phone: 800-858-1840
Fax: 405-225-9230
Email: studentinfo@osrhe.edu
Website: http://www.okhighered.org
Purpose: To provide financial assistance to low-income students attending institutions in the Oklahoma State system.
Eligibility: Applicants must be Oklahoma residents who are enrolled full-time in an undergraduate program at an Oklahoma State System institution. They must also meet low-income criteria.
Target applicant:
    College students
    Adult students
Minimum GPA: None.
Amount: Up to full tuition.
Number of awards: Varies.
Scholarship may be renewable.
Deadline: Varies.
How to apply: Students must be nominated by their college's president.

(1935) · William Winter Teacher Scholarship

Mississippi Office of Student Financial Aid
3825 Ridgewood Road
Jackson, MS 39211
Phone: 800-327-2980

Fax: 601-432-6527
Email: sfa@ihl.state.ms.us
Website: http://www.ihl.state.ms.us
Purpose: To increase the supply of teachers for public schools in Mississippi.
Eligibility: Applicants must be enrolled as full-time students in programs leading to a Class 'A' teaching license and must have a high school GPA of 3.0 or higher and an ACT score of 21 or higher. Sophomores, juniors, seniors and persons seeking a second baccalaureate degree leading to a Class "A" teaching license must have a cumulative college GPA of 2.5 or higher. Applicants must also agree to serve for one year in any Mississippi public school for each year they receive the scholarship. Awards are made on a first come, first served basis.
Target applicant:
    High school students
    College students
    Adult students
Minimum GPA: Varies.
Amount: $1,000-$3,000.
Number of awards: Varies.
Scholarship may be renewable.
Deadline: March.
How to apply: Contact the Mississippi Office of Student Financial Aid for an application.

(1936) · Willis HRH Scholarship

Virginia Foundation for Independent Colleges
8010 Ridge Road
Suite B
Richmond, VA 23229-7288
Phone: 800-230-6757
Fax: 804-282-4635
Email: info@vfic.org
Website: http://www.vfic.org/scholarship/scholarships_applications.html
Purpose: To provide assistance for students attending VFIC colleges and find qualified interns for Willis HRH.
Eligibility: Applicants must be full-time students at a VFIC college or university. They must be in the first semester of their junior year and have a GPA of 3.0 or higher. They must be majoring or intend to major in marketing, business, economics, finance, mathematics or a related field. Financial need is required, as is evidence of leadership in college extracurricular activities. Winners must apply for a paid internship with Willis HRH. Students who can speak a second language or have work experience in sales, customer relations or retail will be given special consideration.
Target applicant:
    College students
    Adult students
Minimum GPA: 3.0
Amount: $2,500.
Number of awards: 6.
Scholarship may be renewable.
Deadline: November 1.
How to apply: Applications are available online.

(1937) · Wisconsin Foundation for Independent Colleges Scholarship

Wisconsin Foundation for Independent Colleges
4425 North Port Washington Road
Suite 402

Glendale, WI 53212
Phone: 414-273-5980
Email: wfic@wficweb.org
Website: http://www.wficweb.org
Purpose: To support students who are attending private colleges in Wisconsin.
Eligibility: Students must meet various college-specific requirements for each scholarship including residency, GPA and area of study.
Target applicant:
   High school students
   College students
   Adult students
Minimum GPA: None.
Amount: Varies.
Number of awards: Varies.
Deadline: Varies.
How to apply: Applications are available at college financial aid offices.

(1938) · Wisconsin National Guard Scholarships

Department of Military Affairs
WING-SBF
P.O. Box 14587
Madison, WI 53708-14587
Phone: 800-292-9464
Fax: 608-242-3154
Email: education@wi.ngb.army.mil
Website: http://dma.wi.gov
Purpose: To help Wisconsin National Guard members with their education.
Eligibility: Applicants must be Wisconsin National Guard enlisted members and warrant officers in good standing who do not have a bachelor's degree. Recipients may use the grant at any campus of the University of Wisconsin System, a public institution of higher education under the Minnesota-Wisconsin student reciprocity agreement or an accredited institution of higher education in Wisconsin.
Target applicant:
   High school students
   College students
   Adult students
Minimum GPA: 2.0
Amount: Varies.
Number of awards: Varies.
Scholarship may be renewable.
Deadline: Varies.
How to apply: Applications are available online.

(1939) · Wisconsin Oratorical Contest

American Legion, Department of Wisconsin
2930 American Legion Drive
P.O. Box 388
Portage, WI 53901
Phone: 608-745-1090
Fax: 608-745-0179
Email: info@wilegion.org
Website: http://www.wilegion.org
Purpose: To enhance high school students' experience with and understanding of the U.S. Constitution. The contest will help develop students' leadership skills and civic appreciation, as well as the ability to deliver thoughtful, insightful orations regarding U.S. citizenship and its inherent responsibilities.

Eligibility: Applicants must be high school students under the age of 20 who are U.S. citizens or legal residents and residents of the state. Students first give an oration within their state and winners compete at the national level. The oration must be related to the Constitution of the United States focusing on the duties and obligations citizens have to the government. It must be in English and be between eight and ten minutes. There is also an assigned topic which is posted on the website, and it should be between three and five minutes.
Target applicant:
   High school students
Minimum GPA: None.
Amount: Varies.
Number of awards: Varies.
Deadline: February 3.
How to apply: Application information is available by contacting the local American Legion Post.

(1940) · Wisconsin Region Student Leadership Scholarship

National Association for Campus Activities
13 Harbison Way
Columbia, SC 29212
Phone: 803-732-6222
Fax: 803-749-1047
Email: info@naca.org
Website: http://www.naca.org
Purpose: To help students who are working toward undergraduate or graduate degrees that lead to careers in student activities or services.
Eligibility: Applicants must be undergraduate or graduate students taking at least six credits per semester and be enrolled in or have previously earned a degree from a college or university in Wisconsin or the Upper Peninsula of Michigan. Applicants must also have demonstrated leadership and service to their campus community.
Target applicant:
   College students
   Graduate school students
   Adult students
Minimum GPA: None.
Amount: Varies.
Number of awards: Varies.
Deadline: January 15.
How to apply: Applications are available online.

(1941) · Women in Science and Technology Scholarship

Virginia Business and Professional Women's Foundation
P.O. Box 4842
McLean, VA 22103-4842
Phone: 800-525-3729
Email: bpwfoundation@act.org
Website: http://www.vabpwfoundation.org
Purpose: To support women who are pursuing careers in science and technology.
Eligibility: Applicants must be at least 18 years of age, and they must be officially accepted into a bachelor's, master's or doctoral program in the state of Virginia. Students must be majoring in biology, bio-engineering, chemistry, computer science, dentistry, engineering, mathematics, medicine, physics or similar scientific and technical fields. Applicants must show financial need and have concrete plans to use their education in a science or technical career. Recipients must complete their course of study within two years.

Target applicant:
High school students
College students
Graduate school students
Adult students
Minimum GPA: None.
Amount: $500-$1,000.
Number of awards: Varies.
Deadline: April 1.
How to apply: Applications are available online.

(1942) · Workforce Incentive Program

New Hampshire Postsecondary Education Commission
3 Barrell Court
Suite 300
Concord, NH 03301
Phone: 603-271-2555 x352
Fax: 603-271-2696
Email: jknapp@pec.state.nh.us
Website: http://www.state.nh.us/postsecondary
Purpose: To encourage New Hampshire students to enter career shortage areas in special education, foreign language, mathematics, chemistry, science, physics and nursing. The scholarship repays education loans.
Eligibility: Applicants must have completed at least one year of service in an approved shortage area for each year of repayment.
Target applicant:
College students
Graduate school students
Adult students
Minimum GPA: 3.0
Amount: $1,500-$3,000.
Number of awards: Varies.
Scholarship may be renewable.
Deadline: October 31.
How to apply: Applications are available online.

(1943) · Workforce Shortage Student Assistance Grant Program

Maryland Higher Education Commission
Office of Student Financial Assistance
839 Bestgate Road, Suite 400
Annapolis, MD 21401
Phone: 800-974-1024
Fax: 410-260-3200
Email: osfamail@mhec.state.md.us
Website: http://www.mhec.state.md.us
Purpose: To support students in Maryland who plan to work in jobs which are needed on a statewide or regional basis.
Eligibility: Applicants must be currently enrolled or planning to enroll in a Maryland postsecondary school. Dependent students must have parents who also live in Maryland. Eligible majors are chosen to address current state or regional needs and usually include the following: child care, human services, teaching, nursing, physical and occupational therapy and public service. Students must agree to begin working within that employment field within one year of graduation at a rate of one year for every year that the scholarship was granted.
Target applicant:
High school students
College students
Graduate school students
Adult students

Minimum GPA: None.
Amount: $2,000-$4,000.
Number of awards: Varies.
Scholarship may be renewable.
Deadline: July 1.
How to apply: Applications are available online in January.

(1944) · World of Expressions Scholarship - Music

Random House Inc. Creative Writing Competition
c/o Scholarship America
One Scholarship Way
P.O. Box 297
St. Peter, MN 56082
Phone: 888-369-3434
Fax: 212-940-7590
Email: worldofexpression@randomhouse.com
Website: http://www.worldofexpression.org
Purpose: To recognize students of New York City Public High Schools for creativity in music.
Eligibility: Applicants must be seniors in a New York City Public High School who are 21 years old or younger and must not have family members employed by Bertelsmann or its subsidiaries. They should submit original literary compositions in one of the following ways: poetry/spoken work, fiction/drama, personal essay/memoir or graphic novel. Compositions are judged based on technical merit, but artistic expression is the main criterion.
Target applicant:
High school students
Minimum GPA: None.
Amount: $500-$10,000.
Number of awards: Varies.
Deadline: February 9.
How to apply: Applications are available online.

(1945) · World Trade Center Memorial Scholarship

New York State Higher Education Services Corporation (HESC)
99 Washington Avenue
Albany, NY 12255
Phone: 888-697-4372
Email: hescwebmail@hesc.org
Website: http://www.hesc.com
Purpose: To support the families and dependents of those who were injured or died as a result of the attacks on September 11, 2001.
Eligibility: Applicants must be full-time undergraduate students. Students must attend school in the state of New York, but they may be residents of any state or country.
Target applicant:
College students
Adult students
Minimum GPA: None.
Amount: Varies.
Number of awards: Varies.
Scholarship may be renewable.
Deadline: Varies.
How to apply: Applications are available online.

(1946) · WSTLA President's Scholarship

Washington State Trial Lawyers Association
1809 7th Avenue #1500
Seattle, WA 98101-1328

Phone: 206-464-1011
Fax: 206-464-0703
Email: wstla@wstla.org
Website: http://www.wstla.org
Purpose: To provide assistance to needy Washington students who have overcome challenges.
Eligibility: Applicants must be residents of Washington state who are attending high school at the time of application and have achieved advanced placement toward a degree. They must have financial need, and they must have overcome a disability, handicap or similar challenge. They must plan to use their education to help people.
Target applicant:
   High school students
Minimum GPA: None.
Amount: Up to $2,000.
Number of awards: Varies.
Deadline: March 21.
How to apply: Applications are available online.

(1947) · You've Got a Friend in Pennsylvania Scholarship

American Radio Relay League Foundation
225 Main Street
Newington, CT 06111
Phone: 860-594-0397
Fax: 860-594-0259
Email: foundation@arrl.org
Website: http://www.arrl.org
Purpose: To support Pennsylvania students who are involved in amateur radio.
Eligibility: Applicants must have an amateur radio license in General Class or higher and an active American Radio Relay League membership.
Target applicant:
   High school students
   College students
   Adult students
Minimum GPA: None.
Amount: $2,000.
Number of awards: 1.
Deadline: February 1.
How to apply: Applications are available online.

(1948) · Youth for Adolescent Pregnancy Prevention-Leadership Recognition Program

California Health and Welfare Agency - Office of Statewide Health Planning and Development
Health Professions Education Foundation
818 K Street, Room 210
Sacramento, CA 95814
Phone: 916-324-6500
Fax: 916-324-6585
Email: hpef@oshpd.state.ca.us
Website: http://www.healthprofessions.ca.gov
Purpose: To assist California students who promote teen pregnancy prevention and healthy adolescent sexuality.
Eligibility: Applicants must be California residents between the ages of 16 and 24, have either a high school diploma or GED and plan to be or are already be enrolled in a health profession program. Recipients must

sign a two-year service agreement to work in a medically underserved area within six months following graduation from the program.
Target applicant:
   High school students
   College students
Minimum GPA: None.
Amount: $25,000.
Number of awards: Varies.
Deadline: November.
How to apply: Applications are available online.

(1949) · YouthLaunch Scholarship for Outstanding Service

YouthLaunch
7756 Northcross Drive
Suite 203
Austin, TX 78757
Phone: 512-342-0424
Email: info@youthlaunch.org
Website: http://www.youthlaunch.org
Purpose: To honor Texas students who are leaders in their communities and inspire their peers.
Eligibility: Applicants must be high school students or recent graduates who have attended school in the state of Texas. They must plan to begin their post-secondary education within one year of graduation. Current high school students must have completed at least 50 hours of community service during their final year of high school and at least 400 hours during their entire high school career. Recent graduates must have completed at least 100 hours of community service after graduation.
Target applicant:
   High school students
Minimum GPA: None.
Amount: $3,000.
Number of awards: 3.
Deadline: February 28.
How to apply: Applications are available online.

(1950) · Zagunis Student Leader Scholarship

National Association for Campus Activities
13 Harbison Way
Columbia, SC 29212
Phone: 803-732-6222
Fax: 803-749-1047
Email: info@naca.org
Website: http://www.naca.org
Purpose: To provide financial assistance to student leaders.
Eligibility: Applicants must hold a significant campus leadership position, demonstrate significant leadership skills and abilities and make significant contributions through on- or off-campus volunteering. Students must attend school in Kentucky, Michigan, Ohio, West Virginia or Western Pennsylvania.
Target applicant:
   College students
   Adult students
Minimum GPA: 3.0
Amount: Varies.
Number of awards: Varies.
Deadline: November 1.
How to apply: Applications are available online.

(1951) · Zeta Jones-Haldin Endowment

Epsilon Sigma Alpha Foundation
P.O. Box 270517
Fort Collins, CO 80527
Phone: 970-223-2824
Fax: 970-223-4456
Email: kloyd@knoxy.net
Website: http://www.esaintl.com/esaf
Purpose: To provide financial assistance to Florida residents.
Eligibility: Applicants may attend any college or university and pursue any major. Selection is based on scholastic ability (30 percent), financial need (30 percent), leadership (20 percent), character (10 percent) and service (10 percent).
Target applicant:
   High school students
   College students
   Adult students
Minimum GPA: None.
Amount: $500.
Number of awards: 1.
Deadline: February 1.
How to apply: Applications are available online.

MEMBERSHIP

(1952) · Academic Financial Services FFA Scholarship

National FFA Organization
P.O. Box 68960
6060 FFA Drive
Indianapolis, IN 46268-0960
Phone: 317-802-6060
Fax: 317-802-6051
Email: scholarships@ffa.org
Website: http://www.ffa.org
Purpose: To support students who are in the FFA.
Eligibility: Applicants must be current FFA members and high school seniors or college students planning to enroll or currently enrolled full-time. Students only need to complete the online application one time to be considered for all FFA-administered scholarships. The application requires information about the students' activities and a 1,000-word essay. Awards may be used for books, supplies, tuition, fees and room and board.
Target applicant:
   High school students
   College students
   Adult students
Minimum GPA: None.
Amount: $1,000.
Number of awards: 5.
Deadline: February 15.
How to apply: Applications are available online.

(1953) · AFL-CIO Skilled Trades Exploring Scholarship

Explorers Learning for Life
P.O. Box 152079
Irving, TX 75015
Phone: 972-580-2433
Fax: 972-580-2137
Email: pchestnu@lflmail.org
Website: http://www.learningforlife.org/exploring
Purpose: To assist explorers in obtaining an education that will help them start a career in skilled trades.
Eligibility: Applicants must be graduating seniors who plan to attend an accredited public or proprietary institution or a union apprentice program. They must provide three recommendations and a 500-word essay.
Target applicant:
   High school students
Minimum GPA: None.
Amount: $1,000.
Number of awards: 2.
Deadline: April 30.
How to apply: Applications are available online.

(1954) · AFSA Financial Aid Scholarships

American Foreign Service Association (AFSA)
2101 East Street NW
Washington, DC 20037
Phone: 202-944-5504
Fax: 202-338-6820
Email: dec@afsa.org
Website: http://www.afsa.org/essaycontest

Purpose: To provide financial aid to university students who are the children or dependents of Foreign Service employees.

Eligibility: Applicants must be dependents of U.S. government Foreign Service employees with a minimum 2.0 GPA. Students must attend or plan to attend full-time an undergraduate U.S. college, university, community college, art school, conservatory or other post-secondary institution. Applicants must submit applications, transcripts and financial need reports. Recipients must complete their undergraduate degree within four years and must demonstrate financial need.

Target applicant:
High school students
College students
Adult students

Minimum GPA: 2.0

Amount: $1,000-$3,500.

Number of awards: 55.

Scholarship may be renewable.

Deadline: February 6.

How to apply: Applications are available after November 1.

(1955) · AFSA/AAFSW Merit Award

American Foreign Service Association (AFSA)
2101 East Street NW
Washington, DC 20037
Phone: 202-944-5504
Fax: 202-338-6820
Email: dec@afsa.org
Website: http://www.afsa.org/essaycontest

Purpose: To recognize the academic and artistic achievements of high school seniors who are the children or dependents of Foreign Service employees.

Eligibility: Applicants must be dependents of U.S. government Foreign Service employees who are members of AFSA or AAFSW. Students must be high school seniors with a minimum 2.0 GPA. Applicants can also submit an art entry under the categories of visual arts, musical arts, drama, dance or creative writing. Awards are based on GPA, SAT scores, a two-page essay, letters of recommendation and extra-curricular activities.

Target applicant:
High school students

Minimum GPA: 2.0

Amount: $500-$1,500.

Number of awards: Varies.

Deadline: February 6.

How to apply: Applications are available online after November 1.

(1956) · AFSCME Family Scholarship Program

American Federation of State, County and Municipal Employees (AFSCME), AFL-CIO
Attn: Education Department
1625 L Street NW
Washington, DC 20036-5687
Phone: 202-429-1000
Fax: 202-429-1293
Email: education@afscme.org
Website: http://www.afscme.org

Purpose: To offer financial assistance to the dependents of AFSCME members.

Eligibility: Applicants must be graduating high school seniors who are the daughters, sons or financially dependent grandchildren of AFSCME members who intend to enroll in a full-time, four-year degree program

in any accredited college or university. Applicants should submit applications, essays, transcripts, test scores and recommendation letters. Selection is based on information provided on the application form, high school transcript, SAT/ACT scores and a required essay.

Target applicant:
High school students

Minimum GPA: None.

Amount: $2,000.

Number of awards: 13.

Scholarship may be renewable.

Deadline: December 31.

How to apply: Applications are available online and by written request.

(1957) · AFTRA/Heller Memorial Foundation Scholarships

American Federation of Television and Radio Artists
260 Madison Avenue
7th Floor
New York, NY 10016
Phone: 212-532-0800
Fax: 212-532-2242
Email: info@aftra.com
Website: http://www.aftra.com

Purpose: To support AFTRA members and their children.

Eligibility: Applicants must be AFTRA members in good standing with five years of membership or the children of members. Scholarships are awarded based on academic achievement and financial need and can be used to study any academic field or for professional training in the performing arts at an accredited higher education institution.

Target applicant:
High school students
College students
Graduate school students
Adult students

Minimum GPA: None.

Amount: Up to $2,500.

Number of awards: 12-15.

Deadline: May 1.

How to apply: Applications are available online.

(1958) · AGCO Corporation FFA Scholarship

National FFA Organization
P.O. Box 68960
6060 FFA Drive
Indianapolis, IN 46268-0960
Phone: 317-802-6060
Fax: 317-802-6051
Email: scholarships@ffa.org
Website: http://www.ffa.org

Purpose: To support students in select majors who are in the FFA.

Eligibility: Applicants must be current FFA members and high school seniors or college students planning to enroll or currently enrolled full-time. They must have one of the following undergraduate majors: agronomy, crop science, general agriculture, agricultural communications, education, journalism, extension, public relations, business management, economics, sales and marketing, engineering, mechanization, agriculture power and equipment or welding. Students only need to complete the online application one time to be considered for all FFA-administered scholarships. The application requires information about the students' activities and a 1,000-word essay. Awards may be used for books, supplies, tuition, fees and room and board. Students must show financial need and evidence of community service participation.

Target applicant:
  High school students
  College students
  Adult students
Minimum GPA: None.
Amount: $2,400.
Number of awards: 8.
Deadline: February 15.
How to apply: Applications are available online.

(1959) · AGDATA Inc. FFA Scholarship

National FFA Organization
P.O. Box 68960
6060 FFA Drive
Indianapolis, IN 46268-0960
Phone: 317-802-6060
Fax: 317-802-6051
Email: scholarships@ffa.org
Website: http://www.ffa.org
Purpose: To support students who are members of the FFA.
Eligibility: Applicants must be current FFA members and high school seniors or college students planning to enroll or currently enrolled full-time. They must be majoring in one of the following subject areas: agronomy and crop science, animal nutrition, animal/dairy/poultry science, agricultural communications, business management, education, economics, finance, engineering, animal breeding and genetics, biochemistry, biological sciences, family and ranch management, horticulture, computer science in agriculture, entomology, environmental engineering, turf management, general agriculture, plant pathology or soil science. Students only need to complete the online application one time to be considered for all FFA-administered scholarships. The application requires information about the students' activities and a 1,000-word essay. Awards may be used for books, supplies, tuition, fees and room and board. Applicants must show financial need.
Target applicant:
  High school students
  College students
  Adult students
Minimum GPA: None.
Amount: $2,500.
Number of awards: 2.
Deadline: February 15.
How to apply: Applications are available online.

(1960) · Agrium U.S. Inc. FFA Scholarship

National FFA Organization
P.O. Box 68960
6060 FFA Drive
Indianapolis, IN 46268-0960
Phone: 317-802-6060
Fax: 317-802-6051
Email: scholarships@ffa.org
Website: http://www.ffa.org
Purpose: To support students who are members of the FFA.
Eligibility: Applicants must be current FFA members and high school seniors or college students planning to enroll or currently enrolled full-time. They must have at least a 3.0 GPA and be pursuing a bachelor's degree in one of the following subjects: agricultural sales, marketing, engineering, agronomy or crop science. Students only need to complete

the online application one time to be considered for all FFA-administered scholarships. The application requires information about the students' activities and a 1,000-word essay. Awards may be used for books, supplies, tuition, fees and room and board. Applicants must show proof of community service participation.
Target applicant:
  High school students
  College students
  Adult students
Minimum GPA: 3.0
Amount: $1,000.
Number of awards: 5.
Deadline: February 15.
How to apply: Applications are available online.

(1961) · Agway Foundation FFA Scholarship

National FFA Organization
P.O. Box 68960
6060 FFA Drive
Indianapolis, IN 46268-0960
Phone: 317-802-6060
Fax: 317-802-6051
Email: scholarships@ffa.org
Website: http://www.ffa.org
Purpose: To support FFA members who are studying agriculture.
Eligibility: Applicants must be residents of one of the following states: Connecticut, Delaware, Maine, Massachusetts, New Hampshire, New Jersey, New York, Pennsylvania, Rhode Island or Vermont. They must be current FFA members and high school seniors or college students planning to enroll or currently enrolled full-time. They may be pursuing a two-year or four-year degree in any major related to agriculture. Students only need to complete the online application one time to be considered for all FFA-administered scholarships. The application requires information about the students' activities and a 1,000-word essay. Awards may be used for books, supplies, tuition, fees and room and board.
Target applicant:
  High school students
  College students
  Adult students
Minimum GPA: None.
Amount: $1,000.
Number of awards: 9.
Deadline: February 15.
How to apply: Applications are available online.

(1962) · All-Teke Academic Team

Tau Kappa Epsilon Educational Foundation
8645 Founders Road
Indianapolis, IN 46268
Phone: 317-872-6533
Fax: 317-875-8353
Email: tef@tke.org
Website: http://www.tkefoundation.org
Purpose: To recognize the scholastic achievement of the top ten members academically.
Eligibility: Applicants must be initiated Tau Kappa Epsilon members in good standing and full-time students. Applicants must also have a GPA of at least 3.0 and demonstrate outstanding positive contributions to their chapter, campus and community. A statement describing how they have benefited from TKE membership is required.

Target applicant:
 College students
 Adult students
Minimum GPA: 3.0
Amount: $300.
Number of awards: 10.
Deadline: March 16.
How to apply: Applications are available online.

(1963) · Allan Jerome Burry Scholarship

United Methodist Church
Office of Loans and Scholarships
P.O. BOX 340007
Nashville, TN 37203-0007
Phone: 615-340-7344
Fax: 615-340-7367
Email: umscholar@gbhem.org
Website: http://www.gbhem.org
Purpose: To support students in ministry or chaplaincy programs who are members of the United Methodist Church.
Eligibility: Applicants must show evidence of financial need, leadership qualities, academic excellence and church participation. They must have a GPA of 3.0 or higher. Students must have been active members of the United Methodist Church for at least three years and be nominated by the campus chaplain or minister.
Target applicant:
 College students
 Graduate school students
 Adult students
Minimum GPA: 3.0
Amount: Varies.
Number of awards: Varies.
Deadline: February 1.
How to apply: Applications are available from campus ministers or chaplains.

(1964) · ALPA Scholarship Program

Air Line Pilots Association
1625 Massachusetts Avenue NW
Washington, DC 20036
Phone: 703-689-2270
Website: http://www.alpa.org
Purpose: To support the children of medically retired, long-term disabled or deceased pilot members of the Air Line Pilots Association.
Eligibility: Applicants must be pursuing a baccalaureate degree. Selection is based on academic achievements and financial need. The award is renewable for four years with a minimum 3.0 GPA.
Target applicant:
 High school students
 College students
 Adult students
Minimum GPA: 3.0
Amount: $3,000.
Number of awards: 1.
Scholarship may be renewable.
Deadline: April 1.
How to apply: Applications are available by mail.

(1965) · Alpha Gamma Rho Educational Foundation

National FFA Organization
P.O. Box 68960
6060 FFA Drive
Indianapolis, IN 46268-0960
Phone: 317-802-6060
Fax: 317-802-6051
Email: scholarships@ffa.org
Website: http://www.ffa.org
Purpose: To support male students who are majoring in agriculture.
Eligibility: Applicants must be current FFA members and high school seniors or college students planning to enroll or currently enrolled full-time. Students must enroll in a college which has an Alpha Gamma Rho chapter, and they should be pursuing a four-year degree in any field related to agriculture. Students only need to complete the online application one time to be considered for all FFA-administered scholarships. The application requires information about the students' activities and a 1,000-word essay. Awards may be used for books, supplies, tuition, fees and room and board.
Target applicant:
 High school students
 College students
 Adult students
Minimum GPA: None.
Amount: $1,000.
Number of awards: 1.
Deadline: February 15.
How to apply: Applications are available online.

(1966) · Alvin E. Heaps Memorial Scholarship

Retail, Wholesale and Department Store Union District Council (RWDSU)
30 E. 29th Street
New York, NY 10016
Phone: 212-684-5300
Fax: 212-779-2809
Website: http://www.rwdsu.info
Purpose: To provide scholarships for RWDSU members and their children.
Eligibility: Applicants must be RWDSU members or their children. Recipients are determined through consideration of academic performance, involvement in extracurricular activities and completion of a 500-word essay.
Target applicant:
 High school students
 College students
 Adult students
Minimum GPA: None.
Amount: Varies.
Number of awards: Varies.
Deadline: June 15.
How to apply: Applications are available online or by written request.

(1967) · American Family Insurance FFA Scholarship

National FFA Organization
P.O. Box 68960
6060 FFA Drive
Indianapolis, IN 46268-0960
Phone: 317-802-6060
Fax: 317-802-6051

Email: scholarships@ffa.org
Website: http://www.ffa.org
Purpose: To support students who are members of the FFA.
Eligibility: Applicants must be current FFA members and high school seniors or college students planning to enroll or currently enrolled full-time. They may be pursuing a four-year degree in any major in the state of Wisconsin, Minnesota or Missouri. Students only need to complete the online application one time to be considered for all FFA-administered scholarships. The application requires information about the students' activities and a 1,000-word essay. Awards may be used for books, supplies, tuition, fees and room and board.
Target applicant:
   High school students
   College students
   Adult students
Minimum GPA: None.
Amount: $1,000.
Number of awards: 3.
Deadline: February 15.
How to apply: Applications are available online.

(1968) · American Legion Eagle Scout of the Year

American Legion
Attn.: Americanism and Children and Youth Division
P.O. Box 1055
Indianapolis, IN 46206
Phone: 317-630-1249
Fax: 317-630-1369
Website: http://www.legion.org
Purpose: To provide scholarships for Eagle Scouts.
Eligibility: Applicants must be registered, active members of a Boy Scout Troop, Varsity Scout Team or Venturing crew chartered to an American Legion Post or Auxiliary or Scouts who are the sons or grandsons of Legionnaires or Auxiliary Members. Applicants must receive the Eagle Scout Award, be active members of their religious institutions, receiving the appropriate Boy Scouts religious emblem, demonstrate citizenship, be at least 15 years old and be high school students.
Target applicant:
   High school students
Minimum GPA: None.
Amount: $2,500-$10,000.
Number of awards: 4.
Deadline: March 1.
How to apply: Applications are available online.

(1969) · American Veterinary Medical Association FFA Scholarship

National FFA Organization
P.O. Box 68960
6060 FFA Drive
Indianapolis, IN 46268-0960
Phone: 317-802-6060
Fax: 317-802-6051
Email: scholarships@ffa.org
Website: http://www.ffa.org
Purpose: To support students who are pursuing degrees related to animal science.
Eligibility: Applicants must be current FFA members and high school seniors or college students planning to enroll or currently enrolled full-time. They must be pursuing a four-year degree in one of the following subject areas: animal nutrition; animal, dairy, equine or poultry science;

animal breeding and genetics; animal pathology or veterinary sciences. Preference will be given to students who are planning to work in the fields of veterinary medicine and veterinary food supply. Students only need to complete the online application one time to be considered for all FFA-administered scholarships. The application requires information about the students' activities and a 1,000-word essay. Awards may be used for books, supplies, tuition, fees and room and board.
Target applicant:
   High school students
   College students
   Adult students
Minimum GPA: None.
Amount: $1,000.
Number of awards: 2.
Deadline: February 15.
How to apply: Applications are available online.

(1970) · AMVETS National Ladies Auxiliary Scholarship

AMVETS Auxiliary
4647 Forbes Boulevard
Lanham, MD 20706
Phone: 301-459-6255
Website: http://www.amvetsaux.org
Purpose: To promote educational opportunities for students interested in or involved with a national service organization.
Eligibility: Applicants must be the child or grandchild of a current member of the AMVETS Ladies Auxiliary.
Target applicant:
   High school students
   College students
   Adult students
Minimum GPA: None.
Amount: $500-$1,000.
Number of awards: 12.
Deadline: June 1.
How to apply: Applications are available by mail.

(1971) · Anderson Foundation FFA Scholarship

National FFA Organization
P.O. Box 68960
6060 FFA Drive
Indianapolis, IN 46268-0960
Phone: 317-802-6060
Fax: 317-802-6051
Email: scholarships@ffa.org
Website: http://www.ffa.org
Purpose: To support students who are majoring in agriculture.
Eligibility: Applicants must be current FFA members and high school seniors or college students planning to enroll or currently enrolled full-time. They must be pursuing a four-year degree in agriculture in the state of Illinois, Indiana, Michigan or Ohio. Applicants must show proof of community service participation. Students only need to complete the online application one time to be considered for all FFA-administered scholarships. The application requires information about the students' activities and a 1,000-word essay. Awards may be used for books, supplies, tuition, fees and room and board.
Target applicant:
   High school students
   College students
   Adult students

Minimum GPA: None.
Amount: $1,250.
Number of awards: 2.
Deadline: February 15.
How to apply: Applications are available online.

(1972) · Anthony J. DeAndrade Scholarship

Graphic Communications International Union
1900 L Street NW
Washington, DC 20036
Phone: 202-462-1400
Fax: 202-721-0600
Website: http://www.gciu.org
Purpose: To provide scholarships for the dependents of members of the GCIU.
Eligibility: Applicants must be dependents of a member of GCIU, be graduating from high school during the year of the award or be a recent graduate who by Oct. 1 will not have completed more than one-half year of college.
Target applicant:
  High school students
Minimum GPA: None.
Amount: $500.
Number of awards: 10.
Deadline: February.
How to apply: Applications are available by contacting your local union office or by filling out an online request form.

(1973) · ARA Scholarship

ARA Scholarship Foundation Inc.
ARA Scholarship Advisor
109 Defiant Way
Grass Valley, CA 95945
Phone: 703-385-1001
Email: arascholar@sbcglobal.net
Website: http://www.a-r-a.org
Purpose: To support the children of Automotive Recyclers Association (ARA) members.
Eligibility: Applicants must be high school seniors and/or planning to attend college full-time and have earned a minimum 3.0 GPA in their last educational program. Applicants must also be the children of employees of a Direct Member of ARA who were hired at least one year prior to March 15 of the application year. Scholarships are based on academic merit, not financial need.
Target applicant:
  High school students
  College students
  Graduate school students
  Adult students
Minimum GPA: 3.0
Amount: Varies.
Number of awards: Varies.
Scholarship may be renewable.
Deadline: March 15.
How to apply: Applications are available online and by email request.

(1974) · Archer Daniels Midland Company FFA Scholarship

National FFA Organization
P.O. Box 68960

6060 FFA Drive
Indianapolis, IN 46268-0960
Phone: 317-802-6060
Fax: 317-802-6051
Email: scholarships@ffa.org
Website: http://www.ffa.org
Purpose: To support students who are majoring in agriculture.
Eligibility: Applicants must be current FFA members and high school seniors or college students planning to enroll or currently enrolled full-time in an agriculture program. They must have at least a 2.8 GPA and a history of leadership and community service. Students only need to complete the online application one time to be considered for all FFA-administered scholarships. The application requires information about the students' activities and a 1,000-word essay. Awards may be used for books, supplies, tuition, fees and room and board.
Target applicant:
  High school students
  College students
  Adult students
Minimum GPA: 2.8
Amount: $1,000.
Number of awards: 80.
Deadline: February 15.
How to apply: Applications are available online.

(1975) · Armstrong Achievement Scholarships

Armstrong Foundation
2500 Columbia Avenue
Lancaster, PA 17603
Phone: 717-396-5536
Fax: 717-396-6124
Email: foundation@armstrongfoundation.com
Website: http://www.armstrongfoundation.com
Purpose: The Armstrong Foundation awards four-year awards for college to children of employees and retirees of Armstrong and its subsidiaries.
Eligibility: Applicants must be sons or daughters of full-time or retired employees of Armstrong or its subsidiaries. Eligible students must also meet all requirements for participation in the Merit Program as sponsored by the National Merit Scholarship Corporation.
Target applicant:
  High school students
Minimum GPA: None.
Amount: $2,000.
Number of awards: Varies.
Scholarship may be renewable.
Deadline: January 27.
How to apply: Applications are available online.

(1976) · Arysta LifeScience North America FFA Scholarship

National FFA Organization
P.O. Box 68960
6060 FFA Drive
Indianapolis, IN 46268-0960
Phone: 317-802-6060
Fax: 317-802-6051
Email: scholarships@ffa.org
Website: http://www.ffa.org
Purpose: To support students in the FFA who are studying agriculture or business.

Eligibility: Applicants must be current FFA members and high school seniors or college students planning to enroll or currently enrolled full-time. They must be majoring in one of the following subject areas: agronomy, crop science, horticulture, nursery and landscape management, plant science, turf management, agricultural communications, public relations or sales and marketing, entomology or plant pathology. Applicants must have at least a 3.0 GPA. Students only need to complete the online application one time to be considered for all FFA-administered scholarships. The application requires information about the students' activities and a 1,000-word essay. Awards may be used for books, supplies, tuition, fees and room and board.

Target applicant:
   High school students
   College students
   Adult students
Minimum GPA: 3.0
Amount: $1,100.
Number of awards: 5.
Deadline: February 15.
How to apply: Applications are available online.

(1977) · Ashby B. Carter Memorial Scholarship

National Alliance of Postal and Federal Employees (NAPFE)
1628 11th Street NW
Washington, DC 20001
Phone: 202-939-6325
Email: headquarters@napfe.org
Website: http://www.napfe.com
Purpose: To aid the dependents of National Alliance members in furthering their education.
Eligibility: Applicants must be dependents of members of the National Alliance of Postal and Federal Employees who have been in good standing for at least three years. Applicants must take the Aptitude Test of the College Board Entrance Examination at their local high school before March 1 and be high school seniors.
Target applicant:
   High school students
Minimum GPA: None.
Amount: $2000-$5,000.
Number of awards: 6.
Deadline: April 1.
How to apply: Applications are available online.

(1978) · Association of Flight Attendants Annual Scholarship

Association of Flight Attendants
501 Third Street NW
Washington, DC 20001
Phone: 202-434-1300
Email: afatalk@afanet.org
Website: http://www.afanet.org
Purpose: To provide financial assistance to the children of members of the AFA.
Eligibility: Applicants must be the dependents of AFA members in good standing. Applicants must also be in the top 15 percent of their class, have or expect to have excellent SAT/ACT scores, demonstrate financial need and provide a 300-word essay along with the completed application.
Target applicant:
   High school students

Minimum GPA: None.
Amount: $5,000.
Number of awards: 1.
Scholarship may be renewable.
Deadline: April 10.
How to apply: Applications are available online.

(1979) · Astrid G. Cates Scholarship Fund and the Myrtle Beinhauer Scholarship

Sons of Norway
1455 W. Lake Street
Minneapolis, MN 55408
Phone: 800-945-8851
Fax: 612-827-0658
Email: foundation@sofn.com
Website: http://www.sofn.com
Purpose: To support the members and children and grandchildren of members of the Sons of Norway.
Eligibility: Applicants must have a certificate of completion from high school and be enrolled in post-secondary training or education (college, vocational school or trade school) and be current members of Sons of Norway or the children or grandchildren of current Sons of Norway members in Sons of Norway districts 1-6. Students must also have strong financial need. Selection is based on financial need, a statement of education and career goals, applicants' grade-point averages, a letter of recommendation and applicants' extracurricular involvements.
Target applicant:
   College students
   Adult students
Minimum GPA: None.
Amount: $1,000-$3,000.
Number of awards: 2.
Deadline: March 1.
How to apply: Applications are available online and by mail.

(1980) · Awards of Excellence Scholarship Program

International Order of the Golden Rule
Education Department
P.O. Box 28689
St. Louis, MO 631461189
Phone: 800-637-8030
Fax: 314-209-7213
Email: jgabbert@ogr.org
Website: http://www.ogr.org
Purpose: To provide aid for students in mortuary science and who intend to pursue a career in the funeral service profession.
Eligibility: Applicants must be currently enrolled in a mortuary science school and have a minimum 3.0 GPA. The award is based on community service, honors, grades and potential contributions to the funeral service profession.
Target applicant:
   College students
   Adult students
Minimum GPA: 3.0
Amount: $500-$2,500.
Number of awards: 3.
Deadline: October 1.
How to apply: Applications are available online or by email.

(1981) · BCTGM Scholarship Program

Bakery, Confectionery, Tobacco Workers and Grain Millers
International Union
10401 Connecticut Avenue
Kensington, MD 20895
Phone: 301-933-8600
Fax: 301-946-8452
Website: http://www.bctgm.org
Purpose: To provide scholarships for the members and families of members of BTGCM.
Eligibility: Applicants must be members of the BCTGM in good standing or the children of such members. The scholarships are also open to office employees and children of those employed at the International Union office. Applicants must be high school students who will be attending an accredited college, technical college or vocational school for the first time, high school graduates who have never attended college or BCTGM members who have never applied to the program before who are currently enrolled or planning to begin or resume their studies in the fall. All applicants are required to take the SAT or an equivalent, such as the ACT.
Target applicant:
    High school students
    College students
    Graduate school students
    Adult students
Minimum GPA: None.
Amount: $1,000.
Number of awards: 10.
Deadline: March 31.
How to apply: Applications are available through your local BCTGM union office.

(1982) · Beatrice S. Jacobson Memorial Fund

American Guild of Musical Artists
1430 Broadway, 14th Floor
New York, NY 10018
Phone: 212-265-3687
Fax: 212-262-9088
Email: agma@musicalartists.org
Website: http://www.musicalartists.org
Purpose: To provide scholarships to AGMA members.
Eligibility: Applicants must be AGMA members in good standing for at least two years who are full- or part-time, traditional or adult students working toward either undergraduate or graduate degrees. The award is based on financial need and GPA. Applicants don't have to be music majors.
Target applicant:
    College students
    Graduate school students
    Adult students
Minimum GPA: None.
Amount: Varies.
Number of awards: Varies.
Deadline: April 1.
How to apply: Applications are available by written request.

(1983) · Bernard Rotberg Memorial Scholarship Fund

Jewish War Veterans of the USA
1811 R Street NW
Washington, DC 20009
Phone: 202-265-6280
Fax: 202-234-5662
Email: jwv@jwv.org
Website: http://www.jwv.org
Purpose: To provide scholarships for descendents of members of the Jewish War Veterans of the USA.
Eligibility: Applicants must be a direct descendent of a JWV member in good standing. Candidates must also have been accepted to an accredited college, university or nursing school, be in the upper 25 percent of their class and be active in activities at school and within the Jewish community.
Target applicant:
    High school students
Minimum GPA: None.
Amount: $1,000.
Number of awards: 1.
Deadline: May 3.
How to apply: Applications are available online and should be submitted by the applicant's school to the department commander in the local post.

(1984) · Biblical Common Knowledge Challenge

Common Knowledge Scholarship Foundation
P.O. Box 290361
Davie, FL 33329-0361
Phone: 954-262-8553
Email: info@cksf.org
Website: http://www.cksf.org
Purpose: To support students who are knowledgeable about the Bible.
Eligibility: Students must register with CKSF and take several online quizzes about the Bible. The student with the most points from correct answers and the shortest time that it takes to answer the questions wins the scholarship.
Target applicant:
    High school students
    College students
    Graduate school students
    Adult students
Minimum GPA: None.
Amount: $250.
Number of awards: 1.
Deadline: April 13.
How to apply: Applications are available online.

(1985) · Bill Moon Scholarship

NATSO Foundation
Heather Mooney
c/o Bill Moon Scholarship Committee
60 Main Street
Farmington, CT 06032
Phone: 703-549-2100
Fax: 703-684-9667
Website: http://www.natsofoundation.org
Purpose: To assist Truck Stop Operators industry employees and their families.
Eligibility: Applicants must be Truck Stop Operators industry employees or their family members and must submit applications, essays, recommendation letters, transcripts and financial information. The award is based on academic merit, financial need, community activities and essays.

Target applicant:
    High school students
    College students
    Graduate school students
    Adult students
Minimum GPA: None.
Amount: Varies.
Number of awards: 12.
Deadline: April 14.
How to apply: Applications are available online.

(1986) · Blanche Fearn Memorial High School Senior Essay Contest

Freedom from Religion Foundation
P.O. Box 750
Madison, WI 53701
Phone: 608-256-5800
Email: info@ffrf.org
Website: http://www.ffrf.org
Purpose: To support students who write an essay on a topic related to freedom from religion.
Eligibility: Applicants must be high school seniors in the U.S. or Canada and write a three to four page essay on the topic provided. The topic and an explanation of it are listed on the website.
Target applicant:
    High school students
Minimum GPA: None.
Amount: $100-$2,000.
Number of awards: 4.
Deadline: June 1.
How to apply: There is no application form. In addition to the essay on the topic provided, students must also include a biography with their permanent and campus address (if known), email address, phone number, name and city of high school, name and location of college or university that they plan to attend in the fall and intended major and interests. Applicants should not send a resume.

(1987) · BLET Auxiliary Scholarships

Brotherhood of Locomotive Engineers and Trainmen
3341 S. 112th Street
Omaha, NE 68144-4709
Phone: 402-330-6348
Email: bunziegia@cox.net
Website: http://www.ble.org
Purpose: To provide scholarships to the children of members of the BLE.
Eligibility: Applicants must be the children of both a Grand International Auxiliary (GIA) and BLE member (living or deceased) and enrolled or accepted by an accredited university, college or institute of higher learning. If the applicant is a graduate student or returning to school as a sophomore, junior or senior, he or she must have a minimum 3.0 GPA. Selection is based on academic record, leadership, character and personal achievement. Applicants must have a parent participating in the IWC.
Target applicant:
    High school students
    College students
    Graduate school students
    Adult students
Minimum GPA: 3.0
Amount: $1,000.

Number of awards: Varies.
Scholarship may be renewable.
Deadline: April 1.
How to apply: Applications are available online and by written request through your local GIA auxiliary or BLE division.

(1988) · BNSF Railway Company FFA Scholarship

National FFA Organization
P.O. Box 68960
6060 FFA Drive
Indianapolis, IN 46268-0960
Phone: 317-802-6060
Fax: 317-802-6051
Email: scholarships@ffa.org
Website: http://www.ffa.org
Purpose: To support FFA members who are majoring in agriculture.
Eligibility: Applicants must be current FFA members and high school seniors or college students planning to enroll or currently enrolled full-time. Students must be pursuing a four-year degree in one of the following agricultural fields: business management, economics, sales and marketing or finance. They must be residents of California, Illinois, Iowa, Kansas, Minnesota, Montana, Nebraska, North Dakota, South Dakota or Texas. Applicants must have at least a 3.0 GPA. Students only need to complete the online application one time to be considered for all FFA-administered scholarships. The application requires information about the students' activities and a 1,000-word essay. Awards may be used for books, supplies, tuition, fees and room and board.
Target applicant:
    High school students
    College students
    Adult students
Minimum GPA: 3.0
Amount: $5,000.
Number of awards: 10.
Scholarship may be renewable.
Deadline: February 15.
How to apply: Applications are available online.

(1989) · Boilermakers, Iron Ship Builders, Blacksmiths, Forgers and Helpers, International Brotherhood of (IBB) Scholarship Awards

Boilermakers, Iron Ship Builders, Blacksmiths, Forgers and Helpers, (IBB)
753 State Avenue
Suite 570
Kansas City, KS 66101
Phone: 913-371-2640
Website: http://www.boilermakers.org
Purpose: To provide scholarships to the children of members of the International Brotherhood.
Eligibility: Applicants must be the children or dependents of members of the IBB and high school seniors who will be entering their first year of college as full-time students within one year of graduation from high school. U.S. applicants are required to take the SAT or ACT. Recipients are selected on the basis of academic achievement, career goals, extracurricular activities, outside school activities and essay.
Target applicant:
    High school students
Minimum GPA: None.
Amount: $2,000-$5,000.
Number of awards: Varies.

Deadline: March 31.
How to apply: Applications are available by written request.

(1990) · Boys and Girls Clubs of America National Youth of the Year Award

Boys and Girls Clubs of America
1275 Peachtree Street NE
Atlanta, GA 30309
Phone: 404-487-5700
Email: info@bgca.org
Website: http://www.bgca.org
Purpose: To reward club members who demonstrate good academic performance, perform services for both their club and community and who are active in both family and spiritual life.
Eligibility: Applicants must be a member of a BGCA and be selected by their local club to compete for the regional and national scholarships.
Target applicant:
    High school students
Minimum GPA: None.
Amount: $5,000-$10,000.
Number of awards: Varies.
Deadline: Varies.
How to apply: Contact your local club for more information.

(1991) · BRIDGE Endowment Fund FFA Scholarship

National FFA Organization
P.O. Box 68960
6060 FFA Drive
Indianapolis, IN 46268-0960
Phone: 317-802-6060
Fax: 317-802-6051
Email: scholarships@ffa.org
Website: http://www.ffa.org
Purpose: To support disabled students who are studying agriculture.
Eligibility: Applicants must be current FFA members and high school seniors or college students planning to enroll or currently enrolled full-time. They must be physically disabled or handicapped. Students only need to complete the online application one time to be considered for all FFA-administered scholarships. The application requires information about the students' activities and a 1,000-word essay. Awards may be used for books, supplies, tuition, fees and room and board.
Target applicant:
    High school students
    College students
    Adult students
Minimum GPA: None.
Amount: $5,000.
Number of awards: 1.
Deadline: February 15.
How to apply: Applications are available online.

(1992) · Bridgestone/Firestone Trust Fund FFA Scholarship

National FFA Organization
P.O. Box 68960
6060 FFA Drive
Indianapolis, IN 46268-0960
Phone: 317-802-6060
Fax: 317-802-6051
Email: scholarships@ffa.org
Website: http://www.ffa.org
Purpose: To support students from families that are involved in farming.
Eligibility: Applicants must be current FFA members and high school seniors or college students planning to enroll or currently enrolled full-time. They must live on the family farm and show financial need, leadership skills and community service participation. Students only need to complete the online application one time to be considered for all FFA-administered scholarships. The application requires information about the students' activities and a 1,000-word essay. Awards may be used for books, supplies, tuition, fees and room and board.
Target applicant:
    High school students
    College students
    Adult students
Minimum GPA: None.
Amount: $2,500.
Number of awards: 5.
Deadline: February 15.
How to apply: Applications are available online.

(1993) · Bruce B. Melchert Scholarship

Tau Kappa Epsilon Educational Foundation
8645 Founders Road
Indianapolis, IN 46268
Phone: 317-872-6533
Fax: 317-875-8353
Email: tef@tke.org
Website: http://www.tkefoundation.org
Purpose: To award a member of Tau Kappa Epsilon for outstanding academic achievement and leadership within the chapter as a recruitment chair, prytanis, major officer or leader in IFC or other organizations.
Eligibility: Applicants must have a GPA of at least 3.0, be sophomores or above and be seeking an undergraduate degree in political science or government. Applicants must also plan to pursue a career in political or government service. Preference is first given to members of the Beta-Theta Chapter.
Target applicant:
    College students
    Adult students
Minimum GPA: 3.0
Amount: $500.
Number of awards: 1.
Deadline: March 16.
How to apply: Applications are available online.

(1994) · Buckingham Memorial Scholarship

Air Traffic Control Association
Attn.: Scholarship Fund
1101 King Street, Suite 300
Alexandria, VA 22134
Phone: 703-299-2430
Fax: 703-299-2437
Email: info@atca.org
Website: http://www.atca.org
Purpose: To provide education assistance for children of ATCA Specialists.
Eligibility: Applicants must be U.S. citizens who are half- or full-time students enrolled in an accredited institution of higher learning. They may pursue an undergraduate degree in any major.

Target applicant:
High school students
College students
Adult students
Minimum GPA: None.
Amount: $600.
Number of awards: 4-8.
Deadline: May 1.
How to apply: Applications are available from the ATCA.

(1995) · Business Achievement Awards

Golden Key National Honour Society
Scholarship Program Administrators
Golden Key Scholarships/Awards
P.O. Box 23737
Nashville, TN 37202-3737
Phone: 800-377-2401
Email: scholarships@goldenkey.org
Website: http://www.goldenkey.org
Purpose: To support Golden Key members who are studying business.
Eligibility: Applicants must be undergraduate, graduate or post-graduate members who are currently attending classes in a degree-granting program. The award is based on academic achievement and a business-related paper or report.
Target applicant:
College students
Graduate school students
Adult students
Minimum GPA: None.
Amount: $500-$1,000.
Number of awards: 2.
Deadline: March 1.
How to apply: Applications are available online.

(1996) · Carrol C. Hall Memorial Scholarship

Tau Kappa Epsilon Educational Foundation
8645 Founders Road
Indianapolis, IN 46268
Phone: 317-872-6533
Fax: 317-875-8353
Email: tef@tke.org
Website: http://www.tkefoundation.org
Purpose: To award a member of Tau Kappa Epsilon for outstanding academic achievement and for leadership within the organization, campus or community.
Eligibility: Applicants must have a minimum 3.0 GPA and be undergraduates seeking a degree in education or science with the intention of pursuing a career in teaching or the sciences.
Target applicant:
College students
Adult students
Minimum GPA: 3.0
Amount: $700.
Number of awards: 1.
Deadline: March 16.
How to apply: Applications are available online.

(1997) · Casey's General Stores Inc. FFA Scholarship

National FFA Organization
P.O. Box 68960
6060 FFA Drive
Indianapolis, IN 46268-0960
Phone: 317-802-6060
Fax: 317-802-6051
Email: scholarships@ffa.org
Website: http://www.ffa.org
Purpose: To support agriculture students.
Eligibility: Applicants must be current FFA members and high school seniors or college students planning to enroll or currently enrolled full-time. They must be pursuing a two-year or four-year degree in agriculture and have plans to work in agriculture or agribusiness. Applicants must be residents of one of the following states: Illinois, Indiana, Iowa, Kansas, Minnesota, Missouri, Nebraska, South Dakota or Wisconsin. Students only need to complete the online application one time to be considered for all FFA-administered scholarships. The application requires information about the students' activities and a 1,000-word essay. Awards may be used for books, supplies, tuition, fees and room and board.
Target applicant:
High school students
College students
Adult students
Minimum GPA: None.
Amount: $1,000.
Number of awards: 3.
Deadline: February 15.
How to apply: Applications are available online.

(1998) · Catholic Aid Association College Tuition Scholarship

Catholic Aid Association
Scholarship Program
3499 Lexington Avenue North
St. Paul, MN 55126
Phone: 800-568-6670
Email: caa@catholicaid.org
Website: http://www.catholicaid.com
Purpose: To award scholarships to members of the Catholic Aid Association.
Eligibility: Applicants must be members of the Catholic Aid Association for at least two years prior to the date of application, have completed high school and be entering their first or second year in any accredited college, university, state college or technical college other than a private, non-Catholic college/university.
Target applicant:
High school students
College students
Adult students
Minimum GPA: None.
Amount: $300-$500.
Number of awards: Varies.
Deadline: February 16.
How to apply: Applications are available online.

(1999) · Catholic Workman Scholarship

Catholic Workman Fraternal Benefit Society
Attn.: Scholarships
P.O. Box 47

New Prague, MN 56071
Phone: 800-346-6231
Email: info@catholicworkman.org
Website: http://www.catholicworkman.org
Purpose: To assist insured members of Catholic Workman.
Eligibility: Applicants must be insured members of Catholic Workman for at least 12 months prior to application. Applicants may apply during their senior year in high school or any year thereafter. Applicants must have a minimum GPA of 2.5.
Target applicant:
    High school students
    College students
    Adult students
Minimum GPA: 2.5
Amount: $500-$1,000.
Number of awards: 20.
Scholarship may be renewable.
Deadline: July 1.
How to apply: Applications are available online.

(2000) · Chairman's Award

National Association of Blacks in Criminal Justice
North Carolina Central University
P.O. Box 19788
Durham, NC 27707
Phone: 919-683-1801
Fax: 919-683-1903
Email: office@nabcj.org
Website: http://www.nabcj.org
Purpose: To support an individual who has shown leadership, dedication and made contributions to NABCJ at the chapter or regional level.
Eligibility: Applicants must be nominated by a member of NABCJ.
Target applicant:
    College students
    Adult students
Minimum GPA: None.
Amount: Varies.
Number of awards: 1.
Deadline: May 1.
How to apply: Nomination applications are available online.

(2001) · Charles Bradley Memorial Scholarship

Harness Horse Youth Foundation
16575 Carey Road
Westfield, IN 46074
Phone: 317-867-5877
Fax: 317-867-5896
Email: ellen@hhyf.org
Website: http://www.hhyf.org
Purpose: To support the children and relatives of horse racing officials.
Eligibility: Applicants must be related to a member of the North American Judges and Stewards Association or a licensed USTA pari-mutuel official in one of the following areas: presiding judges, associate judges, paddock judges and starters. Students must be at least in their senior year of high school. Applicants must submit an essay and two letters of recommendation.
Target applicant:
    High school students
    College students
    Adult students

Minimum GPA: None.
Amount: Varies.
Number of awards: Varies.
Deadline: April 30.
How to apply: Applications are available online.

(2002) · Charles J. Trabold Scholarship

Tau Kappa Epsilon Educational Foundation
8645 Founders Road
Indianapolis, IN 46268
Phone: 317-872-6533
Fax: 317-875-8353
Email: tef@tke.org
Website: http://www.tkefoundation.org
Purpose: To recognize academic achievement and leadership in members.
Eligibility: Applicants must be initiated Tau Kappa Epsilon members in good standing and full-time students with a GPA of at least 3.0. They must also demonstrate outstanding leadership and include a statement describing how they have benefited from TKE membership. First preference will be given to members of Kappa-Kappa Chapter.
Target applicant:
    College students
    Adult students
Minimum GPA: 3.0
Amount: $1,500.
Number of awards: 1.
Deadline: March 16.
How to apply: Applications are available online.

(2003) · Charles R. Walgreen Jr. Leadership Award

Tau Kappa Epsilon Educational Foundation
8645 Founders Road
Indianapolis, IN 46268
Phone: 317-872-6533
Fax: 317-875-8353
Email: tef@tke.org
Website: http://www.tkefoundation.org
Purpose: To honor Charles R. Walgreen's support of Tau Kappa Epsilon by recognizing academic achievement in members.
Eligibility: Applicants must be initiated Tau Kappa Epsilon members in good standing and full-time students. They must have a GPA of at least 3.0 and demonstrate leadership in their chapter, campus and community. Applicants must also include a statement describing how they have benefited from TKE membership.
Target applicant:
    College students
    Adult students
Minimum GPA: None.
Amount: $2,500.
Number of awards: 1.
Deadline: March 16.
How to apply: Applications are available online.

(2004) · Charlie Logan Scholarship Program for Dependents

Seafarers International Union of North America
Mr. Lou Delma, Administrator
Seafarers Welfare Plan Scholarship Program
5201 Auth Way

Camp Springs, MD 20746
Phone: 301-899-0675
Fax: 301-899-7355
Website: http://www.seafarers.org
Purpose: To offer scholarships to the dependents of members of the SIU.
Eligibility: Applicants must be the dependent children or spouses of members of the Seafarers International Union. The union member must be eligible for the Seafarer's Plan and must have credit for 3 years with an employer who is obligated to make a contribution to the Seafarer's Plan on behalf of the employee. Recipients may attend any U.S. accredited institution. Selection is based upon review of secondary school records, SAT or ACT test scores, college transcripts, if any, character references, extracurricular activities and autobiography.
Target applicant:
    High school students
    College students
    Adult students
Minimum GPA: None.
Amount: $5,000.
Number of awards: 4.
Scholarship may be renewable.
Deadline: April 15.
How to apply: Applications are available by written request.

(2005) · Chevron Corporation FFA Scholarship
National FFA Organization
P.O. Box 68960
6060 FFA Drive
Indianapolis, IN 46268-0960
Phone: 317-802-6060
Fax: 317-802-6051
Email: scholarships@ffa.org
Website: http://www.ffa.org
Purpose: To support students from Florida and Georgia who are in the FFA.
Eligibility: Applicants must be current FFA members and high school seniors or college students planning to enroll or currently enrolled full-time. They must be pursuing a degree in one of the following areas: agricultural engineering, biochemistry, biotechnology, conservation, soil science or soil or water conservation. Applicants must also show leadership skills and community service participation. Students only need to complete the online application one time to be considered for all FFA-administered scholarships. The application requires information about the students' activities and a 1,000-word essay. Awards may be used for books, supplies, tuition, fees and room and board.
Target applicant:
    High school students
    College students
    Adult students
Minimum GPA: None.
Amount: $1,000.
Number of awards: 2.
Deadline: February 15.
How to apply: Applications are available online.

(2006) · Chief Industries FFA Scholarship
National FFA Organization
P.O. Box 68960
6060 FFA Drive
Indianapolis, IN 46268-0960

Phone: 317-802-6060
Fax: 317-802-6051
Email: scholarships@ffa.org
Website: http://www.ffa.org
Purpose: To support FFA members who are majoring in agriculture.
Eligibility: Applicants must be current FFA members and high school seniors or college students planning to enroll or currently enrolled full-time. They must be residents of Indiana, Iowa or Nebraska. Students only need to complete the online application one time to be considered for all FFA-administered scholarships. The application requires information about the students' activities and a 1,000-word essay. Awards may be used for books, supplies, tuition, fees and room and board.
Target applicant:
    High school students
    College students
    Adult students
Minimum GPA: None.
Amount: $1,000.
Number of awards: 1.
Deadline: February 15.
How to apply: Applications are available online.

(2007) · Christian Connector Undergraduate Scholarship
Christian Connector Inc.
627 24 1/2 Road
Suite D
Grand Junction, CO 81505
Phone: 800-667-0600
Website: http://www.christianconnector.com
Purpose: To provide financial assistance for students attending Christian or Bible colleges.
Eligibility: Applicants must be enrolling as a first-time student at a Christ-centered Christian or Bible college, including but not limited to CCCU, NACCAP or AABC member institutions, within 16 months of winning the scholarship. To enter the drawing, the student must fill out an information request form.
Target applicant:
    High school students
Minimum GPA: None.
Amount: $2,500.
Number of awards: 1.
Deadline: Varies.
How to apply: Applications are available online.

(2008) · Christopher Grasso Scholarship
Tau Kappa Epsilon Educational Foundation
8645 Founders Road
Indianapolis, IN 46268
Phone: 317-872-6533
Fax: 317-875-8353
Email: tef@tke.org
Website: http://www.tkefoundation.org
Purpose: To recognize a member of Tau Kappa Epsilon for outstanding leadership in the local chapter or community.
Eligibility: Applicants must have a GPA of at least 2.5. Preference is first given to members of the Alpha-Tau Chapter.
Target applicant:
    College students
    Adult students
Minimum GPA: 2.5

Amount: $300.
Number of awards: 1.
Deadline: March 16.
How to apply: Applications are available online.

(2009) · Church and Dwight Company Inc. FFA Scholarship

National FFA Organization
P.O. Box 68960
6060 FFA Drive
Indianapolis, IN 46268-0960
Phone: 317-802-6060
Fax: 317-802-6051
Email: scholarships@ffa.org
Website: http://www.ffa.org
Purpose: To support FFA members who are pursuing degrees related to agricultural science or business.
Eligibility: Applicants must be current FFA members and high school seniors or college students planning to enroll or currently enrolled full-time. They must be majoring in one of the following areas: animal nutrition, animal or dairy science, agricultural business management, finance, sales and marketing or agricultural engineering. Students must have at least a 3.0 GPA. Preference will be given to applicants who show strong leadership skills and an interest in pursuing a dairy-related career. Students only need to complete the online application one time to be considered for all FFA-administered scholarships. The application requires information about the students' activities and a 1,000-word essay. Awards may be used for books, supplies, tuition, fees and room and board.
Target applicant:
    High school students
    College students
    Adult students
Minimum GPA: 3.0
Amount: $1,000.
Number of awards: 2.
Deadline: February 15.
How to apply: Applications are available online.

(2010) · Cindy Shemansky Travel Scholarship

National Gerontological Nursing Association (NGNA)
7794 Grow Drive
Pensacola, FL 32514
Phone: 800-723-0560
Fax: 850-484-8762
Email: ngna@puetzamc.com
Website: http://www.ngna.org
Purpose: To provide assistance to NGNA members who wish to attend the annual convention but who need financial assistance with travel expenses.
Eligibility: Applicants must have been members of NGNA for at least one year.
Target applicant:
    College students
    Adult students
Minimum GPA: None.
Amount: $1,000.
Number of awards: Varies.
Deadline: June 1.
How to apply: Applications are available online.

(2011) · Clara Abbott Foundation Educational Grant Program

Clara Abbott Foundation
1505 South White Oak Drive
Waukegan, IL 60085
Phone: 800-972-3859
Fax: 847-938-6511
Website: http://clara.abbott.com/
Purpose: To help children of eligible Abbott employees and retirees worldwide receive a college-level education by providing scholarships on the basis of financial need.
Eligibility: Applicants must be full- or part-time students at an accredited college, university, community college, vocational school or trade school. Applicants must also be 24 years of age or younger, be the children or dependents of retirees or full-time/part-time employees with at least a year's service to Abbott Laboratories and be residents of the United States or Puerto Rico. Scholarships are awarded according to financial need. Applicants may first apply as high school seniors.
Target applicant:
    High school students
    College students
Minimum GPA: None.
Amount: Varies.
Number of awards: Varies.
Scholarship may be renewable.
Deadline: March 15.
How to apply: Applications are available online.

(2012) · Collegian of the Year

Delta Sigma Pi
330 S. Campus Avenue
Oxford, OH 45056
Phone: 513-523-1907
Fax: 513-523-7292
Email: centraloffice@dspnet.org
Website: http://www.dspnet.org
Purpose: To honor the most outstanding collegian member of Delta Sigma Pi who exemplifies the ideals of the organization.
Eligibility: Nominees must be members in good standing and be nominated by their chapter by October 15. Demonstrated fraternity involvement, demonstrated college/university and/or community involvement, demonstrated pursuit of professional development and scholastic average will all be considered along with other desirable characteristics like moral character and professional attitude.
Target applicant:
    College students
    Adult students
Minimum GPA: None.
Amount: $3,000.
Number of awards: 1.
Deadline: November 15.
How to apply: Applications are available online.

(2013) · Community Service Award

Golden Key National Honour Society
Scholarship Program Administrators
Golden Key Scholarships/Awards
P.O. Box 23737
Nashville, TN 37202-3737
Phone: 800-377-2401

Email: scholarships@goldenkey.org
Website: http://www.goldenkey.org
Purpose: To support a Golden Key member who has served the community.
Eligibility: Applicants must be undergraduate or graduate Golden Key members who were enrolled during the previous academic year. Selection is based on the impact of the community service. Applicants must provide an essay of up to 500 words describing the community service project, recommendation letters and list of extracurricular activities.
Target applicant:
　College students
　Graduate school students
　Adult students
Minimum GPA: None.
Amount: $250.
Number of awards: 1.
Deadline: February 15.
How to apply: Applications are available online.

(2014) · Continuing Education Grant/Loan Program
Presbyterian Church (USA)
100 Witherspoon Street
Louisville, KY 40202
Phone: 888-728-7228 x5776
Email: fcook@ctr.pcusa.org
Website: http://www.pcusa.org
Purpose: To aid Presbyterian Church (U.S.A.) members pursuing post graduate educations.
Eligibility: Applicants must be enrolled in a Ph.D. or equivalent ATS accredited postgraduate program in religious studies, or an applicant must be a Presbyterian Church minister or lay professional serving a congregation of at most 150 people. Eligible events must be at least three days in duration and the applicant may be required to document expenses prior to distribution of award. The awards are these two categories: (1) The Continuing Education Grant—Events $100-$500 and (2) Continuing Education Grant—DMin $500-$1,000.
Target applicant:
　Graduate school students
　Adult students
Minimum GPA: None.
Amount: $100-$1,000.
Number of awards: Varies.
Deadline: November 15.
How to apply: Applications are available online.

(2015) · Continuing Education Scholarships
Federation of American Consumers and Travelers (FACT)
P.O. Box 104
318 Hillsboro Avenue
Edwardsville, IL 62025
Phone: 800-872-3228
Email: cservice@fact-org.org
Website: http://www.fact-org.org
Purpose: To help FACT members and their families.
Eligibility: Applicants must be FACT members or their immediate families in the following categories: current high school seniors, students already in college, students who graduated from high school four or more years ago or students planning to attend a trade or technical school.
Target applicant:
　High school students
　College students

Graduate school students
Adult students
Minimum GPA: None.
Amount: $10,000.
Number of awards: Varies.
Deadline: Varies.
How to apply: Contact the organization for more information.

(2016) · CTA Scholarship for Dependent Children
California Teachers Association (CTA)
CTA Human Rights Department
P.O. Box 921
Burlingame, CA 94011-0921
Phone: 650-697-1400
Fax: 650-552-5001
Website: http://www.cta.org
Purpose: To support the children of CTA members.
Eligibility: Students must be the dependents of active, retired or deceased California Teachers Association members. Applicants must have a 3.5 high school GPA or high academic achievement in college, although there is the opportunity to explain any extenuating circumstances affecting grades. Scholarships are based on a personal statement, school and community activities and letters of recommendation.
Target applicant:
　High school students
　College students
　Graduate school students
　Adult students
Minimum GPA: 3.5
Amount: $2,000.
Number of awards: 25.
Deadline: January 27.
How to apply: Applications are available online.

(2017) · CTA Scholarship for Members
California Teachers Association (CTA)
CTA Human Rights Department
P.O. Box 921
Burlingame, CA 94011-0921
Phone: 650-697-1400
Fax: 650-552-5001
Website: http://www.cta.org
Purpose: To support CTA members as they further their education.
Eligibility: Applicants must be current active members of the California Teachers Association who are attending college. Their coursework must show high academic achievement, although they may explain any extenuating circumstances affecting their grades. Scholarships are awarded based on a personal statement, school and community activities and letters of recommendation.
Target applicant:
　College students
　Graduate school students
　Adult students
Minimum GPA: None.
Amount: $2,000.
Number of awards: 5.
Deadline: January 27.
How to apply: Applications are available online.

(2018) · Cunat Visionary Scholarship

Circle K International
3636 Woodview Trace
Indianapolis, IN 46268
Website: http://www.circlek.org
Purpose: This scholarship, provided by Kiwanis International Past President Brian Cunat and Miki Cunat, was established to recognize Kiwanis members who aspire to make a difference in people's lives and create a better world for all.
Eligibility: Applicants must be either college-attending Circle K International members or graduating Key Club members.
Target applicant:
   High school students
   College students
   Adult students
Minimum GPA: None.
Amount: $2,500.
Number of awards: 2.
Deadline: April 15.
How to apply: Applications are available online.

(2019) · CWA Joe Beirne Foundation Scholarship

Communications Workers of America
Attn.: George Kohl
501 Third Street NW
Washington, DC 20001
Phone: 202-434-1158
Fax: 202-434-1139
Email: kadams@cwa-union.org
Website: http://www.cwa-union.org
Purpose: To provide scholarships for CWA members and their families.
Eligibility: Applicants may be Communications Workers of America (CWA) members, their spouses, their children or their grandchildren. Applicants must be high school graduates or at least high school students who will graduate during the year in which they apply. Winners are selected by a lottery drawing. This is a two-year scholarship.
Target applicant:
   High school students
   College students
   Graduate school students
   Adult students
Minimum GPA: None.
Amount: $3,000.
Number of awards: 30.
Scholarship may be renewable.
Deadline: March 31.
How to apply: Contact a CWA Local or write (referencing CWA local number, member name and Social Security number) for an application. Applications are available online.

(2020) · Delta Gamma Foundation Scholarship

Delta Gamma Foundation
3250 Riverside Drive
P.O. Box 21397
Columbus, OH 43221
Phone: 614-481-8169
Fax: 614-481-0133
Email: dgscholarships08@aol.com
Website: http://www.deltagamma.org

Purpose: To support student members.
Eligibility: Applicants must be initiated members of Delta Gamma, have maintained a 3.0 GPA and have completed three semesters or five quarters of college coursework. Applicants should also be active participants in chapter, campus and community leadership activities. Awards are based on academic achievement and participation in activities.
Target applicant:
   College students
   Adult students
Minimum GPA: 3.0
Amount: $1,000.
Number of awards: Varies.
Deadline: February 15.
How to apply: Applications are available online.

(2021) · Delta Phi Epsilon Educational Foundation Scholarship

Delta Phi Epsilon Educational Foundation
16A Worthington Drive
Maryland Heights, MO 63043
Phone: 314-275-2626
Fax: 314-275-2655
Email: fausbury@dphie.org
Website: http://www.dphie.org
Purpose: To award members of Delta Phi Epsilon.
Eligibility: Applicants must be members or the sons or daughters of members of Delta Phi Epsilon who are applying for undergraduate or graduate study. The award is based on service and involvement, academics and financial need. Applicants should submit transcripts, letters of introduction and financial need, autobiographical sketches, two recent photos, at least two letters of recommendation and the contact information of the financial aid director for the school.
Target applicant:
   High school students
   College students
   Graduate school students
   Adult students
Minimum GPA: None.
Amount: Varies.
Number of awards: Varies.
Deadline: April 15.
How to apply: Applications are available online.

(2022) · Diocese of the Armenian Church of America (Eastern) Scholarships

Diocese of the Armenian Church of America (Eastern)
630 Second Avenue
New York, NY 10016
Phone: 212-686-0710
Fax: 212-686-0245
Email: info@armenianchurch.net
Website: http://www.armenianchurch.net
Purpose: To support young Armenian Church members who are seeking higher education.
Eligibility: Applicants must be Armenian Americans who currently attend or plan to attend a four-year college or university. Preference is given to applicants who are U.S. citizens and are active in the Armenian Church.

Target applicant:
High school students
College students
Adult students
Minimum GPA: None.
Amount: Varies.
Number of awards: Varies.
Deadline: June 15.
How to apply: Applications are available from the Diocese of the Armenian Church of America (Eastern).

(2023) · Don Forsyth "Circle K" Scholarship Fund

Community Foundation for the Greater Capital Region
6 Tower Place
Albany, NY 12203
Phone: 518-446-9638
Fax: 518-446-9708
Email: info@cfgcr.org
Website: http://www.cfcr.org/grants_scholarships/scholarships.htm
Purpose: To provide recognition and financial assistance for outstanding Circle K members.
Eligibility: Applicants must be members of Circle K clubs at New York colleges who are in good standing with the club and their schools. They must have an exceptional community service record and be enrolled in college full-time.
Target applicant:
College students
Adult students
Minimum GPA: None.
Amount: $4,200.
Number of awards: 1.
Deadline: March 24.
How to apply: Applications are available online.

(2024) · Donald A. and John R. Fisher Memorial Scholarship

Tau Kappa Epsilon Educational Foundation
8645 Founders Road
Indianapolis, IN 46268
Phone: 317-872-6533
Fax: 317-875-8353
Email: tef@tke.org
Website: http://www.tkefoundation.org
Purpose: To recognize academic achievement and leadership in honor of father and son members Donald A. and John R. Fisher.
Eligibility: Applicants must be initiated Tau Kappa Epsilon members in good standing and full-time students with a GPA of at least 3.0. They must demonstrate outstanding leadership in their chapter, campus and community. Applicants must also include a statement describing how they have benefited from TKE membership.
Target applicant:
College students
Adult students
Minimum GPA: 3.0
Amount: $1,500.
Number of awards: 1.
Deadline: March 16.
How to apply: Applications are available online.

(2025) · Doris and Elmer H. Schmitz, Sr. Memorial Scholarship

Tau Kappa Epsilon Educational Foundation
8645 Founders Road
Indianapolis, IN 46268
Phone: 317-872-6533
Fax: 317-875-8353
Email: tef@tke.org
Website: http://www.tkefoundation.org
Purpose: To award a member of Tau Kappa Epsilon for academic achievement and outstanding leadership within the organization as a chapter officer.
Eligibility: Applicants must have a GPA of at least 2.5. First preference is given to applicants from Wisconsin.
Target applicant:
College students
Adult students
Minimum GPA: 2.5
Amount: $600.
Number of awards: 1.
Deadline: March 16.
How to apply: Applications are available online.

(2026) · Drug, Chemical and Allied Trades Association (DCAT) Scholarship

Drug, Chemical, and Allied Trades Association (DCAT)
One Washington Boulevard, Suite 7
Robbinsville, NJ 08691
Phone: 800-640-3228
Fax: 609-448-1944
Email: dorothy@dcat.org
Website: http://www.dcat.org
Purpose: To benefit the children of DCAT member employees.
Eligibility: Applicants must be high school seniors with a parent employed full-time by a DCAT member company, which are companies that manufacture, distribute or provide services to the pharmaceutical, chemical, nutritional and related industries. Selection is based on leadership, academic achievement and the application essay.
Target applicant:
High school students
Minimum GPA: None.
Amount: $10,000 over four years.
Number of awards: 6.
Scholarship may be renewable.
Deadline: February 7.
How to apply: Applications are available online during the application period.

(2027) · Duke Energy Scholars

Duke Energy Corporation
526 S. Church Street
Charlotte, NC 28202-1904
Phone: 704-594-6200
Email: contactus@duke-energy.com
Website: http://www.duke-energy.com
Purpose: To support the children of Duke Energy employees and retirees.
Eligibility: Applicants should be children of Duke Energy employees and retirees who are undergraduates at accredited, two-year technical schools or community colleges or four-year colleges or universities in

the U.S. and Canada. The awards are based on academics, references, community service and financial need.
Target applicant:
    College students
    Adult students
Minimum GPA: None.
Amount: $5,000.
Number of awards: 15.
Scholarship may be renewable.
Deadline: Varies.
How to apply: Contact the company for more information.

(2028) · Dwayne R. Woerpel Memorial Scholarship
Tau Kappa Epsilon Educational Foundation
8645 Founders Road
Indianapolis, IN 46268
Phone: 317-872-6533
Fax: 317-875-8353
Email: tef@tke.org
Website: http://www.tkefoundation.org
Purpose: To award a member of Tau Kappa Epsilon for oustanding academic achievement and leadership within the fraternity, civic and religious communities.
Eligibility: Applicants must have a GPA of at least 3.0. Preference is first given to graduates of the TKE Leadership Academy.
Target applicant:
    College students
    Adult students
Minimum GPA: 3.0
Amount: $500.
Number of awards: 1.
Deadline: March 16.
How to apply: Applications are available online.

(2029) · E. Craig Brandenburg Scholarship
United Methodist Church
Office of Loans and Scholarships
P.O. BOX 340007
Nashville, TN 37203-0007
Phone: 615-340-7344
Fax: 615-340-7367
Email: umscholar@gbhem.org
Website: http://www.gbhem.org
Purpose: To support adult students who are members of the United Methodist Church.
Eligibility: Applicants must be at least 35 years old, and they must have been members of the United Methodist Church for at least one year. Students may be pursuing undergraduate or graduate degrees.
Target applicant:
    College students
    Graduate school students
    Adult students
Minimum GPA: None.
Amount: Varies.
Number of awards: Varies.
Deadline: March 1.
How to apply: Applications are available online.

(2030) · Eagle Scout Scholarship
National Society of the Sons of the American Revolution
1000 S. Fourth Street
Louisville, KY 40203
Phone: 502-589-1776
Email: contests@sar.org
Website: http://www.sar.org
Purpose: To reward exceptional students who have reached the status of Eagle Scout.
Eligibility: Applicants must have reached Eagle Scout status, must currently be registered in an active unit and can't have reached their 19th birthday during the year of application. Applicants can apply multiple years as long as they are under the age limit, but the maximum award amount is $8,000. Applicants usually apply at the chapter level. Applicants will be required to submit an essay and four-generation ancestor chart with their application.
Target applicant:
    Junior high students or younger
    High school students
Minimum GPA: None.
Amount: $2,000-$8,000.
Number of awards: 3.
Deadline: December 31.
How to apply: Applications are available online.

(2031) · Edith M. Allen Scholarship
United Methodist Church
Office of Loans and Scholarships
P.O. BOX 340007
Nashville, TN 37203-0007
Phone: 615-340-7344
Fax: 615-340-7367
Email: umscholar@gbhem.org
Website: http://www.gbhem.org
Purpose: To support African American students who are attending United Methodist colleges.
Eligibility: Applicants must have been active members of the United Methodist Church for at least three years. They must be majoring in education, social work, medicine or other health fields. Students may be pursuing undergraduate or graduate degrees. They must have at least a B+ average.
Target applicant:
    High school students
    College students
    Graduate school students
    Adult students
Minimum GPA: 3.3
Amount: Varies.
Number of awards: Varies.
Deadline: May 1.
How to apply: Applications are available online.

(2032) · Education Achievement Awards
Golden Key National Honour Society
Scholarship Program Administrators
Golden Key Scholarships/Awards
P.O. Box 23737
Nashville, TN 37202-3737
Phone: 800-377-2401
Email: scholarships@goldenkey.org
Website: http://www.goldenkey.org

Purpose: To support members studying education.
Eligibility: Applicants must be undergraduate, graduate or post-graduate Golden Key members who are taking classes in a degree-granting program. Selection is based on academic achievement and education-related paper or report.
Target applicant:
    College students
    Graduate school students
    Adult students
Minimum GPA: None.
Amount: $500-$1,000.
Number of awards: 2.
Deadline: March 1.
How to apply: Applications are available online.

(2033) · Elks' Eagle Scout Scholarship

Boy Scouts of America, Eagle Scout Service
1325 West Walnut Hill Lane
P.O. Box 152079
Irving, TX 75015-2079
Phone: 972-580-2401
Fax: 972-580-2413
Website: http://www.learningforlife.org/exploring/
Purpose: To support Boy Scouts who have achieved Eagle Scout rank.
Eligibility: Applicants must be registered Boy Scouts with an Eagle rank, have a minimum SAT score of 1090 and/or an ACT score of 26, be high school seniors and demonstrate financial need.
Target applicant:
    High school students
Minimum GPA: None.
Amount: $1,000-2,000.
Number of awards: 8.
Scholarship may be renewable.
Deadline: February 28.
How to apply: Applications are available from the local Scout Council Service Center and online.

(2034) · Emergency Educational Fund Grants

Elks National Foundation (IL)
2750 North Lakeview Avenue
Chicago, IL 60614
Phone: 773-755-4732
Fax: 773-755-4733
Email: scholarship@elks.org
Website: http://www.elks.org
Purpose: To assist children of deceased and incapacitated Elks.
Eligibility: Applicants must be the children of deceased or incapacitated Elks who were/are members in good standing for at least one year, unmarried, under 23 years old and full-time undergraduate students at a U.S. school. Applicants must also demonstrate financial need.
Target applicant:
    High school students
    College students
Minimum GPA: None.
Amount: Up to $4,000.
Number of awards: Varies.
Scholarship may be renewable.
Deadline: December 31.
How to apply: Applications are available from the local Elks Lodge or by phone or e-mail request.

(2035) · Engineering/Technology Achievement Awards

Golden Key National Honour Society
Scholarship Program Administrators
Golden Key Scholarships/Awards
P.O. Box 23737
Nashville, TN 37202-3737
Phone: 800-377-2401
Email: scholarships@goldenkey.org
Website: http://www.goldenkey.org
Purpose: To support members who are studying engineering or technology.
Eligibility: Applicants must be undergraduate, graduate or post-graduate members who are taking classes in a degree-granting program. Selection is based on academic achievement and engineering-related paper or report.
Target applicant:
    College students
    Graduate school students
    Adult students
Minimum GPA: None.
Amount: $500-$1,000.
Number of awards: 2.
Deadline: March 1.
How to apply: Applications are available online.

(2036) · Ethnic Minority Scholarship

United Methodist Church
Office of Loans and Scholarships
P.O. BOX 340007
Nashville, TN 37203-0007
Phone: 615-340-7344
Fax: 615-340-7367
Email: umscholar@gbhem.org
Website: http://www.gbhem.org
Purpose: To support minority students who belong to the United Methodist Church.
Eligibility: Applicants must belong to one of the following minority groups: Native American, Asian, African American, Hispanic or Pacific Islander. They must have been members of the United Methodist Church for at least one year. Students must be currently pursuing their first undergraduate degree at an accredited school in the United States, and they must be attending school full-time with a GPA of at least 2.5.
Target applicant:
    High school students
    College students
    Adult students
Minimum GPA: 2.5
Amount: Varies.
Number of awards: Varies.
Deadline: May 1.
How to apply: Applications are available online.

(2037) · Eugene C. Beach Memorial Scholarship

Tau Kappa Epsilon Educational Foundation
8645 Founders Road
Indianapolis, IN 46268
Phone: 317-872-6533
Fax: 317-875-8353
Email: tef@tke.org
Website: http://www.tkefoundation.org

Purpose: To award a member of Tau Kappa Epsilon for outstanding academic achievement and leadership within the chapter, campus and community.
Eligibility: Applicants must have a minimum GPA of 3.0.
Target applicant:
  College students
  Adult students
Minimum GPA: 3.0
Amount: $400.
Number of awards: 1.
Deadline: March 16.
How to apply: Applications are available online.

(2038) · Fadel Educational Foundation Annual Award Program

Fadel Educational Foundation
P.O. Box 212135
Augusta, GA 30917-2135
Phone: 866-705-9495
Fax: 866-705-9495
Email: afadel@bww.com
Website: http://www.fadelfoundation.org
Purpose: To support Muslim U.S. citizens and permanent residents.
Eligibility: Applicants must be non-incarcerated students pursuing higher education. Selection is based on need and merit. Applicants should provide application forms, two teacher recommendation forms, one masjid official recommendation letter and financial need reports.
Target applicant:
  High school students
  College students
  Graduate school students
  Adult students
Minimum GPA: None.
Amount: $2,000.
Number of awards: Varies.
Deadline: April 20.
How to apply: Applications are available online.

(2039) · Faith and Education Scholarship Fund

Faith and Education Scholarship Fund
P.O. Box 25555
San Mateo, CA 94402
Phone: 650-341-8702
Email: chris@faithandeducation.org
Website: http://www.faithandeducation.org
Purpose: To support students who are active members of churches of Christ.
Eligibility: Applicants must be active members of churches of Christ and be enrolled full-time at four-year liberal arts colleges or universities. Students must submit the application form, transcripts, copy of SAT or ACT scores from high school applicants and a recommendation letter from a leader of their congregation.
Target applicant:
  High school students
  College students
  Adult students
Minimum GPA: None.
Amount: $5,000.
Number of awards: Varies.
Deadline: April 28.
How to apply: Applications are available online.

(2040) · FEEA Scholarship

Federal Employee Education and Assistance Fund
8441 W. Bowles Avenue
Suite 200
Littleton, CO 80123
Phone: 303-933-7580
Fax: 303-933-7587
Website: http://www.feea.org
Purpose: The FEEA scholarship program aids postal employees and their family members.
Eligibility: Applicants must be current civilian federal and postal employees with three years of service or their children or spouses. Applicants must also be enrolled or plan to enroll in an accredited post secondary school, have a minimum 3.0 GPA and may be high school seniors, college students or graduate students.
Target applicant:
  High school students
  College students
  Graduate school students
  Adult students
Minimum GPA: 3.0
Amount: $300-$1,500.
Number of awards: Varies.
Deadline: March.
How to apply: Applications are available online or by sending a self-addressed and stamped envelope.

(2041) · Fellowship of United Methodists in Music and Worship Arts Scholarship

Fellowship of United Methodists in Music and Worship Arts
Robert A. Schilling
4702 Graceland Avenue
Indianapolis, IN 46208-3504
Phone: 800-952-8977
Fax: 615-749-6874
Email: info@fummwa.org
Website: http://www.fummwa.org
Purpose: To support students who want to pursue church music and/or worship arts as a career.
Eligibility: Applicants must be full-time music students pursuing a career in sacred music who are either entering freshmen or already enrolled in an accredited college, university or school of theology or pursuing an academic education in worship; be members of the United Methodist Church or be employed in the United Methodist Church for at least a year before applying and show Christian character and participation in Christian activities. Students must also demonstrate musical or other artistic talent and leadership potential. Applicants must submit applications, transcripts, personal statements and three reference letters.
Target applicant:
  High school students
  College students
  Graduate school students
  Adult students
Minimum GPA: None.
Amount: Varies.
Number of awards: Varies.
Deadline: March 1.
How to apply: Applications are available online.

(2042) · Fleet Reserve Association Scholarship

Fleet Reserve Association
FRA Scholarship Administrator
125 N. West Street
Alexandria, VA 22314
Phone: 800-372-1924
Website: http://www.fra.org

Purpose: To provide financial support for post-secondary education to FRA members and their dependents and grandchildren.

Eligibility: Applicants must be either FRA members or the dependents or grandchildren of an FRA member who is in good standing or was in good standing at time of death. Applicants are judged on the basis of leadership skills, financial need, academic record and character.

Target applicant:
   High school students
   College students
   Graduate school students
   Adult students

Minimum GPA: None.
Amount: Varies.
Number of awards: Varies.
Deadline: April 15.
How to apply: Applications are available online.

(2043) · Ford Motor Company Business and Leadership Scholarship

Golden Key National Honour Society
Scholarship Program Administrators
Golden Key Scholarships/Awards
P.O. Box 23737
Nashville, TN 37202-3737
Phone: 800-377-2401
Email: scholarships@goldenkey.org
Website: http://www.goldenkey.org

Purpose: To provide opportunities for undergraduate and graduate students majoring in business.

Eligibility: Applicants must be Golden Key members and must be majoring in business. The award is based on academic achievement, leadership, Golden Key involvement and extracurricular activities.

Target applicant:
   College students
   Graduate school students
   Adult students

Minimum GPA: None.
Amount: $10,000.
Number of awards: 1.
Deadline: March 1.
How to apply: Applications are available online.

(2044) · Ford Motor Company Engineering and Leadership Scholarship

Golden Key National Honour Society
Scholarship Program Administrators
Golden Key Scholarships/Awards
P.O. Box 23737
Nashville, TN 37202-3737
Phone: 800-377-2401
Email: scholarships@goldenkey.org
Website: http://www.goldenkey.org

Purpose: To provide opportunities for undergraduate and graduate students majoring in engineering.

Eligibility: Applicants must be Golden Key members and must be majoring in engineering. Award is based on academic achievement, leadership, Golden Key involvement and extracurricular activities.

Target applicant:
   College students
   Graduate school students
   Adult students

Minimum GPA: None.
Amount: $10,000.
Number of awards: 1.
Deadline: March 1.
How to apply: Applications are available online.

(2045) · Ford Truck Scholarship Program

National FFA Organization
P.O. Box 68960
6060 FFA Drive
Indianapolis, IN 46268-0960
Phone: 317-802-6060
Fax: 317-802-6051
Email: scholarships@ffa.org
Website: http://www.ffa.org

Purpose: To provide educational assistance to FFA members.

Eligibility: Applicants must be high school seniors who plan to pursue a two- or four-year degree in any major. They must apply online and obtain a signature and dealer code from a local participating Ford Truck dealer. If there is no participating Ford dealer in the applicant's area, he or she may obtain a signature from any local Ford dealer and be eligible for one of five national scholarships.

Target applicant:
   High school students

Minimum GPA: None.
Amount: $1,000.
Number of awards: Up to 705.
Deadline: February 17.
How to apply: Applications are available online.

(2046) · Ford Trucks/Built Ford Tough FFA Scholarship Program

National FFA Organization
P.O. Box 68960
6060 FFA Drive
Indianapolis, IN 46268-0960
Phone: 317-802-6060
Fax: 317-802-6051
Email: scholarships@ffa.org
Website: http://www.ffa.org

Purpose: To support students who are members of the FFA.

Eligibility: Applicants must be current FFA members and high school seniors or college students planning to enroll or currently enrolled full-time. Students only need to complete the online application one time to be considered for all FFA-administered scholarships. The application requires information about the students' activities and a 1,000-word essay. Awards may be used for books, supplies, tuition, fees and room and board. Applicants must obtain a signature from a local Ford dealer.

Target applicant:
   High school students
   College students
   Adult students

Minimum GPA: None.
Amount: $1,000.
Number of awards: 705.
Deadline: February 15.
How to apply: Applications are available online.

(2047) · Foundation Scholars Program

United Methodist Church
Office of Loans and Scholarships
P.O. BOX 340007
Nashville, TN 37203-0007
Phone: 615-340-7344
Fax: 615-340-7367
Email: umscholar@gbhem.org
Website: http://www.gbhem.org
Purpose: To support students attending a United Methodist-related school.
Eligibility: Applications and nominations will be accepted for candidates who have been active members of the UMC for at least one year and who will be enrolled in full-time study at a two- or four-year United Methodist-related school, college or university. A scholarship will be given to an applicant of each grade level at each school.
Target applicant:
    College students
    Adult students
Minimum GPA: None.
Amount: $1,000.
Number of awards: 420.
Deadline: September 1.
How to apply: Applications may be obtained from your UM-related institution.

(2048) · Foundation Scholarship Program

Kappa Alpha Theta Foundation
Attn.: Undergraduate Scholarship Application
8740 Founders Road
Indianapolis, IN 46268
Phone: 888-526-1870 x119
Fax: 317-876-1925
Email: cthoennes@kappaalphatheta.org
Website: http://www.kappaalphatheta.org
Purpose: To provide merit-based scholarships for undergraduate, graduate and alumna Kappa Alpha Theta members.
Eligibility: The award is based on academics, fraternity activities, campus and community activities and references.
Target applicant:
    College students
    Graduate school students
    Adult students
Minimum GPA: None.
Amount: Varies.
Number of awards: Varies.
Deadline: February 1.
How to apply: Applications are available online.

(2049) · Fourth Degree Pro Deo and Pro Patria Scholarships

Knights of Columbus
Department of Scholarships
P.O. Box 1670
New Haven, CT 06507
Phone: 203-752-4000
Email: info@kofc.org
Website: http://www.kofc.org
Purpose: To provide aid to members or the children of members of the Knights of Columbus.
Eligibility: Applicants must be members or the children of current or deceased members of the Knights of Columbus or, in some cases, be members of the Columbian Squires. Applicants must be entering their freshmen year at a U.S. Catholic college.
Target applicant:
    High school students
    College students
    Adult students
Minimum GPA: None.
Amount: $1,500.
Number of awards: 62.
Scholarship may be renewable.
Deadline: March 1.
How to apply: Applications are available by mail.

(2050) · Francis J. Flynn Memorial Scholarship

Tau Kappa Epsilon Educational Foundation
8645 Founders Road
Indianapolis, IN 46268
Phone: 317-872-6533
Fax: 317-875-8353
Email: tef@tke.org
Website: http://www.tkefoundation.org
Purpose: To recognize academic achievement and chapter leadership in members pursuing degrees in mathematics and education.
Eligibility: Applicants must be initiated Tau Kappa Epsilon members in good standing and full-time undergraduate students pursuing a degree in mathematics or education. They must have a GPA of at least 2.75 and demonstrate outstanding chapter leadership. Applicants must also include a statement describing how they have benefited from TKE membership. First preference will be given to members of Theta-Sigma Chapter.
Target applicant:
    College students
    Adult students
Minimum GPA: 2.75
Amount: $1,400.
Number of awards: 1.
Deadline: March 16.
How to apply: Applications are available online.

(2051) · Gaston/Nolle Scholarships

Alpha Chi
Harding University Box 12249
915 E. Market Avenue
Searcy, AR 72149-2249
Phone: 800-477-4225
Fax: 501-279-4589
Email: dorgan@harding.edu
Website: http://www.harding.edu/alphachi/scholarships.htm
Purpose: To assist Alpha Chi members who are entering their senior year of undergraduate study.
Eligibility: Applicants must be members of Alpha Chi who are enrolled full-time in a bachelor's degree program.

Target applicant:
    College students
    Adult students
Minimum GPA: None.
Amount: $1,500-$2,500.
Number of awards: 12.
Deadline: February 22.
How to apply: Application requirements are available online, and applicants must be nominated by the faculty sponsor.

(2052) · GCSAA Legacy Awards

Golf Course Superintendents Association of America Foundation
GCSAA Career Development Department
GCSAA Scholars Competition
1421 Research Park Drive
Lawrence, KS 66049
Phone: 800-472-7878
Email: infobox@gcsaa.org
Website: http://www.gcsaa.org
Purpose: To support the children and grandchildren of GCSAA members.
Eligibility: The applicants' parents or grandparents must have been GCSAA members for five or more consecutive years. Applicants must also be full-time college students or high school seniors already accepted into a postsecondary school.
Target applicant:
    High school students
    College students
    Adult students
Minimum GPA: None.
Amount: $1,500.
Number of awards: Varies.
Deadline: April 15.
How to apply: Applications are available by contacting Pam Smith, 800-472-7878, x3678.

(2053) · GEICO Life Scholarship

Golden Key National Honour Society
Scholarship Program Administrators
Golden Key Scholarships/Awards
P.O. Box 23737
Nashville, TN 37202-3737
Phone: 800-377-2401
Email: scholarships@goldenkey.org
Website: http://www.goldenkey.org
Purpose: To support undergraduate students who balance family, career or other life commitments with pursuing a degree.
Eligibility: Applicants must be members of Golden Key, be enrolled in a baccalaureate program and have completed at least 12 hours at the time of application. The award is based on academic achievement, extracurricular activities and family and/or career commitments.
Target applicant:
    College students
    Adult students
Minimum GPA: None.
Amount: $1,000.
Number of awards: 10.
Deadline: April 1.
How to apply: Applications are available online.

(2054) · General Conference Women's Ministries Scholarship Program

General Conference of Seventh-Day Adventists Women's Ministries
12501 Old Columbia Pike
Silver Spring, MD 20904
Phone: 301-680-6672
Fax: 301-680-6600
Email: womensministries@gc.adventist.org
Website: http://wm.gc.adventist.org
Purpose: To support female Seventh-day Adventists who are pursuing Christian education.
Eligibility: Applicants must be women who are planning to study at a Seventh-day Adventist college in their division. Students in their final two years of study will be given preference. Applicants must show financial need, academic achievement and willingness to serve the Lord.
Target applicant:
    High school students
    College students
    Graduate school students
    Adult students
Minimum GPA: None.
Amount: Varies.
Number of awards: Varies.
Deadline: Varies.
How to apply: Applications are available online and from Women's Ministries Directors in each division.

(2055) · George W. Woolery Memorial Scholarship

Tau Kappa Epsilon Educational Foundation
8645 Founders Road
Indianapolis, IN 46268
Phone: 317-872-6533
Fax: 317-875-8353
Email: tef@tke.org
Website: http://www.tkefoundation.org
Purpose: To award a member of Tau Kappa Epsilon for academic achievement and outstanding leadership within the chapter and campus.
Eligibility: Applicants must have a GPA of at least 2.5 and must be seeking an undergraduate degree in marketing or communications. Preference is first given to members of the Beta-Sigma Chapter.
Target applicant:
    College students
    Adult students
Minimum GPA: 2.5
Amount: $600.
Number of awards: 1.
Deadline: March 16.
How to apply: Applications are available online.

(2056) · Girl Scout Achievement Award

American Legion Auxiliary
8945 N. Meridian Street
Indianapolis, IN 46260
Phone: 317-569-4500
Fax: 317-569-4502
Email: alahq@legion-aux.org
Website: http://www.legion-aux.org
Purpose: To reward Girl Scout Gold Award winners.

Eligibility: Applicants must be Cadet or Senior Girl Scouts who have received the Girls Scout Gold Award, be active members of their religious institution and have received the appropriate religious emblem, and demonstrate citizenship. Applicants must submit four letters of recommendation from a religious institution, school, the community and scouting.
Target applicant:
  High school students
Minimum GPA: None.
Amount: Varies.
Number of awards: Varies.
Deadline: February 11.
How to apply: Applications are available online.

(2057) · Glass, Molders, Pottery, Plastics and Allied Workers Memorial Scholarship Fund

Glass, Molders, Pottery, Plastics and Allied Workers International Union
608 E. Baltimore Pike
P.O. Box 607
Media, PA 19063
Phone: 610-565-5051
Fax: 610-565-0983
Email: gmpiu@ix.netcom.com
Website: http://www.gmpiu.org
Purpose: To provide financial assistance to the children of members.
Eligibility: Applicants must be children, step-children or legally-adopted children of Glass, Molders, Pottery, Plastics and Allied Workers members.
Target applicant:
  High school students
Minimum GPA: None.
Amount: $4,000.
Number of awards: Varies.
Scholarship may be renewable.
Deadline: November 1.
How to apply: Applications are available by written request or by contacting your local union office.

(2058) · Golden Key Graduate Scholar Award

Golden Key National Honour Society
Scholarship Program Administrators
Golden Key Scholarships/Awards
P.O. Box 23737
Nashville, TN 37202-3737
Phone: 800-377-2401
Email: scholarships@goldenkey.org
Website: http://www.goldenkey.org
Purpose: To support Golden Key members' graduate studies at accredited universities in the U.S. or abroad.
Eligibility: Applicant must be a Golden Key member. Selection is based on academic achievement, involvement in Golden Key and extracurricular activities.
Target applicant:
  College students
  Graduate school students
  Adult students
Minimum GPA: None.
Amount: $10,000.
Number of awards: 12.

Deadline: January 20.
How to apply: Applications are available online.

(2059) · Grange Insurance Group Scholarship

Grange Insurance Association
Scholarship Committee
P.O. Box 21089
Seattle, WA 98111-3089
Phone: 800-247-2643
Website: http://www.grange.com
Purpose: To help those associated with Grange Insurance Group.
Eligibility: Applicants must be current Grange Insurance Group (GIG) policyholders (or children or grandchildren of GIG policyholders) in California, Colorado, Idaho, Oregon, Washington or Wyoming; Grange members (or children or grandchildren of Grange members) or children or grandchildren of current GIG employees and residents in California, Colorado, Idaho, Oregon, Washington and Wyoming. Applicants can apply for scholarships in either academic or vocational studies. Three of the awards will be for students wishing to pursue vocational studies and 22 will be for academic studies. The top scoring student in each category receives $1,500 and each additional winner receives $1,000. Scholarships may be used toward a certificate or degree in a recognized profession or vocation, including community colleges, business colleges and technical institutes, as well as institutions offering an academic degree program. Vocational scholarships are intended for use at community colleges, technical or business schools or other institutions that offer vocational training which does not lead to a two- or four-year academic degree. Selection is based on academic achievement and essays.
Target applicant:
  High school students
  College students
  Adult students
Minimum GPA: None.
Amount: $1,000-$1,500.
Number of awards: 25.
Deadline: April 15.
How to apply: Applications are available online.

(2060) · Grant Programs for Medical Studies

Presbyterian Church (USA)
100 Witherspoon Street
Louisville, KY 40202
Phone: 888-728-7228 x5776
Email: fcook@ctr.pcusa.org
Website: http://www.pcusa.org
Purpose: To aid Presbyterian Church (U.S.A.) members pursuing a post graduate education in a medical profession.
Eligibility: Applicants must be PCUSA church members who demonstrate financial need and are in good academic standing at an accredited institution at which they are enrolled full-time. A recommendation by a church pastor and an academic advisor from their institution is required.
Target applicant:
  Graduate school students
  Adult students
Minimum GPA: None.
Amount: $100-$1,000.
Number of awards: Varies.
Scholarship may be renewable.
Deadline: May 15.
How to apply: Applications are available online.

(2061) · Guy and Gloria Muto Memorial Scholarship

Guy and Gloria Muto Memorial Scholarship Foundation Inc.
P.O. Box 60159
Sacramento, CA 95860
Email: ggmuto@aol.com
Website: http://www.ggmuto.org
Purpose: To provide scholarships for pool and spa industry employees and their immediate families.
Eligibility: Applicants or their immediate family must have been employed full-time in the pool and spa industry for at least one year. Students must have the endorsement of an officer of a chapter of a recognized pool and spa association. Scholarships may be used for college, graduate school, trade school or vocational education.
Target applicant:
    High school students
    College students
    Graduate school students
    Adult students
Minimum GPA: None.
Amount: Varies.
Number of awards: Varies.
Deadline: May 31.
How to apply: Applications are available online.

(2062) · HANA Scholarship

United Methodist Church
Office of Loans and Scholarships
P.O. BOX 340007
Nashville, TN 37203-0007
Phone: 615-340-7344
Fax: 615-340-7367
Email: umscholar@gbhem.org
Website: http://www.gbhem.org
Purpose: To support students in the United Methodist Church who are of Hispanic, Asian, Native American or Pacific Island parentage.
Eligibility: Applicants must be in at least their junior year of college or in graduate school, and they must have at least a 2.85 GPA. They must have been members of the United Methodist Church for at least three years. Students must plan to take on leadership roles in their church and ethnic communities.
Target applicant:
    College students
    Graduate school students
    Adult students
Minimum GPA: 2.85
Amount: Varies.
Number of awards: Varies.
Deadline: April 1.
How to apply: Applications are available online.

(2063) · Harold Davis Memorial Scholarship

National FFA Organization
P.O. Box 68960
6060 FFA Drive
Indianapolis, IN 46268-0960
Phone: 317-802-6060
Fax: 317-802-6051
Email: scholarships@ffa.org
Website: http://www.ffa.org
Purpose: To provide financial assistance to students who have livestock backgrounds and are seeking degrees in animal science, agricultural education and agribusiness.
Eligibility: Applicants must be current FFA members and high school seniors or college students planning to enroll or currently enrolled full-time. Students only need to complete the online application one time to be considered for all FFA-administered scholarships. The application requires information about the students' activities and a 1,000-word essay. Awards may be used for books, supplies, tuition, fees and room and board.
Target applicant:
    High school students
    College students
    Adult students
Minimum GPA: None.
Amount: $400.
Number of awards: Varies.
Deadline: February 15.
How to apply: Applications are available online.

(2064) · Harry C. Bates Merit Scholarships

International Union of Bricklayers and Allied Craftworkers (BAC)
Education Department
1776 Eye Street NW
Washington, DC 2006
Phone: 888-880-8222 x3111
Email: askbac@bacweb.org
Website: http://www.bacweb.org
Purpose: To award scholarships to the children of BAC members.
Eligibility: U.S. applicants must be the children of a member, living or deceased, of BAC and among the semifinalists in the PSAT/NMSQT.
Target applicant:
    High school students
Minimum GPA: None.
Amount: $800-$2,000.
Number of awards: 3.
Scholarship may be renewable.
Deadline: Varies.
How to apply: For U.S. students: There is no application. NMSQT semi-finalists should notify their local BAC office. The application for Canadian students is available online.

(2065) · Harry J. Donnelly Memorial Scholarship

Tau Kappa Epsilon Educational Foundation
8645 Founders Road
Indianapolis, IN 46268
Phone: 317-872-6533
Fax: 317-875-8353
Email: tef@tke.org
Website: http://www.tkefoundation.org
Purpose: To honor the "father" of the TKE Educational Foundation by recognizing outstanding current members.
Eligibility: Applicants must be initiated Tau Kappa Epsilon members in good standing and full-time students. They must be undergraduate students in accounting or graduate students in law and plan to be full-time students in the following academic year. Applicants must have a GPA of at least 3.0, demonstrate outstanding leadership in their chapter, campus and community and include a statement describing how they have benefited from TKE membership.

Target applicant:
- College students
- Graduate school students
- Adult students

Minimum GPA: 3.0
Amount: $1,000.
Number of awards: 1.
Deadline: March 16.
How to apply: Applications are available online.

(2066) · Helping Hands of WSC Endowment

Epsilon Sigma Alpha Foundation
P.O. Box 270517
Fort Collins, CO 80527
Phone: 970-223-2824
Fax: 970-223-4456
Email: kloyd@knoxy.net
Website: http://www.esaintl.com/esaf
Purpose: To provide financial assistance to Epsilon Sigma Alpha members.
Eligibility: Applicants must be female residents of the states of Alaska, Arizona, California, Oregon or Washington or of Australia. They may pursue any major at any institution of higher learning. Selection is based equally on character, leadership, service, financial need and scholastic ability.
Target applicant:
- High school students
- College students
- Adult students

Minimum GPA: None.
Amount: $500.
Number of awards: 1.
Deadline: February 1.
How to apply: Applications are available online.

(2067) · Highway Worker Memorial Scholarship Program

American Road and Transportation Builders Association
1219 28th Street NW
Washington, DC 20007
Phone: 202-289-4434
Email: rbritton@artba.org
Website: http://www.artba.org
Purpose: To support the children of injured or deceased highway workers.
Eligibility: Students must have a parent who was killed or seriously injured in a highway construction zone accident, and the parent must have been employed by a transportation construction firm or a transportation public agency at the time of the accident. Applicants must demonstrate financial need, and they must have at least a 2.5 GPA.
Target applicant:
- High school students
- College students
- Adult students

Minimum GPA: 2.5
Amount: Up to $2,000.
Number of awards: Varies.
Deadline: February 28.
How to apply: Applications are available online.

(2068) · Himmel Scholarship

Circle K International
3636 Woodview Trace
Indianapolis, IN 46268
Website: http://www.circlek.org
Purpose: This scholarship is in memory of Harry S. Himmel, deceased President Emeritus of the Kiwanis International Foundation. Recipients should demonstrate dedication and leadership within the organization.
Eligibility: Applicants must be Key Club or Circle K members who appear on the international roster, are currently enrolled in college or are college-bound and have completed 100 service hours with the organization. Key Club members must have also held an elected officer position within the organization.
Target applicant:
- High school students
- College students
- Adult students

Minimum GPA: 3.0
Amount: $500.
Number of awards: 2.
Deadline: February 13.
How to apply: Applications are available online.

(2069) · Howard Coughlin Memorial Scholarship Fund

Office and Professional Employees International Union
1660 L Street NW
Suite 801
Washington, DC 20036
Phone: 202-393-4464
Fax: 202-347-0649
Website: http://www.opeiu.org
Purpose: To offer scholarships to OPEIU members and their children.
Eligibility: Applicants must either be members of OPEIU in good standing, or the children, stepchildren or legally adopted children of an OPEIU member in good standing or associate members. Applicants must also be high school seniors, high school graduates entering a college, university or a recognized technical or vocational post-secondary school as full-time students or presently in a college, university or a recognized technical or vocational post-secondary school as a full-time or part-time student. Part-time scholarships are defined as a minimum of three credits and no more than two courses. Selection is based on transcripts, high school class rank and SAT/ACT scores or evidence of an equivalent exam by a recognized technical or vocational post-secondary school.
Target applicant:
- High school students
- College students
- Adult students

Minimum GPA: None.
Amount: $2,400-$6,000.
Number of awards: 18 (12 full-time, 6 part-time).
Scholarship may be renewable.
Deadline: March 31.
How to apply: Applications are available at the local union office, at the secretary-treasurer's office of the International Union or online.

(2070) · Imagine America II

Imagine America Foundation
1101 Connecticut Avenue NW
Suite 901

Washington, DC 20036
Phone: 202-336-6724
Fax: 202-408-8102
Email: kerryt@career.org
Website: http://www.imagine-america.org
Purpose: To help Imagine America scholarship recipients.
Eligibility: Students do not apply for these scholarships and must be nominated by a participating career college. Applicants must also be adult students currently attending career colleges in the United States and Puerto Rico, have been an Imagine America (high school) scholarship recipient, have a 95 percent or higher attendance record and obtain a written recommendation.
Target applicant:
  College students
  Graduate school students
  Adult students
Minimum GPA: 3.5
Amount: Varies.
Number of awards: Varies.
Deadline: May 31.
How to apply: Nomination forms are available online.

(2071) · International Association of Machinists and Aerospace Workers Scholarship for Members

International Association of Machinists and Aerospace Workers
9000 Machinists Place
Room 117
Upper Marlboro, MD 20772
Phone: 301-967-4500
Website: http://www.iamaw.org
Purpose: To offer scholarships to members of the International Association of Machinists and Aerospace Workers (IAM).
Eligibility: Applicants must have two years of continuous good standing membership and must be working for a company under contract with the IAM. Applicants may be entering college or vocational/technical school as a freshman or at a higher level with some college credits already completed. Grades, attitude, references, test scores, activities and participation in local lodge are considered in selecting scholarship recipients.
Target applicant:
  High school students
  College students
  Adult students
Minimum GPA: None.
Amount: $2,000.
Number of awards: Varies.
Deadline: Last Friday of February.
How to apply: Applications are available by written request.

(2072) · International Association of Machinists and Aerospace Workers Scholarship for Members' Children

International Association of Machinists and Aerospace Workers
9000 Machinists Place
Room 117
Upper Marlboro, MD 20772
Phone: 301-967-4500
Website: http://www.iamaw.org
Purpose: To offer scholarships to children of the members of the IAM.

Eligibility: Applicants' parent member must have two years of continuous good standing membership, and applicants must be in their senior year of high school. Selection is based on grades, attitude, references, test scores and activities outside of school.
Target applicant:
  High school students
Minimum GPA: None.
Amount: $1,000-$2,000.
Number of awards: Varies.
Deadline: Last Friday of February.
How to apply: Applications are available by written request.

(2073) · International Organization of Masters, Mates and Pilots Scholarship

International Organization of Masters, Mates and Pilots
700 Maritime Boulevard
Linthicum Heights, MD 21090
Phone: 410-850-8700
Website: http://www.bridgedeck.com
Purpose: To provide financial assistance to the children of members of the MMP.
Eligibility: Applicants must be the children of an eligible offshore active or deceased member or eligible pensioner of the International Organization of Masters, Mates and Pilots. Recipients are chosen on the basis of high school records, extracurricular activities, SAT scores, character and leadership.
Target applicant:
  High school students
  College students
  Adult students
Minimum GPA: None.
Amount: $5,000.
Number of awards: 6.
Scholarship may be renewable.
Deadline: November 30.
How to apply: Applications are available by written request.

(2074) · Isabella M. Gillen Memorial Scholarship Fund

Aviation Boatswain Mates Association (ABMA)
Scholarship Chairman
Lanny Vines
144 CR 1515
Alba, TX 75410
Email: secretary@abma-usn.org
Website: http://www.abma-usn.org
Purpose: To support family members of ABMA.
Eligibility: Applicants must be the spouses or dependent children of ABMA members who have paid dues for at least two years. In addition to the application, applicants must write a letter stating their professional goals and how they plan to reach them.
Target applicant:
  High school students
  College students
  Graduate school students
  Adult students
Minimum GPA: None.
Amount: $2,500.
Number of awards: 1.
Deadline: June 1.
How to apply: Applications are available online.

(2075) · IUE-CWA International Paul Jennings Scholarship

IUE-CWA
1275 K Street NW
Suite 600
Washington, DC 20005
Phone: 202-513-6300
Fax: 202-513-6357
Website: http://www.iue-cwa.org
Purpose: To provide scholarships for the children and grandchildren of local IUE-CWA union elected officials.
Eligibility: Applicants must be the children or grandchildren of IUE-CWA members who are now or have been local union elected officials. Applicants must also be accepted for admission or already enrolled as full-time students at an accredited college, university, nursing school or technical school offering college credit courses. All study must be completed at the undergraduate level. Applicants should demonstrate an interest in equality, improving the quality of life of others and community service. Applicants will also be evaluated on character, leadership and a desire to improve.
Target applicant:
    High school students
    College students
    Adult students
Minimum GPA: None.
Amount: $3,000.
Number of awards: 1.
Deadline: March 31.
How to apply: Applications are available online.

(2076) · J. Robert Ashcroft National Youth Scholarship

Assemblies of God
1445 N. Boonville Avenue
Springfield, MO 65802
Phone: 417-862-2781
Email: colleges@ag.org
Website: http://www.ag.org
Purpose: To provide financial assistance to college-bound seniors who attend Assemblies of God churches.
Eligibility: Applicants must be high school seniors who attend an Assemblies of God church, either in the United States or abroad as dependents of Assemblies of God missionaries or chaplains. Applicants must also attend an institution of higher learning that is endorsed by the Assemblies of God the fall immediately following their high school graduation.
Target applicant:
    High school students
Minimum GPA: None.
Amount: $1,000-$5,000.
Number of awards: 3.
Deadline: March 31.
How to apply: Applications are available online.

(2077) · J. Russel Salsbury Memorial Scholarship

Tau Kappa Epsilon Educational Foundation
8645 Founders Road
Indianapolis, IN 46268
Phone: 317-872-6533
Fax: 317-875-8353
Email: tef@tke.org
Website: http://www.tkefoundation.org
Purpose: To award a member of Tau Kappa Epsilon for outstanding academic achievement and leadership within the chapter, campus or community.
Eligibility: Applicants must have a GPA of at least 3.0.
Target applicant:
    College students
    Adult students
Minimum GPA: 3.0
Amount: $300.
Number of awards: 1.
Deadline: March 16.
How to apply: Applications are available online.

(2078) · J. Walker Field Endowed Scholarship

Circle K International
3636 Woodview Trace
Indianapolis, IN 46268
Website: http://www.circlek.org
Purpose: The scholarship is in memory of J. Walker Field, a former Kiwanis governor and dedicated Circle K supporter who allowed no obstacle to stand between him and his Circle K'ers. The recipient should demonstrate similar commitment to the organization.
Eligibility: Applicants must be Circle K members who appear on the international roster, are currently enrolled in college and have completed 100 service hours with the organization.
Target applicant:
    College students
    Adult students
Minimum GPA: 3.0
Amount: $1,000.
Number of awards: 1.
Deadline: February 13.
How to apply: Applications are available online.

(2079) · James C. Borel FFA Leaders Scholarship Fund

National FFA Organization
P.O. Box 68960
6060 FFA Drive
Indianapolis, IN 46268-0960
Phone: 317-802-6060
Fax: 317-802-6051
Email: scholarships@ffa.org
Website: http://www.ffa.org
Purpose: To support FFA officers who are studying agriculture.
Eligibility: Applicants must be current FFA members and high school seniors or college students planning to enroll or currently enrolled full-time. They must have served as a chapter, state or national FFA officer, and preference will be given to students who have demonstrated leadership skills. Applicants must have at least a 3.5 GPA, and they must show proof of community service participation. Students only need to complete the online application one time to be considered for all FFA-administered scholarships. The application requires information about the students' activities and a 1,000-word essay. Awards may be used for books, supplies, tuition, fees and room and board.
Target applicant:
    High school students
    College students
    Adult students
Minimum GPA: 3.5
Amount: $1,000.
Number of awards: 1.

Deadline: February 15.
How to apply: Applications are available online.

(2080) · James McPherson Memorial Endowment Scholarship

Epsilon Sigma Alpha Foundation
P.O. Box 270517
Fort Collins, CO 80527
Phone: 970-223-2824
Fax: 970-223-4456
Email: kloyd@knoxy.net
Website: http://www.esaintl.com/esaf
Purpose: To support undergraduate members who are residents of Virginia.
Eligibility: Students may attend any U.S. college or university and study any major. Selection is based on character (20 percent), leadership (20 percent), service (20 percent), financial need (20 percent) and scholastic ability (20 percent).
Target applicant:
High school students
College students
Adult students
Minimum GPA: None.
Amount: $1,000.
Number of awards: 1.
Deadline: February 1.
How to apply: Applications are available online.

(2081) · Jerry Harvey Endowment Scholarship

Epsilon Sigma Alpha Foundation
P.O. Box 270517
Fort Collins, CO 80527
Phone: 970-223-2824
Fax: 970-223-4456
Email: kloyd@knoxy.net
Website: http://www.esaintl.com/esaf
Purpose: To support members who are residents of Texas.
Eligibility: Applicants may major in any subject area and attend any college or university. Students must show financial need and scholastic achievement. Selection is based on character (10 percent), leadership (20 percent), service (10 percent), financial need (30 percent) and scholastic ability (30 percent).
Target applicant:
High school students
College students
Adult students
Minimum GPA: None.
Amount: $2,000.
Number of awards: 1.
Deadline: February 1.
How to apply: Applications are available online.

(2082) · Joe Jaegers Family Endowment Scholarship

Epsilon Sigma Alpha Foundation
P.O. Box 270517
Fort Collins, CO 80527
Phone: 970-223-2824
Fax: 970-223-4456
Email: kloyd@knoxy.net
Website: http://www.esaintl.com/esaf

Purpose: To support undergraduate members.
Eligibility: Applicants must reside in one of the following states: California, Colorado, Missouri, Indiana, North Carolina, Oklahoma or Texas. Students must have a GPA of 3.0 to 3.5 and may attend any school or study any major. Selection is based on character (25 percent), leadership (25 percent), service (20 percent), financial need (15 percent) and scholastic ability (15 percent).
Target applicant:
High school students
College students
Adult students
Minimum GPA: 3.0
Amount: $1,000.
Number of awards: 1.
Deadline: February 1.
How to apply: Applications are available online.

(2083) · John A. Courson Top Scholar Award

Tau Kappa Epsilon Educational Foundation
8645 Founders Road
Indianapolis, IN 46268
Phone: 317-872-6533
Fax: 317-875-8353
Email: tef@tke.org
Website: http://www.tkefoundation.org
Purpose: To recognize academic achievement in members.
Eligibility: Applicants must be initiated Tau Kappa Epsilon members in good standing and full-time students with a GPA of 3.0 or higher. They must include a statement describing how they have benefited from TKE membership and demonstrate leadership on their campus, in their community and in their chapter.
Target applicant:
College students
Adult students
Minimum GPA: 3.0
Amount: $3,000.
Number of awards: 1.
Deadline: March 16.
How to apply: Applications are available online.

(2084) · John H. Lyons, Sr., Scholarship Program

Iron Workers, International Association of Bridge, Structural, Ornamental and Reinforcing
1750 New York Avenue NW
Suite 400
Washington, DC 20006
Phone: 203-383-4000
Fax: 202-638-4856
Website: http://www.ironworkers.org
Purpose: To offer scholarships to the children of members of the Iron Workers Union.
Eligibility: Applicants must be the children, stepchildren or adopted children of an active member of the Iron Workers who has had five or more years of continuous membership. Children of deceased members who were in members in good standing at the time of their death are also eligible. Applicants must also be in their senior year of high school and rank in the upper half of their graduating classes. Selection is based on academic record, SAT/ACT scores, extracurricular activities, references, leadership and citizenship.
Target applicant:
High school students

Minimum GPA: None.
Amount: Up to $2,500.
Number of awards: 2.
Scholarship may be renewable.
Deadline: Varies.
How to apply: Applications are available by written request.

(2085) · John Kelly Labor Studies Scholarship Fund

Office and Professional Employees International Union
1660 L Street NW
Suite 801
Washington, DC 20036
Phone: 202-393-4464
Fax: 202-347-0649
Website: http://www.opeiu.org
Purpose: To offer scholarships to OPEIU members and associate members.
Eligibility: Applicants must be members of OPEIU in good standing or associate members for at least two years, and applicants must be either undergraduate or graduate students in one of the following areas of study: labor studies, industrial relations, union leadership and administration or non-degree programs sponsored by the National Labor College at the George Meany Center or similar institution. The selections shall be based on recommendations of an academic scholarship committee.
Target applicant:
 College students
 Graduate school students
 Adult students
Minimum GPA: None.
Amount: $3,000.
Number of awards: 10.
Deadline: March 31.
How to apply: Applications are available by phone or written request from the local union office, at the secretary-treasurer's office of the International Union or online.

(2086) · John L. Dales Scholarship Fund

Screen Actors Guild Foundation
5757 Wilshire Boulevard
7th Floor
Los Angeles, CA 90036
Phone: 323-549-6649
Fax: 323-549-6710
Email: dlloyd@sag.org
Website: http://www.sagfoundation.org
Purpose: To award scholarships to the families of the SAG.
Eligibility: Applicants must be members of the Screen Actors Guild or children of members. Members applying for a scholarship must have been members of the Guild for five years; however, the parent of an applicant must have been a member for ten years. Members must have a lifetime earnings of at least $30,000, earned in the guild's jurisdiction, while parents of an applicant must have lifetime earnings of at least $60,000, earned in the guild's jurisdiction. Applicants must be either students accepted by an accredited institution of higher learning or students already enrolled for at least 12 credit hours per quarter or semester at such an institution. Recipients will be chosen based upon SAT scores, high school/college academic record, a statement of family income and an essay of not less than 250 words.
Target applicant:
 High school students

College students
Adult students
Minimum GPA: None.
Amount: Varies.
Number of awards: Varies.
Deadline: March 15.
How to apply: Applications are available online.

(2087) · John Sarrin Scholarship

Society of Friends (Quakers)
Attn.: Dinah Geiger
2757 South 1050 East
Indianapolis, IN 46231
Phone: 765-962-7573
Fax: 765-966-1293
Email: info@usfwi.org
Website: http://www.usfwi.org
Purpose: To support the education of ministers, missionaries, the children of ministers and other Friends who aspire to full-time Christian service.
Eligibility: Applicants must belong to the Society of Friends. They must be committed to staying drug and alcohol free, and they must agree to never join the armed forces of any country. Students must possess good moral character in order to receive and keep the scholarship.
Target applicant:
 Junior high students or younger
 High school students
 College students
 Graduate school students
 Adult students
Minimum GPA: None.
Amount: Varies.
Number of awards: Varies.
Deadline: Varies.
How to apply: Applications are available by written request.

(2088) · John W McDevitt (Fourth Degree) Scholarship Fund

Knights of Columbus
Department of Scholarships
P.O. Box 1670
New Haven, CT 06507
Phone: 203-752-4000
Email: info@kofc.org
Website: http://www.kofc.org
Purpose: To provide financial assistance to college students who are Knights of Columbus members or family members of a member.
Eligibility: Applicants must be a Knights of Columbus member or the wife, widow or child of a member in good standing. New applicants must also be entering their freshman year at a Catholic college or university.
Target applicant:
 High school students
 College students
 Adult students
Minimum GPA: None.
Amount: $1,500.
Number of awards: Varies.
Scholarship may be renewable.
Deadline: March 1.
How to apply: Applications are available by mail.

(2089) · Jones-Laurence Award for Scholastic Achievement

Sigma Alpha Epsilon (SAE)
Dave Sandell
Sigma Alpha Epsilong Foundation Scholarships
1856 Sheridan Road
Evanston, IL 60201-3837
Phone: 800-233-1856 x234
Fax: 847-475-2250
Email: dsandell@sae.net
Website: http://www.sae.net
Purpose: To improve scholarship among active Sigma Alpha Epsilon members.
Eligibility: Applicants must be brothers of Sigma Alpha Epsilon in good standing and either must have junior standing or higher or must be pursuing full-time graduate study. This award is merit-based, with an emphasis on combining academic excellence, leadership, service and campus involvement. Applicants are nominated by their chapters and have a minimum 3.9 GPA.
Target applicant:
    College students
    Graduate school students
    Adult students
Minimum GPA: 3.9
Amount: $1,000-$3,000.
Number of awards: 2.
Deadline: February 28.
How to apply: Applications are available online.

(2090) · JWV Grant

Jewish War Veterans of the USA
1811 R Street NW
Washington, DC 20009
Phone: 202-265-6280
Fax: 202-234-5662
Email: jwv@jwv.org
Website: http://www.jwv.org
Purpose: To provide scholarships for descendents of members of the Jewish War Veterans of the USA.
Eligibility: Applicants must be direct descendents of a JWV member in good standing. Candidates must also have been accepted to an accredited college, university or nursing school, be in the upper 25 percent of their class and be active in activities at school and within the Jewish community.
Target applicant:
    High school students
Minimum GPA: None.
Amount: $500.
Number of awards: 1.
Deadline: May 3.
How to apply: Applications are available online and should be submitted by the applicant's school to the department commander in the local post.

(2091) · Kenneth L. Duke, Sr., Memorial Scholarship

Tau Kappa Epsilon Educational Foundation
8645 Founders Road
Indianapolis, IN 46268
Phone: 317-872-6533
Fax: 317-875-8353

Email: tef@tke.org
Website: http://www.tkefoundation.org
Purpose: To award a member of Tau Kappa Epsilon for academic achievement and outstanding leadership within the chapter, campus or community.
Eligibility: Applicants must have a GPA of at least 2.5.
Target applicant:
    College students
    Adult students
Minimum GPA: 2.5
Amount: $300.
Number of awards: 1.
Deadline: March 16.
How to apply: Applications are available online.

(2092) · Koven L. Brown Scholarship Program

International Order of the Golden Rule
Education Department
P.O. Box 28689
St. Louis, MO 631461189
Phone: 800-637-8030
Fax: 314-209-7213
Email: jgabbert@ogr.org
Website: http://www.ogr.org
Purpose: To assist mortuary science students with financial need.
Eligibility: Applicants must be studying mortuary science and have a minimum 3.0 GPA. The award is based on community service, honors, grades and potential contributions to the funeral service profession.
Target applicant:
    College students
    Adult students
Minimum GPA: 3.0
Amount: Varies.
Number of awards: Varies.
Deadline: October 1.
How to apply: Applications are available online.

(2093) · L. Gordon Bittle Memorial Scholarship for Student CTA (SCTA)

California Teachers Association (CTA)
CTA Human Rights Department
P.O. Box 921
Burlingame, CA 94011-0921
Phone: 650-697-1400
Fax: 650-552-5001
Website: http://www.cta.org
Purpose: To support members of the Student California Teachers Association.
Eligibility: Applicants must be planning to work in public education and have a minimum 3.5 high school GPA or show high academic achievement in college coursework, explaining any special circumstances affecting their grades. Scholarships are based on a personal statement, school and community activities and letters of recommendation.
Target applicant:
    High school students
    College students
    Graduate school students
    Adult students
Minimum GPA: 3.5
Amount: $2,000.
Number of awards: 3.

Deadline: January 27.
How to apply: Applications are available online.

(2094) · Legacy Award

Elks National Foundation (IL)
2750 North Lakeview Avenue
Chicago, IL 60614
Phone: 773-755-4732
Fax: 773-755-4733
Email: scholarship@elks.org
Website: http://www.elks.org
Purpose: To assist the descendants of Elk members.
Eligibility: Applicants must be children or grandchildren (including step-children/grandchildren and legal wards) of Elk members in good standing and be high school seniors planning to attend accredited U.S. postsecondary institutions (with the exception of some non-U.S. Elks Lodges). Applicants must also take or have taken the SAT or ACT. The selection committee will evaluate applicants on the core values of knowledge, charity, community and integrity. Financial need is not a consideration.
Target applicant:
    High school students
Minimum GPA: None.
Amount: $1,000.
Number of awards: Up to 500.
Deadline: January 11.
How to apply: Applications are available from local Elks Lodges, online or by written request.

(2095) · Lenwood S. Cochran Scholarship

Tau Kappa Epsilon Educational Foundation
8645 Founders Road
Indianapolis, IN 46268
Phone: 317-872-6533
Fax: 317-875-8353
Email: tef@tke.org
Website: http://www.tkefoundation.org
Purpose: To award a member of Tau Kappa Epsilon for outstanding academic achievement and leadership within the chapter, including serving as an officer.
Eligibility: Applicants must have a GPA of at least 3.0. Preference is first given to members of the Gamma-Mu Chapter.
Target applicant:
    College students
    Adult students
Minimum GPA: 3.0
Amount: $400.
Number of awards: 1.
Deadline: March 16.
How to apply: Applications are available online.

(2096) · Leonard M. Perryman Communications Scholarship for Ethnic Minority Students

United Methodist Church
Office of Loans and Scholarships
P.O. BOX 340007
Nashville, TN 37203-0007
Phone: 615-340-7344
Fax: 615-340-7367
Email: umscholar@gbhem.org
Website: http://www.gbhem.org

Purpose: To assist undergraduate Christian students who intend on pursuing a career in religion journalism.
Eligibility: Applicants must be undergraduate students entering their junior or senior year of college, be Christian students who are pursuing a career in religion journalism and must major in religion journalism or communications. One scholarship will be given to the best Methodist applicant and one will be given to best overall. Applicants must submit letters of recommendation, a personal statement, photograph and three samples of journalism work.
Target applicant:
    College students
    Adult students
Minimum GPA: None.
Amount: $2,500.
Number of awards: 2.
Deadline: March 15.
How to apply: Applications are available online and by request.

(2097) · Life Members' Scholarship

American Atheists
P.O. Box 5733
Parsippany, NJ 07054
Phone: 908-276-7300
Fax: 908-276-7402
Email: info@athiests.org
Website: http://www.atheists.org
Purpose: To support Atheist students who are activists.
Eligibility: Applicants must be high school seniors or college students who are Atheists, have a minimum 2.5 GPA and be student activists. The award is based on the level of activism and requires a 500- to 1,000-word essay. In addition to the scholarship, the winner will receive a free trip to the American Atheists National Convention.
Target applicant:
    High school students
    College students
    Adult students
Minimum GPA: 2.5
Amount: $2,000.
Number of awards: 1.
Deadline: January 31.
How to apply: Applications are available online.

(2098) · Lillian and Arthur Dunn Scholarship

National Society Daughters of the American Revolution
1776 D Street NW
Washington, DC 20006-5303
Phone: 202-628-1776
Website: http://www.dar.org
Purpose: To assist the children of members with their education.
Eligibility: Applicants must be sons or daughters of current women members of NSDAR, must be U.S. citizens and plan to attend an accredited U.S. college or university. All applicants must obtain a letter of sponsorship from their local DAR chapter.
Target applicant:
    High school students
    College students
    Adult students
Minimum GPA: None.
Amount: $2,000.
Number of awards: 1.
Scholarship may be renewable.

Deadline: February 15.
How to apply: Applications are available by written request.

(2099) · Literacy Grants

Honor Society of Phi Kappa Phi
P.O. Box 16000
Louisiana State University
Baton Rouge, LA 70893
Phone: 800-804-9880
Fax: 225-388-4900
Email: awards@phikappaphi.org
Website: http://www.phikappaphi.org
Purpose: To award grants to Phi Kappa Phi members and chapters to offer literacy programs.
Eligibility: The project leader must be a member of Phi Kappa Phi. Previous winners have provided books and book bags to literacy programs, organized literacy fairs and conducted research on literacy.
Target applicant:
   College students
   Graduate school students
   Adult students
Minimum GPA: None.
Amount: Up to $2,500.
Number of awards: Varies.
Deadline: February 1.
How to apply: Applications are available online.

(2100) · Literary Achievement Awards

Golden Key National Honour Society
Scholarship Program Administrators
Golden Key Scholarships/Awards
P.O. Box 23737
Nashville, TN 37202-3737
Phone: 800-377-2401
Email: scholarships@goldenkey.org
Website: http://www.goldenkey.org
Purpose: To support members who demonstrate literary talents.
Eligibility: Applicants must be undergraduate, graduate or post-graduate members who are taking classes in a degree-granting program. Selection is based on an original composition. One winner is selected in each of four categories: fiction, non-fiction, poetry and news writing.
Target applicant:
   College students
   Graduate school students
   Adult students
Minimum GPA: None.
Amount: $1,000.
Number of awards: 4.
Deadline: April 1.
How to apply: Applications are available online.

(2101) · Lorin E. Kerr Scholarship Fund

United Mine Workers of America/BCOA T.E.F.
8315 Lee Highway
Fairfax, VA 22031-2215
Phone: 703-208-7200
Website: http://www.umwa.org
Purpose: To offer scholarships to UMWA members and their families.

Eligibility: Applicants must be UMWA members or dependents who pursue undergraduate degrees. Selection is based on academic potential and financial need.
Target applicant:
   High school students
   College students
   Adult students
Minimum GPA: None.
Amount: $2,500.
Number of awards: 2.
Deadline: February 15.
How to apply: Applications are available online.

(2102) · Louis S. Silvey Grant

Jewish War Veterans of the USA
1811 R Street NW
Washington, DC 20009
Phone: 202-265-6280
Fax: 202-234-5662
Email: jwv@jwv.org
Website: http://www.jwv.org
Purpose: To provide scholarships for descendents of members of the Jewish War Veterans of the USA.
Eligibility: Applicants must be direct descendents of a JWV member in good standing. Candidates must also have been accepted to an accredited college, university or nursing school, be in the upper 25 percent of their class and be active in activities at school and within the Jewish community.
Target applicant:
   High school students
Minimum GPA: None.
Amount: $750.
Number of awards: 1.
Deadline: May 3.
How to apply: Applications are available online and should be submitted by the applicant's school to the department commander in the local post.

(2103) · Maids of Athena Scholarships

American Hellenic Education Progressive Association
1909 Q Street NW
Suite 500
Washington, DC 20009
Phone: 202-232-6300
Fax: 202-232-2140
Email: ahepa@ahepa.org
Website: http://www.ahepa.org
Purpose: To support members of the Maids of Athena.
Eligibility: Students must demonstrate financial need and academic achievement. Applicants must be high school seniors, college undergraduates or graduate students. Selection is based on academic achievement, financial need and participation in the organization.
Target applicant:
   High school students
   College students
   Graduate school students
   Adult students
Minimum GPA: None.
Amount: $1,000.
Number of awards: 3.
Deadline: Varies.
How to apply: Applications are available online.

(2104) · Martin Luther King, Jr. Memorial Scholarship

California Teachers Association (CTA)
CTA Human Rights Department
P.O. Box 921
Burlingame, CA 94011-0921
Phone: 650-697-1400
Fax: 650-552-5001
Website: http://www.cta.org
Purpose: To encourage ethnic minority students to become teachers and support the continuing education of ethnic minority teachers.
Eligibility: Applicants must be African American, American Indian/Alaska Native, Asian/Pacific Islander or Hispanic students pursuing a teaching-related career in public education. Candidates must also be active members of the California Teachers Association or Student California Teachers Association or the dependents of an active, retired-life or deceased California Teachers Association member.
Target applicant:
    High school students
    College students
    Graduate school students
    Adult students
Minimum GPA: None.
Amount: Varies.
Number of awards: Varies.
Deadline: March 15.
How to apply: Applications are available online.

(2105) · Michael Hakeem Memorial College Essay Contest

Freedom from Religion Foundation
P.O. Box 750
Madison, WI 53701
Phone: 608-256-5800
Email: info@ffrf.org
Website: http://www.ffrf.org
Purpose: To assist current college students who write an essay about freedom from religion.
Eligibility: Applicants must write a four- to five-page essay on the provided topic. Recent topic choices have been, "Why I am an atheist/agnostic/unbeliever," "Growing up a freethinker" or "Rejecting religion." More details about the topic are available online.
Target applicant:
    College students
    Adult students
Minimum GPA: None.
Amount: $100-$2,000.
Number of awards: 4.
Deadline: July 1.
How to apply: There is no application form. In addition to the essay, applicants must submit a one-paragraph biography and should not include a resume.

(2106) · Michael J. Morin Memorial Scholarship

Tau Kappa Epsilon Educational Foundation
8645 Founders Road
Indianapolis, IN 46268
Phone: 317-872-6533
Fax: 317-875-8353
Email: tef@tke.org
Website: http://www.tkefoundation.org

Purpose: To award a member of Tau Kappa Epsilon for outstanding academic achievement and leadership within the chapter, community and campus.
Eligibility: Applicants must have a GPA of at least 3.0.
Target applicant:
    College students
    Adult students
Minimum GPA: 3.0
Amount: $500.
Number of awards: 1.
Deadline: March 16.
How to apply: Applications are available online.

(2107) · Michael J. Quill Scholarship Fund

Transport Workers Union of America
1700 Broadway, Second Floor
New York, NY 10019-5905
Website: http://www.twu.org
Purpose: To provide financial assistance to the dependents of TWU members.
Eligibility: Applicants must be high school seniors and may be the children of present, retired or deceased TWU members in good standing or meet other eligibility requirements. Recipients are selected by a public drawing.
Target applicant:
    High school students
Minimum GPA: None.
Amount: $1,200.
Number of awards: 15.
Scholarship may be renewable.
Deadline: May 1.
How to apply: Applications are available from local unions and the union publication. They're also available online.

(2108) · Michelin/TIA Scholarship Program

Tire Association of North America
Michelin/TIA Scholarship Program
P.O. Box 1465
Taylors, SC 29687-0031
Phone: 864-268-3363
Email: susanjlee@bellsouth.net
Website: http://www.tireindustry.org
Purpose: To offer financial assistance to children of full-time TIA employees and part-time TIA employees.
Eligibility: Applicants must be part-time employees or dependent children of full-time employees of the Tire Industry Association. Applicants must also be seniors in high school with a minimum 3.0 GPA and be pursuing further education at an accredited two-year or four-year school. Academic achievement, scholarship performance, scholastic aptitude, essays and leadership skills will all be considered.
Target applicant:
    High school students
Minimum GPA: 3.0
Amount: $1,250-$2,500.
Number of awards: 3.
Scholarship may be renewable.
Deadline: March 31.
How to apply: Applications are available online.

(2109) · Miles Gray Memorial Scholarship

Tau Kappa Epsilon Educational Foundation
8645 Founders Road
Indianapolis, IN 46268
Phone: 317-872-6533
Fax: 317-875-8353
Email: tef@tke.org
Website: http://www.tkefoundation.org
Purpose: To award a member of Tau Kappa Epsilon for outstanding academic achievement and leadership within the chapter, campus and community.
Eligibility: Applicants must have a GPA of at least 3.0.
Target applicant:
    College students
    Adult students
Minimum GPA: 3.0
Amount: $500.
Number of awards: 1.
Deadline: March 16.
How to apply: Applications are available online.

(2110) · Mitchell-Beall Scholarship

NASA Federal Credit Union
Mitchell-Beall Memorial Scholarship
P.O. Box 1588
Bowie, MD 20717-1588
Phone: 888-627-2328
Fax: 301-249-0799
Email: support@nasafcu.com
Website: http://www.nasafcu.com
Purpose: To assist younger members of the NASA FCU to further their educations.
Eligibility: Applicants must be the primary owners of NASA Federal Credit Union accounts, high school seniors under the age of 21 and have a minimum 2.0 GPA.
Target applicant:
    High school students
Minimum GPA: 2.0
Amount: $3,000-$7,000.
Number of awards: Varies.
Deadline: February 5.
How to apply: Applications are available online.

(2111) · Moris J. and Betty Kaplun Scholarship

Kaplun Foundation
Essay Contest Committee
P.O. Box 234428
Great Neck, NY 11023
Website: http://www.kaplunfoundation.org
Purpose: To award essays about Jewish-related topics.
Eligibility: Applicants must be in grades 7 through 12. Grades 7 through 9 are level one, and grades 10 through 12 are level two. Applicants must submit essays on Jewish-related topics listed on the website, and essays must be typed, double-spaced and a minimum of 250 words. Level one essays may not be more than 1,000 words. Level two essays may not be more than 1,500 words. A recent level one topic has been, "What person of importance to the Jewish people, past or present, would you like to meet and why?" A recent level two topic has been, "Antisemitism plagues all Jews regardless of religious adherence. How do you see yourself reacting to it?"

Target applicant:
    Junior high students or younger
    High school students
Minimum GPA: None.
Amount: $1,800.
Number of awards: 12.
Deadline: March 15.
How to apply: Essays must be submitted by mail.

(2112) · Mortin Scholarship

Triangle Education Foundation
Chairman, Scholarship and Loan Committee
120 S. Center Street
Plainfield, IN 46168-1214
Phone: 317-837-9640
Fax: 317-837-9642
Email: scholarships@triangle.org
Website: http://www.triangle.org
Purpose: To help deserving active members of Triangle Fraternity in completing their education.
Eligibility: Applicants must be active members of the Triangle Fraternity, enrolled in a course of study leading to a degree. Applicants must have at least a 3.0 GPA, have completed at least two full academic years of school and be undergraduates in the year following their application. Selection is based on financial need, grades and participation in campus and Triangle activities.
Target applicant:
    College students
    Adult students
Minimum GPA: 3.0
Amount: $2,500.
Number of awards: 1.
Deadline: February 15.
How to apply: Applications are available online.

(2113) · National Beta Club Scholarship

National Beta Club
151 Beta Club Way
Spartanburg, SC 29306-3012
Phone: 800-845-8281
Fax: 864-542-9300
Email: jburnett@betaclub.org
Website: http://www.betaclub.org
Purpose: To award outstanding Beta Club members.
Eligibility: Applicants must be active National Beta Club members who are registered with the national headquarters by June 3 of the application year, high school seniors and nominated by their chapters. Awards are based on factors including academic excellence, leadership, character and school and community service.
Target applicant:
    High school students
Minimum GPA: None.
Amount: $1,000-$15,000.
Number of awards: 210.
Deadline: December 10.
How to apply: Applications are available from your Beta Club sponsor.

(2114) · National Eagle Scout Scholarship

Boy Scouts of America, Eagle Scout Service
1325 West Walnut Hill Lane
P.O. Box 152079
Irving, TX 75015-2079
Phone: 972-580-2401
Fax: 972-580-2413
Website: http://www.learningforlife.org/exploring/
Purpose: To support Jewish Boy Scouts who have received their Eagle Scout award based on their commitment to scouting ideals and community and religious service.
Eligibility: Applicants must be seniors in high school and active members of the Boy Scouts or Varsity Scouts who have received the Eagle Scout award. In addition, applicants must be an active member of a synagogue or have received the Ner Tamid or Etz Chaim religious emblem.
Target applicant:
    High school students
Minimum GPA: None.
Amount: $500-$1,000.
Number of awards: Varies.
Scholarship may be renewable.
Deadline: February 28.
How to apply: Applications are available online.

(2115) · National Honor Society Scholarship

National Honor Society
c/o National Association of Secondary School Principals
1904 Association Drive
Reston, VA 20191
Phone: 703-860-0200
Fax: 703-476-5432
Email: nhs@nhs.us
Website: http://www.nhs.us
Purpose: To recognize NHS members.
Eligibility: Each high school chapter may nominate two senior members. Nominees must demonstrate character, scholarship, service and leadership.
Target applicant:
    High school students
Minimum GPA: None.
Amount: $1,000.
Number of awards: 200.
Deadline: January 21.
How to apply: Nomination forms are available from your local NHS chapter adviser.

(2116) · National Presbyterian College Scholarship

Presbyterian Church (USA)
100 Witherspoon Street
Louisville, KY 40202
Phone: 888-728-7228 x5776
Email: fcook@ctr.pcusa.org
Website: http://www.pcusa.org
Purpose: To recognize young students preparing to enter as full-time incoming freshmen in one of the participating colleges related to the Presbyterian Church.
Eligibility: Applicants must be members of the Presbyterian Church, U.S. citizens or permanent residents and high school seniors planning to attend a participating college related to PCUSA. Applicants must also demonstrate financial need and take the SAT or ACT exam no later than December 15 of their senior year in high school. Applicants must have recommendations from both their church pastors and high school guidance counselors.
Target applicant:
    High school students
Minimum GPA: 3.0
Amount: Varies.
Number of awards: Varies.
Scholarship may be renewable.
Deadline: January 31.
How to apply: Applications are available online.

(2117) · National Scholars and Awards Program

Girls Inc.
120 Wall Street
New York, NY 10005
Phone: 800-374-4475
Website: http://www.girlsinc.org
Purpose: To support young members of Girls Incorporated.
Eligibility: Applicants must be young women who are in their junior or senior year of high school and members of a Girls Incorporated affiliate.
Target applicant:
    High school students
Minimum GPA: None.
Amount: Varies.
Number of awards: Varies.
Deadline: Varies.
How to apply: Applications are available by written request.

(2118) · National Temperance Scholarship

United Methodist Higher Education Foundation
P.O. Box 340005
Nashville, TN 37203-0005
Phone: 615-340-7385
Fax: 615-340-7330
Email: umscholar@gbhem.org
Website: http://www.gbhem.org
Purpose: To provide financial assistance for Methodist students.
Eligibility: Applicants must have been members of the United Methodist Church for at least one year and be enrolled or plan to enroll in a United Methodist-affiliated institution of higher learning. They must have a GPA of 3.0 or higher and be U.S. citizens or permanent residents.
Target applicant:
    High school students
    College students
    Adult students
Minimum GPA: 3.0
Amount: Varies.
Number of awards: Varies.
Deadline: May 15.
How to apply: Applications are available online.

(2119) · NIADA Scholarship

National Independent Automobile Dealers Association
2521 Brown Boulevard
Arlington, TX 76006-5203
Phone: 817-640-3838
Fax: 817-649-5866
Email: rachel@niada.com
Website: http://www.niada.com

Purpose: To support high school seniors with academic achievement and ties to NIADA members.

Eligibility: Applicants must be the son, daughter or grandchild of a NIADA member, have an excellent high school academic record and have high SAT or ACT scores. Applications, transcripts, test scores and a maximum of five recommendation letters are required.

Target applicant:
    High school students

Minimum GPA: None.

Amount: $2,500.

Number of awards: 4.

Deadline: January 31.

How to apply: Applications are available online and should be submitted to the state association.

(2120) · NPC Foundation Regional Scholarships

National Panhellenic Conference
8777 Purdue Road
Suite 117
Indianapolis, IN 46268
Phone: 317-872-3185
Fax: 317-872-3192
Email: npccentral@npcwomen.org
Website: http://www.npcwomen.org/foundation/scholarships.aspx

Purpose: To provide financial assistance to NPC members.

Eligibility: Requirements vary by region. Some regions require applicants to have graduated from certain high schools while others require attendance at specific colleges or residence in certain counties.

Target applicant:
    High school students
    College students
    Adult students

Minimum GPA: None.

Amount: Varies.

Number of awards: Varies.

Deadline: Varies.

How to apply: Applications are available online.

(2121) · Oliver and Esther R. Howard Scholarship

Fleet Reserve Association
FRA Scholarship Administrator
125 N. West Street
Alexandria, VA 22314
Phone: 800-372-1924
Website: http://www.fra.org

Purpose: To provide financial aid to the dependent children of FRA members or LA FRA members.

Eligibility: Applicants must be the dependent children of members of either the Fleet Reserve Association or the Ladies' Auxiliary of the Fleet Reserve Association who are in good standing. This scholarship is alternated between male and female recipients each year (males - odd years) (females - even years). Recipients must be high school seniors or college undergraduates pursuing undergraduate degrees and are selected on the basis of academic record, financial need, leadership skills and character.

Target applicant:
    High school students
    College students
    Adult students

Minimum GPA: None.

Amount: Varies.

Number of awards: Varies.

Deadline: April 15.

How to apply: Applications are available online.

(2122) · Opportunity Scholarships for Lutheran Laywomen

Women of the Evangelical Lutheran Church in America
8765 W. Higgins Road
Chicago, IL 60631
Phone: 800-638-3522 x2730
Fax: 773-380-2419
Email: women.elca@elca.org
Website: http://www.womenoftheelca.org

Purpose: To assist Lutheran women in studying for careers other than ordained ministry.

Eligibility: Applicants must be U.S. citizens, members of the Evangelical Lutheran Church and at least 21 years of age. They must also have had an interruption in education of two years or more since graduating from high school.

Target applicant:
    College students
    Graduate school students
    Adult students

Minimum GPA: None.

Amount: Varies.

Number of awards: Varies.

Deadline: February 15.

How to apply: Applications are available online.

(2123) · Outstanding Scouts Awards

Veterans of Foreign Wars
406 W. 34th Street
Kansas City, MO 64111
Phone: 816-756-3390
Fax: 816-968-1149
Email: info@vfw.org
Website: http://www.vfw.org

Purpose: To recognize outstanding Boy Scouts and support the common bonds between the Boy Scouts of America and the VFW: belief in God, respect for others, honesty and patriotism.

Eligibility: Applicants must be nominated as the top Scout by a VFW organization.

Target applicant:
    Junior high students or younger
    High school students

Minimum GPA: None.

Amount: $1,000-$5,000.

Number of awards: 3.

Deadline: March 1.

How to apply: Applications are available online.

(2124) · Owens-Bell Award

National Association of Blacks in Criminal Justice
North Carolina Central University
P.O. Box 19788
Durham, NC 27707
Phone: 919-683-1801
Fax: 919-683-1903
Email: office@nabcj.org
Website: http://www.nabcj.org

Purpose: To award an individual NABCJ member for outstanding chapter development and leadership.
Eligibility: Applicants must be nominated by a member of NABCJ.
Target applicant:
   College students
   Adult students
Minimum GPA: None.
Amount: Varies.
Number of awards: 1.
Deadline: May 1.
How to apply: Nomination applications are available online.

(2125) · Phi Kappa Phi Fellowship

Honor Society of Phi Kappa Phi
P.O. Box 16000
Louisiana State University
Baton Rouge, LA 70893
Phone: 800-804-9880
Fax: 225-388-4900
Email: awards@phikappaphi.org
Website: http://www.phikappaphi.org
Purpose: To provide fellowships for Phi Kappa Phi members entering their first year of graduate or professional studies.
Eligibility: Applicants may enter any professional or graduate field and must not have completed one full term of graduate study. Selection is based on academic achievement, service, leadership, letters of recommendation, personal statement and career goals.
Target applicant:
   College students
   Graduate school students
   Adult students
Minimum GPA: None.
Amount: $5,000.
Number of awards: 60.
Deadline: February 1.
How to apply: Applications are available online.

(2126) · Phyllis J. Jones Memorial Scholarships for Head Start Graduates

National Head Start Association
1651 Prince Street
Alexandria, VA 22314
Phone: 703-739-0875 x7507
Fax: 703-739-0878
Email: chutchinson@nhsa.org
Website: http://www.nhsa.org/program/program_scholarship.htm
Purpose: To honor the memory of Phyllis J. Jones, former NHSA president.
Eligibility: Applicants must be Head Start graduates of an NHSA program or individual members of NHSA. They must prove acceptance or enrollment at a college or university. Three letters of reference are required.
Target applicant:
   High school students
   College students
   Adult students
Minimum GPA: None.
Amount: $1,500.
Number of awards: Varies.
Deadline: December 28.
How to apply: Applications are available online.

(2127) · Power Systems Professional Scholarship

National Strength and Conditioning Association (NSCA) Foundation
1885 Bob Johnson Drive
Colorado Springs, CO 80906
Phone: 800-815-6826
Fax: 719-632-6367
Email: nsca@nsca-lift.org
Website: http://www.nsca-lift.org
Purpose: To support students interested in becoming strength and conditioning coaches.
Eligibility: Applicants must be undergraduate or graduate students and be working under a coach in the school's athletic department. Applicants must be members of the National Strength and Conditioning Association for one year prior to applying for a scholarship. Applications must include a resume, transcript, personal essay and letter from the head strength coach. The application must also be submitted by the head strength coach.
Target applicant:
   College students
   Adult students
Minimum GPA: None.
Amount: $1,000.
Number of awards: 1.
Deadline: March 15.
How to apply: Applications are available online.

(2128) · Priscilla R. Morton Scholarship

United Methodist Higher Education Foundation
P.O. Box 340005
Nashville, TN 37203-0005
Phone: 615-340-7385
Fax: 615-340-7330
Email: umscholar@gbhem.org
Website: http://www.gbhem.org
Purpose: To help students who are members of the United Methodist Church.
Eligibility: Applicants must be active, full members of the United Methodist Church for at least a year before applying and enrolled or planning to enroll in an accredited institution working towards a degree full-time. The scholarship may be used for undergraduate, graduate or professional study. Applicants should provide application forms, transcripts, references, membership proof and essays. A minimum 3.5 GPA and financial need are required. Preference is given to students who enroll at a United Methodist-related college, university, seminary or theological school.
Target applicant:
   High school students
   College students
   Graduate school students
   Adult students
Minimum GPA: 3.5
Amount: $1,000.
Number of awards: 35.
Deadline: May 15.
How to apply: Applications are available online.

(2129) · Professional and Technical Engineers, International Federation Scholarship

International Federation of Professional and Technical Engineers
8630 Fenton Street
Suite 400

Silver Spring, MD 20910
Phone: 301-565-9016
Fax: 301-565-0018
Email: gjunemann@ifpte.org
Website: http://www.ifpte.org
Purpose: To offer scholarships to the children and grandchildren of IFPTE members.
Eligibility: Applicants must be high school seniors who are the children or grandchildren of IFPTE members.
Target applicant:
    High school students
Minimum GPA: None.
Amount: $1,500.
Number of awards: 3.
Deadline: March 15.
How to apply: Applications are available online.

(2130) · Pryor Fellowships

Alpha Chi
Harding University Box 12249
915 E. Market Avenue
Searcy, AR 72149-2249
Phone: 800-477-4225
Fax: 501-279-4589
Email: dorgan@harding.edu
Website: http://www.harding.edu/alphachi/scholarships.htm
Purpose: To assist alumni and graduate Alpha Chi members who are seeking doctoral, master's or first professional degrees.
Eligibility: Applicants must be Alpha Chi members who are enrolled full-time in a doctoral, terminal master's or first professional degree program.
Target applicant:
    Graduate school students
    Adult students
Minimum GPA: None.
Amount: $3,000-$5,000.
Number of awards: 2.
Deadline: February 1.
How to apply: Applications are available online.

(2131) · Racial/Ethnic History Research Grant

General Commission on Archives and History, The United Methodist Church
P.O. Box 127
36 Madison Avenue
Madison, NJ 07940
Phone: 973-408-3189
Fax: 973-408-3909
Email: research@gcah.org
Website: http://www.gcah.org
Purpose: To promote excellence in research and writing in the history of Asians, Blacks, Hispanics and Native Americans in The United Methodist Church.
Eligibility: Applicants must submit an application in English which includes biographical information, a detailed description of the project, the expected date of completion, a budget and letters of recommendation.
Target applicant:
    Junior high students or younger
    High school students

College students
Graduate school students
Adult students
Minimum GPA: None.
Amount: $750-$1,500.
Number of awards: 1-2.
Deadline: December 31.
How to apply: Submit materials to the General Secretary at the address listed.

(2132) · Rev. Dr. Karen Layman Gift of Hope 21st Century Scholars Program

United Methodist Church
Office of Loans and Scholarships
P.O. BOX 340007
Nashville, TN 37203-0007
Phone: 615-340-7344
Fax: 615-340-7367
Email: umscholar@gbhem.org
Website: http://www.gbhem.org
Purpose: To support students who have demonstrated leadership within the United Methodist Church.
Eligibility: Applicants must have been members of the United Methodist Church for at least three years. They must be full-time undergraduates with at least a 3.0 GPA.
Target applicant:
    High school students
    College students
    Adult students
Minimum GPA: 3.0
Amount: $1,000.
Number of awards: Varies.
Deadline: May 1.
How to apply: Applications are available online.

(2133) · Richard F. Walsh, Alfred W. DiTolla, Harold P. Spivak Foundation Award

International Alliance of Theatrical Stage Employees, Artists and Allied Crafts of the U.S.
1430 Broadway
20th Floor
New York, NY 10018
Website: http://www.iatse-intl.org
Purpose: To provide scholarships for the children of IATSE members.
Eligibility: Applicants must be the sons or daughters of IATSE members in good standing, be high school seniors and apply for admission to an accredited college or university full-time leading towards a bachelor's degree.
Target applicant:
    High school students
Minimum GPA: None.
Amount: $1,750.
Number of awards: 2.
Scholarship may be renewable.
Deadline: December 31.
How to apply: Applications are available by written request (through an online form).

(2134) · Robert G. Porter Scholars Program for Members

American Federation of Teachers
555 New Jersey Avenue NW
Washington, DC 20001
Phone: 202-879-4400
Website: http://www.aft.org
Purpose: To provide grants to AFT members.
Eligibility: Applicants must be AFT members who have been in good standing for at least one year and intend to pursue courses in their field of work. Applicants must submit an essay on a labor-related topic.
Target applicant:
    Graduate school students
    Adult students
Minimum GPA: None.
Amount: $1,000.
Number of awards: 10.
Deadline: March 31.
How to apply: Applications are available by written request.

(2135) · Robert G. Porter Scholars Program for Members' Dependents

American Federation of Teachers
555 New Jersey Avenue NW
Washington, DC 20001
Phone: 202-879-4400
Website: http://www.aft.org
Purpose: To provide scholarships to AFT members' dependents.
Eligibility: Applicants must be graduating high school seniors. The award is merit-based and will consider academics, community service and performance on the required labor-related essay. Applicants' parents or guardians must be AFT members for at least one year.
Target applicant:
    High school students
Minimum GPA: None.
Amount: $8,000.
Number of awards: 4.
Scholarship may be renewable.
Deadline: March 31.
How to apply: Applications are available by written request.

(2136) · Ronald Reagan Leadership Award

Tau Kappa Epsilon Educational Foundation
8645 Founders Road
Indianapolis, IN 46268
Phone: 317-872-6533
Fax: 317-875-8353
Email: tef@tke.org
Website: http://www.tkefoundation.org
Purpose: To honor Ronald Reagan's dedication and loyalty as a Tau Kappa Epsilon member.
Eligibility: Applicants must be initiated Tau Kappa Epsilon members in good standing and full-time students. Applicants must also have a GPA of at least 3.0 and demonstrate leadership in their chapter, campus and community. A statement describing how they have benefited from TKE membership is required.
Target applicant:
    College students
    Adult students

Minimum GPA: 3.0.
Amount: $2,000.
Number of awards: 1.
Deadline: March 16.
How to apply: Applications are available online.

(2137) · Rosalie Bentzinger Scholarship

United Methodist Church
Office of Loans and Scholarships
P.O. BOX 340007
Nashville, TN 37203-0007
Phone: 615-340-7344
Fax: 615-340-7367
Email: umscholar@gbhem.org
Website: http://www.gbhem.org
Purpose: To support United Methodist students who are pursuing doctoral degrees in Christian education.
Eligibility: Applicants must be attending a graduate school of theology which is approved by the University Senate. They must be full-time students with at least a B+ grade average. Students must have been members of the United Methodist Church for at least three years, and they must have attained one of the following positions: deacon in full connection, diaconal minister or deaconess.
Target applicant:
    Graduate school students
    Adult students
Minimum GPA: 3.3.
Amount: $5,000.
Number of awards: 1.
Deadline: February 1.
How to apply: Applications are available online.

(2138) · Rust Scholarship

Triangle Education Foundation
Chairman, Scholarship and Loan Committee
120 S. Center Street
Plainfield, IN 46168-1214
Phone: 317-837-9640
Fax: 317-837-9642
Email: scholarships@triangle.org
Website: http://www.triangle.org
Purpose: To help deserving active members of Triangle Fraternity in completing their education.
Eligibility: Applicants must be active members of the Triangle Fraternity who have completed at least two full academic years of school and will be undergraduates in the school year following their application. Selection is based on financial need, grades and participation in campus and Triangle activities. Preference is given to applicants in engineering and the hard sciences. Applicants must have at least a 3.0 GPA.
Target applicant:
    College students
    Adult students
Minimum GPA: 3.0.
Amount: $5,500.
Number of awards: 1.
Deadline: February 15.
How to apply: Applications are available online.

(2139) · S. Frank Bud Raftery Scholarship

International Union of Painters and Allied Trades of the United States and Canada
1750 New York Avenue NW
Washington, DC 20006
Website: http://www.iupat.org
Purpose: To provide scholarships for the children of IUPAT members.
Eligibility: Applicants must be the children or legally-adopted dependents of an IUPAT member in good standing. Selection is based on a 1,000- to 2,000-word essay on a subject chosen by the IUPAT.
Target applicant:
High school students
College students
Graduate school students
Adult students
Minimum GPA: None.
Amount: $2,000.
Number of awards: 10.
Deadline: Varies.
How to apply: Applications are available by written request.

(2140) · Sam Rose Memorial Scholarship

Ladies Auxiliary of the Fleet Reserve Association
125 N. West Street
Alexandria, VA 22314
Phone: 800-372-1924 x123
Email: mserfra@fra.org
Website: http://www.la-fra.org
Purpose: To support the descendants of Fleet Reserve Association members.
Eligibility: Applicants must have a deceased father or grandfather who was a member of the Fleet Reserve Association or was eligible for membership at the time of death.
Target applicant:
High school students
College students
Adult students
Minimum GPA: None.
Amount: Varies.
Number of awards: Varies.
Deadline: April 15.
How to apply: Applications are available online.

(2141) · Schuyler S. Pyle Award

Fleet Reserve Association
FRA Scholarship Administrator
125 N. West Street
Alexandria, VA 22314
Phone: 800-372-1924
Website: http://www.fra.org
Purpose: To support members of the FRA, their spouses and their dependent children or grandchildren.
Eligibility: Applicants must be members of the FRA in good standing or the spouse or dependent children/grandchildren of a member who is in good standing or was in good standing at time of death. Recipients are determined on the basis of academic record, leadership skills, character and financial need.
Target applicant:
High school students
College students

Graduate school students
Adult students
Minimum GPA: None.
Amount: Varies.
Number of awards: Varies.
Deadline: April 15.
How to apply: Applications are available online.

(2142) · SEIU-Jesse Jackson Scholarship Program

Service Employees International Union
c/o Scholarship Program Administrators Inc.
P.O. Box 23737
Nashville, TN 37202-3737
Phone: 800-424-8592
Website: http://www.seiu.org
Purpose: To honor the Rev. Jesse Jackson by giving a scholarship to those SEIU members and their children who exemplify his values in the pursuit of social justice.
Eligibility: Applicants must be members or the children of members of the SEIU and must be enrolled in an accredited two- or four-year college or university. The scholarship is for undergraduate work only.
Target applicant:
High school students
College students
Adult students
Minimum GPA: None.
Amount: $5,000.
Number of awards: 1.
Scholarship may be renewable.
Deadline: March 1.
How to apply: Applications are available online.

(2143) · Service Employees International Union Scholarships

Service Employees International Union
c/o Scholarship Program Administrators Inc.
P.O. Box 23737
Nashville, TN 37202-3737
Phone: 800-424-8592
Website: http://www.seiu.org
Purpose: To give financial assistance to members of the SEIU and their children.
Eligibility: For the $1,000 scholarship, applicants must be members or the children of members of SEIU who have been in good standing for at least three years. Applicants must also be enrolled in an accredited college or university and should not have completed more than one year of college. For the $1,500 scholarship, applicants must be members or the children of members of SEIU returning full time to an accredited college or university as a sophomore, junior or senior or attending an accredited community college, trade or technical school. This scholarship is not renewable. All applicants must read a report online and answer questions.
Target applicant:
High school students
College students
Adult students
Minimum GPA: None.
Amount: $1,000-$1,500.
Number of awards: 48.
Deadline: March 1.
How to apply: Applications are available online.

(2144) · Sheet Metal Workers' International Scholarship Fund

Sheet Metal Workers' International Association
1750 New York Avenue NW
6th Floor
Washington , DC 20006-5389
Phone: 202-783-5880
Email: scholarship@smwia.org
Website: http://www.smwia.org
Purpose: To provide scholarships for members of the SMWIA and their families.
Eligibility: Applicants must be SMWIA members, covered employees, or dependent spouses or children under the age of 25 of SMWIA members or covered employees. Applicants must also be full-time students or accepted to be full-time students at an accredited college or university. Only qualified applicants from local unions that participate in the one-cent check off are eligible for these four-year scholarships. Selection is based on information on SMWIA membership, including information on the local union's jurisdiction and family member's SMWIA membership, high school transcript, SAT/ACT scores or college transcript if already enrolled in college, an essay on the importance of SMWIA to the applicant's family and a letter of recommendation.
Target applicant:
  High school students
  College students
  Adult students
Minimum GPA: None.
Amount: $4,000.
Number of awards: 30.
Scholarship may be renewable.
Deadline: March 1.
How to apply: Applications are available by email and written request.

(2145) · Shopko Scholarships

ShopKo Stores, Inc.
Website: http://www.shopko.com
Purpose: To provide educational opportunities for Shopko employees and their families.
Eligibility: Applicants must be Shopko employees who have been with the company for at least one year or their dependents under the age of 24. Factors considered include academic record, leadership and community activities, honors, work experience and future goals.
Target applicant:
  High school students
  College students
  Adult students
Minimum GPA: None.
Amount: Up to $2,500.
Number of awards: Varies.
Deadline: March 1.
How to apply: Applications are available online or from Shopko stores.

(2146) · Shropshire Scholarship

Civitan
Civitan International Foundation
P.O. Box 130744
Birmingham, AL 35213-0744
Phone: 205-591-8910
Fax: 205-592-6307
Email: civitan@civitan.org
Website: http://www.civitan.org
Purpose: The Shropshire Scholarship assists deserving Civitan members who will pursue careers that further the ideals of Civitan International, such as working toward world peace and unity, fighting for justice and building better citizenship.
Eligibility: Applicants must be Civitans or a Civitan's immediate family member, have been Civitan or Junior Civitan members for at least two years, be enrolled in a college or university and pursue careers which help further the ideals of Civitan International.
Target applicant:
  College students
  Graduate school students
  Adult students
Minimum GPA: None.
Amount: Up to $1,000.
Number of awards: Varies.
Deadline: January 31.
How to apply: Applications are available online.

(2147) · Sledge/Benedict Fellowships

Alpha Chi
Harding University Box 12249
915 E. Market Avenue
Searcy, AR 72149-2249
Phone: 800-477-4225
Fax: 501-279-4589
Email: dorgan@harding.edu
Website: http://www.harding.edu/alphachi/scholarships.htm
Purpose: To assist Alpha Chi members who are entering their first year of graduate study.
Eligibility: Applicants must be Alpha Chi members in their final year of undergraduate study and must be enrolled full-time as a graduate student the following fall semester.
Target applicant:
  College students
  Adult students
Minimum GPA: None.
Amount: $2,500-$3,500.
Number of awards: 12.
Deadline: February 22.
How to apply: Application requirements are available online, and applicants must be nominated by the faculty advisor.

(2148) · Stanfield and D'Orlando Art Scholarship

Unitarian Universalist Association
25 Beacon Street
Boston, MA 02108
Phone: 617-742-2100
Email: info@uua.org
Website: http://www.uua.org
Purpose: To help graduate and undergraduate Unitarian Universalist artists.
Eligibility: Applicants must be preparing for a career in fine arts which includes painting, drawing, photography and sculpture. Applicants must submit applications, transcripts, recommendations, slide portfolios and a list of works.
Target applicant:
  College students
  Graduate school students
  Adult students

Minimum GPA: None.
Amount: Varies.
Number of awards: Varies.
Deadline: February 15.
How to apply: Applications are available online.

(2149) · Stanley A. Doran Memorial Scholarship

Fleet Reserve Association
FRA Scholarship Administrator
125 N. West Street
Alexandria, VA 22314
Phone: 800-372-1924
Website: http://www.fra.org
Purpose: To provide financial aid to the dependents of FRA members.
Eligibility: Applicants must be the dependent children of a member in good standing of the FRA or a member who was in good standing at time of death. Recipients are selected on the basis of academic achievement, leadership skills, financial need and character.
Target applicant:
    High school students
    College students
    Graduate school students
    Adult students
Minimum GPA: None.
Amount: Varies.
Number of awards: Varies.
Deadline: April 15.
How to apply: Applications are available online.

(2150) · Steven J. Muir Scholarship

Tau Kappa Epsilon Educational Foundation
8645 Founders Road
Indianapolis, IN 46268
Phone: 317-872-6533
Fax: 317-875-8353
Email: tef@tke.org
Website: http://www.tkefoundation.org
Purpose: To recognize a member of Tau Kappa Epsilon for academic achievement and outstanding leadership within the organization.
Eligibility: Applicants must be sophomores or above and have at least a 3.0 GPA. Members must be seeking an undergraduate degree in engineering or another of the pure sciences. Applicants must have served as a chapter officer or committee chair; preference will be given to a member of the Beta-Eta Chapter.
Target applicant:
    College students
    Adult students
Minimum GPA: 3.0
Amount: $1,000.
Number of awards: 1.
Deadline: March 16.
How to apply: Applications are available online.

(2151) · Student CEC Graduation Awards

Council for Exceptional Children
1110 North Glebe Road
Suite 300
Arlington, VA 22201
Phone: 888-232-7733
Fax: 703-264-9494
Email: mbrship@cec.sped.org
Website: http://www.cec.sped.org
Purpose: To provide financial aid to student members transitioning to professional membership status in the Council for Exceptional Children.
Eligibility: Applicants must be undergraduate or graduate students enrolled at an accredited college or university graduating in the academic year the award is given. Applicants must be members of the Student CEC with a minimum 3.0 GPA. Selection is based on an essay, GPA, letters of recommendation and extracurricular activities.
Target applicant:
    College students
    Graduate school students
    Adult students
Minimum GPA: 3.0
Amount: $350.
Number of awards: 2.
Deadline: November 1.
How to apply: Applications are available online.

(2152) · Student Leader Award

Golden Key National Honour Society
Scholarship Program Administrators
Golden Key Scholarships/Awards
P.O. Box 23737
Nashville, TN 37202-3737
Phone: 800-377-2401
Email: scholarships@goldenkey.org
Website: http://www.goldenkey.org
Purpose: To support student members who have demonstrated leadership.
Eligibility: Applicants must be currently or previously involved in Golden Key and be currently enrolled in an undergraduate or graduate program at an accredited college or university. There are awards for both U.S. and international students. U.S. applicants must submit an application form, personal statement, description of Golden Key involvement, list of activities, recommendation letter and transcript.
Target applicant:
    College students
    Graduate school students
    Adult students
Minimum GPA: None.
Amount: $500.
Number of awards: 10.
Deadline: June 1.
How to apply: Applications are available online.

(2153) · Study Abroad Scholarships

Golden Key National Honour Society
Scholarship Program Administrators
Golden Key Scholarships/Awards
P.O. Box 23737
Nashville, TN 37202-3737
Phone: 800-377-2401
Email: scholarships@goldenkey.org
Website: http://www.goldenkey.org
Purpose: To assist members who study abroad.
Eligibility: Applicants must be undergraduate members who plan to be or are currently enrolled in a study abroad program. Selection is based on academic achievement and relevance of the study abroad program to the applicant's major.

Target applicant:
   College students
   Adult students
Minimum GPA: None.
Amount: $1,000.
Number of awards: 10.
Deadline: April 15 and October 20.
How to apply: Applications are available online.

(2154) · Subway Scholarship Fund

Subway Restaurants
Susan Lee
Center for Scholarship Administration, Subway Scholarship Fund
P.O. Box 1465
Taylors, SC 29687-0031
Phone: 864-268-3363
Fax: 864-268-7160
Email: susanjlee@bellsouth.net
Website: http://www.subway.com
Purpose: To provide scholarships for Subway employees.
Eligibility: Applicants must be either high school seniors or full-time college students and must be Subway employees who work a minimum of 15 hours a week and have worked at least six months prior to December 31. Academic achievement, scholarship performance, scholastic aptitude, essays and letters of recommendation will be considered.
Target applicant:
   High school students
   College students
   Adult students
Minimum GPA: 2.75
Amount: $1,000.
Number of awards: Varies.
Deadline: November 30.
How to apply: Applications are available online.

(2155) · T.J. Schmitz Scholarship

Tau Kappa Epsilon Educational Foundation
8645 Founders Road
Indianapolis, IN 46268
Phone: 317-872-6533
Fax: 317-875-8353
Email: tef@tke.org
Website: http://www.tkefoundation.org
Purpose: To award a member of Tau Kappa Epsilon for oustanding academic achievement and leadership within the organization, campus and community.
Eligibility: Applicants must have a GPA of at least 3.0.
Target applicant:
   College students
   Adult students
Minimum GPA: 3.0
Amount: $800.
Number of awards: 1.
Deadline: March 16.
How to apply: Applications are available online.

(2156) · Tall Club International Kae Sumner Einfeldt Scholarship

Tall Clubs International
6770 River Terrace Drive
Franklin, WI 53132
Phone: 888-468-2552
Email: info@tcifoundation.org
Website: http://www.tall.org
Purpose: To support students of tall stature.
Eligibility: Applicants must be high school seniors or college students under the age of 21 attending or planning to attend a two- or four-year institution of higher learning. Female applicants must meet the height requirement of 5'10" and male applicants must meet the requirement of 6'2". Applicants must live within the geographic area of a participating club.
Target applicant:
   High school students
   College students
Minimum GPA: None.
Amount: Varies.
Number of awards: Varies.
Deadline: Varies.
How to apply: Applications are available online.

(2157) · Tau Beta Pi Scholarships

Tau Beta Pi Association
Attn.: D. Stephen Pierre Jr., P.E.
Alabama Power Company
150 Joseph Street, P.O. Box 2247
Mobile, AL 36652-2247
Phone: 865-546-4578
Fax: 865-546-4579
Email: fellowships@tbp.org
Website: http://www.tbp.org
Purpose: To assist members who are studying engineering.
Eligibility: Applicants must be undergraduate members of Tau Beta Pi and be juniors at the time of application who are planning to remain in or return to school for a senior year of full-time study in engineering.
Target applicant:
   College students
   Adult students
Minimum GPA: None.
Amount: $2,000.
Number of awards: 135.
Deadline: March 1.
How to apply: Applications are available online.

(2158) · Terrill Graduate Fellowship

Phi Sigma Kappa International Headquarters
2925 E. 96th Street
Indianapolis, IN 46240
Phone: 317-573-5420
Fax: 317-573-5430
Email: vershun@phisigmakappa.org
Website: http://www.phisigmakappa.org
Purpose: To award money to graduating senior and alumni members entering graduate school or members already enrolled in graduate school.
Eligibility: Applicants must graduate from college by August of the year during which they apply, plan to begin graduate or professional

study during the next academic year or already be in graduate school and have a minimum B GPA for all undergraduate work. Scholarships are awarded based on scholastic performance.

Target applicant:
    College students
    Graduate school students
    Adult students
Minimum GPA: 3.0
Amount: $3,000.
Number of awards: 1.
Deadline: January 31.
How to apply: Applications are available online.

(2159) · Thomas H. Dunning, Sr., Memorial Scholarship

Tau Kappa Epsilon Educational Foundation
8645 Founders Road
Indianapolis, IN 46268
Phone: 317-872-6533
Fax: 317-875-8353
Email: tef@tke.org
Website: http://www.tkefoundation.org
Purpose: To award a member of Tau Kappa Epsilon for academic achievement and service within the chapter as an officer or committee chair.
Eligibility: Applicants must have a GPA of at least 2.75 and be at least sophomores. Applicants must also be undergraduates seeking a degree in engineering, computer science or any of the pure sciences. Preference is first given to members of the Beta-Eta Chapter and then to other Tekes at colleges/universities in Indiana or Missouri.
Target applicant:
    College students
    Adult students
Minimum GPA: 2.75
Amount: $600.
Number of awards: 1.
Deadline: March 16.
How to apply: Applications are available online.

(2160) · Timothy L. Taschwer Scholarship

Tau Kappa Epsilon Educational Foundation
8645 Founders Road
Indianapolis, IN 46268
Phone: 317-872-6533
Fax: 317-875-8353
Email: tef@tke.org
Website: http://www.tkefoundation.org
Purpose: To award a member of Tau Kappa Epsilon for academic achievement and outstanding leadership within the organization as a chapter officer.
Eligibility: Applicants must have a GPA of at least 2.75 and be seeking an undergraduate degree in natural resources, earth sciences or similar fields. Preference is first given to graduates of the TKE Leadership Academy.
Target applicant:
    College students
    Adult students
Minimum GPA: 2.75
Amount: $500.
Number of awards: 1.
Deadline: March 16.
How to apply: Applications are available online.

(2161) · Tri Delta Graduate Scholarship

Tri Delta
Delta Delta Delta Foundation
P.O. Box 5987
Arlington, TX 76005
Phone: 817-633-8001
Fax: 817-652-0212
Email: info@trideltaeo.org
Website: http://www.tridelta.org
Purpose: To offer scholarships to graduate student members.
Eligibility: The Mary Margaret Hafter Fellowship, Luella Akins Key Scholarship, Second Century Graduate Scholarship, Margaret Stafford Memorial Scholarship and Sarah Shinn Marshall Scholarship may be awarded to Tri Delta members who are admitted or current graduate students. Applicants to the Durning Sisters Scholarship must be unmarried Tri Delta members who have completed at least 12 graduate credits and who will be continuing graduate study during the year in which the award is given. There is usually one winner for each award.
Target applicant:
    College students
    Graduate school students
    Adult students
Minimum GPA: None.
Amount: $3,000.
Number of awards: 8.
Deadline: March 15.
How to apply: Applications are available online.

(2162) · Tri Delta Undergraduate Scholarship

Tri Delta
Delta Delta Delta Foundation
P.O. Box 5987
Arlington, TX 76005
Phone: 817-633-8001
Fax: 817-652-0212
Email: info@trideltaeo.org
Website: http://www.tridelta.org
Purpose: To offer scholarships to undergraduate members.
Eligibility: Applicants must be sophomores or juniors in good standing with the organization.
Target applicant:
    College students
    Adult students
Minimum GPA: None.
Amount: $500-$1,500.
Number of awards: 50.
Deadline: March 15.
How to apply: Applications are available online.

(2163) · Tuition Exchange Scholarships

Tuition Exchange
1743 Connecticut Avenue NW
Washington, DC 20009
Phone: 202-518-0135
Email: info@tuitionexchange.org
Website: http://www.tuitionexchange.org
Purpose: To assist the children or other family members of the faculty and staff at participating colleges and universities to encourage employment of parents and guardians in higher education.

Eligibility: Eligibility varies by institution. Applicants must be family members of the home institution where they are applying. However specific details about employment status, years of service or other requirements are determined solely by the home institution.

Target applicant:
High school students
College students
Adult students

Minimum GPA: None.

Amount: Varies.

Number of awards: Varies.

Scholarship may be renewable.

Deadline: Varies.

How to apply: Applications are available from the liaison officer at the home institution.

(2164) · UCC Seminarian Scholarship

United Church of Christ
700 Prospect Avenue
Cleveland, OH 44115
Phone: 216-736-3839
Email: jeffersv@ucc.org
Website: http://www.ucc.org
Purpose: To support members of the United Church of Christ who are preparing for ministry.
Eligibility: Applicants must be members of a United Church of Christ congregation for at least one year prior to receipt of the scholarship. They must be currently enrolled in an ATS accredited seminary in a course of study to become an ordained minister, and they must maintain at least a B average to receive and keep the scholarship. Applicants should be able to show that they have demonstrated leadership abilities in a church or academic environment. Students must also agree to serve the United Church of Christ or one of its partners after the completion of their studies.

Target applicant:
High school students
College students
Graduate school students
Adult students

Minimum GPA: 3.0

Amount: Varies.

Number of awards: Varies.

Scholarship may be renewable.

Deadline: Varies.

How to apply: Applications are available by mail.

(2165) · UFCW Suffridge Scholarship

United Food and Commercial Workers Union
Scholarship Program - Education Office
1775 K Street NW
Washington, DC 20006
Email: scholarship@ufcw.org
Website: http://www.ufcw.org/scholarship
Purpose: To provide financial assistance for members of the UFCW and their children.
Eligibility: Applicants must be members of good standing of the UFCW with a membership of one continuous year or more or the unmarried children of a member. Applicants must also be graduating high school in the year of the competition and be less than 20 years old. Academic achievement, community involvement and essays are part of the selection process.

Target applicant:
High school students

Minimum GPA: None.

Amount: $2,000.

Number of awards: 14.

Scholarship may be renewable.

Deadline: March 15.

How to apply: Applications are available online.

(2166) · UMWA/BCOA Training and Education Fund

United Mine Workers of America/BCOA T.E.F.
8315 Lee Highway
Fairfax, VA 22031-2215
Phone: 703-208-7200
Website: http://www.umwa.org
Purpose: To offer scholarships to UMWA members and their families.
Eligibility: Applicants must be miners unemployed from the coal industry with at least five years in classified employment. The spouses or children (below age 25) of eligible unemployed or working miners are also eligible for benefits. Grants are awarded based on the recommendation of one or more panels chosen by UMWA and the Bituminous Coal Association.

Target applicant:
High school students
College students
Graduate school students
Adult students

Minimum GPA: None.

Amount: Varies.

Number of awards: Varies.

Deadline: Varies.

How to apply: Applications are available by phone or written request.

(2167) · Undergraduate Fellows Program

Fund for Theological Education Inc.
825 Houston Mill Road, Suite 250
Atlanta, GA 30329
Phone: 404-727-1450
Fax: 404-727-1490
Email: fte@thefund.org
Website: http://www.thefund.org
Purpose: To support students who are considering ministry as a possible career.
Eligibility: Applicants must be juniors or seniors in an accredited undergraduate program at a North American college or university who are considering ministry as a career, have a minimum 3.0 GPA and be citizens of the U.S. or Canada. Applicants are evaluated on the basis of ability and character.

Target applicant:
College students
Adult students

Minimum GPA: 3.0

Amount: $2,000.

Number of awards: Up to 70.

Deadline: March 1.

How to apply: Applicants must be nominated by a college faculty member, administrator, campus minister or chaplain or current pastor. Nomination forms and application forms are available online.

(2168) · Undergraduate Research Grants

Golden Key National Honour Society
Scholarship Program Administrators
Golden Key Scholarships/Awards
P.O. Box 23737
Nashville, TN 37202-3737
Phone: 800-377-2401
Email: scholarships@goldenkey.org
Website: http://www.goldenkey.org
Purpose: To assist members in their thesis research or in presenting their research at a professional conference.
Eligibility: Applicants must be undergraduate student members. Selection is based on academic achievement and the quality of the research.
Target applicant:
    College students
    Adult students
Minimum GPA: None.
Amount: $500.
Number of awards: 10.
Deadline: April 15 and October 20.
How to apply: Applications are available online.

(2169) · Undergraduate Scholarship

Delta Sigma Pi
330 S. Campus Avenue
Oxford, OH 45056
Phone: 513-523-1907
Fax: 513-523-7292
Email: centraloffice@dspnet.org
Website: http://www.dspnet.org
Purpose: To assist student members.
Eligibility: Applicants must be members in good standing of Delta Sigma Pi with at least one semester or quarter of undergraduate studies remaining. Applicants are judged on scholastic achievement, financial need, fraternal service, service activities, letters of recommendation and overall presentation of required materials.
Target applicant:
    College students
    Adult students
Minimum GPA: None.
Amount: $500-$1,250.
Number of awards: 10.
Deadline: June 30.
How to apply: Applications are available online.

(2170) · Undergraduate Scholarships

American Baptist Churches USA
P.O. Box 851
Valley Forge, PA 19482
Phone: 800-222-3872
Fax: 610-768-2453
Email: karen.drummond@abc-usa.org
Website: http://www.nationalministries.org
Purpose: To support American Baptist students pursuing educational opportunities.
Eligibility: Applicants must be members of an American Baptist church for at least one year before applying for aid, be enrolled at an accredited educational institution in the U.S. or Puerto Rico, be U.S. citizens and retain a 2.75 GPA to remain eligible for the scholarships.

Target applicant:
    High school students
    College students
    Adult students
Minimum GPA: 2.75
Amount: $1,000-$2,000.
Number of awards: Varies.
Scholarship may be renewable.
Deadline: May 31.
How to apply: Applications are available by request.

(2171) · Union Women Summer School Scholarships

Service Employees International Union
c/o Scholarship Program Administrators Inc.
P.O. Box 23737
Nashville, TN 37202-3737
Phone: 800-424-8592
Website: http://www.seiu.org
Purpose: To award scholarships to the female members of the SEIU.
Eligibility: Applicants must be female members of SEIU local unions, have demonstrated a committed level of activity in the local union and have the support of the local union president.
Target applicant:
    College students
    Adult students
Minimum GPA: None.
Amount: Full tuition plus room and board.
Number of awards: Varies.
Deadline: Varies.
How to apply: Applications are available by written request.

(2172) · United Methodist General Scholarship

United Methodist Church
Office of Loans and Scholarships
P.O. BOX 340007
Nashville, TN 37203-0007
Phone: 615-340-7344
Fax: 615-340-7367
Email: umscholar@gbhem.org
Website: http://www.gbhem.org
Purpose: To support students who are members of a United Methodist Church.
Eligibility: Applicants must be active, full members of a United Methodist Church for at least one year prior to applying, be admitted to a full-time degree program in an accredited college or university and have a minimum 2.5 GPA. Students must also be U.S. citizens or permanent residents and be undergraduate, graduate or doctoral students.
Target applicant:
    College students
    Graduate school students
    Adult students
Minimum GPA: 2.5
Amount: Varies.
Number of awards: Varies.
Deadline: May 15.
How to apply: Applications are available online.

(2173) · United Transportation Union Scholarships

United Transportation Union Insurance Association
UTUIA Scholarship Program
14600 Detroit Avenue
Cleveland, OH 44107-4250
Website: http://www.utuia.org
Purpose: To provide financial aid to the children and grandchildren of UTU/UTUIA members.
Eligibility: Applicants must be at least high school seniors or the equivalent and be age 25 or less. Applicants must also be UTU or UTUIA-insured members, the children or grandchildren of a UTU or UTUIA-insured member or the children of a deceased UTU or UTUIA-insured member. UTU or UTUIA-insured members must be U.S. residents. Applicants must be accepted for admittance or already enrolled for at least 12 credit hours per quarter or semester at a recognized institution of higher learning (university, college or junior college, nursing or technical school offering college credit). Scholarships are awarded on the basis of chance, not grades. A UTUIA scholar, however, is expected to maintain a satisfactory academic record to keep the scholarship for the full four years.
Target applicant:
    High school students
    College students
Minimum GPA: None.
Amount: $500.
Number of awards: 50.
Scholarship may be renewable.
Deadline: Last workday in March.
How to apply: Applications are available from the UTU news or by written request.

(2174) · Utility Workers Union of America Scholarships

Utility Workers Union of America
815 16th Street NW
Washington, DC 20006
Phone: 202-974-8200
Fax: 202-974-8201
Email: webmaster@uwua.net
Website: http://www.uwua.net
Purpose: To offer scholarships to the children of UWUA members.
Eligibility: Applicants must be the sons or daughters of active Utility Workers Union members. Recipients are selected from those who participate in the National Merit Scholarship Competition by taking the PSAT/NMSQT as high school juniors, complete high school and are enrolled in a regionally accredited college in the United States.
Target applicant:
    High school students
Minimum GPA: None.
Amount: $500-$2,000.
Number of awards: Varies.
Scholarship may be renewable.
Deadline: December 31.
How to apply: Applications are available online.

(2175) · VFW Scout of the Year Scholarship

Veterans of Foreign Wars
406 W. 34th Street
Kansas City, MO 64111
Phone: 816-756-3390
Fax: 816-968-1149
Email: info@vfw.org
Website: http://www.vfw.org
Purpose: To reward an outstanding Boy Scout, Venture Scout or Sea Scout.
Eligibility: Applicants must have received the Eagle Scout Award, the Venture Silver Award or the Sea Scout Quartermaster Award and demonstrated practical citizenship. Applicants must also have reached their 15th birthday and be enrolled in high school.
Target applicant:
    High school students
Minimum GPA: None.
Amount: $5,000.
Number of awards: 1.
Deadline: March 1.
How to apply: Applications are available online.

(2176) · Visual and Performing Arts Achievement Awards

Golden Key National Honour Society
Scholarship Program Administrators
Golden Key Scholarships/Awards
P.O. Box 23737
Nashville, TN 37202-3737
Phone: 800-377-2401
Email: scholarships@goldenkey.org
Website: http://www.goldenkey.org
Purpose: To assist members who are talented in the visual and performing arts.
Eligibility: Applicants must be undergraduate, graduate or post-graduate members who are currently taking classes at a degree-granting program. Selection is based on the work submitted. For the visual arts, students must submit a slide or slides of their artwork. For the performing arts, students must submit a videotape or DVD of a performance up to 10 minutes. The competition categories are: painting, drawing, photography, sculpture, computer-generated art/graphic design/illustration, mixed media, instrumental performance, vocal performance and dance.
Target applicant:
    College students
    Graduate school students
    Adult students
Minimum GPA: None.
Amount: $500.
Number of awards: 9.
Deadline: April 1.
How to apply: Applications are available online.

(2177) · Vocations Scholarship Funds

Knights of Columbus
Department of Scholarships
P.O. Box 1670
New Haven, CT 06507
Phone: 203-752-4000
Email: info@kofc.org
Website: http://www.kofc.org
Purpose: To support theology students on their path to the priesthood.
Eligibility: Applicants must be males studying with ecclesiastical approval at a major seminary for a diocese or religious institute in the United States, its territories and Canada. The Father Michael J. McGivney Vocations Scholarship Fund awards scholarships based on financial need, and applicants must provide proof of need. The Bishop

Thomas V. Daily Scholarships Fund awards recipients on the basis of merit, and applicants must submit their most recent transcript and two letters of recommendation. Both funds give preference to Knights of Columbus members and their sons, but membership is not required.

Target applicant:
High school students
College students
Graduate school students
Adult students
Minimum GPA: None.
Amount: $2,500.
Number of awards: Varies.
Scholarship may be renewable.
Deadline: June 1.
How to apply: Applications are available from seminary rectors and diocesan vocations directors starting in February.

(2178) · W. Allan Herzog Scholarship

Tau Kappa Epsilon Educational Foundation
8645 Founders Road
Indianapolis, IN 46268
Phone: 317-872-6533
Fax: 317-875-8353
Email: tef@tke.org
Website: http://www.tkefoundation.org
Purpose: To assist Tau Kappa Epsilon members entering the fields of accounting and finance.
Eligibility: Applicants must be initiated Tau Kappa Epsilon members in good standing and full-time undergraduate students majoring in accounting or finance. They must have a GPA of at least 2.75 and demonstrate a record of leadership in their chapter and other campus organizations. Applicants must also include a statement describing how they have benefited from TKE membership.
Target applicant:
College students
Adult students
Minimum GPA: 2.75
Amount: $3,000.
Number of awards: 1.
Deadline: March 16.
How to apply: Applications are available online.

(2179) · Wallace G. McCauley Memorial Scholarship

Tau Kappa Epsilon Educational Foundation
8645 Founders Road
Indianapolis, IN 46268
Phone: 317-872-6533
Fax: 317-875-8353
Email: tef@tke.org
Website: http://www.tkefoundation.org
Purpose: To award a member of Tau Kappa Epsilon for outstanding academic achievement who has participated in developing and improving alumni relations and participation.
Eligibility: Applicants must have a GPA of 3.0 and be in the junior or senior year. If no "alumni relations" applicants are recognized, the GPA requirement will be 2.5 and the award will be given in honor of academic achievement and chapter or community leadership.
Target applicant:
College students
Adult students
Minimum GPA: 3.0

Amount: $600.
Number of awards: 1.
Deadline: March 16.
How to apply: Applications are available online.

(2180) · Walter L. Mitchell Memorial Scholarship Awards

Chemical Workers Union Council, International, of the UFCW
Research and Education Department
1799 Akron Peninsula Road
Akron, OH 44313
Phone: 330-926-1444
Fax: 330-926-0816
Website: http://www.icwuc.org
Purpose: To offer scholarships to the children or step-children of members of the UFCW.
Eligibility: Applicants must be children or step-children of members of at least a year who intend to enter college the fall following application. Recipients are selected on the basis of biographical information, ACT/SAT scores and high school records.
Target applicant:
High school students
Minimum GPA: None.
Amount: $1,500.
Number of awards: 13.
Deadline: March 2.
How to apply: Applications are available online.

(2181) · Wenderoth Undergraduate Scholarship

Phi Sigma Kappa International Headquarters
2925 E. 96th Street
Indianapolis, IN 46240
Phone: 317-573-5420
Fax: 317-573-5430
Email: vershun@phisigmakappa.org
Website: http://www.phisigmakappa.org
Purpose: To give financial aid to college sophomore and junior members.
Eligibility: Applicants must be sophomores or juniors in college for the year that the scholarship will apply to, have completed two semesters or three quarters of study and have a minimum B GPA. Scholarships are awarded on the basis of academic accomplishments and essays.
Target applicant:
College students
Adult students
Minimum GPA: 3.0
Amount: $1,750-$4,000.
Number of awards: 4.
Deadline: January 31.
How to apply: Applications are available online.

(2182) · William C. Doherty Scholarship Fund

National Association of Letter Carriers
100 Indiana Avenue NW
Washington, DC 20001-2144
Phone: 202-393-4695
Email: nalcinf@nalc.org
Website: http://www.nalc.org
Purpose: To offer scholarships to the children of members of the Letter Carriers Union.

Eligibility: Applicants must be the children or legally adopted children of an active, retired or deceased letter carrier and high school seniors. Applicants' parents must be members in good standing at least one year prior to applying. Selection is based on SAT/ACT scores, high school transcript and questionnaire.
Target applicant:
    High school students
Minimum GPA: None.
Amount: $4,000.
Number of awards: 5.
Scholarship may be renewable.
Deadline: December 31.
How to apply: Preliminary applications are available online.

(2183) · William V. Muse Scholarship
Tau Kappa Epsilon Educational Foundation
8645 Founders Road
Indianapolis, IN 46268
Phone: 317-872-6533
Fax: 317-875-8353
Email: tef@tke.org
Website: http://www.tkefoundation.org
Purpose: To award a member of Tau Kappa Epsilon for outstanding academic achievement and leadership within the organization as a chapter officer.
Eligibility: Applicants must have a GPA of at least 3.0 and must have earned at least 30 semester-credit hours. Preference is first given to members of the Epsilon-Upsilon Chapter.
Target applicant:
    College students
    Adult students
Minimum GPA: 3.0
Amount: $700.
Number of awards: 1.
Deadline: March 16.
How to apply: Applications are available online.

(2184) · William Wilson Memorial Scholarship
Tau Kappa Epsilon Educational Foundation
8645 Founders Road
Indianapolis, IN 46268
Phone: 317-872-6533
Fax: 317-875-8353
Email: tef@tke.org
Website: http://www.tkefoundation.org
Purpose: To award a member of Tau Kappa Epsilon for outstanding academic achievement who has participated in developing and improving alumni relations and participation.
Eligibility: Applicants must have a GPA of 3.0 and be in the junior or senior year. If no "alumni relations" applicants are recognized, the GPA requirement will be 2.5 and the award will be given in honor of academic achievement and chapter or community leadership.
Target applicant:
    College students
    Adult students
Minimum GPA: 3.0
Amount: $600.
Number of awards: 1.
Deadline: March 16.
How to apply: Applications are available online.

(2185) · Wilson W. Carnes Scholarship
National FFA Organization
P.O. Box 68960
6060 FFA Drive
Indianapolis, IN 46268-0960
Phone: 317-802-6060
Fax: 317-802-6051
Email: scholarships@ffa.org
Website: http://www.ffa.org
Purpose: To support students who are majoring in agricultural communications.
Eligibility: Applicants must be current FFA members and high school seniors or college students planning to enroll or currently enrolled full-time. Students only need to complete the online application one time to be considered for all FFA-administered scholarships. The application requires information about the students' activities and a 1,000-word essay. Awards may be used for books, supplies, tuition, fees and room and board.
Target applicant:
    High school students
    College students
    Adult students
Minimum GPA: None.
Amount: $300.
Number of awards: 1.
Deadline: February 15.
How to apply: Applications are available online.

(2186) · Women in Sports Media Scholarship/Internship Program
Association for Women in Sports Media
P.O. Box 601557
Dallas, TX 75360
Email: awsmintern@hotmail.com
Website: http://www.awsmonline.org
Purpose: To encourage females interested in sports media careers.
Eligibility: Applicants must be female students working full-time toward a graduate or undergraduate degree with the goal of becoming a sports writer, editor, broadcaster or public relations representative. Applicants must submit a resume, an essay on a memorable experience in sports or sports media, three references, two letters of recommendation and up to five samples of their work. Application fee is waived for AWSM members. It is highly recommended that you research the scholarship and awarding organization before applying for a scholarship with a fee. There are many scholarships that do not require a fee.
Target applicant:
    College students
    Graduate school students
    Adult students
Minimum GPA: None.
Amount: $1,000-$2,000+internship pay and expenses for convention attendance.
Number of awards: Varies.
Deadline: October 20.
How to apply: Applications are available online.

(2187) · Women in United Methodist History Research Grant

General Commission on Archives and History, The United Methodist Church
P.O. Box 127
36 Madison Avenue
Madison, NJ 07940
Phone: 973-408-3189
Fax: 973-408-3909
Email: research@gcah.org
Website: http://www.gcah.org
Purpose: To provide seed money for research projects relating specifically to the history of women in the United Methodist Church.
Eligibility: Applicants must submit an application that includes a resume, a description of the project, a timetable for the project, a budget and letters of recommendation.
Target applicant:
Junior high students or younger
High school students
College students
Graduate school students
Adult students
Minimum GPA: None.
Amount: $500-$1,000.
Number of awards: 1-2.
Deadline: December 31.
How to apply: Submit materials to the General Secretary at the address listed.

(2188) · Women in United Methodist History Writing Award

General Commission on Archives and History, The United Methodist Church
P.O. Box 127
36 Madison Avenue
Madison, NJ 07940
Phone: 973-408-3189
Fax: 973-408-3909
Email: research@gcah.org
Website: http://www.gcah.org
Purpose: To reward research and writing on the history of women in The United Methodist Church.
Eligibility: Applicants must submit completed, original manuscripts no longer than 20 double-spaced, typewritten pages with footnotes and bibliography about the history of women in the United Methodist Church or its antecedents.
Target applicant:
Junior high students or younger
High school students
College students
Graduate school students
Adult students
Minimum GPA: None.
Amount: $250.
Number of awards: 1.
Deadline: May 1.
How to apply: Send manuscript to the General Secretary at the address listed.

(2189) · Youth of the Year Award

National Exchange Club
3050 Central Avenue
Toledo, OH 43606
Phone: 800-924-2643
Fax: 419-535-1989
Email: info@nationalexchangeclub.org
Website: http://www.nationalexchangeclub.org
Purpose: To recognize students who excel in academics, leadership and community service.
Eligibility: Applicants are chosen by their local Exchange Clubs. The process begins with Youth of the Month Awards. At the end of the year, a Youth of the Year nominee is selected from Youth of the Month winners. Applicants are judged based on participation in activities, community service, special achievements/awards, grades and a required essay. To be eligible to win, applicants must be able to attend national convention to accept the award.
Target applicant:
High school students
Minimum GPA: None.
Amount: $10,000.
Number of awards: 1.
Deadline: Varies.
How to apply: Applications are available online.

(2190) · Youth Partners Accessing Capital

Alpha Kappa Alpha
5656 S. Stony Island Avenue
Chicago, IL 60637
Phone: 800-653-6528
Fax: 773-947-0277
Email: akaeaf@akaeaf.net
Website: http://www.akaeaf.org
Purpose: To provide financial assistance to Alpha Kappa Alpha members with exceptional academic achievement or extreme financial need.
Eligibility: Applicants must be Alpha Kappa Alpha members who are in their sophomore year of college or higher with a GPA of 3.0 or higher. They must have either high academic achievement or extreme financial need, and they must participate in leadership, volunteer, civic or campus activities.
Target applicant:
College students
Adult students
Minimum GPA: 3.0
Amount: Up to $3,000.
Number of awards: Varies.
Deadline: April 15.
How to apply: Applications are available online.

ETHNICITY / RACE / GENDER

(2191) · A.T. Anderson Memorial Scholarship
American Indian Science and Engineering Society
P.O. Box 9828
Albuquerque, NM 87119-9828
Phone: 505-765-1052
Fax: 505-765-5608
Website: http://www.aises.org
Purpose: To provide scholarships for Native American and Alaskan Native students majoring in science, engineering, medicine, natural resources, math and technology.
Eligibility: Applicants must be full-time undergraduate or graduate students at an accredited college or university. Applicants must also be members of a Native American tribe or Alaskan Native and members of AISES.
Target applicant:
    College students
    Graduate school students
    Adult students
Minimum GPA: 2.7
Amount: $1,000-$2,000.
Number of awards: Varies.
Deadline: June 15.
How to apply: Applications are available online.

(2192) · AAJA Newhouse National Scholarship And Internship Awards
Asian American Journalists Association
1182 Market Street
Suite 230
San Francisco, CA 94102
Phone: 415-346-2051
Fax: 415-346-6343
Email: lilac@aaja.org
Website: http://www.aaja.org
Purpose: Offers monetary assistance to print journalism college students from historically underrepresented Asian Pacific American groups.
Eligibility: The AAJA encourages students from historically underrepresented Asian Pacific American groups, including Vietnamese, Cambodians, Hmong and other Southeast Asians, South Asians and Pacific Islanders to apply. Applicants must demonstrate a commitment to the field of journalism, sensitivity to Asian American issues as demonstrated by community involvement, journalistic ability, scholastic ability and financial need. Applicants may be high school seniors, college students or graduate students.
Target applicant:
    High school students
    College students
    Graduate school students
    Adult students
Minimum GPA: None.
Amount: $5,000.
Number of awards: Varies.
Deadline: March 27.
How to apply: Applications are available online.

(2193) · AAUW Educational Foundation Career Development Grants
American Association of University Women (AAUW) Educational Foundation
Dept. 60
301 ACT Drive
Iowa City, IA 52243-4030
Phone: 319-337-1716 x60
Fax: 202-872-1425
Email: aauw@act.org
Website: http://www.aauw.org
Purpose: To support college-educated women who need additional training to advance their careers, re-enter the workforce or change careers.
Eligibility: Applicants must be U.S. citizens, hold a bachelor's degree and enroll in courses at a regionally-accredited program related to their professional development, including two- and four-year colleges, technical schools and distance learning programs. Special preference is given to women of color, AAUW members and women pursuing their first advanced degree or credentials in a nontraditional field.
Target applicant:
    Graduate school students
    Adult students
Minimum GPA: None.
Amount: $2,000-$8,000.
Number of awards: Varies.
Deadline: December 15.
How to apply: Applications are available online from August 1-December 15.

(2194) · Actuarial Scholarships for Minority Students
Casualty Actuarial Society/Society of Actuaries
475 N, Martingale Road, Suite 600
Schaumburg, IL 60173-2226
Phone: 847-706-3501
Fax: 847-706-3599
Email: kwiener@soa.org
Website: http://www.beanactuary.org
Purpose: To provide scholarships at the undergraduate or graduate level for minority students who are interested in pursuing actuarial careers.
Eligibility: This award is available to the following groups interested in an actuarial career: African American, Hispanic and Native North American. Applicants must be admitted to a college or university offering either a program in actuarial science or courses that will serve to prepare the student for an actuarial career. In addition, applicants must have taken either the SAT or ACT. They should submit applications, two nomination forms, student aid reports, proof of college expenses, transcripts and test scores.
Target applicant:
    High school students
    College students
    Graduate school students
    Adult students
Minimum GPA: None.
Amount: Varies.
Number of awards: Varies.
Scholarship may be renewable.
Deadline: January 17.
How to apply: Applications are available online.

(2195) · Adolph Van Pelt Scholarship

Association on American Indian Affairs
Lisa Wyzlic, Scholarship Coordinator
966 Hungerford Drive, Suite 12-B
Rockville, MD 20850
Phone: 240-314-7155
Fax: 240-314-7159
Email: general.aaia@verizon.net
Website: http://www.indian-affairs.org
Purpose: To assist American Indian students based on merit and financial need.
Eligibility: Applicants must be full-time students and provide proof of tribal enrollment, a Certificate of Indian Blood (showing 1/4 Indian blood) and an essay on educational goals.
Target applicant:
College students
Graduate school students
Adult students
Minimum GPA: None.
Amount: $500-$800.
Number of awards: Varies.
Scholarship may be renewable.
Deadline: July 20.
How to apply: Applications are available online.

(2196) · Afro-Academic, Cultural, Technological and Scientific Olympics (ACT-SO)

National Association for the Advancement of Colored People
The United Negro College Fund
Scholarships and Grants Administration
8260 Willow Oaks Corporate Drive
Fairfax, VA 22031
Phone: 703-205-3400
Website: http://www.naacp.org
Purpose: To recognize and reward the academic and cultural achievements of African American high school students.
Eligibility: Students must be in grades 9 through 12, 19 years of age or younger and of African-American descent. They must compete in one of 25 categories including business, sciences, humanities and performing and visual arts. Winners receive scholarships, internships and apprenticeships.
Target applicant:
High school students
Minimum GPA: None.
Amount: Up to $2,000.
Number of awards: Varies.
Deadline: March 15.
How to apply: Applications are available from the NAACP.

(2197) · AGBU Scholarship Program

Armenian General Benevolent Union (AGBU)
55 E. 59th Street, 7th Floor
New York, NY 10022-1112
Phone: 212-319-6383
Fax: 212-319-6507
Email: scholarship@agbu.org
Website: http://www.agbu.org
Purpose: To help students of Armenian descent.
Eligibility: Applicants should be international full-time students or high school seniors of Armenian descent who attend academic institutions and graduate programs. Applications, two recommendation letters, transcripts, college acceptance letters, financial award letters, resumes and photographs are required.
Target applicant:
High school students
College students
Graduate school students
Adult students
Minimum GPA: None.
Amount: Varies.
Number of awards: Varies.
Scholarship may be renewable.
Deadline: May 15.
How to apply: Applications are available online.

(2198) · Agnes Jones Scholarship

National Association for the Advancement of Colored People
The United Negro College Fund
Scholarships and Grants Administration
8260 Willow Oaks Corporate Drive
Fairfax, VA 22031
Phone: 703-205-3400
Website: http://www.naacp.org
Purpose: To reward NAACP members with financial need.
Eligibility: Students must be members of the NAACP, U.S. citizens and attending an accredited U.S. college. Undergraduates must attend college full-time, while graduates may be full- or part-time students. High school seniors and undergraduates must have a minimum 2.5 GPA while graduate students must have a minimum 3.0 GPA. Applicants must demonstrate financial need according to the formula in the application form.
Target applicant:
High school students
College students
Graduate school students
Minimum GPA: 2.5 for high school seniors and undergraduates; 3.0 for graduate students
Amount: $1,500-$2,500.
Number of awards: Varies.
Scholarship may be renewable.
Deadline: Last Friday in March.
How to apply: Applications are available online.

(2199) · Agnes Missirian Scholarship

Armenian International Women's Association
65 Main Street
#3A
Watertown, MA 02472
Phone: 617-926-0171
Email: aiwainc@aol.com
Website: http://www.aiwa-net.org/scholarshipinfo.html
Purpose: To honor the memory of Professor Agnes Missirian and assist Armenian women in obtaining higher education.
Eligibility: Applicants must be full-time students at accredited colleges or universities who are females of Armenian descent. They must be juniors, seniors or graduate students.
Target applicant:
College students
Graduate school students
Adult students
Minimum GPA: None.
Amount: $2,000.

Number of awards: Varies.
Deadline: April.
How to apply: Applications are available online.

(2200) · Al Muammar Scholarships for Journalism

Arab American Institute Foundation
1600 K Street NW
Suite 600
Washington, DC 20006
Phone: 202-429-9210
Email: saltaf@aaiusa.org
Website: http://www.aaiusa.org
Purpose: To support Arab American journalism majors.
Eligibility: Applicants must be full-time Arab American college students majoring in journalism at an accredited U.S. college or university or college seniors who have been accepted to a graduate journalism school. Students must have a demonstrated commitment to print or broadcast journalism and to pursuing journalism as a career. The applicants' sensitivity to Arab American issues, social advocacy and community involvement are seriously considered, as well as financial need and academic achievement.
Target applicant:
    College students
    Adult students
Minimum GPA: 3.3
Amount: $5,000.
Number of awards: 4.
Deadline: February 15.
How to apply: Applications are available online.

(2201) · Alliance Data Scholarship

United Negro College Fund (UNCF)
8260 Willow Oaks Corporate Drive
P.O. Box 10444
Fairfax, VA 22031-8044
Phone: 800-331-2244
Website: http://www.uncf.org
Purpose: To assist African American students who are enrolled at a UNCF institution.
Eligibility: Applicants must have a minimum 3.0 GPA, complete the Free Application for Federal Student Aid (FAFSA) and have unmet financial need that is verified by the college or university financial aid office. UNCF students are encouraged to complete the UNCF General Scholarship application to be matched with scholarships for which they meet the criteria.
Target applicant:
    High school students
    College students
    Adult students
Minimum GPA: 3.0
Amount: $5,000.
Number of awards: 1.
Deadline: Varies.
How to apply: Applications are available online.

(2202) · Allogan Slagle Memorial Scholarship

Association on American Indian Affairs
Lisa Wyzlic, Scholarship Coordinator
966 Hungerford Drive, Suite 12-B
Rockville, MD 20850

Phone: 240-314-7155
Fax: 240-314-7159
Email: general.aaia@verizon.net
Website: http://www.indian-affairs.org
Purpose: To assist college students who are members of American Indian tribes that are not recognized by the government.
Eligibility: Applicants must submit a financial need analysis form, Certificate of Indian Blood or documents proving their lineal descent, proof of tribal enrollment, essay, two letters of recommendation, current financial aid award letter, transcripts and class schedule.
Target applicant:
    College students
    Adult students
Minimum GPA: None.
Amount: $1,500.
Number of awards: 4.
Deadline: July 1.
How to apply: Applications are available online.

(2203) · Alton and Dorothy Higgins MD Scholarship

United Negro College Fund (UNCF)
8260 Willow Oaks Corporate Drive
P.O. Box 10444
Fairfax, VA 22031-8044
Phone: 800-331-2244
Website: http://www.uncf.org
Purpose: To assist UNCF students or UNCF graduates in attending medical school.
Eligibility: The award may be used for tuition, room and board, books or to repay a federal student loan.
Target applicant:
    College students
    Graduate school students
    Adult students
Minimum GPA: None.
Amount: Varies.
Number of awards: Varies.
Deadline: Varies.
How to apply: Applications are available online.

(2204) · America's Junior Miss Scholarship Program

America's Junior Miss
P.O. Box 2786
Mobile, AL 36652
Phone: 251-438-3621
Fax: 251-431-0063
Email: lynne@ajm.org
Website: http://www.ajm.org
Purpose: To provide scholarship opportunities and encourage personal development for high school girls through a competitive pageant stressing academics and talent as well as poise and fitness.
Eligibility: Teen girls are selected from state competitions to participate in a national pageant. Contestants are judged on a combination of scholastics, personal interview, talent, fitness and poise. Applicants should be a high school student at least in their sophomore year.
Target applicant:
    High school students
Minimum GPA: None.
Amount: Varies.
Number of awards: Varies.
Deadline: Varies.

How to apply: Applications are available from the local Junior Miss Program offices. A list of local contacts is available online.

(2205) · American Chemical Society Minority Scholars Program

National Urban League
120 Wall Street
New York, NY 10005
Phone: 888-839-0467
Email: info@nul.org
Website: http://www.nul.org
Purpose: To aid minority students with a strong interest in chemistry.
Eligibility: Applicants must be high school seniors planning to attend college, college students who are currently pursuing or planning to pursue full-time study in a chemically related field, community college graduates and transfer students who plan to attain a baccalaureate degree in chemistry, biochemistry, chemical engineering or a chemically related field or community college freshmen majoring in a two-year chemical technology program.
Target applicant:
  High school students
  College students
  Adult students
Minimum GPA: None.
Amount: Varies.
Number of awards: 200.
Deadline: February 15.
How to apply: Applications are available by request.

(2206) · American Chemical Society Scholars Program

American Chemical Society
1155 16th Street NW
Washington, DC 20036
Phone: 800-227-5558
Fax: 202-872-6067
Email: scholars@acs.org
Website: http://www.chemistry.org
Purpose: To encourage minority students to pursue careers in the sciences and to help them acquire the skills necessary for success in these fields.
Eligibility: Applicants must be African American, Hispanic/Latino or American Indian and graduating high school seniors or college freshmen, sophomores or juniors enrolled full-time at an accredited institution. Students must major in chemistry, biochemistry, chemical engineering or a chemically-related science and plan to work in a chemistry-related field. Those entering pre-med programs or pursuing pharmacy degrees are not eligible. A minimum GPA of 3.0 or "B" or better with high academic achievement in chemistry or science is required. Students must also demonstrate financial need through the Free Application for Federal Student Aid (FAFSA).
Target applicant:
  High school students
  College students
  Adult students
Minimum GPA: 3.0
Amount: Up to $3,000.
Number of awards: Varies.
Scholarship may be renewable.
Deadline: March 1.
How to apply: Applications are available online.

(2207) · American Dream Scholarship

Sallie Mae Fund
12061 Bluemont Way
Reston, VA 20190
Phone: 703-810-3000
Website: http://www.thesalliemaefund.org
Purpose: To support African-American students based on academic merit and financial need.
Eligibility: Applicants must have financial need, meet Pell Grant eligibility criteria and intend to be enrolled full-time at two- or four-year schools.
Target applicant:
  High school students
  College students
  Adult students
Minimum GPA: 2.5
Amount: $500-$5,000.
Number of awards: Varies.
Deadline: April 15.
How to apply: Applications are available online.

(2208) · American Geological Institute Minority Scholarship

American Geological Institute
4220 King Street
Alexandria, VA 22302
Phone: 703-379-2480
Fax: 703-379-7563
Website: http://www.agiweb.org
Purpose: To increase the number of minority students in the geosciences by providing financial awards and mentorship.
Eligibility: Applicants must be black, Latino or Native American (American Indian, Eskimo, Hawaiian or Samoan) and full-time students with demonstrable financial need who are currently majoring in geoscience at the undergraduate or graduate level.
Target applicant:
  College students
  Graduate school students
  Adult students
Minimum GPA: None.
Amount: Varies.
Number of awards: Varies.
Deadline: March 10.
How to apply: Applications available online.

(2209) · American Hotel Management Foundation Scholarship

United Negro College Fund (UNCF)
8260 Willow Oaks Corporate Drive
P.O. Box 10444
Fairfax, VA 22031-8044
Phone: 800-331-2244
Website: http://www.uncf.org
Purpose: To promote the study of hotel management.
Eligibility: Applicants must be major in hotel management at United Negro College Fund (UNCF) member colleges and universities. Students must also have a minimum 2.5 GPA, complete the Free Application for Federal Student Aid (FAFSA) and have unmet financial need that is verified by the college or university financial aid office. UNCF students are encouraged to complete the UNCF General Scholarship application to be matched with scholarships for which they meet the criteria.

Target applicant:
 High school students
 College students
 Adult students
Minimum GPA: 2.5
Amount: $1,500.
Number of awards: 1.
Deadline: Varies.
How to apply: Applications are available online.

(2210) · American Indian Scholarship

National Society Daughters of the American Revolution
1776 D Street NW
Washington, DC 20006-5303
Phone: 202-628-1776
Website: http://www.dar.org
Purpose: To assist Native American students.
Eligibility: Applicants must be Native Americans with papers proving Native American blood, have a minimum 2.75 GPA and demonstrate financial need and academic achievement. Preference is given to undergraduate students.
Target applicant:
 College students
 Graduate school students
 Adult students
Minimum GPA: 2.75
Amount: $500.
Number of awards: Varies.
Deadline: April 1 and October 1.
How to apply: Applications are available by written request.

(2211) · American Society of Criminology Fellowships for Ethnic Minorities

American Society of Criminology
Department of Sociology and Criminal Justice C.O. Ronet Bachman
University of Delaware
Newark, DE 19717-5242
Email: ronet@udel.edu
Website: http://www.asc41.com
Purpose: To encourage minorities to study criminology or criminal justice.
Eligibility: Applicants must be African American, Asian American, Latino or Native American. Recipients must have been accepted into a doctoral studies program. Selection is based on curriculum vitae, college transcripts, financial need, references and letter describing career plans, experiences and interest in criminology.
Target applicant:
 College students
 Graduate school students
 Adult students
Minimum GPA: None.
Amount: $6,000.
Number of awards: 3.
Deadline: March 1.
How to apply: Applications are available by written request.

(2212) · Amtrak Travel Scholarship

United Negro College Fund (UNCF)
8260 Willow Oaks Corporate Drive
P.O. Box 10444

Fairfax, VA 22031-8044
Phone: 800-331-2244
Website: http://www.uncf.org
Purpose: To assist African American students with their college-related travel expenses.
Eligibility: Applicants must be enrolled at one of the following schools: Bennett College for Women, Bethune-Cookman College, Claflin University, Clark Atlanta University, Dillard University, Edward Waters College, Johnson C. Smith University, Lane College, LeMoyne-Owen College, Morehouse College, Philander Smith College, Shaw University, Spelman College, Tougaloo College, Virginia Union University, Wiley College, Xavier University, Howard University or Hampton University. Selected students will be given the opportunity to travel to any destination serviced by Amtrak.
Target applicant:
 High school students
 College students
 Adult students
Minimum GPA: 2.5
Amount: $750.
Number of awards: 185.
Deadline: October 30.
How to apply: Applications are available online.

(2213) · APA Planning Fellowships

American Planning Association
122 S. Michigan Avenue
Suite 1600
Chicago, IL 60603
Phone: 312-431-9100
Fax: 312-431-9985
Website: http://www.planning.org
Purpose: To foster increased minority interest in the study of urban planning at the graduate level.
Eligibility: Applicants must be African American, Hispanic American or Native American, be U.S. citizens and demonstrate financial need. Applicants must also be students enrolled or accepted for enrollment in a graduate planning program that has been accredited by the Planning Accreditation Board. Selection is based on personal background statement, academic performance, letters of recommendation, financial need and geographic diversity. Applicants must be first or second-year graduate students.
Target applicant:
 Graduate school students
 Adult students
Minimum GPA: None.
Amount: Varies.
Number of awards: Varies.
Deadline: May 15.
How to apply: Applications are available online.

(2214) · Armenian Educational Foundation Scholarships

Armenian Educational Foundation Inc.
600 W. Broadway
Suite 130
Glendale, CA 91204
Phone: 818-242-4154
Email: aef@aefweb.org
Website: http://www.aefweb.org
Purpose: To support Armenian students throughout the world.

Eligibility: Students must be of Armenian descent either on their mother's side, father's side or both. Selection is based on academic performance and financial need. Applicants must be at least college sophomores or graduate students who attend the colleges or universities listed on the website.
Target applicant:
    College students
    Graduate school students
    Adult students
Minimum GPA: None.
Amount: Varies.
Number of awards: Varies.
Deadline: October 8.
How to apply: Applications are available online.

(2215) · Armenian Relief Society Undergraduate Scholarship

Armenian Relief Society Of North America Inc.
80 Bigelow Avenue
Watertown, MA 02472
Phone: 617-926-5892
Fax: 617-926-4855
Email: ars1910@aol.com
Website: http://www.ars1910.org
Purpose: To provide merit and need-based scholarships for students of Armenian ancestry.
Eligibility: Applicants must be of Armenian ancestry and not related to the ARS Central Executive or Eremian Scholarship Committee members. Specific requirements may vary by region.
Target applicant:
    Junior high students or younger
    High school students
    College students
    Adult students
Minimum GPA: None.
Amount: Varies.
Number of awards: Varies.
Deadline: Varies.
How to apply: Applications are available by mail.

(2216) · ASA Scholarships

Armenian Students' Association of America
333 Atlantic Avenue
Warwick, RI 02888
Phone: 401-461-6114
Email: asa@asainc.org
Website: http://www.asainc.org
Purpose: To provide scholarships for students of Armenian descent.
Eligibility: Applicants must be college sophomores or beyond in the year of application and be of Armenian descent.
Target applicant:
    College students
    Graduate school students
    Adult students
Minimum GPA: None.
Amount: Varies.
Number of awards: Varies.
Deadline: March 15.
How to apply: Request forms for applications are available online.

(2217) · Asian American Scholarship Fund

U.S. Pan Asian American Chamber of Commerce
1329 18th Street NW
Washington, DC 20036
Phone: 800-696-7818
Fax: 202-296-5225
Email: info@uspaacc.com
Website: http://www.uspaacc.com
Purpose: To support the higher education goals of Asian American students.
Eligibility: Applicants must be U.S. citizens or permanent residents and Asian American high school seniors who will pursue post-secondary educations at an accredited institution in the U.S. Selection is based on academic achievement, leadership in extracurricular activities, community service and financial need. A minimum 3.3 GPA required. Applicant must be able to attend the annual conference.
Target applicant:
    High school students
Minimum GPA: 3.3
Amount: $5,000.
Number of awards: 1.
Deadline: February 22.
How to apply: Applications are available online.

(2218) · Asian and Pacific Islander American Scholarships

Asian and Pacific Islander American Scholarship Fund
1900 L Street NW
Suite 210
Washington, DC 20036-5002
Phone: 202-986-6892
Fax: 202-530-0643
Email: info@apiasf.org
Website: http://www.apiasf.org
Purpose: To provide financial assistance to Asian and Pacific Island Americans.
Eligibility: Applicants must be of Asian or Pacific Islander ethnicity as defined by the U.S. Census, and they must be legal citizens, nationals or permanent residents of the United States. Citizens of the Marshall Islands, Micronesia and Palau are also eligible. Applicants must be enrolling full-time as a first-year degree-seeking student in an accredited college or university in the U.S. They must have a GPA of 2.7 or higher or have earned a GED, and they must apply for federal financial aid.
Target applicant:
    High school students
Minimum GPA: 2.7
Amount: $2,500.
Number of awards: Varies.
Deadline: January 19.
How to apply: Applications are available online.

(2219) · Berbeco Senior Research Fellowship

United Negro College Fund (UNCF)
8260 Willow Oaks Corporate Drive
P.O. Box 10444
Fairfax, VA 22031-8044
Phone: 800-331-2244
Website: http://www.uncf.org
Purpose: To encourage African Americans to conduct independent research internationally.

Eligibility: Applicants must be college juniors who attend United Negro College Fund (UNCF) member colleges or universities. The need-based award is for students to work on their senior thesis or research projects outside the U.S. during the summer between their junior and senior years.

Target applicant:
  College students
  Adult students
Minimum GPA: 2.5
Amount: Varies.
Number of awards: Varies.
Deadline: December 12.
How to apply: Applications are available online.

(2220) · Bernadette Wong-Yu Scholarship

U.S. Pan Asian American Chamber of Commerce
1329 18th Street NW
Washington, DC 20036
Phone: 800-696-7818
Fax: 202-296-5225
Email: info@uspaacc.com
Website: http://www.uspaacc.com
Purpose: To support the higher education goals of Asian American students.
Eligibility: Applicants must be U.S. citizens or permanent residents and be students of Asian or Pacific Heritage planning to enroll or currently enrolled in post-secondary education at an accredited institution in the U.S. or China. Selection is based on academic excellence, community service involvement and financial need. Minimum 3.3 GPA and Chinese Language or Chinese Studies major required. Applicants must be able to attend the Excellence Awards and Scholarships Dinner during the CelebrAsian Annual Conference (in May).

Target applicant:
  High school students
  College students
  Adult students
Minimum GPA: 3.3
Amount: Up to $3,000.
Number of awards: 1.
Deadline: February 28.
How to apply: Applications are available online.

(2221) · Bessie Irene Smith Trust Scholarship

United Negro College Fund (UNCF)
8260 Willow Oaks Corporate Drive
P.O. Box 10444
Fairfax, VA 22031-8044
Phone: 800-331-2244
Website: http://www.uncf.org
Purpose: To help African American students attending United Negro College Fund (UNCF) member colleges and universities.
Eligibility: Applicants must have a minimum 2.5 GPA, complete the Free Application for Federal Student Aid (FAFSA) and have unmet financial need that is verified by the college or university financial aid office. Students are encouraged to complete the UNCF General Scholarship application to be matched with scholarships for which they meet the criteria.

Target applicant:
  High school students
  College students
  Adult students

Minimum GPA: 2.5
Amount: Varies.
Number of awards: Varies.
Deadline: Varies.
How to apply: Applications are available online.

(2222) · Best Buy Scholarship Program

United Negro College Fund (UNCF)
8260 Willow Oaks Corporate Drive
P.O. Box 10444
Fairfax, VA 22031-8044
Phone: 800-331-2244
Website: http://www.uncf.org
Purpose: To help African Americans majoring in business- and computer science-related fields.
Eligibility: There are two programs, one for employees and one for non-employees. Employee awards are $2,500 while non-employee awards are $5,000. To qualify for the employee program, applicants must have worked for six consecutive months at Best Buy. For both programs, applicants must be undergraduates at United Negro College Fund (UNCF) member colleges or universities or Florida A&M University and must demonstrate financial need. Students must major in business, finance, accounting, marketing, communications, computer science or advertising. A transcript, resume, two recommendation letters and essay are required.

Target applicant:
  High school students
  College students
  Adult students
Minimum GPA: 3.0
Amount: $5,000.
Number of awards: Varies.
Deadline: November 5.
How to apply: Applications are available online.

(2223) · Brown Foundation Scholarships

Brown Foundation Scholarship Program
P.O. Box 4862
Topeka, KS 66604
Phone: 785-235-3939
Fax: 785-235-1001
Email: brownfound@juno.com
Website: http://www.brownvboard.org/foundatn/sclrbroc.htm
Purpose: To help minority students who are either high school seniors or college juniors who want to teach.
Eligibility: High school seniors should have a demonstrated desire to enter a teacher education program through volunteer experience, work experience, and/or references and should plan to enroll in college at least half-time. The high school senior scholarship is $300 for the freshman year. College juniors must be accepted to a teacher education program and attend at least half-time. The college award is $500 per year for two academic years. Selection for both awards is based on GPA, school, community and extracurricular activities, career plans and goals in education, essays and two recommendations.

Target applicant:
  High school students
  College students
  Adult students
Minimum GPA: 3.0
Amount: $300-$500.
Number of awards: 2.
Scholarship may be renewable.

Deadline: April 1.
How to apply: Applications are available from high school counselors, from departments of education at participating colleges, from the Brown Foundation and online.

(2224) · Bruce Lee Scholarship

U.S. Pan Asian American Chamber of Commerce
1329 18th Street NW
Washington, DC 20036
Phone: 800-696-7818
Fax: 202-296-5225
Email: info@uspaacc.com
Website: http://www.uspaacc.com
Purpose: To support the higher education goals of Asian American students.
Eligibility: Applicants must be U.S. citizens or permanent residents and be high school seniors of Asian or Pacific Heritage who will pursue post-secondary educations at an accredited institution in the U.S. Selection is based on character, the ability to persevere over adversity, academic excellence with at least a 3.0 GPA, community service involvement and financial need. Applicants must be able to attend the Excellence Awards and Scholarships Dinner during the CelebrAsian Annual Conference (in May).
Target applicant:
  High school students
Minimum GPA: 3.0
Amount: $5,000.
Number of awards: 1.
Deadline: February 28.
How to apply: Applications are available online.

(2225) · Bureau of Reclamation Scholarship and Internship

American Indian Science and Engineering Society
P.O. Box 9828
Albuquerque, NM 87119-9828
Phone: 505-765-1052
Fax: 505-765-5608
Website: http://www.aises.org
Purpose: To provide scholarships for Native American and Alaskan Native students seeking bachelor's degrees in science or engineering related to water resources and/or the environment.
Eligibility: Applicants must be enrolled full-time at an accredited college or university, seeking a degree in science or engineering related to water resources and/or the environment. Students must belong to a federally recognized Indian tribe and must be members of AISES. Recipients must complete an eight- to ten-week internship with the Bureau of Reclamation.
Target applicant:
  College students
  Adult students
Minimum GPA: 2.5
Amount: $5,000 per year.
Number of awards: Varies.
Scholarship may be renewable.
Deadline: June 15.
How to apply: Applications are available online.

(2226) · Burlington Northern Santa Fe (BNSF) Foundation Scholarship

American Indian Science and Engineering Society
P.O. Box 9828
Albuquerque, NM 87119-9828
Phone: 505-765-1052
Fax: 505-765-5608
Website: http://www.aises.org
Purpose: To provide a four-year scholarship for an American Indian student attending an accredited four-year college or university in a state where Burlington Northern Santa Fe operates.
Eligibility: Applicants must reside in one of the following states: Arizona, California, Colorado, Kansas, Minnesota, Montana, New Mexico, North Dakota, Oklahoma, Oregon, South Dakota or Washington. Applicants must also major in one of the following areas: business, engineering, math, medicine/health administration, natural/physical sciences, technology or education and belong to AISES.
Target applicant:
  High school students
  College students
  Adult students
Minimum GPA: 2.0
Amount: $2,500 per year.
Number of awards: Varies.
Scholarship may be renewable.
Deadline: April 15.
How to apply: Applications are available online.

(2227) · Burton G. Bettingen Foundation Scholarship

United Negro College Fund (UNCF)
8260 Willow Oaks Corporate Drive
P.O. Box 10444
Fairfax, VA 22031-8044
Phone: 800-331-2244
Website: http://www.uncf.org
Purpose: To support higher education among African American students.
Eligibility: Applicants must attend United Negro College Fund (UNCF) member colleges and universities, have a minimum 2.5 GPA, complete the Free Application for Federal Student Aid (FAFSA) and have unmet financial need that is verified by the college or university financial aid office. UNCF students are encouraged to complete the UNCF General Scholarship application to be matched with scholarships for which they meet the criteria.
Target applicant:
  High school students
  College students
  Adult students
Minimum GPA: 2.5
Amount: Varies.
Number of awards: Varies.
Deadline: Varies.
How to apply: Applications are available online.

(2228) · C-SPAN Scholarship Program

United Negro College Fund (UNCF)
8260 Willow Oaks Corporate Drive
P.O. Box 10444
Fairfax, VA 22031-8044
Phone: 800-331-2244
Website: http://www.uncf.org

Purpose: To assist African American students in communications- and social science-related fields.

Eligibility: Applicants must be sophomores or juniors at United Negro College Fund (UNCF) member colleges and universities and must major in radio/television/film, communications, journalism, political science, English or history. This program also offers a paid summer internship.

Target applicant:
    College students
    Adult students
Minimum GPA: 3.0
Amount: $2,000.
Number of awards: 1.
Deadline: March 28.
How to apply: Applications are available online.

(2229) · California Chafee Grant Program

California Student Aid Commission
P.O. Box 419026
Rancho Cordova, CA 95741-9026
Phone: 888-224-7268
Fax: 916-464-8002
Email: studentsupport@csac.ca.gov
Website: http://www.csac.ca.gov

Purpose: To provide educational assistance for students who have been in foster care in California.

Eligibility: Applicants must be current or former foster youth who are under 22 years of age as of July 1 of the award year. Dependency must have been established by the court between the ages of 16 and 18. Financial need is required. Applicants must enroll at least half-time in a program that is at least one academic year long, and they must attend class regularly and maintain good grades.

Target applicant:
    High school students
    College students
Minimum GPA: None.
Amount: Varies.
Number of awards: Varies.
Scholarship may be renewable.
Deadline: Varies.
How to apply: Applications are available online.

(2230) · Career Advancement Scholarship

Business and Professional Association Foundation
Career Advancement Scholarship Program
P.O. Box 4030
Iowa City, IA 52243-4030
Phone: 800-525-3729
Fax: 202-861-0298
Email: bpwfoundation@act.org
Website: http://www.bpwusa.org

Purpose: To support disadvantaged women who wish to advance in their career or enter the workforce.

Eligibility: Applicants must be female U.S. citizens who are at least 25, demonstrate financial need, have clear career plans, be officially accepted in an accredited institution in the U.S., Puerto Rico or the Virgin Islands and graduate within 12 to 24 months of the grant.

Target applicant:
    College students
    Graduate school students
    Adult students
Minimum GPA: None.

Amount: $1,000-$2,000.
Number of awards: 50-100.
Deadline: April 15.
How to apply: Applications are available online.

(2231) · Carmen E. Turner Scholarship

Conference of Minority Transportation Officials
818 18th Street NW, Suite 850
Washington, DC 20006
Phone: 202-530-0551
Fax: 202-530-0617
Email: comto@comto.org
Website: http://www.comto.org

Purpose: To support students who are members of COMTO.

Eligibility: Applicants must have been COMTO members in good standing for at least the past year. Students must be enrolled in an undergraduate or graduate program for at least six credits per semester with at least a 2.5 GPA.

Target applicant:
    College students
    Graduate school students
    Adult students
Minimum GPA: 2.5
Amount: $3,500.
Number of awards: Varies.
Deadline: April 4.
How to apply: Applications are available online.

(2232) · Carolyn Bailey Thomas Scholarship

United Negro College Fund (UNCF)
8260 Willow Oaks Corporate Drive
P.O. Box 10444
Fairfax, VA 22031-8044
Phone: 800-331-2244
Website: http://www.uncf.org

Purpose: To help African Americans attending United Negro College Fund (UNCF) member colleges and universities.

Eligibility: Applicants must have a minimum 3.0 GPA, complete the Free Application for Federal Student Aid (FAFSA) and have unmet financial need that is verified by the college or university financial aid office. Students are encouraged to complete the UNCF General Scholarship application to be matched with scholarships for which they meet the criteria.

Target applicant:
    High school students
    College students
    Adult students
Minimum GPA: 3.0
Amount: Varies.
Number of awards: Varies.
Deadline: Varies.
How to apply: Applications are available online.

(2233) · Cary C. and Debra Y.C. Wu Scholarship

U.S. Pan Asian American Chamber of Commerce
1329 18th Street NW
Washington, DC 20036
Phone: 800-696-7818
Fax: 202-296-5225
Email: info@uspaacc.com
Website: http://www.uspaacc.com

Purpose: To support the higher education goals of Asian American students.

Eligibility: Applicants must be U.S. citizens or permanent residents and be high school seniors of Asian or Pacific Heritage who will pursue post-secondary educations at an accredited institution in the U.S. Selection is based on academic excellence, leadership in extracurricular activities, community service involvement and financial need. Minimum 3.5 GPA required. Applicants must be able to attend the Excellence Awards and Scholarships Dinner during the CelebrAsian Annual Conference.

Target applicant:
   High school students
Minimum GPA: 3.5
Amount: Up to $5,000.
Number of awards: 1.
Deadline: February 28.
How to apply: Applications are available online.

(2234) · Catherine W. Pierce Scholarship

United Negro College Fund (UNCF)
8260 Willow Oaks Corporate Drive
P.O. Box 10444
Fairfax, VA 22031-8044
Phone: 800-331-2244
Website: http://www.uncf.org

Purpose: To help African American students majoring in art or history.

Eligibility: Applicants must have a minimum 3.0 GPA, complete the Free Application for Federal Student Aid (FAFSA) and have unmet financial need that is verified by the college or university financial aid office. UNCF students are encouraged to complete the UNCF General Scholarship application to be matched with scholarships for which they meet the criteria.

Target applicant:
   High school students
   College students
   Adult students
Minimum GPA: 3.0
Amount: Up to $5,000.
Number of awards: Varies.
Deadline: Varies.
How to apply: Applications are available online.

(2235) · CDM Scholarship/Internship

United Negro College Fund (UNCF)
8260 Willow Oaks Corporate Drive
P.O. Box 10444
Fairfax, VA 22031-8044
Phone: 800-331-2244
Website: http://www.uncf.org

Purpose: To support African Americans studying engineering, science or construction disciplines.

Eligibility: Applicants must be undergraduates majoring in engineering, science or construction fields, such as chemical, civil, electrical, environmental, geotechnical, geology/hydrogeology, geography, GIS, mechanical, mining and structural or must be planning to pursue a master's degree in one of these disciplines at United Negro College Fund (UNCF) member colleges and universities. A minimum 3.0 GPA is required. There is also an internship as a part of the program.

Target applicant:
   High school students
   College students

   Graduate school students
   Adult students
Minimum GPA: 3.0
Amount: $6,000.
Number of awards: 6.
Deadline: April 6.
How to apply: Applications are available online.

(2236) · CHCI Scholarship Award

Congressional Hispanic Caucus Institute Inc.
911 2nd Street NE
Washington, DC 20002
Phone: 202-543-1771
Email: shernandez@chci.org
Website: http://www.chci.org

Purpose: To award Latino students for public service activities in their communities.

Eligibility: Applicants must be Latinos who have actively participated in public service; be accepted as full-time students into an accredited community college, four-year university or a graduate/professional program; demonstrate financial need and have good writing skills. Students should submit applications, resumes, essays, Student Aid Reports, two recommendation letters, transcripts and a self-addressed stamped postcard to be notified when application is received.

Target applicant:
   College students
   Graduate school students
   Adult students
Minimum GPA: None.
Amount: $5,000.
Number of awards: Varies.
Deadline: March 1.
How to apply: Applications are available online.

(2237) · Cherokee Nation PELL Scholarship

Cherokee Nation
Cherokee Nation Undergraduate Scholarship Programs
Attn.: Higher Education
P.O. Box 948
Tahlequah, OK 74465
Phone: 918-456-0671
Email: highereducation@cherokee.org
Website: http://www.cherokee.org

Purpose: To support students who are Cherokee Nation Members.

Eligibility: Applicants must be high school senior Cherokee Nation tribal members planning to attend an institution of higher education.

Target applicant:
   High school students
Minimum GPA: None.
Amount: Varies.
Number of awards: Varies.
Deadline: June 17.
How to apply: Applications are available online.

(2238) · Chickasaw Nation Education Foundation Program

Chickasaw Nation Education Foundation
P.O. Box 1726
Ad, OK 74821
Phone: 580-421-9031
Website: http://www.chickasaw.net

Purpose: To assist Chickasaw students who demonstrate academic excellence, community service, dedication to learning and a commitment to Native Americans.

Eligibility: Applicants must be full-time Chickasaw students. Other eligibility requirements vary by scholarship.

Target applicant:
- High school students
- College students
- Graduate school students
- Adult students

Minimum GPA: None.

Amount: Varies.

Number of awards: 29.

Deadline: June 1.

How to apply: Applications are available online.

(2239) · Chief Manuelito Scholarship Program

Office of Navajo Nation Scholarship and Financial Assistance

Website: http://www.onnsfa.org

Purpose: The scholarship was created to help high-achieving Navajo students.

Eligibility: Students must be enrolled members of the Navajo nation, submit a Certificate of Indian Blood, attend a regionally-accredited school and complete a FAFSA form. Students must also complete a Navajo Government course (available online).

Target applicant:
- High school students
- College students
- Graduate school students
- Adult students

Minimum GPA: None.

Amount: $5,000.

Number of awards: Varies.

Scholarship may be renewable.

Deadline: Varies by term.

How to apply: Applications are available online and must be submitted to your agency, which is listed online.

(2240) · Chinn Scholarship

American Atheists

P.O. Box 5733

Parsippany, NJ 07054

Phone: 908-276-7300

Fax: 908-276-7402

Email: info@athiests.org

Website: http://www.atheists.org

Purpose: To support gay or lesbian Atheist students.

Eligibility: Applicants must be high school seniors or college students who are Atheists, have a minimum 2.5 GPA and be student activists. The award is based on the level of activism and requires a 500- to 1,000-word essay. In addition to the scholarship, the winner will receive a free trip to the American Atheists National Convention.

Target applicant:
- High school students
- College students
- Adult students

Minimum GPA: 2.5

Amount: $1,000.

Number of awards: 1.

Deadline: January 31.

How to apply: Applications are available online.

(2241) · Chrysler Corporation Scholarship

United Negro College Fund (UNCF)

8260 Willow Oaks Corporate Drive

P.O. Box 10444

Fairfax, VA 22031-8044

Phone: 800-331-2244

Website: http://www.uncf.org

Purpose: To help African Americans attending United Negro College Fund (UNCF) member colleges and universities.

Eligibility: Applicants must have a minimum 2.5 GPA, complete the Free Application for Federal Student Aid (FAFSA) and have unmet financial need that is verified by the college or university financial aid office. UNCF students are encouraged to complete the UNCF General Scholarship application to be matched with scholarships for which they meet the criteria.

Target applicant:
- High school students
- College students
- Adult students

Minimum GPA: 2.5

Amount: $3,900.

Number of awards: 10.

Deadline: Varies.

How to apply: Applications are available online.

(2242) · Citigroup Fellows Program

United Negro College Fund (UNCF)

8260 Willow Oaks Corporate Drive

P.O. Box 10444

Fairfax, VA 22031-8044

Phone: 800-331-2244

Website: http://www.uncf.org

Purpose: To assist sophomores at United Negro College Fund (UNCF) member colleges and universities who plan to pursue business careers.

Eligibility: Applicants must major in business, finance, economics, accounting, information systems, computer science/MIS, computer science, banking, business-related, information technology, business (sales interest), computer engineering, management or management information systems. The program also provides access to Citigroup professionals as mentors and professional development conferences.

Target applicant:
- College students
- Adult students

Minimum GPA: 3.0

Amount: $6,400.

Number of awards: Varies.

Scholarship may be renewable.

Deadline: April 1.

How to apply: Applications are available online.

(2243) · Citizen Potawatomi Nation Tribal Scholarship

Citizen Potawatomi Nation

1601 S. Gordon Cooper

Shawnee, OK 74801

Phone: 405-275-3121

Email: hownikan@potawatomi.org

Website: http://www.potawatomi.org

Purpose: To provide financial assistance to tribal members who are studying in undergraduate or graduate programs, vocational technical career courses or other accredited educational programs.

Eligibility: Applicants must be tribal members who maintain a GPA of 2.0 and meet requirements for financial aid.
Target applicant:
   High school students
   College students
   Graduate school students
   Adult students
Minimum GPA: 2.0
Amount: Varies.
Number of awards: Varies.
Scholarship may be renewable.
Deadline: August 15.
How to apply: Applications are available online.

(2244) · Colgate-Palmolive Company/UNCF Scholarship

United Negro College Fund (UNCF)
8260 Willow Oaks Corporate Drive
P.O. Box 10444
Fairfax, VA 22031-8044
Phone: 800-331-2244
Website: http://www.uncf.org
Purpose: To help African American sophomores, juniors and seniors majoring in business with a concentration in marketing.
Eligibility: Applicants must have a minimum 3.0 GPA and attend United Negro College Fund (UNCF) member colleges and universities. Students must complete the Free Application for Federal Student Aid (FAFSA) and have unmet financial need that is verified by the college or university financial aid office. UNCF students are encouraged to complete the UNCF General Scholarship application to be matched with scholarships for which they meet the criteria.
Target applicant:
   College students
   Adult students
Minimum GPA: 3.0
Amount: Varies, based on need.
Number of awards: Varies.
Deadline: Varies.
How to apply: Applications are available online.

(2245) · College Scholarship Program

Hispanic Scholarship Fund (HSF)
55 Second Street
Suite 1500
San Francisco, CA 94105
Phone: 877-473-4636
Fax: 415-808-2302
Email: scholar1@hsf.net
Website: http://www.hsf.net
Purpose: To advance the college education of Hispanic Americans. Over the past 25 years, HSF has awarded more than 68,000 scholarships.
Eligibility: Applicants must be of Hispanic heritage (one parent must be fully Hispanic or both parents must be half Hispanic), be U.S. citizens or permanent residents and be eligible to apply and receive Title IV funds. Selection is based on academic achievement, letter of recommendation, personal statement and financial need.
Target applicant:
   College students
   Adult students
Minimum GPA: 2.7
Amount: Varies.

Number of awards: Varies.
Deadline: August.
How to apply: Applications are available online.

(2246) · Community College Transfer Scholarship Program

Hispanic Scholarship Fund (HSF)
55 Second Street
Suite 1500
San Francisco, CA 94105
Phone: 877-473-4636
Fax: 415-808-2302
Email: scholar1@hsf.net
Website: http://www.hsf.net
Purpose: To support students of Hispanic heritage who plan to transfer from a community college program to a four-year college or university.
Eligibility: Applicants must be of Hispanic heritage (one parent fully Hispanic or each parent half-Hispanic) and be a part-time or full-time community college student with a minimum 3.0 GPA. Applicants must plan to transfer to a four-year college or university the following academic year.
Target applicant:
   College students
   Adult students
Minimum GPA: 3.0
Amount: $1,000-$2,500.
Number of awards: Varies.
Deadline: January 2.
How to apply: Applications are available online.

(2247) · Community College Transfer Scholarships

Sallie Mae Fund
12061 Bluemont Way
Reston, VA 20190
Phone: 703-810-3000
Website: http://www.thesalliemaefund.org
Purpose: To help Hispanic students attending community college attend a four-year college.
Eligibility: Applicants must be Hispanic, apply for federal financial aid and be part-time or full-time community college students. Applicants must also intend to be full-time students at a four-year college.
Target applicant:
   College students
   Adult students
Minimum GPA: 3.0
Amount: $1,000-$2,500.
Number of awards: Varies.
Deadline: February 1.
How to apply: Applications are available online.

(2248) · Consortium Fellowship

Consortium for Graduate Study in Management
5585 Pershing
Suite 240
St. Louis, MO 63112-4621
Phone: 314-877-5500
Email: frontdesk@cgsm.org
Website: http://www.cgsm.org
Purpose: To support graduate business students at member schools.

Eligibility: Applicants must be African Americans, Hispanic Americans or Native Americans and U.S. citizens and U.S. permanent residents of other races and ethnicities who fulfill the Consortium's mission. Applicants must have a bachelor's degree, and the degree may be in any academic discipline from an accredited institution recognized by Consortium member schools. The fellowship supports full-time graduate business studies at member schools only. Applicants must submit two references, transcripts, copies of GMAT scores and application fees. All applicants must also interview with a Consortium representative. It is highly recommended that you research the scholarship and awarding organization before applying for a scholarship with a fee. There are many scholarships that do not require a fee.

Target applicant:
    Graduate school students
    Adult students
Minimum GPA: None.
Amount: Varies.
Number of awards: Varies.
Deadline: January 15.
How to apply: Applications are available online.

(2249) · Continuing Education Award

Slovenian Women's Union of America
Mary Turvey, SWUA Scholarship Director
52 Oakridge Drive
Marquette, MI 49855
Email: mturvey@aol.com
Website: http://www.swua.org
Purpose: To promote Slovenian culture.
Eligibility: Applicants must be returning to an accredited college in the fall as full- or part-time students and must have been a member of the SWUA for at least three years or an active participant. Students must include a photograph, resume, FAFSA, income tax return and a letter of recommendation from their SWU branch president or secretary. The awards committee considers life goals and involvement in school, church and community.
Target applicant:
    College students
    Graduate school students
    Adult students
Minimum GPA: None.
Amount: $500.
Number of awards: Varies.
Deadline: March 1.
How to apply: Applications are available online and from SWUA branch secretaries.

(2250) · CosmoGirl! Of The Year Award

CosmoGirl!
300 W. 57th Street
20th Floor
New York, NY 10019
Email: cgoftheyear@cosmogirl.com
Website: http://www.cosmogirl.com
Purpose: To recognize girls and young women who have made contributions to the world.
Eligibility: Applicants must be age 11 to 25 and send an essay of up to 300 words about how they are a CosmoGirl along with a photo of themselves. Only females from the U.S. and Canada may enter. In addition to the monetary prize, the winner receives a trip to New York City to the awards ceremony.

Target applicant:
    Junior high students or younger
    High school students
    College students
    Graduate school students
Minimum GPA: None.
Amount: $20,000.
Number of awards: 1.
Deadline: July 26.
How to apply: Applications are available online. Applications may be sent by postal mail or through an email instead of an online application. Applicants who are 11 and 12 must enter by postal mail.

(2251) · Coy G. Eklund Scholarship

United Negro College Fund (UNCF)
8260 Willow Oaks Corporate Drive
P.O. Box 10444
Fairfax, VA 22031-8044
Phone: 800-331-2244
Website: http://www.uncf.org
Purpose: To help African Americans majoring in business at United Negro College Fund (UNCF) Member Colleges and Universities.
Eligibility: Applicants must have a minimum 2.5 GPA, complete the Free Application for Federal Student Aid (FAFSA) and have unmet financial need that is verified by the college or university financial aid office. UNCF students are encouraged to complete the UNCF General Scholarship application to be matched with scholarships for which they meet the criteria.
Target applicant:
    High school students
    College students
    Adult students
Minimum GPA: 2.5
Amount: Varies.
Number of awards: Varies.
Deadline: Varies.
How to apply: Applications are available online.

(2252) · Darden Restaurants Hallmark Scholarship

US Pan Asian American Chamber of Commerce
13229 18th Street NW
Washington, DC 20036
Phone: 800-696-7818
Fax: 202-296-5225
Email: info@uspaac.com
Website: http://www.uspaacc.com/web/programs/scholarship_programs.htm
Purpose: To provide financial assistance to Asian-American students.
Eligibility: Applicants must be high school seniors of Asian or Pacific heritage who are at least 16 years of age. They must be U.S. citizens or permanent residents and plan to enroll full-time in an accredited U.S. college or university in the fall following graduation. A GPA of 3.3 or higher is required, and applicants should demonstrate academic excellence, leadership, community service involvement and financial need.
Target applicant:
    High school students
Minimum GPA: 3.3
Amount: Up to $5,000.
Number of awards: Varies.
Deadline: February 28.
How to apply: Applications are available online.

(2253) · David Risling Emergency Aid Scholarship

Association on American Indian Affairs
Lisa Wyzlic, Scholarship Coordinator
966 Hungerford Drive, Suite 12-B
Rockville, MD 20850
Phone: 240-314-7155
Fax: 240-314-7159
Email: general.aaia@verizon.net
Website: http://www.indian-affairs.org
Purpose: To provide emergency financial assistance to Native Americans who face temporary circumstances which would prevent them from going to school.
Eligibility: Applicants must be full-time students in the continental U.S. or Alaska, and they must not be in a technical, trade or seminary program.
Target applicant:
   College students
   Adult students
Minimum GPA: None.
Amount: Up to $400.
Number of awards: Varies.
Deadline: Varies.
How to apply: Applications are available online.

(2254) · Displaced Homemaker Scholarship

Association on American Indian Affairs
Lisa Wyzlic, Scholarship Coordinator
966 Hungerford Drive, Suite 12-B
Rockville, MD 20850
Phone: 240-314-7155
Fax: 240-314-7159
Email: general.aaia@verizon.net
Website: http://www.indian-affairs.org
Purpose: To provide financial assistance toward child care, transportation, living expenses or educational costs for men and women who would be unable to attend college due to family responsibilities.
Eligibility: Applicants must be full-time students able to prove financial need, proof of tribal enrollment and Certificate of Indian Blood (showing 1/4 Indian blood).
Target applicant:
   College students
   Graduate school students
   Adult students
Minimum GPA: None.
Amount: $1,000.
Number of awards: Varies.
Deadline: July 20.
How to apply: Applications are available online.

(2255) · Donald Malcolm MacArthur Scholarship

St. Andrew's Society of Washington, DC
Charity and Education Committee
P.O. Box 372
Glen Echo, MD 20812
Email: secretary@saintandrewsociety.com
Website: http://www.saintandrewsociety.com
Purpose: To encourage foster study between the U.S. and Scotland, monies are awarded to third and fourth year college students and full-time graduate students who are either Scots wishing to study in the U.S. or U.S. students intending to study in Scotland.

Eligibility: Eligible U.S. candidates must live or attend school within a 200 mile radius of Washington, DC and be of Scottish descent.
Target applicant:
   College students
   Graduate school students
   Adult students
Minimum GPA: None.
Amount: $2,500.
Number of awards: Varies.
Deadline: April 30.
How to apply: Applications are available online.

(2256) · Doris and John Carpenter Scholarship

United Negro College Fund (UNCF)
8260 Willow Oaks Corporate Drive
P.O. Box 10444
Fairfax, VA 22031-8044
Phone: 800-331-2244
Website: http://www.uncf.org
Purpose: To help African Americans with the most financial need.
Eligibility: Applicants must be freshmen at United Negro College Fund (UNCF) member colleges or universities and must have a minimum 2.5 GPA.
Target applicant:
   High school students
Minimum GPA: 2.5
Amount: $2,000-$5,000.
Number of awards: Varies.
Deadline: Varies.
How to apply: Applications are available online.

(2257) · Dorothy N. McNeal Scholarship

United Negro College Fund (UNCF)
8260 Willow Oaks Corporate Drive
P.O. Box 10444
Fairfax, VA 22031-8044
Phone: 800-331-2244
Website: http://www.uncf.org
Purpose: To support students interested in pursuing community service careers.
Eligibility: Applicants must be African American students attending a UNCF member college or university with a GPA of at least 2.5. Students must complete the Free Application for Federal Student Aid (FAFSA) and have unmet financial need that is verified by the college or university financial aid office. Applicants are encouraged to complete the UNCF General Scholarship application to be matched with scholarships for which they meet the criteria.
Target applicant:
   High school students
   College students
   Adult students
Minimum GPA: 2.5
Amount: Varies.
Number of awards: Varies.
Deadline: Varies.
How to apply: Applications are available online.

(2258) · Dr. James M. Rosin Scholarship

United Negro College Fund (UNCF)
8260 Willow Oaks Corporate Drive

P.O. Box 10444
Fairfax, VA 22031-8044
Phone: 800-331-2244
Website: http://www.uncf.org
Purpose: To help African American students pursuing bachelor's degrees in the health sciences and who plan for careers in the health sciences field.
Eligibility: Applicants must have a minimum 3.0 GPA, complete the Free Application for Federal Student Aid (FAFSA) and have unmet financial need that is verified by the college or university financial aid office. UNCF students are encouraged to complete the UNCF General Scholarship application to be matched with scholarships for which they meet the criteria. Applicants must show dedication to personal growth, helping others and education.
Target applicant:
   High school students
   College students
   Adult students
Minimum GPA: 3.0
Amount: $5,000.
Number of awards: 1.
Deadline: Varies.
How to apply: Applications are available online.

(2259) · Dr. Joe Ratliff Challenge

United Negro College Fund (UNCF)
8260 Willow Oaks Corporate Drive
P.O. Box 10444
Fairfax, VA 22031-8044
Phone: 800-331-2244
Website: http://www.uncf.org
Purpose: To help African American students attending United Negro College Fund (UNCF) Member Colleges and Universities and majoring in religion.
Eligibility: Applicants must have a minimum 2.5 GPA, complete the Free Application for Federal Student Aid (FAFSA) and have unmet financial need that is verified by the college or university financial aid office. Students are encouraged to complete the UNCF General Scholarship application to be matched with scholarships for which they meet the criteria.
Target applicant:
   High school students
   College students
   Adult students
Minimum GPA: 2.5
Amount: Up to $3,000.
Number of awards: Varies.
Deadline: Varies.
How to apply: Applications are available online.

(2260) · Dr. Richard Chinn Scholarship

American Atheists
P.O. Box 5733
Parsippany, NJ 07054
Phone: 908-276-7300
Fax: 908-276-7402
Email: info@athiests.org
Website: http://www.atheists.org
Purpose: To provide educational assistance to gay and lesbian atheists.

Eligibility: Applicants must be current college students or high school students who will be entering college the following academic year. They must be Atheists with a GPA of 2.5 or higher. Membership in American Atheists Inc. is required to accept the prize but not to apply.
Target applicant:
   High school students
   College students
   Adult students
Minimum GPA: 2.5
Amount: $1,000.
Number of awards: 1.
Deadline: February 28.
How to apply: Applications are available online.

(2261) · Dr. Scholl Foundation Scholarship

United Negro College Fund (UNCF)
8260 Willow Oaks Corporate Drive
P.O. Box 10444
Fairfax, VA 22031-8044
Phone: 800-331-2244
Website: http://www.uncf.org
Purpose: To help African American students attending United Negro College Fund (UNCF) member colleges and universities.
Eligibility: Applicants must have a minimum 2.5 GPA, complete the Free Application for Federal Student Aid (FAFSA) and have unmet financial need that is verified by the college or university financial aid office. Students are encouraged to complete the UNCF General Scholarship application to be matched with scholarships for which they meet the criteria.
Target applicant:
   High school students
   College students
   Adult students
Minimum GPA: 2.5
Amount: Varies.
Number of awards: Varies.
Deadline: Varies.
How to apply: Applications are available online.

(2262) · Drs. Poh Shien and Judy Young Scholarship

U.S. Pan Asian American Chamber of Commerce
1329 18th Street NW
Washington, DC 20036
Phone: 800-696-7818
Fax: 202-296-5225
Email: info@uspaacc.com
Website: http://www.uspaacc.com
Purpose: To support the higher education goals of Asian American students.
Eligibility: Applicants must be U.S. citizens or permanent residents and be high school seniors of Asian or Pacific Heritage who will pursue post-secondary educations at an accredited institution in the U.S. Selection is based on academic excellence, leadership in extracurricular activities, community service involvement and financial need. Minimum 3.5 GPA required. Applicants must be able to attend the Excellence Awards and Scholarships Dinner during the CelebrAsian Annual Conference (in May).
Target applicant:
   High school students
Minimum GPA: 3.5
Amount: Up to $4,000.

Number of awards: 1.
Deadline: February 22.
How to apply: Applications are available online.

(2263) · Earl and Patricia Armstrong Scholarship

United Negro College Fund (UNCF)
8260 Willow Oaks Corporate Drive
P.O. Box 10444
Fairfax, VA 22031-8044
Phone: 800-331-2244
Website: http://www.uncf.org
Purpose: To promote the health sciences among African American students.
Eligibility: Applicants must major in pre-medicine, biology or health, have a minimum 3.0 GPA, complete the Free Application for Federal Student Aid (FAFSA) and have unmet financial need that is verified by the college or university financial aid office. UNCF students are encouraged to complete the UNCF General Scholarship application to be matched with scholarships for which they meet the criteria.
Target applicant:
　High school students
　College students
　Adult students
Minimum GPA: 3.0
Amount: Up to $3,000.
Number of awards: 1.
Deadline: Varies.
How to apply: Applications are available online.

(2264) · Earl Graves Scholarship

National Association for the Advancement of Colored People
The United Negro College Fund
Scholarships and Grants Administration
8260 Willow Oaks Corporate Drive
Fairfax, VA 22031
Phone: 703-205-3400
Website: http://www.naacp.org
Purpose: The NAACP created its scholarships to promote equal opportunity in education.
Eligibility: Applicants must be junior or senior business majors or accepted into a business master's or doctoral program at an accredited U.S. college or university, in the top 20 percent of their class and attend school full-time.
Target applicant:
　College students
　Graduate school students
　Adult students
Minimum GPA: None.
Amount: $5,000.
Number of awards: Varies.
Deadline: The last Friday in the month of March.
How to apply: Applications are available online and by written request.

(2265) · Edward and Hazel Stephenson Scholarship

United Negro College Fund (UNCF)
8260 Willow Oaks Corporate Drive
P.O. Box 10444
Fairfax, VA 22031-8044

Phone: 800-331-2244
Website: http://www.uncf.org
Purpose: To help African American seniors at United Negro College Fund (UNCF) member colleges or universities.
Eligibility: Applicants must have a minimum 2.5 GPA, complete the Free Application for Federal Student Aid (FAFSA) and have unmet financial need that is verified by the college or university financial aid office. Students are encouraged to complete the UNCF General Scholarship application to be matched with scholarships for which they meet the criteria.
Target applicant:
　College students
　Adult students
Minimum GPA: 2.5
Amount: $1,000-$3,000.
Number of awards: Varies.
Deadline: Varies.
How to apply: Applications are available online.

(2266) · Edward D. Grigg Scholarship

United Negro College Fund (UNCF)
8260 Willow Oaks Corporate Drive
P.O. Box 10444
Fairfax, VA 22031-8044
Phone: 800-331-2244
Website: http://www.uncf.org
Purpose: To support needy African American students.
Eligibility: Applicants must have a minimum 2.5 GPA, complete the Free Application for Federal Student Aid (FAFSA) and have unmet financial need that is verified by the college or university financial aid office. Applicants must be UNCF students and are encouraged to complete the UNCF General Scholarship application to be matched with scholarships for which they meet the criteria.
Target applicant:
　High school students
　College students
　Adult students
Minimum GPA: 2.5
Amount: Varies.
Number of awards: Varies.
Deadline: Varies.
How to apply: Applications are available online.

(2267) · Edward N. Ney Scholarship

United Negro College Fund (UNCF)
8260 Willow Oaks Corporate Drive
P.O. Box 10444
Fairfax, VA 22031-8044
Phone: 800-331-2244
Website: http://www.uncf.org
Purpose: To support African American students at UNCF member schools.
Eligibility: Applicants must have a minimum 3.5 GPA, complete the Free Application for Federal Student Aid (FAFSA) and have unmet financial need that is verified by the college or university financial aid office. Students are encouraged to complete the UNCF General Scholarship application to be matched with scholarships for which they meet the criteria.

Target applicant:
  High school students
  College students
  Adult students
Minimum GPA: 3.5
Amount: Varies.
Number of awards: Varies.
Deadline: Varies.
How to apply: Applications are available online.

(2268) · Elizabeth and Sherman Asche Memorial Scholarship

Association on American Indian Affairs
Lisa Wyzlic, Scholarship Coordinator
966 Hungerford Drive, Suite 12-B
Rockville, MD 20850
Phone: 240-314-7155
Fax: 240-314-7159
Email: general.aaia@verizon.net
Website: http://www.indian-affairs.org
Purpose: To provide financial assistance to American Indians who are seeking undergraduate or graduate degrees in public health or science.
Eligibility: Applicants must be American Indians who are studying full-time in public health or science programs. They must be full-time students and must not be enrolled in a technical or trade program or seminary. The scholarship is open to undergraduate and graduate students.
Target applicant:
  High school students
  College students
  Graduate school students
  Adult students
Minimum GPA: None.
Amount: $1,500.
Number of awards: 6.
Deadline: July 1.
How to apply: Applications are available online.

(2269) · Ella Fitzgerald Charitable Foundation Scholarship

United Negro College Fund (UNCF)
8260 Willow Oaks Corporate Drive
P.O. Box 10444
Fairfax, VA 22031-8044
Phone: 800-331-2244
Website: http://www.uncf.org
Purpose: To support music students as a testament to Ella Fitzgerald's love of music.
Eligibility: Applicants must be African American students majoring in music with a minimum 2.5 GPA. Students must attend a UNCF member college or university and demonstrate financial need.
Target applicant:
  High school students
  College students
  Adult students
Minimum GPA: 2.5
Amount: Varies.
Number of awards: Varies.
Deadline: Varies.
How to apply: Applications are available online.

(2270) · Emilie Hesemeyer Memorial Scholarship

Association on American Indian Affairs
Lisa Wyzlic, Scholarship Coordinator
966 Hungerford Drive, Suite 12-B
Rockville, MD 20850
Phone: 240-314-7155
Fax: 240-314-7159
Email: general.aaia@verizon.net
Website: http://www.indian-affairs.org
Purpose: To provide financial assistance to Native Americans, especially those who are studying education.
Eligibility: Applicants must be Native Americans who are full-time students from the continental U.S. or Alaska. Preference is given to those who are studying education.
Target applicant:
  High school students
  College students
  Adult students
Minimum GPA: None.
Amount: $1,500.
Number of awards: Varies.
Scholarship may be renewable.
Deadline: July 1.
How to apply: Applications are available online.

(2271) · Eunice Walker Johnson Endowed Scholarship

United Negro College Fund (UNCF)
8260 Willow Oaks Corporate Drive
P.O. Box 10444
Fairfax, VA 22031-8044
Phone: 800-331-2244
Website: http://www.uncf.org
Purpose: To assist African American students attending UNCF member colleges or universities or Selma University.
Eligibility: Applicants must have a minimum 3.0 GPA, complete the Free Application for Federal Student Aid (FAFSA) and have unmet financial need that is verified by the college or university financial aid office. UNCF students are encouraged to complete the UNCF General Scholarship application to be matched with scholarships for which they meet the criteria.
Target applicant:
  High school students
  College students
  Adult students
Minimum GPA: 3.0
Amount: $2,000-$5,000.
Number of awards: Varies.
Deadline: Varies.
How to apply: Applications are available online.

(2272) · Explorations Summer Research Fellowships

American Physiological Society
Education Office
9650 Rockville Pike
Bethesda, MD 20814-3991
Phone: 301-634-7787
Fax: 301-634-7241
Email: education@the-aps.org
Website: http://www.the-aps.org

Purpose: To support undergraduate Native American students in summer research programs focusing on biomedical research and physiology.

Eligibility: Applicants must be Native American undergraduate students with little or no research experience in life sciences or physiology not including coursework. Students have the opportunity to participate in a major scientific meeting.

Target applicant:
College students
Adult students

Minimum GPA: None.

Amount: Up to $4,000, plus living and travel expenses.

Number of awards: Varies.

Deadline: February 3.

How to apply: Applications are available online.

(2273) · Fannie Mae Foundation Scholarship

United Negro College Fund (UNCF)
8260 Willow Oaks Corporate Drive
P.O. Box 10444
Fairfax, VA 22031-8044
Phone: 800-331-2244
Website: http://www.uncf.org

Purpose: To help African American rising juniors planning careers in the fields of housing and community development.

Eligibility: Applicants must be full-time students attending Benedict College, Bethune-Cookman College, Johnson C. Smith University, LeMoyne-Owen College or United Negro College Fund (UNCF) Member Colleges and Universities. Students should have community development/community service experience, financial need and a minimum 3.0 GPA. Applicants must also submit transcripts, essays, two recommendation letters and small photos.

Target applicant:
College students
Adult students

Minimum GPA: 3.0

Amount: Varies.

Number of awards: 12.

Deadline: November 5.

How to apply: Applications are available online.

(2274) · Fedex Hallmark Scholarship

US Pan Asian American Chamber of Commerce
13229 18th Street NW
Washington, DC 20036
Phone: 800-696-7818
Fax: 202-296-5225
Email: info@uspaac.com
Website: http://www.uspaacc.com/web/programs/scholarship_programs.htm

Purpose: To provide financial assistance to Asian American students.

Eligibility: Applicants must be high school seniors at least 16 years of age who are of Asian or Pacific heritage. They must be U.S. citizens or permanent residents and plan to enroll full-time at an accredited college or university in the United States in the fall following graduation. A minimum GPA of 3.3 is required, and applicants should demonstrate academic excellence, leadership, community service involvement and financial need.

Target applicant:
High school students

Minimum GPA: 3.3

Amount: Up to $5,000.

Number of awards: 1.

Deadline: Varies.

How to apply: Applications are available online.

(2275) · Financial Services Institution

United Negro College Fund (UNCF)
8260 Willow Oaks Corporate Drive
P.O. Box 10444
Fairfax, VA 22031-8044
Phone: 800-331-2244
Website: http://www.uncf.org

Purpose: To help African Americans majoring in Finance at United Negro College Fund (UNCF) Member Colleges and Universities.

Eligibility: Applicants must have a minimum 2.5 GPA, complete the Free Application for Federal Student Aid (FAFSA) and have unmet financial need that is verified by the college or university financial aid office. UNCF students are encouraged to complete the UNCF General Scholarship application to be matched with scholarships for which they meet the criteria.

Target applicant:
High school students
College students
Adult students

Minimum GPA: 2.5

Amount: Varies.

Number of awards: Varies.

Deadline: Varies.

How to apply: Applications are available online.

(2276) · First in My Family Scholarship

Sallie Mae Fund
12061 Bluemont Way
Reston, VA 20190
Phone: 703-810-3000
Website: http://www.thesalliemaefund.org

Purpose: To award Hispanic students who are the first in their family to go to college based on academic merit and financial need.

Eligibility: Applicants must be Hispanic full-time undergraduate students studying in the U.S. or Puerto Rico and have financial need. Qualified applicants need to write an essay and send a recommendation letter, financial verification form, transcript and proof of citizenship.

Target applicant:
College students
Adult students

Minimum GPA: 3.0

Amount: $500-$5,000.

Number of awards: Varies.

Deadline: April 15.

How to apply: Applications are available online.

(2277) · Florence Young Memorial Scholarship

Association on American Indian Affairs
Lisa Wyzlic, Scholarship Coordinator
966 Hungerford Drive, Suite 12-B
Rockville, MD 20850
Phone: 240-314-7155
Fax: 240-314-7159
Email: general.aaia@verizon.net
Website: http://www.indian-affairs.org

Purpose: To provide financial assistance to Native Americans who are working toward a master's degree in art, public health or law.
Eligibility: Applicants must be full-time students from the continental U.S. or Alaska.
Target applicant:
  Graduate school students
  Adult students
Minimum GPA: None.
Amount: $1,500.
Number of awards: Varies.
Deadline: July 1.
How to apply: Applications are available online.

(2278) · Forum for Concerns of Minorities Scholarship

American Society for Clinical Laboratory Science
6701 Democracy Boulevard, Suite 300
Bethesda, MD 20817
Phone: 301-657-2768
Fax: 301-657-2909
Email: ascls@ascls.org
Website: http://www.ascls.org
Purpose: To assist minority students in becoming clinical laboratory scientists and clinical laboratory technicians.
Eligibility: Applicants must be minority students accepted to an NAACLS-accredited Clinical Laboratory Science/Medical Technology program or a Clinical Laboratory Technician/Medical Laboratory Technician program. They must also demonstrate financial need.
Target applicant:
  High school students
  College students
  Graduate school students
  Adult students
Minimum GPA: None.
Amount: Varies.
Number of awards: 2.
Deadline: April 1.
How to apply: Applications are available online.

(2279) · Foundation Scholarships

CIRI Foundation
3600 San Jeronimo Drive
Suite 256
Anchorage, AK 99508-2870
Phone: 800-764-3382
Fax: 907-793-3585
Email: tcf@thecirifoundation.org
Website: http://www.thecirifoundation.org
Purpose: To provide financial aid for Alaska Natives.
Eligibility: Applicants must be qualified Alaska Native beneficiaries who plan to attend or are currently attending undergraduate or graduate institutions. There are a number of awards based on field of study or career goal. Applicants must submit applications, proof of eligibility, reference letter, transcripts, purpose statements and proof of enrollment.
Target applicant:
  High school students
  College students
  Graduate school students
  Adult students
Minimum GPA: None.
Amount: $500-$20,000.

Number of awards: Varies.
Scholarship may be renewable.
Deadline: Varies.
How to apply: Applications are available online.

(2280) · Frances Crawford Marvin American Indian Scholarship

National Society Daughters of the American Revolution
1776 D Street NW
Washington, DC 20006-5303
Phone: 202-628-1776
Website: http://www.dar.org
Purpose: To assist Native American students.
Eligibility: Applicants must be Native Americans able to prove Native American blood, demonstrate financial need and academic achievement, be enrolled full-time at a college or university and have a minimum 3.0 GPA.
Target applicant:
  College students
  Graduate school students
  Adult students
Minimum GPA: 3.0
Amount: Varies.
Number of awards: 1.
Deadline: February 1.
How to apply: Applications are available by written request.

(2281) · Frederick D. Patterson Scholarship

United Negro College Fund (UNCF)
8260 Willow Oaks Corporate Drive
P.O. Box 10444
Fairfax, VA 22031-8044
Phone: 800-331-2244
Website: http://www.uncf.org
Purpose: To help African Americans attending United Negro College Fund (UNCF) Member Colleges and Universities.
Eligibility: Applicants must have a minimum 2.5 GPA, complete the Free Application for Federal Student Aid (FAFSA) and have unmet financial need that is verified by the college or university financial aid office. Students are encouraged to complete the UNCF General Scholarship application to be matched with scholarships for which they meet the criteria.
Target applicant:
  High school students
  College students
  Adult students
Minimum GPA: 2.5
Amount: Varies.
Number of awards: Varies.
Deadline: Varies.
How to apply: Applications are available online.

(2282) · GAP Foundation Scholarship

United Negro College Fund (UNCF)
8260 Willow Oaks Corporate Drive
P.O. Box 10444
Fairfax, VA 22031-8044
Phone: 800-331-2244
Website: http://www.uncf.org
Purpose: To support future retailers and fashion designers.

Eligibility: Applicants must be African American sophomores or juniors attending a UNCF member college or university, majoring in business, fashion design, merchandise management or retail management. Applicants must have a GPA of at least 3.0 and demonstrate financial need.

Target applicant:
    College students
    Adult students
Minimum GPA: 3.0
Amount: Up to $5,000.
Number of awards: Varies.
Deadline: January 12.
How to apply: Applications are available online.

(2283) · GAPA's George Choy Memorial Scholarship

Horizons Foundation
870 Market Street
Suite 728
San Francisco, CA 94102
Phone: 415-398-2333
Fax: 415-398-4733
Email: info@horizonsfoundation.org
Website: http://www.horizonsfoundation.org
Purpose: To assist Bay Area gay, lesbian, bisexual and transgender Asian and Pacific Islander graduating high school students.
Eligibility: Applicants should have at least 25 percent Asian/Pacific Islander ancestry, plan to attend or currently attend a post-secondary institution as a freshman or sophomore and reside in one of the nine Bay Area counties (Alameda, Contra Costa, Marin, San Francisco, San Mateo, Santa Clara, Napa, Sonoma or Solano). Preference is given to those who are lesbian, gay, bisexual or transgender or who are involved in the LGBT community.
Target applicant:
    High school students
    College students
    Adult students
Minimum GPA: 2.75
Amount: $1,000.
Number of awards: Varies.
Deadline: Varies.
How to apply: Applications are available by phone.

(2284) · Gates Millennium Scholars Program

Gates Foundation
P.O. Box 10500
Fairfax, VA 22031
Phone: 877-690-4677
Website: http://www.gmsp.org
Purpose: To provide outstanding minority students with opportunities to complete their undergraduate college educations.
Eligibility: Applicants must be African American, American Indian/Alaska Native, Asian Pacific Islander American or Hispanic American students with a minimum 3.3 GPA, enter an accredited college or university and have significant financial need. Applicants must also be eligible for federal Pell Grants.
Target applicant:
    High school students
Minimum GPA: 3.3
Amount: Varies.
Number of awards: 1000.

Deadline: January 12.
How to apply: Students are nominated by teachers, principals or other education professionals. Nomination materials are available online.

(2285) · GEM Fellowship Program

National Consortium for Graduate Degrees for Minorities in Engineering and Science Inc. (GEM)
GEM Consortium
P.O. Box 537
Notre Dame, IN 46556
Phone: 574-631-7771
Fax: 574-287-1486
Website: http://www.gemfellowship.org
Purpose: To provide fellowships for minority students pursuing graduate degrees in engineering, physical science or natural science.
Eligibility: Applicants must be college sophomore, junior or senior or graduate student majors in engineering, physical science or natural science and be members of one of the following minority groups: African American, Native American or Puerto Rican, Latino or other Hispanic American.
Target applicant:
    College students
    Graduate school students
    Adult students
Minimum GPA: None.
Amount: Varies.
Number of awards: Varies.
Deadline: November 1.
How to apply: Applications are available online.

(2286) · Gena Wright Memorial Scholarship

United Negro College Fund (UNCF)
8260 Willow Oaks Corporate Drive
P.O. Box 10444
Fairfax, VA 22031-8044
Phone: 800-331-2244
Website: http://www.uncf.org
Purpose: To support students interested in working with children.
Eligibility: Applicants must be African American students interested in working with children. They must attend a UNCF member college or university, have a GPA of at least 3.0 and demonstrate financial need.
Target applicant:
    High school students
    College students
    Adult students
Minimum GPA: 3.0
Amount: Varies.
Number of awards: 2.
Deadline: Varies.
How to apply: Applications are available online.

(2287) · General Mills Technology Scholars Award

United Negro College Fund (UNCF)
8260 Willow Oaks Corporate Drive
P.O. Box 10444
Fairfax, VA 22031-8044
Phone: 800-331-2244
Website: http://www.uncf.org
Purpose: To recognize outstanding students in technology-related fields.

Eligibility: Applicants must be African American undergraduate students majoring in engineering, information systems, computer science/MIS, computer science, food service, information technology or management information systems. They must have a GPA of at least 3.0 and demonstrate financial need. Academics, career aspirations, leadership and achievement will be considered in awarding the scholarship.

Target applicant:
   College students
   Adult students

Minimum GPA: 3.0

Amount: $5,000.

Number of awards: 1.

Deadline: March 15.

How to apply: Applications are available online.

(2288) · General Motors Engineering Scholarship

American Indian Science and Engineering Society

P.O. Box 9828

Albuquerque, NM 87119-9828

Phone: 505-765-1052

Fax: 505-765-5608

Website: http://www.aises.org

Purpose: To provide scholarships for members of AISES who are American Indian or Alaskan Native and who are pursuing undergraduate or graduate degrees in engineering.

Eligibility: Applicants must be full-time undergraduate or graduate students at an accredited college or university, members of an American Indian tribe or Alaskan Native and members of AISES. Preference is given to those majoring in electrical, industrial or mechanical engineering.

Target applicant:
   College students
   Graduate school students
   Adult students

Minimum GPA: 3.0

Amount: $3,000.

Number of awards: Varies.

Deadline: June 15.

How to apply: Applications are available online.

(2289) · Gerald W. and Jean Purmal Endowed Scholarship

United Negro College Fund (UNCF)

8260 Willow Oaks Corporate Drive

P.O. Box 10444

Fairfax, VA 22031-8044

Phone: 800-331-2244

Website: http://www.uncf.org

Purpose: To help African Americans attending United Negro College Fund (UNCF) Member Colleges and Universities.

Eligibility: Applicants must have a minimum 2.5 GPA, complete the Free Application for Federal Student Aid (FAFSA) and have unmet financial need that is verified by the college or university financial aid office. Students are encouraged to complete the UNCF General Scholarship application to be matched with scholarships for which they meet the criteria.

Target applicant:
   High school students
   College students
   Adult students

Minimum GPA: 2.5

Amount: $1,000-$4,000.

Number of awards: Varies.

Deadline: Varies.

How to apply: Applications are available online.

(2290) · Gillette/National Urban League Scholarship and Intern Program for Minority Students

National Urban League

120 Wall Street

New York, NY 10005

Phone: 888-839-0467

Email: info@nul.org

Website: http://www.nul.org

Purpose: To recognize outstanding undergraduates majoring in engineering and business fields.

Eligibility: Applicants must be African American undergraduate juniors studying engineering, marketing, manufacturing operations, finance, business administration or human resource management or related fields. Applicants must be in the top 25 percent of their class and must show proof of work experience, extracurricular activities, leadership skills and volunteer work.

Target applicant:
   College students
   Adult students

Minimum GPA: None.

Amount: $5,000.

Number of awards: Varies.

Scholarship may be renewable.

Deadline: January 15.

How to apply: Applications are available by request.

(2291) · GlaxoSmithKline Company Science Achievement Award

United Negro College Fund (UNCF)

8260 Willow Oaks Corporate Drive

P.O. Box 10444

Fairfax, VA 22031-8044

Phone: 800-331-2244

Website: http://www.uncf.org

Purpose: To support graduate-level science students.

Eligibility: Applicants must be African American graduates of a UNCF member college with a science-related degree pursuing a graduate degree in science. They must have a GPA of at least 3.0 and demonstrate financial need.

Target applicant:
   Graduate school students
   Adult students

Minimum GPA: 3.0

Amount: $3,000.

Number of awards: 4.

Deadline: February 8.

How to apply: Applications are available online.

(2292) · Goodyear Tire and Rubber Company Scholarships

Brown Foundation for Educational Equity, Excellence and Research

P.O. Box 4862

Topeka, KS 66604

Website: www.brownvboard.org/foundation/scholarships/goodyear

Purpose: To provide financial assistance to minority education majors.

Eligibility: Applicants must be high school seniors or college juniors who are enrolled in or plan to enroll in an institution of higher learning in an accredited education program. They must enroll at least half-time and have a GPA of 3.0 or higher. Two recommendations are required.

Target applicant:
 High school students
 College students
 Adult students

Minimum GPA: 3.0

Amount: Up to $1,000.

Number of awards: Varies.

Scholarship may be renewable.

Deadline: April 1.

How to apply: Applications are available from your high school counselor, financial aid office or the Brown Foundation.

(2293) · Google Scholarship

United Negro College Fund (UNCF)
8260 Willow Oaks Corporate Drive
P.O. Box 10444
Fairfax, VA 22031-8044
Phone: 800-331-2244
Website: http://www.uncf.org

Purpose: To encourage diversity in the computer field.

Eligibility: Applicants must be African American students who are juniors at a UNCF member school or HBCU. They must be computer science or computer engineering majors with a GPA of at least 3.5 and demonstrate financial need.

Target applicant:
 College students
 Adult students

Minimum GPA: 3.5

Amount: $5,000.

Number of awards: Varies.

Deadline: October 6.

How to apply: Applications are available online.

(2294) · Hagiwara Student Aid Award

Japanese American Citizens League (JACL)
National Scholarship Awards
1765 Sutter Street
San Francisco, CA 94115
Phone: 415-921-5225
Email: jacl@jacl.org
Website: http://www.jacl.org

Purpose: To aid students who otherwise would have to delay or terminate their education due to lack of financing.

Eligibility: Applicants must be National JACL members and must be attending a college, university, trade school, business school or any other institution of higher learning. A personal statement, letter of recommendation, academic performance, work experience and community involvement are considered. Applicants should have extreme financial need.

Target applicant:
 College students
 Graduate school students
 Adult students

Minimum GPA: None.

Amount: Varies.

Number of awards: Varies.

Deadline: April 1.

How to apply: Applications are available online.

(2295) · Harry C. Jaecker Scholarship

United Negro College Fund (UNCF)
8260 Willow Oaks Corporate Drive
P.O. Box 10444
Fairfax, VA 22031-8044
Phone: 800-331-2244
Website: http://www.uncf.org

Purpose: To assist pre-medical students attending a UNCF member school.

Eligibility: Applicants must be African American, have a minimum 2.5 GPA, complete the Free Application for Federal Student Aid (FAFSA) and have unmet financial need that is verified by the college or university financial aid office. Students are encouraged to complete the UNCF General Scholarship application to be matched with scholarships for which they meet the criteria.

Target applicant:
 High school students
 College students
 Adult students

Minimum GPA: 2.5

Amount: $2,000-$5,000.

Number of awards: Varies.

Deadline: Varies.

How to apply: Applications are available online.

(2296) · Harvey H. and Catherine A. Moses Scholarship

United Negro College Fund (UNCF)
8260 Willow Oaks Corporate Drive
P.O. Box 10444
Fairfax, VA 22031-8044
Phone: 800-331-2244
Website: http://www.uncf.org

Purpose: To support African American students at UNCF member schools.

Eligibility: Applicants must have a minimum 2.5 GPA, complete the Free Application for Federal Student Aid (FAFSA) and have unmet financial need that is verified by the college or university financial aid office. UNCF students are encouraged to complete the UNCF General Scholarship application to be matched with scholarships for which they meet the criteria.

Target applicant:
 High school students
 College students
 Adult students

Minimum GPA: 2.5

Amount: Varies.

Number of awards: Varies.

Deadline: Varies.

How to apply: Applications are available online.

(2297) · Hawaiian Homes Commission Scholarship

Hawaii Community Foundation - Scholarships
1164 Bishop Street, Suite 800
Honolulu, HI 96813
Phone: 888-731-3863
Fax: 808-521-6286

Email: scholarships@hcf-hawaii.org
Website: http://www.hawaiicommunityfoundation.org
Purpose: To provide financial assistance to students of Hawaiian ancestry.
Eligibility: Applicants must be native Hawaiians or homestead lessees but do not have to live in Hawaii. They must be enrolled full-time at an accredited college or university as classified students and have a minimum GPA of 2.0 (3.0 if graduate students). Additional awards are available for students with high academic achievement and a proven commitment to the native Hawaiian community.
Target applicant:
 High school students
 College students
 Graduate school students
 Adult students
Minimum GPA: 2.0 for undergraduates; 3.0 for graduate students
Amount: Varies.
Number of awards: Varies.
Deadline: March 1.
How to apply: To apply, register online, complete the online application and select the scholarships to which you wish to apply. In addition, mail the supporting materials: printed confirmation page from the online application, personal statement, copy of Student Aid Report (SAR) available at www.fafsa.ed.gov and official transcript.

(2298) · Hellenic Times Scholarship

Hellenic Times Scholarship Fund
823 Eleventh Avenue
Attn.: Nick Katsoris
New York, NY 10019
Fax: 212-977-3662
Email: htsfund@aol.com
Website: http://www.htsfund.org
Purpose: To financially help Greek American students.
Eligibility: Applicants must be undergraduate or graduate students of Greek descent between the ages of 17 and 25 and may not win any other full scholarships. Applicants must submit transcripts and may be required to submit tax returns.
Target applicant:
 College students
 Graduate school students
Minimum GPA: None.
Amount: Varies.
Number of awards: Varies.
Deadline: January 16.
How to apply: Applications are available online.

(2299) · Herbert Lehman Scholarships

NAACP Legal Defense and Educational Fund
99 Hudson Street, Suite 1600
New York, NY 10013
Phone: 212-965-2200
Email: mbagley@naacpldf.org
Website: http://www.naacpldf.org
Purpose: To support African American students who are attending college for the first time.
Eligibility: Applicants must have a strong academic record and clear educational goals, and they must show leadership potential through involvement in school and extracurricular activities. Students must show good character through positive recommendations from teachers, employers or community representatives.

Target applicant:
 High school students
 College students
 Adult students
Minimum GPA: None.
Amount: $2,000.
Number of awards: Varies.
Scholarship may be renewable.
Deadline: April 30.
How to apply: Applications are available by sending a written request.

(2300) · HIAS Scholarship

Hebrew Immigrant Aid Society
333 Seventh Avenue, 16th Floor
New York, NY 10001-5004
Phone: 212-613-1358
Fax: 212-967-4483
Email: scholarship@hias.org
Website: http://www.hias.org
Purpose: To award scholarships to Jewish immigrant students.
Eligibility: Applicants must have completed one year of high school or college in the United States and have arrived in the United States after January 1, 1992. Selection is based on academic achievement, financial need and service within the Jewish community.
Target applicant:
 High school students
 College students
 Graduate school students
 Adult students
Minimum GPA: None.
Amount: Varies.
Number of awards: Varies.
Deadline: March 15.
How to apply: Applications are available online.

(2301) · High School Scholarship Program

Hispanic Scholarship Fund (HSF)
55 Second Street
Suite 1500
San Francisco, CA 94105
Phone: 877-473-4636
Fax: 415-808-2302
Email: scholar1@hsf.net
Website: http://www.hsf.net
Purpose: To assist high school students of Hispanic descent with college expenses. Over the past 25 years, HSF has provided more than 68,000 scholarships.
Eligibility: Applicants must be of Hispanic heritage (one parent fully Hispanic or each parent half Hispanic) and graduating high school seniors with a minimum 3.0 GPA. Students must have definite plans to attend a college or university the following fall semester after graduation.
Target applicant:
 High school students
Minimum GPA: 3.0
Amount: $1,000-$2,500.
Number of awards: Varies.
Deadline: December 15.
How to apply: Applications are available online.

(2302) · Higher Education Grant

Bureau of Indian Affairs
1849 C Street NW/MS-3512 MIB
Washington, DC 20240-0001
Phone: 202-208-6123
Fax: 202-208-3312
Email: gking@bia.edu
Website: http://www.doi.gov/bia
Purpose: To assist American Indian and Alaska Native students obtaining their undergraduate degrees.
Eligibility: Applicants must be members of a tribe or at least one-quarter degree Indian blood descendents of members of an American Indian tribe, be accepted into a college or another similar institution that provides an associate's or bachelor's degrees and show financial need.
Target applicant:
   High school students
   College students
   Adult students
Minimum GPA: None.
Amount: Varies.
Number of awards: Varies.
Deadline: Varies.
How to apply: Applications are available through tribes.

(2303) · Hispanic College Fund Scholarships

Hispanic College Fund
1301 K Street NW
Suite 450-A
Washington, DC 20005
Phone: 800-644-4223
Fax: 202-296-3774
Email: hcf-info@hispanicfund.org
Website: http://www.hispanicfund.org
Purpose: To develop future Hispanic business leaders by aiding students who have demonstrated excellence and potential.
Eligibility: Applicants must be Hispanic students applying to or enrolled at a college or university in the U.S. or Puerto Rico. Applicants must be U.S. citizens or permanent residents, plan to attend school full-time during the next academic year and have a minimum 3.0 GPA. Selection is based on academics and financial need. Some specific awards have additional eligibility requirements.
Target applicant:
   High school students
   College students
   Adult students
Minimum GPA: 3.0
Amount: Varies.
Number of awards: Varies.
Scholarship may be renewable.
Deadline: April 15.
How to apply: Applications are available online.

(2304) · Hispanic Heritage Youth Awards

Hispanic Heritage Awards Foundation
2600 Virginia Avenue NW
Suite 406
Washington, DC 20037
Phone: 202-861-9797
Fax: 202-861-9799
Email: contact@hispanicheritageawards.org
Website: http://www.hispanicawards.org

Purpose: To promote Hispanic excellence and recognize the contributions of Hispanic American youth.
Eligibility: Applicants must be high school seniors who are U.S. citizens or permanent residents, reside in Chicago, Denver, Dallas, Los Angeles, Miami, New York City, Philadelphia, Phoenix, San Antonio, San Diego, San Jose and Washington DC and have Hispanic parentage (Hispanic parentage can be one parent of Mexican, Central American, Cuban, Puerto Rican, South American, Spanish or Caribbean Hispanic descent). Selection criteria include achievement in the applicant's discipline, involvement in community, ability to overcome adversity and character. The disciplines are: Academic Excellence, Sports, the Arts, Literature/Journalism, Mathematics, Leadership/Community Service and Science and Technology.
Target applicant:
   High school students
Minimum GPA: None.
Amount: $2,000-$5,000.
Number of awards: Varies.
Deadline: March 6.
How to apply: Applications are available by request.

(2305) · Hispanic Outlook Scholarship

Hispanic Outlook Magazine
Scholarship Fund
210 Route 4 East
Suite 310
Paramus, NJ 07652
Website: http://www.hispanicoutlook.com
Purpose: To support Hispanic students who are pursuing higher education.
Eligibility: Applicants must be high school seniors who are Hispanic.
Target applicant:
   High school students
Minimum GPA: None.
Amount: Varies.
Number of awards: 2.
Deadline: May 1.
How to apply: Applications are available by sending a self-addressed, stamped envelope to the organization.

(2306) · Hopi Scholarship

Hopi Tribe Grants and Scholarship Program
P.O. Box 123
Kykotsmovi, AZ 86039
Phone: 800-762-9630
Fax: 928-734-9575
Email: info@hopi.nsn.us
Website: http://www.hopieducationfund.org
Purpose: To help Hopi students with academic achievement.
Eligibility: Applicants must be enrolled members of the Hopi tribe, be high school graduates or have earned a GED, have been accepted to a regionally accredited college and plan to attend full-time and have completed the Free Application for Federal Student Aid. Students must be in top 10 percent of their high school class or score 930 on the SAT or 21 on the ACT as entering freshmen; have a minimum 3.0 GPA as undergraduates or have a minimum 3.2 GPA as graduate, post graduate or professional degree students. Applications, statements of goals, financial needs analysis, proof of Hopi enrollment and transcripts are required.
Target applicant:
   High school students
   College students

Graduate school students
Adult students
Minimum GPA: 3.0 for undergraduates; 3.2 for graduate students
Amount: Varies.
Number of awards: Varies.
Deadline: Varies.
How to apply: Applications are available by mail.

(2307) · Houghton Mifflin Company Fellows Program/ Internship

United Negro College Fund (UNCF)
8260 Willow Oaks Corporate Drive
P.O. Box 10444
Fairfax, VA 22031-8044
Phone: 800-331-2244
Website: http://www.uncf.org
Purpose: To introduce college students to careers in the publishing industry.
Eligibility: Applicants must be African American juniors with a GPA of at least 3.0 interested in the publishing industry. They must attend a UNCF member college or university and demonstrate financial need. The scholarship will be awarded upon successful completion of a summer internship.
Target applicant:
    College students
    Adult students
Minimum GPA: 3.0
Amount: $3,700+internship pay.
Number of awards: Varies.
Deadline: Varies.
How to apply: Applications are available online.

(2308) · HSF/General Motors Scholarship

Hispanic Scholarship Fund (HSF)
55 Second Street
Suite 1500
San Francisco, CA 94105
Phone: 877-473-4636
Fax: 415-808-2302
Email: scholar1@hsf.net
Website: http://www.hsf.net
Purpose: To help Latinos pursuing degrees in engineering and business.
Eligibility: Applicants must be of Hispanic heritage, enrolled full-time at a four-year U.S. accredited college or university in the U.S., Puerto Rico or U.S. Virgin Islands and major in engineering (electrical, industrial, manufacturing or mechanical) or business (accounting, business administration, economics or finance). Applicants or their families must have ethnic backgrounds from Spain, Mexico, Guatemala, Honduras, El Salvador, Costa Rica, Nicaragua, Panama, Colombia, Venezuela, Ecuador, Peru, Argentina, Chile, Bolivia, Uruguay, Paraguay, Brazil, Cuba, Puerto Rico or the Dominican Republic. Students from Belize, Guyana, Suriname and French Guiana are ineligible. Semifinalists must complete the GM online assessment.
Target applicant:
    High school students
    College students
    Adult students
Minimum GPA: 3.0
Amount: $2,500.
Number of awards: Varies.

Deadline: June 30.
How to apply: Applications are available online.

(2309) · Ida M. Pope Memorial Scholarship

Hawaii Community Foundation - Scholarships
1164 Bishop Street, Suite 800
Honolulu, HI 96813
Phone: 888-731-3863
Fax: 808-521-6286
Email: scholarships@hcf-hawaii.org
Website: http://www.hawaiicommunityfoundation.org
Purpose: To assist female students of Hawaiian ancestry in obtaining higher education.
Eligibility: Applicants must attend an accredited college or university and have a GPA of 3.0 or higher.
Target applicant:
    High school students
    College students
    Adult students
Minimum GPA: 3.0
Amount: Varies.
Number of awards: Varies.
Deadline: March 1.
How to apply: To apply, register online, complete the online application and select the scholarships to which you wish to apply. In addition, mail the supporting materials: printed confirmation page from the online application, personal statement, copy of Student Aid Report (SAR) available at www.fafsa.ed.gov and official transcript.

(2310) · Jack and Jill of America Foundation Scholarship

United Negro College Fund (UNCF)
8260 Willow Oaks Corporate Drive
P.O. Box 10444
Fairfax, VA 22031-8044
Phone: 800-331-2244
Website: http://www.uncf.org
Purpose: To help African American high school seniors attend college.
Eligibility: Applicants must plan to attend college full-time, have a minimum 3.0 GPA, complete the Free Application for Federal Student Aid (FAFSA) and have unmet financial need that is verified by the college or university financial aid office. UNCF students are encouraged to complete the UNCF General Scholarship application to be matched with scholarships for which they meet the criteria.
Target applicant:
    High school students
Minimum GPA: 3.0
Amount: $1,500-$2,500.
Number of awards: Varies.
Deadline: March 14.
How to apply: Applications are available online.

(2311) · Jackie Chan Scholarship

U.S. Pan Asian American Chamber of Commerce
1329 18th Street NW
Washington, DC 20036
Phone: 800-696-7818
Fax: 202-296-5225
Email: info@uspaacc.com
Website: http://www.uspaacc.com

Purpose: To support the higher education goals of Asian American students.

Eligibility: Applicants must be U.S. citizens or permanent residents and be high school seniors of Asian or Pacific Heritage who will pursue post-secondary educations at an accredited institution in the U.S. Selection is based on academic excellence, leadership in extracurricular activities, community service involvement and financial need. Minimum 3.3 GPA required. Applicants must be able to attend the Excellence Awards and Scholarships Dinner during the CelebrAsian Annual Conference (in May).

Target applicant:
    High school students
Minimum GPA: 3.3
Amount: Up to $8,000.
Number of awards: 2.
Deadline: February 28.
How to apply: Applications are available online.

(2312) · Jackie Robinson Scholarship

Jackie Robinson Foundation
3 W. 35th Street
11th Floor
New York, NY 10001
Phone: 212-290-8600
Fax: 212-290-8081
Email: general@jackierobinson.org
Website: http://www.jackierobinson.org
Purpose: To help minority students who have shown leadership skills in their communities.

Eligibility: Applicants must be minority high school seniors with demonstrated financial need and academic achievement and who have already been accepted to a four-year college or university.

Target applicant:
    High school students
Minimum GPA: None.
Amount: $6,000.
Number of awards: Varies.
Deadline: April 1.
How to apply: Applications are available online, by email to requests@jackierobinson.org or by mail.

(2313) · Japanese American Citizens League Creative and Performing Arts Awards

Japanese American Citizens League (JACL)
National Scholarship Awards
1765 Sutter Street
San Francisco, CA 94115
Phone: 415-921-5225
Email: jacl@jacl.org
Website: http://www.jacl.org
Purpose: To recognize and encourage performing arts and creative projects among JACL members.

Eligibility: Applicants must be National JACL members and must be attending a college, university, trade school, business school or any other institution of higher learning. A personal statement, letter of recommendation, academic performance, work experience and community involvement are considered. Professional artists are not allowed.

Target applicant:
    College students

Graduate school students
Adult students
Minimum GPA: None.
Amount: Varies.
Number of awards: 2.
Deadline: April 1.
How to apply: Applications are available online or by sending a self-addressed, stamped envelope.

(2314) · Japanese American Citizens League Entering Freshman Awards

Japanese American Citizens League (JACL)
National Scholarship Awards
1765 Sutter Street
San Francisco, CA 94115
Phone: 415-921-5225
Email: jacl@jacl.org
Website: http://www.jacl.org
Purpose: To recognize and encourage education as a key to greater opportunities among JACL members.

Eligibility: Applicants must be National JACL members and must be planning to attend a college, university, trade school, business school, or any other institution of higher learning at the undergraduate level. A personal statement, letter of recommendation, academic performance, work experience and community involvement will all be considered.

Target applicant:
    High school students
Minimum GPA: None.
Amount: Varies.
Number of awards: 11.
Deadline: March 1.
How to apply: Applications are available through local JACL chapters, regional offices, National JACL Headquarters and website.

(2315) · Japanese American Citizens League Graduate Awards

Japanese American Citizens League (JACL)
National Scholarship Awards
1765 Sutter Street
San Francisco, CA 94115
Phone: 415-921-5225
Email: jacl@jacl.org
Website: http://www.jacl.org
Purpose: To provide monetary assistance for graduate studies to JACL members.

Eligibility: Applicants must be National JACL members and must attend a college or university at the graduate level. A personal statement, letter of recommendation, academic performance, work experience and community involvement are considered.

Target applicant:
    Graduate school students
    Adult students
Minimum GPA: None.
Amount: Varies.
Number of awards: 8.
Deadline: April 1.
How to apply: Applications are available online and by sending a self-addressed, stamped envelope.

(2316) · Japanese American Citizens League Law Scholarships

Japanese American Citizens League (JACL)
National Scholarship Awards
1765 Sutter Street
San Francisco, CA 94115
Phone: 415-921-5225
Email: jacl@jacl.org
Website: http://www.jacl.org
Purpose: To help JACL members who are studying law.
Eligibility: Applicants must be National JACL members and must be studying law at a college or university. A personal statement, letter of recommendation, academic performance, work experience, and community involvement will all be considered.
Target applicant:
    Graduate school students
    Adult students
Minimum GPA: None.
Amount: Varies.
Number of awards: 3.
Deadline: April 1.
How to apply: Applications are available online and by sending a self-addressed, stamped envelope.

(2317) · Japanese American Citizens League Undergraduate Awards

Japanese American Citizens League (JACL)
National Scholarship Awards
1765 Sutter Street
San Francisco, CA 94115
Phone: 415-921-5225
Email: jacl@jacl.org
Website: http://www.jacl.org
Purpose: To recognize and encourage education as a key to greater opportunities among JACL members.
Eligibility: Applicants must be National JACL members and must be attending a college, university, trade school, business school or any other institution of higher learning at the undergraduate level. A personal statement, letter of recommendation, academic performance, work experience and community involvement will all be considered.
Target applicant:
    College students
    Adult students
Minimum GPA: None.
Amount: Varies.
Number of awards: 10.
Deadline: April 1.
How to apply: Applications are available through local JACL chapters, regional offices, National JACL Headquarters and website.

(2318) · Jeannette Rankin Foundation Award

Jeannette Rankin Foundation
P.O. Box 6653
Athens, GA 30604-6653
Phone: 706-208-1211
Fax: 706-548-0202
Email: info@rankinfoundation.org
Website: http://www.rankinfoundation.org
Purpose: To support the education of low-income women 35 years or older.

Eligibility: Applicants must be women 35 years of age or older, plan to obtain an undergraduate or vocational education and meet maximum household income guidelines.
Target applicant:
    College students
    Adult students
Minimum GPA: None.
Amount: $2,000.
Number of awards: Varies.
Scholarship may be renewable.
Deadline: March 1.
How to apply: Applications are available online or by sending a self-addressed and stamped envelope to the foundation.

(2319) · Jeffry and Barbara Picower Foundation Scholarship

United Negro College Fund (UNCF)
8260 Willow Oaks Corporate Drive
P.O. Box 10444
Fairfax, VA 22031-8044
Phone: 800-331-2244
Website: http://www.uncf.org
Purpose: To help African American students attending United Negro College Fund (UNCF) Member Colleges and Universities.
Eligibility: Applicants must have a minimum 3.0 GPA, complete the Free Application for Federal Student Aid (FAFSA) and have unmet financial need that is verified by the college or university financial aid office. Students are encouraged to complete the UNCF General Scholarship application to be matched with scholarships for which they meet the criteria.
Target applicant:
    High school students
    College students
    Adult students
Minimum GPA: 3.0
Amount: $5,000.
Number of awards: 3.
Deadline: Varies.
How to apply: Applications are available online.

(2320) · Jesse Jones, Jr. Scholarship

United Negro College Fund (UNCF)
8260 Willow Oaks Corporate Drive
P.O. Box 10444
Fairfax, VA 22031-8044
Phone: 800-331-2244
Website: http://www.uncf.org
Purpose: To assist business students at UNCF member schools.
Eligibility: Applicants must be African American, have a minimum 2.5 GPA, complete the Free Application for Federal Student Aid (FAFSA) and have unmet financial need that is verified by the college or university financial aid office. UNCF students are encouraged to complete the UNCF General Scholarship application to be matched with scholarships for which they meet the criteria.
Target applicant:
    High school students
    College students
    Adult students
Minimum GPA: 2.5
Amount: $2,000-$5,000.

Number of awards: Varies.
Deadline: Varies.
How to apply: Applications are available online.

(2321) · Jimi Hendrix Endowment Fund Scholarship

United Negro College Fund (UNCF)
8260 Willow Oaks Corporate Drive
P.O. Box 10444
Fairfax, VA 22031-8044
Phone: 800-331-2244
Website: http://www.uncf.org
Purpose: To assist students studying music at UNCF member schools.
Eligibility: Applicants must have a minimum 2.5 GPA, complete the Free Application for Federal Student Aid (FAFSA) and have unmet financial need that is verified by the college or university financial aid office. Students are encouraged to complete the UNCF General Scholarship application to be matched with scholarships for which they meet the criteria.
Target applicant:
    High school students
    College students
    Adult students
Minimum GPA: 2.5
Amount: $2,000-$5,000.
Number of awards: Varies.
Deadline: Varies.
How to apply: Applications are available online.

(2322) · John Lennon Scholarship

United Negro College Fund (UNCF)
8260 Willow Oaks Corporate Drive
P.O. Box 10444
Fairfax, VA 22031-8044
Phone: 800-331-2244
Website: http://www.uncf.org
Purpose: To support communications and performing arts students at UNCF member schools.
Eligibility: Applicants must be African American, have a minimum 3.0 GPA, complete the Free Application for Federal Student Aid (FAFSA) and have unmet financial need that is verified by the college or university financial aid office. UNCF students are encouraged to complete the UNCF General Scholarship application to be matched with scholarships for which they meet the criteria.
Target applicant:
    High school students
    College students
    Adult students
Minimum GPA: 3.0
Amount: $5,000.
Number of awards: 1.
Deadline: February 16.
How to apply: Applications are available online.

(2323) · Jos. L. Muscarelle Foundation Scholarship

United Negro College Fund (UNCF)
8260 Willow Oaks Corporate Drive
P.O. Box 10444
Fairfax, VA 22031-8044

Phone: 800-331-2244
Website: http://www.uncf.org
Purpose: To support African American students at UNCF member schools.
Eligibility: Applicants must have a minimum 2.5 GPA, complete the Free Application for Federal Student Aid (FAFSA) and have unmet financial need that is verified by the college or university financial aid office. UNCF students are encouraged to complete the UNCF General Scholarship application to be matched with scholarships for which they meet the criteria.
Target applicant:
    High school students
    College students
    Adult students
Minimum GPA: 2.5
Amount: $1,000-$2,500.
Number of awards: Varies.
Deadline: Varies.
How to apply: Applications are available online.

(2324) · Juanita Robles-Lopez Scholarship

National Association of Hispanic Nurses
Attn: Maria Castro, NAHN Awards and Scholarship Committee Chair
1501 Sixteenth Street NW
Washington, DC 20036
Phone: 202-387-2477
Fax: 202-483-7183
Email: info@thehispanicnurses.org
Website: http://www.thehispanicnurses.org
Purpose: To support graduate students enrolled in a maternal-child nursing program.
Eligibility: Students must be members of NAHN although they may apply for membership at the time of application. Selection is based on an essay describing the maternal-child needs in Hispanic communities and the applicant's potential leadership in this field, recommendations, academic achievement and application form.
Target applicant:
    Graduate school students
    Adult students
Minimum GPA: 3.0
Amount: $2,000.
Number of awards: 1.
Deadline: March 14.
How to apply: Applications are available online or by mail.

(2325) · Julianne Malveaux Scholarship

National Association of Negro Business and Professional Women's Clubs Inc.
1806 New Hampshire Avenue NW
Washington, DC 20009-3298
Phone: 202-483-4206
Email: info@nanbpwc.org
Website: http://www.nanbpwc.org
Purpose: To award scholarships to college students majoring in journalism, economics or a related field.
Eligibility: Applicants must be enrolled as sophomores or juniors at an accredited college or university and have a minimum 3.0 GPA. Students may major in related fields such as public policy or creative writing.
Target applicant:
    College students
    Adult students

Minimum GPA: 3.0
Amount: $1,000.
Number of awards: Varies.
Deadline: April 30.
How to apply: Applications are available online.

(2326) · Kuntz Foundation Scholarship

United Negro College Fund (UNCF)
8260 Willow Oaks Corporate Drive
P.O. Box 10444
Fairfax, VA 22031-8044
Phone: 800-331-2244
Website: http://www.uncf.org
Purpose: To support African American college students at UNCF member colleges and universities.
Eligibility: Applicants must have a minimum 2.5 GPA, complete the Free Application for Federal Student Aid (FAFSA) and have unmet financial need that is verified by the college or university financial aid office. Students are encouraged to complete the UNCF General Scholarship application to be matched with scholarships for which they meet the criteria.
Target applicant:
    High school students
    College students
    Adult students
Minimum GPA: 2.5
Amount: Varies.
Number of awards: Varies.
Deadline: Varies.
How to apply: Applications are available online.

(2327) · Letty Garofalo Scholarship

United Negro College Fund (UNCF)
8260 Willow Oaks Corporate Drive
P.O. Box 10444
Fairfax, VA 22031-8044
Phone: 800-331-2244
Website: http://www.uncf.org
Purpose: To support students in need of financial assistance.
Eligibility: Applicants must have a minimum 2.5 GPA, complete the Free Application for Federal Student Aid (FAFSA) and have unmet financial need that is verified by the college or university financial aid office. UNCF students are encouraged to complete the UNCF General Scholarship application to be matched with scholarships for which they meet the criteria.
Target applicant:
    High school students
    College students
    Adult students
Minimum GPA: 2.5
Amount: Varies.
Number of awards: Varies.
Deadline: Varies.
How to apply: Applications are available online.

(2328) · Limited Inc. and Intimate Brands Inc. Scholarship

United Negro College Fund (UNCF)
8260 Willow Oaks Corporate Drive
P.O. Box 10444
Fairfax, VA 22031-8044
Phone: 800-331-2244
Website: http://www.uncf.org
Purpose: To support students at UNCF member schools in Ohio.
Eligibility: Applicants must be African American students, have a minimum 2.5 GPA, complete the Free Application for Federal Student Aid (FAFSA) and have unmet financial need that is verified by the college or university financial aid office. UNCF students are encouraged to complete the UNCF General Scholarship application to be matched with scholarships for which they meet the criteria.
Target applicant:
    High school students
    College students
    Adult students
Minimum GPA: 2.5
Amount: Varies.
Number of awards: Varies.
Deadline: Varies.
How to apply: Applications are available online.

(2329) · Linc Telacu Scholarships

LINC TELACU Education Foundation
5400 E.Olympic Boulevard
Los Angeles, CA 90022
Phone: 323-721-1655
Fax: 323-724-3372
Email: info@telacu.com
Website: http://www.telacu.com/english/graphic_version/scholarship_program/index.asp
Purpose: To provide financial and other support to aspiring college students.
Eligibility: Applicants must be first-generation Latino college students from low income families. They must have a GPA of 2.5 or higher, and they must be residents of New York State, the Greater Chicagoland area, San Antonio or Austin Texas or certain areas of California.
Target applicant:
    High school students
    College students
    Adult students
Minimum GPA: 2.5
Amount: Varies.
Number of awards: Varies.
Deadline: March 29.
How to apply: Applications are available online.

(2330) · Louis Dreyfus Natural Gas Company Scholarship

United Negro College Fund (UNCF)
8260 Willow Oaks Corporate Drive
P.O. Box 10444
Fairfax, VA 22031-8044
Phone: 800-331-2244
Website: http://www.uncf.org
Purpose: To support African American college students at UNCF member colleges and universities.
Eligibility: Applicants must have a minimum 2.5 GPA, complete the Free Application for Federal Student Aid (FAFSA) and have unmet financial need that is verified by the college or university financial aid office. Students are encouraged to complete the UNCF General Scholarship application to be matched with scholarships for which they meet the criteria.

Target applicant:
  High school students
  College students
  Adult students
Minimum GPA: 2.5
Amount: Varies.
Number of awards: Varies.
Deadline: Varies.
How to apply: Applications are available online.

(2331) · Louis Stokes Scholarship

National Association for the Advancement of Colored People
The United Negro College Fund
Scholarships and Grants Administration
8260 Willow Oaks Corporate Drive
Fairfax, VA 22031
Phone: 703-205-3400
Website: http://www.naacp.org
Purpose: To promote equal opportunity in education.
Eligibility: Applicants must be incoming freshman at an accredited Historically Black College or University in the U.S., must major in engineering, computer science or science and demonstrate financial need. Membership in the NAACP is not required, but highly recommended.
Target applicant:
  High school students
Minimum GPA: 2.5
Amount: $2,000.
Number of awards: Varies.
Deadline: The last Friday in the month of March.
How to apply: Applications are available online and by mail.

(2332) · LULAC GE Scholarship

League of United Latin American Citizens
2000 L Street NW
Suite 610
Washington, DC 20036
Phone: 202-835-9646
Fax: 202-835-9685
Email: scholarships@lnesc.org
Website: http://www.lnesc.org
Purpose: To assist minority students who are majoring in business or engineering.
Eligibility: Applicants must be entering their sophomore year of college at an accredited institution and majoring in business or engineering.
Target applicant:
  College students
  Adult students
Minimum GPA: None.
Amount: $5,000.
Number of awards: Varies.
Deadline: July 15.
How to apply: Applications are available from LULAC.

(2333) · LULAC General Awards

League of United Latin American Citizens
2000 L Street NW
Suite 610
Washington, DC 20036
Phone: 202-835-9646

Fax: 202-835-9685
Email: scholarships@lnesc.org
Website: http://www.lnesc.org
Purpose: To provide assistance to Hispanic students who are seeking or plan to seek degrees.
Eligibility: Students must have applied to or be enrolled in a two- or four-year college or graduate school and be U.S. citizens or legal residents. Grades and academic achievement may be considered, but emphasis is placed on motivation, sincerity and integrity as demonstrated by the interview and essay.
Target applicant:
  High school students
  College students
  Graduate school students
  Adult students
Minimum GPA: None.
Amount: Varies.
Number of awards: Varies.
Deadline: March 31.
How to apply: Applications are available from LULAC.

(2334) · LULAC Honors Awards

League of United Latin American Citizens
2000 L Street NW
Suite 610
Washington, DC 20036
Phone: 202-835-9646
Fax: 202-835-9685
Email: scholarships@lnesc.org
Website: http://www.lnesc.org
Purpose: To provide assistance to all levels of degree seeking Latino students.
Eligibility: Applicants must be U.S. citizens or legal residents, have applied to or attend a college or graduate school and have a GPA of 3.25 or better. Applicants who are entering freshmen must also have an ACT score of 23 or higher or an SAT score of 1000 or higher.
Target applicant:
  High school students
  College students
  Graduate school students
  Adult students
Minimum GPA: 3.25
Amount: Varies.
Number of awards: Varies.
Deadline: March 31.
How to apply: Applications are available from LULAC.

(2335) · LULAC National Scholastic Achievement Awards

League of United Latin American Citizens
2000 L Street NW
Suite 610
Washington, DC 20036
Phone: 202-835-9646
Fax: 202-835-9685
Email: scholarships@lnesc.org
Website: http://www.lnesc.org
Purpose: To aid Hispanic students attending colleges, universities and graduate schools.
Eligibility: Applicants must have applied to or be enrolled in a college, university or graduate school and be U.S. citizens or legal residents.

Students must also have a minimum 3.5 GPA and if entering freshmen a minimum ACT score of 29 or minimum SAT score of 1350. Eligible candidates cannot be related to scholarship committee members, the Council President or contributors to the Council funds. Since applications must be sent from local LULAC Councils, students without LULAC Councils in their states are ineligible.

Target applicant:
  College students
  Graduate school students
  Adult students
Minimum GPA: 3.5
Amount: $250-$2,000.
Number of awards: Varies.
Deadline: March 31.
How to apply: Applications are available online.

(2336) · Mae Maxey Memorial Scholarship

United Negro College Fund (UNCF)
8260 Willow Oaks Corporate Drive
P.O. Box 10444
Fairfax, VA 22031-8044
Phone: 800-331-2244
Website: http://www.uncf.org
Purpose: To provide assistance to African American students at UNCF member colleges and universities who are interested in poetry.
Eligibility: Applicants must have a minimum 2.5 GPA, complete the Free Application for Federal Student Aid (FAFSA) and have unmet financial need that is verified by the college or university financial aid office. Students are encouraged to complete the UNCF General Scholarship application to be matched with scholarships for which they meet the criteria.
Target applicant:
  High school students
  College students
  Adult students
Minimum GPA: 2.5
Amount: $1,000-$5,000.
Number of awards: Varies.
Deadline: Varies.
How to apply: Applications are available online.

(2337) · MAES Scholarship Program

Society of Mexican American Engineers and Scientists Inc. (MAES)
711 W. Bay Area Boulevard
Suite #206
Webster, TX 77598-4051
Phone: 281-557-3677
Fax: 281-557-3757
Email: execdir@maes-natl.org
Website: http://www.maes-natl.org
Purpose: To assist Hispanic students in the fields of science and engineering.
Eligibility: Applicants must be current Hispanic MAES student members who are full-time undergraduate and graduate students in an accredited U.S. college or university majoring in science or engineering. Community college applicants must be enrolled in majors that are transferable to a four-year institution offering bachelor's degrees. There are various scholarships in the program. Some sponsors require students to be U.S. citizens or permanent residents. Awards are based on financial need, academic achievement, personal qualities, strengths and leadership abilities. Applicants should submit applications, financial information, recommendations and transcripts.

Target applicant:
  College students
  Graduate school students
  Adult students
Minimum GPA: None.
Amount: $3,000.
Number of awards: 5.
Deadline: October 6.
How to apply: Applications are available online.

(2338) · Malcolm X Scholarship for Exceptional Courage

United Negro College Fund (UNCF)
8260 Willow Oaks Corporate Drive
P.O. Box 10444
Fairfax, VA 22031-8044
Phone: 800-331-2244
Website: http://www.uncf.org
Purpose: To assist students who attend UNCF member colleges and universities and have overcome extreme circumstances and hardships.
Eligibility: Applicants must be African American students, have a minimum 2.5 GPA, complete the Free Application for Federal Student Aid (FAFSA) and have unmet financial need that is verified by the college or university financial aid office. Students are encouraged to complete the UNCF General Scholarship application to be matched with scholarships for which they meet the criteria. Academic excellence and leadership on campus and in the community are also required.
Target applicant:
  College students
  Adult students
Minimum GPA: 2.5
Amount: $4,000.
Number of awards: 1.
Deadline: Varies.
How to apply: Applications are available online.

(2339) · Margaret Mcnamara Memorial Fund Fellowships

Margaret Mcnamara Memorial Fund
1818 H Street NW, MSN H2-204
Washington, DC 20433
Phone: 202-473-8751
Fax: 202 522-3142
Email: familynetwork@worldbank.org
Website: http://www.worldbank.org/yournet
Purpose: To provide financial assistance to women from developing countries who are currently studying to earn a college degree in the U.S.
Eligibility: Applicants must be from an eligible nation, have a record of community service in their country and be U.S. or Canadian residents at the time of application, while intending to return to their country of origin with two years. Individuals under the age of 25 and relatives of World Bank employees are not eligible.
Target applicant:
  College students
  Graduate school students
  Adult students
Minimum GPA: None.
Amount: $11,000.
Number of awards: 6.
Deadline: February 10.
How to apply: Applications are available online.

(2340) · Maria Elena Salinas Scholarship Program

National Association of Hispanic Journalists
Scholarship Committee
1000 National Press Building
Washington, DC 20045
Phone: 202-662-7145
Fax: 202-662-7144
Email: ntita@nahj.org
Website: http://www.nahj.org
Purpose: To support Spanish speaking students who plan to become broadcast journalists.
Eligibility: Applicants must be high school seniors, undergraduates or first-year graduate students who plan to pursue careers in journalism in Spanish-language television or radio. The award includes an opportunity to intern with the news division of Univision or an affiliate. Applicants must write an essay in Spanish outlining their career goals and provide Spanish-language samples of their work.
Target applicant:
　High school students
　College students
　Graduate school students
　Adult students
Minimum GPA: None.
Amount: $5,000.
Number of awards: 2.
Scholarship may be renewable.
Deadline: Last Friday in January.
How to apply: Applications are available online.

(2341) · Marriott Scholars Program

United Negro College Fund (UNCF)
8260 Willow Oaks Corporate Drive
P.O. Box 10444
Fairfax, VA 22031-8044
Phone: 800-331-2244
Website: http://www.uncf.org
Purpose: To assist future hospitality industry professionals.
Eligibility: Applicants must be incoming African American students majoring in hotel management, restaurant management or a similar hospitality field. They must have a GPA of at least 3.0 and demonstrate financial need.
Target applicant:
　High school students
Minimum GPA: 3.0
Amount: Up to $9,000+mentoring and internships.
Number of awards: Varies.
Scholarship may be renewable.
Deadline: April 1.
How to apply: Applications are available online.

(2342) · Mary E. Scott Memorial Scholarship

United Negro College Fund (UNCF)
8260 Willow Oaks Corporate Drive
P.O. Box 10444
Fairfax, VA 22031-8044
Phone: 800-331-2244
Website: http://www.uncf.org
Purpose: To help African American students attending United Negro College Fund (UNCF) member colleges and universities.

Eligibility: Applicants must have a minimum 2.5 GPA, complete the Free Application for Federal Student Aid (FAFSA) and have unmet financial need that is verified by the college or university financial aid office. Students are encouraged to complete the UNCF General Scholarship application to be matched with scholarships for which they meet the criteria.
Target applicant:
　High school students
　College students
　Adult students
Minimum GPA: 2.5
Amount: $1,500-$5,000.
Number of awards: Varies.
Deadline: Varies.
How to apply: Applications are available online.

(2343) · Mary Moy Quan Ing Memorial Scholarship

Asian American Journalists Association
1182 Market Street
Suite 230
San Francisco, CA 94102
Phone: 415-346-2051
Fax: 415-346-6343
Email: lilac@aaja.org
Website: http://www.aaja.org
Purpose: Monetary assistance is awarded to a high school senior pursuing college studies that lead to a journalism career.
Eligibility: Applicants must be high school seniors intending to major in journalism. Applicants must also demonstrate a commitment to the field of journalism, sensitivity to Asian American issues as demonstrated by community involvement, journalistic ability, scholastic ability and financial need.
Target applicant:
　High school students
Minimum GPA: None.
Amount: $1,500.
Number of awards: 1.
Deadline: March 27.
How to apply: Applications are available online.

(2344) · MasterCard Worldwide Special Support Program

United Negro College Fund (UNCF)
8260 Willow Oaks Corporate Drive
P.O. Box 10444
Fairfax, VA 22031-8044
Phone: 800-331-2244
Website: http://www.uncf.org
Purpose: To support African American college students.
Eligibility: Applicants must have a minimum 2.5 GPA, complete the Free Application for Federal Student Aid (FAFSA) and have unmet financial need that is verified by the college or university financial aid office. Students are encouraged to complete the UNCF General Scholarship application to be matched with scholarships for which they meet the criteria.
Target applicant:
　High school students
　College students
　Adult students
Minimum GPA: 2.5
Amount: $2,000-$3,000.

Number of awards: Varies.
Deadline: February 5.
How to apply: Applications are available online.

(2345) · MCCA Lloyd M. Johnson, Jr. Scholarship Program

United Negro College Fund (UNCF)
8260 Willow Oaks Corporate Drive
P.O. Box 10444
Fairfax, VA 22031-8044
Phone: 800-331-2244
Website: http://www.uncf.org
Purpose: To support first-year entering law students.
Eligibility: Applicants must be African American students entering their first year of law school at an accredited institution. They must have a GPA of at least 3.0 and demonstrate financial need.
Target applicant:
    College students
    Graduate school students
    Adult students
Minimum GPA: 3.0
Amount: $10,000-$30,000.
Number of awards: 13.
Scholarship may be renewable.
Deadline: June 1.
How to apply: Applications are available online.

(2346) · McClare Family Trust Scholarship

United Negro College Fund (UNCF)
8260 Willow Oaks Corporate Drive
P.O. Box 10444
Fairfax, VA 22031-8044
Phone: 800-331-2244
Website: http://www.uncf.org
Purpose: To provide funding to humanities students.
Eligibility: Applicants must be African American college freshmen at a UNCF member college or university majoring in the humanities, with an interest in English literature. Students must have a GPA of at least 3.0 and demonstrate financial need.
Target applicant:
    College students
    Adult students
Minimum GPA: 3.0
Amount: Varies.
Number of awards: Varies.
Deadline: October 29.
How to apply: Applications are available online.

(2347) · McDonald's Scholarship

US Pan Asian American Chamber of Commerce
13229 18th Street NW
Washington, DC 20036
Phone: 800-696-7818
Fax: 202-296-5225
Email: info@uspaac.com
Website: http://www.uspaacc.com/web/programs/scholarship_programs.htm
Purpose: To provide financial assistance to outstanding Asian American students.

Eligibility: Applicants must be high school seniors of Asian Pacific Island descent who are 16 years of age or older at the time of application. They must be U.S. citizens or permanent residents and plan to begin study at an accredited institution of higher learning full-time in the fall following application. A GPA of 3.3 or higher, financial need and participation in extracurricular activities and community service are required.
Target applicant:
    High school students
Minimum GPA: 3.3
Amount: Up to $3,000.
Number of awards: Varies.
Deadline: February 22.
How to apply: Applications are available online.

(2348) · Medicus Student Exchange

Swiss Benevolent Society of New York
Scholarship Committee
500 Fifth Avenue, Room 1800
New York, NY 10110
Website: http://www.swissbenevolentny.com
Purpose: To provide need and merit-based scholarships for students from Swiss-American backgrounds.
Eligibility: Applicants or one of their parents must be a Swiss national. The Medicus grant for study in Switzerland is only open to U.S. residents and is a need-based award. Applicants must be college juniors or seniors or graduate-level students accepted to a Swiss university or the Federal Institute of Technology.
Target applicant:
    College students
    Graduate school students
    Adult students
Minimum GPA: None.
Amount: Varies.
Number of awards: Varies.
Deadline: January 31.
How to apply: Applications are available online.

(2349) · Medtronic Foundation Scholarship

United Negro College Fund (UNCF)
8260 Willow Oaks Corporate Drive
P.O. Box 10444
Fairfax, VA 22031-8044
Phone: 800-331-2244
Website: http://www.uncf.org
Purpose: To support African American sophomores and juniors at UNCF member colleges and universities majoring in a science, engineering or medical field.
Eligibility: Eligible majors include: engineering, pre-medicine, science, chemistry, biochemistry, biology, microbiology, biomedical research, medicine, physical sciences, electrical engineering, civil engineering, chemical engineering and mechanical engineering. Applicants must have a GPA of at least 3.3 and demonstrate financial need.
Target applicant:
    College students
    Adult students
Minimum GPA: 3.3
Amount: $5,000.
Number of awards: Varies.
Deadline: April 15.
How to apply: Applications are available online.

(2350) · Memorial Scholarships for American Indian Students

Center for Native American Studies
Berger Scholarship Selection Committee
P.O. Box 172340 / 2-179 Wilson Hall
Bozeman, MT 59717-2340
Phone: 406-994-3881
Email: zna7001@montana.edu
Website: http://www.montana.edu/wwwnas
Purpose: To promote academic excellence among American Indians.
Eligibility: Applicants must be freshmen, transfer students from a tribally-controlled community college or graduate students who are enrolled members of a federally-recognized tribe or a member of the Little Shell Band of Chippewa Crees. Candidates must be graduates of an accredited high school or tribally-controlled community college.
Target applicant:
　　High school students
　　College students
　　Graduate school students
　　Adult students
Minimum GPA: None.
Amount: $1,000.
Number of awards: Varies.
Scholarship may be renewable.
Deadline: March 3.
How to apply: Applications are available online, by phone and by email.

(2351) · MESBEC Program

Catching the Dream
Attn.: Scholarship Affairs Office
8200 Mountain Road NE
Suite 203
Albuquerque, NM 87110
Phone: 505-262-2351
Email: nscholarsh@aol.com
Website: http://www.catchingthedream.org
Purpose: To provide scholarships to high-achieving American Indians in the fields of math, engineering, science, business, education and computers.
Eligibility: Applicants must be 1/4 or more degree American Indian, enrolled in a tribe and attend or plan to attend college full-time. Students must apply to all other sources of funding at the same time they apply for this scholarship. Selection is based on grades, SAT or ACT scores, work experience, leadership, clear goals, commitment to the American Indian community and the potential to improve the lives of American Indian people.
Target applicant:
　　High school students
　　College students
　　Graduate school students
　　Adult students
Minimum GPA: None.
Amount: $500-$5,000.
Number of awards: Varies.
Deadline: March 15, April 15 and September 15.
How to apply: Applications are available online.

(2352) · Michael and Donna Griffith Scholarship

United Negro College Fund (UNCF)
8260 Willow Oaks Corporate Drive
P.O. Box 10444
Fairfax, VA 22031-8044
Phone: 800-331-2244
Website: http://www.uncf.org
Purpose: To support African American college students.
Eligibility: Applicants must have a minimum 2.5 GPA, complete the Free Application for Federal Student Aid (FAFSA) and have unmet financial need that is verified by the college or university financial aid office. Applicants must be UNCF students and are encouraged to complete the UNCF General Scholarship application to be matched with scholarships for which they meet the criteria.
Target applicant:
　　High school students
　　College students
　　Adult students
Minimum GPA: 2.5
Amount: $1,000-$2,500.
Number of awards: Varies.
Deadline: Varies.
How to apply: Applications are available online.

(2353) · Michael Jackson Scholarship

United Negro College Fund (UNCF)
8260 Willow Oaks Corporate Drive
P.O. Box 10444
Fairfax, VA 22031-8044
Phone: 800-331-2244
Website: http://www.uncf.org
Purpose: To assist students majoring in communications, English or performing arts.
Eligibility: Applicants must be African American students at a UNCF member college or university majoring in communications, English or performing arts. Applicants must have a GPA of at least 3.0 and demonstrate financial need.
Target applicant:
　　High school students
　　College students
　　Adult students
Minimum GPA: 3.0
Amount: Up to $4,000.
Number of awards: Varies.
Deadline: Varies.
How to apply: Applications are available online.

(2354) · Mike and Stephanie Bozic Scholarship

United Negro College Fund (UNCF)
8260 Willow Oaks Corporate Drive
P.O. Box 10444
Fairfax, VA 22031-8044
Phone: 800-331-2244
Website: http://www.uncf.org
Purpose: To assist African American students with financial need.
Eligibility: Applicants must attend United Negro College Fund (UNCF) member colleges and universities, have a minimum 2.5 GPA, complete the Free Application for Federal Student Aid (FAFSA) and have unmet financial need that is verified by the college or university financial aid office. UNCF students are encouraged to complete the UNCF General

Scholarship application to be matched with scholarships for which they meet the criteria.

Target applicant:
- High school students
- College students
- Adult students

Minimum GPA: 2.5
Amount: Varies.
Number of awards: Varies.
Deadline: Varies.
How to apply: Applications are available online.

(2355) · Minority Affairs Committee Award for Outstanding Scholastic Achievement

American Institute of Chemical Engineers - (AIChE)
3 Park Avenue
New York, NY 10016
Phone: 212-591-7634
Fax: 212-591-8890
Email: awards@aiche.org
Website: http://www.aiche.org

Purpose: Recognizes outstanding achievements by a chemical engineering student who serves as a role model for minority students.
Eligibility: Applicants must be ethnic minorities, major in chemical engineering and be undergraduate or graduate students.

Target applicant:
- College students
- Graduate school students
- Adult students

Minimum GPA: None.
Amount: $1,500.
Number of awards: 1.
Deadline: April 15.
How to apply: Applications are available online or by telephone or written request.

(2356) · Minority Scholarship

National Strength and Conditioning Association (NSCA) Foundation
1885 Bob Johnson Drive
Colorado Springs, CO 80906
Phone: 800-815-6826
Fax: 719-632-6367
Email: nsca@nsca-lift.org
Website: http://www.nsca-lift.org

Purpose: To encourage minorities to enter the field of strength and conditioning.
Eligibility: Applicants must be African American, Hispanic, Asian American or Native American students working toward a graduate degree related to strength and conditioning. Students must be NSCA members for one year before applying and be pursuing careers in strength and conditioning. Applications are evaluated based on grades, courses, experience, honors, recommendations and involvement in the community and with NSCA.

Target applicant:
- College students
- Graduate school students
- Adult students

Minimum GPA: None.
Amount: $1,000.
Number of awards: 2.
Deadline: March 15.
How to apply: Applications are available with membership.

(2357) · Minority Scholarship and Training Program

LinTV
8 Elm Street
New Haven, CT 06510
Phone: 203-784-8958
Email: gail.brekke@lintv.com
Website: http://www.lintv.com

Purpose: To help educate outstanding minority students who plan to enter the television broadcast field.
Eligibility: Applicants must have a minimum 3.0 GPA, major in journalism or a related broadcast field at an accredited university or college, be college sophomores, be U.S. citizens and of non-white origin.

Target applicant:
- College students
- Adult students

Minimum GPA: 3.0
Amount: $20,000.
Number of awards: Varies.
Deadline: March 15.
How to apply: Applications are available online.

(2358) · Minority Scholarship Awards for College Students

American Institute of Chemical Engineers - (AIChE)
3 Park Avenue
New York, NY 10016
Phone: 212-591-7634
Fax: 212-591-8890
Email: awards@aiche.org
Website: http://www.aiche.org

Purpose: To offer financial aid to minority students in chemical engineering.
Eligibility: Applicants must be AIChE national student members, undergraduates in chemical engineering, and members of a minority group (i.e., African American, Hispanic, Native American or Alaskan Native) that is underrepresented in chemical engineering. Selection is based on academic record, participation in AIChE student and professional activities, career objectives and financial need.

Target applicant:
- College students
- Adult students

Minimum GPA: None.
Amount: $1,000.
Number of awards: 10.
Deadline: May 15.
How to apply: Applications are available online or by telephone or written request.

(2359) · Minority Scholarship Awards for Incoming College Freshmen

American Institute of Chemical Engineers - (AIChE)
3 Park Avenue
New York, NY 10016
Phone: 212-591-7634
Fax: 212-591-8890
Email: awards@aiche.org
Website: http://www.aiche.org

Purpose: To offer financial aid to minority students in chemical engineering.

Eligibility: Applicants must be members of a minority group (i.e. African American, Hispanic, Native American or Alaskan Native) that is underrepresented in chemical engineering. Applicants must also be high school graduates during the academic year of application and plan to enroll in a four-year college or university. Applicants are encouraged to major in science or engineering. Selection is also based on academic record, reason for choosing science or engineering, work or activities and financial need.

Target applicant:
　　High school students
Minimum GPA: None.
Amount: $1,000.
Number of awards: 10.
Deadline: May 15.
How to apply: Applications are available online or by telephone or written request.

(2360) · Minority Scholarships

American Institute for Foreign Study
AIFS College Division
River Plaza
9 W. Broad Street
Stamford, CT 06902
Phone: 800-727-2437
Fax: 203-399-5597
Email: info@aifs.com
Website: http://www.aifsabroad.com
Purpose: To help increase the participation of ethnic minority college students in study abroad programs.
Eligibility: Applicants must be African-Americans, Asian-Americans, Native-Americans, Hispanic-Americans or Pacific Islanders who are currently enrolled as undergraduates at a U.S. institution. Applicants must also meet the admission requirements of the AIFS program selected, demonstrate financial need, have a minimum 3.0 GPA and be involved in community or extra-curricular activities focused on multicultural or international issues.

Target applicant:
　　College students
　　Adult students
Minimum GPA: 3.0
Amount: Full tuition or $2,000.
Number of awards: Varies.
Deadline: April 15 and October 15.
How to apply: Applications are available online.

(2361) · Mitsubishi Motors U.S.A. Foundation Leadership Awards

United Negro College Fund (UNCF)
8260 Willow Oaks Corporate Drive
P.O. Box 10444
Fairfax, VA 22031-8044
Phone: 800-331-2244
Website: http://www.uncf.org
Purpose: To support African American students at UNCF member schools who have leadership roles in their communities.
Eligibility: Applicants must have a minimum 2.5 GPA, complete the Free Application for Federal Student Aid (FAFSA) and have unmet financial need that is verified by the college or university financial aid office. Students are encouraged to complete the UNCF General Scholarship application to be matched with scholarships for which they meet the criteria.

Target applicant:
　　College students
　　Adult students
Minimum GPA: 2.5
Amount: $2,000.
Number of awards: 39.
Deadline: October 29.
How to apply: Applications are available online.

(2362) · Morgan Stanley Scholarship/Internship

United Negro College Fund (UNCF)
8260 Willow Oaks Corporate Drive
P.O. Box 10444
Fairfax, VA 22031-8044
Phone: 800-331-2244
Website: http://www.uncf.org
Purpose: To help African American students attending United Negro College Fund (UNCF) member colleges and universities who are majoring in finance or banking.
Eligibility: Applicants must have a minimum 2.5 GPA, complete the Free Application for Federal Student Aid (FAFSA) and have unmet financial need that is verified by the college or university financial aid office. Students are encouraged to complete the UNCF General Scholarship application to be matched with scholarships for which they meet the criteria. This program includes a summer internship. Funds may be used for tuition, room and board, books or to repay a federal student loan.

Target applicant:
　　High school students
　　College students
　　Adult students
Minimum GPA: 2.5
Amount: Up to $10,000.
Number of awards: Varies.
Deadline: Varies.
How to apply: Applications are available online.

(2363) · Multicultural Affairs Scholarship Program

Public Relations Student Society of America
33 Maiden Lane
11th Floor
New York, NY 10038
Phone: 212-460-1474
Fax: 212-995-0757
Email: prssa@prsa.org
Website: http://www.prssa.org
Purpose: To assist minority communications majors.
Eligibility: Applicants must be of African American, Hispanic, Asian, Native American, Alaskan Native or Pacific Islander ancestry, be at least college juniors studying communications in an undergraduate program and have a minimum 3.0 GPA. Applicants are required to submit a typed, double-spaced essay no more than three pages in length about workplace diversity or a similar topic.

Target applicant:
　　College students
　　Adult students
Minimum GPA: 3.0
Amount: $1,500.
Number of awards: 2.
Deadline: April 16.
How to apply: Applications are available online.

(2364) · NAACP/HBCU Scholarship Fund

United Negro College Fund (UNCF)
8260 Willow Oaks Corporate Drive
P.O. Box 10444
Fairfax, VA 22031-8044
Phone: 800-331-2244
Website: http://www.uncf.org
Purpose: To support incoming freshmen at HBCUs.
Eligibility: Applicants must be incoming African American freshmen at a Historically Black College or University (HBCU). Students must have a GPA of at least 2.5 and demonstrate financial need.
Target applicant:
    High school students
Minimum GPA: 2.5
Amount: $2,000.
Number of awards: 1.
Deadline: March 30.
How to apply: Applications are available online.

(2365) · NAHJ Scholarships

National Association of Hispanic Journalists
Scholarship Committee
1000 National Press Building
Washington, DC 20045
Phone: 202-662-7145
Fax: 202-662-7144
Email: ntita@nahj.org
Website: http://www.nahj.org
Purpose: To support Hispanic students who plan to enter the journalism field.
Eligibility: Applicants must be high school seniors, college undergraduate or graduate students majoring in print, photo, online or broadcast journalism.
Target applicant:
    High school students
    College students
    Graduate school students
    Adult students
Minimum GPA: None.
Amount: Varies.
Number of awards: Varies.
Deadline: Last Friday in January.
How to apply: Applications are available online.

(2366) · NAHN Scholarship

National Association of Hispanic Nurses
Attn: Maria Castro, NAHN Awards and Scholarship Committee Chair
1501 Sixteenth Street NW
Washington, DC 20036
Phone: 202-387-2477
Fax: 202-483-7183
Email: info@thehispanicnurses.org
Website: http://www.thehispanicnurses.org
Purpose: To aid Hispanic nursing students who demonstrate the potential to make contributions to the nursing profession and who will act as positive role models for other nursing students.
Eligibility: Applicants must be members of the NAHN and be enrolled in a diploma, associate, baccalaureate, graduate or practical/vocational nursing program.

Target applicant:
    College students
    Graduate school students
    Adult students
Minimum GPA: 3.0
Amount: $1,000.
Number of awards: Varies.
Deadline: March 14.
How to apply: Applications are available online or by mail.

(2367) · NAJA Scholarship Fund

Native American Journalists Association
555 Dakota Street
Al Neuharth Media Center
Vermillion, SD 57069
Phone: 605-677-5282
Fax: 866-694-4262
Email: info@naja.com
Website: http://www.naja.com
Purpose: To assist Native American students pursuing journalism degrees.
Eligibility: Applicants must be current members of NAJA.
Target applicant:
    College students
    Adult students
Minimum GPA: None.
Amount: $1,000-$3,000.
Number of awards: Varies.
Deadline: May 15.
How to apply: Applications are available online.

(2368) · NANBPWC National Scholarships

National Association of Negro Business and Professional Women's Clubs Inc.
1806 New Hampshire Avenue NW
Washington, DC 20009-3298
Phone: 202-483-4206
Email: info@nanbpwc.org
Website: http://www.nanbpwc.org
Purpose: To provide assistance to African American students who wish to pursue higher education.
Eligibility: Applicants must be graduating African American high school seniors with a GPA of 3.0 or higher. A 300-word essay is required.
Target applicant:
    High school students
Minimum GPA: 3.0
Amount: Varies.
Number of awards: Varies.
Deadline: March 1.
How to apply: Applications are available online.

(2369) · National AAJA General Scholarship Awards

Asian American Journalists Association
1182 Market Street
Suite 230
San Francisco, CA 94102
Phone: 415-346-2051
Fax: 415-346-6343
Email: lilac@aaja.org
Website: http://www.aaja.org

Purpose: Monetary assistance is awarded to students pursuing studies that lead to careers in print, broadcast or photo journalism.
Eligibility: Applicants must demonstrate a commitment to the field of journalism, sensitivity to Asian American issues demonstrated by community involvement, journalistic ability, scholastic ability and financial need. Applicants may be high school seniors, college students or graduate students.
Target applicant:
  High school students
  College students
  Graduate school students
  Adult students
Minimum GPA: None.
Amount: $2,000.
Number of awards: Varies.
Deadline: March 27.
How to apply: Applications are available online.

(2370) · National and District Scholarships

American Hellenic Education Progressive Association
1909 Q Street NW
Suite 500
Washington, DC 20009
Phone: 202-232-6300
Fax: 202-232-2140
Email: ahepa@ahepa.org
Website: http://www.ahepa.org
Purpose: To support projects furthering the goals of AHEPA: studies concerning Hellenism, Hellenic culture or Greek-American life.
Eligibility: Applicants must be high school seniors, college students, post-graduate students or adult students of Greek descent.
Target applicant:
  High school students
  College students
  Graduate school students
  Adult students
Minimum GPA: None.
Amount: Up to $5,000.
Number of awards: Varies.
Scholarship may be renewable.
Deadline: June 1.
How to apply: Applications are available online.

(2371) · National Association of Black Accountants Scholarship Program

National Association of Black Accountants
7249-A Hanover Parkway
Greenbelt, MD 20770
Phone: 301-474-NABA
Fax: 301-474-3114
Website: http://www.nabainc.org
Purpose: To support African Americans and other minorities in the accounting and finance professions.
Eligibility: Applicants must be ethnic minorities currently enrolled as full-time undergraduates in accounting, finance or business or as graduate students in a Master's of Accountancy program. Applicants must also be NABA members and have a minimum 2.5 GPA.
Target applicant:
  College students
  Graduate school students
  Adult students

Minimum GPA: 2.5
Amount: $500-$6,000.
Number of awards: Varies.
Deadline: December 31.
How to apply: Applications are available online.

(2372) · National Association of Black Journalists Scholarship Program

National Association of Black Journalists
Scholarship Program
8701-A Adelphi Road
Adelphi, MD 20783
Phone: 301-445-7100
Fax: 301-445-7101
Email: warren@nabj.org
Website: http://www.nabj.org
Purpose: To support African American students who are planning to pursue careers in journalism.
Eligibility: Applicants must be African American high school seniors, college students or graduate students who plan to pursue careers in journalism and who are journalism majors or in staff positions on the school newspaper or campus television, radio or website.
Target applicant:
  High school students
  College students
  Graduate school students
  Adult students
Minimum GPA: None.
Amount: Varies.
Number of awards: Varies.
Deadline: Varies.
How to apply: Applications are available online.

(2373) · National Foster Parent Association Vocational/Job Training Scholarship

National Foster Parent Association
7512 Stanich Avenue #6
Gig Harbor, WA 98335
Phone: 800-557-5238
Fax: 253-853-4001
Email: info@nfpainc.org
Website: http://www.nfpainc.org
Purpose: To support foster youth in furthering their education through technical or vocational programs.
Eligibility: Applicants must be foster children at least 17 years old planning to enroll in vocational, job training or correspondence courses, including the GED.
Target applicant:
  High school students
  College students
  Adult students
Minimum GPA: None.
Amount: $1,000.
Number of awards: 5.
Deadline: March 31.
How to apply: Applications are available online.

(2374) · National Leadership Grant

Order Sons of Italy in America (OSIA)
219 East Street NE
Washington, DC 20002
Phone: 202-547-5106
Fax: 202-546-8168
Email: scholarships@osia.org
Website: http://www.osia.org
Purpose: To provide awards to college students of Italian descent.
Eligibility: Applicants must be enrolled in an undergraduate or graduate program at a four-year university and of Italian descent. Students must submit official transcripts, test scores, letters of recommendation and an essay. Awards are given based on academic merit. There is a non-refundable $30 processing fee. It is highly recommended that you research the scholarship and awarding organization before applying for a scholarship with a fee. There are many scholarships that do not require a fee.
Target applicant:
    College students
    Graduate school students
    Adult students
Minimum GPA: None.
Amount: $5,000-$25,000.
Number of awards: 10-13.
Deadline: February 28.
How to apply: Applications are available online.

(2375) · National Scholarship

National Association of Negro Business and Professional Women's Clubs Inc.
1806 New Hampshire Avenue NW
Washington, DC 20009-3298
Phone: 202-483-4206
Email: info@nanbpwc.org
Website: http://www.nanbpwc.org
Purpose: To award scholarships to aspiring business and professional college or university students.
Eligibility: Applicants must be graduating high school seniors and have a minimum 3.0 GPA. Students must submit a transcript, an application form, two letters of recommendation and an essay that is at least 300 words on "Why is education important to me?"
Target applicant:
    High school students
Minimum GPA: 3.0
Amount: Up to $1,000.
Number of awards: Varies.
Deadline: March 1.
How to apply: Applications are available online.

(2376) · National Urban League Scholarships

National Urban League
120 Wall Street
New York, NY 10005
Phone: 888-839-0467
Email: info@nul.org
Website: http://www.nul.org
Purpose: To recognize young people who exhibit potential for success at the highest levels and provide them with financial aid in their higher education.
Eligibility: Applicants must be African American high school seniors. Selection is based on academic and personal achievement, community service and leadership.
Target applicant:
    High school students
Minimum GPA: 2.7
Amount: Varies.
Number of awards: Varies.
Scholarship may be renewable.
Deadline: January 31.
How to apply: Applications are available online.

(2377) · Native American Education Grant

Presbyterian Church (USA)
100 Witherspoon Street
Louisville, KY 40202
Phone: 888-728-7228 x5776
Email: fcook@ctr.pcusa.org
Website: http://www.pcusa.org
Purpose: To aid Alaska Natives and Native Americans pursuing full-time post-secondary education.
Eligibility: Applicants must be U.S. citizens who are high school graduates or G.E.D. recipients and demonstrate financial need. They must be recommended by a church pastor. Applicants must present proof of tribal membership, and preference will be given to active members of the Presbyterian Church.
Target applicant:
    College students
    Adult students
Minimum GPA: 2.5
Amount: $200-$3,000.
Number of awards: Varies.
Deadline: June 15.
How to apply: Subscribe to the list serve to get an application.

(2378) · Native American Leadership Education Program

Catching the Dream
Attn.: Scholarship Affairs Office
8200 Mountain Road NE
Suite 203
Albuquerque, NM 87110
Phone: 505-262-2351
Email: nscholarsh@aol.com
Website: http://www.catchingthedream.org
Purpose: To increase the number of American Indian teachers in American Indian schools.
Eligibility: Applicants must be at least 1/4 degree American Indian, enrolled in a tribe and current paraprofessionals in an American Indian school who are attending or plan to attend college full-time studying education, counseling or school administration. Students are required to apply for all other sources of funding at the same time as applying for this scholarship. Scholarships are based on grades, ACT or SAT scores, work experience, leadership, commitment to the American Indian community, goals and potential to improve the lives of American Indian people.
Target applicant:
    College students
    Graduate school students
    Adult students
Minimum GPA: None.

Amount: $500-$5,000.
Number of awards: Varies.
Deadline: March 15, April 15 and September 15.
How to apply: Applications are available online.

(2379) · Nelnet Scholarship

United Negro College Fund (UNCF)
8260 Willow Oaks Corporate Drive
P.O. Box 10444
Fairfax, VA 22031-8044
Phone: 800-331-2244
Website: http://www.uncf.org
Purpose: To support African American students attending UNCF member schools.
Eligibility: Applicants must have a minimum 2.5 GPA, complete the Free Application for Federal Student Aid (FAFSA) and have unmet financial need that is verified by the college or university financial aid office. Students are encouraged to complete the UNCF General Scholarship application to be matched with scholarships for which they meet the criteria.
Target applicant:
   High school students
   College students
   Adult students
Minimum GPA: 2.5
Amount: $1,000.
Number of awards: 1.
Deadline: Varies.
How to apply: Applications are available online.

(2380) · Newhouse Scholarship Program

National Association of Hispanic Journalists
Scholarship Committee
1000 National Press Building
Washington, DC 20045
Phone: 202-662-7145
Fax: 202-662-7144
Email: ntita@nahj.org
Website: http://www.nahj.org
Purpose: To support Hispanic students who plan to enter the journalism field.
Eligibility: Applicants must be current college sophomores. Recipients are required to intern at a Newhouse newspaper the summer following their junior year. The program provides a stipend to attend NAHJ's annual convention.
Target applicant:
   College students
   Adult students
Minimum GPA: None.
Amount: $5,000.
Number of awards: Varies.
Scholarship may be renewable.
Deadline: Last Friday in January.
How to apply: Applications are available online.

(2381) · OCA/UPS Gold Mountain Scholarship

Organization of Chinese Americans (OCA)
1322 18th Street NW
Washington, DC 20036-1803
Phone: 202-223-5500

Fax: 202-296-0540
Email: oca@ocanatl.org
Website: http://www.ocanatl.org
Purpose: To support first generation Asian American students.
Eligibility: Applicants must be Asian Pacific Americans who intend to begin college in the fall of the year of application and must demonstrate significant financial need. Applicants must also be the first in their family to attend college and have a minimum 3.0 GPA.
Target applicant:
   High school students
Minimum GPA: 3.0
Amount: $2,000.
Number of awards: 12.
Deadline: Varies.
How to apply: Applications are available online or by written request.

(2382) · Office Depot Scholarship

United Negro College Fund (UNCF)
8260 Willow Oaks Corporate Drive
P.O. Box 10444
Fairfax, VA 22031-8044
Phone: 800-331-2244
Website: http://www.uncf.org
Purpose: To help African American students attending United Negro College Fund (UNCF) member colleges and universities who have performed service to the community.
Eligibility: Applicants must have a minimum 2.5 GPA, complete the Free Application for Federal Student Aid (FAFSA) and have unmet financial need that is verified by the college or university financial aid office. Students are encouraged to complete the UNCF General Scholarship application to be matched with scholarships for which they meet the criteria. Applicants should submit two recommendation letters, a personal statement, a transcript, a resume and a small photo.
Target applicant:
   High school students
   College students
   Adult students
Minimum GPA: 2.5
Amount: $2,000-$3,000.
Number of awards: Varies.
Deadline: March 31.
How to apply: Applications are available online.

(2383) · Office of Hawaiian Affairs Scholarship Fund

Hawaii Community Foundation - Scholarships
1164 Bishop Street, Suite 800
Honolulu, HI 96813
Phone: 888-731-3863
Fax: 808-521-6286
Email: scholarships@hcf-hawaii.org
Website: http://www.hawaiicommunityfoundation.org
Purpose: To support students of Hawaiian ancestry.
Eligibility: Students may attend any two- or four-year college in the United States. Ancestry must be verified through the office's Hawaiian Registry Program, which is available online.
Target applicant:
   High school students
   College students
   Adult students
Minimum GPA: None.

Amount: Varies.
Number of awards: Varies.
Deadline: March 1.
How to apply: To apply, register online, complete the online application and select the scholarships to which you wish to apply. In addition, mail the supporting materials: printed confirmation page from the online application, personal statement, copy of Student Aid Report (SAR) available at www.fafsa.ed.gov and official transcript.

(2384) · Oscar and Mildred Larson Award

Vasa Order of America
597 West Walbrook Drive
San Jose, CA 95129
Website: http://www.vasaorder.com
Purpose: To provide financial assistance to Swedish students.
Eligibility: Applicants must be students of Swedish ancestry or who were born in Sweden and are now residents of the United States, Canada or Sweden. They must be attending an accredited four-year institution of higher learning in the United States pursuing an undergraduate or graduate degree.
Target applicant:
   High school students
   College students
   Graduate school students
   Adult students
Minimum GPA: None.
Amount: $3,000.
Number of awards: 1.
Deadline: February 10.
How to apply: Applications are available online or from the VASA Vice Grand Master.

(2385) · P.A. Margaronis Scholarships

American Hellenic Education Progressive Association
1909 Q Street NW
Suite 500
Washington, DC 20009
Phone: 202-232-6300
Fax: 202-232-2140
Email: ahepa@ahepa.org
Website: http://www.ahepa.org
Purpose: To support undergraduate and graduate students who are of Greek descent.
Eligibility: Applicants must submit an essay and two letters of recommendation.
Target applicant:
   High school students
   College students
   Graduate school students
   Adult students
Minimum GPA: None.
Amount: $500-$2,000.
Number of awards: Varies.
Deadline: March 31.
How to apply: Applications are available online.

(2386) · P.E.O. Program for Continuing Education

P.E.O. Sisterhood
3100 Grand Avenue
Des Moines, IA 50312-2899

Phone: 515-255-3153
Fax: 515-255-3820
Website: http://www.peointernational.org
Purpose: To assist women whose education has been interrupted.
Eligibility: Applicants must be women who are resuming studies to improve their marketable skills due to changing demands in their lives. They must have financial need and cannot use the funds to pay living expenses or repay educational loans. They must be sponsored by a P.E.O. chapter and be citizens and students of the United States or Canada. They must have had at least two consecutive years as a non-student in their adult lives and be able to complete their educational goals in two consecutive years or less. Doctoral degree students are not eligible.
Target applicant:
   College students
   Graduate school students
   Adult students
Minimum GPA: None.
Amount: Varies.
Number of awards: Varies.
Scholarship may be renewable.
Deadline: Varies.
How to apply: Applications are available online or from the P.E.O.

(2387) · Palmer B. Carson-PFLAG Scholarship for LGBT Advocacy

Parents, Families and Friends of Lesbians and Gays
1726 M Street NW
Suite 400
Washington, DC 20036
Phone: 202-467-8180
Fax: 202-467-8194
Email: info@pflag.org
Website: http://www.pflag.org
Purpose: To provide financial assistance to gay, lesbian, bisexual and transgender students and their allies.
Eligibility: Applicants must be graduating seniors or prior-year graduates who have applied to an accredited institution of higher learning. Students must be attending college for the first time. They must be a member or ally of, and demonstrate interest in service to, the LGBT community. An essay and reference are required.
Target applicant:
   High school students
Minimum GPA: None.
Amount: $5,000.
Number of awards: 1.
Deadline: March 15.
How to apply: Applications are available online.

(2388) · Parents without Partners International Scholarship Program

Parents without Partners
1650 S. Dixie Highway, Suite 510
Boca Raton, FL 33432
Phone: 561-391-8833
Fax: 561-395-8557
Website: http://www.parentswithoutpartners.org
Purpose: To aid children raised by single parents.
Eligibility: Applicants should be the dependent children of Parents without Partners members and be no more than 25 years old. Students must be seniors applying to a college or trade school or current undergraduates.

Target applicant:
    High school students
    College students
Minimum GPA: None.
Amount: $250-$500.
Number of awards: Up to 10.
Deadline: March 15.
How to apply: Applications are available with membership in the organization.

(2389) · Parents, Families and Friends of Lesbians and Gays General Scholarships

Parents, Families and Friends of Lesbians and Gays
1726 M Street NW
Suite 400
Washington, DC 20036
Phone: 202-467-8180
Fax: 202-467-8194
Email: info@pflag.org
Website: http://www.pflag.org
Purpose: To provide educational opportunities for the GLBT community.
Eligibility: Applicants must identify themselves as gay, lesbian, bisexual or transgender or be an ally of the GLBT community. Students must be graduating from high school in the year of application or have graduated the previous year. They must have applied to an accredited college or university to attend for the first time, and they must demonstrate interest in serving the GLBT community.
Target applicant:
    High school students
Minimum GPA: None.
Amount: $1,000.
Number of awards: 8.
Deadline: March 1.
How to apply: Applications are available online.

(2390) · PBS&J Achievement Scholarship

Conference of Minority Transportation Officials
818 18th Street NW, Suite 850
Washington, DC 20006
Phone: 202-530-0551
Fax: 202-530-0617
Email: comto@comto.org
Website: http://www.comto.org
Purpose: To support high school, undergraduate and graduate students who are pursuing careers in transportation.
Eligibility: High school and undergraduate students must have at least a 2.0 GPA. Undergraduate students must be enrolled in at least 12 credits per semester. Undergraduate and graduate students must have majors related to transportation.
Target applicant:
    High school students
    College students
    Graduate school students
    Adult students
Minimum GPA: 2.0
Amount: $4,000.
Number of awards: Varies.
Deadline: April 4.
How to apply: Applications are available online.

(2391) · PEO International Peace Scholarship

PEO International Peace Scholarship Fund
3700 Grand Avenue
Des Moines, IA 50312
Phone: 515-255-3153
Fax: 515-255-3820
Website: http://www.peointernational.org
Purpose: Women from countries other than the U.S. or Canada are assisted in their graduate studies within North America.
Eligibility: Applicants must be female, attend a North American graduate school or Cottey College and be from a country other than the U.S. or Canada.
Target applicant:
    Graduate school students
    Adult students
Minimum GPA: None.
Amount: $6,000.
Number of awards: Varies.
Scholarship may be renewable.
Deadline: January 31.
How to apply: Applicants must first submit an eligibility form, available online. If found eligible, students will be mailed application materials.

(2392) · Polish National Alliance Scholarship

Polish National Alliance
Educational Department
6100 Cicero Avenue
Chicago, IL 60646
Phone: 800-621-3723
Email: pna@pna-znp.org
Website: http://www.pna-znp.org
Purpose: To assist members of the Polish National Alliance with their undergraduate studies.
Eligibility: Applicants must be college sophomores, juniors or seniors and have been paying members in good standing with the Polish National Association for at least three years. If the applicant has been in good standing with the PNA for at least two years, his or her parents must have been paying PNA members for at least five years.
Target applicant:
    College students
    Adult students
Minimum GPA: None.
Amount: Varies.
Number of awards: Varies.
Scholarship may be renewable.
Deadline: April 15.
How to apply: Applications are available by email at mary.srodon@pna-znp.org.

(2393) · Possible Woman Foundation International Scholarship

Possible Woman Enterprises
P.O. Box 924137
Norcross, GA 30010-4137
Email: info@possiblewomanfoundation.org
Website: http://www.possiblewomanfoundation.org
Purpose: To provide financial assistance to women who are returning to school to change or further their careers and to stay-at-home moms who wish to return to school.

Eligibility: Applicants must be women at least 25 years of age who plan to study in the United States. Students from other countries are eligible but must be referred by an educational institution or organization. An essay is required. Applicants should not be eligible for significant funding from other sources.

Target applicant:
  College students
  Adult students

Minimum GPA: None.

Amount: Varies.

Number of awards: Varies.

Deadline: January 23.

How to apply: Applications are available online.

(2394) · Premedical Summer Institute Program/ Internship

United Negro College Fund (UNCF)
8260 Willow Oaks Corporate Drive
P.O. Box 10444
Fairfax, VA 22031-8044
Phone: 800-331-2244
Website: http://www.uncf.org

Purpose: To help African American students attending United Negro College Fund (UNCF) Member Colleges and Universities who are pre-med and who are interested in medical careers.

Eligibility: Applicants must have a minimum 3.0 GPA, complete the Free Application for Federal Student Aid (FAFSA) and have unmet financial need that is verified by the college or university financial aid office. Students are encouraged to complete the UNCF General Scholarship application to be matched with scholarships for which they meet the criteria. The program allows access to pre-med education through an eight-week internship during the summer.

Target applicant:
  High school students
  College students
  Adult students

Minimum GPA: 3.0

Amount: $1,000.

Number of awards: Varies.

Deadline: March 1.

How to apply: Applications are available online.

(2395) · Prince Kuhio Hawaiian Civic Club Scholarship

Prince Kuhio Hawaiian Civic Club
P.O. Box 4728
Honolulu, HI 96812
Email: cypakele@ksbe.edu
Website: http://www.pkhcc.com/scholarship

Purpose: To provide funds for higher education to Hawaiians.

Eligibility: Applicants must be high school seniors or current college students from Hawaii. Preference is given to students who have some Hawaiian ancestry and have participated in community service or volunteer work. Studies of Hawaiian language, studies and culture, journalism and education are encouraged. Applicants must enroll full-time at a two- or four-year institution.

Target applicant:
  High school students
  College students
  Adult students

Minimum GPA: None.

Amount: Up to $1,000.

Number of awards: Varies.

Scholarship may be renewable.

Deadline: April 1.

How to apply: Applications are available online or by mail.

(2396) · Private High School Scholarship

Hopi Tribe Grants and Scholarship Program
P.O. Box 123
Kykotsmovi, AZ 86039
Phone: 800-762-9630
Fax: 928-734-9575
Email: info@hopi.nsn.us
Website: http://www.hopieducationfund.org

Purpose: To help Hopi students who plan to attend an accredited private high school.

Eligibility: Applicants must be enrolled members of the Hopi tribe and should submit applications, statements of goals, financial needs analysis, proof of Hopi enrollment and transcripts.

Target applicant:
  Junior high students or younger
  High school students

Minimum GPA: None.

Amount: Varies.

Number of awards: Varies.

Deadline: Varies.

How to apply: Applications are available by mail.

(2397) · Raymond W. Cannon Memorial Scholarship

United Negro College Fund (UNCF)
8260 Willow Oaks Corporate Drive
P.O. Box 10444
Fairfax, VA 22031-8044
Phone: 800-331-2244
Website: http://www.uncf.org

Purpose: To help African American student leaders.

Eligibility: Applicants must be juniors majoring in pharmacy or pre-law at United Negro College Fund (UNCF) member colleges or universities or Historically Black Colleges or Universities (HBCU Schools) and who have shown leadership in high school and college.

Target applicant:
  College students
  Adult students

Minimum GPA: 2.5

Amount: $2,000-$5,000.

Number of awards: Varies.

Deadline: Varies.

How to apply: Applications are available online.

(2398) · Reader's Digest Scholarship

United Negro College Fund (UNCF)
8260 Willow Oaks Corporate Drive
P.O. Box 10444
Fairfax, VA 22031-8044
Phone: 800-331-2244
Website: http://www.uncf.org

Purpose: To help African American students attending United Negro College Fund (UNCF) Member Colleges and Universities and majoring in communications, journalism or English who have shown an interest in print journalism.

Eligibility: Applicants must have a minimum 3.0 GPA, complete the Free Application for Federal Student Aid (FAFSA) and have unmet financial need that is verified by the college or university financial aid office. Students are encouraged to complete the UNCF General Scholarship application to be matched with scholarships for which they meet the criteria. Funds may be used for tuition, room and board, books or to repay a federal student loan.

Target applicant:
  High school students
  College students
  Adult students
Minimum GPA: 3.0
Amount: $5,000.
Number of awards: Varies.
Deadline: November 17.
How to apply: Applications are available online.

(2399) · Rhea and Louis Spieler Scholarship Program

United Negro College Fund (UNCF)
8260 Willow Oaks Corporate Drive
P.O. Box 10444
Fairfax, VA 22031-8044
Phone: 800-331-2244
Website: http://www.uncf.org
Purpose: To help African American students who are pursuing higher education.
Eligibility: Applicants must have a minimum 2.5 GPA, complete the Free Application for Federal Student Aid (FAFSA) and have unmet financial need that is verified by the college or university financial aid office. UNCF students are encouraged to complete the UNCF General Scholarship application to be matched with scholarships for which they meet the criteria.

Target applicant:
  High school students
  College students
  Adult students
Minimum GPA: 2.5
Amount: Varies.
Number of awards: Varies.
Deadline: Varies.
How to apply: Applications are available online.

(2400) · Richard R. Tufenkian Memorial Scholarship

Armenian Educational Foundation Inc.
600 W. Broadway
Suite 130
Glendale, CA 91204
Phone: 818-242-4154
Email: aef@aefweb.org
Website: http://www.aefweb.org
Purpose: To support Armenian undergraduate students.
Eligibility: Applicants must be full-time undergraduate students of Armenian descent at U.S. universities, have a minimum 3.0 GPA, demonstrate financial need and be involved in the Armenian community. Tax returns, transcripts, two reference letters, essays and applications are required.
Target applicant:
  College students
  Adult students
Minimum GPA: 3.0
Amount: $2,000.

Number of awards: 5.
Deadline: July 30.
How to apply: Applications are available online.

(2401) · Robert Dole Scholarship for Disabled Students

United Negro College Fund (UNCF)
8260 Willow Oaks Corporate Drive
P.O. Box 10444
Fairfax, VA 22031-8044
Phone: 800-331-2244
Website: http://www.uncf.org
Purpose: To help physically and/or mentally challenged African Americans at United Negro College Fund (UNCF) member colleges or universities.
Eligibility: Applicants must have a minimum 2.5 GPA, complete the Free Application for Federal Student Aid (FAFSA) and have unmet financial need that is verified by the college or university financial aid office. UNCF students are encouraged to complete the UNCF General Scholarship application to be matched with scholarships for which they meet the criteria.
Target applicant:
  High school students
  College students
  Adult students
Minimum GPA: 2.5
Amount: $3,000.
Number of awards: Varies.
Deadline: November 30.
How to apply: Applications are available online.

(2402) · Robert Half International

United Negro College Fund (UNCF)
8260 Willow Oaks Corporate Drive
P.O. Box 10444
Fairfax, VA 22031-8044
Phone: 800-331-2244
Website: http://www.uncf.org
Purpose: To support African American business and accounting students.
Eligibility: Applicants must be majoring in business or accounting at a UNCF member college or university. They must have a GPA of at least 2.5 and demonstrate financial need.
Target applicant:
  High school students
  College students
  Adult students
Minimum GPA: 2.5
Amount: $1,000-$1,750.
Number of awards: Varies.
Deadline: Varies.
How to apply: Applications are available online.

(2403) · Ron Brown Scholar Program

CAP Charitable Foundation
Ron Brown Scholar Program
1160 Pepsi Place
Suite 206
Charlottesville, VA 22901
Phone: 434-964-1588
Fax: 434-964-1589

Email: franh@ronbrown.org
Website: http://www.ronbrown.org
Purpose: To award scholarships to academically talented, highly motivated African American high school seniors.
Eligibility: Applicants must be African American collegebound high school seniors. Selection is based on academic promise, leadership, communication skills, school and community involvement and financial need.
Target applicant:
   High school students
Minimum GPA: None.
Amount: $10,000.
Number of awards: Varies.
Scholarship may be renewable.
Deadline: January 9.
How to apply: Applications are available online.

(2404) · Rosa L. Parks Scholarship

Conference of Minority Transportation Officials
818 18th Street NW, Suite 850
Washington, DC 20006
Phone: 202-530-0551
Fax: 202-530-0617
Email: comto@comto.org
Website: http://www.comto.org
Purpose: To support graduating high school students whose parents are COMTO members and college or graduate students who are studying fields related to transportation.
Eligibility: Applicants must have at least a 3.0 GPA. High school students must be accepted into a college or technical school, and their parents must have been COMTO members in good standing for at least the past year. College students must have at least 60 credits, and graduate students must have at least 15 credits.
Target applicant:
   High school students
   College students
   Graduate school students
   Adult students
Minimum GPA: 3.0
Amount: $4,500.
Number of awards: Varies.
Deadline: April 4.
How to apply: Applications are available online.

(2405) · Roy Wilkins Scholarship

National Association for the Advancement of Colored People
The United Negro College Fund
Scholarships and Grants Administration
8260 Willow Oaks Corporate Drive
Fairfax, VA 22031
Phone: 703-205-3400
Website: http://www.naacp.org
Purpose: The NAACP created its scholarships to promote equal opportunity in education.
Eligibility: Students must be entering college freshmen at an accredited U.S. college and be full-time students. Membership in the NAACP is not required, but highly recommended.
Target applicant:
   High school students
   College students
   Adult students

Minimum GPA: 2.5
Amount: $1,000.
Number of awards: Varies.
Deadline: The last Friday in the month of March.
How to apply: Applications are available online or by mail.

(2406) · Ruth Mu-Lan Chu and James S.C. Chao Scholarship

U.S. Pan Asian American Chamber of Commerce
1329 18th Street NW
Washington, DC 20036
Phone: 800-696-7818
Fax: 202-296-5225
Email: info@uspaacc.com
Website: http://www.uspaacc.com
Purpose: To support the higher education goals of Asian American students.
Eligibility: Applicants must be female U.S. citizens or permanent residents and be high school seniors of Asian or Pacific heritage who will pursue post-secondary educations at an accredited institution in the U.S. Selection is based on academic excellence, community service involvement and financial need. A minimum 3.5 GPA required. Applicants must be able to attend the Excellence Awards and Scholarships Dinner during the CelebrAsian Annual Conference (in May).
Target applicant:
   High school students
Minimum GPA: 3.5
Amount: Up to $3,000.
Number of awards: 1.
Deadline: February 22.
How to apply: Applications are available online.

(2407) · Scholarships for Social Justice

Higher Education Consortium for Urban Affairs
2233 University Avenue W, Suite 210
St. Paul, MN 55114
Phone: 651-646-8832
Email: info@hecua.org
Website: http://www.hecua.org/scholarships.php
Purpose: To support students from low-income families, students from ethnic minorities and students who are the first in their families to attend college.
Eligibility: Students must have submitted an application to one of HECUA's semester programs, and they must be enrolled at an HECUA member institution. A list of member institutions is available online.
Target applicant:
   College students
   Adult students
Minimum GPA: None.
Amount: $1,500.
Number of awards: 2.
Deadline: April 15.
How to apply: Applications are available online. An essay, letter of recommendation and Student Aid Report from completing the Free Application for Federal Student Aid are required.

(2408) · Sequoyah Graduate Fellowships for American Indian and Alaskan Natives

Association on American Indian Affairs
Lisa Wyzlic, Scholarship Coordinator

966 Hungerford Drive, Suite 12-B
Rockville, MD 20850
Phone: 240-314-7155
Fax: 240-314-7159
Email: general.aaia@verizon.net
Website: http://www.indian-affairs.org
Purpose: To provide graduate fellowships for students of American Indian and Alaskan Native heritage.
Eligibility: Applicants must be full-time students who can provide proof of tribal enrollment, a Certificate of Indian Blood (showing 1/4 Indian blood) and an essay on educational goals.
Target applicant:
  Graduate school students
  Adult students
Minimum GPA: None.
Amount: $1,500.
Number of awards: Varies.
Deadline: July 20.
How to apply: Applications are available online.

(2409) · Siemens Teacher Education Scholarship Program

United Negro College Fund (UNCF)
8260 Willow Oaks Corporate Drive
P.O. Box 10444
Fairfax, VA 22031-8044
Phone: 800-331-2244
Website: http://www.uncf.org
Purpose: To help African American students who are rising juniors or seniors who plan to teach in science, technology or math.
Eligibility: Applicants must plan to teach and may major in mathematics, science, information systems, education, chemistry, biology, science technology, computer engineering or chemical engineering. Applicants must have a minimum 2.75 GPA, complete the Free Application for Federal Student Aid (FAFSA) and have unmet financial need that is verified by the college or university financial aid office. UNCF students are encouraged to complete the UNCF General Scholarship application to be matched with scholarships for which they meet the criteria.
Target applicant:
  College students
  Adult students
Minimum GPA: 2.75
Amount: $2,500.
Number of awards: Varies.
Scholarship may be renewable.
Deadline: October 16.
How to apply: Applications are available online.

(2410) · Sikh Education Aid Fund

Association of Sikh Professionals
2917 Oak Brook Hills Road
Oak Brook, IL 60523
Email: contact@sikhprofessionals.org
Website: http://www.sikhprofessionals.org
Purpose: To recognize Sikh students for academic achievement.
Eligibility: Applicants must be accepted by or attend an accredited U.S. institution. Recipients are usually high school seniors or college students. Financial documents, a photo, copies of recent transcripts, essays and names and addresses of five Sikhs in the community are required. Financial need is the most important criteria, but academic

ability and involvement in Sikh activities is also considered. Candidates may be interviewed.
Target applicant:
  High school students
  College students
  Graduate school students
  Adult students
Minimum GPA: None.
Amount: $2,500.
Number of awards: Varies.
Scholarship may be renewable.
Deadline: June 1.
How to apply: Applications are available online.

(2411) · Siragusa Foundation Scholarship

United Negro College Fund (UNCF)
8260 Willow Oaks Corporate Drive
P.O. Box 10444
Fairfax, VA 22031-8044
Phone: 800-331-2244
Website: http://www.uncf.org
Purpose: To help African American students attending United Negro College Fund (UNCF) member colleges and universities.
Eligibility: Applicants must have a minimum 2.5 GPA, complete the Free Application for Federal Student Aid (FAFSA) and have unmet financial need that is verified by the college or university financial aid office. Students are encouraged to complete the UNCF General Scholarship application to be matched with scholarships for which they meet the criteria.
Target applicant:
  High school students
  College students
  Adult students
Minimum GPA: 2.5
Amount: $2,000.
Number of awards: Varies.
Deadline: Varies.
How to apply: Applications are available online.

(2412) · Slovenian Women's Union of America Scholarship Program

Slovenian Women's Union of America
Mary Turvey, SWUA Scholarship Director
52 Oakridge Drive
Marquette, MI 49855
Email: mturvey@aol.com
Website: http://www.swua.org
Purpose: To promote Slovenian culture.
Eligibility: Students must be high school seniors or current college students at an accredited school. Applicants must have been members of the SWUA for at least three years. High school senior applications must include a photo, FAFSA, a letter of recommendation from high school principal or teacher, brief autobiography, including personal and educational goals, a high school transcript including SAT and ACT scores, a letter of recommendation from an SWUA branch officer and a financial statement from their parents. College student applications must include a photo, FAFSA, a brief autobiography including personal and educational goals, letters of recommendation from a college professor/instructor and an SWUA branch officer and grade transcripts from the last two semesters. The committee considers life goals, scholastic achievement, financial need and involvement in school, church and community.

Target applicant:
High school students
College students
Graduate school students
Adult students
Minimum GPA: None.
Amount: $1,000-$2,000.
Number of awards: Varies.
Deadline: March 1.
How to apply: Applications are available online and from SWUA branch secretaries.

(2413) · Sodexho Scholarship

United Negro College Fund (UNCF)
8260 Willow Oaks Corporate Drive
P.O. Box 10444
Fairfax, VA 22031-8044
Phone: 800-331-2244
Website: http://www.uncf.org
Purpose: To help African American freshmen, especially those who have helped with community service programs dealing with hunger, attending Historically Black Colleges and Universities (HBCU) or United Negro College Fund (UNCF) member colleges and universities.
Eligibility: Applicants must have a minimum 3.0 GPA, complete the Free Application for Federal Student Aid (FAFSA) and have unmet financial need that is verified by the college or university financial aid office. UNCF students are encouraged to complete the UNCF General Scholarship application to be matched with scholarships for which they meet the criteria. Priority will be given to students who have participated in community service programs dealing with hunger. Applicants must submit a transcript, two recommendation letters, an essay and college or university acceptance letters.
Target applicant:
High school students
College students
Adult students
Minimum GPA: 3.0
Amount: up to $3,500.
Number of awards: Varies.
Deadline: August 22.
How to apply: Applications are available online.

(2414) · Standardized Test Fee Scholarship

Hopi Tribe Grants and Scholarship Program
P.O. Box 123
Kykotsmovi, AZ 86039
Phone: 800-762-9630
Fax: 928-734-9575
Email: info@hopi.nsn.us
Website: http://www.hopieducationfund.org
Purpose: To help Hopi students who are required to take an entrance exams or career certification tests.
Eligibility: Applicants must be enrolled members of the Hopi tribe, be high school graduates or have earned a GED, have been accepted to and plan to attend full-time a regionally accredited college and have completed the Free Application for Federal Student Aid. Applications, statements of goals, financial needs analysis, proof of Hopi enrollment and transcripts are required. The award provides assistance with the Graduate Record Exam, Law School Admission Test, Arizona Teachers Proficiency Exam, Bar Exam and others. Applications should be submitted 30 days before the test date.

Target applicant:
High school students
College students
Graduate school students
Adult students
Minimum GPA: None.
Amount: Varies.
Number of awards: Varies.
Deadline: Varies.
How to apply: Applications are available by mail.

(2415) · Sterling Bank Scholarship

United Negro College Fund (UNCF)
8260 Willow Oaks Corporate Drive
P.O. Box 10444
Fairfax, VA 22031-8044
Phone: 800-331-2244
Website: http://www.uncf.org
Purpose: To help African American students attending United Negro College Fund (UNCF) member colleges and universities.
Eligibility: Applicants must have a minimum 2.5 GPA, complete the Free Application for Federal Student Aid (FAFSA) and have unmet financial need that is verified by the college or university financial aid office. Students are encouraged to complete the UNCF General Scholarship application to be matched with scholarships for which they meet the criteria.
Target applicant:
High school students
College students
Adult students
Minimum GPA: 2.5
Amount: Varies.
Number of awards: Varies.
Deadline: Varies.
How to apply: Applications are available online.

(2416) · Student CEC Ethnic Diversity Scholarship

Council for Exceptional Children
1110 North Glebe Road
Suite 300
Arlington, VA 22201
Phone: 888-232-7733
Fax: 703-264-9494
Email: mbrship@cec.sped.org
Website: http://www.cec.sped.org
Purpose: To recognize a student CEC member from an ethnically diverse background who is currently pursuing a degree in special education.
Eligibility: Applicants must be U.S. or Canadian citizens, junior, senior or graduate students enrolled in an accredited college or university, members of an ethnically diverse group and pursuing a degree in special education. Students must be student CEC members in good standing with a minimum 2.5 GPA. Applicants must also submit a list of their Student CEC activities and/or other involvement with those with disabilities and a short autobiography focusing on their interest in special education.
Target applicant:
College students
Graduate school students
Adult students
Minimum GPA: 2.5
Amount: $500.

Number of awards: 1.
Deadline: November 1.
How to apply: Applications are available online.

(2417) · Student CEC/Black Caucus Scholarship

Council for Exceptional Children
1110 North Glebe Road
Suite 300
Arlington, VA 22201
Phone: 888-232-7733
Fax: 703-264-9494
Email: mbrship@cec.sped.org
Website: http://www.cec.sped.org
Purpose: To recognize an African American student who is a student CEC member and pursuing a degree in special education.
Eligibility: Applicants must be African American and junior, senior or graduate students enrolled in an accredited college or university and be U.S. or Canadian citizens. Applicants must also be student CEC members in good standing and majoring in special education with a minimum 2.5 GPA. Applicants must submit a list of their Student CEC activities and/or other involvement with programs for those with disabilities and a short autobiography focusing on their interest in special education.
Target applicant:
  College students
  Graduate school students
  Adult students
Minimum GPA: 2.5
Amount: $500.
Number of awards: 1.
Deadline: November 1.
How to apply: Applications are available online.

(2418) · Sutton Scholarship

National Association for the Advancement of Colored People
The United Negro College Fund
Scholarships and Grants Administration
8260 Willow Oaks Corporate Drive
Fairfax, VA 22031
Phone: 703-205-3400
Website: http://www.naacp.org
Purpose: To support African Americans entering the field of education.
Eligibility: Applicants must be education majors at an accredited college and U.S. citizens. Undergraduates must be full-time students with a GPA of 2.5, while graduates may be full- or part-time students and must maintain a GPA of 3.0. NAACP membership is not required but is highly desirable.
Target applicant:
  High school students
  College students
  Graduate school students
  Adult students
Minimum GPA: 2.5 for undergraduates; 3.0 for graduate students
Amount: $1,000-$2,000.
Number of awards: Varies.
Scholarship may be renewable.
Deadline: Last Friday in March.
How to apply: Applications are available online.

(2419) · Suzanne Jourdan Memorial Scholarship

Epsilon Sigma Alpha Foundation
P.O. Box 270517
Fort Collins, CO 80527
Phone: 970-223-2824
Fax: 970-223-4456
Email: kloyd@knoxy.net
Website: http://www.esaintl.com/esaf
Purpose: To assist single mothers in obtaining higher education.
Eligibility: Applicants must be single moms between the ages of 18 and 35. They must be Florida residents and have a GPA of at least 2.0. Selection is based on financial need (50 percent), scholastic ability (25 percent), character (10 percent), leadership (10 percent) and service (5 percent).
Target applicant:
  High school students
  College students
  Adult students
Minimum GPA: None.
Amount: $500.
Number of awards: 1.
Deadline: February 1.
How to apply: Applications are available online.

(2420) · Sylvia Shapiro Scholarship

United Negro College Fund (UNCF)
8260 Willow Oaks Corporate Drive
P.O. Box 10444
Fairfax, VA 22031-8044
Phone: 800-331-2244
Website: http://www.uncf.org
Purpose: To help African American students attending United Negro College Fund (UNCF) member colleges and universities.
Eligibility: Applicants must have a minimum 2.5 GPA, complete the Free Application for Federal Student Aid (FAFSA) and have unmet financial need that is verified by the college or university financial aid office. Students are encouraged to complete the UNCF General Scholarship application to be matched with scholarships for which they meet the criteria.
Target applicant:
  High school students
  College students
  Adult students
Minimum GPA: 2.5
Amount: Varies.
Number of awards: Varies.
Deadline: Varies.
How to apply: Applications are available online.

(2421) · Telamon Scholarship

U.S. Pan Asian American Chamber of Commerce
1329 18th Street NW
Washington, DC 20036
Phone: 800-696-7818
Fax: 202-296-5225
Email: info@uspaacc.com
Website: http://www.uspaacc.com
Purpose: To support the higher education goals of Asian American students.
Eligibility: Applicants must be U.S. citizens or permanent residents and be high school seniors of Asian or Pacific heritage who will pursue post-

secondary educations at an accredited institution in the U.S. Selection is based on academic excellence, leadership in extracurricular activities, community service involvement and financial need. A minimum 3.3 GPA required. Applicants must be able to attend the Excellence Awards and Scholarships Dinner during the CelebrAsian Annual Conference (in May).

Target applicant:
  High school students
Minimum GPA: 3.3
Amount: Up to $2,000.
Number of awards: 1.
Deadline: February 22.
How to apply: Applications are available online.

(2422) · The Black History Common Knowledge Challenge

Common Knowledge Scholarship Foundation
P.O. Box 290361
Davie, FL 33329-0361
Phone: 954-262-8553
Email: info@cksf.org
Website: http://www.cksf.org
Purpose: To support students who are knowledgeable about black history.
Eligibility: Applicants must register online with CKSF. Students must take several online quizzes on black history. The student with the most points from correct answers and the shortest time that it takes to answer the questions wins the scholarship.
Target applicant:
  High school students
  College students
  Graduate school students
  Adult students
Minimum GPA: None.
Amount: $250.
Number of awards: 1.
Deadline: February 17.
How to apply: Applications are available online.

(2423) · The Maureen L. & Howard N. Blitman, P.E., Scholarship

National Society of Professional Engineers
1420 King Street
Alexandria, VA 22314-2794
Phone: 703-684-2885
Fax: 703-836-4875
Email: memserv@nspe.org
Website: http://www.nspe.org
Purpose: To encourage minority students to pursue careers in engineering.
Eligibility: Applicants must be African-American, Hispanic or Native American high school seniors who have been accepted into an accredited engineering program at a four-year institution. Students are evaluated based on academic achievement, community involvement and recommendations and must have a minimum 3.5 GPA.
Target applicant:
  High school students
Minimum GPA: 3.5
Amount: $5,000.
Number of awards: 1.
Deadline: March 1.
How to apply: Applications are available online.

(2424) · Thomas G. Neusom Scholarship

Conference of Minority Transportation Officials
818 18th Street NW, Suite 850
Washington, DC 20006
Phone: 202-530-0551
Fax: 202-530-0617
Email: comto@comto.org
Website: http://www.comto.org
Purpose: To support college students who are members of COMTO.
Eligibility: Applicants must have been COMTO members in good standing for at least the past year. Students must be enrolled in at least six credits per semester at a college, vocational school or graduate school. They must have at least a 2.5 GPA. Applicants must submit a short essay and two letters of recommendation.
Target applicant:
  College students
  Graduate school students
  Adult students
Minimum GPA: 2.5
Amount: $5,500.
Number of awards: Varies.
Deadline: April 4.
How to apply: Applications are available online.

(2425) · Thurgood Marshall Scholarship Fund Scholarship

Thurgood Marshall Scholarship Fund
80 Maiden Lane
Suite 2204
New York, NY 10038
Phone: 212-573-8888
Fax: 212-573-8497
Email: studentinfo@tmsf.org
Website: http://www.thurgoodmarshallfund.org
Purpose: To provide support to the nation's 45 historically black public colleges and universities by offering merit-based scholarships.
Eligibility: Applicants must be currently enrolled or planning to enroll as full-time students at one of the 45 TMSF member schools, have a minimum 3.0 high school GPA and have a minimum SAT score of 1100 or ACT score of 25. Applicants must demonstrate a commitment to academic excellence and community service and show financial need. Winners need to maintain a 3.0 GPA for the duration of the scholarship. Applicants must submit a head shot photograph, letters of recommendation, essay and resume.
Target applicant:
  High school students
  College students
  Adult students
Minimum GPA: 3.0
Amount: Varies.
Number of awards: Varies.
Scholarship may be renewable.
Deadline: Varies.
How to apply: Applications are available through the member schools.

(2426) · Time Warner Scholars Program

United Negro College Fund (UNCF)
8260 Willow Oaks Corporate Drive
P.O. Box 10444
Fairfax, VA 22031-8044

Phone: 800-331-2244
Website: http://www.uncf.org
Purpose: To help African American sophomores attending historically black colleges and universities.
Eligibility: Applicants must attend historically black colleges and universities (HBCU): Benedict College, Bennett College for Women, Bethune-Cookman College, Claflin University, Clark Atlanta University, Dillard University, Edward Waters College, Fisk University, Florida Memorial College, Huston-Tillotson University, Johnson C. Smith University, Lane College, LeMoyne-Owen College, Livingstone College, Miles College, Morehouse College, Morris College, Oakwood College, Paine College, Paul Quinn College, Philander Smith College, Rust College, Saint Augustine's College, Saint Paul's College, Shaw University, Spelman College, Stillman College, Talladega College, Tougaloo College, Tuskegee University, Virginia Union University, Voorhees College, Wilberforce University, Wiley College, Xavier University, Florida A & M University or Norfolk State University. Applicants must also have a minimum 3.0 GPA, complete the Free Application for Federal Student Aid (FAFSA) and have unmet financial need that is verified by the college or university financial aid office.
Target applicant:
  College students
  Adult students
Minimum GPA: 3.0
Amount: $2,500.
Number of awards: Over 100.
Deadline: Varies.
How to apply: Applications are available online.

(2427) · Trailblazer Scholarship
Conference of Minority Transportation Officials
818 18th Street NW, Suite 850
Washington, DC 20006
Phone: 202-530-0551
Fax: 202-530-0617
Email: comto@comto.org
Website: http://www.comto.org
Purpose: To support undergraduate and graduate students in the field of transportation.
Eligibility: Students must be in an undergraduate or graduate program enrolled in at least six credits per semester, and they must have at least a 2.5 GPA.
Target applicant:
  College students
  Graduate school students
  Adult students
Minimum GPA: 2.5
Amount: $2,500.
Number of awards: 2.
Deadline: April 4.
How to apply: Applications are available online.

(2428) · Tribal Business Management Program
Catching the Dream
Attn.: Scholarship Affairs Office
8200 Mountain Road NE
Suite 203
Albuquerque, NM 87110
Phone: 505-262-2351
Email: nscholarsh@aol.com
Website: http://www.catchingthedream.org

Purpose: To support American Indian students majoring in business, finance, management, economics, banking, hotel management and related fields who plan to work in economic development for tribes.
Eligibility: Applicants must be 1/4 or more degree American Indian, enrolled in a U.S. tribe and attending or planning to attend college full-time. Candidates are required to apply for all other forms of funding in addition to applying for this scholarship. Scholarships are based on grades, SAT or ACT scores, work experience, leadership, commitment to the tribe, personal goals and potential to improve the lives of American Indian people.
Target applicant:
  High school students
  College students
  Graduate school students
  Adult students
Minimum GPA: None.
Amount: $500-$5,000.
Number of awards: Varies.
Deadline: March 15, April 15 and September 15.
How to apply: Applications are available online.

(2429) · Tribal Priority Scholarship
Hopi Tribe Grants and Scholarship Program
P.O. Box 123
Kykotsmovi, AZ 86039
Phone: 800-762-9630
Fax: 928-734-9575
Email: info@hopi.nsn.us
Website: http://www.hopieducationfund.org
Purpose: To encourage Hopi college students to obtain bachelor's and graduate degrees in subject areas of priority interest to the Hopi Tribe.
Eligibility: Applicants must be Hopi college juniors, seniors and graduate students who would like to obtain bachelor's or graduate degrees in specific subject areas. Contact the scholarship program for more information.
Target applicant:
  College students
  Graduate school students
  Adult students
Minimum GPA: None.
Amount: Varies.
Number of awards: Varies.
Scholarship may be renewable.
Deadline: Varies.
How to apply: Applications are available by mail.

(2430) · Trull Foundation Scholarship
United Negro College Fund (UNCF)
8260 Willow Oaks Corporate Drive
P.O. Box 10444
Fairfax, VA 22031-8044
Phone: 800-331-2244
Website: http://www.uncf.org
Purpose: To help African American students attending United Negro College Fund (UNCF) member colleges and universities.
Eligibility: Applicants must have a minimum 2.5 GPA, complete the Free Application for Federal Student Aid (FAFSA) and have unmet financial need that is verified by the college or university financial aid office. Students are encouraged to complete the UNCF General Scholarship application to be matched with scholarships for which they meet the criteria.

Target applicant:
- High school students
- College students
- Adult students

Minimum GPA: 2.5
Amount: Varies.
Number of awards: Varies.
Deadline: Varies.
How to apply: Applications are available online.

(2431) · Truman D. Picard Scholarship

Intertribal Timber Council
Attn.: Education Committee
1112 NE 21st Avenue
Portland, OR 97232
Phone: 503-282-4296
Fax: 503-282-1274
Email: itc1@teleport.com
Website: http://www.itcnet.org
Purpose: To promote the field of natural resources.
Eligibility: Applicants must be high school seniors or college students and must pursue the natural resources field. Applicants must submit a resume, letters of reference, validated enrollment in Tribe/Native Alaska Corporation, letter about interest in natural resources, education, academics and financial need.

Target applicant:
- High school students
- College students
- Graduate school students
- Adult students

Minimum GPA: None.
Amount: $1,200-$1,800.
Number of awards: Varies.
Deadline: January 30.
How to apply: There is no official application form.

(2432) · Tuition and Book Scholarship

Hopi Tribe Grants and Scholarship Program
P.O. Box 123
Kykotsmovi, AZ 86039
Phone: 800-762-9630
Fax: 928-734-9575
Email: info@hopi.nsn.us
Website: http://www.hopieducationfund.org
Purpose: To assist Hopi students pursuing post-secondary education.
Eligibility: Applicants should be pursuing post-secondary education because of personal growth, career enhancement or change, continuing education, as part-time students or as students without financial need. Students must be enrolled members of the Hopi tribe, be high school graduates or GED recipients and have been accepted to regionally accredited colleges. Applicants should submit applications, statements of goals, proof of Hopi enrollment and transcripts.

Target applicant:
- High school students
- College students
- Graduate school students
- Adult students

Minimum GPA: None.
Amount: Varies.
Number of awards: Varies.
Deadline: Varies.
How to apply: Applications are available by mail.

(2433) · UNCF-Foot Locker Foundation Inc. Scholarship

United Negro College Fund (UNCF)
8260 Willow Oaks Corporate Drive
P.O. Box 10444
Fairfax, VA 22031-8044
Phone: 800-331-2244
Website: http://www.uncf.org
Purpose: To support African American students attending UNCF member schools.
Eligibility: Applicants must be high school seniors or current college students planning to attend or attending a UNCF member college or university. Students must also have a minimum 2.5 GPA, complete the Free Application for Federal Student Aid (FAFSA) and have unmet financial need that is verified by the college or university financial aid office. Students are encouraged to complete the UNCF General Scholarship application to be matched with scholarships for which they meet the criteria.

Target applicant:
- High school students
- College students
- Adult students

Minimum GPA: 2.5
Amount: Up to $5,000.
Number of awards: Varies.
Deadline: April 1.
How to apply: Applications are available online.

(2434) · UNCF/Merck Graduate Science Research Dissertation Fellowships

United Negro College Fund (UNCF)
8260 Willow Oaks Corporate Drive
P.O. Box 10444
Fairfax, VA 22031-8044
Phone: 800-331-2244
Website: http://www.uncf.org
Purpose: To assist African American graduate students completing dissertations in biomedically-related life or physical sciences.
Eligibility: Applicants must be full-time Ph.D. students in a life or physical science or M.D./Ph.D. candidates who are within one to three years of completing their dissertation research. Students must also be U.S. citizens or permanent residents. Selection is based on academic record, accomplishments and proposed doctoral research plan. Recipients are mentored by a Merck scientist.

Target applicant:
- Graduate school students
- Adult students

Minimum GPA: None.
Amount: Up to $52,000.
Number of awards: 12.
Deadline: December 17.
How to apply: Applications are available online.

(2435) · United Negro College Fund Cargill Scholarship-Internship Program

Cargill
The College Fund/UNCF
8260 Willow Oaks Corporate Drive
Fairfax, VA 22031
Phone: 952-742-7874

Email: cargill@ffa.org

Website: http://www.cargill.com/commun/grantmk.htm

Purpose: To help minority students majoring in engineering, information technology, finance or science.

Eligibility: Applicants must be African American, American Indian, Asian American, Hispanic American or other minority students at a UNCF institution or one of the Cargill-specified schools. Students must also be rising freshmen, sophomores or juniors majoring in engineering (chemical, mechanical), information technology (MIS, computer science), accounting/finance or science (chemistry, biochemistry food science, microbiology and agricultural and animal science), show financial need and be able to work in the U.S. Applicants should submit transcripts, resumes, recommendation letters and essays and may need to do a phone interview. Recipients may participate in a summer internship at selected Cargill locations throughout the United States.

Target applicant:
   High school students
   College students
   Adult students

Minimum GPA: 3.0

Amount: $5,000.

Number of awards: 6.

Deadline: February 28.

How to apply: Applications are available online.

(2436) · United Negro College Fund Scholarships

United Negro College Fund (UNCF)

8260 Willow Oaks Corporate Drive

P.O. Box 10444

Fairfax, VA 22031-8044

Phone: 800-331-2244

Website: http://www.uncf.org

Purpose: To enhance the quality of education by providing financial assistance to deserving students.

Eligibility: The UNCF general scholarship eligibility criteria are: Students must have a minimum 2.5 GPA and must have unmet financial need as verified by the Financial Aid Director. Students must also complete a Financial Aid Form (FAF) or a Family Financial Aid Statement (FFS) and request that the Student Aid Report (SAR) be sent to the financial aid office at their college or university.

Target applicant:
   College students
   Graduate school students
   Adult students

Minimum GPA: 2.5

Amount: Varies.

Number of awards: Varies.

Scholarship may be renewable.

Deadline: Varies.

How to apply: Applications are available online.

(2437) · United Parcel Service Foundation

United Negro College Fund (UNCF)

8260 Willow Oaks Corporate Drive

P.O. Box 10444

Fairfax, VA 22031-8044

Phone: 800-331-2244

Website: http://www.uncf.org

Purpose: To provide financial assistance to African American students at UNCF member schools.

Eligibility: Applicants must have a minimum 2.5 GPA, complete the Free Application for Federal Student Aid (FAFSA) and have unmet financial need that is verified by the college or university financial aid office. Students are encouraged to complete the UNCF General Scholarship application to be matched with scholarships for which they meet the criteria.

Target applicant:
   High school students
   College students
   Adult students

Minimum GPA: 2.5

Amount: Varies.

Number of awards: Varies.

Deadline: Varies.

How to apply: Applications are available online.

(2438) · United Parcel Service Scholarship for Minority Students

Institute of Industrial Engineers (IIE)

3577 Parkway Lane

Suite 200

Norcross, GA 30092

Phone: 800-494-0460

Fax: 770-441-3295

Email: bcameron@iienet.org

Website: http://www.iienet.org/studentcenter

Purpose: To help minority undergraduate students in industrial engineering.

Eligibility: Applicants must be full-time undergraduate minority students enrolled in a college in the United States, Canada or Mexico with an accredited industrial engineering program, major in industrial engineering and be active members. Students may not apply directly for this scholarship and must be nominated. The award is based on academic ability, character, leadership, potential service to the industrial engineering profession and financial need.

Target applicant:
   College students
   Adult students

Minimum GPA: 3.4

Amount: $4,000.

Number of awards: 1.

Deadline: February 15.

How to apply: Nomination forms are available online.

(2439) · USA Funds Scholarship

United Negro College Fund (UNCF)

8260 Willow Oaks Corporate Drive

P.O. Box 10444

Fairfax, VA 22031-8044

Phone: 800-331-2244

Website: http://www.uncf.org

Purpose: To help African American students attain a post-secondary education at a UNCF member college or university.

Eligibility: Applicants must have a minimum 2.5 GPA, complete the Free Application for Federal Student Aid (FAFSA) and have unmet financial need that is verified by the college or university financial aid office. Students are encouraged to complete the UNCF General Scholarship application to be matched with scholarships for which they meet the criteria.

Target applicant:
  High school students
  College students
  Adult students
Minimum GPA: 2.5
Amount: Varies.
Number of awards: Varies.
Deadline: Varies.
How to apply: Applications are available online.

(2440) · USENIX Association Scholarship

United Negro College Fund (UNCF)
8260 Willow Oaks Corporate Drive
P.O. Box 10444
Fairfax, VA 22031-8044
Phone: 800-331-2244
Website: http://www.uncf.org
Purpose: To encourage African American computer science and information systems students.
Eligibility: Applicants must major in computer science, computer science/MIS or information systems at a UNCF member college or university. Applicants must have a minimum 3.5 GPA, complete the Free Application for Federal Student Aid (FAFSA) and have unmet financial need that is verified by the college or university financial aid office. Students are encouraged to complete the UNCF General Scholarship application to be matched with scholarships for which they meet the criteria.
Target applicant:
  High school students
  College students
  Adult students
Minimum GPA: 3.5
Amount: Up to $10,000.
Number of awards: Varies.
Deadline: Varies.
How to apply: Applications are available online.

(2441) · Wells Fargo Scholarship

United Negro College Fund (UNCF)
8260 Willow Oaks Corporate Drive
P.O. Box 10444
Fairfax, VA 22031-8044
Phone: 800-331-2244
Website: http://www.uncf.org
Purpose: To support African American students at HBCUs.
Eligibility: Applicants must be college sophomores or juniors or first-year MBA students, have a minimum 2.5 GPA, complete the Free Application for Federal Student Aid (FAFSA) and have unmet financial need that is verified by the college or university financial aid office. Students may major in business, finance, accounting, architecture, electrical engineering, computer engineering or systems engineering. UNCF Students are encouraged to complete the UNCF General Scholarship application to be matched with scholarships for which they meet the criteria.
Target applicant:
  College students
  Adult students
Minimum GPA: 2.5
Amount: $2,000.
Number of awards: Varies.
Deadline: October 31.
How to apply: Applications are available online.

(2442) · Wendell Scott, Sr./NASCAR Scholarship

United Negro College Fund (UNCF)
8260 Willow Oaks Corporate Drive
P.O. Box 10444
Fairfax, VA 22031-8044
Phone: 800-331-2244
Website: http://www.uncf.org
Purpose: To provide financial support for upper-level African American students at UNCF member colleges or universities.
Eligibility: Applicants must be juniors, seniors or graduate students. Graduate students may be part-time students. Applicants must have a GPA of at least 3.0 for undergraduates and at least 3.2 for graduate students and demonstrate financial need.
Target applicant:
  College students
  Graduate school students
  Adult students
Minimum GPA: 3.0 for undergraduates; 3.2 for graduate students
Amount: $1,500-$2,000.
Number of awards: Varies.
Deadline: April 28.
How to apply: Applications are available online.

(2443) · Willems Scholarship

National Association for the Advancement of Colored People
The United Negro College Fund
Scholarships and Grants Administration
8260 Willow Oaks Corporate Drive
Fairfax, VA 22031
Phone: 703-205-3400
Website: http://www.naacp.org
Purpose: To encourage African-American males in scientific and technical fields.
Eligibility: Students must be males majoring in engineering, chemistry, physics or mathematical sciences. Applicants must be U.S. citizens attending an accredited U.S. school. Undergraduates must be full-time students with a 2.5 GPA. Graduate students may be full- or part-time students and must maintain a 3.0 GPA. Students must display financial need according to the chart included in the application materials. Membership in the NAACP is not required but preferred.
Target applicant:
  High school students
  College students
  Graduate school students
  Adult students
Minimum GPA: 2.5 for undergraduates; 3.0 for graduate students
Amount: $2,000-$3,000.
Number of awards: Varies.
Deadline: Last Friday in March.
How to apply: Applications are available online.

(2444) · William Randolph Hearst Endowed Scholarship for Minority Students

Aspen Institute
Nonprofit Sector Research Fund
Attn.: John Russell, Program Coordinator
One Dupont Circle, Suite 700
Washington, DC 20036
Phone: 202-736-5800
Fax: 202-293-0525

Email: hearstinfo@aspeninstitute.org
Website: http://www.nonprofitresearch.org
Purpose: To provide fellowships for minority students interested in philanthropy, volunteerism and the nonprofit sector.
Eligibility: Applicants must be undergraduate or graduate students belonging to a minority group. Hearst fellows work as interns at the Fund, providing assistance with research and outreach programs. Awards are based on academic excellence and financial need.
Target applicant:
    College students
    Graduate school students
    Adult students
Minimum GPA: None.
Amount: Up to $5,000.
Number of awards: Varies.
Deadline: March 15, July 15, December 15.
How to apply: Application information is available online.

(2445) · William Wrigley Jr. Scholarship/Internship

United Negro College Fund (UNCF)
8260 Willow Oaks Corporate Drive
P.O. Box 10444
Fairfax, VA 22031-8044
Phone: 800-331-2244
Website: http://www.uncf.org
Purpose: To support African American engineering, business and chemistry students with scholarships and paid internships.
Eligibility: Applicants must be sophomores or juniors at a UNCF member college or university. They must demonstrate financial need and have a GPA of at least 3.0.
Target applicant:
    College students
    Adult students
Minimum GPA: 3.0
Amount: Up to $3,000.
Number of awards: Varies.
Deadline: Varies.
How to apply: Applications are available online.

(2446) · Women's Opportunity Awards Program

Soroptimist International
1709 Spruce Street
Philadelphia, PA 19103
Phone: 215-893-9000
Fax: 215-893-5200
Email: siahq@soroptimist.org
Website: http://www.soroptimist.org
Purpose: To assist women entering or re-entering the workforce with educational and skills training support.
Eligibility: Applicants must be attending or been accepted by a vocational/skills training program or an undergraduate degree program. Applicants must be the women heads of household who provide the primary source of financial support for their families and demonstrate financial need. Applicants must submit their application to the appropriate regional office.
Target applicant:
    College students
    Adult students
Minimum GPA: None.
Amount: Varies.
Number of awards: 31.

Deadline: December 1.
How to apply: Applications are available online.

(2447) · Writers of Passage Scholarship

Sallie Mae Fund
12061 Bluemont Way
Reston, VA 20190
Phone: 703-810-3000
Website: http://www.thesalliemaefund.org
Purpose: To support students attending black colleges or universities.
Eligibility: Applicants must be enrolled as full-time undergraduate students at a black institution of higher learning, have financial need and apply for federal student aid. Applicants must also send an essay about how they have overcome difficulties, an application, a transcript and a copy of the Student Aid Report. The colleges of the winners also receive $20,000 grants.
Target applicant:
    College students
    Adult students
Minimum GPA: 2.5
Amount: $5,000.
Number of awards: Varies.
Deadline: March 3.
How to apply: Applications are available online.

(2448) · Young Women in Public Affairs Fund

Zonta International
557 West Randolph Street
Chicago, IL 60661-2206
Phone: 312-930-5848
Fax: 312-930-0951
Email: zontafdtn@zonta.org
Website: http://www.zonta.org
Purpose: To encourage young women to participate in politics and public service.
Eligibility: Applicants must be pre-college women between the ages of 16 and 20. District award winners receive at least $500, and international award winners receive $1,000. Selection is based on volunteerism, volunteer leadership and dedication to "advancing the status of women worldwide."
Target applicant:
    High school students
Minimum GPA: None.
Amount: $500-$1,000.
Number of awards: 30.
Deadline: February 28.
How to apply: Applications are available online or from your local Zonta Club.

DISABILITY / ILLNESS

(2449) · AG Bell College Scholarship Program

Alexander Graham Bell Association
Manager, AG Bell Financial Aid and Scholarship Programs
3417 Volta Place NW
Washington, DC 20007
Phone: 202-337-5220
Fax: 202-337-8314
Email: info@agbell.org
Website: http://www.agbell.org
Purpose: To recognize students with moderate to profound hearing loss who have academically excelled.
Eligibility: Applicants must have moderate to profound hearing loss since birth or before learning to speak with a hearing loss of 60 dB or greater. Students must use spoken communication as their primary means of communicating and be enrolled in an accredited mainstream university. The TTY phone number is 202-337-5221.
Target applicant:
    High school students
    College students
    Graduate school students
    Adult students
Minimum GPA: None.
Amount: $1,000-$5,000.
Number of awards: 20.
Deadline: February 15.
How to apply: Applications are available online.

(2450) · American Council of the Blind Scholarships

American Council of the Blind
Scholarship Program
1155 15th Street NW
Suite 1004
Washington, DC 20005
Phone: 202-467-5081
Fax: 202-467-5085
Email: info@acb.org
Website: http://www.acb.org
Purpose: To reward outstanding blind students.
Eligibility: Students must be legally blind in both eyes and admitted full-time to a post-secondary academic or vocational program. A minimum GPA of 3.3 is required, except in extenuating circumstances. Students who work full-time and attend school part-time may apply for the John Hebner Memorial Scholarship. Scholarship recipients are expected to attend a national convention if they are over 18.
Target applicant:
    High school students
    College students
    Graduate school students
    Adult students
Minimum GPA: 3.3
Amount: Varies.
Number of awards: Over two dozen.
Deadline: March 1.
How to apply: Applications are available online and by phone.

(2451) · Andre Sobel Award

Andre Sobel River of Life Foundation
8899 Beverly Boulevard
Suite 11
Los Angeles, CA 90048
Phone: 310-276-7111
Fax: 310-276-0244
Email: info@andreriveroflife.org
Website: http://www.andreriveroflife.org
Purpose: To provide financial assistance for young survivors of catastrophic illness.
Eligibility: Applicants must be between the ages of 12 and 21 as of June 30 of the year of application. They must be survivors of cancer or some other critical or life-threatening illness. Friends, family members and caregivers of those who meet these qualifications may also participate. All applicants must be United States residents. An essay is required.
Target applicant:
    Junior high students or younger
    High school students
    College students
Minimum GPA: None.
Amount: Up to $5,000.
Number of awards: Varies.
Deadline: August 29.
How to apply: Applications are available online.

(2452) · Ann and Matt Harbison Scholarship

P. Buckley Moss Society
20 Stoneridge Drive, Suite 102
Waynesboro, VA 22980
Phone: 540-943-5678
Fax: 540-949-8408
Email: society@mosssociety.org
Website: http://www.mosssociety.org
Purpose: This scholarship recognizes the persistence and dedication to academic or extracurricular pursuits of students with a learning disability.
Eligibility: Applicants must be nominated by a P. Buckley Moss Society member, have a language-related learning difference and pursue a post-secondary education.
Target applicant:
    High school students
Minimum GPA: None.
Amount: $1,000.
Number of awards: 1.
Scholarship may be renewable.
Deadline: March 31.
How to apply: Applications are available online.

(2453) · Anne Ford Scholarship Program

National Center for Learning Disabilities
381 Park Avenue South, Suite 1401
New York, NY 10016-8806
Phone: 888-575-7373
Fax: 212-545-9665
Email: afscholarship@ncld.org
Website: http://www.ncld.org
Purpose: To provide financial assistance to students with learning disabilities who plan to pursue undergraduate degrees.
Eligibility: Applicants must be U.S. citizens who are academically successful in public or private secondary schools and with an identified learning disability. Financial need is considered.
Target applicant:
    High school students

Minimum GPA: 3.0
Amount: $10,000.
Number of awards: 1.
Deadline: December 31.
How to apply: Applications are available online.

(2454) · Association of Blind Citizens Scholarships

Association of Blind Citizens
P.O. Box 246
Holbrook, MA 02343
Email: scholarship@blindcitizens.org
Website: http://www.blindcitizens.org/abc_scholarship.htm
Purpose: To assist blind individuals who wish to pursue higher education.
Eligibility: Applicants must be legally blind U.S. residents who have been accepted to an accredited institution of higher learning or vocational program. A 300- to 500- word autobiographical sketch, a certificate of legal blindness, a letter from an ophthalmologist and two letters of reference are required.
Target applicant:
    High school students
    College students
    Adult students
Minimum GPA: None.
Amount: $1,000-$2,000.
Number of awards: 9.
Deadline: April 15.
How to apply: Applications are available online.

(2455) · Award of Excellence Asthma Scholarship Program

American Academy of Allergy, Asthma and Immunology
555 E. Wells Street
Suite 1100
Milwaukee, WI 53202-3823
Phone: 414-272-6071
Email: info@aaaai.org
Website: http://www.aaaai.org
Purpose: The AAAAI provides college scholarships to graduating high school seniors with asthma to recognize their achievements in a wide variety of areas, including academic and extracurricular.
Eligibility: Applicants must be asthmatic students who will attend college or an accredited technical school within three years of graduating from high school.
Target applicant:
    High school students
Minimum GPA: None.
Amount: $1,000.
Number of awards: 23.
Deadline: January 7.
How to apply: Applications are available online.

(2456) · Career Incentive Award

Lighthouse International
111 E. 59th Street
New York, NY 10022
Phone: 212-821-9200
Fax: 212-821-9707
Email: info@lighthouse.org
Website: http://www.lighthouse.org

Purpose: To assist blind or partially-sighted collegiate or college-bound students.
Eligibility: Applicants must be blind or have low vision capabilities in one of four categories: college-bound high school student, undergraduate college student, undergraduate student returning to college at least 10 years after high school or graduate student.
Target applicant:
    High school students
    College students
    Graduate school students
    Adult students
Minimum GPA: None.
Amount: $5,000.
Number of awards: 4.
Deadline: March 31.
How to apply: Applications are available by phone, fax or email to kboyle@lighthouse.org.

(2457) · Chair Scholars Scholarship

Chair Scholars Foundation Inc.
16101 Carencia Lane
Odessa, FL 33556-3278
Phone: 813-920-0544
Fax: 813-920-7661
Email: chairscholars@tampabay.rr.com
Website: http://www.chairscholars.org
Purpose: To allow financially disadvantaged, physically challenged students a chance to obtain a college education.
Eligibility: Applicants must be significantly physically challenged (although not necessarily in a wheelchair), demonstrate severe financial need (such that they could not attend college without financial aid) and have at least a B+ average in previous scholastic work. Applicants must also be under age 21 and be high school seniors or college freshmen with previous community contributions. Applicants must submit applications, parents'/guardians' tax returns, test scores, photos, three recommendations and transcripts.
Target applicant:
    High school students
    College students
Minimum GPA: 3.33
Amount: $3,000-$5,000.
Number of awards: 15 to 20.
Scholarship may be renewable.
Deadline: February 21.
How to apply: Applications are available online.

(2458) · Chairscholars Foundation National Scholarships

Chair Scholars Foundation Inc.
16101 Carencia Lane
Odessa, FL 33556-3278
Phone: 813-920-0544
Fax: 813-920-7661
Email: chairscholars@tampabay.rr.com
Website: http://www.chairscholars.org
Purpose: To provide educational opportunities for physically challenged students.
Eligibility: Applicants must have major disabilities and serious financial difficulties that would prevent them from going to college without financial aid. They must have a B+ or higher average. They must be high school seniors or college freshmen age 21 or younger, and they

must have participated in some form of major community service or other social contribution.

Target applicant:
High school students
College students
Minimum GPA: 3.3
Amount: Up to $20,000.
Number of awards: 15-20.
Scholarship may be renewable.
Deadline: February 28.
How to apply: Applications are available online.

(2459) · Challenge Met Scholarship

American Radio Relay League Foundation
225 Main Street
Newington, CT 06111
Phone: 860-594-0397
Fax: 860-594-0259
Email: foundation@arrl.org
Website: http://www.arrl.org
Purpose: To provide assistance to amateur radio operators with learning disabilities.
Eligibility: Applicants must be licensed amateur radio operators who are accepted to or enrolled in a two- or four-year college, technical school or university. Preference is given to students with documented learning disabilities who are putting forth effort.
Target applicant:
High school students
College students
Adult students
Minimum GPA: None.
Amount: $500.
Number of awards: Varies.
Deadline: February 1.
How to apply: Applications are available online.

(2460) · CRS Scholarship

Christian Record Services
Melisa Welch
4444 S. 52nd Street
Lincoln, NE 68516-1302
Phone: 402-488-0981
Fax: 402-488-7582
Email: info@christianrecord.org
Website: http://www.christianrecord.org
Purpose: To assist legally blind youths in obtaining a college education.
Eligibility: Applicants must be legally blind and intend to attend undergraduate institutions to gain independence and self sufficiency. Applicants should submit application forms and character reference forms.
Target applicant:
High school students
College students
Adult students
Minimum GPA: None.
Amount: $500.
Number of awards: 10.
Deadline: April 1.
How to apply: Applications are available online.

(2461) · Cystic Fibrosis Foundation Scholarship

Cystic Fibrosis Scholarship Foundation
1555 Sherman Avenue #116
Evanston, IL 60201
Phone: 847-328-0127
Fax: 847-328-0127
Email: mkbcfsf@aol.com
Website: http://www.cfscholarship.org
Purpose: To aid to students with cystic fibrosis.
Eligibility: Applicants must be high school seniors or college undergraduates who have cystic fibrosis. Recipients are chosen on the basis of academic achievement, leadership skills and financial need.
Target applicant:
High school students
College students
Adult students
Minimum GPA: None.
Amount: $1,000.
Number of awards: Varies.
Deadline: March 8.
How to apply: Applications are available online.

(2462) · Cystic Fibrosis Scholarships

Cystic Fibrosis Scholarship Foundation
1555 Sherman Avenue #116
Evanston, IL 60201
Phone: 847-328-0127
Fax: 847-328-0127
Email: mkbcfsf@aol.com
Website: http://www.cfscholarship.org
Purpose: To provide educational opportunities for young adults with cystic fibrosis.
Eligibility: Applicants may be high school seniors or current college students. A doctor's note indicating a diagnosis of cystic fibrosis is required. Criteria for selection include financial need, academic achievement and leadership.
Target applicant:
High school students
College students
Adult students
Minimum GPA: None.
Amount: $1,000.
Number of awards: Varies.
Scholarship may be renewable.
Deadline: March 21.
How to apply: Applications are available online.

(2463) · Dr. Mae Davidow Memorial Scholarship

American Council of the Blind
Scholarship Program
1155 15th Street NW
Suite 1004
Washington, DC 20005
Phone: 202-467-5081
Fax: 202-467-5085
Email: info@acb.org
Website: http://www.acb.org
Purpose: To provide financial assistance for visually impaired students.

Eligibility: Applicants must be blind or visually impaired. They must submit letters of recommendation, autobiographical sketches, and copies of their academic transcripts.

Target applicant:
  High school students
  College students
  Adult students
Minimum GPA: None.
Amount: $1,500.
Number of awards: 1.
Deadline: March 1.
How to apply: Applications are available online.

(2464) · Duane Buckley Memorial Scholarship

American Council of the Blind
Scholarship Program
1155 15th Street NW
Suite 1004
Washington, DC 20005
Phone: 202-467-5081
Fax: 202-467-5085
Email: info@acb.org
Website: http://www.acb.org
Purpose: To assist students who work to overcome challenges.
Eligibility: Applicants must be legally blind college freshmen. A letter of recommendation, autobiographical sketch and copies of transcripts are required.
Target applicant:
  College students
  Adult students
Minimum GPA: None.
Amount: $1,000.
Number of awards: 1.
Deadline: March 1.
How to apply: Applications are available online.

(2465) · Eden Services Charles H. Hoens, Jr., Scholars Program

Autism Society of America
7910 Woodmont Avenue, Suite 300
Bethesda, MD 20814-3067
Phone: 800-328-8476
Email: chapters@autism-society.org
Website: http://www.autism-society.org
Purpose: To assist an autistic student in completing a post-secondary program.
Eligibility: Applicants must have autism and be accepted into an accredited post-secondary educational or vocational program. Nominations must be made by members of the ASA.
Target applicant:
  College students
  Adult students
Minimum GPA: None.
Amount: $1,000.
Number of awards: 1.
Deadline: March 14.
How to apply: Applications are available online.

(2466) · Educator of Tomorrow Award

National Federation of the Blind
Anil Lewis
1800 Johnston Street
Baltimore, MD 21230
Phone: 404-371-1000
Email: scholarships@nfb.org
Website: http://www.nfb.org
Purpose: To assist legally blind education students.
Eligibility: Applicants must be legally blind, full-time post-secondary students pursuing a career in education at any level. Academic excellence, financial need and community service involvement will be considered. Applicants must submit a personal letter, letters of recommendation, transcripts, a letter from a Federation state president or designee and test score reports for high school seniors.
Target applicant:
  High school students
  College students
  Adult students
Minimum GPA: None.
Amount: $3,000.
Number of awards: 1.
Deadline: March 31.
How to apply: Applications are available online.

(2467) · Eric Dostie Memorial College Scholarship

NuFACTOR
41093 County Center Drive
Temecula, CA 92591
Phone: 800-323-6832
Fax: 951-296-2565
Website: http://www.kelleycom.com
Purpose: To assist students who suffer from hemophilia or related bleeding disorders as well as their immediate families.
Eligibility: Applicants must be individuals with hemophilia or related to said individuals, enrolled full-time in an accredited college or university and demonstrate academic achievement, financial need and a history of community service.
Target applicant:
  College students
  Adult students
Minimum GPA: None.
Amount: $1,000.
Number of awards: 10.
Deadline: March 1.
How to apply: Applications are available after November 1 by telephone or mail.

(2468) · Ethel Louise Armstrong Foundation Scholarship

Ethel Louise Armstrong Foundation
2460 N. Lake Avenue, PMB #128
Altadena, CA 91001
Phone: 626-398-8840
Email: executivedirector@ela.org
Website: http://www.ela.org
Purpose: To promote the inclusion of people with disabilities and to expand the opportunities of female graduate students with disabilities.
Eligibility: Applicants must be female with a physical disability, active in a disability organization, currently enrolled in or applying to a graduate

school in the U.S. and willing to work with the foundation on future research work.

Target applicant:
Graduate school students
Adult students

Minimum GPA: None.

Amount: $500-$2,000.

Number of awards: Varies.

Deadline: June 1.

How to apply: Applications are available online.

(2469) · Ferdinand Torres Scholarship

American Foundation for the Blind Scholarship Committee
11 Penn Plaza
Suite 300
New York, NY 10001
Phone: 800-232-5463
Fax: 212-502-7771
Email: afbinfo@afb.net
Website: http://www.afb.org

Purpose: The foundation addresses the issues of literacy, independent living, employment and access for visually impaired Americans.

Eligibility: Applicants must be full-time, post-secondary students with proof of legal blindness. Students must reside in the U.S. and provide evidence of economic need. Preference is given to applicants living in the New York metropolitan area and new immigrants to the U.S. Applicants must submit applications, essays, transcripts, enrollment letters, and two recommendation letters.

Target applicant:
College students
Graduate school students
Adult students

Minimum GPA: None.

Amount: $1,500.

Number of awards: 1.

Deadline: March 31.

How to apply: Applications are available online.

(2470) · Fred Scheigert Scholarships

Council of Citizens with Low Vision International
1155 15th Street NW
Suite 1004
Washington, DC 20005
Phone: 800-733-2258
Email: ncclv@yahoo.com
Website: http://www.cclvi.org/scholarship.html

Purpose: To provide educational assistance for students with low vision.

Eligibility: Applicants must be registered in a full-time undergraduate or graduate course of study at a college, trade or vocational school. They must have a GPA of 3.2 or higher. Those with extenuating circumstances may be exempt from these requirements. Applicants must have 20/70 or worse vision in the better eye with the best possible correction, or a field of vision of 30 degrees or less.

Target applicant:
High school students
College students
Graduate school students
Adult students

Minimum GPA: 3.2

Amount: Varies.

Number of awards: Varies.

Deadline: March 1.

How to apply: Applications are available online.

(2471) · Hemophilia Resources of America

Hemophilia Resources of America
Attn.: Scholarships 4
45 Route 46 East, Suite 609
P.O. Box 2011
Pine Brook, NJ 07058
Phone: 973-276-0254
Fax: 973-276-0998
Email: mscudiery@hrahemo.com
Website: http://www.hrahemo.com

Purpose: To provide financial assistance to individuals living with hemophilia or von Willebrand disease, or their children.

Eligibility: Applicants must have either hemophilia or von Willebrand disease or be the child of an individual with one of these two diseases. Applicants must also demonstrate financial need as well as a record of academic excellence and community service.

Target applicant:
High school students
College students
Adult students

Minimum GPA: 2.5

Amount: $1,000.

Number of awards: 20.

Deadline: May 15.

How to apply: Applications are available online or by calling 800-549-2654.

(2472) · Immune Deficiency Foundation Scholarship

Immune Deficiency Foundation
40 W. Chesapeake Avenue
Suite 308
Towson, MD 21204
Phone: 800-296-4433
Email: idf@primaryimmune.org
Website: http://www.primaryimmune.org

Purpose: To provide financial assistance to undergraduate students afflicted with a primary immune deficiency disease.

Eligibility: Applicant must have been admitted or must currently be enrolled in an accredited college or university as an undergraduate student. Applicants must also have demonstrated financial need and a record of community involvement.

Target applicant:
High school students
College students
Adult students

Minimum GPA: None.

Amount: $750-$1,000.

Number of awards: Varies.

Scholarship may be renewable.

Deadline: March 31.

How to apply: Applications are available online, by email or by telephone.

(2473) · Ina Brudnick Scholarship Award

Great Comebacks Award Program
100 Headquarters Park Drive
Skillman, NJ 08558
Phone: 858-259-2092
Email: professional.services@bms.com
Website: http://www.greatcomebacks.com
Purpose: To support students who have undergone ostomy surgery or are suffering from inflammatory bowel disease.
Eligibility: Students must be 24 years old or younger, and they must be planning to attend an institution of higher education.
Target applicant:
    High school students
    College students
Minimum GPA: None.
Amount: $1,000.
Number of awards: 4.
Deadline: July 15.
How to apply: Applications are available online.

(2474) · Incight Go-Getter Scholarship

Incight Company
310 S.W. 4th Avenue
Suite 530
Portland, OR 97204
Phone: 971-244-0305
Fax: 971-244-0304
Email: questions@incight.org
Website: http://www.incight.com/incight/edul.html
Purpose: To support students with physical or learning disabilities.
Eligibility: Applicants must have a documented disability that may include physical, learning or cognitive. Students must also attend a trade school, college or university on a full-time basis and have at least a 2.5 GPA. Recipients are placed with internships related to their field of study.
Target applicant:
    High school students
    College students
    Adult students
Minimum GPA: 2.5
Amount: $750.
Number of awards: Varies.
Scholarship may be renewable.
Deadline: Varies.
How to apply: Applications are available online.

(2475) · Kafoury and McDougal Personal Injury Scholarship

Epsilon Sigma Alpha Foundation
P.O. Box 270517
Fort Collins, CO 80527
Phone: 970-223-2824
Fax: 970-223-4456
Email: kloyd@knoxy.net
Website: http://www.esaintl.com/esaf
Purpose: To provide financial assistance for disabled students.
Eligibility: Applicants must have been disabled by an accidental injury. They may be residents of any state who are pursuing any major at any school. Selection is based equally on character, leadership, service, financial need and scholastic ability.

Target applicant:
    High school students
    College students
    Adult students
Minimum GPA: None.
Amount: $375.
Number of awards: 1.
Deadline: February 1.
How to apply: Applications are available online.

(2476) · Karen D. Carsel Memorial Scholarship

American Foundation for the Blind Scholarship Committee
11 Penn Plaza
Suite 300
New York, NY 10001
Phone: 800-232-5463
Fax: 212-502-7771
Email: afbinfo@afb.net
Website: http://www.afb.org
Purpose: The foundation addresses the issues of literacy, independent living, employment and access for visually impaired Americans.
Eligibility: Applicants must be full-time graduate students who are legally blind and can present evidence of financial need. Students must submit applications, transcripts, enrollment letters, proof of U.S. citizenship, proof of legal blindness, two letters of recommendation and a typed statement describing educational and personal goals, work experience, extracurricular activities and how the scholarship funds will be used.
Target applicant:
    Graduate school students
    Adult students
Minimum GPA: None.
Amount: $500.
Number of awards: 1.
Deadline: March 31.
How to apply: Applications are available online.

(2477) · Keppra Family Epilepsy Scholarship Program

Hudson Medical Communications
200 White Plains Road
Tarrytown, NY 10591
Phone: 866-825-1920
Email: questions@hudsonmc.com
Website: http://www.ucbepilepsyscholarship.com
Purpose: To provide financial assistance to people with epilepsy who wish to obtain higher education.
Eligibility: Applicants must be U.S. citizens or legal and permanent residents who have epilepsy or family members or caregivers of persons with epilepsy. They must be graduating high school in the year of application or have already graduated and be enrolled in or awaiting acceptance from a U.S. institution of higher learning. They must have demonstrated academic achievement, participate in extracurricular activities and be positive role models.
Target applicant:
    High school students
    College students
    Adult students
Minimum GPA: None.
Amount: $5,000.
Number of awards: 30.

Deadline: May 2.
How to apply: Applications are available online.

(2478) · Kermit B. Nash Academic Scholarship

Sickle Cell Disease Association of America
231 E. Baltimore Street
Suite 800
Baltimore, MD 21202
Phone: 800-421-8453
Fax: 410-528-1495
Email: scdaa@sicklecelldisease.org
Website: http://www.sicklecelldisease.org
Purpose: To encourage individuals with sickle cell disease to pursue their educational goals.
Eligibility: Applicants must be U.S. citizens or permanent residents who have sickle cell disease. They must be graduating high school seniors with a GPA of 3.0 or higher (unless they can demonstrate special hardship), a record of leadership and community service and SAT scores. An essay is required.
Target applicant:
  High school students
Minimum GPA: 3.0
Amount: $5,000.
Number of awards: 1.
Scholarship may be renewable.
Deadline: May 31.
How to apply: Applications are available online.

(2479) · Kevin Child Scholarship

National Hemophilia Foundation
116 W. 32nd Street
11th Floor
New York, NY 10001
Phone: 212-328-3700
Fax: 212-328-3777
Email: webmaster@hemophilia.org
Website: http://www.hemophilia.org
Purpose: To support students who have been diagnosed with hemophilia or von Willebrand disease.
Eligibility: Applicants must be high school seniors or enrolled undergraduate students.
Target applicant:
  High school students
  College students
  Adult students
Minimum GPA: None.
Amount: $1,000.
Number of awards: 1.
Deadline: June 27.
How to apply: Applications are available online.

(2480) · Kyle Lee Foundation Scholarship

Kyle Lee Foundation Inc.
c/o Arnold Uy
85 Sansovino
Ladera Ranch, CA 92694
Phone: 714-433-3204
Email: foundation@kylelee28.com
Website: http://www.kylelee28.com

Purpose: To provide financial assistance to college-bound cancer survivors, especially survivors of Ewing's sarcoma.
Eligibility: Applicants must be cancer survivors who have taken the SAT, ACT or GRE and plan to attend an institution of higher learning.
Target applicant:
  High school students
  College students
  Graduate school students
  Adult students
Minimum GPA: None.
Amount: Varies.
Number of awards: Varies.
Deadline: May 15.
How to apply: Applications are available online.

(2481) · Lawrence Madeiros Scholarship

Adirondack Spintacular
P.O. Box 11
Mayfield, NY 12117
Phone: 518-661-6005
Email: carol@adirondackspintacular.com
Website: http://www.adirondackspintacular.com/pages/scholarship.html
Purpose: To support students who are living with a bleeding disorder or other chronic disorder.
Eligibility: Applicants must be graduating high school seniors.
Target applicant:
  High school students
Minimum GPA: None.
Amount: Varies.
Number of awards: Varies.
Deadline: June 1.
How to apply: Applications are available online.

(2482) · Lilly Moving Lives Forward Reintegration Scholarships

Center for Reintegration Inc.
609 72nd Street
Floor 1
North Bergen, NJ 07047
Phone: 201-869-2333
Fax: 201-869-2123
Email: reintegration@reintegration.com
Website: http://www.reintegration.com/resources/scholarships/scholarship.asp
Purpose: To encourage people with schizophrenia and similar disorders to obtain higher education.
Eligibility: Applicants must be diagnosed with schizophrenia, schizophreniform, schizoaffective disorder or bipolar disorder and be receiving treatment for the disease. They must be involved in reintegrative efforts such as work, school or volunteer programs. Three recommendations and an essay are required.
Target applicant:
  High school students
  College students
  Adult students
Minimum GPA: None.
Amount: Varies.
Number of awards: Varies.
Deadline: Varies.
How to apply: Applications are available online.

(2483) · Lilly Reintegration Scholarship

Lilly Reintegration Programs
PMB 327
310 Busse Highway
Park Ridge, IL 60068
Phone: 800-809-8202
Email: lillyscholarships@reintegration.com
Website: http://www.reintegration.com
Purpose: To provide aid to students with schizophrenia or similar disorders who are seeking to advance themselves academically and vocationally.
Eligibility: Applicants must have been diagnosed with schizophrenia, schizophreniform, schizoaffective disorder or bipolar disorder, be undergoing medical treatment for their disease(s) and be involved in other rehabilitative efforts, such as working part-time or volunteering with a civic organization.
Target applicant:
    High school students
    College students
    Graduate school students
    Adult students
Minimum GPA: None.
Amount: Varies.
Number of awards: Varies.
Deadline: February 15.
How to apply: Applications are available online or by phone, mail or email.

(2484) · Manne Family Foundation Scholarships

SuperSibs!
4300 Lincoln Avenue
Suite 1
Rolling Meadows, IL 60008
Phone: 866-444-7427
Fax: 847-776-7084
Website: http://www.supersibs.org
Purpose: To provide education opportunities for siblings of cancer patients.
Eligibility: Applicants must be siblings of children who have or have had cancer. They must be U.S. residents who are graduating high school in the year of application. A minimum GPA of 3.5 is required. Applicants must have financial need and plan to attend a four-year college or university immediately following high school.
Target applicant:
    High school students
Minimum GPA: 3.5
Amount: $5,000.
Number of awards: 4.
Deadline: February 1.
How to apply: Applications are available online.

(2485) · Marion Huber Learning Through Listening Awards

Recording for the Blind and Dyslexic
20 Roszel Road
Princeton, NJ 08540
Phone: 866-RFBD-585
Fax: 609-520-7990
Email: custserv@rfbd.org
Website: http://www.rfbd.org
Purpose: To assist learning-disabled high school seniors.
Eligibility: Applicants must demonstrate leadership skills, scholarship and a desire to help others and attend a two- or four-year college or vocational school. Students must have a specific learning disability and be registered with RFB&D for at least one year prior to the application deadline.
Target applicant:
    High school students
Minimum GPA: 3.0
Amount: $2,000-$6,000.
Number of awards: 9.
Deadline: February 20.
How to apply: Applications are available online.

(2486) · Mary Ellen Locher Foundation Scholarship

Mary Ellen Locher Foundation
P.O. Box 4032
Chattanooga, TN 37405
Website: http://www.maryellenlocherfoundation.org
Purpose: To provide scholarship assistance to children whose mothers have died of breast cancer and children whose mothers are breast cancer survivors.
Eligibility: Applicants must have lost a parent to breast cancer or complications of the disease or have a parent who has survived breast cancer. They must be high school seniors who have been accepted as a full-time student at an accredited college or university.
Target applicant:
    High school students
Minimum GPA: None.
Amount: Varies.
Number of awards: Varies.
Deadline: February 15.
How to apply: Applications are available online.

(2487) · Mary P. Oenslanger Scholastic Achievement Awards

Recording for the Blind and Dyslexic
20 Roszel Road
Princeton, NJ 08540
Phone: 866-RFBD-585
Fax: 609-520-7990
Email: custserv@rfbd.org
Website: http://www.rfbd.org
Purpose: Assistance for graduate study is awarded to blind college senior students who have shown leadership skills, scholarship and a desire to help others.
Eligibility: Applicants must be legally blind, have been registered with RFB&D for at least one year prior to the application deadline and hold a bachelor's degree from an accredited U.S. college or university.
Target applicant:
    Graduate school students
    Adult students
Minimum GPA: 3.0
Amount: $1,000-$6,000.
Number of awards: 9.
Deadline: February 20.
How to apply: Applications are available online.

(2488) · Michael A. Hunter Memorial Scholarship Fund

Orange County Community Foundation
30 Corporate Park, Suite 410
Irvine, CA 92606
Phone: 949-553-4202
Fax: 949-553-4211
Email: rho@oc-cf.org
Website: http://www.oc-cf.org
Purpose: To support those who have been affected by leukemia as they pursue an education.
Eligibility: Applicants must be high school seniors or current college students who are leukemia patients and/or are the children of non-surviving leukemia patients. Applicants must be full-time students with a GPA of at least 3.0 and demonstrate financial need. They must submit an essay describing how leukemia has impacted their life, a doctor's note verifying the leukemia diagnosis and two letters of recommendation.
Target applicant:
  High school students
  College students
  Adult students
Minimum GPA: 3.0
Amount: $5,000.
Number of awards: 2.
Deadline: February 28.
How to apply: Applications are available online.

(2489) · Mike Hylton and Ron Niederman Scholarships

Factor Support Network Pharmacy
900 Avenida Acaso, Suite A
Camarillo, CA 93012
Phone: 877-376-4968
Fax: 805-482-6324
Email: scholarships@factorsupport.com
Website: http://www.factorsupport.com/scholarships.htm
Purpose: To support men with hemophilia or von Willebrand disease and their families.
Eligibility: Students must provide proof of diagnosis by a physician. Applicants must submit an essay and two letters of recommendation.
Target applicant:
  High school students
  College students
  Adult students
Minimum GPA: None.
Amount: $1,000.
Number of awards: 5.
Deadline: April 30.
How to apply: Applications are available online.

(2490) · Millie Gonzales Memorial Scholarships

Factor Support Network Pharmacy
900 Avenida Acaso, Suite A
Camarillo, CA 93012
Phone: 877-376-4968
Fax: 805-482-6324
Email: scholarships@factorsupport.com
Website: http://www.factorsupport.com/scholarships.htm
Purpose: To support women with hemophilia or von Willebrand Disease.

Eligibility: Students must provide proof of diagnosis by a physician. Applicants must submit an essay and two letters of recommendation.
Target applicant:
  High school students
  College students
  Adult students
Minimum GPA: None.
Amount: $1,000.
Number of awards: 2.
Deadline: April 30.
How to apply: Applications are available online.

(2491) · Minnie Pearl Scholarship

EAR Foundation
P.O. Box 330867
Nashville, TN 37203
Phone: 800-545-HEAR
Fax: 615-627-2728
Email: info@earfoundation.org
Website: http://www.earfoundation.org
Purpose: To help integrate hearing impaired persons into mainstream society through education.
Eligibility: Applicants must be high school seniors with a minimum 3.0 GPA and be accepted to a college, university or technical school and be planning to attend full-time. Applicants must also be U.S. citizens, be mainstreamed hearing impaired students and have significant bilateral hearing impairment.
Target applicant:
  High school students
Minimum GPA: 3.0
Amount: Up to $2,500.
Number of awards: Varies.
Deadline: February 15.
How to apply: Applications are available online.

(2492) · National Collegiate Cancer Foundation Scholarship

National Collegiate Cancer Foundation
P.O. Box 14190
Silver Spring, MD 20911
Phone: 717-215-0943
Email: info@collegiatecancer.org
Website: http://www.collegiatecancer.org
Purpose: To provide financial assistance to college students who have been diagnosed with cancer.
Eligibility: Applicants must demonstrate financial need. Selection is based on financial need, quality of essay and recommendations, demonstrating a "will win" attitude and overall story of cancer survivorship.
Target applicant:
  College students
  Adult students
Minimum GPA: None.
Amount: $1,000.
Number of awards: Varies.
Deadline: September 15.
How to apply: Applications are available online.

(2493) · National Federation of the Blind Scholarship

National Federation of the Blind
Anil Lewis
1800 Johnston Street
Baltimore, MD 21230
Phone: 404-371-1000
Email: scholarships@nfb.org
Website: http://www.nfb.org
Purpose: The National Federation of the Blind offers thirty scholarships to exceptional blind scholars.
Eligibility: Applicants must be legally blind and pursue a full-time postsecondary study in the following semester in the U.S. One scholarship may be given to a part-time student. There are no additional restrictions for most of the scholarships. However, a few require study in certain fields and the Michael and Marie Marucci Scholarship requires competence in a foreign language. Awards are based on academic excellence, community service and financial need. Applicants must participate in the entire NFB national convention and in all scheduled scholarship program activities.
Target applicant:
    High school students
    College students
    Graduate school students
    Adult students
Minimum GPA: None.
Amount: $3,000-$12,000.
Number of awards: 30.
Deadline: March 31.
How to apply: Applications are available online.

(2494) · National MS Society Scholarship Program

National Multiple Sclerosis Society
733 Third Avenue
New York, NY 10017
Phone: 800-344-4867
Website: http://www.nationalmssociety.org
Purpose: To provide educational opportunities for students affected by multiple sclerosis.
Eligibility: Applicants must be high school seniors or graduates who have MS, or who have a parent with MS, and will be attending college for the first time. They must be U.S. citizens or legal residents who plan to enroll in an undergraduate program at an accredited institution of higher learning. Applicants must take at least six credit hours per semester, and the courses taken must lead to a degree, license or certificate.
Target applicant:
    High school students
Minimum GPA: None.
Amount: $1,000-$3,000.
Number of awards: 500.
Deadline: January 15.
How to apply: Applications are available online.

(2495) · NFMC Hinda Honigman Award for the Blind

National Federation of Music Clubs (NC)
Regina Einig
864 Schoolhouse Road
Carbondale, IL 62902-7928
Phone: 618-549-5082
Fax: 317-638-0503
Email: reinig@siu.edu
Website: http://www.nfmc-music.org

Purpose: To support blind instrumentalists or vocalists.
Eligibility: Applicants must be between the ages of 16 and 25, be an instrumentalist or vocalist and submit an affidavit from an ophthalmologist stating that they are blind. Applicants must also be affiliated with the National Federation of Music Clubs.
Target applicant:
    High school students
    College students
    Graduate school students
Minimum GPA: None.
Amount: $350-$650.
Number of awards: 2.
Deadline: February 1.
How to apply: Applications are available online.

(2496) · Optimist International Communications Contest

Optimist International
4494 Lindell Boulevard
St. Louis, MO 63108
Phone: 314-371-6000
Fax: 314-371-6006
Email: programs@optimist.org
Website: http://www.optimist.org
Purpose: To reward students based on their communications performance.
Eligibility: Applicants must be students up to grade 12 in the U.S. and Canada, to CEGEP in Quebec and to grade 13 in the Caribbean who are recognized by their schools as deaf or hard of hearing.
Target applicant:
    High school students
Minimum GPA: None.
Amount: $1,500.
Number of awards: Varies.
Deadline: September.
How to apply: Contact your local Optimist Club.

(2497) · Pfizer Epilepsy Scholarship

Pfizer Epilepsy Scholarship Award
c/o The Eden Communications Group
515 Valley Street
Suite 200
Maplewood, NJ 07040
Phone: 800-292-7373
Email: czoppi@edencomgroup.com
Website: http://www.epilepsy-scholarship.com
Purpose: To recognize outstanding students who demonstrate how they have overcome the challenge of epilepsy in their lives.
Eligibility: Applicants must be high school seniors or college undergraduates currently under a physician's care for epilepsy, demonstrate achievement in academic and extracurricular activities and submit verification of academic status and two letters of recommendation. Selection is made by a panel of judges composed of opinion leaders in the fields of medicine and education.
Target applicant:
    High school students
    College students
    Adult students
Minimum GPA: None.
Amount: $3,000.
Number of awards: 25.

Deadline: March 1.
How to apply: Applications are available online.

(2498) · Project Red Flag Academic Scholarship for Women with Bleeding Disorders

National Hemophilia Foundation
116 W. 32nd Street
11th Floor
New York, NY 10001
Phone: 212-328-3700
Fax: 212-328-3777
Email: webmaster@hemophilia.org
Website: http://www.hemophilia.org
Purpose: To assist women with bleeding disorders in pursuing higher education.
Eligibility: Applicants must be female U.S. residents who have a bleeding disorder that has been diagnosed by a hematologist. Preference is given to those who have participated in community service or volunteer work pertaining to bleeding disorders. The funds may be used to pay for undergraduate or graduate studies.
Target applicant:
    High school students
    College students
    Graduate school students
    Adult students
Minimum GPA: None.
Amount: $2,500.
Number of awards: 2.
Deadline: May 16.
How to apply: Applications are available online.

(2499) · Robert Guthrie PKU Scholarship and Awards

National PKU News
6869 Woodlawn Avenue NE #116
Seattle, WA 98115-5469
Email: schuett@pkunews.org
Website: http://www.pkunews.org
Purpose: In honor of the doctor who created the newborn screening test for PKU, the scholarship gives support to bright students living with PKU.
Eligibility: Students must have PKU, follow the diet and attend an accredited school. Financial need is considered along with academic excellence.
Target applicant:
    High school students
    College students
    Graduate school students
Minimum GPA: None.
Amount: Varies.
Number of awards: Varies.
Deadline: November 1.
How to apply: Applications are available by mail.

(2500) · Roger and Rhea Weaver Endowment for Cancer Survivors or Catastrophic Diseases Scholarship

Epsilon Sigma Alpha Foundation
P.O. Box 270517
Fort Collins, CO 80527

Phone: 970-223-2824
Fax: 970-223-4456
Email: kloyd@knoxy.net
Website: http://www.esaintl.com/esaf
Purpose: To provide financial assistance for young students who have overcome adversity.
Eligibility: Applicants must be under 21 years of age and must have survived cancer or another catastrophic disease. Selection is based on the following characteristics: character (10 percent), leadership (20 percent), service (10 percent), financial need (30 percent) and scholastic ability (30 percent).
Target applicant:
    High school students
    College students
Minimum GPA: None.
Amount: $500.
Number of awards: 1.
Deadline: February 1.
How to apply: Applications are available online.

(2501) · Sara Conlon Memorial Scholarship

Foundation for Exceptional Children
1110 N. Glebe Road
Suite 300
Arlington, VA 22201
Phone: 800-224-6830
Email: yesican@cec.sped.org
Website: http://www.cec.sped.org
Purpose: To help disabled students who major in special education.
Eligibility: Applicants must be enrolled in two- or four-year undergraduate college programs or vocational, technical or fine arts training programs. Students should submit the application form, transcript, three letters of recommendation, goals statement, statement verifying disability and statement verifying financial need.
Target applicant:
    High school students
    College students
    Adult students
Minimum GPA: None.
Amount: $500.
Number of awards: 1.
Deadline: February 1.
How to apply: Applications are available online.

(2502) · SBAA Four-Year Scholarship

Spina Bifida Association of America
4590 MacArthur Boulevard NW
Suite 250
Washington, DC 20007-4226
Phone: 800-621-3141
Fax: 202-944-3295
Email: tcoogan@sbaa.org
Website: http://www.sbaa.org
Purpose: To create opportunities for high school students with spina bifida to attend a four-year college that is otherwise outside of the applicants' financial reach.
Eligibility: Applicants must have spina bifida with a statement of disability from a physician and be high school seniors at the time of application. Awards are based on academic record, financial need, work history, community service, leadership and commitment to personal goals.

Target applicant:
    High school students
Minimum GPA: None.
Amount: Up to $5,000.
Number of awards: 1.
Scholarship may be renewable.
Deadline: March 7.
How to apply: Applications are available online.

(2503) · Scholarships for Survivors

Patient Advocate Foundation
Ruth Anne Reed, Vice President of Special Programs
700 Thimble Shoals Boulevard
Suite 200
Newport News, VA 23606
Phone: 800-532-5274
Fax: 757-873-8999
Email: help@patientadvocate.org
Website: http://www.patientadvocate.org
Purpose: This group of scholarships seeks to assist students whose educations have been delayed due to life-threatening illness.
Eligibility: Eligible students must be survivors of life-threatening diseases. If awarded a scholarship, the student must maintain a 3.0 GPA, be enrolled full time and perform 20 hours of community service each year.
Target applicant:
    High school students
    College students
    Graduate school students
    Adult students
Minimum GPA: None.
Amount: $5,000.
Number of awards: 8.
Scholarship may be renewable.
Deadline: May 1.
How to apply: Applications are available online.

(2504) · School Age Financial Aid Awards

Alexander Graham Bell Association
Manager, AG Bell Financial Aid and Scholarship Programs
3417 Volta Place NW
Washington, DC 20007
Phone: 202-337-5220
Fax: 202-337-8314
Email: info@agbell.org
Website: http://www.agbell.org
Purpose: To assist students who are deaf or hard of hearing.
Eligibility: Applicants must be students with pre-lingual hearing loss between the ages of 6 and 21 who are enrolled in parochial, independent or private schools.
Target applicant:
    Junior high students or younger
    High school students
Minimum GPA: None.
Amount: Varies.
Number of awards: Varies.
Deadline: March 15.
How to apply: Applications are available online.

(2505) · Sertoma Hearing Impaired Scholarship

Sertoma International
1912 E. Meyer Boulevard
Kansas City, MO 64132
Phone: 816-333-8300
Fax: 816-333-4320
Email: infosertoma@sertomahq.org
Website: http://www.sertoma.org
Purpose: The organization's focus is to concentrate on communicative disorders.
Eligibility: Applicants must be entering or continuing as full-time undergraduates in the U.S., show proof that they have a clinically significant (40dB) bilateral hearing loss and have a minimum 3.2 GPA for all high school and college courses.
Target applicant:
    High school students
    College students
    Adult students
Minimum GPA: 3.2
Amount: $1,000.
Number of awards: Varies.
Deadline: May 1.
How to apply: Applications are available online.

(2506) · Soozie Courter Sharing a Brighter Tomorrow Hemophilia Scholarship

Wyeth Pharmaceuticals
Hemophilia Scholarship Program (Bioanalytical Solutions)
P.O. Box 26825
Collegeville, PA 19426-0825
Phone: 888-999-2349
Website: http://www.hemophiliavillage.com
Purpose: To provide financial assistance to students with hemophilia.
Eligibility: Applicants must be high school seniors or graduates, GED recipients or college or vocational school students who have been diagnosed with hemophilia A or B.
Target applicant:
    High school students
    College students
    Adult students
Minimum GPA: None.
Amount: Up to $7,500.
Number of awards: 20.
Deadline: April 4.
How to apply: Applications are available online.

(2507) · Stanley E. Jackson Scholarship Awards

Foundation for Exceptional Children
1110 N. Glebe Road
Suite 300
Arlington, VA 22201
Phone: 800-224-6830
Email: yesican@cec.sped.org
Website: http://www.cec.sped.org
Purpose: To honor the memory of Mr. Stanley E. Jackson through the provision of funds to disabled students.
Eligibility: Applicants must be U.S. citizens who are enrolling for the first time in full-time post-secondary education or training in the coming year. The scholarship is composed of four awards, and different recipients are selected for each category. For Award #1, applicants

must be disabled. For Award #2, applicants must be disabled and be a member of a minority ethnic group such as African American, Native American, Hispanic or Asian American. For Award #3, applicants must be disabled and must demonstrate a gift or talent in general intellectual ability, specific academic aptitude, creativity, leadership or the visual or performing arts. For Award #4, applicants must be disabled, be a member of a minority ethnic group and display ability in one of the fields mentioned in Award #3.

Target applicant:
   High school students
Minimum GPA: None.
Amount: $500.
Number of awards: 4-10.
Deadline: February 1.
How to apply: Applications are available online.

(2508) · The Barbara Palo Foster Memorial Scholarship

Ulman Cancer Fund for Young Adults
4725 Dorsey Hall Drive, Suite A
Ellicott City, MD 21042
Phone: 410-964-0202
Email: scholarship@ulmanfund.org
Website: http://www.ulmanfund.org
Purpose: To support students who have a parent with cancer and those who have lost a parent to cancer.
Eligibility: Students must show financial need, community service participation, commitment to education and career goals and how they have used their experience to help others.
Target applicant:
   High school students
   College students
   Adult students
Minimum GPA: None.
Amount: $2,500.
Number of awards: Varies.
Deadline: May 10.
How to apply: Applications are available online.

(2509) · The Marilyn Yetso Memorial Scholarship

Ulman Cancer Fund for Young Adults
4725 Dorsey Hall Drive, Suite A
Ellicott City, MD 21042
Phone: 410-964-0202
Email: scholarship@ulmanfund.org
Website: http://www.ulmanfund.org
Purpose: To support students who have a parent with cancer and those who have lost a parent to cancer.
Eligibility: Students must show financial need, community service participation, commitment to education and career goals and how they have used their experience to help others.
Target applicant:
   High school students
   College students
   Adult students
Minimum GPA: None.
Amount: $2,500.
Number of awards: Varies.
Deadline: May 10.
How to apply: Applications are available online.

(2510) · The Vera Yip Memorial Scholarship

Ulman Cancer Fund for Young Adults
4725 Dorsey Hall Drive, Suite A
Ellicott City, MD 21042
Phone: 410-964-0202
Email: scholarship@ulmanfund.org
Website: http://www.ulmanfund.org
Purpose: To support students who are cancer survivors and students whose parents have been afflicted with cancer.
Eligibility: Students must show financial need, community service participation, personal or family medical hardship, commitment to education and career goals and how they have used their experience to help others.
Target applicant:
   High school students
   College students
   Adult students
Minimum GPA: None.
Amount: $2,500.
Number of awards: Varies.
Deadline: May 10.
How to apply: Applications are available online.

(2511) · TPA Scholarship Trust for the Deaf and Near Deaf

TPA Scholarship Trust for the Deaf and Near Deaf
3755 Lindell Boulevard
St. Louis, MO 63108-3476
Phone: 314-371-0533
Fax: 314-371-0537
Email: support@tpahq.org
Website: http://www.tpahq.org
Purpose: To provide financial aid to children and adults who are deaf or hearing impaired and who need assistance in obtaining mechanical devices, treatment or specialized education.
Eligibility: Applicants must suffer from deafness or hearing impairment.
Target applicant:
   Junior high students or younger
   High school students
   College students
   Graduate school students
   Adult students
Minimum GPA: None.
Amount: Varies.
Number of awards: Varies.
Deadline: March 1.
How to apply: Applications are available by request or online.

(2512) · Will to Win Scholarship

Schering-Plough
P.O. Box 6503
Carlstadt, NJ 07072
Phone: 800-724-3746
Email: requests@schering-ploughwilltowin.com
Website: http://www.schering-ploughwilltowin.com
Purpose: To demonstrate that asthma need not affect one's ability to excel in life.
Eligibility: Applicants must be high school seniors with asthma who demonstrate outstanding performance and achievements in performing

arts, community service, athletics, visual arts or science. They must plan to attend college in the fall following application. A GPA of 3.5 or higher and at least one award related to entry category are required.
Target applicant:
     High school students
Minimum GPA: 3.5
Amount: $5,000.
Number of awards: 10.
Deadline: October 31.
How to apply: Applications are available online.

(2513) · William and Dorothy Ferrell Scholarship
Association for Education and Rehabilitation of the Blind and Visually Impaired
1703 N. Beauregard Street
Suite 440
Alexandria, VA 22311
Phone: 877-493-2708
Fax: 703-671-6391
Website: http://www.aerbvi.org
Purpose: To assist visually-impaired students who plan to assist others who are visually impaired.
Eligibility: Applicants must be legally blind, with a vision of 20/200 or less in the best eye or 20 degrees or less in the visual field. Applicants must also study in college or a similar institution and must be in the field of services for the blind or visually impaired. Scholarships are only awarded in the even numbered years.
Target applicant:
     College students
     Graduate school students
     Adult students
Minimum GPA: None.
Amount: Varies.
Number of awards: 2.
Deadline: February 15.
How to apply: Applications are available online or by phone request.

(2514) · Young Soloists Awards
VSA Arts
818 Connecticut Avenue NW
Suite 600
Washington, DC 20006
Phone: 800-933-8721
Fax: 202-429-0868
Email: info@vsarts.org
Website: http://www.vsarts.org
Purpose: To award promising young musicians with disabilities with scholarship funds and a chance to perform in Washington, DC, at the John F. Kennedy Center for the Performing Arts.
Eligibility: Applicants must be instrumentalists or vocalists no older than 25 years of age and have physical or mental disabilities that limit one or more of their major life activities. Applicants need to include audio or videocassette recordings of three musical selections along with a one-page biography explaining why they feel they should be selected for the award. Awards are based on technique, tone, intonation, rhythm and interpretation from the taped performances.
Target applicant:
     Junior high students or younger
     High school students
     College students
     Graduate school students

Minimum GPA: None.
Amount: Varies.
Number of awards: 2.
Deadline: November 1.
How to apply: Applications are available online.

Scholarship Indexes

What would you rather do: read the description of every single scholarship in this book or use an index to quickly zero in on scholarships that fit you? That's what we thought, which is why we put together a set of indexes that make it easy for you to find the perfect scholarships. We strongly recommend that you use all of the indexes. This is because every scholarship can be categorized in numerous ways and often the decision is unavoidably subjective. So to make sure that you don't miss out on a great scholarship, spend the time to consult each of the following indexes:

GENERAL CATEGORY INDEX

This is one of the most useful indexes since it organizes the scholarships by common fields of study or career areas. It does not list any state specific scholarships since there is another index just for state of residence. Here are the general categories:

Academics/General
Accounting/Finance
Aerospace/Aviation
Agriculture/Horticulture/Animals
Architecture/Landscape
Athletics/Outdoors
Biological Sciences/Life Sciences
Business/Management
Chemistry
Communications
Computer and Information Science
Construction Trades
Culinary Arts
Dentistry
Disability/Illness
Education/Teaching
Engineering
English/Writing
Ethnic and Area Studies
Food Services
Foreign Language
Forestry/Wildlife
Graphic Arts
Hospitality/Travel/Tourism
Journalism/Broadcasting
Law
Leadership
Library Science
Marketing
Mathematics
Medicine/Nursing/Health Professions
Military/Police/Fire
Organizations/Clubs/Employers
Performing Arts/Music/Drama/Visual Arts
Psychology
Public Administration/Social Work
Public Service/Community Service
Race/Ethnicity/Gender/Family Status
Real Estate
Religion and Churches
Sciences/Physical Sciences
Social Science/History
Unions
Vocational/Technical

ACADEMICS/GENERAL
Also See Scholarships Listed Under:
Leadership
Public Service/Community Service
$1,000 Gen and Kelly Tanabe Parent Scholarship • 1
$1,000 Gen and Kelly Tanabe Student Scholarship • 2
Academic Competitiveness Grant • 3
AFSA National Essay Contest • 4
AG Bell College Scholarship Program • 2449

Akademos / TextbookX.com Scholarship • 5
All-Ink Scholarship • 6
Alpha Kappa Alpha Financial Need Scholars • 7
American Fire Sprinkler Association Scholarship Program • 9
Arlene Schlosser Memorial Endowment • 13
Asian American Scholarship Fund • 2217
AXA Achievement Scholarships • 15
Ayers/Gallatin Endowment • 16
Blogging for Progress • 21
Blogging Scholarship • 22
Burger King Scholars Program • 27
Chinese American Citizens Alliance Foundation Essay Contest • 30
Church Hill Classics "Frame My Future" Scholarship • 31
CIA Undergraduate Scholarship Program • 32
CKSF Intern Challenge • 33
CKSF Movie Scholarships • 34
Coca-Cola Scholars Program • 35
Coca-Cola Two-Year College Scholarship • 36
College Insider TV $500 Scholarship • 37
College Match Program • 38
College Prep Scholarship for High School Juniors • 39
College Prowler Essay Scholarship • 40
College Scholarship Program • 2245
CollegeNET Scholarship • 41
CollegeWeekLive.com $3,500 Scholarship • 42
Congressional Black Caucus Spouses Education Scholarship • 43
CosmoGirl! Of The Year Award • 2250
CrossLites Scholarship Contest • 44
Cultural Ambassadorial Scholarships • 45
Davidson Fellows Award • 47
Davis-Putter Scholarship Fund • 48
Dell Scholars Program • 49
Dennis Schlosser Endowment • 50
DiscoverScholars.org Scholarship • 53
Dollars for Scholars Scholarship • 57
Dr. Arnita Young Boswell Scholarship • 59
Dr. Wynetta A. Frazier "Sister to Sister" Scholarship • 60
Educational Advancement Foundation Merit Scholarship • 62
ESA Foundation Endowment • 63
Family Common Knowledge Challenge • 65
FiSCA Scholarship • 66
Floyd Gray Endowment • 67
Fulbright Grants • 69
General Scholarships • 71
Global Action Awards • 74
Global Citizen Awards • 75
GPA Isn't Everything Scholarship • 77
Graduate Scholarship • 79
Graduate Studies Scholarship • 80
Hagiwara Student Aid Award • 2294
HANDS Essay Contest • 81
Hayek Fund for Scholars • 83
High School Internet Challenge • 84
Hispanic Heritage Youth Awards • 2304
Holocaust Remembrance Project Essay Contest • 503
Horatio Alger Association Scholarship Program • 86
Humane Studies Fellowships • 88

Japanese American Citizens League Entering Freshman Awards • 2314
Japanese American Citizens League Undergraduate Awards • 2317
Jeanne Parker Honorarium Endowment • 91
John F. Kennedy Profile in Courage Essay Contest • 538
Josephine De Karman Fellowship • 94
KFC Colonel's Scholars Program • 95
Lauretta M. Roberts Memorial Endowment • 98
Life Lessons Essay Contest • 100
Linda Riddle/SGMA Scholarship • 101
Margaret Jesser Memorial Endowment • 102
Marshall Memorial Fellowship • 105
Maxine Wirth Graduate Studies Endowment • 106
Mensa Education & Research Foundation Scholarship Program • 107
Most Valuable Student Scholarships • 108
My Turn Essay Competition • 109
Nancy Reagan Pathfinder Scholarships • 113
National Beta Club Scholarship • 2113
National D-Day Museum Online Essay Contest • 595
National Honor Society Scholarship • 2115
National Merit Scholarship Program and National Achievement Scholarship Program • 116
National Oratorical Contest • 117
Nelnet $1 Million Scholarship Giveaway • 121
New America Foundation Essay Contest • 122
Off to College Scholarship Sweepstakes • 125
Parent Answer Scholarship Sweepstakes • 126
Past International Council President's Endowment • 127
Patricia M. McNamara Memorial Scholarship • 128
Patriot's Pen Essay Contest • 129
Patriot's Pen Youth Essay Contest • 294
Paul and Daisy Soros Fellowships for New Americans • 130
Phoenix Scholarship Program • 132
Rhodes Scholar • 135
RMHC National Scholarship Program • 136
Rosagene Huggins Memorial Endowment • 137
Russ Griffith Memorial Scholarship • 138
Ruth Gregg Memorial Endowment • 139
Sallie Mae $1,000 Scholarship • 140
Salvatore J. Natoli Dissertation Award in Geographic Education • 141
Sam Walton Community Scholarship • 142
Scholarship Drawing for $1000 • 145
Scholarship Lucky Draw • 146
Scholarship Program for Students in Cargill Communities • 147
September 11th Scholarship • 149
Shepherd Scholarship • 150
Simon Youth Foundation Community Scholarship • 151
Stokes Educational Scholarship Program • 153
Stuck at Prom Scholarship • 155
Study Abroad Grants • 157
Summer Graduate Research Fellowships • 158
SuperCollege.com Student Scholarship • 159
Swackhamer Peace Essay Contest • 315
Talbots Women's Scholarship Fund • 160
Telluride Association Summer Programs • 161

NSA Scholarship Foundation • 623

Pat Roberts Intelligence Scholars Program for Global Network Analysts • 629

Pat Roberts Intelligence Scholars Program for Intelligence Analysts • 630

Princess Cruises and Princess Tours Scholarship • 638

Professional Engineers In Government (PEG) • 1014

Professional Scholarships • 639

Professor Sidney Gross Memorial Award • 640

Ritchie-Jennings Memorial Scholarship • 648

Simmons Scholarship • 660

Southern California Chapter/Pleasant Hawaiian Holidays Scholarship • 663

SSPI Scholarship Program • 666

Stuart Cameron and Margaret McLeod Memorial Scholarship • 669

Summer Graduate Research Fellowships • 158

Transatlantic Fellows Program • 685

Undergraduate Scholarship • 2169

United Negro College Fund Cargill Scholarship-Internship Program • 2435

William Randolph Hearst Endowed Scholarship for Minority Students • 2444

CHEMISTRY (PHYSICAL SCIENCES)

Also See Scholarships Listed Under:
Biological Sciences/Life Sciences
Engineering (Includes Chemical Eng.)
Medicine/Nursing/Health Professions
Sciences/Physical Sciences

ACIL Scholarship • 717

American Chemical Society Minority Scholars Program • 2205

American Chemical Society Scholars Program • 2206

American Electroplaters and Surface Finishers Society Scholarship • 743

American Plastics Council (APC)/SPE Plastics Environmental Division Scholarship • 744

AMS/Industry/Government Graduate Fellowships • 749

ARM Undergraduate Student Fellowships • 767

Astronaut Scholarship • 786

Canadian Section Student Award • 805

Chemistry Common Knowledge Challenge • 810

Composites Division/Harold Giles Scholarship • 816

Davidson Fellows Award • 47

Donald F. and Mildred Topp Othmer Foundation • 834

Gladys Anderson Emerson Scholarship • 872

Industrial Electrolysis and Electrochemical Engineering Division H.H. Dow Memorial Student Award • 897

Intel Science Talent Search • 899

John J. McKetta Scholarship • 914

Larson Aquatic Research Support (LARS) • 927

Members-at-Large Reentry Award • 956

Minority Affairs Committee Award for Outstanding Scholastic Achievement • 2355

Minority Scholarship Awards for College Students • 2358

Minority Scholarship Awards for Incoming College Freshmen • 2359

National Student Design Competition • 978

NDSEG Fellowship Program • 985

Polymer Modifiers and Additives Division Scholarships • 1011

Science and Technology Scholarship • 1812

SemiZone E-Learning Fellowships • 1035

Siemens Westinghouse Competition in Math, Science and Technology • 1039

Society of Plastics Engineers (SPE) General Scholarships • 1043

Student Poster Session Awards • 1051

Ted Neward Scholarship • 1057

Thermoforming Division Memorial Scholarships • 1060

Thermoset Division/James I. MacKenzie Memorial Scholarship • 1061

Undergraduate Award for Excellence in Chemistry • 1070

United Negro College Fund Cargill Scholarship-Internship Program • 2435

Vinyl Plastics Division Scholarship • 1079

Willems Scholarship • 2443

COMMUNICATIONS

Also See Scholarships Listed Under:
English/Writing
Journalism/Broadcasting

AFCEA Ralph W. Shrader Scholarships • 724

ARRL Scholarship Honoring Senator Barry Goldwater, K7UGA • 393

BI-LO Minority Scholarship Program • 1159

Bill Gove Scholarship • 209

Bill Salerno, W2ONV, Memorial Scholarship • 399

Bodie McDowell Scholarship • 401

Carole J. Streeter, KB9JBR Scholarship • 411

Cavett Robert Scholarship • 215

CCNMA Scholarships • 1202

Charles & Lucille King Family Foundation Scholarship • 415

Charles Clarke Cordle Memorial Scholarship • 417

Charles N. Fisher Memorial Scholarship • 421

Chicago FM Club Scholarships • 423

Dayton Amateur Radio Association Scholarship • 438

Distinguished Service Award for Students • 439

Donald Riebhoff Memorial Scholarship • 444

Dr. James L. Lawson Memorial Scholarship • 446

Earl I. Anderson Scholarship • 448

Earl Nightengale Scholarship • 234

Edmond A. Metzger Scholarship • 451

Electronic Document Systems Foundation Scholarship Awards • 456

Eugene Gene Sallee, W4YFR Memorial Scholarship • 461

Francis Walton Memorial Scholarship • 469

Frank del Olmo Memorial Scholarship • 1340

Fred R. McDaniel Memorial Scholarship • 471

Fund for American Studies Internships • 475

Future Teacher Scholarship • 477

Gary Wagner, K3OMI Scholarship • 479

General Fund Scholarships • 483

Grants for Research in Broadcasting • 491

Hispanic Heritage Youth Awards • 2304

IFEC Scholarships Award • 512

IRARC Memorial Joseph P. Rubino WA4MMD Scholarship • 522

Jean Cebik Memorial Scholarship • 530

Joel Garcia Memorial Scholarship • 1456

Julianne Malveaux Scholarship • 2325

K2TEO Martin J. Green, Sr. Memorial Scholarship • 545

L. Phil Wicker Scholarship • 549

Literary Achievement Awards • 2100

Mary Lou Brown Scholarship • 569

Milk Marketing Scholarship • 963

Multicultural Affairs Scholarship Program • 2363

NCDXF Scholarship • 613

NEMAL Electronics Scholarship • 615

New England FEMARA Scholarships • 616

Nido Qubein Scholarship • 290

Optimist International Communications Contest • 2496

Optimist International Oratorical Contest • 625

Parsons Brinckerhoff –Golden Apple Scholarship • 628

Pat Roberts Intelligence Scholars Program for Global Network Analysts • 629

Pat Roberts Intelligence Scholars Program for Intelligence Analysts • 630

Paul and Helen L. Grauer Scholarship • 631

Perry F. Hadlock Memorial Scholarship • 633

PHD ARA Scholarship • 634

Print and Graphics Scholarship • 299

Public Relations Scholarship • 642

Ray, NRP & Katie, WKTE Pautz Scholarship • 643

Richard W. Bendicksen Memorial Scholarship • 647

Rolling Stone Annual College Journalism Competition • 649

Seth Horen, K1LOM Memorial Scholarship • 657

SSPI Scholarship Program • 666

Student Journalist Impact Award • 671

Student with a Disability Scholarship • 674

TLMI Four Year Colleges/Full-Time Students Scholarship • 681

Tom and Judith Comstock Scholarship • 683

Transatlantic Fellows Program • 685

William R. Goldfarb Memorial Scholarship • 698

Yasme Foundation Scholarship • 704

Young Communicators Fellowships • 706

Youth Scholarship • 707

Zachary Taylor Stevens Memorial Scholarship • 708

COMPUTER AND INFORMATION SCIENCE

Also See Scholarships Listed Under:
Engineering
Mathematics
Sciences/Physical Sciences

AFCEA General Emmett Paige Scholarships • 353

AFCEA General John A. Wickham Scholarships • 723

AFCEA Ralph W. Shrader Scholarships • 724

AFCEA ROTC Scholarships • 354

AFCEA Sgt Jeannette L. Winters, USMC Memorial Scholarship • 355

AGA Scholarships • 357

AOC Scholarships • 758

ARM Undergraduate Student Fellowships • 767

Astronaut Scholarship • 786

ENGINEERING

Also See Scholarships Listed Under:
Aerospace/Aviation
Computer and Information Science
Sciences/Physical Sciences

MILITARY/POLICE/FIRE (INCLUDES PROTECTIVE SERVICES WHICH IS MAIN CIP)

Also See Scholarships Listed Under:
Leadership

ORGANIZATIONS/CLUBS/EMPLOYERS

Also See Scholarships Listed Under:
Unions

P.E.O. Program for Continuing Education • 2386
Palmer B. Carson-PFLAG Scholarship for LGBT Advocacy • 2387
Parents without Partners International Scholarship Program • 2388
Parents, Families and Friends of Lesbians and Gays General Scholarships • 2389
PBS&J Achievement Scholarship • 2390
PEO International Peace Scholarship • 2391
Polish National Alliance Scholarship • 2392
Possible Woman Foundation International Scholarship • 2393
Premedical Summer Institute Program/Internship • 2394
Prince Kuhio Hawaiian Civic Club Scholarship • 2395
Private High School Scholarship • 2396
Raymond W. Cannon Memorial Scholarship • 2397
Reader's Digest Scholarship • 2398
Rhea and Louis Spieler Scholarship Program • 2399
Richard R. Tufenkian Memorial Scholarship • 2400
Robert Dole Scholarship for Disabled Students • 2401
Robert Half International • 2402
Ron Brown Scholar Program • 2403
Rosa L. Parks Scholarship • 2404
Roy Wilkins Scholarship • 2405
Ruth Mu-Lan Chu and James S.C. Chao Scholarship • 2406
Scholarships for Social Justice • 2407
Scholarships to Oslo International Summer School • 303
Sequoyah Graduate Fellowships for American Indian and Alaskan Natives • 2408
Siemens Teacher Education Scholarship Program • 2409
Sikh Education Aid Fund • 2410
Siragusa Foundation Scholarship • 2411
Slovenian Women's Union of America Scholarship Program • 2412
Sodexho Scholarship • 2413
Standardized Test Fee Scholarship • 2414
Sterling Bank Scholarship • 2415
Student CEC Ethnic Diversity Scholarship • 2416
Student CEC/Black Caucus Scholarship • 2417
Sutton Scholarship • 2418
Suzanne Jourdan Memorial Scholarship • 2419
Sylvia Shapiro Scholarship • 2420
Telamon Scholarship • 2421
The Black History Common Knowledge Challenge • 2422
The Maureen L. & Howard N. Blitman, P.E., Scholarship • 2423
Thomas G. Neusom Scholarship • 2424
Thurgood Marshall Scholarship Fund Scholarship • 2425
Time Warner Scholars Program • 2426
Trailblazer Scholarship • 2427
Tribal Business Management Program • 2428
Tribal Priority Scholarship • 2429
Trull Foundation Scholarship • 2430
Truman D. Picard Scholarship • 2431

Tuition and Book Scholarship • 2432
Tuition Scholarship Program • 320
UNCF-Foot Locker Foundation Inc. Scholarship • 2433
UNCF/Merck Graduate Science Research Dissertation Fellowships • 2434
Undergraduate Scholarship and Construction Crafts Scholarship • 1072
United Negro College Fund Cargill Scholarship-Internship Program • 2435
United Negro College Fund Scholarships • 2436
United Parcel Service Foundation • 2437
United Parcel Service Scholarship for Minority Students • 2438
USA Funds Scholarship • 2439
USENIX Association Scholarship • 2440
Violet Richardson Award • 181
Wells Fargo Scholarship • 2441
Wendell Scott, Sr./NASCAR Scholarship • 2442
Willems Scholarship • 2443
William L. Hastie Award • 697
William Randolph Hearst Endowed Scholarship for Minority Students • 2444
William Wrigley Jr. Scholarship/Internship • 2445
Women in Need Scholarship • 701
Women in Transition Scholarship • 702
Women's Opportunity Awards Program • 2446
Writers of Passage Scholarship • 2447
Young Women in Public Affairs Fund • 2448

REAL ESTATE (BUSINESS/MGT.)
Also See Scholarships Listed Under:
Business/Management
George M. Brooker Collegiate Scholarship for Minorities • 487
Minorities and Women Educational Scholarship • 581

RELIGION AND CHURCHES
Also See Scholarships Listed Under:
Academics/General
Allan Jerome Burry Scholarship • 1963
Biblical Common Knowledge Challenge • 1984
Blanche Fearn Memorial High School Senior Essay Contest • 1986
Broome and Allen Boys Camp and Scholarship Fund • 212
California Masonic Foundation Scholarship • 1181
Catholic Aid Association College Tuition Scholarship • 1998
Catholic Workman Scholarship • 1999
Christian Connector Undergraduate Scholarship • 2007
Continuing Education Grant/Loan Program • 2014
Diocese of the Armenian Church of America (Eastern) Scholarships • 2022
E. Craig Brandenburg Scholarship • 2029
Edith M. Allen Scholarship • 2031
Ethnic Minority Scholarship • 2036
Fadel Educational Foundation Annual Award Program • 2038
Faith and Education Scholarship Fund • 2039
Fellowship of United Methodists in Music and Worship Arts Scholarship • 2041
Foundation Scholars Program • 2047

General Conference Women's Ministries Scholarship Program • 2054
Grant Programs for Medical Studies • 2060
HANA Scholarship • 2062
J. Robert Ashcroft National Youth Scholarship • 2076
John Sarrin Scholarship • 2087
Leonard M. Perryman Communications Scholarship for Ethnic Minority Students • 2096
Life Members' Scholarship • 2097
Michael Hakeem Memorial College Essay Contest • 2105
Moris J. and Betty Kaplun Scholarship • 2111
National Presbyterian College Scholarship • 2116
National Temperance Scholarship • 2118
Opportunity Scholarships for Lutheran Laywomen • 2122
Otto M. Stanfield Legal Scholarship • 626
Priscilla R. Morton Scholarship • 2128
Racial/Ethnic History Research Grant • 2131
Rev. Dr. Karen Layman Gift of Hope 21st Century Scholars Program • 2132
Rosalie Bentzinger Scholarship • 2137
Stanfield and D'Orlando Art Scholarship • 2148
UCC Seminarian Scholarship • 2164
Undergraduate Fellows Program • 2167
Undergraduate Scholarships • 2170
United Methodist General Scholarship • 2172
Vocations Scholarship Funds • 2177
Women in United Methodist History Research Grant • 2187
Women in United Methodist History Writing Award • 2188

SCIENCES/PHYSICAL SCIENCES
Also See Scholarships Listed Under:
Engineering
Chemistry
Computer and Information Science
Mathematics
ACIL Scholarship • 717
AFCEA General Emmett Paige Scholarships • 353
AFCEA General John A. Wickham Scholarships • 723
AFCEA Ralph W. Shrader Scholarships • 724
AFCEA ROTC Scholarships • 354
AFCEA Sgt Jeannette L. Winters, USMC Memorial Scholarship • 355
AIAA Foundation Undergraduate Scholarship Program • 729
American Chemical Society Scholars Program • 2206
American Electroplaters and Surface Finishers Society Scholarship • 743
AMS Graduate Fellowship in the History of Science • 746
AMS Undergraduate Scholarships • 747
AMS/Industry Minority Scholarships • 748
AMS/Industry/Government Graduate Fellowships • 749
ANS Graduate Scholarship • 755
ANS Undergraduate Scholarship • 756
Antoinette Lierman Medlin Scholarship • 757
APS Minority Scholarship • 765
ARM Undergraduate Student Fellowships • 767
ASM Foundation Scholarship Awards • 776

ASM Foundation Technical and Community College Scholarship Awards • 777
ASM Outstanding Scholars Awards • 778
ASNE Scholarship Program • 780
Association for Women in Science College Scholarship • 782
Association for Women in Science Predoctoral Awards • 783
Astronaut Scholarship • 786
Barry M. Goldwater Scholarship and Excellence in Education Program • 793
Battery Division Student Research Award • 794
Collegiate Inventors Competition • 814
Corrosion Division Morris Cohen Graduate Student Award • 819
Davidson Fellows Award • 47
DuPont Challenge Science Essay Award • 840
Explorations Summer Research Fellowships • 2272
Fellowship Award • 850
Freshman Undergraduate Scholarship • 859
GBT Student Support Program • 864
GEM Fellowship Program • 2285
GeoEye Award • 867
George A. Roberts Scholarships • 869
Graduate Student Research Grants • 875
Graduate Summer Student Research Assistantship • 877
Herbert Levy Memorial Scholarship • 888
Hertz Foundation's Graduate Fellowship Award • 889
Hispanic Heritage Youth Awards • 2304
HORIZONS Foundation Scholarship • 506
Industrial Electrolysis and Electrochemical Engineering Division H.H. Dow Memorial Student Award • 897
Industrial Electrolysis and Electrochemical Engineering Division Student Achievement Awards • 898
Intel Science Talent Search • 899
International Science and Engineering Fair • 900
ISS Scholarship Foundation • 904
Jack Horkheimer Award • 905
John and Muriel Landis Scholarship • 911
Len Assante Scholarship Fund • 930
MAES Scholarship Program • 2337
Marliave Fund • 943
Michael Kidger Memorial Scholarship • 959
Minnesota Academic Excellence Scholarship • 1588
National Young Astronomer Award • 981
NDSEG Fellowship Program • 985
Nicholas J. Grant Scholarship • 991
Payzer Scholarship • 1003
Peggy Dixon Two-Year Scholarship • 1004
Robert E. Altenhofen Memorial Scholarship • 1023
Robert E. Thunen Memorial Scholarships • 1024
Rust Scholarship • 2138
Science and Technology Scholars Program • 1032
Science and Technology Scholarship • 1812
SEA Scholarship Contest • 1034
SemiZone E-Learning Fellowships • 1035
Shlemon Awards • 1038
Siemens Westinghouse Competition in Math, Science and Technology • 1039

Society of Exploration Geophysicists (SEG) Scholarship • 1041
SPS Future Teacher Scholarship • 665
SPS Leadership Scholarships • 1046
Student Poster Session Awards • 1051
Student Travel Contingency Grants • 1055
The Father James B. Macelwane Annual Awards in Meteorology • 1058
Tilford Fund • 1065
Travel Grants • 1067
Undergraduate Student Research Grants • 1073
Undergraduate Student Summer Research Fellowships • 1074
Undergraduate Summer Student Research Assistantship • 1075
William A. Fischer Memorial Scholarship • 1082
William Park Woodside Founder's Scholarship • 1084
Young Naturalist Awards • 1088

SOCIAL SCIENCE/HISTORY
Also See Scholarships Listed Under:
Education/Teaching
English/Writing
Foreign Language
Ethnic and Area Studies
ABC-CLIO America: History and Life Award • 339
ACOR-CAORC Fellowships • 349
Adelle and Erwin Tomash Fellowship in the History of Information Processing • 350
AGA Scholarships • 357
American History Scholarship, Enid Hall Griswold Memorial Scholarship, J.E. Caldwell Centennial Scholarship • 377
American Society of Criminology Fellowships for Ethnic Minorities • 2211
ARIT Fellowships for Research in Turkey • 387
Association for Women in Science Predoctoral Awards • 783
BSA Research Fellowship • 406
CaGIS Scholarships • 407
College/University Excellence of Scholarship Awards • 432
Contemplative Practice Fellowship Program • 434
DAAD/AICGS Research Fellowship Program • 228
Darrel Hess Community College Geography Scholarship • 436
Davidson Fellows Award • 47
Donald Groves Fund • 443
Donald Riebhoff Memorial Scholarship • 444
Fellowship in Aerospace History • 851
Fellowships for Regular Program • 239
Florence C. and Robert H. Lister Fellowship • 467
Frances M. Schwartz Fellowship • 468
Fund for American Studies Internships • 475
Gamma Theta Upsilon-Geographical Honor Society • 478
Gene Carte Student Paper Competition • 482
George and Viola Hoffman Award • 486
German Studies Research Grant • 245
Grades 7-12 Excellence of Scholarship Awards • 490
Hagley-Winterthur Fellowships in Arts and Industries • 492

Harrell Family Fellowship • 493
Harry S. Truman Research Grant • 495
Harry S. Truman Undergraduate Student Grant • 496
Henry Belin du Pont Dissertation Fellowship • 499
Herbert Hoover Presidential Library Association Travel Grant Program • 501
Holocaust Remembrance Project Essay Contest • 503
Horace Samuel and Marion Galbraith Merrill Travel Grants in Twentieth-Century American Political History • 505
Humane Studies Fellowships • 88
Huntington Fellowships • 508
Huntington-British Academy Fellowships for Study in Great Britain • 509
J. Franklin Jameson Fellowship in American History • 524
Jennifer C. Groot Fellowship • 531
John F. Kennedy Profile in Courage Essay Contest • 538
Joseph S. Rumbaugh Historical Oration Contest • 543
Julianne Malveaux Scholarship • 2325
Junior Fellowships • 544
Lou Hochberg Awards • 561
Lyndon B. Johnson Foundation Grants-in-Aid Research • 564
Minnesota Academic Excellence Scholarship • 1588
Minority Fellowship Program • 582
National D-Day Museum Online Essay Contest • 595
National History Day Contest • 597
NIH Undergraduate Scholarship Program • 992
NIH Undergraduate Scholarship Program for Students from Disadvantaged Backgrounds • 993
Pat Roberts Intelligence Scholars Program for Intelligence Analysts • 630
Pi Sigma Alpha Washington Internship Scholarships • 635
Pierre and Patricia Bikai Fellowship • 636
Predoctoral Fellowships for Historians of American Art to Travel Abroad • 637
Racial/Ethnic History Research Grant • 2131
Robert G. Porter Scholars Program for Members' Dependents • 2135
Rural Poverty Research Center Undergraduate Fellowships • 650
Samuel H. Kress Foundation Paired Fellowship for Research in Conservation and the History of Art • 651
Student Travel Award • 673
Summer Fellowship Program • 675
Summer Graduate Research Fellowships • 158
W.M. Keck Foundation Fellowships for Young Scholars • 694
Wesley-Logan Prize • 695
Women in Geographic Education Scholarship • 700
Women in United Methodist History Research Grant • 2187
Women in United Methodist History Writing Award • 2188
Young Communicators Fellowships • 706

FIELD OF STUDY INDEX

This index organizes the scholarships by fields of study. It lists both general areas of study (in bold) as well as specific areas of study. If you cannot find a specific area of study that matches your major simply look at the scholarships under the closest matching general area.

In addition to this index be sure to use the Career Index since many scholarships are targeted to specific careers but do not have specific field of study requirements.

ACCOUNTING
AGDATA Inc. FFA Scholarship • 1959
BNSF Railway Company FFA Scholarship • 1988
Candon, Todd and Seabolt Scholarship Fund • 1187
Charles B. Atchison, Jr. Endowment • 1206
Charles Foy Jr. Scholarship Fund • 419
Church and Dwight Company Inc. FFA Scholarship • 2009
Citigroup Fellows Program • 2242
Financial Services Institution • 2275
Financial Women International Scholarship • 1328
Hawaii Society of Certified Public Accountants Scholarship Fund • 1383
Jane M. Klausman Women in Business Scholarship Fund • 529
Laurel Fund • 553
LULAC GE Scholarship • 2332
Maine State Chamber of Commerce Scholarship • 1539
Miller Brewing Scholarship • 580
Morgan Stanley Scholarship/Internship • 2362
Robert Half International • 2402
Washington State Auto Dealers Association Awards • 1923
Wells Fargo Scholarship • 2441
William R. Goldfarb Memorial Scholarship • 698
William Wrigley Jr. Scholarship/Internship • 2445
Willis HRH Scholarship • 1936
Women in Need Scholarship • 701
Women in Transition Scholarship • 702

ACTING
Charline E. McCue Memorial Endowment • 1213
Japanese American Citizens League Creative and Performing Arts Awards • 2313
John Lennon Scholarship • 2322
Michael Jackson Scholarship • 2353
Thespian Scholarships • 318

ADVERTISING
AGCO Corporation FFA Scholarship • 1958
AGDATA Inc. FFA Scholarship • 1959
John Lennon Scholarship • 2322
Lebanese American Heritage Club Scholarships • 1495
Michael Jackson Scholarship • 2353
Mississippi Scholarship • 1597
NEMAL Electronics Scholarship • 615

NMPRSA Scholarship • 1646
Philippine Cultural Foundation of Hawai'i Scholarship Fund • 1713
Shirely McKown Scholarship Fund • 1822
Wilson W. Carnes Scholarship • 2185

AEROSPACE, AERONAUTICAL AND ASTRONAUTICAL ENGINEERING
AGCO Corporation FFA Scholarship • 1958
Air Force ROTC Express Scholarships • 361
Amelia Earhart Fellowships • 741
David Alan Quick Scholarship • 825
Ellison Onizuka Memorial Scholarship Fund • 1312
Gary Wagner, K3OMI Scholarship • 479
Hansen Scholarship • 880
High Technology Scholar/Intern Tuition Waiver • 1395
Hoku Scholarship Fund • 1402
LTK Engineering Services Scholarship • 938
LULAC GE Scholarship • 2332
Medtronic Foundation Scholarship • 2349
National Science & Mathematics Access to Retain Talent Grant • 977
Parsons Brinckerhoff – Engineering Scholarship • 999
Perry F. Hadlock Memorial Scholarship • 633
RBC Dain Rauscher Colorado Scholarships • 1732
Sallie Mae Bank Scholarships • 1802
SEA Scholarship Contest • 1034
The Maureen L. & Howard N. Blitman, P.E., Scholarship • 2423
William R. Goldfarb Memorial Scholarship • 698
William R. Kimel, P.E., Engineering Scholarship • 1085
William Wrigley Jr. Scholarship/Internship • 2445
Women in Science and Technology Scholarship • 1941
Yasme Foundation Scholarship • 704

AGRICULTURAL ANIMAL BREEDING
AGDATA Inc. FFA Scholarship • 1959
Agway Foundation FFA Scholarship • 1961
Alpha Gamma Rho Educational Foundation • 1965
American Veterinary Medical Association FFA Scholarship • 1969
Anderson Foundation FFA Scholarship • 1971
Archer Daniels Midland Company FFA Scholarship • 1974
Arysta LifeScience North America FFA Scholarship • 1976
BNSF Railway Company FFA Scholarship • 1988
BRIDGE Endowment Fund FFA Scholarship • 1991
Casey's General Stores Inc. FFA Scholarship • 1997
Chevron Corporation FFA Scholarship • 2005
Chief Industries FFA Scholarship • 2006
Church and Dwight Company Inc. FFA Scholarship • 2009
Darling International Inc. FFA Scholarship • 824
Good Eats Scholarship Fund • 1362
Harold Davis Memorial Scholarship • 2063

James C. Borel FFA Leaders Scholarship Fund • 2079
SEA Scholarship Contest • 1034
Walter and Ruby Behlen Memorial Scholarship • 1916
Wilson W. Carnes Scholarship • 2185

AGRICULTURE AND RELATED SCIENCES (ALL AREAS)
AOS Master's Scholarship Program • 760
Arysta LifeScience North America FFA Scholarship • 1976
ASEV Scholarships • 772
ASF Olin Fellowships • 773
Association of Food and Drug Officials Scholarship Award • 784
BNSF Railway Company FFA Scholarship • 1988
BRIDGE Endowment Fund FFA Scholarship • 1991
Carville M. Akehurst Memorial Scholarship • 807
Casey's General Stores Inc. FFA Scholarship • 1997
Chevron Corporation FFA Scholarship • 2005
Chicago Mercantile Exchange FFA Scholarship • 811
Chief Industries FFA Scholarship • 2006
Church and Dwight Company Inc. FFA Scholarship • 2009
Dairy Student Recognition Program • 822
Darling International Inc. FFA Scholarship • 824
FIRST Scholarship • 853
Freehold Soil Conservation District Scholarship • 1342
Freshman and Sophomore Scholarships • 858
GCSAA Scholars Program • 865
GCSAA Student Essay Contest • 866
Good Eats Scholarship Fund • 1362
Graduate Fellowships • 873
Harness Tracks of America Scholarship Fund • 881
Harold Davis Memorial Scholarship • 2063
HOPE General Scholarship • 1408
James C. Borel FFA Leaders Scholarship Fund • 2079
Junior and Senior Scholarships • 921
Klussendorf Scholarship • 925
Marshall E. McCullough Scholarship • 945
Masonic-Range Science Scholarship • 949
Milk Marketing Scholarship • 963
National FFA College and Vocational/Technical School Scholarship Program • 972
National Garden Clubs Scholarship • 973
Scotts Company Scholars Program • 1033
SEA Scholarship Contest • 1034
Spring Meadow Nursery Scholarship • 1045
United Negro College Fund Cargill Scholarship-Internship Program • 2435
W. Malcolm Harding Scholarship, Philip F. French Scholarship and Owen Hallberg Scholarship • 1080
Walter and Ruby Behlen Memorial Scholarship • 1916
Wilson W. Carnes Scholarship • 2185
Yanmar/SAE Scholarship • 1087

AGRONOMY AND CROP SCIENCE
AGCO Corporation FFA Scholarship • 1958

AGDATA Inc. FFA Scholarship • 1959
Agrium U.S. Inc. FFA Scholarship • 1960
Agway Foundation FFA Scholarship • 1961
Alpha Gamma Rho Educational Foundation • 1965
Anderson Foundation FFA Scholarship • 1971
Archer Daniels Midland Company FFA Scholarship • 1974
Arysta LifeScience North America FFA Scholarship • 1976
BNSF Railway Company FFA Scholarship • 1988
BRIDGE Endowment Fund FFA Scholarship • 1991
Casey's General Stores Inc. FFA Scholarship • 1997
Chevron Corporation FFA Scholarship • 2005
Chicago Mercantile Exchange FFA Scholarship • 811
Chief Industries FFA Scholarship • 2006
Church and Dwight Company Inc. FFA Scholarship • 2009
Darling International Inc. FFA Scholarship • 824
Good Eats Scholarship Fund • 1362
Harold Davis Memorial Scholarship • 2063
James C. Borel FFA Leaders Scholarship Fund • 2079
Monsanto Company/The National Association of Farm Broadcasters Commitment to Agriculture Scholarship • 967
SEA Scholarship Contest • 1034
Walter and Ruby Behlen Memorial Scholarship • 1916
Wilson W. Carnes Scholarship • 2185

AIRLINE/COMMERCIAL/PROFESSIONAL PILOT AND FLIGHT CREW

Eugene S. Kropf Scholarship • 847
Gary Kiteley Executive Director Scholarship • 863
H.P. Milligan Aviation Scholarship • 879
Herbert L. Cox Memorial Scholarship • 887
Joseph Frasca Excellence in Aviation Scholarship • 919

ANIMAL SCIENCES

AGDATA Inc. FFA Scholarship • 1959
Agway Foundation FFA Scholarship • 1961
Alpha Gamma Rho Educational Foundation • 1965
American Veterinary Medical Association FFA Scholarship • 1969
Anderson Foundation FFA Scholarship • 1971
Archer Daniels Midland Company FFA Scholarship • 1974
Arysta LifeScience North America FFA Scholarship • 1976
BNSF Railway Company FFA Scholarship • 1988
BRIDGE Endowment Fund FFA Scholarship • 1991
Casey's General Stores Inc. FFA Scholarship • 1997
Chevron Corporation FFA Scholarship • 2005
Chief Industries FFA Scholarship • 2006
Church and Dwight Company Inc. FFA Scholarship • 2009

Darling International Inc. FFA Scholarship • 824
Good Eats Scholarship Fund • 1362
Harold Davis Memorial Scholarship • 2063
James C. Borel FFA Leaders Scholarship Fund • 2079
SEA Scholarship Contest • 1034
Walter and Ruby Behlen Memorial Scholarship • 1916
Wilson W. Carnes Scholarship • 2185

ANIMAL TRAINING

American Veterinary Medical Association FFA Scholarship • 1969
Arysta LifeScience North America FFA Scholarship • 1976
BNSF Railway Company FFA Scholarship • 1988
BRIDGE Endowment Fund FFA Scholarship • 1991
Casey's General Stores Inc. FFA Scholarship • 1997
Chevron Corporation FFA Scholarship • 2005
Chief Industries FFA Scholarship • 2006
Church and Dwight Company Inc. FFA Scholarship • 2009
Darling International Inc. FFA Scholarship • 824
Good Eats Scholarship Fund • 1362
Harold Davis Memorial Scholarship • 2063
James C. Borel FFA Leaders Scholarship Fund • 2079
SEA Scholarship Contest • 1034
Walter and Ruby Behlen Memorial Scholarship • 1916
Wilson W. Carnes Scholarship • 2185

APPLIED HORTICULTURE AND HORTICULTURAL BUSINESS SERVICES

AGCO Corporation FFA Scholarship • 1958
AGDATA Inc. FFA Scholarship • 1959
Agway Foundation FFA Scholarship • 1961
Alpha Gamma Rho Educational Foundation • 1965
Anderson Foundation FFA Scholarship • 1971
Archer Daniels Midland Company FFA Scholarship • 1974
Arysta LifeScience North America FFA Scholarship • 1976
BNSF Railway Company FFA Scholarship • 1988
BRIDGE Endowment Fund FFA Scholarship • 1991
Casey's General Stores Inc. FFA Scholarship • 1997
Chevron Corporation FFA Scholarship • 2005
Chief Industries FFA Scholarship • 2006
Church and Dwight Company Inc. FFA Scholarship • 2009
Darling International Inc. FFA Scholarship • 824
Emily M. Hewitt Memorial Scholarship • 1315
Good Eats Scholarship Fund • 1362
Harold Davis Memorial Scholarship • 2063
James C. Borel FFA Leaders Scholarship Fund • 2079
Monsanto Company/The National Association of Farm Broadcasters Commitment to Agriculture Scholarship • 967
Rain Bird Scholarship • 1016

SEA Scholarship Contest • 1034
Timothy Bigelow and Palmer W. Bigelow, Jr. Scholarship • 1066
Usrey Family Scholarship • 1077
Walter and Ruby Behlen Memorial Scholarship • 1916
Wilson W. Carnes Scholarship • 2185

AQUACULTURE

Arysta LifeScience North America FFA Scholarship • 1976
BNSF Railway Company FFA Scholarship • 1988
BRIDGE Endowment Fund FFA Scholarship • 1991
Casey's General Stores Inc. FFA Scholarship • 1997
Chevron Corporation FFA Scholarship • 2005
Chief Industries FFA Scholarship • 2006
Church and Dwight Company Inc. FFA Scholarship • 2009
Darling International Inc. FFA Scholarship • 824
Emily M. Hewitt Memorial Scholarship • 1315
Good Eats Scholarship Fund • 1362
Harold Davis Memorial Scholarship • 2063
James C. Borel FFA Leaders Scholarship Fund • 2079
SEA Scholarship Contest • 1034
Walter and Ruby Behlen Memorial Scholarship • 1916
Wilson W. Carnes Scholarship • 2185

ARABIC LANGUAGE AND LITERATURE

Critical Need Language Supplement • 227
JTG Scholarship in Scientific and Technical Translation or Interpretation • 262
National Science & Mathematics Access to Retain Talent Grant • 977

ARCHEOLOGY

Fellowships for Regular Program • 239
Samuel H. Kress Foundation Paired Fellowship for Research in Conservation and the History of Art • 651

ARCHITECTURE AND RELATED SERVICES (ALL AREAS)

ACI Student Fellowship Program • 715
AIA/AAF Minority/Disadvantaged Scholarship • 728
APA Planning Fellowships • 2213
AWA Scholarships • 1148
Carville M. Akehurst Memorial Scholarship • 807
FIRST Scholarship • 853
James L. Shriver Scholarship • 1444
National Garden Clubs Scholarship • 973
Predoctoral Fellowships for Historians of American Art to Travel Abroad • 637
Rain Bird Scholarship • 1016
Raymond E. Page Scholarship • 1019
Robert E. Thunen Memorial Scholarships • 1024
RTKL Traveling Fellowship • 1027
Spring Meadow Nursery Scholarship • 1045
William J. Locklin Scholarship • 1083
Worldstudio Foundation Scholarship Program • 328

AREA, ETHNIC, CULTURAL AND GENDER STUDIES (ALL AREAS)

Bernadette Wong-Yu Scholarship • 2220

Botany/Plant Biology

AGDATA Inc. FFA Scholarship • 1959

Arysta LifeScience North America FFA Scholarship • 1976

Get Ready for Math and Science Conditional Scholarship Program • 1357

Medtronic Foundation Scholarship • 2349

National Science & Mathematics Access to Retain Talent Grant • 977

SEA Scholarship Contest • 1034

Siemens Teacher Education Scholarship Program • 2409

UNCF/Merck Graduate Science Research Dissertation Fellowships • 2434

Women in Science and Technology Scholarship • 1941

Broadcast Journalism

AGDATA Inc. FFA Scholarship • 1959

C-SPAN Scholarship Program • 2228

Charles & Lucille King Family Foundation Scholarship • 415

Guy P. Gannett Scholarship • 1381

John Lennon Scholarship • 2322

Lebanese American Heritage Club Scholarships • 1495

Michael Jackson Scholarship • 2353

Mississippi Scholarship • 1597

NEMAL Electronics Scholarship • 615

NMPRSA Scholarship • 1646

Philippine Cultural Foundation of Hawai'i Scholarship Fund • 1713

Wilson W. Carnes Scholarship • 2185

Business Administration and Management

AGCO Corporation FFA Scholarship • 1958

BNSF Railway Company FFA Scholarship • 1988

Charles B. Atchison, Jr. Endowment • 1206

Charles Foy Jr. Scholarship Fund • 419

Church and Dwight Company Inc. FFA Scholarship • 2009

Citigroup Fellows Program • 2242

Financial Women International Scholarship • 1328

GAP Foundation Scholarship • 2282

George Mason Business Scholarship Fund • 1353

Jane M. Klausman Women in Business Scholarship Fund • 529

LULAC GE Scholarship • 2332

Maine State Chamber of Commerce Scholarship • 1539

Miller Brewing Scholarship • 580

Morgan Stanley Scholarship/Internship • 2362

Peggy Jacques Memorial Scholarship • 1707

Robert Half International • 2402

Washington State Auto Dealers Association Awards • 1923

Wells Fargo Scholarship • 2441

William R. Goldfarb Memorial Scholarship • 698

William Wrigley Jr. Scholarship/Internship • 2445

Willis HRH Scholarship • 1936

Business, Management and Marketing (All Areas)

Accountemps/American Institute Of Certified Public Accountants Student Scholarship • 344

Actuarial Scholarships for Minority Students • 2194

AGA Scholarships • 357

Allstudentloan.org College Scholarship Program for Business Students • 371

American Legion Auxiliary, Department of California $1,000 Scholarships • 1128

American Legion Auxiliary, Department of California $2,000 Scholarships • 1129

Avis Scholarship • 395

Best Buy Scholarship Program • 2222

Betsy Plank/PRSSA Scholarship • 397

BI-LO Minority Scholarship Program • 1159

Burlington Northern Santa Fe (BNSF) Foundation Scholarship • 2226

Business Achievement Awards • 1995

Charles B. Atchison, Jr. Endowment • 1206

Charles Earp Memorial Scholarship • 418

Charles Foy Jr. Scholarship Fund • 419

College Scholarships • 431

Consortium Fellowship • 2248

Coy G. Eklund Scholarship • 2251

Donald W. Fogarty International Student Paper Competition • 445

Earl Graves Scholarship • 2264

Ecolab Scholarship Competition • 449

Edmund S. Muskie Graduate Fellowship Program • 452

Electronic Document Systems Foundation Scholarship Awards • 456

Esther R. Sawyer Scholarship Award • 460

Executive Women International Scholarship Program • 462

Financial Women International Scholarship • 1328

Fisher Broadcasting Scholarships for Minorities • 466

Ford Motor Company Business and Leadership Scholarship • 2043

Fund for American Studies Internships • 475

Gary Yoshimura Scholarship • 480

George M. Brooker Collegiate Scholarship for Minorities • 487

George W. Woolery Memorial Scholarship • 2055

Gillette/National Urban League Scholarship and Intern Program for Minority Students • 2290

Harry A. Applegate Scholarship • 494

Harry J. Donnelly Memorial Scholarship • 2065

Henry B. Gonzalez Award • 498

Henry Belin du Pont Dissertation Fellowship • 499

Hispanic College Fund Scholarships • 2303

HOPE General Scholarship • 1408

HORIZONS Foundation Scholarship • 506

HSF/General Motors Scholarship • 2308

HSMAI Foundation Scholarship • 507

Humane Studies Fellowships • 88

IFEC Scholarships Award • 512

IMA Memorial Education Fund Scholarship • 515

James A. Turner, Jr. Memorial Scholarship • 526

James J. Hill Research Grants • 528

James L. Shriver Scholarship • 1444

Jane M. Klausman Women in Business Scholarship Fund • 529

Jesse Jones, Jr. Scholarship • 2320

Jessica King Scholarship • 532

Joe Perdue Scholarship • 535

Lawrence G. Foster Award for Excellence in Public Relations • 554

Lodging Management Program (LMP) • 559

LULAC GE Scholarship • 2332

Maine State Chamber of Commerce Scholarship • 1539

MESBEC Program • 2351

Milk Marketing Scholarship • 963

Minorities and Women Educational Scholarship • 581

Multicultural Affairs Scholarship Program • 2363

National Association of Black Accountants Scholarship Program • 2371

National Business School High School Scholarship • 594

National Defense Transportation Association, St. Louis Area Chapter Scholarship • 596

National Scholarship • 2375

National Society of Hispanic MBAs Scholarship • 601

NCCPAP Scholarship • 612

NSA Scholarship Foundation • 623

Pat Roberts Intelligence Scholars Program for Global Network Analysts • 629

Pat Roberts Intelligence Scholars Program for Intelligence Analysts • 630

Professor Sidney Gross Memorial Award • 640

Public Relations Scholarship • 642

Ritchie-Jennings Memorial Scholarship • 648

SSPI Scholarship Program • 666

Steven Hymans Extended Stay Scholarship • 667

Stuart Cameron and Margaret McLeod Memorial Scholarship • 669

Summer Fellowship Program • 675

Summer Graduate Research Fellowships • 158

Transatlantic Community Foundation Fellowship • 166

Transatlantic Fellows Program • 685

Tribal Business Management Program • 2428

United Negro College Fund Cargill Scholarship-Internship Program • 2435

W. Allan Herzog Scholarship • 2178

William R. Goldfarb Memorial Scholarship • 698

William Randolph Hearst Endowed Scholarship for Minority Students • 2444

William Wrigley Jr. Scholarship/Internship • 2445

Central/Middle and Eastern European Studies

Clan MacBean Foundation Grant Program • 219

DAAD/AICGS Research Fellowship Program • 228

Fellowships for Regular Program • 239

Graduate and Postgraduate Study and Research in Poland • 248

Lilly Lorénzen Scholarship • 1515

Malmberg Scholarship and Fellowship • 272

Metchie J.E. Budka Award • 273

Short-Term Travel Grants (STG) • 305

Year Abroad Program • 331

Chemical Engineering

AGCO Corporation FFA Scholarship • 1958

AGDATA Inc. FFA Scholarship • 1959

Agrium U.S. Inc. FFA Scholarship • 1960

American Chemical Society Scholars Program • 2206

Gary Wagner, K3OMI Scholarship • 479

High Technology Scholar/Intern Tuition Waiver • 1395

Hoku Scholarship Fund • 1402

LTK Engineering Services Scholarship • 938

LULAC GE Scholarship • 2332

Medtronic Foundation Scholarship • 2349

National Science & Mathematics Access to Retain Talent Grant • 977

Parsons Brinckerhoff – Engineering Scholarship • 999

Perry F. Hadlock Memorial Scholarship • 633

RBC Dain Rauscher Colorado Scholarships • 1732

Sallie Mae Bank Scholarships • 1802

SEA Scholarship Contest • 1034

The Maureen L. & Howard N. Blitman, P.E., Scholarship • 2423

William R. Goldfarb Memorial Scholarship • 698

William R. Kimel, P.E., Engineering Scholarship • 1085

William Wrigley Jr. Scholarship/Internship • 2445

Women in Science and Technology Scholarship • 1941

Yasme Foundation Scholarship • 704

CHEMISTRY

ACIL Scholarship • 717

AGDATA Inc. FFA Scholarship • 1959

American Chemical Society Scholars Program • 2206

Canadian Section Student Award • 805

Chemistry Common Knowledge Challenge • 810

Chevron Corporation FFA Scholarship • 2005

Elizabeth and Sherman Asche Memorial Scholarship • 2268

Get Ready for Math and Science Conditional Scholarship Program • 1357

GlaxoSmithKline Company Science Achievement Award • 2291

Medtronic Foundation Scholarship • 2349

National Science & Mathematics Access to Retain Talent Grant • 977

NC Student Loan Program for Health, Science and Mathematics • 1615

RBC Dain Rauscher Colorado Scholarships • 1732

San Francisco Section Daniel Cubicciotti Student Award • 1803

SEA Scholarship Contest • 1034

Siemens Teacher Education Scholarship Program • 2409

UNCF/Merck Graduate Science Research Dissertation Fellowships • 2434

William James and Dorothy Bading Lanquist Fund • 1932

William R. Goldfarb Memorial Scholarship • 698

William Wrigley Jr. Scholarship/Internship • 2445

Women in Science and Technology Scholarship • 1941

Yasme Foundation Scholarship • 704

CHINESE LANGUAGE AND LITERATURE

Critical Need Language Supplement • 227

JTG Scholarship in Scientific and Technical Translation or Interpretation • 262

National Science & Mathematics Access to Retain Talent Grant • 977

U.S. Department of Education Fulbright-Hays Project Abroad Scholarship for Programs in China • 321

CHINESE STUDIES

American Association of Japanese University Women Scholarship Program • 1123

Philippine Cultural Foundation of Hawai'i Scholarship Fund • 1713

Short-Term Travel Grants (STG) • 305

CHIROPRACTIC (DC)

Carole J. Streeter, KB9JBR Scholarship • 411

Chiropractic Education Assistance Scholarship • 1220

Congressional Black Caucus Spouses Cheerios Brand Health Initiative Scholarship • 817

Cora Aguda Manayan Fund • 1248

Dr. Hans and Clara Zimmerman Foundation Health Scholarships • 1289

Dr. James M. Rosin Scholarship • 2258

Edith M. Allen Scholarship • 2031

Elizabeth and Sherman Asche Memorial Scholarship • 2268

Eloise Collins Endowment • 1313

Florence Young Memorial Scholarship • 2277

Robanna Fund • 1742

Women in Science and Technology Scholarship • 1941

Workforce Shortage Student Assistance Grant Program • 1943

CIVIL ENGINEERING

AGCO Corporation FFA Scholarship • 1958

AGDATA Inc. FFA Scholarship • 1959

Agrium U.S. Inc. FFA Scholarship • 1960

Air Force ROTC Express Scholarships • 361

AIST Ronald E. Lincoln Memorial Scholarship • 732

AIST William E. Schwabe Memorial Scholarship • 733

CDM Scholarship/Internship • 2235

Gary Wagner, K3OMI Scholarship • 479

High Technology Scholar/Intern Tuition Waiver • 1395

Hoku Scholarship Fund • 1402

LTK Engineering Services Scholarship • 938

LULAC GE Scholarship • 2332

Medtronic Foundation Scholarship • 2349

Milton F. Lunch Research Fellowship • 964

National Science & Mathematics Access to Retain Talent Grant • 977

Parsons Brinckerhoff – Engineering Scholarship • 999

Perry F. Hadlock Memorial Scholarship • 633

RBC Dain Rauscher Colorado Scholarships • 1732

Sallie Mae Bank Scholarships • 1802

SEA Scholarship Contest • 1034

The Maureen L. & Howard N. Blitman, P.E., Scholarship • 2423

William R. Goldfarb Memorial Scholarship • 698

William R. Kimel, P.E., Engineering Scholarship • 1085

William Wrigley Jr. Scholarship/Internship • 2445

Women in Science and Technology Scholarship • 1941

Yasme Foundation Scholarship • 704

COMMUNICATION AND JOURNALISM (ALL AREAS)

AAJA Newhouse National Scholarship And Internship Awards • 2192

Abe Schechter Graduate Scholarship • 340

AGDATA Inc. FFA Scholarship • 1959

Al Muammar Scholarships for Journalism • 2200

Al Neuharth Free Spirit Scholarship and Conference Program • 370

Best Buy Scholarship Program • 2222

BI-LO Minority Scholarship Program • 1159

Bill Gove Scholarship • 209

Bodie McDowell Scholarship • 401

Broadcast Education Association Scholarship Program • 405

C-SPAN Scholarship Program • 2228

Carole Simpson Scholarship • 412

Cavett Robert Scholarship • 215

CCNMA Scholarships • 1202

DJNF Summer Internships • 441

Dr. James L. Lawson Memorial Scholarship • 446

Ed Bradley Scholarship • 450

Edmund S. Muskie Graduate Fellowship Program • 452

Edward J. Nell Memorial Scholarships in Journalism • 454

Edward Payson and Bernice Piilani Irwin Scholarship • 1308

Electronic Document Systems Foundation Scholarship Awards • 456

Felix Morley Journalism Competition • 464

Fisher Broadcasting Scholarships for Minorities • 466

Frank del Olmo Memorial Scholarship • 1340

Fred R. McDaniel Memorial Scholarship • 471

Fund for American Studies Internships • 475

Future Teacher Scholarship • 477

George W. Woolery Memorial Scholarship • 2055

Grants for Research in Broadcasting • 491

HOPE General Scholarship • 1408

IFEC Scholarships Award • 512

IHS Journalism Internships • 514

Joel Garcia Memorial Scholarship • 1456

John Bayliss Radio Scholarship • 536

John Lennon Scholarship • 2322

Julianne Malveaux Scholarship • 2325

Ken Kashiwahara Scholarship • 547

Lebanese American Heritage Club Scholarships • 1495

Leonard M. Perryman Communications Scholarship for Ethnic Minority Students • 2096

Literary Achievement Awards • 2100

Lou and Carole Prato Sports Reporting Scholarship • 560

Maria Elena Salinas Scholarship Program • 2340

Marshall E. McCullough Scholarship • 945

Mary Moy Quan Ing Memorial Scholarship • 2343

Michael Jackson Scholarship • 2353

Mike Reynolds Scholarship • 576

Milk Marketing Scholarship • 963

Minority Scholarship and Training Program • 2357

Women in Science and Technology Scholarship • 1941

Yasme Foundation Scholarship • 704

ELEMENTARY EDUCATION AND TEACHING

AGCO Corporation FFA Scholarship • 1958

AGDATA Inc. FFA Scholarship • 1959

Alma White - Delta Kappa Gamma Scholarship • 1117

Bill Kane Scholarship, Undergraduate • 798

Christa McAuliffe Scholarship • 1222

Dr. Hans and Clara Zimmerman Foundation Education Scholarship • 1288

Early Childhood Educators Scholarship • 1297

Edith M. Allen Scholarship • 2031

Elsie M. Vogler / Lois E. Carter Memorial Teaching • 1314

Future Educators Academy • 1345

Future Teachers Conditional Scholarship • 1346

Gilbert Matching Student Grant • 1358

Goodyear Tire and Rubber Company Scholarships • 2292

Hope Baney Memorial Endowment • 1406

Ichiro and Masako Hirata Scholarship • 1412

Jack Kinnaman Scholarship • 525

Kay Mills Memorial Scholarship • 1479

Maine State Chamber of Commerce Scholarship • 1539

Mathematics and Science Teachers Scholarship Program • 1564

Melvin and Anne Tracy Endowment • 572

Minority Teacher/Special Education Services Scholarship • 1594

Olive Griffith Memorial Scholarship • 1673

Paraprofessional Teacher Preparation Grant • 1689

Sallie Mae Bank Scholarships • 1802

Siemens Teacher Education Scholarship Program • 2409

WaMu Future Teachers of Color Scholarships • 1917

Worda Russell Memorial Endowment • 703

Workforce Shortage Student Assistance Grant Program • 1943

ENGINEERING (ALL AREAS)

A.O. Putnam Memorial Scholarship • 709

A.T. Anderson Memorial Scholarship • 2191

Abel Wolman Fellowship • 712

Academic Achievement Award • 713

ACI Student Fellowship Program • 715

ACI-James Instruments Student Award for Research on NDT of Concrete • 716

ACIL Scholarship • 717

ACSM - AAGS - NSPS Scholarships • 718

Adams Scholarship Grant • 720

ADDC Education Trust Scholarship • 721

AFCEA General Emmett Paige Scholarships • 353

AFCEA General John A. Wickham Scholarships • 723

AFCEA Ralph W. Shrader Scholarships • 724

AFCEA ROTC Scholarships • 354

AFCEA Sgt Jeannette L. Winters, USMC Memorial Scholarship • 355

AGC Graduate Scholarships • 726

AGCO Corporation FFA Scholarship • 1958

AIST Benjamin F. Fairless Scholarship (AIME) • 731

AIST Willy Korf Memorial Fund • 734

American Electroplaters and Surface Finishers Society Scholarship • 743

American Legion Auxiliary, Department of California $1,000 Scholarships • 1128

American Legion Auxiliary, Department of California $2,000 Scholarships • 1129

American Plastics Council (APC)/SPE Plastics Environmental Division Scholarship • 744

Amtrol Inc. Scholarship • 752

ARM Undergraduate Student Fellowships • 767

ASAE Foundation Scholarship • 768

ASAE Student Engineer of the Year Scholarship • 769

ASDSO Dam Safety Scholarships • 771

ASHRAE Scholarship Program • 775

ASM Foundation Scholarship Awards • 776

ASM Foundation Technical and Community College Scholarship Awards • 777

ASM Outstanding Scholars Awards • 778

ASME Foundation Scholarships • 779

ASNE Scholarship Program • 780

ASNT Fellowship • 781

Association for Women in Science College Scholarship • 782

Association for Women in Science Predoctoral Awards • 783

Astronaut Scholarship • 786

Automotive Hall of Fame Scholarships • 789

AWA Scholarships • 1148

Banatao Filipino American Education Fund • 1152

Baroid Scholarship • 792

Barry M. Goldwater Scholarship and Excellence in Education Program • 793

Battery Division Student Research Award • 794

Ben Everson Scholarship • 796

Benjamin Willard Niebel Scholarship • 797

Black and Veatch Scholarships • 799

Bureau of Reclamation Scholarship and Internship • 2225

Burlington Northern Santa Fe (BNSF) Foundation Scholarship • 2226

C.B. Gambrell Undergraduate Scholarship • 802

CaGIS Scholarships • 407

Canadian Section Student Award • 805

Composites Division/Harold Giles Scholarship • 816

Corrosion Division Morris Cohen Graduate Student Award • 819

Davidson Fellows Award • 47

Doctoral Scholars Forgivable Loan Program • 831

Donald F. and Mildred Topp Othmer Foundation • 834

Dorothy M. and Earl S. Hoffman Award • 837

Dwight D. Gardner Scholarship • 842

E.J. Sierieja Memorial Fellowship • 843

Earl I. Anderson Scholarship • 448

Engineering and Land Surveying Scholarships • 1316

Engineering Undergraduate Award • 846

Engineering/Technology Achievement Awards • 2035

F.W. Beichley Scholarship • 848

Ford Motor Company Engineering and Leadership Scholarship • 2044

Frank and Dorothy Miller ASME Auxiliary Scholarships • 857

Freehold Soil Conservation District Scholarship • 1342

Garland Duncan Scholarships • 861

Gary Wagner, K3OMI Scholarship • 479

GEM Fellowship Program • 2285

General Mills Technology Scholars Award • 2287

General Motors Engineering Scholarship • 2288

George A. Roberts Scholarships • 869

Gilbreth Memorial Fellowship • 871

Gillette/National Urban League Scholarship and Intern Program for Minority Students • 2290

Graduate Research Award (GRA) • 874

Hertz Foundation's Graduate Fellowship Award • 889

High Technology Scholar/Intern Tuition Waiver • 1395

Hispanic College Fund Scholarships • 2303

Hoku Scholarship Fund • 1402

Holly Cornell Scholarship • 892

HORIZONS Foundation Scholarship • 506

HSF/General Motors Scholarship • 2308

IEEE Presidents' Scholarship • 895

IIE Council of Fellows Undergraduate Scholarship • 896

Industrial Electrolysis and Electrochemical Engineering Division H.H. Dow Memorial Student Award • 897

Industrial Electrolysis and Electrochemical Engineering Division Student Achievement Awards • 898

Intel Science Talent Search • 899

International Science and Engineering Fair • 900

ISS Scholarship Foundation • 904

James L. Shriver Scholarship • 1444

John and Elsa Gracik Scholarships • 910

John J. McKetta Scholarship • 914

John L. Imhoff Scholarship • 915

John S.W. Fargher Scholarship • 916

Joseph C. Johnson Memorial Grant • 918

Joseph M. Parish Memorial Grant • 920

Kenneth Andrew Roe Scholarship • 924

Larson Aquatic Research Support (LARS) • 927

Lisa Zaken Award For Excellence • 934

LTK Engineering Services Scholarship • 938

LULAC GE Scholarship • 2332

MAES Scholarship Program • 2337

Marliave Fund • 943

Marvin Mundel Memorial Scholarship • 946

Medtronic Foundation Scholarship • 2349

Melvin R. Green Scholarships • 955

MESBEC Program • 2351

Minority Affairs Committee Award for Outstanding Scholastic Achievement • 2355

Minority Scholarship Awards for College Students • 2358

Minority Scholarship Awards for Incoming College Freshmen • 2359

NAMEPA Scholarship Program • 969

National Network for Environmental Management Studies Fellowship Program • 974

National Science & Mathematics Access to Retain Talent Grant • 977

National Student Design Competition • 978
NDSEG Fellowship Program • 985
Nellie Yeoh Whetten Award • 988
Nicholas J. Grant Scholarship • 991
Parsons Brinckerhoff – Engineering Scholarship • 999
Paul H. Robbins, P.E., Honorary Scholarship • 1002
Payzer Scholarship • 1003
Perry F. Hadlock Memorial Scholarship • 633
Polymer Modifiers and Additives Division Scholarships • 1011
Professional Engineers In Government (PEG) • 1014
Professional Engineers In Industry (PEI) Scholarship • 1015
Raymond Davis Scholarship • 1018
RBC Dain Rauscher Colorado Scholarships • 1732
Robert B. Oliver ASNT Scholarship • 1022
Robert E. Thunen Memorial Scholarships • 1024
Robert F. Sammataro Pressure Vessel Piping Division Scholarship • 1025
Russell and Sigurd Varian Award • 1028
SAE Engineering Scholarships • 1030
Sallie Mae Bank Scholarships • 1802
Science and Technology Scholars Program • 1032
SEA Scholarship Contest • 1034
SemiZone E-Learning Fellowships • 1035
Siemens Westinghouse Competition in Math, Science and Technology • 1039
Small Cash Grant Program • 1040
Society of Exploration Geophysicists (SEG) Scholarship • 1041
Society of Naval Architects and Marine Engineers Undergraduate Scholarships • 1042
Society of Plastics Engineers (SPE) General Scholarships • 1043
SSPI Scholarship Program • 666
Steven J. Muir Scholarship • 2150
Stokes Educational Scholarship Program • 153
Student Poster Session Awards • 1051
Ted Neward Scholarship • 1057
The Maureen L. & Howard N. Blitman, P.E., Scholarship • 2423
Thermoforming Division Memorial Scholarships • 1060
Thermoset Division/James I. MacKenzie Memorial Scholarship • 1061
Thomas H. Dunning, Sr., Memorial Scholarship • 2159
Thomas M. Stetson Scholarship • 1062
Thomas R. Camp Scholarship • 1063
Tilford Fund • 1065
United Negro College Fund Cargill Scholarship-Internship Program • 2435
United Parcel Service Scholarship for Female Students • 1076
United Parcel Service Scholarship for Minority Students • 2438
Vertical Flight Foundation Engineering Scholarships • 1078
Vinyl Plastics Division Scholarship • 1079
Willems Scholarship • 2443
William Park Woodside Founder's Scholarship • 1084

William R. Goldfarb Memorial Scholarship • 698
William R. Kimel, P.E., Engineering Scholarship • 1085
William Wrigley Jr. Scholarship/Internship • 2445
Women in Science and Technology Scholarship • 1941
Yanmar/SAE Scholarship • 1087
Yasme Foundation Scholarship • 704

ENGLISH LANGUAGE AND LITERATURE (ALL AREAS)

Amy Lowell Poetry Travelling Scholarship • 200
Bill Gove Scholarship • 209
BSA Research Fellowship • 406
C-SPAN Scholarship Program • 2228
Cavett Robert Scholarship • 215
Davidson Fellows Award • 47
Edna Meudt Memorial Award and the Florence Kahn Memorial Award • 235
Film and Fiction Scholarships • 241
HOPE General Scholarship • 1408
Huntington Fellowships • 508
Huntington-British Academy Fellowships for Study in Great Britain • 509
IFEC Scholarships Award • 512
Jeanne S. Chall Research Fellowship • 259
Julianne Malveaux Scholarship • 2325
Literary Achievement Awards • 2100
McClare Family Trust Scholarship • 2346
Michael Jackson Scholarship • 2353
Minnesota Academic Excellence Scholarship • 1588
National Ten Minute Play Contest • 286
Nido Qubein Scholarship • 290
Playwright Discovery Award • 296
Reader's Digest Scholarship • 2398
Taylor/Blakeslee University Fellowships • 316
W.M. Keck Foundation Fellowships for Young Scholars • 694

ENTOMOLOGY

AGDATA Inc. FFA Scholarship • 1959
Arysta LifeScience North America FFA Scholarship • 1976
Get Ready for Math and Science Conditional Scholarship Program • 1357
Medtronic Foundation Scholarship • 2349
National Science & Mathematics Access to Retain Talent Grant • 977
SEA Scholarship Contest • 1034
Siemens Teacher Education Scholarship Program • 2409
UNCF/Merck Graduate Science Research Dissertation Fellowships • 2434
Women in Science and Technology Scholarship • 1941

ENTREPRENEURSHIP/ENTREPRENEURIAL STUDIES

Charles B. Atchison, Jr. Endowment • 1206
Charles Foy Jr. Scholarship Fund • 419
Financial Women International Scholarship • 1328
Jane M. Klausman Women in Business Scholarship Fund • 529
LULAC GE Scholarship • 2332
Maine State Chamber of Commerce Scholarship • 1539
Robert Half International • 2402

Washington State Auto Dealers Association Awards • 1923
William R. Goldfarb Memorial Scholarship • 698
William Wrigley Jr. Scholarship/Internship • 2445

EUROPEAN STUDIES/CIVILIZATION

Clan MacBean Foundation Grant Program • 219
DAAD/AICGS Research Fellowship Program • 228
Fellowships for Regular Program • 239
Graduate and Postgraduate Study and Research in Poland • 248
Lilly Lorénzen Scholarship • 1515
Malmberg Scholarship and Fellowship • 272
Metchie J.E. Budka Award • 273
Short-Term Travel Grants (STG) • 305
Year Abroad Program • 331

FAMILY AND CONSUMER SCIENCES / HUMAN SCIENCES (ALL AREAS)

ADAF Student Scholarship • 719
Association of Food and Drug Officials Scholarship Award • 784
BI-LO Minority Scholarship Program • 1159
Golden Gate Restaurant Association Scholarship • 489
HOPE General Scholarship • 1408
IEHA Scholarship • 511
IFEC Scholarships Award • 512
IFSEA Worthy Goal Scholarship • 513
National Foster Parent Association Vocational/Job Training Scholarship • 2373

FAMILY PRACTICE NURSE/NURSE PRACTITIONER

AfterCollege/AACN Nursing Scholarship Fund • 725
Alice / Jeanne Wagner Endowment • 735
AMT Student Scholarship • 751
Annual NBNA Scholarships • 754
Bachelor's Scholarships • 791
Carole J. Streeter, KB9JBR Scholarship • 411
Caroline E. Holt Nursing Scholarship • 806
Congressional Black Caucus Spouses Cheerios Brand Health Initiative Scholarship • 817
Cora Aguda Manayan Fund • 1248
Dr. Hans and Clara Zimmerman Foundation Health Scholarships • 1289
Dr. James M. Rosin Scholarship • 2258
Edith M. Allen Scholarship • 2031
Elizabeth and Sherman Asche Memorial Scholarship • 2268
Eloise Collins Endowment • 1313
Filipino Nurses' Organization of Hawaii Scholarship • 1327
Florence Young Memorial Scholarship • 2277
Gilbert Matching Student Grant • 1358
Health Professional Scholarship • 1388
Health Resources and Services Administration-Bureau of Health Professions Scholarships for Disadvantaged Students • 884
Linda Moore Scholarship • 933
Lydia's Professional Uniform/AACN Excellence in Academics Nursing Scholarship • 940
NC Student Loan Program for Health, Science and Mathematics • 1615
Nurse Education Scholarship Loan Program • 1658

MARINE BIOLOGY AND BIOLOGICAL OCEANOGRAPHY

Elizabeth and Sherman Asche Memorial Scholarship • 2268

Get Ready for Math and Science Conditional Scholarship Program • 1357

GlaxoSmithKline Company Science Achievement Award • 2291

Medtronic Foundation Scholarship • 2349

National Science & Mathematics Access to Retain Talent Grant • 977

RBC Dain Rauscher Colorado Scholarships • 1732

Rockefeller State Wildlife Scholarship • 1793

SEA Scholarship Contest • 1034

Siemens Teacher Education Scholarship Program • 2409

UNCF/Merck Graduate Science Research Dissertation Fellowships • 2434

William James and Dorothy Bading Lanquist Fund • 1932

William R. Goldfarb Memorial Scholarship • 698

Women in Science and Technology Scholarship • 1941

Yasmc Foundation Scholarship • 704

MARKETING/MARKETING MANAGEMENT, GENERAL

AGCO Corporation FFA Scholarship • 1958

American Express Scholarship Competition • 374

Annual Logistics Scholarship Competition • 382

Charles B. Atchison, Jr. Endowment • 1206

Charles Foy Jr. Scholarship Fund • 419

Donald W. Fogarty International Student Paper Competition • 445

Ecolab Scholarship Competition • 449

Electronic Document Systems Foundation Scholarship Awards • 456

Financial Women International Scholarship • 1328

Harry A. Applegate Scholarship • 494

HOPE General Scholarship • 1408

HORIZONS Foundation Scholarship • 506

HSMAI Foundation Scholarship • 507

IFEC Scholarships Award • 512

James L. Shriver Scholarship • 1444

Jane M. Klausman Women in Business Scholarship Fund • 529

Lodging Management Program (LMP) • 559

LULAC GE Scholarship • 2332

Maine State Chamber of Commerce Scholarship • 1539

Malcolm Baldrige Scholarship • 1545

Steven Hymans Extended Stay Scholarship • 667

Tribal Business Management Program • 2428

William R. Goldfarb Memorial Scholarship • 698

William Wrigley Jr. Scholarship/Internship • 2445

MATERIALS ENGINEERING

AGCO Corporation FFA Scholarship • 1958

AIST Benjamin F. Fairless Scholarship (AIME) • 731

AIST Ronald E. Lincoln Memorial Scholarship • 732

AIST William E. Schwabe Memorial Scholarship • 733

AIST Willy Korf Memorial Fund • 734

Ferrous Metallurgy Education Today (FeMET) • 852

Gary Wagner, K3OMI Scholarship • 479

High Technology Scholar/Intern Tuition Waiver • 1395

Hoku Scholarship Fund • 1402

LTK Engineering Services Scholarship • 938

LULAC GE Scholarship • 2332

Medtronic Foundation Scholarship • 2349

Michael Kidger Memorial Scholarship • 959

National Science & Mathematics Access to Retain Talent Grant • 977

Parsons Brinckerhoff – Engineering Scholarship • 999

Perry F. Hadlock Memorial Scholarship • 633

RBC Dain Rauscher Colorado Scholarships • 1732

Sallie Mae Bank Scholarships • 1802

Samuel H. Kress Foundation Paired Fellowship for Research in Conservation and the History of Art • 651

SEA Scholarship Contest • 1034

STEEL Engineering Education Link Initiative • 1048

The Maureen L. & Howard N. Blitman, P.E., Scholarship • 2423

William R. Goldfarb Memorial Scholarship • 698

William R. Kimel, P.E., Engineering Scholarship • 1085

William Wrigley Jr. Scholarship/Internship • 2445

Women in Science and Technology Scholarship • 1941

Yasme Foundation Scholarship • 704

MATHEMATICS AND STATISTICS (ALL AREAS)

A.T. Anderson Memorial Scholarship • 2191

Actuarial Scholarships for Minority Students • 2194

AFCEA General Emmett Paige Scholarships • 353

AFCEA General John A. Wickham Scholarships • 723

AFCEA Ralph W. Shrader Scholarships • 724

AFCEA ROTC Scholarships • 354

AFCEA Sgt Jeannette L. Winters, USMC Memorial Scholarship • 355

Alice T. Schafer Prize • 736

AMS Undergraduate Scholarships • 747

Astronaut Scholarship • 786

AWM Biographies Contest • 790

Barry M. Goldwater Scholarship and Excellence in Education Program • 793

Burlington Northern Santa Fe (BNSF) Foundation Scholarship • 2226

Collegiate Inventors Competition • 814

D.W. Simpson Actuarial Science Scholarship • 820

Davidson Fellows Award • 47

Francis J. Flynn Memorial Scholarship • 2050

Frank and Brennie Morgan Prize for Outstanding Research in Mathematics by an Undergraduate Student • 856

Gertrude Cox Scholarship For Women In Statistics • 870

Get Ready for Math and Science Conditional Scholarship Program • 1357

Hertz Foundation's Graduate Fellowship Award • 889

Hoku Scholarship Fund • 1402

HORIZONS Foundation Scholarship • 506

Intel Science Talent Search • 899

International Science and Engineering Fair • 900

John Culver Wooddy Scholarships • 912

MESBEC Program • 2351

Minnesota Academic Excellence Scholarship • 1588

National Science & Mathematics Access to Retain Talent Grant • 977

NC Student Loan Program for Health, Science and Mathematics • 1615

NDSEG Fellowship Program • 985

Payzer Scholarship • 1003

Shuichi, Katsu and Itsuyo Suga Scholarship • 1827

Siemens Teacher Education Scholarship Program • 2409

Siemens Westinghouse Competition in Math, Science and Technology • 1039

Steven J. Muir Scholarship • 2150

Stokes Educational Scholarship Program • 153

Thomas H. Dunning, Sr., Memorial Scholarship • 2159

Willems Scholarship • 2443

Willis HRH Scholarship • 1936

Women in Science and Technology Scholarship • 1941

MECHANIC AND REPAIR TECHNOLOGIES / TECHNICIANS (ALL AREAS)

California - Hawaii Elks Association Vocational Grants • 408

John and Anne Clifton Scholarship • 1458

Louis B. Russell, Jr. Memorial Scholarship • 1524

Maine Metal Products Association Scholarship • 1537

Medallion Fund • 1567

National Science & Mathematics Access to Retain Talent Grant • 977

Perry F. Hadlock Memorial Scholarship • 633

Technical Award • 1862

Wachovia Technical Scholarship • 1915

Washington Award for Vocational Excellence • 1918

MECHANICAL ENGINEERING

AGCO Corporation FFA Scholarship • 1958

AGDATA Inc. FFA Scholarship • 1959

Agrium U.S. Inc. FFA Scholarship • 1960

Air Force ROTC Express Scholarships • 361

AIST Ronald E. Lincoln Memorial Scholarship • 732

AIST William E. Schwabe Memorial Scholarship • 733

CDM Scholarship/Internship • 2235

Gary Wagner, K3OMI Scholarship • 479

High Technology Scholar/Intern Tuition Waiver • 1395

Hoku Scholarship Fund • 1402

LTK Engineering Services Scholarship • 938

LULAC GE Scholarship • 2332

Medtronic Foundation Scholarship • 2349

Milton F. Lunch Research Fellowship • 964

National Science & Mathematics Access to Retain Talent Grant • 977

NNM American Society of Mechanical Engineers Scholarship • 1647

The Ultimate Scholarship Book 2010
Field of Study Index

Eloise Collins Endowment • 1313
Filipino Nurses' Organization of Hawaii Scholarship • 1327
Florence Young Memorial Scholarship • 2277
Gilbert Matching Student Grant • 1358
Health Professional Scholarship • 1388
Health Resources and Services Administration-Bureau of Health Professions Scholarships for Disadvantaged Students • 884
Linda Moore Scholarship • 933
Lydia's Professional Uniform/AACN Excellence in Academics Nursing Scholarship • 940
NC Student Loan Program for Health, Science and Mathematics • 1615
Nurse Education Scholarship Loan Program • 1658
Nurse Educator Scholarship Program (NESP) • 1659
Nurse Support Program II - Graduate Nursing Faculty Scholarship • 1660
Nursing Education Scholarship Program • 1661
Nursing Scholarship • 996
Paulina L. Sorg Scholarship • 1706
Predoctoral Research Training Fellowship • 1012
Robanna Fund • 1742
Sallie Mae Bank Scholarships • 1802
Tuition Reduction for Non-Resident Nursing Students • 1887
William R. Goldfarb Memorial Scholarship • 698
Women in Science and Technology Scholarship • 1941
Workforce Shortage Student Assistance Grant Program • 1943

PHYSICS, GENERAL
ACIL Scholarship • 717
APS Minority Scholarship • 765
Elizabeth and Sherman Asche Memorial Scholarship • 2268
Get Ready for Math and Science Conditional Scholarship Program • 1357
GlaxoSmithKline Company Science Achievement Award • 2291
Hoku Scholarship Fund • 1402
Medtronic Foundation Scholarship • 2349
National Science & Mathematics Access to Retain Talent Grant • 977
RBC Dain Rauscher Colorado Scholarships • 1732
SEA Scholarship Contest • 1034
Shuichi, Katsu and Itsuyo Suga Scholarship • 1827
Siemens Teacher Education Scholarship Program • 2409
UNCF/Merck Graduate Science Research Dissertation Fellowships • 2434
William James and Dorothy Bading Lanquist Fund • 1932
William R. Goldfarb Memorial Scholarship • 698
Women in Science and Technology Scholarship • 1941
Yasme Foundation Scholarship • 704

PHYSIOLOGY, PATHOLOGY AND RELATED SCIENCES
Get Ready for Math and Science Conditional Scholarship Program • 1357
Medtronic Foundation Scholarship • 2349
National Science & Mathematics Access to Retain Talent Grant • 977

SEA Scholarship Contest • 1034
Siemens Teacher Education Scholarship Program • 2409
UNCF/Merck Graduate Science Research Dissertation Fellowships • 2434
Women in Science and Technology Scholarship • 1941

PLANETARY ASTRONOMY AND SCIENCE
AGDATA Inc. FFA Scholarship • 1959
Elizabeth and Sherman Asche Memorial Scholarship • 2268
Get Ready for Math and Science Conditional Scholarship Program • 1357
GlaxoSmithKline Company Science Achievement Award • 2291
Medtronic Foundation Scholarship • 2349
National Science & Mathematics Access to Retain Talent Grant • 977
RBC Dain Rauscher Colorado Scholarships • 1732
SEA Scholarship Contest • 1034
Siemens Teacher Education Scholarship Program • 2409
William James and Dorothy Bading Lanquist Fund • 1932
William R. Goldfarb Memorial Scholarship • 698
Women in Science and Technology Scholarship • 1941
Yasme Foundation Scholarship • 704

POLISH STUDIES
Clan MacBean Foundation Grant Program • 219
DAAD/AICGS Research Fellowship Program • 228
Fellowships for Regular Program • 239
Graduate and Postgraduate Study and Research in Poland • 248
Lilly Lorénzen Scholarship • 1515
Malmberg Scholarship and Fellowship • 272
Metchie J.E. Budka Award • 273
Short-Term Travel Grants (STG) • 305
Year Abroad Program • 331

POLITICAL SCIENCE AND GOVERNMENT, GENERAL
American History Scholarship, Enid Hall Griswold Memorial Scholarship, J.E. Caldwell Centennial Scholarship • 377
C-SPAN Scholarship Program • 2228
Henry A. Zuberano Scholarship • 1391

POLYMER/PLASTICS ENGINEERING
AGCO Corporation FFA Scholarship • 1958
Gary Wagner, K3OMI Scholarship • 479
High Technology Scholar/Intern Tuition Waiver • 1395
Hoku Scholarship Fund • 1402
LTK Engineering Services Scholarship • 938
LULAC GE Scholarship • 2332
Medtronic Foundation Scholarship • 2349
National Science & Mathematics Access to Retain Talent Grant • 977
Parsons Brinckerhoff – Engineering Scholarship • 999
Perry F. Hadlock Memorial Scholarship • 633
RBC Dain Rauscher Colorado Scholarships • 1732
Sallie Mae Bank Scholarships • 1802
SEA Scholarship Contest • 1034

The Maureen L. & Howard N. Blitman, P.E., Scholarship • 2423
William R. Goldfarb Memorial Scholarship • 698
William R. Kimel, P.E., Engineering Scholarship • 1085
William Wrigley Jr. Scholarship/Internship • 2445
Women in Science and Technology Scholarship • 1941
Yasme Foundation Scholarship • 704

PORTUGUESE LANGUAGE AND LITERATURE
Fellowships for Regular Program • 239
JTG Scholarship in Scientific and Technical Translation or Interpretation • 262
National Science & Mathematics Access to Retain Talent Grant • 977
Tadeusz Sendzimir Fund • 1860

PRECISION PRODUCTION (ALL AREAS)
Arc Welding Awards • 386
Corporate Leadership Scholarships • 225
Electronic Document Systems Foundation Scholarship Awards • 456
FFTA Scholarship Competition • 240
GEF Resource Center Scholarships • 243
Gravure Catalog and Insert Council Scholarship • 249
Hallmark Graphic Arts Scholarship • 250
James L. Shriver Scholarship • 1444
TLMI Four Year Colleges/Full-Time Students Scholarship • 681
Werner B. Thiele Memorial Scholarship • 325

PSYCHOLOGY (ALL AREAS)
APF/COGDOP Graduate Research Scholarships • 383
APF/TOPSS Scholars Competition • 384
Behavioral Sciences Student Fellowship • 795
Eileen J. Garrett Scholarship • 455
Henry Hecaen and Manfred Meier Neuropsychology Scholarships • 886
HOPE General Scholarship • 1408
Predoctoral Research Training Fellowship • 1012

PUBLIC ADMINISTRATION AND SOCIAL SERVICE PROFESSIONS (ALL AREAS)
AGA Scholarships • 357
Behavioral Sciences Student Fellowship • 795
Charles G. Koch Summer Fellow Program • 420
Edmund S. Muskie Graduate Fellowship Program • 452
Fellowship on Women and Public Policy • 1326
Freehold Soil Conservation District Scholarship • 1342
Harry S. Truman Undergraduate Student Grant • 496
Henry A. Zuberano Scholarship • 1391
HOPE General Scholarship • 1408
Julianne Malveaux Scholarship • 2325
Transatlantic Community Foundation Fellowship • 166
Transatlantic Fellows Program • 685
William Randolph Hearst Endowed Scholarship for Minority Students • 2444
Workforce Shortage Student Assistance Grant Program • 1943
Young Communicators Fellowships • 706

657

Fellowship of United Methodists in Music and Worship Arts Scholarship • 2041

FFTA Scholarship Competition • 240

Film and Fiction Scholarships • 241

GEF Resource Center Scholarships • 243

Glenn Miller Scholarship Competition • 247

Gravure Catalog and Insert Council Scholarship • 249

Hagley-Winterthur Fellowships in Arts and Industries • 492

Hallmark Graphic Arts Scholarship • 250

Henry Luce Foundation/ACLS Dissertation Fellowships in American Art • 253

HOPE General Scholarship • 1408

Huntington Fellowships • 508

IDSA Undergraduate Scholarships • 255

IFEC Scholarships Award • 512

Japanese American Citizens League Creative and Performing Arts Awards • 2313

Joel Polsky Academic Achievement Award • 260

Mabelle Wilhelmina Boldt Scholarship • 271

Mildred and Albert Panowski Playwriting Award • 275

Minnesota Academic Excellence Scholarship • 1588

MMT New Play Competition • 276

Morton Gould Young Composer Award • 277

Music Committee Scholarship • 1610

NFMC Wendell Irish Viola Award • 289

Nido Qubein Scholarship • 290

Omaha Symphony Guild International New Music Competition • 291

Optimist International Oratorical Contest • 625

Playwright Discovery Award • 296

Poster Contest for High School Students • 297

Princess Grace Awards • 298

Print and Graphics Scholarship • 299

Stanfield and D'Orlando Art Scholarship • 2148

Stillman-Kelley Awards • 311

Student Design Competition • 313

Urban Outreach Grants • 323

Visual and Performing Arts Achievement Awards • 2176

Werner B. Thiele Memorial Scholarship • 325

Young Communicators Fellowships • 706

Young Jazz Composer Award • 333

Youth Free Expression Network Film Contest • 334

ZOOLOGY/ANIMAL BIOLOGY

AGDATA Inc. FFA Scholarship • 1959

Get Ready for Math and Science Conditional Scholarship Program • 1357

Medtronic Foundation Scholarship • 2349

National Science & Mathematics Access to Retain Talent Grant • 977

SEA Scholarship Contest • 1034

Siemens Teacher Education Scholarship Program • 2409

Theodore Gordon Flyfishers, Inc. Founders Fund Scholarship • 1874

UNCF/Merck Graduate Science Research Dissertation Fellowships • 2434

Women in Science and Technology Scholarship • 1941

CAREER INDEX

This index organizes the scholarships by common career fields. If you cannot find your specific career listed simply look at the scholarships under the closest matching career area.

In addition to this index be sure to use the Major Index since many scholarships are targeted to fields of study but do not have specific career requirements.

ACADEMIA

ACLS Digital Innovation Fellowships • 347

ACLS Fellowships • 348

ACOR-CAORC Fellowships • 349

BSA Research Fellowship • 406

Charles A. Ryskamp Research Fellowships • 416

Contemplative Practice Fellowship Program • 434

Frederick Burkhardt Residential Fellowships for Recently Tenured Scholars • 473

Harry S. Truman Research Grant • 495

Harry S. Truman Undergraduate Student Grant • 496

Henry Belin du Pont Dissertation Fellowship • 499

Herbert Hoover Presidential Library Association Travel Grant Program • 501

Huntington Fellowships • 508

Huntington-British Academy Fellowships for Study in Great Britain • 509

Jeanne S. Chall Research Fellowship • 259

Robert E. Thunen Memorial Scholarships • 1024

Transatlantic Fellows Program • 685

W.M. Keck Foundation Fellowships for Young Scholars • 694

ACCOUNTING/FINANCE

Accountemps/American Institute Of Certified Public Accountants Student Scholarship • 344

AGA Scholarships • 357

Best Buy Scholarship Program • 2222

BI-LO Minority Scholarship Program • 1159

Carl W. Christiansen Scholarship • 1194

Charles Earp Memorial Scholarship • 418

Cheryl A. Ruggiero Scholarship • 1214

Entrepreneurial Scholarship from the McKelvey Foundation • 457

Harry J. Donnelly Memorial Scholarship • 2065

Hispanic College Fund Scholarships • 2303

HSF/General Motors Scholarship • 2308

IMA Memorial Education Fund Scholarship • 515

James L. Shriver Scholarship • 1444

National Association of Black Accountants Scholarship Program • 2371

NCCPAP Scholarship • 612

NSA Scholarship Foundation • 623

Parsons Brinckerhoff –Golden Apple Scholarship • 628

Ritchie-Jennings Memorial Scholarship • 648

Stuart Cameron and Margaret McLeod Memorial Scholarship • 669

Tribal Business Management Program • 2428

United Negro College Fund Cargill Scholarship-Internship Program • 2435

W. Allan Herzog Scholarship • 2178

ADVERTISING/PR

Best Buy Scholarship Program • 2222

BI-LO Minority Scholarship Program • 1159

Entrepreneurial Scholarship from the McKelvey Foundation • 457

J.D. Edsal Advertising Scholarship/Women's Advertising Club Scholarship • 1440

Parsons Brinckerhoff –Golden Apple Scholarship • 628

PRSA-Hawaii/Roy Leffingwell Public Relations Scholarship • 1721

Public Relations Scholarship • 642

AGRICULTURE/FARMING

ASEV Scholarships • 772

ASF Olin Fellowships • 773

Association of Food and Drug Officials Scholarship Award • 784

Carville M. Akehurst Memorial Scholarship • 807

Entrepreneurial Scholarship from the McKelvey Foundation • 457

FIRST Scholarship • 853

GCSAA Scholars Program • 865

GCSAA Student Essay Contest • 866

Harness Tracks of America Scholarship Fund • 881

Masonic-Range Science Scholarship • 949

National FFA College and Vocational/Technical School Scholarship Program • 972

Scotts Company Scholars Program • 1033

United Negro College Fund Cargill Scholarship-Internship Program • 2435

W. Malcolm Harding Scholarship, Philip F. French Scholarship and Owen Hallberg Scholarship • 1080

ARCHEOLOGISTS

Florence C. and Robert H. Lister Fellowship • 467

Harrell Family Fellowship • 493

Jennifer C. Groot Fellowship • 531

Pierre and Patricia Bikai Fellowship • 636

ARCHITECTURE/DESIGN

ACI Student Fellowship Program • 715

AIA/AAF Minority/Disadvantaged Scholarship • 728

American Architectural Foundation and Sir John Soane's Museum Foundation Traveling Fellowship • 742

APA Planning Fellowships • 2213

AWA Scholarships • 1148

Hagley-Winterthur Fellowships in Arts and Industries • 492

James L. Shriver Scholarship • 1444

National Garden Clubs Scholarship • 973

Robert E. Thunen Memorial Scholarships • 1024

RTKL Traveling Fellowship • 1027

Student Design Competition • 1050

William J. Locklin Scholarship • 1083

ARTIST

American Architectural Foundation and Sir John Soane's Museum Foundation Traveling Fellowship • 742

Animoids 3D Animation Contest • 201
Congressional Black Caucus Spouses Visual Arts Scholarship • 223
Hagley-Winterthur Fellowships in Arts and Industries • 492
IDSA Undergraduate Scholarships • 255
Poster Contest for High School Students • 297
Stacey Scholarship Fund • 309
Stanfield and D'Orlando Art Scholarship • 2148
Visual and Performing Arts Achievement Awards • 2176

ASTRONOMERS
Association for Women in Science College Scholarship • 782
Association for Women in Science Predoctoral Awards • 783
GBT Student Support Program • 864
Graduate Summer Student Research Assistantship • 877
International Science and Engineering Fair • 900
Jack Horkheimer Award • 905
MESBEC Program • 2351
National Young Astronomer Award • 981
Undergraduate Summer Student Research Assistantship • 1075

ATHLETES AND SPORTS
Challenge Scholarship • 29
Entrepreneurial Scholarship from the McKelvey Foundation • 457
Ethnic Minority and Women's Enhancement Scholarship • 64
GNC Nutritional Research Grant • 76
Graduate Research Grant - Master and Doctoral • 78
High School Scholarship • 85
Minority Scholarship • 2356
NATA Scholarship • 114
Undergraduate Research Grant • 170
Women's Scholarship • 1086

AUTOMOTIVE INDUSTRY
Automotive Hall of Fame Scholarships • 789
James L. Shriver Scholarship • 1444
Specialty Equipment Market Association (SEMA) Memorial Scholarship • 664

AVIATION/AEROSPACE/SPACE
AIAA Foundation Undergraduate Scholarship Program • 729
Air Traffic Control Association Scholarship Program • 730
Bud Glover Memorial Scholarship • 801
Dan L. Meisinger Sr. Memorial Learn to Fly Scholarship • 823
David Arver Memorial Scholarship • 826
Donald Burnside Memorial Scholarship • 833
Dutch and Ginger Arver Scholarship • 841
Garmin Scholarship • 862
James L. Shriver Scholarship • 1444
Johnny Davis Memorial Scholarship • 917
Lee Tarbox Memorial Scholarship • 929
Lowell Gaylor Memorial Scholarship • 937
McAllister Memorial Scholarship • 950
Mid-Continent Instrument Scholarship • 961
National Aviation Explorer Scholarships • 971
Pioneers of Flight • 1010

BANKING/FINANCIAL INDUSTRY
BI-LO Minority Scholarship Program • 1159
Entrepreneurial Scholarship from the McKelvey Foundation • 457
Pat Roberts Intelligence Scholars Program for Global Network Analysts • 629
Pat Roberts Intelligence Scholars Program for Intelligence Analysts • 630
Tribal Business Management Program • 2428

BIOLOGISTS
AOS Master's Scholarship Program • 760
ARM Undergraduate Student Fellowships • 767
ASAE Foundation Scholarship • 768
ASAE Student Engineer of the Year Scholarship • 769
ASF Olin Fellowships • 773
Association for Women in Science College Scholarship • 782
Association for Women in Science Predoctoral Awards • 783
Astronaut Scholarship • 786
Barry M. Goldwater Scholarship and Excellence in Education Program • 793
Carrol C. Hall Memorial Scholarship • 1996
David S. Bruce Awards for Excellence in Undergraduate Research • 827
Davidson Fellows Award • 47
Don King Student Fellowship • 832
Gaige Fund Award • 860
GEM Fellowship Program • 2285
George A. Hall / Harold F. Mayfield Award • 868
Hertz Foundation's Graduate Fellowship Award • 889
HSA Research Grants • 894
Intel Science Talent Search • 899
International Science and Engineering Fair • 900
John Henry Comstock Graduate Student Awards • 913
Louis Agassiz Fuertes Award • 936
MAES Scholarship Program • 2337
MESBEC Program • 2351
National Garden Clubs Scholarship • 973
National Wildlife Federation Ecology Fellowship • 980
NDSEG Fellowship Program • 985
NIH Undergraduate Scholarship Program • 992
NIH Undergraduate Scholarship Program for Students from Disadvantaged Backgrounds • 993
Normand R. Dubois Memorial Scholarship • 995
Paul A. Stewart Awards • 1000
Raney Fund Award • 1017
Science and Technology Scholarship • 1812
Stan Beck Fellowship • 1047
Stoye and Storer Awards • 1049
Student Research Scholarships • 1053
Thomas H. Dunning, Sr., Memorial Scholarship • 2159
Undergraduate Scholarship • 1071
Youth Activity Grant • 1089
Youth Incentive Award • 1090

BIOMEDICAL SCIENCES/BIOTECHNOLOGY
Carrol C. Hall Memorial Scholarship • 1996
HDSA Research Fellowships • 882
MESBEC Program • 2351

BUSINESS AND MANAGEMENT
Accountemps/American Institute Of Certified Public Accountants Student Scholarship • 344
Allstudentloan.org College Scholarship Program for Business Students • 371
American Legion Auxiliary, Department of California $1,000 Scholarships • 1128
American Legion Auxiliary, Department of California $2,000 Scholarships • 1129
Annual Logistics Scholarship Competition • 382
Best Buy Scholarship Program • 2222
Betsy Plank/PRSSA Scholarship • 397
BI-LO Minority Scholarship Program • 1159
Burlington Northern Santa Fe (BNSF) Foundation Scholarship • 2226
Business Achievement Awards • 1995
Coca-Cola USA Scholarship • 429
Consortium Fellowship • 2248
Donald W. Fogarty International Student Paper Competition • 445
Earl Graves Scholarship • 2264
Entrepreneurial Scholarship from the McKelvey Foundation • 457
Esther R. Sawyer Scholarship Award • 460
Executive Women International Scholarship Program • 462
Ford Motor Company Business and Leadership Scholarship • 2043
Fund for American Studies Internships • 475
Gary Yoshimura Scholarship • 480
Henry B. Gonzalez Award • 498
Henry Belin du Pont Dissertation Fellowship • 499
Hispanic College Fund Scholarships • 2303
HORIZONS Foundation Scholarship • 506
HSF/General Motors Scholarship • 2308
HSMAI Foundation Scholarship • 507
Humane Studies Fellowships • 88
James J. Hill Research Grants • 528
James L. Shriver Scholarship • 1444
Joe Perdue Scholarship • 535
Lawrence G. Foster Award for Excellence in Public Relations • 554
MESBEC Program • 2351
Minorities and Women Educational Scholarship • 581
Multicultural Affairs Scholarship Program • 2363
National Association of Black Accountants Scholarship Program • 2371
National Business School High School Scholarship • 594
National Defense Transportation Association, St. Louis Area Chapter Scholarship • 596
National Scholarship • 2375
National Society of Hispanic MBAs Scholarship • 601
NSA Scholarship Foundation • 623
Pat Roberts Intelligence Scholars Program for Global Network Analysts • 629
Pat Roberts Intelligence Scholars Program for Intelligence Analysts • 630
Professor Sidney Gross Memorial Award • 640
Ritchie-Jennings Memorial Scholarship • 648
SSPI Scholarship Program • 666
Summer Graduate Research Fellowships • 158
Transatlantic Fellows Program • 685

Chesapeake Urology Associates Scholarship • 1215

Cindy Shemansky Travel Scholarship • 2010

Clinical Research Pre-Doctoral Fellowship • 812

Collins Scholarship • 815

Continuing Education Award • 818

Dade-Behring/Coordinating Council on the Clinical Laboratory Workforce Scholarship • 821

David S. Bruce Awards for Excellence in Undergraduate Research • 827

Dorothy Budnek Memorial Scholarship • 835

Earl and Patricia Armstrong Scholarship • 2263

Eight and Forty Lung and Respiratory Nursing Scholarship Fund • 844

Ellen R. Clayton Scholarship for Nursing Students • 1311

ENA Foundation Undergraduate Scholarship • 845

Explorations Summer Research Fellowships • 2272

FA Davis Student Award • 849

Fellowship Award • 850

Forum for Concerns of Minorities Scholarship • 2278

Foundation for Surgical Technology Advanced Education/Medical Mission Scholarship • 854

Foundation for Surgical Technology Student Scholarship • 855

Gillette/National Urban League Scholarship and Intern Program for Minority Students • 2290

Grant Programs for Medical Studies • 2060

Grotto Scholarships • 878

HDSA Research Fellowships • 882

Health Careers Scholarship • 883

Health Professional Loan Repayment • 1387

Health Professions Education Scholarship Program • 1389

Health Sciences Student Fellowship • 885

Henry Hecaen and Manfred Meier Neuropsychology Scholarships • 886

HHMI-NIH Research Scholars (Cloister Program) • 890

Hobble (LPN) Nursing Scholarship • 1401

International Science and Engineering Fair • 900

James L. Shriver Scholarship • 1444

James P. Dearing Scholarship • 906

Jerry W. Richmond Memorial Scholarship • 908

Karen O'Neil Endowed Advanced Nursing Practice Scholarship • 923

Leadership Development Award • 928

Loan Assistance Repayment Program Primary Care Services • 1518

Mary Gibbon Scholarship • 947

Mary Opal Wolanin Scholarship • 948

McNeil Rural Health Scholarship • 952

Medical Student Summer Research Training in Aging Program • 953

Medtronic Physio-Control Advanced Nursing Practice Scholarship • 954

Merit Scholarships and Educational Loans • 957

Michael Dunaway Scholarship • 958

NAHN Scholarship • 2366

National Nursing Scholarship - College • 975

National Nursing Scholarship - High School • 976

National Student Nurses' Association Scholarship • 979

Need-Based Scholarship Program • 986

NEHA/AAS Scholarship Awards • 987

NIH Undergraduate Scholarship Program • 992

NIH Undergraduate Scholarship Program for Students from Disadvantaged Backgrounds • 993

NNF Scholarship Program • 994

Past Presidents' Parley Nursing Scholarships • 1702

Perfusion Student Scholarship • 1005

Physician Assistant Foundation Scholarship • 1008

Pioneer in Perfusion Scholarship • 1009

Pre-Nursing Scholarship Program • 1719

Premedical Summer Institute Program/Internship • 2394

Presidential Scholarship • 1013

Regents Health Care Opportunity Scholarships in Medicine and Dentistry • 1734

Research Training Fellowships for Medical Students (Medical Fellows Program) • 1021

Sandra R. Spaulding Memorial Scholarship • 1031

Shirley C. Titus Scholarship Fund • 1824

State Nursing Scholarship • 1845

Surgical Technology Scholarships • 1056

Thompson Delmar Learning Student Scholarship • 1064

Tylenol Scholarship • 1069

Undergraduate Student Summer Research Fellowships • 1074

Wilhelm-Frankowski Scholarship • 1081

Workforce Incentive Program • 1942

Youth for Adolescent Pregnancy Prevention-Leadership Recognition Program • 1948

ECONOMISTS

AGA Scholarships • 357

Entrepreneurial Scholarship from the McKelvey Foundation • 457

Fund for American Studies Internships • 475

Julianne Malveaux Scholarship • 2325

Tribal Business Management Program • 2428

EDUCATION/TEACHING

A. Harry Passow Classroom Teacher Scholarship • 336

Achievement Award • 345

ACLS Digital Innovation Fellowships • 347

ACLS Fellowships • 348

American Legion Auxiliary, Department of California $1,000 Scholarships • 1128

Antonio Cirino Memorial Art Education Fellowship • 1134

Association of Food and Drug Officials Scholarship Award • 784

Brown Foundation Scholarships • 2223

Burlington Northern Santa Fe (BNSF) Foundation Scholarship • 2226

Career Advancement Program Tuition Waiver • 1191

Carrol C. Hall Memorial Scholarship • 1996

Charles A. Ryskamp Research Fellowships • 416

Charles McDaniel Teacher Scholarship • 1209

Child Care Provider Scholarship • 1218

Coca-Cola USA Scholarship • 429

Collaborative Teachers Tuition Waiver • 1229

Community Scholarship Fund • 1243

Contemplative Practice Fellowship Program • 434

Critical Needs Teacher Program • 1252

Critical Teacher Shortage Loan Forgiveness Program • 1253

Critical Teacher Shortage Tuition Reimbursement Program • 1254

Dottie Martin Teachers Scholarship • 1281

Education Achievement Awards • 2032

Educator of Tomorrow Award • 2466

Francis J. Flynn Memorial Scholarship • 2050

Frederick Burkhardt Residential Fellowships for Recently Tenured Scholars • 473

Future Teacher of America Scholarship--High School • 476

Future Teacher Scholarship • 477

Future Teachers Conditional Scholarship • 1346

Future Teachers Scholarship • 1347

Golden Apple Scholars of Illinois (Illinois Scholars Program) • 1360

Incentive Program for Aspiring Teachers • 1427

International Order of Alhambra Scholarship • 521

James L. Shriver Scholarship • 1444

Jewel Gardiner Memorial Scholarship • 1452

John Blanchard Memorial Scholarship • 1459

Leadership for Diversity Scholarship • 1493

Learning and Leadership Grants • 555

Library Media Teacher Scholarship • 1512

Litherland Scholarship • 558

Maley Teacher Scholarship • 565

Martin Luther King, Jr. Memorial Scholarship • 2104

MESBEC Program • 2351

NACA East Coast Graduate Student Scholarship • 591

Native American Leadership Education Program • 2378

Paraprofessional-to-LMT Scholarship • 1690

Robert E. Thunen Memorial Scholarships • 1024

Robert G. Porter Scholars Program for Members • 2134

Sara Conlon Memorial Scholarship • 2501

Shields-Gillespie Scholarship • 659

Siemens Teacher Education Scholarship Program • 2409

SPS Future Teacher Scholarship • 665

Student Achievement Grants • 670

Teacher of the Year Award • 678

Tobin Sorenson Physical Education Scholarship • 682

Tomorrow's Teachers Scholarship Program • 1876

Truman Scholar • 167

TSA-Sponsored ITEA Scholarship • 688

Undergraduate Scholarship • 690

William Winter Teacher Scholarship • 1935

Wisconsin Region Student Leadership Scholarship • 1940

Women in Geographic Education Scholarship • 700

Workforce Incentive Program • 1942

ENGINEERING

A.O. Putnam Memorial Scholarship • 709

A.T. Anderson Memorial Scholarship • 2191

Abel Wolman Fellowship • 712

Academic Achievement Award • 713

ACI Student Fellowship Program • 715

INTERESTS INDEX

This index lists awards that are geared toward students who are active in specific pasttimes and hobbies.

SPECIAL CIRCUMSTANCE

This index lists a variety of special circumstances that are used as eligibility limits for these scholarships.

Alliance Data Scholarship • 2201
Alton and Dorothy Higgins MD Scholarship • 2203
American Hotel Management Foundation Scholarship • 2209
Amtrak Travel Scholarship • 2212
Berbeco Senior Research Fellowship • 2219
Bessie Irene Smith Trust Scholarship • 2221
Best Buy Scholarship Program • 2222
Burton G. Bettingen Foundation Scholarship • 2227
C-SPAN Scholarship Program • 2228
Carolyn Bailey Thomas Scholarship • 2232
CDM Scholarship/Internship • 2235
Chrysler Corporation Scholarship • 2241
Citigroup Fellows Program • 2242
Colgate-Palmolive Company/UNCF Scholarship • 2244
Coy G. Eklund Scholarship • 2251
Doris and John Carpenter Scholarship • 2256
Dorothy N. McNeal Scholarship • 2257
Dr. Joe Ratliff Challenge • 2259
Dr. Scholl Foundation Scholarship • 2261
Edward and Hazel Stephenson Scholarship • 2265
Edward D. Grigg Scholarship • 2266
Edward N. Ney Scholarship • 2267
Ella Fitzgerald Charitable Foundation Scholarship • 2269
Eunice Walker Johnson Endowed Scholarship • 2271
Fannie Mae Foundation Scholarship • 2273
Financial Services Institution • 2275
Frederick D. Patterson Scholarship • 2281
Gena Wright Memorial Scholarship • 2286
Gerald W. and Jean Purmal Endowed Scholarship • 2289
GlaxoSmithKline Company Science Achievement Award • 2291
Google Scholarship • 2293
Harry C. Jaecker Scholarship • 2295
Harvey H. and Catherine A. Moses Scholarship • 2296
Houghton Mifflin Company Fellows Program/Internship • 2307
Jeffry and Barbara Picower Foundation Scholarship • 2319
Jesse Jones, Jr. Scholarship • 2320
Jimi Hendrix Endowment Fund Scholarship • 2321
John Lennon Scholarship • 2322
Jos. L. Muscarelle Foundation Scholarship • 2323
Kuntz Foundation Scholarship • 2326
Letty Garofalo Scholarship • 2327
Limited Inc. and Intimate Brands Inc. Scholarship • 2328
Louis Dreyfus Natural Gas Company Scholarship • 2330
Mae Maxey Memorial Scholarship • 2336
Malcolm X Scholarship for Exceptional Courage • 2338
Marriott Scholars Program • 2341
Mary E. Scott Memorial Scholarship • 2342
MasterCard Worldwide Special Support Program • 2344
McClare Family Trust Scholarship • 2346
Medtronic Foundation Scholarship • 2349

Michael and Donna Griffith Scholarship • 2352
Michael Jackson Scholarship • 2353
Mike and Stephanie Bozic Scholarship • 2354
Mitsubishi Motors U.S.A. Foundation Leadership Awards • 2361
Morgan Stanley Scholarship/Internship • 2362
NAACP/HBCU Scholarship Fund • 2364
Nelnet Scholarship • 2379
Office Depot Scholarship • 2382
Premedical Summer Institute Program/Internship • 2394
Raymond W. Cannon Memorial Scholarship • 2397
Reader's Digest Scholarship • 2398
Robert Dole Scholarship for Disabled Students • 2401
Robert Half International • 2402
Siragusa Foundation Scholarship • 2411
Sodexho Scholarship • 2413
Sterling Bank Scholarship • 2415
Sylvia Shapiro Scholarship • 2420
Time Warner Scholars Program • 2426
Trull Foundation Scholarship • 2430
UNCF-Foot Locker Foundation Inc. Scholarship • 2433
United Parcel Service Foundation • 2437
USA Funds Scholarship • 2439
USENIX Association Scholarship • 2440
Wells Fargo Scholarship • 2441
Wendell Scott, Sr./NASCAR Scholarship • 2442
William Wrigley Jr. Scholarship/Internship • 2445

VEGETARIAN
VRG Scholarship • 184

This index lists awards that are restricted to students who are residence of the state or who are planning to study in the state.

ALABAMA
Alabama Past President's Memorial Scholarship • 1105
Alabama Student Grant Program • 1106
Cargill Community Scholarship Program • 1193
Charles Clarke Cordle Memorial Scholarship • 417
Dixie Boys Baseball Scholarship Program • 54
Dixie Youth Scholarship Program • 55
Dr. Donald L.Moak Scholarship • 1286
Family District 1 Scholarships • 1324
First in Family Scholarship • 1330
Jimmy Rane Foundation Scholarships • 1453
Linda Moore Scholarship • 933
NACA Southeast Region Student Leader Scholarship • 1613
NEMAL Electronics Scholarship • 615
SERC Endowment • 1818
Two-Year College Academic Scholarship Program • 1891

ALASKA
Alaska State Council Endowment • 1108
Atsuhiko Tateuchi Memorial Scholarship • 1147
GEAR UP ALASKA Scholarship Program • 1349
Helping Hands of WSC Endowment • 2066
Lori Rhett Memorial Scholarship • 1520
Mary Lou Brown Scholarship • 569
Raymond & Catherine Brizzolari Memorial • 1729
Robert C. Byrd Honors Scholarship Program - Alaska • 1743

ARIZONA
Alpha Omichrom - Arizona Endowment • 1119
Arizona BPW Foundation Annual Scholarships • 1135
Arizona Chapter MOAA Educational Scholarships • 1136
Arizona Council Endowment Scholarship • 1137
Arizona Non-Traditional Education for Women Scholarships • 1138
Arizona Private Postsecondary Education Student Financial Assistance Program (PFAP) • 1139
BLET Auxiliary Scholarships • 1987
Burlington Northern Santa Fe (BNSF) Foundation Scholarship • 2226
Central Arizona DX Association Scholarship • 1203
Charles N. Fisher Memorial Scholarship • 421
Corporate Leadership Scholarships • 225
Elsie M. Vogler / Lois E. Carter Memorial Teaching • 1314
GEF Resource Center Scholarships • 243
Hallmark Graphic Arts Scholarship • 250
Helping Hands of WSC Endowment • 2066
Leveraging Educational Assistance Partnership (LEAP) • 1508
Robert C. Byrd Honors Scholarship Program - Arizona • 1744

Governor's Postsecondary Merit Scholarship • 1367

Governor's Postsecondary Merit-At-Large Scholarship • 1368

Lori Rhett Memorial Scholarship • 1520

Mary Lou Brown Scholarship • 569

MHEG- Montana Higher Education Grant • 1574

Montana State ESA Council Scholarship • 1606

Montana University System Honor Scholarship • 1607

MTAP - Montana Tuition Assistance Program/ Baker Grant • 1608

National Defense Transportation Association, St. Louis Area Chapter Scholarship • 596

Olive Griffith Memorial Scholarship • 1673

Robert C. Byrd Honors Scholarship Program - Montana • 1767

Sara E. Jenne Scholarship • 1805

Treacy Company Scholarship • 1881

NEBRASKA

Access College Early Scholarship • 1098

BNSF Railway Company FFA Scholarship • 1988

Cargill Community Scholarship Program • 1193

Casey's General Stores Inc. FFA Scholarship • 1997

Charles B. Washington Scholarship • 1207

Chief Industries FFA Scholarship • 2006

Darling International Inc. FFA Scholarship • 824

Jennings and Beulah Haggerty Scholarship • 1450

Jimmy Rane Foundation Scholarships • 1453

MARC Endowment • 1548

Midwest Student Exchange Program • 1582

Money to Learn Scholarship • 1605

Multicultural Association Scholarship • 1609

National Defense Transportation Association, St. Louis Area Chapter Scholarship • 596

Nebraska ESA Endowed Scholarship • 1616

Nebraska State Grant • 1617

Nebraska Veterans' Aid Fund Waiver of Tuition • 1618

Nebraskans of World War II Scholarships • 1619

Norman & Ruth Good Educational Endowment • 1649

Paul and Helen L. Grauer Scholarship • 631

PHD ARA Scholarship • 634

Postsecondary Education Award Program (PEAP) • 1718

Ray, NRP & Katie, WKTE Pautz Scholarship • 643

Robert C. Byrd Honors Scholarship Program - Nebraska • 1768

Scholarship Assistance Program (SAP) • 1809

State Scholarship Award Program (SSAP) • 1848

Walter and Ruby Behlen Memorial Scholarship • 1916

NEVADA

ABC Stores Jumpstart Scholarship • 1093

BLET Auxiliary Scholarships • 1987

Nevada Millennium Scholarship • 1623

Nevada Women's Fund Scholarships • 1624

Robert C. Byrd Honors Scholarship Program - Nevada • 1769

NEW HAMPSHIRE

Agway Foundation FFA Scholarship • 1961

Buddy Pelletier Surfing Foundation Scholarship • 26

Dr. James L. Lawson Memorial Scholarship • 446

Future Educators Academy • 1345

Granite State Scholars Program • 1374

Leveraged Incentive Grant Program • 1506

Medallion Fund • 1567

New England FEMARA Scholarships • 616

New England Regional Student Program • 1626

New Hampshire Charitable Foundation Adult Student Aid Program • 1627

New Hampshire Charitable Foundation State-wide Student Aid Program • 1628

New Hampshire Incentive Program • 1629

Robert C. Byrd Honors Scholarship Program - New Hampshire • 1770

Scholarships for Orphans of Veterans • 1811

Shaw-Worth Memorial Scholarship • 1037

Timothy Bigelow and Palmer W. Bigelow, Jr. Scholarship • 1066

Veterinary Education Program • 1899

Workforce Incentive Program • 1942

NEW JERSEY

Agway Foundation FFA Scholarship • 1961

Bego Fund Scholarships • 1155

Buddy Pelletier Surfing Foundation Scholarship • 26

Carolina Rice Scholarship Program • 1197

Clanseer and Anna Johnson Scholarships • 1227

Dana Christmas Scholarship for Heroism • 1259

Dominique Lisa Pandolfo Scholarship • 1275

Educational Opportunity Fund • 1303

Educational Opportunity Fund (EOF) Grant • 1304

Edward J. Bloustein Distinguished Scholars • 1307

Freehold Soil Conservation District Scholarship • 1342

Luterman Scholarship • 1530

NACA East Coast Graduate Student Scholarship • 591

NACA East Coast Undergraduate Scholarship for Student Leaders • 1612

New Jersey Oratorical Contest • 1630

New Jersey School Counselor Association Scholarships • 1631

New Jersey State Elks Handicapped Children's Scholarship • 1632

NJ Student Tuition Assistance Reward Scholarship • 1642

NJ Student Tuition Assistance Reward Scholarship II • 1643

NJVVM Scholarship Program • 1644

Part-Time Tuition Aid Grant • 1699

Perry F. Hadlock Memorial Scholarship • 633

Robert C. Byrd Honors Scholarship Program - New Jersey • 1771

Safety Essay Contest • 1801

Stutz Scholarship • 1857

The Heart of a Marine Foundation Scholarship • 1872

Tuition Aid Grant • 1883

Urban Scholars Award • 1894

NEW MEXICO

3 Percent Scholarships • 1092

Alan Johnston Memorial Scholarship • 1107

Albuquerque ARC/Toby Cross Scholarship • 1112

BLET Auxiliary Scholarships • 1987

Burlington Northern Santa Fe (BNSF) Foundation Scholarship • 2226

College Affordability Grant • 1231

Competitive Scholarships • 1244

Deborah Humphrey Scholarship • 1264

Excel Staffing Companies Scholarships for Excellence in Continuing Education • 1321

Fred R. McDaniel Memorial Scholarship • 471

Leadership Scholarship • 1494

Legislative Endowment Scholarships • 1498

Legislative Lottery Scholarships • 1501

Los Alamos Employees' Scholarship • 1521

Los Alamos National Laboratory Foundation • 1522

Markley Scholarship • 103

New Mexico Children of Deceased Veterans Scholarships • 1633

New Mexico Scholars • 1634

New Mexico State Council Road Runner Endowment • 1635

NMASBO Scholarship • 1645

NMPRSA Scholarship • 1646

NNM American Society of Mechanical Engineers Scholarship • 1647

Philip P. Barker Memorial Scholarship • 1712

Rae Lee Siporin Award • 1725

Ralph and Ruth Strother Scholarship • 1726

Regional College Scholarship • 1736

Robert C. Byrd Honors Scholarship Program - New Mexico • 1772

Science or Other Studies Scholarship • 1813

Student Incentive Grants • 1856

Sussman-Miller Educational Assistance Award • 1859

Toby Wright Scholarship • 1875

UC Nonresident Fee Scholarship • 1892

Vietnam Veterans' Scholarship • 1902

NEW YORK

Agway Foundation FFA Scholarship • 1961

Aid for Part-Time Study • 1104

Bego Fund Scholarships • 1155

Buddy Pelletier Surfing Foundation Scholarship • 26

Carolina Rice Scholarship Program • 1197

Corporate Leadership Scholarships • 225

Don Forsyth "Circle K" Scholarship Fund • 2023

Dr. James L. Lawson Memorial Scholarship • 446

Fellowship on Women and Public Policy • 1326

GEF Resource Center Scholarships • 243

Hallmark Graphic Arts Scholarship • 250

Linc Telacu Scholarships • 2329

Maryann K. Murtha Memorial Scholarship • 1558

Math and Science Teaching Incentive Scholarships • 1563

Memorial Scholarships • 1571

Military Service Recognition Scholarship • 1586

NACA East Coast Graduate Student Scholarship • 591

Dorothy Campbell Memorial Scholarship • 1280

Federal Chafee Educational and Training Grant • 1325

Ford Opportunity Program Scholarship • 1337

Ford Scholars Scholarship • 1338

Grange Insurance Group Scholarship • 2059

Hazel Knapp Endowment • 1386

Helping Hands of WSC Endowment • 2066

Hope Baney Memorial Endowment • 1406

Jerome B. Steinbach Scholarship • 1451

Lori Rhett Memorial Scholarship • 1520

Mary Lou Brown Scholarship • 569

ORCA Bob Hasson Memorial Scholarship Fund • 1676

Oregon Association of Student Councils Scholarships • 1677

Oregon National Guard State Tuition Program • 1678

Oregon Nursing Services Program • 1679

Oregon Opportunity Grant • 1680

Oregon Scholarship Fund Community College Student Award • 1681

Oregon State Council Endowment • 1682

Robert C. Byrd Honors Scholarship Program - Oregon • 1778

Scan|Design Foundation by Inger and Jens Bruun Scholarship for Study in Denmark • 1806

Pennsylvania

Agway Foundation FFA Scholarship • 1961

Bego Fund Scholarships • 1155

Big 33 Scholarship Foundation Scholarships • 1160

Buddy Pelletier Surfing Foundation Scholarship • 26

Commonwealth "Good Citizen" Scholarships • 1240

NACA East Coast Graduate Student Scholarship • 591

NACA East Coast Undergraduate Scholarship for Student Leaders • 1612

Pennsylvania Educational Gratuity for Veterans' Dependents • 1708

Pennsylvania Knights Templar Educational Foundation Scholarships • 1709

Pennsylvania Oratorical Contest • 1710

Robert C. Byrd Honors Scholarship Program - Pennsylvania • 1779

State Grant Program • 1841

Tese Caldarelli Memorial Scholarship • 1867

You've Got a Friend in Pennsylvania Scholarship • 1947

Zagunis Student Leader Scholarship • 1950

Puerto Rico

NACA Southeast Region Student Leader Scholarship • 1613

Rhode Island

Agway Foundation FFA Scholarship • 1961

Antonio Cirino Memorial Art Education Fellowship • 1134

Bach Organ and Keyboard Music Scholarship • 1150

Buddy Pelletier Surfing Foundation Scholarship • 26

Carl W. Christiansen Scholarship • 1194

Cheryl A. Ruggiero Scholarship • 1214

CollegeBoundfund Academic Promise Scholarship • 1233

Dr. James L. Lawson Memorial Scholarship • 446

J.D. Edsal Advertising Scholarship/Women's Advertising Club Scholarship • 1440

James J. Burns and C.A. Haynes Scholarship • 1443

Lily and Catello Sorrentino Memorial Scholarship • 1516

New England FEMARA Scholarships • 616

New England Regional Student Program • 1626

Rhode Island Foundation Association of Former Legislators Scholarship • 1739

Robert C. Byrd Honors Scholarship Program - Rhode Island • 1780

Shaw-Worth Memorial Scholarship • 1037

State Grant Program • 1842

Timothy Bigelow and Palmer W. Bigelow, Jr. Scholarship • 1066

South Carolina

Corporate Leadership Scholarships • 225

Dixie Boys Baseball Scholarship Program • 54

Dixie Youth Scholarship Program • 55

Family District 1 Scholarships • 1324

GEF Resource Center Scholarships • 243

Hallmark Graphic Arts Scholarship • 250

James. F. Byrnes Scholarships • 1447

Jimmy Rane Foundation Scholarships • 1453

Kittie M. Fairey Educational Fund Scholarships • 1486

L. Phil Wicker Scholarship • 549

Legislative for Future Excellence (LIFE) Scholarship Program • 1500

Linda Moore Scholarship • 933

Lottery Tuition Assistance Program • 1523

NACA Southeast Region Student Leader Scholarship • 1613

NEMAL Electronics Scholarship • 615

Palmetto Fellows Scholarship Program • 1687

Robert C. Byrd Honors Scholarship Program - South Carolina • 1781

SERC Endowment • 1818

Sherman and Nancy Reece Scholarship • 1821

South Carolina Hope Scholarship • 1831

South Carolina Sheriffs' Association Scholarships • 1832

South Carolina Tuition Grants Program • 1833

State Need-based Grants • 1844

Werner B. Thiele Memorial Scholarship • 325

South Dakota

Alert Scholarship • 1113

BNSF Railway Company FFA Scholarship • 1988

Burlington Northern Santa Fe (BNSF) Foundation Scholarship • 2226

Cargill Community Scholarship Program • 1193

Casey's General Stores Inc. FFA Scholarship • 1997

Cora E. and Royal L. Scott Family Endowment • 1249

Dr. Sidney E. Milburn Memorial Scholarship • 1290

Joe Foss, An American Hero Scholarship • 1454

MARC Endowment • 1548

Marlin R. Scarborough Memorial Scholarship • 1552

National Defense Transportation Association, St. Louis Area Chapter Scholarship • 596

Parr Family Memorial Endowment • 1691

Robert C. Byrd Honors Scholarship Program - South Dakota • 1782

South Dakota Free Tuition for Veterans and Others Who Perfomed War Service • 1834

Treacy Company Scholarship • 1881

Vincent L. Hawkinson Scholarship for Peace and Justice • 1903

Tennessee

Aspire Award • 1145

Christa McAuliffe Scholarship • 1222

Dixie Boys Baseball Scholarship Program • 54

Dixie Youth Scholarship Program • 55

Family District 1 Scholarships • 1324

Gary Wagner, K3OMI Scholarship • 479

General Assembly Merit Scholarship • 1351

James M. and Virginia M. Smyth Scholarship • 90

Jimmy Rane Foundation Scholarships • 1453

Linda Moore Scholarship • 933

NACA Southeast Region Student Leader Scholarship • 1613

Ned McWherter Scholars Program • 1620

NEMAL Electronics Scholarship • 615

Robert C. Byrd Honors Scholarship Program - Tennessee • 1783

SERC Endowment • 1818

Student Assistance Award Program • 1853

Tennessee HOPE Access Grant • 1865

Tennessee HOPE Lottery Scholarship • 1866

Wilder-Naifeh Technical Skills Grant • 1927

Texas

Baccalaureate Scholarship • 1149

BNSF Railway Company FFA Scholarship • 1988

Career Colleges and Schools of Texas Scholarship Program • 1192

Cargill Community Scholarship Program • 1193

Collegiate Scholarship • 1234

Courageous Heart Scholarship • 1251

Dallas Morning News Annual Teenage Citizenship Tribute • 1258

Dixie Boys Baseball Scholarship Program • 54

Dixie Youth Scholarship Program • 55

Don't Mess with Texas Scholarship • 1276

Fred R. McDaniel Memorial Scholarship • 471

J.A. Knowles Memorial Scholarship • 1439

James M. and Virginia M. Smyth Scholarship • 90

Jerry Harvey Endowment Scholarship • 2081

Jimmy Rane Foundation Scholarships • 1453

Joe Jaegers Family Endowment Scholarship • 2082

Johnnie and Tom Moseley Memorial Endowment • 1462

Kay Mills Memorial Scholarship • 1479

License Plate Insignia Scholarship • 1513

Markley Scholarship • 103

Mary Karele Milligan Scholarship • 1554

Robert C. Byrd Honors Scholarship Program - Texas • 1784

Science and Technology Scholars Program • 1032

Technical Certification Scholarship • 1863

Texas Oratorical Contest • 1868

MILITARY RELATED INDEX

Most of the awards in this index require that you have a parent or grandparent who has served in the military. There are also awards if you want to enter the armed services.

ETHNICITY AND RACE INDEX

This index lists awards for members of minority and non-minority ethnic groups.

AFRICAN AMERICAN

Drs. Poh Shien and Judy Young Scholarship • 2262

Ethnic Minority Scholarship • 2036

Fedex Hallmark Scholarship • 2274

Forum for Concerns of Minorities Scholarship • 2278

GAPA's George Choy Memorial Scholarship • 2283

Gates Millennium Scholars Program • 2284

Goodyear Tire and Rubber Company Scholarships • 2292

HANA Scholarship • 2062

Jackie Robinson Scholarship • 2312

Jimmy A. Young Memorial Education Recognition Award • 909

Kansas Ethnic Minority Scholarship • 1474

Leadership for Diversity Scholarship • 1493

Legal Opportunity Scholarship Fund • 556

Louis B. Russell, Jr. Memorial Scholarship • 1524

Martin Luther King, Jr. Memorial Scholarship • 2104

McDonald's Scholarship • 2347

Minorities and Women Educational Scholarship • 581

Minority Fellowship Program • 582

Minority Scholarship and Training Program • 2357

Minority Scholarships • 2360

MLA Scholarship for Minority Students • 585

MLA/NLM Spectrum Scholarship • 586

Multicultural Affairs Scholarship Program • 2363

National AAJA General Scholarship Awards • 2369

OCA/UPS Gold Mountain Scholarship • 2381

PBS&J Achievement Scholarship • 2390

Rosewood Family Scholarship Program • 1798

Ruth Mu-Lan Chu and James S.C. Chao Scholarship • 2406

Student CEC Ethnic Diversity Scholarship • 2416

Telamon Scholarship • 2421

Tongan Cultural Society Scholarship • 1877

Trailblazer Scholarship • 2427

United Parcel Service Scholarship for Minority Students • 2438

POLISH

Polish National Alliance Scholarship • 2392

Tuition Scholarship Program • 320

Year Abroad Program • 331

PORTUGUESE

Forum for Concerns of Minorities Scholarship • 2278

Louis B. Russell, Jr. Memorial Scholarship • 1524

Luso-American Education Foundation General Fund Scholarship • 1529

Portuguese Foundation Scholarships • 1716

PUERTO RICAN

California Community Service Scholarship Program • 1175

Chicana/Latina Foundation Scholarship • 1217

Forum for Concerns of Minorities Scholarship • 2278

GEM Fellowship Program • 2285

Jose Marti Scholarship Challenge Grant • 1464

Leadership for Diversity Scholarship • 1493

Legal Opportunity Scholarship Fund • 556

Louis B. Russell, Jr. Memorial Scholarship • 1524

Martin Luther King, Jr. Memorial Scholarship • 2104

Minority Fellowship Program • 582

Minority Scholarship • 2356

National Society of Hispanic MBAs Scholarship • 601

Need-Based Scholarship Program • 986

Student CEC Ethnic Diversity Scholarship • 2416

ROMANIAN

Louis B. Russell, Jr. Memorial Scholarship • 1524

SAMOAN

American Geological Institute Minority Scholarship • 2208

Asian American Scholarship Fund • 2217

Asian and Pacific Islander American Scholarships • 2218

Atsuhiko Tateuchi Memorial Scholarship • 1147

Costco Wholesale Scholarships • 1250

Darden Restaurants Hallmark Scholarship • 2252

Drs. Poh Shien and Judy Young Scholarship • 2262

Fedex Hallmark Scholarship • 2274

Forum for Concerns of Minorities Scholarship • 2278

Goodyear Tire and Rubber Company Scholarships • 2292

Jackie Robinson Scholarship • 2312

Leadership for Diversity Scholarship • 1493

Legal Opportunity Scholarship Fund • 556

Louis B. Russell, Jr. Memorial Scholarship • 1524

Martin Luther King, Jr. Memorial Scholarship • 2104

McDonald's Scholarship • 2347

Minority Fellowship Program • 582

Ruth Mu-Lan Chu and James S.C. Chao Scholarship • 2406

Student CEC Ethnic Diversity Scholarship • 2416

Telamon Scholarship • 2421

SCOTTISH

Clan MacBean Foundation Grant Program • 219

Donald Malcolm MacArthur Scholarship • 2255

SOUTHEAST ASIAN

Asian American Scholarship Fund • 2217

Asian and Pacific Islander American Scholarships • 2218

Atsuhiko Tateuchi Memorial Scholarship • 1147

CLA Scholarship for Minority Students in Memory of Edna Yelland • 426

Costco Wholesale Scholarships • 1250

Darden Restaurants Hallmark Scholarship • 2252

Drs. Poh Shien and Judy Young Scholarship • 2262

Fedex Hallmark Scholarship • 2274

Forum for Concerns of Minorities Scholarship • 2278

Goodyear Tire and Rubber Company Scholarships • 2292

Jackie Robinson Scholarship • 2312

Jimmy A. Young Memorial Education Recognition Award • 909

Leadership for Diversity Scholarship • 1493

Legal Opportunity Scholarship Fund • 556

Louis B. Russell, Jr. Memorial Scholarship • 1524

Martin Luther King, Jr. Memorial Scholarship • 2104

McDonald's Scholarship • 2347

Minority Fellowship Program • 582

Minority Scholarship • 2356

OCA/UPS Gold Mountain Scholarship • 2381

Ruth Mu-Lan Chu and James S.C. Chao Scholarship • 2406

Student CEC Ethnic Diversity Scholarship • 2416

Telamon Scholarship • 2421

SPANISH

Chicana/Latina Foundation Scholarship • 1217

Forum for Concerns of Minorities Scholarship • 2278

Jose Marti Scholarship Challenge Grant • 1464

Martin Luther King, Jr. Memorial Scholarship • 2104

Minority Scholarship • 2356

National Society of Hispanic MBAs Scholarship • 601

Student CEC Ethnic Diversity Scholarship • 2416

SWEDISH

Oscar and Mildred Larson Award • 2384

SWISS

Medicus Student Exchange • 2348

MEMBERSHIP INDEX

If you or your parents are members of any of the groups in this index, you may qualify for a scholarship.

693

AMERICAN ATHEISTS
Chinn Scholarship • 2240
Dr. Richard Chinn Scholarship • 2260
Life Members' Scholarship • 2097

AMERICAN BAPTIST CHURCHES USA
Undergraduate Scholarships • 2170

AMERICAN BAR ASSOCIATION
ABA Essay and Writing Competitions • 338
Legal Opportunity Scholarship Fund • 556

AMERICAN BOARD OF FUNERAL SERVICE EDUCATION
National Scholarship Program • 600

AMERICAN CENTER OF ORIENTAL RESEARCH (ACOR)
ACOR-CAORC Fellowships • 349
Harrell Family Fellowship • 493
Jennifer C. Groot Fellowship • 531
Pierre and Patricia Bikai Fellowship • 636

AMERICAN CHEMICAL SOCIETY
American Chemical Society Scholars Program • 2206

AMERICAN CONCRETE INSTITUTE ACI-JAMES INSTRUMENTS STUDENT AWARD
ACI-James Instruments Student Award for Research on NDT of Concrete • 716

AMERICAN CONCRETE INSTITUTE STUDENT FELLOWSHIP PROGRAM
ACI Student Fellowship Program • 715

AMERICAN CONGRESS ON SURVEYING AND MAPPING (ACSM)
ACSM - AAGS - NSPS Scholarships • 718
CaGIS Scholarships • 407

AMERICAN COUNCIL OF INDEPENDENT LABORATORIES
ACIL Scholarship • 717

AMERICAN COUNCIL OF LEARNED SOCIETIES (ACLS)
ACLS Digital Innovation Fellowships • 347
ACLS Fellowships • 348
Charles A. Ryskamp Research Fellowships • 416
Contemplative Practice Fellowship Program • 434
Frederick Burkhardt Residential Fellowships for Recently Tenured Scholars • 473
Henry Luce Foundation/ACLS Dissertation Fellowships in American Art • 253

AMERICAN COUNCIL OF THE BLIND
American Council of the Blind Scholarships • 2450
Dr. Mae Davidow Memorial Scholarship • 2463
Duane Buckley Memorial Scholarship • 2464

AMERICAN CRIMINAL JUSTICE ASSOCIATION
ACJA/Lambda Alpha Epsilon Scholarship • 346
Student Paper Competition • 672

AMERICAN DARTS ORGANIZATION
American Darts Organization Memorial Scholarships • 8

AMERICAN DENTAL ASSOCIATION FOUNDATION
Allied Dental Health Scholarships • 738
Dental Student Scholarship • 830
Minority Dental Student Scholarship • 965

AMERICAN DENTAL HYGIENISTS' ASSOCIATION (ADHA) INSTITUTE FOR ORAL HEALTH
ADHA Institute Scholarship Program • 722

Cadbury Adams Community Outreach Scholarships • 803
Colgate "Bright Smiles, Bright Futures" Minority Scholarships • 813
Dr. Alfred C. Fones Scholarship • 838
Dr. Harold Hillenbrand Scholarship • 839
Irene E. Newman Scholarship • 902
Margaret E. Swanson Scholarship • 942
Marsh Affinity Group Services Scholarships • 944
Oral-B Laboratories Dental Hygiene Scholarships • 998
Pfizer Inc. Scholarships • 1006

AMERICAN DIETETIC ASSOCIATION FOUNDATION
ADAF Student Scholarship • 719

AMERICAN FEDERATION FOR AGING RESEARCH (AFAR)
Medical Student Summer Research Training in Aging Program • 953

AMERICAN FEDERATION OF STATE, COUNTY AND MUNICIPAL EMPLOYEES (AFSCME), AFL-CIO
AFSCME Family Scholarship Program • 1956

AMERICAN FEDERATION OF TEACHERS
Robert G. Porter Scholars Program for Members • 2134
Robert G. Porter Scholars Program for Members' Dependents • 2135

AMERICAN FEDERATION OF TELEVISION AND RADIO ARTISTS
AFTRA/Heller Memorial Foundation Scholarships • 1957

AMERICAN FIRE SPRINKLER ASSOCIATION
American Fire Sprinkler Association Scholarship Program • 9

AMERICAN FOREIGN SERVICE ASSOCIATION (AFSA)
AFSA Financial Aid Scholarships • 1954
AFSA National Essay Contest • 4
AFSA/AAFSW Merit Award • 1955

AMERICAN FOUNDATION
Angus Foundation Scholarship • 753

AMERICAN FOUNDATION FOR THE BLIND SCHOLARSHIP COMMITTEE
Ferdinand Torres Scholarship • 2469
Karen D. Carsel Memorial Scholarship • 2476

AMERICAN FOUNDATION FOR UROLOGIC DISEASE INC.
AUA Foundation Research Scholars Program • 787

AMERICAN GEOLOGICAL INSTITUTE
American Geological Institute Minority Scholarship • 2208

AMERICAN GROUND WATER TRUST
Amtrol Inc. Scholarship • 752
Baroid Scholarship • 792
Ben Everson Scholarship • 796
Thomas M. Stetson Scholarship • 1062

AMERICAN GUILD OF MUSICAL ARTISTS
Beatrice S. Jacobson Memorial Fund • 1982

AMERICAN HEALTH INFORMATION MANAGEMENT ASSOCIATION
Merit Scholarships and Educational Loans • 957

AMERICAN HELLENIC EDUCATION PROGRESSIVE ASSOCIATION
Family District 1 Scholarships • 1324
Maids of Athena Scholarships • 2103
National and District Scholarships • 2370
P.A. Margaronis Scholarships • 2385

AMERICAN HISTORICAL ASSOCIATION
Fellowship in Aerospace History • 851
J. Franklin Jameson Fellowship in American History • 524
Wesley-Logan Prize • 695

AMERICAN HOLISTIC NURSES' ASSOCIATION
Charlotte McGuire Scholarship • 808

AMERICAN HOTEL AND LODGING EDUCATIONAL FOUNDATION (AH&LEF)
American Express Scholarship Competition • 374
Ecolab Scholarship Competition • 449
Lodging Management Program (LMP) • 559
Steven Hymans Extended Stay Scholarship • 667

AMERICAN INDIAN SCIENCE AND ENGINEERING SOCIETY
A.T. Anderson Memorial Scholarship • 2191
Bureau of Reclamation Scholarship and Internship • 2225
Burlington Northern Santa Fe (BNSF) Foundation Scholarship • 2226
General Motors Engineering Scholarship • 2288

AMERICAN INSTITUTE FOR CONTEMPORARY GERMAN STUDIES - (AICGS)
DAAD/AICGS Research Fellowship Program • 228

AMERICAN INSTITUTE FOR ECONOMIC RESEARCH
Summer Fellowship Program • 675

AMERICAN INSTITUTE FOR FOREIGN STUDY
International Scholarships • 257
Minority Scholarships • 2360

AMERICAN INSTITUTE OF AERONAUTICS AND ASTRONAUTICS
AIAA Foundation Undergraduate Scholarship Program • 729

AMERICAN INSTITUTE OF CERTIFIED PUBLIC ACCOUNTANTS
Accountemps/American Institute Of Certified Public Accountants Student Scholarship • 344

AMERICAN INSTITUTE OF CHEMICAL ENGINEERS - (AICHE)
Donald F. and Mildred Topp Othmer Foundation • 834
John J. McKetta Scholarship • 914
Minority Affairs Committee Award for Outstanding Scholastic Achievement • 2355
Minority Scholarship Awards for College Students • 2358
Minority Scholarship Awards for Incoming College Freshmen • 2359
National Student Design Competition • 978

AMERICAN INSTITUTE OF INDIAN STUDIES
Junior Fellowships • 544

AMERICAN KENNEL CLUB
Junior Scholarship Program • 922

701

The Ultimate Scholarship Book 2010
Sponsor Index

National Science & Mathematics Access to Retain Talent Grant • 977

FEDERATION OF AMERICAN CONSUMERS AND TRAVELERS (FACT)
Continuing Education Scholarships • 2015

FELLOWSHIP OF UNITED METHODISTS IN MUSIC AND WORSHIP ARTS
Fellowship of United Methodists in Music and Worship Arts Scholarship • 2041

FINANCIAL MARKETS CENTER
Henry B. Gonzalez Award • 498

FINANCIAL SERVICE CENTERS OF AMERICA
FiSCA Scholarship • 66

FISHER COMMUNICATIONS INC.
Fisher Broadcasting Scholarships for Minorities • 466

FLEET RESERVE ASSOCIATION
Fleet Reserve Association Scholarship • 2042
Oliver and Esther R. Howard Scholarship • 2121
Schuyler S. Pyle Award • 2141
Stanley A. Doran Memorial Scholarship • 2149

FLEXOGRAPHIC TECHNICAL ASSOCIATION
FFTA Scholarship Competition • 240

FLORICULTURE INDUSTRY RESEARCH AND SCHOLARSHIP TRUST
FIRST Scholarship • 853

FLORIDA ASSOCIATION OF POSTSECONDARY SCHOOLS AND COLLEGES
Florida Association of Postsecondary Schools and Colleges Scholarship Program • 1333

FLORIDA DEPARTMENT OF EDUCATION
Access to Better Learning and Education Grant Program • 1099
Critical Teacher Shortage Loan Forgiveness Program • 1253
Critical Teacher Shortage Tuition Reimbursement Program • 1254
Ethics in Business Scholarship Program • 1319
First Generation Matching Grant Program • 1329
Florida Bright Futures Scholarship Program • 1334
Florida Student Assistance Grant Program • 1336
Jose Marti Scholarship Challenge Grant • 1464
Mary McLeod Bethune Scholarship Program • 1556
Robert C. Byrd Honors Scholarship Program - Florida • 1750
Rosewood Family Scholarship Program • 1798
William L. Boyd, IV, Florida Resident Access Grant • 1933

FLORIDA'S OFFICE OF CAMPUS VOLUNTEERS
Excellence in Service Award • 1322

FOREST ROBERTS THEATRE AT NORTHERN MICHIGAN UNIVERSITY
Mildred and Albert Panowski Playwriting Award • 275

FORT COLLINS SYMPHONY
Annual Young Artist Competition • 202
Junior Competition • 264

FOUNDATION FOR EXCEPTIONAL CHILDREN
Sara Conlon Memorial Scholarship • 2501
Stanley E. Jackson Scholarship Awards • 2507

FOUNDATION FOR SURGICAL TECHNOLOGY
Surgical Technology Scholarships • 1056

FOUNDATION OF THE FIRST CAVALRY DIVISION ASSOCIATION
First Cavalry Division Association Scholarship • 465

FRANCIS OUIMET SCHOLARSHIP FUND
The Francis Ouimet Scholarship Fund • 1871

FRATERNAL ORDER OF EAGLES
Fraternal Order of Eagles Memorial Foundation • 470

FREDRIKSON AND BYRON, P.A.
Minority Scholarship Program • 583

FREEDOM FORUM
Al Neuharth Free Spirit Scholarship and Conference Program • 370

FREEDOM FROM RELIGION FOUNDATION
Blanche Fearn Memorial High School Senior Essay Contest • 1986
Michael Hakeem Memorial College Essay Contest • 2105
Student Activist Awards • 156

FREEHOLD SOIL CONSERVATION DISTRICT
Freehold Soil Conservation District Scholarship • 1342

FRESH START SCHOLARSHIP FOUNDATION
Fresh Start Scholarship • 1343

FUND FOR AMERICAN STUDIES
Fund for American Studies Internships • 475

FUND FOR THEOLOGICAL EDUCATION INC.
Undergraduate Fellows Program • 2167

FUNERAL SERVICE FOUNDATION
FSF Scholarship Program • 474

GAMMA THETA UPSILON
Gamma Theta Upsilon-Geographical Honor Society • 478

GATES FOUNDATION
Gates Millennium Scholars Program • 2284

GEN AND KELLY TANABE PARENT SCHOLARSHIP PROGRAM
$1,000 Gen and Kelly Tanabe Parent Scholarship • 1

GEN AND KELLY TANABE SCHOLARSHIP PROGRAM
$1,000 Gen and Kelly Tanabe Student Scholarship • 2

GENERAL COMMISSION ON ARCHIVES AND HISTORY, THE UNITED METHODIST CHURCH
Racial/Ethnic History Research Grant • 2131
Women in United Methodist History Research Grant • 2187
Women in United Methodist History Writing Award • 2188

GENERAL CONFERENCE OF SEVENTH-DAY ADVENTISTS WOMEN'S MINISTRIES
General Conference Women's Ministries Scholarship Program • 2054

GEOLOGICAL SOCIETY OF AMERICA
Antoinette Lierman Medlin Scholarship • 757
Graduate Student Research Grants • 875
Shlemon Awards • 1038
Travel Grants • 1067
Undergraduate Student Research Grants • 1073

GEORGIA STUDENT FINANCE COMMISSION
Charles McDaniel Teacher Scholarship • 1209
Georgia Tuition Equalization Grant • 1356
Governor's Scholarship Program • 1370
HOPE Scholarship Program • 1409
Leveraging Educational Assistance Partnership (LEAP) Grant • 1509
Robert C. Byrd Honors Scholarship Program - Georgia • 1751

GERMAN ACADEMIC EXCHANGE SERVICE
German Studies Research Grant • 245

GERMAN MARSHALL FUND OF THE UNITED STATES
Marshall Memorial Fellowship • 105
Transatlantic Community Foundation Fellowship • 166
Transatlantic Fellows Program • 685

GINA BACHAUER INTERNATIONAL PIANO FOUNDATION
Junior Competition • 263

GIRLS INC.
National Scholars and Awards Program • 2117

GLAMOUR
Top Ten College Women Competition • 164

GLASS, MOLDERS, POTTERY, PLASTICS AND ALLIED WORKERS INTERNATIONAL UNION
Glass, Molders, Pottery, Plastics and Allied Workers Memorial Scholarship Fund • 2057

GLENN MILLER BIRTHPLACE SOCIETY
Glenn Miller Scholarship Competition • 247

GOCOLLEGE.COM
Scholarship Lucky Draw • 146

GOLDEN GATE RESTAURANT ASSOCIATION
Golden Gate Restaurant Association Scholarship • 489

GOLDEN KEY NATIONAL HONOUR SOCIETY
Business Achievement Awards • 1995
Community Service Award • 2013
Education Achievement Awards • 2032
Engineering/Technology Achievement Awards • 2035
Ford Motor Company Business and Leadership Scholarship • 2043
Ford Motor Company Engineering and Leadership Scholarship • 2044
GEICO Life Scholarship • 2053
Golden Key Graduate Scholar Award • 2058
Literary Achievement Awards • 2100
Student Leader Award • 2152
Study Abroad Scholarships • 2153
Undergraduate Research Grants • 2168
Visual and Performing Arts Achievement Awards • 2176

GOLF COURSE SUPERINTENDENTS ASSOCIATION OF AMERICA FOUNDATION
GCSAA Legacy Awards • 2052
GCSAA Scholars Program • 865

706

SOCIETY OF AUTOMOTIVE ENGINEERS (SAE)
Doctoral Scholars Forgivable Loan Program • 831
Long-Term Member Sponsored Scholarship • 935
SAE Engineering Scholarships • 1030
Yanmar/SAE Scholarship • 1087

SOCIETY OF BROADCAST ENGINEERS
Youth Scholarship • 707

SOCIETY OF EXPLORATION GEOPHYSICISTS
Society of Exploration Geophysicists (SEG) Scholarship • 1041

SOCIETY OF FRIENDS (QUAKERS)
John Sarrin Scholarship • 2087

SOCIETY OF MEXICAN AMERICAN ENGINEERS AND SCIENTISTS INC. (MAES)
MAES Scholarship Program • 2337

SOCIETY OF NAVAL ARCHITECTS AND MARINE ENGINEERS
Society of Naval Architects and Marine Engineers Undergraduate Scholarships • 1042

SOCIETY OF NUCLEAR MEDICINE
Paul Cole Scholarship Award • 1001

SOCIETY OF PHYSICS STUDENTS
Herbert Levy Memorial Scholarship • 888
Peggy Dixon Two-Year Scholarship • 1004
SPS Future Teacher Scholarship • 665
SPS Leadership Scholarships • 1046

SOCIETY OF PLASTICS ENGINEERS
American Plastics Council (APC)/SPE Plastics Environmental Division Scholarship • 744
Composites Division/Harold Giles Scholarship • 816
Polymer Modifiers and Additives Division Scholarships • 1011
Society of Plastics Engineers (SPE) General Scholarships • 1043
Ted Neward Scholarship • 1057
Thermoforming Division Memorial Scholarships • 1060
Thermoset Division/James I. MacKenzie Memorial Scholarship • 1061
Vinyl Plastics Division Scholarship • 1079

SOCIETY OF SATELLITE PROFESSIONALS INTERNATIONAL (SSPI)
SSPI Scholarship Program • 666

SONS OF NORWAY
Astrid G. Cates Scholarship Fund and the Myrtle Beinhauer Scholarship • 1979
General Heritage and Culture Grants • 244
King Olav V Norwegian-American Heritage Fund • 267
Scholarships to Oslo International Summer School • 303

SONS OF UNION VETERANS OF THE CIVIL WAR
Sons of Union Veterans of the Civil War Scholarships • 662

SOROPTIMIST INTERNATIONAL
Violet Richardson Award • 181
Women's Opportunity Awards Program • 2446

SOUTH CAROLINA BOARD FOR TECHNICAL AND COMPREHENSIVE EDUCATION
Lottery Tuition Assistance Program • 1523

SOUTH CAROLINA COMMISSION ON HIGHER EDUCATION
Legislative for Future Excellence (LIFE) Scholarship Program • 1500
Palmetto Fellows Scholarship Program • 1687
South Carolina Hope Scholarship • 1831
State Need-based Grants • 1844

SOUTH CAROLINA DEPARTMENT OF EDUCATION
Robert C. Byrd Honors Scholarship Program - South Carolina • 1781

SOUTH CAROLINA SHERIFFS' ASSOCIATION
South Carolina Sheriffs' Association Scholarships • 1832

SOUTH CAROLINA TUITION GRANTS COMMISSION
South Carolina Tuition Grants Program • 1833

SOUTH DAKOTA BOARD OF REGENTS
Marlin R. Scarborough Memorial Scholarship • 1552
South Dakota Free Tuition for Veterans and Others Who Perfomed War Service • 1834

SOUTH DAKOTA DEPARTMENT OF EDUCATION AND CULTURAL AFFAIRS
Robert C. Byrd Honors Scholarship Program - South Dakota • 1782

SOUTHERN SCHOLARSHIP FOUNDATION
Southern Scholarship Foundation Scholarship • 1835

SOUTHWEST VIRGINIA HIGHER EDUCATION CENTER
Southside Tobacco Forgiveness Loan • 1836

SPECIAL LIBRARIES ASSOCIATION
Affirmative Action Scholarship • 356
SLA Scholarship • 661

SPECIALTY EQUIPMENT MARKET ASSOCIATION
Specialty Equipment Market Association (SEMA) Memorial Scholarship • 664

SPINA BIFIDA ASSOCIATION OF AMERICA
SBAA Four-Year Scholarship • 2502

ST. ANDREW'S SOCIETY OF WASHINGTON, DC
Donald Malcolm MacArthur Scholarship • 2255

STATE COUNCIL OF HIGHER EDUCATION FOR VIRGINIA
College Scholarship Assistance Program • 1232
Graduate and Undergraduate Assistance Program • 1372
Part-Time Assistance Program • 1693
Virginia Commonwealth Award Program • 1904
Virginia Guaranteed Assistance Program • 1905
Virginia Tuition Assistance Grant Program (VTAG) • 1908

STATE EMPLOYEES ASSOCIATION OF NORTH CAROLINA
State Employees Association of North Carolina (SEANC) Scholarships • 1840

STATE OF ALABAMA
Alabama Student Grant Program • 1106
Two-Year College Academic Scholarship Program • 1891

STATE OF NEW JERSEY DEPARTMENT OF EDUCATION
Robert C. Byrd Honors Scholarship Program - New Jersey • 1771

STATE OF WISCONSIN HIGHER EDUCATIONAL AIDS BOARD
Academic Excellence Scholarship • 1095
Higher Education Grant • 1398
Talent Incentive Program (TIP) Grant • 1861
Tuition Grant • 1886

STATE STUDENT ASSISTANCE COMMISSION OF INDIANA
Frank O'Bannon Grant Program • 1341
GEAR UP Summer Scholarship • 1350
Hoosier Scholar Award • 1405
Minority Teacher/Special Education Services Scholarship • 1594
Nursing Scholarship Fund • 1662
Part-Time Grant Program • 1695
Robert C. Byrd Honors Scholarship Program - Indiana • 1755
Twenty-first Century Scholars Program • 1890

STONEHOUSE PUBLISHING COMPANY
Stonehouse Golf Youth Scholarship • 154

STUDENT ASSISTANCE FOUNDATION OF MONTANA
MHEG- Montana Higher Education Grant • 1574
MTAP - Montana Tuition Assistance Program/ Baker Grant • 1608

SUBWAY RESTAURANTS
Subway Scholarship Fund • 2154

SUNTRUST
Off to College Scholarship Sweepstakes • 125

SUPERCOLLEGE.COM
SuperCollege.com Student Scholarship • 159

SUPERSIBS!
Manne Family Foundation Scholarships • 2484

SWISS BENEVOLENT SOCIETY OF NEW YORK
Medicus Student Exchange • 2348

TAG AND LABEL MANUFACTURERS INSTITUTE INC.
TLMI Four Year Colleges/Full-Time Students Scholarship • 681

TAILHOOK ASSOCIATION
Tailhook Educational Foundation Scholarship • 676

TALBOTS
Talbots Women's Scholarship Fund • 160

TALL CLUBS INTERNATIONAL
Tall Club International Kae Sumner Einfeldt Scholarship • 2156

TAU BETA PI ASSOCIATION
Tau Beta Pi Scholarships • 2157

TAU KAPPA EPSILON EDUCATIONAL FOUNDATION
All-Teke Academic Team • 1962
Bruce B. Melchert Scholarship • 1993
Carrol C. Hall Memorial Scholarship • 1996
Charles J. Trabold Scholarship • 2002
Charles R. Walgreen Jr. Leadership Award • 2003
Christopher Grasso Scholarship • 2008
Donald A. and John R. Fisher Memorial Scholarship • 2024
Doris and Elmer H. Schmitz, Sr. Memorial Scholarship • 2025
Dwayne R. Woerpel Memorial Scholarship • 2028
Eugene C. Beach Memorial Scholarship • 2037

The Ultimate Scholarship Book 2010
Sponsor Index

J.A. Knowles Memorial Scholarship • 1439
Leonard M. Perryman Communications Scholarship for Ethnic Minority Students • 2096
Rev. Dr. Karen Layman Gift of Hope 21st Century Scholars Program • 2132
Rosalie Bentzinger Scholarship • 2137
United Methodist General Scholarship • 2172

UNITED METHODIST HIGHER EDUCATION FOUNDATION
National Temperance Scholarship • 2118
Priscilla R. Morton Scholarship • 2128

UNITED MINE WORKERS OF AMERICA/BCOA T.E.F.
Lorin E. Kerr Scholarship Fund • 2101
UMWA/BCOA Training and Education Fund • 2166

UNITED NATIONS ASSOCIATION OF THE UNITED STATES OF AMERICA
National High School Essay Contest • 278

UNITED NEGRO COLLEGE FUND (UNCF)
Alliance Data Scholarship • 2201
Alton and Dorothy Higgins MD Scholarship • 2203
American Hotel Management Foundation Scholarship • 2209
Amtrak Travel Scholarship • 2212
Berbeco Senior Research Fellowship • 2219
Bessie Irene Smith Trust Scholarship • 2221
Best Buy Scholarship Program • 2222
Burton G. Bettingen Foundation Scholarship • 2227
C-SPAN Scholarship Program • 2228
Carolyn Bailey Thomas Scholarship • 2232
Catherine W. Pierce Scholarship • 2234
CDM Scholarship/Internship • 2235
Chrysler Corporation Scholarship • 2241
Citigroup Fellows Program • 2242
Colgate-Palmolive Company/UNCF Scholarship • 2244
Coy G. Eklund Scholarship • 2251
Doris and John Carpenter Scholarship • 2256
Dorothy N. McNeal Scholarship • 2257
Dr. James M. Rosin Scholarship • 2258
Dr. Joe Ratliff Challenge • 2259
Dr. Scholl Foundation Scholarship • 2261
Earl and Patricia Armstrong Scholarship • 2263
Edward and Hazel Stephenson Scholarship • 2265
Edward D. Grigg Scholarship • 2266
Edward N. Ney Scholarship • 2267
Ella Fitzgerald Charitable Foundation Scholarship • 2269
Eunice Walker Johnson Endowed Scholarship • 2271
Fannie Mae Foundation Scholarship • 2273
Financial Services Institution • 2275
Frederick D. Patterson Scholarship • 2281
GAP Foundation Scholarship • 2282
Gena Wright Memorial Scholarship • 2286
General Mills Technology Scholars Award • 2287
Gerald W. and Jean Purmal Endowed Scholarship • 2289
GlaxoSmithKline Company Science Achievement Award • 2291
Google Scholarship • 2293
Harry C. Jaecker Scholarship • 2295

Harvey H. and Catherine A. Moses Scholarship • 2296
Houghton Mifflin Company Fellows Program/Internship • 2307
Jack and Jill of America Foundation Scholarship • 2310
Jeffry and Barbara Picower Foundation Scholarship • 2319
Jesse Jones, Jr. Scholarship • 2320
Jimi Hendrix Endowment Fund Scholarship • 2321
John Lennon Scholarship • 2322
Jos. L. Muscarelle Foundation Scholarship • 2323
Kuntz Foundation Scholarship • 2326
Letty Garofalo Scholarship • 2327
Limited Inc. and Intimate Brands Inc. Scholarship • 2328
Louis Dreyfus Natural Gas Company Scholarship • 2330
Mae Maxey Memorial Scholarship • 2336
Malcolm X Scholarship for Exceptional Courage • 2338
Marriott Scholars Program • 2341
Mary E. Scott Memorial Scholarship • 2342
MasterCard Worldwide Special Support Program • 2344
MCCA Lloyd M. Johnson, Jr. Scholarship Program • 2345
McClare Family Trust Scholarship • 2346
Medtronic Foundation Scholarship • 2349
Michael and Donna Griffith Scholarship • 2352
Michael Jackson Scholarship • 2353
Mike and Stephanie Bozic Scholarship • 2354
Mitsubishi Motors U.S.A. Foundation Leadership Awards • 2361
Morgan Stanley Scholarship/Internship • 2362
NAACP/HBCU Scholarship Fund • 2364
Nelnet Scholarship • 2379
Office Depot Scholarship • 2382
Premedical Summer Institute Program/Internship • 2394
Raymond W. Cannon Memorial Scholarship • 2397
Reader's Digest Scholarship • 2398
Rhea and Louis Spieler Scholarship Program • 2399
Robert Dole Scholarship for Disabled Students • 2401
Robert Half International • 2402
Siemens Teacher Education Scholarship Program • 2409
Siragusa Foundation Scholarship • 2411
Sodexho Scholarship • 2413
Sterling Bank Scholarship • 2415
Sylvia Shapiro Scholarship • 2420
Time Warner Scholars Program • 2426
Trull Foundation Scholarship • 2430
UNCF-Foot Locker Foundation Inc. Scholarship • 2433
UNCF/Merck Graduate Science Research Dissertation Fellowships • 2434
United Negro College Fund Scholarships • 2436
United Parcel Service Foundation • 2437
USA Funds Scholarship • 2439
USENIX Association Scholarship • 2440
Wells Fargo Scholarship • 2441

Wendell Scott, Sr./NASCAR Scholarship • 2442
William Wrigley Jr. Scholarship/Internship • 2445

UNITED STATES BOWLING CONGRESS
Billy Welu Scholarship • 20
Earl Anthony Memorial Scholarships • 61
Gift for Life Scholarships • 73
USBC Alberta E. Crowe Star of Tomorrow • 175
USBC Annual Zeb Scholarship • 176
USBC Chuck Hall Star of Tomorrow • 177
USBC Earl Anthony Memorial Scholarships • 178
USBC Gift for Life Scholarships • 179
USBC Youth Ambassador of the Year • 180

UNITED STATES PUBLIC HEALTH SERVICE
Health Resources and Services Administration-Bureau of Health Professions Scholarships for Disadvantaged Students • 884

UNITED TRANSPORTATION UNION INSURANCE ASSOCIATION
United Transportation Union Scholarships • 2173

UNIVERSITY AVIATION ASSOCIATION (UAA)
Gary Kiteley Executive Director Scholarship • 863
Joseph Frasca Excellence in Aviation Scholarship • 919

UNIVERSITY AVIATION ASSOCIATION EUGENE S. KROPF SCHOLARSHIP
Eugene S. Kropf Scholarship • 847

UNIVERSITY OF HAWAII
Charles R. Hemenway Memorial Scholarship • 1210

URBAN LEAGUE OF NEBRASKA INC.
Charles B. Washington Scholarship • 1207
Multicultural Association Scholarship • 1609

US PAN ASIAN AMERICAN CHAMBER OF COMMERCE
Darden Restaurants Hallmark Scholarship • 2252
Fedex Hallmark Scholarship • 2274
McDonald's Scholarship • 2347

USA FUNDS
USA Funds Access to Education Scholarships • 174

UTAH HIGHER EDUCATION ASSISTANCE AUTHORITY
Leveraging Educational Assistance Partnership (LEAP) Grants • 1510
Utah Centennial Opportunity Program for Education (UCOPE) Grants • 1895

UTAH STATE BOARD OF REGENTS
New Century Scholarship • 1625

UTAH STATE BUSINESS AND PROFESSIONAL WOMEN
Business and Professional Women Utah Foundation Scholarship • 1170

UTAH STATE OFFICE OF EDUCATION
Robert C. Byrd Honors Scholarship Program - Utah • 1785

UTILITY WORKERS UNION OF AMERICA
Utility Workers Union of America Scholarships • 2174

VASA ORDER OF AMERICA
Oscar and Mildred Larson Award • 2384

720

SCHOLARSHIP NAME INDEX

More Books and
Resources from
SuperCollege

GET THE MONEY YOU NEED TO PAY FOR COLLEGE!

- Insider tips from top scholarship winners and judges
- Secrets to writing applications and essays that win
- Where to find the best scholarships
- Techniques for maximizing your financial aid package

Get your copy at bookstores nationwide or from www.supercollege.com

ISBN13: 978-1-932662-35-1

Price: $19.95

EVERY CONCEIVABLE WAY TO PAY FOR COLLEGE

- Where to find the best scholarships

- Pay in-state tuition even if you're an out-of-state student

- Jump-start your college savings

- Get your share of the $143 billion in financial aid available

- Have your state pay for your college education

- Get your student loans forgiven

- And much, much more!

---

*Get your copy at bookstores nationwide
or visit www.supercollege.com*

ISBN: 978-1-932662-38-2

$19.95

LEARN HOW TO GO BACK TO SCHOOL WITHOUT GOING BROKE

- Insider tips from top scholarship winners and judges

- Details every conceivable way to pay for college

- Where to find the best scholarships just for adults

- Proven strategies for applying for federal financial aid

- Take advantage of federal and state retraining programs

- Claim valuable tax credits and deductions

- Get your employer to pay for your education

- Earn credit for life and work experiences

- Have your student loans forgiven

Get your copy at bookstores nationwide or from www.supercollege.com

ISBN13: 978-1-932662-33-7

Price: $17.95

A COLLEGE GUIDE FOR STUDENTS WITHOUT STRAIGHT A'S

- Complete profiles of 150 great colleges that welcome students like you

- Information on academics, majors and what the colleges seek

- Admission tips for overcoming less than perfect grades or test scores

- Inside advice from students, counselors and admission officers

Get your copy at bookstores nationwide or from www.supercollege.com

ISBN13: 978-1-932662-22-1

Price: $19.95

GET MORE TOOLS AND RESOURCES AT SUPERCOLLEGE.COM

Visit **www.supercollege.com** for more free resources on college admission, scholarships, and financial aid. And, apply for the SuperCollege Scholarship.

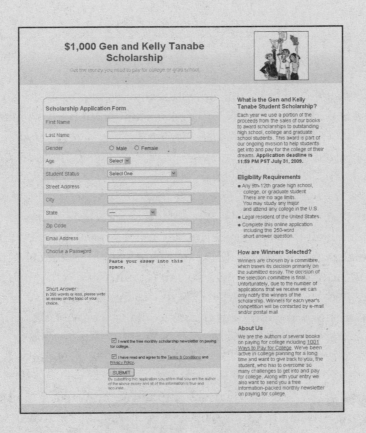

APPLY FOR THE GEN AND KELLY TANABE SCHOLARSHIP

Visit **www.genkellyscholarship.com** to win a scholarship for college or graduate school. The award is open to 9th-12th grade high school, college or graduate students.

Plus, parents can win too! Parents, win a scholarship to help pay for your child's education. The Gen and Kelly Tanabe Parent Scholarship is open to parents of current high school or college students. Apply at **www.parentscholarship.com**.

ABOUT THE AUTHORS

Harvard graduates and husband and wife team Gen and Kelly Tanabe are the founders of SuperCollege and award-winning authors of twelve books including: *Get Free Cash for College, 1001 Ways to Pay for College, How to Write a Winning Scholarship Essay, Get into Any College, Accepted! 50 Successful College Admission Essays, 501 Ways for Adult Students to Pay for College* and *Accepted! 50 Successful Business School Admission Essays*.

Together, Gen and Kelly were accepted to every school to which they applied, including all the Ivy League colleges and won over $100,000 in merit-based scholarships. They were able to graduate from Harvard debt-free.

Gen and Kelly give workshops across the country and write the nationally syndicated "Ask the SuperCollege Experts" column. They have made hundreds of appearances on television and radio and have served as expert sources for *USA Today*, the *New York Times*, *U.S. News & World Report*, *New York Daily News*, *San Jose Mercury News*, *Chronicle of Higher Education*, *CNN* and *Seventeen*.

Gen grew up in Waialua, Hawaii. A graduate of Waialua High School, he was the first student from his school to be accepted at Harvard, where he graduated magna cum laude with a degree in both History and East Asian Studies.

Kelly attended Whitney High School, a nationally ranked public high school in her hometown of Cerritos, California. She graduated magna cum laude from Harvard with a degree in Sociology.

The Tanabes approach financial aid from a practical, hands-on point of view. Drawing on the collective knowledge and experiences of students, they provide real strategies students can use to pay for their education.

Gen and Kelly live in Belmont, California with their son Zane and dog Sushi.